EX LIBRIS

Reader's Digest Complete Book of the Garden

Third Printing: 1968

Library of Congress Catalog Card No.: 66-15517
Printed in the United States of America

Reader's Digest
Complete Book of the Garden

The Reader's Digest Association,
Pleasantville, New York

The Reader's Digest Association Ltd.,
Montreal, Canada

Elizabeth C. Hall, Associate Curator of Education, The New York Botanical Garden, Bronx, N.Y.

Dr. P. Pirone, Senior Plant Pathologist, The New York Botanical Garden, Bronx, N.Y.; author of *Diseases and Pests of Ornamental Plants* and *Tree Maintenance*

Dr. Robert W. Schery, Director, The Lawn Institute, Kansas City, Mo.; author of *Plants for Man, The Lawn Book* and *The Householder's Guide to Outdoor Beauty*

Dr. George L. Slate, Professor of Pomology, New York State Agricultural Experiment Station, Cornell University, Geneva, N.Y.

Jerald P. Stowell, President of the Bonsai Society of Greater New York

CONTRIBUTORS:

E. B. Anderson, M.SC., V.M.H.

Alan Bloom

Miles Hadfield

Vera Higgins, M.A., F.L.S., V.M.H.

Will Ingwersen, V.M.H.

Keith Paisley, DIP. HORT. (WYE), A.M.I. BIOL., A.I.AGR.E.

S. A. Pearce, A.H.R.H.S., F.INST.P.A.

Robert F. Pearson

Frances Perry, M.B.E., F.L.S.

Gerald Perry

Thomas Rochford

W. E. Shewell-Cooper, M.B.E., N.D.H., DIP. HORT. (WYE), F.L.S., F.R.S.L., D. LITT.

Brian Walkden

Stanley B. Whitehead, D.SC.

ARTISTS:

William Abbot	Arthur Henderson Hall	Frederick Middlehurst
Will Bryant	Lowell Hess	Joan Milroy
Ruth Connor	David Hutter	Charles Raymond
David Cook	James Lucas	Eric Saunders
Gretel Dalby	Ernest Mansell	Kathleen Smith
Gordon Davies	Gloria McKeown	Darrell Sweet
Bill Goldsmith	Wesley McKeown	Elsie Wrigley
Roy Grubb	Eve Melady	Elly Zappert

Contents

For Everyone
Who Loves a Garden

The Garden of Eden was said to contain "every tree that is pleasant to the sight and good for food." All through the ages, gardens have been the symbol of fertility and loveliness. The Hanging Gardens of Babylon so astonished travelers that they were ranked as one of the Seven Wonders of the World. Even before the days of European horticulture, ancient Mexican gardens were watered by aqueducts and their flowers scientifically arranged.

Gardens are our private refuges, where we can satisfy our need for beauty, tranquillity and achievement. They are worlds of nature we help to create; tending plants, we share with the sun, the rain and the soil the task of transforming an area of earth into leaf and blossom. The successful gardener—the one who reaps a bounty of these satisfactions—understands basic principles, and can adapt himself to changing conditions. He need not be an expert. But he should glean from experts the knowledge that will guide him.

The Complete Book of the Garden offers the information that leads to such mastery—authoritative descriptions of every kind of gardening, indoors and out. Some of the most attractive plants of the world flourish in the dry heat of an apartment, by the light of windows. Sections of the book deal with the habits and care of the most widely known and reliable flowers and vegetables, trees and shrubs. But the full story of gardening embraces plants from many climes and countries, and these are included, too. A plumy astilbe or dusky gaillardia is no more troublesome to grow than a chrysanthemum. The cleome deserves a season's place in the sun as much as the universal zinnia.

Garden practices change. Effective as they were, the methods of yesterday have been superseded by new, less arduous ways that employ the latest scientific advances and recently developed materials. In this single volume is the distillation of the experience and thought of a group of the most highly regarded experts of the United States and Canada. In all the main phases of gardening, their recommendations are given: for choosing among the many varieties of plants available, for the making of lawns, for garden design, for indoor gardening and greenhouse culture. Here are the finest ways of creating distinctive areas: Japanese gardens and water gardens, rock gardens and gardens for the difficult conditions of seaside and city. An important part of this book is devoted to the more unusual climates of both North and South, with a calendar of garden work for each of them. Outstanding authorities have contributed chapters on five such great special zones.

Many other topics are presented, explaining the "business" side of gardening in detail: how plants live and grow; what soil consists of and how it can be adapted and enriched; how to prevent disease and to control pests and weeds. The editors have endeavored to cover every aspect of gardening that will prove useful and bring reality to the gardener's vision.

Emerson called his garden "an honest place," where every tree and vine told by its appearance what treatment it had received.

And Kipling wisely wrote:

Such gardens are not made
By singing, "Oh, how beautiful!"
And sitting in the shade.

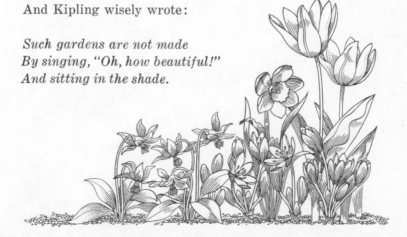

PART I

Flowers and Plants in the Home

Growing plants indoors in homes and small greenhouses affords pleasure to millions of us in North America. This hobby we share with the peoples of the world. Wherever you may travel, you find windows and balconies filled with plants—cultivated in clay pots, sections of bamboo, coconut hulls, seashells, jardinieres — in whatever will hold the roots.

The front windows of homes in Holland, Germany, France, England and other European countries are gay with geraniums and begonias. In Lima, Santiago, Buenos Aires and Rio, house plants are popular decorations. In Japan and in the most crowded parts of Hong Kong, you notice the carefully tended potted flowers. People proudly exhibit house plants in the windows of the living quarters of Chinese junks.

Never was it easier to cultivate plants in the home, and never has such an infinite variety been available. Botanists and horticulturists have searched the world for new species; plant breeders and hybridists have produced new and wonderful kinds. Nurserymen, florists and specialists in house plants offer them to the public everywhere. Growing plants and displaying flowers in the house have become one of the most satisfying aspects of modern living.

12

Cissus rhombifolia. See page 24.
(Grape Ivy)

Ficus elastica decora. See page 30.
(Rubber Plant)

HOW TO GROW
HOUSE PLANTS

Temperature, Humidity, Light—Watering—Fertilizing—63 Recommended Plants and Their Care

IN GENERATIONS PAST, a few ferns, palms, aspidistras and seasonal-flowering pot plants were the only ones available for interior decoration.

Then, in recent decades, a tremendous interest in house plants arose. Both those grown for their flowers and those valued for their foliage, in great variety, found favor and are cultivated in vast number in houses, apartments, offices and other places of business. Thanks to improved lighting

Aechmea fasciata (a bromeliad). See page 19.

and heating, many plants formerly able to flourish only in conservatories or hothouses now thrive as house plants. With proper climate control, assuring favorable temperatures and humidity, many delicate flowering kinds will keep in bloom for weeks, and a number of the foliage plants, such as grape ivy, will last for years. Some of the more popular varieties of house plants are described in this chapter.

CHOOSING HOUSE PLANTS

When choosing plants, consider first their shape, habit, texture and coloring for the place they will occupy and in relation to one another. For a group of plants, choose a tall specimen to give height (dracaena or schefflera), a climbing variety (philodendron), several bushy varieties (begonia or pilea) and a trailing vine to cascade over the edges of the container. Try also for good contrasts of leaf shape and color, choosing the fresh and subtle green-leaved plants for outstanding specimens in key positions. Use multiple wall brackets rather than the type of bracket that holds a single plant, to allow scope for grouping and massing.

TEMPERATURE

A chief consideration is the temperature of the room in which the plants are to live. If the night temperature falls to between 45° and 50° F., choose only the hardiest kinds. If the minimum night temperature is maintained at 50° to 60° F., intermediate plants may be used. Temperatures of 60° to 70° F. at night are adequate for even the most tropical kinds. Day temperatures should be 5° to 10° above recommended night temperatures; this may be attained with the common automatic house thermostat. In summer both day and night temperatures are likely to be higher, which is natural and suitable to the growing season.

HUMIDITY

Humidity is linked with temperature. The relative humidity of the air increases as the temperature falls. As the temperature rises, unless additional moisture is added to the air, it becomes drier. Modern heating provides good warmth but often dries the atmosphere. It is important, therefore, to keep all plants away from sources of dry heat, such as hot radiators. Never place a plant directly above such heat. All house plants prefer fairly high humidity, and the delicate ones must have it. Naturally a home cannot be turned into a steaming jungle, but plants can be helped in many ways without interfering with personal comfort.

An easy way to provide additional humidity is to dampen the leaves occasionally with water, using a very fine spray for the purpose. Fresh air is not essential to house plants, but opening the windows on a mild, calm day will serve the purpose of raising humidity; be careful, however, to avoid creating drafts.

Another means of providing humidity is to place a layer of small pebbles or gravel in the bottom of a shallow tray or saucer about 1 in. deep. Fill this with water just below the surface of the pebbles and stand the plant in its pot on the pebbles. Evaporation will create the humid "microclimate" the plant thrives in. When the plant is watered, the surplus will drain through to the pebble base, but care should be taken that the plant does not stand with its roots in water.

Plants that are grouped usually suffer somewhat less from atmospheric dryness than plants standing alone. Together they give off more water vapor from their soil and foliage than does a single plant, continuously moistening the air in the immediate vicinity.

LIGHT

Light is an important factor regulating plant growth, and the closer natural conditions can be simulated, the greater will be the success in growing house plants. Many varieties originate from the floors of great tropical forests, where the sunlight is filtered through the canopy of branches and leaves overhead. As house plants they, therefore, prefer shade or semi-shade. In winter, the deciduous forest trees shed their leaves, and more, though less intense, light reaches the floor of the forest. And in winter, when the days are short, such house plants need all the light they can get. During the day they should be moved as close as possible to a window, without endangering them from winter cold penetrating through the glass.

Generally speaking, green-leaved foliage plants prefer shade, and many will tolerate quite dark areas of a room. The colored-leaved kinds require more light, but a south-facing window, which receives the strongest summer sun, is not an ideal position for many kinds of house plants, unless the sunlight is filtered by net curtaining or a venetian blind. Conservatories or greenhouses containing house plants should be shaded in spring and summer as a protection against strong sunlight. Remove all shading, however, during the fall and winter, so that the plants receive maximum light.

Some varieties of house plants, especially certain of those that flower, such as geraniums, are sun lovers and thrive best with full exposure at all seasons. With these, care must be taken in summer that temperatures behind glass do not become too high. To prevent this in hot weather, either the window in which the plants are

grown should be opened or it should be lightly shaded.

PLANTERS

A metal-lined trough or pottery bowl makes a good container for several plants, or, for those who prefer something a little more unusual, a deep copper pan or antique container can be used. Fill the planter with moist peat moss, and plunge the plants into the peat up to the rims of their pots. Keep the plants in their pots so that they may be watered and fertilized according to their particular individual requirements.

Be sure that the peat in the container is moist but not soaked. The moisture will then evaporate slowly, forming the beneficial humid "microclimate" around the plants, which will form an umbrella of leaves over the container. This will help to prevent the moisture from evaporating too rapidly. For a single plant, choose an attractive pot, tub or other container with a larger diameter than that of the original pot, place some gravel or other drainage material in its bottom, stand the pot containing the plant inside it, and pack moist peat in the space between the two containers.

DRAINAGE

Good drainage is important in the cultivation of practically all plants grown in containers. Soil should be sufficiently porous to permit the free passage of water, and the bottoms of the containers should have holes through which surplus water may drain. The drainage holes may be covered with a layer of crocks (pieces of broken flowerpots), gravel, charcoal or coarse coal cinders. Then cover these with a layer of peat moss, newly fallen tree leaves, straw or similar material that will prevent the soil from washing down and clogging the openings. The adequate drainage of planters in which pots are buried is quite as important as drainage of the soil in the individual pots. Stagnant water actually drowns the roots of plants and is fatal to most kinds.

WATERING

Correct watering is of supreme importance and largely determines the indoor gardener's success or failure with house plants.

There are no cheap and reliable instruments for measuring the water content of the soil in the pot, but gardeners and horticulturists have evolved some simple, practical methods. With experience, one can quickly tell from the weight of the pot whether the soil is wet or dry, but a sharp rap on the side of a clay pot with a small wooden mallet or a heavy wooden stick, such as a wooden trowel handle, will confirm this. If the sound is a hollow ringing tone, the soil is dry; if it is a dull thud, the soil is wet. If the plant is in a plastic pot, the difference in weight and the condition of the surface soil must be relied upon. When wet, the color of the surface soil is black or dark; when the soil dries out, it becomes a grayish-white. Also, by pressing the tips of the fingers into the topsoil one can learn whether it is wet and soggy, moist, or hard and dry, from the resistance offered by the soil. The two extremes of wet and dry soil should always be avoided, the ideal being an intermediate, evenly moist condition.

The amount of water required by most house plants changes with the season, and even from one home to another. All but desert or bog types of plants require the same general care in watering. During the period of vigorous growth in spring and summer, they require plenty of water, and the soil should not be allowed to dry out too much between waterings. In autumn, when growth slows down, the soil should be kept somewhat drier. In winter, particularly during very cold weather, the greatest care should be taken, as many plants then have almost ceased to grow. In this semi-dormant period, allow the soil almost to dry out before watering again. Give only sufficient water to maintain life, but never permit the soil to become so dry that the foliage wilts or the stems shrivel. At usual room temperature— 70° F. or higher—the air is comparatively dry, and frequent watering of smaller pots even in winter may be needed to prevent prolonged drying. The golden rule at all times, particularly in winter, is *never water when the soil is wet.* Make a practice of watering early in the day, and drain off all surplus water before replacing the pot in position. When water is applied, always give enough to saturate thoroughly the whole mass of soil. Never follow a period of dryness with repeated heavy watering, as this can cause the loss of the lower leaves, but return gradually to normal watering. Black or brown wet patches on the leaves or stem are often a sign of overwatering in winter. If the lower part of the stem is affected, the plant may die. If the leaves are affected, keep the plant almost dry for a while. Some leaves will certainly fall, but the plant may be saved.

In winter, delicate varieties should be given tepid water of room temperature—about 70° F. This treatment also benefits the easily grown varieties.

Where the room temperature drops sharply at night during cold weather, always remove a plant that is moist or wet to a warmer place. Plants left on windowsills, between the curtains and the window, are in danger of being damaged or killed by cold, perhaps even frozen.

Before going away for any lengthy period in spring or summer, water all house plants thoroughly. Insert two small stakes in each pot, slightly taller than the plant, one at each side of the pot. Slip a polyethylene bag over the stakes and fasten it to the sides of the pot with a rubber band in such a way that water draining down the inside of the bag will be conducted to the soil. Place the plants in a position where they will not be exposed to strong sunlight. While you are away, moisture will evaporate from the leaves, condense on the walls of the polyethylene bag and run down. The plants will be in an ideal atmosphere, with enough humidity and a simple self-watering device.

FERTILIZING

Fertilizing is beneficial during the period of active growth from spring through summer to early autumn. In late autumn and winter, discontinue fertilizing altogether.

There are many good brands of house-plant fertilizer available from florists or garden supply stores. Always follow the manufacturer's instructions, for exceeding the stated dosage will only harm the plants. The small bottles of liquid fertilizer are perhaps the most convenient to use in the home.

A trap into which many inexperienced house-plant enthusiasts fall is that of attributing the unhealthy appearance of a plant to starvation. Try to determine first whether the unhealthy symptoms are caused by damage from cold, overwatering or excessive dryness. If these possibilities can be excluded, take the soil out of the pot to make sure that the roots are healthy and undamaged. This can be done by spreading the fingers of one hand on either side of the stem between the lower leaves and the top of the pot. Invert the pot, and tap the rim sharply two or three times. The soil ball will then fall out into the hand. If all is well with the roots, fer-

tilize the plant. Remember that feeding a sick plant will make it worse.

Pale green leaves usually indicate the need for fertilizing, particularly if the plant is pot-bound (that is, the pot is full of roots).

REPOTTING

Frequent repotting of house plants is quite unnecessary, and generally plants placed in containers 5 in. or larger in diameter can stay in the same pots for 12 to 18 months. Most kinds will thrive in pots that appear too small for them, and many that have filled their pots with roots will grow satisfactorily if they are fertilized regularly. Late spring or early summer is the right time for repotting, as the roots then have time to become established in the new soil before winter.

Top-heavy growth should be the main signal for repotting, but before repotting, inspect the ball of soil. If the roots are obviously overcrowded or tangled around the outside of the soil ball, transferring to a pot one size larger is probably necessary. Cover the drainage hole of the larger pot with crocks, put some potting soil in the bottom, stand the soil ball in the center, then fill up with potting soil and pack it moderately firmly.

If repotting is unnecessary, drop the ball back into the same pot and tap the base sharply once or twice. The plant should then be firmly in place, but if it is not, firm the soil with both thumbs.

A good potting compost, suitable for most house plants, contains: 2 parts turfy loam (loam containing undecayed grass roots), 1½ parts leaf mold or peat moss, 1 part washed coarse sand, ¼ part dried manure (all parts by volume).

The reaction should be slightly acid with a pH of 5½ to 6 (see page 741 concerning the pH factor of soils).

Add bone meal at the rate of 1 pt. to each bushel of soil mixture. For plants that need soil especially rich in organic matter, such as African violets, begonias and flame violets, double the proportion of leaf mold or peat moss. Plants of the pineapple family (bromeliads) thrive best in a loose, porous mixture that contains a large proportion of pieces of orchid peat (osmunda) or orchid fir bark, rough half-decayed leaves and lumps of charcoal, mixed with some turfy soil.

At potting time the soil mixture and the ball of the plant should be just moist. After repotting, it should be watered sparingly for a few weeks to encourage the roots to grow into the new soil.

PRUNING AND TRAINING

In the winter months some house plants tend to make long, thin, weak growth with small leaves. In spring, when vigorous growth resumes, this poor growth should be cut back as far as the good-sized, healthy leaves. The appearance and shape of the plant will improve as healthier and more robust side shoots soon grow.

The variegated climbing and trailing kinds easily revert to all green leaves during the winter when the light is inadequate. In spring this green growth should be cut back to the last well-variegated leaf in order to encourage variegated side shoots.

If a plant is growing too tall and a bushier shape is required, stop the growing shoots by breaking off the tips with finger and thumb (known as "pinching" or "pinching back"). This encourages the growth of side shoots, and bushiness will soon result.

House plants are quite frequently trained up bamboo or trellis to form a partial screen or divider in a large room, and the climbing and trailing varieties lend themselves well to this practical and decorative use. The foliage of many climbing plants, particularly members of the arum family, such as philodendron, is improved by training the plants up a stake.

CLEANING

Regular sponging of the leaves with tepid water helps to prevent attacks by insect pests and provides the wash that indoor plants cannot get from rain. To impart a gloss to smooth-leaved varieties, sponge with a mixture of equal parts of milk and water.

House plants are not usually much affected by fungus or other diseases, but they do become infested with mites and such insect pests as aphids, mealybugs and scale insects. A close watch should be maintained for the first signs of insects and prompt remedial measures taken. These will usually be the application of an insecticide (insect-killing spray) or miticide (mite-killing spray). Follow carefully the manufacturer's directions.

Clean the leaves of hairy-leaved plants with a soft brush such as a paintbrush, or blow off accumulated dust. The same treatment is recommended for the leaves of varieties with silvery-gray peltate scales. These scales form the attractive silvery bandings on many members of the pineapple family and are easily damaged by rubbing, so that the appearance of the plant is spoiled.

POPULAR VARIETIES

The plants which may be successfully cultivated as house plants are very numerous. Some of the best will be described here. Others useful for growing indoors, such as the many tender bulbs, ferns and cactuses and other succulents, are described elsewhere in this book.

The genus name of each plant is spelled when it first appears with its species name; thereafter the genus name is abbreviated. (For example, in

Aglaonema, Aglaonema commutatum is the first reference, then *A. modestum*, and so on.)

ABUTILON (FLOWERING MAPLE)

Both variegated and plain green-leaved varieties of these graceful flowering plants are very decorative. They produce their hanging, bell-shaped flowers of cream, yellow, orange or red over a long summer season. For their successful cultivation they need cool conditions; a night temperature of 50° F. is adequate. They require well-drained fertile soil, watered often enough to keep it always moist but not constantly saturated, and full sun, except that in high summer a little shade from very strong direct sun is beneficial. Plants that have filled their pots with healthy roots benefit from an application of dilute liquid fertilizer every week or two from spring through fall. Pinching back the shoots occasionally encourages desirable bushy growth.

AECHMEA FASCIATA

This highly decorative and popular bromeliad, or member of the pineapple family, grows as a dense rosette of leaves, each leaf being 2 to 3 in. wide and 1 to 1½ ft. long, with a saw-toothed edge. The leaves vary considerably in color, but usually either have alternate bands of green and silver-gray or are almost entirely silver-gray. The silver-gray effect is produced by a mealy substance on the surface and underside of the leaves, and should never be rubbed off. Dust on the leaves may be blown off. A rosy-pink flower scape grows up from the center of the rosette to about 1½ ft., ending in rose-pink spiky bracts, between which red and violet-blue flowers emerge. When the flowers die, pluck them from the scape, which will then remain pink for six to nine months. At about flowering time, the plant produces one to three offshoots. Leave these on the plant, which will die down after flowering and should be cut off near the base. The offshoots will then grow on the root system of the parent plant and will flower again in two to three years. See illustration, page 13.

Many other kinds of aechmeas make very good house plants.

AESCHYNANTHUS PULCHER

With its tiny green leaves covering the entire length of the long stems, this is one of the best trailing house plants, either for a hanging pot or small hanging basket. It produces brilliant scarlet and yellow tubular flowers in spring, which soon drop in a hot, dry atmosphere. The plant prefers 60° F. and humidity in a semi-shaded location. Keep the soil moist in summer, but allow it nearly to dry out between waterings in winter.

AFRICAN VIOLET. See *Saintpaulia*.

AGLAONEMA PSEUDOBRACTEATUM

A decorative, bushy plant, this has spear-shaped leaves, about 9 in. long and 2 in. across, on short stems. Irregular golden-yellow markings appear along the center of the leaf and give way to gray-green and finally to dark green on the border of the leaf. Rather delicate, the plant requires constant warmth and humidity in a draft-free, shady place. It needs plenty of water in summer but careful watering in winter, and a minimum temperature of 55° F. It should be fed regularly with a liquid fertilizer in spring and summer.

Other good aglaonemas are *Aglaonema commutatum*, *A. modestum* (Chinese evergreen), and *A. treubii*. All require the same care. The Chinese evergreen withstands unfavorable growing conditions better than the others.

The two plants shown here illustrate some of the striking contrasts of color and leaf shape to be found among house plants: the fanlike foliage of Begonia rex-cultorum, hairy and richly colored; and the graceful, arching leaves, striped with cream, of Chlorophytum comosum picturatum (spider plant).

Begonia rex-cultorum
(Rex Begonia)

ALUMINUM PLANT. See *Pilea.*

AMARYLLIS. See *Hippeastrum.*

ANTHURIUM

These handsome tropical plants are suitable only for growing in highly humid air and with shade from direct sun. *Anthurium scherzerianum*, which has red flowers, is useful for cultivating in terrariums and bottle gardens.

APHELANDRA SQUARROSA LOUISAE

Purchased in bud or flower, the aphelandra should be regarded as a flowering plant which will have some decorative value when the flowers have fallen off. When purchased as a foliage plant, not in flower, it may last quite well as a house plant. The aphelandra has large lance-shaped leaves, which grow in pairs from the upright stem. The leaves are about 9 in. long and 4½ in. across, of a very dark, shiny green, the main rib

and side veins being emphasized by ivory-colored stripes. The tubular yellow flowers grow in spikes at the top of the main stem or stem branches, and they emerge from between colored bracts, forming a head shaped like a four-cornered pyramid. Aphelandras will grow under a variety of conditions, but ideally they like a semishaded location and should be kept evenly moist and warm. When caring for an aphelandra, remember that the pot must be full of roots with very little soil, for until the plant has become pot-bound and starved, it will not flower. It will need frequent watering to keep it evenly moist; in winter, however, give only enough water to keep the soil just moist. The leaves have a natural droop, but this will become exaggerated if the plant is too dry. Sponging will keep the leaves fresh and free of dust, but take care not to injure the leaves, or brown patches will appear. Regular feeding

Chlorophytum comosum picturatum (Spider Plant)

with a liquid fertilizer is essential to maintain the dark green color of the leaves.

Other varieties of *Aphelandra squarrosa* are quite as attractive as *A.s. louisae*.

ARALIA. See *Fatsia japonica*.

ARAUCARIA EXCELSA
(NORFOLK ISLAND PINE)
Having the appearance of a beautiful, stylized Christmas tree, this decorative foliage plant thrives only under fairly cool conditions. Temperatures of 45° to 50° F. at night are adequate. It requires good light with a little protection from strong, direct sun in summer. A fertile, peaty, sandy soil suits it best, and this should be kept always moist but not in a constant state of saturation. Well-established specimens benefit from watering with dilute liquid fertilizer at two-week intervals.

ASPARAGUS (ASPARAGUS FERNS)
These are not true ferns but are botanical relatives of the lilies. They are, however, fernlike in appearance and are grown for the beauty of their foliage. The two most popular kinds are *Asparagus sprengeri* and *A. plumosus*. Both require the same care. Asparagus ferns thrive in any fertile soil that is efficiently drained. When well rooted they respond to frequent feeding with dilute liquid fertilizer. Although they are by no means bog plants, their soil should never be permitted to become really dry. They are at their best in good light without strong, direct sun. Temperatures of 50° to 60° F. suit them well.

ASPIDISTRA (CAST-IRON PLANT)
One of the toughest house plants, this has paddle-shaped leaves arising from rhizomes lying horizontally at about ground level. It thrives in ordinary soil in cool or warm conditions and

stands much shade. Propagation is by division. Both plain green and variegated-leaved varieties are grown.

AZALEA. See *Rhododendron*.

BABY'S TEARS. See *Helxine soleirolli*.

BEGONIA
This important genus of plants includes hundreds of kinds that are suitable for cultivating indoors. They are classified as tuberous and non-tuberous according to whether or not they possess a bulblike tuber and are completely dormant in winter or whether they have no tubers and are evergreen. The nontuberous group include some that have thick, prostrate horizontal stems or rhizomes resembling those of bearded iris. These are called rhizomatous begonias and they include the *Begonia rex-cultorum* varieties, notable for their magnificently colored foliage. Most of the begonias are fairly easy to grow provided they are given a soil that contains an abundance of decayed organic matter (leaf mold, humus or peat moss), which is porous. Night temperatures should be about 55° to 60° F. From fall through spring the atmosphere should not become excessively dry. Too dry air, sudden drops in temperature, and drafts are likely to cause serious leaf dropping. Except for tuberous kinds during their season of dormancy, the soil of all begonias should be kept always reasonably moist, but none will long stand a saturated, stagnant soil. Free drainage is important. They respond to mild fertilization after their pots are well filled with roots, but the application of excessively strong fertilizer solutions can soon bring disaster. The wax begonia (*B. semperflorens*) and its varieties thrive in full sun. However, all others need some shade from strong summer sun, but not dense shade. In winter all benefit from exposure to maximum light.

Tuberous begonias may be raised from seed but are more usually grown from purchased tubers. These are planted in late winter or early spring and started into growth in a humid atmosphere in a temperature of 70° to 75° F. As growth develops they are successively transplanted to larger pots. They thrive best where summer nights are fairly cool, and they are excellent for the decoration of shaded porches. Before fall frost they are gradually dried off and the tubers are stored in dry sand or peat moss at about 55° F. over winter.

B. rex-cultorum varieties may also be raised from seed but are often grown from leaf cuttings, which root easily and soon produce young plants. Varieties of this group need a more humid atmosphere than most and are best accommodated in a terrarium. (See illustration, page 20.)

Of other kinds of begonias, almost all are usually propagated from cuttings, except the wax begonias (see Begonia, page 126), which are most often raised from seed. Begonia seeds are extremely small and are sown on the surface of finely sifted soil that contains an abundance of humus or peat moss and are merely pressed into the surface without being covered with soil. The growth habits of different kinds of begonias vary tremendously. With many it is desirable to pinch the shoots occasionally to induce branching. Many need careful attention to staking and tying to afford the shoots needed support.

BELOPERONE GUTTATA
(SHRIMP PLANT)
Under favorable conditions this plant blooms almost continuously. Its common name derives from the cluster of bracts that are colored and shaped like shrimps. These surround the

lower parts of the white flowers and form the conspicuous parts of the dense flower spikes. The shrimp plant prospers in any good potting soil in a temperature of about 60° F. It needs good light and an atmosphere that is not too dry. Unless its shoots are pinched regularly it tends to develop into a straggly, unkempt-looking specimen. Staking is usually necessary. Specimens that have filled their containers with roots should be fed with dilute liquid fertilizer. This species is very subject to infestations of red spider mites.

BILLBERGIA NUTANS
All kinds of billbergia require the same care and are excellent bromeliads for the house. *Billbergia nutans* forms dense clusters of rosettes of narrow, erect, stiff, silver-bronze leaves. From the center of each rosette is produced an arching flower stem furnished with rose-pink bracts and bearing nodding flowers that have violet-edged green petals. The flowers remain exotically attractive for long periods. Like all members of the pineapple family this needs a soil containing an abundance of organic matter and a coarse soil so that water and air percolate freely through it. Grow in full sun or very light shade, and water moderately; keep the cup formed by the bases of the leaves filled. Temperatures of 60° to 70° F. are appropriate.

BLOOD LEAF. See *Iresine*.

CALAMONDIN. See *Citrus mitis*.

CALATHEA MAKOYANA
Of the many kinds of these tropical foliage plants, this one is sometimes cultivated in terrariums and bottle gardens. It requires the same culture as *Maranta*.
    Calathea makoyana has rosettes of paddle-shaped leaves prettily pat-terned in light green and olive-green and red on their undersides.

CAPE JASMINE. See Gardenia.

CAPSICUM FRUTESCENS
(CHRISTMAS PEPPER)
Grown for their attractive red, purple or cream-colored fruits. Remarks and culture as for *Solanum pseudo-capsicum* (Jerusalem cherry).

CHLOROPHYTUM COMOSUM PICTURATUM
(SPIDER PLANT)
An easy and popular variety, it grows as a dense cluster of narrow, gracefully arching leaves, each having a cream stripe down the center. It will grow almost anywhere in the home, but requires plenty of water. The plant should be repotted when the tubers begin to push it up out of its pot. When the plant is mature in a 5-in. pot, it will produce what appear to be flower stems with little clusters of leaves at the ends, making an attractive hanging plant. These are the young plants which may be used for increasing stock. Peg them down into small pots of soil as for the runners of a strawberry plant, and wait until they root before cutting the stem joined to the parent plant. Keep the soil in the small pots fairly dry until the young plants have rooted. (See illustration, page 21.)
    Several other varieties of *Chlorophytum* differ chiefly in the patterns of their leaf variegations. All are easy.

CHRISTMAS PEPPER. See *Capsicum*.

CINERARIA. See *Senecio*.

CISSUS
    Cissus antarctica (kangaroo vine) is an easy plant, popular for its climbing habit. The stems will readily attach themselves to trellis, cane or string supports by means of tendrils, and

have been known to reach a length of 40 ft. or more. The dark green leaves are 2 to 3 in. long and 1 to 1½ in. wide, with serrated edges similar to an oak leaf. It tolerates almost any condition except cold below 45° F. and prefers a semishaded place and liberal watering in summer, with more light and less water in winter. Regular feeding in spring and summer promotes growth and keeps the foliage a healthy green.

C. rhombifolia (grape ivy), is an undemanding, bushy, vigorous climber or trailer, which grows best up a trellis or framework of strings. It produces many climbing stems from which spring the leaf stalks, each with three leaflets on individual stalks. The deep green leaves are nearly rhomboidal in shape, with toothed edges, and are about 2½ to 3 in. long and 2 in. wide. The growing tips are covered by a fine silvery down, which becomes brown a little beyond, before it disappears. An ideal plant for cool, shady places in summer, it prefers some warmth in winter. The leaves will turn pale or yellow in strong light. Keep the soil just moist, but take care not to overwater in winter. Pinching back the growing tips will make the plant bushy and improve its shape. It benefits from regular feeding during the summer months.(See illustration, page 12.)

CITRUS

Several kinds of citrus are useful house plants. They need a sunny location, ordinary well-drained soil watered often enough to keep it moderately moist and, after their pots are well filled with roots, applications of dilute liquid fertilizer at biweekly intervals from spring through fall. Their night temperature should be about 50° F. in winter and a few degrees warmer during the day, and they benefit from being put outdoors in summer. Plants can be raised from seeds of oranges, lemons and grapefruits, but such plants rarely, if ever, reach fruiting size under house conditions. It is better to grow dwarf varieties which are known to fruit when small and which have been propagated from cuttings. Some of the best of these are described below.

Citrus limonia Ponderosa, a large-fruited lemon, has fruit that is excellent for pies.

C. meyeri is a nearly thornless hybrid between the lemon and sweet orange. It has attractive, fragrant, lavender-tinged white flowers and acid edible fruit.

C. mitis (calamondin) is spineless with small, white, fragrant flowers and loose-skinned, edible, acid, orange-colored fruits.

C. taitensis (Otaheite orange) has waxy white flowers tinged pink and tiny oranges that are acid-flavored.

CODIAEUM (CROTON)

These plants, always referred to as crotons, are usually regarded as hot-house plants, but they will last for a considerable time in a warm room. Planted in a bowl or in a planter as part of a mixed arrangement, they receive the humidity they require, and have been known to remain in good condition for more than two years. This colorful and beautiful group includes numerous varieties, leaf shapes and color combinations. Leaf shapes range from long, narrow and curling (corkscrew varieties) to wider and irregularly pointed (oak-leaf varieties) and elongated and oval (broad-leaf varieties). Colors range from bright yellow and green, through red and green, red and pink, orange and red, to almost black, orange and red. The midrib and side veins determine the pattern in some varieties, but other intricate patterns have no regular form. All require warmth, humidity and good light, but not direct strong sunlight. Keep evenly moist at all times and provide a minimum temperature of 60° F. in winter. Feed during the growing season.

COLEUS

There are many named varieties of these quick-growing plants, and seedlings produce a great variety of differ-

ent leaf patterns and colors—red, bronze, brown, yellow, cream and shades of green. Plants sometimes bear spikes of small blue-purple flowers but the chief attraction is their beautiful foliage. Coleuses are easily raised from seed or cuttings and they thrive in any ordinary potting soil. They are sun lovers, and a temperature of 55° to 60° F. suits them well.

Codiaeum (Croton)

A moderately humid atmosphere and generous supplies of water (the soil must be porous and well drained) are necessary. Feeding with liquid fertilizer at weekly intervals promotes good growth of specimens when their roots have filled their containers. To encourage bushy growth, shoots must be pinched back from time to time.

COLLINIA ELEGANS. See *Neanthe*.

CORN PLANT. See *Dracaena fragrans massangeana*.

CREEPING FIG. See *Ficus pumila*.

CROTON. See *Codiaeum*.

CRYPTANTHUS
Cryptanthus bivittatus minor is a small bromeliad ideal for planting in bowls or dish gardens, as it provides a contrast in height and form. The leaves, 3 to 6 in. long, are striped longitudinally in pale and medium green, have crinkled edges and form a flat, star-shaped rosette. When moved to a light position, the leaves become richly suffused with pale pink and deep maroon. This process can be reversed by putting the plant in a dark or shady place. The plant will survive for a long time without water. Ideally, keep the soil just moist in summer and on the dry side in winter. Stock is easily increased by removing and potting up the side shoots that appear after flowering. When a side shoot measures about 1½ in. in diameter, remove it by tugging the tip of its lowest leaf.
C. bromelioides tricolor is perhaps the most popular of all cryptanthuses for its grace and coloring. A star-shaped rosette is formed by the graceful, arching leaves, which are 1 in. wide and 6 to 10 in. long. Colored cream with narrow green longitudinal stripes, they become richly suffused

with bright pink at the edges and base in good light in spring and summer. Should the leaves turn brown at the edges, remove the affected area carefully with scissors. The plant prefers warmth, ideally 60° F., but it will tolerate small variations in temperature and survive for long periods without water. However, for the best results keep the soil moderately moist and the plant in a light position.

There are several other kinds of cryptanthuses; all need care.

CYCLAMEN
Cyclamen, with flowers of white, pink and red, grown and brought into bloom in greenhouses, may be used as temporary house plants in winter and spring. Most houses are too warm and dry for them to remain in good condition long, but under exceptional circumstances (for instance in a bright window in a cool room where the air is not too dry) they may remain attractive for a month or two. After flowering is finished these plants are of no further use. They need light shade from strong sun and plenty of water.

DEVIL'S IVY. See *Scindapsus aureus*.

DIEFFENBACHIA (DUMB CANE)
Dieffenbachias are severely irritating to mucous membranes, and their leaves or stems should not be chewed or eaten. An old legend says that chewing the plant causes dumbness for several days, and that it was given to slaves as a punishment.
Dieffenbachia amoena forms a good free-standing specimen with large, nearly oblong leaves varying from 6 to 10 in. in width and from 14 to 20 in. in length, and branching alternately from a thick stem. The medium green leaves have irregular yellow and cream markings along the lines of the lateral veins. This species is "tougher" than other dieffenbachias. It will with-

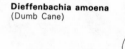

Dieffenbachia amoena
(Dumb Cane)

stand temperatures down to 50° F., although it grows better under warmer conditions. Like other dieffenbachias, this plant prefers humidity and warmth to maintain growth. It will shed its lower leaves from time to time with age, but this loss is more than compensated by the production of new leaves at the top.

D. picta requires warmth and moderately high humidity. Provide a minimum temperature of 60° F. and a semishaded or shaded position. Lance-shaped leaves grow from a thick stem or trunk. The dark green leaves, about 6 in. wide and 12 in. long, have cream markings between the side veins which form an almost completely cream area toward the center vein. The bottom leaves will turn yellow and fall off naturally, but will be compensated by growth at the top, making an interesting treelike plant. There are many varieties of D. picta. Some of the best are D.p. barraquiniana, which has a strong white midrib and a few white spots on its leaves; D.p. jenmannii, with ivory-white diagonal bands marking its leaves; and D.p. Rudolph Roehrs, which has chartreuse leaves with dark midribs and blotches of ivory-white.

D. seguine is a vigorous species with dark green leaves marked with prominent midribs and depressed veins. It requires the same growing conditions as D. picta, but its varieties are more commonly grown than D. seguine itself. Chief among these are *D.s. decora*, with its leaves marked with clear white spots and its leaf-stalks white, and *D.s. irrorata*, which has white leafstalks and yellow-green leaves with darker blotchings.

Other worthwhile dieffenbachias, some of which are hybrids, are *D. bausei*, with its pale foliage variegated with dark green and white spots; *D. memoria-corsii*, which has grayish leaves with darker veins and a few white spots; and *D. Exotica*, a compact kind with rather small leaves that are handsomely variegated with creamy-white. All require the same culture as *D. picta*.

DRACAENA

Dracaena fragrans massangeana is the old-fashioned "corn plant." It grows vigorously and without difficulty in almost any indoor environment where it receives fairly good light and where the temperature ranges between 55° and 70° F. The long, broad leaves arch downward and are striped light green and yellow along their centers. Water this kind often enough to keep its soil moderately moist, and give it an application of dilute fertilizer about once a month.

D. sanderiana is quite different

Dracaena terminalis tricolor (Ti Plant)

from the many other varieties of dracaena. The leaves, about 1 in. across and 6 to 8 in. long, grow at intervals from the straight stem somewhat like wheat. The center of the leaf is grayish-green and the margin ivory-cream. This plant needs semishade, a temperature of 60° to 70° F. and sufficient water to keep the soil evenly moist. It is often used in mixed arrangements in planters.

D. terminalis (syn. *Cordyline terminalis*) is the ti plant of Hawaii, which will tolerate home conditions for many months, and in a planter arrangement may last for a year. The coloring of the leaves ranges from irregular patterns of bright red and green to pale pink and green.

Plants 1½ to 2 ft. high are usually available in 5-in. pots. They should be put in a light place out of direct sunlight, or in semishade. Ideally, they should have a temperature of 60° to 70° F., but they will withstand temperatures a few degrees lower. Keep evenly moist and provide humidity if possible by plunging in peat moss or by placing in a planter arrangement.

This species is prone to attack by red spider mites, especially when it is in a hot, dry atmosphere.

D.t. tricolor has broad leaves with large areas of cream on green and vivid flashes of bright pink.

DUMB CANE. See *Dieffenbachia.*

EASTER LILY. See *Lilium.*

EPISCIA (FLAME VIOLET)
These relatives of African violets are trailers with attractive, usually variegated, hairy foliage and red, orange-red, lilac or white flowers. They are especially useful for hanging baskets and planters. Episcias need good light with shade from strong sun and a humid or fairly humid atmosphere.

The soil for them should contain an abundance of organic matter, such as leaf mold or peat moss, and be well drained. At all times it should be kept fairly moist. Too much wetness and poor aeration of the soil quickly causes the death of these plants.

EUPHORBIA PULCHERRIMA
(POINSETTIA)
To maintain these popular Christmas plants in good condition in bloom as long as possible, keep them out of drafts, in good light but out of direct sun, in temperatures between 58° and 70° F., spray their foliage with water daily and keep the soil always moist. Poinsettias may be kept over for the following year but rarely do they flower satisfactorily when grown under house conditions. If kept, let them dry completely after flowering and remain dry until May. Then, prune to within 6 in. of the soil, shake them free of old soil and repot in new, fertile, porous soil. Place them in full sun, minimum temperature 60° F., and resume regular watering. Pinch tips out of new shoots when 6 to 8 in. long, and again in late July. Pot them into larger containers if the old ones are well filled with roots. Fertilize well-rooted specimens regularly. They may be kept outdoors, in full sun, during summer, but bring indoors before cold nights arrive, and grow them in full sun. Poinsettias will not bloom unless they get 14 hours of complete darkness each night. Artificial light during this period prevents blooming.

FATSHEDERA LIZEI
This bigeneric hybrid resulted from a cross between *Fatsia* and *Hedera* (English ivy). It is of erect, wiry growth on a single stem that requires support. The dark green leaves are shaped rather like those of the *Fatsia* or *Aralia* but are smaller and have

five points. One of the easiest of
house plants, it is tolerant of almost
any treatment and condition, even
when the temperature goes down to
45° or 50° F. at night. Keep moist, in
semishade, and feed regularly during
the growing season. Repot in spring
or summer when the plant becomes
too tall for the pot in which it is
growing.

Fatshedera lizei variegata. This has
a broad cream margin around the
edges of the leaves. It is not quite as
hardy as the green variety. In poor
light in winter, in a hot, dry atmosphere, or if the plant is allowed to
dry out, the lower leaves tend to turn
brown and fall off.

FATSIA JAPONICA
(syn. ARALIA SIEBOLDII)
One of the easiest house plants, its
leaves are large and shaped like the
palm of a hand, with seven to nine
lobes. Frequent feeding when in active growth keeps the leaves a good
dark green. Attractive when about
1½ to 2 ft. high in a 5-in. pot, the
plant prefers semishade, but can be
gradually acclimatized to almost full
light. Keep well watered in summer,
but give less water in winter.

Fatsia japonica variegata, an intermediate plant, is more delicate than
the green-leaved variety. The variegation occurs at the tips of the lobes
and leaf edges and this form can be
propagated only from cuttings.

FICUS
If protected from drafts, ficus will
tolerate both low and high temperatures, but it thrives best in a temperature of 55° to 70° F. It will
grow in a wide variety of locations
but if in a light place should be
moved to shade when new leaves
emerge, as too much sunlight will
cause the leaves to be hard and small.
Keep it evenly moist in spring and

summer, but take care not to overwater in winter. Sponging the leaves
not only benefits the plant, but also
improves the glossy appearance.

Ficus benjamina is attractive and
highly individual. The upright woody
stem and numerous branches covered
with small dark green leaves give the
impression of a graceful, weeping
tree. It should always be kept moist
in summer, but allowed almost to
dry out between waterings. This
plant prefers a semishaded position
out of direct sunlight. Some yellowing and dropping of the leaves
may occur naturally in winter, but
this loss will be more than replaced
in the growing season.

F. elastica decora (rubber plant) is
a great improvement over the old-
fashioned rubber plant. The dark
green, leathery leaves grow spirally
from an upright stem, each leaf being
attached by a thin stalk about 1 in.
long. The leaves are about 9 to 12 in.
in length and 5 to 7 in. wide. During
the growing months, the sheath containing the furled new leaf at the
growing tip of the plant is colored
bright red, but it turns brown and
falls off when the new leaf emerges. If
it fails to do so, it should be removed,
as it may cause the new leaf to rot.
(See illustration, page 12.)

F.e. doescheri (variegated rubber
plant) is the only large-leaved variegated ficus. It is similar in appearance
to *F.e. decora,* but the leaves are
longer and narrower. The young
leaves have broad, irregularly shaped
cream markings round the edges,
which become narrower as the leaf
matures. The center of the leaf is of
two shades of green in irregular
patches. A striking and highly decorative though somewhat delicate
plant, it requires warmth and humidity. Place in a light location out of
direct sunlight. Keep moist in summer and rather dry in winter; if the

soil becomes very dry, however, the leaves will droop and may fall off. Take care also not to overwater this plant, or the edges of the leaves will turn brown. If this should happen, trim off the brown edges with scissors, and allow it to dry out almost completely before attempting to water it again.

F. pumila (creeping fig). This climbing, creeping or trailing plant, with its thin stems and thick growth of elongated, heart-shaped leaves, is quite unlike other members of the family. The leaves are about ½ in. across and 1 in. long. Unlike most house plants, it should always be kept moist. Never let the soil dry out. An occasional spraying over the leaves and regular feeding during the growing season are beneficial. The plant will withstand moderate to cool temperatures, and in a cool sunroom will climb a wall rapidly, supported by its aerial roots. It prefers a shaded or semishaded location.

F.p. variegata. This variegated form of the creeping fig is dainty and good-looking. The leaves are blotched with white, and although they tend to revert to green during the winter, the new growth in spring and summer will be variegated. Treatment and conditions are the same as for *F. pumila*, but it should have more light (not direct sunlight).

FITTONIA ARGYRONEURA
A tropical plant, a prostrate grower, *Fittonia argyroneura* is rather delicate. The leaves are roundish, about 3 to 4 in. long, and of a medium green with silver veins, which give the effect of an intricate silver net over the leaf. The plant prefers deep shade and must be kept humid and warm (minimum 55° F.). It will quickly die if allowed to dry out, but overwatering will have the same effect. Best results are obtained when this sensi-

tive plant is grown in a terrarium.
F. verschaffeltii is similar to *F. argyroneura*, but the leaf veins are pink.

FLAME VIOLET. See *Episcia*.

FLOWERING MAPLE. See *Abutilon*.

FUCHSIA
These graceful, summer-blooming plants may be had in wide variety. Their hanging flowers are single or double and come in various shades and combinations of pink, red, blue, purple and white. They need cool growing conditions and in winter must be kept almost dormant. Then, night temperatures of 40° to 50° F. are adequate. With the coming of spring, temperatures may be increased by 5° or 10°. A humid atmosphere at all times is essential; fuchsias will not stand hot, dry conditions. From spring through fall they need light shade from strong, direct sun. In winter only enough water should be given to them to prevent the stems from shriveling; between waterings the soil should be allowed to become almost completely dry. At other seasons liberal watering should be the rule, if the soil is sufficiently porous to avoid stagnation. Occasional pinching back of the tips in the growing season induces bushy growth, and in late winter or early spring old specimens may be pruned back rather severely and at the same time repotted. Well-rooted specimens will respond to regular fertilizing throughout the summer.

GARDENIA (CAPE JASMINE)
Some people succeed in growing florist's gardenias as house plants; most who try do not. Gardenia requirements are exacting—acid soil, good light, a humid atmosphere, temperatures between 60° and 70° F., sufficient watering to keep the soil al-

ways moist (not constantly saturated) and moderate fertilizing. The florist's gardenia is *Gardenia jasminoides veitchii* and its varieties. These exotic plants are chiefly winter and spring bloomers.

Easier to grow as a house plant is *G. jasminoides* (commonly planted outdoors in the South). Smaller-flowered and summer-blooming, this kind can be kept in a fairly cool, light cellar over winter and be flowered in a sun porch or window or on an outdoor terrace in summer.

GERANIUM. See *Pelargonium.*

GLOXINIA. See *Sinningia.*

GRAPE IVY. See *Cissus rhombifolia.*

HEDERA (IVY)
All varieties make easy house plants, and most are hardy out of doors except in regions of very severe winters.

THE GREEN-LEAVED IVIES
Place these ivies in a shady spot. During the growing season feed regularly with a liquid fertilizer, and keep moist. Allow the soil almost to dry out between waterings in winter. All of the numerous varieties will tolerate a great deal of neglect or ill-treatment.

Hedera helix cristata (parsley ivy). The leaves are almost round in shape with a heavily fringed edge similar to parsley. This variety, though unusual, is not especially decorative.

H.h. Green Ripples is an increasingly popular variety, because of its remarkably pointed and dainty leaves.

H.h. hibernica (commonly called English ivy) is a most popular house plant, mainly because of its vigorous growth and its ability to take rough treatment. It can be grown either as a climber or as a trailer and benefits from restrictive pruning in the growing season. It has a rather large leaf.

H.h. minima has a profusion of very small, thin leaves.

H.h. My Heart has attractive medium-large, dark green glossy leaves, almost heart-shaped and slightly pointed.

H.h. sagittaefolia (arrowhead ivy), a popular variety with arrow-shaped leaves, has central lobes that are elongated and triangular.

THE VARIEGATED-LEAVED IVIES
These are slightly less tolerant of neglect than the green-leaved varieties, although they may still be classified as easy house plants. Keep them away from any source of dry heat. As with most other variegated-leaved varieties, they prefer good light, particularly in winter, but not direct sunlight. Feed regularly in the growing season with a good liquid fertilizer and keep moist, but allow them almost to dry out between waterings in winter. Overwatering at this season often causes the variegated section of the leaf to turn brown. Some variegated varieties revert to green growth during the winter, and in early spring produce thin, spindly growth. Prune this as soon as the plant is growing vigorously. Pruning improves the shape of the plant and encourages self-branching. There are many variegated varieties of ivy.

Hedera canariensis variegata is one of the showiest and most popular varieties. Its large, almost heart-shaped leaves have irregular markings of dark green, and are gray-green in the center with a pale cream margin. A slow grower, it should not be overwatered or the leaves will soon turn brown.

H. helix Glacier. The small leaves of this ivy are an effective silver-gray with a cream margin. It makes a good trailer, will withstand frost and is therefore a fine subject for window boxes out of doors. If the plant becomes straggly in the autumn, let it dry out and stand it outside in a sheltered place for the winter. Bring it back into the house early in March, and water sufficiently to start growth again, increasing watering as growth progresses. The woody stems that have hardened outside during the winter will eventually produce masses of tiny new leaves along their whole length.

H.h. hibernica variegata has large green leaves with irregular cream-white variegation.

H.h. Goldheart is a fascinating ivy with small leaves, each with a golden center surrounded by a dark green margin. Normally a slow-growing variety, it seems to grow more quickly under cool conditions and in full light, but growth will then be rather thin with a long section of stem between the leaves.

H.h. lutzii. The basic coloring of the leaves of this small-leaved, bushy ivy varies from medium green to a very light green, densely mottled with deeper green.

H.h. sagittaefolia variegata (variegated arrowhead ivy). Similar in shape and size to the green-leaved *sagittaefolia*, this ivy has leaves that are mainly pale cream with green markings in spring and summer. In the autumn and winter months the leaves may become rather green, because of poor light. They grow quite close together on the stem, giving a dense, bushy effect.

HELXINE SOLEIROLII (BABY'S TEARS)
This creeping green mosslike plant provides a suitable carpet for terrariums and bottle gardens. Needs ordinary soil, kept moderately moist; shade from strong sun.

HIPPEASTRUM (AMARYLLIS)
This tropical bulb is one of the most gorgeous of flowering house plants. In winter or spring it produces one or more massive stalks that bear two to five huge lily-shaped flowers, white, pink, red or striped. The leaves are strap-shaped and dark green. Amaryllises should rest and stay dry in a temperature of about 55° F. from late fall until new growth begins to develop spontaneously early in the year. At other times water them freely and, if their pots are well filled with roots, feed them generously with dilute liquid fertilizer. They need a rich, porous soil and free drainage. Established specimens should be repotted every three or four years only, at the beginning of their growing season. A temperature of about 70° F. is suitable, and the atmosphere should be reasonably moist with good light, and shade from strong summer sun. New bulbs have no roots and every effort must be made to develop a good root system the first year. To encourage this take special care not to keep the soil too wet until roots fill the container, and avoid fertilizing.

HOYA CARNOSA (WAX PLANT)
An interesting fleshy-leaved vine that bears clusters of star-shaped, very delicate pink flowers. It needs an exceptionally open porous soil and should be contained in a pot fairly small for the size of the plant; one too large is harmful. During the winter allow the soil to become nearly dry between waterings, and lower the temperature to 50° to 60° F. At other times the soil must be always moderately moist and temperatures between 60° and 70° F. Good light is needed but with some shade from strong summer sun.

HYDRANGEA
White-, pink-, lavender-, blue- and purple-flowered varieties of *Hydrangea macrophylla* are forced by florists and used as temporary house plants.

They last longest in bloom if kept in a cool, light place out of direct sun. They need plenty of water. After bloom is finished, keep them growing in a cool, sunny place; and, in areas where they are winter-hardy, plant outdoors after danger of frost is past.

IMPATIENS (PATIENCE PLANT, PATIENT LUCY, SULTANA)
These are quick-growing bushy plants that bear white, pink or red flat blooms almost continuously. Both taller-growing and dwarf varieties are available. A rich, porous, fairly moist soil and temperatures from 50° to 60° F. suit them. They withstand moderate shade but thrive in sun and must have good light to induce blooming. When in active growth they are improved by having their shoots pinched occasionally and by being given dilute liquid fertilizer at weekly or biweekly intervals.

IRESINE (BLOOD LEAF)
Attractive tropical foliage plants. They thrive in ordinary, well-drained soil kept moderately moist, in sun or light shade. They need a humid atmosphere. Pinch shoots regularly to induce bushiness. Propagate this from cuttings.

Iresine herbstii has roundish leaves, green or purplish with yellow veins.

I.h. reticulata is brighter-colored green or greenish-red, with yellow veins.

I. lindenii has narrow, pointed deep red leaves.

IVY. See *Hedera*.

JERUSALEM CHERRY. See *Solanum*.

KANGAROO VINE. See *Cissus antarctica*.

LEMON. See *Citrus limonia* Ponderosa.

LILIUM LONGIFLORUM (EASTER LILY)
Temporary house plants. To maintain them in bloom as long as possible water freely and keep in 55° to 60° F., in good light, out of direct sun. After blooming keep watered, in cool light place; plant in the outdoor garden, with the top of bulb 6 in. below the soil surface, after danger of frost is past. They will bloom again in summer. In the South, and if well mulched as far north as New York, they will live outdoors throughout the winter and bloom in succeeding years.

MARANTA LEUCONEURA KERCHOVEANA (PRAYER PLANT)
This is an attractive but rather delicate plant requiring a little extra care. The leaves grow in a fairly dense rosette, the mature leaves lying prostrate and the new leaves standing furled and upright. About 5 in. long and 3 in. wide, the leaves are medium green with symmetrical blotches of maroon-red on either side of the midrib between the side veins. Always keep the plant moist, warm and humid, in a shady, draft-free place. If subjected to too much light, the leaves will turn yellow. It is a good terrarium plant.

MEXICAN BREADFRUIT. See *Monstera deliciosa*.

MONSTERA DELICIOSA (MEXICAN BREADFRUIT)
An accommodating and popular plant, *Monstera* has a thick round stem and dark green leaves, which have prominent stalks about 12 to 15 in. long. The leaves are about 12 in. long and 10 in. wide, and are an elongated heart-shape. They are deeply cut between the side veins almost to the midrib, and mature plants will, ideally, produce holes in the leaves near the midrib between

Monstera deliciosa
(Mexican Breadfruit)

the cuts. The serration of the leaves causes the plant to throw intriguing shadows when subjected to angled lighting. Thick aerial roots in search of support and moisture grow from the stem, opposite to the leaf stems. Those near the bottom should be trained down into the soil in the pot; those farther up the stem should be trained up a stake.

Frequent repotting is unnecessary unless the plant becomes top-heavy, and should then only be carried out in spring or early summer. If fed and watered regularly, a monstera will continue to grow in a small pot for a long time.

The plant likes shade or semishade, and should be moist but never too wet, particularly in winter. A temperature of 60° F. or over is ideal, but it will withstand lower temperatures. Feed regularly during the growing season with a liquid fertilizer, but do not fertilize in the winter. In the early part of the year some leaves will be without cuts or perforations, and although these will appear in leaves produced later, they may be less numerous if the plant is grown in the house than if it is raised in a greenhouse.

MOSES-IN-A-BOAT. See *Rhoeo discolor*.

NEANTHE BELLA (COLLINIA ELEGANS)
This slow-growing miniature palm can be quite easily grown in the home. It has feathered leaves ranging from 4 to 8 in. in length and composed of individual leaves that become larger and coarser as the plant grows. It tolerates quite a variety of conditions, but drafts will cause the leaves to go brown at the edges. Warmth, semishade, and humidity are congenial to neanthe. Keep the soil evenly moist, but allow it to dry out almost completely between waterings during the winter.

NEOREGELIA CAROLINAE TRICOLOR
A dense rosette in the form of a spray flattens out prior to the flowering of this bromeliad. The strap-shaped leaves are 12 to 15 in. long and about 1 to 1½ in. wide. They are green with a cream center and striped at the edges with fine green lines. The cream variegation becomes suffused with pink before the rosette flattens out. At the time of flowering, the short leaves and the base of the larger leaves around the cup-shaped depression in the center of the plant become a brilliant red. Even after its small pale lilac-blue flowers have died, the plant will retain its brilliant red center for 12 months or more, and side shoots will grow up between the leaves. If left on the parent plant, these will flower again in one or two years, according to conditions.

This is an easy plant, which prefers warmth and semishade or shade, but will tolerate a dryish atmosphere. Keep the center cup filled with water and the soil in the pot just moist, but allow the soil to dry out between waterings in winter, when tepid water should be used. As the flowers die off, wash out the center cup thoroughly every day, or a pungent odor will arise.

NORFOLK ISLAND PINE. See *Araucaria excelsa*.

ORANGE. See *Citrus taitensis*.

PATIENCE PLANT. See *Impatiens*.

PATIENT LUCY. See *Impatiens*.

PELARGONIUM (GERANIUM)
Botanically the indoor plants called geraniums belong in the genus *Pelargonium*. They are classed in four main groups, the familiar "fish" or "bedding" geraniums, the ivy-leaved geraniums, scented-leaved geraniums and the Lady Washington or Martha

Washington geraniums. Each group includes numerous varieties. All need full sun, a fertile, rather heavy but well-drained soil and fairly cool growing conditions. From fall through spring, night temperatures of 45° to 50° F. are adequate and day temperatures should not be more than 5° or 10° higher. They all are easily propagated from cuttings and need pinching occasionally during their growing seasons to develop as shapely specimens. The "bedding" geraniums come with flowers in white and various shades and combinations of pinks and reds and in single- and double-flowered varieties. Blooms may be borne in the winter but primarily in spring, summer and fall. Ivy-leaved geraniums are similar in most respects to the bedding kinds but have more or less trailing stems and ivy-shaped leaves.

Scented-leaved geraniums, such as *Pelargonium graveolens* (rose geranium), *P. limoneum* (lemon geranium), *P. odoratissimum* (nutmeg geranium), and *P. quercifolium* (oakleaf geranium) have much smaller flowers than those of the bedding and the ivy-leaved kinds. These plants are grown chiefly for their aromatic foliage.

Quite different from any of the above are Lady Washington geraniums. These have heads of large pansylike flowers in a wide variety of colors and combinations and bloom for a comparatively short season in spring. After they have finished flowering they should be rested by being kept completely dry until August, when they should be pruned back quite severely, repotted and restarted into growth.

In addition to the geraniums mentioned, there are a few semisucculent kinds which are grown under conditions suitable for cactuses and other succulents.

PEPEROMIA

Most peperomias appear as a short bush of thick, fleshy leaves, indicating that they can store water and will withstand periods of dryness. Many of them produce several thin, erect flower spikes like little tails, which stand some 6 to 8 in. above the leaves and add considerable interest to the form of the plant. The flower spikes are whitish-cream and are occasionally branched. Peperomias prefer moist soil but must be allowed to dry out between waterings. In winter, keep them as dry as possible without causing damage to the roots. When water is necessary it should be tepid. The green- and gray-leaved varieties prefer shaded conditions, while the variegated-leaved varieties need more light, but not strong sunlight. All of these plants need a minimum temperature of 60° to 65° F.

Peperomia caperata produces a dense mass of small, heart-shaped leaves 1 to 1½ in. long. They are irregularly corrugated, dark green and purple in the "valleys" of the corrugations, and bright emerald-green on the "hills." The leafstalks are pink, and the overall effect is of a rich velvet. An interesting plant, producing upright whitish-cream flowers, it has varieties called Little Fantasy and Emerald Ripple.

P. glabella variegata grows as a bush, with pinkish, trailing stems that may be 6 to 8 in. long. The leaves are green with a cream margin. Requires warmth and humidity, and is not as easy to grow as the green-leaved variety.

P. hederaefolia is similar in leaf and habit to *P. caperata*. The heart-shaped leaves are crinkled and some 2 in. long and wide. They are pale gray, and dark olive-green main veins form the "valleys" of the corrugations. Prefers shade and humidity.

P. magnoliaefolia, a shrubby va-

Peperomia obtusifolia variegata

riety tolerant of varying conditions, produces side shoots. The oval leaves are medium green, about 2 in. long and 1¾ in. wide.

P. obtusifolia has fleshy, dark green obovate dark green leaves with narrow red margins.

P. o. variegata differs from *P. obtusifolia* in that its leaves have irregular patches of dark and light green on a yellowish-cream background.

P. sandersii (watermelon peperomia) forms a dense bush of leaves that are almost round but taper to a point at the end. The mature leaves are fleshy, and are about 3 in. long and 2 in. wide. They are silver with a dark green band along the main vein, forming an attractive plant that requires more attention than most. Keep evenly moist with tepid water, and allow almost to dry out between each watering. Keep warm and fairly

dry in winter, but never allow to dry out completely. Cold and overwatering will cause the leaves to turn black and rot off.

PHILODENDRON

Philodendron bipinnatifidum is an easy, compact plant. The medium green triangular leaves have an irregular serrated edge and rise from a central point. They are usually about 12 in. long and 9 in. across, but sometimes much larger. Place the plant in a semishaded place in summer, and give it more light, though not direct sunlight, in winter. Keep evenly moist in summer, but allow almost to dry out between waterings in winter. Feed regularly during the growing season. This species grows slowly and the lower leaves may turn yellow and fall off, but are replaced by new and larger leaves.

P. melanochrysum. This delicate climbing plant may be trained to grow up a stake.

Its heart-shaped leaves vary from 3 to 5 in. in length and have a most exotic appearance, with a velvety, very dark green, almost black surface and a deep golden underside. The plant requires moist conditions, a minimum temperature of 55° F. and a semishaded, draft-free position. Always water this philodendron with tepid water.

P. oxycardium is a popular and attractive climbing plant which produces aerial roots at every leaf joint and will grow larger leaves if trained up a stake. It has heart-shaped, dark green leaves some 3 to 4 in. long and 2½ to 3 in. wide, although they can be much larger in mature specimen plants. This plant will survive in almost any conditions, but thrives best in warmth and humidity in a semishaded or shaded location and will tolerate quite dark places. It prefers moderate watering and regular feed-

Philodendron bipinnatifidum

ing during the summer. Keep the plant fairly dry in winter if in a cool location. During winter and early spring it tends to make weak, thin growth (elongated with small leaves), which should be removed to encourage fresh "breaks" and stronger growth.

P. o. variegatum. The variegation is usually confined to one half of each leaf and consists of green splashes on an almost white background. This variegation often causes severe distortion of the variegated half of the leaf and is surely virus-induced.

P. selloum. Although this is almost indistinguishable from *P. bipinnati-*

fidum when small, and is often sold as the same plant, it forms a trunk when larger, and has larger leaves, with deeper serrations.

P. wendlandii (bird's-nest philodendron) is quite unlike other philodendrons in habit and leaf shape. The long, lance-shaped leaves are a glossy dark green, and stand up stiff and erect round a central point. The leaves of specimens in 6- or 7-in. pots reach a length of 20 to 24 in. and are some 3 to 3½ in. wide. Often an exciting cluster of two or three beautiful cream-and-deep-red flowers appears in the center of the cone of leaves. The flower has a stem about 3 in. long, and lasts for only about 24 hours when cut. The plant requires a semi-shaded position away from direct sunlight, and should be kept moist. Feed during the growing season, and never subject the plant to a temperature of less than 55° F.

PIGGYBACK PLANT. See *Tolmiea menziesii*.

PILEA CADIEREI NANA
(ALUMINUM PLANT, WATERMELON PILEA)
This dwarf variety has replaced the larger *P. cadierei* in popularity, as it will tolerate temperatures down to 50° F. and a variety of conditions. It grows as a low bush, and its leaves are 1½ to 2 in. long and about 1 in. across. They are dark green with bright silver markings on the raised areas of the quilted surface. This vigorous plant requires regular feeding.

If it becomes straggly, cut well back with scissors and pinch out the growing tips to keep the plant bushy. Place in a semishaded or shaded place that is out of strong light, and water liberally.

PODOCARPUS
Several kinds are occasionally cultivated as foliage plants and thrive in ordinary well-drained soil in good light with shade from strong, direct sun. The most popular variety is the following:
Podocarpus macrophylla maki, which becomes a tall tree but with pruning can be kept low. The leaves are dark green and narrow.

POINSETTIA. See *Euphorbia*.

POMEGRANATE. See *Punica*.

POTHOS. The name is often mistakenly applied to *Scindapsus*.

PRAYER PLANT. See *Maranta leuconeura kerchoveana*.

PRIMROSE. See *Primula*.

PRIMULA (PRIMROSE)
Greenhouse-grown, late winter- and spring-flowering primroses, especially *Primula malacoides*, *P. obconica*, with pink, red or white flowers, and *P. kewensis*, with yellow flowers, are sometimes used when in bloom as temporary house plants. Unless given cool and humid conditions (impossible to maintain in most houses), they soon wilt and die. They are of no further use once they are through blooming. They need plenty of water and shade from strong sun.

PUNICA (POMEGRANATE)
Punica granatum nana is a dwarf variety that does not exceed 6 ft. in height and blooms and fruits when very much smaller. It has bright green leaves and orange-scarlet flowers followed by orange-red edible fruits. Propagated by cuttings, it will grow readily in any ordinary, well-drained soil in full sun in a cool room.

RHODODENDRON (AZALEA)
The plants called azaleas are an important group of the genus *Rhododendron*. Some are popular as house plants. They succeed if they can be accorded cool conditions. Their cultural needs are described on page 92 in "Your Own Greenhouse."

RHOEO DISCOLOR (MOSES-IN-A-BOAT)
This relative of *Tradescantia* is easy to grow and has attractive, fleshy leaves that are green above and purple on their undersides. Of interest are its small, three-petaled white flowers which arise from a boat-shaped container formed of two leafy bracts. Any ordinary soil is suitable

if well drained and kept just moderately moist. It should have good light and a little shade from strong direct sun. Temperatures should be 60° to 70° F.

RUBBER PLANT. See *Ficus elastica decora*.

SAINTPAULIA IONANTHA
(AFRICAN VIOLET)
One of the most popular flowering house plants, this species is available in countless varieties and in a wide range of colors. Both single- and double-flowered varieties are grown. The leaves vary considerably in size according to variety, but on a 3-in. stem they are usually about 2½ in. long and nearly 2 in. wide. The most popular flower colors are violet-blue, pink and white. Pinch out the flowers as they die off, and keep the soil somewhat dry for a period of four to six weeks until more flower buds appear, then return to normal watering. This method will produce several flowerings in a season. Always use tepid water, and lift the leaves gently before pouring the water onto the soil in the pot. If water touches the leaves it may cause unsightly marks. African violets quickly succumb to overwatering but do well if plunged, in their pots, into a container of moist peat moss. A minimum temperature of 55° F. and a shaded place are essential.

SANSEVIERIA TRIFASCIATA LAURENTII
(SNAKE PLANT)
This is a well-known plant with stiff, upright, sword-shaped leaves, which have irregular horizontal bands of dark green and gray-green and a clearly defined yellow margin. They are thick and fleshy and range from 6 in. long in a 3-in. pot to 24 in. long in a 5-in. pot, and from 2 to 3 in. wide. The rhizomatous roots will persist-

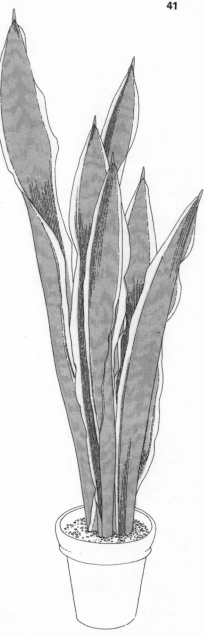

Sansevieria trifasciata laurentii
(Snake Plant)

ently throw up side shoots, which may be left to grow in the same pot or can be cut off with as much root as possible and potted separately. Never remove a side shoot until it is 10 to 12 in. long, and then tie it to a stick for support until rooted in its new pot. Tolerant of prolonged periods of neglect, the plant is happy in a sunny or a shaded area and thrives in a hot, dry atmosphere. In an average room it may be watered once a week in the summer and usually less often in the winter, although in a hot, dry atmosphere more frequent watering is necessary. The only hazard in growing this variety is the rotting of the leaves if the plant is exposed to frost or a combination of very low temperatures and wet soil. There are several other attractive kinds of sansevieria, including the dwarf *S. trifasciata hahnii*, which is useful for dish gardens and bottle gardens.

SCHEFFLERA ACTINOPHYLLA
The leaves of young plants are divided into three small leaflets, and of larger plants into five leaflets; these spring from the center of the leaf stem rather like sun rays. They are a pleasant medium green, oval and from 4 to 6 in. long and 1½ to 2 in. wide. The plant likes humidity, a temperature of 55° to 70° F. and a semishaded location away from strong sunlight. Keep just moist in summer but allow almost to dry out between waterings in winter. It will shed its leaves if allowed to dry out. Feed regularly during the growing season.

SCINDAPSUS AUREUS (DEVIL'S IVY)
A climbing or trailing plant somewhat similar to the philodendron and often misnamed *Pothos*. The leaves are roundish heart-shaped, about 3½ in. long and 3 in. wide, and have a dark green background flecked with yellow. The leaves will be larger and more luxuriant if the plant's aerial roots are trained up a stake.

Full light in winter will help the plant to maintain its variegation. In a warm, humid, draft-free location in semishade, keep moist in summer, but take care not to overwater in winter. If the leaves droop when the soil is moist, allow to dry out before watering again.

Scindapsus a. Marble Queen is a variety with almost entirely white leaves flecked with green. Half of each leaf often provides a striking contrast by reverting to green. The variegated half of the leaf is nearly always smaller than the green half and sometimes slightly distorted, indicating that the variegation is virus-induced. Conditions and treatment should be the same as for *S. aureus*, except that Marble Queen requires more light, or the leaves will revert to all green. Avoid strong, direct sunlight. Green leaves may be cut out.

SEDUM SIEBOLDII FOLLIS-MEDIO-
VARIEGATIS
This extremely easy and attractive plant is widely used in hanging baskets and out-of-doors window boxes in summer. It is bushy with long, thin stems surrounded at intervals by round, blue-gray leaves, variegated cream at the center. If the plant becomes dry out of doors in hot sunshine, the leaves take on a deep reddish tinge. Pinkish-red flowers appear in the autumn before the plant dies down. It may then be left dry for the winter in a cool greenhouse or sunroom. In early March put it in a pot one size larger and water, and growth will recommence. It will withstand any conditions and treatment, from sunlight to part shade and from overwatering to drought, but ideally the soil should be kept just moist and allowed to dry out completely between waterings. Keep the plant in a cool

place, as it will not prosper in warm rooms.

SENECIO CRUENTUS (CINERARIA)
Winter- and spring-flowering plants with large heads of daisylike flowers in many brilliant colors and combinations of colors and white. Greenhouse-grown specimens in bloom may be used temporarily as house plants but unless given cool, humid conditions (impossible to provide in most houses) they soon wilt and die. They are of no further use once they finish blooming. They need watering generously and shading from strong sun.

SHRIMP PLANT. See *Beloperone guttata.*

SINNINGIA (GLOXINIA)
Botanists call these well-known choice bulbous plants, which are commonly known as gloxinias, *Sinningia.* They can be grown only where the atmosphere is quite humid, as in a terrarium. A temperature of about 70° F. and good light without strong direct sun are needed. Gloxinias bear huge, velvety trumpet flowers in summer—white, pink, red, lavender, blue or violet. The bulbs are started into growth in late winter or spring. A well-drained soil that contains an abundance of organic matter (peat moss or leaf mold) favors good growth and this should be kept evenly moist throughout the growing season. Shade from strong sun must be provided. In the fall, watering is gradually reduced, and through the winter the plants are kept quite dry. In the spring, the bulbs are shaken free of the old soil and restarted into growth again in fresh soil. Gloxinias can be raised from seeds sown in sandy peaty soil and cultivated in the same manner as begonias. They need humid conditions, shade from direct sun and should be kept at a temperature of about 70° F.

SNAKE PLANT. See *Sansevieria trifasciata laurentii.*

SOLANUM PSEUDO-CAPSICUM
(JERUSALEM CHERRY)
Grown for its attractive yellow or red fruits. Although it may grow well after its berries drop, it rarely fruits again under house conditions and is best regarded as a temporary plant to be discarded after it ceases to be decorative. Full sun, cool temperature (50° F. at night) and watering often enough to keep the soil moderately moist provide suitable conditions.

SPATHIPHYLLUM WALLISII
With dark green shiny lance-shaped leaves, 5 to 6 in. long and 1 to 1½ in. wide, with thin, pointed tips, this plant is grown chiefly for its delicate white bracts ("flowers") which rise up between the leaves on thin stems, and appears at intervals from spring to autumn. It prefers shade, warmth and humidity, but it will tolerate temperatures down to 50° F. and even a fairly warm, dry atmosphere. Keep moist in winter; give more water in summer; feed regularly.

SPIDER PLANT. See *Chlorophytum.*

SULTANA. See *Impatiens.*

TOLMIEA MENZIESII
(PIGGYBACK PLANT)
This interesting foliage plant has rosettes of soft, lobed green leaves. Young plantlets develop on top of the older leaves, piggyback fashion, and can be detached and rooted as new individuals. Ordinary soil kept fairly moist, good light with shade from strong sun and night temperatures between 40° and 50° F. are satisfactory.

TRADESCANTIA
These plants, like *Zebrina,* are often called wandering Jew. Several attrac-

tive variegated kinds make excellent trailing house plants, and can also be used in window boxes or hanging baskets outside in summer. All of them will tolerate a wide range of temperature and retain their variegation best in good light away from direct strong sun. Ideally, keep moist, but an occasional period of dryness will not harm them. If the growth reverts to green in poor light, cut out the affected shoots, and move the plant to a lighter position. If the plant becomes thin and straggly, prune out the weak growth and push the growing tips, about 3 in. in length, into the soil to take root in the same pot. In both cases the plant will soon become bushy again. Always grow tradescantias in poor soil and do not feed them.

Tradescantia fluminensis has ovate green leaves about 1½ in. long by ¾ in. across. It bears small white flowers.

T. f. albo-vittata. The leaves are striped white on a medium green background and are longer than those of *T. f. variegata*.

T. f. variegata has leaves 1½ in. long and ¾ in. across, variegated with creamy yellow longitudinal stripes.

T. viridis Loekenensis Rainbow is a very popular variety. The leaf markings are white stripes suffused with delicate pink.

VRIESIA SPLENDENS

This really easy plant has, like many bromeliads, a rosette of strap-shaped leaves about 12 in. long and up to 3 in. wide. The leaves are dark green with irregular transverse bands of chocolate-maroon on the underside. The plant takes several years to grow to flowering size from seed, but then produces a spectacular head of flowers and colored bracts. Each head develops on a stalk from the center funnel of leaves, and is composed of many segments; between these the yellow tubular flowers emerge. Keep the center funnel filled with water and the roots just moist. The plant will tolerate periods of drought and varying light conditions except strong, direct sunlight, but prefers semishade. It will withstand temperatures down to 50° F. if it is kept fairly dry at the roots, but temperatures of 60° to 70° F. and a humid atmosphere are best.

WANDERING JEW. See *Tradescantia* and *Zebrina*.

WATERMELON PEPEROMIA. See *Peperomia sandersii*.

WAX PLANT. See *Hoya carnosa*.

ZEBRINA

Several varieties of these plants are similar in habit and leaf structure to the tradescantias and require the same conditions and treatment. Like *Tradescantia* they are commonly called wandering Jew.

Zebrina pendula. The leaves are about 2½ in. long and 1¼ in. wide, silvery gray-green with a deep green margin and a broad purple stripe down the center.

Z. p. quadricolor is a magnificent plant with leaves striped in a silvered pinkish cream, rosy purple, dark green and silvery green. Keep it warm and in good light, as the leaves tend to revert easily to the ordinary *Z. pendula*. This will usually happen in winter, but the brilliant colors may reappear in the new spring growth.

Z. purpusii is a beautiful plant for a hanging basket where both the reddish-purple upper side and the more vivid purple underside of its leaves may be seen. Keep in a good light, and do not overwater or the leaves may become green. The delicate bluish-purple flowers develop in autumn.

INDOOR GARDENING

Forcing Bulbs—Gardens: Miniature,
Bottle and Dish—Plants from Fruits—
Planters Great and Small

MORE AND MORE people are discovering the pleasures of indoor gardening, not only those who live in apartments, but those with gardens too. Keeping a room supplied with cut flowers is one way of bringing the garden indoors. But perhaps more satisfying is the cultivation of house plants and the making of miniature gardens in bottles, planters, bowls and various other containers.

BULBS

Early Bloom, or Forcing

Hardy bulbs grown indoors give special pleasure, since their development can be watched from start to finish and their blooms appear at times when flowers in the garden are scarce. They are showy and beautiful and often delightfully fragrant.

For forcing, choose bulbs that are solid, heavy and free from blemish. They need not be top size, but make sure that the tips are undamaged and that the thin outer skins or tunics are reasonably intact. Be particularly careful about this when choosing tulips. Those that look skinned may have been mishandled; such bulbs will probably do well enough in a garden, but avoid them for growing indoors.

When available, choose bulbs that have been specially treated to flower early in the season. A hardy bulb normally requires a long period at low temperatures after it has been planted, followed by warmth as it reaches the flowering period. By artificially simulating these natural conditions, through subjecting the bulbs to heat or cold treatment, bulb growers are able to vary the length of the waiting period. In this way they can influence the time of year at which a bulb will bloom. The grower may then ship bulbs to any part of the world, and the indoor gardener may buy, with confidence, bulbs that have been specially prepared to flower earlier than unprepared bulbs.

Planting

These bulbs may be forced in different kinds of containers filled with one of a variety of growing mediums.

The beginner will probably wish to use flowerpots filled with soil. A mixture of peat moss, vermiculite and pea-sized charcoal is a suitable medium in which to set bulbs planted in bowls. The bowls should have one or more holes at the bottom—with lumps of charcoal over each hole—to insure drainage. There are special pots made of terra-cotta, with holes punched out at intervals around the sides. Fill the pots gradually with the peat moss–vermiculite–charcoal mixture or with vermiculite alone, and poke the tip of a crocus corm through each hole from the inside as the work proceeds; plant several more on the top. Each crocus pot holds about a dozen corms and makes a delightful picture when all come to flower, with blossoms around the sides of the pot as well as on top.

Most bulbs can be grown in the mixture described above, or in vermic-

Hyacinth Bulbs and Crocus Corms

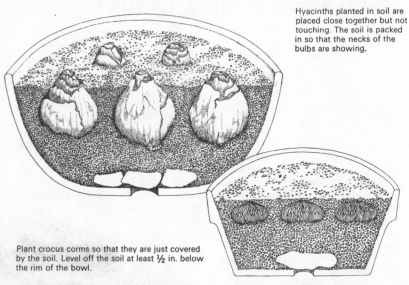

Hyacinths planted in soil are placed close together but not touching. The soil is packed in so that the necks of the bulbs are showing.

Plant crocus corms so that they are just covered by the soil. Level off the soil at least ½ in. below the rim of the bowl.

ulite, gravel or water (see page 47).

The chief essential is to maintain an even amount of moisture. The planting material must never become waterlogged and never dry out. Food is of less consequence, since a bulb usually stores enough within itself to bring it to flower.

If soil is to be used as the planting medium, make up a mixture of equal parts of sifted topsoil, coarse sand and peat. The soil must be firm in the pots but not hard-packed.

Plunging Bulbs

After the bulbs are planted in their bowls, put them into a dark place where a temperature as close as possible to between 35° and 40° F. is maintained. Keep them there 10 to 12 weeks to encourage good root formation, without which there cannot be success. Most bulb failures are caused by bringing the bowls into the light and warmth too soon.

Ideally, the bowls should be plunged under a 6-in. layer of ashes, sand or porous soil in the garden. If they cannot be plunged in a garden, the bowls should be put in a cool but frostproof place such as a basement or garage. First wrap the bowls in *black* polyethylene, which keeps out the light and prevents them from drying out. Bowls wrapped in polyethylene will not need watering throughout the plunge period. If they are not wrapped, they should be looked at occasionally and supplied with sufficient water to keep the rooting medium just moist.

Examine the containers from time to time. When the bulb shoots are about 1 in. high, root growth is sufficiently strong for the bowls to be brought in from the garden or taken from the cellar or garage where they have been placed. Remove the polyethylene wrapping, and then put them in a light, cool place, perhaps near a basement window, at a temperature of 50° to 60° F.

For the first day keep the bowls covered with newspaper to allow the white shoots to accustom themselves to the light. They gradually turn green and grow vigorously, but do not take them into real warmth—higher than 60° F.—until the leaves are well out of the bulbs. At this stage, water more frequently; how often depends on the temperature of the room, but the soil or other rooting medium must never be permitted to dry completely.

A good idea is to sprinkle the container with *Agrostis tenuis* grass seed as soon as it is removed from the plunge bed or wherever the bulbs have been kept during the rooting period. By the time the bulbs come to flower, the surface of the rooting medium will be completely hidden by a green turf carpet.

Common Causes of Bulb Failure

1. Insufficient time in the plunge bed, causing stunted growth.

2. Placing the containers in a draft, which turns the leaves yellow.
3. Insufficient water at the roots, which may result in dead blooms on the flower spike, stunted flower stems shorter than the leaves, or dead foliage.
4. Insufficient light, inducing long, lanky and yellowing leaves.

Growing Bulbs on Water

A few bulbs, notably those of hyacinth, crocus, *Narcissus* Grand Soleil d'Or and *Narcissus* Paper-White, can be grown entirely in water. The bulbs themselves should barely touch the water with their bases or even be slightly above the water surface, so that their roots can go down for moisture. Water-grown bulbs need not be kept in darkness for any time, so their development can be watched daily.

There are two methods of water cultivation. The most usual is in bulb glasses, which can be bought in various sizes. A bulb glass has a restricted

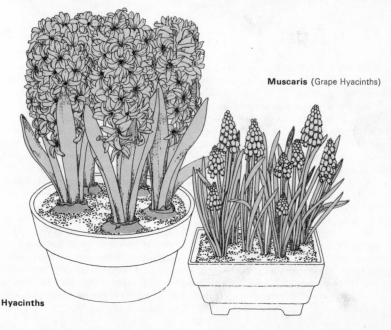

Muscaris (Grape Hyacinths)

Hyacinths

neck in which the bulb perches, sending its roots down to the water below. Always keep a lump of charcoal in the glass.

Rainwater gives much better results than tap water; even in an apartment, rainwater can be trapped in a suitable container placed on a window ledge. Keep the bulb glass filled, also with rainwater.

The other method is to pile washed pebbles in bowls or saucers with water in the bottom. The bulbs are lodged between the stones, which keep them from being too deep in the water.

BULBS FOR FORCING

CROCUSES

All crocuses can be forced.

HYACINTHS

Most of the large-flowered hyacinths force well. They are available in white, red, yellow, pink, blue and purple shades. Roman hyacinths bloom earlier, are smaller and daintier, and produce several spikes from a single bulb; the flowers are usually white, but there is a deep rose-pink variety called Rosalie. Most hyacinths should be planted in September or October.

MUSCARIS (GRAPE HYACINTHS)

All need cool conditions.

NARCISSUSES
(INCLUDING DAFFODILS AND JONQUILS)

For growing in pebbles and water the best are Cragford, Grand Soleil d'Or and Paper-White. All varieties may be forced in soil.

TULIPS

Most double tulips can be forced. Of the single varieties, choose for forcing those listed in bulb catalogues as "single early." Potted in September and October, they will flower in January and February.

Miniature Plant Gardens

A fascinating form of indoor gardening is to construct and cultivate tiny, complete gardens. They can be made in almost any low container of earthenware, porcelain or metal, except copper. Miniature or dish gardens give particular pleasure in winter and early spring, when flowers are scarce and more time is spent indoors.

If the chosen container has drainage holes, so much the better, but they are not essential. With or without them, cover its base with a 1-in. layer of crocks, small stones or pebbles; they drain moisture from the soil above and keep plant roots from standing in water. Next spread a thin layer of leaves, straw or sheet moss to prevent the finer soil from sifting through. Then add the soil—

equal parts of coarse sand, peat moss and topsoil—with some crushed charcoal and broken crocks or brick mixed in to insure porosity.

The miniature garden can be designed in almost as many different ways as an ordinary full-scale garden. If it is to be a miniature rock garden, pile the soil unevenly to give an informal effect, and introduce small pieces of natural stone here and there. If it is to be a formal garden, little paths and sunken beds are constructed around small lawns. Thin pieces of stone or slate are used for walls and pathways, and the lawns are sown with grass seed and kept trim with nail scissors. Some of the loveliest miniature gardens are made in Japanese style with small bridges,

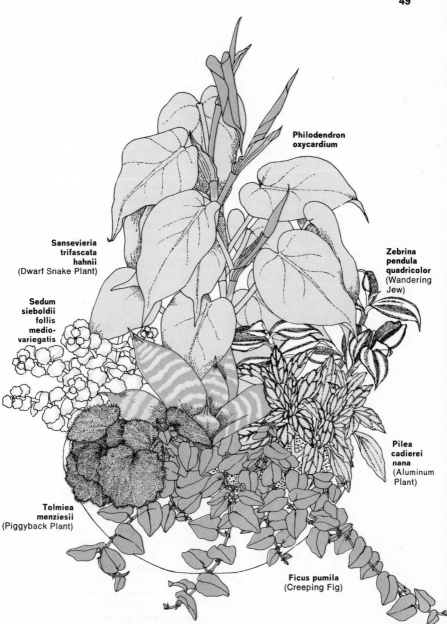

Philodendron
oxycardium

Sansevieria
trifascata
hahnii
(Dwarf Snake Plant)

Sedum
sieboldii
follis
medio-
variegatis

Zebrina
pendula
quadricolor
(Wandering
Jew)

Pilea
cadierei
nana
(Aluminum
Plant)

Tolmiea
menziesii
(Piggyback Plant)

Ficus pumila
(Creeping Fig)

A Plant Arrangement Suitable for a Cool Room

temples and similar ornaments, and sunken pools made from shallow glass containers.

Whichever style is chosen, the aim is to keep trees, plants and stones all in scale. If the miniature garden can be kept in a quite cool place, such as a sunroom where the night temperature is about 50° F., dwarf evergreen spruce (*Picea abies pumila* or *P. a. pygmaea*) form the trees that are to give height to the garden. A tiny conifer of the cypress family, *Chamaecyparis obtusa nana compacta*, makes a dome-shaped tree a few inches high and wide. Oak and beech seedlings, as well as those of other trees, can be planted in the miniature garden and will last for a few years before they grow too big. Another very suitable tree for the miniature garden is a dwarf juniper, *Juniperus communis compressa*.

Most small bulbs look well in miniature gardens. Try particularly *Narcissus asturiensis* (syn. *N. minimus*), snowdrop, dwarf cyclamen and crocus.

Miniature roses can also be included. The dwarf *Rosa roulettii* (also known as *R. chinensis minima*) forms are only a few inches tall, with red, pink, white or yellow flowers.

Other plants for the miniature garden are sedums, sempervivums, the dwarf *Iris cristata*, and *Tolmiea menziesii*, which has rough leaves. *Mentha requienii*, with a minty smell and blue flowers, is one of the smallest of flowering plants. The small thrift, *Armeria caespitosa*, is charming, and there are two delicate varieties of blue-eyed grass, *Sisyrinchium bermudiana* and *S. californicum*, both with small rushlike leaves—the first with blue flowers, the other yellow.

When planting miniature gardens that are to be kept in normal living-room temperatures (70° F. or slightly higher), the same principles of de-

sign, planting and care apply, but the plants used must be subtropical and tropical kinds instead of hardy species and varieties. Among useful kinds are: dwarf citrus, abutilon, podocarpus, *Euonymus japonica*, *Neanthe bella*, *Dracaena sanderiana* (dracena), *Malpighia coccigera*, *Helxine soleirolii* (baby's tears), small-leaved varieties of ivy, dwarf pomegranate, miniature bamboos, iresine, sedums, cryptanthus and the creeping fig, *Ficus pumila*.

BOTTLE GARDENS

A garden in a bottle has the same sort of fascination, and requires much the same kind of ingenuity and dexterity to construct, as a ship in a bottle. But once the bottle garden is established, it can be left for months without attention; it will not even need watering.

More than a hundred years ago, a London physician named Nathaniel Ward discovered that ferns and mosses, which never grew satisfactorily in the industrial dry air of the city, would flourish if grown in the protection of glass-sided cases. It is from Ward's experiments that bottle gardens have been developed.

Use any large bottle (a carboy, used especially for holding acids, is ideal), wash and dry it and, through a paper funnel, pour in several inches of dry, sandy soil mixed with a little crushed charcoal. Damp soil will not go through the neck of the bottle easily and will cling to its sides.

Only small plants should be introduced, for it is the planting that needs dexterity (see illustration, page 52). Even if this is not done very efficiently, however, the plants will, after watering, soon reroot in the humidity of the container. After planting, water is introduced by means of a tube or fine spray.

Once planting is finished, cork the

A Bottle Garden

Dracaena
sanderiana
(Dracena)

Aglaonema
commutatum

Zebrina pendula
(Wandering Jew)

Ficus
pumila
(Creeping
Fig)

Maranta
leuconeura
kerchoveana
(Prayer Plant)

Cryptanthus
bivittatus

Peperomia tithymaloides

Useful tools for bottle gardening: a paper
funnel so that the soil can be introduced
easily, and a spoon and fork lashed
to bamboo canes to move the soil

bottle tightly. The idea is to establish a completely closed atmosphere
which is virtually self-watering; moisture passed off from the leaves con-
denses on the glass sides of the bottle
and returns to the roots. For this
reason a bottle garden needs watering
very rarely—once a year is probably
sufficient.

Stand the bottle in a good light
but not in direct sun.

Bottle-Garden Plants

Specimens for the bottle garden are
those that naturally like close, moist
conditions, such as:

Aglaonema commutatum, dark green
leaves with silver-gray spots.

Begonia foliosa, a shrubby plant
with small, glossy dark green leaves.

Billbergia nutans, stiff, grayish
leaves, very showy pink bracts, and
purple and green flowers.

Cryptanthus bivittatis minor, pink
leaves with cream stripes, which
turn light and dark green in shade.

Dracaena godseffiana, dark green
leaves thickly spotted with cream.

D. sanderiana, grayish-green leaves
with ivory-cream margins.

Ficus pumila (creeping fig), dark
green heart-shaped leaves.

Fittonia verschaffeltii, a trailing
dwarf with dark green leaves netted
with carmine.

Maranta leuconeura kerchoveana
(prayer plant), medium green leaves
with blotches of maroon-red.

Peperomia obtusifolia, dark green
fleshy leaves with a purple edge.

P. rotundifolia, round, stalked
leaves and creeping, threadlike stems.

P. tithymaloides, medium green
leaves with an irregular cream margin.

Pilea microphylla (artillery plant),
minute blue-green leaves.

Saintpaulia ionantha (African violet). Varieties have flowers ranging in
color from white to deep violet.

Tradescantia fluminensis (wandering Jew), perennial trailer, shiny
leaves and stems, and small white
flowers.

Zebrina pendula (wandering Jew),
silvery gray-green leaves with a dark
green margin and a purple stripe
down the center.

The following ferns are also suitable for the bottle garden:

Adiantum cuneatum (Delta maidenhair fern), delicate, light green fronds.

Asplenium nidus (bird's-nest fern),
a shiny dark green strap-shaped fern.

Davallia bullata (ball fern), broad,
leathery dark green leaves.

Pteris cretica, straw-colored or pale brown fronds. Small varieties of this species are suitable.

PLANTS FROM FRUIT SEEDS

Charming small plants can be grown from fruit seeds. Seeds of dates, avocado pears and the citrus fruits are the ones to choose. Plant them in a rather sandy soil, and keep them if possible at a temperature of 65° to 70° F.

An avocado seed will germinate more quickly if it is soaked in water for 48 hours before it is planted— large end down, tip above the surface.

GROWING PINEAPPLE TOPS

A pineapple plant is interesting to grow. Cut off the leafy top of a pineapple with a thin segment of the upper rind, and leave it for a day or so to dry. Then pot it carefully in very sandy soil and put it in a warm place to root. A terrarium is suitable, or the newly potted top may be placed in a box, with an inch or two of moist peat moss in its bottom and its top covered with a sheet of glass or polyethylene plastic film to conserve humidity. Another method is to enclose the potted pineapple top in a polyethylene bag. Requisite conditions for rooting are warmth, humidity and good light but no direct sun. Not every top "takes," but if one does, put it in fairly rich soil and keep it in a warm, light place out of direct sun. Do not overwater. A pineapple plant grown in this way in the house is unlikely to fruit, but in a warm greenhouse it may do so.

DISH GARDENS

House plants that may not be in themselves particularly striking gain greatly in effect if they are combined in mixed plant gardens in large bowls or dishes. Any attractive deep-dish pottery or metal containers except copper will do. Many house plants do better in such a community than individually in pots.

Fill the container with porous soil to which crushed charcoal has been added, and arrange the plants on the surface to get some idea of composition before turning them out of their pots. The plants themselves should be chosen for contrasting shapes and textures, as well as colors. It is important, of course, to use in any one container only kinds that need approximately the same growing conditions. The container should have drainage holes, but often surprisingly good results can be obtained in undrained dishes. When there are no drainage holes, special care with watering must be given so that the roots of the plants are not immersed for long periods in standing water. It may be possible after watering to tilt the dish and its contents carefully so that surplus water drains away without disturbing the soil or plants.

Set the plants firmly, interspersing a few small pieces of rock if desired; then cover the surface of the soil with coarse sand or granite chippings. Take great care not to overwater, especially during the winter months; dish gardens that are kept in warm rooms will, of course, need more water than those kept in cooler places.

Indoor Garden Planters

Modern houses make possible and often necessary a new kind of indoor gardening—the use of indoor garden planters. These troughs, boxes and beds serve as integral architectural and furnishing units and challenge artistic abilities and horticultural skills. When well planned and well managed, they add immensely to the appearance and livability of a home.

The need for the bold effects and patterns that living plants can create results largely from the architectural simplicity and sometimes severity of modern interiors. Expanses of plain wall, picture windows and extensive surfaces of glass brick invite the use of vegetation as contrast and relief. Ample light from generous window space, up-to-date heating and humidifying systems, absence of coal-burning furnaces and the possibilities of fluorescent light combine to afford favorable growing conditions for a wide variety of plants.

Modern homes afford places for planters against various backgrounds and in many different settings. Glassed-in and skylighted areas are especially favorable. The base of a picture window is an ideal place for a planter. If the window extends to the bottom of the wall, a built-in bed, level with or only slightly higher than the floor, is ideal. Such a bed may connect directly with the soil beneath the house. A complementary planter on the outside of the window makes it possible to relate plants growing outside with those inside and achieve a most convincing transition from indoors to outdoors. Planters are effective as room dividers, as screens and as features that supply interesting patterns of stems and foliage. They do much to bring indoors a feeling of the outdoors.

Planters can be of any dimensions and shapes appropriate to their locations. Some enthusiasts have floor-level bed-type planters large enough to include a fountain and perhaps a path to make servicing them easier. These are truly indoor gardens! But most planters are less elaborate. They may be built-in or portable, at floor

level or raised. They may be of wood, masonry or other appropriate material. Their interior depth should be from 8 to 12 in., or more in exceptional circumstances—as, for instance, a built-in ground bed that is to contain large "trees." Whatever the material of which the planter is constructed, it should have holes in its bottom to assure adequate drainage and its inside should be covered with two or three coats of asphalt paint. If desired, a liner box—also with drainage holes—of zinc, aluminum or galvanized steel, but not copper, can be used.

Before setting the plants, an inch or more of coarse gravel or cinders is placed in the bottom of the planter to encourage drainage. The plants may then, without being removed from their pots, be arranged—raised if necessary on blocks of wood so that the rims of the pots are not more than an inch below the surface after peat moss or vermiculite has been poured in between the pots. Or the planter may be filled with porous soil and the plants set in it after they are removed from their pots. The first method makes it easier to replace a plant that is failing and to rearrange the plants to provide change; moreover, somewhat better control of watering is achieved if plants with different needs are used in the same planter. All in all, this is the best method of handling garden planters.

Arranging the plants gives opportunity for artistic expression. So far as is possible, in any one planter use plants having the same general requirements. Do not, for example, mix cactuses and African violets, or moisture- and shade-loving ferns with a plant that prefers dry soil and sun, like the crown of thorns.

Plants of varying sizes, some almost ceiling-high, others low ground covers, may be used in the same arrangement. Trailing plants are especially useful for draping the sides of raised planters. Vines—trained to trellises, bamboo stakes or wires—are excellent. For dramatic effect choose large-leaved plants such as dieffenbachias and rubber plants. The modern *Ficus elastica decora*, with broad leaves, is more handsome than the oldtime *F. elastica*.

Care of the plants does not differ materially from that for pot-grown specimens, though less frequent watering will be necessary. Prompt measures must be taken to eliminate any harmful insects that infest the plants. The foliage should be kept clean by sponging it with sudsy water occasionally. Occasional fertilizing and, in some cases pruning, will be needed. Almost any house plants that are reasonably permanent can be used in indoor garden planters.

CHAPTER 3

CACTUSES AND SUCCULENTS—
Camels of the Plant World

How They Store Water—Seasonal Rest —Gardens Indoors and Out—Potting, Soil, Propagation—Pests, Diseases— Descriptive List

PLANTS with green leaves that are left in the sun without water ordinarily wilt in a few hours and die within a few days. Plants that live in hot, dry climates, however, manage to survive. They are able to adapt to their environment, often by passing the dry seasons as leafless shrubs, as dry bulbs or as seeds. Certain other plants continue to live because of their ability to store moisture in the tissues of their stems or leaves or both, during the rainy periods, and in drier periods to lose moisture by transpiration much more slowly than do most other plants. Such plants are called succulents. This term properly includes cactuses (members of the botanical family *Cactaceae*), as well as representatives of several other quite different botanical families.

Succulent plants are not found in very dry areas but in semideserts, where there are long dry periods alternating with shorter wet ones. When rain falls, the plant tissues tend to swell and the moisture is retained in the plant if it has been adapted to prevent evaporation—either by a protective covering such as a layer of wax or hairs, or by a reduction of the surface area. Since the smallest surface area for a given volume is a sphere, succulent plants tend to be spherical.

Many of the cactuses are of this form, at least when young. The stem is swollen but there are no leaves—or only a few small ones which soon fall—when growth begins each year. In an ordinary plant the leaves contain a green substance (chlorophyll) by means of which, in the presence of light, the plant can make use of the various nutrient materials taken in by its roots, as well as carbon dioxide absorbed from the air. When leaves are absent, their functions must be taken over by the stem. Stem succulents are, therefore, usually green, though in age the base portion may become corklike.

In many plants, water is stored in the leaves, which in extreme cases may become spherical. However, as in the case of *Conophytum*, a pair of leaves may be joined so closely into a top-shaped body that only a slit across the top of the body indicates its dual origin.

In leaf succulents, the stem is often much reduced, so that the leaves are crowded together to form a rosette. An advantage of this formation is that the overlapping leaves prevent each other, and also the soil below, from drying out too rapidly.

Apart from the plants in which water storage is definitely in stem or leaf, there are a number of kinds where both stem and leaf are slightly succulent. Many of these show surface adaptations which make them very decorative and well worth growing.

Succulent plants are sometimes found where there is a physiological drought, although not a real one. For instance, plants of succulent character that often occur in salt marshes cannot absorb the amounts of water needed were they not succulent, because of the salt contained in the water. Much the same thing occurs in cold regions where the low temperature prevents the absorption of water; the houseleek (*Sempervivum*) grows in these conditions.

The true desert cactuses are not difficult to recognize; they are almost all stem succulents, without leaves, and generally with spines which arise from special organs known as "areoles." These are small protuberances arranged regularly on the surface of

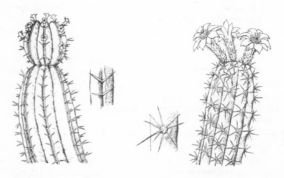

Nondesert succulent (Euphorbia), showing spines in pairs, not originating from areoles

True desert cactus (Cereus), showing spines in groups originating from cushionlike areoles

the plant, generally bearing wool or hairs as well as a number of spines. The spines in the center of an areole may differ from the radial ones and are characteristic of the plant, so that a cactus can often be identified by the spines.

The only plants with which cactuses are likely to be confused are some of the euphorbias (spurges), which may also have round or columnar stems without leaves. When spines are present on euphorbias they do not arise from an areole but appear in pairs or singly at regular positions up the ribs of the stem.

Another type of cactus from tropical forests—known as epiphytic cactuses because they grow on trees—have thinner, more slender stems which, in some species, are flattened. Even in these plants, though the spines are not well developed, they come from small areoles, often in the crenations (scallops) along the edge of the stems. This type is sometimes called "leaf cactus," but this name is misleading, for—despite appearance—the plants consist of leafless stems.

Two genera of cactuses, *Pereskia* and *Pereskiopsis*, do bear and retain normal leaves throughout their growing season. These kinds are often used as understocks upon which to graft Christmas cactus (*Zygocactus truncatus*) and Easter cactus (*Schlumbergera gaertneri*).

OUTDOOR CULTIVATION

In southwestern North America and other regions where warm, dry weather prevails through most of the year and where winters are not excessively cold, a great variety of cactuses and other succulents grow outdoors with great ease. In more humid warm climates, such as the southeastern United States, fewer kinds are likely to succeed. However, a goodly number of the more robust types—agaves, kalanchoes, euphorbias, aloes and so forth—will prosper, provided the soil is very porous and sharply drained and they receive plenty of sun.

Even in the cold northernmost tier of states of the United States and in adjacent Canada, a few hardy kinds of cactuses may be grown outdoors as well as many sedums and sempervivums. These last-named are truly succulents, but their hardy kinds are usually described—as they are in this book—under rock-garden plants. Once again, exposure to full sun and very well-drained soil are the two requisites for successfully growing these hardiest of succulents.

INDOOR CULTIVATION

Cactuses and other succulents are not difficult to grow indoors, in greenhouses or in window gardens. It must be remembered that they need an alternation of wet and dry periods, such as they would get in their native habitats, and they prefer this at the correct time of year, depending on their country of origin. True desert cactuses should be rested from October to March and during this period given little or no water; many of them will stand (and some even prefer) a cool temperature when resting. All but the very hardiest should be protected from freezing.

Plants with very succulent leaves and much reduced stems need a definite resting period of some weeks or months, but this will not necessarily be in winter. Many succulents from South Africa (where the seasons are the reverse of ours) grow during our winter and rest in our summer.

Semisucculents—plants with both stem and leaf slightly succulent—do not need such a definite period of rest but do require less water after flowering.

Even though cactuses are accom-

58

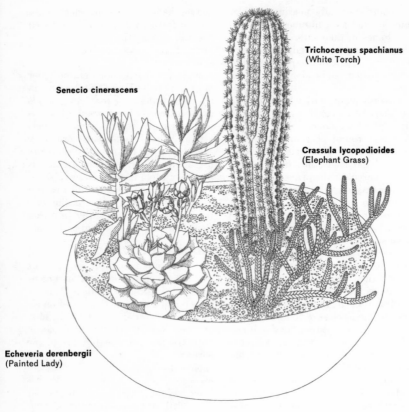

Trichocereus spachianus
(White Torch)

Senecio cinerascens

Crassula lycopodioides
(Elephant Grass)

Echeveria derenbergii
(Painted Lady)

Dish Garden
(For descriptions of these plants see pages 66, 67 and 76.)

modating plants, they need plenty of light. If they are being grown in the house, keep them as near to a window as possible; but give them some ventilation if they are in hot sun, to avoid damage being done to them by burning. Place individual pots in a saucer, or in an ornamental pot containing some gravel, so that the pot does not remain standing in any excess water that runs through. Turn the pots occasionally; otherwise the plants may be drawn toward the light and their shape spoiled.

Potted cactuses benefit from being out of doors in the summer if there is no long wet spell.

Dish Gardens

Surprisingly—although succulents need minimal supplies of water and, when grown as potted specimens, are normally given porous soil and excellent drainage so that excess moisture does not accumulate around the roots—many kinds succeed and live for months or years in undrained dish gardens in relatively heavy soil. The reason seems to be that the amount of soil, compared to the number of plants crowded into it, is small. Because of this it does not lie wet for long. It is good practice to water dish gardens of succulents thoroughly but only when the soil is dry, and immediately after watering to tip the garden carefully so that surplus water drains out of the dish.

POTTING
Pots

Succulent plants are generally grown in pots—either the usual red porous clay type or plastic. In many ways, the plastic pot gives better results provided it is realized that very much less water is required, since there is no evaporation through the sides. In either case there should be a drainage hole at the base. Cover this hole with broken crocks to prevent the soil from washing through.

The pot should be large enough to give the plant sufficient space. However, it should not be too large, or the soil will remain too wet and become unsuitable for plant growth if not penetrated by roots in a few weeks after repotting is done.

Potting Soil

Plants that live in a desert are not necessarily growing in very poor soil; it may be sandy and loose but, since there is not much rain to wash out the nutrients, it is likely to be fairly rich in mineral salts. There is no humus, however, since few shrubs grow whose fallen leaves could enrich the soil. For this reason do not add leaf mold, peat moss or other bulk organic matter to potting soil for desert cactuses. They like an open soil through which water drains rapidly, and this is best made up of good loam mixed with coarse sand or gritty coal cinders.

Most succulent plants do very well in a soil similar to that recommended for desert cactuses but with some organic matter added. Some kinds,

such as kalanchoes and echeverias, benefit from the addition of moderate amounts of dried cow manure.

Repotting

Newly purchased plants will not ordinarily need repotting for some time, but if the soil does not dry out in a few days after watering, turn the plant out and make sure that the roots are sound. They should look clean and "plump"; if they are shriveled they are not healthy roots. Disentangle the roots carefully, remove any damaged portions and repot in fresh soil.

Repot young plants annually, or as soon as their roots have filled the pot, moving them into a larger pot. Do not repot adult plants every year unless it appears necessary, for the root tips, through which the plant absorbs nourishment from the soil, are sure to be damaged during the process and the plant will receive a setback in consequence. Large plants seldom need repotting; it is sufficient to remove the top layer of soil carefully and replace it with fresh soil.

WATERING

This is an important operation and one which often presents difficulties to beginners. It is essential to remember that succulent plants naturally experience alternate wet and dry periods and these should be maintained in cultivation. For very highly adapted plants whose stems and leaves are much thickened, the time of year and the duration of the wet period are important. It must always coincide with the growing period.

Plants grown in a greenhouse, where heat is available in cold weather, can be given what they want when they want it. But for plants grown in the living room, where the temperature and ventilation are arranged to suit the human occupants, a compromise must be effected. Plants such as the desert cactuses, which need resting in winter, are better in cooler conditions; so move them, if possible, to a cool room for the rest period; if they are kept in the living room, occasional watering may be necessary to prevent the stems from shrinking.

The best way to learn how to water is by studying the plant itself. Most plants will start into growth whether they are watered or not; so as soon as new growth is seen, begin to water more frequently. Once they are growing freely, resume normal watering. A good supply once a week is better than frequent driblets, but never give water when the soil is wet. If a plant such as a desert cactus has been kept quite dry for some time, stand the pot in water until the whole ball of soil becomes evenly moist.

Water semisucculents from semi-desert regions throughout the year, but allow longer periods between applications when they are not growing actively, usually after flowering.

PROPAGATION

Seed

Most succulent plants are easily raised from seed, and if the seed is obtained from a reliable source the plants should be true to type.

Sow seeds of most succulents in late winter or spring; seeds of succulents that are natives of South Africa usually produce the best results when sown in August or September. Distribute the seeds evenly over the surface of the soil; if they are larger than pinheads, cover them with a light sifting of fine soil.

As small seedlings are difficult to handle, leave them in the seed pan—provided they are not overcrowded—until the growing period of the following year. Do not allow them to get dry, or growth will be retarded.

If there are a number of seedlings, transplant them together into one pan rather than individually into separate pots. This will make it easier to keep them moist, but when the seedlings are definitely progressing, make the second transplanting into individual pots. Or, if grouping is planned, set several in one pot.

Cuttings

Another method of propagation is by cuttings. Where side branches can be removed without spoiling the parent plant, they can be rooted separately. Break them off at a joint or cut neatly with a sharp knife. If the flesh is moist, leave the cut surfaces to dry for a day or two before putting the cuttings into the rooting medium. The best rooting material is coarse sand or a mixture of peat moss and sand.

If a fair-sized flat or seed pan is filled with this mixture, a number of cuttings of different types can be put in. Label all cuttings with the names of the kinds and with the dates they are planted.

It is not necessary to cover the container with glass, as is usual with soft-leaved plants. Succulents do not wilt easily and there is less danger of rot if there is plenty of air around them. Allow the rooting medium to dry out almost completely between waterings; it must not be constantly wet.

Leaf Cuttings

A number of succulent plants, such as *Echeveria*, *Sedum*, *Crassula* and *Haworthia*, can be propagated from single leaves. Carefully pull the leaves from the stem—do not cut them off. Lay them on the sand and peat-moss mixture so that the base of the leaf is just covered; in time a young plant will develop. Do not detach the old leaf until it has dried up, even if the new plantlet is sufficiently rooted to be potted separately.

Offsets

Some succulents make offsets around the base of the plant, forming a fine clump—the natural way for such a plant to grow. Some of these offsets can be detached to make extra plants; if, as will often be found, they have already made some roots, pot them right away; if there are no roots, treat them as cuttings.

PESTS AND DISEASES

Pests

Succulent plants do not suffer greatly from pests, but if any insects are found, remove them at once with tweezers or a paintbrush.

The commonest pest is the mealybug, a small whitish insect covered with waxy white filaments. It lays eggs in cocoons that look like cotton. Since mealybugs are covered with wax, most insecticides do not kill them; a solution that dissolves wax would do so, but the plant might also be damaged. The best remedy is to remove the bugs with a brush.

An easily recognized insect, the root mealybug, is sometimes found as white threads and nodules among the roots when repotting; brush the roots under running water until all traces of the bugs are removed and then re-pot in fresh soil and a clean pot.

Scale insects may infest some succulents. Remove them immediately, for they are sucking insects and may damage the surface of the plant. This pest is also difficult to kill with an insecticide but is easy to remove with a small blunt instrument.

Red spider mites are not common but can do considerable damage where they occur, especially as the creature is so small that it is rarely noticed until the stem is badly damaged. It usually occurs on plants that have been kept in a very dry atmosphere or have been grown too "soft," either by being kept in an overwarm room or by overwatering. Spraying with water or dusting with rotenone powder will destroy the pest.

Diseases

Diseases are not common among well-grown succulents, but damage caused by accident may set up rot in the tissues. Scrape the damaged part away, treat the surface with dusting sulphur and the wound will generally heal. Where the base of a plant has become rotten through excess water in the soil, it may be found that the roots have also suffered, in which case cut off the top of the plant above the rotten portion, treat with sulphur and reroot as a cutting.

TYPES OF SUCCULENTS

Succulents are classed together because they resemble each other in their adaptation to dry conditions, but they do not all belong to the same plant family. There are 24 families in which some degree of succulence is found but only three—*Cactaceae*, *Crassulaceae* and *Mesembryanthemaceae*—in which all the plants are succulent. A large number of succulents are now grown, and if the generic or first part of the Latin name of a plant is known, some idea of the type of plant can be obtained.

It is impossible to indicate the exact flowering time for most succulents; it will vary according to the treatment given, the weather and especially the amount of light the plant gets. All the species in a genus may not flower at the same time, notably when they come from different geographical regions. This is particularly the case with *Crassula;* there is no time in the year when none of the species is flowering. With succulents it is the plant itself that is of chief importance; if flowers come, they are a welcome addition, but many succulents do not flower regularly and some never reach flowering size when they are grown in pots or other containers.

Similarly, it is impossible to predict the height of many succulents. In cultivation, one can find good representatives of the same plant which vary widely in size according to age and cultural conditions; and to give the height that plants attain when growing in their natural surroundings would be misleading.

ADROMISCHUS
These small South African plants with thick leaves and short woody stems were at one time included in *Cotyledon* but can be distinguished from that genus by their small flowers in slender spikes.

Adromischus cooperi, larger leaves than *A. cristatus*, narrowed toward the base, gray-green with darker markings.

A. cristatus, thick, green, hairy leaves on thin stalks, the wide top edge thinner and wavy; stems short, stout and covered with dry brown aerial roots.

A. leucophyllus, short woody stems bearing thin-edged round or oval leaves covered with a white waxy coating.

AEONIUM
Related to *Sempervivum* but forming shrubs with woody stems, these plants are not hardy in cold climates since they come from the Canary Isles.

Aeonium arboreum, compact rosettes of green leaves on branched stems.

A.a. foliis purpureus, similar to *A. arboreum* but has dark purple leaves.

A. domesticum (syn. *Aichryson domesticum*), shrublet with much-branched stem and small rosettes of roundish, hairy leaves toward the tips; small yellow flowers.

A. tabulaeforme, almost stemless, with numerous leaves symmetrically arranged in flat rosettes up to 10 in. across; a pyramidal inflorescence rises from the center, after which the rosette dies. Can be raised from seed to flower in two or three years.

AGAVE
These natives of the Americas have thick leaves, usually tapering, sometimes with spiny edges; the leaves are in rosettes, frequently on short stems. When fully grown most agaves are extremely large plants, but small specimens are very attractive and grow slowly. They are members of the amaryllis family.

Agave americana (century plant), spreading, grayish-green leaves. Several varieties have yellow, white or pinkish longitudinal stripes along leaves. The century plant got its popular name from the fact that some varieties bloom very rarely indeed, though probably all flower oftener than once in a century.

A. victoriae-reginae, a small kind with very stiff dark green leaves edged with light gray.

AICHRYSON. See *Aeonium domesticum*.

AIR PLANT. See *Kalanchoe pinnata*.

ALOE
Natives of Africa, these plants vary in size, some having stems, others none; some species, where the stem increases in height, become trees in their native habitats. In the tree form, aloes are known for their beautifully grained wood. Varieties of aloe yield incense, several kinds of medicine, rope, cord and a delicate pigment. A Mohammedan returning from the sacred pilgrimage to Mecca places an aloe over his doorway.

The leaves are thick and tapering, sometimes with spiny edges, and are in rosettes; flowers are usually orange or red. Winter growers, the aloes

63

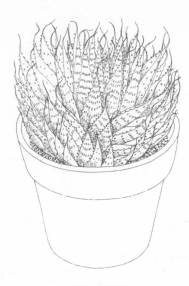

Aloe aristata

APOROCACTUS
One of the cactuses that grow on trees, the plant has long, slender stems that are ribbed and covered with fine spines.

Aporocactus flagelliformis (rattail cactus), usually grown as a hanging plant; slender carmine flowers borne toward the base of the stems.

APRICA. See *Astroloba*.

ASTROLOBA
Formerly called *Aprica*, this genus is closely related to *Haworthia*, the chief difference being in the form of the flower. The leaves are arranged symmetrically up the stem, which may become 6 to 10 in. long.

Astroloba pentagona, five rows of leaves, wide at the base, green, thick,

need less water in summer. Repot sometime in September.

Aloe arborescens. Even young plants develop a stem; slender leaves have stout spines along edges.

A. aristata, one of the smaller species. The stem never lengthens but branches at ground level forming clumps. Numerous small, incurved leaves, dark green with white edges and spines on back and edge. Sometimes mistaken for a haworthia until it produces its annual spike of typical red aloe flowers.

A. saponaria, also short-stemmed and forms offsets, but leaves are fewer and much larger, pale green with white oblong spots arranged in bands.

A. variegata (partridge-breasted aloe), quite distinct, as the leaves stand more or less erect, arranged in three rows, keel-shaped on the outside, dark green with white teeth along edge, and transverse rows of white spots in irregular bands. Red flowers on loose spike about 1 ft. high.

Astroloba pentagona

Aloe variegata

Astrophytum myriostigma
(Bishop's-Cap)

firm and terminating in a sharp tip.

A. spiralis, similar; its five rows of leaves are spiraled and blue-gray in color.

ASTROPHYTUM (STAR CACTUS)
This cactus is low-growing and globular in shape, but may become cylindrical with age. There are usually five to eight ribs only; the areoles are close-set along the ribs and the whole surface is covered with tiny white flakes. The large yellow flowers are borne in the center of the plant.

Astrophytum capricorne has eight ribs, and woolly areoles bearing a number of twisted spines.

A. myriostigma (bishop's-cap), usually four or five ribs but no spines.

BARREL CACTUS. See *Echinocactus grusonii.*

BISHOP'S-CAP. See *Astrophytum myriostigma.*

BRYOPHYLLUM. See *Kalanchoe.*

BURRO'S TAIL. See *Sedum morganianum.*

CANDLE PLANT. See *Senecio articulata.*

CARALLUMA
Related to the stapelias, these plants have stout, four- to six-angled leafless stems and small star-shaped flowers.

Caralluma europaea, the commonest species; with four-angled stems and clusters of small, pale yellow flowers banded with purple.

CARRION FLOWER. See *Stapelia.*

CENTURY PLANT. See *Agave americana.*

CEPHALOCEREUS
A large genus of columnar cactuses normally reaching a considerable height; the ribbed stems are generally hairy.

Cephalocereus senilis (old-man cactus) is best known. Has a green ribbed body wrapped in long white hairs. Decorative even when small.

CEREUS
This name was formerly used to include most columnar cactuses but is now reserved for a few species only, which bear large, funnel-shaped flowers that open at night.

Cereus aethiops and *C. azureus* have a blue waxy coating on young stems; must be about 1 ft. tall before their white flowers are produced.

CEROPEGIA
These are mostly climbing or trailing plants with the exception of two from the Canary Isles: *Ceropegia dichotoma* and *C. fusca.*

C. dichotoma, stout, erect stems, leafless for most of the year; curiously shaped yellow flowers.

C. fusca, similar to *C. dichotoma*, but with chocolate-colored flowers.

C. woodii (string of hearts), a trailing plant with thin stems rising from a corm, and bearing small heart-shaped leaves, dark green with silvery markings and purple undersides.

CHAMAECEREUS

Chamaecereus silvestri (peanut cactus) is a small-growing cereus with prostrate stems, which are brittle and break off easily but can be rerooted. Comparatively large, the plant has erect orange or scarlet flowers.

CHOLLA. See *Opuntia.*

CHRISTMAS CACTUS. See *Zygocactus truncatus.*

CLEISTOCACTUS

This is one of the columnar cereuses with thin, branching stems, the spiny areoles being close together. The flowers are small and do not open wide.

Cleistocactus straussii, stems slender and erect, entirely covered with white spines, flowers carmine.

CONOPHYTUM (CONE PLANT)

These resemble mesembryanthemums, each pair of leaves being so closely joined that a small top-shaped body with a slit across the upper surface is formed; the surface may be flat, curved or lobed. The flowers emerge through the slit, after which the plant divides. Keep the plants completely dry or almost so from December until June, by which time the outer pair of leaves should have dried up to a papery skin which splits when growth begins. This is a large genus of some 200 species.

Conophytum calculus, round green head, without markings, and yellow flowers.

C. frutescens, one of the lobed-top type, and the earliest to bloom. The orange flowers sometimes appear

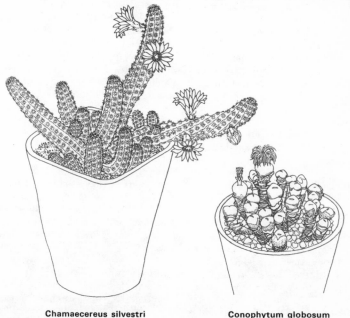

Chamaecereus silvestri
(Peanut Cactus)

Conophytum globosum
(Cone Plant)

66

before regular watering begins again.

C. globosum, similar in color to *C. calculus* but larger and kidney-shaped, with mauve flowers.

CORYPHANTHA

The round or cylindrical plants are a few inches across and grow solitary or in clumps. At one time included in *Mammillaria,* these cactuses are distinguished by the groove on the upper side of each tubercle, or protuberance; one or more of the spines is hooked.

Coryphantha elephantidens, spherical, with large tubercles and white wool on top.

C. vivipara, smaller than *C. elephantidens,* with more cylindrical tubercles; it rapidly makes clumps.

COTYLEDON

Woody shrubs from South Africa with slightly succulent leaves, they are usually attractively colored.

Cotyledon orbiculata, roundish, gray-green leaves with red edges.

C. undulata, leaves rather thicker than *C. orbiculata,* with a wavy edge and covered with white meal. Does not produce its orange or reddish, bell-shaped, hanging flowers until it is a fair size.

CRASSULA

This genus includes a wide variety of types found in South Africa and South West Africa.

Crassula arborescens, a large shrub resembling a cotyledon.

C. argentea (jade plant), a large green shrub, famous as a house plant.

C. cooperi forms mats of small rosettes of prettily marked leaves.

C. falcata, a tall plant with narrow grayish leaves, turned on edge. A wide head of bright red flowers in summer terminates the stem, which later branches.

C. lycopodioides (elephant grass), branching stems covered with over-

Crassula argentea
(Jade Plant)

lapping tiny dark green pointed leaves. (See illustration, page 58.)

C. sarcocaulis, small shrub with tiny blue-green leaves and bunches of pink flowers on ends of branches.

C. schmidtii, low, branching stems with rosettes of leaves, the centers of which elongate into inflorescences bearing small red flowers.

CROWN OF THORNS. See *Euphorbia splendens.*

DOLICHOTHELE

Formerly included in *Mammillaria,* these cactuses have longer tubercles of softer texture than that genus.

Dolichothele longimamma, blue-green (glaucous) protuberances, or tubercles, up to 2 in. long. Produces large yellow flowers freely.

DROSANTHEMUM

This plant is one of the mesembryanthemums (see page 73) characterized by the glistening, nipple-like papillae on the leaves.

Drosanthemum floribundum forms cushions of prostrate stems. Flowers very freely, often in first year, from seed.

EASTER CACTUS. See *Schlumbergera gaertneri.*

ECHEVERIA
In this popular genus the leaves are in rosettes, either stemless or on branching stems. As a rule they have a coating of wax or hairs on the surface, which makes them very decorative; the flowers are red or orange, in loose, few-flowered sprays.

Echeveria derenbergii (painted lady), glaucous blue leaves in rosettes a few inches across with red edges, and bright orange flowers. (See illustration, page 58.)

E. gibbiflora, a much larger plant than *E. derenbergii*, with rosettes carried on branching stems.

E.g. carunculata, similar to type but center of leaf puckered.

E.g. metallica, similar to type but has dark reddish-purple leaves.

E. glauca (sometimes regarded as variety of *E. secunda*), well-known species with compact rosettes about 4 in. across, rounded leaves with short tips, blue-gray with reddish margins.

E. harmsii (once known as *Oliveranthus elegans*), a small, erect shrub with hairy leaves in loose rosettes. Bright red flowers about 1 in. long, one to three together on short stems.

E. leucotricha, hairy leaves, mostly silvery but brown on edges.

E. pulvinata, low, branching stems, rosettes of green hairy leaves with crimson edges, large orange flowers.

ECHINOCACTUS
Echinocactus grusonii (barrel cactus) is the best known of this genus. The stem, at first spherical, becomes cylindrical with age, with many ribs and golden spines. Large specimens are sometimes seen, but even small ones are very attractive.

ECHINOCEREUS
This cactus somewhat resembles the columnar cereuses, but though some species may become cylindrical in time, they never form columns. The flowers are usually large and showy.

Echinocereus delaetii, ribbed, cylindrical stem entirely covered with white hairs; it resembles young specimens of *Cephalocereus senilis.*

E. rigidissimus (rainbow cactus), short, stiff spines flattened against the stem, alternate zones being white and red—hence the common name.

ECHINOPSIS
These spherical cactuses have straight ribs, sometimes divided into tubercles; offsets are produced freely. The flowers are very large with long tubes, white or pink. There has been much hybridization, and it is doubtful if many of the plants now in cultivation are true species.

E. eyriesii, a round plant with flowers up to 10 in. long, white with green throat.

E. multiplex, a globular plant with pink flowers.

E. oxygona, similar to *E. multiplex.*

EPIPHYLLUM (CEREUS)
Formerly known as *Phyllocactus*, these are epiphytic, not desert, cactuses. The stems are flattened, often wavy or notched along the edge, with very small spines (if any) in the notches. The flowers are large and showy; many of the plants in cultivation are hybrids, often with other genera. (See illustration, page 68.)

EUPHORBIA
This large genus is worldwide in its distribution, but only a few of the species are succulent. Some from South Africa are often mistaken for

Epiphyllum Hybrid

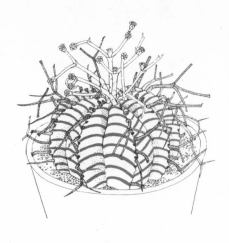

Euphorbia meloformis
(Melon Spurge)

cactuses because of their columnar, spiny stems, but they belong to a quite distinct plant family, as can be seen by their flowers, which are quite small and insignificant. A milky juice or latex exudes if the skin is broken, and in certain cases this is poisonous.

Euphorbia caput-medusae (Medusa's head). Cylindrical, spineless branches rise from a large, spectacular central head, a new ring of branches being formed annually.

E. grandicornis, angular stems, and spines in pairs along the angles.

E. heptagona, ribbed columnar stems with solitary spines along angles.

E. horrida, similar to *E. heptagona*, but much stouter.

E. meloformis (melon spurge) has a low stem, depressed in the center, with about eight wide ribs. The male and female flowers grow on different plants, and the so-called spines are the remains of branching flower stalks that have become woody.

E. obesa, round when young, becoming cylindrical; ribs more prominent at the top, and its gray surface is covered with dull purple transverse lines.

E. pseudocactus, similar to *E. grandicornis*.

E. splendens (crown of thorns) has branching stems with irregularly scattered spines; bright green oval leaves near tips of branches during growing period. Flowers are small, but they are surrounded by two conspicuous bright red bracts.

E. submammillaris, similar to *E. heptagona* but smaller and freely branching.

E. tirucallii (milkbush), erect stems, leafless and spineless.

E. virosa, similar to *E. grandicornis*.

FAUCARIA

These low-growing mesembryanthemums have two or three pairs of thick leaves at right angles to each other; they are keeled (shaped like a keel, or with center ridge) at the back, with a fringe of teeth along each edge.

F. tigrina (tiger jaw), large, stemless, bright yellow flowers, and leaves 1½ to 2 in. long.

F. tuberculosa, similar to *F. tigrina* but the leaves are not so long; short, stout teeth occur on the back as well as on the edges of the leaves.

Faucaria tigrina
(Tiger Jaw)

Gasteria verrucosa

FENESTRARIA
Mesembryanthemums of this type are known as "window plants" because of the translucent upper surface of the erect, cylindrical leaves, which are held in rosettes.

F. aurantiaca has large yellow flowers.

F. rhopalophylla has large white flowers.

FEROCACTUS
These large spherical cactuses do not make offsets. The ribs are well developed and the spines are stout, sometimes flattened, and usually curved or hooked.

F. rectispinus, unusually long spines, up to 5 in.

F. wislizenii, very stout, with flattened central spines.

GASTERIA
Related to the aloes and haworthias, these plants can generally be recognized by the leaves, which are arranged in two ranks instead of in a rosette, with no stem. The flowers are small, tubular with a swollen base, reddish in color with green tips, and hang from long, arching flower stems.

Gasteria lingua, short, broad dark green leaves patterned in white.

G. verrucosa, leaves about 6 in. long and more pointed than *G. lingua*, grayish-green with white dots.

GLOTTIPHYLLUM
These mesembryanthemums have soft-fleshed green leaves closely packed in two ranks along short stems that are often prostrate. The flowers, which appear in September, are very large.

Glottiphyllum depressum, translucent green leaves and yellow flowers up to 2 in. across.

G. linguiforme, wider leaves and larger yellow flowers, but many of the plants which go under this name are hybrids.

GRAPTOPETALUM
This genus from Mexico is closely related to *Echeveria*.

Graptopetalum amethystinum has very thick bluish-gray leaves, flushed with amethyst, on a stout, branching stem; small white flowers are held in a loose cluster.

GYMNOCALYCIUM

Natives of South America, these cactuses form low, spherical plants with wide ribs divided into tubercles characterized by a chinlike projection below the areole; the spines are very variable, and the white, pink or occasionally yellowish flowers are freely produced and usually large.

Gymnocalycium mihanovichii, an interesting species, as the spherical body has alternate zones of light and dark green, resembling *Euphorbia meloformis*. Diameter about 2 in. The variety of this species named *rubra* is an astonishing tomato-red color; it cannot be grown on its own roots but develops only when grafted on another cactus.

G. multiflorum (chin cactus), a large bluish-green plant, about 4 or 5 in. across with eight or nine stout, curved spines in each areole; pink flowers 2 in. across.

G. quehlianum, much smaller than *G. multiflorum*, though flower is large.

Gymnocalycium multiflorum
(Chin Cactus)

HAWORTHIA

This genus from South Africa and South West Africa is related to the aloes, but the plants are smaller, the leaves in rosettes and the small white flowers held in long, loose inflorescences. These plants grow mostly in

winter and need less water in summer. Repot in September.

All of the following except *Haworthia cymbiformis* have thick skins and grow well in the sun.

Haworthia coarctata. Leaves are often reddish and incurved.

H. cymbiformis, very succulent, stemless, with rosettes of softer leaves. Prefers slight shade.

H. margaritifera has dark green leaves with raised white dots on back and front.

H. reinwardtii, similar to *H. margaritifera* but with broader, shorter leaves.

H. tessellata, a distinctive plant; small, low rosettes composed of a few very thick leaves with tips recurved. The surface is covered with a network of fine lines.

INDIAN FIG. See *Opuntia ficus-indica*.

JADE PLANT. See *Crassula argentea*.

KALANCHOE

This genus, which includes plants formerly known as *Bryophyllum*, comes chiefly from Madagascar and other parts of Africa and Asia; the plants need moister conditions than most succulents but grow quite well in a cool greenhouse or living room.

Kalanchoe blossfeldiana, clusters of bright red flowers. By selection a number of distinct varieties have been obtained.

K. daigremontiana produces plantlets along the notched edges of the large triangular leaves. Often seen as small specimens, but if potted in richer soil will grow more freely and flower in a year or two.

K. pinnata (air plant, life plant) has leaves consisting of three to five oval leaflets which produce young plants along their scalloped margins if they are laid on moist soil or even if kept in a light place without soil.

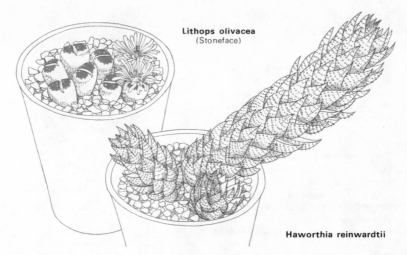

Lithops olivacea
(Stoneface)

Haworthia reinwardtii

Flowers are greenish or yellowish suffused with pink.

K. tomentosa (panda plant), leaves covered with silvery hairs, brown along the edges, and in loose rosettes on branching stems.

K. tubiflora, similar to *K. daigremontiana* but produces plantlets only at the tips of its narrow leaves.

KLEINIA
This name is often used for plants now generally referred to as *Senecio*.

LAMPRANTHUS
A large genus which includes many of the shrubby mesembryanthemums, they are very useful for planting outdoors in warm, dry climates, especially near the sea. The following can all be grown in pots but tend to become straggly, when they should be started again from cuttings.

Lampranthus aureus, yellow flowers.

L. blandus, large pale pink flowers.

L. coccineus taller than *L. blandus*, with red flowers.

LEMAIREOCEREUS
Columnar cereuses are found in both North and South America. They have large felted areoles and numerous stout spines.

Lemaireocereus marginatus (organpipe cactus), dark green stems with five or six ribs along which woolly areoles are very close together.

L. pruinosus. The new growth at the top is blue-green (glaucous). Stout little plants can be obtained from seed in two or three years.

LIFE PLANT. See *Kalanchoe pinnata*.

LITHOPS (STONEFACE)
These plants which resemble mesembryanthemums have one pair of leaves, united to form a top-shaped body. In nature only the upper surface, which is often beautifully marked, appears above the ground, but in cultivation it is safer not to plant so deeply. The flowers, which may be white or yellow, emerge through the slit across the top. The plants should be kept completely dry or nearly so during the resting period, from December to about May.

Lithops bella, pale gray with a sunken brown and yellow patterning on the surface, and white flowers.

L. lesliei has olive-green leaves

72

with red patches, and yellow flowers.

L. *olivacea*, one of the "window plants," the center of each lobe being translucent.

L. *optica* differs from other lithops in having a deep cleft between the two lobes, which gape open and have translucent tips; color normally gray, but there is a purplish-red variety.

LOBIVIA

Formerly included in *Echinopsis*, these cactuses are medium-sized, round or cylindrical, usually very spiny, and make offsets around the base. They flower freely, the flowers being usually yellow, sometimes orange or red.

L. *aurea*, large funnel-shaped yellow flowers.

L. *famatimensis* is variable—flowers may be yellow, orange, pink or blood-red.

L. *pentlandii*, rather larger; branches to form clumps of orange or red flowers.

LOPHOPHORA (MESCAL, PEYOTE)

This curious cactus from Mexico and Texas forms a low head, depressed in the center, on a large taproot. Its few ribs are rounded, divided into low tubercles, and there are no spines in the areoles, only tufts of wool. The small pink or white flowers emerge from the woolly center and are followed by little red fruits. This plant has been used by the Mexican Indians in their rites, for it contains alkaloids that produce hallucinations.

MAMMILLARIA (PINCUSHION)

This chiefly North American genus is a large one; the plants vary in size but are mostly round or cylindrical, sometimes solitary but more often making offsets or forming clumps. They are characterized by spiral rows of tubercles instead of straight ribs. There is an areole on the top of each tubercle and the spines vary in size and color;

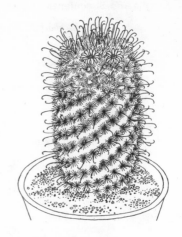
Mammillaria bombycina
(Silken Pincushion)

in some kinds there is wool in the axils as well as in the areoles. The flowers are small and produced in rings around the plant, not in the center. In some the sap is watery but in others milky.

Mammillaria applanata, hemispherical, with large green tubercles and white flowers; milky sap.

M. bombycina (silken pincushion), a slow-growing type, with hooked central spines; attractive, with red flowers; watery sap.

M. echinaria, a small plant, branching freely on the sides to form groups about 3 or 4 in. across; radial spines are white, but centrals, which do not appear until the plant reaches flowering size, are brown; watery sap.

M. elongata, a small type with golden spines. There are a number of varieties in which the color of the spines varies.

M. magnimamma, a variable species with round green stems; white wool in the center and on the areoles; flowers creamy yellow; milky sap.

M. plumosa, a small plant, 1 in. or so across, completely covered with soft feathery spines; it forms clumps but does not flower in cultivation.

MEDUSA'S HEAD. See *Euphorbia caput-medusae.*

MELON SPURGE. See *Euphorbia meloformis.*

MESCAL. See *Lophophora.*

MESEMBRYANTHEMUM
This name is applied to many plants that belong to the family *Mesembryanthemaceae*, especially to the shrubby types. They all come from South Africa and South West Africa. Details of some of the genera into which the family is divided will be found under: *Conophytum, Drosanthemum, Faucaria, Fenestraria, Glottiphyllum, Lampranthus, Lithops* and *Pleiospilos.*

MILKBUSH. See *Euphorbia tirucallii.*

NOTOCACTUS
This South American group includes round and cylindrical cactuses with ribs of tubercles and yellow flowers.
Notocactus apricus, globular, with stout, reddish, central spines.

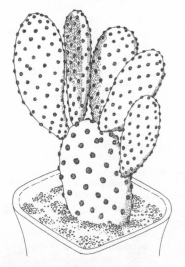

Opuntia microdasya (Bunny Ears)

N. leninghausii (golden ball), a tall-growing plant with golden, bristlelike spines. (See illustration, page 74.)

OLD-MAN CACTUS. See *Cephalocereus senilis.*

OPUNTIA (PRICKLY PEAR, CHOLLA)
This large group of cactuses is found from Canada to the southern tip of South America. The stems are jointed and the joints may be flat, cylindrical or globose. The spines vary in number and type. The characteristic of this genus is that tufts of barbed bristles called "glochids" are also produced in each areole. As these easily become detached, the plants should be handled with care—for, owing to their barbed tips, the glochids are difficult to get out of the skin. To remove, press adhesive plaster over them, and then peel it off, or shave them off with a sharp razor. Many of the flat-jointed plants make large bushes.
Opuntia compressa, native from Ontario to Alabama and Missouri, is hardy, low-growing; has large yellow flowers. Good for seaside plantings.
O. cylindrica (emerald idol), cylindrical stems with lozenge-shaped protuberances bearing areoles but few spines. It bears scarlet flowers. (See illustration, page 74.)
O. ficus-indica (Indian fig), a large plant, cultivated for its edible fruit; its oval pads may be up to 1 ft. long. Flowers yellow.
O. microdasya (bunny ears), smaller than *O. ficus-indica*, with no spines but tufts of glochids that look like plush, and are white, yellow or reddish. Flowers yellow or tinged reddish.
O. polyantha, flat oval pads about 4 in. long, bearing yellow spines; produces yellow flowers regularly.

OREOCEREUS
A genus of columnar cactuses from South America, these plants have

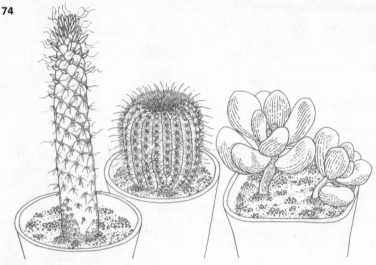

Opuntia cylindrica (Emerald Idol)   **Pachyphytum oviferum** (Moonstone)
Notocactus leninghausii (Golden Ball)

ribbed stems divided into tubercles.
There are few spines but a large number of long hairs which wrap around
the plant.

Oreocereus celsianus, white hairs
and yellow spines.

O. trollii, silky white hairs which
almost cover the plant, and golden-
reddish spines.

ORGAN-PIPE CACTUS. See *Lemaireocereus marginatus*.

PACHYPHYTUM
These Mexican plants are closely related to *Echeveria* but the glaucous
blue leaves are very thick, club-
shaped and arranged in a loose rosette
up a short, stout stem. The flowers
are small.

Pachyphytum compactum, very close
rosettes 1 to 2 in. across, dark red
flowers with greenish tips.

P. oviferum (moonstone), larger
leaves than *P. compactum*, more
loosely arranged, and with a dense
white coating; scarlet flowers.

PANDA PLANT. See *Kalanchoe tomentosa*.

PARODIA
The straight or spiral ribs of these
small South American cactuses are
divided into tubercles, and the areoles near the center have much white
wool; the large flowers are red or
orange, freely produced.

Parodia microsperma, a round plant,
elongated when old; offsets around
the base can be used for propagation.

P. nivosa, an attractive little plant
with snow-white wool at the top. Does
not produce offsets so freely as *P.
microsperma*.

PARTRIDGE-BREASTED ALOE. See *Aloe
variegata*.

PEANUT CACTUS. See *Chamaecereus
silvestri*.

PELARGONIUM
As a group these plants from South
Africa are not markedly succulent;

some have succulent stems, like the common garden geranium, which is a pelargonium; and a few have thick, woody stems which act as storage organs, leaves appearing only in the growing season. Among the latter the following are of special interest:

P. echinatum, thick woody stem; produces hairy, heart-shaped leaves in autumn, which is the beginning of the growing period; flowers are small and lilac-colored.

P. tetragonum, an attractive plant with slender, four-sided stems which stay green throughout the year, even when the small geranium-like leaves have fallen. Large pink flowers, two or three together, at the tips of the branches.

PEYOTE. See *Lophophora*.

PINCUSHION. See *Mammillaria*.

PLEIOSPILOS
These mesembryanthemums usually consist of a single pair of thick leaves which look like chunks of stone; the large yellow flowers appear between the leaves in autumn at the end of the growing season, which starts in the summer. During the resting period keep the plants completely dry. Even when a new pair of leaves begins to grow in the center, give no water until the old pair begins to dry up, having nourished the growing pair.

Pleiospilos bolusii. Its leaves, which are brownish green with dark dots, are about 3 in. long and broad, with the lower side rounded.

P. nelii, similar to *P. bolusii*, but each leaf is the shape of half a sphere.

P. simulans. Leaves are very thick, but spread out on the ground.

PRICKLY PEAR. See *Opuntia*.

RAINBOW CACTUS. See *Echinocereus rigidissimus*.

RATTAIL CACTUS. See *Aporocactus flagelliformis*.

REBUTIA
A South American genus of small, spherical cactuses, this plant usually makes offsets from the base or sides of the plant; the flowers spring from old areoles, near the base in some species.

Rebutia minuscula looks like a small green golf ball; bears a large number of scarlet flowers with slender tubes.

R. senilis, similar to *R. minuscula*, but long white spines surround the plant.

RHIPSALIDOPSIS
An epiphytic type of cactus from Brazil, it has freely branching, short dark green or reddish stems with narrow, flat joints.

Rhipsalidopsis rosea, pink flowers (up to 1 in. across) produced freely at the tips in spring.

SCHLUMBERGERA
This epiphytic cactus has short, flattened, jointed stems with elongated areoles on the top from which flowers and new joints develop.

Schlumbergera gaertneri (Easter cactus) has bright red flowers. There are a number of hybrids and varieties.

SEDUM
Very widely distributed in the northern hemisphere, many of the species are hardy even in cold regions and, even though slightly succulent, are often regarded as rock-garden plants rather than tender succulents. Those that come from warmer countries such as Mexico can be grown out of doors in mild climates only. Some are very attractive, especially if grown in full sun when their coloring is at its best. There are a number of small types not unlike the common stonecrop (*Sedum acre*). Examples of these

Sedum guatemalense
(Christmas Cheer)

are *S. stahlii* and *S. guatemalense*.

S. dasyphyllum, a small plant whose tiny, bluish, succulent leaves tinge red in the sun.

S. guatemalense (Christmas cheer), fat, bronzy leaves about ½ in. long, becoming green if not in sun.

S. morganianum (burro's tail), a hanging plant from Mexico; small cylindrical, close-packed bluish leaves along long stems ending in small bunches of pale pink flowers.

S. pachyphyllum, erect woody stems with slender, club-shaped leaves toward the ends, pale yellow-green with red tips.

S. stahlii, prostrate stems with fat little reddish leaves.

SENECIO
This large genus includes plants of many very different kinds; a small number of the South African species are succulent.

Senecio articulata (syn. *Kleinia articulata*—candle plant). Keep dry or

nearly so from March to September so that stems will remain short and glaucous-blue (watering will make them long and green); leaves and flowers appear when watering is resumed in autumn.

S. cinerascens, slow-growing, lovely plant which branches from the base only; its long cylindrical leaves are wrapped in a felt of white hairs. (See illustration, page 58.)

S. stapeliaeformis, four-angled, dark purplish-green stems. New growths tend to burrow underground before emerging and growing erect, ending in orange-red heads of flowers.

STAPELIA (CARRION FLOWER)
When their flowers open, the unpleasant smell of many of these African plants attracts flies for pollination. The stems are usually angular, leafless and rather soft. Do not give them much water, but do not keep them completely dry when resting.

Stapelia variegata, stems smooth and erect with spreading teeth; five-pointed, star-shaped flowers at base, with wrinkled surface, yellow with purple markings. This kind is not unpleasantly scented.

STAR CACTUS. See *Astrophytum*.

STONEFACE. See *Lithops*.

STRING OF HEARTS. See *Ceropegia woodii*.

TIGER JAW. See *Faucaria tigrina*.

TRICHOCEREUS
These columnar cactuses from South America usually branch from the base; the spines are well developed and the white flowers, which are produced on old specimens only, open at night.

Trichocereus spachianus (white torch), a vigorous grower, used as grafting stock. Areoles close, with curly white wool and yellow-brown spines. Branches at base when about 12 in. high. (See illustration, page 58.)

ZYGOCACTUS

Zygocactus truncatus (Christmas cactus) is a very popular epiphytic cactus with interesting flattened, jointed stems. From their ends, in midwinter, emerge bright carmine two-lipped blooms. Put outside in shade in the summer; give less water in the fall and bring in again before winter frosts; then, if necessary, repot in fresh soil.

CHAPTER 4

YOUR OWN GREENHOUSE

Types of Greenhouses—Construction, Ventilation and Heating—Cold Frames and Hotbeds—Plants for the Greenhouse—Forcing—Care: Watering, Propagation, Potting, Soils—Pest and Disease Control

A GREENHOUSE, however small, opens new vistas and offers the gardener endless possibilities and delights. Under its protection even the most tender plants are well sheltered, whatever the weather, and pot plants and bedding plants flourish. It is possible to pick tomatoes and Bibb lettuce at a time when they are expensive to buy, while other vegetables started in the greenhouse, such as cauliflower, onions and tomatoes, will produce a heavier yield when planted out of doors later. Here chrysanthemums, carnations and snapdragons can be grown to provide a colorful succession of cut flowers, and such diverse kinds of plants as begonias, cactuses and orchids can thrive and prosper.

Not all of these things can be done in one small greenhouse; when possible, the owner should determine what is to be grown before the greenhouse is built. Heating and other facilities can then be tailored to the special needs of the plants.

The merits of a warm greenhouse with its accommodation for tropical and subtropical plants must be weighed against the pleasures afforded by a cool greenhouse which is suitable for alpines, bulbs and hardier cut flowers and pot plants. An intermediate-temperature greenhouse will produce a range wider than either of the others. If the greenhouse is large enough, one or more partitions can be installed to provide diverse climatic conditions. Do not have the compartments too small, however, because the smaller the enclosed volume, the more difficult it is to control and maintain desired temperatures.

There are three principal types of greenhouses in use in North America: the full span, the lean-to and the pit house.

The full span, shaped like a long tent, has an equal amount of roof sloping down from each side of a center ridge and can provide maximum light and growing space. It may be attached to the home and it can be constructed glass-to-ground. It also offers the most flexible floor plan for either ground beds or benches. The latter are waist-high tray tables in which plants are grown or on which pots are stood. The cross-ventilation made possible by the full span is an important consideration with some crops, especially in regions where hot summers are the rule.

The full span also may have waist-high walls on all sides, but it is equipped only with benches, not with ground beds.

The lean-to greenhouse is, in effect, half of a full span with the ridge attached lengthwise to a wall. Adjoining a house, it should have a connecting door, particularly in northern climates. Sliding glass doors or a picture window in the house wall provide a pleasant view into the greenhouse. The lean-to type loses heat at a slower rate than the full span and is cheaper to build because it has only three sides, or in some cases only two. Often it faces south to take full advantage of the sunlight.

The pit house is actually an unheated walk-in greenhouse mostly underground, with a slanting glass roof and most of its side walls below ground level. It is often built into a hillside and is designed to catch the sun's warmth by day and to release it slowly at night. Pit houses are ideal for storing nearly hardy plants over winter as well as for growing the hardier kinds such as camellias and cymbidiums.

In cold climates measures should be taken to keep out frost either by covering the glass with insulating material in very cold weather or by installing some kind of heating. If the pit houses are heated to maintain a minimum temperature of 40° F., a great many cool-temperature crops can be grown in them.

All of these greenhouses can be used anywhere in North America with certain structural variations to meet local climatic needs. Selecting the location of a greenhouse is important. For plants needing maximum light, the lean-to must face approximately south, whereas a freestanding full-span greenhouse is best built on an approximately north-south axis to obtain the greatest amount of light.

The orientation of the greenhouse is of less importance for plants that do not need a large amount of light in winter. It is quite possible to grow a very wide variety of plants in westfacing and in east-facing lean-to greenhouses and in full-span greenhouses that have their axes in any direction. Only north-facing greenhouses seriously limit what can be grown in them and should not be considered except under exceptional circumstances. Artificial illumination has limited possibilities for improving conditions in a greenhouse that does not receive enough natural light. It is always simpler to decrease the illumination by shading than to improve it by lighting. Hence the general rule—locate greenhouses where they receive maximum sun.

STRUCTURE

The kind of foundation needed for a greenhouse varies with geographical location, and may range from concrete blocks or other masonry extending to 3 ft. belowground in the northern areas, to a few inches of gravel for

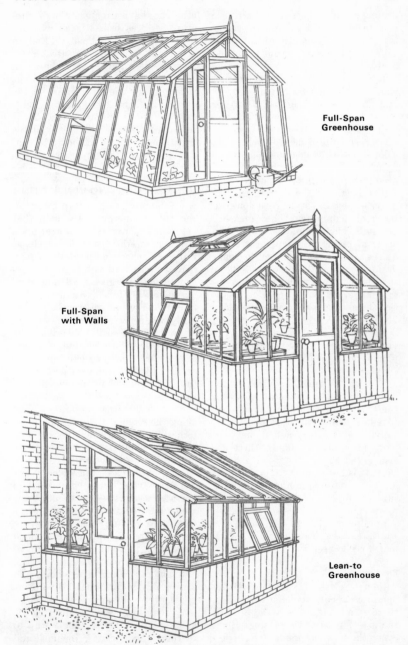

**Full-Span
Greenhouse**

**Full-Span
with Walls**

**Lean-to
Greenhouse**

drainage and a barrier of hardware cloth (a heavy, stiff, galvanized screening) to protect against rodent invasion in the southernmost United States.

Most greenhouses have bearing walls that support the glazed areas and that rise to a height of 2½ ft. or more above the foundations. The material used for the walls can be poured concrete, concrete block, brick, wood or asbestos sheeting. The severity of the climate should be taken into account when making a choice.

The height of the bearing walls is governed by the style greenhouse to be erected on them. The "glass-to-ground" construction (best suited to areas of moderate temperatures) requires no solid walls above the foundation, which may be carried 3 in. or so above ground level. Glass-to-ground greenhouses provide additional growing space under the plant benches. They are ideal for ground beds, which are so useful for raising vines of various types and taller plants such as sweet peas and lantana standards.

Though the greenhouse framework has traditionally been built of wood, the trend now is toward aluminum, to reduce maintenance problems. But, convenient as it is not to have to paint an aluminum house, there are also advantages in the wooden structure. It is better able to hold a good level of atmospheric humidity and is subject to narrower fluctuations of temperature. It is also especially adaptable to all sorts of attachments which can be installed easily with nails or wood screws.

Plastics

Although glass is still favored by operators of commercial greenhouses, there is an increasing trend toward the use of plastics for glazing. However, the flexible kinds (i.e., poly-ethylene) have a tendency to disintegrate after as brief a span as three months in warm climates. And in cold regions they must be used in two layers, with an air space in between, to insure sufficient insulation. The rigid plastics and fiber glass, on the other hand, are acceptable if light-ray distortions are not critical. New, improved plastics become available from time to time and should be considered with an open mind as well as a critical eye.

VENTILATORS AND VENTILATING

A greenhouse is a sun trap. Much of the radiant energy of the light that enters it is converted into heat upon striking interior surfaces, such as walls, benches, paths and plants. Some of this heat is lost by conduction through the glass, walls and framing members of the structure, but in bright and in sunny weather, especially when the outside temperature is not a great deal lower than the temperature desired inside, heat loss is much less than heat buildup. Without ventilation, temperatures inside the greenhouse may become so high that plants are injured or killed. Most commonly, ventilators are situated along the ridge of the greenhouse, alternating on both sides. By opening only those on the leeward side on breezy days, direct drafts damaging to the plants can be avoided. Various devices are currently available to operate these vents—electrically operated units, manually operated gears and, more recently, nonelectric cylinders containing liquid chemicals which expand with heat and open the greenhouse vents through a series of arms.

Usually automatic opening and closing devices are installed to operate the top vents only. Side and bottom vents are usually operated by hand. If the vents are hooked up to thermostatic controls, opening and closing automatically according to preset temperatures, care should be exercised to install the thermostat in a shaded location away from the pipes or the heater itself, so that its reactions are indicative of the *general* atmospheric temperature of the whole greenhouse.

Side vents, placed just above the plant benches in many greenhouses, are of particular value in hot weather and in warm climates for maintaining a free circulation of air.

Bottom vents, located under the plant benches, are less frequently installed. Their principal advantage is that as cold air enters the greenhouse through them, it passes over the hot water (or steam) pipes and is warmed before it comes in contact with the plants; thus air circulation can be assured even on cold days. In warmer weather air enters through the bottom ventilators to replace heated air that passes out through the top ventilators, thus cooling the greenhouse and creating air circulation without direct drafts on the plants.

In some situations, where, for instance, a lean-to greenhouse is protected from prevailing breezes, or where a greenhouse is in an especially warm area, a ventilator fan (mounted overhead or high at one end) is often helpful in maintaining a steady air movement. This fan, like the ventilator itself, can be activated by a thermostatic control. The primary objective in ventilating a greenhouse is to maintain favorable temperatures without subjecting the plants to the excessive chilling or drying effects of drafts. A second purpose is to avoid stagnant, humid air that might cause the development of mildew, damping-off and other disease organisms.

Ordinarily, a minimum night temperature is established for each particular greenhouse and this should be held to as closely as possible. Of course, in summer when outdoor temperatures are far higher than the ideal minimums of 50°, 55°, 60° or 65° F. that are usually set, the night temperature inside a greenhouse will approximate that of the outdoors. At other seasons night temperatures should not vary more than a couple of degrees from the ideal. On extremely cold nights it may, however, be the lesser of two evils to allow a drop of 5° or even more, rather than dry out the atmosphere by using excessive heat.

Daytime temperatures on dull days may be about 5° above night temperatures and on sunny days may exceed night temperatures by as much as 10° to 15°. Ventilating is begun before maximum day temperatures are reached. The ventilators are always opened a little at first and more as the day warms up. So far as is practicable, ventilating is done on the lee (away from the direction of the wind) side of the greenhouse.

Allowing for the variations of seasons, latitudes and kinds of plants, vents are usually partially opened by midmorning and opened still wider by noon. At the first sign of a drop in temperature (about 4 p.m. in summer and 2 p.m. in winter in the Middle Atlantic states) the vents should be closed for the night to conserve heat and avoid the growth-retarding effects of a sudden temperature change.

AIR COOLING AND HUMIDIFYING

All the foregoing ventilating techniques have the effect of reducing moisture in the atmosphere. While this loss is not critical to some kinds of plants—especially those of a succulent nature—plants native to very humid areas are likely to suffer. One answer to this problem is the evaporative cooler, an increasingly popular system for summertime ventilation. Basically it involves a fan that pulls the warm air from the outside into the greenhouse through a set of filters. Cold water dripping down on the filters cools the air as it is pushed inside. The volume of cool air soon forces the warm air out through the top vents of the greenhouse.

The evaporative cooler makes possible true air conditioning of greenhouses. Such air conditioning is not restricted to the southern states but is used as far north as Boston, Mass., to maintain the best growing conditions in summer for such plants as sweet peas, chrysanthemums, cyclamens, primulas and certain orchids. An ordinary home air conditioner *can* be used to cool a small greenhouse, but this type of unit *removes* humidity from the atmosphere and is expensive to operate. Supplementary humidifiers designed to add moisture to the air are available in great variety to suit the cubic dimensions of each greenhouse. These are controlled by humidistats set to meet the needs of the plants.

Despite the techniques and equipment just described, the most usual way of humidifying greenhouses is by "damping down." This calls for the wetting at intervals by hose or watering can of all surfaces—paths, under-bench areas, bench spaces between pots, and interior walls. The timing of these waterings varies according to the plants grown, the temperatures maintained, weather conditions and even the structure of the greenhouse itself.

The higher the interior temperature above the outdoor temperature, the greater the amount of moisture that must be added to the air. Sunny greenhouses need more of this attention than do shaded ones. In humid, cool weather comparatively little damping down is needed; the reverse is true in dry, sunny, warm weather. Damping down may be done once,

twice or more times a day depending upon greenhouse conditions and the plants grown.

Fog nozzles that produce a constant or intermittent mist may be installed in greenhouses where high relative humidity is needed at all times. These can be operated automatically or by hand.

Many crops also benefit from being forcibly sprayed (syringed) with plain water. This is especially true of most tropical plants that have nonhairy leaves. Syringing should be done only when the foliage will dry within an hour or so, never so late in the day that the foliage remains wet all night.

HEATING

In the northern areas of the United States and in Canada, greenhouse heating is the most costly maintenance item. Oil burners connected to a hot-water circulator have been much favored in recent years. Gas heaters are also becoming more and more popular because of their cleanliness, relative dependability and lower initial cost.

Where the greenhouse is connected to the residence, it is wise to utilize an extension of the home heating system. One furnace or burner serves all needs, with an additional "zone control" to provide the right level of heat to the greenhouse. However, this is not always practicable. In some cases it is necessary to install an independent system, at which time *only* the requirements of the greenhouse, cost of operation and practicability need be considered. When this happens the owner of a greenhouse that is 25 ft. long or smaller might well choose one of the recent-model gas heaters that can be vented to the outside, thus avoiding all danger of injurious fumes affecting the plants. This type of heater incorporates an electrically driven fan to circulate the warm air, and can be set so that the fan continues to operate even after the temperature has been brought up to the required level and the heating element has closed down.

Electric heaters are suitable for small greenhouses where winters are not too severe. Areas subject to winter power failures are of course not a good risk for this kind of equipment.

Because an hour or so of either freezing or extremely high temperature can spell rapid disaster to many greenhouse plants, it is advisable to take all possible precautions against heat failure. A good device to have is a temperature alarm. This simple thermostatic device is preset in the greenhouse to make an electrical contact when the temperature is either too high or too low. A bell installed in the home, connected to two dry-cell batteries and independent of any other power source, alerts the owner.

A large greenhouse is usually built with a "head house," which acts as a potting shed and contains the heating plant. In houses over 25 ft. in length, an oil-fired burner supplying hot water to pipes attached against the greenhouse walls (under the plant benches) has the advantage of providing very uniform temperatures.

The pipes remain warm long after the furnace has been turned off, while gas and electric heaters become cold minutes after ceasing to operate. If a boiler of ample size is chosen initially, it is also possible later to add new sections of pipe, should the greenhouse be enlarged.

SHADING

As the sun rises higher across the sky with the approach of spring, greater care must be taken for the protection of foliage, to prevent dehydration and consequent "burning." This can be handled inexpensively by painting or spraying the glass with one of the prepared commercial shading compounds or with a mixture of lime, water and a "sticker" such as kerosene. A light application should be made in late winter, and the density of the compound increased as the days lengthen. Toward fall, the glass surface can be gradually brushed, scraped (leaving stripes) or merely allowed to wear off. This technique is not completely efficient since the shading is constant, even on cloudy days.

The alternative, however, involves a daily chore. A series of rolled wood-lath shades, installed along the ridge

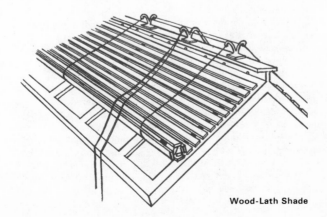

Wood-Lath Shade

of the greenhouse, can be raised and lowered by cords attached through pulleys, to suit the weather of the moment. This system provides the best use of sunlight and prevents a buildup of excessive heat as well as leaf-burning caused by too intense direct rays of the sun.

Most amateur greenhouse gardeners grow a variety of plants which have different shading requirements, and therein lies a challenge. In situations where the majority of plants need full sun while a few require shading of varying degrees, the solution often lies in the judicious placement of individual pots, so that one plant can benefit from the shade of another.

BENCHES AND PATHS

Usually greenhouse plants are placed on the bench tables, which are sometimes fitted with high sides and filled with soil to form beds in which plants are set directly. Not all greenhouses are equipped with benches. In some the plants are grown in ground beds of soil. In others they are put in pots, tubs or other containers and set on the floor. The kinds of benches used are determined by the manner in which the plants are grown. The most versatile and widely used are made of redwood, a long-lasting material that is sufficiently porous to absorb some excess water. This contributes to the desirable atmospheric humidity.

Greenhouses devoted to plants requiring high atmospheric humidity are often plagued by a lack of adequate air circulation. To minimize this problem, benches for pot plants can be constructed with their bottoms made of hardware cloth instead of wood. This type of bench has the additional advantage of not providing breeding places for insect pests. Other materials—especially recommended for their long-lasting qualities—are pre-

formed concrete slabs and sheetrock.

An edge or rim to the bench is desirable, to contain an inch or two of $\frac{1}{4}$-in. gravel as a good drainage base for pot plants.

When bench crops—such as chrysanthemums, carnations, snapdragons, lettuce and tomatoes—are grown directly in soil beds, the benches should have 6-in.-high sides to contain the soil. There must be enough headroom for such crops, which cannot be moved when they touch the glass.

A 3-ft. height is a comfortable working level for benches and a 3-ft. width allows for the tending of each plant.

Paths between greenhouse benches or beds may be of gravel, cinders, crushed stone, concrete, brick or other material. A hard surface such as brick or concrete is cleanest, most attractive in appearance and easiest to walk upon, but a loose surface absorbs moisture better and helps to maintain desirable atmospheric humidity. The areas beneath the benches should always be water-absorbent.

FRAMES AND HOTBEDS

Used very extensively in connection with the greenhouse is the frame, a simple bottomless box made of wood or masonry and fitted with a sloping

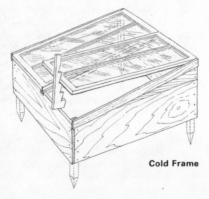

Cold Frame

roof of glass or plastic. This cover is known as a sash and may be slid up or down or removed completely.

A frame extends 6 in. or more above grade in front and is 9 in. higher at the rear. The resulting slant takes care of drainage of rain off the sash. Except for a few very special purposes, such as the propagation of evergreens, frames should be placed so that the front or low side is to the south. The depth of the inside floor of the frame is governed by the height of the plants to be grown, and it may vary from a few inches to 6 ft. (the latter, in effect, a pit greenhouse). In the case of deep frames which have floors considerably lower than the outside grade, the sides or walls should be composed of masonry, not wood. Frames, particularly deep ones, should also be located where good drainage is assured.

If unheated, the frame is called a cold frame. It is particularly useful for "hardening off"—getting plants started in the greenhouse used to cooler temperatures before transferring them to the outdoor garden. In early spring, when there is still danger of frost and the soil temperature is low, the cold frame relieves crowded conditions in the greenhouse. It is valuable also for extending the gardening season in fall, especially in northern latitudes. With its help an additional month can easily be added to the growing season, and plants such as chrysanthemums and lettuce may be harvested long after frost would have destroyed them in the open garden.

If warmed by hot-water pipes or an electric heating cable covered with plastic or lead and controlled by a simple thermostat, the "cold frame" is transformed into a "warm frame" (or "heated frame"). This type of frame will extend the growing season still further and broaden its use. With such slight additional artificial

warmth, the warm frame also functions as a "holding station." It can house those hardy and nearly hardy plants (rhododendrons, azaleas, heaths and so on) which, having been forced into bloom in midwinter, cannot be returned to the outdoors until spring because of their out-of-season soft growth.

The warm frame also provides ideal conditions for the gentle forcing of tulips, daffodils, pansies, primroses and other spring flowers. These are potted in fall and kept cold till late December in the frame—with the glass cover slightly opened on all favorable occasions. The daytime warmth can be captured by closing the cover each afternoon before the temperature drops. Slow, steady growth in light, cool conditions (45° to 55° F.) is ideal for producing long-lasting plants with strong stems and rich flower color. The heating cable acts as an automatic standby emergency system to prevent night temperature from dropping too low during the forcing period.

By putting a network of electric cables under the soil or other planting medium, even greater heat control of a frame is secured, and such a frame is called a "hotbed." At one time beds of fermenting manure provided the source of heat.

Plants are set in frames in three ways, depending upon what kind of bed forms the floor of the frame. If the plants remain growing in pots or flats, the floor of the frame can be of any material that will form a hard, clean surface and drain rapidly. Coal cinders, gravel or crushed stone are suitable.

If the plants are in pots or other containers that are to be plunged (buried to their rims, or in the case of hardy bulbs covered to a depth of several inches), then the floor may be composed of an underbed of gravel, crushed stone or cinders topped with sand, sifted coal cinders, a mixture of peat moss and sand or other porous, fairly fine and easily handled medium.

The third technique is to set the plants directly in a growing bed of soil (or, for propagation, sand or a sand and peat moss mixture). Good drainage must be assured beneath such beds, and it is often advisable to line the frame beneath the bed with hardware cloth to keep out rodents.

GREENHOUSE CROPS

No matter where you live, there is a natural cycle of events which affect plants in greenhouses. Spring, with its longer days and new, heartening surge of growth, comes earlier in Delaware than it does in Connecticut, and winter is shorter in Arizona than in Wisconsin. Although such differences exist and the lengths of the seasons vary considerably, their sequences remain the same. It is not only possible but desirable to prepare a calendar guide for what to do and when to do it in your own greenhouse. Without such a reminder it is easy to forget, for example, that rooted cuttings of poinsettia should be potted in August. Obviously planning is necessary if plants are to be ready and in bloom when wanted.

All plants have a definite growth cycle (some more pronounced than others) which includes a period of most active growth, a blooming season (except, of course, in the case of such plants as ferns) and a time of relative dormancy. The successful gardener tries to understand these cycles as they apply to the plants he grows and to meet the changing needs of his plants during every phase of their growth.

COOL, INTERMEDIATE, HOT

The coolhouse is maintained at a minimum night temperature of 40° to 50° F., the intermediate greenhouse at 50° to 60° F. and the hothouse, or tropical greenhouse, at 60° to 70° F. The category into which any particular greenhouse falls largely determines the kinds of plants that can be successfully grown in it.

Broadly speaking, plants for the greenhouse can be divided into flowering plants, foliage plants (see Recommended Indoor Ferns, page 270) and food plants. It is quite possible to grow some of each category in either a cool, intermediate or tropical greenhouse, provided care is taken to select suitable kinds.

Cut flowers are usually better grown in benches filled with soil than in pots. They develop a more prosperous root system and are less subject to checks to their growth that may result from slight inattentions to watering and fertilizing.

COOLHOUSE CUT FLOWERS

The majority of greenhouse cut flowers are grown in cool greenhouses, with night temperatures (during that part of the year when they can be kept so low) of 40° to 50° F. On all favorable occasions ample ventilation is provided and good air circulation is necessary. These plants are harmed by a warm, humid, dank atmosphere. All of them need full sun with, perhaps, just enough shade to reduce the full intensity of the light in high summer. While directions are given here in most cases for cultivating these crops in benches, ground beds and, in some instances, deep flats, all can be grown to flowering stage in pots. As a matter of fact, although this entails more work, it enables a greater total production from a given area of bench space and so has special appeal to owners of small greenhouses. With pot culture, the young plants are transferred from 2½-in. pots to 4-, 5- or sometimes 6-in. pots.

RECOMMENDED GREENHOUSE CUT FLOWERS

ASTER. See *Callistephus chinensis.*

CALENDULA
These like deep, rich soil and are excellent for ground beds as well as benches. Sow August to March, transplant to 2½-in. pots, plant out 10 by 12 in. apart. Ventilate freely. Pinch out center of plant when first bud appears to encourage branching. Disbud, leaving one flower on each stem. Keep soil dryish in dull weather. Fertilize moderately.

CALLISTEPHUS CHINENSIS
(CHINA ASTER)
China asters thrive in nearly neutral, rich soil. Sow from August to February. Transplant to 2½-in. pots, later to benches, spacing 4 by 4 in. if each plant is disbudded to only one flower; 8 by 8 in. if each plant is to have six or seven branches, each disbudded to one flower. Water freely, but good drainage is essential. Asters bloom only when they have 15 hours of continuous light each day, from start to finish. To achieve this in winter, supplement daylight with artificial illumination.

CARNATION. See *Dianthus caryophyllus.*

CENTAUREA CYANUS (CORNFLOWER)
A plant easy to raise, it is grown in soil of moderate fertility, in deep flats or benches. Sow August to January. Transplant seedlings to 2½-in. pots, later plant 10 by 12 in. apart. Water moderately.

CHRYSANTHEMUM
Cuttings are easily rooted from one's own stock plants, but it is strongly suggested that rooted cuttings be purchased annually from specialists.

This provides opportunity to obtain the newest varieties and insures a disease-free start. The rooted cuttings are set into 3-in. pots in a slightly acid general-purpose soil.

If they are to be grown for cut flowers they may be transplanted later, directly from the 3-in. pots into benches or ground beds. However, if pot plants are the goal, they are repotted successively into larger containers until their "finals," perhaps 6- or 7-in. pots, are attained. For short, bushy varieties many gardeners prefer to grow mums in deep pans (sometimes called three-quarter pots) rather than in pots of regular depth. These are deep enough to provide room for root development but not so high that the well-flowered plant becomes top-heavy. From the time the cuttings are planted either in bench or in pots, steady, gradual growth is desirable.

While most cut flowers are best suited for cool greenhouses, and chrysanthemums can be raised under similar conditions, the latter are grown commercially as an important intermediate-house crop. They bloom when day length is a suitable number of hours. By carefully controlling the hours of light, lengthening their day by giving artificial illumination or shortening it by covering the plants with lightproof black cloth for part of each day, chrysanthemums are brought to bloom at all times of the year.

But such carefully controlled nurture is usually left to commercial growers. Those interested in flowering chrysanthemums out of season by careful control of light and temperature can obtain directions from specialist suppliers of rooted cuttings for this purpose. Most owners of small greenhouses are satisfied to have chrysanthemums during their natural flowering season in fall and early winter. To achieve this the green-house is ventilated as much as possible at all times and in fall and early winter is kept just free of frost. (A night temperature of 40° F. is quite satisfactory.)

Chrysanthemums are heavy feeders and must be fertilized regularly. If bushy growth is desired the young plants should be pinched back to encourage branching when they are 3 or 4 in. high and perhaps once or twice thereafter, with the last pinch being given not later than mid-July.

Sow annual chrysanthemums from August to January. Seedlings should be transplanted to 2½-in. pots, later to benches or ground beds of moderately rich, well-drained soil. Space 6 by 8 or 7 by 7 in. Pinch young plants to encourage branching. Do not allow soil to become dry. (See also Marguerite, page 90.)

CLARKIA
This graceful flower *must* be grown under cool conditions. Sow from September to January, transplant seedlings to 2½-in. pots. Transplant later to benches or deep flats, spacing 6 by 8 in. or, if all side branches are to be pulled off, 4 by 4 in. Avoid keeping too wet. Fertilize moderately.

CORNFLOWER. See *Centaurea cyanus*.

DELPHINIUM (LARKSPUR)
Sow anytime September to January, then transplant seedlings of these plants to 2½-in. pots. Later transfer them to benches or ground beds of rich, loamy soil, spacing them 6 by 12 in. Ventilate freely and take special care not to keep the soil too wet.

DIANTHUS CARYOPHYLLUS (CARNATION)
These are a long-season crop, blooming in all but those months of mid-summer when the vegetative growth for the next season's bloom is made.

Started as rooted cuttings, either purchased from specialists or made at home in November, they are grown in a general purpose soil in 3-in. peat or clay pots and moved to a larger size to keep them growing until the bench is freed by the final cutting in July of the previous crop of summer flowers. At that time, the soil should be reworked as needed with 2½ bu. of superphosphate added every 50 sq. ft. Carnations are not sensitive, and tolerate an acid soil as easily as one that is alkaline.

They are attacked by a variety of fungus diseases and the best precaution is a "clean" soil. As summer is the easiest time to sterilize soil outdoors by gas or liquid means, a sufficient supply can be readied before benching the plants. All the ingredients (peat, manure or humus) must be added *before* sterilization. Plant in benches 6 by 8 in. apart.

Unlike many plants, carnations are best planted higher in the final pot or in the bench than they were in the previous pot. It is even better to allow a few roots to be exposed than to plant them too deeply.

Successful carnation culture requires continuous growth, achieved through thorough watering, periodic feeding (bimonthly), maximum sunlight and free air movement. Watering is best done in the early part of the day with the ventilators open. Neither the foliage nor the stems should be wet more than necessary. The optimum temperature is 50° F. at night with a maximum of 75° F. during the day, although cooler if possible. The growing tips should be pinched out once a month to promote branching.

FREESIA
Good-sized bulbs are planted from September to November in benches or flats of fertile, well-drained soil.

Dianthus caryophyllus (Carnation)

Space 3 by 6 in. apart. Water freely after growth is well started. Dryness results in brown tips of foliage.

GLADIOLUS
Use best-quality corms and plant them in ground beds or benches of light, porous, moderately fertile, well-drained soil—January to March. Space the plants 3 by 6 or 4 by 6 in. apart. Water moderately and avoid overwetness of the soil. Fertilizing is unnecessary.

HYACINTHUS (HYACINTH). See Dutch Bulbs, page 100.

LARKSPUR. See *Delphinium.*

MARGUERITE (BOSTON DAISY)
(CHRYSANTHEMUM FRUTESCENS)
They bloom freely over a long period. Propagate by cuttings; set rooted plants in 2½-in. pots. Later place them 12 by 12 in. apart in ground beds or benches in moderately fertile, approximately neutral soil. Water freely when well rooted. Fertilize regularly. They bloom earlier if short winter days are lengthened by artificial light to provide 16 hours a day.

MARIGOLD, AFRICAN (TAGETES)
These need rich, well-drained soil. Sow August to January, transplant to 2½-in. pots, and later plant 12 by 12 in. apart if the marigolds are to be pinched so that each develops several branches, or 4 by 6 in. if they are to be restricted to one flower to each plant. Fertilize regularly and water moderately.

MIGNONETTE (RESEDA)
Wonderfully fragrant flowers, they are much finer when grown in greenhouses than outdoors. They need approximately neutral, rich soil. If the soil is acid, add lime. Sow August to January. Transplant to 2½-in. pots

and later space them 10 by 12 in. in benches. Water and fertilize them moderately.

NARCISSUS (including DAFFODIL). See Dutch Bulbs, page 100.

PHLOX, ANNUAL
Good in benches or deep flats, they may be sown from August to February. Transplant to rich, porous soil, 8 by 8 in. apart. Do not allow soil to become excessively dry.

SNAPDRAGON (ANTIRRHINUM)
These are easily grown from seeds, which are so small that they germinate readily without a soil covering. Sow seed from May to September. The seedlings are transplanted into flats or 2½-in. pots.

Set the plants in benches or ground beds, 4 by 4 in. apart if each plant is to be restricted to a single stem—the method used for a quick crop with one harvest. If a more abundant cutting over a longer period is the aim, space the plants 8 by 8 in. apart and pinch them just above the third pair of leaves to induce branching.

A soil high in organic material and of a heavy texture suits snapdragons with no more nutrients added than an initial application of superphosphate. Water moderately and fertilize regularly after the soil is well filled with roots. A well-ventilated sunny greenhouse is as necessary for stocky, well-flowered plants as is a minimum night temperature of 45° to 50° F. During the winter high humidity is to be avoided.

STEVIA (PIQUERIA)
Although always called stevia by gardeners this is botanically *Piqueria.* Root cuttings in late spring or early summer, pot into 2½-in. pots and successively into larger ones until they are in 6 in. size. Use rich soil.

During summer stand outdoors and pinch shoots once a month until September. Water and fertilize freely.

STOCK (MATHIOLA)

These fragrant flowers need fertile soil that is neutral or nearly so. To acid soils add lime. Sow seed of columnar varieties from August to February. Pot seedlings in 2½-in. pots; transplant to benches before roots are much crowded, spacing 8 by 8 in. Fertilize generously. Water thoroughly, but do not keep soil constantly saturated.

TULIP. See Dutch Bulbs, page 100.

ZINNIA

Popular annuals such as these are excellent for greenhouse culture. Sow August to March; transplant seedlings to 2½-in. pots and later to benches or deep flats of rich, porous soil, spacing 4 by 6 in. Allow only one flower to develop on each plant. Free air circulation is necessary. Avoid keeping soil excessively wet.

FLOWERING POT PLANTS

The great variety of pot plants which can be grown under glass is often what lures the beginner into greenhouse gardening. Most are so easily propagated from seeds or by cuttings that the amateur is often appalled to find that he is being crowded out of his greenhouse by a tremendous number of cyclamens, solanums or cinerarias that, but a few weeks previous, were tiny seedlings taking up only a few square feet of space. In order to keep the greenhouse and one's home well stocked with decorative flowering plants throughout the year, the best plan is to grow a few pots each of a wide selection. Some—such as hydrangeas, tulips, daffodils and hyacinths—will be in a cold frame or garage until they are actually ready to be forced into growth, thereby placing little demand on valuable greenhouse space.

Cinerarias, with brightly colored daisylike flowers, grown from seed, will flower in eight months in a cool greenhouse (see page 86). Cyclamens bloom from fall into spring and are worth the 14 months they take from seed. Quicker-maturing from seed are *Primula malacoides*, *P. kewensis*, the wax begonias, kalanchoes and numerous others.

Kinds of pot plants that require many months from start to maturity can be purchased as young plants from commercial greenhouses, thereby saving space and avoiding the more demanding processes of sowing, transplanting and potting during their early stages. Among those usually available are African violets, gloxinias, streptocarpuses, poinsettias, hydrangeas, geraniums and pelargoniums (Martha Washington varieties).

Flowering pot plants fall conveniently into two groups: those that are usually raised to blooming size, enjoyed and then discarded; and those that are kept for more than one season and are permanent inhabitants of the greenhouse. In each group are found various kinds suitable for cool, intermediate and hot (or tropical) greenhouses.

In the list that follows, the letters "C," "I" and "H" indicate the type of greenhouse suited for each plant. Plants previously listed under "Coolhouse Cut Flowers" can also be grown as pot plants. For many bulbs which may be grown as pot plants, see "Tender Bulbs," page 249.

ABUTILON (FLOWERING MAPLE) (I)

These have drooping flowers of white, pink, red, yellow or orange. Propagate spring or fall, seeds or cuttings. Pinch young plants to induce branching. Soil ordinary. Shade from strong sun.

Water freely in summer, moderately in winter. Fertilize moderately.

AGERATUM (C)

Compact plants with blue, white or pink flowers, they are best propagated from selected plants or varieties by cuttings, but can be raised from seeds. Propagate anytime, July-August for winter bloom, in ordinary soil. Pinch young plants to encourage branching. Discard after flowering.

ANTHURIUM (H)

Flowers are red, pink or white. Very porous, coarse, rich soil. Shade. Humid atmosphere. Propagate by division or seeds. Water and fertilize freely.

APHELANDRA SQUARROSA (H)

This plant has handsome foliage and yellow flowers. Use rich soil; shade from strong sun; provide humid atmosphere. Propagate by cuttings. Water and fertilize freely.

AZALEA (RHODODENDRON) (C)

Botanically *Rhododendron*, these plants, chiefly white-, pink- or red-flowered, are known as azaleas to gardeners. Greenhouse azaleas are of several distinct types. *Indica* varieties are propagated by grafting, *kurume* varieties by cuttings in summer. All need sandy, peaty, fertile, acid soil, part shade in summer (they may remain outdoors at that season) and always moist soil. Keep in barely frost-free temperatures fall to January or later, then bring into 50° to 60° F. night-temperature greenhouse for forcing into bloom. Fertilize regularly spring through summer.

BEGONIA (I)

There are numerous kinds of this plant with white, pink, red, orange or yellow flowers. Wax begonias (*Begonia semperflorens*) are propagated by seeds or cuttings, others by cut-

tings, leaf cuttings or division. Soil should be porous, with an abundance of organic matter, and kept always evenly moist. Except for wax begonias, which like full sun, give good light with shade from strong sun, and humid atmosphere. For tuberous begonias see page 250 in "Tender Bulbs."

BELOPERONE (I)

Flower bracts are coppery red or yellow in color. Soil should be ordinary, well drained; water and fertilize moderately. Propagate by cuttings. Pinch young plants several times to induce bushiness.

BROWALLIA SPECIOSA (I)

They are charming for pots and baskets. Sow seed July-August, transplant to 2½-in. pots, later to 4- or 5-in. Provide ordinary soil, kept moderately moist; expose to full sun. Pinch to induce branching. Fertilize when well rooted in final pots. Flowers blue-purple or white. Discard after flowering.

CINERARIA (SENECIO) (C)

These winter bloomers have a wide range of flower colors. Sow seed May to August, transplant and pot as growth makes necessary in rich, coarse soil containing abundant organic matter. Provide drainage. Water freely and fertilize liberally when final pots are filled with roots. Shade from strong sun. Keep bed on which pots stand always moist. Spray foliage with water on bright days. Discard after blooming.

CLERODENDRON (H)

Here are both vines and shrubby plants with white and red flowers. All need high humidity, light shade, rich soil, watering generously in summer, moderately in winter. Fertilize moderately spring through fall. Propagate by cuttings.

Cyclamen

CYCLAMEN (C)
These have lovely winter and spring flowers of white, pink or red. The plants take 14 months or more from seed; sow August to December. Grow in light, well-drained, fertile soil. Pot with top of bulb at soil surface. Shade from strong sun. Fertilize moderately. Keep bed on which pots stand always moist. Spray foliage with water on bright days. Discard after blooming.

DAPHNE ODORA (C)
A fragrant, white or lavender winter-flowering shrub, it needs sandy, peaty, acid soil kept always evenly moist. Light shade from strong sun. Propagate by cuttings. Slow-growing.

FUCHSIA (C OR I)
Hanging flowers—white, pink, red, purple and combinations—blossom from this plant (see illustration, page 94). Propagate by cuttings August to April. Pot in rich soil. Pinch to induce branching. Water freely summer, moderately winter; fertilize moderately. Shade from strong sun.

GERANIUM (PELARGONIUM) (C)
Botanically named *Pelargonium*, they have clusters of white, pink or red flowers; some kinds have scented foliage. Propagate by cuttings August to February. Moderately rich, rather heavy soil. Pinch shoots occasionally. Use full sun and water moderately. Fertilize moderately. Ivy-leaved varieties are suitable for baskets.

HYDRANGEA MACROPHYLLA (C OR I)
These can be raised from cuttings May to August, or young plants may be bought from specialists. Pot in rich, coarse soil. Water freely when growing; full sun. In fall store in cold frame or similar place where temper-

94

Fuchsia

ature does not drop below 20° F. Bring into cool greenhouse from January on and gradually increase temperature. Water and fertilize freely when forcing into bloom. Discard forced plants, or plant outdoors after blooming.

IMPATIENS (PATIENCE PLANT) (I)
Flowers are white, pink, red, orange, yellow. Propagate by seeds or cuttings. Pinch young plants to induce branching. Soil rich, well drained, always kept moist. Shade from strong sun. Discard after flowering.

IXORA (H)
Pink, orange-red or red flowers grow in clusters on this shrub. Propagate by cuttings. Soil rich, well drained. Water and fertilize freely; light shade.

JACOBINIA (H)
Flowers are pink or red. Culture as for aphelandra.

KALANCHOE BLOSSFELDIANA (I)
Clusters of small pink or red flowers are showy in winter and spring. Propagate by seeds, cuttings or leaf cuttings. Soil ordinary, well drained; full sun. Discard after flowering.

PELARGONIUM (C)
Zonal, ivy-leaved and scented pelargoniums are treated under Geranium. Here we deal with Martha Washington varieties. Propagate by cuttings in August and September. Pot in porous, rich, neutral or slightly alkaline soil. Pinch to induce branching. Full sun; water freely September to June, keep quite dry in summer. In August prune back, repot and resume watering. Fertilize moderately when in active growth.

PENTAS (I)
The plant has clusters of white, pink or red flowers. Propagate by cuttings. Pinch young plant for branch-

ing. Ordinary soil. Water and fertilize moderately. Sun or light shade.

POINSETTIA
(EUPHORBIA PULCHERRIMA) (H)
Propagate this plant from cuttings, June to August. Pot in 2½-in. pots and later pot singly or several together in larger pots or pans. Use soil rich, well drained. Pinch shoots not later than August. Water moderately; avoid drafts; give full sun and provide humid atmosphere. Fertilize generously when containers are filled with roots. After flowering, dry and store. In April bring into greenhouse, prune back and resume watering for growth to use as cuttings.

PRIMULA (PRIMROSE) (C)
Greenhouse primroses (see illustration, page 96) include *Primula malacoides* and *P. obconica*, with white, pink or red flowers, and *P. kewensis* with yellow flowers; bloom in winter and spring. Sow the seed February to May and cultivate in the same way as cinerarias. Primulas should be kept in a shady corner at 50° F. in the growing season and 55° in the flowering season. Discard after flowering.

SCHIZANTHUS (BUTTERFLY FLOWER, POOR MAN'S ORCHID) (C)
The flowers are white, pink or red. Sow September and January; transplant into 2½-in. pots, then successively into larger ones. Soil should be rich, light, porous. Pinch once or twice to encourage branching. Water, fertilize moderately and expose to full sun. Discard after flowering.

FOLIAGE PLANTS
Plants with foliage more decorative than their flowers are mostly tropical or subtropical, although there are exceptions. A few, such as palms, asparagus ferns, Australian silk oak (*Grevillea robusta*) and blue gum

(*Eucalyptus globulus*), must be grown from seed. Coleus and *Fatsia japonica* can be grown from seed or cuttings (*Fatsia* also by air layering; see page 715 in "How to Raise New Plants").

Foliage plants must never suffer from lack of water, but *Schefflera* is easily harmed by excessive wetness. Umbrella plant (*Cyperus alternifolius*), on the other hand, thrives even if its pot is half immersed. Regular fertilizing from spring through fall is beneficial to all that have filled their pots with roots. Coleus and croton thrive in full sun, but other foliage plants need sufficient shade to prevent their leaves from yellowing or being burned brown by strong sun. Humidity is essential for most (except, for example, Australian silk oak, eucalyptus and English ivy) and on bright days leaves should be sprayed one or more times with water. The chief pests of foliage plants are scale insects, mealybugs and red spider mites. For their control, see Greenhouse and House-Plant Pests, page 825.

FOR COOLHOUSE
Araucaria excelsa . . .
Norfolk Island pine
Asparagus plumosus . . .
asparagus fern
A. sprengeri . . . asparagus fern
Aspidistra elatior . . . cast-iron plant
Eucalyptus globulus . . . blue gum
Fatshedera lizei
Ferns, various kinds
Grevillea robusta . . .
Australian silk oak
Hedera helix, and varieties . . .
English ivy
Tolmiea menziesii . . .
piggyback plant

FOR INTERMEDIATE HOUSE
Coleus blumei
Cyperus alternifolius . . .
umbrella plant

96

Primula malacoides
(Fairy Primrose)

Primula obconica
(Primrose)

Dracaena, various kinds
Fatsia japonica (syn. *Aralia sieboldii*)
Ferns, various kinds
Pilea cadieri . . .
 aluminum plant, watermelon pilea
Zebrina pendula . . .
                              wandering Jew

FOR HOTHOUSE
Acalypha, various kinds
Aglaonema, various kinds
Begonia rex-cultorum, various kinds
Bromeliads, various kinds
Calathea, various kinds
Codiaeum, various kinds . . .
                              croton
Dieffenbachia, various kinds . . .
                              dumb cane
Dracaena, various kinds
Ferns, various kinds
Ficus, various kinds
Fittonia, various kinds
Maranta, various kinds
Peperomia, various kinds
Philodendron, various kinds
Pilea, various kinds
Sansevieria, various kinds

PLANTS FOR HANGING BASKETS
Many foliage and flowering plants lend themselves to growing in hanging baskets. Some of the most successful are: *Columnea, Lantana, Abutilon,* flame violet, *Davallia, Begonia, Browallia, Streptosolen, Fuchsia, Aeschynanthus,* geranium and wandering Jew. Such baskets, made of wire, are offered for sale by dealers in garden supplies. These are lined with sheet moss and then filled with soil of a type suitable for the kind of plants to be set in them. The baskets are then planted, well watered and hung in the shade for a few days.

VINES
A greenhouse can appropriately be furnished with plants which lend not only beauty, but atmosphere as well. No greenhouse can adequately dis-

play the lush growth of the tropics without a few well-placed vines. Several species of *Hoya, Passiflora* (passionflower) and *Thunbergia* make interesting flowering vines as do *Allamanda, Bougainvillea, Clerodendron, Manettia.* Species of *Cissus* are grown primarily for their foliage effects, and so, sometimes, are kinds of philodendrons. All of them are suited to the intermediate house and the hothouse. For cooler temperatures *Plumbago capensis, Solanum jasminoides, Jasminum mesnyi* and hybrid clematis are excellent choices among flowering vines, and various ivies (*Hedera*) among nonflowering kinds. Most vines are heavy feeders and benefit from being treated with fertilizer regularly through their growing seasons. Their containers should be large enough to accommodate a generous amount of roots, with a 10-in. tub being about right for most vines after the first year. Bamboo canes, stiff wire trellis or wires strung under the greenhouse roof will provide adequate support. Self-clinging kinds, such as ivies, will attach themselves to masonry and other supports.

ORCHIDS
Few families exhibit such infinite variety as the *Orchidaceae,* and few hold such fascination for gardeners.

Coolhouse Orchids: The ideal temperature for coolhouse orchids is 60° F., with a minimum night temperature of 50° to 55°.
 The great number of orchids which thrive under cool conditions include some of the most beautiful. Cymbidiums, native to the Himalayas, are grown for their long spikes of pastel wax-textured flowers, which are long-lasting as cut flowers. Miniature varieties are especially suitable for a small greenhouse.
 Odontoglossums are also splendid

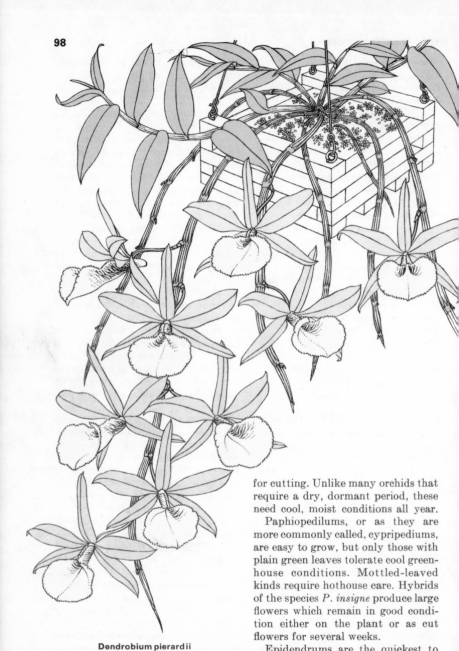

Dendrobium pierardii

for cutting. Unlike many orchids that require a dry, dormant period, these need cool, moist conditions all year.

Paphiopedilums, or as they are more commonly called, cypripediums, are easy to grow, but only those with plain green leaves tolerate cool greenhouse conditions. Mottled-leaved kinds require hothouse care. Hybrids of the species *P. insigne* produce large flowers which remain in good condition either on the plant or as cut flowers for several weeks.

Epidendrums are the quickest to reach flowering stage, with 5-ft.-long stems of many flowers, each about 2 in. in diameter.

Intermediate-House Orchids: In an intermediate greenhouse, with a 60° F.
minimum night temperature, many
different kinds of orchids can be cultivated. Orchids that can be grown
in a warm corner of a cool greenhouse
will have a reasonable chance for success in the coolest area of an intermediate house, and those that will
grow in a cool spot in a tropical house
are likely to prosper in the warmest
part of an intermediate house.

Important among intermediate-
house orchids are cattleyas, with their
tremendous number of beautiful hybrids; those cypripediums having
mottled leaves; and many dendrob-
iums. A handsome variety, *Dendrobium pierardii* (see opposite page), has
rosy-mauve sepals and petals, with
a pale primrose-yellow lip. Miltonias
have beautiful pansylike flowers of
large size and rich colors, and *Laelia
digbyana* is one of the most striking
of all orchids with its deeply fringed
lip, its chartreuse color and heady
perfume.

Other orchids to grow in the intermediate house are:

Angraecum veitchii, developing large
sprays of white star-shaped flowers.

Brassavola nodosa, which becomes
fragrant at night when its clusters of
greenish-white flowers are open.

Brassia longissima, with sprays of
chartreuse and brown flowers, outstanding for its very long sepals.

Pleurothallis roezlii, which has an
unusual deep purple flower.

Hothouse Orchids: Orchids which do best
under hothouse conditions, with a
minimum night temperature of 65°,
include some very dramatic species.
All *Phalaenopsis* must be grown in
high heat and ample humidity in a
tropical greenhouse. Among other important hothouse orchids are vandas,
whose flower spikes emerge from between straplike leathery leaves. The

flowers remain in perfect condition
for well over a month.

VEGETABLES

The luxury of vegetables harvested
from the home greenhouse will never
pose a threat to the local grocer.
However, the pleasure of growing
just a few and the enjoyment of them
may make the venture attractive.
Lettuce, tomatoes, chives, parsley,
radishes, beets, thyme and mint are
some of the easiest crops to raise "out
of season." The requirements are a
loose, fertile soil, abundant water,
regular feeding and as much sunlight as possible.

While a cool greenhouse is best for
most salad vegetables and herbs, it is
certainly possible to grow them in the
coolest part of an intermediate greenhouse, since many varieties are tolerant of higher temperatures. The
globe varieties of radishes are best for
greenhouse cultivation. Sow them in
rows 6 in. apart and thin to 2 in.
Beets are worthwhile, as both the
tops and roots can be enjoyed.

Tomatoes require an intermediate
greenhouse. Select an early variety
especially recommended for forcing
and grow in 10-in. pots, each plant
restricted to a single stem supported
by a bamboo cane. They may also be
raised in benches or ground beds.

Midsummer is the latest sowing
date north of Richmond (Va.), Kansas City and Colorado Springs for a
winter crop, and late March the dead-
line for sowing to produce an early
summer harvest. When the flowers of
the tomato plant open, they should
be brushed daily with a small hair-
brush to insure pollination and setting of fruit. As they are self-fertile,
only the brushing is needed. Alternatively, they may be sprayed with a
hormone-type spray which will insure
fruits forming without pollination.

Parsley seed can be sown in flats or

pots in late summer, or the plants can be carefully dug from the outdoor garden and potted. If maintained as cool as possible and cut regularly, they will produce new growth for several months. Thyme and mint are two other herbs easily grown in pots, but they should be cut continuously to encourage tender growth and prevent flowering and seeding. Swiss chard, grown in the bench of the cool greenhouse, can be used as an alternating crop by starting a new sowing between rows of other crops about to finish their usefulness.

The greenhouse vegetable considered by many to be most welcome is delicately flavored Bibb lettuce. Young plants can be transplanted from seed flats into the bench or be grown in pots until harvesting. Salad Bowl is a good second choice for the greenhouse. For rhubarb and Witloof chicory, see Vegetables, just below.

FORCING

By "forcing," the greenhouse gardener means the procedure of bringing crops to maturity out of season. This is done by using higher temperatures than normal together with comparatively high humidity and generous watering. Fertilizing is of little help.

Vegetables

Witloof chicory or French endive can be forced. Roots are raised from seeds sown outdoors in May. The plants are taken up in the fall, the tops are chopped off to the crown of the roots, and the roots cut to a uniform 6-in. length. They are then planted close together in a mixture of ½ sand and ½ peat moss in a box about 8 in. deep, and are kept until needed for forcing in a frost-free, cool, dark location. Forcing is done by placing the box under the bench and shading to assure total darkness.

In the North, rhubarb is a tasty midwinter luxury and is easily forced. Dug from the outdoor garden in late fall, strong roots are put in bushel baskets or grape crates and covered with leaves. They are placed outdoors in the shade or in a cold frame, then allowed to freeze and become thoroughly dormant. They may be brought into the greenhouse in successive batches after the first of the year. Kept under the benches and shaded, the stalks will be far superior in taste and tenderness to the outdoor crop.

Dutch Bulbs

Among the chief flowering plants that can be forced are the so-called Dutch bulbs—tulips, narcissuses (including daffodils) and hyacinths, as well as such minor bulbs as crocuses, scillas and grape hyacinths.

The technique is simple. The bulbs should be obtained from a florist or garden-supply house as early as possible in the fall. They are then planted in pots, pans or flats, so close together that they almost touch, and with their tips out of the soil. The containers are then buried outdoors or in a cold frame under about 8 in. of sand, sifted ashes, peat moss or sawdust and are left until the bulbs are well rooted, which may take from 8 to 12 weeks. After this the bulbs are brought into the greenhouse in successive batches so that blooms are produced over a long period. If possible, a cool temperature should be maintained for the first week or ten days, then raised. But if necessary the bulbs may be brought into high temperatures from the first.

The production of long flower stems can be encouraged by having the bulbs kept in absolute darkness until their flowers begin to expand. To have flowers as early as possible, late in the year or very early in the new year, purchase "precooled" bulbs which have been especially treated for very early forcing.

Shrubs

Many of the hardy shrubs, in small convenient sizes, may be forced into bloom anytime after mid-January. Lilac, flowering almond, rhododendron, azalea, mock orange, daphne, heath, Japanese flowering quince and, indeed, practically all kinds that normally produce blooms in the spring are easily brought into early bloom. Shrubs for forcing should be potted or tubbed in the early fall. Then they are buried to the rims of their containers in an ash or sand bed in a deep cold frame or outdoors until it is time to bring them into the greenhouse. Start forcing in a cool greenhouse, and move to the warmest location for higher temperature after growth begins. The roots must always be kept moist, and the branches should be sprayed two or three times a day with water. When the flower buds show color, move the plants gradually to areas of cooler and cooler temperatures.

Perennials

Several perennials force easily for late-winter and early-spring bloom. Among the best are astilbe (spirea), variegated-leaved hosta (plantain lily), bleeding heart and lily of the valley. They are treated exactly as are shrubs for forcing. It is possible to buy retarded pips of lily of the valley, especially prepared for forcing. These are planted closely together in pots or flats and may then bloom within three or four weeks.

WATERING

In commercial greenhouses the duty of watering is usually assigned to one of the most experienced men. This is some indication of its importance and of the skill required for what at first seems like a simple mechanical chore.

Whenever watering is done, the soil should be wet thoroughly. When a plant is potted, the soil level should be an inch or so below the rim, and this reservoir should be filled at each watering. A periodic test (by turning the plant out of the pot shortly after watering) will indicate whether a second watering is necessary to moisten thoroughly the *entire* ball of soil. Great numbers of plants are lost through extremes in watering. Too little prevents the deeper roots from absorbing and transmitting nutrients. Overwatering soon forces much-needed oxygen from the soil and causes the slowing down or stoppage of all necessary functions, then death of the roots of ordinary land plants.

The texture and composition of the soil controls, to a great extent, its water-retention characteristics. Also, plants of different kinds may have similar or different moisture requirements. Some may be rootbound in their pots, while others have not yet filled their containers with roots and so will not need frequent watering.

The grouping of plants in a greenhouse affects and to some extent is affected by their water needs. Greenhouse plants are grouped first according to their temperature requirements. In any greenhouse there are variations, and one soon finds cool spots and warm corners for plants with special needs. The next grouping is done according to shade requirements. And the third consideration should be their arrangement, for the sake of efficiency and convenience, according to watering needs. Certainly those plants which have dormant periods must be segregated for proper treatment. When a complete drying-off is called for, as with calla lilies or amaryllises, turning the pot on its side (on top of the bench or on the floor) is the best way of avoiding inadvertent watering. However, to remember not to reduce the amount of watering for some plants, mark the pots with wooden labels dipped in red paint.

Some miscellaneous observations for successful watering are:

1. Never wet the leaves of plants having a velvety texture, such as African violets and *Gynura*. These are best watered carefully, either under the leaves or by placing the pot in a container of water so that the plant absorbs moisture from the bottom up.

2. Improper drainage through the bottom of a pot will eventually, and sometimes very quickly, harm the plant and probably cause its death. Green moss on the soil surface is one indication. In such cases it is more important to correct the cause than to worry about the visible effect, since the moss causes no real damage.

3. Plants should never go into the nighttime hours with their leaves or leaf crowns wet. Wetness together with low temperatures encourages funguses and other diseases. This must be most carefully avoided during the cool months. It is best to water all but small seedling plants *without* a sprinkler attached to the spout of the watering can. Fill the space between the soil and the rim of the pot as many times as necessary to wet the entire body of soil, making sure water is not trapped in the crown of the plant.

4. When watering directly from a hose, it is best to use a special nozzle known as a "water breaker" to prevent washing away the soil, exposing surface roots and compacting the soil. There are devices available to reduce the pressure of the stream without reducing the volume of the flow.

5. Several mechanical devices have been designed that measure the "pull" of the water through the soil and indicate on a dial whether or not watering is necessary. Even these indicate only the degree of wetness of the soil, not the plant's need for more or less moisture. After taking readings decisions must still be made. Most gardeners rely entirely on their own judgment. See also page 16 in "How to Grow House Plants."

GENERAL MANAGEMENT AND CARE

After the first 12-month cycle of attending to a greenhouse, it becomes clear to the new owner that crowded conditions are seasonal and should be anticipated in order to plan properly. In late winter, bench space is needed for propagation by seed and cuttings. Early spring demands that part of this area be available for flats filled with young plants. (At that time temporary shelves supported by sturdy brackets are most useful.)

As the business of potting the plants into larger individual containers progresses, the seedlings that once took up but a few square feet are spread over most of the greenhouse. As soon as practicable, plants that can be moved should be put in heated frames and cold frames for protection. By late spring the greenhouse is almost emptied of the plants grown for outdoor use and attention can once more be directed toward summer cleanup and the growing of fall and winter crops. Many plants are moved out during the summer season for use on porches and terraces. Others spend the summer in the dappled sunlight of a shady tree. When winter arrives many of the larger plants are not returned to the greenhouse, but cuttings are taken to produce new vigorous plants for the season to follow. Then the entire cycle begins again.

Since most activities in a greenhouse are interrelated and frequently continuous, a regular program must be maintained for healthy growing conditions. If at all possible, the greenhouse should be completely emptied once a year, the framework and glass scrubbed with a disinfectant and hosed clean, and painted surfaces given a fresh coat.

PROPAGATION

However small a greenhouse may be, a section should be set up for propagating. Most propagating techniques are best achieved in temperatures between 60° and 70° F., which are impractical to maintain during the fall-through-spring season in a cool greenhouse without special aid. The use of thermostatically controlled plastic- or lead-coated heating cable stretched back and forth across the bench beneath the rooting medium makes the task a simple one. If desired, a cable may be strung around the walls of a propagating case (a small glass- or polyethylene-covered frame inside the greenhouse).

For a house 25 ft. by 10 ft. a bench section 6 ft. long devoted to propagating will probably prove to be productive enough. The 6-ft. length, divided into three areas, with dividers nailed to the top of the bench, allows the use of each section for a different purpose.

For methods of plant increase, see "How to Raise New Plants," page 696.

POTTING AND POTTING SOILS

It is quite possible to prepare an all-purpose potting soil that can be used for a wide variety of plants with reasonable success. However, better results are to be had if soils especially adapted to the needs of particular kinds or groups of plants are used.

Greenhouse soils are composed of good topsoil (loam), leaf mold or peat moss and coarse sand. The most commonly recommended proportions call for equal parts of each. This is a very rough approximation indeed. For plants such as chrysanthemums and geraniums, which like loamy soils, the proportion of topsoil might well be doubled. For African violets, ferns and primroses, which like a woodland soil, the proportion of peat moss or leaf mold can, with advantage, be markedly increased. Many succulent plants thrive in a soil mixture that includes a higher proportion of sand. Also, the amounts of sand and organic matter added to the topsoil when preparing a greenhouse soil should depend upon whether it is heavy and somewhat clayey or is sandy, and whether it contains much or little organic matter.

To raise its fertility, dried cow manure, dried sheep manure and other desiccated organic fertilizers as well as bone meal, superphosphate, unleached wood ashes and complete commercial fertilizers may be mixed in appropriate amounts with greenhouse soils at the time of their preparation. Ground limestone is used to reduce soil acidity; sulphur, more rarely, to increase acidity.

A general-purpose soil for chrysanthemums, geraniums, fuchsias and other strong-rooted plants: 4 parts good garden soil; 2 parts leaf mold, peat moss or humus; 1 part dried cow manure; 2 parts coarse sand. To each bushel of the basic mixture add: 1 pint bone meal, 2 quarts wood ashes, ½ pint complete fertilizer.

A soil of high organic content for plants such as begonias, ferns and others native to woodland and jungle areas: 2 parts good garden soil; 2½ parts leaf mold; ½ part coarse sand; 1 part crushed brick or crocks; ½ part crushed charcoal; 1 part dried cow manure. To each bushel of the basic mixture add 1 pint bone meal.

Important though it be, the initial preparation of soils that are used for potting or bench planting in greenhouses does not assure that what is a good soil at planting or potting time will remain so indefinitely. The character of the soils in which the plants grow changes constantly. The combination of frequent watering and high greenhouse temperatures eventually breaks down the organic material, which results in compaction of the soil, too little aeration and an ever-decreasing level of fertility. It is apparent, therefore, that periodic soil replacement is necessary to provide proper conditions for growth and flowering. A crop of snapdragons or carnations can be grown in bench soil until maturity; the flowers are harvested and the plants pulled up and discarded. Then, if the soil is free of disease organisms and pests, it can be revitalized by mixing in organic material and fertilizers together, perhaps, with a dressing of lime.

Pot plants, however, need periodic attention in the matter of repotting, during which operation they are given some new soil. The frequency of repotting varies greatly. Slow-growing plants may remain for several years in the same pot, while fast-growing kinds may need repotting every few months.

However, if a plant is left to grow in the same pot for more than a year, it should have a little of the old soil poked away from the surface of the root ball and from the outside (a pencil makes an ideal tool) and new soil added before returning it to the old pot. This should be done at the beginning of the plant's growth cycle.

Once a plant is moved from the propagation bench into a pot it should be repeatedly "potted-on" in a bigger pot as more root room is needed, until it is in its "final" pot, a container of adequate size for the plant to grow in to its maturity. With container-grown plants, such as palms, bay trees and oleanders, the final container may be a large tub.

The gradual transfer from a small-sized pot in which the seedling or rooted cutting is planted to the comparatively large-sized container the plant occupies when mature is basic to good pot-plant culture. As an aid in determining whether or not a plant is in need of repotting an inspection can be made. First water the plant thoroughly and let it drain for a while. Then invert the plant in its pot, tap the rim of the pot on the edge of a bench or table and allow the root ball to fall into the palm of the hand. If the roots have taken complete possession of the soil and have filled the pot, it may be time for a larger one.

A first step is the selection of a suitable container, which may be chosen for a particular type of plant. In addition to conventional pots, there are shallow pans, deeper (azalea or bulb) pans, and tubs. They may be of earthenware, wood or plastic. The material of which the container is made affects the frequency of watering that is needed throughout the growth of the plant. Some plants, such as geraniums, fuchsias and clivias, flower better when the roots are allowed little, if any, excess room and are somewhat crowded. Others, including many of the vining plants, require a container of generous proportions in comparison with the size of the root mass.

Flowerpots made of pressed peat are fast gaining favor as containers for annuals and vegetables that are later to be planted outdoors or into greenhouse benches. These pots can be put in the soil without removing the plant, thereby avoiding any setback caused by root damage. Plastic pots are coming into increased use because they are light and inexpensive. However, the traditional earthenware clay pot is still used the most for greenhouse-grown plants. Its porous walls give a certain amount of protection from dangers caused by overwatering.

When a suitable container has been chosen, a shallow layer of crocks (pieces of broken flowerpot) or of cinders covered with coarse leaves, moss or similar material to prevent the soil washing down should be placed in the bottom to insure adequate drainage.

Add some soil, then position the plant with the top of its root ball an inch or so below the pot rim and work additional soil around and on top of the root ball. Pack it rather lightly, moderately firm, or quite firm, depending upon the kind of plant and its needs. When finished, the soil surface should usually be ¾ to 1 in. below the rim, to allow for thorough watering. With very large pots and tubs the space left for water may be more than this; in the case of very small pots, it may be somewhat less.

Every greenhouse or potting shed should maintain a supply of "clean" soil (soil that has been sterilized either chemically or with steam to rid it of weed seeds), sand, peat moss, leaf mold and dried manure, stored in large containers such as plastic garbage cans. The other miscellaneous ingredients used in soil "recipes" in smaller quantities may be kept in covered coffee cans. With these items readily at hand, soils can be prepared for those plants being potted at the moment, eliminating the storage of larger quantities of a number of soil mixtures. (Further information on repotting is given on page 17 in "How to Grow House Plants.")

PEST AND DISEASE CONTROL

Control of pests and diseases in greenhouses requires prompt removal of seriously diseased plants for which effective treatment cannot be provided; the picking and removing of dead flowers and leaves; the eliminating of weeds; and the removal or treatment of infected soil.

But even with the best care of plants and strict control of the greenhouse environment, pests and diseases will be troublesome from time to time.

Pest Control

The greenhouse gardener should be alert to detect the very first evidence of trouble. Indeed, in the case of commoner insects (and for convenience that term is used to include a number of small creatures such as spider mites and slugs, which are not actually insects), preventive treatment plays a considerable part in keeping greenhouse plants free of attack.

In the fall, when garden plants and soil are brought into the greenhouse, care must be taken lest insects be brought in with them. Close inspection and spraying are necessary.

Keeping plants "clean" in spring is especially important because the abundant new spring growth is a tender, succulent haven for many harmful insects.

Greenhouses should be sprayed or fumigated with a "smoke" generator that dispenses a reliable insecticide, such as malathion, about every three weeks. Always use insecticides with the greatest care and strictly according to the manufacturer's directions. And, of course, store them in a locked closet.

Handled carelessly, poison sprays are even more dangerous in the confined area of a greenhouse than outdoors, where dispersal is quicker. For this reason it is well to wear a respirator when preparing and using such sprays. A respirator is *not* a complex, expensive device. It is merely a rubber mask that fits over the nose and mouth, contains a paper and chemical filter and costs perhaps nine or ten dollars.

A pint-bottle sprayer is adequate to treat a few plants. Larger equipment will be needed to spray an entire greenhouse. For fumigating, greenhouse smoke generators are used, and the operator is never in the greenhouse during or after the work, so long as fumes are present. The best time to fumigate is in the evening. By morning all but the odor will have gone, and it is necessary to ventilate only two or three hours before the air is clear and safe to enter. Smoke generators are more expensive on a per-treatment basis than spraying, but placing a canister in the aisle, lighting a fuse and then locking the greenhouse door is the cleanest—and the easiest—way of eliminating many harmful insects.

A list of insects that attack greenhouse plants would be lengthy. However, certain ones are the most common offenders. Each leaves its own distinct "calling card" by way of damage to the plant. Deformed leaves or buds can be caused by aphids; cottony masses at leaf joints are the sap-sucking, plant-yellowing mealybugs. The whitefly, easily set into flight when the plant is touched, causes gradual leaf-yellowing, as do scales, the armadillolike insects that fasten themselves on stem and leaf surfaces, insert their feeding organs, and live out their lives thereafter without moving. Nocturnal-feeding slugs can be a real nuisance. These snails without shells have an appetite for tender new growth including flower buds, and can best be stopped by poisoned bait (readily available in a prepared form). Red spider mites are almost too small to see, but in an excessively dry, warm atmosphere they propagate rapidly, leaving brown- or gray-mottled foliage as a result of their activities. (See also Greenhouse and House-Plant Pests, page 825.)

A regular spray or fumigating program, supplemented by the use of baits when needed, will keep most insects in check, but occasions will arise when special measures other than spraying or fumigating are needed. When defeated by a persistent pest or disease, consult an expert.

Certain plants seem to have an affinity for certain afflictions. *Hoya carnosa* easily falls prey to mealybugs. The Martha Washington pelargoniums are favorite hosts of whitefly. Tuberous begonias are decidedly susceptible to mildew. Careful, frequent inspections will reveal which plants are prone to which pests and diseases. When control becomes too difficult or burdensome, throw the plant out. There are so many wonderful plants that are relatively trouble-free that it is not worthwhile for the amateur greenhouse gardener to nurse the kinds that cause special difficulties.

Disease Control

The chief causes of diseases of greenhouse plants are funguses, bacteria and viruses. Of these the funguses give trouble most often, showing themselves as dark spots on leaves, as molds on plants and soil, as rots and in other ways. Several commercial fungicides are easily applied as liquids or dusts and are effective for fungus control. (See page 787 in "Plant Diseases.")

However, it is a good idea to apply a fungicide (in spray form) every three weeks at the same time that an insecticide is used. A specific recommendation for reasonable control of both disease and insects is a mixture (in 1 gal. water) of 2 tsp. 50-percent carbaryl wettable powder, 3 tsp. Kelthane 18.9 percent wettable powder and 4 tsp. 75-percent folpet wettable powder. This spray should be applied on relatively warm days, with all the vents kept open while spraying.

Diseases are less susceptible to control by following a regular spray program than are insects. A general practice is to delay application of fungicides until the first evidence of infection is detected. Then begin a special spray or dusting program designed to control a specific disease on a particular plant or crop and keep this up until satisfactory control is attained.

PART II

Plants for the Garden –
An Endless Choice

Flower gardens are cultivated for summer recreation
over much of North America. Each garden has individuality. It may be very small, a splash of color asserted
by blue delphiniums and lemon-yellow snapdragons in
a border, pink and white geraniums near a door, huge
blue morning glories on a white lattice. A garden may
be serenely formal, with carefully groomed shrubs, trees
and lawns, or delightfully hodgepodge, full of unexpect-
ed surprises such as poppies close to a rock, hyacinths
in a tub, a curtain of green beans on tall poles. A garden
may be very specialized: all roses, irises or lilies.

Gardening is a challenging occupation involving physical exertion and more than a little mental stimulation.
To grow plants one must know plants. The successful
gardener is sensitive to the varying needs of the kinds
he tends. He is skilled in horticultural techniques and
alert to vary his practices to take full advantage of the
changing seasons.

To plant a row of tiny seeds, small and delicate seedlings, or dusty bulbs in the raw earth of spring and eventually to gather armfuls of flowers and vegetables are a
miracle that causes even the most nonchalant gardener
to be filled with pride.

CHAPTER 5

WHERE THEY CAME FROM

Plants from Afar—Early Plant Description—Traveling Species—Dutch Origins—Explorers—Modern Collectors—Mutations—Hybrids

THE SIMILARITY of this continent's climates and soils to those of such varied places as Europe, the mountains of northern India and western China, the isles of Japan and parts of South America has made it possible to add great variety to North American gardens. A few examples are the potato and runner bean from South America; rhododendrons from southeast Europe, China and Tibet; apples from the continent of Europe; the horse chestnut from the Balkans; and roses from the continents of Europe and Asia. Some of these plants now grow more vigorously here than they do in their natural homes. Some have been hybridized with our own native plants, to produce fine new varieties.

PLANT ORIGINS

In 1548 William Turner, who had a garden near London, compiled a list of plants grown in England. He named a number of them from overseas already well known in cultivation. Such were the black mulberry (*Morus nigra*), now believed to have originated in central China; southernwood or old man (*Artemisia abrotanum*) from southern Europe; the winter cherry (*Physalis alkekengi*) from Europe; the almond and apricot from western Asia; the common white jasmine, which ranges from Persia to Kashmir and China; and the old red peony from southern Europe.

FIRST AMERICAN LISTS

The story of plants in the Americas began early in 1552 in Mexico. An Indian, Martin de la Cruz, wrote in his native language and illustrated in color a beautiful manuscript on native medicinal plants. Translated into Latin, the manuscript was presented to the Pope and it is now in the Vatican Library. Among numerous specimens described are the castor bean, the chocolate tree (*Theobroma cacao*) and the delightful vanilla orchid. Undoubtedly many of the plants were sent home to Spain, distributed through Europe and, sometimes, shipped back across the Atlantic to the North American colonies. Such appears to be the history of the African marigold.

In 1596 John Gerard, an English gardener, added very considerably to the knowledge of the plants then cultivated in England that had come from abroad. His list included the tomato (long grown for decoration but not eaten) from western South America. The manner of the arrival of the potato has been a puzzle. Gerard wrote that it was native to Virginia, but it is a native of South America and was unknown in North America until the 17th century.

EUROPE AND THE NEAR EAST

The horse chestnut, which plays such a lovely part in the spring landscape, arrived in England from Constantinople via France about 1615. It was long believed to have originated in India, but in 1879 was found to be a native of Greece and Albania.

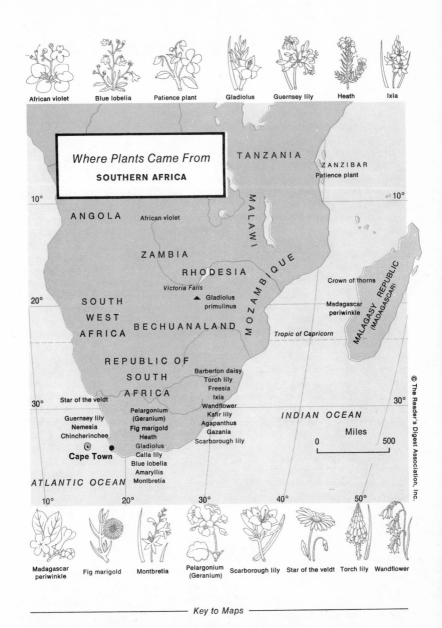

African violet

Blue lobelia

Patience plant

Gladiolus

Guernsey lily

Heath

Ixia

Where Plants Came From
SOUTHERN AFRICA

TANZANIA

ZANZIBAR
Patience plant

10°

ANGOLA

African violet

ZAMBIA

RHODESIA

Victoria Falls

▲ Gladiolus
primulinus

Crown of thorns

Madagascar
periwinkle

20°

SOUTH
WEST
AFRICA

BECHUANALAND

MOZAMBIQUE

MALAWI

MALAGASY REPUBLIC (MADAGASCAR)

Tropic of Capricorn

REPUBLIC OF
SOUTH
AFRICA

Barberton daisy
Torch lily
Freesia
Ixia
Wandflower
Kafir lily
Agapanthus
Gazania
Scarborough lily

INDIAN OCEAN

30°

Star of the veldt

Guernsey lily
Nemesia
Chincherinchee

Cape Town

Pelargonium
(Geranium)
Fig marigold
Heath
Gladiolus
Calla lily
Blue lobelia
Amaryllis
Montbretia

Miles

0   500

ATLANTIC OCEAN

10°   20°   30°   40°   50°

© The Reader's Digest Association, Inc.

Madagascar
periwinkle

Fig marigold

Montbretia

Pelargonium
(Geranium)

Scarborough lily

Star of the veldt

Torch lily

Wandflower

Key to Maps

© Principal botanical gardens through which
plants were distributed

▲ Wild parent of garden varieties

✳ Cultivated form

☆ Important source of cultivated plants

Anchusa
Wallflower
Horned violet
Tulip
Tamarisk
Sweet William
Sweet pea

Anemone

Annual
chrysanthemum

Auricula

Sweet bay

Tussock
bellflower

Candytuft

Carnation

55°   10°   0°   5°   10°

Irish heath
● Edinburgh
Heather

● Dublin
IRELAND
North Sea

50°

Strawberry tree
London pride

English primrose

15°
GREAT BRITAIN
HOLLAND
Leiden
❋ Ten-week s
SAXONY

ATLANTIC OCEAN
● Kew
BELGIUM
GERMAN

Honesty
Winter cherry

NORMANDY
Sweet William
● Paris
Baden-Baden ●

45°

Bay of Biscay
FRANCE
Willow gentian

Martagon lily
Monkshood
German iris AUSTR
SWITZERLAND
Erica ca.
Hepati

Firethorn
Larkspur

Laburnum
Globe thistle
Canterbury bell
Auricula
Padua ●

English iris
Perennial cornflower
Shasta daisy
Cupid's dart
Sweet alyssum
Virginia stock
Lavender
❋ Sweet violet
Aster amellus
Anemone apennina

40°
Tamarisk
Heath
● Montpellier
PYRENEES
ILES D'HYERES
Lavandula stoechas
Florence ●
Florentine iris

Crocuses
Horned violet
Yellow Turk's-cap lily
Carnation
Rosemary
CORSICA
Helleborus corsicus
Rockrose
❋ Anemone
● Rome
Sage
Bladder se

Laurustinus
Portugal broom
Portugal laurel
● Madrid
SPAIN

Tree heath
Annual convolvulus
Spanish broom
Spanish iris
SARDINIA
Parsley

Daffodils and narcissuses

35°
GIBRALTAR
Rhododendron
Mediterranean
SIC.

Crimson flax
Annual chrysanthemum
Viscaria
Mignonette
Iris unguicularis
Chaste tree
Mt. Etna bro
Sweet pea

ALGERIA

MOROCCO

© The Reader's Digest Association, Inc.

Catnip
Christmas rose
Perennial cornflower
Crimson peony
Crocus
Cyclamen
Daffodi

Strawberry tree   Spanish broom   Snowdrop   Sage   Rosemary   Oriental poppy   Parsley

20°

Where Plants Came From
EUROPE AND THE MEDITERRANEAN COASTS

Narcissus

Gypsophila

POLAND

Monkshood

U. S. S. R.

CZECHOSLOVAKIA   Tussock bellflower

CARPATHIANS

Christmas rose

Dwarf almond
Catnip
Blue scabious
Iris reticulata
Anchusa
Pyrethrum
Salvia turkistanica

Mignonette

HUNGARY

▲ Lilac   BANAT

ROMANIA

CRIMEA
Azalea
Snowdrop

Danube

Black Sea

Madonna lily

SLAVIA

BULGARIA

Iris pallida
Anemone
Crocus
Hyacinth

Strawberry tree
Opium poppy

Salonika ●

Madonna lily
Night-scented stock

Sweet bay

GREECE

Wallflower

Corinth ●

Acanthus
Myrtle

AEGEAN
ISLANDS

Tulip
Jerusalem cross
Crown imperial

Istanbul ●   Rose of Sharon

☆   Cherry laurel
Sweet sultan
Pink

Tulip
Mock orange

TURKEY

Glory-of-the-snow
Hyacinth
Cyclamen coum
Lilac

▲ Cyclamen

Rhododendron
Autumn crocus
Oriental poppy
Grape hyacinth

Love-in-a-mist

Weeping willow

● Aleppo

SYRIA

Damask rose

CYPRUS

Rockrose

Cedar

● Damascus

Love-in-a-mist

Lavender

Lilac

CRETE

Oleander
Candytuft
Crimson peony

Sea

20°   25°

0   Miles   250

ISRAEL   Hollyhock

English iris   Erica carnea   Gentian   Globe thistle   Grape hyacinth   Honesty   Hyacinth

Dahlia

California poppy

Cactus (Opuntia)

Cactus

Bloodroot

African marigold

Adam's need

Dutchman's-pipe

Evening primrose

Flowering currant

Gaillardia

Sneezeweed

Morning glory

Beard-tongue

ALASKA

Arctic Circle

Hudson Bay

LABRADOR

Wintergreen

50°

Snowberry

CANADA

Juneberry
Cardinal flower
Bloodroot
Bergamot

Boston

Flowering currant
Fleabane
Holly mahonia
Silk-tassel bush

▲ Long-spurred columbine

R O C K Y   M O U N T A I N S

Great Lakes

Calico bush
Perennial aster ▲
Phlox ▲

▲ Lupine   Cornus nuttallii

OREGON

40°

Camass   Musk

CALIFORNIA

Nemophila insignis
Godetia
Meadow-foam
California poppy
Clarkia
Phacelia
Tree lupine
Ceanothus

Gaultheria

U. S. A.

Beard-tongue

Cactuses and Succulents
Yucca
Penstemon barbatus

ARIZONA

30°

Mexican orange

TEXAS

Mississippi

Dutchman's-pipe

PENNSYLVANIA
OHIO
Virginia creeper
Evening primrose
Mountain rosebay

Spiderwort

VIRGINIA

BERMUD

Coneflower
Helenium
Gaillardia
Goldenrod
Tickseed
Annual phlox
Mealycup sage

Shooting star
Azalea

Blue-eyed gr

CAROLINAS

Trumpet vine
Rose acacia
Carolina allspice
Southern magnolia
Flowering dogwood
Adam's needle

ATLANTIC
OCEAN

Mock orange
Coralroot
African marigold
Cosmos
Zinnia

FLORIDA

Tropic of Cancer

Gulf of Mexico

20°

MEXICO

Tiger flower
Dahlia ▲ ✳
Morning glory
Salvia

WEST INDIES

Poinsettia
Canna

PACIFIC OCEAN

Caribbean Sea

Miles

0   500

10°

110°

100°

90°

Phlox

Coneflower

Salvia

Snowberry

Spiderwort

Virginia creeper

Wintergreen

Passionflower Sunflower Calceolaria Eucryphia Fuchsia Avens Marvel of Peru

Monkey flower

Nasturtium

Oenothera odorata

Orchid (cattleya)

Orchid

Pampas grass

Peruvian lily

Salpiglossis

Where Plants Came From

NORTH AND SOUTH AMERICA

10°
70° 60° 50° 40°

VENEZUELA

COLOMBIA

0°

ECUADOR

Amazon

Sunflower
Nasturtium
Heliotrope

Orchids

Canary creeper
Marvel of Peru
Peruvian lily
Calceolaria

P E R U

B R A Z I L

10°

Alstroemeria
Tropaeolum tricolor
Begonia
Salpiglossis
Monkey flower
Butterfly flower
Fuchsia

B O L I V I A

Blue passionflower
Bougainvillea
Purslane

20°

P A R A G U A Y

Tropic of Capricorn

PACIFIC OCEAN

Plata

30°

A R G E N T I N A

U R U G U A Y

Escallonia
Embothrium
Eucryphia
Tricuspidaria
Barberry

Flowering tobacco
Pampas grass
Zephyr flower
Verbena
Petunia

C H I L E

ATLANTIC OCEAN

40°

I. DE CHILOE

Berberis darwinnii
Gunnera
Avens

Oenothera odorata

Miles

0   500

© The Reader's Digest Association, Inc.

Pernettya
Veronica elliptica

90° 80°

FALKLAND
ISLANDS

50° 40° 30° 20°

Fuchsia magellanica

Zephyr flower Verbena Tropaeolum tricolor Flowering tobacco Butterfly flower Salpiglossis

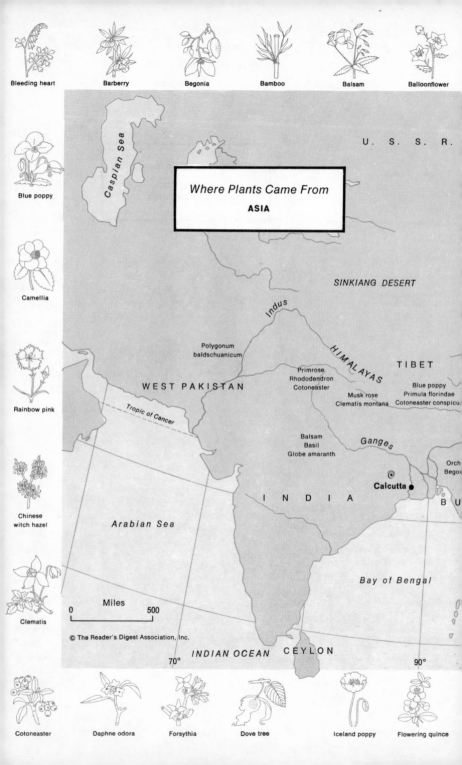

Bleeding heart

Barberry

Begonia

Bamboo

Balsam

Balloonflower

Blue poppy

Camellia

Rainbow pink

Chinese witch hazel

Clematis

Cotoneaster

Daphne odora

Forsythia

Dove tree

Iceland poppy

Flowering quince

Where Plants Came From
ASIA

Caspian Sea

U. S. S. R.

SINKIANG DESERT

Indus

HIMALAYAS

TIBET

Polygonum
baldschuanicum

Primrose
Rhododendron
Cotoneaster

Musk rose
Clematis montana

Blue poppy
Primula florindae
Cotoneaster conspicu

WEST PAKISTAN

Tropic of Cancer

Balsam
Basil
Globe amaranth

Ganges

Orch
Bego

Calcutta

B U

I N D I A

Arabian Sea

Bay of Bengal

Miles
0   500

© The Reader's Digest Association, Inc.

INDIAN OCEAN   CEYLON

70°

90°

Weeping willow
Viburnum fragrans
Viburnum carlesii
Tree peony
Tiger lily
Rhododendron

MANCHURIA

Amur

Iceland poppy

40°

GOBI DESERT

Sea of Japan

Japanese primrose
Balloonflower
Clematis
Cherry
Chrysanthemum
Hydrangea
Camellia
Kurume azalea
Japanese maple
Bamboo   JAPAN
Goldband lily
Japanese wisteria
Star magnolia
Aspidistra elatior
Rambler rose
▲ Flowering quince
Kousa
Mahonia japonica
Pieris japonica
Ligustrum japonicum
Euonymus japonicus
Aucuba japonica

Azalea

KOREA

Prunus triloba
▲ China aster
▲ Rainbow pink
Caryopteris mongholica
Maidenhair tree

▲ Korean chrysanthemum
Viburnum carlesii

Yellow
Sea

Nagasaki ●
☆

30°

Cherry

Gentiana sino-ornata
Clematis macropetala
▲ Tree peony
Viburnum fragrans
▲ Persian lilac
Ceratostigma willmottianum
Barberry
Incarvillea delavayi
Pieris formosa
Camellia reticulata

Hwang Ho

Clematis lanuginosa
Winter jasmine
Bleeding heart
Forsythia
Pompon chrysanthemum
Chinese witch hazel
False plumbago

CHINA

dodendron

Weeping willow
Plume poppy
Senecio clivorum
Dove tree
▲ Butterfly bush
Japanese anemone

Yangtze Kiang

Magnolia yulan
Chrysanthemum
Camellia
Azalea
Peony

TAIWAN

20°

Japanese
primrose

Si-Kiang

● Canton

Daphne odora
Winter sweet
Kerria
China rose

Flowering quince
Chinese wisteria
Tiger lily
Hydrangea

PACIFIC OCEAN

False
plumbago

A

HAINAN

Mekong

V I E T N A M

THAILAND

South China Sea

PHILIPPINES

10°

Primrose

110°

130°

Winter jasmine
Kurume azalea
Star magnolia
Musk rose
Orchid (cymbidium)
Orchid (paphiopedilum)

During the 17th century a number of new plants, including the cedar of Lebanon, were spread by the "Turkey Merchants," an English trading community in Aleppo.

DUTCH EXPLORATION

Much that was new came via Holland, then as now a nation of gardeners. The Dutch established close connections with South Africa and the Dutch East Indies, and they introduced many of the strange and brightly colored Cape bulbs, which can be grown if kept free from frost. Dutch traders were almost the only contact in that era with the largely unapproachable islands of Japan—for centuries the home of wonderful garden art. In 1690 the German traveler Engelbert Kaempfer was attached to the Dutch Embassy in Japan. One result of his two-year stay was the first account of the natural history of Japan, its plants and gardens. The popular and exotic-looking Japanese *Iris kaempferi* is named after him.

From Holland also came the great vogue for the tulip. This remarkable plant arrived in England about 1578 through Holland from Vienna, having been introduced there from Constantinople about 1554.

AMERICAN AND ALPINE COLLECTIONS

The American collector John Bartram, founder of the first botanical garden in America, near Philadelphia, sent to England the first azaleas and rhododendrons to be grown there, as well as maples, magnolias and other North American plants now found in gardens throughout the Temperate Zones.

Many gardens include a rock garden of some kind, or at least a few alpine plants. Rock gardening and the cultivation of alpines are relatively new interests—as late as the end of the 18th

century the common flowers of the European Alps were almost unknown. In 1775 Thomas Blaikie—a Scottish gardener—sent home from the Swiss Alps some 440 packets of plants, seeds and specimens.

Today, the woodlands of Europe include many kinds of trees from the Pacific coast of North America, the home of countless plants that are now common and almost indispensable in the garden. Captain George Vancouver on his voyage of 1791–1795 around the world had with him as surgeon Archibald Menzies, who was also a botanist. From him came the first detailed account of the rich flora to be found along the Pacific coast.

The Horticultural Society of London (now the internationally famous Royal Horticultural Society) was formed in 1807, and its committee felt that a plant-collecting expedition to follow up Menzies' discoveries would be rewarding. In 1824 the young Scot David Douglas sailed for the north Pacific coast and took back the now common mahonia (*Mahonia aquifolium*), the snowberry, clarkia, the musk plant, nemophila, the shrubby garrya, the red flowering currant, and the annual *Limnanthes douglasii*, which carries his name The Douglas fir, discovered by Menzies but introduced by Douglas, is a tree important for lumber.

PLANTS FROM CHINA

Although China was closed to travelers, there was some trade with the ports, and fortunately a certain John Reeves, tea inspector in China for the East India Company, had developed a successful technique for sending plants to England in the care of the company's captains. These plants included peonies, chrysanthemums, camellias and azaleas.

In 1842 a treaty opened additional

ports to the British, and the collector Robert Fortune was helped by a new invention, an airtight plant case produced by the amateur naturalist Dr. Nathaniel Ward. The introduction of plants by seed, even in the days of sail, was not too difficult. The seeds were sealed up in containers and so protected against changes of temperature on a long voyage. But to keep plants alive at sea for weeks on end through changing temperatures and climates was another matter. Ward's invention considerably improved their chances of survival.

Fortune ranged more widely than any previous collector. He had a flair for selecting from the wealth of Chinese plants those that would both thrive and be liked. To him are owed the winter-flowering jasmine; the so-called Japanese anemones; one of the first forsythias; *Prunus triloba; Primula japonica;* and many rhododendrons, azaleas, tree peonies and chrysanthemums. He also obtained the tea plant from China and introduced it into India.

OTHER FAR EASTERN SOURCES

Thomas Lobb was a pioneer collector of orchids. In 1843 he visited parts of India, Burma, Malaya and Borneo, and orchids soon became immensely fashionable.

In the middle of the 19th century the Bavarian Philipp von Siebold was appointed physician and naturalist to the Dutch East India Company, which had a trading station in Japan. He collected and sent to Europe numerous Japanese plants, many of which are popular in North American and European gardens today—notably camellias, azaleas and primulas.

But only the fringes of China and Japan were explored, and plants collected were mostly those grown in gardens. It was realized that many Japanese plants had originated in China,

and later, that the plants in the gardens of China itself had originated far from the coast, in the mountains of western China and Tibet, which were then unknown to Europeans.

Among plants discovered more recently are the butterfly bush (*Buddleia*), now seen everywhere; that great favorite, the regal lily; flowering cherries; clematis; and primulas and poppies. Many of these, although now almost commonplace, are among the most beautiful plants.

MODERN AMERICAN EXPLORATIONS

In the 20th century, explorations in many parts of the world have been sponsored by American institutions, including the Arnold Arboretum, the United States Department of Agriculture and Longwood Gardens. Among those who have journeyed to remote areas are Ernest H. Wilson, Frederick G. Meyer, Joseph F. Rock and John L. Creech.

PLANT CHANGES

Apart from the great number of plants collected, many others have been evolved: first, the unusual variations of form that on rare occasions occur naturally, sometimes producing a plant that is much more desirable than the standard type; and second, variations produced by man.

In the first case, a change takes place within the plant—a mutation—causing an obvious exterior change. These mutations occur very infrequently, and even then usually pass unnoticed, for, as mutants are usually so abnormal as to be weakly, nature soon eliminates them.

A good example of one type of mutant is the double flower—the daffodil and the cherry. From time immemorial observant gardeners have noticed such peculiarities and have nurtured and propagated their growth by one of the numerous means available to man but not found in nature—such as the rooting of cuttings, grafting and budding.

Until recent times man has been unable to produce these "sports," as they are called. Now, however, he can do so to some extent.

One method is by the use of a substance called colchicine, found in the autumn crocus (*Colchicum*). Atomic radiation may also have the same effect. But such methods are very haphazard. Often the embryo plant under treatment is killed, and many of the mutants that do result are useless.

HYBRIDIZATION

The second method of producing new plants occurs sparingly in nature, but has been used by man on an enormous scale, particularly during the last century. If pollen is taken from one kind of plant and is successfully used to fertilize the ovules of a related one, the seedling, or hybrid, will have qualities that are different from those of both its parents.

There are, of course, very severe limitations on the production of hybrids. The parents must be close members of the same flower family. It is often possible to hybridize, or "cross," two kinds of rose, but a rose could never, of course, be crossed with a holly or a lupine.

Hybrids can occur naturally when two kinds of plant grow close together, are compatible with each other, flower simultaneously—with bees, flies or wind carrying the pollen at an appropriate time from one to the other. The hybrid plane tree is a particularly famous example of the almost infinite possibilities of producing new plants, for, strange as it may seem, one parent comes from the New World and the other from the Old. It seems certain that at some time an American plane tree was placed close to an Oriental plane. The wind carried the pollen of one to the female flowers of the other. The seedlings from this union showed variations from both the American and Oriental parents, and the vigorous tree proved to be ideal for growth in smoky cities.

Many hybrids owe their origins to the accidental planting of two varieties of the same family close to each other. For many centuries gardeners unknowingly brought about the necessary conditions by placing plants side by side, and then selected the new plants that arose as seedlings. As far as is known, it was not until the early 18th century that gardeners understood how hybrids arose, and became aware of their power to emulate the process by transferring the pollen themselves.

SCIENTIFIC BREEDING

This was a development of the greatest importance to the human race, for in the hands of scientific breeders plants can be bred to fulfill special conditions—to resist disease, to give bigger and better crops or to produce more showy flowers. Desirable parents may be brought together from any part of the world, or pollen from an early-flowering plant may be kept alive, by means of refrigeration, for use on a plant that flowers at a different season.

That domestic animals could be bred had been known for centuries. Now many skillful men took up the work of breeding plants for a specific purpose. The American Luther Burbank gained great fame as a hybridist. There are few vegetable plants or fruit trees in the garden today that are not hybrids. Among flowers, almost all roses, irises, lupines and many annuals have been developed in this way. A few plants are accidental in their origins, but the majority are the results of purposeful breeding.

ANNUALS FOR COLOR AND CUTTING
These Bloom Quickly From Seed

The Versatile Plant—Soil—Time and Methods of Sowing—Indoor Starting— 127 Plants and Many Varieties

A TRUE ANNUAL is a plant which completes its life cycle from seed sowing to seed setting and dies naturally within 12 months. Many other kinds of plants can, however, be grown as annuals by sowing the seed early in the year, usually indoors to hasten germination, and then, after careful nurturing, planting the seedlings outdoors to flower the same summer.

The great merit of annuals is their adaptability. (See list of annuals beginning on page 121.) They can be used to fill flower beds and gaps in established borders, as trailing plants in hanging baskets, in window boxes and to provide quickly grown, gay flowers in a new garden. The taller kinds may be grown to form a temporary screen or background. In addition, annuals provide an excellent source of cut flowers, and rows can be sown for this purpose. For any of these uses they give quick results at low cost.

Many flowers grown as annuals and commonly called by this name are really tender perennials. In their native lands and in regions where little or no frost occurs they persist from year to year, but in severer climates winter cold kills them. Here belong such plants as snapdragon, scarlet sage (salvia), verbena and many others. Larkspur, calendula and cockscomb are examples of true annuals.

The soil itself may play its part in delaying or hastening flowering. Some plants—for instance the annual lupine and the flowering tobacco plant (nicotiana)—bloom earlier when there are generous amounts of nitrogen in the soil. On the other hand, scarlet salvia and clarkia flower earlier when the soil is poor in nitrogen.

It is possible, therefore, to alter the time of flowering to some extent by using different methods of fertilizing.

PREPARING THE GROUND

Because the great majority of annual seeds are small in size, it is necessary to rake the surface of the soil to as fine a condition as possible prior to sowing them directly outdoors. (For preparation of the soil, see page 745.) Rake the earth backward and forward to crumble the smaller lumps. Crush any obstinate ones by using the teeth of the rake with the handle held upright. If the soil is still not sufficiently fine, rake and crumble it once more.

Where the soil is known to be acid, it may be necessary to apply agricultural lime as a dressing (see page 742), depending on the degree of acidity. This is especially necessary in the case of such annuals as candytuft and love-in-a-mist, which need nearly neutral or alkaline soil for success.

SEED SOWING OUTDOORS
When to Sow

The seeds of all fairly quick-growing annuals can be sown outdoors where the plants are to flower, in the spring—about the time that trees begin to leaf out, or earlier in some cases. A number of the hardiest may also be sown in the autumn; then they will flower much earlier the following spring. Geographical location largely determines which annuals may be autumn-sown. Such sowing is more apt to be successful in regions where winters are fairly mild than where severe winters prevail. To assure a constant supply of cut flowers it is common practice to make two or more successive sowings of the same kinds.

Annuals that require a comparatively long period of growth before they reach blooming size, such as wax begonia, lobelia, verbena and stock, are usually sown indoors from six weeks to three months before the resulting seedlings are planted outdoors. Indoor sowing is also practiced when earlier blooms are wanted from kinds that respond satisfactorily from outdoor sowings, and when the seed of certain varieties is scarce or expensive. (For sowing, see page 700.)

Sowing Broadcast

To make a beautiful border, use a pointed stick to mark out broad, irregularly shaped drifts or patches on the bed where the plants are to flower. Label each with the name of the variety to be planted, bearing in mind that the groups should provide pleasing color combinations and other agreeable associations. Generally speaking, the taller-growing types should be kept to the back of the border, the small or edging annuals to the

front, and those of intermediate size somewhere between the two. Island beds, which can be viewed from all sides, are also attractive. Sprinkle the seeds of each variety within the confines of the marked-out drift and then carefully rake the soil over the seeds so that they are just buried. Do not disturb the outlines of the drifts.

As an alternative to sowing broadcast (that is, dispersing the seeds evenly over each drift or patch area), sow the seeds in shallow drills—little furrows or trenches—spaced 6 to 12 in. apart, within the boundaries of each area. These furrows may be made by using a stake or the end of a rake handle. After the seeds are in place, cover them with soil. This method eases the work of thinning the seedlings and weeding between them.

Sowing for Cut Flowers

There is no simpler way to provide cut flowers for decoration in summer than by sowing annuals. Select a border some distance from the house, where, if the blooms are cut regularly, the general appearance of the garden will not suffer. Make the rows 1 to 1½ ft. apart so that it will be easy to hoe between them later on, and so that the plants will have plenty of room for development.

Sow four rows and then allow a space of 2 ft. before sowing another four rows, and so on. The 2-ft. spaces in between form "picking" paths and will become well tramped down as picking proceeds.

Should the weather remain dry, gentle watering with a fine sprinkler is advisable two days after sowing and again a week later.

Thinning and Weeding

When the seedlings are about 1 in. high, thin out those of small plants—such as sweet alyssum, portulaca and candytuft—so they are about 4 in.

apart, and those of taller and broader kinds—such as calendula, hunnemannia and aster—6 to 9 in. apart. Very large growers, such as dwarf dahlias, celosias, sunflowers and amaranthus, may be allowed 1 to 2 ft. between the plants that remain after thinning out. At the same time remove any weeds that have come up. After thinning, press down the soil firmly where it has been disturbed. It is usually better not to thin autumn-sown seedlings until the following spring, but where they come up too thickly they should be lightly thinned in the fall and fully thinned the following March.

How to Tell Seedlings from Weeds

The easiest way to recognize the seedlings of the varieties sown in the garden is to sow a very small quantity of each indoors, labeling each kind clearly. The seedlings will come up two or three weeks before those sown outside, thus giving the gardener time to become familiar with the appearance of the young plants.

Staking

Stiff-growing annuals, such as vincas and dwarf marigolds, require no staking, and many of the taller-growing ones, such as cosmos, may be strong enough to stand alone. Soft and floppy plants, such as cornflowers and gaillardias, need support. Provide this by inserting small, twiggy brushwood stakes at about 8-in. intervals all over the area, once the seedlings have appeared and have been thinned. Also needing support—best provided by bamboo or strong wooden stakes to which the plants are neatly tied—are such sturdily growing kinds as sunflowers, amaranthus, tall marigolds and tall snapdragons.

Annual vines may be trained up strings or wires stretched taut, on trellises or over pyramids or cones formed of brushwood stakes pushed firmly into the ground.

SEED SOWING INDOORS

Sow annuals which are to be started indoors in flats or pots in late winter or early spring. (See page 701.)

When transplanting annuals that have been raised indoors, space them in the garden as recommended in the list of plants discussed below.

At the correct planting time in spring many kinds of annuals can be bought from nurserymen as seedlings ready for planting out. This makes it possible for gardeners who do not have the interest or facilities to raise their own plants indoors to secure some that will provide a colorful display of early annuals.

Recommended Plants

ABRONIA (SAND VERBENA)

A low-growing and usually trailing tender perennial, this is often grown as an annual. Useful for edging beds, it is sometimes also planted in hanging baskets. Its best scent is in the evening. Sow seed early indoors or in a greenhouse, space seedlings 2 in. apart in flats and harden off before planting in the garden 9 in. apart; or sow seed directly outdoors in spring.

Abronia umbellata, about 6 in. The best-known species; flowers bright rose with white centers from June to September. Fragrant.

ACROCLINIUM. See *Helipterum*.

ADONIS (PHEASANT'S-EYE)

It produces red or yellow flowers con-

sisting of from 5 to 16 petals. Equally
useful in formal and informal gardens,
it prefers soil with plenty of compost
or peat incorporated. Sow seed not
more than ⅛ in. deep in early spring
where plants are to flower. Thin out
plants to 6 in. apart.

Adonis aestivalis (summer adonis),
1½ ft. Crimson flowers 1½ in. across,
in June and July.

A. annua (autumn adonis), 2 ft.
Deep red flowers ¾ in. across, from
June to September.

AETHIONEMA (STONECRESS)

This dwarf plant bears white, pink,
rose or lilac flowers. It likes a light,
sandy soil. Sow seed early under glass,
harden off and plant out 6 in. apart;
or sow directly outdoors in spring.

Aethionema buxbaumii, 6 in. Bears
gray-white leaves and tiny lilac or
pink flowers in June and July.

AFRICAN DAISY. See *Arctotis, Dimorphotheca.*

AGERATUM (FLOSSFLOWER)

Some varieties are dwarf and compact, others are 3 ft. tall. They bear
tassel-like blue, white or pinkish
flowers from June to September. They
need a sunny place and are often used
for summer flower beds. Sow seed indoors or in a greenhouse, harden off,
plant out 6 to 9 in. apart. Seed sown
directly outdoors produces plants that
bloom in late summer.

Ageratum corymbosum. Bright blue
flowers.

A. houstonianum. Heart-shaped
leaves, largish heads of bright blue
flowers. Many named garden varieties are offered in catalogues.

AGROSTIS (BENT GRASS)

These ornamental grasses are raised
chiefly for use in dried flower arrangements. They grow well in sun in ordinary soil. Sow seed directly outdoors
in spring where plants are to bloom.
Thin to 4 to 6 in. apart.

Agrostis hiemalis (hair grass), 2 ft.

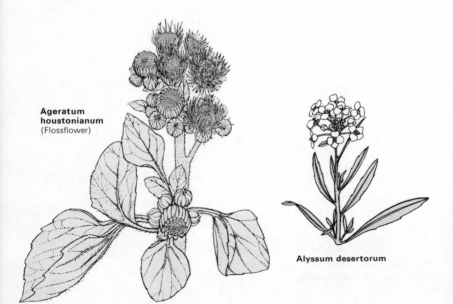

**Ageratum
houstonianum**
(Flossflower)

Alyssum desertorum

Narrow leaves and attractive silky, hairlike panicles.

A. nebulosa (cloud grass), 1 ft. Ornamental panicles with fine, hairlike branches.

ALONSOA (MASK-FLOWER)

The plant has showy red or orange flowers in great profusion in summer and early fall. It likes sunny places, and does badly in wet seasons. Remove dead flower heads and trim back growth for long succession of bloom.

Sow seed in spring where plants are to flower. Thin out to 9 in. apart.

Alonsoa acutifolia, 2 ft. Bushy, deep red flowers from June to October.

A. warscewiczii, 1½ ft. Heart-shaped leaves, brilliant scarlet flowers July to October.

ALYSSUM

Low-growing, gray foliage and small yellow or white flowers. It grows in any soil and prefers sun. Sow seed in spring, and thin out plants to 3 in. apart.

Alyssum desertorum, 4 in. Silvery-gray leaves, pale yellow flowers June to August.

For sweet alyssum, see *Lobularia*.

AMARANTHUS (AMARANTH)

Tall, erect, coarse-growing; some kinds have brilliantly colored foliage. Dense spikes of flowers can be dried and used as "everlastings." Sow seed indoors or in greenhouse, harden off and plant out when weather is warm and settled; or sow directly outdoors after danger from frost is passed.

Amaranthus caudatus (love-lies-bleeding), 2 to 3 ft. Bears drooping spikes and bright red tassels from June to September.

A. hybridus hypochondriacus (prince's-feather), 2 ft. Slender spikes of blood-red flowers from July to September.

A. tricolor, 1½ ft. Leaves greenish purple, bronzy, carmine or reddish violet. Long spikes of deep red flowers from July to September. Various garden varieties are offered, including Molten Fire with upper leaves brilliant crimson, *A.t. splendens* or Joseph's coat, with yellow, green and red leaves, and *A. salicifolia* with narrow orange and bronze leaves.

ANAGALLIS (PIMPERNEL)

Flowers are scarlet, blue or white. A low-growing plant, it is useful for fronts of borders. Sunny location preferred but any soil suitable. Sow seed indoors in spring, harden off in frame and plant out, 6 in. apart, when weather is warm and settled.

Anagallis arvensis (poor man's weatherglass, scarlet pimpernel). Spreading, with small pointed leaves and scarlet, blue or white flowers in summer and autumn, which close at the approach of bad weather.

A. linifolia, 1 ft. Narrow, pointed, dark green leaves, dense clusters of deep blue flowers in July.

A. tenella. Rounded leaves, tiny red bell-shaped flowers in summer. Prefers damp soil.

ANCHUSA (SUMMER FORGET-ME-NOT)

Quick-growing annuals, with bold foliage and clusters of blue or white forget-me-not-like flowers, they prefer fertile, well-drained soil and full sun. Sow seed in spring where plants are to bloom. Thin seedlings to 6 in. apart.

Anchusa officinalis and *A. capensis* (Cape forget-me-not) are similar, 1½ to 2 ft. Bluebird is the best and most commonly grown variety.

ANIMATED OAT. See *Avena sterilis*.

ANTIRRHINUM (SNAPDRAGON)

Really perennials which are commonly treated as annuals, these plants

Antirrhinum majus
(Snapdragon)

produce masses of showy flowers from early June until fall frost. They thrive best in light soil enriched with old compost or peat moss. Bone meal forked in at 5 oz. per sq. yd. prior to planting encourages a good fibrous root system to support a bushy top growth.

Sow the seed indoors or in a greenhouse in early spring, transplant the seedlings into flats, 2 in. apart, and when they are 3 in. high, pinch out the tip of the plant to encourage branching. Plant outdoors as soon as danger from late frost has passed. For earlier flowering, sow seeds out of doors early in August, and transplant the seedlings, 3 in. apart, to cold frames as soon as they are big enough to handle. Protect the frames from winter cold, and in spring set the plants out of doors where they are to bloom.

Antirrhinum majus. The most beautiful garden varieties belong to this species. Most catalogues list many kinds grouped according to height, flower color and other characteristics. Some varieties are resistant to rust disease. The Tetra varieties have especially large flowers. Double-flowered varieties are available. Snapdragons may be had in a wide selection of colors and combinations. Every color except blue is represented.

APHANOSTEPHUS (LAZY DAISY)
Pretty plants with daisylike flowers useful for garden decoration and for cut flowers, they bloom freely for a long period. Sow seed outdoors in spring where plants are to blossom, in a sunny location and in ordinary soil, and thin the seedlings to 8 to 9 in. apart.

Aphanostephus skirrobasis, 1½ ft. Flowers white with yellow centers.

APPLE OF PERU. See *Nicandra physalodes.*

ARCTOTIS (AFRICAN DAISY)
These plants are from South Africa, with white woolly leaves and brilliant yellow, pink, violet or rose daisylike flowers. Splendid for beds and good for cutting. Sow indoors in spring, harden off; plant out 1 ft. apart when weather is warm and settled, to start flowering in July.

Arctotis acaulis, 1½ ft. Flowers yellow above, wine-purple beneath. Deeply cut leaves covered with silver-white hairs.

A. stoechadifolia grandis, 2 to 2½ ft. Flowers white and violet. Leaves toothed.

Seedsmen offer hybrid arctotis which produce flowers in various shades of cream, yellow, apricot, bronze, pink, red or mauve as well as in white.

ARGEMONE
(MEXICAN POPPY, PRICKLY POPPY)
Unusual, coarse plants bearing large yellow, white or purple poppylike flowers and prickly leaves, they prefer dry soil and a sunny spot. Sow seed indoors in spring, harden off, and plant out when fairly warm, settled weather arrives, 1 ft. apart, for midsummer flowering; or, for late flowering, sow out of doors where the plants are to grow.

Argemone grandiflora, 3 ft. Leaves thistlelike. Large, cup-shaped white flowers in July and August.

A. mexicana, 2 ft. Bears scented bright yellow or orange flowers, 2 in. across, in July and August.

ASPERULA (WOODRUFF)
This attractive dwarf plant with small blue or white flowers is suitable for filling gaps in the rock garden. It prefers a moist, shady place. Sow seed in spring where plants are to flower, thin out to 1 in. apart. Flowers last well in water when cut. The only annual species is:

Asperula orientalis, 9 to 10 in. Hairy leaves, clusters of small, tubular sky-blue fragrant flowers in summer.

ASTER. See *Callistephus*.

AUTUMN ADONIS. See *Adonis annua*.

AVENA
Avena sterilis (animated oat), 3 ft. Ornamental grass grown chiefly for dried-flower arrangements, it flourishes best in sunny places in ordinary soil. Sow seed directly outdoors in spring where plants are to bloom. Thin 4 to 6 in. apart. Has curious twisting flower heads which move with changes in the amount of moisture present; this is called hygroscopic action.

BABY BLUE-EYES. See *Nemophila menziesii*.

BABY'S BREATH. See *Gypsophila*.

BACHELOR'S BUTTON. See *Centaurea cyanus*.

BALLOON VINE. See *Cardiospermum halicacabum*.

BALSAM. See *Impatiens balsamina*.

BALSAM APPLE. See *Momordica balsamina*.

BALSAM PEAR. See *Momordica charantia*.

BARTONIA. See *Mentzelia*.

BASELLA (MALABAR NIGHTSHADE)
These are fleshy, twining vines of rampant growth. In the North, start seed indoors and set young plants in garden after settled warm weather arrives. In the South, seed may be sown directly outdoors. Space plants

1 to 1½ ft. apart. Flowers are inconspicuous.

Basella alba. Flowers whitish.

B. rubra. Flowers reddish.

BASKET FLOWER. See *Centaurea americana.*

BEGONIA

Varieties of wax begonia are commonly grown as annuals. They succeed in sun or light shade and bloom continuously throughout the summer. Seed is very fine; sow it in January or February in pots indoors. Do not cover the seeds with soil—simply press them into the surface with a flat tamper or piece of board. Transplant seedlings to sandy, peaty or woodland soil, 2 in. apart, and keep them growing indoors. Harden off and plant outdoors after weather is settled and warm. Excellent for beds, borders, window and porch boxes.

Begonia semperflorens (wax begonia). Numerous varieties. Plants are characteristically bushy, 6 in. to 1½ ft. tall with attractive green, bronze or reddish foliage and a profusion of pink, red or white flowers.

BELLS OF IRELAND. See *Moluccella laevis.*

BENT GRASS. See *Agrostis.*

BINDWEED. See *Convolvulus.*

BIRD'S-EYES. See *Gilia tricolor.*

BLACK-EYED-SUSAN VINE. See *Thunbergia alata.*

BLANKETFLOWER. See *Gaillardia.*

BLUE DAISY. See *Felicia.*

BLUE-EYED MARY. See *Collinsia verna.*

BLUE LIPS. See *Collinsia grandiflora.*

BLUE MARGUERITE. See *Felicia.*

BRACHYCOME

Daisylike flowers of white, blue, lilac or rose blossom from these plants, which form dense, delicately scented carpets. Sow seed indoors in spring and harden off the plants before putting them in the garden after settled warm weather arrives. Plant 4 or 5 in. apart. Brachycome blooms from July on for a long period. Seed can be sown in the open for flowering later.

Brachycome iberidifolia (Swan River daisy), 1½ ft. Many different-colored flowers according to variety, each measuring about 1½ in. across.

BROWALLIA

It bears violet, blue or white flowers in great profusion throughout the summer. Sow seed indoors in spring; harden off and plant seedlings in deep, rich loam, 9 in. apart, after warm, settled weather arrives.

Browallia americana, 1 to 2 ft. Oval, pointed leaves, blue flowers ½ in. across. Plant 9 in. apart.

B. speciosa, 2 to 3 ft., has flowers 2 in. across, blue, violet or white.

Garden varieties, such as Sapphire, Blue Bells and Silver Bells, are especially recommended.

B. viscosa, 1 to 1½ ft. Oval, hairy, sticky leaves, dark blue flowers with white centers, 1 in. across. Plant 6 in. apart.

BROWN-EYED SUSAN. See *Rudbeckia triloba.*

CALANDRINIA (ROCK PURSLANE)

These thrive in hot locations in full sun and in well-drained soil. They withstand dry conditions well. Seed may be sown directly outdoors in spring where the plants are to bloom. The resulting plants should be thinned to 6 in. If preferred, sowing may be done indoors in spring and the young plants set outdoors later. Flowers open only in sunshine.

Calandrinia grandiflora, 15 to 18 in. Pink or red.

C. umbellata, 6 to 8 in. Magenta-crimson.

CALENDULA
There are double and semidouble flowered varieties of this plant which produce large, flat disklike flowers in many beautiful colors from deep orange through yellow to cream. It thrives in a poor soil. Where mild winters prevail, sow mid-September for early summer flowering. Sow outdoors in spring for flowers from early July onward. Thin out to 9 in. apart. Alternatively, sow indoors in spring about six weeks before the plants are to be set out in the garden. A good cut flower, with a unique odor.

Calendula officinalis (pot marigold), up to 3 ft. but usually lower. Many beautiful named varieties of pot marigold are listed in seed catalogues.

C. stellata (star marigold), 2½ ft. Bears yellow flowers 2 in. across, excellent for cutting.

CALIFORNIA POPPY. See *Eschscholtzia californica*.

CALLIOPSIS. See *Coreopsis*.

CALLISTEPHUS (CHINA ASTER)
These produce double or single disklike flowers in varying brilliant pinks, purples or mauves, as well as white. They prefer rich soil and full sun. Sow seed indoors, harden off, plant out about mid-May in the North. Set the plants 8 to 9 in. apart. Excellent results may also be had by sowing directly outdoors in spring, where the plants are to bloom, and thinning out the seedlings.

Callistephus chinensis. Has an incredible number of varieties from the dwarf bedding types to the 3-ft.-tall California Giant and the Giant Crego varieties. Special wilt-resistant strains are offered and are recommended for areas where wilt disease is prevalent. For descriptions of varieties consult seed catalogues.

CALONYCTION (MOONFLOWER)
Tall, twining vines resemble morning glories but they open their large, fragrant white or purple flowers only at night. Propagated by seed sown directly outdoors or can be started in pots indoors and set out later. Soak seed in water for 48 hours before sowing. Plant in area that has sun or part shade. Vines grow to a height of 20 ft. or more.

Calonyction aculeatum. Flowers white or white and green, up to 6 in. diameter.

C. muricatum. Flowers 3 in. across, purple.

CAMPION. See *Silene*.

CANARYBIRD FLOWER. See *Tropaeolum peregrinum*.

CANDYTUFT. See *Iberis*.

CAPE FORGET-ME-NOT. See *Anchusa capensis*.

CAPE MARIGOLD. See *Dimorphotheca*.

CARDINAL CLIMBER. See *Quamoclit sloteri*.

CARDIOSPERMUM (HEARTSEED)
A quick-growing vine, needs fertile, well-drained soil and full sun. Sow seed directly outdoors and thin plants to 1 ft., or start seed indoors six weeks before warm, settled weather is expected and then transplant to open garden.

Cardiospermum halicacabum (balloon vine), 10 ft., with small white flowers and decorative seedpods.

CASTOR BEAN. See *Ricinus*.

CATCHFLY. See *Silene*.

CATHEDRAL BELLS. See *Cobaea scandens*.

CELOSIA (COCKSCOMB)

These are warm-weather annuals. The plumed varieties are commonly grown for planting out; their feathery spikes are interesting for flower arrangements. The crested cockscomb varieties are attractive for garden display and cutting. Sow seed indoors in spring, grow the young plants in a minimum temperature of 60° F., in rich soil. Plant outdoors only after the weather is decidedly warm and settled. Allow about 1 ft. between plants.

Celosias also prosper if seed is sown outdoors during springtime in fertile soil and in a sunny location. Thin the young plants to 9 to 12 in. apart.

Celosia argentea, 3 ft. Narrow, pointed leaves and dense spikes of yellow, orange, red, crimson or purple flowers for most of the summer.

C. a. cristata, 2½ ft. Numerous garden varieties with crested heads, flowering all summer.

CENTAUREA

Attractive blue, purple, white or pink tubular flowers in close heads blossom on these tall plants. Sow seed in fall or spring where plants are to flower. Thin out to 9 in. apart.

Centaurea americana (basket flower), 3 to 4 ft. Flowers 5 in. diameter, pink, lavender or white, in summer. Fine for cutting.

C. cyanus (cornflower, bachelor's button). Many different garden varieties with red, blue, mauve, white or pink flowers. May grow to 3 ft. but dwarf varieties are available.

C. moschata (sweet sultan), 2 ft. Attractive heads of purple, yellow or

Centaurea cyanus
(Cornflower,
Bachelor's Button)

white slightly scented flowers from June to September.

CENTRANTHUS OR KENTRANTHUS (VALERIAN)

Annuals, or perennials treated as annuals, with dense terminal clusters of red or white flowers. Sow seed in spring where the plants are to flower. Thin out to 10 in. apart. They prefer full sun, are not particular as to soil.

Centranthus calcitrapa, 1½ ft. Deeply cut leaves, rosy-purple flowers from midsummer onward.

C. macrosiphon, 2 ft. Oval, toothed leaves, rose-colored tubular flowers from midsummer onward.

CEPHALARIA (GIANT SCABIOUS)

These plants produce small white, blue or yellow flowers with thistlelike heads from June to August. Sow seed

¼ in. deep in spring where plants are to flower. Thin out to 1 ft. apart. They like heavy soil.

Cephalaria syriaca, 1 ft. Prickly stems, pale blue or lilac flowers.

C. transylvanica, 3 ft. Slender stems; flowers creamy white or bluish in globular heads.

CERINTHE (HONEYWORT)

An interesting, good-looking plant that grows well in ordinary soil in full sun. The flowers are attractive to bees. Sow seed directly outdoors in spring and thin plants to 6 to 8 in. apart.

Cerinthe aspera, 18 in. Flowers bell-shaped, drooping, yellow or purple-brown.

CHINA ASTER. See *Callistephus*.

CHINA PINK. See *Dianthus chinensis*.

CHINESE FORGET-ME-NOT. See *Cynoglossum amabile*.

CHINESE HOUSES. See *Collinsia bicolor*.

CHRYSANTHEMUM
(ANNUAL CHRYSANTHEMUM)

These attractive plants bear daisylike flowers from midsummer onward. They are good for cutting. Sow ¼ in. deep in spring where plants are to flower. Thin out to 9 in. apart. When sown in mid-September to winter out of doors in fairly mild climate, it will flower earlier the following summer.

Chrysanthemum carinatum. Deeply cut leaves, white flowers 2 in. across with a purple center and a yellow zone at the base of the petals—hence the obsolete but catalogue name of *C. tricolor*. There are many varieties, with purple-, yellow- or red-banded flowers. All grow 2 ft. high and are excellent for cutting.

C. coronarium (crown daisy), 3 to 4 ft. White, cream or yellow flowers 1½ in. across. There are double-flowered kinds which are particularly good for cutting.

C. segetum (corn marigold), 1½ ft. Sprays of golden-yellow flowers, 2½ in. across. There are many lovely garden varieties.

CIGAR FLOWER. See *Cuphea platycentra*.

CLADANTHUS

The branching, bushy plants are easy to raise from seed sown directly outdoors in ordinary soil at sunny sites during springtime. Thin the seedlings to 9 in. Alternatively, seed can be sown indoors early and the resulting plants set in the garden after all danger of frost is passed.

Cladanthus arabicus, 2 to 3 ft. Flowers yellow, daisylike, 2 in. across.

CLARKIA

Where summers are cool, these showy plants make a wonderful display from July to mid-October with their attractive rose, purple, lilac, pink or white flowers. They will not stand hot, humid weather and prefer well-fertilized, slightly acid soil. Sow seed in spring where plants are to flower and thin out to 6 in. apart. In mild climates seed can be sown mid-September for flowering early in the year. A good cut flower, provided it is put in water immediately after picking.

Clarkia elegans, 3 ft. Best-known species.

C. pulchella, 1½ ft. Double-flowered varieties of both species are the most popular.

CLEOME
(SPIDERFLOWER, SPIDER PLANT)

Interesting and showy, bearing white, rose, yellow or purple flowers from June to killing frost; they are good for cutting. The plant prefers a light, sandy soil and a sunny place. It does not need to be staked, although it reaches a height of 3 to 6 ft. Sow seed indoors in spring, harden off and plant out 1½ ft. apart when weather becomes warm; or sow directly outdoors in spring.

Cleome lutea, 3 ft. Yellow flowers.

C. spinosa has erect hairy stems, covered with spines at the leafstalks. Flowers strongly scented, ranging from white and clear pink to rosy-purple according to variety; stamens protrude up to 4 in. The slender seedpods sticking out from the stem below the flowers give the spidery effect.

CLOUD GRASS. See *Agrostis nebulosa*.

COBAEA (CUP-AND-SAUCER VINE)
A quick-growing vine, it thrives in ordinary soil. Sow seed early indoors and transplant to garden when weather is warm and settled. In the South, sow directly outdoors. Suitable for sun or part shade.

Cobaea scandens (cathedral bells), 20 to 30 ft. Flowers large, bell-shaped, greenish-violet or white.

COCKSCOMB. See *Celosia*.

COIX
To raise this variety of ornamental grass, sow seed indoors about six weeks before weather is settled and, when warm enough, transplant the seedlings to the garden; or sow directly outdoors in spring and thin 6 to 9 in. apart. Requires well-drained soil and full sun.

Coix lacryma-jobi (Job's tears), 3 ft. Forms dense tufts and bears comparatively large pearl-gray seeds.

COLLINSIA
It bears single or clustered violet-rose, violet-blue or white flowers all summer. Best suited for areas where summers are not excessively hot, the plant prefers partial shade and dampish soil. The blooms are very good as cut flowers. Sow seed in mid-September ¼ in. deep. Thin out to 6 in. apart in following spring. Sow again in spring where plants are to flower in the fall; thin to same distance.

Collinsia bicolor (Chinese houses), 2 ft. Slender stems, large showy flowers in August, upper lip white, lower lip rosy-purple or violet. A white-flowered variety is sometimes grown.

C. grandiflora (blue lips), 15 in. Flowers in late spring and early summer, lower lip deep blue, upper lip purple or white. Likes partial shade.

C. verna (blue-eyed Mary), 2 ft. Bears clusters of long-stalked flowers in May with upper lip purple and lower lip vivid blue.

COLLOMIA
A good edging plant with white, red or yellow tubular flowers which attract bees, it likes a sunny location. Sow seed in spring where plants are to flower, and thin out to 6 in. apart. Best suited for regions where summers are not oppressively hot.

Collomia biflora (syn. *C. coccinea*), 2 ft. Narrow, pointed leaves, clusters of bright scarlet flowers in summer.

C. grandiflora, 3 ft. Stout reddish stems, dark green pointed leaves, clusters of orange or buff-colored tubular flowers in summer, each about 1 in. long. Unopened buds are pale green and sticky.

CONEFLOWER. See *Rudbeckia*.

CONVOLVULUS (BINDWEED)
The plant flowers freely throughout the summer until killing frost. It prefers a sunny place, ordinary soil. Sow seed indoors in spring, harden off, and set the plants 1 ft. apart in the garden after danger from frost has passed. For later flowering, sow

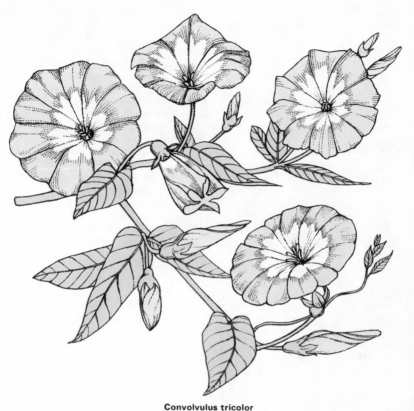

Convolvulus tricolor
(Dwarf Morning Glory)

seed where the plants are to be grown.

Convolvulus pentapetaloides. Narrow pointed leaves, solitary blue flowers; good for covering dry banks.

C. tricolor (dwarf morning glory). Reddish hairy stems, oblong pointed leaves, blue flowers 1½ in. across with a yellow and white throat. There are white, blue and rose-colored varieties.

COREOPSIS (TICKSEED)

The yellow, brown or reddish disklike flowers of this plant are brilliant in summer and early autumn, and make good long-stemmed cut flowers. Sow

seed in fall in regions of mild winters, or in spring, where plants are to flower. Thin out to 9 in. apart. They flourish in ordinary soil in sunny locations. Often listed as *Leptosyne* and as *Calliopsis.*

Coreopsis calliopsidea, 1½ ft. Large golden-yellow flowers 3 in. across. Prefers moist soil.

C. douglasii. Low, tufty plant, bears bright yellow flowers 1½ in. across on 1-ft. stems.

C. stillmanii, 1 ft. Golden-yellow flowers 2 in. across. Prefers dry soil and comes into bloom quickly.

C. tinctoria, 1 to 3 ft. Finely cut

Cosmos bipinnatus

foliage; bright yellow flowers 2 in. across, marked with dark crimson or purple at base. Many varieties.

CORNFLOWER. See *Centaurea cyanus*.

CORN MARIGOLD. See *Chrysanthemum segetum*.

COSMOS
Erect plants 3 to 6 ft., with finely cut leaves, they have white, yellow, rose,

purple or crimson disklike flowers. The foliage is graceful and feathery and the flowers large and colorful. The plants prefer poor soil and a sunny location. Sow seed indoors in spring, and set plants in garden when weather is settled and warm, after hardening them off. Space plants 1½ ft. apart. Where the growing season is short it is advisable to sow the early-flowering kinds.

Cosmos bipinnatus, 4 ft. Bushy,

erect, with white, pink, crimson or rose-colored flowers in late summer. Many single and double-flowered varieties are offered.

C. sulphureus. Has yellow flowers. Varieties grow 3 ft. tall and come in various tones of yellow and orange.

CREPIS (HAWK'S-BEARD)
It is easily grown in full sun in well-drained soil. Sow outdoors in spring directly where plants are to bloom. Thin 5 to 6 in. apart.

Crepis rubra, 6 to 8 in. Flowers resemble pink dandelions.

CROWN DAISY. See *Chrysanthemum coronarium.*

CROWN OF JEWELS. See *Lopezia coronata.*

CUP-AND-SAUCER VINE. See *Cobaea.*

CUPFLOWER. See *Nierembergia.*

CUPHEA (FIRECRACKER PLANT)
These striking plants bear vivid and unusual "firecracker" flowers from June until killing frost. Sow seed indoors in spring, pinch to induce bushiness, harden off and plant out 1 ft. apart in late May.

Cuphea lanceolata, 1½ ft. Quick-growing, lance-shaped leaves; striking deep mauve flowers. Flowers good for cutting.

C. platycentra (syn. *C. ignea*—cigar-flower). Flowers like tiny red cigars with ash-colored tips.

CYNOGLOSSUM (HOUND'S-TONGUE)
A pretty plant with rather coarse, hairy leaves and small blue, white or purple flowers, it likes a light soil but will grow in partial shade or sun. Sow seed mid-September where plants are to flower and thin out to 1 ft. apart the following spring, or sow directly outdoors in spring where plants are

to bloom. They may also be started early indoors and set out later.

Cynoglossum amabile (Chinese forget-me-not), 2 ft. Small, sweetly scented flowers produced freely over a long period from June.

CYPRESS VINE. See *Quamoclit pennata.*

DAHLBERG DAISY. See *Thymophylla.*

DELPHINIUM (LARKSPUR)
This erect and branching plant has large spikes of blue, red, white or purple flowers in summer. Sow seed where the plants are to flower, in spring or in fall. They like a soil which is deep and rich, and should be staked. Excellent as cut flowers, especially Giant Imperial and Giant Steeplechase varieties. Seedsmen's catalogues describe and offer a wide range of varieties of these annual kinds of delphinium, which are more commonly known as larkspur.

Delphinium ajacis (rocket larkspur), 1 to 3 ft. Blue or violet flowers. There is also the giant hyacinth-flowered type which has white or pink, mostly double flowers.

D. consolida flore-pleno (forking larkspur), 3 ft. Narrow leaves and double violet or blue flowers.

DEVIL-IN-THE-BUSH. See *Nigella damascena.*

DIANTHUS (ANNUAL PINK)
An attractive plant that bears brilliant-colored flowers suitable for garden decoration and cutting. Sow seed indoors early, transplant, harden off, and plant outdoors as soon as danger from frost is past; or sow directly outdoors in spring and thin to 6 to 8 in. apart. Well-drained neutral or slightly alkaline soil is preferred, as well as full sun.

Dianthus chinensis (Chinese pink) and its variety *heddewigii* have given rise to numerous color variations, with single or double flowers, the petals often beautifully fringed. Heights vary from 6 in. to 1½ ft. according to variety. Flower colors include white, pink, red, mauve and various combinations.

DIMORPHOTHECA
(CAPE MARIGOLD, AFRICAN DAISY)
The daisylike, brilliant flowers are blue, purple, violet, orange or white with shiny rays. They close at night and in dull weather. Sow seed indoors in spring, harden off, and plant out when weather is warm and settled. These plants need full sun.

Dimorphotheca annua, 15 in. Its flowers are white or yellowish; variety *ringens* has a blue ring around central eye.

D. aurantiaca, 15 in. Produces abundant brilliant orange-yellow flowers over a long period through the summer.

Modern hybrid varieties produce plants that show much variation in flower color.

DWARF MORNING GLORY. See *Convolvulus tricolor.*

ECHIUM (VIPER'S BUGLOSS)
An erect, hairy gray-leaved plant, it has blue, purple, rose or white irregular flowers which are liked by bees. Sow seed in late March where plants are to flower, thin out to 6 in. apart. Useful for beds.

Echium creticum, 2 ft. Brick-red flowers in summer.

E. plantagineum, up to 2 ft. Branching spikes of lilac-blue flowers in June. *E. plantagineum* hybrids produce plants that vary from white to deep blue in flower color.

EMILIA (TASSEL FLOWER)
Often known as *Cacalia coccinea*, this annual is easy to grow from seed sown directly outdoors in spring in ordinary soil with full sun. Thin seedlings to 8 to 9 in. apart. The flowers are good for cutting, may be dried for winter bouquets, and bloom for a long period.

E. sagittata, 12 to 15 in. Flowers in small tassels, orange-scarlet.

ESCHSCHOLTZIA
The plant has finely cut blue-green leaves with masses of glossy, vivid flowers of orange, red or pink from June onward. It likes a poor sandy soil in a sunny location. Sow seed in spring where plants are to grow, thin out to 6 in. apart. For earlier flowering sow in September. These plants frequently seed themselves in gardens.

Eschscholtzia californica (California poppy), 1 to 1½ ft. Saucer-shaped flowers of many brilliant colors in great profusion all summer. Many named varieties exist, some with semi-double flowers.

EUPHORBIA (SPURGE)
These annuals thrive in ordinary soil in full sun. Sow seed in the spring outdoors where plants are to remain, and thin young plants to 9 to 12 in. apart.

Euphorbia heterophylla (annual poinsettia or Mexican fire plant), 2 ft. Has dark green foliage with the upper leaves (bracts) blotched brilliant red.

E. marginata (snow-on-the-mountain), 3 to 4 ft. Leaves margined with white, upper leaves almost all white.

EVERLASTING. See *Helipterum, Xeranthemum.*

FELICIA
(BLUE MARGUERITE, BLUE DAISY)
A low-growing plant, it bears blue or white daisylike flowers from June onward. Sow seed indoors in early March, harden off in mid-April; plant out 9 in. apart when weather is warm and settled.

Felicia affinis, 1 ft. Dark green hairy leaves, yellow-centered blue flowers.

F. bergeriana (kingfisher daisy), 8 to 10 in. With yellow-centered blue flowers in profusion.

FENNELFLOWER. See *Nigella.*

FEVERFEW. See *Matricaria parthenoides.*

FIREBUSH. See *Kochia.*

FIRECRACKER PLANT. See *Cuphea.*

FIVE SPOT. See *Nemophila maculata.*

FLAG-OF-SPAIN. See *Quamoclit lobata.*

FLAX. See *Linum.*

FLOSSFLOWER. See *Ageratum.*

FLOWERING TOBACCO. See *Nicotiana.*

FORKING LARKSPUR. See *Delphinium consolida flore-pleno.*

GAILLARDIA (BLANKETFLOWER)
These are fine for hot, sunny areas and easy to grow in ordinary soil. Sow indoors in spring and set seedlings in the garden after all danger of frost has passed, or sow directly outdoors in spring and thin seedlings 8 to 9 in. apart. Good for cutting.

Gaillardia amblyodon, 1 to 2 ft. Flowers brown-red.

G. pulchella picta (Indian blanket), 1 to 2 ft. Fine garden varieties with large single or double flowers, in various colors and combinations—including sulphur, yellow, orange, maroon and smoky red—are sold by seedsmen.

GIANT SCABIOUS. See *Cephalaria.*

GIANT SUNFLOWER. See *Helianthus annuus.*

GILIA
Easy to grow in sunny locations and light, porous soil, they do not withstand hot weather well. Sow early outdoors and thin plants 6 to 8 in. apart. Foliage is finely dissected.

Gilia achilleaefolia, 1 to 2 ft. Flowers in dense terminal clusters, blue.

G. capitata, 1 to 2 ft. Flowers in heads, light blue.

G. tricolor (bird's-eyes), 1½ to 2 ft. Flowers lilac, pale lavender or white.

GLOBE AMARANTH. See *Gomphrena.*

GLOBE CANDYTUFT. See *Iberis umbellata.*

GODETIA
A charming and valuable garden plant, this does not thrive in hot weather. It flourishes best where fairly cool summers prevail. The gray-green foliage is covered in summer and autumn with delicately scented flowers in pink, purple, crimson or lavender. It likes a slightly acid soil and sun. Sow seed in spring where plants are to flower. Thin out to 10 in. apart.

Godetia grandiflora (satinflower), 1 to 2 ft. Compact, bushy, with dense clusters of red, pink, crimson, carmine or scarlet flowers. There are many different varieties, and new types and colors are frequently introduced. Splendid cut flower. (See illustration on next page.)

GOLDEN AGERATUM. See *Lonas.*

GOLDEN CUP. See *Hunnemannia fumariaefolia.*

GOMPHRENA (GLOBE AMARANTH)
Showy, compact plants, they bear a wealth of attractive, cloverlike heads of bloom throughout the summer. Sow indoors in spring, transplant, and harden off in time to set plants outdoors after weather is warm and set-

Gypsophila elegans
(Baby's Breath)

Godetia grandiflora (Satinflower)

tled. Flowers may be cut and dried and used as everlastings.

Gomphrena globosa, 1½ to 2 ft. Flowers bright magenta, lavender, pink or white.

G. haageana, 2½ ft. Flowers yellow with light red bracts.

GYPSOPHILA (BABY'S BREATH)
Stems and leaves are gray, and the tiny white or pink flowers are produced in summer and later from successive sowing. Choose an open, sunny place and sow in drifts in fall or spring. Thin out to 6 in. apart.

Gypsophila elegans, 1½ ft. Many varieties.

G. muralis, 6 in. Flowers starlike and rose-colored. Suitable for rock gardens.

HAIR GRASS. See *Agrostis hiemalis*.

HAWK'S-BEARD. See *Crepis*.

HEARTSEED. See *Cardiospermum*.

HELIANTHUS (SUNFLOWER)
It produces large or even huge disk-like flowers of yellow, brown or purple. Sow seed in spring where plants are to flower, in full sun. Thin out to 2 ft. apart. Modern garden varieties of sunflowers exhibit wide variations. They range in height from 15 in. to 10 ft. or more; in color from creamy-white through golden-yellow to deepest bronze and chestnut-red; and in diameter of flower may vary from 3 in. to 1½ ft.

Helianthus annuus (giant sunflower), up to 10 ft., bearing huge single yellow flowers with dark disk from July to September. Some forms are double-flowered, others have darker markings on petals.

H. debilis (cucumber-leaved sunflower or miniature sunflower), 3½ ft. Useful border plant, blooming freely from July to September.

HELICHRYSUM (STRAWFLOWER)
The plant has very showy clustered flowers—red, orange, mauve or white—and papery in texture when mature. Sow seed in spring where plants are to flower, and thin out to 6 in. apart. Cut-flowers when half open and hang in bunches to dry for two or three weeks in a dry, dustproof place to provide flowers for decoration all winter.

Helichrysum bracteatum, 1 to 3 ft. Erect plant with flowers 2 in. across, from June to August.

HELIOTROPIUM (HELIOTROPE)
Although truly tender perennials and often propagated from cuttings, these can be easily raised from seed and bloom well the first year. They are valued especially for their fragrant flowers. Sow seed in late winter indoors or in a greenhouse. Pinch out the tips of the seedlings when 3 to 4 in. high, harden off, and plant outdoors only after weather is quite warm and settled. Give them full sun and ordinary well-drained soil.

Heliotropium arborescens, 1 to 3 ft., bears small, fragrant flowers in large, flat-topped heads throughout summer and fall, until killing frost. Named seed varieties, which come reasonably true to color and type, are offered.

HELIPTERUM
(IMMORTELLE, EVERLASTING)
The plant bears white, yellow or rose-colored flowers which may be dried in the same way as helichrysum. It grows well in poor soils but likes sunny location. Sow seed indoors during springtime, harden off, and plant out 9 in. apart when weather is warm and settled. Alternatively, sow directly outdoors where plants are to bloom in spring. *Helipterum* now includes genera previously known as *Rhodanthe* and *Acroclinium*.

Helipterum corymbiflorum, 1 ft.

White, woolly leaves, and clusters of white flowers for most of the summer.

H. manglesii (Swan River everlasting), 15 in. White, pink or rose-colored flowers in summer. There are many named varieties.

H. roseum, 1½ ft., bears rose-colored flowers that close at night and open in the morning, although the double-flowered varieties are less inclined to do so. At its best in July and August and useful as a cut flower.

HONEYWORT. See *Cerinthe*.

HOP. See *Humulus*.

HOUND'S-TONGUE. See *Cynoglossum*.

HUMULUS (HOP)

Popular vine for screening, it is grown primarily for its attractive foliage. Sow seed indoors in spring, transplant, harden off, and set outdoors after danger of frost has passed, or sow directly outdoors in spring. Ordinary soil; sun or light shade.

Humulus japonicus, 10 to 20 ft. Leaves deeply lobed, dark green. Variety *variegatus* has leaves streaked and splashed with white. It comes reasonably true from seed.

HUNNEMANNIA
(MEXICAN TULIP POPPY)

Attractive poppylike plants have finely divided bluish foliage and long-stemmed flowers which are borne throughout the summer and are excellent for cutting. It needs warm, well-drained soil and full sun. Sow seed in spring where plants are to bloom, and thin 6 to 7 in. apart.

Hunnemannia fumariaefolia (golden cup), 2 ft. Flowers clear yellow, 3 in. in diameter. A semidouble-flowered variety is available.

IBERIS (CANDYTUFT)

Beautiful sweet-scented flowers bloom from early summer onward—white, red, purple or lilac. Plants do best in light, well-drained soils in open, sunny areas. Sow seed out of doors; often they will seed themselves in following years. Thin out to 6 in. apart. Need a neutral or somewhat alkaline soil.

Iberis amara (rocket candytuft), 1 ft. Many named garden varieties with various-colored flowers, splendid for cutting.

I. umbellata (globe candytuft), 6 in. to 2 ft. The most popular species, of which there are many lovely named varieties.

IMMORTELLE. See *Helipterum*, *Xeranthemum*.

IMPATIENS (TOUCH-ME-NOT)

Good plants for sun or part shade in ordinary soil that is not excessively dry, they bloom freely all summer. Sow seed indoors in late winter or spring. Grow young plants indoors, harden off and plant outdoors when weather is warm and settled, or sow directly outdoors in spring. Space plants 9 to 12 in. apart.

Impatiens balsamina (balsam), 1 to 2½ ft. Flowers are single or double, borne close to the leafy stems. Many named varieties are offered by seedsmen. Flower colors include white, pink, red, lavender and purple. These are true annuals.

I. holstii (patience plant, sultana), 8 to 18 in. Bushy plants freely bearing flat flowers—white, pink or red—throughout the summer and fall. Garden kinds may be hybrids of this species and *I. sultana*.

INDIAN BLANKET. See *Gaillardia pulchella picta*.

IPOMOEA (MORNING GLORY)

Splendid twining vines for covering posts and other supports, they have attractive foliage and large, funnel-shaped flowers—blue, red, pink, rosy-lavender or white. Double-flowered varieties are offered. The morning glories are day bloomers. The moon-flowers, which are night bloomers, are sometimes catalogued as *Ipomoea* but are more correctly named *Calonyction*. Sow seeds of morning glories in spring in sunny locations, where the plants are to flower. Soak the seed in water for two days before sowing to encourage sprouting.

The many beautiful catalogued varieties of morning glories have been derived from the two species *I. purpurea* and *I. tricolor*.

Ipomoea purpurea, broad, heart-shaped leaves with deep violet flowers in summer. Some varieties have double flowers.

I. p. huberi, rosy-purple or pink flowers.

I. tricolor, heart-shaped leaves and deep blue, white-throated flowers, 5 in. across, from July to August.

JEWEL-OF-THE-VELDT. See *Ursinia anethoides*.

JEWELS OF OPHIR. See *Talinum*.

JOB'S TEARS. See *Coix lacryma-jobi*.

JOSEPH'S COAT. See *Amaranthus tricolor splendens*.

KENTRANTHUS. See *Centranthus*.

KINGFISHER DAISY. See *Felicia bergeriana*.

KOCHIA
(SUMMER CYPRESS, FIREBUSH)
This feathery green bushy plant turns vivid red in the autumn and is often used in flower beds and borders. Sow seed indoors in spring, harden off, and plant out 8 in. apart after settled warm weather arrives.

Kochia scoparia trichophylla, 2 ft.

Dense oval or rounded bush with finely divided, rather delicate foliage that starts the summer a lovely, fresh green and gradually deepens to fiery red.

LACE FLOWER. See *Trachymene*.

LARKSPUR. See *Delphinium*.

LATHYRUS (SWEET PEA)
Choice vines and bush plants bearing beautiful fragrant flowers, sweet peas are very useful for garden ornament and cutting. They need rich, deep soil, always fairly moist. Sweet peas do not thrive in very hot weather; they prosper under the same conditions as do garden peas. Sow seed outdoors—where the plants are to bloom—as early as it is possible to work the ground in spring; or, where winters are not excessively severe, sow in late fall. For the vining varieties provide supports of brushwood, chicken wire or other suitable material. To prolong flower display, pick all blooms before they begin to form seedpods.

Lathyrus odoratus, 1 to 8 ft. Flowers of all colors except good yellows. Numerous named varieties are offered by seedsmen, including bush types that do not exceed 1 ft. in height. (See illustration on next page.)

LAVATERA (TREE MALLOW)
Large, showy, hibiscuslike flowers are produced on tall plants. They prefer a sunny, sheltered place and not too rich a soil. Sow seed in spring where plants are to flower. Thin to 1½ ft. apart.

Lavatera trimestris, 3 ft. This is the most commonly grown species; one of the very best flowering annuals for regions where summer temperatures are not excessively high. Rose-colored flowers are borne in summer and autumn.

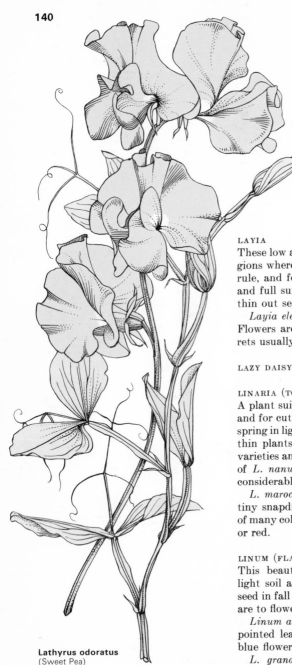

Lathyrus odoratus
(Sweet Pea)

LAYIA

These low annuals are adapted for regions where hot summers are not the rule, and for light, well-drained soils and full sun. Sow seed in spring and thin out seedlings 4 to 5 in. apart.

Layia elegans (tidytips), 1 to 2 ft. Flowers are pale yellow, the ray florets usually tipped with white.

LAZY DAISY. See *Aphanostephus.*

LINARIA (TOADFLAX)

A plant suitable for beds and borders and for cutting. Sow seed outdoors in spring in light soil in a sunny area, and thin plants 4 to 6 in. apart. Garden varieties and some hybrids, especially of *L. nanus* and *L. pubescens*, show considerable color variation.

L. maroccana, 1½ ft. Flowers like tiny snapdragons in garden varieties of many colors—white, pink, lavender or red.

LINUM (FLAX)

This beautiful showy plant prefers light soil and a sunny location. Sow seed in fall or spring where the plants are to flower. Thin out to 4 in. apart.

Linum angustifolium, 2 ft. Narrow pointed leaves and masses of bright blue flowers in June and July.

L. grandiflorum, 2 to 3 ft. Has

pointed leaves, and clear red flowers in June and July. There are many varieties, including a white form and a rose-colored form.

L. usitatissimum (common flax), 4 ft. Brilliant sky-blue flowers in June and July.

LOBELIA

These low, bushy plants are most useful for edgings and for flower boxes and baskets. Sow seed indoors 10 or 12 weeks before the plants are to be planted outdoors. Transplant seedlings in groups of three or four, 2 in. apart in flats. Grow in fairly warm place, harden off and plant out after weather is really warm and settled. Space about 6 in. apart. They will grow in part shade.

Named garden varieties of the following species are available.

Lobelia erinus, 4 to 10 in. Densely covered throughout summer with numerous flowers of blue, pink, white or blue with white throat.

L. tenuior, 1 to 1½ ft. Of looser growth than *L. erinus* and with larger flowers; otherwise similar.

LOBULARIA (SWEET ALYSSUM)

Lobularia maritima, 4 to 9 in. A popular, fragrant-flowered plant that is easily cultivated in any well-drained soil where there is sun. Seed is usually sown directly outdoors. When this is done, the seedlings may be thinned 3 to 4 in. apart. Sometimes the plants are started indoors in flats for about six weeks and later set out 6 in. apart in the garden.

When the flowering branches become straggly they may be sheared back to encourage the development of new flowering shoots. Both white-flowered and violet-flowered varieties are available.

LONAS (GOLDEN AGERATUM)

The common name refers to a general resemblance of this plant to ageratum. It needs ordinary soil and full sun. Its flowers remain attractive on the plant for a long period. Sow seed indoors early and plant outdoors after danger from frost has passed; or sow directly outdoors in spring and thin plants 8 in. apart.

Lonas annua, also called *L. inodora*,

Linum grandiflorum
(Flax)

1½ to 2 ft. Flowers golden-yellow in broad, flattish clusters. Leaves deeply cut, dark green.

LOPEZIA

These dainty plants make a display of blooms over a long period. They need sun and ordinary soil. Sow the seed outdoors in spring and thin the seedlings 10 to 12 in. apart, or start the seed indoors earlier and plant in the garden after all danger from cold weather has passed.

Lopezia coronata (crown of jewels), 2 to 3 ft. Flowers pink or lilac.

LOVE-IN-A-MIST. See *Nigella damascena*.

LOVE-LIES-BLEEDING. See *Amaranthus caudatus*.

LUPINUS (LUPINE)

Quick-growing, erect plants, 1½ to 2½ ft., they have showy spikes of white, pink, yellow or blue flowers. Sow seed in spring 3 to 4 in. apart directly outdoors where plants are to bloom. Thin out 6 to 8 in. apart. Full sun or very light shade and fertile, well-drained soil are needed.

LYCHNIS

The vivid flowers which cover this beautiful plant in the summer vary through shades of mauve from crimson to sky-blue. They last well in water. The plant grows in an open, sunny place in poor soil. Sow seed in spring where plants are to flower; thin out to 6 in. apart.

Lychnis coeli-rosa (rose of heaven), 8 to 15 in., bears large rosy-red, white-centered flowers from June to August. Many varieties—with red, blue, purple or white flowers—are grown.

MACHAERANTHERA

These pretty asterlike plants are suitable for garden decoration and for cut

flowers. Sow seed indoors in spring, harden off, and move young plants outdoors after weather has moderated; or sow directly outdoors in spring or fall. Space plants 8 to 9 in. apart.

Machaeranthera tanacetifolia (Tahoka daisy), 2 ft. Blue or violet-blue daisy flowers with yellow centers.

MADAGASCAR PERIWINKLE. See *Vinca rosea*.

MALABAR NIGHTSHADE. See *Basella*.

MALCOMIA

Malcomia maritima (Virginian stock), 6 in. Many beautiful varieties come from this plant. It makes a good edging plant, especially when mixed with night-scented stock (see *Mathiola bicornis*). Sow seed in spring where plants are to flower in summer. This annual is best suited for regions where summers are fairly cool. Its flowers are produced in a wide range of colors.

MALLOW. See *Malva*.

MALOPE

It produces showy, trumpetlike flowers of pink, red, violet, rose, purple or white from June to September; good for cutting. The plant prefers a sunny situation and soil rich in organic matter. Sow seed in spring out of doors, where plants are to flower. Thin out to 9 in. apart.

Malope trifida, 2 to 3 ft. Branching stems, rose-purple flowers 3 in. across.

M.t. alba, white flowers.

M.t. grandiflora, rose-red flowers.

MALVA (MALLOW)

These rather tall plants bear rose or white five-petaled flowers from June to September. They are useful for backgrounds. Sow seed in spring where plants are to flower. Thin out to 15 in. apart.

Malva crispa, 6 ft. Bears dense clusters of white flowers tinged with purple.

MARIGOLD. See *Tagetes*.

MASK-FLOWER. See *Alonsoa*.

MATHIOLA (STOCK)
This famous cutting flower produces dense spikes of sweetly scented, showy flowers in white and many shades of red, pink, cream, blue and mauve. Likes a deep, well-manured soil and a sunny location, but will tolerate slight shade.

Mathiola bicornis (night-scented stock), up to 1 ft. Pretty and single-flowered, they are good for edging, especially when mixed with Virginian stock (see *Malcomia maritima*). Flowers open in evening and are strongly fragrant. Sow seed in spring where plants are to flower in summer.

M. incana, 1 to 3 ft. The annual varieties derived from this species are known as ten-week stocks, offered in many different types and varieties. Some are freely branching, others—called column stocks—develop single, unbranched, columnlike flower stems. All are delightfully fragrant. They do not thrive in very hot weather but tend at that time to produce much foliage and few or no flowers. Sow seed of ten-week stocks indoors in spring. Harden the young plants off and set them 8 to 10 in. apart in the garden as soon as danger from frost has passed. They like a neutral or slightly alkaline soil.

MATRICARIA
Called by many botanists *Chrysanthemum parthenium*, this perennial species is often grown as an annual for its attractive, ferny foliage and clusters of buttonlike flowers. Sow seed indoors early and harden off before setting plants outdoors, 6 to 8 in. apart, after the weather is warm and settled. They require full sun and ordinary soil.

Matricaria parthenoides (feverfew), 6 in. to 3 ft., bushy and much branched, often with curled leaves. Variety *aureum* (golden feather) is popular. Other named varieties have white, lemon-yellow or golden flowers.

MEALYCUP SAGE. See *Salvia farinacea*.

MENTZELIA
A rather straggling plant, it has coarsely toothed leaves and bright golden-yellow starlike flowers which expand in the evening and remain open until about noon the next day. Sow seed in spring where plants are to bloom. Thin seedlings to 6 in. apart. Needs full sun and well-drained soil. It is often sold as *Bartonia aurea*. A tall variety, Stella Polaris, is one of those offered.

Mentzelia lindleyi, 1 to 4 ft.

MEXICAN FIRE PLANT. See *Euphorbia heterophylla*.

MEXICAN POPPY. See *Argemone*.

MEXICAN SUNFLOWER. See *Tithonia*.

MEXICAN TULIP POPPY. See *Hunnemannia*.

MIGNONETTE. See *Reseda*.

MIMULUS (MONKEY FLOWER)
Thickly covered with vivid two-lipped flowers between May and August, it prefers partial shade and a soil rich in organic matter. Sow in spring where plants are to flower, or set out young plants started indoors. The varieties offered in seed catalogues—sometimes as *M. tigrinus*, but often under fancy varietal names—seem to be hybrids between *M. luteus* (or its varieties) and *M. guttatus*. They grow 6 in. to 1 ft. high and have

showy flowers in a wide range of creams, yellows, reds and browns, often attractively spotted or mottled with contrasting colors.

MOLUCCA BALM. See *Moluccella laevis*.

MOLUCCELLA
These aromatic plants—easy to cultivate—with curious flower spikes, are attractive for flower arrangements and may be dried and used as everlastings. The large green calyxes are the most conspicuous parts of the flowers. Seed may be sown directly outdoors in spring and the seedlings thinned 9 to 12 in. apart; or seed may be started early indoors and the young plants set outdoors after all danger from frost has passed. A well-drained, rather dryish soil and full sun are required.

Moluccella laevis (Molucca balm, bells of Ireland), 1½ to 3 ft. Flowers small, white and fragrant, with enlarged, conspicuous calyxes.

MOMORDICA
Related to gourds and cucumbers, the quick-growing vines are easily raised. Sow the seed directly where plants are to grow, after the weather is quite warm and settled. Alternatively, indoor sowing four to five weeks before the arrival of settled warm weather allows transplanting out of doors. Rich soil, full sun and generous watering during the growing season are needed. Fertilize occasionally after growth is well developed. Provide supports to which the plants may cling with their tendrils.

Momordica balsamina (balsam apple), 10 ft. Grown chiefly for its attractive, egg-shaped orange-colored fruits which open to reveal the seeds.

M. charantia (balsam pear), 10 ft. Has very attractive, warty orange-colored fruits which split to show the bright red seeds.

MONARCH-OF-THE-VELDT. See *Venidium*.

MONKEY FLOWER. See *Mimulus*.

MOONFLOWER. See *Calonyction*.

MORNING GLORY. See *Ipomoea*.

MORNING GLORY, DWARF. See *Convolvulus tricolor*.

NASTURTIUM. See *Tropaeolum majus*.

NEMESIA
It bears brilliant, dainty flowers like miniature snapdragons of orange, red, yellow and blue from July to September. The plant is not adapted for regions of high summer temperatures. Sow seed in greenhouse in spring, harden off, and plant out when 5 or 6 in. high.

Nemesia strumosa, 1 to 2 ft. Erect stems with terminal clusters of yellow, white, orange or purple flowers. Some beautiful named varieties are available.

NEMOPHILA
This plant has narrow leaves and blue-white or purple bell-shaped flowers. It prefers a sandy soil rich in humus, and cool, lightly shaded locations. Cut flowers last well in water. Sow seed in spring where the plants are to flower; thin out to 6 in. apart. In mild regions seed may be sown in mid-September.

Nemophila maculata (five spot), 6 in. Pale green leaves; 2-in. white flowers with five purple spots (one at the tip of each petal), in summer.

N. menziesii (baby blue-eyes), 4 in. Bears masses of blue-and-white flowers in summer, and pale green leaves. There are varieties in other colors.

NICANDRA
An old-fashioned plant of vigorous growth, it is supposed to be repellent

to flies. Sow directly outdoors in
spring; or sow early indoors and transplant outdoors after danger from frost
has passed. Deep, fairly rich, moist
soil is preferred. Space plants 1½ to 2
ft. apart.

Nicandra physalodes (apple of Peru,
shoofly plant), 3 to 4 ft. Spreading
plant with pale-blue, white-throated,
bell-shaped flowers which open for a
few hours only in the middle of the
day. The foliage is quite handsome.

NICOTIANA (FLOWERING TOBACCO)
Rather large hairy leaves grow on the
plant and it bears green, red or white
flowers from July to September. Because the blooms are at their best in
the evening, they are often used for
planting around garden seats and under
windows. They like deep, well-fertilized soil and a sunny place. Sow seed
indoors or in a greenhouse in spring,
harden off, and plant out about 10 in.
apart when all danger from frost has
passed and the weather has become
settled and mild.

Nicotiana alata, 1 to 3 ft. Clusters
of white, tubular flowers 2 in. long
and 2 in. across. There are varieties
with mauve, rose, violet and crimson
flowers. All are free-flowering and
sweet-scented. (The scent is particularly noticeable as the flowers open in
the evening.) Hybrids are available
which do not close their petals during
the day. Dwarf varieties are offered.

N. sanderae, 1 to 3 ft. Bears loose
clusters of flowers 3 in. long, with
greenish-yellow tubes and carmine-
rose mouths. There are a number of
varieties.

NIEREMBERGIA (CUPFLOWER)
Dainty, bushy plants bloom freely all
summer in sunny locations and well-
drained soils. Sow seed early indoors;
grow young plants in greenhouse,
pinching out tips of young shoots
when 3 in. tall. Harden off; plant out-

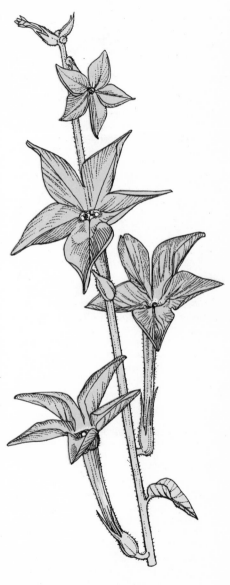

Nicotiana alata
(Flowering Tobacco)

doors, 6 to 8 in. apart, after warm and settled weather arrives.

Nierembergia caerulea, 9 in. Flowers shallow, cup-shaped, blue.

N. frutescens, 2 ft. Flowers shallow, cup-shaped; lilac or white.

NIGELLA (FENNELFLOWER)
Delightful white, blue or yellow flowers are produced from July to September. Good for cutting. Sow seed in spring in open, sunny area where plants are to flower; can be sown in mid-September in regions where winters are not excessively severe. Thin out plants to 9 in. apart. The balloon-like seed heads and spiky leaves can be used for floral decoration and may be gilded for Christmas. These plants grow best in a neutral or slightly alkaline soil.

Nigella damascena (love-in-a-mist, devil-in-the-bush), 1 to 2 ft. Finely divided leaves, showy bluish-white flowers surrounded with green tracing. Miss Jekyll is the best-known variety, with semidouble flowers of blue or white.

N. hispanica, 2 ft. Dark green leaves; scented deep blue flowers, 2½ in. across. The seed heads are large and particularly valuable for winter decoration. There are purple and wine-colored varieties.

NIGHTSHADE. See *Solanum*.

ORNAMENTAL CORN. See *Zea*.

OXYPETALUM
From June to October it produces lovely flowers on somewhat twining, arching stems. The plant flourishes in a warm, sunny location and fertile, well-drained soil. Sow seed indoors early and grow under warm conditions until settled warm weather allows planting outside. Or sow in spring directly outdoors, where the plants are to bloom.

Oxypetalum caeruleum, 1 to 1½ ft. Flowers star-shaped, blue, long-lasting.

PAINTED TONGUE. See *Salpiglossis*.

PAPAVER (POPPY)
A showy plant with large, somewhat flimsy, open flowers, it prefers a sunny spot and a light soil. Sow seed in fall or in spring where plants are to flower. Thin out 9 or 10 in. apart. The plants often seed themselves prolifically.

Papaver macrostomum, 1 to 1½ ft. Deeply cut leaves. In June has semidouble purple-red flowers, 2 in. across, with shiny black centers. Good for cutting.

P. pavoninum (peacock poppy), 1 ft. Finely divided leaves; in summer has glossy, scarlet flowers spotted with black at base.

P. rhoeas (corn poppy), 1 to 2 ft. Branching plant with many red, purple, white or white-and-red flowers in

Phlox drummondii

summer. This is the poppy the World War I poet John McCrae wrote about—"In Flanders fields the poppies blow/Between the crosses, row on row." Many splendid garden varieties, including the well-known and beautiful Shirley poppy, are derived from this species.

P. somniferum (opium poppy), 2 ft. Pearl-gray, lobed leaves; large (5-in.) pink, red, white or purple floppy flowers in the summer. Numerous superb varieties are available, some with double flowers.

PATIENCE PLANT. See *Impatiens holstii.*

PERILLA

An interesting foliage plant, it is easily raised from seed sown outdoors in the spring, or can be started early indoors and transplanted to the open garden after warm weather arrives. It somewhat resembles coleus. *Perilla* needs ordinary soil, full sun and a reasonable amount of moisture in summer.

Perilla frutescens crispa, 1½ to 3 ft. Foliage dark metallic purple, crisped and crinkled. A number of named garden varieties are described in seed catalogues.

PETUNIA

Very extensively used for summer displays, these plants make a wonderful show of salver-shaped flowers in many different colors from early summer to killing frost. They prefer well-drained, slightly acid soil in a sunny area. Sow seed in spring in a greenhouse, harden off, and plant out 1 ft. apart after the weather is warm and settled.

Petunia hybrida, the only kind cultivated, but in numerous distinct varieties. Sticky-leaved plants; some forms are compact in growth and others more sprawling. There are giant

forms, fringed types, and varieties with striped flowers, in many colors.

PHACELIA

Attractive bell-shaped flowers bloom in great profusion from June to September. It prefers a sunny location. Sow seed in spring where plants are to flower. Thin out to 9 in. apart.

Phacelia campanularia, 8 to 9 in. Reddish stems; royal blue, bell-shaped flowers 1 in. across. Likes poor, dry soil.

P. congesta, 1 ft. Erect stems; pale green, hairy leaves; clusters of tiny pale lavender-blue flowers. Prefers a heavy soil.

P. minor (syn. *Whitlavia grandiflora*—California bluebell), 6 to 8 in., with violet-blue bells 1 in. long and 1 in. wide.

P. viscida, 1 to 2 ft. Pale green, heart-shaped, hairy leaves; white-centered gentian-blue flowers 1 in. across, which are attractive to bees. Foliage when crushed has a distinct smell. Sometimes offered as *Eutoca viscida*.

PHEASANT'S-EYE. See *Adonis.*

PHLOX

Beautiful plants for bedding out, they produce flat flowering heads of red, pink, purple, blue or white. A sunny place and rich, slightly acid soil are preferred. Sow seed indoors, harden off, and plant out 9 in. apart after settled warm weather arrives; or sow directly outdoors where plants are to bloom in spring and thin out seedlings 4 to 5 in. apart.

Phlox drummondii, 6 to 18 in. White, yellow, pink, red or pale purple flowers from July onward. Many varieties available: some with starlike flowers (*P.d. stellaris*); some dwarf forms (*P.d. compacta*); some with large, broad-petaled flowers (*P.d. rotundata*).

PIMPERNEL. See *Anagallis*.

PINCUSHION FLOWER. See *Scabiosa*.

PINK, ANNUAL. See *Dianthus*.

POINSETTIA, ANNUAL. See *Euphorbia heterophylla*.

POLYGONUM
Vigorous species are easily raised from seed sown in spring directly where the plants are to grow. Full sun and good soil. Space 1½ to 2 ft. apart.
Polygonum orientale (prince's-feather, prince's-plume), 6 ft. This plant branches freely. It produces bright pink flowers in drooping, branched spikes.

POOR MAN'S WEATHERGLASS. See *Anagallis arvensis*.

POPPY. See *Papaver*.

PORTULACA
These are low-growing, fleshy plants with red, yellow, rose or white flowers from July to September. They prefer a rather dry, poor soil and do best in a hot, dry summer. Sow seed in spring outdoors, where plants are to bloom, and thin 3 to 4 in. apart.
Portulaca grandiflora (rose moss). Gray-green cylindrical leaves; brilliantly colored flowers 1 in. across. Many varieties of different colors. May be single- or double-flowered.

POT MARIGOLD. See *Calendula officinalis*.

PRICKLY POPPY. See *Argemone*.

PRINCE'S-FEATHER. See *Amaranthus hybridus hypochondriacus* and *Polygonum orientalis*.

PRINCE'S-PLUME. See *Polygonum orientalis*.

QUAMOCLIT
Fast-growing, summer-flowering vines such as these are suitable for screens or for covering posts, fences and other supports. They are easy to cultivate. Sow seed indoors in spring and set the young plants in the garden after assured warm weather comes; or, in the South, sow seed directly outdoors in spring, where the plants are to grow.
Quamoclit coccinea (star ipomoea), 10 ft. Heart-shaped or lobed leaves; scarlet-and-yellow, yellow or orange-yellow flowers.
Q. lobata (flag-of-Spain), 20 ft. Often sold as *Mina lobata*. Leaves deeply three-lobed. Flowers crimson, changing to pale yellow.
Q. pennata (cypress vine), 20 ft. Has fine, feathery foliage and funnel-shaped scarlet or white flowers.
Q. sloteri (cardinal climber), 15 to 20 ft. A hybrid, with lobed leaves; flowers are crimson with a white throat.

RESEDA (MIGNONETTE)
Grown for its sweet scent, seed should be sown in the spring in a sunny place where plants are to flower; thin out to 6 in. apart. Prefers slightly alkaline soil.
Reseda odorata, 1½ ft. Bears loose spikes of heavily scented yellowish-white flowers from June to October. Many varieties.

RICINUS (CASTOR BEAN)
A vigorous foliage plant of tropical appearance, it is useful for screens and giving accents in the landscape. It can be very easily raised from seed sown directly outdoors after the soil is warm and the weather settled, or from seed sown indoors early and transplanted outdoors when suitable warm weather arrives. The plant needs deep, rich soil and a place sheltered from sweeping winds. Plenty of water should be supplied during summer. As

the large seeds are poisonous, take care that children do not have access to them.

Ricinus communis, 6 to 12 ft. Leaves large, hand-shaped, green, dark brown, bronze or red according to variety. Seed catalogues offer and describe several varieties.

ROCKET CANDYTUFT. See *Iberis amara.*

ROCKET LARKSPUR. See *Delphinium ajacis.*

ROCK PURSLANE. See *Calandrinia.*

ROSE OF HEAVEN. See *Lychnis coelirosa.*

RUDBECKIA (CONEFLOWER)
This striking plant has orange-brown to purple daisylike flowers with prominent dark, raised center. It prefers a good soil and a sunny location. Sow seed indoors or in a greenhouse in spring, harden off, and plant out 1 ft. apart in May.

Rudbeckia bicolor, 1 to 2 ft. The yellowish flowers with black centers bloom in July. There are semidouble varieties.

R. triloba (brown-eyed Susan), 2 to

5 ft. Brownish centers and orange-purple flowers from July to September.

Many fine garden varieties are grown, including the large-flowered tetraploids (kind with four layers of petals) called "gloriosa daisies."

SALPIGLOSSIS (PAINTED TONGUE)
Beautiful trumpet-shaped flowers from the plant are splendid for cutting. It prefers a rich soil and a sunny location. Sow seed indoors in spring, harden off, and plant out 1 ft. apart when settled warm weather comes.

Salpiglossis sinuata, 1½ to 3 ft. Bears pale green, hairy leaves and flowers 2 in. long and 2 in. across in summer. There are reds, yellows, blues—often splashed with gold.

SALVIA
Excellent plants for summer display in sunny locations, they need only ordinary soil, where drainage is good. Sow seed in spring indoors; transplant seedlings, pinching out their tips when they are 3 to 4 in. high to encourage branching. Seed sown directly outdoors in spring (the seedlings later thinned 8 to 9 in. apart) will produce satisfactory but later-flowering plants—a method which is best re-

Rudbeckia bicolor
(Coneflower)

stricted to *S. farinacea* and its varieties.

S. farinacea (mealycup sage), 2 to 4 ft. Has an abundance of slender spikes of blue-purple or white flowers with conspicuous white, mealy calyxes.

S. splendens (scarlet sage), 1 to 3 ft. Despite the common name there are varieties, listed in seed catalogues, which have purple, lavender, pink, salmon or white flowers, as well as varieties with blooms of brilliant scarlet. All are good. The flowers are borne in erect spikes and contrast well with the handsome green foliage. This is a very showy plant for summer beds and window and porch boxes.

SAND VERBENA. See *Abronia*.

SANVITALIA (CREEPING ZINNIA)
Flowers of this low plant somewhat resemble small zinnias. It is very easily raised from seed and thrives in sun, needs well-drained soil and blooms continuously throughout the summer. In mild climates sow seed outdoors in September and again in spring; where severe winters occur, depend upon spring sowing. Sow directly where the plants are to bloom and thin the seedlings 3 to 4 in. apart.

Sanvitalia procumbens, 6 to 8 in. Flowers yellow with dark purple centers, or yellow and fully double.

SATINFLOWER. See *Godetia grandiflora*.

SCABIOSA (PINCUSHION FLOWER)
Lovely flowers in many different colors that are good for cutting bloom on this plant from the beginning of summer to September. It prefers light soil and a sunny position. Seed should be sown in early April where plants are to flower. Thin out to 6 in. apart. May also be sown out of doors in early fall for late spring flowering.

Scabiosa atropurpurea (sweet scabious), 2 to 3 ft. Bears the typical pincushion flowers and has beautiful

varieties in colors from scarlet to pink, and blue, yellow, white.

SCARLET PIMPERNEL. See *Anagallis arvensis*.

SCARLET SAGE. See *Salvia splendens*.

SHOOFLY PLANT. See *Nicandra physalodes*.

SILENE (CATCHFLY, CAMPION)
Brilliant flowers—pink, red, purple, white or rose—beautify this plant. It likes a slightly acid soil and a sunny spot. Sow seed in early April where plants are to flower; thin out to 8 in. apart.

Silene pendula, 9 in. Soft, hairy leaves, pale pink flowers from May to September. There are many good varieties with single or double flowers.

SNAPDRAGON. See *Antirrhinum*.

SNOW-ON-THE-MOUNTAIN. See *Euphorbia marginata*.

SOLANUM (NIGHTSHADE)
Producing bell-shaped flowers and large ornamental fruits, the plant prefers a sunny spot and rich soil. Sow indoors in late February, harden off in April and plant out in late May; or sow directly outdoors after weather is warm and settled.

Solanum integrifolium (tomato eggplant), 3 ft. Small white flowers in summer followed by long scarlet or yellow tomatolike fruits in autumn.

SPIDER FLOWER. See *Cleome*.

SPIDER PLANT. See *Cleome*.

SPURGE. See *Euphorbia*.

STAR IPOMOEA. See *Quamoclit coccinea*.

STAR MARIGOLD. See *Calendula stellata*.

STOCK. See *Mathiola.*

STONECRESS. See *Aethionema.*

STRAWFLOWER. See *Helichrysum.*

SULTANA. See *Impatiens holstii.*

SUNFLOWER. See *Helianthus.*

SWAN RIVER DAISY. See *Brachycome iberidifolia.*

SWAN RIVER EVERLASTING. See *Helipterum manglesii.*

SWEET ALYSSUM. See *Lobularia.*

SWEET PEA. See *Lathyrus.*

SWEET SCABIOUS. See *Scabiosa atropurpurea.*

SWEET SULTAN. See *Centaurea moschata.*

TAGETES
(AFRICAN and FRENCH MARIGOLDS)
Easy to grow, these plants have brilliantly colored yellow or bronzy flowers. The foliage often has a somewhat objectionable scent when bruised. They are much used for beds and cut flowers. Sow seed indoors in spring, harden off young plants, plant out when weather is warm and settled. Numerous varieties of both African and French marigolds and hybrids in many heights, forms and colors, are listed and described by seedsmen.

TAHOKA DAISY. See *Machaeranthera tanacetifolia.*

TALINUM (JEWELS OF OPHIR)
Good for hot, sunny locations and dryish soils, the seed is sown outdoors in spring where plants are to grow. Thin the seedlings 6 to 8 in. apart; or sow seed indoors early and transplant

Tagetes
(French Marigold)

outdoors after weather is warm.
Talinum paniculatum, 1 to 2 ft. Has fleshy leaves and airy sprays of small pink flowers which open in the afternoon and close the following morning. A constant succession of bloom is maintained. The small ruby-colored seedpods are attractive.

TASSEL FLOWER. See *Emilia.*

THUNBERGIA
This twining vine has handsome flowers throughout the season. Useful for flower beds, low trellises, hanging baskets and other purposes, it is easily raised from seed sown indoors or in a greenhouse in late winter or spring. The young plants should not be set in the garden until the weather is quite warm and settled. Space them 12 to 18 in. apart. In the South seed may be sown directly outdoors in spring.
Thunbergia alata (black-eyed-Susan vine), 3 to 6 ft. Flowers orange, yellow, cream or white, usually with a dark central eye.

T. gibsonii, 3 to 6 ft. Similar to *T. alata*, but with larger orange-colored flowers.

THYMOPHYLLA (DAHLBERG DAISY)
An excellent low plant which blooms freely all summer, it is especially suitable for edgings and rock gardens. This daisy stands hot weather well and prefers well-drained soil in full sun. Sow seed outdoors in spring where plants are to bloom, and thin to 6 in. apart; or sow early indoors and transplant to garden when all danger from frost has passed.

Thymophylla tenuiloba, 6 to 12 in. This species has aromatic, ferny foliage and a multitude of small yellow daisy flowers.

TICKSEED. See *Coreopsis*.

TIDYTIPS. See *Layia elegans*.

TITHONIA (MEXICAN SUNFLOWER)
Known for their good summer and fall bloom, these plants are most useful for garden decoration and cutting. They withstand hot weather well and need full sun and ordinary soil. Excessively rich soil encourages coarse growth and may inhibit flowering. Seed may be sown directly outdoors where the plants are to bloom as soon in spring as the ground is fairly warm and the weather settled; or an early start may be had by sowing indoors six to seven weeks before warm weather allows transplanting outdoors. Space 2 to 3 ft. between individuals.

Tithonia rotundifolia (sometimes called *T. speciosa*), 6 to 12 ft. Flowers resembling single dahlias, brilliant orange-red. Named varieties—some of which are lower-growing, some earlier-blooming, than the typical species—are available.

TOADFLAX. See *Linaria*.

TORENIA (WISHBONE FLOWER)
A very pretty plant which blooms all summer, it stands hot weather well and is adapted for sun or light shade and ordinary soil. Easily raised from seed sown indoors in spring, the young plants are transplanted to flats, hardened off, then planted outdoors when settled warm weather is assured. In the South may be grown from seeds sown directly outdoors. Plants in the garden should stand about 8 in. apart.

Torenia fournieri, 8 to 12 in. Bushy plants with an abundance of showy flowers either blue-and-white, blue-and-yellow, or white-and-yellow according to variety.

TOUCH-ME-NOT. See *Impatiens*.

TRACHYMENE (LACE FLOWER)
Often grown under the name *Didiscus*, this is an attractive plant for garden display and for use as a cut flower. It thrives in full sun and fertile soil but does not prosper in very hot weather. Sow seeds in spring directly outdoors where plants are to bloom, and thin seedlings 6 to 8 in. apart. In the North, seed may be sown indoors during springtime and later, as soon as all danger from frost has passed, the young plants may be transferred to the open garden.

Trachymene caerulea (blue lace flower), $1\frac{1}{2}$ to 2 ft. Branching with lacy foliage; flowers, similar to Queen Anne's lace, are pale blue, delicate pink or white.

TREE MALLOW. See *Lavatera*.

TROPAEOLUM
Tropaeolums have showy, often scented flowers, in both dwarf and climbing types. The latter are used to cover fences and other supports. Sow seed in spring where plants are to flower; thin out to 6 in. apart.

Tropaeolum majus (garden nasturtium), a summer-flowering plant, climbing and trailing, with yellow- or orange-spurred flowers 2 in. across. There are many beautiful varieties of almost every conceivable shade of red, orange, yellow, scarlet, purple, white, as well as double hybrids.

T. peregrinum (canarybird flower). Climbs up to 7 ft. and looks attractive on a trellis. Golden-yellow, green-spurred flowers in summer.

URSINIA

These members of the daisy family come in brilliant colors—orange-yellow, orange-scarlet, and bright orange with crimson-red. The plants are at their best from June to September in full sun. Sow seed in greenhouse in mid-March; harden off in April; plant out in early May, 6 in. apart.

Ursinia anethoides (jewel-of-the-veldt), 1½ ft. Finely cut leaves; orange-yellow flowers 2 in. across.

U. anthemoides, 1 ft. Long-stemmed bright yellow flowers.

U. pulchra, 9 in Bushy annual with strongly scented leaves and bright orange flowers with purple zones. There are several named varieties, all good for the front of the border.

VALERIAN. See *Centranthus.*

VENIDIUM (MONARCH-OF-THE-VELDT)

Brilliant orange-yellow, daisylike flowers bloom in great profusion during the summer and are excellent for cutting. Sow seed in greenhouse in spring, harden off, and plant out after all danger of frost is passed; or sow directly outdoors in the spring. This plant does not withstand hot, humid weather.

Venidium fastuosum, 2 to 3 ft. Brilliant orange flowers 4 in. across with large, shiny black central disks. Leaves and buds covered with silvery-white hairs. There are varieties with larger flowers and varied colors.

VERBENA

Good plants for beds, borders and window boxes, they have brilliant red, blue, pink, lilac or white flowers throughout the summer and until killing frost. Sow seed in greenhouse in late winter, harden off. Plant outdoors after danger of frost is passed.

Verbena hortensis, 6 to 12 in., is really a perennial but is grown as an annual. Bushy or trailing plants producing clusters of blue, lilac, salmon, purple, rose, scarlet, yellow or white flowers all summer long. Numerous splendid named varieties are offered by seedsmen.

V. rigida (syn. *V. venosa*), 12 to 18 in. A rather stiff-growing plant with lavender or rosy-purple flowers.

VINCA

This warm-weather plant blooms freely throughout the summer in full sun or very light shade. Sow seed indoors in late winter or spring. Transplant and keep growing in warm greenhouse. Pinch out tips of shoots when 3 to 4 in. tall. Harden off and plant outdoors after really warm, settled weather is assured. Space plants 8 to 10 in. apart.

Vinca rosea (Madagascar periwinkle), 1 to 1½ ft. Attractive, glossy foliage, and flat phloxlike flowers about 1½ in. across; rosy-purple, white or white with a red eye.

VIPER'S BUGLOSS. See *Echium.*

VIRGINIAN STOCK. See *Malcomia maritima.*

WISHBONE FLOWER. See *Torenia.*

WOODRUFF. See *Asperula.*

XERANTHEMUM
(IMMORTELLE, EVERLASTING)

Pretty "everlastings" are easily grown from seed and, when dried, are very useful for winter bouquets. Sow seed directly outdoors in spring where the plants are to bloom; or raise plants from seed indoors and set them out as soon as danger from frost is passed. A sunny place and porous soil are needed. Space plants 2 to 3 in. apart.

Xeranthemum annuum (common immortelle), 1½ to 2 ft. Flowers are papery; may be single or double; white, pink or red.

YOUTH-AND-OLD-AGE. See *Zinnia*.

ZEA (ORNAMENTAL CORN)
Certain varieties of corn are cultivated for their ornamental foliage or for their brightly hued grain. The colorfully seeded ears are dried and used as winter decorations. Sow seed directly outdoors in spring after soil has warmed and weather is settled,

at the same time as sweet corn is sown.

Zea mays, 4 to 6 ft. Named varieties are offered by seedsmen.

ZINNIA (YOUTH-AND-OLD-AGE)
Very popular for garden decoration and cut flowers, these are easy to grow either from seed sown in spring outdoors where the plants are to bloom or from seed sown indoors about six weeks before the weather becomes settled and warm. At this time the plants may be transferred to the garden. They need full sun and fertile soil. Space plants 6 to 12 in. apart, according to variety.

Zinnia elegans, 1 to 3 ft. Stiff-stemmed plants with rather flat-topped flowers turned upward. Offered in numerous garden varieties, in a wide range of colors, heights and forms. Flowers are single or double.

CHAPTER 7

PRACTICAL AND PERMANENT PERENNIALS

Soil and Site—Types of Borders and Beds—Season of Bloom—Selecting Plants—Planting—Care—Diseases and Pests—Propagation—Recommended Hardy Perennials

WITH THEIR almost limitless variety in kind, height, color and season of flower, hardy perennials offer the

gardener a most satisfying return for his time and outlay. Although more expensive to buy than bedding plants or other annuals, perennials are less costly in the long run. Once planted, they live on from year to year, and most of them increase in number. If a reasonably large selection is grown, there will be bloom from early spring to late fall. Early, midseason and late-flowering kinds should be planted. Either choose varieties that can adapt themselves to a given site, or choose a site suitable for the plants selected.

Until the end of the last century, there had been little scope in gardens for the use of hardy perennials. Because they were so varied, they could not be restricted to the formal garden styles of former eras. So the perennial border, called the herbaceous border in England, emerged as a compromise, with plants growing more freely but within straight lines. This became the conventional method of displaying perennials. Recent developments in design have proved to be more satisfying. In Great Britain there is a marked trend toward planting perennials in "island beds" that can be viewed from all sides. Of course a goodly number will grow and flower almost anywhere; but, depending on their adaptability to soil and shade, many will fall short of their natural perfection.

LIGHT AND AIR

Conventional perennial borders tend to encourage weak growth. A hedge as backing, nearby trees or shrubs and overcrowding may all be harmful. Not only is light often restricted, but so is the free circulation of air. These conditions cause stem weakness and encourage disease.

Another disadvantage of the conventional border is that many plants may be much too tall for a narrow strip. Perennials, if adequately spaced in beds that receive light from all sides, and are exposed to free circulation of air, increase in number of stems from year to year, yet keep to their normal height. In a narrow strip, with a wall, hedge or tree backing, they grow taller in their search for sun and air, becoming weak and

leggy and out of balance with shorter plants in the same border.

Exposure

Most perennial borders face one way only, and the direction they face is very important. Since most hardy perennials are sun-loving plants, they should face more or less south if possible. If only a north-facing border is possible, it may be filled with plants that prefer partial shade. There is a considerable number of these to choose from, but a wide variety of shade-tolerant perennials may be difficult to obtain. Most nurserymen keep a larger stock of the more popular sun-loving varieties.

Wind, particularly a sudden storm or gale, can play havoc with plants. A border located in what might prove to be a funnel for strong winds—such as an opening between buildings or between screens of trees or evergreens—needs more staking than a border in a completely open or a completely sheltered place. Far less staking is needed if island beds for perennials are set in unenclosed areas.

SOIL

Most hardy perennials are very adaptable as to soil. Some kinds prefer a richer or moister soil than others, but there is sufficient variety available for almost any situation. It is possible to have perennials flourishing in any garden, even in city yards.

Essentially all of the perennials listed at the end of this chapter must have freely drained soil; they will not grow in waterlogged or badly drained locations.

In only a few cases is the acidity of the soil a matter of prime consideration. The great majority of garden perennials are tolerant of a fairly wide pH range (see page 741 in "The Soil"). All will grow in a neutral or near-neutral soil. Wherever a fair selection of garden vegetables and annuals can be successfully cultivated, a wide range of hardy perennials may also be grown.

SITE

If possible, choose a site where sun and air are not restricted. Aim for the maximum width of bed or border that is practicable. If space permits, 10 ft., or even 12 ft., is not excessive, but very good results may be had with narrower areas. Destroy all perennial weeds through the use of chemicals before the border is planted; or by thorough digging, removing the roots of the most persistent by hand. Many weeds can be killed by burying them as the digging proceeds. This may not be easy. With a spade, skim off the few inches of topsoil that contain the weed roots, upturn it in the bottom of a trench, 8 to 10 in. deep. Stamp it down and cover with weed-free soil from just below the surface.

IMPROVING THE SOIL

In general, hardy perennials do not demand extraordinarily rich earth; but most certainly, if the soil is poor, it should be improved by mixing in manure, rotted compost or peat moss together with some bone meal or other organic fertilizer. This is done during the preparatory spading or rotary tilling. If the natural soil is dark with humus or is of good, loamy texture, organic fertilizer alone may prove satisfactory and give the plants the good start that is important to them. If the soil is excessively acid—a fact to be determined by having a soil test made—it should be corrected by liming (see page 742).

TYPES OF PLANTINGS

Traditional Borders

A traditional perennial border is one planted against a hedge, shrubbery, wall or fence. These may of course be curving or straight, even or varying in width.

There is no doubt that most excellent effects may be had from these traditional plantings, especially when there is enough area to permit planting width of 8 ft. or more. With a 6-ft.-wide border, the *effective* width for plants is only 3 to 4 ft. However, even narrower strips can be planned and planted most attractively.

One cannot plant as close to a hedge or to shrubbery as to a wall or a fence; some hedges have roots that can take nourishment and moisture from 3 ft. or more on either side, especially in light sandy soil. Because of this, allow 2 to 3 ft. of space between the hedge and the perennials planted closest to it.

A fence or wall does not take moisture or nutrients from the soil, although it will interfere with light and air circulation and sometimes will reflect heat. Plants that are taller than a foot or two naturally lean away from any kind of backing as they reach up to flower. The closer they are planted to the backing, the more they will lean.

Low and medium-height plants usually look better than tall kinds in a narrow border. A safe guide is to limit the selection of plants to those of heights not more than half the effective width of the border. For example, if the effective width is 6 ft., it should contain very few plants taller than about 3 ft. Apply this ratio to all borders less than 12 ft. wide, and place the plants more or less in order of height, with the shorter-growing ones in front.

Island Beds

Island borders or beds can be approached and viewed from all around. Light and air are less restricted, growth is stronger, and normal heights are maintained. Given adequate spacing and reasonable planning, perfection can be attained with the least effort and care.

If the garden is laid out generally in straight lines, a formal shape, such as oblong or oval, is best. But there are no rules against informal shapes that follow the configuration of surrounding trees and shrubs. An island bed sometimes fits in perfectly with a group of shrubs and may form a promontory into a lawn, with only a narrow path between the shrubs and the perennial plants in the beds.

Island beds may be small and devoted to one or two kinds of perennials, or they may be large and planted with many kinds arranged in groups of varying size to give maximum effect.

Mixed Beds and Borders

Many perennials bloom magnificently if only for a comparatively short period. In those parts of America where summers are hot, it is not possible to have a continuous and lavish display of bloom from spring through fall from a planting of perennials alone. To give additional color, many gardeners make mixed plantings of perennials and annuals and sometimes biennials. Bulbs, which of course are truly perennials although usually classed separately by gardeners, are also used.

Well planned and cared for, a mixed bed or border can be very satisfactory. It is important that adequate spaces be left at suitable intervals between the patches of perennials to receive annual and biennial plants. Such spaces should be not less than 5 sq. ft. This permits the soil to be forked and fertilized each year shortly before planting time. Good results cannot be had by setting annuals in among perennials where they will be crowded together at the peak of the growing season. Add color to mixed beds and borders by choosing those annuals that remain in bloom for long periods: marigolds, zinnias, petunias, ageratum, sweet alyssum, globe amaranths, nicotiana and dwarf dahlias.

Special-Purpose Plantings

Midget beds or borders, which can be as little as 5 ft. wide, offer considerable scope to those with small gardens. Many hardy perennials are normally seen only in rock gardens, but they can be effectively used as frontal groups in small beds. With heights ranging from 6 in. to $2\frac{1}{2}$ ft., they can produce effects that are both varied and very charming.

It is possible to select perennials not only for different soils and situations, for flowering at required periods and for cutting, but also for fragrance, for flowers attractive to bees and for silver or gray variegated foliage. A fairly wide range of ground-cover perennials flourish among flowering shrubs or trees. Some, especially those with an overall symmetry or stateliness, such as kniphofias and heucheras, look well between or in front of shrubs. The gardener must be careful, however, to avoid indiscriminate planting that will result in harmful competition for light and space.

PLANNING

Before deciding what plants you will set out, gain as wide an acquaintance as you can with the many possibilities. Visit other gardens and nurseries in your area, not just once but at various times from spring through fall. Study the catalogues of seedsmen and nurserymen who specialize in perennials. Weigh all factors—time of flowering, season of bloom, ease of culture, color preferences, usefulness for cutting, suitability for your region and location and so on.

When you have settled on the kinds and varieties of plants you intend to grow in your border, make a rough plan to scale on graph paper showing where each is to be located. In deciding this, take into consideration the habits of growth and decorative qualities of each variety.

Only in rare instances should a single plant be set out. Usually three or more specimens of the same variety are planted together to form a group. The areas of the groups should be varied and in scale with the bed. Wide and extensive beds will be more effective if the plant groups are comparatively large; small and narrow borders should have more limited groups. Always allow a greater distance between groups than between individual plants that comprise a group. This not only gives the plants a better chance to develop their special habits and characteristics, but it also makes for easier access to tend the garden.

Avoid an even flatness or a too regular grading of heights from dwarf to tall. The best effect is gained from having adjoining groups of somewhat irregular heights. With plants that differ widely in form or shape when in flower, intersperse the bushy or flat-topped varieties with spiky plants, such as delphiniums, lythrums (loosestrifes) and sidalceas.

A few initial errors may be made, but these can be easily remedied. A misplaced group, for example, will show itself in the first flowering season, and may be transferred in autumn or spring. No one yet knows everything about the cultivation or arrangement of plants, so do not be afraid to make experiments. Juggling groups is part of the pleasure.

SEASON OF BLOOM

It is possible to plan a border that provides some bloom throughout the entire season. Even though a short-season border provides a blaze of color at the chosen time, most people prefer to aim for maximum continuity, and thus they particularly like the plants which have a long flowering period.

Some perennials flower for several weeks, while others, such as irises and peonies, are past their best period after two or three weeks. Planning for continuity calls for careful placing. Do not plant in adjacent groups the kinds that flower about the same time. Put those that make a brief show and then have to be cut back or remain untidy behind or beside such plants as chrysanthemums, which become bush-like as the season advances and flower later.

Some people plan adjoining groups that give color contrast; others prefer an overall effect of color blending. The use of white flowers in a border helps to tie together and bring into harmony colors that might otherwise tend to clash. Discordant effects are less likely if plants of similar habit and time of flowering are well interspersed with others of different form which bloom later or earlier.

SPREAD

Some kinds grow and spread faster than others. Discretion in selection and planning contributes greatly to success. The more robust kinds such as monardas (Oswego tea or bee balm), phlox and heleniums may exceed the annual spread of others three times over; if planted in groups adjacent to much-slower-growing kinds, they will give trouble later on. They are better left out altogether if space is limited, particularly where variety and continuity are desired.

In the second season after planting, a fast spreader may encroach upon a group less robust; such aggression calls for annual curbing. The slowest-spreading kinds are often the choicest.

IMPROVING AN EXISTING BORDER

Borders that were poorly planned in the first place can usually be improved. Very often the cause of the trouble is that the border is too narrow for the tall plants it contains, or that light and air have become restricted. The remedy may be simply to take out overtall plants and replace them with others of lower stature. But the border may need a complete overhaul, with thorough spading and soil conditioning, using again only those plants that are adaptable to the site, and filling out with fresh and more suitable kinds.

SELECTING PLANTS

Do not buy cheap plants from questionable sources, as these may well consist of divisions of older, less vigorous stock, or may be immature or nondescript; such will certainly prove disappointing.

Because hardy perennials are so adaptable and of such infinite variety, they offer enormous possibilities.

Visit a good nurseryman to make a selection of quality plants, or order from reliable dealers. Such specialists have or can obtain the best varieties in the widest range. Most of them offer preselected collections for border planting. Be sure that a collection made to fit a stereotyped plan is suitable for your particular needs. It may be better to make your own selection.

PLANTING TIME

The best time for planting most hardy perennials is early fall, while the soil is warm and quick establishment is easy. This allows the most time for new roots to develop and assures the best possible display the following year. Spring planting can also be done successfully. But there is then some danger from overdry soil following planting; this is seldom true in autumn.

Some plants, such as scabious and pyrethrum, are better set out in spring, and in extremely cold regions spring planting may be preferable for all. A dependable nurseryman should deliver plants at the correct time for planting.

Avoid too much treading on damp soil; otherwise forking over will be necessary and, if the soil is heavy, even this will not correct the damage done. If the soil is very dry and clotty or dusty before the plants are set out, give the site a soaking a day or so before planting. If the weather becomes quite dry after planting, water the area thoroughly with a fine spray.

When planting, spread the roots in their natural positions and make the soil firm about them. The drier the soil, the heavier the firming should be, but on no account should wet, sticky soil be tightly packed.

Care of a perennial border in the first season differs somewhat from that of subsequent years. More attention must be given to watering because the plants have not yet struck their roots deeply into the earth. There should be no need to fertilize, since the initial preparation of the soil will be adequate to carry the plants through their first year without additional nutrients.

WEED CONTROL

Weed control is essential. Hoe annual weeds when they are tiny. Perennial weeds should not appear at all if the site is well prepared, but it is better to uproot a plant or two rather than allow a really pernicious perennial weed to gain a hold and become completely intergrown with choice perennials. Do not use chemical weed killers after the border has been planted.

STAKING

Nothing detracts more from the beauty of perennials than sticks and stakes carelessly and untidily used as supports, and no chore is more troublesome than staking. Support only those plants that will become floppy or top-heavy when in flower, putting in the stakes well before growth reaches that stage. Do not try to impose rigidity on plants that are naturally a little floppy. For tall plants such as delphiniums, use the attractive bamboo stakes for each spike. All supports should be used as sparingly as possible, and should be of a height that is appropriate to that of the plants. Well before buds open, place the supports in position and, wherever necessary, tie the stems to them with soft twine or other material that will not cut into the soft growth. Make the ties loose enough to allow for natural thickening of the stems without strangulation.

FERTILIZING AND MULCHING

Perennials vary in their need for nourishment. Give them a good start, and they should not need additional fertilizing during the first season. After that, depending on the quality of the soil, fork in old manure, rotted compost or peat, together with an organic fertilizer each fall or early spring, or fork in the manure, compost or peat each fall and fertilize in spring. Apply a mulch to the soil surface in late spring or early summer before the onset of hot weather. Be sure that the ground is weed-free before spreading the mulch. Peat moss, buckwheat hulls, rotted sawdust and similar materials are excellent for this purpose. The mulch will retain moisture and keep down weeds.

Mulching is also helpful to certain plants that tend to lift out of the ground. Every three or four years it may be necessary to dig up, divide and replant them more deeply, especially such plants as monarda and perennial aster, which make a rapid surface spread and exhaust their vigor. For replanting, use only the younger parts, the outer edges of the clumps, and discard the rest.

WATERING

During dry weather, it is helpful to soak the plantings with water to a minimum depth of 6 to 8 in. Sprinklings that merely wet the surface are of little value because they encourage roots to develop in the top inch or two of soil, and these are soon destroyed by subsequent drying and by cultivation. A deep soaking at weekly intervals is much to be preferred to more frequent, less thorough applications. It takes a long time to wet dry soil to the depth recommended; when you think you have accomplished this, dig down in a few spots chosen at random as a check. Soil-soaker types of hoses often afford a practical means of thoroughly watering perennial beds.

WINTER PROTECTION

In colder sections, winter protection should be given in the form of a light covering of salt-marsh hay, branches of evergreens or some other material that permits free access of air and does not become wet and soggy. This is especially true where a lasting snow cover cannot be depended upon.

When the ground freezes, the water in it will expand, causing plants to "heave" upward. Subsequent thawing and freezing make the situation worse. But the protection of mulch minimizes heaving and saves plant roots from being torn and exposed. The cover should be put on after the ground has frozen to a depth of 2 or 3 in. and should be gradually removed in spring just as new growth is beginning.

DISEASES AND PESTS

Like most other plants, hardy perennials may suffer from various diseases and pests. The gardener must maintain a constant lookout for the first signs of infection or infestation and take prompt action (see Pests of Decorative Plants, page 829 in "Plant

Pests"). Be sure to cut down all stems and foliage killed by frost. Consign it all to the compost heap, or burn it if soil-borne pests or diseases have affected the plants. Diseased weeds growing nearby should be destroyed as well.

REPLANTING

A well-planned and planted perennial border or bed will go several years without a complete job of lifting and replanting. Nevertheless, it is advisable to undertake this task every fourth or fifth year. It gives an opportunity to rehabilitate the soil, which becomes somewhat exhausted. Undertake this work in early fall. Lift all perennials except the very few—such as peonies—which are known to resent root disturbance strongly. Label them carefully and heel them in temporarily by covering their roots in a trench in an out-of-the-way shaded corner while the soil preparation is completed.

Before the plants are reset, separate or divide the clumps into pieces, retaining only the most vigorous and discarding all old, worn-out parts.

In the years between the major overhauls, a certain amount of dividing and replanting will probably be desirable to check excessive growth of some kinds of plants that crowd out their neighbors. To give their roots a chance to become reestablished, attend to this in early fall or as early in the spring as possible.

PROPAGATION

Many perennials can be raised from seed. This is true of nearly all natural species (the kinds that occur wild and are not the result of plant breeding or hybridizing) as well as of some horticultural varieties, such as delphiniums. But a great many garden varieties of perennials cannot be propagated from seed because they do not produce seed or because they will not breed true from seed.

The commonest method of increasing perennials is by division. Many can be grown from cuttings; some, such as anchusas and phlox, by root cuttings. (See "How to Raise New Plants," page 696.)

Recommended Hardy Perennials

Each plant in this list has been graded for spread and should be planted as shown in the following chart. Gradings include the spread of summer-flowering growth.

Unless some regard is paid to this important factor, unfair competition may result in losses or trouble. Although it should be remembered that both soil and climate play a part in growth spread, these gradings can serve for purposes of comparison.

Grading	No. of plants per sq. yd.	Approx. spacing in group (no. of in. apart)	No. of in. required between adjoining groups
S/1	6–9	6–10	12–18
S/2	5	10–12	18–20
S/3	4	12–14	20–24
S/4	3–4	14–16	24–28
S/5	3	16–18	28–30

AARON'S ROD. See *Thermopsis caroliniana*.

ACANTHUS (BEAR'S-BREECH)

These plants are fine for isolated positions where the handsome foliage and tapering spikes can be seen to advantage. They associate well with shrubs, are drought-resistant, deep-rooting and long-lived. They like sun or partial shade and cannot tolerate damp, heavy soil. Where winters are severe, plant them in protected locations only and cover well in winter.

Acanthus mollis, S/4. Large dark green leaves and 3- to 4-ft. spikes of whitish, hooded flowers in summer.

A. spinosus, S/4. Freer-flowering than *A. mollis*. Purple-white flowers, each protected by a sharp spine, on 3- to 4-ft. spikes from June to August. Leaves appear prickly, but are not so.

ACHILLEA (YARROW, MILFOIL)

Varies in height and appearance, but all kinds have pungent foliage; best in sun and well-drained soil. Divide in spring. Good for cutting.

Achillea clypeolata, S/3. Forms clumpy plants of silver-gray leaves, with flat heads of deep yellow flowers on about 20-in. stems for many weeks, June to August. Likes dry places in sun. Not worth attempting in damp soil, as overexuberant growth in summer leads to rotting off in winter.

A. filipendulina (syn. *A. eupatorium*), S/3–4. One of the most reliable of tall border plants, reaching 5 ft. without supports. Deep yellow flowers between June and September, continuity being encouraged by cutting. Green filigree leaves. Not fussy as to soil and seldom needs replanting.

Coronation Gold, S/3–4. 3 ft. This excellent hybrid has bright golden-yellow flower heads, smaller than those of Gold Plate, which are produced very freely from July to August. Good for cutting.

Gold Plate, S/3–4. 5 ft. The best-known variety has deep golden-yellow flowers from July to August.

Moonshine, S/3–4. 2 ft. Rather like a more robust *A. taygetea*, it has much broader heads of glistening light yellow between May and July.

A. millefolium (yarrow), S/3. 1½–2 ft. This is not worthy of cultivating as a garden decorative perennial, but several named varieties of it, all characterized by pink or cerise-red flowers, have value as border plants and for cutting. They have green or grayish fernlike foliage and erect stems which bear flat-topped heads of

Achillea
(Yarrow, Milfoil)

small daisylike flowers. All thrive with little care and flourish in dry soil and full sun. Among named varieties offered are Cerise Queen, Crimson Beauty, Fire King and Rose Beauty.

A. ptarmica Perry's White, S 4. Double white flowers ½ in. across on 3-ft. stems, which branch near the top, from June to August. Good for cutting. Often needs staking. Divide every three or four years or flowers will deteriorate.

A.p. The Pearl, S/4. Similar to *A.p.* Perry's White.

A. taygetea, S/2. Gray foliage, stiff 1½-ft. stems of light yellow flowers on broad heads from late May to July. Divide and replant every three to four years. Some named varieties and some crosses between this species and those mentioned above are good garden plants.

ACONITUM (MONKSHOOD)
The following are all adaptable for a wide range of soils. Most of them will grow in semishade as well as sun, and although finer spikes come when they are replanted in enriched soil every three or four years, they can remain without attention for a long time. Staking is not usually needed. Roots are poisonous if eaten, and care should be taken in the handling of these plants, especially if there are cuts or abrasions on the hands. Good for cutting.

Aconitum arendsii, S/2–3. An intermediate cross with *A. wilsonii* and *A. fischeri* combining the best features of both. Blue flowers from August to early October. Spikes are erect, reaching 4 to 4½ ft. on unbranched stems.

A. fischeri (syn. *A. carmichaelii*), S/2. A fine autumn-flowering plant with sturdy 3-to-4-ft. spikes carrying large hooded flowers of amethyst blue near the top. Stems are well clothed with shiny, jagged leaves. Needs good, moist soil.

A. napellus bicolor, S/2. 3½ ft. A first-rate plant with branching spikes carrying very pretty blue and white flowers in June and July.

Bressingham Spire, S/2. 3 ft. This has deep violet-blue flowers on tapering spikes in July and August, and dark green shiny leaves covering the stem.

Newry Blue, S/2–3. Similar in color to Bressingham Spire but a little taller and earlier to flower, with spikes more loosely branched.

Spark's Variety, S/2–3. 4 ft. Even more branching habit than Newry Blue. Deep violet-blue flowers in June and July.

A. wilsonii, S/2–3. Best in Barker's Variety. Spikes often exceed 6 ft. and need supports. Large, glistening lavender-blue flowers in September and October.

AJUGA (BUGLEWEED)
These plants make excellent ground cover, the tallest being only about 1 ft. high in flower. Ajugas flourish even in dry, shady places and need very little attention. They may also be effectively used in the front of open beds or borders. If vigor flags after a few years, topdress with rich compost or lift and replant.

Ajuga genevensis, S/4. 6 to 12 in. Blue, rose or white flowers in late spring.

A. pyramidalis, S/2–3. The finest for flowering, having 9-in. spikes of gentian blue from May to July. Likes some shade and prefers soil that is not too dry.

A. reptans, S/5. 6 to 12 in. Purple flowers in late spring.

A.r. Rainbow, S/4. Leaves are bronze with buff and purple markings. Blue flowers on 6-in. spikes in late spring.

A.r. variegata, S/4. Pretty, with variegated leaves. Blue flowers on stubby 6-in spikes in late spring.

ALTHAEA

Althaea rosea (hollyhock), S/5. 6 to 9 ft. There are many garden varieties of this popular, stately early-summer bloomer with single or double, white, pink, red, maroon, purple or yellow flowers. Excellent for providing vertical lines and accents in the landscape. They thrive in fertile, well-drained soil in sun or part shade. Because these plants are subject to a serious, disfiguring fungus rust disease, the best results are often had by growing them as biennials, instead of retaining them after their second year.

ALYSSUM

Excellent low-growing, spring-blooming plants for associating with tulips and other spring-flowering bulbs, and for planting at the front of borders, they bloom freely. Need full sun and ordinary soil. All S 2.

Alyssum saxatile (basket-of-gold). 1 ft. Has grayish foliage and golden-yellow flowers.

A.s. citrinum (syn. *A.s.* Silver Queen). 1 ft. Similar to *A. saxatile*, but has pale-yellow flowers.

A.s. compactum flore-pleno, 1 ft. This is similar to *A. saxatile*, but has fully double flowers.

AMERICAN IPECAC. See *Gillenia stipulata*.

AMSONIA

Easy-to-grow plants for light shade or sun in ordinary soil, they form bushy, round clumps with numerous erect stems and a profusion of star-shaped flowers in summer. This plant is rarely troubled by pests or diseases.

Amsonia tabernaemontana, S/3. 2½ to 3½ ft. Flowers pale gray-blue.

ANAPHALIS (EVERLASTING)

These easy-to-grow gray- or silver-leaved plants carry heads or sprays of whitish daisy flowers of crisp, ever-lasting texture. Although flowering best in sun and dryish soils, they will flourish happily in some shade. They form quite effective ground cover. Good for cutting. When propagating these, divide them in spring.

Anaphalis margaritacea (pearly everlasting), S/4. 2 to 3 ft. Robust. Silver-gray leaves and loose heads of off-white flowers on 15-in. stems in late summer.

A. nubigena, S/3, *A. triplinervis*, S/3. Both are smaller and more compact than *A. margaritacea*. Flower in high summer.

A. yedoensis, S/4. 2 to 2½ ft. Slowly creeping underground shoots run to flower quite erectly in crisp, flat white heads, useful for cutting in summer. Stems become massed, and plants are pleasing, with their silvery leaves, from spring onward.

ANCHUSA (BUGLOSS)

The brightest of the anchusas are the least reliable. Although the varieties of *A. azurea* (syn. *A. italica*) are popular, they are not very long-lived, and are best in sun and dryish soils. Roots are thick and fleshy; leaves and stems are rough, hairy, and they may need supporting. The colorful show they make in early summer is apt to leave an unsightly gap when flowering is over in July. The plant often named *A. myosotidiflora* is really *Brunnera macrophylla*.

The five varieties listed below are all forms of *A. azurea*:

Dropmore, S/3. 3 ft. Beautiful gentian-blue flowers in early summer.

Loddon Royalist, S/3. Deeper blue and smaller than Morning Glory.

Morning Glory, S/3. 4 ft. Heavy, branched spikes of bright-blue flowers.

Opal, S/3. Light blue, taller than Morning Glory.

Royal Blue, S/3. Deeper blue and smaller than Morning Glory.

A. angustifolia (syn. *A. caespitosa*),

Anchusa
(Bugloss)

S/2. Not long-lived or easy to increase, but still worthwhile for the sheer brilliance and continuity of its display of blue for much of the summer. Flowers are small, but hundreds develop on 12-in. sprays arching out from a compact, deep-rooting plant. At its best and longest-lived in poor, dry soil in full sun.

ANEMONE (WINDFLOWER)
From the species *Anemone japonica* have been derived many fine garden varieties called Japanese anemones. They bloom in fall and provide excellent cut flowers. They need deep, fertile soil that contains an abundance of organic matter and is fairly moist but well drained; avoid stagnant water. Light shade from strong sun is advantageous. Winter protection is

desirable; in areas of very severe winter cold they are not reliably hardy. Among the best varieties, all 2 to 3 ft. tall, are:

A.j. alba, S/2. Pure white flowers, one of the hardiest.

A.j. Alice, S/2. Flowers rose pink with lilac centers.

A.j. Margarette, S/2. Double rose-pink flowers.

A.j. Profusion, S/2. Flowers deep rose-pink.

A.j. September Charm, S/2. Flowers silvery pink, shaded with deeper pink.

A. pulsatilla (pasqueflower), S/1. 9 to 12 in. Has finely divided silvery foliage and large lavender, violet, purple or white flowers in spring, followed by attractive, silky seed heads. Suitable for front of flower border. Needs full sun and porous soil.

A. vitifolia, S/2. Very similar to *A. japonica* and needing the same culture, but able to withstand considerably lower temperatures.

A.v. robustissima, S/2. 2½ ft. Silvery-pink flowers. Begins blooming in early fall.

A.v. r. rubra, S/2. 2½ to 3 ft. Flowers deeper pink than *A.v. robustissima*.

ANTHEMIS
These members of the daisy family need full sun and well-drained soil. Bright, free-flowering and good for cutting, but some are untidy in growth. Cut hard back after flowering to encourage their basal growth for overwintering.

Anthemis sancti-johannis, S/3. 1½ ft. Bright gold flowers between June and September, but smaller-flowered, more compact and longer-lived than *A. tinctoria* and its varieties. Easy to grow from seed.

A. tinctoria, S/4. 2 to 2½ ft. Has ferny foliage and an abundance of light yellow daisylike flowers in summer. The parent of several varieties, the best of which are:

Beauty of Grallagh, S/3. A little larger and deeper yellow than Grallagh Gold. Flowers from June to September. Not reliably perennial, although behavior seems to vary according to locality.

Grallagh Gold, S/3. Rich yellow and gold flowers, 2 in. across, carried loosely on rather floppy bushy growth to 2 ft. or so for many weeks between June and September. Not reliably perennial, although behavior seems to vary according to locality.

A.t. kelwayi, S/3. 2 to 2½ ft. Also known as Kelway's Variety, this is an old and reliable kind with slightly gray-green ferny foliage and pale yellow flowers.

Moonlight, S/3. 2½ ft. Best of the light yellow varieties, flowering from May to September. Flowers are 2½ in. across and are superb for cutting. They last well in water. This is a plant of neat and attractive habit.

ANTHERICUM

Anthericum liliago (St. Bernard's lily), S/1. 2 ft. Compact and trouble-free, this pretty plant has narrow, rushy leaves and small white trumpet flowers from smooth stems. Blooms in June; likes sun or semishade. Its flowering is brief, followed by period of dormancy. A related plant, *Paradisea liliastrum* (St. Bruno's lily), is often confused with this.

AQUILEGIA (COLUMBINE)

Although many species exist, inter-breeding makes it difficult to keep aquilegias true to name or character, since they can be increased only by seed. Seedlings flower in their second year. Once they have flowered, vitality decreases, so be prepared with replacements. Good mixed strains exist, as well as selected varieties, which come almost true from seed. Groups of any of the following add much to the gaiety of early summer gardens.

Plant in sun or partial shade. Good for cutting.

Aquilegia caerulea, S/2. 2 to 3 ft. The lovely Colorado columbine has handsome blue and white blooms, each 2 in. in diameter. It flowers in early summer. A variety of this species, *A.c. candidissima*, has pure white flowers.

A. canadensis, S/2. 2 to 3 ft. A red or red and yellow native American species that grows naturally in woodlands but is easy to cultivate in ordinary flower borders. It appreciates part shade. A variety of this species named *flavescens* has yellow flowers.

A. chrysantha, S/2. 3 to 4 ft. Native of the Rocky Mountains and Texas, this much-branched species produces bright yellow flowers with 2½-in.-long spurs.

A. hybrida. This group name includes hybrids involving several species. The seeds are usually sold under varietal or strain names.

A.h. Crimson Star, S/2. 1½ ft. Large red and pale pink flowers.

Blue King, Celestial Blue, Coral Pink, S/2. Similar height and form to Crimson Star.

A.h. McKana Hybrid, S/2. 3 ft. Has now ousted the once-popular Scott Elliott strain. From mixed seeds it has a wide variation in color and long-spurred flowers. Plant in good soil.

A. longissima, S/2. 2 to 3 ft. This kind has pale yellow flowers which have slender spurs up to 5 in. long. It is a native of the Southwest and of Mexico.

ARABIS (ROCK CRESS)

Thrives in full sun or part shade in well-drained soil. It blooms in spring. As soon as the flowers fade, the plants should be sheared lightly. All S/1.

Arabis albida, 8 to 12 in. tall. Flowers white. This plant is often grown as *A. alpina*.

A.a. flore-pleno. Identical with *A. albida*, but blooms slightly later and has double flowers. An exceptionally fine variety.

ARMERIA (THRIFT)

Reliable for the front of a border, all form tufty, evergreen clumps or mats from which come drumstick heads of flowers in early summer. Plant in a sunny place. They are good for cutting.

Armeria Bee's Ruby, S/2. 15 in. First-rate in every respect, with heads of glistening pink from early June till late August.

A. Glory of Holland, S/2. 1 to 1½ ft. Has good pink flowers.

A. Royal Rose, S/2. 15 in. Has bright pink flowers and neat, rounded clumps of foliage.

A. maritima alba, S/3. White, similar in growth to *A.m.* Vindictive.

A.m. laucheana, S/2. 9 to 10 in. Bright-pink flowers. A good variety for edgings to beds and borders.

A.m. Vindictive, S/3. 6 to 8 in. Rosy-red flowers. A fine edging plant.

A. pseud-armeria, S/2. 10 to 12 in. A broad-leaved kind with large heads of pink flowers. Sometimes called *A. cephalotes*. Its variety *rubra* has deep pink flowers.

ARTEMISIA

Only one of these, *Artemisia lactiflora*, is of value as a flowering plant, but others are most effective for foliage in summer. All are of easy culture and have aromatic foliage. The silver-leaved species prefer sun and poor or dry soil, and can be used effectively to set off flowering plants.

Artemisia abrotanum (southernwood, old man), S/3–4. Makes a sizable bush up to 3 ft., but where cold winters occur, it dies back to a compact woody root in winter.

A. albula (syn. Silver King), S/2. 3–3½ ft. Silvery-white foliage. Good

for contrast with strong colors and for cutting.

A. discolor, S/2. 2 ft. Beautiful silver filigree foliage.

A. frigida, S/1. 1½ ft. Attractive silvery-gray foliage.

A. lactiflora (white mugwort), S/2. Ranks highly because of its plumes of creamy-white flowers which reach 4 or 5 ft. Stems are well clothed with jagged leaves. No supports are needed. Plant in good, moist soil.

A. schmidtiana nana (syn. Silver Mound), S/1. 9 in. Makes a compact mound of finely divided silver-gray foliage.

A. stelleriana (dusty miller, old woman), S/4. Silvery foliage but leaves broader than *A. discolor*. Spreads rather quickly. Especially suitable for seaside gardens and sandy soils.

A. versicolor, S/1. 1½ to 2 ft. A very distinct and delightful border plant producing a charming foliage pattern of silvery gray-green.

ARUNCUS (GOATSBEARD)

Aruncus sylvester (syn. *Spiraea aruncus*), S/4. 5 ft. A plant of noble appearance, it has strong, erect plumes of tiny milk-white flowers in June. Although an adaptable plant, it prefers good, moist soil with some shade.

A.s. kneiffii, S/2. 2 ft. Needs shade and moisture to show off its drooping plumes of creamy flowers to full advantage in June. Leaves also droop and are very prettily laced.

ASCLEPIAS (MILKWEED)

Asclepias tuberosa (butterfly weed), S/1. 2 ft. Summer-flowering, it has erect stems topped by flat clusters of bright orange-colored flowers. Needs full sun and very well-drained soil. Attractive to butterflies.

ASTER (MICHAELMAS DAISY)

The perennial asters are less appreciated here than they are in Europe, where a great many varieties are grown under the common name of Michaelmas daisies. However, our gardeners are becoming interested in them, and with increasing frequency we find wide selections offered in nursery catalogues. A majority of the kinds cultivated are native North American species, as well as varieties and hybrids of them—the results of the efforts of European plant breeders, though American breeders have raised a goodly number in recent years. As a group, the perennial asters are easy to grow. They appreciate good drainage, moderately rich soil and full sun. They are easily increased by division in spring or fall and by cuttings.

Aster acris, S/2. 2½ ft. in the type, rather less in the dwarf form *nanus*, S/1. Makes an effective neat bushy mound of small light blue starry flowers in August and September. Likes sun.

A. alpinus, S/1. 6 to 9 in. Single blue, mauve or pinkish flowers in May and June. Useful near front of border but not spectacular.

A. amellus, S/2–3. This, a Euro-

pean species, is the parent of a number of garden varieties that form what is called the *amellus* group of hardy asters. Most are less adaptable to conditions in many parts of America than are varieties that have been derived from American species. Where they do thrive, they are of real value for late summer and autumn. Stems are rather short and erect; flowers are often 2 in. across, with rayed petals from yellow centers. Heights vary from 20 to 30 in. Plants grow very compactly and, once established, should be allowed to remain a few years. Divide in spring.

A. cordifolius, S/2. 4 ft. Grows compactly as a plant, but stems are willowy and often need support. Small, graceful flowers in September and October. Stake carefully. Garden varieties of this species are offered in seed catalogues.

A. ericoides, S/2–3. 2½ to 3 ft. Sturdy bushes covered with tiny pale starry flowers in autumn. Needs no staking. Garden varieties of this species are offered in catalogues.

A. farreri, S/2–3. 1 to 2 ft. Forms a

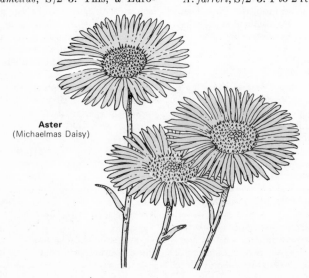

Aster
(Michaelmas Daisy)

low carpet of foliage and has lilac-
blue flowers with golden centers.
Hardy and easy to grow. Excellent
for cutting. A variety named Berg-
garten is particularly good.

A. frikartii, S/2–3. 2 ft. A hybrid
that blooms very freely throughout
the summer. Its lavender-blue flowers are 2 to 2½ in. in diameter and
have yellow centers. An especially
fine variety of this hybrid is Wonder
of Staffa. The cut flowers last well.

A. novi-belgii, S/3–4. Varieties of
this American species are among the
kinds most commonly called Michaelmas daisies. They need rather frequent attention as to dividing and
replanting to give of their best. Finest
flowers come from young plants. To
overcome the deterioration that sets
in after the first season or two, replant
vigorous outer shoots and discard the
remainders of old plants. Great advances have been made in range of
height and color and in size of flower.
Flowers in autumn. The tallest varieties need careful staking, but several
varieties exist in the 1- to 2½-ft.
height range which need no staking.

A. subcaeruleus, A/2–3. The best
known of early-flowering asters. Large
blue, orange-centered flowers on 1- to
1½-ft. stems from matlike growth in
late May and June. The best known
is Napsbury, S/2–3, and this, more
than others, needs dividing and replanting every second year to retain
vitality. It is sometimes listed as *A.
yunnanensis* Napsbury.

ASTILBE (SPIREA)
These superb plants prefer light shade
and moisture. They are hardy, long-
lived, with graceful spikes of flowers,
often brilliantly colored, and very attractive foliage. Plants form woody
crowns and may become quite massive
growing in good, moist soil. Much-
divided leaves emerge in spring—
bronze or purplish in some varieties;

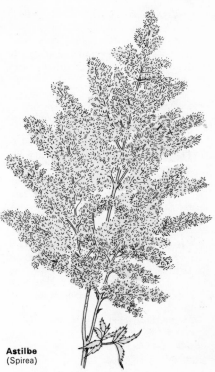

Astilbe
(Spirea)

by June the plants make graceful but
dense mounds, with stems that spray
out into delicate, tapering or pendant
spikes of countless tiny flowers. They
are excellent waterside plants and can
be left undisturbed for years when
doing well. Provide extra moisture by
sinking a deep pot or a drainpipe into
the soil between the plants, and fill
this occasionally with water to percolate to the roots of the plants.

These vary in height from a few
inches to several feet. Good varieties
of *Astilbe* include:

Deutschland, S/2. Salmon-pink
flowers.

Europa, S/2. Clear pink flowers.

Fanal, S/2. Deep red flowers.

Gladstone, S/3. White flowers.

Salmon Queen, S/3–4. Salmon-pink
flowers.

A. chinensis pumila, S/2–3. 12 to 15 in. Lilac-rose.

A. simplicifolia rosea, S/2–3. 5 in. Makes a very fine plant and adapts to dryish soil better than other dwarf varieties.

ASTRANTIA (MASTERWORT)
These are curious, charming and rare plants, which do not, however, produce any appreciable show of color. They are suitable for any but dry situations, adaptable for shade and flower from June to August. Good for cutting.

Astrantia biebersteinii, S/3–4. Silvery, starry flowers on erect, freely branching stems.

A. carniolica, S/3; *A. major*, S/3–4. Greenish starry flowers, tinged with pink, on erect stems branching at about 2 ft. to form a loose head.

A. maxima, S/3–4. 3 ft. Heads of rosy flowers of considerable appeal.

AVENS. See *Geum*.

BABY'S BREATH. See *Gypsophila paniculata*.

BALLOONFLOWER. See *Platycodon*.

BAPTISIA (FALSE INDIGO)
Has attractive foliage and flowers, is easy to grow in any ordinary soil in sun and is generally pest- and disease-free. All varieties S/2.

Baptisia australis, 3 to 6 ft. Flowers indigo-blue, summer.

B. tinctoria, 4 ft. Flowers bright yellow, summer.

BASKET-OF-GOLD. See *Alyssum saxatile*.

BEARD-TONGUE. See *Penstemon barbatus*.

BEAR'S-BREECH. See *Acanthus*.

BEE BALM. See *Monarda*.

BELAMCANDA (BLACKBERRY LILY)
The foliage of this plant somewhat resembles that of iris; the flowers, on branched stems, are like small, upturned lily blooms. Individual flowers are short-lived, but a succession is maintained over a long period.

Belamcanda chinensis, S/1. 2 to 3 ft. Flowers orange-yellow with red spots, summer.

B. flabellata, S/1. 2 to 3 ft. Flowers yellow without spots, bloom in summer or fall.

BELLFLOWER. See *Campanula*.

BELLWORT. See *Uvularia*.

BERGENIA
The chief attractions of bergenias (which are sometimes called megaseas and sometimes saxifragas) are their heavy spikes of pink flowers in very early spring and their quite large dark green leaves. They are fine for shady places but will do just as well in sun, and remain, slowly spreading, for many years. They are best for frontal positions and for planting near rocks.

Bergenia cordifolia, S/3. 9 in. The most common species, it has large reddish-pink flowers in spring, and more or less heart-shaped leaves 9 in. across.

BETONY. See *Stachys*.

BLACKBERRY LILY. See *Belamcanda*.

BLANKETFLOWER. See *Gaillardia*.

BLAZING STAR. See *Liatris scariosa*.

BLEEDING HEART. See *Dicentra*.

BLUE MISTFLOWER. See *Eupatorium coelestinum*.

BOCCONIA. See *Macleaya cordata*.

BOLTONIA (FALSE CHAMOMILE)
An asterlike plant, this is easily grown in ordinary soil and full sun. All varieties are summer- and fall-blooming, and all are S/2.

Boltonia asteroides, 6 to 8 ft. Flowers purplish-pink to white.

B. latisquama, 6 to 8 ft. Flowers purplish-pink to white, larger than those of *B. asteroides*.

BOUNCING BET. See *Saponaria officinalis*.

BUGBANE. See *Cimicifuga*.

BUGLEWEED. See *Ajuga*.

BURNET. See *Sanguisorba*.

BURNING BUSH. See *Dictamnus*.

BUTTERCUP. See *Ranunculus*.

BUTTERFLY WEED. See *Asclepias tuberosa*.

CALLIRHOE (POPPY MALLOW)
Callirhoe involucrata, S/4–5. 9 to 12 in. This plant has prostrate stems and large saucer-shaped flowers, crimson-purple to cherry-red, in summer and fall. A good plant for a bank of dryish, porous soil in full sun.

CAMPANULA (BELLFLOWER)
A genus generally thriving best in sun and well-drained soil. There are many kinds differing in height, color, size and shape of flowers, and in other ways. Most are easy to grow. Propagated by division and by seeds.

Campanula alliariaefolia, S/2. 2 ft. Creamy-white flowers from late May to August. Very free-flowering; flourishes in sun and even in rather poor soil. May not live for more than two or three years, but this kind is easy to raise from seed, and self-sown seedlings usually appear.

C. carpatica, S/2. 9 to 18 in. Ideal for the front of the border. Named varieties, all having sizable saucer-shaped flowers on neat, bushy growth from June to August, are offered in dealers' catalogues. Flower colors range from pure white through paler and deeper lavenders, blues and purples to deep purple.

C. glomerata, S/2. 1 to 2 ft. Flowers between late May and August and needs no staking or special soil, although it grows best in sunny places. The flowers, rich purple in color, are borne crowded together in dense heads at the terminations of main stems and side branches and in the leaf axils. In addition to the type, the following varieties are specially recommended:

C.g. acaulis, S/2. A dwarf variety with spikes only 9 in. high.

C.g. alba, S/2. White. Similar to *C.g. acaulis*.

C.g. dahurica, S/3–4. 1½ to 2 ft. Similar to *C.g. superba*.

C.g. superba, S/3–4. The best variety. Rich violet clustering heads on stout stems, reaching 3 ft. in good soil. Good for cutting.

C. lactiflora, S/2–3. Heights vary from 2½ to 4 ft. Quite happy in sun but does well with some shade. A very good deep-rooted plant with somewhat willowy stems carrying open-petaled bells in terminal sprays between June and September. The flowers come in various shades of pale blue, lavender and white. This is a choice plant. Named varieties are sometimes offered. Among the best of these are:

C.l. Loddon Anna, S/3. 4 ft. or more. Flesh-pink flowers. A distinctive plant.

C.l. Pritchard's Variety, S/2. The deepest shade. Grows compactly to 2½ ft.

C. latifolia (syn. *C. macrantha*), S/3. 2½ to 3½ ft. Stems come from a stocky root and carry pendant bells on clustered spikes in June and July. Less continuous-blooming than some campanulas, but more adaptable and does not mind shade. Good for cutting. Variations include:

C.l. alba, S/3. White flowers.

C.l. Brantwood, S/3. One of the best violet-blue varieties.

C.l. lilacina, S/3. Has pale mauve flowers.

C.l. macrantha, S/3. Deep violet flowers.

C. latiloba (syn. *C. grandis*), S/4. 3 ft. Surface-rooting, with quite erect stems carrying 2-in. saucer-shaped flowers along most of their length in June and July. Best in sun. Good for cutting.

C.l. alba, S/4. White, not so free-flowering as other varieties.

C. persicifolia, S/2–3. Thin, erect stems carry wide-open flowers along most of their length from mid-June to August. Basal leaves are narrow and pointed and grow in surface-rooting tufts which form clumps that spread and often deteriorate with age, so that dividing and replanting are needed every two or three years. Color of flowers varies, and some kinds are more or less double-flowered. The flowers come in white and in pale and deeper blues. Although they are gay and graceful, high winds may damage them, and excessive wet may tarnish those with double flowers, especially. Notable varieties are:

C.p. alba, S/2–3. 2 to 3 ft. Flowers white.

C.p. caerulea, S/2–3. 2 to 3 ft. Flowers blue.

C.p. Telham Beauty, S/2–3. 2 to 3 ft. Very large blue flowers.

C. rapunculoides, S/2–3. 2 to 4 ft. Of vigorous growth, this species bears an abundance of purple-blue flowers in one-sided spikes in summer. Very easily cultivated.

C. trachelium, S/2–3. 2 to 3 ft. Vigorous and easy to grow. Has bell-shaped purple or white flowers in summer. A double-flowered variety exists.

CAMPION. See *Lychnis*.

CARDAMINE (LADY'S-SMOCK)
Cardamine are spring-blooming perennials which associate well with calthas and primulas. They need moist or wet soil.

Cardamine pratensis, 1 ft. Flowers pale purple to white from April to May.

C.p. flore-pleno, pale lilac, double blooms, borne on showy spikes.

CARDINAL FLOWER. See *Lobelia cardinalis*.

CARNATION. See *Dianthus*.

CASSIA (SENNA)
Cassia marilandica, S/3. 3 to 4 ft. The plant has light green foliage and bright yellow flowers in loose clusters in summer. It requires full sun or light shade in ordinary soil. Disease- and pest-resistant, this perennial is hardy into southern New England.

CATANANCHE (CUPID'S DART)
Is like a perennial cornflower. The petals are papery in texture although not everlasting. Flowers come in great profusion on wiry 2-ft. stems from June to September. Full sun and very well-drained soil are essential for longevity. Plants may be propagated by seeds and root cuttings. Branches spread considerably and often need tying in. Plant in spring. Good for cutting.

Catananche caerulea bicolor, S/3. Blue and white petals. Usually raised from seed.

C.c. Blue Giant, S/3. An especially good variety with fine blue flowers.

C.c. major, S/3. Light cornflower-blue flowers.

CENTAUREA (CENTAURY, KNAPWEED)
All centaureas love sun and are generally best in well-drained soil. Some
varieties spread aggressively.

Centaurea dealbata, S/4. 2-ft. stems
carrying rosy-purple cornflower-type
flowers from June to August emerge
from ample grayish foliage. Robust.
Good for cutting.

C. d. steenbergii, S/4. 2½ ft. A showy,
long-lived plant, rather more robust
than *C. dealbata* and with deeper pink
flowers which it produces in June,
July and August.

C. macrocephala, S/4. 4 to 5 ft.
Erect. Has big yellow terminal flow-
ers in July and large green leaves.
Very long-lived.

C. montana, S/4–5. 1½ to 2 ft.
Makes spreading mats of gray leaves
and has shaggy fork-rayed flowers
that flop over and are not easy to keep
tidy. Pretty, easy to grow and early-
flowering. Typical flower color is rich
violet-blue, but there are many variations—pink, violet-purple, white and
deep rose.

C. ruthenica, S/3. Slender but strong
stems often 4 ft. tall, branching to
carry lemon-yellow flowers from June
to late August. Foliage is deep green
and shiny. A good species, deep-rooted
and not invasive. These are good for
cutting.

CENTAURY. See *Centaurea*.

CENTRANTHUS (VALERIAN)
Centranthus ruber, S/4. 2 to 3 ft.
This perennial has deep pink or
reddish flowers which keep coming
for weeks between May and August.
Plants themselves may not live more
than two or three years, but self-sown
seedlings usually appear freely. Likes
sun and poor soil.

CEPHALARIA
Cephalaria tatarica, S/4–5. 6 ft. Is
the species usually available. Pale

yellow pincushion flowers from July
to September. Rather too large for
small gardens, but useful where something tall, massive and erect is needed.
It is long-lived. Likes ordinary soil
and sun or partial shade. Good for
cutting.

CERASTIUM
Cerastium tomentosum (snow-in-
summer), S/2. 1 ft. A billowing plant,
it is covered with a multitude of small
white flowers in the spring. Prefers
full sun and well-drained soil.

CHELONE (TURTLEHEAD)
These are moisture-loving plants suitable for growing in wild gardens and
for the fronts of borders. One plant
sometimes called *Chelone barbata* is
Penstemon barbatus.

C. glabra, S/2. 2 to 3 ft. Similar to
C. obliqua, but the flowers are white
or delicate pink.

C. lyonii, S/2. 2 to 3 ft. Long-
flowering, rosy-lilac flowers from leafy
stems between July and September.

C. obliqua, S/2. 2 ft. Pretty lilac-
rose flowers on erect stems in late
summer. Long-lived, spreading by underground shoots that come through
in spring. An unusual plant and even
less common in the white form *alba*.
Good for cutting.

CHRISTMAS ROSE. See *Helleborus niger*.

CHRYSANTHEMUM
Botanists include in *Chrysanthemum*
some groups of perennials which gardeners usually know by other names,
notably the pyrethrums or painted
daisies (varieties of *C. coccineum*) and
the Shasta daisies (*C. maximum* varieties). These are discussed below. In
addition, a few natural species are
cultivated. The plants usually known
as chrysanthemums to gardeners and
nurserymen, however, are a vast number of varieties of hybrid origin which

Border Chrysanthemum

are identified by the group name of *C. morifolium*.

Chrysanthemum coccineum (pyrethrum or painted daisy). These early-summer-flowering daisies with their carrotlike leaves are splendid for flower borders and for cutting. All are S/2–3 and attain 2 to 3 ft. in height. They sometimes need supporting, and where this is necessary, stake well before flowering time. Plant in ordinary soil in early spring or early fall—rich or moist soil is not advised. An open place and good drainage are essential to avoid floppiness and winter rotting. Cutting back after flowering often produces a second crop. Flow-

ers are in every shade from white to pink, magenta and crimson-red, in both doubles and singles, but the doubles are usually less vigorous and erect.

The plants are propagated by seeds or by dividing the roots. The last-mentioned method is essential to perpetuate choice kinds. Among the best named varieties are:

Buckeye, double rose-scarlet flowers.

Helen, double, light pink with darker center.

Robinson's Red, single, crimson.

Robinson's Rose, single, rose-pink.

Chrysanthemum maximum (Shasta daisy). 2 to 3 ft. White double or single flowers from June to August. Prefers sun and well-drained soil. Divide and replant every two or three years. Good for cutting. Reliable varieties of Shasta daisies, all S/2–3, are:

Alaya, large double flowers with fringed petals.

Majestic, large flowers with double row of petals and small yellow center.

Mount Hood, large white asterlike flowers.

Mount Shasta, pure white, fully double flowers.

Thomas Killin, a double row of white petals and a crested, golden-yellow center.

Wirral Pride, anemone-type flower, with a small yellow center.

C. morifolium (border chrysanthemum or hardy chrysanthemum). Some varieties of *C. morifolium* are suitable only for growing indoors or in greenhouses, but others are well adapted for outdoor cultivation. All are late-summer or fall bloomers. They have flowers of single, double, pompon, anemone, spoon and other distinctive forms, and come in almost all colors except blue and true purple. They vary in height from 1 to 3 ft. or more and provide splendid material for garden decoration and cut flowers. Because varieties are so numerous and listings change constantly as new ones are introduced, a list of hardy chrysanthemums is not given here. When making selections, consult the catalogues of specialists.

Hardy or border chrysanthemums need deep, fertile, well-drained soil and full sun. They are less winter-hardy when planted in heavy clay soils than in those that are more sandy and porous. For the best results, new plants should be propagated each spring either by cuttings or by dividing old clumps; use only single shoots (rooted) for replanting in newly spaded and fertilized soil. It is best to change the location of chry-

santhemums periodically so that they are not grown on the same ground for more than two or three years. If this cannot be done, it is well to sterilize the soil each year to reduce danger of damage by pests and diseases. Space S/4 or S/5.

To encourage bushiness, pinch back the tips of the main shoots and succeeding side branches every time they attain a length of 6 in. until the middle of July. Water copiously during dry weather, and mulch the soil or keep it shallowly cultivated throughout the summer. Staking and tying must be done with all except low-growing varieties such as the cushion chrysanthemums. Flowers more perfect and of greater size may be obtained from large-flowering varieties if they are disbudded by removing most side shoots. Only a limited number of shoots, usually five to nine, should be allowed to develop on each plant. Pinch off, while they are yet small, all flower buds except the terminal one on each shoot.

After the plants have been killed by frost, cut them to the ground and later provide protection by covering them lightly with salt-marsh hay, branches of evergreens or other cover that permits free circulation of air. In very cold climates, dig up plants in the fall and winter them in a well-protected cold frame or similar place.

C. nipponicum (Nippon daisy), S/3–4. 2 ft. Really a subshrub. Branches do not die to the ground but persist through the winter. Flowers are white with yellow centers, daisylike; late-fall-blooming. Needs ordinary soil and full sun.

C. rubellum, S/3. 1½ to 3 ft. Compact; flowers pink, single. Needs same culture as *C. morifolium*. Very hardy. Good varieties of this species are:

C. r. Clara Curtis, 1 to 1½ ft. Spreading habit, flowers salmon-pink, in late summer and early fall.

C.r. Royal Command, 2 ft. Flowers wine-red, in fall.

C. uliginosum, S/4. 4 to 5 ft. Large white flowers like the Shasta daisy, blooming in fall.

CIMICIFUGA (BUGBANE)
These are really worthwhile plants for not-too-dry soil. Slender, tapering spikes set closely with small, fluffy white flowers in late summer or autumn are attractive. Jagged dark green leaves show prettily for months before flowers appear. Stems are strong and wiry. Slow-growing and need no attention for years. Adaptable, but happiest in partial shade and good, deep soil. They are all S/2–3 and are good for cutting.

Cimicifuga americana, 3 to 5 ft. Dainty spikes of creamy-white flowers from late August to October.

C. davurica. Up to 5 ft. Later-blooming than *C. americana.*

C. racemosa, 4 to 7 ft. Abundant shiny foliage, with gracefully erect plumes from August to September.

C. simplex, 2 to 3 ft. This is perhaps the choicest kind. It has arching, dense spikes of nearly pure white flowers in late summer and fall. Excellent for cutting. One of the finest of fall-flowering perennials.

CINQUEFOIL. See *Potentilla.*

CLEMATIS
Bush varieties of *Clematis* are excellent for perennial borders. They prosper in fertile, well-drained soil in full sun or part shade. All are S/4 or S/5.

Clematis hereacleaefolia, 4 ft. Flowers light blue, in clusters.

C. h. davidiana, 4 ft. Flowers bright blue, fragrant, in clusters.

C. integrifolia, 1½ to 2½ ft. Flowers solitary, rather dull blue-purple.

C. recta, 2 to 3 ft. Flowers white, fragrant, in large, many-flowered clusters.

C. r. mandshurica, 3 ft. Flowers white, fragrant, in large, loose, many-flowered clusters. This variety is good for cutting, like *C. recta,* which it closely resembles.

COLUMBINE. See *Aquilegia.*

CONEFLOWER. See *Rudbeckia.*

CONVALLARIA (LILY OF THE VALLEY)
Several varieties of this well-known fragrant-flowered plant are grown. All are worthwhile. They succeed best in rich soil that contains an abundance of organic matter and does not dry excessively, and in shade. Fertilize established plantings annually. All are 8 to 9 in. high and all S/1. (See illustration, page 542.)

Convallaria majalis. Flowers white.

C. m. flore-pleno. Double flowers, white.

C. m. rosea. Flowers delicate pink.

C. m. variegata. Has striped leaves with yellow and white flowers.

CORALBELLS. See *Heuchera.*

COREOPSIS (TICKSEED)
These popular plants produce bright yellow flowers of the daisy type for many weeks in summer. They are good cut flowers.

Coreopsis auriculata, S/4. Growth spreads out and up from a smallish rootstock to 1½ ft. or so. The 2-in. flowers often have a maroon blotch at the base of each fringed-ray floret. Low-growing with a long succession of flowers, but not always reliably perennial. It prefers sun and light soil.

C. grandiflora, S/4, and *C. lanceolata,* S/4, 1 to 2 ft. Easily raised from seed but often do not live more than two or three years. It is advisable to grow a few new plants from seed each year. Growth is dark green and vigorous, and flowers are carried singly on wiry stems from June to

September. Best in full sun. Both single- and double-flowered varieties of the two species are cultivated.

C. verticillata, S/2–3. Starry yellow flowers nestle on shapely 1½-ft. plants from June to August. Distinctive, with finely divided foliage, it likes reasonably good soil.

C.v. grandiflora, S/4. Similar to *C. verticillata*, but 6 in. taller and with flowers of deeper gold.

CORONILLA

Coronilla varia (crown vetch), S/2. 1 to 1½ ft. Vigorous plant with more or less trailing stems, ferny foliage and dense heads of pink or white flowers in summer. Suitable for covering banks or for fronts of borders in full sun where soil is very well drained. Succeeds in poor soil.

CRANESBILL. See *Geranium*.

CROWFOOT. See *Ranunculus*.

CROWN VETCH. See *Coronilla varia*.

CUPID'S DART. See *Catananche*.

CYNOGLOSSUM (HOUND'S-TONGUE)

Cynoglossum nervosum, S/2–3. 1½ to 2 ft. A stocky plant with abundant deep green slightly hairy leaves through which unfurls a lengthy succession of intense blue flowers from June to August. A long-lived relative of forget-me-not, this is a useful plant, adaptable for sun or partial shade and not fussy as to soil. Cynoglossum is easily propagated by seed and root cuttings.

DAY LILY. See *Hemerocallis*.

DELPHINIUM (PERENNIAL LARKSPUR)
Considerable care is needed to bring these noble plants to perfection. They like rich soil but quickly exhaust it, so dig deeply and fertilize before plant-

Delphinium
(Perennial Larkspur)

ing, and mulch in subsequent seasons. Thin out the weaker shoots in April or May on older, larger plants; if they are left, there will be too many spikes, resulting in poor ones and premature withering of the plant's lower leaves.

If massive spikes are to be grown, support each spike with a strong stake well before flowering. To allow the plants to mature, carefully remove old spikes after flowering. In regions of cool summers they usually remain vigorous for three to four years after seedlings are planted. Where hot summers prevail, however, the plants are likely to last only one or two years, and new stocks must be raised frequently from seed. Many gardeners treat delphiniums as biennials, and they can even be handled as annuals. If seeds are sown in January indoors or in a greenhouse and planted outdoors in early spring, they will bloom well the first year. Plant all delphiniums S/3.

Seed-raised plants of *Delphinium hybridum* always vary somewhat in color and may range from pale to deep blue, rosy lilac or mauve to deep purple and white. Heights vary from 3½ to 7 ft. depending on soil fertility as well as on the strain of seed. The tendency nowadays is to breed lower-growing types, available as named varieties.

A smaller-flowered type exists under the name Belladonna, and this is less demanding than the larger-flowered kinds. Leaves are smaller and more deeply cut, and spikes are shorter and loosely branched. Belladonna has grace and charm of a less massive kind. Bellamosa is similar to Belladonna, but the flowers are of a much darker blue.

DIANTHUS (PINK AND CARNATION)
In addition to many kinds of *Dianthus* grown in rock gardens, two

groups of horticulturally developed varieties are suitable for the fronts of flower borders and for cutting. These are the border pinks and carnations. The former are derived from *D. plumarius* and perhaps other species, the latter from varieties of *D. caryophyllus*. All pinks are hardy, but this is not true of all varieties of carnations; some can be grown outdoors only in mild climates, or indoors. These plants are remarkable for their scent and their profusion of bloom. They have bluish-gray, somewhat grassy foliage, and flower stems are wiry.

Pinks and carnations need full sun and fertile, rather sandy, well-drained soil that is nearly neutral or slightly alkaline. Plant in spring or fall S/1. Cutting back the old stems immediately after flowering is helpful, and mulching at that time or in spring with a mixture of light soil and added bone meal is good practice. Increase by cuttings rather than by dividing old plants, although some respond to division and replanting in autumn. Good mixtures can be raised from seed to give a colorful and long-lasting display, but choice named varieties are superior. Among the best of these are:

Blanche, perpetual-flowering type, white.

Cynthia, shrimp-pink, a carnation.

Dinah, old rose with maroon center.

Doris, perpetual-flowering type, salmon-pink with darker center.

Evangeline, soft Persian rose-pink.

Helen, perpetual-flowering type, salmon-pink.

Ian, perpetual-flowering type, dark red shading to almost black.

Lucia, rose-pink shaded salmon, a carnation.

Old Spice, salmon-pink, one of the best.

Robin, perpetual-flowering type, orange-scarlet.

DICENTRA (BLEEDING HEART)

Old-fashioned favorites such as these are easy to grow. In addition to the species, a few named kinds, presumably of hybrid origin, are now available.

Dicentra Bountiful, S/3. 1½ ft. A fine hybrid having dark blue-green foliage and deep pink flowers. It blooms freely in spring and early summer, and again in fall.

D. Debutante, S/3. 12 to 15 in. A vigorous hybrid with light silvery-green foliage and blush-pink flowers produced freely throughout the summer months.

D. Silversmith, S/3. 8 to 9 in. A compact-growing hybrid with deep blue-green foliage and white to ivory-white flowers. Blooms more or less continuously through the summer.

D. Summer Beauty, S/3. 12 to 15 in. A good hybrid with light green foliage and pink flowers, which blooms freely throughout the summer.

D. eximia, S/4. 1½ ft. This species produces an abundance of green leaves and a long succession of pinkish flowers from April to June and even later. Adaptable to most soils and locations, but appreciates light shade.

D. formosa, S/4. Similar to *D. eximia* but with blue-green leaves.

D. spectabilis, S/3. 2 ft. In spring and early summer, pink and red locket-shaped flowers dangle from arching stems decked in delightful greenery. Plants have deep, fleshy roots and need soil of good depth, as well as a fairly sheltered location for protection from strong winds. Good for cutting. The foliage dies down in early summer.

DICTAMNUS
(BURNING BUSH, GAS PLANT)

Strong-smelling and very hardy, these perennials succeed in any fertile, well-drained soil. They dislike trans-

Dicentra (Bleeding Heart)

planting and should not be moved unless necessary. They prefer full sun but will stand some shade. On hot, still summer evenings, they give off a resinous volatile substance, which may be ignited, without harm to the plant, by holding a lighted match near them.

Dictamnus albus, S/2–3. 2½ ft. Lilac or rosy-mauve flowers on stiff stems in June and July. The dark, shiny leaves are of ash-tree form. A well-proportioned, long-lived plant which needs full sun and good drainage. A white variety exists.

D. a. caucasicus, S/2–3. 2½ ft. Has larger and more showy flowers.

DIGITALIS (FOXGLOVE)
Most foxgloves are biennial and are useful for setting in odd corners rather than in the border. A few, however, are perennial:

Digitalis ambigua, S/2. 2½ ft. One of the best. Soft-yellow flowers from June to August. Not likely to live for more than about three years, but seedlings are easy to raise.

D. lutea, S/2. 2 ft. Yellowish flowers (smaller than *D. ambigua*) close to the stem in July.

DORONICUM (LEOPARD'S-BANE)
These yellow daisy-flowered plants are bright and useful for early color. Easy to grow in ordinary soil in sun or partial shade, they begin flowering long before reaching the heights given, and are good for cutting. Divide and replant every two years in early fall or spring.

Doronicum Madame Mason, S/3. Bright yellow flowers 3 in. across on 1½ ft. stems from March to late May. Unlike the other varieties, this seldom needs dividing.

D. caucasicum, S/3. 2 ft. Flowers are bright yellow.

D. c. magnificum, S/3. 2 to 2½ ft. A robust variety with somewhat

larger flowers than the type itself.

D. plantagineum (syn. *D. excelsum*), S/3. 5 ft. The largest-flowered of all, with golden-yellow flowers from April to May.

DUSTY MILLER. See *Artemisia stelleriana*.

ECHINOPS (GLOBE THISTLE)
Although easy to grow, some are rather coarse and overlarge for small gardens. All are deep-rooted with grayish, spreading, thistly leaves and globular drumstick heads on stiff stems from June to August. Prefer sun and soil that is not too rich or moist. Good for cutting.

Echinops humilis. Best variety of this species is Taplow Blue, S/3, which reaches about 4 ft. when established.

E. nivalis, S/4–5. 5 to 6 ft. Whitish flowers.

E. ritro, S/3. 3 ft. Bright blue flowers. Of neat habit.

E. sphaerocephalus, S/5. 5 to 6 ft. Similar to *E. nivalis* but with silver-gray flowers.

EREMURUS (FOXTAIL LILY)
A stately plant with thick, fleshy roots, this perennial has a basal rosette of broad leaves. From the center of this rosette, in early summer, grow sturdy, erect stems that bear hundreds of star-shaped flowers in dense, cylindrical spikes of great size. The plants need rich, well-drained soil and an abundant supply of water when in foliage, but no watering after the leaves die down soon after flowering. New growth begins very early in spring and should be protected by covering with a box on nights when frost threatens. Some varieties can be grown as far north as New York and southern New England, but they cannot be regarded as hardy in the coldest parts of North America. Winter protection may be

given by covering them with a water-tight box filled with hay, straw or dry leaves.

Foxtail lilies resent root disturbance, so do not transplant them unnecessarily if they are thriving. When planting, take care not to damage the brittle roots; spread and cover them in their natural horizontal positions, and set them with the crown bud not more than 2 in. beneath the surface. Plant in fall and space the plants 1½ to 2½ ft. apart.

Eremurus Himrob, 6 to 8 ft. Pale pink flowers.

E. bungei, 4 to 6 ft. Yellow flowers.

E. himalaicus, 5 to 6 ft. Flowers white; one of the hardiest.

E. olgae, 4 to 6 ft. Flowers white, tinted pink.

E. robustus, 6 to 9 ft. Flowers pale pink. One of the hardiest.

E. shelfordii, 6 to 8 ft. Copper-yellow flowers.

E. tubergenii, 5 to 6 ft. Sulphur-yellow flowers.

E. warei, 4 to 6 ft. Flowers yellowish buff.

ERIGERON (FLEABANE)
Members of this attractive genus are rather like summer-flowering perennial asters. The earliest bloom in May, and although some continue on and off all summer, their best period is June. Not fussy as to soil, they prefer sun and good drainage. Cut back hard after flowering. Many named garden varieties are grown in Europe, and from time to time some of these are offered by nurseries on this continent.

ERYNGIUM (SEA HOLLY)
These are striking plants with blue teazlelike flowers of varying size. In some kinds the blue coloring extends down the stems. All have deep, fleshy roots and are best in sun and well-drained soil. Good for cutting.

Eryngium alpinum, S/3. 2 ft. Large, bristly light blue flowers on heavy stems from June to August. Leaves are deeply jagged.

E. amethystinum. The plant cultivated under this name is usually *E. planum*.

E. bourgatii, S/2. Seldom exceeds 2 ft. in height. Blue flowers in July and August. The whole plant has a silvery-blue, neatly shaggy appearance. Very effective.

E. planum, S/2–3. 2½ to 3½ ft. Blue flowers in July and August. This is very leafy and has branching stems which may need supporting. The blue color is confined to the flowers. This species is often cultivated under the name *E. amethystinum*.

E. tripartitum, S/2–3. 3 ft. Green-leaved. Flowers are small, but the stem branches widely and attractively, giving a real show in July and August.

EUPATORIUM
Eupatorium coelestinum (blue mist-flower), S/4. 1½ to 2½ ft. This North American native is perhaps the finest eupatorium for flower beds and borders. It has large, flattish, ageratumlike heads of lavender-blue flowers in late summer and fall. A selection called Wayside Variety is offered.

E. purpureum (Joe-Pye weed), S/3. 5 to 6 ft. Broad, deep purple-lilac flower heads in autumn, on stiff, strong stems which are well clothed in greenery. A statuesque plant that likes space, depth and not too dry soil.

E. rugosum (syn. *E. fraseri*—white snakeroot), S/4. 4 ft. Makes a stout, erect, very leafy bush which is smothered with flattish heads of white fluffy flowers in July and August. An easy, vigorous plant, best where not too dry. Likes sun or partial shade.

EUPHORBIA (SPURGE)

Euphorbia epithymoides (syn. *E. polychroma*), S/3. Sulphur-yellow bracted flower shoots appear above-ground in early spring and within a month make a bright little bushy plant 1½ ft. high, which gradually fades to green for the rest of the summer. A first-class perennial, easy and reliable in ordinary soil and in sun or partial shade.

E. palustris, S/4. 3 ft. Large sulphur-yellow flowers in early summer. Showy, easy and out-of-the-ordinary, it prefers somewhat moister conditions than other euphorbias.

EVENING PRIMROSE. See *Oenothera*.

EVERLASTING. See *Anaphalis*.

FALSE CHAMOMILE. See *Boltonia*.

FALSE INDIGO. See *Baptisia*.

FALSE SUNFLOWER. See *Heliopsis*.

FILIPENDULA (MEADOWSWEET)

Most filipendulas are moisture lovers and prefer a little shade, but will grow quite well in full sun, in soil that does not dry out quickly.

Filipendula hexapetala flore-pleno, S/3. 2 ft. White flower heads in June and July, and dark ferny leaves. Very dainty. Will grow in moderately dry soils.

F. purpurea (syn. *Spiraea palmata rubra*), S/2–3. 2 to 4 ft. Carmine-red heads in July. Bushy growth, beautiful flowers. Must have moist soil.

F. rubra (queen-of-the-prairie), S/3–4. 4 to 5 ft. Broad heads of glistening pink flowers from June to August. Needs moist soil.

F. ulmaria (queen-of-the-meadow), S/3–4. 3 to 5 ft. Large, toothed leaves and heads of small creamy-white flowers. A double-flowered variety, *F. u. plena*, is grown.

FLAX. See *Linum*.

FLEABANE. See *Erigeron*.

FOXGLOVE. See *Digitalis*.

FOXTAIL LILY. See *Eremurus*.

FUNKIA. See *Hosta*.

GAILLARDIA (BLANKETFLOWER)

Showy flowers of this plant need full sun and light, well-drained soil. They grow from 2 to 3 ft. according to soil and season. Losses may occur after three or four years, so replace with named varieties or seedlings. If cut regularly, gaillardias flower for many weeks between June and November. Usually they need supporting. Good for cutting. Several fine named varieties are grown in Europe and some are offered from time to time in nursery catalogues. Among the best of these are the following, all S/2–3:

Croftway Yellow, self-colored.

Ipswich Beauty, deep yellow, crimson-zoned flowers 3 in. across.

Mandarin, suffused orange-flame.

Wirral Flame, browny-orange.

GALEGA (GOAT'S RUE)

These make bushy, pea-green growth up to 4 ft., with short spikes of pea-type flowers in June and July. Sun and good drainage and even poor soil give best results. Named varieties, all S/4, include:

Galega officinalis, dense clusters of purple-blue flowers.

G. o. albiflora, white flowers.

G. o. hartlandii, lilac flowers and leaves which are variegated when young.

Lady Wilson, mauve-pink flowers.

GAS PLANT. See *Dictamnus*.

GAY FEATHER. See *Liatris*.

GENTIANA (GENTIAN)

The following summer-flowering species can be well recommended for planting in flower borders. They respond to deep, well-drained soil that contains an abundance of organic matter and that never becomes excessively dry.

Gentiana asclepiadea (willow gentian), S/1. 20 to 24 in. Azure-blue trumpets on slender, willowy stems in July and August. Prefers some shade. Good for cutting.

G. makinoi, S/1. Clusters of rich blue, closed bell-like flowers on erect 15-in. stems in late summer.

G. septemfida, S/1. 6 to 9 in. Brilliant blue trumpets for several weeks from July. Makes a fine show and is excellent for planting at the front of a border. Easy to grow. Prefers sun.

GERANIUM (CRANESBILL)

Hardy geraniums are among the most adaptable garden perennials and are quite distinct from what are generally known as geraniums. (The red- pink- and white-flowered plants commonly called geraniums and popular in house and garden are, botanically, pelargoniums.) All thrive in sun or partial shade and are long-lived.

A. T. Johnson, S/3, light pink.

Johnson's Blue, S/3, a bright, showy hybrid. Does not flower so continuously as A. T. Johnson or Wargrave Pink.

Wargrave Pink, S/3, light pink.

Geranium armenum, S/3. The tallest, reaching 3 ft. in moist soil, but less where dry. Flowers are vivid magenta, continuing from June to August.

G. endressii, S/4. Best in named varieties. All make bushy mounds 15 to 20 in. high and flower for a long time from early June.

G. grandiflorum, S/4. 1 to 2 ft. The blue salver-shaped flowers are $1\frac{1}{2}$ to 2 in. in diameter and are often veined and zoned with deeper shades. Flowers May to July.

Geranium (Cranesbill)

G. ibericum, S/4. About 20 in. Rich, deep violet-blue flowers in June and July. This is a plant of neat habit.

G. macrorrhizum, S/3. 1½ ft. Blue-lavender or blue-purple flowers at midsummer. Of stiff growth. Flowers pink.

G. pratense, S/3. 1½ ft. Blue-lavender or blue-purple flowers at midsummer.

G. renardii, S/3. 10 in. Has pretty lobed and puckered grayish leaves and a rather brief show of silvery lavender-blue flowers in early summer.

G. sanguineum, S/4. Low-growing and spreading with a long succession of purple-red flowers in summer.

G.s. prostratum (syn. *G. s. lancastriense*), S/3. Light pink, makes low mounds only a few inches high.

GERBERA (TRANSVAAL DAISY)
These lovely natives of South Africa are hardy only in California and in other regions where winters are quite mild. They bloom over a very long season and the flowers last a long time when cut. They need full sun and a fairly moist, peaty soil that is well-drained.

Gerbera jamesonii, S/3. Has given rise to many beautiful single- and double-flowered varieties and hybrids in a wide range of colors including pink, salmon, light red, orange and yellow. These form basal rosettes of foliage and carry their daisylike flowers singly on 1½-ft. stems.

GERMAN CATCHFLY. See *Lychnis viscaria*.

GEUM (AVENS)
These make tufty, leafy clumps blooming in early summer, but those with the largest flowers and brightest colors are often the shortest-lived. The best known, easy to grow from seed, are the short-lived:

Geum coccineum Lady Stratheden, S/1–2. Near-double yellow flowers spraying up and out on 2-ft. branching stems. Seldom flowers a third season.

G.c. Mrs. Bradshaw, S/1–2, red. Similar to Lady Stratheden.

Longer-living species, best in sun and well-drained soil, include:

G. borisii, S/2. 9 in. Makes leafy clumps and carries bright orange flowers in summer. A very adaptable plant.

G. bulgaricum, S/2. 15 to 18 in. Orange flowers from May to July.

G. heldreichii, S/2. Similar to *G. bulgaricum*, but more vigorous.

GILLENIA
Suitable for partial shade where the soil is fairly moist.

Gillenia stipulata (American ipecac), S/2. 2 to 4 ft. Flowers white.

G. trifoliata (Indian physic), S/2. 2 to 4 ft. Has white flowers slightly larger than those of *G. stipulata*.

GLOBEFLOWER. See *Trollius*.

GLOBE THISTLE. See *Echinops*.

GOATSBEARD. See *Aruncus*.

GOAT'S RUE. See *Galega*.

GOLDENROD. See *Solidago*.

GOLDEN GLOW. See *Rudbeckia laciniata*.

GOLDILOCKS. See *Linosyris vulgaris*.

GREEK VALERIAN. See *Polemonium caeruleum*.

GYPSOPHILA
All gypsophilas like sun and light, and, preferably, limy soil.

Gypsophila paniculata (baby's breath), S/5. 2½ ft. Has clouds of tiny white flowers from June to August. Not easy to fit in with other flowers because of its expansive, branching habit. The summer spread, from deep, fanglike roots, is considerable, but it dies back each autumn. Very reliable. Good for cutting.

G.p. Bristol Fairy, S/4–5. 2½ ft. Double white flowers. Makes a better show than *G. paniculata.*

G.p. compacta plena, S/4. Compact, double white flowers from June to August. Less tall and spreading than *G. paniculata.*

Perfect is similar to Bristol Fairy, but flowers are about twice as big. Excellent for cutting.

Pink Star, S/3–4. Newer and neater than Rosy Veil. Makes a low mound 1 to 1½ ft. high; is quite charming.

Rosy Veil, S/4. 1½ to 2 ft. Light pink double flowers, June to August. Makes considerable surface spread.

HELENIUM (SNEEZEWEED)
Flowers of rich yellow, orange and crimson-brown; blooms from June to October. Heights vary from 2 to 5 ft. Easy to grow, long-lived. Produces better heads of flowers if shoots are thinned out from older plants in May. Lower leaves wither if the soil becomes too dry. Support for taller kinds may be needed in wet weather. Good for cutting. Recommended varieties, all S/3–4, are:

Bruno, 3½ ft. Dark brown-red flowers in September.

Butterpat, 3½ ft. Golden-yellow flowers in September.

Chippersfield Orange, 4 ft. Has large heads of copper and golden-yellow flowers.

Moerheim Beauty, 3 ft. Crimson-brown flowers from June to August.

Riverton Gem, 3 ft. Free-blooming, flowers red-brown and yellow.

Helenium autumnale pumilum, 2½ to 3 ft. Yellow flowers from June to August.

H. bigelovii, 3 ft. Flowers yellow with brown centers, in summer.

H. hoopesii, 2 to 3 ft. Flowers yellow, in early summer.

H. peregrinum, 3 ft. Large dark mahogany flowers, their edges seamed with yellow.

HELIANTHUS (SUNFLOWER)
The following are fully perennial, some making tidy but massive bushes, others with rather too much spread from running roots. Leaves wither if the soil becomes excessively dry.

Helianthus Loddon Gold, S/3–4. 4 to 5 ft. Erectly bushy, with fine golden-yellow double flowers 3 to 4 in. across from July to September. The finest double variety.

H. atrorubens (syn. *sparsifolius*), Monarch, S/5. 5 to 6 ft. with 4- to 6-in. golden flowers on leafy stems in September and October.

H. decapetalus flore-pleno, S/3. 4 to 5 ft. A fine, easy-to-grow kind with golden-yellow flowers, most of which are fully double but a few of which are single or only partly double. *H. d. grandiflorus* and *H. d. maximus* are similar. The plant called *H. multiflorus* also belongs here. It has clear yellow flowers that resemble small dahlias, and it grows about 4 ft. high.

H. multiflorus. See *H. decapetalus flore-pleno.*

HELIOPSIS (FALSE SUNFLOWER)
Akin to sunflowers, these long-lived plants are really valuable for sun and almost any soil. All have yellow flowers from midsummer to September and a moderate S/3 spread. Wet weather tends to tarnish flowers of double varieties and sometimes makes branches sag.

Heliopsis Golden Plume, 3 ft. Gorgeous double flowers 3 in. across on branching stems.

Gold Greenheart, 3 ft. The lemon-

yellow double flowers are tinged with
green in the center.

Light of Loddon, 3½ ft. Single
yellow-gold flowers.

Patula, 3 ft. Single yellow-gold
flowers.

H. helianthoides pitcheriana, 4 ft.
Deep-yellow flowers. A very free-
blooming variety.

H. scabra incomparabilis, 2½ to
3 ft. Deep yellow double flowers with
petals overlapping as with zinnias.

HELLEBORUS

This leathery-leaved plant needs
deep, rich, fairly moist soil that is
well drained, with liberal amounts
of organic matter. It also requires
shade and, because it resents root
disturbance, should not be transplanted oftener than absolutely necessary. Water freely in dry weather.
Mulch with leaf mold, compost or
well-rotted manure in fall. All S/4.

Helleborus niger (Christmas rose),
about 1 ft. Leaves evergreen. Flowers
white fading to pink in winter.

H.n. altifolius, similar to *H. niger*
but earlier-blooming, probably the
kind most reliable to flower at Christmas or sooner.

H. orientalis (Lenten rose), similar
to *H. niger*, but flowers appear in
spring and are greenish suffused with
purple. This kind stands hot weather
better than *H. niger* and is easier to
transplant.

HEMEROCALLIS (DAY LILY)

Day lilies are among the most satisfactory perennials for American and
Canadian gardens. They withstand
heat and dry weather better than
most garden flowers and can be grown
in practically all parts of North
America. The plants make few demands on the skill of the gardener
and thrive with minimum care in sun
or light shade in any reasonably fertile, well-drained soil. Propagation is

Hemerocallis
(Day Lily)

easily accomplished by division of the roots in early spring or early fall.

By planting a selection of varieties, day lilies may be kept in bloom from early summer until killing frost. Each plant bears a succession of blooms on branching stems. The individual flowers last only a day, but follow each other in close succession over a long period. They are carried on graceful 1½- to 4-ft. stems, which arise from among fresh green leaves. Several species exist, but these have been outmoded for garden planting by many named varieties. From the original orange and yellow types, colors now include near-pink and near-red shades. The latter are mostly ruby, purple, mahogany or copper rather than true red. The list of varieties is so wide that no specific recommendations can be made. Choose varieties from the catalogues of specialists. Evergreen kinds are best for warm climates. They average S/3 in spread.

HEUCHERA (CORALBELLS)

Very long-lived and drought-resistant, these plants make good ground covers. Dainty, small, bell-shaped flowers on wiry 1½- to 2½-ft. stems come in every shade from white through pink to bright red from May to July and often later, and are good for cutting. Their only need is well-drained, reasonably good soil. They tend to lift out of the ground with age, but this can be remedied by replanting them more deeply or by mulching between the crowns to encourage fibrous roots to form so as to renew vigor and freedom of flowering. Modern varieties bear more blooms than older sorts; the freest to flower are the Bressingham Hybrids. These also provide the best range of colors. Many garden varieties of *Heuchera* are of hybrid origin. They should be planted about 1 ft. apart.

Heuchera
(Coralbells)

Bressingham Hybrids, 2 to 3 ft. All colors from pale pink to deep red.

Heuchera brizoides. 1 ft., rose-pink.

H.b. Firefly. 2 ft.

H.b. Girandole. 2 ft., salmon-pink.

H.b. Marie Rose, 2 ft., pink.

H.b. Perry's white, 15 in., white.

H.b. Pluie de Feu, 1 ft., red.

H.b. Rosamundi, 2 to 2½ ft., coral-pink.

H. sanguinea, 15 in., red.

H.s. Scarlet Sentinel, 2 to 3 ft., scarlet-vermilion.

H.s. White Cloud, 1½ to 2 ft., white.

HEUCHERELLA

This is the cross between *Heuchera* and its relative *Tiarella*.

Heucherella tiarelloides, S/4. A useful plant, it makes excellent ground cover but has a rather short season. 10-in. sprays of light pink flowers in May and June and golden-green foliage. Good for cutting.

HIBISCUS (ROSE MALLOW)

Modern giant herbaceous hibiscus has been derived from *Hibiscus moscheutos*, a native of swampy places in northeastern America. Numerous named varieties are cultivated. They grow 3½ to 7 ft. tall and need full sun and rich, fairly moist soil. Plant them up to 3 ft. apart. Among the best are:

Clown, pink, white and red.

Fresno, silvery-pink, deepening toward petal margins and with red centers.

Pink Giant, pale pink with red eye.

Satan, dark velvety crimson.

Snow White, pure white with cream centers.

HOLLYHOCK. See *Althaea rosea.*

HOSTA (PLANTAIN LILY, FUNKIA)

Hardy, long-lived, these plants have decorative flowers and foliage, are adaptable for shade or sun and are not fussy as to soil, but grow quite luxuriantly where fairly moist. Most hostas have attractive mauve or lavender lilylike flowers in late summer on smooth 1½- to 2½-ft. stems. Good for cutting. All are capable of making quite large clumps in time, but the majority would have to be left alone in good soil for three years to reach S/3 in spread. Some have green leaves, but there are also many variegated forms. Confusion exists regarding their identification and naming, and where possible they should be seen before ordering. Recommended kinds are:

Hosta erromena. A robust kind with dark green foliage and pale lilac blooms. Does well in sun.

H. fortunei. Large glaucous (blue-green) leaves. Flowers lavender-blue. The variety *marginato-alba* has leaves margined with white; varieties *gigantea* and *robusta* are larger and more vigorous than the type.

H. glauca (syn. *H. sieboldiana*). Fine blue-green leaves. Flowers faintly lilac-colored. Foliage colors best in full sun.

H. lancifolia (syn. *H. japonica*). Rather narrow green leaves and lilac or pale lavender flowers. Variety *albo-marginata* has leaves margined with white; variety *tardiflora* is dwarf and late-blooming.

H. plantaginea (syn. *H. subcordata*). Large green leaves and fragrant white or pinkish flowers.

H. Thomas Hogg. Large green leaves with narrow white margins.

HOUND'S-TONGUE. See *Cynoglossum.*

INCARVILLEA

They are exotic-looking plants with reddish-pink, trumpetlike flowers in early summer, easy to grow in sun and well-drained soil that never becomes excessively dry. Roots are fanglike.

Although new growth is slow to appear in spring, they quickly come into flower. They are not suited for areas where very severe winters prevail.

Incarvillea delavayi, S/2. Flowers and leaves reach up to 18 to 20 in. by midsummer.

I. grandiflora, S/1. Flowers begin about ground level in May before dark green toothed leaves appear. Never attain more than 10-in. height in flower.

INDIAN PHYSIC. See *Gillenia trifoliata*.

INULA

These members of the daisy family are all yellow-flowered and easy to grow. All prefer sun.

Inula ensifolia, S/2. Makes a neat bush about 2 ft. high, well set with golden daisies for many weeks from July to September.

Golden Beauty, S/3. Similar to *I. ensifolia* with larger, clear golden-yellow flowers. 1½ to 2 ft.

I. hookeri, S/4. 1 to 2 ft. Lemon-yellow rayed flowers, 2 in. across, from August to October. Growth is dense, leafy and spreading.

I. orientalis S/2. The orange-yellow flowers are wide-rayed and bloom on stiff 1½-ft. stems in June and July.

IRIS

This is a vast genus, and only the principal types suitable for garden decoration and cut flowers can be mentioned here. Horticultural varieties are not named because they are so numerous, and because so many new ones are introduced each year that any listing is soon outdated. It is well, when making selections for planting, to consult the catalogues of specialists.

In addition to the iris types referred to here, all of which should be set at planting distances S/2 or S/3,

Iris germanica
(Bearded Iris)

there are lesser-known ones occasionally cultivated by fanciers, rock gardeners and other enthusiasts. There are also true bulbous irises, which are discussed on page 237, "Hardy Bulbs."

Most popular of the commonly cultivated irises are the bearded varieties. These come in a wide range of colors from white through lavender and blue to deepest purple, as well as cream, yellow, bronze and tones of pink. They are essentially spring and early-summer bloomers. Bearded irises are divided into three groups: the dwarfs, varieties of *Iris pumila*, which bloom first and are less than 1 ft. tall; the intermediates, chiefly varieties of *I. germanica*, which range in height from 1 to 1½ ft.; and the tall bearded, also varieties of *I. germanica* and allied species, which vary in height from 1½ to 3 ft.

Bearded irises grow best in full sun, in well-drained soil of moderate fertility that is not excessively acid; applications of lime periodically are usually beneficial. They are propagated by division of the rhizomes, preferably shortly after they are through blooming. At planting time the rhizomes should be only about half covered with soil.

The most important groups of beardless irises cultivated are the Japanese, varieties of *I. kaempferi* and *I. laevigata*; the Siberian, varieties of *I. sibirica*; and the Louisiana irises, varieties derived from a complex of species native to bogs in Louisiana.

Japanese irises have huge flowers of white, lavender, blue, purple, lavender-pink and intermediate shades. They require rich soil, constantly moist in summer but not saturated in winter, and full sun. They are propagated by division after blooming.

Siberian irises have grassy foliage

and white or blue flowers on slender stems. They grow in moderately dry soils, provided they have ample moisture in spring; they are also useful for planting by the banks of streams. When clumps become too large, they should be divided and replanted in spring or early fall.

Louisiana irises come in a wide range of lovely colors. In the Deep South they are permanent, even in bog soil; elsewhere they thrive better with drier conditions in winter but with ample moisture in spring and summer. The soil should be rich and contain ample amounts of organic matter. Propagate by division in spring.

Other beardless irises of importance are the water-loving, semiaquatic *I. pseudacorus*, with yellow flowers, and *I. versicolor*, which has blue-purple blooms. These are best divided and planted in spring or early fall.

JACOB'S LADDER. See *Polemonium caeruleum*.

JOE-PYE WEED. See *Eupatorium purpureum*.

JOINTWEED. See *Polygonum*.

KNAPWEED. See *Centaurea*.

KNIPHOFIA (RED-HOT POKER, TRITOMA, TORCH LILY)
These stately flowering plants provide their best display where the whole plant can be seen, and are especially handsome against a background of evergreens. They are drought-resistant, grow best in light soil and full sun and are good for cutting. Following severe winters they are best left undisturbed till new growth begins. A selection of varieties can be had to flower in every month between May and October, but never cram them in among taller, bushier plants

or shrubs, as this weakens their growth and spoils their appearance.

Coral Sea, small-flowered, coral-red suffused with rose-pink.

Earliest of All, large-flowered, coral-rose. The earliest to bloom and probably the hardiest.

Goldmine, large-flowered, golden-yellow, summer and fall.

Primrose Beauty, large-flowered, primrose-yellow, early summer.

Springtime, large-flowered. Lower flowers ivory-yellow; upper flowers, coral-red, summer.

White Fairy, small-flowered, white, early summer.

Kniphofia galpinii, S/2, and *K. macowanii*, S/2, both 2 ft., are specially good dwarfs. Both have orange flowers in August.

K. rufa, S/2. An earlier-flowering dwarf. Light yellow flowers in June and July.

KNOTWEED. See *Polygonum*.

LADY'S-SMOCK. See *Cardamine*.

LAMB'S EARS. See *Stachys lanata*.

LARKSPUR. See *Delphinium*.

LATHYRUS

Lathyrus vernus (syn. *Orobus vernus*), S/2. An easy, early-flowering plant which grows bushily to 12 to 15. in. and is covered with little creamy-white, pink, purple or blue lupine-like flowers in April and May.

LENTEN ROSE. See *Helleborus orientalis*.

LEOPARD'S-BANE. See *Doronicum*.

LIATRIS (GAY FEATHER)

These striking plants are easy to grow in sun and well-drained soil. They have dark, narrow leaves and brightly colored rosy-lilac poker spikes which begin flowering at the top and continue downward. Good for cutting. Roots are fleshy and cormlike just below the ground surface.

Liatris Kobalt Blue, S/1–2. 2 ft. A good variety with deep mauve-pink flowers.

L. pycnostachya, S/1–2. 3 to 4 ft. Flowers from July to September. A white-flowered variety, *alba*, is offered.

L. scariosa (blazing star), S/1–2. 3 to 6 ft. Flowers bluish-purple. Good varieties of this species are *alba*, with white flowers; September Glory, an excellent variety which has flowers open all along the stem at one time; White Spire, a superb white-flowered variety; and Silver Tips, flowers lavender with a silver sheen.

L. spicata, S/1–2. 2 ft. Flowers blue-purple. Variety *alba* has white flowers.

LIGULARIA

Closely related to *Senecio*, they are very ornamental, growing massively with big, cabbagelike leaves and branching spikes of yellow or orange flowers in July and August. They dislike dry conditions. Excellent for planting beside ponds, lakes and streams. They do not require frequent dividing.

Ligularia clivorum, S/4. 4 ft. Flowers orange-yellow with darker centers.

L.c. Gregynog Gold, S/4. 3½ ft. Orange flowers.

L.c. hessei, S/5. 5 ft. Flowers deep yellow.

L.c. Othello, S/5. 4 ft. Orange-gold flowers and purplish leaves.

L. wilsoniana, S/4. 4 ft. A bold and stately kind; golden-yellow flowers.

LILY OF THE VALLEY. See *Convallaria*.

LIMONIUM (SEA LAVENDER, STATICE)

These plants produce masses of small flowers which may be cut and dried as everlastings. They thrive in well-drained sandy soils in full sun and are among the best plants for seaside gardens.

Limonium latifolium, S/4. 2 to 3 ft. Has widely branching sprays of tiny lavender-blue flowers from July to September. When at their best can be cut and dried. Leaves are long and leathery. Tough, deep roots withstand drought and are not readily moved when old. Established plants need space to grow well. Good for cutting.

L.l. Collier's Pink, S/4. 2 ft. Flowers pink.

L.l. Violetta, S/4. 2 to 3 ft. Flowers violet-blue.

L. tataricum angustifolium (syn. *L. incanum*), S/3. 15 in. Grayish foliage and flattish broad heads of small pale pink flowers from July to September. Good for cutting.

LINOSYRIS

Linosyris vulgaris (goldilocks), S/2. A neat plant carrying heads of pretty golden fluffy flowers on willowy 2-ft. stems in August and September. Easy in ordinary soil in sun.

LINUM (FLAX)

All linums are sun lovers and prefer light soil. They appreciate the presence of lime in the soil. Although the individual flowers last but a short time, a succession of bloom is maintained over a long period.

Linum flavum, S/2. 10 to 15 in. Golden-yellow, short-stemmed flowers from bushy plants from June to August. Showy and good in full sun and dryish soil.

L. lewisii, S/2. 1½ ft. Flowers sky-blue. Very similar to *L. perenne* but somewhat more robust.

L. narbonense, S/2. 1½ ft. Azure-blue with white. Flowers from May to July. Grows more erectly than *L. perenne*. Best from seed. A white-flowered variety is *album*.

L. paniculatum, S/2. Similar to *L. flavum*, but foliage bluish-green.

L. perenne, S/2. Easy and pretty with a profusion of slender, arching 20-in. sprays of sky-blue flowers from June to September. Best from seed. *L.p. album* has white flowers.

LOBELIA

Late-summer- and fall-blooming. They grow well in rich, fairly moist soil and full sun or part shade. Showy flowers in erect spikes.

Lobelia cardinalis (cardinal flower), S/2. 3 to 4 ft. Flowers cardinal-red.

L. siphilitica, S/2. 2 to 3 ft. Blue flowers.

L.s. alba, S/2. 2 to 3 ft. White flowers.

L. vedariensis, S/2. 2 to 2½ ft. Flowers violet-purple.

LOOSESTRIFE. See *Lysimachia*.

LUNGWORT. See *Pulmonaria*.

LUPINUS (LUPINE)

Modern perennial lupines are excellent showy, hardy border plants, although longevity is not their strong point. They do not care for rich manuring and are adaptable for town gardens and partial shade. They grow best where the atmosphere is always fairly humid and are likely to be disappointing where they are subjected to hot, dry summer winds.

The perennial lupines of gardens, varieties and hybrids of *Lupinus polyphyllus*, are all S/3, varying in height from 2½ to 3 ft. and with colors ranging from white to shades of pale pink, yellow, orange and red, as well as blue and purple. The blue, purple and pale pinks predominate in time if seed is indiscriminately saved or allowed to self-germinate. To avoid this, remove flower spikes as soon as color has gone, and sow only seed of the finest strains obtained from reliable sources. Early removal of faded flower spikes encourages secondary spikes to flower

Lupinus (Lupine)

S/2–3. Has heads of small scarlet flowers on leafy 2- to 3-ft. stems in June and July. Compact, easy to grow. Best where not starved or dry.

L. coronaria (mullein pink, rose campion), S/3. Makes a gray-leaved clump; a long succession of intense magenta-red flowers on 1½-ft. branching stems from late June to August. Best in full sun and light soil. White and pale pink varieties are also grown.

L. haageana, S/2–3. A hybrid; orangered flowers about 2 in. in diameter.

L. viscaria (German catchfly), S/3. This plant, 1½-ft. tall, has spikes of bright magenta-red flowers with sticky areas on the stems beneath the blooms. Needs full sun and well-drained soil. For best results divide and replant every third year. The double-flowered *L.v. flore-pleno* is especially showy.

LYSIMACHIA (LOOSESTRIFE)

Lysimachia clethroides, S/4. Prettily curved spikes of white flowers on erect 3-ft. stems in summer; slowly creeping roots. A very fine plant for a fairly moist, rich soil.

L. ephemerum, S/3. 4 ft. White flowers in summer. Stately and erect. Needs the same conditions as *L. clethroides*.

L. punctata, S/4–5. Whorls of yellow flowers for much of the summer on leafy 3-ft. spikes. Robust and easy. Best in moist soil.

L. vulgaris, S/4–5. Similar to *L. punctata*, but flowers in terminal leafy panicles.

LYTHRUM (PURPLE LOOSESTRIFE)

Bright-flowered summer bloomers that bear a profusion of flower spikes and are of easiest cultivation in fairly moist soil and sun. They flower over a long period. Good garden varieties, all S/2, are:

Lythrum Lady Sackville, 5 ft. Flowers are a splendid bright rose-pink.

over a longer period. Lupines bloom in June and July, and seed sown early will often produce plants to flower the same year.

LYCHNIS (CAMPION)

Included here are plants sometimes listed under *Agrostemma*, *Melandrium* and *Viscaria*.

Lychnis chalcedonica (Maltese cross),

L. Morden Pink, 3 to 4 ft. Flowers deep pink.

L. Robert, 2 to 3 ft. Flowers fuchsia-pink.

MACLEAYA

Macleaya cordata (syn. *Bocconia cordata*—plume poppy), S/5. 6 to 8 ft. Of noble appearance and vigorous growth, this plant is cultivated as much for its handsome bluish-green foliage as for the plumes of small creamy flowers it produces in summer. The flowers are succeeded by a multitude of small decorative seedpods. Both flowers and seedpods are useful for flower arrangements. It thrives in sun and any ordinary soil.

MALLOW. See *Malva*.

MALTESE CROSS. See *Lychnis chalcedonica*.

MALVA (MALLOW)

Malva alcea, S/3. 3 to 4 ft. Similar to *M. moschata* but with larger flowers. Blooms almost all summer. Flowers are deep pink to white. Easy, and excellent for hot, dry, sunny locations.

M. moschata (musk mallow), S/3. 1½ to 2½ ft. Flowers pink. Blooms freely throughout summer. Requires same conditions as *M. alcea*.

M.m. alba. Is identical with *M. moschata* except that the flowers are pure white. A very good plant.

MASTERWORT. See *Astrantia*.

MEADOW RUE. See *Thalictrum*.

MEADOWSWEET. See *Filipendula*.

MEGASEA. See *Bergenia*.

MERTENSIA

Mertensia virginica (Virginia bluebells, Virginia cowslip), S/2. 1 to 2 ft. A native of eastern North America,

this beautiful plant is excellent for semishade and moderately moist soil. The flower buds are pink, the flowers blue, produced in spring. Stems and foliage die down in early summer.

MICHAELMAS DAISY. See *Aster*.

MILFOIL. See *Achillea*.

MILKWEED. See *Asclepias*.

MONARDA (BEE BALM, OSWEGO TEA)

Monardas are native American plants. The kinds cultivated in gardens are improved varieties which have been developed by plant breeders. They make stout 3-ft. bushy plants with aromatic foliage rising from spreading, matlike roots and bloom for many weeks from June to August. Not difficult to curb, but replanting every two or three years is advised. Flowers are bright and of a curious form. The stem leaves wither if soil is too dry. Recommended varieties, all S/4–5, are:

Adam Scarlet. By many considered superior to the older variety Cambridge Scarlet.

Blue Stocking, purple-blue.
Cambridge Scarlet, scarlet.
Croftway Pink, cerise-pink.
Mahogany, deep mahogany-red.
Magnifica, purple-blue.
Melissa, cerise-pink.
Prairie Glow, salmon.
Snow Witch, white.

MONKSHOOD. See *Aconitum*.

MUGWORT. See *Artemesia lactiflora*.

MULLEIN. See *Verbascum*.

MULLEIN PINK. See *Lychnis coronaria*.

MUSK MALLOW. See *Malva moschata*.

NEPETA

These aromatic plants have gray-green foliage and are easy to grow in full sun and well-drained soil. They succeed even in soils that are rather low in fertility. All S/3.

Nepeta Blue Beauty (syn. *N.* Souvenir d'André Chaudron), 2 ft.; blue-lavender flowers in summer.

N. faassenii (syn. *N. mussinii*), 1 to 1½ ft. Forms billowy mounds of attractive foliage and in early summer has a profusion of lavender flowers. After the first blooming, shear the plants lightly to encourage intermittent flowering later.

N. tatarica, 2½ ft. Of erect growth and blooming freely in summer. Large trusses of lilac flowers.

NIPPON DAISY. See *Chrysanthemum nipponicum*.

OBEDIENT PLANT. See *Physostegia*.

OENOTHERA (EVENING PRIMROSE)
Those with bright yellow cup-or salver-shaped flowers make a fine show and are long-lived. They are plants for full sun and porous, not-too-rich soils. Recommended are:

O. fruticosa, S/2. 1 to 2 ft. Flowers are clear yellow, 2 to 3 in. wide, from June to August. The variety *youngii* is a very profuse bloomer; the variety Yellow River, S/2, bears canary-yellow flowers and is first-rate.

O. missouriensis, S/4. Best on a fairly dry slope, but must have room to trail. Spreads from fanglike root; long succession of large lemon-yellow salverlike flowers in summer.

O. tetragona hybrids, S/2. 1½ ft. Bronzy-green tufty leaves and fine yellow flowers following red buds from June to August. Similar in growth to *O. fruticosa*.

OSWEGO TEA. See *Monarda*.

PAEONIA (PEONY)
Herbaceous peonies are among the

Paeonia (Peony)

most permanent of plants and need careful site selection, soil preparation and planting. For best results set them in rich, deep soil in full sun in early fall, with the buds at the crown of the roots only 2 in. below the surface when firmed and settled. They need space and airiness, for an old plant may cover a square yard when in flower. Although better in full sun, peonies will stand a little shade; they should not be planted, however, where they are forced to compete with the roots of nearby trees or shrubs.

Newly planted peonies often take two years or more before they become really established and bloom well. Specimens that are thriving should not be transplanted unless there is good reason for so doing. Propagation is by division of roots in early September. This operation requires digging up plants. Each division should consist of a portion of root with three to five buds or "eyes" attached.

During dry summer weather peonies need copious watering, and a summer mulch is beneficial. Larger flowers are obtained if the plants are disbudded by removing all side flower buds when quite small, leaving only the central one on each stem to develop. No special winter protection is needed, and under no circumstances should a winter covering of manure, peat moss or other moisture-holding material be applied, because this encourages disease.

Very few species or wild types of peonies are grown in gardens, but immense numbers of horticultural varieties are cultivated. These include single-flowered and double-flowered kinds in a wide variety of whites, pinks and reds. The flowers of some are very fragrant. Only a few of the best are listed below; for a wider selection of peonies consult the catalogues of specialists. Plants need S/4 spacing.

Felix Crousse, brilliant crimson, an old and dependable variety.

Festiva Maxima, white with a few crimson markings; early, a fine old variety.

Hermione, apple-blossom pink; flowers on strong stems.

Isani-Gidui, single-flowered, white with golden center.

Krinkled White, large single-flowered white.

Le Cygne, large flower, creamy white tinged green at center.

Mary Brand, a distinctive red with good keeping qualities when cut.

Mikado, single-flowered, red with yellow center.

Nick Shaylor, light pink with a few red markings.

Sea Shell, single-flowered, bright pink with yellow center.

Walter Faxon, pure rose-pink, one of the best.

P. mlokosewitschii, S/3. 1½ ft. Lovely yellow flowers in April and early May. Not difficult, but not commonly available.

P. officinalis, S/4. 2 to 3 ft. The old-fashioned, early-flowering kind. Its double varieties are *alba plena*, white; *rubra plena*, red; and *rosea superba*, pink.

P. tenuifolia, S/4. 2 ft. Decorative, finely divided foliage. Flowers are dark red.

PAINTED DAISY. See *Chrysanthemum coccineum*.

PAPAVER (POPPY)

Only some varieties of *Papaver orientale*, all S/3, are recommended as hardy and reliably perennial, but even these are apt to suffer rot damage to the roots in overrich or overmoist soil. They prefer a deep, porous, moderately fertile, loamy soil, but will tolerate a fairly wide variation of soil types. Plant them in early fall or early spring. Water them freely if dry periods occur before they bloom. Poppies require full sun. Their big, resplendent flowers make a brave show in early summer, but are apt to leave a gap afterward when stems and foliage die down for a rather lengthy period in summer, and therefore they need careful siting. Some grow only 20 in. high, others reach 3 ft., but most need staking. A few good varieties of poppies are:

Barr's White, 2½ ft. Single, white with purplish black spots at bases of petals.

Cowichan, 3 ft. Substantial flowers of fine turkey red. Of easy culture.

Crimson Pompon, 2 ft. Fully double, red, profuse.

Helen Elizabeth, 3 ft. A lovely pink without dark spots. One of the best.

Peter Pan, dwarf double. Orange-scarlet.

Salmon Glow, 2½ ft. Exceptionally large salmon-orange flowers.

Sultana, 3 ft. Single, clear pink.

PARADISEA

Paradisea liliastrum (St. Bruno's lily), S/1. 1 to 2 ft. Grassy-leaved plants with slender, erect stems bearing white starlike flowers in early summer. Of easy cultivation in ordinary soil. In gardens this plant is often misnamed *Anthericum*.

PASQUEFLOWER. See *Anemone pulsatilla*.

PENSTEMON

Perennial penstemons include both subshrubby and truly herbaceous kinds, some having brilliant colors and all with tubular flowers. All are S/3.

Penstemon barbatus (syn. *Chelone barbata*—beard-tongue). Drooping bright pink or scarlet tubular flowers along 2- to 3-ft. stems from June to August. Plants flower so freely in sunny positions that they tend to exhaust themselves. Encourage longevity by cutting back hard after flowering, or by dividing and replanting more deeply in spring.

P. diffusus. Makes ample, bushy growth with spikes of lilac-blue flowers, 1½ ft. tall, from June to August. Is longer-lived than most.

P. grandiflorus, 2 to 4 ft. Flowers white or pink.

P.g. Firebird, 1½ to 2 ft. Ruby-crimson.

P.g. Newberry, 12 to 15 in. Light purple-blue.

P.g. Prairie Dusk, 2 ft. Dark purple-blue.

P. subglaber, 1½ to 2 ft. Blue or violet.

PEONY. See *Paeonia*.

PEROVSKIA (RUSSIAN SAGE)

Perovskia atriplicifolia, S/3 or S/4. Somewhat shrubby. Has gray foliage; in late summer, panicles (pyramid-shaped clusters) of blue flowers develop, which are useful for cutting.

Needs full sun and well-drained soil that is not too rich.

PHLOX

In addition to several kinds of phlox that are of special interest to rock gardeners (see page 535 in "Rock Gardens"), the following are grown for general garden decoration:

Phlox divaricata (wild sweet William), S/2. 9 to 18 in., a profusion of lavender-blue or sometimes white flowers in spring. Prefers rich, fairly moist soil and part shade. Excellent for associating with tulips and other bulbs.

P. paniculata, in many splendid named garden varieties, all S/3. 2 to 3½ ft.

No garden in regions where phlox can be grown is complete without some of these tall, summer-flowering phlox, which produce gay panicles or heads of bright, delicately fragrant flowers from July to September. They range widely in color and fit in perfectly with most other plants. Adaptable as they are, they respond to good cultivation. They do best in light soil and appreciate fertility and moisture. Where soil is dry, heavy or poor, apply a mulch of peat moss or compost; a fertilizer applied in spring is also helpful.

Thin out some of the shoots, if these are crowded, in May. Unfortunately, these phlox are sometimes difficult to grow well in regions where hot summers are the rule; they seem to rebel against hot nights especially. They should be divided and replanted every second or third year, and faded flower heads should be removed promptly to avoid seed formation. When watering, avoid wetting the foliage because this encourages the fungus disease called mildew.

There are numerous splendid varieties of phlox, and new ones are introduced each year. When making selections, consult up-to-date catalogues of specialists or visit nurseries where these plants are grown during their blooming season.

Phlox suffruticosa Miss Lingard, S/2–3. 2 to 2½ ft. Has pure white flowers in early summer and again in fall. Very reliable. Needs same culture as other summer-flowering phlox.

PHYSOSTEGIA (OBEDIENT PLANT)
These plants produce tapering spikes set closely with lipped flowers. Their stems are well foliaged with dark green pointed leaves. They are easily grown in almost any soil and do not mind some shade. Good for cutting.

Physostegia virginiana, S/4. Up to 4 ft. Flesh-colored or rosy-purple flowers from July to September. Roots tend to run, forming close mats.

P.v. alba has white flowers and is more compact and not as tall as *P. virginiana*.

P.v. Summer Snow, S/4. 3 ft. Pretty white flowers in July and August.

P.v. Summer Spire, S/4. 3½ ft. Lilac-purple flowers bloom in July and August.

P.v. Vivid, S/4. Shorter, later and deeper-colored than other varieties. Color of flowers, deep rose-pink. Wandering roots make annual lifting and replanting advisable.

PINCUSHION FLOWER. See *Scabiosa*.

PINK. See *Dianthus*.

PLANTAIN LILY. See *Hosta*.

PLATYCODON (BALLOONFLOWER)
Closely related to the bellflower (*Campanula*), these are excellent summer bloomers for sunny places and porous, well-drained soil. Once planted and established, they should not be transplanted unless necessary. All S/3.

Platycodon grandiflorum, 1½ to 2 ft. Deep blue flowers.

P.g. album, 1½ to 2 ft. White.
P.g. semi-plenum, 1½ to 2 ft. Blue; semidouble.

PLUME POPPY. See *Macleaya cordata*.

POLEMONIUM
These charming plants have pretty leaves and blue, or sometimes white, attractive flowers; they are not always very long-lived.

Polemonium Blue Pearl, S/3. Makes a 1-ft.-high mound set with deep-blue flowers from May to June.

P. Sapphire, S/2. 1½ ft. Reliable, flowering in May and June.

P. caeruleum (Jacob's ladder, Greek valerian), S/3. 2 to 3 ft. Flowers blue, in early summer. A white-flowered variety, *album*, is also cultivated.

P. foliosissimum, S/3. 2 ft. A good species. Bushy growth, and white or blue flowers in June and July.

P. richardsonii, S/3. 1 to 2 ft. Its flowers are blue-purple; blooms in early summer.

POLYGONATUM (SOLOMON'S SEAL)
Excellent subjects for shady places and deep soil that contains an abundance of organic matter and is fairly moist. They bloom in late spring and early summer. Variegated-leaved varieties are grown. All are S/2.

Polygonatum biflorum (small Solomon's seal), 2 to 3 ft. Flowers are greenish-white.

P. commutatum (great Solomon's seal), 3 to 6 ft. Flowers greenish-white.

P. multiflorum, 3 ft. Flowers greenish-white.

POLYGONUM (JOINTWEED, KNOTWEED)
This is a large genus of wide variations, the best of which deserve to be more extensively grown. Most polygonums like fairly moist conditions but are surprisingly adaptable. Some, not mentioned, are weedy, and caution is advised.

Polygonum affine Darjeeling Red, S/5. 9 in. Has spikes of bright pink flowers. Makes an excellent ground cover even in poor soil.

P. bistorta superbum, S/3–4. Grows a clump of sorrel-like leaves, with a profusion of clear pink flower heads on 3-ft. wiry stems in early summer.

P. capitatum, S/2. 6 in. Prostrate plant with small, rounded heads of pink flowers. For mild climates only.

P. reynoutria, S/3–4. 1 to 2 ft. A vigorous spreader best adapted for using as a ground cover. Best in full sun but will stand some shade. Its flowers are pink and are arranged in numerous sprays. In fall its foliage turns brilliant red.

POPPY. See *Papaver.*

POPPY MALLOW. *See Callirhoe.*

POTENTILLA (CINQUEFOIL)
A genus offering a wide selection of brightly flowered, mostly dwarfish plants. All like sun but are not fussy as to soil. Their flowers and in some

Potentilla
(Cinquefoil)

cases their foliage reveal their kinship to the strawberry.

Potentilla argyrophylla, S/3–4. 2 to 3 ft. Good silvery foliage and floppy masses of yellow or red flowers in May and June.

P. nepalensis Miss Willmott, S/3. Masses of cherry-pink flowers on 1½-ft. branching stems in July and August.

P.n. Roxana is similar to Miss Willmott, with buff-rose flowers.

P. recta (syn. *P. warrensii*), S/2. 1½ ft. More erect than *P. nepalensis*, with ample foliage and yellow flowers from June to August.

P.r. Gibson's Scarlet, S/2. 1½ ft. Single, red.

P.r. Lady Rollisson, S/2. 1½ ft. Flame-orange flowers and vigorous, strawberrylike foliage.

POTERIUM. See *Sanguisorba obtusa.*

PRIMROSE. See *Primula.*

PRIMULA (PRIMROSE)
This large group includes several kinds which, in especially favored locations, are suitable for growing in shade and moist soils. There are few, however, that can be considered generally useful in beds and borders. These few need shade from strong, direct sun. They require fertile soil that contains an abundance of organic matter and is fairly moist.

Primula polyantha (polyanthus primrose), S/1. 6 to 12 in. Has rosettes of basal leaves and many flower stems, each terminated by a cluster of flowers, which may be white or one of many shades of cream, yellow, orange, bronze, maroon or red; blooms in spring and early summer. Double-flowered forms occur.

P. vulgaris (English primrose), S/1. 6 to 9 in. Similar to *P. polyantha*, but having only one flower on each stem. Flower colors include blue, purple, lavender and yellow. Double-flowered varieties are cultivated. Needs same culture as *P. polyantha*.

PULMONARIA (LUNGWORT)
They thrive best in part shade but are quite adaptable, needing only ordinary soil and the minimum of attention. If provided with adequate moisture, they will also grow well in full sun. Their chief value is their early-flowering habit—they are at their best in early spring.

Pulmonaria angustifolia azurea, S/2–3. 9 in. Half-prostrate sprays of gentian-blue flowers show well before the tongue-shaped leaves appear.

P. saccharata, S/4. 1 ft. Variable, some having blue and pink flowers (due to fading) on the same plant from April to June. Leaves are attractively spotted with white.

PURPLE LOOSESTRIFE. See *Lythrum*.

PYRETHRUM. See *Chrysanthemum coccineum*.

QUEEN-OF-THE-MEADOW. See *Filipendula ulmaria*.

QUEEN-OF-THE-PRAIRIE. See *Filipendula rubra*.

RAGWORT. See *Senecio*.

RANUNCULUS (BUTTERCUP, CROWFOOT)
The following species are well worth cultivating. All like sun and good drainage. Good for cutting.

Ranunculus acris flore-pleno, S/3. A bright, trouble-free plant for sun, with fully double yellow flowers ½ in. across on 2-ft. branching stems in May and June.

R. bulbosus flore-pleno, S/2. 1 ft. Double yellow flowers in May and June. Leafier and larger-flowered than *R.a. flore-pleno*.

R. gramineus, S/1. 6 to 12 in. Brilliant golden single flowers in spring, and grayish narrow leaves. Grows in a neat clump.

R. repens pleniflorus, S/3. 2 ft. A creeping plant which bears many double yellow flowers on branched stems in early summer.

RED-HOT POKER. See *Kniphofia*.

ROCK CRESS. See *Arabis*.

ROSE CAMPION. See *Lychnis coronaria*.

ROSE MALLOW. See *Hibiscus*.

RUDBECKIA (CONEFLOWER)
Most rudbeckias, except a few fully double-flowered kinds, are distinguished by a central cone, above rayed petals. They are easy to grow in sun, but thrive best where not too dry.

Rudbeckia Goldsturm, S/3. 2½ ft. Has a mat growth of moderate spread. Erect stems carry finely rayed golden flowers with black centers from late summer into fall.

R. Herbstsonne, S/4–5. 6 ft. Large, rich golden-yellow flowers from July to September. Too tall for narrow beds or borders.

R. laciniata (golden glow), S/4–5. 6 ft. Produces double chrome-yellow flowers from July to September. Too tall for narrow beds or borders.

R.l. Goldquelle, S/2–3. Fully double golden-yellow flowers from July to September. Makes a neat bush 2½ to 3 ft. high.

R. purpurea, S/2. Purplish-rose flowers, with petals often drooping, grow on stiff 2½- to 3-ft. stems in late summer.

R.p. The King. Deep purple-rose flowers on 3-ft. stems.

R.p. Robert Bloom, 3 ft. Glowing crimson-purple. Compact, bushy growth.

R.p. White Lustre, 3 ft. White with

centers of a metallic quality resembling old brass.

RUSSIAN SAGE. See *Perovskia.*

SAGE. See *Salvia.*

ST. BERNARD'S LILY. See *Anthericum liliago.*

ST. BRUNO'S LILY. See *Paradisea liliastrum.*

SALVIA (SAGE)

There are over 500 species of salvia; the following are recommended hardy plants, easy to grow in ordinary soil in sun or semishade:

Salvia azurea, S/3. 3 to 5 ft. Good blue flowers for late summer and fall. Tends to be a little straggly, needs careful staking.

S.a. grandiflora (syn. *S.a. pitcheri*), similar to above but flowers larger and in more compact spikes.

S. haematodes, S/3. 4 ft. A handsome plant with light blue flowers on sturdy branching stems in summer.

S. superba (syn. *S. nemerosa*), S/3. 3½ ft. The finest of all. In the type, erect tapering spikes are massed in bush form, each carrying many tiny violet-purple flowers in summer. Even when faded these are attractive.

S. uliginosa, S/4. 3 to 5 ft. Spikes of light blue flowers mass bushily in fall. This would be really good except that it sometimes becomes top-heavy. Not reliable in very severe winters.

SANGUISORBA (BURNET)

Sanguisorba obtusa, S/2–3. 2 to 3 ft. Often called *Poterium*, this species thrives in ordinary soil in sun. Foliage is of good decorative value. Flowers are pink, in dense heads, and are useful for cutting.

SAPONARIA (SOAPWORT)

Saponaria officinalis flore-pleno

(bouncing Bet), S/2. 1½ to 2 ft. This, the common double-flowered form, is an aggressive spreader and should be planted only where its tendency to take possession of adjacent areas can be checked. Flowers pale pink in spring and early summer. Thrives in ordinary or poor soil in sun or light shade. Sometimes called *S. caucasica.*

SAXIFRAGA. See *Bergenia.*

SCABIOSA
(SCABIOUS, PINCUSHION FLOWER)

Scabiosa caucasica, S/2–3. 1½ to 2½ ft. This and its varieties are not reliably hardy where winter temperatures approach 0° F. In favored climates, they are excellent for garden decoration and for cutting. Among the best varieties are:

S.c. Bressingham White. Flowers from June to September, the best white-flowered variety.

S.c. Clive Greaves. This is the most reliable. Blue open flowers on wiry stems come freely from June to September. The more they are cut, the

Scabiosa
(Scabious, Pincushion Flower)

more they flower. They do best in light soil and sun and like lime. Plant in spring from young plants, not pieces of old, unthrifty clumps, and divide a third of the total number of plants each year to maintain vigor.

SCABIOUS. See *Scabiosa*.

SEA HOLLY. See *Eryngium*.

SEA LAVENDER. See *Limonium*.

SEDUM (STONECROP)
All the following sedums like sun and light soil. In addition to the kinds listed here, other sedums, some of which are useful for the fronts of flower borders and similar locations, are described on page 537 in "Rock Gardens" and on page 75 in "Cactuses and Succulents."
    Sedum maximum atropurpureum, S/3. 2 to 3 ft. A handsome plant with bronze-purple stems and foliage and creamy-pink flowers in large heads in late summer.
    S. spectabile, S/3. 1½ to 2 ft. tall, with attractive fleshy blue-green foliage. In late summer each stem terminates in a wide, flat head of glistening pink flowers.
    S.s. Brilliant, 1½ ft. Bright pink flowers.
    S.s. Carmen, 1½ ft. Deeper pink flowers than *S.s.* Brilliant.
    S.s. Meteor, 1½ ft. Rosy-red flowers.
    S.s. variegatum, same as *S. spectabile*, but its leaves are variegated with yellow.
    S. *telephium* Autumn Joy, S/3. 1½ to 2 ft. Flower heads open pale copper-red and change to salmon-rose. Late summer.

SENECIO (RAGWORT)
    Senecio doronicum, S/2. Very neat, slowly forming surface mats set with orange-gold daisies on 10-in. stems in spring.

S. pryzwalskii, S/3–4. 4 ft. Has tapering spikes of small, shaggy golden flowers on stiff black stems in summer, and deeply jagged leaves. A noble plant, but needs moisture for development to perfection.

SENNA. See *Cassia*.

SHASTA DAISY. See *Chrysanthemum maximum*.

SIDALCEA
These near relatives of mallow make well-foliaged spikes in the mass, set with 1-in. open flowers along much of each stem in summer. Easy and reasonably long-lived, but best planted where they receive full sun and in soil that is always moderately moist. Only some of the varieties listed appear to be cultivated in North America, but all are popular in Europe and are likely to be imported. They are all S/2–3.
    Sidalcea Croftway Red, 3 ft., red.
    Elsie Heugh, Mrs. Alderson, Rev. Page Roberts, Sussex Beauty. These are all in shades of light pink on slender 4-ft. spikes.
    Wensleydale, 4 ft., deep rose.
    William Smith, 3 ft., rose-tinged salmon.

SILVER KING. See *Artemisia albula*.

SNEEZEWEED. See *Helenium*.

SNOW-IN-SUMMER. See *Cerastium tomentosum*.

SOAPWORT. See *Saponaria*.

SOLIDAGO (GOLDENROD)
Although popular abroad, the goldenrods until recently were essentially ignored by North American gardeners. The belief that they are responsible for causing hay fever is not supported by facts. Magnificent improved varieties

of native American species have been developed in Europe, and some are now offered by nurseries here: Available in colors from primrose-yellow to deep gold. Good for cutting.

The following neat-growing varieties all grow between 2 and 3 ft., flower in late summer and have good foliage and habit.

Golden Falls. S/2.

Goldenmosa, S/2.

Golden Shower, S/2.

Lemore, S/2.

Lena, S/2.

Lesden, S/2.

Good varieties growing only 10 to 12 in. high: Queenie, S/1; Tom Thumb. S/1.

Crown of Rays, S/3. 2½ ft. Wide heads of bright yellow in July.

Mimosa, S/3. 4 ft. Has handsome golden plumes in July and August. One of the better tall varieties.

Peter Pan, S/3. Has spreading heads on stiff 3-ft. stems in July.

SOLOMON'S SEAL. See *Polygonatum*.

SOUTHERNWOOD. See *Artemisia abrotanum*.

SPEEDWELL. See *Veronica*.

SPIDERWORT. See *Tradescantia*.

SPIREA. See *Astilbe*.

SPURGE. See *Euphorbia*.

STACHYS (BETONY)

Stachys grandiflora superba, S/3. 2 ft. Also known as *Betonica grandiflora superba*. Lilac-rose lipped flowers in June and July. A first-rate plant which has no special needs. Suitable for sun or partial shade.

S. lanata (lamb's ears), S/3–4. Thickly felted silver leaves and 1½-ft. stems carrying deep-pink flowers in July. A good plant for hot, dry places.

STATICE. See *Limonium*.

STOKE'S ASTER. See *Stokesia*.

STOKESIA (STOKE'S ASTER)

Stokesia laevis (syn. *S. cyanea*), S/1. Less than 1 ft. Has dark, leathery leaves close to the ground and very large mauve-blue flowers with quilled centers for many weeks between June and September. Best in sun. Good for cutting.

S.l. Blue Star, S/2. A few inches taller than *S. laevis*, with bluer flowers for many weeks between June and September. Best in sun. Good for cutting.

STONECROP. See *Sedum*.

SUNFLOWER. See *Helianthus*.

THALICTRUM (MEADOW RUE)

All thalictrums have dainty foliage, but the best are the most difficult to grow. None of them likes a hot, dry position. Good for cutting.

Thalictrum aquilegifolium, S/2–3. Up to 4 ft. Clouds of fluffy mauve flower heads on fairly erect, branching stems in late spring or early summer. Shiny blue-green foliage. This plant is easy to grow in fairly good soil and a little shade.

T. dipterocarpum, all S/1–2. A fine array of small mauve, yellow-centered flowers appears from July to September. Given good, deep soil, this is a superb plant, although it needs support for its 4- to 5-ft. stems. Choice varieties are:

T.d. album, 3 to 4 ft. This kind bears pretty white flowers in August and September.

T.d. Hewitt's Double, 3 to 4 ft., with violet-mauve flowers in August and September. Really choice but demands richer soil than *T. dipterocarpum*.

T. flavum, S/2. 4 ft. Lemon-yellow

fluffs on strong stems in summer. Handsome deep green foliage.

T. glaucum, S/2. Rather similar to *T. flavum* but with glaucous blue-green leaves.

THERMOPSIS

Thermopsis caroliniana (Aaron's rod), S/2. 3 to 4 ft. Lupinelike, with bright yellow flowers in summer. Well adapted for full sun and dryish soil.

T. montana, S/1–2. 2 to 2½ ft. Similar to *T. caroliniana,* but less hardy to winter cold and useful only where winters are fairly mild.

THRIFT. See *Armeria.*

TICKSEED. See *Coreopsis.*

TORCH LILY. See *Kniphofia.*

TRADESCANTIA (SPIDERWORT)

Tradescantia virginiana. 1½ to 2 ft. Soft-leaved plants topped by three-petaled flowers in early summer and fall. This species is a native American, but modern garden varieties are such great improvements over the wild type that only they are really worth cultivating. All thrive in light shade in reasonably moist and fertile soil. For a short period in summer, the foliage dies down and looks a little untidy. Individual flowers last only a brief time, but a succession is maintained over a long period. Varieties, all S/2–3, include:

Blue Stone, medium blue.

Iris Pritchard, white, flecked blue.

Isis, large-flowered, deep blue.

Osprey, white with a central blue crest.

Pauline, orchid-mauve.

Purple Dome, purple.

Double blue and double red-purple varieties exist, but flowers are smaller than in the singles.

TRANSVAAL DAISY. See *Gerbera.*

TRITOMA. See *Kniphofia.*

TROLLIUS (GLOBEFLOWER)

These plants make a fine show with their big, globular buttercuplike flowers in late spring and early summer. They are moisture-loving, but will flourish in any fertile, deep soil that is not too dry. Good for cutting. The following varieties, all about 2½ ft. high and all S/2, have been derived from *Trollius europaeus* and *T. caucasicus.* These named kinds may not at present be available from nurseries in North America, but they are very likely to be introduced and offered in the future.

Canary Bird, light yellow.

Earliest of All, golden-yellow, strong-growing.

Feuertroll, orange-yellow.

Goldquelle, fine pure yellow.

Lemon Queen, light yellow.

Orange Princess, orange-yellow.

Pritchard's Giant, golden-yellow, strong-growing.

T. ledebouri, 2 to 3 ft. This flowers in summer with prominent deep-orange stamens on more open orange flowers.

TURTLEHEAD. See *Chelone.*

UVULARIA (BELLWORT)

Attractive spring-blooming plants for shaded locations, they require soil that is fertile and not excessively dry. All S/1.

Uvularia grandiflora, 1 to 1½ ft. Flowers pale yellow.

U. perfoliata, 1 to 1½ ft. Flowers pale yellow.

VALERIAN. See *Centranthus.*

VERBASCUM (MULLEIN)

These plants make big rosettes of woolly foliage and have tapering spikes set closely with cup-shaped flowers often more than 1 in. across in early summer. They are very decorative and do best in sun and well-drained or even dry soil.

Verbascum broussa, S/3. 4 to 5 ft. Very handsome. Stems and foliage silver, hairy. Flowers yellow.

V. chaixii (syn. *V. vernale*), S/3. 4 to 5 ft. Yellow flowers on strong, branching stems with docklike leaves. Reliably perennial.

V. hartleyi, S/4. Yellow flowers suffused with plum-purple on massive 5-ft. spikes; grayish foliage.

V. thapsiforme, S/3. 4 to 5 ft. Very erect, with deep-yellow flowers. Similar to *V. chaixii*, but spikes more closely set.

In addition to the above-mentioned species, many hybrid varieties are available. Among the best of these are:

Cotswold Gem, S/3, 4 ft. The flowers have pale amber petals and purple centers. They are borne on many branching stems.

Gainsborough, S/2. 3 ft. Spikes of light yellow flowers and gray leaves.

Pink Domino, S/3. 3½ ft. Purplish-rose flowers. Good.

VERONICA (SPEEDWELL)

Veronica exaltata, S/3. 5 ft. Has countless small, light blue flowers in late summer and autumn, on fine, tapering spikes which are well covered with pointed leaves. Easy to grow. Does not need staking.

V. gentianoides, S/2–3. Makes a fine, if rather brief, show in spring with dainty 2-ft. spikes of light blue flowers from close-growing, evergreen glossy-leaved plants. Easy to grow in sun or part shade.

V. incana, S/2. 1½ ft. Violet-blue flowers in summer, and charming ash-gray leaves close to the ground. Best in sun and drier places.

V. longifolia, *S*/2, and its varieties carry no foliage over winter. Has blue or white flowers on 2-ft. fairly erect spikes from July to September. It

likes good soil that is not too dry.

V.l. subsessilis, S/2. Rich deep blue flowers on spikes that grow at a tangent from 1½-ft. bushes of dark green pointed leaves in summer, from July to September.

V. spicata, S/2. These summer-flowering plants are surface-rooting, and they are best divided every two to three years. They need plenty of sun and good drainage, or winter losses may ensue. Recommended varieties are:

V.s. Barcarolle, S/2. A little taller than Minuet, rose-pink flowers and close-set tapering spikes.

V.s. Minuet, S/2. 1½ ft. Pink flowers and gray foliage. A very effective plant.

V.s. Romily Purple, S/2. 2 ft. Dark blue.

V. teucrium. This species and its varieties lose all foliage over winter. In spring they send up massed new shoots developing into loose mounds covered with short spikes and bright blue flowers. They are easy in ordinary soil, sun or part shade and flower in early summer. Recommended varieties are:

V.t. Crater Lake Blue, S/3. 15 in.

V.t. Icicle, S/3. 15 in.

V.t. Royal Blue, S/3. 1½ ft.

V.t. Shirley Blue, S/2. 1 ft.

VIRGINIA BLUEBELLS, VIRGINIA COWSLIP. See *Mertensia virginica*.

WHITE SNAKEROOT. See *Eupatorium rugosum*.

WILD SWEET WILLIAM. See *Phlox divaricata*.

WILLOW GENTIAN. See *Gentiana asclepiadea*.

WINDFLOWER. See *Anemone*.

YARROW. See *Achillea*.

CHAPTER 8

ROSES
Our Favorite Flower

What Roses to Grow—Bush, Tree or Standard—Ramblers and Climbers, Miniatures—Pruning—Care—Winter Protection—Pests and Diseases

ANYONE CAN GROW ROSES—and grow them almost anywhere. The number of types and varieties is so vast that there are roses to suit all tastes and all climates.

Not all roses are universally adaptable. Some that thrive in the far South are not hardy in the North. On the other hand, varieties bred to withstand subzero temperatures will not grow well where winters are frost-free. Fortunately, the great majority of bush and climbing roses are reliable in most parts of the United States and Canada except for the coldest regions. When there is any doubt about the reliability of certain kinds, consult local authorities such as nurserymen, botanical gardens, park superintendents, experienced rosarians or the department of horticulture of your state university.

Most roses will grow and flower with relatively little attention. They will, however, give much better results, increasing in both size and beauty for a number of years, with extra care. This is well within the scope of the average gardener, even if he is growing roses for the first time.

In selecting the site for roses, one should be aware that the roots of most trees extend at least as far as the outermost tips of the branches. Roots of trimmed hedges grow well beyond their width. Shrubs will fill the soil with a mass of fibrous roots. In every instance, roses set too close to any of these woody plants cannot compete with them to get the moisture and food they need to survive. Make allowance in the beginning for the ultimate size of nearby ornamentals.

Most roses attain normal growth when they get full sun for at least half the day. For richly colored hybrid teas and roses in other classes, morning sun is preferred to afternoon sun, particularly in climates where sunlight is intense and temperatures are high. The colors of many roses burn, bleach or become unattractive, even in one afternoon, under intense sunlight. Exposed only to morning sun, flowers will keep in good condition until the petals drop.

An average soil will support roses, but the better the soil, the less preparation is needed to make it acceptable. The quality of soil around the grounds may vary considerably from one part to another. Therefore, in selecting the site for a bed of roses, choose the best soil—provided the location fits into the plan for the layout of the garden.

Good drainage is vital. Low areas where rainwater collects and stands for a long time or ice forms in winter are not suited to roses. In some cases the soil remains soggy and damp because underlying layers of clay or hardpan keep water from draining into the subsoil. It is better to select another location for the roses rather than undertake the hard work of laying drain tiles (see page 743).

PLANTING

Preparation for Planting

Complete the soil preparation about three weeks before planting in order to allow the ground to settle. For spring planting, it is even suggested that the rose bed be prepared the preceding fall. Beds for hybrid teas, floribundas and grandifloras are best prepared by digging the whole area, mixing in humus and fertilizer in the process. Nearly all soils, especially sandy or clay soils, are improved by the addition of up to a 4-in. layer of compost, peat moss or other form of organic matter, thoroughly mixed with the soil to a depth of 12 in. Well-rotted manure is excellent where available. Add agricultural lime in amounts indicated by a soil test to correct strong soil acidity, but not to an alkaline soil (see page 742). Little plant food is needed at first by rosebushes. Small amounts of specially prepared rose fertilizer mixed completely into the soil will suffice. Organic plant foods are good.

The soil for individual plants set out as specimens in a flower border is made ready by digging separate holes and mixing plant food and humus thoroughly with the existing soil. Coarse materials, like rough compost and well-rotted manure, must be crumbled to make them fine, and mixed throughout the soil so they are not left in layers.

Rose beds may be of any shape. The length is immaterial, but the width does affect care and maintenance of the plants. Avoid excessively wide beds, since reaching between the thorny plants will be difficult.

When to Plant

Dormant rosebushes can be planted in late fall or early spring in most parts of the United States and some parts of southern Canada. The season selected depends upon several factors. One is the soil. In heavy soils which hold much moisture, planting in early spring often is more successful. The climate is of prime importance. Wherever winter temperatures rarely go below zero, or do not constantly fluctuate, fall planting is as good as spring. In the North, spring planting is preferred. This applies also to places exposed to cold winds. In southern states and in areas that have mild winters, midwinter planting is best.

Dormant roses shipped by nurseries are packed in several ways, and in each case the protective wrapping or package is designed to hold moisture around the roots and stems and to prevent the plant from drying during shipment. Stems of dormant roses may be coated with a waxlike substance to keep the bark, which is thin, from shriveling. The roots may be surrounded by moist moss or other absorbent material, or the whole plant tightly wrapped with a sheet of polyethylene film inside a carton. Packaged dormant roses in stores or nurseries also are enclosed and protected from dry air. Often these plants are held out of cold storage in stores or nurseries so long that top growth has started. The longer the shoots have grown inside the container, the weaker the plants.

If possible, plant roses as soon as they arrive. If for some reason they cannot be set out at once, leave them in the carton or package in a frost-proof cool place, out of sunlight. They may be held this way for a few days.

When bushes cannot be planted soon after arrival, unpack them and find a sheltered spot in the garden. Dig a trench and place them in it, on a slight slant, in a single row so that they can eventually be lifted a few at a time without disturbing the remainder. Cover the roots and most of the stems with soil, pressing it over the plants with the foot so it will not be loose. This is called "heeling in," and with this treatment the plants can safely be left for several weeks.

How to Plant

When plants are unpacked, plunge their roots in a pail of water. Cut off dead or broken roots and decayed or twiggy shoots. If the stems are at all shriveled, leave the whole plant in water for several hours, when it will usually freshen up.

Make the planting hole 15 to 18 in. wide and, except for tree roses, no deeper than will be required to bring the budding union (a bulge where the main stem starts) about level with the surface soil. Make a mound of fine soil in the middle of the hole. Hold the bush in the center of the hole and spread the roots out without bending or twisting them. Work in plenty of fine soil with the fingers, shaking the bush a little so that the soil falls through the roots and there are no air gaps left. Fill in more soil until the hole is half full and press it down firmly all around with the foot. Pour half a bucket of water around each bush. After this settles, replace the rest of

the soil. When this has been done the budding union should be level with the surface or not more than 1 in. beneath it. Always plant firmly, because loose planting encourages the development of suckers or wild growths from the stock on which the rose was budded. Deep planting is detrimental because subsequent manuring, feeding and mulching will gradually raise the soil level.

Newly planted dormant bushes need protection against drying. Hills of soil, drawn around the stems to a height of 6 to 8 in., are enough in most climates. This soil is left on all winter with fall-planted bushes, or until new shoots have sprouted after spring planting. In the coldest areas, additional winter cover of loose straw, salt hay or evergreen boughs will give plants extra protection.

Potted Roses

Rosebushes, growing in various kinds of containers—clay or plastic pots, pressed fiber or tin cans—can be planted at almost any time from spring to fall. These plants are useful in filling bare spaces in rose beds or other parts of the garden. Plants making healthy, vigorous growth and having two or more stems are the best; they may be fully grown and in bud or in bloom. Transplanting from

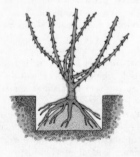

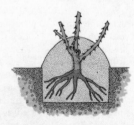

(Left) Proper planting of a rosebush
(Right) Pruning and protective mounding

pots to the garden is not hard to do, provided the ball of soil around the roots is kept intact during the process.

WHAT TO GROW

First decide on the types of roses to be grown. Nowadays the color range is very wide, probably greater than in any other flower. Roses of one color, two colors and multicolors are available in innumerable shades. One can choose from bush roses, standards or trees, climbers, ramblers, miniatures or shrub roses. The last class is dealt with on page 441 in "Shrubs and Flowering Small Trees."

Roses come in so many types, plant sizes and forms that an entire landscape planting could be made from roses alone. The best way to judge roses for oneself is to see them growing. There are hundreds of public gardens, botanical gardens and parks which contain rose collections. Information on varieties is supplied also in the publications of the American Rose Society.

Many people want to grow only fragrant roses and one often hears that modern varieties are scentless. There have always been roses with little or no scent, and many present-day varieties are just as fragrant as the old-timers. Almost all rose blooms will seem scentless unless the weather and atmospheric conditions are just right, for fragrance depends on the volatilization, or vaporization, of essential oils, which occurs chiefly in a warm, humid atmosphere. During cold, wet spells even the most highly scented varieties may have little or no fragrance.

Rose hybridists do not ignore fragrance when breeding new varieties, but unfortunately fragrance is a recessive, not a dominant, characteristic. If a new plant has vigor, color, abundance of bloom and all the other virtues but is merely lacking in scent,

the hybridist would be foolish to pass it over. On the other hand, if he has one which is strongly scented but is a weak grower, he will not offer it to the public.

Many new varieties of roses are introduced each year. No rose is released unless it is known to be superior to other varieties in its class. Qualities considered are color—its novelty, clarity, richness and stability during extremes in weather—bud form, flower form, doubleness, flower size, amount of bloom, strength and length of stem, foliage, disease resistance, plant habit and hardiness.

Some firms have established an elaborate testing system through which, one or more years prior to introduction, promising seedlings are sent for observation to rosarians located in all parts of the country. Based on reports, the grower may judge whether his seedling will thrive under all sorts of climatic conditions. A rose that is good only in a limited geographical area will not be very profitable.

There is also the All-America Rose Selections testing program, operated by leading commercial rosebush growers, in which professional judges score numbered entries in trial gardens located in major climatic regions. Seedlings that score sufficiently high over a two-year period are given the A.A.R.S. award, which is noted in catalogues and on name tags. Most introducers also patent their new roses, and the patent number appears on tags and with descriptions. A patent protects the grower against unscrupulous competition, but it is no guarantee that the variety has exceptional quality.

Hybridists must continue to offer new rose varieties regularly, not only because the public demands them but also to replace those that fall by the wayside. As with other products of which new models must be advertised each year, so with roses. Occasionally a newly introduced rose proves to be sensational and sets the style for future novelties. Such roses were the hybrid teas Peace and Charlotte Armstrong and the floribunda Fashion. So successful were these varieties that breeders have used them as parents for scores of introductions during the last 20 years. Examples of hybrid teas with a long record of reliability include red Crimson Glory and Etoile de Hollande, pink Radiance and Dainty Bess (single) and yellow- and pink-tinted Peace.

Bush Roses

These vary in height from 1½ to 6 ft. or so, according to variety and method of pruning. They are represented by hybrid teas, floribundas and grandifloras as well as the informal shrub types or species, usually grown as single specimens and not in formal beds.

Hybrid teas are the mainstay of gardens. Their blooms are borne either singly or in twos and threes. Where roses of real quality are desired, they are the first choice. They vary in height between 1½ and 5 ft.

The floribundas, formerly known as hybrid polyanthas, carry their blooms in clusters or trusses. They flower profusely, are excellent for cutting and are exceptionally hardy even where prolonged low temperatures are experienced. Heights differ considerably, from moderately vigorous varieties up to 2 ft., which are suitable for fronts of borders, to the taller kinds, which may reach 5 ft. or so with light pruning.

Floribunda dwarfs are bushy, unusually low-growing varieties. They vary in height from about 12 to 20 in., and some are ideal for edging.

The flowers of grandifloras are larger than those of floribundas. Sev-

Hybrid Tea

Floribunda

eral are clustered on long stems. Plants grow upright and taller than floribundas, often exceeding 6 ft.

Most kinds of bush roses can be spaced 20 in. apart, the compact growers rather closer, say 16 to 18 in., and the very vigorous varieties farther apart, say up to 2 ft. In southern gardens, vigorous varieties may need 3 ft. or more. Bush roses are more effective when they are staggered rather than planted in straight rows.

Tree or Standard Roses

Hybrid teas and floribundas are also grown in tree form. Buds or "eyes" are taken from the chosen variety and budded onto brier, *Rosa rugosa* or other hardy stems about 3½ ft. tall (see Budding of Tree Roses, page 218). Only the more vigorous hybrid teas, such as Tropicana, John S. Armstrong, Peace and Kordes' Perfecta, make really effective standards, especially if they have a bushy, spreading habit of growth.

Before planting rose trees, treat stakes with a wood preservative from the bottom to a couple of inches above ground level; then drive them firmly into the ground at least 6 ft. apart. After planting, tie each tree to its stake in three places, making one tie just below the budding union at the top of the stem or trunk, another halfway up and a third toward the base.

Ramblers and Climbers

These are often slow starters and will not produce a profusion of flowers for at least two years after planting. They are, however, very long-lived. They can be grown on pillars, arches, pergolas, fences and walls.

There is a basic difference between ramblers and climbers. Ramblers are very vigorous, somewhat lax growers, and bear a heavy crop of small flowers in clusters. Climbers make fewer basal shoots; the growths are stiffer, the flowers are individual and much larger. Some varieties bloom more or less continuously.

If the plants are to be grown against walls or fences, place them not less than 10 ft. apart, so that their long shoots can spread out properly. If climbers are to grow on house walls, plant them 15 in. away from the house to allow moisture to reach the roots. Keep the surrounding soil clear of other plants for about 18 in. in all directions. If a rose is to be grown up a pillar or post, plant the rose 12 in. away from it and tie it loosely to the post. Pruning is very important, as all ramblers and some climbers bloom on shoots which have grown during the previous year (see page 214).

Miniature Roses

These range from 6 to 15 in. high. The tiny individual blooms are often perfect replicas of hybrid teas. The foliage is also proportionately smaller. All varieties are excellent for edgings of beds of floribundas or hybrid teas, as well as for window boxes or rock gardens.

For limited periods they can be grown in the living room in pots or planter boxes with some success. They dislike a dry atmosphere and normal house temperatures. One method is to raise them in a greenhouse until the buds are showing, then transfer them to a really cool room and spray them night and morning with clear water. As soon as the first crop of bloom is over, return them to the greenhouse until more buds appear. As an experiment in keeping them indoors all year, stand each pot in a large pan or saucer containing at least 1 in. of damp peat moss. Keep the peat moss fairly moist except in winter, and take the pots out of doors during summer showers.

For the garden, choose a sunny place, and soil which is reasonably retentive of moisture but is perfectly drained. If the soil is on the dry side, work in plenty of damp peat moss or compost. Since the plants are very small, do not let them become crowded by taller roses.

Filling Gaps in Old Rose Beds

Countless disappointments have been caused by planting new rosebushes in an established bed, to replace plants that have died, without changing the existing soil. Preparing a hole is not sufficient. Soil which has grown roses for many years gradually becomes "rose-sick" since all roses take considerable quantities of plant nutrients from the soil. The existing roses will, however, continue to flourish for many years because their roots are constantly spreading to new areas which have untapped supplies of plant foods.

If a gap is to be filled, first remove the soil for each new bush to at least 12 in. deep and 18 in. across and exchange it for soil from another part of the garden where roses have not been grown. (In the case of well-established climbers and ramblers make the hole 18 in. deep and not less than 2 ft. across.) Then prepare the ground in the usual way. This is hard work but it is a basic necessity. Empty spaces that exist in early spring or late fall can be filled with dormant plants. During the growing season use potted roses.

Moving Roses Out of Season

Roses may be successfully moved at any time of the year, even in full flower and when the soil is dry, provided certain precautions are taken.

Remove all buds and flowers, but do not cut them with long stems. Lift each plant carefully, cutting back any extra long roots. There is

no need to lift with a ball of soil, but cover the roots and lower portions of the stems with damp burlap, since it is even more important in the summer than during the normal planting season that the roots are never allowed to become dry. Replant the roses in their new location as soon as possible, having first removed all leaves and "puddled" the roots—that is, dipped the roots in a bucket containing water and enough fine soil to form mud.

Firm planting is vital. Water freely if the soil is dry, and continue watering if dry weather persists. Spray the entire plant with clear water two or three times a day until fresh growth has started. A 2-in. mulch of damp peat moss spread around the base of the plant is also helpful.

Do not prune until new growth appears; then cut away any dead shoots. Some dieback invariably occurs, but there is no cause for anxiety.

Of course, when there is a choice, it is much safer to transplant roses when they are dormant, either in early spring or fall. Very old climbers and other heavy-growing kinds may be so deeply rooted as to make transplanting impractical, in or out of season.

PRUNING

For general instructions about pruning, see "Principles of Pruning," page 766.

The most common error made in pruning roses is the location of the cut in relation to the dormant eyes or buds on the stems. Every rose stem, either on a bush in a dormant state or on one in full growth, has a number of growing points, or buds, often hardly visible to the eye, which are capable of producing new stems. They are located at each joint along the stem. On dormant, leafless plants, the buds, hardly bigger than the

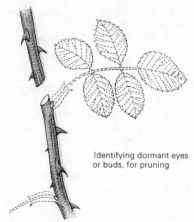

Identifying dormant eyes or buds, for pruning

point of lead in a pencil, may extend from a ringlike mark around the stem. On plants in leaf, the buds are in the angle formed by the leaf stem and the main stem.

New growth must originate from dormant buds. There are no growing points between joints or nodes along the stem. When a long section of stem above a bud is left after pruning, it must eventually die back to the next node below, and in doing so often becomes diseased, destroying the whole cane or stem. This is why cuts should be made no more than ¼ to ½ in. above a dormant bud, using sharp shears and being careful not to tear the bark or bruise the bud. Cuts made near nodes heal over in time, closing the wound.

Buds near the tops of stems grow first. When stems are left long, branches will be high aboveground; conversely, low pruning induces basal branching. In time, however, plants growing well may send up new stems from the base or crown.

The shape of a bush rose may be controlled to some extent by pruning so as to force new stems to grow away from the center of the plant. It is desirable to open up the middle of a bush to admit sunlight and air. By making all cuts just above dormant buds that face outward, the new shoots will extend away from the center.

Pruning Newly Planted Roses

Dormant bushes, shipped by nurseries, should require little pruning at planting time. All dead material, either root or stem, is pruned back to sound, healthy growth. Shorten very long roots. Stems thinner than a lead pencil should be pruned back to the base or to a main branch. Cut back remaining branches of hybrid teas, floribundas and grandifloras to not more than 12 in. high, if this was not done by the nursery. Make fresh cuts wherever long stubs have been left above nodes or dormant buds. Less pruning is required by climbing and shrub roses, because the original stems will be pruned off at the base one to two years after planting to make space for the new growth which bears the flowers. All dormant roses planted in fall are left unpruned until spring, since some branches may partially die back during winter.

Packaged dormant roses are pruned as for plants shipped by mail. If any rose plant has been in storage long enough to grow pale-colored sprouts, these should be snipped back to the main stem. It is easiest to do all pruning before the bushes are planted rather than afterward.

Potted rosebushes in full foliage need very little pruning, but spindly stems should be removed.

Tree or standard roses: Hybrid tea and floribunda trees generally have been pruned before delivery. The tops of dormant plants should be balanced, with the stems that form the head of the tree being nearly equal in length. Side shoots on the main stem below the head or at the base must be cut off.

214

Pruning Established Roses

Hybrid teas: Prune hybrid teas in early spring when new growth shows signs of starting. The basic idea is to encourage the plant to make a reasonably open, cup-shaped bush. This admits light and air, reducing danger of mildew and black-spot diseases. Remove wood several years old, which tends to harbor diseases and pests. The bark of winter-damaged stems generally is brown or discolored and must be cut back to healthy wood, which is indicated by white or greenish-white pith.

Remove soft wood, easily identified by gently pressing the thorns on the stem. If the wood is soft, the thorns break off with effort, but on ripe growth they will snap off readily.

Cut back the remaining shoots to half their length, more or less, leaving strong ones decidedly longer than thin, weak ones. The garden effect desired must be considered; hard pruning results in fewer, longer-stemmed blooms than light pruning. If it is necessary to encourage fresh basal growth, reduce an occasional old shoot to within 3 or 4 in. of its base.

Hybrid perpetuals: Prune as recommended for hybrid teas but leave stems approximately 2 ft. long.

Floribundas and grandifloras: Prune these early in spring. First remove all dead, diseased and damaged wood. Crisscross shoots should also be cut right out. Leave the remaining shoots at various lengths to help insure continuity of bloom. Center stems may be left taller than outer ones to form a well-shaped plant.

Ramblers: When flowering is over, cut out at their bases as many of the old flowering canes as can be spared (all of them, if enough new shoots are developing from the bottom of the plant to replace those that have bloomed) and train and tie the new shoots into place. If there are not enough strong new shoots to replace all of the old canes, retain some of the youngest and the more vigorous of the old ones, cut back their side branches to within 2 or 3 in. of their bases, and tie them into place, including as many of the new shoots as there are present.

Climbers: These have a potential for blooming more than once during the summer. Some produce only a light second crop of flowers; others are a little more profuse. The final pruning of these can be delayed until spring, but some cutting out may have to be done in summer to assure light and air for new shoots developing low on the canes.

Pruning is a modified form of that recommended for ramblers. The modification consists of retaining more second- and even third-year shoots (their side branches trimmed back as advised for ramblers), because they do not produce strong new shoots from the base nearly as freely as do ramblers. Climber varieties differ a great deal in vigor and freedom and continuity of bloom, but the general rule is to spare the knife. Climbing sports of hybrid teas in particular resent hard pruning. Never allow them to grow upward; train the main shoots fanwise or horizontally, because most blooms are produced on the laterals.

Prune climbers trained on pillars as described for regular climbers, except that old stems which are too tall should be pruned to the height of the post, and as new growth gets too long, it may be shortened at any time of year.

Miniatures: Miniature roses need little pruning. Simply trim the plants to

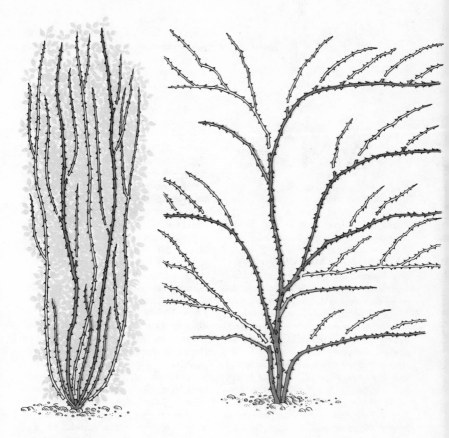

Rambler pruned after blooming

Spring pruning of a leafless climber

the desired shape and cut back to half their length any strong shoots which emerge from below soil level. When branches stop flowering, snip them back to a new side shoot.

Suckers

These are growths from the stock on which the rose has been budded. They occur not only on bush roses, but also on climbers, ramblers and even tree roses. As all suckers come from below the budding union they can be easily identified by drawing soil away to check this point. Also, the color and number of leaflets is different from that of the cultivated variety. Cut the suckers right out at the point of origin on the roots or neck of the stock. Use a sharp knife, which will make a cleaner cut than shears. All side shoots along the

To obtain large terminal blooms,
pinch out the side buds.

trunk of a tree rose should be removed as soon as they appear.

FEEDING AND MANURING

Some amateurs underfeed rather than
overfeed their roses. When this is the
case, one should not hesitate to give a
"boost" to any established rosebush
which is reluctant to make fresh
growth. It is often said that aphids
and other pests thrive on the soft,
sappy shoots produced by the heavy
use of chemical fertilizers, but heavy
infestations are by no means confined to such growth. It is advisable
not to use commercial fertilizers on
newly planted roses until they are
fully rooted in.

The main elements concerned with
plant growth are nitrogen, phosphorus, potash and, to a lesser extent,
minor or "trace" elements such as
magnesium. Roses rarely suffer from
nitrogen deficiency, which can be
recognized by pale green leaves and
weak growth. Typical signs of phosphorus deficiency are bronze or purplish markings on the foliage, as well
as fewer, smaller blooms. Shortage
of available potash is more evident
on light, sandy soil. It causes rose-

bushes to look scorched, with browning on the edges of the leaves.

Rose Fertilizers

These usually contain nitrogen, phosphorus and potash in varying proportions, and minor elements as well.
The proportions required by roses are
not vital and almost any brand-name
fertilizer will give good results if applied according to the manufacturer's
instructions. A conventional 5-10-5
commercial fertilizer can be used, or
one made especially for roses. Do not
apply during a drought unless the
roses will be watered regularly afterward. Spread fertilizer between the
bushes, so that it can be washed in
by the rain or with the hose and reach
the feeding rootlets which are concentrated away from the base of the
stems. All chemical fertilizers should
be regarded as supplementary to organic materials like rotted farmyard
manure and compost.

Foliar Feeding

The spraying of foliage with liquid
plant food instead of applying it to
the roots has recently achieved some
popularity among rose growers. It is
not an alternative to conventional
feeding methods, if only because considerably more applications would be
needed during the growing season.
Young foliage seems to take up nutrients more readily than older leaves.
Temporary nutrient deficiencies—of
magnesium and iron, for instance—
can be corrected as they appear by
foliar, or leaf, feeding, but exact directions for their use cannot be given
here. Experiment by trying one of the
foliar plant foods now available, taking care to follow the manufacturer's
instructions.

MULCHING

Do not spread compost or old farmyard manure around rosebushes in

winter, since this keeps the ground cold and wet. Instead, use it as a summer mulch to conserve moisture. Many other products are available to mulch roses, including ground corncobs, buckwheat hulls, shredded tree bark and peat moss.

If the mulching of roses is unsuccessful, it is because the mulch has been carelessly applied. Timing is important. Wait until new growth is well along and the soil is rapidly warming up. Remove all traces of weeds and thoroughly wet the soil immediately before mulching. Cultivate fertilizer into the soil. Spread the mulch loosely to permit free circulation of air, the depth depending upon the product. Keep lawn mowings very loose and no deeper than 1 in. when they have settled; they tend to pack down tightly and may introduce weeds.

Leave the mulch undisturbed until early October. At this time, organic materials such as old manure may be worked into the soil. Remove coarse materials prior to hilling soil around the stems for winter protection.

WINTER PROTECTION

Bush roses such as hybrid teas, floribundas and grandifloras are winter-hardy in all but the coldest northern states, mountain areas and some parts of Canada, when they are given conventional winter protection. This consists of a hill of soil banked against the base of the plant to a height of 8 to 10 in. late in fall after growth has stopped and most leaves have dropped off. Even though the tops of some canes may freeze back, sections below soil level will survive and be the source of new flowering stems next year.

Where subzero temperatures prevail, these roses need more cover. This should be light, airy material, such as cut evergreen boughs, coarse straw, salt hay or dry oak leaves. These are worked between the plants in such a way as to protect upper parts of the plant from wind and sun during winter. Where necessary, fence in rose beds with 1-ft.-high wire cloth to confine these materials.

Stems of bush roses taller than 3 ft. should be shortened somewhat in late fall. This makes it easier to work between the plants and also lessens winter breakage from ice and snow. Other bush roses, including types such as rugosa hybrids, species like *Rosa hugonis* and most hybrid perpetuals, can stand severe cold.

It is hard to winter over climbing roses that are grown to the north of their natural range of hardiness. Commercial firms generally use discretion and will not ship tender varieties into northern areas. Within some classes of climbers, varieties differ in their degree of hardiness. As an example, among hybrid teas, the climbing forms of Peace, Talisman and Crimson Glory are reasonably hardy wherever the bush forms will grow, whereas climbing sports of other hybrid teas may do well only in southern states and on the West Coast. Climbers of doubtful hardiness should be sheltered. Plants against south-facing walls or fences need to be shielded against the sun and wind with burlap tied over or around the plants. Other loose materials can be used, but avoid tight covers such as polyethylene film. In extreme climates take climbers off their support in late fall, bend them over to the ground and cover the entire plant with soil.

South of New York, tree roses can stand out over winter with limited protection. Shorten the branches of the head first, and wrap the whole top in burlap sacking. Then wrap the entire trunk in heavy paper. Make sure the trunk is securely tied to its supporting stake. Wherever winter temperatures drop toward zero or below, dig tree roses carefully to get up all the roots and bury the whole tree in a shallow trench. Choose a place where drainage is good. Dig and replant trees in spring when there is no longer any danger of hard frost.

WATERING

Watering is seldom needed on heavy soils, except in very dry weather. On light soils watering is often necessary, especially during long spring and summer droughts and where roses are grown alongside walls.

Choose a watering method, such as porous hose, that will wet the soil but not the foliage. Diseases spread rapidly when the leaves remain wet. When overhead sprinklers must be used, water roses in the morning so that the foliage will have dried off by nightfall.

Give each plant plenty of water. Do not just sprinkle the surface soil; this will only encourage the feeding rootlets to come to the surface, where they can easily become dried up. Where only a few rosebushes are grown, a good plan is to sink a flowerpot in the soil about 9 in. from each plant, setting the rim level with the soil surface. Fill each pot several times and replenish every two or three days until the drought breaks.

PROPAGATION

Budding

Roses bought from the nurseryman have all been grown as budded plants. Budding consists of taking a bud or "eye" of the chosen variety and inserting it in the bark of a vigorous selected form such as *R. multiflora*. This is known as the stock and it provides the roots of the new plant, which is sold by the nurseryman about 15 months later. The details of budding, described and illustrated in "How to Raise New Plants" (see page 696), can be followed exactly for budding bush roses, climbers and ramblers.

Budding of Tree Roses

Several different kinds of rose stock are used for the trunk and root system of tree roses, including *rugosa* and a selected strain of *multiflora*. For these the actual budding is the same as for bush roses, although the buds are inserted in a different position. Understocks are trained to have a clean trunk with no side branches lower than 3½ ft. This trunk is tied to a stake to hold it erect. Two or more buds are inserted in different positions around the main stem, directly under the top growths. Usually these will remain dormant until the following spring, when the top of the understock is pruned just above the buds. Hybrid teas, floribundas and even trailing-type roses will all make very good trees.

Cuttings

Propagation by cuttings is generally not as successful as by budding. Commercially the method is quite impracticable since a shoot which provides several buds yields only one cutting, and budding is much quicker. Even if the cutting should root, it may subsequently die or fail to make a sizable bush. Hybrid teas are usually failures in northern states, though in the South they often do well. Floribundas are likelier to succeed, the crimson-scarlet Frensham in particular making an acceptable plant in most cases. Climbers, ramblers and many of the old-fashioned varieties such as the albas, centifolias, gallicas and Bourbons, root fairly readily and eventually make satisfactory plants.

The period immediately following spring bloom is the best time to take cuttings. Use the stems that have just flowered, before new side shoots start to grow. The procedure is described in "How to Raise New Plants," page 696. Leave the cuttings in the soil for about 15 months, then move them to their permanent quarters, where they may be expected to bloom the following summer.

PESTS AND DISEASES

Insects that attack roses may be divided into several groups. Those such as aphids suck plant juices from tender new growth and young flower buds, which must be covered with what is called a "contact insecticide" as soon as the insects appear. When more of these insects occur, spraying must be repeated. Systemic insecticides also show promise of controlling sucking insects.

Chewing insects (including Japanese beetles), which eat leaves, flower buds and blooms, form another group. They are controlled by keeping all parts of the plant covered with insecticide. By learning when to expect these pests and following a regular application program, a rose grower can prevent these insects from disfiguring the plants. Numerous products will maintain a protective coating satisfactorily, though they vary as to the length of time during which they are potent (see page 807 in "Plant Pests").

Pests attack plants in other ways, including boring down through the center of the stem. Once inside, the pest is beyond the reach of an insecticide, and the hollowed stems eventually die. At signs of weakened stems, prune them back to solid wood, thus eradicating the pest. To avoid further attacks, cover exposed ends of stems with a tree paint after pruning.

Major diseases are black spot, mildew and rust. Black spot may appear at first as yellowish areas on leaves, darkening later. Lower leaves are infected first. Mildew often starts to show on young new foliage as a whitish coating. The leaves curl or become crippled. Rust is serious in a few areas, such as the West Coast. Its symptom is the appearance of orange spots on the leaves.

Canker is a disease of the stems. Areas of bark turn brown; when they encircle the stem it dies. In general, canker disease enters the stems through bark injury and winter frost damage. Pruning stems back to green wood helps to restore plants to health and eliminate the disease.

Technical advances in developing effective fungicides and insecticides have simplified the problem of disease and pest control. The sprays and dusts available include separate materials to control specific rose enemies (see "Plant Diseases," page 774 and "Plant Pests," page 806), and proprietary mixtures of insecticides and fungicides. Though the cost may be higher, usually it is most satisfactory to use a complete rose spray or dust on a regular application program. Then it is unnecessary to attempt to identify each pest or disease and select a product for its control.

To be effective, spray should cover both upper and lower surfaces of the leaves with a fine mist. It is particularly important, for black-spot control, to cover the bottom leaves. For aphids, the spray must cover the insects, including young ones which hide under the foliage and in between new leaves.

Dusts weigh less than liquids and can be applied with little effort, but they must cover all leaf surfaces to be effective. They do blow in the wind, and should be put on when the air is still or toward evening. Dusts cannot be used in wet weather; sprays can. The best dusters eject the dust as a cloud of fine particles that envelop the plant.

Complete control of pests and diseases is possible through repeated applications of reliable materials, beginning when the first leaves reach maturity and continuing through the summer. Applications may be every seven to ten days, depending upon the frequency of rains.

COMPANIONS FOR ROSES

Ideally, roses should be planted in beds or borders where there is little or no competition from other flowers and shrubs, even in winter. If, however, space is limited, other flowers may be combined with them either by widening the rose bed to leave space in the foreground, or by planting rosebushes and flowers in alternate groups. With care, the results can be very pleasing. Avoid strong-growing, spreading plants; there are plenty of other intriguing possibilities. For interplanting with beds of hybrid teas and floribundas or as edgings to rose beds, try dwarf annuals such as the deep blue *Phacelia campanularia*, or candytuft in mixed colors or *Ne-*

mophila menziesii (baby blue-eyes), sky-blue with white center. *Ageratum* Fairy Pink is a pleasing salmon-rose and *Alyssum* Violet Queen is compact, as is the white variety Carpet of Snow. The most compact types of petunias are good, too.

Pinks are sometimes used for edgings and are also very effective when planted in between tree roses grown in rows. A groundwork of violas or pansies is equally satisfactory.

Tulips, daffodils and other spring-flowering bulbs will add color to rose beds in advance of the rose bloom. They can be planted in open soil in the forepart of a rose bed or in open spaces between groups of bushes. For later color, interplant annuals between clusters of bulbs.

Tall-growing lilies are also suitable, particularly where there is space for them to the rear of a rose bed.

CHAPTER 9

BIENNIALS

Popular Biennials—Seed Sowing— Care of Seedlings—Planting Out— Winter Protection

BIENNIALS take two years from the seedling stage to the production of ripe seed. They grow during the first year; flower, fruit and die in the second. In addition to true biennials, it is convenient, for one reason or

another, to grow a few kinds of perennial plants as if they were biennials and to discard them after their first blooming. These plants are often listed as biennials.

Seeds of biennials are sown in the open or in a cold frame any time from about the middle of May to the end of July. The earlier sowings generally give better results because they produce sizable plants which are well established before winter. On the other hand, in some cases, as with pansies and wallflowers, if the plants are too large in the fall they may winter badly. Trials of different sowing dates may be made to determine the best for any particular locality. The seeds of biennials are sown in rows and later are transplanted to nursery beds or to cold frames. Finally the plants are moved into their permanent quarters either in the fall, if winters are comparatively mild, or in early spring.

POPULAR BIENNIALS

ALTHAEA (HOLLYHOCK)

Hollyhocks are perennials, but because they are so very susceptible to a disfiguring fungus rust disease it is often most satisfactory to grow them as biennials. Tall and stately, with single or double flowers in white, pink, red, maroon, purple or yellow, they are excellent for providing accents in a flower border, along a fence, against a building or in other places where strong, vertical lines are attractive. They bloom in early to midsummer. They thrive best in full sun but will stand a little shade. They should be spaced about 2 ft. apart in any fertile, well-drained garden soil. Hollyhocks are varieties of *Althaea rosea*.

BACHELOR'S BUTTON. See *Bellis*.

BELLFLOWER. See *Campanula*.

BELLIS

(ENGLISH DAISY, BACHELOR'S BUTTON)
Varieties of *Bellis perennis* are low rosette plants which for a long period in spring bear numerous solitary flower heads, each 1 to 2 in. in diameter, on 6-in. stalks. In the varieties commonly grown the flowers are double, although a small proportion

of single-flowered or semidouble-flowered individuals are likely to occur. The colors are white, pink and crimson. English daisies prefer full sun and a moderately rich, well-drained loamy soil. Where winter temperatures drop to as low as 10° above zero F. it is best to winter the plants in cold frames. They are excellent for edging flower beds and for use as underplantings for spring bulbs such as tulips. Set the plants 8 to 9 in. apart.

BLANKETWEED. See *Verbascum*.

CAMPANULA (BELLFLOWER)

The most popular biennial campanula is the Canterbury bell. Like other kinds, it prefers a deep soil rich in humus, and an open, semisunny place. Fork in bone meal lightly at 4 oz. per sq. yd.

Campanula medium (Canterbury bell), 1 to 4 ft., flowers in March and April in the South, in May or June farther north. There are a number of varieties, usually listed under their colors. Some have cup-and-saucer-like flowers and some bear double blooms. Dean's Hybrids are vigorous and produce flowers in mixed shades of blue, pink and white. Most of them have double flowers. Plant Canterbury bells 1 to 1½ ft. apart.

C. pyramidalis (chimney bellflower) may grow to 4 ft. when planted in a sheltered place. Produces pale blue or white saucer-shaped flowers each measuring 1 in. or more in diameter, blooming in succession from late spring until late summer. This kind is suitable for growing outdoors only where winters are nearly frost-free; elsewhere it must be regarded as a greenhouse plant. Set plants 1½ to 2 ft. apart.

CANTERBURY BELL. See *Campanula medium*.

CHEIRANTHUS (WALLFLOWER)
These bushy plants grow up to 2 ft. high, with spikes of velvety flowers in reds or yellows. There are many different types—dwarf and tall. All are grown as spring bedding plants.

Cheiranthus allionii (syn. *Erysimum asperum*—Siberian wallflower). A splendid plant, about 1 ft. high, for early summer bedding, especially for interplanting with tulips. It flowers a little later than the English wallflower and lasts longer. Good varieties are Orange Queen and Golden Bedder. Plant 10 to 12 in. apart.

C. cheiri (English wallflower), 1 to 2 ft. Decidedly useful for spring bedding; very sweetly scented. Named varieties have orange, yellow, red, pink or brown flowers in spring and early summer. They prefer well-limed soils and will bloom in partial shade or full sun. It is a good plan to transplant the young plants twice during their early growth to encourage the

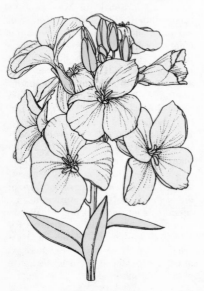

Cheiranthus cheiri
(English Wallflower)

development of plenty of fibrous roots, and to pinch back the tops with thumb and forefinger once or twice to insure bushiness. English wallflowers are slightly tender and in climates where winter temperatures reach as low as 15° above zero F. it is wise to winter them in protected cold frames. Plant them out 10 to 12 in. apart.

C. kewensis, 9 in., the winter-flowering hybrid with darkish orange flowers fading to purple. Blooms during mild periods from January onward. It is adapted only for regions of quite mild winters. Set plants 9 to 10 in. apart.

CHIMNEY BELLFLOWER. See *Campanula pyramidalis*.

CHINESE FORGET-ME-NOT. See *Cynoglossum amabile*.

COMMON FOXGLOVE. See *Digitalis purpurea*.

CYNOGLOSSUM (HOUND'S-TONGUE)
Similar to the forget-me-not but taller, with arching sprays of tiny flowers and rough leaves, this plant thrives in any ordinary soil. Sow the seed in June and plant out 10 to 12 in. apart either in September or in April.

Cynoglossum amabile (Chinese forget-me-not), 2 ft., produces masses of bright blue, pink or white flowers in early summer.

DAME'S VIOLET. See *Hesperis*.

DIANTHUS (PINK)
The plants produce large, flattish heads of sweet-scented, velvety flowers. They do equally well in partial shade or sun.

Dianthus barbatus (sweet William), 1 to 2 ft. There are many varieties, such as Crimson Beauty, Pink Beauty,

Scarlet Beauty, Newport Pink and
the very striking *"oculatus marginatus"* strain, the flowers of which have
white central eyes surrounded by
bands of other colors. Space plants 10
to 12 in. apart. In climates such as
that of New York City, sweet Williams
should be overwintered in cold frames;
in milder climates they will live
through the winter outdoors and may
be safely planted in their flowering
quarters in fall.

DIGITALIS (FOXGLOVE)
The biennial foxgloves are tall, erect
plants bearing long tubular white,
purple or rose-colored flowers. They
prefer a moderately rich soil and a
partially shaded location and often
seed themselves. Because of this,
quite often there is no need to sow
seed each year to maintain a continuity of display. Set the plants 9 to
12 in. apart.

Digitalis ferruginea, 5 ft., oblong
leaves and long spikes of brownish-
red flowers in summer.

D. purpurea (common foxglove),
3 to 6 ft., bears large purple- or red-
spotted flowers in June and July.
There are some excellent hybrids
(such as Excelsior) with white, yellow or red flowers carried all around
the stem. The Shirley strain of this
plant is magnificent and produces
blotched and spotted flowers of great
beauty.

ENGLISH DAISY. See *Bellis*.

ENGLISH WALLFLOWER. See *Cheiranthus cheiri*.

FORGET-ME-NOT. See *Myosotis*.

FOXGLOVE. See *Digitalis*.

HESPERIS
(SWEET ROCKET, DAME'S VIOLET)
It is grown for its delightfully scented

Digitalis purpurea
(Common Foxglove)

white or purple flowers that are at their best from June to September. The most commonly grown is *Hesperis matronalis*. Plant 1 ft. apart.

Hesperis matronalis, really a perennial but grown as a biennial, 3 ft.; beautiful erect plant of which there are a number of varieties.

H.m. alba, 1½ to 2 ft., pure white. A dwarf white-flowered variety sometimes called *nana candidissima* is offered by seedsmen.

H.m. purpurea, 1½ to 2 ft., deep mauve.

HOLLYHOCK. See *Althaea*.

HONESTY. See *Lunaria*.

HOUND'S-TONGUE. See *Cynoglossum*.

ICELAND POPPY. See *Papaver nudicaule*.

LUNARIA (HONESTY, SILVER DOLLAR) These erect plants, 2½ to 3 ft. high, have attractive large purple or violet flowers, followed by flat, disk-shaped seedpods, which are known as "silver dollars." When stripped, these are silvery; they are widely used for winter decoration. Set plants 1 ft. apart.

Lunaria annua, quick-growing, with pink or purple sweet-scented flowers.

L.a. alba, white.

L.a. Munstead Purple.

MATHIOLA (STOCK)

Mathiola incana. Brompton stocks and Midlothian stocks are biennials suitable for growing outdoors where there is only a little winter frost. In more severe regions they can be wintered in well-protected cold frames. They form bushy plants 1 to 1½ ft. high, and bear erect spikes of fragrant, mostly double, flowers—white, pink, red, lavender or purple, in late spring. The plants like sun and a well-drained soil that contains lime. Set them 9 to 12 in. apart.

MOTH MULLEIN. See *Verbascum blattaria*.

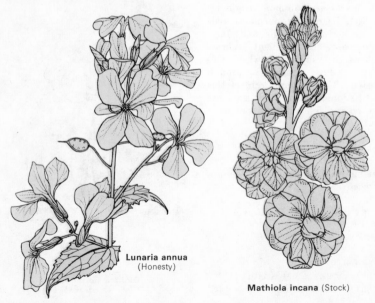

Lunaria annua
(Honesty)

Mathiola incana (Stock)

MULLEIN. See *Verbascum*.

MYOSOTIS (FORGET-ME-NOT)
A popular bedding plant because it produces a dense carpet of small sky-blue, pink or white flowers. Prefers a sunny or lightly shaded place. Likes a slightly acid soil, rich with humus. Plant 6 to 8 in. apart. Excellent as a ground cover beneath spring bulbs.
Myosotis alpestris, 6 to 10 in., spring-flowering; good varieties are Blue Bird, Victoria, Ruth Fisher and Pink Beauty.

PANSY. See *Viola*.

PAPAVER (POPPY)
Poppies are mostly perennials but a few kinds are treated as biennials. Sow the seed where the plants are to flower, because these plants resent disturbance. Thin the seedlings in two stages: to about 3 or 4 in. apart as soon as they are big enough to handle, and, two to three weeks later, to 6 to 9 in. apart.

Myosotis alpestris
(Forget-Me-Not)

Papaver alpinum, 6 to 8 in. An attractive rock-garden or edging plant with white flowers.
P. nudicaule (Iceland poppy) is the most important species grown as a biennial. It bears flower stems 1 ft. high and flowers in a range of colors from white through yellow to orange. There is a crimson-flowered variety called Red Cardinal; the best orange-flowered ones are Golden and Coonara Tangerine. The flowers are excellent for cutting.

PINK. See *Dianthus*.

POPPY. See *Papaver*.

SIBERIAN WALLFLOWER. See *Cheiranthus allionii*.

SILVER DOLLAR. See *Lunaria*.

STOCK. See *Mathiola*.

SWEET ROCKET. See *Hesperis*.

SWEET WILLIAM. See *Dianthus barbatus*.

VERBASCUM
(MULLEIN or BLANKETWEED)
Tall, erect plants with woolly leaves and spikes of yellow, red, purple or white flowers, they are good for planting toward the rear of a flower border. Prefer a moderately rich soil and, with the exception of the purple mullein, a sunny spot. Set plants 10 to 12 in. apart.
Verbascum blattaria (moth mullein), 4 ft., huge spikes of bright yellow flowers with purple stamens. Blooms in summer.
V. bombyciferum, 4 to 5 ft. Stems and leaves gray, downy. Flowers beautiful pale yellow.
V. hybridum, 6 ft., pure yellow flowers all summer; the best-known form is the Harkness Hybrid.

VIOLA (PANSY)

Both pansies (varieties of *Viola tricolor*) and garden violas (varieties and hybrids of *V. cornuta*) are truly perennials but are very widely grown as biennials for spring and early-summer flower display. They grow 6 to 8 in. high and produce a long succession of attractively colored flat-faced flowers. These plants prosper in any good garden soil and in full sun. A fertile soil rich in humus and not excessively dry is ideal.

The violas prefer cool conditions and are less tolerant of hot weather than are pansies. Both may be had in a wide variety of flower colors and combinations. Viola and pansy seed should not be sown before the end of July. When transplanted the seedlings should be set in well-drained soil, since excessive wetness in winter is very harmful. Where winters are severe the protection of a cold frame is very useful or even necessary. The flowering season of these plants is much prolonged if all faded blooms are picked promptly. Space these plants 8 to 9 in. apart.

WALLFLOWER. See *Cheiranthus*.

SEED SOWING OF BIENNIALS

Prepare a seedbed as for annuals or vegetables. Once the seedbed is level and the surface of the soil is fine, use a sturdy stake or the corner of a hoe blade against a taut line to make drills or furrows 1 in. deep and 9 in. apart. Soak the bottom of each drill with water carefully poured into it from the spout of a watering can or from a slowly running hose, before sowing. Sow the seeds thinly, then use the back of the rake to cover them.

CARE OF BIENNIAL SEEDLINGS

As soon as the seedlings show above the ground, cultivate lightly between the rows to keep down weeds. When the seedlings have developed their second pair of leaves, transplant them into nursery beds either in the open or in cold frames, allowing about 6 to 8 in. between individual plants. These transplanting beds should be prepared in the same way as the seedbeds but with some dried manure and bone meal added and thoroughly mixed with the soil.

PLANTING OUT

If practicable, plant out biennials during cloudy weather. If you must move the plants in sunny weather, spraying them with an antitranspirant (antidesiccant) before they are lifted is helpful.

When the time comes for planting out, dig up the plants from their nursery beds with balls of soil as big as possible. This is easier to do if the ground is well watered the day before. Put the plants with their balls of soil into shallow flats (boxes) so that they can be carried without breaking the soil. Prepare good-sized holes with the trowel so that the ball of soil may be inserted with a minimum of disturbance. Pack soil firmly around each plant and rake afterward to remove footmarks.

Water the plants thoroughly with a can fitted with a sprinkler, or soak the entire area with a sprinkler-fitted hose for at least half an hour. It may be necessary to water again two or three days later if the weather is dry. If the weather is sunny, shading for a few days immediately after moving assists recovery. Subsequent care consists of regular shallow cultivation, watering during dry weather and—when they are through blooming in the second year—pulling up the plants and consigning them to the compost heap.

Grow the young plants in as cool a place as possible throughout the summer and early fall to encourage development of sturdy, winter-resistant specimens. (Do not keep biennials growing in cold frames covered with glass or plastic sash during the summer and fall growing periods.) Keep weeds down by frequent surface cultivation, hand pulling close to the plants themselves. Watch out for aphids and other insects, and take prompt measures against them should infestations appear.

WINTER PROTECTION OF BIENNIALS

In sections where winter cold is likely to damage types that are not quite hardy and where their roots may be harmed by alternate freezing and thawing, some form of winter protection is recommended. After the ground has frozen to a depth of an inch or two, cover outdoor beds with a protectant that will admit some light as well as a reasonably free circulation of air. Pine and other evergreen branches and salt-marsh hay make good coverings.

Superior winter protection is afforded by cold frames, but great care must be exercised in ventilating these through the winter to make sure that the inside temperature is not too high. Whenever the outside temperature is above freezing, the frames should be aired freely. On very cold nights extra protection in the form of mats, wooden shutters or other suitable devices is helpful. A snow covering on frames gives good protection and should not be removed unless it lasts so long that plants begin to suffer from lack of light.

CHAPTER 10

HARDY BULBS

Bulbs and Corms—Uses—Planting—Kinds and Varieties

HARDY BULBS are a great asset to the garden, for they provide some of the earliest and the latest blooms, beginning with snowdrops and winter aconites and finishing with autumn cyclamens and autumn crocuses and colchicums. Such bulbs may be used in many different ways—in formal beds, in flower borders and rock gardens, between shrubs and under small trees. Many can be naturalized in rough grass or near the margins of lawns, where their foliage will not be mowed after blooming.

With hardy-bulb plants we have a vast choice, including not only the well known, but many kinds of lesser importance, though certainly not of less interest. Among them will be found both exotic and native American species—some of the easiest culture, some more demanding. There are kinds for rock gardens, for wild gardens, for planting beneath shrubs and trees and for other landscape purposes. There are kinds that bloom in spring, in summer, in fall, and those for different types of soil.

The term "bulb" has been used generally in this chapter to include both bulbs and corms as well as certain tuberous-rooted plants.

When a tulip bulb and a crocus corm are cut in half, the difference between a bulb and a corm is immediately apparent (see illustration below).

PLANTING

Bulbs normally like a good, well-drained loam. If the soil in which they are to be grown is not good, add well-rotted manure, well-rotted compost, peat moss or other organic material. Never add fresh manure when preparing soil for bulbs. If the soil is very heavy, add compost or peat moss as well as gritty coal cinders or coarse sand. In addition fork in a liberal dressing of bone meal, say 6 to 8 oz. per sq. yd., before planting. (Apply

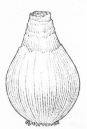

A bulb is composed of fleshy scales, like an onion, protecting a bud at the base.

A corm has the bud at the top and is a solid mass of starchy material.

bone meal as a topdressing each winter to bulbs which are not lifted.) Brand-name fertilizers, specially compounded for bulbs, can also be used.

Plant the bulbs, with the exception of the shade lovers, where they will get all the sun possible and where they will be sheltered from sweeping winds. Where bulbs are to be planted in grass, or when hundreds are to be planted, use a tool known as a "bulb planter." Otherwise make the holes with a trowel, but flatten them at the bottom so that the bulb sits on the soil and not on a pocket of air.

Most bulbs will increase in number if their conditions of cultivation are satisfactory. After three to five years lift and divide the clumps, or else there will be few flowers. Do this as soon as the leaves have died down, or better still, after the leaves have turned half yellow, as it is then easier to see where the bulbs are.

As a rule, bulbs require ample watering during the season when their foliage is green and growing actively, and much drier conditions during their periods of summer dormancy. Great care should be taken not to remove any foliage until it has died down naturally. When cutting flowers, leave as much foliage as possible: the leaves are the food-manufacturing organs, and it is their function to prepare food enough to be transported to and stored in the bulbs to insure sturdy growth and flower production the following year.

RECOMMENDED HARDY BULBS

ADDER'S-TONGUE. See *Erythronium*.

ALLIUM

Some of the members of the onion genus, despite the odor they emit when bruised or cut, are very decorative in the garden and quite easy to grow in almost any soil. The smaller ones are useful for rock gardens and flower from May to July. Others are good for cutting. When stems are cut, immerse them in plenty of cold water overnight, and the smell will have disappeared by the next day.

Plant anywhere, except in full shade, in fall—the large bulbs with their tips 3 or 4 in. deep and the bulbs about 1 ft. apart, and the small ones 2 in. deep and 2 to 6 in. apart.

Allium albopilosum grows to a height of 1 to 1½ ft. and has nearly globular heads, 8 in. in diameter, of star-shaped lilac-colored flowers. It is useful for cutting.

A. beesianum, 6 to 12 in., with clear blue flowers. Likes a moister soil than the others.

A. caeruleum (syn. *A. azureum*), 1 to 2 ft., sky-blue. Plant in well-drained, dryish soil.

A. farreri, 3 in., the smallest of all, with drooping heads of small, red-purple blossoms.

A. flavum, gray leaves, golden flowers on 6-in. stems.

A. giganteum is an amazing and very ornamental kind which attains a height of 4 to 5 ft. and in July bears colossal heads of rosy-violet flowers which last a long time when cut.

A. karataviense, 8 in., pink. Lovely leaves, but flowers rather straggly for the garden though good for dry winter bouquets.

A. moly, 9 to 12 in., has broad leaves and umbels of bright yellow flowers in June. This kind thrives in light shade. It is excellent for naturalizing and for flower arrangements.

A. neapolitanum is not reliably hardy in regions of severe winters, but where it will survive is one of the best for naturalizing. Its pure white flowers are fine for cutting.

A. odorum, a late-summer or early-fall bloomer. This is one of the best. It forms dense leafy clumps and produces numerous erect stems 1½ to 2 ft. tall, each topped by a cluster of pure white, very fragrant flowers that are especially attractive to butterflies. A fine plant for the perennial border.

A. ostrowskianum is a dwarf species well suited for rock gardens. Its large heads of rosy-purple flowers are carried on 6-in. stems in June.

A. rosenbachianum is a tall-growing, handsome plant that bears large, dense heads of rich purple-rose flowers in May. The flowering stems are 3 to 4 ft. tall.

A. r. album is identical with the above except that the flowers are white.

A. zebanense is a white-flowered kind, 1 to 1½ ft. high, which blooms in May or early June and is excellent for naturalizing.

AMIANTHIUM

Native American bulb related to *Zigadenus*, not very showy but of interest for planting in wild gardens. Plant in fall 6 to 12 in. apart and 3 to 4 in. deep. Prefers light shade and rich woodland soil.

Amianthium muscaetoxicum (fly poison), 2 to 4 ft., racemes of small white flowers in summer.

ANEMONE (WINDFLOWER)

Several tuberous anemones are suitable for rock gardens and wild gardens; they flourish in light shade and rich, moderately moist woodland soil. All are spring bloomers. Plant in early fall.

Anemone apennina, 3 to 6 in., blue, pink and white. Similar to *A. blanda* in appearance.

A. blanda, 3 to 6 in., blue, violet, pink and white. Stands considerable sun. See illustration, next page.

A. nemorosa (European wood anemone), 6 to 8 in. Comes in various colors—white, purple, lavender, blue and pink.

A. quinquefolia (American wood anemone), 4 to 8 in. Similar to *A. nem-*

Anemone blanda (Windflower)

orosa, but has smaller white flowers.

A. ranunculoides (yellow wood anemone), 4 to 6 in. A delightful plant of easy culture. Has bright yellow 1-in. flowers.

ANEMONELLA

Anemonella thalictroides (rue anemone), 3 to 6 in. A North American woodland plant suitable for naturalizing and for rock gardens. Needs rich, fairly moist, woodland soil. Plant 2 or 3 in. deep and 3 to 6 in. apart, in shaded places in naturalistic colonies. The delicate foliage and white or light pink flowers appear in spring.

ARISAEMA

These are tuberous-rooted plants with oddly colored calla-lily-type flower heads, and spikes of bright red berries. Jack-in-the-pulpit is the best known. They are adapted for planting in shaded and woodland areas where the soil is rich with leaf mold or other decayed organic matter, deep and moderately moist.

Arisaema candidissimum, 1 to 2 ft., white or tinged pink.

A. dracontium (dragonroot), 2 to 3 ft., green or greenish.

A. triphyllum (jack-in-the-pulpit), 1 to 2 ft. The spathe is green striped with purple.

ARUM

Relatives of the calla lily, these are suitable for partly shaded places in rock gardens and woodland gardens. Give them rich soil that contains an abundance of reasonably moist humus. Plant in fall, 4 in. deep and 8 to 10 in. apart. The red berries of these plants are poisonous.

Arum italicum, 1 to 1½ ft., creamy-white.

A. maculatum, 6 to 9 in., yellowish-green spotted with purple.

AUTUMN CROCUS. See *Colchicum;* see also *Crocus.*

BEGONIA

Only one species of begonia is hardy and even that, when grown in such northern locations as New York City, requires a sheltered location and the protection of a suitable mulch.

Begonia evansiana, 1 to 2 ft., a branching plant with attractive foliage and small but charming pink flowers in summer.

B.e. alba, the same as above but with white flowers.

BRODIAEA

Mostly natives of western North America, these cormous plants are mostly better adapted for growing in gardens in the West than in the East or Midwest. However, a few, including those listed below, may be persuaded to make themselves at home over a wider geographical area. They are primarily subjects for rock gardens and, in regions where they prosper without difficulty, for naturalizing. Brodiaeas need sun and porous soil. They have scant foliage and should be planted 3 to 4 in. deep in drifts or colonies with the individuals rather close to one another. The plant previously called *Brodiaea uniflora* is *Ipheion uniflora* (see page 237).

Brodiaea californica, 1 ft., violet-purple.

B. capitata (blue dicks), 1½ to 2 ft., blue.

B. coronaria (syn. *B. grandiflora*, 1½ ft., violet-purple.

B. ixioides (pretty face), 1½ ft., buff yellow.

B. lactea (wild hyacinth), 1½ ft., white or lilac.

B. laxa (triplet lily), 1 to 2 ft., white or purple.

B. stellaris, 6 in., violet-purple.

BULBOCODIUM
A bulb rather difficult to grow, it bears its flowers in spring before its leaves appear. Needs gritty, porous, fertile soil and full sun; for rock gardens.

Bulbocodium vernum, 6 in., lavender-pink.

BUTTERFLY TULIP. See *Calochortus*.

CALOCHORTUS
These native western American bulbs are of great interest and beauty but are mostly short-lived and difficult to establish in gardens in the Midwest and in eastern North America. They are best suited for rock gardens, where they flourish easily when naturalized. *Calochortus* is divided into three distinct groups. The fairy lantern or globe tulip kinds have nodding, globular flowers and enjoy a porous, gritty soil that contains an abundance of humus. They require light shade; and a mulch of leaves, pine branches or other suitable material put in place after the ground freezes is helpful. Set the bulbs so that they are covered with soil to about twice their depth. Good kinds in this group are:

Calochortus albus, 1 to 2 ft., white or pink.

C. amabilis, 1 to 1½ ft., golden-yellow.

C. amoenus, 1 to 1½ ft., rosy-purple.

The kinds known as cat's-ears, owl's-ears and star tulips have flowers that open wide, face upward, and are conspicuously hairy inside. They need the same cultural conditions as those recommended for the previous group. Good kinds are:

C. caeruleus, 6 in., blue.

C. maweanus, 6 to 8 in., white or white tinged purple. Varieties of this species are *grandiflorus*, *purpurescens* and *rosea*.

C. monophyllus, 6 to 8 in., bright yellow with brown at bases of petals.

C. uniflorus, 8 to 9 in., lilac.

The group of *Calochortus* called butterfly tulips or mariposa lilies have upturned, brilliantly colored flowers 3 to 4 in. across and are very good for cutting. These kinds need the same culture as the other groups except that they appreciate full sun. Among the best are:

C. clavatus, 1½ to 2 ft., yellow lined with brown.

C. gunnisonii, 1 to 1½ ft., white tinged with lavender.

C. leichtlinii, 9 to 12 in., white tinted purple and with yellow and a darker spot at bases of petals.

C. luteus, 1½ to 2 ft., yellow or orange-yellow lined with brown.

C. nutallii, 1½ ft., white lined with purple and with purple spots at bases of petals.

C. venustus, 9 to 12 in., white, yellow, pink, lavender or purple with conspicuous contrasting markings or dark centers.

CAMASS. See *Camassia*.

CAMASSIA (QUAMASH, CAMASS)
These plants grow from 1½ to 3 ft. or higher, have star-shaped flowers of light blue, white or purplish-blue, and are excellent in early summer. Plant

in early autumn, 4 to 5 in. deep and 6 to 8 in. apart in a moist soil, or even heavy clay soil provided it is not waterlogged.

Camassia cusickii, 2 to 3 ft., produces spikes of pale blue flowers.

C. esculenta, 2 ft., has spikes of rich blue flowers, each up to 2 in. across.

C. leichtlinii, 1½ to 2 ft., has flowers dark blue to almost white.

C. quamash, 2½ to 3½ ft., has flowers from deep blue to nearly white.

CAT'S-EARS. See *Calochortus*.

CHIONODOXA (GLORY-OF-THE-SNOW)
These neat plants grow up to 6 in. high and make a wonderful display in the spring. There are blue, pink and white varieties. Plant in autumn, 2 in. deep and 2 to 3 in. apart, in sandy loam, anywhere except in full shade. They are well suited for planting in rock gardens and under and between shrubs and trees. The best are:

Chionodoxa luciliae, blue with white center, or pink or white.

C. sardensis, gentian-blue, without a white eye.

C. tmolusii, dark blue, smaller and later than *C. luciliae*, very good.

CLAYTONIA (SPRING BEAUTY)
Native American tuberous plants, they bloom in spring and are attractive for naturalizing and for planting in rock gardens. Their needs are for part shade and a rich woodland soil that tends to be damp.

Claytonia caroliniana, 4 to 8 in., pink to white; foliage dies down soon after bloom is finished.

C. virginica is similar to above except in botanical details.

COLCHICUM (AUTUMN CROCUS)
Despite the common name, some kinds of *Colchicum* bloom in spring, others flower in late summer and fall. The leaves appear in early spring.

These bulbs, called "autumn crocuses," are quite distinct from certain true crocuses which bloom in fall and belong to the genus *Crocus*.

Colchicums are best suited for naturalizing in informal parts of the garden and for planting in rock gardens. In more tailored places their large leaves are apt to look a little untidy when they are dying down. A deep, porous soil enriched with leaf mold or compost, reasonably moist but not wet, is ideal; they grow well in partial shade or in sun. Plant in August with the tops of the bulbs 2 to 3 in. beneath the soil surface. Do not transplant as long as the plants continue to bloom satisfactorily. When in foliage these plants should never be permitted to suffer from lack of moisture. Except when noted, all the following are fall bloomers.

Colchicum agrippinum, 4 in., lavender-purple and white.

C. autumnale, 8 to 9 in., rosy-purple. White-flowered and double-flowered varieties of this species are grown.

C. bornmuelleri, 9 to 12 in., rosy-lilac.

C. luteum, 4 in., yellow, spring-flowering.

C. speciosum, 6 in., lilac-purple. A white-flowered variety is cultivated as well.

A number of beautiful hybrid colchicums are also available.

CORAL LILY. See *Lilium pumilum*.

CROCOSMIA
In gardens the name *montbretia* is most commonly applied to a group of hybrids to which belongs the botanical name *Crocosmia crocosmaeflora*. They are useful for late-summer color and are ideal for cutting. Their flowers grow to 1½ in. in diameter on 1½- to 3-ft. stems, and the colors vary from yellow through orange to red. They

are not reliably hardy north of Philadelphia, and there only if they are well protected over winter. Plant in spring, 4 in. deep and 3 in. apart in well-drained loamy soil. If the plants are thriving they soon spread into clumps and appreciate a topdressing of well-rotted manure in early spring. Be sure to divide the clumps every three or four years.

C. masonorum, 3 ft., flaming orange.

CROCUS

The large-flowered varieties of *Crocus vernus*, sometimes called Dutch crocuses, are among the best-known spring-flowering bulbs (corms). There are also many wild species which flower in the spring or fall, as well as some which bloom in winter in mild climates. Note that the common name autumn crocus is also applied to *Colchicum*.

Plant the spring-flowering kinds in the autumn, and the autumn-flowering species in August, not closer than 2 or 3 in. apart and about 2 in. deep. Best effects are usually obtained by spacing them casually to obtain a naturalistic effect, rather than by setting them at even distances as is done when planting beds of hyacinths or tulips. Plant in rough grass as well as at the edge of borders, between shrubs and beneath small trees. Because moles and mice love to eat crocus corms, plant a few more than are really needed. Sift naphthalene over the places where they are planted, or bury a mothball with each corm when planting, to discourage these little animals from eating them. Some gardeners plant their choice crocus corms inside baskets or boxes made of wire mesh and buried in the ground. Others surround the planted area with wire mesh set vertically in the ground with its upper edge just buried, then cover over the top with wire mesh spread horizontally barely below the soil surface.

Although the foliage is untidy after flowering, do not cut it off until it dies naturally. If the bulbs multiply and become crowded, lift, separate and replant them after the foliage dies.

Consult dealers' catalogues for varieties of Dutch crocus.

Plant the wild species in a choice, sunny, well-drained spot by themselves. These are admirable in rock gardens among creeping thyme or other low, surface-rooting ground cover.

The collection below will give a lot of pleasure and interest over a long period. Plant as for the garden forms

Spring-Flowering Crocus

Autumn-Flowering Crocus

but be still more vigilant for mice.

Autumn-Flowering

Crocus longiflorus, soft lilac, scented.
C. medius, lilac-blue.
C. salzmannii, lavender.
C. speciosus, bright blue.
C. zonatus (syn. *C. kotschyanus*), pale lavender-pink.

Spring-Flowering—Early and Late

Crocus aureus, dark orange-yellow.
C. biflorus, very variable in color, but all variations are good.
C. dalmaticus, soft lilac-blue.
C. olivieri, golden-yellow.
C. sieberi, lavender.
C. tomasinianus, pale lavender.
C. versicolor picturatus, white.

CROCUS, AUTUMN. See *Colchicum*.

CROWN IMPERIAL. See *Fritillaria imperialis*.

CYCLAMEN
The hardy cyclamens are miniatures of the greenhouse kinds and are most valuable for places in shade or semi-shade. Unfortunately they are rather difficult to raise in most parts of North America. They grow from 2 to 3 in. high. The flowers are attractive and the leaves often beautifully marbled with silver. Some varieties root from the top of the tuber, and others from the bottom. Plant in August or September in shade or semishade in a limy soil with some leaf mold added, 2 in. deep and 6 in. apart, though *C. neapolitanum* should be particularly well spaced as the tubers may grow to as much as 6 in. across.
Cyclamen coum, 4 in., has red, pink or white flowers in early spring.
C. europaeum, 3 in., has sweet-scented, deep pink flowers about August, or sometimes earlier. Likes a woodland location. Roots from the top of the tuber.

C. neapolitanum, 3 in., has rose-pink flowers in September or October. Its marbled leaves follow later and last until May or June. Roots from the top of the tuber.
C. repandum, 3 in., has bright crimson flowers in spring, is not so reliably hardy as the others and needs a sheltered place. Roots from the bottom of the tuber.

DAFFODIL. See *Narcissus*.

DOGTOOTH VIOLET. See *Erythronium dens-canis*.

DRAGONROOT. See *Arisaema dracontium*.

ENGLISH BLUEBELL. See *Scilla nonscripta*.

ERANTHIS (WINTER ACONITE)
Winter aconites are hardy plants and grow up to 6 in. Their bright yellow flowers appear in late winter or early spring and are long-lasting. Plant anywhere in ordinary soil, in August or as early as the bulbs can be obtained from the supplier. Early planting encourages the plants to make roots before the hard weather comes. Set the bulbs 2 in. deep and in groups of at least half a dozen in the rock garden, or in more generous masses beneath trees or shrubs. The bulbs should be spaced 3 to 4 in. apart. Lift and replant only when the plants seem to show evidences of deteriorating.
Eranthis cilicica, 3 to 4 in., darker yellow than *E. hyemalis* and flowers later.
E. hyemalis, 3 to 6 in., yellow.
E. tubergenii, 3 to 6 in., large, fragrant yellow flowers. Increases more slowly than the other kinds.

ERYTHRONIUM (ADDER'S-TONGUE)
These are mostly native American plants suitable for woodlands and shaded places in rock gardens. Not all

of those that are natives of the West are easy to grow or are long-lived when planted in other regions, but most can be persuaded to grow and bloom and to stay for at least a few years if they are well located and skillfully cared for. They need a deep, loose woodland soil that is not waterlogged but is always moist. It is important that the bulbs be planted as early in the fall as they are procurable; delay is very detrimental. A mulch of very well-rotted manure, good compost or leaf mold spread over the soil surface in late fall is highly beneficial. Set the bulbs 3 to 4 in. deep and 2 to 3 in. apart. In dry weather keep the soil well watered.

Erythronium americanum (trout lily), 6 to 10 in., a native of eastern North America, is a shy bloomer and does not produce any flowers until it is very well established. Its flowers are yellow, its leaves green mottled with brown.

E. californicum (fawn lily), 6 to 10 in., yellow and cream. This is one of the easiest of the erythroniums to cultivate.

Eranthis hyemalis (Winter Aconite)

E. citrinum, 6 to 8 in., cream and light yellow.

E. dens-canis (dogtooth violet), 6 in., leaves mottled; flowers rose-purple.

E. grandiflorum, 1 to 1½ ft., bright yellow. A variety of this named *album* has white flowers.

E. hendersonii, 6 to 12 in., pinkish-lilac. Leaves mottled.

E. multiscapoideum, 6 in., white or cream and yellow.

E. revolutum, 9 to 12 in., lavender, purple, pink or white.

E. tuolumnense, 9 to 12 in., golden-yellow; greenish at bases of petals.

FAWN LILY. See *Erythronium californicum.*

FLY POISON. See *Amianthium muscaetoxicum.*

FRITILLARIA
Fritillarias include 2- to 3-ft.-high crown imperials and many lower-growing species; all bloom in spring. Plant in early autumn in a rich, deep soil, in sun or light shade. Late planting is very detrimental. The smaller kinds are well suited for rock gardens, the others for woodland gardens and similar locations. Most fritillarias are rather unpredictable and capricious and tend to deteriorate and gradually die out despite best efforts to satisfy their needs, but they are well worth attempting. With the exception of *F. imperialis* and its varieties, plant the bulbs 3 to 6 in. apart and 3 to 4 in. deep. In fall mulch them with leaf mold, compost or very old rotted manure. Avoid transplanting established bulbs unless absolutely necessary. Water freely during periods of dry weather.

Fritillaria camschatcensis, 1 to 1½ ft., very dark, almost black-purple.

F. glauca, 6 to 8 in., purple and greenish yellow.

F. imperialis (crown imperial),

many varieties with flowers ranging
from yellow to red. These prefer a
limy, alkaline soil but even then they
do not flourish in all gardens. Plant 6
in. deep and 6 to 8 in. apart. Do not
plant near the house as they have a
foxy odor.

F. lanceolata, 1½ to 2 ft., purple
mottled with greenish yellow.

F. meleagris (snake's head), 9 to 12
in., usually with solitary flowers, purple with white checkering or white
with green veins. Can be naturalized
in rough grass. Plant 3 in. deep and 3
to 4 in. apart.

F. pluriflora, 1 ft., pinkish-purple.

F. pudica, 9 in., yellow or orange-
yellow tinged with purple.

GALANTHUS (SNOWDROP)

Snowdrops are easy to grow, and
flower very early in the year. The
blooms are white, with the ends and
sometimes the bases of the inner petals marked with green or, in a few
varieties, yellow.

Plant in early autumn, 2 to 3 in.
deep and 2 to 4 in. apart, in good light
soil in groups or drifts, preferably in
half-shaded places where the soil is
deep and mellow and not markedly
dry. Mulch each fall with leaf mold,
humus or good well-rotted compost.
Fertilize in spring. When the plants
have increased sufficiently for division, divide them after flowering when
the tips of the leaves have become
yellow.

Galanthus byzantinus, 6 to 9 in.,
white with green spots.

G. elwesii, 8 to 12 in., white with
green markings.

G. nivalis (common snowdrop), 4 to
8 in., white with green markings.

G.n. flavescens, 4 to 8 in., white with
yellow markings.

G.n. flore-pleno, 4 to 8 in., double
white flowers with green markings.

G. plicatus, 6 to 12 in., white with
yellow markings.

GALTONIA

Galtonia candicans (syn. *Hyacinthus
candicans*) is a stately plant for the
summer border. The 3- to 4-ft. stems
carry 15 or more drooping fragrant
white bells which flower in late summer. Plant in the spring, 6 in. deep
and 6 in. apart, in a well-drained soil
in a sunny location. If well protected
over winter, this fine South African
native is hardy in climates as severe
as that of Philadelphia.

GLORY-OF-THE-SNOW. See *Chionodoxa*.

GRAPE HYACINTH. See *Muscari*.

HERMODACTYLUS (SNAKE'S-HEAD IRIS)

Hermodactylus tuberosus (syn. *Iris
tuberosus*), 6 to 12 in., flowers green
and black. A distinct plant of curious
irislike appearance, suitable for well-
drained fertile soil in sun.

HYACINTHUS (HYACINTH)

The Dutch hyacinths were so named
not because they are natives of Holland (actually they are derived from a
species that occurs as a wild plant
from Greece to Syria and Asia Minor),
but because the commercial production of these bulbs is almost a mo-
nopoly of the Netherlands. For the
best results Dutch hyacinths require
a deep, fertile, well-drained soil, preferably of a somewhat sandy character. The first spring after they are
planted they are likely to produce a
satisfactory display in almost any soil,
provided it is not waterlogged. However, in most parts of North America
the quality of the bulbs and flowers
gradually deteriorates even given the
best soil conditions, and replacements
are needed every two, three or four
years. Among Dutch hyacinths there
is a wide range of varieties and colors.

A plan that finds favor with many
gardeners is to buy new bulbs each
year for formal flower beds, where

uniformity of height and size of flower spikes is important. Carefully lift them after they have flowered and "heel them in" (plant them closely together temporarily) in a lightly shaded place and keep them watered until the foliage has completely died. Then the bulbs are stored through the summer in a dry, airy cellar or similar place and are replanted in fall at the fronts of shrubberies and similar locations where they can remain undisturbed to bloom for as many succeeding seasons as they may. These later flowerings will consist of spikes less massive and less regular in size and color than those of the first season after planting. For this very reason they are especially delightful in areas where formality is not important.

Plant hyacinth bulbs in September or as early as they can be obtained in fall. For outdoor gardening the "bedding size" is adequate; "exhibition-size" bulbs should be reserved for indoor forcing. Set the bulbs 6 to 8 in. apart and with their tips 4 to 5 in. beneath the surface. In regions of cold winters cover with branches of evergreens, salt-marsh hay or other protective material.

The following species of *Hyacinthus* have much smaller bulbs, foliage and flower spikes than the Dutch hyacinths. Their chief use is in rock gardens, but they may also be grouped at the front of perennial borders or in suitable spaces at the fronts of shrub plantings. Set them in early fall with the tops of the bulbs 2 in. beneath the surface and spaced 2 to 3 in. apart.

Hyacinthus amethystinus, 6 in., light blue.

H.a. albus, 6 in., white.

H. ciliatus (syn. *H. azureus*), 8 to 12 in., pale blue. This plant is sometimes called *Muscari azureum*.

IPHEION (SPRING STARFLOWER)
This charming little plant forms dwarf tufts of leaves and bears large star-shaped flowers, in spring. It is sweet-scented, but if crushed the leaves smell of onions. Plant in autumn, 2 to 3 in. deep and 2 to 3 in. apart, in rich, sandy loam. Height, 6 to 8 in.

Ipheion uniflora, white or violet-tinged flowers.

IRIS
The Dutch, English and Spanish irises all have true bulbs and are essentially plants for the summer border. The Dutch flower in May or early June, the Spanish, which are scented, about two weeks later and the English at the end of June and in early July. All grow to 1½ to 2 ft. high and are excellent for cutting. If cut while in bud they will open indoors to perfect blooms.

Plant in October, 4 in. deep and 6 in. apart, except the smaller bulbs of the Spanish varieties, which are more effective at 4 in. apart. In cold sections give winter protection.

The Dutch and Spanish prefer a light, sandy soil, but the English iris should be planted in a heavier, moister soil. All require an open, fairly sunny place. Flower colors include white, lavender, blue, purple, yellow and bronze.

In addition to the showy flower-garden Dutch, English and Spanish irises, there are a number of smaller bulbous kinds that are excellent for rock gardens. These are wild species, a few hybrids, and varieties of species that have been left unchanged or only slightly changed by plant breeders. All succeed best in gritty, fertile, well-drained soil in full sun. Plant the bulbs in early fall 3 in. deep and about 3 in. apart. Lift and replant them every three or four years. If preferred they may be set among some low ground cover such as creeping thyme or muehlenbeckia. Planting them near crocuses provides an interesting com-

Iris bulb

Iris reticulata

bination in early spring. Among the best of these small irises are:

Iris bakeriana, 4 to 6 in. A charming, early-flowering kind with pale blue flowers which have a deep purple blotch on each outer petal.

I. danfordiae, 4 to 6 in., bright canary-yellow. After the first year these bulbs take several years to build up to flowering size again.

I. histrio, 6 to 9 in., similar to *I. reticulata* but blooms earlier (in midwinter in mild climates). Flowers are lilac-blue and purple with a gold band on outer petals.

I. histrioides major, 9 in., Oxford blue. This plant is very early-flowering.

I. reticulata, 6 to 9 in., violet-scented with violet-blue flowers in late winter. This species includes many varieties and some hybrids, described in seed catalogues.

I. tuberosa. The plant sometimes known in gardens by this name is *Hermodactylus tuberosus*.

IXIOLIRION

Ixiolirions are best in a well-drained, sunny rock garden or similar location in light, fairly rich soil. They grow to about 15 in. tall and have a number of blue flowers on each stem. The foliage is rather scanty. Plant the bulbs about 4 in. apart and 3 in. deep in fall.

Ixiolirion montanum (syn. *I. ledebourii*), porcelain-blue flowers in May.

I.m. pallasii, deep blue flowers in June.

JACK-IN-THE-PULPIT. See *Arisaema triphyllum*.

LEOPARD LILY. See *Lilium pardalinum*.

LEUCOJUM (SNOWFLAKE)

The snowflakes bloom in spring, summer and autumn and are easy to grow in any good soil in sun or half shade. The bell-shaped white flowers of the spring and summer bloomers are spotted on the outside with green. Plant in late summer or early autumn, 2 to 3 in. deep to the top of the bulb and 3 to 4 in. apart, except *L. autumnale*, which should be set 1 to 2 in. apart.

Leucojum aestivum (summer snowflake), 18 in., flowers in April and May, has four or more bells. The Gravetye form is better than the original type. It likes a moist soil and grows well in full shade.

L. autumnale, 4 in., flowers in September and October, has slender grassy foliage and pink-flushed white bells, which appear before the leaves. Plant in light soil in full sun 1 to 2 in. apart.

L. vernum, 6 in., has large single bells in very early spring, will grow in part shade. In the trade *L. aestivum* is often misnamed *L. vernum*.

LILIUM

Gardeners are pleasantly surprised when they discover the enormous variety of this lovely group. Besides the classic Madonna lily and other trumpet lilies, there are those with cup-shaped, upright flowers of orange, yellow or red; others, called Turk's cap, with small, sharply reflexed petals somewhat resembling those of a cyclamen, which can be mauve, yellow, white, scarlet, lilac-pink or crimson-purple; and some with great bowl-shaped, fragrant flowers. Some lilies are small enough for rock gardens, while others soar to 8 ft. or more. Many are delightfully scented.

Lilies belong in the genus *Lilium*. Other plants have "lily" as part of their common names, but are not botanically lilies—such as lily of the valley and day lily.

Lilies include a wide variety of splendid hardy garden plants, some difficult to grow, others easy. All grow from scaly bulbs; all bloom in summer.

As a group, lilies thrive in deeply prepared, well-drained, fertile, neutral or slightly acid soil; a few grow well in alkaline soils. Some prosper in full sun, others in part shade; many grow best if the soil and bases of the stems are shaded by low shrubs or other plants. Many kinds produce roots from the stems which grow from the tips of their bulbs; they also produce roots from the bulb bottoms. Such kinds are planted deeply, with their tips 4 to 6 in. beneath the surface. Those that are not stem-rooting are planted with their tips about 2 in. deep. The best planting season is fall.

Most lilies can be grown from seed, but hybrids and varieties may not reproduce true to type when so propagated. Some seeds make little bulbs but do not show aboveground for a year or more. Some lilies, such as regals, are fairly quick to flower from seed; others take five to seven years.

Lilies can also be increased from bulb scales, bulbils (little purplish-black or greenish pealike bodies developing in the angles between the stem and leaves—the axils) and bulb-lets. Leave lilies from seeds, scales and bulbils undisturbed in flats about a year, and plant out in early autumn or spring just as is done with older bulbs, but more shallowly.

Some strong-growing lilies split into two or more bulbs nearly every year. It is often necessary to lift and replant them every four years or so.

Lilies suffer from soil pests, particularly cutworms and slugs. Regular use of baits, dusts or sprays will take care of slugs; dusts such as chlordane discourage other soil pests. Aphids are a severe problem because they transmit deadly virus diseases. Lily diseases are few but serious (see page 801 in "Plant Diseases").

Of the numerous *Lilium* species only a few of the easiest to grow are listed here. For others, consult the catalogues of specialists.

Lilium canadense (meadow lily), 4 ft., flowers hanging, bell-shaped, yellow to orange-red, early summer. Stem-rooting. For acid soil.

L. candidum (Madonna lily), 5 ft., flowers white, early summer. Foliage produced in fall remains all winter. Not stem-rooting. Somewhat capricious; does not always succeed. The variety *salonikae* flowers earlier and is easier. Both prefer fairly heavy soil, neutral or somewhat alkaline.

L. cernuum, 2 ft., flowers lilac-pink, Turk's-cap-shaped; foliage grasslike. Stem-rooting. Tolerates slightly alkaline soil. Very hardy.

L. hansonii, 4 ft., flowers orange-yellow, spotted brown. Turk's-cap-shaped, in July. Stem-rooting. Thrives in ordinary soil. Best in part shade.

L. henryi, 6 ft., flowers apricot-yellow, petals recurved, in August. Stem-rooting. Best in neutral or slightly alkaline soil in part shade.

L. pardalinum (leopard lily), 5 ft., flowers red with yellow centers and dark spots, Turk's-cap-shaped, in July. Not stem-rooting. For rich,

Lilium regale (Regal Lily)

moist, peaty and somewhat acid soils.

L. pumilum (syn. *L. tenuifolium*) (coral lily), 1½ ft., flowers coral-red to yellow-orange, in June. Stem-rooting. For full sun and light, well-drained soil. Flowers quickly from seed.

L. regale (regal lily), 6 ft., flowers trumpet-shaped, white with yellow in throat, purplish outside. Stem-rooting. For ordinary soil in full sun. Grows easily and quickly from seed.

L. speciosum, 4 ft., flowers with recurved petals, white overlaid with crimson with darker raised spots, in August. Stem-rooting. Needs slightly acid soil and slight shade. Several color variations occur. Unfortunately, much subject to diseases.

L. tigrinum (tiger lily), 4 ft.; flowers orange with purplish-black spots, flat with recurved petals, in August and September. Stem-rooting. Produces bulbils. For neutral or acid soils.

Hybrid Lilies

Until the present century there were

but few hybrid lilies, and not until after World War I did the great era of breeding and development begin. Now numerous kinds are available in a very wide range of forms, colors, heights and blooming times.

American and Canadian breeders have pioneered much of this hybridization. For the most part the hybrids are better garden plants and are easier to grow than many of the natural species. Among the most important of the hybrid types are those listed below. Gardeners should consult catalogues of specialists to keep up to date.

L. aurelianense. The new *L. aurelianense* (aurelians) vary in shape and color. All are beautiful summer bloomers for part shade. Stem-rooting.

Bellingham hybrids, 4 to 8 ft. These increase quickly and flower in July. Plant 5 in. deep in moist, well-drained soil mixed with peat moss and coarse sand.

Fiesta hybrids, 3 to 5 ft. These are gay Turk's caps, flowering in June and very vigorous. Plant 5 to 6 in. deep in ordinary garden soil in sun.

Golden Chalice hybrids, 1½ to 3 ft. They resemble *L. hollandicum.* Plant bulbs 6 in. deep in good soil in sun. They bloom in May and are drought-resistant.

Green Mountain hybrids, 5 to 7 ft., are trumpet lilies prevailingly white with green throats and brown-shaded exteriors. Plant in good soil in light shade. Plant bulbs 6 to 8 in. deep.

Harlequin hybrids, 3 to 5 ft., vary in color from ivory-white to purple with a wide variety of intermediate shades. Plant 6 to 8 in. deep.

L. hollandicum, useful and attractive hybrids, 1½ to 3 ft. The cup-shaped flowers come in many colors, in June and July. Stem-rooting.

L. maculatum, 2 ft. These bear cup-shaped flowers in June and July in shades ranging from lemon to crimson. They are stem-rooting and easy to

grow, but are not tolerant of lime.

Midcentury hybrids, 3 to 5 ft. Vigorous; specially bred to be easy to grow in a wide variety of situations. Plant 6 to 8 in. deep.

Olympic hybrids, 5 to 7 ft. Trumpet lilies, the flowers white or pinkish suffused with brown or green on their outsides. Set bulbs 6 to 8 in. deep in fertile, well-drained soil.

Patterson hybrids, 2 to 5 ft. Midsummer-flowering lilies of Canadian origin produced from work on particularly cold-resistant species to endure the bitter winters of Saskatchewan. Stem-rooting; easy to grow; a neutral soil is recommended.

Preston hybrids, 2 to 5 ft. Pretty, vigorous, free-flowering and quick to increase. Stem-rooting, for sun or semishade.

L. testaceum (Nankeen lily), 5 ft., has large recurved, fragrant flowers of delicate apricot-yellow in early July. Likes lime in soil and a well-drained location in full sun.

LYCORIS

Lycoris squamigera (syn. *Amaryllis hallii*), 2 ft. Known as the hardy amaryllis, this species produces its flower stalks in August and September, after foliage is gone. The lilylike lavender-pink flowers are fragrant and very handsome and are borne in umbels of 8 to 12. Attractive strap-shaped leaves develop in spring and remain until July.

L. squamigera often takes a year or two to become established and may not bloom until then. Do not transplant bulbs which are thriving unless absolutely necessary. Plant the bulbs in early fall, so that they are covered to a depth of 5 or 6 in. and spaced 8 or 9 in. apart, in deep, fertile soil that is well drained but not excessively dry. In cold climates, provide a winter cover of leaves, salt-marsh hay or other appropriate material.

MADONNA LILY. See *Lilium candidum*.

MARIPOSA LILY. See *Calochortus*.

MEADOW LILY. See *Lilium canadense*.

MONTBRETIA. See *Crocosmia*.

MUSCARI (GRAPE HYACINTH)
Grape hyacinths are among the easiest and most satisfactory of spring-flowering bulbs. They will grow in a wide variety of situations, except in deep shade, and in ordinary soil. They have spikes of little pinched-mouthed, bell-shaped flowers in conical heads, often sweet-scented. All grow 6 to 8 in. and flower in early spring. The plant known as *M. azureum* is *Hyacinthus azureus*.

Grape hyacinths are splendid for rock gardens, and for planting beneath shrubs and trees. Often they develop foliage in fall which remains all winter and on to early summer. Plant the bulbs in fall, 2 to 3 in. apart and at a depth of about 2 in.

Muscari armeniacum, brilliant blue, scented.

M. a. Cantab, clear light blue.

M. botryoides, blue.

M.b. album, white.

M. comosum, greenish, purple-tipped spikes.

M. c. monstrosum; has shredded petals which produce a feathery effect; bluish-violet.

M. latifolium, lower flowers on spike dark blue, upper flowers light blue.

M. moschatum, greenish-yellow tinged with violet. Musk-scented.

M. paradoxum, blue-black.

M. tubergenianum, top flowers light blue, lower flowers dark blue.

NANKEEN LILY. See *L. testaceum*.

NARCISSUS
Narcissus is the generic name for one of the oldest known plants and includes daffodils, jonquils and the flowers generally known as narcissuses. There are nine main classes or divisions besides the wild species.

The name jonquil most properly belongs to varieties of *N. jonquilla;* these are very fragrant and have slender, cylindrical, rushlike leaves. "Daffodil" is, perhaps, best reserved for varieties with large trumpets, but there is a present-day tendency to apply the names indiscriminately.

Narcissus bulbs prefer moister soil than tulips and they will grow well in partial shade. In fact, the bright orange varieties keep their color better in semishady locations.

They are useful for planting between shrubs and under small trees, and look lovely in grass. Do not cut the grass until the leaves have died down; otherwise the bulbs are weakened and future flowering is impaired.

Narcissuses are less formal in appearance than hyacinths or tulips and may be planted so that they appear to have grown spontaneously from self-sown seeds. This effect may be attained by strewing the bulbs by handfuls over the ground surface and planting them where they fall, taking care to leave some open spaces without bulbs, or with very few bulbs, between drifts of greater density.

Plant in mid-August or as early as the bulbs can be obtained from the dealer, 6 in. deep and 6 to 9 in. apart, preferably in moist, sandy loam that has good subsurface drainage. There is no need to lift narcissuses until they become crowded. Keep their locations well weeded and forked over as the foliage decays, because the narcissus fly lays its eggs in the holes left by the dead foliage, or in cracks in the soil nearby. As soon as the leaves are dead, shallowly cultivate the ground to fill up these holes, and dust with an insecticide to kill the grubs as they hatch.

Classification by Flower Shape

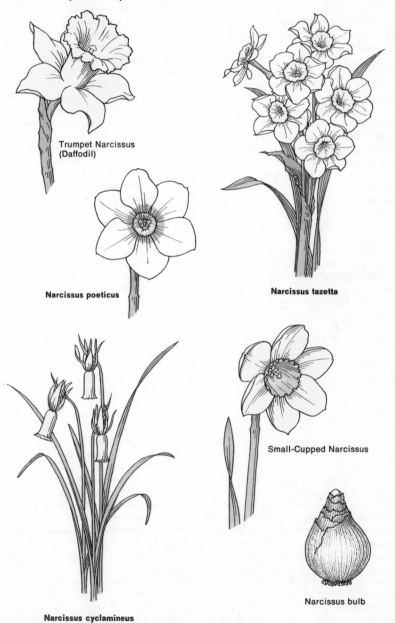

Trumpet Narcissus
(Daffodil)

Narcissus poeticus

Narcissus tazetta

Small-Cupped Narcissus

Narcissus bulb

Narcissus cyclamineus

If any bulbs come up in the spring with discolored or distorted foliage, dig them up immediately and burn them. Also burn any bulbs which are soft when lifted.

Even in cold areas it is rarely necessary to provide winter protection for narcissuses when they are planted in grass, but when the soil is bare of ground cover it is advisable to protect them with a winter protection of evergreen branches or other suitable material in regions where severe cold is experienced. This is especially so the first winter after planting. The one group of *Narcissus* that is not hardy in the North are a few varieties of *N. tazetta*. These—Chinese Sacred Lily, Paper-White and Soleil d'Or—are suitable for planting outdoors in the Deep South only; elsewhere they are valued for forcing indoors.

The horticultural varieties of narcissuses are exceedingly numerous and are listed and described in catalogues of bulb dealers.

Other Narcissuses

The growing of the dwarf wild species and dwarf hybrids is a special interest, as some of them require conditions different from those in the ordinary garden. Two which can be grown in the very front of a border or in a rock garden without special care are:

Narcissus obvallaris (Tenby daffodil), 8 in., single flowers, clear golden-yellow.

W. P. Milner, 8 in., single flowers, dainty sulphur-yellow.

The following species and varieties are especially suitable for growing in rock gardens. They prosper in sandy, peaty, fertile soil that is never waterlogged but that is constantly moist from early spring until the foliage dies down naturally in early summer. In cold localities winter protection is very desirable or even necessary. This may be provided by covering with evergreen branches, salt-marsh hay or other similar material.

Narcissus bulbocodium citrinus, similar to *N. b. conspicuus* but with sulphur-yellow flowers.

N.b. conspicuus, rushlike leaves and dainty golden-yellow flowers with large, conspicuous trumpet.

N.b. monophyllus, similar to *N.b. citrinus* but with white flowers.

N. cyclamineus, hanging yellow flowers which have narrow, tubular trumpets and strongly reflexed petals.

N. minimus, a miniature yellow-flowered trumpet daffodil.

N. nanus, a beautiful tiny trumpet daffodil with yellow flowers.

N. triandrus albus (angel's-tears daffodil), a slender kind that bears clusters of creamy-white flowers with globular trumpets and somewhat turned-back petals.

N.t. concolor, similar to above but the flowers are yellow.

ORNITHOGALUM

The hardy kinds are well adapted for naturalizing in informal parts of the garden and for planting in rock gardens. They grow well in any fairly good soil in sun or light shade. Plant in fall, 3 to 4 in. apart and 3 to 4 in. deep.

Ornithogalum nutans, 1½ to 2 ft. Flowers are white within and green without, in spring.

O. pyramidale, a good plant for the border, bears spikes of star-shaped white, green-backed flowers on 2-ft. stems in June. Ideal for cutting.

O. umbellatum (star-of-Bethlehem), 8 in., flowers white within, green-striped white without, in May. Plant this kind with discretion; it may become a weed.

OWL'S-EARS. See *Calochortus*.

PUSCHKINIA

Puschkinia scilloides (syn. *P. li-*

banotica), 4 in., a scilla-like plant that grows anywhere in sun. The whitish hyacinthlike flowers have a deep blue line down the center of each petal and bloom in early spring. There is also a pure white form. Plant in October or November, 2 in. deep and 2 to 3 in. apart, in well-drained soil.

REGAL LILY. See *Lilium regale.*

QUAMASH. See *Camassia.*

RUE ANEMONE. See *Anemonella tha-lictroides.*

SCILLA (SQUILL)
Scillas are easy to grow in any reasonable soil. Plant as early as possible in fall, the smaller bulbs 3 in. deep and 2 to 3 in. apart, and the larger bulbs 5 to 6 in. deep and 4 in. apart. These are admirable for rock gardens and for planting under trees and shrubs where it is not excessively shady. The soil should be well drained and not extremely dry in spring.

Scilla amoena (star hyacinth), 6 in., spring, blue-purple.

S. autumnalis, 6 in., rosy lavender, in late summer or fall.

S. bifolia, 6 in., deep blue, in early spring.

S.b. alba, same as *S. bifolia*, but flowers are white.

S.b. rosea, soft rose-pink flowers.

S. chinensis, 6 to 9 in., lilac-pink, late summer.

S. hispanica (syn *S. campanulata*— Spanish bluebell), 1 to 2 ft., blue, in spring. Variety *alba* has white flowers, variety *rosea*, pink flowers. These thrive in light shade in deep woodland soil. Good as cut flowers. There are a number of especially fine varieties of this species.

S. nonscripta (syn. *S. nutans*—English bluebell), late spring, violet-blue, also comes in white-flowered and pink-flowered varieties. Needs shade

Scilla sibirica (Siberian Squill)

and deep woodland soil. Blooms are good for cutting.

S. pratensis, 6 to 8 in., blue-purple, the buds marked with green, fragrant, late spring.

S.p. amethystina, similar to above but a little larger.

S. sibirica (Siberian squill), 4 to 6 in., dark blue, in spring.

S.s. alba, same as above but pure white.

S.s. atrocaerulea (syn. *S.s.* Spring Beauty), large-flowered, blue.

S. tubergiana, 6 in., very pale blue with dark median stripes on each petal, early spring.

SIBERIAN SQUILL. See *Scilla sibirica.*

SNAKE'S HEAD. See *Fritillaria melea-gris.*

SNAKE'S-HEAD IRIS. See *Hermodac-tylus.*

SNOWDROP. See *Galanthus.*

SNOWFLAKE. See *Leucojum.*

SPANISH BLUEBELL. See *Scilla his-panica.*

SPRING BEAUTY. See *Claytonia*.

SPRING STARFLOWER. See *Ipheion*.

SQUILL. See *Scilla*.

STAR HYACINTH. See *Scilla amoena*.

STAR-OF-BETHLEHEM. See *Ornithogalum umbellatum*.

STAR TULIP. See *Calochortus*.

STERNBERGIA

These grow to 8 in. and bear large golden crocuslike flowers in autumn, long before the leaves. Plant in August in a somewhat heavy soil, in a sheltered sunny place, 4 to 6 in. deep and 6 in. apart.

Sternbergia lutea, flowers regularly only in warm, dry locations.

S.l. angustifolia, has narrow leaves, an excellent variety producing its flowers every fall in any reasonably sunny place.

TIGER LILY. See *Lilium tigrinum*.

TRILLIUM (WAKE-ROBIN)

The cultivated kinds are all spring-blooming native Americans. They grow naturally in woodlands, and in cultivation require light shade and deep, fairly moist but not wet soil that contains an abundance of humus. Plant immediately after blooming or in very early fall, 3 to 6 in. apart, covered to a depth equal to about four times the diameter of the bulbs. In fall, mulch with good compost or leaf mold. Among the best are:

Trillium cernuum, 9 to 18 in., white or pink.

T. erectum, 9 to 15 in., maroon-red flowers, ill-smelling.

T. grandiflorum, 9 to 12 in., has very beautiful large, upturned white flowers which become pink or pinkish as they age.

T. nivale, 3 to 6 in., white, becoming pink with age.

T. recurvatum, 6 to 18 in., brown-purple.

T. sessile, 4 to 12 in., red-purple or green.

TROUT LILY. See *Erythronium americanum*.

TULIPA (TULIP)

In most parts of North America tulips are less permanent than narcissuses but more so than hyacinths; nevertheless it is not unknown for vigorous varieties to thrive and bloom regularly for 10 to 20 years. Most kinds remain productive and healthy for much shorter periods.

Tulips prefer a sandy to medium loamy soil with sharp underdrainage but they will grow and bloom (at least for one, two, three or more years) in almost any soil that is not waterlogged. While in general they are sun lovers, light shade for a part of the day does them no appreciable harm.

Unless the bulbs are to be set quite deeply, say at 7 to 8 in. below the surface, it is a mistake to plant them before late October or early November. Darwin, cottage, breeder and other May-flowering tulips do very well even when planted 9 to 10 in. deep, provided there is an ample depth of good soil beneath the bulbs. Such deep planting restrains to some degree the tendency of the bulbs to split into several smaller ones that produce only foliage or, at the best, small leaves and inferior blooms. This depth also makes it possible to plant a wide variety of summer annuals over them without lifting the bulbs and without harming them.

Bulbs that are lifted after blooming should be planted temporarily close together in a lightly shaded "reserve" area of the garden and kept watered until the foliage has completely rip-

Classification by Flower Shape

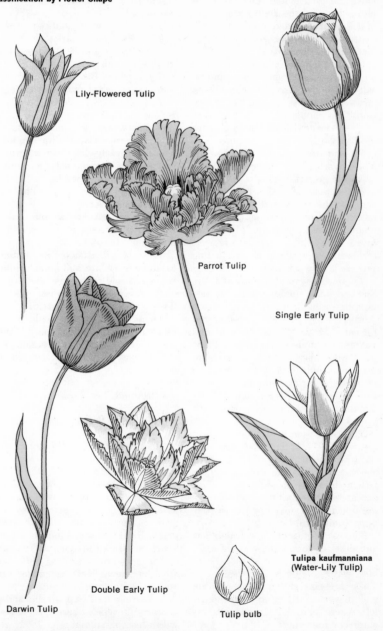

Lily-Flowered Tulip

Parrot Tulip

Single Early Tulip

Double Early Tulip

Darwin Tulip

Tulip bulb

Tulipa kaufmanniana
(Water-Lily Tulip)

ened and died. Then they should be cleaned, sorted to size (for uniformity of flower size), and kept in a dry, well-ventilated cellar or similar storage place until fall planting time.

Tulips planted in areas of severe winters benefit from a covering of salt-marsh hay, evergreen branches, straw, dry leaves or similar protection. This should not be put in place until the ground is frozen to a depth of 2 or 3 in.; otherwise mice and other rodents may be troublesome. The covering is removed gradually as spring growth begins.

If the weather is dry between the time the shoots break through the soil in spring and the time the plants bloom, water copiously. Always remove faded blooms promptly; the formation of seeds is an exhausting process that weakens the bulbs.

There are several classes of tulip. Start with the single and double earlies, flowering from middle to late April, the cottage and lily-flowered for early May, and the Darwins and parrots for mid- to late May. Plant in late October, 5 to 6 or more in. deep and about 6 in. apart; or 8 to 9 in. apart if spring-bedding biennials, such as pansies, forget-me-nots and English daisies, are to be used with them.

Tulips are usually lifted every year; but if the soil is good and the bulbs are healthy, most tulips, with the exception of the earlies, can be left in the same place for more than a year, provided all dead and decaying foliage is removed at the earliest opportunity and burned.

The catalogues of bulb dealers list and describe numerous varieties.

Wild Species ("Botanical") Tulips

These are best grown in raised beds and in rock gardens and should be left where planted. Good kinds include the following:

Tulipa chrysantha, yellow inside, red outside.

T. clusiana, white and red.

T. eichleri, pure scarlet.

T. fosteriana and its varieties, 8 in., all in some shade of vivid scarlet.

T.f. Rockery Beauty, 8 in., brilliant scarlet, the best of the dwarf varieties.

T. kaufmannia, cream, yellow and red.

T. kaufmanniana (water-lily tulip), from Central Asia, of dwarf habit— 6 to 8 in., early-flowering with large ivory-white flowers with a crimson stain on the outer petals.

T.k. The First, creamy-yellow with vivid red exterior.

T. orphanidea, bronze and orange.

T. praestans, orange-scarlet, several flowers on one stem.

T. tarda (*T. dasystemon* in many catalogues), white and yellow, sometimes suffused with pink.

T. turkestanica, several creamy flowers together on one stem.

There are many other wild species but they should be tried only if they can be given very good drainage, full sun and no artificial watering in the summer.

WAKE-ROBIN. See *Trillium*.

WINDFLOWER. See *Anemone*.

WINTER ACONITE. See *Eranthis*.

ZIGADENUS

Though not especially showy, these are interesting subjects for wild gardens and similar developments. They will grow in sun or part shade in rich, decidedly moist soil. Plant 4 to 8 in. apart and 3 to 4 in. deep, in full sun.

Zigadenus elegans, 2 to 3 ft. Has starlike greenish-white flowers on spikes, in summer.

Z. freemontii, 2 to 3 ft. Has spikes of starry flowers that are white tinged with green, in summer.

TENDER BULBS

Corms, Rhizomes and Tubers—Kinds of Tender Bulbs—Dormancy and Storage—Lists of Bulbs by Type

TENDER BULBS—and we use "bulbs" to include plants having such bulblike structures as corms, fleshy rhizomes, tubers and the like—are many and interesting. They afford excellent opportunities to add exotic colors, forms and fragrances to outdoor gardens, greenhouses and window gardens. Some are excellent as cut flowers. Many summer-blooming kinds can be as successfully cultivated in gardens in the colder parts of North America as in subtropical areas; most are among the easiest of plants to grow.

Of necessity, the term "tender bulb" is arbitrary. There are borderline cases between "hardy" and "tender," the borderlines determined to a large degree by the location of the garden. In Montreal, Canada, as well as in Boston, Mass., all the kinds dealt with here are tender; none survives outdoors over winter. Generally these bulbs cannot be cultivated as permanent outdoor garden plants in regions of severe winters. Their aboveground portions are damaged by severe freezing and in some instances by slight frost; but in a few cases the plants survive, provided the bulbs themselves are not frozen. In some places this can be prevented by protecting them with a heavy winter covering of hay, straw, dry leaves or similar material, or by cultivating them in well-protected cold frames.

Tender bulbs may be classified into two main groups. The first includes all

kinds that lend themselves to being taken from the soil during their dormant seasons, and stored, usually without roots, in bags or boxes. The second group consists of kinds that retain their roots during their seasons of rest and which ordinarily are left undisturbed in the soil where they were planted. Both groups may be subdivided into those which rest in summer and those which rest in winter. Included in the second group are some evergreen kinds that are never completely dormant, although they do have a season of partial rest.

BULBS STORED OUT OF THE GROUND WHEN DORMANT

Members of this group that are dormant in winter and in active growth from spring through fall are as suitable for outdoor gardens in the North as they are for those in the South. They are planted in spring, dug up and stored in a frostproof cellar or similar place over winter.

The kinds that are dormant in summer, begin growing in fall, continue through the winter and bloom in late winter, spring or early summer are suitable for outdoor cultivation in very favored winter climates only, such as parts of the West Coast and the far South. These are splendid greenhouse plants anywhere, and some are suitable for sunny window gardens.

Bulbs Dormant in Winter

ACIDANTHERA

Closely related to gladioluses and requiring the same culture, these fragrant-flowered fall bloomers need a long growing season. Where frost comes early, they may be grown in pots or tubs outdoors and brought into a cool greenhouse or sunroom before frost, to develop their flowers.

Acidanthera bicolor murieliae, 1 to 2 ft., white with magenta-purple throat.

BASKET FLOWER. See *Hymenocallis*.

BEGONIA, TUBEROUS

Tuberous begonias come in a wide range of colors and flower types. Most gardeners purchase bulbs in spring, start them into growth in warm, humid, light conditions indoors and have them well established in 4- or 5-in. pots ready to plant in beds and window boxes when the weather is warm and settled. They bloom all summer and are attractive as pot plants for any place in good light with little or no direct sunlight.

They enjoy light shade, loose, fertile, well-drained soil that contains an abundance of organic matter and is

Tuberous Begonia

always reasonably moist, and thrive best where summer nights are cool.

In fall, just before killing frost, dig up entire plants with earth attached, put them in a warm, dry place, clean the tubers after the tops have completely died and store in temperature of 50° to 55° F.

BOUSSINGAULTIA
(MADEIRA VINE; MIGNONETTE VINE)
This tuberous-rooted twining vine is hardy outdoors as far north as Washington, D.C. In colder climates, dig roots in fall and store in peat moss, sand or dry soil in temperature of 35° to 40° F. Grows in any ordinary, well-drained soil. Suitable for trellises, porches, etc.

Boussingaultia baselloides, 10 to 20 ft.; flowers fragrant, white, in late summer or fall.

CALADIUM (FANCY-LEAVED CALADIUM)
Easy-to-grow, highly colored foliage plants, 1 to 2 ft. Have heart-shaped leaves beautifully variegated with green, pink, red and white in a great variety of patterns. Attractive for summer beds, window boxes and as indoor pot plants. They need warm, humid conditions with light shade, shelter from wind and rich, fairly loose soil, always reasonably moist but not constantly saturated.

In the Deep South, plant tubers directly outdoors, 2 to 3 in. deep, in spring as soon as settled warm weather arrives. Elsewhere, start tubers into growth indoors two months before plants are set outdoors, which should not be until late spring, when settled warm weather is assured. Tubers may be initially placed in a peat moss and sand mixture in flats. When 2-in. roots have developed, plant tubers individually in 5-in. pots and grow in warm, moist atmosphere. Lift plants after first frost, dry and clean tubers of dead foliage and store in vermiculite or

Canna

dry sand—temperature 60° to 65° F.

CANNA
These are very showy, gorgeous flowering plants for beds, borders, porch boxes and tubs. Canelike stems, 2½ to 5 ft. tall, are furnished with large, paddle-shaped, green or bronze leaves and bear massive clusters of large cream, yellow, orange, pink or red flowers, often decorated with darker spots, throughout summer and fall. They thrive best in deep, fertile, fairly moist soil in full sun, spaced 1½ to 2 ft. apart.

Tuber divisions may be planted directly outdoors when it is safe to plant corn and tomatoes; or, as is more commonly done in the North, they may be started indoors four to eight weeks before planting-out time and set outdoors when settled warm weather arrives. Plant with tops of tubers 2 in. beneath surface. After killing frost, cut tops down, dig tubers with soil adhering to roots, pack in dry soil or sand, store in temperature of 40° to 50° F. In the Deep South plants may remain in the ground all year. Modern canna varieties are great improvements over many of the older kinds.

COLOCASIA (ELEPHANT'S EAR)

Colocasia antiquorum, often called *Caladium esculentum*, grows 6 to 9 ft. tall, has enormous, heart-shaped, dark green leaves. For beds and borders; the foliage is especially attractive by the waterside. Needs deep, rich, moist soil, shelter from wind; prefers light shade. In the Deep South plant tubers directly outdoors, 3 to 6 ft. apart in spring; elsewhere start tubers into growth in pots of soil indoors or in a greenhouse eight to ten weeks before setting plants outdoors in late spring after settled warm weather arrives. Water freely in summer. Plants may remain undisturbed through winter in the Deep South; elsewhere, lift after the first killing frost and store in the same manner as cannas.

CROCOSMIA

The plants commonly called montbretia as well as the related *Crocosmia masonorum* are useful for summer beds and cut flowers. If well covered with leaves or similar protection, winter-hardy about as far north as Philadelphia. Elsewhere, dig after the first frost and, without separating, pack bulbs closely together in shallow boxes of soil and store in temperature of 40° to 50° F. In spring, separate the bulbs and plant 2 to 3 in. apart, 3 to 4 in. deep, in fertile, well-drained sandy soil.

Crocosmia crocosmaeflora (montbretia), 2 to 3 ft., flowers yellow to copper-red.

C. masonorum, 2½ to 3 ft., orange-flame.

DAHLIA

Showy and summer-blooming, these tuberous plants exhibit tremendous variation in height, flower form and color. Striking as cut blooms and as garden decoration, they appeal also to growers of exhibition flowers. They can survive with little care, but respond to good cultivation, blooming over a long period.

Dahlias are propagated by seeds, tuber division and cuttings. Increase by seeds is restricted to the breeding of new varieties, except for dwarf or bedding dahlias, which make such a gay show from midsummer until killing frost. It is quite practicable to sow seed directly outdoors, but more usual to sow indoors six to eight weeks before the young plants are set out in the garden, at about the time it is safe to set out tomatoes and geraniums.

Cuttings, taken from tubers started early indoors, produce "green plants" in pots for planting out at that time too. It is simpler to divide old clumps of tubers in spring to single tubers, each with a small piece of old stem attached. Plant outdoors in late spring in holes 6 in. deep, cover with 3 in. soil. Fill holes later.

Any ordinary, well-drained soil is suitable, but everything at all possible should be done to enrich it and bring it to a high state of fertility. Dahlias prefer sun but stand part shade. Spacing must be determined by the mature size and may vary from 1½ to 4 ft. apart. For tall-growing kinds stout stakes should be driven, one to each plant, before the plants are set. The stems should be tied to the stakes.

After planting, care includes pinching out the tip of the young plant when its second or third pair of leaves is formed and, with all except short-stemmed varieties, giving a second pinching above the first pair of leaves on each branch. In some cases thinning out the branches that subsequently develop is desirable so that no more than six to nine are retained. Dahlias grown for the production of large flowers are disbudded by removing all flower buds except the central or terminal one from each stem while they are tiny. Disbranching to insure long, clean flower stems is done by re-

Classification by Flower Shape

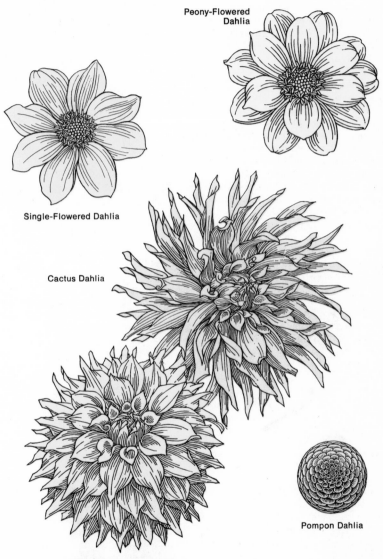

Peony-Flowered
Dahlia

Single-Flowered Dahlia

Cactus Dahlia

Pompon Dahlia

Formal Decorative Dahlia

moving young shoots from the leaf axils.

Shallow surface cultivation is necessary until hot weather arrives, then a mulch may be applied. In July an application of a complete fertilizer is helpful. During dry periods water copiously at four- to six-day intervals.

Aphids, caterpillars, slugs, leafhoppers, borers and other pests attack dahlias; the gardener must be constantly alert to take preventive or remedial action. The chief diseases are viruses, for which there is no cure. Infected plants should be destroyed.

In fall, after killing frost, cut off the stems at a length of 6 in. and carefully dig up the tubers. Remove surplus soil and turn them upside down in a warm, dry place. After they have dried store in dry sand, peat moss or vermiculite in a temperature of about 45° F.

Dahlias come in all flower colors except blue. There are single-flowered, double-flowered, semidouble-flowered, narrow-petaled varieties, and all manner of other variations. Catalogues of specialists describe and offer a wide selection of varieties.

ELEPHANT'S EAR. See *Colocasia*.

GALTONIA (SUMMER HYACINTH)
Often called *Hyacinthus candicans*, but more correctly *Galtonia candicans*, the summer hyacinth—if protected with a covering of leaves or salt hay— may be left in the ground permanently where winters are not more severe than those of Philadelphia. Elsewhere plant 5 to 6 in. deep, 1½ to 2 ft. apart, in spring. Dig bulbs after killing frost and store in a dry, dark, airy place, at a temperature of 40° to 50° F. This plant has erect spikes of large, fragrant white flowers in summer.

GLADIOLUS
With swordlike leaves, the erect spikes of handsome flowers open in

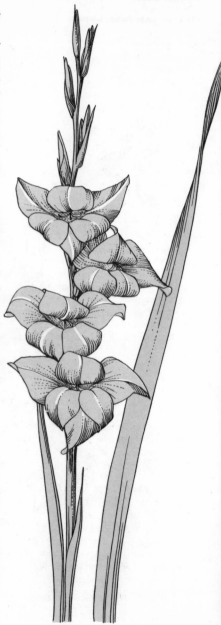

Gladiolus (Small-Flowered Hybrid)

succession from below upward. They are chiefly summer-flowering, easy to grow and most desirable for garden beds and cut flowers. Modern varieties vary from 2 to 3 ft. in height, with individual flowers ranging from 2 to almost 6 in. in diameter. The flowers are white or any color except blue. Catalogues of specialists present hundreds of varieties. and new ones are added each year.

Gladioluses thrive in any fertile, well-drained soil, in sun and, preferably, where air circulation is good. The corms (bulbs) are planted as soon as danger from frost is past, usually in early May. To extend the season of bloom, plantings are spaced out at two-week intervals until ten weeks before first fall frosts are expected. Set the corms 4 to 5 in. deep, about 4 in. apart, in rows 18 in. apart for cut flowers; or space them 8 in. apart in groups in flower beds. In exposed locations staking will be needed to prevent wind damage. Shallow cultivation or mulching will keep them free of weeds. During dry periods the soil should always be kept fairly moist. Harvest the flower spikes when the bottom flower on the spike is half open. If the corms are to be kept for another year, do not cut any of the large leaves with the flower.

At the end of the growing season when the foliage naturally dies, and before severe frost, dig up the plants carefully. Cut the foliage off half an inch above the new corms that have formed on top of the old ones, and let the corms air in a cool, frost-free place. When they are quite dry, clean off and discard the shriveled old corms and roots and store the new corms in dry conditions at about 50° F. If thrips have been troublesome or suspected, dust the corms before storing with 5 percent DDT dust.

In addition to the well-known summer-flowering gladioluses, there are a few that are planted in fall in greenhouses, or outdoors in very mild climates for spring bloom. Here belong *Gladiolus tristis*, a delightfully fragrant kind, and *G. colvillei*, the so-called baby gladiolus. These require the same treatment as freesias, described below under Bulbs Dormant in Summer.

GLORIOSA (GLORY LILY)
Twining vines with handsome lilylike flowers in summer and fall, they may be grown permanently outdoors in the Deep South. Elsewhere start tubers indoors in pots of well-drained soil in a minimum temperature of 65° to 70° F. and humid atmosphere from February to April, planting them horizontally; transplant them to sunny or lightly shaded places outdoors after warm weather arrives. Water well in dry weather. Provide supports for tendrils to cling to. Lift before killing frost, being especially careful not to damage tubers, dry, and store packed in peat moss, vermiculite or sand in temperature of 55° to 65° F.

Gloriosa rothschildiana, 6 to 10 ft., red and yellow.

G. superba, 6 to 10 ft., yellow-orange changing to red.

G. virescens, 5 to 7 ft., orange and greenish yellow.

Gloriosa
(Glory Lily)

GLOXINIA. See *Sinningia*.

HYMENOCALLIS (syn. ISMENE)
Ismenes or, as they are also called, basket flower and Peruvian daffodil, may be grown outdoors permanently in the South but in the North should be lifted after frost, keeping as many roots as possible intact. Store in a dry place, at a temperature of 60° F., with dry soil packed about the roots. After weather is warm and settled, plant in deep, rich soil containing an abundance of organic matter, and in full sun. Water freely in dry weather. Some other kinds of *Hymenocallis* are suited only to permanent cultivation in pots or beds in greenhouses or outdoors in the Deep South (see page 262).

Hymenocallis amancaes, 1½ to 2 ft., yellow and green.

H. calathina, white.

H. c. Advance, white, more vigorous than *H. calathina*.

H. Sulphur Queen, pale yellow.

Hymenocallis calathina (Ismene)

ISMENE. See *Hymenocallis*.

MADEIRA VINE. See *Boussingaultia*.

MEXICAN SHELLFLOWER. See *Tigridia*.

MIGNONETTE VINE. See *Boussingaultia*.

MONTBRETIA. See *Crocosmia crocosmaeflora*.

PERUVIAN DAFFODIL. See *Hymenocallis*.

POLIANTHES (TUBEROSE)
Very fragrant, white-flowered, summer bloomers for garden decoration and cutting, they require a warm location, full sun and rich, well-drained soil. Plant 6 in. apart, 3 in. deep, after weather is warm and settled, or start indoors in pots of soil six to eight weeks before transplanting the started plants outdoors. Dig up before killing frost, air, and store in a dry place at 60° to 65° F. Bulbs often fail to bloom satisfactorily the second year, especially if they are stored in too cool a place.

Polianthes tuberosa, 2½ to 4 ft. Single and double-flowered varieties are grown.

SINNINGIA (GLOXINIA)
See page 43 in "House Plants."

SUMMER HYACINTH. See *Galtonia*.

TIGRIDIA (MEXICAN SHELLFLOWER)
Large, brilliantly colored, bowl-shaped flowers, the individuals last only one day but give a succession of bloom throughout the summer. For beds, borders and cutting. They need a warm, sunny place and rich, well-drained soil. Plant 3 in. deep, 5 to 6 in. apart, after weather is warm in spring. Mulch when shoots are 3 to 4 in. high. Dig up before killing frost and store in temperature of 50° to 55° F.

Tigridia pavonia, 1 to 2 ft., scarlet, red, pink, yellow, orange or white flowers, oddly blotched with carmine, mahogany or purple. The showy blooms are up to 6 in. across.

TUBEROSE. See *Polianthes*.

Bulbs Dormant in Summer

With the exception of the anemones and ranunculuses, which are natives of the Mediterranean region, the bulbs in this group originated in South Africa. In North America they rest in summer, grow from fall through spring. None is tropical or suitable for very humid conditions; all thrive in airy, cool temperatures (night, 45° to 50° F.; day, a little higher), sunny greenhouses and outdoors in a climate like that of southern California.

All these bulbs require essentially the same culture. In late summer or early fall they are planted directly outdoors or in cold frames in favorable, mild climates; or, for greenhouse culture, in pots of porous, fertile soil. Those kinds that are grown for cut flowers are planted in benches or ground beds. For greenhouse culture cover tops of bulbs with 1 in. of soil; for outdoor culture, with 2 to 3 in. When planted outdoors they are usually spaced apart about twice the distance suggested for pot culture. At first the newly planted bulbs are watered sparingly, more freely as foliage develops. When they are well rooted, dilute liquid fertilizer is occasionally applied. After the bulbs have flowered, watering is continued until the foliage begins to die naturally; then it is gradually withheld. When the foliage is completely dead, the bulbs are removed from the soil and stored in paper or cheesecloth bags, flats or shallow boxes, in a cool, dry cellar or similar place.

ANEMONE

Varieties and hybrids of *Anemone coronaria* (poppy anemone), *A. fulgens* and *A. hortensis* are colorful spring flowers, 6 to 8 in. high and ideal for cutting. The main kinds are de Caen (giant poppy) anemone and its double St. Brigid forms. For outdoor cultivation they are best adapted for the U.S. Pacific Northwest. They are excellent for pot or bench culture in greenhouses. Plant 4 to 6 in. apart in medium loamy soil in a sheltered, sunny place. Although the plants can be left undisturbed for several years— provided the ground is good and they are fertilized—it is better to lift and store them over summer. It is better still to buy new corms each year, since they are quite inexpensive.

BABIANA (BABOON FLOWER)

These are somewhat like freesias but not fragrant; they bloom in late winter and spring. Plant in pots in autumn, 1½ to 2 in. apart.

Babiana disticha, 9 in., pale lilac.

B. rubro-cyanea, 9 in., blue and red.

B. stricta, 12 in., red or purple.

BERMUDA BUTTERCUP. See *Oxalis cernua.*

CAPE COWSLIP. See *Lachenalia.*

CORN LILY. See *Ixia.*

FREESIA

These delightful, fragrant flowers come in a wide color range, including white, yellow, lavender and pink, 1 to 2 ft. tall, and they are excellent for cutting. Named varieties are offered. In pots, plant about 2 in. apart. Winter- and spring-blooming.

IXIA (CORN LILY)

Very graceful and colorful, the flowers of this plant appear in late winter and spring, expand fully only in sun or good light. In pots, plant 2 in. apart.

Ixia maculata, 1½ to 2 ft., cream, yellow or pinkish with dark purple center.

I. viridiflora, 2 ft., pale green with black center.

LACHENALIA (CAPE COWSLIP)

These delightful scillalike flowers are

Ixia (Corn Lily)

for winter and spring bloom. In pots, plant 1½ to 2 in. apart.

Lachenalia contaminata, 9 to 12 in., white.

L. nelsonii, yellow tipped with green.

L. purpureo-caerulea, 9 to 12 in., blue and purple.

L. quadricolor, red and yellow tipped with green.

L. roodeae, 9 to 12 in., blue and purple.

L. tricolor, 9 to 12 in., red and yellow.

OXALIS

Adapted for growing in pots in sunny windows, the flowers close at night and in dull weather. Blooms late winter and early spring. In pots, plant 2 to 3 in. apart.

Oxalis bowieana, 6 to 10 in., large pink flowers.

O. cernua (Bermuda buttercup), 1 ft., yellow.

O.c. flore-pleno, has double yellow flowers.

O. variabilis (Grand Duchess), 1 ft., lavender-pink and red.

RANUNCULUS

Turban and Persian varieties, 1 to 1½ ft., are horticultural varieties of *Ranunculus asiaticus*. Their flowers, white, yellow, orange, pink or red, are splendid for cutting and for outdoor beds in climates such as that of the U.S. Pacific Northwest. They bloom in spring. Cultivate in same way as for poppy anemones.

SPARAXIS (WANDFLOWER)

Similar to *Ixia*, but lower and with larger blooms. Spring-blooming. In pots, plant 2 in. apart.

Sparaxis tricolor, 9 to 12 in., orange, yellow and black.

WANDFLOWER. See *Sparaxis*.

WATSONIA

Resembling gladioluses in their growth, these leafy plants produce flowers that are slender and tubular or with

Watsonia

wide-spreading petals like those of gladioluses. Spring- and summer-blooming. In pots, plant 3 to 4 in. apart.

Watsonia aletroides, 1½ to 2 ft., deep pink to scarlet.

W. ardernei (syn. *W. o'brienii*), 3 to 4 ft., white.

W. meriana, 2 to 3 ft., pink to rose-red.

BULBS LEFT DORMANT IN SOIL

The roots of these plants are fleshy and perennial. The bulbs—instead of being shaken free of soil, cleaned and stored separately through their dormant period—remain in the soil. With deciduous kinds the soil is kept quite dry from the time the foliage dies down naturally until growth begins again. With evergreen types the amount of water given is greatly reduced during the resting period. All need rich, porous soil, ample water when in active growth, and fertilizing with dilute liquid fertilizer every week or two during that period. Ordinarily these bulbs are repotted or replanted every two or three years, or less often. In intervening years, some surface soil is removed and replaced with a rich mixture at the beginning of each growing season. Some of these kinds are dormant in winter, others are dormant in summer.

Bulbs Dormant in Winter

AGAPANTHUS (LILY OF THE NILE)
These are not true bulbs but somewhat bulbous, fleshy-rooted perennials. They are useful garden plants for mild climates but will not stand severe winter cold. Their straplike leaves are evergreen. The leafless flower stems, which are freely produced in summer, carry many-flowered heads of blue trumpet-shaped flowers, long-lasting both on the plant and as cut flowers. In good soil, not too dry, these plants grow best. They thrive in full sun or very light shade.

Agapanthuses are excellent summer-blooming tub plants to stand on terraces, steps, etc. In northern gardens they must be wintered in a light place indoors in temperatures of 35° to 50° F. and be watered sparingly at that time. From spring through fall, water freely and fertilize regularly. They need rich, loamy, well-drained soil.

ALSTROEMERIA
Deciduous, summer-blooming tuberous-rooted plants for beds and cut flowers, they are not reliably hardy in climates colder than that of Washington, D.C. Best suited for regions of cool, moist summers. They require well-drained, fertile, sandy soil and full sun. Water freely in dry weather. May be grown in sunny, cool greenhouses in light, fertile soil. Water freely when in leaf, but keep quite dry

Agapanthus (Lily of the Nile)

when dormant. Fertilize regularly during growing season.

Alstroemeria aurantiaca, 3 ft., yellow, spotted brown.

A. caryophyllea, 9 to 12 in., red.

A. chilensis, 3 to 4 ft., rose-pink or red.

A. ligtu, 2 ft., white, lilac, pink or purplish.

A. pelegrina, 1 ft., lilac, spotted red-purple.

A. pulchella, 3 ft., dark red petals tipped with green.

AMARCRINUM. See *Crinodonna*.

AMARYLLIS

The plants commonly grown as house plants of this name are described under *Hippeastrum* on page 33. Here we consider the deciduous, summerflowering *Amaryllis belladonna* (syn. *Brunsvigia rosea*, *Callicore rosea*), which somewhat resembles *Lycoris squamigera*. Amaryllises are suitable for garden beds and borders but they are not generally hardy in climates which are any more severe than that of Washington, D.C.

Amaryllis belladonna (belladonna lily), 1½ to 2 ft., fragrant. Many color forms occur, from white to deep pink. Plant in deep, well-drained, fertile, sandy soil, 9 to 10 in. deep, 12 in. apart, in early fall. Water freely in dry weather. Protect with winter covering. Do not transplant unless absolutely necessary.

AMAZON LILY. See *Eucharis*.

ATAMASCO LILY. See *Zephyranthes atamasco*.

AZTEC LILY. See *Sprekelia*.

BELLADONNA LILY. See *Amaryllis belladonna*.

BLOOD LILY. See *Haemanthus*.

CLIVIA (KAFIR LILY)

Somewhat bulbous, fleshy-rooted evergreens with strap-shaped leaves and large clusters of lilylike or tubular flowers in spring, these are excellent for large pots or tubs and for outdoor gardens in very mild climates. They need rich, porous soil, good light with some shade from strong, direct sun, minimum temperatures (when grown indoors) of 45° to 50° F. in winter, increased to 55° to 65° F. in spring. Water freely from spring through fall and more sparsely in winter. Well-rooted specimens benefit from regular fertilizing, spring through fall.

Clivia caulescens, tubular flowers, brilliant red with green tips.

C. cyrtanthiflora, tubular flowers, orange-red and green.

C. miniata, salmon-orange.

In addition to those listed above, there are a number of magnificent hybrids and selected forms with larger flowers; also a yellow-flowered variety and one with variegated foliage.

Clivia miniata (Kafir Lily)

CRINODONNA (AMARCRINUM)

This is a deciduous or semievergreen hybrid between *Crinum moorei* and *Amaryllis belladonna*. Blooms in late summer and fall and is useful for outdoor cultivation in mild climates, elsewhere for growing in large pots or tubs. Culture as for *Crinum*.

Crinodonna Delkin's Find, similar to *C. howardii* but has smaller parts.

C. howardii, 3 ft., pink, fragrant.

CRINUM

Large bulbs with evergreen or deciduous foliage and lilylike, usually fragrant flowers, mostly in summer. Hardy in the South, and some kinds (*C. longifolium*, *C. moorei*, *C. powellii* and their varieties) flourish as far north as Washington, D.C. May also be grown in large pots or tubs in cool greenhouses. They require full sun, well-drained, fertile soil, plenty of water from spring through fall; the deciduous kinds should not be watered during their winter resting period. Fertilize well-rooted specimens regularly through summer. Plant bulbs outdoors with tips 2 to 3 in. beneath surface, indoors with upper third above soil. Do not repot or replant oftener than necessary.

Crinum americanum (swamp lily), 1½ to 2 ft., white.

C. asiaticum (poison bulb), 3 to 5 ft., white, evergreen.

C. longifolium, 1½ to 2 ft., white or pink. One of the hardiest.

C. moorei, 2 to 3 ft., deep pink.

C. m. album, white.

C. powellii, 2 to 3 ft., pink.

C. p. album, 2 to 3 ft., white.

C. p. Cecil Houdyshel, 2 to 3 ft., deep pink.

C. p. Ellen Bonsanquet, 2 to 3 ft., wine-rose.

EASTER LILY. See *Lilium longiflorum*.

EUCHARIS (AMAZON LILY)

These tropical evergreens have handsome foliage and beautiful, fragrant flowers; for tropical greenhouses. They need rich, porous soil, generous fertilizing, a minimum temperature of 60° to 65° F., high humidity and shade from strong sun. Plant with tips of bulbs 1 to 2 in. below surface. Repot at intervals of several years only, topdress with rich soil each spring. Water freely from spring through fall, moderately in winter.

Eucharis grandiflora, 1½ to 2 ft., white, blooms in spring, and often again in summer.

EUCOMIS (PINEAPPLE FLOWER)

Deciduous, summer-blooming, these grow outdoors in mild climates, in pots elsewhere. Hardy outdoors at Washington, D.C., if well protected over the winter. Flowers of some kinds fragrant, in cylindrical spikes topped by crowns of small leaves. Full sun and fertile, well-drained soil suit them. Plant outdoors 9 in. apart with bulb tips 4 to 6 in. deep, indoors with bulbs barely covered. Water and fertilize freely from spring through fall. Keep indoor specimens dry during the winter.

Eucomis bicolor, 1 to 1½ ft., pale green, petals margined lilac.

HAEMANTHUS (BLOOD LILY)

Best for pot culture, but may be grown outdoors in very mild climates only. Plant in rich, loamy, well-drained soil. They need sun or, in summer, light shade. Summer- and autumn-flowering; but bloom in spring or early summer if started indoors or in frames. Water freely when in leaf; keep deciduous kinds dry when dormant, evergreen kinds rather dry in winter. Minimum night temperature indoors 50° to 55° F. Fertilize regularly in growing season.

Haemanthus albiflos, 9 to 12 in., deciduous, flowers white, red berries.

H. coccineus, 1 to 2 ft., deciduous, bright red.

H. katharinae, 1 to 2 ft., evergreen, salmon-red.

H. puniceus, 1 ft., deciduous, pink.

HIPPEASTRUM (AMARYLLIS)
See page 33 in "House Plants."

HYMENOCALLIS (SPIDER LILY)
These are evergreen and deciduous
and mostly summer-blooming. Those
discussed here are for outdoor culture
in the Deep South, and in greenhouses
elsewhere. (For kinds called ismenes,
see page 256.) They need deep, rich
soil containing an abundance of organic matter, plenty of water from
spring through fall. Give deciduous
kinds no water in winter, evergreens
less water. All require full sun with
light shade in summer, and regular fertilizing during the growing season.
Tropical kinds need a minimum night
temperature of 65° F., temperate
kinds 50° F. Plant with tips of bulbs
just beneath the ground, or pot with
tips above surface.
Hymenocallis caribaea, 1 to 2 ft.,
white, tropical.
H. occidentalis, 1½ ft., white, a
temperate kind.
H. speciosa, 1½ to 2 ft., white,
tropical.

JACOBEAN LILY. See *Sprekelia*.

KAFIR LILY. See *Clivia*.

LILIUM
Lilium longiflorum (Easter lily)
flowers in July and August outdoors.
It is much planted in the South and is
hardy about as far north as Washington, D.C. It is stem-rooting. There are
several named varieties such as Croft,
Creole and Estate.
This lily is also commonly grown in
pots in greenhouses. It is easily flowered for Easter by forcing. For this
purpose the bulbs are potted in fall,
kept in a temperature of 40° to 50° F.
for four to six weeks or longer, and
then are moved to a greenhouse—
temperature at night about 60° F. and
in daytime several degrees higher.

LILY OF THE NILE. See *Agapanthus*.

PINEAPPLE FLOWER. See *Eucomis*.

POISON BULB. See *Crinum asiaticum*.

SPIDER LILY. See *Hymenocallis*.

SPREKELIA
(JACOBEAN LILY; AZTEC LILY)
This deciduous summer bloomer is
hardy outdoors in mild climates and
elsewhere suited for pot culture in
greenhouses and window gardens.
Plant outdoors in spring in sandy, fertile soil 3 to 4 in. deep, 4 to 6 in. apart.
Indoor culture as for *Hippeastrum*.
Sprekelia formosissima, 1 ft., crimson-red.

SWAMP LILY. See *Crinum americanum*.

ZEPHYRANTHES (ZEPHYR FLOWER)
Deciduous, crocuslike bulbs, most of
which are generally not hardy in climates severer than that of Washington, D.C. For full sun and sandy,
well-drained soils. Plant in early fall,
3 to 4 times depth of bulb, 2 to 3 in.
apart, for summer and autumn bloom.
Easily grown indoors in pans of
porous, fertile soil in cool, sunny
greenhouse or window garden.
Zephyranthes atamasco (atamasco
lily), 6 to 9 in., white or delicate pink.
Z. candida, 3 in., white.
Z. citrina, 5 to 9 in., yellow.
Z. grandiflora, 4 to 8 in., pink.
In addition to these listed above,
several named horticultural varieties
are offered by specialists.

ZEPHYR FLOWER. See *Zephyranthes*.

Bulbs Dormant in Summer
ALBUCA
This is adaptable for outdoor cultivation in a climate such as that of
southern California, and as a pot plant
elsewhere. Fragrant blooms appear in

spring and early summer. Needs full
sun and fertile, porous soil. Plant or
pot in early fall and repot at intervals
of several years only. When cultivated
in pots, keep upper half of bulbs above
soil. Water freely and fertilize regularly, fall through spring; withhold
water during summer dormancy.

Albuca fastigiata, 1½ to 2 ft., white,
with green or brown tips on petals.

A. major, 3 ft., yellow, with green
stripe on each petal.

A. minor, 1½ ft., white, with center stripe of brick-red on each petal.

ALLIUM

Allium neapolitanum, 1 ft., white,
fragrant. In pots, space 1½ to 2 in.
apart, outdoors 2 to 3 in. A delightful
late winter- or spring-blooming bulb.

CALLA LILY. See *Zantedeschia*.

CHINCHERINCHEE. See *Ornithogalum
thyrsoides*.

CLIMBING ONION. See *Schizobasopsis
volubilis*.

GUERNSEY LILY. See *Nerine sarniensis*.

NERINE

When grown in a pot this autumn-
flowering bulb should be planted with
its upper half aboveground. Space so
that the bulbs nearly touch. Unless
needed for propagation, pull out all
small side bulbs that appear. There
are many fine named hybrids.

Nerine bowdenii, 15 to 18 in., pink,
the hardiest kind.

N. curvifolia, 1 to 1½ ft., scarlet.

N. c. fothergillii, more robust than
N. curvifolia, scarlet.

N. flexuosa, 1½ to 2 ft., pink.

N. humilis, 6 to 18 in., lavender-
pink.

N. sarniensis (Guernsey lily), 1½ to
2 ft., salmon-pink.

N. s. corusca, 1½ to 2 ft., scarlet.

N. undulata, 1 to 1½ ft., pale pink.

ORNITHOGALUM

These are attractive for outdoor gardens in mild, dry climates. Elsewhere
they may be grown in sunny, cool
greenhouses. Spring- and summer-
blooming varieties. Plant most kinds
in fall, *O. caudatum* in late winter, in
porous, fertile soil. Grow indoors in
minimum temperature 40° to 50° F.
(55° F. for *O. thyrsoides aureum*.) Water freely and fertilize regularly during the growing season. Gradually dry
off when leaves die down; keep quite
dry during dormant period. Repot
every four years only. Set bulbs of
O. caudatum two-thirds above soil.

Ornithogalum arabicum, 1½ to 2½
ft., creamy-white with black pistils,
fragrant.

O. caudatum, 3 ft., green and white.

O. lacteum, 2 ft., white.

O. thyrsoides (chincherinchee), 1 to
2 ft., white.

O. t. aureum, 1 to 1½ ft., yellow.

O. umbellatum (star-of-Bethlehem),
1 ft., white with green margins.

SCHIZOBASOPSIS (syn. BOWIEA)

Curious aboveground bulbs, like
onions, develop branched, intricate,
twining, leafless stems in the fall
which have tiny green flowers. For
outdoors in dry, warm climates; elsewhere as window or greenhouse plant.
Very easy in porous soil. Pot or plant
in fall with only base of bulb in soil.
Water moderately when stems are
green; keep dry when dormant. Repot
every few years only.

Schizobasopsis volubilis (climbing
onion), 3 ft., green.

STAR-OF-BETHLEHEM. See *Ornithogalum umbellatum*.

VELTHEIMIA

These flourish outdoors in very mild

Veltheimia

or very light shade from strongest
sun. Repot every few years only.

Veltheimia glauca, 12 to 15 in.,
white or yellowish; red or purple spots.

V. viridifolia, deep flesh-pink.

ZANTEDESCHIA (CALLA LILY)
For outdoor gardens in regions of little or no frost; elsewhere these plants
are grown in greenhouses. Excellent
for cut flowers. They need rich soil,
plenty of moisture and regular fertilizing during the growing period. *Z.
aethiopica* and its varieties grow indoors in minimum temperature of 45°
to 50° F., others in a minimum of
55° to 65° F. If grown indoors, give
light shade from strong sun. Plant
or pot in fall. When flowering is finished and foliage dies naturally, gradually reduce water supply and finally
dry completely; keep plants in cool
place until time to start into growth
again. They are primarily winter and
spring bloomers.

Zantedeschia aethiopica, 2 to 3 ft.,
white.

Z. a. childsiana (baby calla), 1 ft.,
white.

Z. a. godefreyana, 1½ to 2 ft.,
white.

Z. albo-maculata, 1½ to 2 ft.,
creamy-white with purple throat,
white-spotted leaves.

Z. elliottiana, 1½ ft., yellow, leaves
spotted white.

Z. rehmannii, 9 to 12 in., pink or
purplish.

climates and may be used elsewhere
for window gardens and greenhouses.
Pot or plant in early fall, in rich,
porous soil. Spring- and summer-
blooming. Water moderately at first,
freely when in full growth; dry off
gradually when foliage begins to die
naturally; finally, keep quite dry during dormant period. Fertilize well-
rooted specimens regularly through
growing season. Grow in night temperature of 50° to 55° F. in full sun,

FERNS—Cool Greenery

Hardy Ferns and Their Cultivation—
Recommended Outdoor Ferns—Ferns
Indoors—The Fern Greenhouse—List
of Indoor Ferns

FERNS HAVE A WIDE geographical distribution, their 10,000 different species and varieties being found almost throughout the whole world. From those growing sparsely in the Arctic to varieties burgeoning in the tropics, these flowerless plants prefer island and coastal areas to those inland.

HARDY FERNS

However well planned a garden may be, some areas that might be developed and enjoyed are likely to be on the north sides of buildings or shaded by trees. There are few gardens without such an unpromising region, and here ferns might well flourish. While there are a few ferns that will tolerate a certain amount of direct sun, there are none which require it.

Many beautiful hardy fern varieties were originally found growing in the wild among their more common relatives. Others have originated as sporelings in the nurseries of growers. Some of these varieties are so fine and lacy in appearance that they rival the choicest exotic ferns that are nursed in greenhouses.

The greatest attribute of hardy ferns is their undemanding nature. It is possible for some specimens to remain undisturbed in the garden for 20 years. An annual cutting away of the previous year's fronds, occasional weeding and an autumn topdressing of leaf mold, sifted peat moss and wood

ash at ¼ lb. per sq. yd. are the main cultural requirements. Yet from early spring, when the young fronds begin to unfurl, until autumn frosts cut down the deciduous kinds—such as osmundas, athyriums and lastreas—they reveal fresh charm almost daily. Polypodiums, phyllitises and polystichums, being evergreen, retain their beauty far into the winter.

Choose a site that is not only protected from strong sun but is also sheltered from cold spring winds that may damage the tender young fronds. Drought is the greatest enemy of most ferns and probably the major cause of disappointment to growers.

Preparation of the Ground

Careful preparation of the soil before planting is essential. Remember that ferns are woodland plants and in nature grow in a spongy carpet of rotted leaf humus that has accumulated through the years. They cannot stand a heavy soil and most of them dislike lime, which should never be added to their compost. Dig the soil deeply, and incorporate with it a liberal supply of organic material so that food and moisture are conserved. Decayed garden compost, peat moss or well-rotted leaves are ideal. Well-rotted sawdust may also be used.

Planting

Plant all hardy ferns during the dormant period, normally in early fall or early spring. Small specimens can be moved with care at other seasons, but do not disturb any fern while the new fronds are unfurling. At this critical period the young, tender stems are very fragile and easily damaged.

Plant ferns that have rhizomatous rootstocks so that the rhizomes are on the surface of the soil and fibrous roots underneath are covered. Keep the rhizomes in position with large stones until established. Plant the nonrhizomatous kind so that the crowns are just level with the soil surface. Never plant any fern with its old planting mark below the soil.

Management

As the plants become established, frequent topdressing with any of the organic materials mentioned above will help to maintain moisture and at the same time supply natural plant food. Never apply inorganic fertilizers in any form. These quickly react on the plants, which grow luxuriantly for a time but may then turn brown and die.

Give an occasional dressing of unleached wood ash and an annual application of dried sheep manure, or other organic fertilizer, to improve both color and size of fronds. The nearer the approach to the natural conditions in which the plants grow wild, the greater will be the success and the fewer the disappointments.

Propagation

Many kinds of ferns can be propagated by division, a few by means of plantlets that develop on the mature fronds. Ferns are also increased by spores. (They do not form seeds; the spores are sown and can be treated as very fine seeds, except that the soil or other medium on which they are sown must be sterilized by heat or other means before sowing.) With some kinds of ferns the spores are developed on special fertile fronds only, and all other fronds are sterile (nonspore-bearing), but most ferns may bear spores on the undersides of all mature fronds. The ripe spores fall to the ground and produce small, flat plant bodies quite different in appearance to the parent fern; these in turn produce ferns as we know them. But

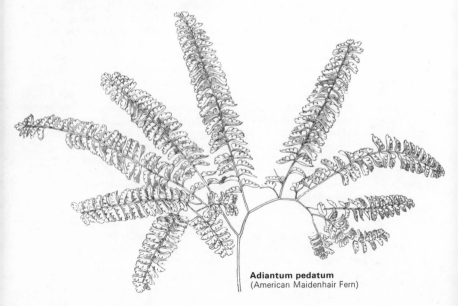

Adiantum pedatum
(American Maidenhair Fern)

the propagation of ferns from spores is complicated, for the specialist only.

RECOMMENDED OUTDOOR FERNS

ADIANTUM

Adiantum pedatum (American maidenhair fern), 12 to 18 in., a graceful plant, is considered by many to be the most beautiful of all hardy ferns. The young, delicate, light green fronds appear very early in the spring and are carried on slender chestnut-brown stems arising from a slowly creeping rootstock. Needs rich soil and considerable shade.

AMERICAN MAIDENHAIR FERN. See *Adiantum pedatum.*

AMERICAN PARSLEY FERN. See *Cryptogramma crispa acrostichoides.*

ATHYRIUM

Athyrium filix-femina (lady fern), one of the loveliest of all ferns, is seen at its best when planted in colonies and interspersed with anemones and rosy cranesbills. It grows freely when well established, the lacy pale green fronds rising at times to 3 or 4 ft. Many of its forms are even more beautiful than the type and have crested, tasseled, finely cut hairlike segments, or congested and mossy fronds. This plant needs shade and rich soil.

CHRISTMAS FERN. See *Polystichum acrostichoides.*

CINNAMON FERN. See *Osmunda cinnamomea.*

COMMON POLYPODY. See *Polypodium vulgare.*

CRYPTOGRAMMA

Cryptogramma crispa acrostichoides (American parsley fern), about 6 in., an elegant little plant, bright and green during summer with a resemblance to parsley at first sight, it has two kinds of fronds: the fertile, nearly

Cryptogramma crispa acrostichoides
(American Parsley Fern)

Dryopteris filix-mas (Male Fern)

triangular in outline, and the barren, broad and flat. The stems are rather slender and very brittle.

DENNSTAEDTIA

Dennstaedtia punctilobula (hay-scented fern) is another North American species. The 3-ft. fronds are feathery and when dry have the refreshing smell of new-mown hay. This species increases by underground runners, a dense mat quickly forming whether it grows in sun or part shade.

DRYOPTERIS

Dryopteris filix-mas (male fern). One of the best known of all hardy ferns, it derives its common name from its robust, sturdy growth. A well-grown specimen is particularly handsome, with graceful, delicate pale green fronds attaining a height of 2½ to 4 ft. In early spring, when they start to develop the fronds are curled around like the flutings of a snail shell and are protected from rain and wind

by their large, chaffy, light brown hairs.

D. noveboracensis (New York fern), has leaves somewhat clustered from creeping rootstocks. It prefers wet soil and forms a good ground cover.

D. spinulosa (spiny wood fern), a handsome North American species that exists in several varieties, of which *intermedia* is best known.

HART'S-TONGUE FERN. See *Phyllitis scolopendrium.*

HAY-SCENTED FERN. See *Dennstaedtia punctilobula.*

INTERRUPTED FERN. See *Osmunda claytoniana.*

LADY FERN. See *Athyrium filix-femina.*

MALE FERN. See *Dryopteris filix-mas.*

NEW YORK FERN. See *Dryopteris noveboracensis.*

ONOCLEA

Onoclea sensibilis (sensitive fern). This delightful North American plant grows in fairly dry shade or moist sunny conditions, but preferably by the waterside, where its creeping rhizomes (which carry two kinds of fronds) can scramble in and out of the water. Its sterile fronds are dark and broadly segmented. The fertile fronds are 1½ to 2½ ft. high with the segments rolled up into beadlike bodies.

OSMUNDA

Osmunda cinnamomea (cinnamon fern), fronds 2 to 3 ft. long and 6 to 8 in. broad, a native of United States and Canada. Prefers rich, moist soil.

O. claytoniana (interrupted fern), fronds 1 ft. long and 8 to 12 in. broad, also a native of North America. Thrives by the waterside in shade.

O. regalis (royal fern), the most conspicuous of all native hardy ferns, attains majestic proportions. Easily cultivated in any moist place, such as the side of a lake, stream or pool. Its fronds—a delicate pale green in spring, changing with the approach of autumn to light russet-brown—are of two kinds: the fertile, approximately 3 ft. long, and the barren, which are more numerous, 5 ft. or more long.

OSTRICH FERN. See *Pteretis nodulosa.*

PHYLLITIS

Phyllitis scolopendrium (syn. *Scolopendrium vulgare*—hart's-tongue fern), readily distinguishable by its evergreen, strap-shaped leaves, which vary in length from 1 to 1½ ft. and contrast beautifully with the feathery appearance of other ferns. One of the most adaptable ferns, it is at home on walls, by the waterside or in the border (either in full sun or part shade). Can also be grown as a pot plant in the house. Of the many varieties, *P.s. crispum* is the most commonly grown.

P.s. crispum, 1½ ft., paler green, more delicate in texture, and beautifully crimped along the leaf margins. There are also forms with baby plantlets on the fronds. These are easily separated and can, with care, be grown to adult stage.

POLYPODIUM

Polypodium vulgare (common polypody) forms low, spreading mats of foliage and occurs in many interesting and beautiful varieties.

POLYSTICHUM

Polystichum aculeatum, 2 to 3 ft., is one of the best ferns for the shady garden. Its luxuriant evergreen fronds arise from a nest of rusty membranous scales. The many varieties and forms of this elegant plant are all good, and since they are unaffected by extreme seasonal variations, they increase in size and beauty year after year.

P. acrostichoides (Christmas fern) is an evergreen, mat-forming variety, adaptable to growing in rock crevices and on rock ledges. The fronds are up to 2 ft. long.

PTERETIS

Pteretis nodulosa (ostrich fern) is a distinct fern of bold, stately appearance that is easy to grow in moist soil. Its fronds may be 6 to 9 ft. long.

ROYAL FERN. See *Osmunda regalis.*

SENSITIVE FERN. See *Onoclea sensibilis.*

SPINY WOOD FERN. See *Dryopteris spinulosa.*

FERNS INDOORS

Ferns of the tropics and subtropics are the greenhouse ferns of temperate zones and include a number of kinds suitable for use as house plants. To cultivate them successfully it is desirable to imitate the environment in which they grow naturally, and to provide the moist, humid, sunless but light conditions so essential to their well-being. Although household climates do not maintain as high humidity as conditions in a greenhouse, some ferns—notably the sword fern (*Nephrolepis exaltata*), the holly fern (*Cyrtomium falcatum*) and the squirrel's-foot fern (*Davallia bullata*)—will succeed as house plants.

The minimum temperature of a greenhouse where tropical ferns are grown should be 55° F., but many subtropical kinds will thrive with a minimum temperature of 45° to 50° F. As in the case of hardy ferns, propagation (other than by division) is a job for the specialist, and most amateurs will buy their specimens already potted. The ferns will, however, need repotting from time to time. In a greenhouse this can be done at any season of the year, though spring is most opportune.

When a fern has completely filled its pot with roots, move it on to the next size pot. Be sure the pot is clean inside and out, and place crocks in the bottom to insure good drainage. Use soil similar to that in which the plant would grow in its natural surroundings. It should be light, fibrous, spongy and capable of retaining moisture without becoming soggy or solid. Good materials are a combination of clean fibrous loam, peat moss, leaf mold, coarse sand and granulated charcoal or brick rubble in roughly equal proportions. Experience will show what proportions are best for a particular type of fern. Always plant loosely.

RECOMMENDED INDOOR FERNS

The plants listed below are all suitable for growing under the conditions described. Too often the range of ferns seen in an amateur's greenhouse consists solely of the plants most commonly offered in flower shops, includ-

ing *Pteris cretica, Cyrtomium falcatum* (holly fern), *Asplenium bulbiferum* and *Adiantum cuneatum*, all excellent plants. Although they provide a good backbone for a collection, some of the following will add interest.

ADIANTUM (MAIDENHAIR FERN)

These ferns, 6 in. to 3 ft. high, with their graceful habit and pleasing color tones, are probably the most popular in cultivation. (See also page 267.)

Adiantum caudatum, one of the smaller species, with graceful fronds not exceeding 1 ft. in length, beautifully cut and fringed, with baby plantlets at the tips of the mature leaves. These plantlets can be pegged down to form new plants and later severed from the parent and potted separately. Excellent for greenhouse hanging baskets, for pedestals or other special places that set off a display of pendulous greenery.

A. cuneatum (delta maidenhair) is the most commonly grown of tender maidenhair ferns. All of its many varieties are extremely graceful.

A. decorum, fronds up to 15 in. long, delicate rosy-red when young, changing to bright green, rather erect and stiff in growth.

A. flabellulatum reaches majestic proportions, the fronds ascending to 2 ft. or more and nearly 1 ½ ft. across.

A. roseum, a dwarf kind, with fronds 4 to 6 in. long. Worthy of consideration for its color tones, it is a pleasing pink when young, changing to delicate green later.

ASPLENIUM

There are nearly 800 members of this genus scattered throughout the world, many making excellent greenhouse plants. The fronds are evergreen and have a leathery texture.

Asplenium bulbiferum, 1 to 2 ft., the commonest variety. This kind freely forms young plantlets on its fronds that can be used for propagation. Practical as a house plant in a fairly cool room.

A. nidus (bird's-nest fern), forms a basket-shaped plant of erect, flaring, undivided fronds arising from a common crown. Attractive and distinctive.

BIRD'S-NEST FERN. See *Asplenium nidus.*

BLECHNUM

Blechnum gibbum is one of the best of this extensive family, the long, arching fronds often reaching 2½ to 3 ft. in length.

B.g. bellii, forked fronds, each densely tasseled at the apex.

B.g. tinctum. Young fronds are tinged with pink.

BOSTON FERN. See *Nephrolepis exaltata bostoniensis.*

CLIFF BRAKE. See *Pellaea.*

COFFEE FERN. See *Pellaea andromedaefolia.*

CYRTOMIUM

In common with most ferns from Japan, this plant is evergreen.

Cyrtomium falcatum (holly fern); bears thick, tough, spiny leaves with a polished surface, which normally reach about 1½ ft. high. This fern is one of the best for cultivating as a house plant.

DAVALLIA

All the davallias are beautiful plants of easy cultivation in a greenhouse. They also are satisfactory as house plants if the air is not extremely dry. The following are good subjects for hanging baskets and are rhizomatous.

Davallia bullata (squirrel's-foot fern), up to 1 ft. high.

D. canariensis (rabbit's-foot fern), 1 to 1½ ft., owes its common name to the appearance of the growths of the rootstock, which curve over the sides of the pot.

ELKHORN FERN. See *Platycerium.*

HARE'S-FOOT FERN. See *Polypodium aureum.*

HOLLY FERN. See *Cyrtomium falcatum.*

LYGODIUM

A remarkable genus of climbing ferns, making especially attractive growths when allowed to twine on wires or strings in the greenhouse.

Lygodium japonicum, attractive and easily managed, with almost leaf-like fronds. Can scramble from 8 to 10 ft.

L. scandens, similar to *L. japonicum;* fronds bluish-green.

L. volubile, 10 ft.; its fronds are about 1 ft. long.

MAIDENHAIR FERN. See *Adiantum.*

MICROLEPIA

Plants with very finely divided, broadly toothed foliage carried on hairy stems. There are about 25 sorts, of which the following are the best to try indoors:

Microlepia marginata, 1½ to 2 ft.

M. platyphylla, 2 to 3 ft.

NEPHROLEPIS (SWORD FERN)

One of the most popular of greenhouse ferns; can also be grown as a house plant. Excellent for growing outdoors in shady areas of the Deep South.

Nephrolepis cordifolia has erect, narrow, bright green fronds. There are several varieties of this handsome species.

N. exaltata. This fern has fronds 2 ft. long and from 3 to 6 in. broad, and it is the one most suitable for general cultivation. Its many beauti-

272

Nephrolepis exaltata bostoniensis
(Boston Fern)

ful varieties, including *N.e. bostoniensis* (Boston fern), adapt very well to hanging baskets.

PELLAEA (CLIFF BRAKE)

A very interesting group of low-growing ferns with leathery fronds, of neat habit and easy cultivation.

Pellaea andromedaefolia (coffee fern), a native of the United States, has very scaly, reddish-brown stems about 1 ft. long.

P. atropurpurea, 6 to 12 in., purple stems; a native of North America. A very slow grower.

P. dealbata, 6-in. chestnut-brown stems and pale green foliage, which appears to be heavily dusted with white powder beneath.

P. rotundifolia, charming, with dark green fronds and brown hairy stems.

PLATYCERIUM
(ELKHORN FERN, STAGHORN FERN)

These are among the most beautiful and distinctive of all ferns. The fronds are forked, giving the plants a noble antlerlike appearance, which with their epiphytal character (they live on nutrients from air and rain) attracts immediate attention. Most of them originate in the tropics.

Platycerium bifurcatum (syn. *P. alicorne*), the easiest to cultivate, makes a good house plant, and can exist for years on a branch of wood if sprayed frequently with water. This kind originated in Australia.

POLYPODIUM

A few members of this extensive family are well adapted to greenhouse cultivation, chiefly *Polypodium aureum* and its varieties.

Polypodium aureum (hare's-foot fern), from Australia, has creeping stems clothed with bright rusty scales, and handsome lobed foliage which may easily exceed 2 ft. in length. The plant itself may spread to 10 ft. across.

PTERIS (BRAKE)

Pteris cretica comes in many varieties, all graceful, with individual fronds up to 1 ft. long. Its many outstanding varieties include *P.c. albo-lineata*, with a white stripe down the center of each frond, and *P.c. wimsettii*, with crested fronds. They make good house plants where the atmosphere is not too dry.

RABBIT'S-FOOT FERN. See *Davallia canariensis*.

SQUIRREL'S-FOOT FERN. See *Davallia bullata*.

STAGHORN FERN. See *Platycerium*.

SWORD FERN. See *Nephrolepis*.

Platycerium bifurcatum
(Staghorn Fern)

Pteris cretica
(Brake)

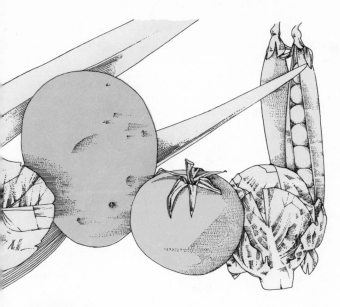

CHAPTER 13

VEGETABLES—
Especially Good
When You Grow Them Yourself

The Advantages of Home Growing—Planning the Vegetable Garden—Preparation of Soil—Planting—Popular Vegetables

CREATING A HOME GARDEN can be a particularly rewarding experience, likely to increase in value from season to season and with considerable adventure and challenge. It is healthy exercise to help plants grow, and fascinating to watch them develop and produce. Probably the greatest satisfaction of all is dining on the harvest. It is a very short trip from the garden

to the kitchen, and no market product can come close to matching the flavor and tenderness of a vegetable picked at exactly the right moment and cooked or processed without delay. The best varieties for the finest taste, for canning or for freezing are not usually available in the markets. Moreover, many vegetables that are rarely found in stores are easily grown in the garden and add zestful interest to the menu. By raising their own produce, large families can make substantial savings in the food budget. And then there is an esthetic bonus when the landscape close to home includes a vegetable garden with its greenery of lettuce, the red-veined deep green of beet tops, the green gusto of cabbage, the big soft leaves of sprawling squash. Reddening tomatoes and great orange pumpkins add joyous color to the ripening garden that has meant well-being to Americans since the day of the first Thanksgiving.

GARDEN PLANNING

To be successful, a vegetable garden should be planned in advance and held to a manageable size. The indispensable requirements are suitable site and soil, good management and the control of weeds, insects and diseases.

It is helpful to diagram the prospective location of each vegetable and how many feet of row are to be allotted to it. Vegetables that are better fresh from the garden than from the store should be given space in preference to those that may readily be purchased in good condition, such as root crops. In deciding how much to grow, consider whether the garden is to provide vegetables only for table use, or for freezing and canning as well. It is important to schedule successive plantings of such vegetables as lettuce, radishes and corn, which are in good condition for only a short time. Too often, a single large planting is made, and much of the crop is not used because it becomes overmature. The family vacation period should be anticipated so that crops will not be ready for harvesting at that time. When canning or freezing is a consideration, the crop should mature at a convenient period for processing it.

Vegetable plants vary greatly in the space they occupy. To make efficient use of the garden area, planning should take into account these diverse growth habits. Radishes, lettuce and spinach need very little space and mature rapidly, so that each planting occupies the ground for only a few weeks. The cucurbit vine crops—cucumber, muskmelon, watermelon, pumpkin and squash—sprawl over many square yards and require a full growing season to mature. Corn also takes much room, grows tall and shades its neighbors.

The perennial vegetables—rhubarb, asparagus and horseradish—should be grown at one side of the garden, where they can remain for many years without interfering with soil preparation for the other vegetables. The small, rapid-maturing radishes, lettuce, spinach, carrots, beets, chard, parsley, onions and parsnips should be in one section, with space left for successive plantings. If the same garden plot is used for vegetables each year, rotation of crops should be followed so that the crops are in different places during the next growing season.

SOIL PREPARATION

When a garden site is used for many years, continuous cultivation depletes the soil of organic matter; it should be replenished from time to time for good tilth and soil fertility. (See "Fertilizers and Manures," page 749, and "Composting and Green Manuring," page 761.)

When vegetables are being raised in a new area, the acidity of the soil should be determined and adjusted to the crops to be grown (see page 741). The County Agricultural Extension Service or other government source will arrange for soil tests and make recommendations.

Fitting, or preparing, the soil depends upon the size of the garden. Usually in larger areas the ground is plowed and worked with a springtooth harrow or rototillers of various types. In small areas hand spading works very well. The gardener's aim in fitting the soil is to work it to a fine, mellow condition with the sod well turned under and chewed up. The structure of sandy soils is not injured by working them when wet, but the heavier soils will become compacted and cloddy and remain that way all summer. Plowing or spading in late fall, followed by final working in the spring, is sound practice.

PLANTING

The time of planting depends upon the vegetable and the local climate. Hotbeds and cold frames are useful in a large garden if many plants are to be raised in advance of warm weather (see page 84).

Plant bands or paper collars obtainable from seed and garden stores, as well as small peat pots, assure late transplanting without disturbing the roots of the young plants.

Some vegetables are very tolerant of cold and may be planted as soon as the condition of the soil permits. Among those that may be sown or planted four to six weeks before the frost-free date are broccoli, cabbage, lettuce, onions, peas, potatoes, spinach and turnips (see map, page 850). Beets, carrots, chard, mustard, parsnips and radishes may be sown two to four weeks before the frost-free date.

Vegetables that are sensitive to cold include snap beans, okra, New Zealand spinach, squash, sweet corn and tomatoes. Those that require prevailing hot weather and a warm soil are lima beans, eggplants, peppers, sweet potatoes, cucumbers, muskmelons and watermelons.

Helpful protectors from late frost are hot caps, or small paper tents. The heat inside the hot cap also brings the plant along faster.

In planting, the space between the rows must depend largely on the method of tillage. If a garden tractor or rototiller is used for cultivation, the rows must be farther apart than if a wheel hoe and hand hoe are to do the job. Space is wasted when rows are far apart; the heaviest yields are obtained from close planting. If the garden is small, most of the cultivation can be done with a hand hoe.

Most vegetable seeds are sown in shallow drills or trenches, the depth depending on the size of the seeds (see page 700).

The date of planting and the variety name should be recorded on a label at the beginning of each row. When seed is reserved for later plantings, it is helpful to note each seeding date on the envelope before filing it.

Germinating seeds require a moist soil; if soil dries out, little seedlings may die. If the soil is not moist at planting time, water each row as soon as seeds are planted. Corn and bean seeds are dropped in a 2-in.-deep furrow, watered and then covered. This watering will usually be enough, but if the weather is hot and dry, extra waterings may be needed.

The finer seeds require frequent light watering unless a cloudy, rainy period follows planting. It is best to water in early evening, but if the weather is hot, dry and windy an additional watering at noon may be needed. Lettuce is difficult to get up in midsummer, but shading the row with cheesecloth keeps the soil moist longer. A board may be used over the seed to encourage germination. Daily inspections are necessary so that it may be removed as soon as the seedlings begin to come up.

Plants of tomato, pepper, eggplant, cabbage, broccoli, cauliflower and muskmelon are sometimes transplanted to the garden. The soil should be well firmed around the roots, and if the weather is hot and dry, the plants should be watered at once. Better yet,

How to Use a Dibber
Make a perpendicular hole (top, left) large enough to hold the plant's roots, then make a hole (top, right) at an angle of about 40° at one side of each plant and lever upward (bottom, left) to firm the roots. If necessary, fill the depression (bottom, right) at the side of the plant with water, both at the time of planting and again a few days later during very dry periods.

a starter solution made with one cupful of 5–10–5 fertilizer in 3 gal. of water may be applied to the newly set plants at the rate of one cup of solution to each plant. As long as the weather is hot and dry, irrigate daily until the plants begin to grow; shading is also helpful.

WEED AND DISEASE CONTROL

After the seedlings are up, the important job is weed control. A hoe is the most useful implement; the small garden can hardly afford the space

needed by a tractor. In any event, the hoe, wheel hoe or hand weeder will be needed frequently for working close to small plants.

Cultivation should be as shallow as possible to avoid root injury to the vegetables, and frequent enough to control the weeds, which are destroyed most easily while they are very small. Heavy infestations of perennial weeds such as quack (witch) grass, bindweed and Canada thistle should be eliminated as soon as possible, as they greatly increase the labor of maintaining the garden. Herbicides are useful for getting rid of them. Small patches may be smothered with black polyethylene. Frequent cultivation and hoeing for one season also discourage the marauders.

Perennial weeds not only crowd a garden's rightful occupants but often harbor viruses which weaken or kill vegetables and garden flowers. Among plants that are known to harbor viruses are milkweed, burdock, plantain, biennial crucifer and horse nettle. Various garden flowers also carry viruses; thus beans grown near gladioluses often fail.

Mulches can be very useful, especially with the larger vegetable plants. For tomatoes and vine crops, a black plastic, hay or other mulch is very effective. Cover the space between the rows soon after the plants are large enough to work around. This will prevent blossom-end rot of tomatoes, inhibit weed growth and keep the fruit clean. Usually mulched crops are larger than those cultivated. A mulch is especially useful when the gardener is on vacation, as it controls weeds and postpones the need for

watering. In dry seasons when the public water supply is short and watering of the garden is limited, a mulch is indispensable and should be applied early in the season.

Even in normal seasons, there will be times when rainfall is inadequate for the best growth of vegetables, especially the shallow-rooted types. If there is no rain, substantial increases in yield result from irrigation—about an inch of water once a week.

QUALITY OF PLANTS

Many vegetables may be grown with very little attention to controlling insects and diseases. See Vegetable Pests, page 811, and Vegetable Diseases, page 804. In general, the quality of vegetable seeds from a reliable seed firm is good.

The vegetables suggested in the following section are currently good for the northeastern quarter of the United States and adjacent Canada. Detailed recommendations for any part of the country are usually available from the county agricultural extension services, other government sources or colleges of agriculture.

Thinning Out Seedlings
As soon as the seedlings are large enough to handle, thin them out. Make sure the ground is wet before thinning, and afterward firm the soil to discourage egg-laying flies. Do not leave discarded seedlings on the ground to decay and attract pests.

Recommended Vegetables

ASPARAGUS

Asparagus is the first vegetable from the garden. The plants are perennial, and a planting is productive for 15 to 20 years. Asparagus grows best where the soil freezes somewhat during the winter; this limits its culture to the territory north of Georgia.

The soil should be fertile and well drained with the pH (see page 741) maintained at 6.0 or above. Since the planting is long-lived, it should be started with an abundance of organic matter, from manure or from plowing under a heavy sod.

Asparagus plants may be purchased and introduced into the garden as soon as the soil can be worked, or the gardener may sow his own seeds and put the plants in permanent places the following spring. Only the largest plants should be used; the smaller ones are less productive.

The plants, or crowns, should be set in trenches 6 in. deep, spaced 18 to 30 in. in rows 3 ft. apart. Cover the crowns to a depth of three inches, and gradually work the soil into the trench as the plants increase in size. During the summer, control the weeds by cultivation to permit vigorous growth.

Asparagus should not be cut for two years, to give the plants time to build up large crowns. During the third season, the asparagus may be cut clean for a month. In future years, the cutting season may be extended to two months. For the remainder of the summer, the plants must be allowed to grow and store food for the next season's crop. The planting should be fertilized near the end of the cutting season with a 10–10–10 formula at the rate of 4 lb. to 50 ft. of row.

BEANS

Beans are warm-weather crops and

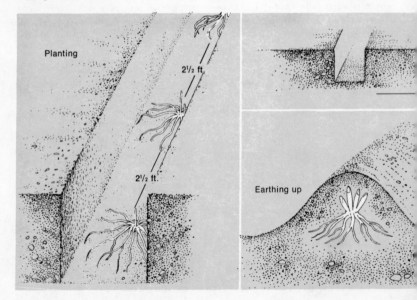

Planting

2½ ft.

2½ ft.

Earthing up

should be planted no earlier than a few days before the average date of the last killing frost. One may gamble on an earlier planting, but the crop may not be hastened, for beans do not grow well until the soil is warm.

Snap beans are one of the mainstays of the home garden. The plants yield heavily, are easily grown and produce throughout the summer if successive plantings are made every two or three weeks. Plant the seeds of bush beans about an inch apart in rows 2 to 2½ ft. apart. Water in dry weather. Excessive use of nitrogen should be avoided. Pole beans require sturdy supports (see illustration on page 282).

Lima beans need a growing season about four months long with a high temperature, and should not be planted until stable warm weather arrives. Again, the bush types are easier to manage than the pole types.

The beans should be harvested while young and tender. If picked often, the plants will yield fruit for a longer period.

BEETS

Beet tops are a delightful bonus to the root crop. The thinnings with the small roots and young leaves may be used as greens; beets themselves should be used while young and tender. Successive sowings should be made every three weeks to provide a continuous supply of small beets.

The first planting may be made as early as the ground can be prepared. The soil should be kept moist and shaded during germination.

BROCCOLI

Broccoli is as easy to grow as cabbage and has the same soil and cultural requirements. It forms a loose flower head on a fleshy, branching stalk instead of a compact head like cauliflower, and it will continue to produce these loose heads throughout the summer.

The head or edible part of the plant is a dense cluster of flower buds, which should be harvested before the buds open. After the main cluster is cut

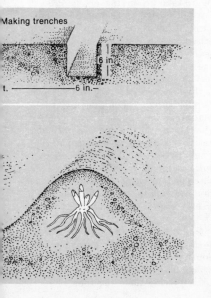

Making trenches

6 in.

t. ——————— 6 in.—

Planting Asparagus
After digging the trenches,
set the crowns in them,
carefully spreading out the roots,
and cover the crowns firmly with
3 in. of good soil. In the third year,
make a 5-in.-high ridge of soil over
each row to blanch the stalks.

Methods of Training Pole Beans

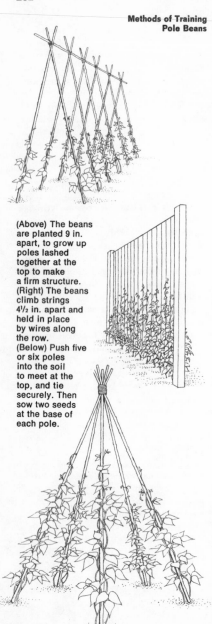

(Above) The beans are planted 9 in. apart, to grow up poles lashed together at the top to make a firm structure. (Right) The beans climb strings 4½ in. apart and held in place by wires along the row. (Below) Push five or six poles into the soil to meet at the top, and tie securely. Then sow two seeds at the base of each pole.

with a stem about 6 in. long, small branches continue to bud throughout the growing season and should be harvested as ready. The plants will bear until severe cold weather.

BRUSSELS SPROUTS

Brussels sprouts are grown like cabbage. The seeds are started in an outdoor seedbed in late May, and the plants are set in the garden in midsummer for a fall crop. The sprouts are borne in the axils where the leaves join the stem. As they begin to crowd the leaf below, sprouts are broken off to give them more room and facilitate harvesting. The top leaves should be left to nourish the plant and its crop.

The plants may be stored for winter use, set close together in a cold frame or cold cellar with soil around the roots. If kept in a shed or garage under hay, the sprouts will last all winter.

CABBAGE

Cabbages are ordinarily grown from plants started in the greenhouse or hotbed, or from southern-grown plants shipped north for spring planting. If raised in the North, seed should be planted a month to six weeks before the plants are to be set in the garden.

The soil should have a pH of 5.5 or higher (see page 741). Acid soils should be limed. High fertility is essential, as rapid growth means better quality. Fertilizers high in nitrogen and potash should be used at planting time. These should be supplemented with a nitrogenous fertilizer every three or four weeks. Shallow cultivation to avoid injury to the roots, and weekly irrigations during dry weather, are essential.

Collards are a type of cabbage that does not head and is grown in the South for its large rosette of leaves, which may be blanched for tenderness by tying them together.

Brussels Sprouts
The sprouts on the left are of good quality; each "button" is tight and firm and is well placed on the stem. Those on the right are badly grown, loose and broken.

CABBAGE, CHINESE

Chinese cabbage is a delicately flavored member of the same genus as the cabbage, and forms elongated, compact heads. The stems may be eaten raw like celery or cooked like asparagus.

A rich soil and plenty of moisture are required to produce a good crop. The seeds should be sown in place, for Chinese cabbage does not transplant well. Plants should be thinned to from 12 to 15 in. apart. Chinese cabbage should not be sown before July 1 or the plants will go to seed without heading.

CARROTS

Carrots may be sown as early as the soil can be worked. The seeds germinate slowly, and the ground should be watered daily until the seedlings are up; shade to prolong the moisture. Carrots are best when young and crisp, so successive plantings should be made every three weeks. Thin seedlings to an inch apart in the row.

CAULIFLOWER

Cauliflower is a more difficult crop to grow than cabbage because it is less tolerant to extreme heat in the summer or severe freezing in the fall. A cool, moist climate and a fertile soil with the pH above 6.0 but not over 7.2 suit this crop.

Plants are set as early as cabbage plants for the summer crop. The fall-crop plants should be set to mature when the weather is cool, but before a hard frost. When the head has reached a diameter of 2 to 3 in., the outside leaves must be tied together over the head to blanch it white and tender. The heads should be harvested when still firm and before they open up. Cauliflower does not keep long when mature.

CELERIAC

Celeriac (celery root, knob celery, root celery or turnip-rooted celery) is celery that has been developed for the root instead of the top. It grows more slowly than celery and may be harvested whenever the root is large enough. Plants may be set out as early as April. The late summer crop may be sown in the garden from May to June and be stored for winter use. To store, pull up, twist off the tops, clean off the side roots and bury in moist sand in a moderately cool place.

CELERY

To grow celery, cool weather, an abundant moisture supply and a deep, fertile soil, well supplied with organic matter, are required. In the North, it is sown in late winter or early spring.

Plants may be purchased, or they may be raised from seed in a hotbed or in the house. The seeds germinate slowly and should be started about ten weeks before the plants are to be set in the garden. The seedlings should be transplanted once in the seed flat or seedbed, and then to the garden, 1 ft. apart in rows 18 in. apart. Frequent watering is essential if rainfall is less than an inch a week. Side dressings of a nitrogenous fertilizer—on the soil or dissolved in water—should be made at three-week intervals.

Celery may be used green, or it may

Planting and Earthing Up Celery
Plant the seedlings 1 ft. apart along prepared trenches, then tamp the roots in well and half-fill each trench with water to encourage firmness. When the plants are 1 ft. high, begin earthing up so that the celery stalks are covered with soil.

be blanched by excluding the light with boards, paper or drain tiles, or by wrapping newspaper around the individual plants. Late-fall blanching may be done by mounding the plants with earth.

Celery harvested late may be kept for winter use by banking with earth and covering the tops with straw or leaves. It may also be dug and stored in a cold frame or cool cellar with the roots in moist soil.

CELERY ROOT. See *Celeriac.*

CHARD

Chard, or Swiss chard, is a type of beet that has been developed for its top, which is used as a cooked green. The leaves, picked off while young and tender, are rapidly replaced by new leaves. Water and nitrogen fertilizer keep the chard growing well throughout the summer and early fall.

Sow the seed where the plants are to grow; space chard 6 in. or more apart in the row. One planting will last through the growing season.

CHICORY, WITLOOF

Witloof chicory is grown for its roots; it provides edible greens in the winter. The seed is sown in the spring, and the plants spaced 6 to 8 in. apart. In autumn the roots are lifted and planted in a box or bed of moist soil in a warm cellar. If the soil is watered occasionally, the heads of white leaves will be ready for the table in a few weeks; the roots are of no further use.

CITRON MELONS. See *Watermelons.*

COLLARDS. See *Cabbage.*

CORN, SWEET

Sweet corn requires more space than is usually available in small gardens, but homegrown corn of a high-quality variety, cooked and eaten within a few minutes after it is picked, is such a delicious vegetable that it should be in every garden that can find room for it. The large-cobbed, heavy-yielding varieties that are grown for market are far inferior to home-garden corn.

Sweet corn is a warm-weather crop, but relatively cold-resistant. The first planting may be made two weeks or more before the average date of the last frost. If it is frosted, the loss is not great, but if no frost occurs, the corn is off to an early start. The leaves turn yellow if the weather is cold after the corn is up, but become green the first warm day; corn grows most rapidly in higher temperatures.

The first planting should be three varieties—early, midseason and late. Thereafter, the late variety, usually the best in quality, should be planted every five to seven days. In regions similar to central New York, the first planting may be made in late April and the last planting about July 12. Corn will thus be available most of the time from late July to mid-October. Since poor pollination causes scantily filled ears, each planting should be in blocks of three rows to provide for wind pollination. The rows should be $2\frac{1}{2}$ to 3 ft. apart with the plants spaced 1 ft. apart in the row.

A complete fertilizer (10–10–10) when the ground is fitted may be supplemented later with a nitrogenous fertilizer. Corn is susceptible to drought and should be watered when rainfall is deficient. Commercial corn growers use atrazine to control weeds, but its use is not advisable in a small garden unless the same area is to be planted with corn for several years.

To enjoy sweet corn at its best, do not pick it until the pot is actually on the stove. As every devotee knows, one walks to the garden, but runs back to the kitchen with the corn. Corn should be harvested in the "milk stage." To test, push the thumbnail into a kernel; if the liquid that comes out is milky, the corn is ready for picking.

Sweet-corn varieties are nearly all hybrids, and the old open-pollinated varieties are no longer grown. There are many hybrids available, and local advice should be sought as to which are best for the garden. The hybrids are very uniform in all characteristics including time of ripening; in fact, the period during which a hybrid is in good eating condition is a week or less.

CUCUMBERS

Cucumbers do well on a wide range of soils if they are in good tilth and well supplied with organic matter. Stable manure may be mixed with the top 8 to 10 in. of soil at the rate of 3 or 4 wheelbarrowfuls to 50 ft. of row. If manure is not easy to obtain, compost and commercial fertilizers will help produce good crops.

For an early crop, start cucumber seeds in pots, plant bands (see Planting, page 277) or berry boxes in the house or hotbed; transplant seedlings to the garden after danger of frost is past. Good crops can be produced by direct seeding in drills or furrows. More seeds should be planted than are needed, to allow for casualties from insects and diseases. The final spacing may be reached after two or three thinnings, with a plant every 2 to 3 ft. in rows 6 ft. apart.

Cucumbers are also grown on hills or mounds 6 ft. from one another. Two or three plants are grouped close together on each hill.

It is best to start cucumbers under cheesecloth, supported by a frame and enclosed at the sides, to keep away destructive insects until the plants are well established. Remove the cloth when the plants begin to bloom.

Healthy growth is encouraged by a mulch of black plastic, hay or other material, which should be laid before the plants start to run. Prompt harvesting before the seeds harden will prolong the fruiting period.

Two types of cucumbers are grown: the large, long varieties for slicing and the small-size varieties for pickling.

EGGPLANT

Eggplant belongs to the same family as the tomato and has similar soil and climatic requirements, except that the growing season should be somewhat longer and hotter than is required by the early-ripening tomato varieties. The plants should be set out only when the soil is well warmed up. Half a dozen will produce enough fruit for the average family.

ENDIVE

Endive has the same cultural requirements and uses as lettuce. However, it is more tolerant of heat.

When the plants are large and nearly ready for use, the heads should be blanched to remove the bitter flavor. Draw the outside leaves together over the heart and tie them with a string or rubber band. The heads will be ready to use in two or three weeks.

FENNEL, FLORENCE

The valuable part of Florence fennel is its enlarged, flattened leafstalk. It is a summer crop in the North and an autumn and winter crop in the South. The stalks are blanched by mounding them with earth when they are about 2 in. in diameter.

HORSERADISH

Horseradish is grown for its roots, which are ground and used as a condiment with beef, oysters and other foods. The plants thrive in any good garden soil; in fact, they often become weedy unless kept under control.

Root cuttings, 6 to 8 in. long, are planted in a sunny area and are ready to harvest the first fall. Pieces of roots left in the soil after harvesting are sufficient to maintain the stock.

KALE

Kale belongs to the cabbage genus, but does not form a head. The leaves are used as greens. Kale is most often grown as a late fall crop, the seed being sown in early or midsummer. The rows are spaced 18 in. apart with plants 1 ft. apart in the row. The larger leaves are harvested while young and tender; they toughen with age.

KNOB CELERY. See *Celeriac*.

KOHLRABI

The edible portion of kohlrabi is the swollen stem. Cultivate like cabbage, but sow the seed where the plants are to remain. Kohlrabi grows rapidly and must be harvested when the edible portion is about 2 in. in diameter; it soon becomes tough.

LEEKS

Relatives of the onion, these are raised from seed. Instead of a bulb, a thick, tasty stem is produced.

LETTUCE

Lettuce thrives on any good soil, preferably with a pH of 6.0 or higher. It is a cool-weather crop, growing best in early spring or fall. The seeds are usually planted in place, but the first crop may be started inside or in the hotbed and transplanted to the garden. The spacing should be 1 ft. between rows and 6 in. between plants. The plants from direct seeding should be thinned promptly to avoid crowding, which checks growth. Water and shade for growth in hot, dry weather.

Lettuce plants mature quickly; successive sowings at two-week intervals should be made for continuous supply. As soon as any unpicked plants are overmature, they should be destroyed to prevent certain viruses, to which they are susceptible, from spreading to the younger plants.

Leaf lettuce is much easier to grow than head lettuce and is preferred for home gardens. There are many good varieties; consult catalogues for those especially heat-resistant.

LIMA BEANS. See *Beans*.

MUSKMELONS

Muskmelons have soil, climatic and cultural requirements similar to those for cucumbers, but they grow better in lighter soil. However, they may be grown in most good garden soils of high fertility and a pH of 6.0 or higher (see page 741). Ample soil moisture should be maintained by irrigation or by mulching.

The melons are ready to harvest when they will slip easily from the stem with a slight twist.

Fusarium is a serious disease of muskmelons. It is best to choose one of the resistant varieties, available from most seed houses.

MUSTARD

A rapid-growing plant that is used for greens; the young inner leaves are choice. Mustard will grow on any good soil. Plant 5 or 6 in. apart in row; sow at intervals through August. Do not allow greens to seed.

OKRA

Okra is a hot-weather vegetable belonging to the mallow family, and it thrives where cucumbers and tomatoes are grown. The seed is sown in rows after the weather is warm, and the seedlings thinned to a spacing of 18 in. to 2 ft. apart in the row.

The seedpods are the edible part of the plant and should be picked every day while young and tender. The older pods soon become woody and tough, and if many remain unharvested, the plants soon stop bearing.

ONIONS

The scallion or green onion is grown from seeds or sets (small onions grown from seed the previous year). Small green plants raised in seedbeds in the South and shipped north are also used. Sets and young plants are preferred for home-garden use, but seed can be satisfactory under favorable conditions. In any case onions should be planted as early as possible, every 3 in. in rows about 1 ft. apart. Choose fertilizer high in phosphorus and potash.

If onion sets are planted closely, every other plant may be pulled after a few weeks' growth and used as green onions, leaving the rest to mature.

"Top" or "tree" onions do not produce seeds but are raised from small onions borne in clusters at the top of the stem. These are planted in the fall and will come up in the spring.

OYSTER PLANT. See *Salsify*.

PARSLEY

Parsley thrives best in cool weather; it should be started as soon as the soil can be worked in the spring. If an early crop is desired, the seeds may be started inside and the seedlings transplanted to the garden. Germination is slow, so the soil should be kept moist by frequent watering or by covering the ground with a board until the first seedlings appear.

PARSLEY, TURNIP-ROOTED

This is a type of parsley with a large, edible root. The seeds should be planted very early, as they germinate with difficulty in hot, dry weather. The roots may be dug and stored for winter use. Hamburg is the variety commonly grown.

PARSNIPS

Parsnips, the perfect vegetable to accent hearty stews, grow well over much of the United States and parts of Canada. The seeds require a long growing season but should not be planted until warm weather. Since germination is slow, the soil must be kept moist until the seedlings appear. Light mulching or shading will keep the soil moist longer after watering.

Parsnips are not ready for use until two or three weeks after the near-freezing temperatures of late fall. They may be left in the ground over winter and dug for use at any time that the ground is not frozen. They may also be dug before the ground freezes and stored in a cold cellar or pit.

PEAS

Peas are a cool-weather crop; they should be planted as early in the spring as the soil can be worked. Late plantings are successful where the climate is cool in midsummer. The quality of the crop will be improved if several varieties maturing at different times are planted together.

The seeds are sown in a shallow furrow about 2 in. deep with the rows about 2 to 4 ft. apart, depending on the height of the variety. Irrigate if the weather is hot and dry.

The peas should be picked and used just as soon as they reach the desired size. They are delicious when small and tender, but tough if overmature.

Peas are available in dwarf and tall varieties, but the dwarf varieties are easier to manage and do not need support. The tall varieties must be supported by small branches inserted in the ground along the row or by a trellis of chicken wire about 4 ft. high.

PEPPERS

Peppers belong to the same family as do tomatoes and have identical cultural requirements, except that plants are not seeded in the garden. They should be started indoors; plant out after settled warm weather arrives.

Peppers are even more sensitive than tomatoes to too much nitrogen, which must be used with care or the plants will grow with great vigor but produce very little fruit. Plastic mulch encourages growth.

POTATOES

Potatoes are always readily available in the markets, so home gardeners with limited space should probably forget them.

A cool-season crop, potatoes thrive in the northern half of the United States and in southern Canada. They are planted as soon as the soil can be fitted in the spring. Since they take two or three weeks to come up, they usually escape late frosts. If injured, they outgrow the damage.

Potatoes are raised from pieces of the tuber or potato, and not from seed. These pieces are called seed potatoes. Before planting, potatoes are cut into chunky pieces, each with an eye, which sprouts and becomes the top of the plant. The seed pieces are planted 4 in. deep, about 1 ft. apart in rows $2\frac{1}{2}$ ft. apart.

Potatoes respond to heavy fertilization; 5-8-5 or a similar formula applied at the rate of $7\frac{1}{2}$ to 15 lb. to a 100-ft. row is indicated. Mix it with the soil at planting time, but be sure that it is not in contact with the seed pieces. Mulching is a good practice; in a dry season irrigation will increase the crop.

Potatoes should not be dug until the vines begin to die; the late crop should not be harvested until the vines are dead. To prevent bruising, leave freshly dug potatoes on the ground in the sun for a full day. They should then be stored in the dark at a temperature of 45° to 50° F.

Two varieties are needed, an early one to provide potatoes for summer use and a late one for storage and winter use.

POTATOES, SWEET

The sweet potato, though usually considered a vegetable for the South, may also be grown in regions of the North where the growing season is warm and at least 150 days in length. Northern yields may not be as heavy as where the growing season is longer and hotter, but this should not discourage home gardeners.

The roots of sweet-potato plants should be started in a hotbed. The shoots ("draws" or "sets") which arise from the roots may be pulled when a few inches high and planted in the garden when weather is warm.

Sandy loam soils of medium fertility are best. Set the plants on top of ridges $3\frac{1}{2}$ to 4 ft. apart, about 1 ft. apart in the row. Control weeds by cultivation until the vines have covered the ground.

Sweet potatoes must be dug carefully to avoid bruising, and after they have dried, they should be cured for ten days at 85° F. and then stored at 50° to 60° F.

PUMPKINS

Pumpkins are very sensitive to frost and require too much room for a small garden, but as they are somewhat tolerant of partial shade, they may be grown between rows of corn, spaced 8 to 10 ft. apart in every third or fourth row. The seeds are usually planted directly in the garden.

Pumpkins should be gathered and stored before a hard frost. Suitable storage is a well-ventilated place where the temperature is a little above 50° F.

RADISHES

Radishes are a cool-weather crop that must be grown rapidly for good flavor and succulence. They come early; most varieties are ready to use in less than four weeks from sowing. The seeds may be planted with slower-germinating crops; they are often sown between the rows of later com-ers. Plantings should be made every week in spring while the weather is cool and again in the autumn.

RHUBARB

Rhubarb, sometimes known as pie-plant, is grown for its large, thick, acid leafstalks, which are popular for tangy pies and sauce. The leaves are poisonous and should not be eaten. A harbinger of spring, rhubarb is ready at least a month before strawberries ripen. A cool, moist summer and win-ters cold enough to freeze the soil to a depth of a few inches are required for good plant growth. The region north of the latitude of Washington, D.C., is best for rhubarb culture.

Rhubarb thrives in fertile loams and clay loams and prefers them to light, sandy soils. Lots of organic mat-ter such as rotted manure, decayed leaves and compost should be incor-porated in the soil before planting.

Six to eight plants set 4 ft. apart in a row will provide enough rhubarb for average family use. The plants may be set in the autumn or spring; mulch well if fall-planted. The stalks should be pulled out of the crown, not cut off; they should not be pulled at all the first year, and only sparingly the second year. By the third year, the stalks may be harvested for about two months; then allow the plant to build up a large crown for the following year.

Heavy fertilization, or about 1 lb. of 10–10–10 to each plant, is recom-mended for vigor. Well-fertilized, heavily mulched plants will produce good crops indefinitely.

It is best to remove the flower stalks and not let them produce seeds, as seed production saps the energy of the plant. Propagation is by division of the root. Each division planted should contain a bud and a piece of the root.

ROOT CELERY. See *Celeriac*.

RUTABAGAS. See *Turnips*.

SALSIFY

Salsify, also called vegetable oyster or oyster plant, has the same cultural requirements as parsnips except that a slightly longer growing season is needed. The seed may be sown early in the spring. The roots may be left in the ground over winter, or lifted and stored like other root crops.

SCALLIONS. See *Onions*.

SOYBEANS

Soybeans are a vegetable crop that is becoming very popular. The food value is great. However, soybeans re-quire a long growing season; three to five months are needed from planting to maturity. The plants are large, so space 3 ft. between rows.

Harvest the pods when the seeds are fully grown but not yet yellow. Boil or steam them five minutes to loosen the beans. Consult your cookbook for versatile ways to use soybeans.

SPINACH

Spinach is a cool-weather crop; it thrives in early spring and late fall in the North and in the winter in the South. Caution: Spinach does not grow well on an acid soil. The pH should be brought up to 6.0 to 6.7 by the use of lime, if necessary.

Seed spinach in early spring as soon as the soil can be worked, in rows 1 ft. apart; thin seedlings to 4 in. apart. If rainfall is less than an inch a week, the plants should be irrigated. Spin-ach goes to seed quickly, so the crop should be used promptly when ready. Small successive plantings will make the tender leaves available through the growing season. Plant in late summer, for autumn harvest.

SPINACH, NEW ZEALAND

This vegetable is not a true spinach

but is a larger plant that is used for greens during midsummer when ordinary spinach does not thrive. The seed is sown later than spinach, after danger of frost is past. One planting is enough; new shoots are produced as the tips are harvested.

SQUASHES

Squashes are warm-weather plants with cultural requirements similar to the other vine crops. They are usually seeded directly in the field. The bush types should be grown in rows 4 to 5 ft. apart or in hills 4 to 5 ft. apart each way; the running types should be planted 3 to 4 ft. apart in rows 8 to 10 ft. apart.

There are two general basic categories: the summer squashes, which should be used while small and tender before the seeds ripen or the rinds harden; and the winter squashes, which have hard rinds and should be well matured when harvested. The winter squashes may be stored in a dry, moderately warm place, where they may keep until midwinter.

SWISS CHARD. See *Chard*.

TOMATOES

Tomatoes are one of the most rewarding vegetables for the home garden. They are easily grown and produce heavy crops in a small area. Tomato plants are very sensitive to frost, however, and must not be set out until weather is reliably warm unless they are protected. Cool weather slows growth so the advantage of planting early is not very great.

Plants may be bought from greenhouses and nurseries or grown from seeds started indoors, four to six weeks before the plants are to be set in the garden. If started in a seed flat, they are usually transplanted once to a spacing of 2 to 3 in. between plants, and then to the garden.

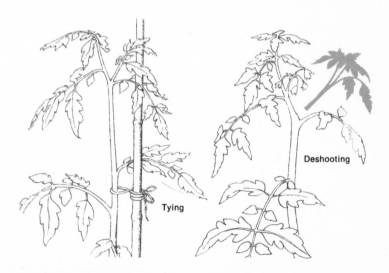

Tying and Deshooting Tomatoes
After planting tomatoes, push a strong bamboo cane into the ground at the side of each root ball. As the plant grows, tie its stem to the cane. Remove side shoots that appear where the leaves join the main stem, to keep the plant to a single main stem.

Planting the seeds directly in the garden is satisfactory except where the growing season is too short to produce a good crop. In many areas, a few plants of a very early variety may be purchased to produce some early fruit. The main crop may be had from seed sown in the garden and thinned to a suitable spacing. The directly seeded plants grow rapidly, without the setback which occurs when they are transplanted.

Tomato plants may be grown on stakes or allowed to sprawl on the ground. However, staked plants are easier to work around and occupy less space in the garden. The stakes should be 6 ft. long, set 1 ft. in the ground. As the plants grow, they are tied to the stakes with soft twine or strips of cloth, and the side shoots are pinched off as they appear.

Staked tomato plants are spaced 2 ft. apart in the row and 3 to 4 ft. between rows. Unstaked plants are set 3 ft. apart in rows 4 to 5 ft. apart.

When the plants are set, they may be watered with a "starter" solution made with 1 oz. of fertilizer to 1 gal. of water. If the weather is dry, the plants should be watered regularly until they begin to grow.

Tomatoes respond well to mulching, and for this purpose black plastic mulch is excellent. Set the plants in a straight row and lay the plastic on each side of the row, holding in place with soil. Blossom-end rot, a disorder of tomato fruits during drought, is much less serious when the plants are mulched. Aside from black plastic, helpful mulches are leaves, hay and sawdust. Much less watering is necessary with mulching.

Fertilizers should be used judiciously, as too much nitrogen stimulates such vigorous growth that the flowers do not set fruit very well and the crop will be light or late. In addition to a general application when the

soil is fitted, or prepared, ½ tbsp. of ammonium nitrate may be worked into the soil a few inches away from each plant.

Tomato varieties are numerous and changing rapidly as the breeders introduce new ones. The small-fruited cherry types are increasing in popularity, and more compact plants are being developed.

TURNIPS AND RUTABAGAS
Turnips and rutabagas are cool-season crops; they are grown in spring and autumn in the North, and through the winter, as well, in the South. They may be planted after an early crop of peas, spinach or potatoes. Turnips need 60 to 80 days to mature, and rutabagas a month longer.

TURNIP GREENS
Turnips are sometimes grown for use as greens, especially in the South.

VEGETABLE OYSTER. See *Salsify*.

WATERMELONS
Watermelon vines grow very vigorously, requiring at least 8 ft. between the hills. Like the muskmelons, they grow better on light, sandy soils with plenty of added manure or complete fertilizer. The plants may be started in small containers and transplanted to the field when warm weather arrives, but direct seeding is the usual practice if varieties suitable for the area are planted. Black plastic, hay or other mulch is preferable to cultivation for weed control.

It is not easy for the novice to determine when a watermelon is ripe, as the skin color does not change at maturity. One test of maturity is to thump the melon with the finger. A muffled or dead sound indicates ripeness; a metallic sound indicates lack of maturity.

The commercial watermelon crop is grown largely in the South, where the growing season is long and hot. Early-ripening varieties have been developed for the shorter and cooler growing season in the North, and these may be hastened along by starting the plants in hotbeds or the greenhouse a month before they can be set in the garden.

The citron melon is a preserving type that is not eaten raw; candied citron, however, is quite different: it is the peel of the fruit of a citrus tree.

CHAPTER 14

HERBS—
For Flavor and Fragrance

What and Where to Grow—Soil, Planning and Propagation—Harvesting, Storage and Use—Recommended Herbs

EARLY EUROPEANS were not familiar with the exotic aromatic plants grown in the East, but they used the herbs that they discovered growing wild around them and learned how to employ them for both flavoring and medicine. Herbs are usually grown for their interesting associations, for their beauty and fragrance, and for their great importance to the art of cooking. It is well worth finding a small place for them in any garden.

WHAT TO GROW

Many herb plants proliferate rapidly, and the garden can soon look untidy and neglected if the useful parts of the plants are not harvested as they become available, or if more herbs are planted than are needed or are cared for. Which herbs can be grown depends on the size and location of the garden, but a few plants of borage, chives, fennel, mint, parsley, rosemary, sorrel, summer savory, tarragon, thyme and sage will provide a representative and varied collection for the flavoring of salads and cooked dishes.

Borage, thyme and chives grow well even in window boxes, and parsley will also thrive on city sills, as long as the air is not too polluted.

Herbs should be planted in a sunny place that is sheltered from wind and frost. The part of the garden immediately outside the kitchen door, which is often thought to be the most convenient place, is therefore sometimes impracticable.

SOIL

Most herbs thrive in well-drained, light soil; many, including marjoram

and thyme, will flourish in alkaline soil; while angelica, bergamot, chamomile, chervil and mint prefer heavier soils. Herbs on the whole, however, are not fussy about soil and will generally succeed in any garden.

Prepare the ground well, being particularly careful to get rid of perennial weeds such as quack grass. Soil that is heavy or sticky can be lightened by forking in sand, coarse coal cinders or rough wood ashes, but generally no special preparation is needed.

PLANNING

Herbs can be grown in a border, or in rows as in a vegetable garden, but if many different herbs are to be grown in the same part of the garden, care should be taken to plant taller herbs, such as angelica, fennel, rosemary and sage, at the back, and smaller ones, such as chives, balm, marjoram, mint and thyme, near the front.

Irregularly shaped patches dovetailing with one another can be filled with individual plants, though for effect patches of herbs that flower at the same time should be planted well apart.

A pleasing arrangement can be obtained by growing the plants in square blocks arranged like a chessboard. Plants that vary in height can then be grown in squares near one another without encroaching upon or overshadowing their neighbors. Each plot should be about 1 yd. square.

Alternatively, plants of the same botanical family can be grouped in one bed and those of other families in separate beds. For example, beds could be devoted to the family *Labiatae* (basil, lavender, marjoram, mint and sage), and other beds to *Umbelliferae* (angelica, caraway, coriander, dill and fennel).

If the plot is large, a paved herb garden is probably the most attractive, not only because so many fascinating plants can be introduced between the flagstones, but also because the color of the stones provides a perfect background for the herbs. The beds within the paved area can be circular, square, triangular or any other pleasing geometric shape.

PROPAGATION

Some herbs, such as anise, borage, chervil, coriander, dill and summer savory, are treated as annuals, and the seed is freshly sown each spring.

When the soil is warm enough, usually in April or early May, draw drills 8 in. apart and sow the seed sparingly along each drill. When the seedlings are large enough to handle, thin them out so that they are 3 in. apart, and later from 6 in. to 2 or 3 ft. apart, according to the ultimate size of the plants. If the herbs are to be used decoratively, sow the seeds broadcast and rake them in. Thin the seedlings in two stages.

Most herbs, other than annuals, are propagated by cuttings in summer—sage, lavender, rosemary, thyme and winter savory are examples.

The mints can be propagated in a simpler way—by division. They form long runnerlike growths, which creep along just under the surface of the soil and produce little groups of roots at each node. In early spring, uproot the runners, break them off from the parent plant and plant them in the soil on their own.

The crowns of such herbs as tansy and tarragon can also be divided and replanted in spring or autumn. Instructions in propagation by division are given in "How to Raise New Plants" (see page 711).

MANAGEMENT

Occasional weeding in summer is the principal task in the herb garden. Twiggy plants with aromatic leaves, such as lavender, sage and thyme, do not usually need watering, but some herbs with soft growth and leaves, such as angelica and the mints, may require added moisture in dry weather.

HARVESTING

If herbs are harvested incorrectly or at the wrong time, their value is lost. It is important to know exactly which part of the plant is to be used later, and this information is given in the list of recommended herbs.

When the particular part of the plant is ready, choose a dry day, and do not work until dew has dried off.

Collect the herbs in a flat box or basket to avoid crushing and bruising them, and do not gather more than can be dealt with at the time, because they do not retain their fragrance for long once they are cut. Most herbs can be used either fresh or dried, although chervil, chives, mint, rosemary and sage should be taken fresh from the garden if possible.

Roots

Lift (take up) the roots carefully in autumn when they are mature, wash free from soil and immediately drain off all water. Trim off any underground stems or fibrous roots.

Whole Plant

If both roots and aboveground parts are to be used, lift the plant when it is in bloom and wash soil from roots.

Herb

The parts of the plant growing aboveground are known as the herb. When this is mature—after the plant has flowered—cut it off at ground level with a really sharp knife. Only clean and healthy plants are useful.

Leaves

Harvest leaves just before the flowers are fully open, for at this time the plant is bursting with life. Choose leaves that are perfect and not those damaged by insects.

Flowers

Nip off the flower heads the day before maturity (if this can be judged), in order to make sure that the essential oils have not been lost. The blooms should be perfect so that they do not deteriorate while drying and spoil the perfume of the potpourri or other product for which they are used. They should be as free from insects as possible, and if they are destined to float in drinks or be used in candymaking, wash them carefully to be sure no animal life remains.

Seed

It is difficult to tell when some kinds of seeds are mature. Color is usually the best indication, and experience will enable the gardener to decide.

To extract the seed, cut off the whole flower head and tie the stems at the mouth of a paper bag; then hang the bag in a light, airy place so that the seeds will fall into it as the head dries. This method insures that the seeds will remain free from dust and that those of different plants will not get mixed together. Sometimes the seeds have to be shaken or rubbed out of seed capsules. Do this over a clean box or other container with deep sides, after the plants have dried.

Drying

Herbs should be dried indoors. The necessary conditions are: (a) good ventilation, (b) shade, except for roots, which should be dried in full sun, and (c) a steady initial temperature of about 90° F.

The best places for drying are a well-shaded greenhouse, a spare room, a garage or a dry basement. Do not use a kitchen, laundry or bathroom—all of these are too humid.

Dry the herbs as soon as they are harvested, to prevent decomposition. Spread the plants or parts collected in a shallow box without a lid, or on trays, cheesecloth or wire mesh. Space the plants or parts so that they lie flat and do not overlap. Keep one kind of herb separate from another.

Some plants, such as artemisia and sage, can be hung upside down in small bunches from the rafters of an airy shed, garage or greenhouse, or indoors on a rod or cord in a cool, dry

room, such as an enclosed porch. So that the air can circulate freely among the plants, the bunches should not be large or tied tightly.

The object of good drying is to reduce the moisture in the plant before it starts to die. It is important to maintain a temperature at 90° F. or slightly above for the first 24 hours, and then to reduce it without letting it fall below 72° F.; otherwise the drying process will not be completed satisfactorily and the plants will reabsorb moisture from the atmosphere. Turn the plants once or twice during the first 24 hours and once a day thereafter. Inadequate drying results in partly decomposed or rotted material, and hurried or excessive drying in brittle, parched, useless material.

Roots take the longest time to dry, and stems take longer than leaves or flowers. The herbs are sufficiently dry when they snap readily without much pressure.

STORING

After crumbling the dried herbs between the hands to remove twiggy pieces, and discarding the stems if not required (as with sage, for example), store the herbs at once before dust collects on them. Use airtight containers such as wooden bins, boxes, bottles or jars.

SPECIAL MIXTURES OF HERBS

Fines herbes is a cooking term indicating basil, chervil, chives, parsley, tarragon and thyme, finely chopped.

Bouquet garni is a bunch of herbs—usually parsley, thyme, bay, tarragon and sometimes marjoram—tied with thread and added to stock or water during cooking. Dried herbs may be tied in a small piece of muslin. Remove the herbs before serving.

Herb Tea

Herb teas or tisanes have been drunk

for many centuries, and their various uses are listed in herbalists' catalogues. They are not only taken as a medicine but also for their refreshing flavor, pleasant aroma and color. To make a tisane, pour boiling water over the fresh or dried plants, and let the infusion stand for seven to ten minutes before drinking. Tisanes are sometimes bottled, but this is not a common practice.

Sachet

Lavender or rose petals are dried to fill small bags placed in drawers to impart a gentle scent, especially among lingerie or handkerchiefs.

Potpourri

A potpourri is a mixture of flower heads and leaves preserved with some of their essential oils and certain additives. It is usually kept in a place where its scent can pervade a room or a closet.

Many different mixtures can be made of flowers and leaves that hold their scent when dried, such as roses, lavender, rosemary, bergamot, verbena and geranium leaves. A potpourri can be expensive to make, but the following recipe will produce a satisfactory result:

Mix together 1 oz. allspice, 1 oz. cloves, 1 oz. ground nutmeg and 4 oz. orrisroot; add the juice and grated rind of 3 lemons. Add any or all of these: 1½ oz. oil of geranium, 1 oz. essence of lemon, ½ oz. oil of bergamot, ½ oz. spirit of lavender.

Make a separate mixture of handfuls of rose petals that have been dried for an hour or two in the sun, and scatter a few pinches of salt and saltpeter for each handful of petals. Let the two mixtures stand for a few hours, and then stir them together. Put this aromatic combination into a tightly fastened container and, as more scented flowers and leaves be-

come available, add them without drying them first. The mixture should remain moist; sprinkle on more salt if it tends to dry out. At the end of the season, when no more plants are to be included, stir the potpourri again and put it into a bowl. Its perfume will last for a long time.

RECOMMENDED HERBS

Unlike most English plant names, those given to herbs are remarkably consistent everywhere. The herbs are therefore listed here under their English names as they are in herbalists' and seedsmen's catalogues, and their Latin names follow in parentheses.

ANGELICA (ANGELICA ARCHANGELICA)
Annual. Sow thickly because the seed is not very viable, and choose a damp and partly shady place. Thin seedlings to 1½ ft. apart. Harvest the stems in May and June while they are tender, or cut from side shoots as late as mid-August. Crystallize the stems for use in confectionery, or use them fresh with rhubarb in compote

Angelica

or jam to reduce the acidity and to add flavor. Essential oil from the seed is an ingredient of liqueurs.

ANISE (PIMPINELLA ANISUM)

Annual. Grow 1 ft. apart in sunny bed in porous, light, fairly rich soil. Gather seed in August, dry and use for sprinkling over cakes, pancakes, salads, soups and young carrots.

ARTEMISIA OR WORMWOOD
(ARTEMISIA SPICATA)

The whole herb is used. Propagate by division. Use either fresh or dried for flavoring, or include in a mixture of aromatic leaves. *A. abrotanum* is called southernwood.

BALM (MELISSA OFFICINALIS)

Propagate by division. Plant 1 ft. apart in any fairly good garden soil. Use leaves fresh or powdered in fish sauces, stuffing or as a substitute for lemons. Fresh leaves are piquant in salads and summer drinks.

BASIL, SWEET (OCIMUM BASILICUM)

Annual. Sow indoors early and set young plants in sunny location in ordinary garden soil when danger of frost is passed, or sow directly outdoors later. Space plants 1 ft. apart. Use the leaves of this clove-scented plant sparingly to flavor soups—especially tomato and mock turtle—and in tomato dishes, salads, omelets, sausages and chopped meat.

BERGAMOT, RED (MONARDA DIDYMA)

Propagate by division or cuttings. Plant in sun, in deep rich soil, 1 ft. apart. Use leaves, or leaves and flowers, as a flavoring. The red flowers make an attractive decoration for a salad, and can be floated in punches and added to fruit cups. Red bergamot is also called bee balm, Oswego tea and fragrant balm.

BORAGE (BORAGO OFFICINALIS)

Annual. Grow in poor, stony or sandy soil, 2 ft. apart. The leaves flavor

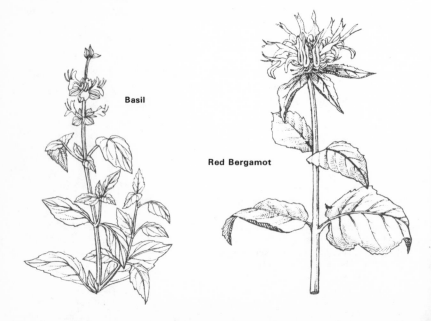

Basil

Red Bergamot

claret cup and soft drinks. A tea made of the fresh or dried leaves, allowed to cool and served with ice, makes a refreshing drink and looks most attractive with the blue borage flowers in it. Flowers can be candied.

CARAWAY (CARUM CARVI)
Annual. Grow in any ordinary soil, where sunny, 1 ft. apart. Dried seeds are used in cakes, breads, salads and mixed with cream cheeses. Can be sprinkled on lamb or pork chops before cooking to enhance the flavor.

CHAMOMILE (ANTHEMIS NOBILIS)
Perennial. Grow in rich soil 9 in. apart. The flowers, either dried or fresh, make chamomile tea, a drink said to have value for alleviating insomnia and as a tonic. Dry flowers quickly for use in tonics and shampoos.

CHERVIL (ANTHRISCUS CEREFOLIUM)
Annual. Make successive sowings from spring to fall, thin seedlings to 6 to 8 in. apart, and water in dry weather. To produce good leaves, discourage the plant from flowering by keeping it growing vigorously and pinching off any buds that appear. Cut the leaves six to eight weeks after sowing. Fresh chopped leaves impart an anise flavor to salads, sauces (tartar sauce) and soups. Use the dried leaves in stuffings. Chervil vinegar is made in the same way as tarragon vinegar and is an alternative to cider or wine vinegar in the preparation of salad dressings.

CHIVES (ALLIUM SCHOENOPRASUM)
Tops are used. Perennial but needs dividing every four or five years. Plant 1 ft. apart in spring. Pot a few plants in early fall and grow in a sunny window to provide winter picking. Fresh leaves are very popular as a seasoning that imparts a mild onion flavor to salads, egg and cheese dishes. They are used in tartar sauce and *fines herbes*.

Chamomile

Chervil

COMFREY (SYMPHYTUM OFFICINALE)
Propagate by seed or division. Grow in damp soil 2 ft. apart. The leaves were formerly used to alleviate pain and reduce the swelling that follows breaks and sprains. After they have been blanched, the young shoots can be eaten like asparagus.

CORIANDER (CORIANDRUM SATIVUM)
Annual. Sow seed at monthly intervals throughout the summer, thin seedlings to 1 ft. apart, and gather the leaves when young to season soups and salads. Flavor is like that of dried orange peel. Use the seeds on cakes and breads, and in curries and chutneys, milk puddings and cream cheeses.

DILL (ANETHUM GRAVEOLENS)
Annual. Grow in any garden soil. Space plants 6 in. apart. Dill water was formerly used for soothing babies. The seeds lend a sharp flavor to pickles and soups and, if soaked in wine vinegar for a few days, produce dill vinegar, a popular ingredient for pickling cucumbers. Chopped leaves may be added to sauces for fish, sprinkled on boiled potatoes or fresh salmon and, with other herbs, mixed into omelets and salads. Use with restraint.

FENNEL (FOENICULUM VULGARE)
Sow seed in a sunny place. Sometimes grows to 6 ft. Use fresh or dried leaves for fennel tea or to add interest to sauces, particularly those served with oily fish. Blanch the fresh leaves in hot salted water and then chop finely. Seed can be sprinkled in soup and pastry fillings, but the anise flavor is strong. Cook the thick, fleshy stalks like celery or use shredded in salad.

GARLIC (ALLIUM SATIVUM)
Plant sets in light soil 9 in. apart in spring. Use the cloves (sections of the bulb) of garlic with discretion in meats, sauces and salads.

HYSSOP (HYSSOPUS OFFICINALIS)
Propagate by cuttings. Plant in a sunny place in dry soil 1 ft. apart. Hyssop is an evergreen shrub with blue-, pink- or white-flowered varieties. It is now grown chiefly for garden decoration. Once, its shoots were used to make hyssop tea, valued as a remedy for the relief of coughs, colds and sore throats.

Hyssop

LAVENDER (LAVANDULA OFFICINALIS)
Propagate by cuttings. Plant in sun and poor soil 2 to 3 ft. apart. It has a pleasing nostalgic aroma, and is used commercially for the distillation of lavender water, and domestically as a moth deterrent and ingredient of potpourri. The flowers can be candied. For use in lavender bags, cut the flower stalks in summer when the flowers are almost mature, to capture most of the essential oils. Dry in the

usual way (see Drying, p. 296) and
then rub the flowers from the stalks
between the hands or on a hard board.

MARJORAM, SWEET
(MAJORANA HORTENSIS)
Leaves are used. Grow from seed.
Plant in hot, dry place 1 ft. apart.
Used in vinegars, soups, egg dishes
and dressings.

MINT OR SPEARMINT (MENTHA SPICATA)
Propagate by division. Plant in shade

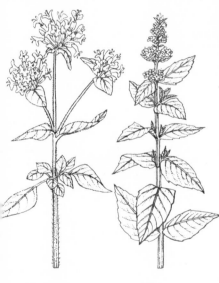

Marjoram   **Mint**

in damp soil 1 ft. apart. Essential for
mint sauce, jelly, butter and tea;
place sprigs in iced drinks or cook
with young vegetables. Mint can be
dried for winter use. It is an ingredient of some potpourris and a basis for
hair tonics. Applemint (*Mentha rotundifolia*) may be substituted for
spearmint.

NASTURTIUM (TROPAEOLUM MAJUS)
Annual. Grow in poor soil. Space

plants 6 in. apart. Season salads with
leaves and flowers. The seeds, if picked
when young, are a good substitute for
capers.

PARSLEY
(PETROSELINUM CRISPUM)
Grow in damp soil in light shade or
sun. Sow seed in spring where plants
are to remain. Thin out seedlings to 8
to 10 in. apart. Used fresh for flavoring salads and vegetables, and fresh
or dried in stuffings. Parsley tea, butter and jelly are also known. To prepare parsley as an accompaniment to
fried fish or ham, scatter it into fat
and cook for a minute over low heat,
then drain on paper before serving.

Parsley does not dry if treated in
the usual way for curing leaves. Wash
the leaves—preferably the tender un-
curled French type (*P.c. latifolium*)—
dip them in boiling water and put on
a baking tray in a very hot oven for
just a minute. Bottle at once.

PENNYROYAL (MENTHA PULEGIUM)
Propagate by division. Plant in moist,
shady place 6 in. apart. Use tender
tips of shoots sparingly to add peppermint flavor to salads.

PEPPERMINT (MENTHA PIPERITA)
Propagate by division. Plant in rich,
moist soil 9 in. apart. Dry for flavoring sweets and for making peppermint tea.

ROSEMARY
(ROSEMARINUS OFFICINALIS)
Propagate by cuttings. Plant in sunny
place in porous soil 3 ft. apart. Use
the sprigs as cut flowers in early summer. Rosemary, an evergreen shrub
not winter-hardy in cold climates, is
the herb of remembrance. Use the
leaves fresh for flavoring lamb and
rabbit and in veal stuffing—only one
small sprig is needed for each dish.
Rosemary tea is a pungent and re-

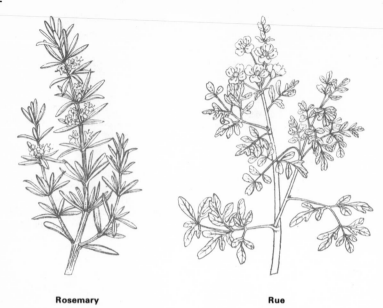

Rosemary   Rue

freshing tisane that was formerly made for the treatment of head colds.

RUE (RUTA GRAVEOLENS)
Propagate by seed or cuttings. Grow in dryish soil, 2 ft. or more apart. Rue, or herb of grace, makes a rounded evergreen bush with deeply divided leaves of a dark blue-green, which have a bitter, acrid taste. It is not hardy in regions of severe winters. Rue provides medicine for poultry and cattle diseases. Long ago, rue tea was used for the relief of indigestion.

SAGE (SALVIA OFFICINALIS)
Plant 2 ft. apart in a light soil and a well-drained location. Sage is a spreading gray-leaved evergreen shrub, which can be propagated from spring or summer cuttings and from seed sown directly outdoors in spring. Old and leggy branches may be pegged down onto a mound of soil and they will root themselves. Sever these layers

from the parent plant in May. Dried leaves are traditional in stuffings for pork, turkey, duck and goose.

SAVORY, SUMMER (SATUREJA HORTENSIS) AND WINTER (S. MONTANA)
Summer savory is an annual, while winter savory is a perennial propagated by cuttings. Grow in rather poor soil, 6 in. apart. Use fresh leaves of either kind for flavoring snap beans and fresh or dried in fish, cheese and egg dishes, stuffings and soups.

SORREL (RUMEX ACETOSA)
Propagate by seed or division. Grow in deep, moist soil 1 ft. apart. Use the acid-tasting young leaves in salads before the plant has flowered. Bring a few crowns into the greenhouse or put in a sunny window for forcing to maintain a winter supply, or plant some in cold frames for early-spring use. The French sorrel (R. scutatus) is sometimes used to flavor soups.

Sage

Tansy

SPEARMINT. See *Mint*.

SOUTHERNWOOD. See *Artemisia*.

SUNFLOWER (HELIANTHUS ANNUUS)
Sow seed early indoors; when weather
is warm and settled and all danger
from frost is past, set young plants
outdoors in rich soil in full sun, 2½ ft.
apart. Or sow seed directly in garden
in spring. Plants should be tied to tall,
stout stakes. Sunflowers form a quick-
growing screen and are gross feeders.
The leaves are harvested as fodder for
rabbits, horses and cattle or, dried, as
an herb tobacco. The flower buds may
be cooked and eaten as a vegetable in
the same way as artichokes. Oil is extracted from the seed and used in the
manufacture of soap and cattle feed.
The seeds have versatile values as
food for poultry and as an attraction
for wild birds; they may be roasted
and then ground to make sunflower
coffee.

TANSY (TANACETUM VULGARE)
Leaves are used. Propagate by division. Plant in any ordinary garden
soil 1 ft. apart. An old-world plant
with coarse, well-divided leaves and
an unpleasant smell, tansy produces
yellow buttonlike flowers in July and
spreads rapidly unless checked. The
variety *T.v. crispum* has especially attractive foliage. Tansy was formerly
used as a potherb and in tansy cake
for Easter. Tansy wine was once considered an excellent tonic, but is too
bitter for present-day palates.

TARRAGON
(ARTEMISIA DRACUNCULUS)
Propagate by division. Plant in sunny
location in dryish soil, 2 ft. apart. Use
fresh leaves in *bouquet garni* and in
tarragon vinegar; in tartar sauces and
in omelets as *fines herbes*. Tarragon
leaves are sometimes added to chutneys and are also dried for winter use.
To make tarragon vinegar, wash the

fresh leaves and barely cover them with white wine vinegar in a bowl. Cover the bowl and soak leaves for two weeks. Strain carefully and bottle.

THYME (THYMUS VULGARIS)
Propagate by cuttings or by seed sown directly in the garden in spring;

or sow indoors early and set out young plants after danger of frost has passed. Plant in sunny place in dryish, porous soil 1 ft. apart. Use fresh or dried in stuffings for veal, poultry and fish, and in stews and casseroles.

WORMWOOD. See *Artemisia*.

CHAPTER 15

FRUITS—
Challenges for the Gardener

Air and Full Sun—Soils and Drainage—How to Select and Plant—Pest Control—Causes of Fruit Failure—Recommended Kinds and Care

FROM THE PLUMP, heart-shaped strawberry to the velvet peach or cluster of shining cherries, fruits are as decorative as they are delicious. At every season—from the time of budding and blossoming to bearing—fruit-producing plants, shrubs and trees are beautiful to behold.

Fortunately, most temperate-zone fruits can be grown successfully wherever peach trees thrive and the warm season lasts long enough to mature Concord grapes. Record-breaking winters that occur infrequently and occasional unseasonable frosts should not discourage the gardener from planting fruits. A newcomer to an area should study the weather record.

Rainfall east of the Mississippi River is usually adequate for established fruit plants, except for strawberries, which are especially susceptible to drought. Agricultural extension services in most counties, at the state universities and at agricultural colleges can be very helpful in providing full information about fruit regions and recommending the most successful kinds and varieties of fruit for each area.

SITE
A gardener cannot change an unsuitable site, and he should not attempt to grow fruit in impossible situations. For preference choose a gentle to moderate slope; on such a slope the cold air will move downward on frosty nights, concentrating in the hollow at the bottom. Frost pockets, perhaps surrounded by a barrier of buildings

or closely planted trees and shrubbery, are not good locations for growing fruit; winter temperatures there are always lower and more damaging.

A location with good air circulation will favor rapid drying of the foliage and fruit, thus tending to reduce damage from fungus diseases such as fruit rots. All fruit needs full exposure to the sun from morning to night. Large trees have extensive and hungry roots. Therefore, they should be set well away from competing plants.

Old fruit plants, especially raspberries, harbor viruses and insects which can ruin a new planting. These should be removed before setting out young fruit plants. Garden sites which have recently grown tomatoes, peppers, potatoes and eggplants should be avoided for three or four years, as the soil may be infested with the fungus of verticillium wilt, a serious root disease of strawberries, black and purple raspberries and sweet cherries.

SOIL

This should be fertile, deep and well drained. It is not necessary to depend on natural fertility, since nutrients come cheaply in a fertilizer sack. Good drainage is a must, however, as fruit plants will not thrive where the water table is at or near the surface for more than a few hours after a heavy rain. During the growing season the water table should be at least 3 ft. beneath the surface. A gravelly, porous subsoil favors the rapid removal of surplus moisture. Drainage is usually better on slopes, but seepage on a slope with a hardpan base can create soggy spots. Sometimes poor drainage can be corrected by installing land drains (see Soil Drainage, page 742).

Sandy loams are preferred, but soils both lighter and heavier are suitable if well drained and in good tilth. Organic matter is valuable. For small areas peat moss and farm manure

may be used; the simplest and most economical way to add organic matter to any extensive area is by green manuring. (See "Composting and Green Manuring," page 764.)

SOIL FERTILITY

Fertilizer ordinarily should not be applied the first summer. If hay is used as a mulch, it will provide nutrients as it rots; if used liberally, it will eliminate the need for fertilizer. In soils of average fertility, nitrogen is apt to be the element most needed for fruit plants. Leaves that are small and yellowing indicate a lack of nitrogen. It may be applied at the rate of 60 to 80 lb. to the acre. There is enough phosphorus in most soils for fruit plants. Sandy and gravelly soils of low fertility may need potash. Sulphate of potash is superior to muriate of potash for many fruits, especially grapes, raspberries, currants and gooseberries. Sulphate of potash may be used at the rate of 300 to 400 lb. to the acre, or at twice that rate the first year if potash-deficiency symptoms (commonly, marginal browning or scorching of leaves) are severe. Potash applied under mulch becomes available to the plants much more quickly than if broadcast on the bare ground.

If only a few fruit plants are to be fertilized, one may apply the complete fertilizer that is used elsewhere in the garden, such as a 5-10-5 or 10-10-10 formula. (For general use of fertilizers, see "Fertilizers and Manures," page 749.)

The pH—acidity or alkalinity of the soil—is not of great importance to most fruits except blueberries, which require an acid soil with a pH of about 4.5 (see page 741). Lime should not be added to soil without consulting an expert.

BUYING PLANTS

Fruit plants should be purchased

from specialized nurseries; some produce only strawberry plants, grapevines or blueberries, while others offer tree fruits. Nearby nurseries can provide plants more freshly dug, at lower transportation cost. Plants from a southern firm are not less hardy than the same variety grown in the North. The order should be placed in the fall as nurseries may be sold out of the desired varieties by spring. The varieties sought should always be specified in the order, and the choice not left to the nursery. The rootstock for apples and sweet cherries should be named.

Virus-free stocks of some varieties, especially new ones, are gradually becoming available from research programs at the agricultural experiment stations. These are often much superior in vigor and productiveness.

Care of Plants on Arrival

Examine the plants immediately. The bark should be plump and fresh. Nick it with a knife to be sure the inner bark is a bright green. Strawberry plants should have bright roots and firm crowns and the leaves should not be rotten. Plants that are dried out are worthless.

Plants that are not to be set at once should be "heeled in" in a cool, shady spot. Dig a trench deep and wide enough to hold the root systems. Separate each plant and place it in the trench, allowing a little space between plants; then work moist soil in among the roots and several inches over them.

PLANTING

Plant in the spring as soon as the soil is dry enough to work without packing. Early planting is best; plants set late, after leaves have appeared, may encounter hot, dry weather and get off to a poor start, or even fail to grow. Fall planting is often superior to spring planting, except in the northern tier of states and Canada.

Prior to planting the small fruits, the soil should be plowed and harrowed; small areas may be spaded. Weeds should be strictly eliminated, as it is a hopeless task to clean quack grass out of a strawberry bed or a raspberry planting.

Before setting out trees and grapevines, prepare 4-ft.-wide strips and leave the grass between them. For each tree or vine dig a hole big enough to hold the root system without bending the roots. Clean off broken roots and ragged ends with sharp shears, but retain all sound roots. It is helpful, especially in a dry spring, to mix the soil that is to be filled in around the roots half-and-half with wet peat moss. This will help the tree get off to a better start. Set the tree with the graft union (a slight bulge in the trunk) a few inches above the ground. Jiggle the tree up and down as the hole is filled in, and work the mixed soil and wet peat moss around the roots with the fingers. Stepping on the soil as the hole is filled will pack it firmly around the roots. Unless the soil is moist, pour a pailful of water in the hole when it is partly filled. No air spaces should be left, and the tree should withstand a firm tug without loosening.

Care of the Planting

After planting apply a mulch. A 3-ft. square of black polyethylene may be fitted around the tree and held in place with soil, or cover the area with a thick layer of sawdust or peat moss. If the tree is not mulched, weeds must be kept down by frequent hoeing. In a dry summer, water at weekly intervals until rainfall is adequate.

PRUNING

Fruit trees should be pruned after the severe cold of winter is past, but before growth begins. Trees of somewhat tender varieties such as peaches,

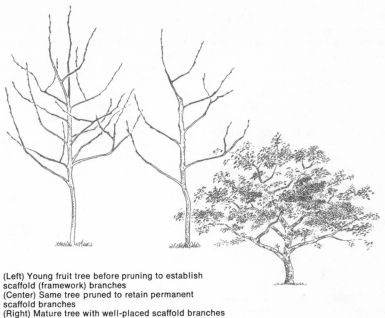

(Left) Young fruit tree before pruning to establish scaffold (framework) branches
(Center) Same tree pruned to retain permanent scaffold branches
(Right) Mature tree with well-placed scaffold branches

sweet cherries, and the less hardy apples (Baldwin, for example) may be injured if early pruning is followed by unseasonably cold weather. In areas where the trees are barely winter-hardy, pruning should always be light. Summer pruning is not necessary except for the removal of unwanted sprouts as they appear.

The principal objective in pruning young fruit trees is to make a structurally strong tree that will support a heavy crop without breakage. The scaffold branches, or main limbs of the tree, should be about a foot apart and point in different directions. When two limbs of equal size grow at the same level on the trunk, they break easily under the stress of a heavy crop, high wind or ice. Eliminate such weakness by removing one limb completely from the tree while it is still young. In an older tree, such a limb may be cut back each year until its load of fruit is lightened, often avoiding the removal of an entire limb.

After fruit trees begin to bear, remove dead and broken branches as well as those in the interior, because shading keeps them weak and unproductive. With very vigorous trees some thinning may be necessary to control the crop. Inhibit them from growing too high by cutting back tall limbs to become side branches.

Pruning invigorates that part of a tree near the cut. However, it tends to dwarf the tree somewhat, which is desirable if a smaller tree is wanted, but the price of a severe pruning is a delay in bearing. (See "Principles of Pruning," page 766.)

PESTS

Insects cause deformed and wormy fruits. They eat the leaves and suck their juice out. Borers tunnel under the bark and kill or greatly weaken the tree. Control is essential if usable fruit is to be produced. Sprays in the correct concentration must be applied at the right time. (See Fruit Pests, page 816.)

Birds will gobble blueberries, sweet cherries, blackberries and strawberries; they peck peaches, especially the early varieties. The only control measure that really works is to cover the bush or tree with netting when the fruit is ripening. For this reason, dwarf fruit trees are easy to handle.

Diseases also have to be controlled. (See Fruit Diseases, page 797.)

VARIETIES

A selection of varieties that ripen at different times will supply fruit throughout the summer and fall. Since a single tree may well supply more fruit than can be used at one time, it may be advisable to plant a tree on which several varieties of a fruit, ripening at different times, have been grafted.

FRUIT FAILURE

These are some of the most common causes of failure of trees to bear:

1. The tree may not be old enough. Fruits and their varieties differ greatly in the ages at which they become productive.
2. Dormant buds may be killed or injured by early spring frost—especially after an unseasonably warm period—or by severe winter cold.
3. A self-sterile variety will fail to fruit if a suitable pollinating variety is not near, or because the pollinating variety does not happen to bloom at the same time as the one that is to be pollinated.
4. Pollinating insects may be scarce, or the weather at blossom time too cool for them to fly.
5. The tree may be in low vigor because of winter injury or an unsuitable soil.
6. Insects or diseases may weaken the tree or destroy the fruit before it ripens.
7. Severe pruning may delay the fruiting.
8. Some varieties fruit heavily only in alternate years.
9. The shade of taller trees or buildings may delay fruiting and result in light crops.

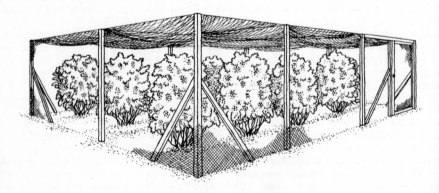

To protect cane fruits, bush fruits and dwarf cherry trees from birds, make a
wire-mesh cage, as large as necessary, 6 ft. high and with a gate. The top may
be of plastic mesh to save expense and to prevent rust from dropping on the bushes.

RECOMMENDED TREE FRUITS

APPLES

Apples are hardier than most fruits and are grown extensively east of the Mississippi Valley and in the Pacific Northwest. In the latitude of New York, a succession of varieties of apples will provide fresh fruit from late July to midwinter or later, if stored.

Rootstocks: Apple trees are propagated by grafting the desired varieties on vigorous rootstocks. In North America until recently, seedlings of normal-sized trees were used as rootstocks.

When mature, such trees grew nearly 20 ft. tall and 40 ft. wide, an overwhelming size for an average home fruit garden. Dwarfing rootstocks, developed at the East Malling Research Station in England and designated by numbers, are now available, however, and trees grafted on them are much smaller than those grown on seedling understocks. Rootstock E. M. IX produces trees about 8 ft. tall at maturity. These may be planted 12 ft. apart in a row and are the best for a home garden.

One-year whips without branches or two-year-old trees are recommended for planting. Older so-called "bearing age" transplants will not prove as strong as younger trees which have had a few years to grow at the sites where they will eventually bear their fruit.

Planting: The soil for apples should be 4 to 6 ft. deep and well drained at all times. Trees on E. M. IX and E. M. VII should be planted with the bud union about 4 in. above the ground. If the bud union is at, or below, the ground level, the rootstock or "scion" variety may develop its own root system and grow into a full-sized standard tree, too large for the garden.

E. M. IX root system is brittle, and the trees tip over easily with a heavy crop. To prevent this a stout stake should be driven into the ground at planting time and the tree should remain tied to it with strong cord.

At planting time unbranched whips should be cut back to a height of about 30 in. At the beginning of the second year select three or four well-spaced branches and a leader and remove the rest of the branches. Thereafter only corrective pruning is needed. The advantage of keeping the tree low is that pruning, spraying, thinning and harvesting can all be done without ladders.

Seasonal Care: Spraying is essential in the production of a good crop. Control weeds by cultivation or mulching. No fertilizer should be used the first year. Thereafter a complete garden fertilizer, such as 5-10-5, may be applied in early spring, at the rate of a pound for each year of the tree's age. If a hay mulch is used, less fertilizer or none at all need be applied. Oversize, coarse, poorly colored apples and very large dark green leaves indicate that there is too much nitrogen.

When apple trees overbear, the fruit is small, poorly colored and of inferior flavor. About three weeks after the trees begin to bloom the surplus small fruit should be picked off, leaving the remaining apples about 6 to 8 in. apart along the branches.

Mice often girdle young fruit trees under the snow during the winter. To prevent this, clear grass, weeds or mulch away from the trunk. A mound of coarse gravel or crushed stone 6 to 8 in. high around the tree will protect it. A cylinder of hardware cloth about a foot high, circling the trunk and inserted slightly into the soil, is also good protection. Beware of rabbits when the snow is deep; they may eat the lower twigs.

APRICOTS

Apricot trees are sturdy and vigorous; handsome in flower, they are among the first fruit trees to bloom. The buds are slightly hardier than those of the peach, but early flowering and consequent risk of frost injury limit the area where apricots may be grown.

Commercial apricot culture is confined to fruit-growing areas of the West Coast where winter temperatures and spring frost are not troublesome. Seedlings of the Russian apricot, hardier than the other varieties in the Northeast, are grown by some home gardeners but tend to be inferior in size and quality to those cultivated commercially on the West Coast.

In general, soils suitable for peaches are suitable for apricots; the site should be as frost-free as possible. Pruning should be less severe than that required by peach trees, and less nitrogen is needed. Mature trees should be spaced 25 ft. apart.

Apricots are budded on seedlings of apricots, peaches and Myrobalan plums; apricot seedlings are preferred, however. The unique rich flavor is not developed until the fruit is fully ripe; premature harvesting is undesirable.

CHERRIES

Sweet cherries are a popular dessert fruit; they are also used for canning, including the processing of maraschino cherries. Sour cherries are used primarily for cooking.

Sweet cherries are somewhat hardier than peaches, but less so than sour cherries, pears and European varieties of plums. They thrive in the vicinity of the Great Lakes and in the cooler parts of the Pacific Coast. Scattered trees are found in dooryards in the northern states east of the Mississippi. They do not thrive in the South.

Cherries bloom early and are susceptible to frost injury, hence a sloping site with good air drainage is essential for regular crops. The trees are very sensitive to poor water drainage and soon die if the water table is too high during the growing season.

Cherry trees are best planted in the fall in any good, well-drained farm soil after the leaves have dropped. Spring-planted trees, if they have been stored in a nursery cellar, often do not survive. The sooner a tree is planted after it is dug by the nursery, the better are its chances of survival. Spacing for sour cherry trees is 20 ft. apart, for the sweet varieties 25 to 30 ft.

Weed control by cultivation or mulching is essential for young trees. Later they may be grown in a closely mown sod. Watering may be necessary the year the trees are set. Some varieties, even when well established, seem to be quite susceptible to drought. Trees that appear to be suffering from a lack of moisture when the fruit is ripening should receive the equivalent of an inch of rain each week. Nitrogen fertilizers are the best.

Cherries are propagated by budding on Mazzard or Mahaleb cherry seedlings. The Mazzard cherry is the sweet cherry, *Prunus avium;* trees of this rootstock are larger, longer-lived and somewhat slower in coming into bearing than the Mahaleb-rooted trees. The Mahaleb rootstock may be suitable for sour cherries, or for sweet varieties on very well-drained soils, but usually the Mazzard root is preferred. No satisfactory dwarfing rootstock for cherries is available. When cherry trees are ordered from the nursery, specify the rootstock. To check— the bark of the root of the Mazzard cherry is bitter to the taste, the Mahaleb root bark is not.

Bearing sweet-cherry trees are pruned less than other fruit trees. After planting, the pruning should be little and corrective, just sufficient to maintain a structurally sound tree.

Sour cherry trees of bearing age require more pruning than the sweet cherry. However, thinning of the weaker growth and some cutting back of the taller branches to keep the tree low enough for spraying and easy harvesting are all that is needed.

Cherries do not ripen after they are removed from the tree; hence they must be fully ripe at harvest if the full flavor is to be had. The fruit keeps fairly well in storage at 32° F.

The main problem is to keep birds away. Scaring devices are only partially effective; the only sure protection is complete enclosure of the crop with cheesecloth or a mesh that birds cannot enter or peck through.

CHERRIES, DWARF

The Western sand cherry, *Prunus besseyi*, a shrub 3 to 4 ft. high with silvery-green foliage, has fruits that are purplish-black and often bitter and astringent, though sweet and palatable forms are known. Cross-pollination is necessary. Sand cherries are very hardy and drought-resistant and grow well in the Great Plains.

The Chinese dwarf cherry or Nanking cherry, *P. tomentosa*, grows to 8 ft. and bears bright red, pleasantly flavored small cherries. This handsome and hardy tree blooms very early. Cross-pollination is needed.

The Korean cherry, *P. japonica*, is 4 ft. high and bears cherrylike fruits, the size of sour cherries but much firmer. This tree of modest size is very hardy.

MULBERRIES

The mulberry is a large, spreading, rapid-growing tree that produces an abundance of soft, sweet, blackberry-shaped fruits that are eaten by several species of birds. A mulberry tree should not be planted near a house or sidewalk, as the ripe fruits drop and are messy underfoot. New American is the best variety, but it is not commonly available from nurseries. Russian mulberry seedlings are commonly sold, but the fruit is inferior.

NECTARINES

The nectarine is identical with the peach in tree and fruit except that the skin is smooth. The fruits were originally smaller, but in recent varieties the size is much larger. Nectarines arise as bud sports or variations on peach trees and also from peach seeds.

The culture of nectarine trees is identical to that of peaches. However, the smooth skin makes them more susceptible to plum curculio and brown rot, and thorough spraying is necessary to control these troubles.

PAPAWS

The papaw, also spelled pawpaw (*Asimina triloba*), is the only member of the *Annonaceae* (custard apple family) that is hardy in the northern United States. It is native in the eastern half of the United States from New York to the Gulf Coast. The papaw is a small tree, 20 to 30 ft. tall, with large, long, glossy leaves. Suckers grow from the roots so that a single tree eventually becomes a thicket. The fruits are 4 to 6 in. long and yellowish in color, with a custardlike flesh in which are embedded numerous large seeds. The flavor is sweet, rich and highly perfumed. Superior types have been discovered, but are so difficult to propagate that they are not generally available. The familiar variety of papaw seedlings are available from some nurseries.

PEACHES

Among temperate-zone fruits, the peach at its best is unsurpassed in juiciness and richness of flavor. Tree-ripened fruits of the best varieties are far superior to the marketed peaches that have been harvested long before they were ripe, and have been softened off the tree.

Wherever winter temperatures drop to −15° F. peach growing is hazardous. However, if the onset of severe cold is slow, the fruit buds of some very hardy varieties may survive at −18° to −20° F. A sudden drop in temperature after a mild spell may injure peach buds, especially those of less hardy varieties. A sloping site that permits cold air to flow to lower levels on still, frosty nights is essential.

In the Deep South and southern California, where winter temperatures are mild, the rest period of many peach varieties may not be fully broken. In these areas, varieties with a low chilling requirement must be planted.

Planting: Peaches thrive on well-drained soils, especially sandy and medium loams. Heavier soils, if well drained and in good physical condition, are adequate. In the North, early spring is the preferred planting time. In the South, late fall or early winter is best. One-year-old trees are preferred for planting. Set the standard trees 20 ft. apart.

Propagation: Peach trees are usually budded on peach seedlings. Nematode-resistant rootstocks are available for infested areas. Dwarfed or small peach trees are produced by using as the rootstock the Western sand cherry, *Prunus besseyi*, and Chinese bush cherry, *Prunus tomentosa*. The beach plum, *Prunus maritima*, is also a successful alternative.

Seasonal Care: Young trees should be mulched or cultivated for two or three years, preferably longer. In the garden a mulch or closely and frequently mowed sod may be used between the trees. Fertilizers should be applied in early spring. Nitrogen fertilizers are helpful and may be applied to one-year-old trees at the rate of a few ounces of ammonium nitrate per tree to 2 or 3 lb. on mature trees; or equivalent amounts of other nitrogen fertilizers may be substituted. Enough nitrogen should be used to produce 12 to 15 in. of new growth each year. Excessive nitrogen causes poorly colored fruit and possible immaturity of the wood, which may winter-kill more easily than well-ripened shoots. Fall growth, particularly, will not survive extensive freezing. Potash may be needed on light soils at the rate of 3 lb. of sulphate of potash for a mature tree.

If weeds are controlled by repeated surface cultivation, this should be discontinued by mid-July and the weeds allowed to grow from then to the end of the season.

Pruning: Peach trees require careful pruning because they fruit on wood produced the previous year. An unpruned tree becomes leggy and the branches are easily broken by wind or by a heavy crop. Pruning is also necessary to keep the tree compact and stocky, and partially to thin the crop.

The newly planted tree is headed at 18 to 30 in. The remaining laterals are cut to short stubs with one or two buds each. As these buds start to grow, the scaffold or framework branches are selected. Other shoots are removed during the first season. Thereafter, until the tree is in bearing, only light corrective pruning is needed.

A standard tree is in full bearing at six to eight years of age and 8 to 10 ft. in height. Pruning should then be fairly heavy to keep the tree low and stimulate vigorous fruiting wood. This is done by removing upright branches, thinning out weaker shoots and removing from the scaffold branches the two- and three-year-old wood.

Pruning in the North should be done after the severe cold of winter has passed. If very low winter temperatures have injured the wood, avoid severe pruning; it may cause serious damage or death of the tree.

Fruit Thinning: Peach trees normally set far more fruits than the tree can ripen properly. On an overloaded tree the fruit is small, of inferior flavor and color, and limb breakage may be excessive. To prevent this and produce large, well-flavored peaches it is necessary to reduce the number of fruits by thinning or removing the excess a few weeks after bloom. Drastic thinning reduces the number of fruits but not the amount of fruit, because those remaining are much larger and of better flavor. An added advantage is that the fruit buds produced by a tree that has had its fruits thinned early may be somewhat hardier the following winter.

Thin by picking off the small green fruits soon after the June drop (a natural shedding of immature fruits in June) for the later varieties, and before for the early varieties. The fruits that remain should be 6 to 8 in. apart on the branches.

Harvesting: For maximum quality the fruit should be harvested when it begins to soften, or a day or two earlier. Fruit for market is often harvested prematurely and never develops its flavor potential.

PEARS

Pear trees are often long-lived and may endure many years of neglect that would kill other fruit trees, but good care produces fine crops in the same way as with other kinds. The pear is somewhat more tolerant than other fruits of soil that is not well drained, but for the trees' vigorous growth and longer life, drainage should be good.

Either late fall or early spring is suitable for planting, but spring is preferable in the colder parts of the northern states. Trees on seedling rootstocks should be spaced 20 ft. apart each way. Dwarf pear trees on quince rootstock may be set 6 to 8 ft. apart in a row, with a somewhat greater distance between rows.

The common European varieties of pear are very susceptible to fire blight. This highly infectious disease is more serious on trees that are making very vigorous growth; hence the soil

should be managed so that the trees grow at a moderate rate. Nitrogen fertilizers should be used with caution, and tree growth may be checked by maintaining a sod cover over the ground, which should be mowed several times during the summer to reduce competition for moisture.

After the scaffold or framework branches of the young tree have been formed, little or no pruning is necessary. Any that is done thereafter should be corrective only, and all cuts should be of small branches. Heavy pruning induces too much growth, which makes trees very susceptible to fire blight.

Pears should be budded on seedlings of the common cultivated pear to produce standard trees. Seedlings of the Bartlett variety are commonly

used. Various Oriental pear species have been used in the past, but as the trees age a physiological disorder of the fruit, known as black end, develops. Trees on Oriental rootstocks have also recently proved susceptible to an insect-borne virus disease.

Dwarf pear trees are produced by using the Angers quince Type A as the rootstock. Some pear varieties, Bartlett, Bosc and Clapp's Favorite, are incompatible with quince rootstock and short-lived if grafted onto it. With these varieties a compatible interstock is used which is budded directly on the quince rootstock. A year later the varieties that are incompatible with quince are budded on the interstock. Hardy and Old Home (blight-resistant) varieties are good interstocks.

Comice Pears

Pears, unlike other fruits, must be harvested partially immature and ripened off the tree to develop maximum texture and flavor. Tree-ripened pears develop grit cells and break down rapidly. Fruit picked for ripening should be exposed to a temperature of 65° F. and high humidity, but can be held in storage at 30° to 32° F. for a few weeks before this is done.

PERSIMMONS, AMERICAN

The native American persimmon, *Diospyros virginiana*, is a common tree in the eastern half of the United States south of central Pennsylvania. It grows to 50 ft. in height and is clothed with lustrous dark green leaves. The fruits are usually less than 2 in. in diameter, yellow, or orange with a blushed cheek, and have a distinctive sweet, rich flavor. The species is dioecious, having separate male and female plants; a male, or staminate, tree should be nearby to provide pollen.

PERSIMMONS, ORIENTAL

The Oriental persimmon is a handsome tree that stands from 15 to 25 ft. tall. The red, orange and yellow fruits are the size of large tomatoes. It is generally grown in the South and Southwest.

PLUMS

There are delicious types of plums that will grow in many of the climatic regions of the United States and southern Canada. Most of the European plums (varieties of *Prunus domestica*) are better suited to the fruit-growing regions of the Pacific Coast and the vicinity of the Great Lakes. The Japanese varieties (derivatives of *P. salicina*) thrive in California, but a few of the hardier sorts are grown in the Northeast.

Plums—especially the Japanese varieties—bloom early, hence sloping

sites with good air circulation are desirable to avoid spring frosts. Brown rot of the fruit is less troublesome where air circulation is adequate. Plums will tolerate heavier soil than is needed for peaches, but it should be well drained.

In the colder regions spring planting is preferable to the fall planting usual in the milder sections. Trees should be spaced about 20 ft. apart.

Weeds should be controlled by cultivation during the first two or three years. Nitrogen fertilizers are usually needed, and in some soils potash deficiency may occur. It can be corrected with sulphate of potash and a hay or straw mulch.

Plum trees may be propagated on several rootstocks. In the northeastern states Myrobalan or cherry plum seedlings are chosen; the Marianna plum is used in California. If the trees are to be grown on sandy soils, peach seedlings are sometimes used. For the native American plum varieties the American plum is useful as an understock.

Being of relatively small size, plum trees are less in need of dwarfing than apple trees, but if a smaller tree is desired, the Western sand cherry, *P. besseyi*, can be used as a dwarfing rootstock.

At planting time, four or five scaffold branches 6 in. or more apart and pointing in different directions should be selected and retained. Remove other branches. Thereafter, until the trees are in bearing, only corrective pruning to prevent a bad crotch from developing is necessary.

Bearing trees will need only light corrective pruning and moderate thinning out of the weak wood to keep the tree from becoming too dense. Older trees that are declining in vigor may need more severe pruning to stimulate vigorous growth.

All black-knot galls should be

removed whenever seen, and burned.

Many plum varieties overbear, with small size and poor quality of fruit, limb breakage, decreased vigor and possible susceptibility to injury in a severe winter. Plums that are borne in dense clusters are much more likely to rot. With most of the Japanese plum varieties and some of the gage types, thin out the green fruits to a space of 3 to 4 in. soon after the June drop (a natural dropping of some of the immature fruits in June). Stanley and Italian prune varieties are not likely to profit from thinning. The home gardener should plant two varieties of most plums to provide cross-pollination.

The Japanese plums are useful because they ripen early, with fruits red or yellow. Cross-pollination should be provided by planting two Japanese varieties in proximity to each other.

The Damson plum is very productive and hardy. It is used only for plum jam and jelly, and the fruits are small, blue and tart. Shropshire and French are good sorts. Sweet yellow damsons known as Mirabelle plums are sometimes grown.

Several American plum species have provided superior types selected from wild trees; but these have mostly been superseded by hybrids between the American plum, *P. americana*, and the Japanese plum, *P. salicina*. These are larger than the American plum, of better flavor and nearly as hardy, suitable for the Middle West and the Great Plains. Cross-pollination is needed and the following are the best pollenizers for this group: Surprise, Kaga, Toka and South Dakota.

Plums for home use should be fully ripe when picked if the full characteristic flavor is desired.

PLUMS, DWARF
The beach plum, *P. maritima*, grows on the sand dunes of the Atlantic Coast. The tree is handsome in bloom, tolerant of salt spray and bears fruit famous for jelly. It is very useful for seaside landscaping where few plants will thrive. Cross-pollination is needed.

QUINCES
The raw quince is not edible, but quince jelly and quince preserves are highly prized delicacies. The small tree is glorious in bloom; its late blossoms escape frost. The quince should never be planted where winter temperatures are too cold for peaches. The trees are slow-growing and shallow-rooted. The soil should be well drained and moderately fertile. Soils that are too fertile stimulate lush growth, which is very susceptible to fire-blight disease.

Newly set trees should be cultivated until well established; thereafter a mowed sod should be maintained beneath them and nitrogen fertilizers used sparingly. Pruning should be very light and corrective only. The fruit moth is another scourge of this tree, and if usable fruit is to be produced the moth must be controlled; spray with all-purpose mixture when the blossom petals fall.

Quince trees are propagated by grafting superior varieties on quince rootstocks raised from seeds, layers or cuttings. The flowers are self-fruitful, so provision for cross-pollination is not necessary. Orange and Smyrna are good varieties.

Nut Trees

A number of kinds and varieties of nut trees may be grown in most of the United States and southern Canada, except in the deserts and colder areas of the Great Plains. In marginal areas of the North, the lowest winter temperatures and the shortness of the growing season limit the choice to the hardier and early-maturing varieties.

Many of the species, especially the walnuts, hickories and pecans, are noble trees of great stature and beauty. Their size limits them to large gardens and country places where they have ample room. Nut trees have no special demands as to soil except that it be well drained and moderately fertile. The site should have good air circulation, as frosts are disastrous: in late spring they can destroy the flowers and young leaves; when untimely in fall they destroy the leaves so that development stops and the kernels are shriveled. The foliage of nut trees must function normally throughout the growing season.

The only pruning needed is to shape the tree while young so that weak crotches do not develop. Severe pruning may cause winter injury of trees, especially those that are not very hardy.

Nitrogen fertilizers may be needed, and if soil is deficient in potash or minor elements, these deficiencies should be corrected.

ALMONDS

Almonds are less winter-hardy than peach trees. Their culture is confined to California. Cross-pollination is necessary.

CHESTNUTS

The native American chestnut has been destroyed by blights, and no trees are known that are resistant enough to be worth planting. The Chinese chestnut is very blight-resistant and it succeeds where the winters are not too cold for peaches. Some trees of this kind may even be slightly hardier than peach trees.

The best varieties bear heavy crops of well-flavored nuts that are much larger than the American chestnuts. Grafted and budded trees are sometimes short-lived, possibly because of stock-scion incompatibility. For this reason, seedling trees are often planted in spite of their variability and inferiority to the best named varieties. Nanking seedlings are preferred; plant two or more varieties of seedlings to provide for cross-pollination.

The Japanese chestnut is less winter-hardy than the Chinese chestnut and somewhat less blight-resistant. The very large nuts are of poor quality raw, but good when cooked.

The European chestnut, which produces the large nuts seen in the markets before Thanksgiving, is very susceptible to blight. It is not satisfactory for cultivation in gardens or orchards in North America.

FILBERTS

In Oregon and Washington the European filbert is an important crop. A few are occasionally grown in gardens in the East, where they will perform reasonably well in peach-growing areas. Growing to about 15 ft. under favorable circumstances, it produces many suckers and is usually cultivated as a large bush; but if the suckers are removed at frequent intervals, the plant may become a small tree.

Hybrids between the native American hazelnut, *Corylus americana*, and the European filbert are available as Jones Hybrids. The gardener should always grow two varieties near each other to provide for cross-pollination.

HICKORIES

Several species of hickory are native in the eastern United States. All are large, majestic trees, but the shagbark hickory is the only one esteemed for highly flavored nuts. The hickory is difficult to transplant and establish owing to the long taproot which extends deep into the ground even from young trees. With good varieties the kernels may be extracted in halves when the nut is cracked.

PECANS

Grown commercially throughout the South, pecan trees also make excellent shade trees on the home grounds. Hybrids between the pecan and hickory, known as hicans, grow rapidly and make handsome shade trees, but they usually bear very light crops of nuts.

PISTACHIOS

Pistachios grow best in the hot interior valleys and desert regions of California and Arizona. Cross-pollination is needed as the species is dioecious; a male or staminate tree must be near pistillate or female trees to provide pollen.

WALNUTS

The black walnut, a native American tree, has long been prized for its richly flavored nuts. The best varieties yield the kernels in quarters.

The trees require at least a 60-ft. spacing when mature. The roots produce a substance that is injurious to some garden plants, so the trees should not be planted near shrubs, vegetables or flowers.

The Persian or English walnut has long been present in the fruit-growing regions of the eastern United States as seedling trees, mostly in dooryards. Many of these, even in areas suitable for peaches, have winter-killed in severe cold spells. During the 1930's and later, seedling trees from Poland were widely planted. Some have proved winter-hardy and are the best available in the North.

The butternut is the hardiest member of the walnut family, but the trees may be short-lived because of disease.

The Japanese walnut makes a handsome, large-spreading tree that grows rapidly. The heartnut, a variant of the Japanese walnut, has a similar tree form, but the nut is heart-shaped and the kernel is extracted easily.

Subtropical and Tropical Trees

AVOCADOS

Three races of avocados are known: the Mexican, which is as cold-tolerant as the orange; the Guatemalan, about as hardy as the lemon; and the West Indian, which is similar to the lime in cold tolerance. There are many varieties. Avocados are grown in southern Florida and southern California, each having its own varieties.

These are unlike other fruits in that the stored food contained in them is fat rather than sugar or starch. The ripe fruit hangs on the tree a long time without deteriorating.

The pollination requirements of avocados are rather complicated. A planting of several varieties should fruit well. Because of the many varieties, a planter should seek advice from his state agricultural extension service.

CITRUS FAMILY

Citrus fruits are subtropical in their climatic requirements and grow best in central and southern California and central and southern Florida in areas where freezing temperatures are neither severe nor prolonged. A few are somewhat more cold-tolerant and may be grown north of these areas.

There are many varieties of citrus, among them very attractive dual-purpose trees, ornamental as well as productive. Insect and disease problems are not ordinarily serious, and cultural requirements are simple. Pruning is very light and consists of removing dead or broken limbs. Fertilization varies according to the soil, so advice should be sought from the local agricultural extension service or other government source.

Publications of the California and Florida agricultural extension services describe interesting citrus fruits, the names of preferred varieties and detailed cultural instructions.

FIGS

Fig trees are grown in California and in the East as far north as Virginia, although they are frequently frozen back when winter temperatures go below normal. Figs may be grown farther north—even as far north as New York City in sheltered locations—if the trees are bent to the ground and covered with several inches of earth or if they are well wrapped up before severe cold arrives.

The root-knot nematode is a serious pest of figs in sandy soils, but heavy mulching tends to control it.

GUAVAS

A large tropical evergreen shrub, the guava bears fruit used to make a popular jelly. The vitamin-C content of the fruit is unusually high. Two species are grown from seedlings—the common, or lemon, guava and the Cattley guava.

LITCHIS OR LYCHEES

The litchi tree may be grown in central and southern Florida, and where the humidity is high and the summer long and hot. The fruits look like large ripe strawberries; a brittle shell encloses a delicious white pulp.

LOQUATS

This evergreen tree is somewhat hardier than other subtropical trees; it will grow well in southern Florida and

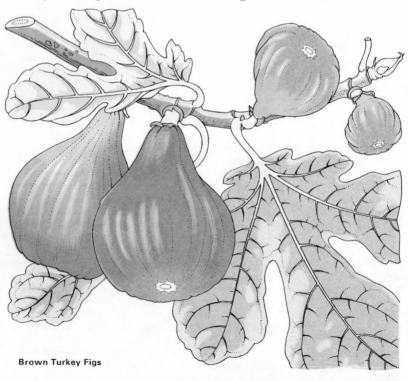

Brown Turkey Figs

most parts of California except the mountains and desert. The fruit is about the size and shape of a small egg, orange-yellow in color, sweet and rich.

MANGOES

The mango is one of the important fruit plants of the tropics, where it is grown in many varieties. The tree is strictly tropical in its requirements and grows satisfactorily only in southern Florida and the warmest parts of California. Even light frost will injure the tree and its flowers. Seedling trees, which are common, produce fruits with stringy flesh and a turpentine flavor, but selected varieties bear delicious and very handsome fruits of red, yellow and purple.

OLIVES

The olive tree can tolerate winter temperatures down to 12° F., but it grows best in the hot interior valleys and desert regions of California.

PAPAYAS

This is a rapidly growing tropical herb without woody tissue. The fruits resemble melons in taste and appearance and weigh from 1 to 5 lb. The plants, which have erect stems, bloom at five months from seed and bear fruit eight months later. After three or four years, the plants must be cut down and replaced with new seedlings. Some seedlings are perfect-flowered, others are either male or female. To make sure that pollination is provided, several seedlings should be planted.

POMEGRANATES

The pomegranate thrives in the hot valleys and desert regions of California. An attractive small tree or large shrub with big red flowers and red fruits, it will withstand temperatures of 10° to 15° F.

BUSH FRUITS

BLUEBERRIES

The highbush blueberry is an excellent shrub that combines beauty with fruit production. It is winter-hardy in all of the United States except the colder portions of the northern states, such as northern New England and the Adirondack region of New York. Usually the plants bloom late enough to escape spring frost.

An open site with good air circulation is the best, as there is less injury from mummy berry, a fungus disease. Full sun is essential.

The blueberry is unique among fruit plants in its specialized soil requirement; it must be acid, with a pH of 4.0 to 4.8 (for explanation of pH, see page 741). If the pH is above 5.5 the soil can be acidified by scattering powdered sulphur over a 3-ft. circle and incorporating it in the upper 10 in. of soil. On light soils 2 lb. of sulphur will be needed for ten plants; on medium loams 4 lb. will be needed. It is also helpful to work several inches of peat moss into the area where the bushes are to be set. Ideally, the soil should be sandy, but medium loams will do if they are acid and supplied with plenty of organic matter of a peaty nature.

The plants may be set in spring or in late fall if they are protected against heaving by winter freezing and thawing of the soil. Incorporate wet peat moss in the soil to be put around the roots at the rate of a pailful for each plant. Additional peat moss may be worked into the bed.

Blueberry plants have shallow roots which are easily injured by cultivation, and they suffer quickly from dry rot. During the first two seasons the plants should be watered if the weather is dry.

Experiments have shown that sawdust mulch, several inches deep and replenished when needed, is much superior to surface cultivation of the soil. Use peat moss if sawdust is not available. Strips of black polyethylene will help to conserve moisture and control weeds. Sulphate of ammonia is the preferred fertilizer and tends to keep the soil acid. One oz. is applied to each bush for each year of age of the plants up to eight years; if a sawdust mulch is used, double the amount of fertilizer.

Blueberry plants are propagated by hardwood or greenwood cuttings rooted in peat moss. Considerable experience is needed, as cuttings sometimes have difficulty rooting.

During the first three years little or no pruning is required. Thereafter annual pruning is necessary because unpruned plants overbear; their berries are small, ripen late and are of disappointing flavor. Pruning consists of moderately thinning out the weaker laterals, which have fewer fruit buds than the vigorous laterals. Occasionally one or two of the old canes should be removed at the base to stimulate the rest of the plant; remove the weaker shoots at the base also, leaving two or three for replacement of old canes.

Blueberries turn blue before they are fully ripe. If picked when those near the ground are not yet fully colored, the berries will taste too tart. The berries weather well on the plants after they are ripe, so prompt harvesting is not as essential as it is with raspberries and strawberries. They also keep very well in the refrigerator.

A blueberry crop must be protected from birds. The bushes may be wrapped in cheesecloth, or a permanent structure of poultry netting may be erected over them. Such measures should be kept in mind when the bushes are planted.

Cross-pollination of blueberry varieties should be provided by planting two or more varieties near each other.

CRANBERRIES, HIGHBUSH

The highbush cranberry (*Viburnum trilobum*), a large, vigorous shrub, produces clusters of bright red fruits that are used for jelly in the colder regions of the United States and Canada.

CURRANTS AND GOOSEBERRIES

Currants and gooseberries require the cool, moist climate of the northern states and Canada, and do not thrive south of Washington, D.C. Very winter-hardy, they are not injured by spring frosts.

Medium to heavy soils well supplied with organic matter are most suitable for these fruits. In lighter soils the plants should be fertilized more heavily and be mulched. If peat moss is used, it should be deep enough to control weeds. Black polyethylene is a good alternative. Somewhat tolerant of light shade, they may be grown between grapevines and small fruit trees if space is scarce.

Plant currants and gooseberries in the fall or early spring. Fall-set plants should be mounded with soil to prevent heaving by frost action the first winter. The plants may be set 3 to 5 ft. apart in the row.

Ammonium nitrate at the rate of $\frac{1}{4}$ lb. per plant may be applied each spring after the first year, or an equivalent amount of nitrogen may be provided by using other fertilizers. If marginal browning of the leaves occurs, potash may be needed. Sulphate of potash is superior to muriate of potash for these fruits, and may be applied at the rate of $\frac{1}{2}$ lb. per plant. It is more effective if used with a mulch, but need not be given every year.

Hardwood cuttings of currants are set in the spring; gooseberries are increased by mound layering. To mound gooseberries the plants are cut to the ground in the spring. As the new shoots grow, soil is heaped among them. Some canes will have roots the

Blackberries

first fall, but better plants will be obtained if the mound is left through the second season.

During the first two or three years no pruning is needed except the removal of broken, prostrate or borer-infested canes. The bushes should be gone over thoroughly each year to detect, remove and burn canes with borers. When pruning older plants remove the weaker canes, leaving equal numbers of one-, two- and three-year-old canes.

ELDERBERRIES

The American elder, *Sambucus canadensis*, is a common native shrub of roadsides and the edge of woods. The fruit has long been used to make jelly, pie and homemade wine.

JUNEBERRIES

The dwarf Juneberry, also known as serviceberry and Saskatoon (*Amelanchier alnifolia*), is a small shrub useful for its little purplish-blue berries that are esteemed in the Great Plains for pies and preserves. Robins are very fond of the fruit.

CANE FRUITS

BLACKBERRIES

Stable, named varieties of this delicious midsummer fruit have only recently been available. Until now it has been of mixed parentage, sometimes the only kind that commercial growers could offer.

East of the Rocky Mountains, bush blackberries have about the same cultural requirements as red raspberries.

The hardier blackberries may be grown in the milder parts of the United States and Canada. The trailing blackberries of the Pacific Coast are not winter-hardy elsewhere. Trailing or semierect plants are trained on trellises made of two wires, the lower one 3 ft. from the ground, the upper 5 ft. A cane, or stem, is tied horizontally along each wire, or fanned out and attached to both wires.

The new shoots are topped at about 3 ft. to make them branch. The following spring the branches should be cut back to 12 in.

The tarnished plant bug often feeds on the open flowers so that they fail to develop into normal berries. A DDT spray just before the first blackberry flowers open will control this insect.

RASPBERRIES

Raspberries have not been grown much for the fresh-fruit market as they do not hold up well in shipping, so they have become almost a basic plant for the home garden. Raspberries are northern, with few exceptions, thriving best north of the latitude of Washington, D.C., and the Ohio River valley. They are especially susceptible to virus diseases, which are prevalent in wild red raspberries and in run-out plantings of garden raspberries. Such plants should be eliminated if possible for a distance of several hundred feet from the proposed new raspberry planting. Soils in which tomatoes, peppers, eggplants and potatoes have been grown recently should be avoided, as these plants may infect the soil with verticillium wilt, a serious soil-borne disease of black and purple raspberries. Perennial weeds should be destroyed, since some of them, especially quack (witch) grass, are very difficult to remove from an established raspberry planting.

Good soil drainage with the water table not nearer than 30 in. from the surface during the growing season is essential; raspberries soon die in a soggy soil. Soil texture is unimportant if the soil is well supplied with organic matter.

Raspberries may be set in late fall or early spring, fall planting being preferable if plants can be obtained at that time. The red varieties are set 2 ft. apart in rows 7 to 9 ft. apart. The black and purple varieties should be 3 ft. apart in the row. Fall-set plants should be mounded up with soil to prevent them from being heaved out by frost action during the winter. The stub should be cut off at ground level before growth starts in the spring to prevent fruiting the first year.

Red-raspberry plants produce many sucker plants, which may soon become a thicket much too wide for good fruit production and convenient management. The fruiting row should not be over a foot wide. Sucker plants arising outside of that spacing should be hoed off as they appear.

Nitrogen is the most useful fertilizer and may be applied each spring at the rate of ½ lb. to each sq. ft. On light soils potash may be needed occasionally at the rate of 1 lb. of sulphate of potash to 100 sq. ft.

Propagation: Red raspberries are naturally propagated from the sucker plants which spring up around the old plants. These may be taken up and transplanted when dormant. Black and red raspberries may also be propagated by tip-layering. The tip of the current season's shoot is inserted vertically in the soil to a depth of 6 in. in late August. Roots develop on the tip, which may be severed from the mother plant the following spring and transplanted.

Pruning: Raspberry canes are biennial; they grow one year, fruit the following year, then die and are replaced by a new set of canes from the same root system. In August, after the canes have fruited, pull them out altogether. The following spring, thin the remaining red-raspberry canes to a spacing of 6 in. between plants in the row. Cut back those which remain to fruit, removing approximately the upper fourth of each cane.

Black raspberries are handled differently. When the new shoot is about 18 in. tall the tip is pinched; this causes the shoot to branch and makes a sturdy self-supporting plant instead of the long sprawling canes that result when the tip is not removed. The following spring the branches are cut back to about 8 in.

Purple raspberry shoots are topped at 2 ft. and the laterals are cut back to 10 or 12 in.

The autumn-fruiting or so-called everbearing red raspberries are pruned the same as the one-crop varieties. They bear one crop in the fall on new shoots produced during the current season and a second crop from the same canes the following summer. After the summer crop is over, the canes that bore it are cut out.

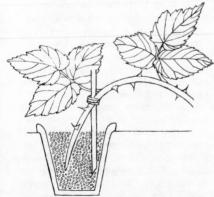

Propagation by Tip Layering
Plant the end of a growing shoot in a pot buried beside the plant. The shoot will take on new roots and can be separated and planted out in the fall or spring.

VINES

GRAPES

Grapes have been a favorite fresh fruit for centuries; they are indispensable for jelly, juice and wines. On trellises, fences and arbors they lend a special beauty to walks and areas of privacy. There are varieties suitable for most of the United States. The date of the first killing frost determines whether late-ripening or only early-ripening varieties can be raised in a given locality.

North of the latitude of Virginia, American varieties are derived from *Vitis labrusca*. Commercially they are usually grown near large bodies of water which temper the climate. Southward the bunch grapes are less successful because of their susceptibility to diseases. The muscadine grape (varieties of *Vitis rotundifolia*) is pre-eminent in the South. In California and in similar climates the European grape (varieties of *Vitis vinifera*) is commonly cultivated.

The good air circulation of a sloping site lessens the damage from fungus diseases. It also delays the first frost so that later-ripening varieties may be grown. A southern slope or the south side of a building or wall receives more heat from the sun, hastening maturity, which is particularly helpful for late-ripening varieties.

Grapes may be grown on a wide range of soils, but good drainage is essential or the vines will fail. Medium and lighter loams are preferred. Very fertile soils may stimulate too vigorous growth that will winter-kill easily.

Planting: Grapevines may be planted in the spring or fall. Earth should be mounded around fall-planted vines for protection against heaving by frost action during the first winter. The largest-size one-year-old vines are better for planting than two-year vines. Most varieties should be spaced

8 ft. apart in the row, but vigorous varieties in fertile soils may need 10 ft.

If phylloxera or nematodes (eelworms) are a problem, the vines should be grafted on rootstocks resistant to these pests. Among resistant rootstocks are those identified by the numbers 3309 and 3306. Other special rootstocks are available, but seek professional advice to determine whether they are needed.

Seasonal Care: Control weeds by clean cultivation or with a mulch if only a few vines are involved. Herbicides are being used extensively now in commercial vineyards, as they eliminate cultivator damage to the trunks and roots. After the vines are on a trellis, a contact herbicide DNBP may be used about three times during the summer to kill the aboveground parts of the weeds. For all-summer weed control with one application, Karmex is successful. Caution: grapevines are very sensitive to 2, 4-D and 2,4,5-T; never use these herbicides on plants growing near grapes.

The amount of fertilizer should depend on the vigor of the vine—growth, leaf size and color, and crop size and maturity. For a bearing vine, apply 4 to 6 oz. of ammonium nitrate or an equivalent amount of other nitrogen fertilizer in the spring before growth starts. With lighter soils, if the edges of the leaves turn brown, sulphate of potash should be applied at $\frac{1}{2}$ lb. per vine; size and frequency of the applications should be determined by the appearance of the leaves.

Propagation and Training: Plant hardwood cuttings in the spring. They are sometimes grafted on phylloxera-resistant or nematode-resistant rootstocks. If only a vine or two is wanted, it may be had by layering; bend down a shoot and cover it with soil. When it takes root, it can be transplanted.

A number of training systems have been devised, but the umbrella Kniffen System is now considered to be among the best for the American-type grapes, Concord and similar varieties. The trellis of this training plan consists of two wires of No. 9 gauge—the lower $2\frac{1}{2}$ to 3 ft. above the ground, the upper $5\frac{1}{2}$ to 6 ft. The object is to have the foliage well displayed to the sun and a vine that is easy to manage.

According to this system, the young vine may lie on the ground the first year. At planting time it is pruned to a single cane. As soon as the new growth is 1 in. long, all shoots except the two topmost are removed. When a cane reaches the top wire, it is tied firmly to it to serve as the trunk of the vine. In succeeding years the vine consists of this trunk and one or more arms arising near the top of the trunk. These are bent sharply over the top wire and extend down to the lower wire where they are tied.

Pruning: At the end of the growing season a vine trained in the umbrella Kniffen manner consists of a number of canes growing from the arms. The canes must be limited by pruning or the vine will overbear with small clusters and fruit that does not ripen well; it may also suffer from frost. The number of buds left for fruiting depends upon the vigor of the vine. Remove and weigh all of the previous year's growth except about 60 buds on several of the more vigorous canes. For the first pound of prunings leave 30 buds; for each additional pound of prunings leave 10 more buds. Thus for a vine with 3 lb. of prunings, 30 plus 10 plus 10 (or 50) buds are left on the canes. A two-bud spur should be retained near the base of each cane to provide new growth for the next year.

Pruning European-Type Grapes: Head pruning is used for varieties that fruit well on short spurs. The vine is developed as a trunk 1 to 3 ft. tall, with several spurs of two to four buds each. An old vine may have from 10 to 20 spurs after pruning.

Thompson Seedless and some wine varieties are cane-pruned. Under this system the vine consists of a short trunk with several canes trained in a fan-shaped manner along the trellis, with 8 to 15 buds each. The trellis wires are 3 and 4 ft. above the ground with a stake at each vine.

Cordon training is used for table-grape varieties. A lower wire is 3 ft. above the ground; the upper wire is 4 ft. from ground level. The mature vine consists of a trunk with an arm each side of the trunk along the lower wire. Two to three bud spurs are spaced 8 to 12 in. apart along each arm. During the growing season the shoots from the spurs are tied to the upper wires.

With any of these systems, if it appears that the vines may overbear, some of the flower clusters should be removed at the end of the blooming period.

Harvesting: Grapes do not ripen after they are removed from the vine; consequently they should not be picked early. Some varieties, especially those that are derived from the species *Vitis labrusca*, deteriorate rapidly after ripening and must be used quickly. Others, such as the European or *V. vinifera* grape, keep well on the vine and after picking. These may be left until frost threatens and then harvested for storage in a cool place.

Some grape varieties, especially those early and sweet-flavored, are taken by birds as soon as they ripen. Protect them by enclosing the clusters in white paper bags fastened together at the top with a stout pin. Brown paper bags should not be used, as they impart a bad taste to the grapes.

STRAWBERRIES

The strawberry is the favorite of all fruits for the home garden. It is first to ripen, does not require much space and is easy to grow. There are strawberry varieties suitable for culture in every state of the Union and much of Canada. Strawberries will grow on a wide range of soil types if they are well drained and in good physical condition. Where winters are severe, a mulch and snow provide the protection needed.

Good air circulation, as on a slope, minimizes frost injury to the flowers on still, cold nights in the spring. It also reduces losses from red-stele root rot, which can result where the berries dry off too slowly after rain and dew.

Perennial weeds must be eliminated before the plants are set out, as it is impossible to remove them in a matted row full of plants. If quack grass becomes firmly established, the bed may as well be abandoned. Grass sods harbor white grubs that feed on strawberry roots. Destroy the grubs by using chlordane before planting.

Planting: The soil should be prepared as for a vegetable garden. Dormant plants from cold storage are superior to freshly dug plants. The latter are satisfactory if dug and planted early, before much growth has taken place. Early spring, as soon as the ground can be worked, is the best time to set strawberries. August is the poorest time. They should be set with a spade or trowel, making sure that the crown of the plant is at ground level and the roots are firm in the soil.

Strawberries are usually grown in matted rows. The plants are set 18 in. apart in rows 3½ ft. apart. The runner plants fill in the space between and alongside the mother plants. In fertile soil, runner plants are produced so freely that the fruiting row is often overcrowded. It is much better to space the runner plants around the mother plants about 6 in. from each other, until the row is 18 in. wide. Thereafter all new runner plants that develop are removed. A row of spaced plants is much more productive the next year than an overcrowded one.

Another system is to set the plants in beds of two, three or four rows, 1 ft. between rows and 1 ft. between plants, and remove all runner plants as they appear. A bed of hill-system plants, as these are called, is the most productive way of growing strawberries.

During the spring in which planting is done, all flower clusters should be removed to prevent fruiting; the plants should not be permitted to crop until their second season. Weeds must be controlled from the outset or the bed will be a failure. Hoeing may be supplemented by using a herbicide such as sesone, dacthal or diphenamid.

Strawberries are sometimes grown under a black polyethylene mulch to keep the berries clean and conserve moisture. The plants are set through holes in the polyethylene, or it is laid on the ground close to the row of plants.

Seasonal Care: Strawberry plants are shallow-rooted and need an ample supply of moisture for good growth and fruit production. In a dry season or location, the plants should receive a total of 1 in. of water a week during the spring through fall growing season. Good irrigation for the plants is far more important than fertilizer.

On infertile soils the plants should receive a side-dressing of ammonium nitrate at the rate of ½ lb. to 100 ft. of row; other nitrogen fertilizers applied at an equivalent rate are also suitable. In August a second application may be made, broadcast in pellet form over the dry plants. Brush it off immediately with a broom or brush.

In late fall, after the plants have experienced two or three hard frosts

but before temperatures drop below 20° F., the bed should be mulched to protect the crowns of the plants from severe freezing and from adverse frost action during the winter when there is no snow cover. The straw, 3 to 4 in. thick, should be as free of weed seeds as possible. In more southerly gardens, where heavy protection from very low temperatures is not needed, a mulch of straw or pine needles may be applied later—to keep the berries clean.

In the spring, just as growth starts, pull part of the straw off the plants to permit the leaves and flower clusters to push through. Spray the plants with DDT just before the first flowers open, to prevent tarnished plant bugs feeding on the flowers and causing the berries to be seedy-ended nubbins.

Everbearing Strawberries: Everbearing strawberries do not grow well south of the latitude of Washington, D.C., but in the North they are very productive. The plants should be grown in hills with all runner plants removed. Plants mulched with sawdust after the first hoeing bear more fruit than those grown where the soil surface is repeatedly cultivated. A polyethylene mulch will prove satisfactory if sawdust is not available. The blossoms should be picked off until about July 1 the first year; those that develop thereafter will fruit in about a month and continue until stopped by cold weather in the fall.

Varieties: Many good strawberry varieties are available, and new ones are introduced each year. Varieties tend to be specific in their soil and climatic requirements. Consult local county agricultural agents, agricultural experiment stations or other government sources for specific recommendations. Virus-free plants of most kinds are available and should be ordered instead of plants of unknown health.

PART III

Your Home in a Garden Setting

Gardens don't just happen — at least not the best ones. They result from careful planning and, usually, a certain amount of trial and error. From the earliest stages decisions must be made on the choice of plants and their placement. Do the grounds need to be contoured or terraced? Should there be hedges or fences, shade trees or light-leaved lawn trees? These are perplexities for the landscaper; they are matters basic to good design.

Some families move into a new house rising on bull-dozed rubble, where even weeds hesitate to grow. With a little labor and care, the homeowner can transform this desolation. Today he is blessed with a vast array of plants that have never been available before except to botanical gardens. By following a program of first things first, he can, within a very few seasons, create grounds that are beautiful and balanced. In time his home will appear comfortably ensconced in a green and growing world that seems always to have been there.

CHAPTER 16

THE GARDEN PLAN

Existing Features—An Individual Design—Space for Family Needs—Plants: Their Ultimate Shapes and Sizes—Paths, Steps, Walls—Terraces and Patios—Fences, Screens, Gates, Pergolas, Bridges

MOST PROPERTY OWNERS can successfully plan the landscaping of the grounds around their homes. Such a project challenges creative ability and is a most interesting and rewarding task. Planning a garden presents specific problems and involves making many decisions; it takes thought and time and energy. The objective, of course, is a landscape that is esthetically satisfying as well as functional, that is composed of plants suitable to the climate and that can be maintained with minimum work and expense. To achieve all these ends is not easy, but it is unwise to aim for less. Designing a landscape is comparable to furnishing a house. A great many selections must be made, with the goal a livable environment, satisfying to the eye.

But there the similarities cease. House furnishings are more or less static. A couch or chair does not increase in size from year to year like a tree or shrub, nor does it shed its fabric each fall or vary its color with changing seasons. The planner of gardens deals not only with shapes and masses and colors as they are; he must know what they will become with time.

INITIAL SURVEY

The planning of a home landscape may involve starting from scratch, beginning where the builder left off, or it may consist of making over and adapting an existing garden. In either case, the first thing to do is to survey and study the property, carefully appraising its possibilities as well as its limitations. This should not be done hurriedly. Indeed if there are a considerable number of trees, shrubs or other permanent plants of possible landscape value already on the place, it is well to allow sufficient time to elapse to identify them correctly, to evaluate them in leaf and in flower, in every season, before making any irrevocable moves.

The survey should include existing features, such as boundaries, location of the house and driveway, topography—level, sloping or irregular surface—outcropping rocks, streams or ponds and other individual characteristics. A prospective designer should take a thoughtful inventory of all living trees, shrubs or other plants that may have value in the finished picture if they remain undisturbed or, in some cases perhaps, if they are transplanted to new locations.

Consider, too, the character of the soil, its depth and quality. Is it adequately drained, not only by surface runoff but through subsoil porosity? Where are shady areas and where sunny ones? Is the site exposed to sweeping winds or is it adequately sheltered? In which directions are the best views and vistas? Are there objectionable features that need screening out? All these and other matters should receive attention and careful thought as a result of the survey.

MAKE A PLAN

To simplify decisions, a scale drawing or plan should first be prepared, showing all important features in their relative positions and proportionate sizes. This need not be elaborate or of landscape-architect quality, but it must be accurate. A large sheet of graph paper affords the easiest way of developing such a working drawing. Let the side of each small square on the paper represent a uniform distance on the ground—say, one square equals one foot, or some such equivalent. Just one important point to remember—all measurements between points on the ground must be taken on a dead level, not up or down a slope. For instance, two trees planted on a steep hillside, one considerably higher than the other, may measure 20 ft. apart along the line of the ground. However, the actual distance between them to be shown on the plan (which is the distance between them as measured along a line held perfectly horizontally) will be decidedly less than 20 ft.

BASIC DESIGN

Once the ground plan is prepared, the next step is the development of a fundamental design. So far nothing has been said about the kinds of plants to be used, and this is as it should be. At this stage we are simply dealing with spatial relationships, with the advantageous locating of masses representing trees, evergreens, shrubs, etc., and of open areas to be carpeted with grass, ground covers and paving materials.

It is much too early yet to decide which kinds of plants will produce the desired effects. All too often amateurs mar their landscaping efforts by first deciding that they simply must have a red-leaved Japanese maple because it looked so brilliant in a nursery, or a shrub because they remember it from childhood—whether or not they are suitable from a designer's point of view. Always begin with the overall concept and gradually refine the plan by filling in detail.

Formal or Informal

Broadly speaking, landscapes fall into two main groups: the formal and geometric; the informal, asymmetric and naturalistic. Formal gardens are obviously imposed on the landscape by man. They are characterized by straight lines, by regular curves and by symmetrical balance. Many of the plants used are likely to be highly developed products of plant breeders—choice hybrid roses, begonias and tulips, hybrid lilacs and delphiniums, geraniums and annuals. Plants may be trained to artificial shapes to form strictly sheared hedges, archways and espaliers. Many of the plants are obviously of exotic (using the word in its true sense of being "not native") origin; they could not have occurred naturally in the locations they occupy. Accessories to the formal garden, such as masonry features, paving, seats, fountains, statues and the like, should be sophisticated. Cut stone, brick, rectangular paving, concrete (carefully and skillfully used) and dressed and finished wood are some of the many suitable materials. Scrupulous neatness and tidiness are needed to maintain formal gardens.

Informal gardens, too, ordinarily show evidences of man's handiwork, especially on close inspection. But the impression is that here man has not relentlessly imposed his wishes. Instead, he has worked together with nature to develop a landscape of unaffected charm, one that epitomizes natural beauties.

Asymmetrical balance and irregular curves of natural appearance characterize informal gardens. Straight lines are rarely part of them, nor, except in naturally flat country, will broad, level areas occur.

If the garden is naturalistic, the plants used will to a large extent be natives or at least will look as though they could be denizens of the region. In informal gardens not intended to be naturalistic, nonnatives may be used more freely, but still will not be planted to achieve symmetrical balance as in a formal garden. They will not be closely sheared or trained to artificial shapes. Trees and shrubs that fit well into the local natural landscape will predominate. Single-flowered shrub roses, naturalized perennials, narcissuses and shrubs such as azaleas, sweet pepperbush and crab apples, and suitable ground covers will be emphasized. Materials used in accessories may include field stone, uncut stone, random paving, tanbark, rustic wood and the like.

Less meticulous garden housekeeping is demanded by informal gardens, especially if they are naturalistic in style. A few leaves unswept, an old stump still in the ground, even a few casual "weeds" lend character.

Often, especially when the ground surrounding the house is more than a small lot, the landscape development may well embody formal, semiformal, informal and even completely natural or wild areas (such as a stand of undeveloped woodland). In such cases the most formal areas should usually be in the immediate vicinity of the house and the more natural ones farther away, ordinarily with a gradual transition from one to the other.

ALLOTMENT OF SPACE

Consider carefully the purposes that the land surrounding the house must satisfy, and allot suitable space to each. Of great importance is what might be called the public area. This consists chiefly of the land between the street and the house, often called the front yard. It forms the setting or framework for the house and as such can greatly enhance or detract from the appearance and value of the property. Much of it will probably be visible from the street. This part of the landscape provides the guest, the visitor, the newcomer, with a first impression of your home and reveals something about its occupants.

The very practical matter of providing a service area is no less important. Unlike the public area, this will ordinarily be screened or at least fitted into the landscape as inconspicuously as possible. It may make provision for a laundry yard, garbage-disposal unit, delivery of fuel and other supplies, possibly a separate garage or tool shed, and—more in the public view than some of the items listed—a driveway giving access to the service area. An efficient service area is important to the smooth functioning of a house.

The third major division to be considered is the private area. Here are located the outdoor living spaces such as terraces and other sitting places, lawns, possibly a swimming pool, and flower gardens. Here, too, if attractively laid out and maintained, may be included a cut-flower and vegetable garden, although these are usually placed on the fringe of the private area, perhaps bordering the service area. The private area may have to be screened. In many ways it is the garden proper, and may be used for relaxing, eating and other enjoyments when weather permits, and to provide pleasant views from the house.

The allotment of space to the three suggested divisions of the property will depend, of course, on the needs of the family and on the topography, especially the location of existing trees and shrubs of value. But it is these three major areas that set the fundamental framework for the design.

A close fence will act as a windbreak and insure privacy.

First, then, indicate on the outline plan the locations of the public, private and service areas. Then begin designing. Make your initial efforts at layout on tracing paper placed over the plan; this simplifies making changes.

The Public Area

Unless, as occasionally happens, the house is built in thinned woodland and the front yard is informal and fairly heavily shaded, the public area should consist primarily of trees placed to frame the building and to cast some shade, an open lawn area and sufficient foundation planting to soften architectural lines and "marry" the structure to the ground. Boundary plantings, hedges or fences may be desirable, especially to screen the service and private areas.

If neighboring properties are pleasant, it is wise to plan the front yard so that it fits well with them and is not incongruous. In all cases restraint is important. It is better to set out too few plants than too many. Often a few sizable specimens, well placed, will be more useful, and not much more expensive, than a greater number of small plants.

The locating of shade trees, and possibly tall evergreens, to frame the house, needs first consideration. To accomplish this, stroll in front of the house, on the sidewalk or road, and then toward it as you would if approaching the front door. Partly close your eyes and visualize where high masses of foliage might be introduced to improve the picture. Trees used for framing may or may not be fairly close to the house. Sometimes specimens at quite a distance away, even perhaps on other properties, will partially serve the purpose. Framing trees may be in front, to the sides or even behind the building, with their tops showing above the ridgeline. For very narrow lots it is often useful to use street trees, planted between the sidewalk and the road, as framers.

In any case, having determined where masses of high greenery should be and their approximate heights and outlines (at maturity), mark on the plan the locations of trees that are to provide these effects. It is of great help also to make perspective sketches or to have photos taken from different viewpoints, and to use these as elevations over which you can place tracing paper and sketch in the foliage masses you would like to have. When space permits, it is usually better to use three or more trees to frame a building.

Following decisions regarding the placement of the framing trees, consider the foundation planting. Modern houses built on low or ground-level foundations do not need the somewhat solid bank of tall shrubbery favored in the past. Foundation planting can do much for the appearance of a house. By carrying it outward from either end to form wing plantings, the apparent length of the structure is increased; by installing corner groupings, harsh vertical lines are softened, and the front door is pleasantly emphasized and made more inviting if the planting on either side of it is appropriate.

Except where windows wrap around the corners of a house, it is a basic rule that the foundation planting should be taller at the corners than elsewhere; its ultimate height at those points should be approximately one-half the distance between ground and eaves.

Of equal importance to the corner or wing groupings are the plants that flank the front door. These should support and add strength to the entrance. What goes between the corner plantings and door-side details will vary greatly with the architecture of the house, placement and height of windows and so forth.

The finished appearance must be one of stability and equilibrium. This does not mean that the identical landscaping must be repeated, plant for plant, on either side of the center. That is usually the worst kind of foundation planting. A balanced effect is obtained by providing equal interest and apparent weight of material on one side of the chief center of interest as on the other. And the chief center of interest need not be the center line of the house; it may very well be an off-center front door.

In developing the public area, you will, of course, be faced with the necessity for access walks and perhaps a driveway. The basic rule here is: If these are under 50 or 60 ft. in length, keep them as straight as possible. Curves should usually be introduced only when the necessity for skirting some obstruction, such as a tree or rock outcrop, is involved or the ground contours make walking in other than a straight line logical.

It is better not to divide a narrow lot with a path leading directly from front door to street; this emphasizes its narrowness. A better plan is to run the driveway along one side of the lot and make a walking path from the driveway to the door. Paths that parallel the building should not be closer than 6 ft. to it, and it is more attractive if there is a greater distance between house and path.

Of great importance to the tranquil appearance of the public area is the maintenance of a goodly sweep of open lawn. This should not be interrupted by spot plantings of shrubs, small trees or flower beds and most certainly not by such distracting elements as gazing globes, sundials, birdbaths or ceramic gnomes, ducks, flamingos or other pretensions. Driveway lamps should be in character with the

(Above) An unsatisfactory landscape results from poor selection and placement of plants. A large evergreen obstructs one window. The poplar is too close to the house, provides little shade and may clog drains with its roots. Sheared shrubs and formal beds produce a spotty effect.

(Below) Here, the same house is framed by a graceful honey locust and a flowering crab. The foundation planting of informal evergreens and ground covers directs attention to the front door and softens the corners of the house. An uncluttered lawn provides a foreground.

architecture of the house and name plates or similar accessories are a matter of personal taste. The purpose of the public area is to provide a pleasing setting for the house, which is the focal point of the picture, and nothing should distract from this ideal.

The North American tradition, contrary to that of European countries, calls for leaving the front of the lot open to public view whenever this is possible. Surely if the house is one of a number along a street, all of which are unfenced, it would be a mistake to introduce a barrier. But sometimes partial or even complete enclosure is necessary and suitable, as, for example, when undesirable views must be screened, or trespassing animals or people kept out. A severe change of grade between one's own lot and the land beyond may prove to be such a hazard that a low wall or a fence is necessary.

Enclosures should not be of obviously forbidding character, such as chain-link fences. If these must be used for security, they should be masked by shrubs or hedges.

Shrubs planted informally, perhaps with small trees interspersed, are usually very satisfactory as boundary screens. Along the front of the property, low hedges, informal or formal, are usually more gracious than fences, although simple open fences and low stone walls with vines spilling along or over them can be friendly and attractive.

It is sometimes useful to provide flowers in the public area, but this must be done with extreme discretion. Groups of carefully chosen kinds in front of the foundation planting may be appropriate, and so may borders of flowers against boundary plantings of shrubs. Whether to use flowers or not depends entirely on the answer to the question: Do they really contribute to the picture as a whole?

The Service Area

Primarily utilitarian, the service area need not be unpleasing. It must blend with the landscape so that incongruity does not result. Ordinarily, the service area should be screened in whole or in part. Screening may be effected by the use of fences or walls, the outside surfaces of which are backgrounds for vines, shrubs or other plants. Hedges, formal or informal, or masses of shrubs will serve, too. Access to the service area from other parts of the garden and from the house should be easy and natural.

Usually the placement and design of the house itself will determine the location of the service area. It may include the kitchen and side doors, cellar entrance and, often, entrance to the garage. However, there is no advantage in allotting more space to this area than is necessary. In addition to providing for the functioning of a lived-in house, the service area may also have space for a children's playpen and possibly for a compost heap and a cold frame, although these can sometimes be more conveniently situated in out-of-the-way parts of the private area.

The Private Area

Here is the greatest opportunity to express individuality, to achieve a design appropriate to the way of life and interests of the family and to establish sympathetic contact with the surrounding landscape. At the planning stage, we are tentatively considering design, the advantageous placement of plants, plant groups and other features to create satisfying pictures and an overall effect, without regard for the exact types or kinds of plants we shall use to achieve it. We are interested in views and vistas, privacy, easy access to all parts of the garden, the provision for shade where needed, as, for example, on the terrace during the afternoon and early evening, and for places to enjoy the sun. We are concerned with placing trees, shrubs, hedges and vines to produce mass and line effects, to hide or reveal, to create patterns.

Special thought must be given to the unique activities and interests of the family: Will it enjoy an outdoor terrace? Is a swimming pool practicable? What about areas for games? How about a barbecue setup? Would a cut-flower or a vegetable garden appeal to family members? If there are avid gardeners, do their interests run to specialties such as native plants, rock gardens, herb gardens or roses?

If the garden is to be formal, it is wise to keep the center open. The main axis may begin at a door or window of the house or at some other logical starting point, and should end with a strong feature. This could be a framed view of a distant natural element, such as the sea, a pond or a mountain, but more often it must be introduced: a seat, a fountain, a bird-bath or a gate. This terminal feature should be quite dominant. In a strictly formal garden, whatever is put on one side of the main axis is repeated on the other. In a semiformal garden, the effect of symmetrical balance will prevail, although minor variations between one side and the other of the chief axis exist.

The open center of a formal garden should be longer than it is wide; it may be rectangular, elliptical or of any other regular geometric form. The center should not be interrupted by any prominent or high-standing shape; but a pool that is flush with the ground or beds of low flowers may be appropriate. One or more axes at right angles to the main axis of the garden may be terminated by features subordinate in importance.

Formal gardens are especially suitable for level sites and those that slope gently and evenly in one direction. To develop them on irregular ground usually necessitates grading operations. However, although installed on level ground, the garden itself need not be all on one grade; varying levels may be used to add interest. Gradations are often necessary in hilly regions and can be contrived in flat country. A formal garden with a sunken central panel, the sides supported by stone walls—cemented or laid dry—and abloom with rock plants, can be very attractive.

When a level formal garden is developed on a sloping or irregular site, great care must be given to planting the immediate surroundings. The new development must be fitted into place without any suggestion that violence has been done to the landscape.

If informality is to characterize the garden, there should be no symmetrical balance on either side of the central axis. Nevertheless, good views or vistas should be emphasized or developed, and a feeling of balance achieved by plantings that complement each other asymmetrically. If possible, the element of surprise should be introduced by new and pleasing views encountered after one turns a corner, passes through a gate or rounds a group of shrubs or trees.

Informal landscapes may be developed on level as well as on topographically irregular properties. They are especially suited to the latter, however, because they enable the gardener to take advantage of every change of grade and other variation, and because they demand minimum contouring of the ground. Changes of grade give opportunities for rustic steps, winding paths, undulating lawns, rock gardens and waterfalls.

Whether the landscape be formal or informal or include both types, if the property is sufficiently large, there will probably be need for a certain amount of compartmenting. Open areas with special features can be isolated by screens of trees, shrubs, hedges and the like, creating in effect a series of outdoor rooms. Consideration must always be given to easy means of access between them—paths or lawn areas.

SELECTING THE PLANTS

At this point, basic decisions of design have been made. Driveway and paths, service features, outdoor terrace, barbecue area, swimming pool have been located on the landscape and entered on the plan. We know where there is to be open lawn, and where masses of foliage will be provided by trees, shrubs and hedges. We have allowed for vegetable and cut-flower garden, rose garden, herb garden, rock garden and the like. It is time to choose the kinds of plants to secure the best effects.

Suggestions that follow must be carried out by each architect-gardener with plants that are adapted to the climate and idiosyncrasies of his particular landscape.

The first basic rule of plant selection is to create all important design features with trees, shrubs and other plants that are reliably hardy. If choice or rare plants of a doubtful hardiness are chosen, place them where the overall appearance of the landscape will not suffer if they are lost.

Soil and locations for prospective planting should be realistically appraised. Admittedly, soils can, and indeed should, be improved before planting, but the chances are all against a gardener if he sets moisture-loving plants in porous, dry soils; dry-land plants in wet or boggy places; neutral-soil plants in excessively acid soil or, above all, acid-soil plants in alkaline soil. He will court disaster or at least disappointment if he sets plants such as rhododendrons and camellias, which need sheltered locations, in open, windswept places, or sun lovers such as roses and buddleias in deep shade. Contrariwise, many plants, including *Acanthopanax* and English ivy, need shade or at least tolerate it, and many pines and junipers prosper exceedingly in open, windswept places.

It is important to compose the landscape of quality plants of choice char-

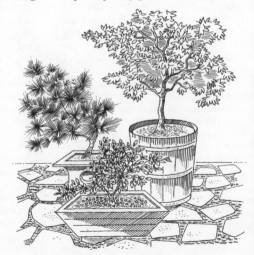

Mobile Plants
Containers of varying shapes and sizes can bring the charm of foliage and flowers to a paved terrace, and they can be moved to achieve new effects.

acter. This does not mean exclusively the newest introductions or the most widely advertised. Plants are like people; some are basically fine, others less admirable. The kinds to seek are those that grow sturdily, are attractive in form and foliage, have no tendency to weediness of habit and are not excessively subject to pests or diseases. Among plants that display these qualities are most pines, rhododendrons, camellias, hollies, oaks, crab apples, azaleas and fothergillas, to mention just a few. One must beware, however, of outright condemnation of almost any plant. Under some circumstances, in some places, most plants that are quite impossible to use generally can be employed to enhance landscape. This applies to the often despised tree of heaven, *Ailanthus altissima*, which is useful in city yards, and even to the rampant goutweed, *Aegopodium podagraria*, which can cover poor barren ground. There appear to be no virtues in poison oak and poison ivy, though even they are beautiful.

Exercise great restraint in the use of bizarre and exotic-looking specimens, kinds that are conspicuous by reason of their unusual form, color or size of foliage. Even though they may be individually beautiful and interesting, pass them by if they do not fit well with neighboring vegetation. They are likely to compete too forcefully with other features in the landscape, even with the house itself. Also, although attractive at first, they may prove to be hard to live with. Examples of exotic-looking plants are highly colored evergreens such as blue spruce and golden arborvitae, golden-leaved honey locust, brilliant Japanese maple, red-leaved forms of other maples, weeping trees and the mop-headed tree commonly called *Catalpa bungei*. Not that these should never be used. Appropriate places may be found for

all of them. But it takes good judgment to place them advantageously.

Don't make the mistake of using too many different kinds of plants in any one view or picture, and be sure that those you select are kinds that blend well. Too much "one of this and one of that," planted with little consideration of the plants' blending qualities, results in an uneasy, "busy" landscape. This is a common failing of foundation plantings. Another point to bear very much in mind is to group plants whenever possible rather than set them out singly. Plants of the same kind grouped and even somewhat crowded do not offend one's sense of rightness as does a haphazard conglomeration of several kinds.

When choosing plants to fit the various needs of your garden design, remember their effect the year around. Don't be carried away by their beauty during a brief period of bloom or of autumn coloration. Lilacs, lovely in flower, are uninteresting in summer foliage and skeletonlike in winter. They are obviously shrubs to use where they can be visited and enjoyed at flowering time, but should not be too conspicuous at other seasons of the year.

Give thought to using evergreens advantageously. (See "Evergreen Trees," page 388, and "Evergreen Shrubs," page 449.) Over much of North America, we depend upon them for winter greenery. A landscape with too few evergreens looks bleak and forbidding for much of the year. Used effectively, they bring life and warmth to the winter landscape; on the other hand, too many can produce an overplanted and even a funereal appearance. They must be nicely balanced by deciduous plants.

Evergreens offer special advantages for screening because they are effective at all seasons. This applies also to their use as windbreaks. A goodly proportion of the foundation planting should be evergreens to provide a body of foliage throughout the year. Evergreen ground covers planted in bold sweeps are extremely effective. Used beneath shrubs planted as a border, they serve splendidly and give the planting cohesiveness.

SHAPES AND ULTIMATE SIZES OF PLANTS

The outline shapes or forms of plants vary tremendously according to kind, and this must be given careful consideration when deciding what to plant where. Among trees, for example, we encounter all variations from the narrow exclamation mark of the Lombardy poplar and the broad, billowy head and down-flowing branches of weeping beeches and weeping cherries, to the round head of the Chinese scholar tree. See "Shade Trees Enhance Your Grounds," page 368, for shapes of deciduous trees. Among evergreen conifers are narrow, columnar junipers and arborvitaes, conical spruces and firs with their neat tiers of branches, and the looser and more informal hemlocks and pines. The same variations are found among shrubs.

Keep in mind the forms that your chosen trees and shrubs will eventually assume. If possible, visit gardens, nurseries, parks and botanical gardens to see mature specimens of these plants. The sizes of some, such as crab apple and willow, can be controlled to some extent by pruning. Others— pines and spruces, for instance—do not lend themselves to this treatment, and in any case it imposes a need for attention that better selection makes unnecessary.

Some trees and shrubs grow and increase in size slowly, some with remarkable speed. It is usually impracticable to purchase very large specimens at the outset, and so room must be left for growth. A common mistake is to set out young plants too closely for their later increase in size.

The best plan is to obtain a few largish individuals for important locations and elsewhere to use small material sufficiently spaced. Provided soil preparation is well done, and the newly set plants are kept well watered the first season and during dry weather afterward, they will soon "catch up" and will do so without being seriously harmed by crowding each other. The ground between the young plants can be kept neat and tidy by maintaining a mulch or a quick-growing ground cover on its surface. For summer appearance, an annual such as sweet alyssum or portulaca would be suitable.

Few except the smallest garden landscapes are completed with the initial planting. Rather, they are projects to develop over a period of a few years; then the progression of planting is gradual, and the cost is spread over a longer period. This is one of the important reasons for making an overall basic plan at the beginning—not one so rigid, of course, that some changes cannot be made as the project evolves, but one avoiding the costly mistakes requiring major changes later.

GARDEN CONSTRUCTION

Paths and sometimes steps, gates and bridges open the way to various parts of a garden. Terraces and sitting areas may be delightful spots that often call for grading and interesting paving. Walls and fences, screens and pergolas insure privacy and afford protection to delicate plants. These are just a few garden features that can be constructed by a handy homeowner—or by a hired contractor.

PATHS

Attractive paths should link the garden's principal features and provide easy access to areas that require attention. It is advisable to choose materials that will blend with the type of garden, but take advantage of the scope that modern materials provide to produce intriguing designs and patterns. Curving paths are most interesting, and it is a sound rule to keep the number of paths to a minimum.

Main paths should be wide enough to allow two people to walk comfortably side by side, and to take a wheelbarrow easily; a useful width is 3 to 4 ft. None should be less than 2 ft. wide.

Flagstones lend a pleasing effect. They may consist of rectangular slabs of uniform size, of rectangular slabs of varying sizes, or of pieces of irregular random sizes and shapes. The best effect can be achieved by laying out the whole path temporarily first, then setting each piece alongside the site and placing them permanently in concrete or other foundation according to the plan worked out. A pleasant effect can be gained if suitable creeping plants are established in the path. For this purpose, leave gaps in the concrete and between stones, making sure that ample room is allowed for root development.

Prefabricated slabs of artificial stone or concrete for path making are available or can be made at home.

Bricks are better suited for straight than for curved paths, and they should be laid in patterns that involve little or no cutting of the bricks. Use only old or well-weathered bricks with coarse surfaces (new bricks look out of place in the garden and they are expensive).

Although gravel and loose crushed stone are often used for path construction, they are not very satisfactory. They tend to stick to shoes in wet weather and are carried into the house. As they do not remain level, rake frequently. They are usually inexpensive and easy to obtain.

One easy way of laying a path is to use a special bituminous material that is sold in sealed paper bags by dealers in building supplies.

In informal areas, such as paths through woodlands, a surfacing of tanbark, pine needles or sawdust is serviceable and attractive. All of these materials give a springy surface that is handsome and pleasant to walk on.

STEPS

There are two important points to keep in mind when building steps: safety and proportion in design. Do not build steps that are too narrow. Their width should be in proportion to their location, but they must also permit comfortable and safe passage. From the point of view of design, a sound rule is: the longer the flight of steps, the wider it should be.

The proportion of tread (horizontal surface one steps on) to riser (vertical front wall or edge of step that supports the tread) is important. The best proportion is a 12-in. tread and a 6-in. riser. Treads should not be less than 10½ in. wide, risers not more than 7½ in. high.

Large flagstones, concrete slabs— colored, plain or a mixture—are ideal for treads. The risers can be made from flagstone, concrete or bricks.

Steps can also be made completely of bricks, either old or rough-faced types, depending on preference. They can be laid flat or on edge and, if bedded into a base of concrete, will produce very strong, durable steps.

An informal flight of steps can be made with logs of wood as the risers. The treads may consist of packed earth, cinders, tanbark or other suitable material; the log risers are held in position by strong wooden pegs driven in at each end.

Garden steps can often be decorated with low-growing plants, such as creeping thyme, sedum, sempervivum and creeping phlox. Leave spaces or holes in the treads and risers in which to naturalize suitable plants. These holes must lead to soil beneath, and they may have to be allowed for at the foundation-laying stage.

RETAINING WALLS

The strength of any wall depends to a considerable extent on its foundation. The depth of the foundation will depend chiefly upon climate and the type of wall. If the units that form the wall—bricks, stone or concrete blocks—are to be cemented together, the foundation should extend down to below the limit of frost penetration, but dry walls (walls built of boulders, irregular-shaped stones or shaped stones, not cemented together) will stand satisfactorily on a much shallower foundation. The depth of the foundation must also satisfy the requirements determined by the character of the soil and the height the wall is to be. If in doubt, consult a builder or other experienced person.

Constructed without cement, a dry wall is ideal for low features. One used to retain a bank should taper from top to bottom, the base being at least as wide as one third the height of the wall and the top about 18 in. wide. The face of the wall should slope

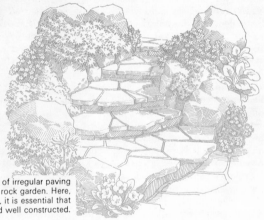

A winding flight of steps of irregular paving helps the "natural" look of a rock garden. Here, among jagged-edged rocks, it is essential that the steps should be safe and well constructed.

Trailing plants will enhance the appearance of walls. They are easy to establish if gaps are left in the stonework. Be sure that there is plenty of soil at the back of the wall into which the roots can penetrate. It is easier to leave these gaps in dry-wall construction; the plants can be inserted as each course is built up. Pot-grown plants are the most suitable as they already have a good root ball.

backward from bottom to top at the rate of 1 in. for each 2 ft. of height.

Retaining walls built of solid masonry (stones laid in cement mortar) should be of the same proportions as given above for dry retaining walls, and must have foundations extending below the frost line. Drainage holes of 4-in. iron pipe or drain tiles that extend through the wall should be installed every 6 ft. to prevent accumulation of water behind the wall. If such water freezes, the wall will lean, earth will fill the aperture, and finally the wall will collapse.

TERRACES AND PATIOS

Between terraces at varying levels, or between a patio and the rest of the garden, steps and low walls may be needed; the location and style of these features will have a great effect on the look of the finished garden.

The work of leveling is the first and most important task in terrace building. It is important that dry and firm flooring be provided for a terrace or patio that is to be used as an outdoor living room. Choose paving material that suits the character of the house. If the house is of modern design, colored flagstones or slabs of artificial stone arranged in simple designs are effective; other properties may be better enhanced by rustic bricks and insets of pebble stones. Random paving is also attractive.

A terrace or patio should have a slight slope away from the house so that rainwater will not collect but be carried away from the house walls. The finished surface must be at least 6 to 12 in. below the top of the house foundation.

FENCES, SCREENS AND PERGOLAS

These provide privacy and shelter from winds, and may be used to divide the garden neatly into sections.

Types of Fences

A solid or close-boarded fence gives complete shelter and privacy, but may be uninteresting. Another type is made from louvered boards. Even fences of more open design will provide a great deal of privacy and shelter if they are clothed with suitable plants. An open lattice design can be constructed quite easily and cheaply. Many interesting fence designs can be produced with different styles and materials: bamboo poles, strips of wood woven between uprights, and concrete blocks of attractive forms.

Gates, Pergolas and Bridges

Well-designed gates add much to the appearance of a house and garden, and they can be purchased in a great variety of styles. Wood is attractive; wrought iron is light, yet strong.

A pergola formed by a series of arches can take the form of a covered walk, or it can be constructed to provide attractive screening or partitioning. Although pergolas are often made of rustic poles of locust, cedar or some other weather-resistant wood, seasoned, squared, stock lumber treated with a wood preservative (not creosote, which is deadly to plants) can be used just as effectively. Clothed with vines, a pergola looks most attractive.

Over a stream or in a rock garden or other suitable setting, well-designed bridges can look charming. A bridge should not be incongruous with its surroundings, so try to incorporate a little of its design and material into the nearby area. If, for example, the bridge is floored with random flagstone paving, insert a few stepping stones of random paving in the garden near the bridge.

Designing a landscape can be a great pleasure; it can express your own personality to visitors even before they enter your house.

CHAPTER 17

LAWNS
and Their Maintenance

Planning a Fine Greensward—Grading—Preparation of Seedbed—Planting—Sprigs and Plugs—Choice of Grass for Northern and Southern Lawns—Care—Aeration—Mowing—Weed and Disease Control

NORTH AMERICA presents so many diverse habitats that no single type of lawn fits all locations. The nearest approach to universality is Kentucky bluegrass and fine fescue mixed with other varieties for cooler climates and higher elevations, and Bermuda grass for the lands southward from Tennessee at lower elevations. Within these broad northern and southern zones, many choices or combinations become possible, conforming to local conditions and preferences. As a starter, the map on page 355 should indicate roughly what kind of lawn is adapted to your location and to the general scheme of care that you wish to follow.

Fortunately, the steps in preparing for a lawn are rather alike, North and South, East and West. There may be regional differences in soil toughness, the timing of cultivation, the type and amount of fertilizer needed and so on. These vary with the soil, climate and availability of products. But adjusting practices somewhat to meet local requirements is relatively simple and easy to understand.

The basic procedures for developing a lawn follow much the same sequence everywhere.

PLANNING A NEW LAWN

Nothing sets off an attractively planted house, showy ornamental beds or fine specimen plants better than a magnificent carpeting of lawn. And only a few lowly relatives of corn, bamboo, wheat, oats, barley and rice have the properties needed to make a fine greensward. What part of the grounds is to be lawn and how it is to be shaped are roughly determined by the position of the house, contour of the land and overall landscape design. In the planning phase, a gardener has a chance to make later lawn tending easier. The layout should avoid as much as possible blind corners difficult to mow, obstructions that slow down mowing, and extravagant use of borders or raised levels that will increase hand trimming. It should not be fragmented or broken into sections without reason. Nor should it be started with kinds of grass you will regret having later; they can be worse to get rid of than weeds.

Spacious properties are often planted informally, with shrub and flower beds taking advantage of natural contours, the borders uneven and sinuous rather than strictly angular, the house landscaped to settle comfortably into its surroundings. Naturalistic plantings with informal lawns are usually more easily maintained. The owner may prefer formalized planting, where geometrical, balanced design prevails. This may well be adapted to smaller properties that can receive detailed attention; an owner who will be regularly tending a large area must remember that a lot of exacting edgings make for more arduous lawn care.

Grading

For most properties, a minimum of grading is suggested, not only to save costs, but also to preserve trees and other native vegetation. Grading that materially raises or lowers the natural land level can hurt underlying root systems. Raising walls to terrace a new level and building wells around grown trees are not always the solution to a grading problem and frequently are not even successful.

Whenever there is home construction, there will be some movement of soil. If the location is one in which good soil is shallow or hard to come by, push aside the topsoil (the top few inches), then dig out the rocky or sticky subsoil as required, spread it and replace the topsoil. This will result in a more fertile, more easily worked seedbed. When topsoil is purchased, it may or may not be superior to the local subsoil, depending upon where it came from and the poverty of the existing subsoil. Almost invariably, purchased topsoil comes from old fields or unweeded diggings and contains weed seeds. Your own subsoil may be weed-free and good enough to grow a lawn if plenty of fertilizer and organic matter is added. In rocky or barren locations, almost any topsoil is better than none. But always, before buying topsoil, consider the reliability of its source. Mere purchase of "topsoil" is not a guarantee of a good lawn or garden, and there are many instances when the money used for buying it might better have been spent on lime, fertilizer and plants.

Common sense dictates that the yard should slope away from the im-

mediate vicinity of the house, so that there will not be seepage into the building. A lawn should also be free of depressions which collect and retain water, incidentally "drowning" grass during rainy weather. Avoid steep or abrupt slopes; they are certain to prove an enduring harassment to mowing, if indeed they are able to sustain acceptable turf at all. The grading should follow the natural slopes and pattern of surface drainage as much as possible. On very flat surfaces or where the land is naturally boggy, drainpipes laid a foot or so deep may help. (See page 743 in "The Soil.")

Tidying Up

During construction of a house, workers often dump debris indiscriminately on the lawn-to-be. Chunks of board, metal trimmings, brick or stone fragments, discarded sand or gravel, leftover cement or plaster and other material may be buried shallowly in the ground. In order to prevent later problems with a lawn, all debris bigger than a golf ball should be removed, and concentrations of smaller stuff scattered. Early during the building, the contractor should be asked not to pour leftover paint or solvents on parts of the property meant to sustain vegetation.

Almost surely, heavy equipment will be used in delivery of construction materials, or for grading and shaping the site. Sandy soils take this pretty well without damage. So do others if they are traveled only during seasons when the ground is quite dry. But with heavier soils, especially when moist, the pressure from vehicles and weighty machinery can so harden the top several inches that the chances for good root penetration by a future lawn are ruined. A constructive measure, following home building and grading, is cultivation some 4 to 6 in. deep wherever heavy equipment has regularly traveled. An agricultural disk drawn behind a tractor is usually sufficient for loosening such soils. In cases of extreme compaction, a preliminary plowing may be necessary. On small properties, rotary tillage (or even spading) by the homeowner may serve to loosen the soil sufficiently.

SEEDBED PREPARATION

Whether the lawn is to be seeded or to be planted with sod or sprigs, the time to get the soil in order is certainly before planting. Once the lawn is growing, not much can be done for the root zone. Adequacy of green leafage aboveground always relates to adequacy of root system in the soil.

Fertility

The homeowner may be aware of the characteristics of the soil in his locality. For specific information, however, soil tests may be obtained through the state agricultural experiment station (check with the County Agricultural Agent) or other government source. In some areas, such as the semiarid western plains, certain elements occur adequately in the native soils—calcium (lime) and potassium especially—and it is possible to purchase fertilizer containing only those elements needed. A little extra fertility is not going to hurt anything, however, and it may prove more economical to purchase a general lawn fertilizer widely used and marketed than to search out custom blends lacking one or more elements (see page 750 in "Fertilizers and Manures").

One chief need for the lawn seedbed is usually phosphorus. In most soils phosphorus is slow to be absorbed, so it cannot be easily introduced into the root zone after the lawn has been planted. Unlike nitrogen, potassium and other major nutrients, phosphorus binds to particles in the soil, becoming insoluble. However, plant roots can release and make use of it when in contact. It is well to stir a phosphatic fertilizer several inches into the seedbed.

Other nutrients can ordinarily be applied later if needed. However, as long as phosphorus is being mixed into the soil, other elements of a complete fertilizer (containing nitrogen and potassium as well) can be included. Liberal use of fertilizer in the seedbed is like banking a savings account—something for the grass to draw upon for months or even years ahead. Good initial provision is especially needed for soils known to be of low fertility; 20 lb. to each 1000 sq. ft. is not too liberal a rate for complete garden or lawn fertilizers of average analysis.

Acid Soil

Lime, or calcium carbonate, has a dual role to serve in the soil. It supplies calcium, a secondary nutrient for plant growth, and it also neutralizes acidity. Since most soils contain sufficient calcium for grass growth, liming is generally a corrective for too much acidity.

Soils tend to be acid where there is abundant rainfall, except perhaps in regions of limestone outcrops. Porous, sandy soils which let water percolate readily through, unfortunately carrying away soluble materials, are often acid. A pH test (measuring acidity) is easily made, so it is best to confirm a need for lime. Soil-testing services can determine this for you, or you can purchase a small home test kit that shows how to gauge the pH (see page 741 in the chapter on "The Soil"). By and large, lawn grasses grow well within the pH range of 6–7½. Mildly acid soils, with a pH not far from 6, can be "sweetened" during seedbed cultivation by adding about

50 lb. of ground limestone to each 1000 sq. ft. of surface area. Double this amount might prove advisable for very acid soils, especially if the texture is heavy. How acid the soil should be depends partly upon the kind of grass being planted. In the humid South, centipede and carpet grasses ordinarily do better on acid soils than on neutral ones, and bent grass is also tolerant.

Alkaline Soil

At the other extreme, where the pH reaches high levels above 8, as on the alkaline flats of the arid West, corrective action may be needed to make the soils more acid. This may be done by adding sulphur or a sulphur-containing compound. The sulphur gradually oxidizes to sulfuric acid, acidifying and neutralizing the alkaline components. The same effect can be obtained more gradually through irrigation with nonalkaline water. Many western soils that originally were alkaline lose some of their alkalinity once they are planted to lawns and regularly watered. Where it is advisable to take chemical precautions against alkalinity, 20 lb. of sulphur for each 1000 sq. ft. of surface area is a suggested rate of application.

Mechanical Condition

Fertility of the seedbed is only half the story; the soil must also accept the seed well and house the young grass adequately, so that it sprouts readily, roots deeply. The physical or mechanical condition of the soil is therefore important. Unless it is properly loose, seed will not find good lodging sites, but rather be perched precariously close to the surface. Unless the root zone is porous enough so that air is admitted for root respiration, deep rooting that results in lasting turf will not occur. Finally, if the seedbed is compact, or alternatively

pulverized into a fine dust, water will not sink into the soil but, instead, "puddle" the surface, clogging the pores of the soil. It then runs off as surface drainage, carrying soil and seed with it.

Whether a desirable condition of a seedbed can be prepared easily depends primarily upon the quality of the soil. Good topsoils that perform well agriculturally generally cultivate nicely to a lawn seedbed. The standard recipe for improving refractory soils is to mix in organic matter. The growing of "green manure" is usually too tedious (see page 764 in "Composting and Green Manuring"). It is more convenient to buy peat moss or humus and till it into the seedbeds where poor soil structure needs improvement. In time, the growing lawn grass with its many fine rootlets will itself improve the soil.

PLANTING THE LAWN

After the seedbed has been fertilized and cultivated, it should, of course, be raked level. For soils that are quite loose, a period of settling through at least one rain or irrigation helps to indicate high or low spots. Raking high points into depressions is all that is ordinarily needed for final touch-up. Rolling may help in firming and leveling the seedbed, although it is suggested only for very fluffy soils where some recompaction is needed. Rolling a heavy soil when wet undoes the benefits of cultivation. In most instances the seedbed will settle tightly enough without rolling, as soon as it is watered.

Seed

Any plant growing in the lawn that the owner does not want there is a weed. Some state seed laws, however, do not always look at it that way. The coarse and clumpy hay grasses have been accepted on a label as "undefined crop," although they are the most troublesome of pests. Fortunately, a combination of legal restrictions, official inspections, trade responsibility and brand competition assures that lawn seed coming to market is reasonably free of bothersome plants. The buyer must acquaint himself with the product to be sure no troublesome "coarse kinds," such as tall fescue (see Northern Lawns, page 354), are included. Paying a fair price for the seed, rather than choosing the cheapest blend, and buying from a reputable source are the best insurance against bringing in weeds with seed.

Sowing Seed

Lawn spreaders are so commonplace around our homes these days that accurate dispersal of lawn seed is usually no problem. The objective, of course, is to scatter seed at a rate appropriate to the particular seed mixture (usually between 2 and 6 lb.

to 1000 sq. ft.). Instructions on the seed box provide a suggested rate, and most spreaders carry instructions giving the approximate setting for mixtures that are primarily bluegrass, fine fescue, bent grass and so on. When in doubt, the safest procedure is to set the spreader on what seems to be a lean rate, and, if necessary, go over the lawn two or more times until the designated quantity of seed is spread. To insure against unseeded blanks, half the seed may be sown in one direction, the other half crosswise to this. Should proper overlap of spreader tracks not be made, the second pass will distribute at least some seed where none fell the first time.

If no spreader is at hand, a passable seeding job can be accomplished by hand sowing. Seed sown at a very light rate, such as Highland bent grass (some 7 million seeds to the pound, so that a pound or less is often sufficient to cover 1000 sq. ft.),

Steps in Sowing a Lawn: (Left) Rototill the area, mixing in manure or compost and fertilizer. (Center) Tread to firm the soil. (Right) Rake any high points into depressions to level off lawn.

may be "extended" with a material of similar particle size. Dry sand, sifted soil, cornmeal, vermiculite, even fertilizer, thoroughly mixed with seed, can be used to increase the volume of seed for hand sowing. The bulked seed then can be scattered more generously, with less fear of overapplication. Extending is ordinarily not necessary for bluegrass-fescue seed mixtures.

With a little experience, it is no trick to cast a handful of seed by letting small dribbles sift between the fingers as the wrist is given a quick flick. This throws the seed in a wide arc so that it falls onto the seedbed well distributed.

Hand sowing is not for a breezy day, and is best accomplished with one's back to the wind, noting carefully where the seed drifts on the air currents. Sowing at half the recommended rate while walking back and forth in one direction, the other half at right angles, offers some assur-

ance of even sowing. Between the half-sowings, tumble the soil by dragging an inverted leaf rake over the surface. This further disperses the seed and works it into the seedbed.

Rolling the bed after it has been planted is as unnecessary as before planting. But sometimes if the soil is very fluffy, it may be necessary to re-pack the ground so that the moist lower soil is in closer contact with the upper portions, establishing capillary connections for rise of water to the surface. Quicker sprouting of the seed will then result.

Raising the Seedlings

On some soils and in favored climates, capillary action and normal rainfall suffice to keep the soil surface sufficiently moist for quick seed sprouting. In most instances, sprouting can be hastened by irrigating and by use of a mulch. Germination depends chiefly upon warmth and humidity. When an ideally warm seedbed (with a tem-

(Left) Sow grass seed, using lawn spreader with correct setting for your particular mixture. (Center) Cover seed by dragging an inverted broom rake over seedbed. (Right) Mulch to retain moisture.

perature of 80° F. by day and 60° by night) is sprinkled frequently and mulched, most grasses sprout to visible proportions within a week or ten days. If the soil temperatures are cooler, growth will, of course, be somewhat slower. To speed up appearance of the grass, mix the seed with damp peat moss or vermiculite and keep it in a plastic bag in the warm indoors some five days until the sprouting process has begun. Then sow it immediately onto the outdoor seedbed. The damp seed will be hard to sow, however, and the infant sprouts will be easily injured.

As soon as dry seed is sowed, the soil, unless moist, should be watered. In the early stages, the main job is to keep the surface soil continuously humid. Frequent light sprinklings are to be recommended over prolonged heavy dosages that run through or off the soil. In dry weather the new seeding may have to be watered both morning and evening. After the seed has sprouted and the grass rootlets have penetrated deeper into the soil, the frequency of watering can be lessened, first to daily, then biweekly, and finally to infrequent watering or none at all.

MULCHING

A loose scattering of any material which allows light, water and air to reach the soil, but forms a partial moisture barrier that prevents the surface from drying out and protects the new planting from rain or wind, makes a satisfactory lawn mulch. Clean, weed-free straw is one of the best inexpensive mulches. It is scattered three or four straws deep over the newly planted lawn and can be left in place as the grass sprouts. It soon becomes invisible and eventually decomposes in the sod.

Where straw is not procurable, garden stores generally carry a wide selection of mulch materials. Stringy sphagnum (peat) moss is fairly good, as are shredded bark, chopped corncobs and excelsior. For large-scale use with powerful sprayers (hydraulic seeding), a wood-pulp mulch is offered. There is also a fiber-glass mat, and plasticlike sprays, though these seem to be more effective in holding the soil in place than in retaining humidity. Chopped twigs from the maintenance trimming of trees are sometimes available. Lawn clippings from another portion of the yard can be utilized also, though care should be taken not to pile them so thick that they mat. It is even possible to stake down a clear polyethylene plastic on especially important spots. This not only maintains humidity but also acts as a miniature "greenhouse," helping to trap sunshine that warms the soil and hastens sprouting. If temperatures rise too high under the covering, wet seed may die. Midday ventilation may be necessary on sunny days.

NURSE GRASSES

An old theory to hasten the appearance of green is to blend into lawn-seed mixtures a fast-sprouting grass. The new lawn looks attractive in a hurry, so the practice has popular appeal with less knowledgeable lawnsmen. But tests have shown that these fast-sprouting grasses are not the ones wanted permanently. They may die out quickly, too, usually leaving behind thin turf that is an invitation to weeds. The quick initial cover creates a poor condition for the wanted grasses. If the so-called nurse grass is very thick, it can so squeeze and shade the slower permanent grasses that the latter scarcely gain a foothold. The lawn expert will usually avoid nurse grasses altogether, or if early green is needed, confine them to a very small percentage of the seed mixture (about 5 percent, not over 10 percent).

Traditionally, annual ryegrass has been the main nurse species. Redtop, a relative of bent grass, has also been used. The danger is that in some climates it may persist, turning quite rank. In northern lawn-seed mixtures containing fine fescues, the fescue seed sprouts with reasonable rapidity and produces a robust seedling; this is a fair substitute for nurse grasses when used with bluegrass. If the fine fescue ends up a permanent component of the lawn, so much the better. Under high fertility, the bluegrass may eventually squeeze the fine fescue into secondary status, but in dry, shady locations and on poor soil, the fine fescue is apt to persist as the main ingredient of the permanent lawn.

STARTING LAWNS VEGETATIVELY

A sod industry has arisen in the North, where expert seeding and culture produce a turf that may be lifted and transplanted. While the purchase of sod is necessarily more expensive than seeding one's own lawn, there are those in our affluent society who are willing to pay a premium for a well-established lawn, which is laid like a carpet.

Sod

Sod, at its worst, is simply lifted from pastures or fields near a metropolitan area. It is seldom sprayed for weeds and often contains coarse field grasses. Such sod is frequently purchased for newly constructed speculative housing to produce a "lawn" immediately.

Growers of quality sod should be sought by the prospective lawn owner. They seed varieties or combinations on level land reasonably near the market area. Expert attention is given to fertilization, water and weed control. Various bluegrasses and bluegrass-fine fescue combinations are

produced for home lawns. Selected bent grasses are also offered.

In the South, it is possible to procure sod of improved Bermuda grasses, zoysia grasses and other elite types, as well as the ubiquitous St. Augustine grass from the mucklands of south-central Florida. But except for the economical St. Augustine grass, lawn costs are usually reduced by planting sprigs and plugs rather than solid sodding (see below). A gardener who purchases sod must be sure that it is freshly gathered. Rolls or squares that have lain in the nursery for some time will show yellowing of the foliage. Bluegrass recovers well, but flourishing sod will suffer no setback that might let weeds gain entry.

Whether grass is sown from seed or planted from live starts, it will flourish only as well as its rooting medium allows. A "sodbed" should be thoroughly cultivated, fertilized and supplied with organic matter before laying the sod. If for any reason grass has failed in a given location, sod will prove only a temporary palliative, growing until exhausted. The basic trouble must be corrected.

It was once felt that thick sod was superior to thinly cut sod, but with modern facilities and mechanization the opposite is more likely to be true. A thick sod will better retain moisture; it will not dry and curl from its soilbed so readily during unfavorable desiccating weather. On the other hand, a thin sod of bluegrass about ¾ in. thick roots more quickly when transplanted than does a thicker sod. Apparently the severance of roots and perhaps the cutting of a few rhizomes as the sod is transplanted stimulates new rooting from the joints and crowns, causing a quicker "take" of the newly laid sod.

Whatever the thickness of sod, it should be carefully laid on a well-prepared soil, firmed in place and watered immediately. A newly sodded lawn should not be given heavy use for several weeks. Water every few days until well rooted. In spring or fall, transplanted bluegrass will anchor itself within four to six weeks.

Lay the necessary number of rolls end to end, usually starting at an extremity of the lawn or from the base of any slope and working upward. Most rolls are rectangular in shape when spread out. Adjacent rows should have the rectangles offset (the common pattern in bricklaying). Roll the sod to firm it into the seedbed, and water it. It is usually well to reserve a few bushels of soil for scattering into the cracks between sod squares or for leveling out any slight depressions in the new surface.

Sprigs and Plugs

In central and southern Florida, it has long been usual to hand-plant small chunks of sod (plugs) or individual stems of grass a few joints in length (sprigs) at spaced intervals around prepared soil. Given reasonable attention, these live starts grow and spread rapidly in that climate. Fast-growing species such as Bermuda grass can form a complete lawn cover within a few months.

Such live plantings are made mostly with lawn grasses for which no true-breeding seed is available, and are confined chiefly to southern grasses. Live plantings are often spaced approximately 1 ft. apart in checkerboard fashion. For quick, economical planting, shallow rows are often hoed across the lawn about a foot apart. The sprigs are laid in the depression, leaving one leafy tip protruding; the stem is partly buried by raking soil back into the depression. The new plantings are firmed by walking on the row, by tamping or by rolling.

In most cases sprigs will spread into adjacent ground more rapidly than

Planting a Lawn with Plugs (above left and center): Cut zoysia turf into 2-in. squares, then plant plugs not more than 1 ft. apart. **Planting a Lawn with Sprigs** (above right and opposite page, left): Using a hoe blade, draw shallow drills 1 ft. apart in soil that is well prepared.

plugs. The sprig, devoid of established roots, is stimulated to new growth hurriedly, whereas a plug, a segment of sod in its own soil, can rest self-contained for some time. Sprigging is more economical than plugging, but sprigs are somewhat more difficult to store and handle, and must be given immediate attention after planting. New sprigging must be watered immediately and be kept as moist as a new seeding until growing well. Plugs can better withstand neglect, although of course they, too, should receive faithful watering.

Stolons

Certain actively growing lawn grasses, such as bent grass in the North and Bermuda grass in the South, can be propagated even more easily by stolons. Botanically, stolons are spreading stems that grow aboveground. Most such stem fragments will root if brought into contact with loose, moist soil and kept well watered. Fresh stolons are simply scattered over the surface of a carefully prepared seedbed. Depending upon cost and type of grass, from as little as two to as many as six bushels of fresh material is recommended for each 1000 sq. ft. A thin layer of soil is ordinarily scattered over the top of the distributed stolons—enough to bury some of the stem but not all the green leafage. The planting is usually rolled for firming in place, and immediately watered.

Newly planted stolons cannot be allowed to dry out; they must be lightly sprinkled even more frequently than a new seeding. Under favorable growing conditions, roots regenerate almost immediately, and within days or at most a few weeks, new growth starts filling in. In favorable weather, this makes a tight cover quickly and economically. Because exact timing and careful handling are required for planting stolons, this method is mostly for

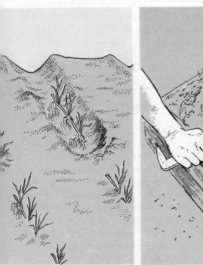

Plant sprigs with upper end of each protruding. **Laying Sod** (above center and right): If the sod is uneven, turn it upside down in a 2½-in.-deep open-ended box, then, with a scythe blade, level the underside of the sod. Lay the sections of sod with joints alternating.

professional use, by golf-course superintendents or experienced contractors. A number of turf nurseries harvest and ship stolon supplies according to an agreed schedule. Cut stolons do not keep well, and often die from delays in transit or planting.

CHOICE OF GRASS

The lawn-grass varieties of North America have different predilections and susceptibilities. Some are injured by certain weed-killing chemicals. Some need more fertilizer, more water or a higher pH. Certain grasses endure well only when mowed high, while others must be cropped close to avoid buildup of thatch. The following are grasses of major importance.

NORTHERN LAWNS

Although "cool-weather grasses" perform well at high elevations as far south as Georgia and Arizona, they are best suited to climates north of Tennessee. Toward the southern limit, they may persist better in light shade than in full sun. They are also planted as "winter grass" throughout the South, chiefly into lawns where Bermuda grass is the permanent species. Bermuda turns dormant about October and is brown until the following spring; many homes enjoy a green lawn through this period, even though the northern grasses will die out the following summer when Bermuda grass revives.

Most states have adopted a nationally suggested labeling requirement for lawn grasses that groups the attractive top-quality lawn species as "fine-textured," while the harsher, although often more durable, species are grouped as "coarse kinds." Grasses of the fine-textured category include the Kentucky bluegrasses, the fine or red fescues, the bent grasses and a few other specialty sorts, mostly *Poa*. All others, including the conventional nurse grasses such as ryegrass and redtop, and various "hay grass" field species such as tall fescue and timothy, fall among the coarse kinds. Beware of even a small percentage of "coarse kind" grasses if these are persistent in your climate. For instance, tall fescue—not to be confused with the fine or red fescues—can be a nuisance, crowding out better grasses that cannot take hold so quickly.

BENT GRASS (AGROSTIS)

The more erect-growing types such as Highland are used for lawns and fairways, numerous creeping types chiefly for golf and bowling greens. Bents make dense, velvety turf, but maintenance is demanding, calling for frequent mowing, generous fertilizing, watering, disease and thatch control. Bents do best in temperate, misty climates—along the Pacific Coast north from San Francisco, around the Great Lakes and in the hills of New England. Highland, Astoria and Exeter, among the "Colonial" or lawn bents, are available as seed; Penncross, Seaside and a few Velvet bent varieties among the creeping types. Bents available from turf nurseries are numerous. Your local golf course can probably steer you to sources.

FINE OR RED FESCUES
(FESTUCA RUBRA)

Fine fescues are very like Kentucky bluegrass, though with thinner, wirier foliage and less abundant rhizomes. They are tolerant of shade, poor soils and dry habitat, and are quicker to sprout than Kentucky bluegrass. Fescues make a good companion for bluegrass, substituting nicely for quick-sprouting impermanent nurse grasses and helping to colonize the less favorable growing locations. Little fertilization is needed. Fine fescues are not good for open, sunny, southerly locations where summers are hot. Estab-

CLIMATIC ZONES FOR LAWN GRASSES

Areas most suitable to various lawn grasses of the United States and lower Canada are indicated below.

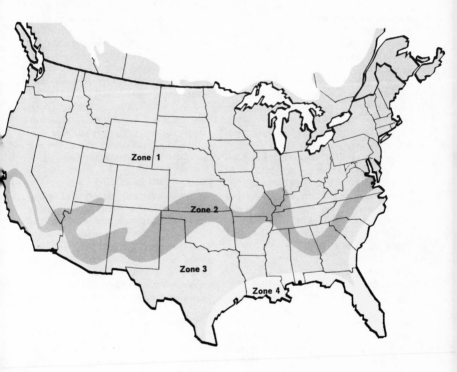

Zone 1—A wide band including the more temperate regions of Canada and the cooler regions of the United States from New England to the Pacific Coast. "Cool-weather" grasses for this area are Kentucky bluegrass, fine fescues and bent grass.

Zone 3—A somewhat restricted band extending from the foothills of the southern states across the plains of South and Southwest. In sun, centipede grass, Bermuda grass and zoysia; in shade and for winter cover, Kentucky bluegrass, fine fescues and bent grass.

Zone 2—A narrow, irregular band across the southern half of the United States from coast to coast. For sunny locations, the best grasses are Bermuda grass and zoysia; Kentucky bluegrass, fine fescues and bent grass may be used for shady locations.

Zone 4—A narrow coastal strip beginning in Virginia and including the Florida peninsula and the Gulf Coast. In sun, use St. Augustine grass and bahia grass. In this zone, zoysia needs extra care. Carpet grass is best for wet, acid soil.

lished varieties include Chewings, Illahee, Pennlawn and Rainier, all produced in Oregon; or the unselected parent type, Creeping Red.

KENTUCKY BLUEGRASSES (POA PRATENSIS)

The most widely used species for lawns, Kentucky bluegrass, yields excellent sod from spreading underground stems called rhizomes. Most varieties are not hard to care for and recover well from damage. Bluegrass has a soft green appearance. It does best on fertile soils, but if mowed reasonably high, survives well with only moderate fertilization and, in most locations, without irrigation. Merion is a somewhat lower-growing variety, very dense and attractive, that requires stepped-up care. Other well-known varieties include Arboretum, C–1, Cougar, Delft, Delta, Newport, Park, Prato and Windsor.

RYEGRASS (LOLIUM)

There are annual and perennial ryegrasses, both labeled "coarse kinds," but the annual is more rank. Both are bunch grasses, not spreading by rhizomes as do the bluegrasses and fine fescues. Ryegrass is sometimes mixed with bluegrass–fine fescue combinations as a "nurse grass," meant to sprout quickly, then disappear. If abundant in a seed mixture, however, its aggressiveness can set back the establishment of preferred grasses.

TALL FESCUE (FESTUCA ARUNDINACEA)

Tall fescue is a tough, clumpy plant, not to be confused with the desirable fine fescues. Kentucky–31 and Alta are two varieties. All are bunch grasses, quite coarse, often used for roadside seeding because of their durability, but unsuitable for lawns. Where used on difficult sites, tall fescue should be densely planted; this alleviates the clumpy look.

Others

Rough bluegrass, *Poa trivialis*, is a "fine-textured" species with runners aboveground. It likes locations that are both shady and moist. Redtop, *Agrostis alba*, is a coarse bent-grass relative, sometimes used instead of ryegrass as a temporary or "nurse grass" species. There are various other pasture grasses akin to tall fescue, such as timothy, orchard grass and bromegrass, none really fit for close-cropped lawns. Clover, *Trifolium repens*—a legume, not a grass—is sometimes planted where its varying texture, white flowers and patchy growth are not felt to be objectionable.

SOUTHERN LAWNS

A longer growing season and warm climate encourage both lawn grasses and a wide diversity of weeds in the South. Most of the specially selected varieties must be planted from live starts, since they do not come true from seed. Notable in this respect are the finer-textured Bermuda and zoysia varieties. The somewhat coarser common Bermuda and zoysia can be seeded, as can Bahia grass, centipede grass and carpet grass (a specialty type for acid, boggy locations). St. Augustine and centipede must be vegetatively planted.

BAHIA GRASS (PASPALUM NOTATUM)

Bahia is utilized chiefly in the Deep South, where the convenience of seeding is important. It is rather coarse, spreads by runners and exists with relatively low maintenance. Seedhead production in spring may be a nuisance for several weeks. The Pensacola variety is most frequently planted. Argentine and Paraguay have comparatively hairy leaves.

BERMUDA GRASSES (CYNODON)

Bermuda grass is the workhorse lawn grass of the upper South. It spreads rapidly by runners and rhizomes, but survives only in the sun. To look well, Bermuda must be given regular attention; some of the named varieties such as are used for golf-green turf are quite demanding, needing certainly as much fertilization, watering, disease control and thatch removal as bent grasses in the North. Varieties considered reasonably hardy as far north as Missouri include Sunturf, U–3 and perhaps Tufcote. Several hybrid types, such as Ormond, Tifgreen, Tifdwarf, Tiflawn and Tifway, are widely used in the South. Texturf selections are utilized chiefly in the Southwest. All of these must be propagated by live starts, but common Bermuda, attractive when reasonably tended, can be started from seed. Seeds with the hulls removed sprout more rapidly.

CENTIPEDE GRASS
(EREMOCHLOA OPHIUROIDES)
Centipede is known as a "poor-soil" grass, seeming to thrive under neglect and with little fertilization. Indeed, forcing it to luxuriant growth with heavy feeding often kills the stand. However, it is prone to chlorosis (yellowing), usually due to an iron deficiency or unfavorable soil pH. Centipede performs best if the soil is moderately acid. Some fairly expensive seed is available; the grass may also be propagated vegetatively. Its widest use is in the southern coastal plain.

ST. AUGUSTINE GRASS
(STENOTAPHRUM SECUNDATUM)
St. Augustine was once the most popular species for the deep South. Its color is attractive although its texture is coarse. This grass is undemanding, notably well adapted to shade. In recent years chinch bug and certain diseases have attacked St. Augustine, so that the constant spraying needed has led to preference for other species.

Seed is not available, but live starts, including sod, are quite inexpensive, especially in Florida. Finer-textured varieties include Bitter Blue and Floratine, a recent release from the University of Florida.

ZOYSIA
Zoysia embraces a broad range of types from the coarser *Z. japonica* sorts (Korean or Japanese lawn grass), through *Z. matrella* (Manila grass), to the even finer-textured *Z. tenuifolia* (mascarene or Korean velvet). Emerald is a variety developed from crossings within the group. Meyer is a fairly coarse but dense and winter-hardy variety for more northerly locations. Midwest is another recent release, coarse and open, for interplanting with Kentucky bluegrass. All zoysias are slow-growing, thus tedious to develop into a complete lawn, but relatively easy to care for later, requiring little mowing. Like the Bermudas, zoysia becomes brown in winter, so it is seldom suitable for planting in more northerly regions, although the hardy types are occasionally used as far north as the Ohio Valley. Zoysia is very resistant to wear, but its toughness also makes it difficult to mow, requiring a heavy-duty machine. Because the vegetation does not decompose readily, the sod may thatch. Recently attacks from billbug have discouraged the zoysia sod industry in parts of Florida. As with most other southern grasses, zoysia spreads by rhizomes and runners. The fine-textured varieties, along with those of Bermuda grass, are used in outstandingly beautiful southern turfs.

SEED MIXTURES
More often than not, several species or varieties are combined for general lawn use. This takes advantage of the differing adaptations of grasses and

broadens the usefulness of a seed blend. For example, with the familiar bluegrass–fine fescue combination, the fescue does well on poorer sites and in the shade, where the bluegrass may be weak, while the bluegrass lends its incomparable sod-forming abilities to those locations where it thrives. There are advantages to growing two grasses side by side in the turf; one may be seasonally stricken by a disease that does not affect the other, or suffer a temporary setback while its companion is not affected. There is a similar advantage in combining varieties of the same species. One variety or strain may be inherently resistant to a disease to which another is susceptible. Nor does an inexperienced lawnkeeper then need to know so exactly what the requirements of a specific variety are.

Components of a mixture should complement one another to the greatest possible degree. Even a little bit of coarse grass would completely offset the attractiveness of the quality species. Nor does one ordinarily mix bent grass with Kentucky bluegrass–fine fescue; bent grass must have close clipping to be attractive, which is not the case with a bluegrass–fine fescue sod. The exact proportion of different components in a suitable mixture is usually not of very great consequence. A little more or less will be of slight influence as to which species or variety will dominate. The prevailing environmental conditions are decisive. For example, whether a bluegrass blend is 30 percent Merion or 50 percent Merion is not so important as whether the lawn is managed to favor the Merion; the very well-fertilized lawn will tend to become mostly Merion, while the underfertilized lawn will probably see Merion drop from competition, no matter how abundant the seed was at the outset.

It is best to adapt a mixture chosen for the climate and type of use. In the North, for sunny locations on good soils, some three fourths of the mixture would probably be bluegrass. In the shade or on sandy outcrops, at least 50 percent might well be fine fescue. And certainly a variety known to be a heavy feeder, such as Merion, should at best be a minor component for lawns that will not be adequately fertilized, although it might be the major component in more favorable northerly climates where heavy feeding is possible without summer injury. Considering the diverse circumstances under which lawns are planted and cared for, seed blending remains more of an art than a science.

CARE OF THE LAWN

The amount of care a lawn needs depends partly upon choice of grass and partly upon the quality of the seedbed. Of primary concern is the required frequency of mowing, fertilization and weed control, and to a lesser degree watering and insect and disease control. Then there are a host of minor attentions which may or may not be worth the effort: checking pH, topdressing, thinning or dethatching, aeration, treatment with wetting agents and so on.

Naturally, having a really lush, blemish-free lawn is going to be more work and entail more expense than getting by with just an average turf. Ironically, intensive care that pushes grass to thick, succulent growth may induce trouble. Such turf is much more susceptible to disease, thatch and loss from drying out than is the lawn that has to shift for itself.

MOWING

Regular mowing is best for the lawn. No phase of lawn attention occupies more of the gardener's time. This repeated activity should be made as pleasurable as possible, with a lawn mower of good quality that is not prone to frustrating breakdowns. Frequency of mowing will vary with the grass, the season and the weather. The generally accepted each-weekend mowing is not unreasonable. Luxuriously kept bent grasses and Bermudas may need mowing twice a week, and even bluegrass can get top-heavy in five days at the height of its spring season. On the other hand, bluegrass may not need mowing oftener than twice a month during summer drought, the usual period with slow-growing zoysia. Centipede, a particularly low, creeping kind, can experience delayed mowing, then withstand a scalping which would severely shock other turfs.

A good rule is to mow whenever the grass adds half again to its customary height after mowing. With this scheme, no more than one third of the foliage is removed at any mowing; more severe clipping can set back the grass. Height of mowing varies. Fine-textured grasses which trail or creep, such as many bent grasses and Bermudas, should be clipped rather low to maintain a compact growth without the appearance of scrawny stems after mowing. For these, mowing heights less than 1 in. are usually suggested. Most other grasses are mowed between 1 and 2 in. in height, and the coarser species, such as St. Augustine and Bahia, 2 in. or even higher. Kentucky bluegrass–fine fescue lawns benefit from higher mowing, for these erect-growing grasses fight their own battles better if allowed to retain ample green leaf. Even in the northerly climates where these species perform at their best, it is not suggested that the lawn be mowed closer than 1½ in. Where summers turn hot, 2 in. or more is better.

Mowing height is often wrongly equated with neatness. In truth, it is the uniformity of the surface that is responsible for an attractive appearance; a freshly mowed lawn looks well whether mowed to 2 in. or only half that. A close mowing may actually encourage unevenness that hastens the need for removing. Low-clipped grass may look clumpy rather than evenly filled, and rapidly growing weeds soon make a lawn look shaggy. It is well documented that low clipping of lawns markedly encourages weeds.

Clippings

Whether grass clippings should be removed or not can be argued either way. The case for their removal is stronger with trailing grasses that thatch readily, for clippings increase the burden of undecomposed vegetation. Any time clippings do not settle deeply into the growing grass, their discoloration as they dry can be quite noticeable. Many authorities believe old clippings serve as a reservoir for fungus spores that spread disease.

Collecting the clippings is, of course, extra work. And their removal does take from the lawn nutrients that the grass built into its tissues. Through a year, the quantity of nutrients removed in grass clippings is about the equivalent of one good fertilizing. If the clippings settle near the soil and quickly decompose, they can be beneficial to soil structure. With the more upright, open-growing grasses such as Kentucky bluegrass and fine fescue, this is often the case. Frequent mowing keeps clippings short, enables them to settle more readily through the grass to the soil. If it is the owner's preference not to leave the clippings on the lawn, both rotary and reel mowers can be equipped with clipping catchers.

Choice of Mower

As with automobiles, there will be individual preferences and a wide range of prices. Machines designed for heavy duty will be more costly. It is almost mandatory for growers of zoysia to procure a heavy-duty machine, preferably a reel type with abundant reel blades. As a general rule, reel-type mowers are best for lawns that are cut low, especially those that are meticulously maintained level and carpetlike. Bent grasses and the improved varieties of Bermuda and zoysia would customarily be mowed by reel mowers. Rotary mowers, which helpfully suck up the grass clippings, are often used for higher mowing.

The reel machine, if in good adjustment, makes the cleaner cut, operating with the scissorslike action of reel blade against bed knife. A rotary, of course, cuts by the sicklelike impact of a whirling blade. Reels may be less hazardous (they will not hurl objects), but a reel is not as versatile as is a rotary, and most models cannot approach borders so closely. Nor are reels easily sharpened and adjusted at home.

Sweeping and Brushing

A pattern of mowing produces certain effects. Inevitably the grass inclines in the direction of frequent mower passage. This creates bands that reflect light differently from adjacent passes in the opposite direction. Some people like the contrasting pattern of adjacent bands mowed in opposite directions. If, after repetitious mowing in the same direction, the grass "leans" markedly, reverse directions or mow crosswise.

The pattern which results from mowing can be obliterated by sweeping or brushing. Of course the sweeper may itself impose a striped effect, but the pattern is apt to be more diffuse. Sweeping also collects clippings and, if vigorous enough, may even loosen

the topmost layer of thatch. In autumn, tree leaves are swept up along with clippings.

There are several different power rakes or lawn brooms, to say nothing of several vacuum devices for sucking up trash. Most sweepers boast rows of brushes rotating in cylindrical fashion.

Rolling

To look well and mow efficiently, a lawn should be level. While rolling to flatten or level the lawn causes little damage to porous, sandy soils, it has proved quite disadvantageous on heavy soils, especially if they are rolled when wet. The soil becomes compacted, and thus all the benefits of nature's winter cultivation through freezing and thawing are undone. Vital pore space is eliminated, air and water penetrate less well, the grass roots grow more shallowly and the turf is prone to damage. There may be some cases where sod patches heave during winter and refirming them into the soil is necessary. But ordinarily soil and sod settle back naturally as thawing occurs. An established sod seldom winter-heaves to any extent.

Where uneven surfaces do occur, it is ordinarily better to elevate the depressions than to smash the mounds. For sizable depressions, sod may have to be cut and lifted back; fertilized soil necessary to achieve proper level is introduced beneath, before the sod is replaced and firmed. In most instances, depressions will be slight. These can be corrected by topdressing with soil, scattering and raking it so that it fills any scars or low areas. As much as a half inch of soil sifted around the crowns of mature grass will not smother them. For such topdressing, use soil similar to that already in the lawn. Also, try to have any topdressing free of weed seeds, either by knowing its source or by fumigating it before spreading. With extremely fine turf mowed low, both topdressing and intelligent rolling may be needed from time to time.

AERATION

The punching of holes through sod into the soil has received wide acceptance in recent years. Yet there is not a great deal of evidence that this materially helps the ordinary lawn. There may be an occasional lawn in which the soil is so tight that water and fertilizers fail to enter, and grass roots become disastrously shallow. Under such circumstances the lawn may respond to aeration. The aerating operation will tear thatch loose—if this is part of the problem. The benefits cited for aeration can in many instances be better attributed to the loosening of thatch.

It hardly pays the average home to maintain an aerating machine. If one is needed, it can usually be rented from a landscape firm, or the service can be hired. Such machines are fairly expensive, and if of a type to core deeply, of course must be powered. Foot models used like a spade are of little value. Unless a core of soil is removed, indentation from a spike will more likely squeeze than loosen soil. Spiked rollers, likewise, probably cause compaction just as often as they achieve loosening. The most recent trend is to economical slicing machines, with blades like a powered buzz saw. They not only thin the sod, but chew inches into the soil, casting loose earth behind as a topdressing. Soil cores cast out behind an aerifier can be broken up and scattered about by dragging a mat over the newly aerated turf.

FERTILIZING

Fertilizing to encourage growth and improve color should be a regular part of lawn maintenance. Even if fertilizer is adequately supplied in the seedbed, its impact is spent in the course of time. Additional applications are needed for continued satisfactory lawn performance.

The deeper green and the faster growth of fertilized grass is largely due to the nitrogen in the fertilizer. Of course if other major nutrients such as phosphorus and potassium are in short supply, grass growth may be limited. If a complete fertilizer, one containing all major nutrients, is used from time to time, and if the clippings are left on the lawn, the grass should be adequately nourished. Nitrogen predominates in fertilizers designed for lawns. Familiar analyses are 35–5–10, 22–10–5, 20–10–10, 12–3–4, etc., nitrogen being always the first-listed percentage, followed by phosphorus and potassium. The chemical symbols of these three major nutrients are, respectively, N, P and K.

Fertilizers may be organic or inorganic. Organic fertilizers are derived from natural plant and animal residues—soybean meal, processed sewage sludge, tankage and other slaughterhouse wastes, fish meal, cottonseed hulls and so on. They are relatively low in nutrient content, being derived from unconcentrated once-living tissue. Organic fertilizers are relatively expensive because much bulk is required. They produce no immediate grass response until they are moistened and the activity of microorganisms ensues. This process is intensified by warm temperatures; organic fertilizers are slow performers in cold weather. But they are generally safe to use, in the sense that they will not burn the grass.

The influence of inorganic fertilizers (see page 749) is felt on the lawn immediately. Often grass will turn deeper green within a day or two after application of an inorganic fertilizer. But by the same token, the risk of burn is greater. If the salts cling to the foliage, the risk is greatly intensified. However, most inorganics are made nowadays as granules with little or no dust; these roll from the grass foliage and are unlikely to burn. In some cases, there is a resinous coating around the granule; the nutrients do not escape until there has been weathering or biological breakdown of the coating, the thickness and formulation of which regulates their release. If an inorganic fertilizer does adhere to the grass foliage, as is likely with trailing grasses such as fine bents and Bermudas, a good precaution against injury is to rinse off the foliage with a hose immediately after application.

Our third category of frequently utilized lawn fertilizers is that of the synthetic organic, primarily designed to provide nitrogen gradually. Synthetic organic fertilizers are free of unpleasant odors and have excellent handling qualities. But they are costly sources of nitrogen because its rate of release may not be efficient. The chief synthetic organic is ureaform.

Application

Applying fertilizers is no different from that described for distribution of seed (see Sowing Seeds, page 700). Spread the product uniformly at the prescribed rate, usually about 1 lb. of elemental nitrogen per 1000 sq. ft. Thus about 3 lb. of a 35-percent nitrogen fertilizer (35–5–10) or 5 lb. of a 20-percent nitrogen fertilizer (20–10–10) would be needed to supply 1 lb. of elemental nitrogen.

Uniform application is most easily achieved by the better mechanical lawn spreaders. The gauges on the spreader set the rate of emission, and many products indicate on the container the suggested rate setting for the more familiar spreaders. If no rate is indicated, a measured amount can be dumped into the spreader and given a trial run to see if it comes close to expected coverage. Obviously, it is better to start with a light setting and gradually increase, rather than to risk fertilizing too heavily. It is easy enough to go over the area a second or third time, but impossible to undo an overapplication. In spreading fertilizer, be careful that adjacent passes of the spreader overlap, so that no strips will be missed; otherwise there will be striping of narrow yellower bands of unfertilized turf between the deep green strips where fertilizer fell.

Timing of fertilization and the recommended amount to be applied over the year vary greatly with kind of lawn, climate and soil. In most cases, only about 1 lb. elemental nitrogen per 1000 sq. ft. is used per application. Bent grasses, improved Bermudas and Merion Kentucky bluegrass are all fairly heavy feeders. They ordinarily receive 6 or more lb. of elemental nitrogen per 1000 sq. ft. a year. Centipede and fine fescues survive nicely on as little as 2 lb. per 1000 sq. ft. a year. Most other grasses range between these extremes. With most soils, 3 lb. per 1000 sq. ft. a year is adequate for average bluegrass performance. At least half of this fertilizer should be applied in autumn and early winter. In the South, with a longer growing season, 4 lb. per 1000 sq. ft. a year is a suggested average, although it is apparent that a great many of the workhorse grasses, such as Bahia, must get along on a lot less.

Chlorosis or blanching for lack of available iron is the chief minor-element deficiency. Spraying soluble iron on the foliage can have an immediate effect, greening the grass at once. Spreading iron salts or chelates may help. Iron sulphate is usually sprayed on grass foliage at the rate of an ounce or so in several gallons of water per 1000 sq. ft. of lawn. Sod or soil applications may require a pound or more per 1000 sq. ft. Iron chelates (Sequestrenes, Versenes) hold the iron chemically available in the soil for a longer period than is the case with soluble iron sulphate or oxalate. The DTPA (330) chelate is suggested for iron chlorosis under acid conditions, fairly frequent with centipede grass; EDDHA (138) chelate is best for alkaline-induced chlorosis, often troublesome in arid western climates. Apply with fertilizer or spray separately, at no less than 1 lb. of chelate per 1000 sq. ft.

WATERING

Irrigation is the only way to have a green lawn during drought. Simplified home watering is becoming more available, with fairly inexpensive underground plastic systems that can be installed by the homeowner himself. Valves and a time clock enable the system to be set for automatic turn-on of any duration. Such installation certainly helps to maintain a lawn that is constantly green; but, surprisingly, unforeseen side effects can arise. Probably more good bluegrass sods are lost from overwatering than from underirrigation. Constantly moist soil causes the same ill effects as does severe soil compaction. Also, frequent irrigation encourages water-loving weeds, and species such as *Poa annua* and *P. trivialis*. Moreover, the constantly humid atmosphere may encourage disease.

Most grasses are well adapted to withstand drought; they may brown completely, yet revive when rains come once again. In fact this is a typical summer cycle in parts of the Midwest, with Kentucky bluegrass–fine fescue turfs. The experience may even be beneficial to the turf, in that

weeds and unwanted plants are much more upset by parching than is the bluegrass–fescue. Over the long haul, this helps give the bluegrass the upper hand. Drought may occasionally be therapeutic, but does not make for attractiveness around the home during dry weather.

Different grasses have somewhat differing water requirements. Bent grasses are well adapted to rainy locations and benefit from frequent irrigation. So do such specialty sorts as *Poa trivialis* and carpet grass in the South. By and large most lawn grasses perform better if they are watered infrequently, but thoroughly. The lawn might well be let dry out almost until wilting occurs, whereupon it is soaked until the whole root zone is wet. Approach of wilting is indicated by a loss of resiliency (footprints show for some time after the grass is walked upon) and by a bluish-gray cast.

On sandy soils in many parts of Florida, turf may have to be watered every second day in bright, dry weather. On the heavier claylike soils of the Corn Belt, the interval may need to be only each ten days or two weeks in default of rain. The sandy soils hold very little water—perhaps only a half inch in the top foot of soil; clay soils may have a reservoir of as much as 3 in. You can soak a half inch of water into a sandy soil in just a few minutes, but you may have to water clay soil slowly for a couple of hours to have it absorb as much as it can contain.

Whatever system of irrigation is used, choose sprinklers which apply the water evenly. This can be checked by spotting tin cans about the lawn, seeing that all fill about equally. In humid areas where rain normally takes care of most irrigation needs, surface sprinklers on the end of the hose usually suffice. In more arid regions, and even for summer use in humid climates, there is a trend toward laying permanent underground piping systems. These are most easily installed at the time the lawn is made, but may be inserted into narrow slit trenches in established lawns. A simple, inexpensive kit is now marketed nationally; the more elaborate systems are probably best installed by professionals.

WEEDS

In the great majority of cases, weeds showing up in the lawn arise from seed that is already present in the soil, or that is blown and tracked in from neighboring grounds. Many weed seeds lie dormant for years and become induced to sprout only when there is thinning of the lawn, or the soil is disturbed. It is not uncommon to have crabgrass or similar weeds show up around the margins of so small a soil disturbance as an aeration hole.

The familiar lawn weeds are fortunately no longer the serious pests they once were because of general susceptibility to the 2,4–D group of weed killers. Included are dandelion, plantain, dock, chickweed, knotweed, spurge, clover, henbit, ground ivy and hordes of a similar sort. Members of the rush, sedge, lily and other allied families, as well as the grasses, may be annual or perennial. In the former category are some weeds with the most nefarious of reputations— particularly crabgrass, goose grass, foxtail, barnyard grass, annual bluegrass and *Poa annua*. The need to go through an annual seedling stage affords a weakness in their life cycle, so such weeds can be controlled with chemical herbicides.

Toughest of all to control are the perennial grasslike weeds, such as tall fescue, timothy, orchard grass, quack grass, nut grass and rushes, for herbicides powerful enough to kill these species are also lethal to lawn grass.

Weed Control

If weeds are abundant in the lawn, nothing short of soil fumigation can eliminate them. This can be accomplished by the use of soil drenches such as Vapam, or, more efficiently, with poisonous fumes such as methyl bromide under a tarpaulin. Professional application may be advisable.

As to the occasional or residual weeds infesting almost every lawn, there are convenient chemical ways of cleaning them out. However, this affords only temporary respite unless the lawn environment encourages the grass to crowd out weeds. The first order of business for maintaining a weed-free lawn is growing the lawn grass well, for if the lawn is thick and tight, there is little chance for weeds to muscle in. Those few that do can be controlled with an occasional herbicide treatment or by hand pulling.

If you have a serious weed problem, first try to determine what has gone wrong with the grass; correct your lawn management rather than relying entirely upon weed killers.

First, however, a gardener must get rid of whatever weeds there are (see "Keep Your Garden Weed-Free," page 839). Crabgrass is a notorious lawn evil. Often crabgrass control fails because some other species has been misidentified and treated with a crabgrass preventive. In recent years many preemergence chemicals have been developed, aimed specifically at checking crabgrass. Chemicals that have proved effective include arsenates, Azak, Bandane, Betasan, Binnel, Dacthal, Tupersan, Zytron and others. Of these, Dacthal and Zytron are best, considering both effectiveness and safety for the lawn grass. Tupersan is relatively new, but seems very promising in that it controls sprouting crabgrass while yet allowing lawn grass seed to come up without damage.

By and large, preemergence herbicides are best used only on lawns old enough to have been mowed. The chemical is spread as a blanket over the lawn, at least in the sunny sections where crabgrass has been a problem. This should be done just before the annual grasses are expected to sprout. Crabgrass usually germinates when soil temperatures approach 60° F., as early as March in the South, but usually not until late June in the North. If the preemergence chemical is evenly spread as recommended at the proper time, crabgrass will be demolished as it sprouts without injury to older perennial lawn grass.

If the incidence of crabgrass is not prevented by preemergence herbicides, other chemicals are able to eliminate it selectively from most lawns. The methyl arsonates (DSMA, AMA) are frequently used. Two applications are needed about a week apart, sprayed on the crabgrass foliage. The same chemicals are fairly effective, too, against goose grass, dallis grass and, in some cases, sedges.

For the perennial grasses there is no really satisfactory answer. Nimblewill (*Muhlenbergia schreberi*), a pest frequent in the Midwest, can often be eliminated without injury to bluegrass by repeat sprayings of liquid zytron. Other perennials can be put at a disadvantage by such simple expedients as letting the lawn dry out occasionally. This helps the lawn grass gain the upper hand over water-loving species such as *Poa trivialis* and sedges. But for the really tough perennial grasses, hand digging, or spot-spraying with a herbicide powerful enough to kill all vegetation, is usually required. Amitrole and dalapon are chemicals recommended for spot-spraying tall fescue, timothy

and quack grass. The chemical is toxic in the soil for some weeks, delaying replanting. Cacodylic acid (Dimethylarsinic acid) is, on the other hand, immediately deactivated upon contact with the soil. Weed killing with this contact chemical permits almost immediate reseeding. Being a contact herbicide, it browns only what it hits, and is not effective on underground parts such as the rhizomes of quack grass. With resilient plants such as tall fescue, follow-up treatments may be needed.

Simazine or atrazine act as preemergents against almost all sprouting weeds and are frequently recommended for spraying newly plugged and sprigged southern lawns of St. Augustine, zoysia and centipede. The crabgrass preemergents can be used, too, but are not so effective under the perpetual onslaught of weeds. The postemergent arsonates can be used selectively on growing Bermuda and zoysia grasses, but are lethal to Bahia and may injure other southern species; 2, 4-D should not be used on St. Augustine, although it will not injure other southern lawn grasses.

MOSS AND ALGAE

Moss and algae are almost never troublesome on flourishing lawns. They can be controlled through improved lawn culture. Moss is most frequently found on underfertilized open turfs in the shade, where the soil is often compacted. Corrective measures include stepped-up fertilization, possibly aeration, high mowing of the grass and improved drainage if there seems to be standing water. The latter is useful for controlling algae, which often disappear naturally as a wet spell subsides.

INSECT PESTS

Most lawns are relatively free of insects. But where outbreaks do occur, inroads can be devastating. A familiar problem with lawns is root damage from grubs such as the Japanese beetle and June beetle in the Northeast. Debilitation and eventual death will result from the sucking of plant sap by chinch bugs and the consumption of lower leaf and crown by sod webworms and larvae of the lawn moth. Occasionally damage from other insects can be important, such as consumption of foliage by caterpillars. Debilitation may also come from leaf hoppers, scales and the eriophyid mite; all suck plant juices. Grass crowns can be consumed by such types as the billbug. Crickets, earthworms, cicada wasps and so on, may burrow into the soil, leaving small, uneven mounds. And in certain regions, the lawn may harbor insects primarily unpleasant to human beings, such as fleas, ticks or chiggers.

Whatever the source of trouble, the cure is essentially the same—application of a broadly effective insecticide. In recent years, populations of chinch bugs and even sod webworms have built up resistance against chemicals such as DDT, chlordane, dieldrin and heptachlor. Where resistance has been developed, newer and more potent insecticides such as the phosphatics and carbamates must be chosen. Diazinon, Trithion, ethion, Sevin and even malathion are recommended where once the inexpensive chlorinated hydrocarbons served well. However, chlordane and its like are often still quite effective for many insects, including those that populate the soil; when the root zone is soaked, grubs may be checked for up to ten years in the future.

All insecticides are toxic to some degree, so their application requires careful handling and exact adherence to product directions. Depending upon the type of insect and its feeding habits, the insecticide may have to be flushed into the soil, applied so as to coat the grass foliage, or worked deep into the grass crowns where the insects may be hidden.

Certain types of nematodes parasitize grass roots, dwarfing and debilitating the plants. Identification is not easy; it is hard to tell whether nematodes are present, except by applying a nematocide and seeing if the grass responds.

Earthworms are seldom killed by insecticides, although the populations may be reduced and the worms encouraged to switch to untreated soil. Snails and slugs are usually controlled by setting out poisoned bait which contains metaldehyde. Moles and other burrowing mammals are partly controllable with poison baits or fumigants in the burrow; it is simpler to reduce their food supply (grubs and other soil insects) by applying insecticides. The moles will then be forced to seek other habitats.

DISEASES

Disease propagules (spores) are ever lurking in soil and vegetation, but they cause infection only when environmental conditions are in their favor. Too much nitrogen, too abundant humidity, or insufficient genetic resistance all encourage epidemics.

With proved lawn grasses, disease is of minor consequence. Although making temporary inroads, it disappears with change of seasons or weather. Depending upon disease and kind of grass, recovery can usually be aided by withholding moisture, temporarily omitting nitrogen fertilization, mowing tall or otherwise favoring the grass. Fungicides may help, but once the disease is rampant, it is almost too late to use them. Fungicides are much better as preventives, applied prior to the expected onset of disease or early in its course. For example, in climates having a snow cover, bent grass is almost certain to suffer snow-mold damage in winter. Use of a mercurial fungicide such as Calo-Clor prior to first snowfall will help to forestall the disease. Where brown patch and other diseases of hot, muggy weather may be anticipated at certain times of the year, a preventive fungicide might well be sprayed whenever such weather prevails. It is more difficult to prevent leaf spot, rust and the like during a lengthy season, but even this is possible to some extent with fungicidal sprays. One difficulty is that when lawn grasses grow vigorously, new foliage, uncoated with fungicide, is produced so rapidly that a spraying one week leaves the lawn unprotected the next. Better choose disease-resistant varieties of grass or combinations which have proved themselves able to ride out the difficulties that are prevalent in the particular locality.

Diagnosing diseases is not easy, even for the expert. In fact, experts theorize that many times several diseases may act in concert, one profiting from another's biochemical activity. A few of the more familiar turfgrass diseases follow.

LEAF SPOT (HELMINTHOSPORIUM)
Shot-hole perforations of the leaves, particularly in spring, may extend to rotting of the crowns and loss of turf. Found on many grasses, but especially noted on bluegrass. Merion and certain other varieties are moderately resistant. To help check, mow high and see that nitrogen levels are not overluxurious. Fungicides such as Dyrene Kromad, maneb, Terson and others are partially preventive.

RUST (PUCCINIA)
Troublesome on Bermudas, ryegrasses and Merion Kentucky bluegrass, manifest as orange pustules covering the blades, typically in late summer. Very difficult to control. The usual treatment is merely fertilization, which stimulates new uninfected leafage and may inhibit the fungus. Severe outbreaks can be avoided by preventive spraying with Acti-dione or Zineb.

BROWN PATCH
(PELLICULARIA, RHIZOCTONIA)
Attacks when temperature and humidity are high. St. Augustine and bent grasses are particularly susceptible, developing brown splotches with a water-soaked appearance. Where the disease is spreading, the brown grass is usually surrounded by a "smoke ring." Fungicides are helpful, as well as reduced fertilization and less watering.

PYTHIUM
Has a number of common names such as "cottony spot." It attacks most grasses, often when weather is muggy and where air ventilation is poor. Fungicides are helpful.

FAIRY RING
(MARASMIUS AND OTHER GENERA)
The fungus grows underground in widening circles, cementing soil and drawing moisture, causing the grass to brown. The grass itself is not attacked. There is no way to kill the fungus short of removing all soil, or using toxicants strong enough to kill the turf. Spiking the hardened soil, watering generously and fertilizing the whole section are suggested palliatives. Fairy ring tends to come and go for no obvious reason. Ordinarily it is easier to live with it than to eradicate it. Mercury- or cadmium-containing fungicides will help to control it. Mushrooms are occasionally produced aboveground.

CHAPTER 18

SHADE TREES
Enhance Your Grounds

Judicious Pruning—Improvement Through Fertilizing—Choosing Shade Trees—Deciduous Trees from Many Lands

SHADE TREES are very important in American and Canadian garden landscapes. Properly selected and located, they add to the value as well as to the appearance and livability of a property. Wherever gardens are made, some kinds of shade trees can be grown—more in regions that were once naturally forested than in such areas as the Great Plains and deserts or semideserts, more in regions of relatively mild climates than those farther to the north. Shade trees, of course, include both evergreen and leaf-losing (deciduous) kinds; here only the latter are considered. For evergreen shade trees see "Evergreen Trees," page 388.

No sharp line of distinction exists between shade trees and the smaller trees dealt with in "Shrubs and Flowering Small Trees," page 449, so check that chapter for deciduous trees not included here. That chapter, too, includes information on buying, treatment after arrival, soil and soil preparation, planting procedures, staking, aftercare and diagnosis of pests and diseases. These practices are also applicable to the trees in this chapter.

PRUNING

Deciduous shade trees normally need no regular pruning once they have developed their main trunks and framework branches, although some kinds, such as plane trees (*Platanus*) and lindens (*Tilia*) may be pruned biannually or annually if the grower desires to shape them or limit their spread. The height and spread of all kinds can be controlled, at least to some extent, by judicious occasional pruning. The removal of dead, broken and ill-placed branches is also a pruning operation that may need attention from time to time. It is not wise for amateurs to engage in any pruning that involves leaving the ground, or to hire labor not fully covered by insurance; the risks of injury and death from falls and other accidents are considerable. When large trees need to be pruned, obtain the services of reliable tree surgeons. At the same time, it is advisable to obtain advice on thinning branches.

All cuts over an inch in diameter should be covered with tree-wound paint. Some trees, such as birches (*Betula*) and maples (*Acer*), "bleed" (lose sap copiously) if they are pruned in late winter or spring. This looks much more serious than it is. Actually what is lost is the sap on its way to the buds and leaves, not the food-containing sap returning from the leaves. However, it is preferable to wait until the foliage is fully out before pruning such trees.

At planting time compensatory pruning, as described on page 416 in "Shrubs and Flowering Small Trees," is applicable to shade trees.

As young specimens, shade trees need formative pruning to establish a good permanent framework of trunk and well-placed branches. It is especially important to prevent the development of bad crotches (angles where branches diverge) that are likely to prove weak and subject to breakage as the branches become heavier. Branches originating opposite each other, especially if they spread at a narrow angle, are most likely to be troublesome.

FERTILIZING

The need for fertilizer is determined by the vigor of the tree. Specimens making good annual growth and abundant foliage need no such attention. Old, starved and even somewhat decrepit trees that make little new growth and poor foliage are often vastly improved by fertilizing or other methods. For thorough rehabilitation, this should be combined with careful pruning and control of diseases and pests.

Fertilizing may be accomplished by using one of the special "tree foods" or a complete garden fertilizer of a type prepared for vegetables. The material may be spread over the surface permeated by the roots, which normally extend beyond the spread of the branches; or holes spaced 18 in. to 2 ft. apart may be made within the feeding-root area, and the fertilizer placed in these and then covered with soil. A mulch of good manure is also a splendid way of providing nourishment.

CHOOSING SHADE TREES

Before selecting shade trees, one should look around the locality and visit nurseries to become familiar with kinds that seem to thrive. Not that one should necessarily confine plantings to kinds already growing in the vicinity, but a thoughtful survey will give some idea of which trees are likely to prove satisfactory.

In recent years much has been accomplished in selecting and propagating, usually by grafting, distinct varieties (or clones, as the horticulturist calls them) of shade trees that possess particular merits. These varieties are given particular names; all trees of the same name are remarkably uniform in appearance and performance. So one can choose, say, not simply the honey locust (*Gleditsia triacanthos*) but the Moraine honey locust or the Shademaster honey locust. Similar opportunities for selection occur with certain maples (*Acer*), ashes (*Fraxinus*) and other trees. Some of these named varieties are listed in the next section of this chapter; others will be found, together with descriptions, in the catalogues of nurserymen.

In using the following lists it is important to remember that heights of different kinds of trees vary greatly in response to geographical location and environmental conditions. The heights given generally represent the maximum or near-maximum height attained at maturity under ideal conditions; in cultivation the trees are often much lower.

Deciduous Trees for Shade

ABELE. See *Populus alba.*

ACER (MAPLE)
A varied group of heavily foliaged

trees, most of which have flowers and fruits of no decorative value. Some assume brilliant leaf colors in fall. The Japanese maples (*Acer palmatum*

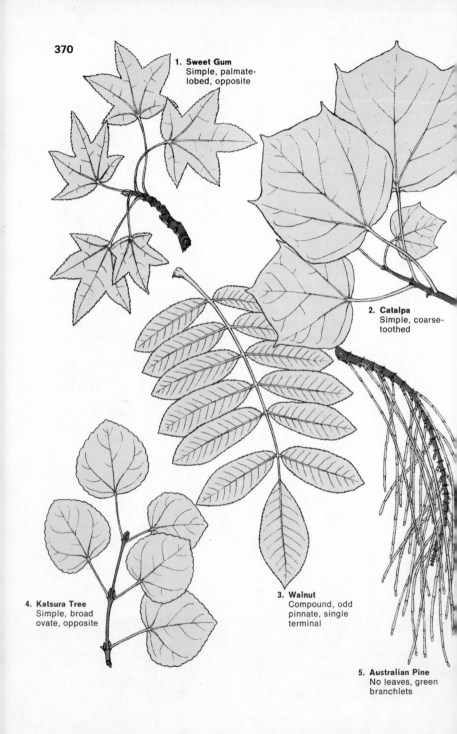

370

1. **Sweet Gum**
Simple, palmate-
lobed, opposite

2. **Catalpa**
Simple, coarse-
toothed

3. **Walnut**
Compound, odd
pinnate, single
terminal

4. **Katsura Tree**
Simple, broad
ovate, opposite

5. **Australian Pine**
No leaves, green
branchlets

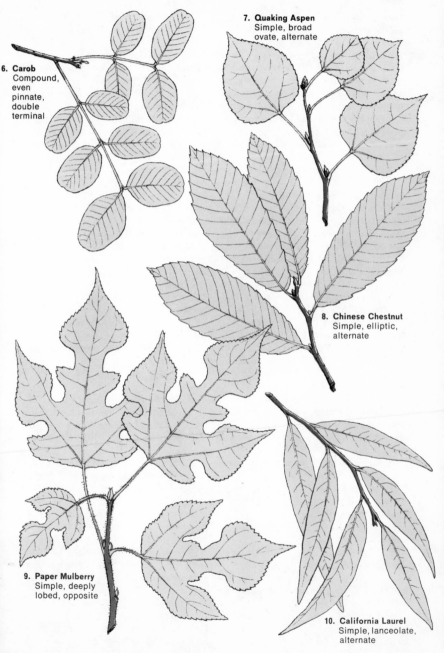

371

6. Carob
Compound,
even
pinnate,
double
terminal

7. Quaking Aspen
Simple, broad
ovate, alternate

8. Chinese Chestnut
Simple, elliptic,
alternate

9. Paper Mulberry
Simple, deeply
lobed, opposite

10. California Laurel
Simple, lanceolate,
alternate

varieties) and some other low-growing kinds are treated under "Shrubs and Flowering Small Trees," page 418.

Maples grow in any good soil. They make abundant surface roots and it is often difficult to grow other plants under mature specimens. Do any necessary pruning in early summer.

Acer cappadocicum (coliseum maple), 45 ft., round-headed.

A. c. aureum, new growth yellow and red.

A. c. rubrum, new growth red.

A. floridanum, 50 ft., round-headed. For Deep South.

A. macrophyllum (Oregon maple), 90 ft., round-headed. Flowers fragrant; leaves very large, turning yellow in fall. Good for Pacific Coast.

A. negundo (box elder), 60 ft., wide-spreading, rapid-growing; branches weak, brittle, subject to storm damage. Withstands dry soil conditions. For regions of very cold winters and hot, dry summers, but elsewhere considered an inferior tree. Variegated-leaved varieties are grown.

A. nikoense, 40 ft., round-headed, rather slow-growing. Foliage bright purple or red in fall.

A. platanoides (Norway maple), 90 ft., round-headed, broad. Foliage very dense, does not color in fall; flowers yellow, conspicuous before leaves unfold in spring.

A. p. columnare, narrow columnar shape, erect branches.

A. p. Crimson King, foliage rich purplish-red throughout the summer, especially bright in spring.

A. p. erectum, narrow pyramidal shape.

A. p. globosum, round-headed, very dense, compact.

A. p. laciniatum, columnar shape; leaf tips turned upward like birds' claws.

A. p. schwedleri (Schwedler's maple), foliage purple-red in spring, turning to dark green later.

A. p. Summershade, fast grower.

A. p. variegatum, margins of leaves white.

A. pseudoplatanus (sycamore maple), 80 ft., wide-spreading; stands seaside conditions well.

A. p. brilliantissima, spring foliage bright yellow.

A. p. leopoldii, young leaves variegated with pink, cream and green.

A. p. pyramidalis, narrow, erect shape.

A. p. spaethii, undersides of leaves burgundy red.

A. p. tricolor, young foliage green and cream above, wine-red on the undersides.

A. p. worleei, foliage at first golden, becoming green later.

A. rubrum (red maple, swamp maple), 120 ft., round-headed. Flowers showy, red, before leaves expand; foliage dense, bright red in fall. Fast-growing, but wood is somewhat weak and subject to storm damage. Suitable for moist—even wet—soils.

A. r. Armstrong, erect, narrow, spirelike.

A. r. columnare, erect and narrow in outline.

A. saccharinum (silver maple), 120 ft., broad-headed. Leaves silvery beneath; foliage clear yellow in fall. Wood brittle, much subject to storm damage.

A. s. laciniatum (Wier's weeping maple), branches pendulous; leaves much divided.

A. saccharum (sugar maple, rock maple), 110 ft., round-headed, dense. Foliage in fall brilliant red, orange and yellow.

A. s. monumentale (sentry maple), erect and narrow in outline; rather slow-growing.

AESCULUS
(BUCKEYE, HORSE CHESTNUT)

Bold-foliaged trees with showy spires of flowers in late spring. They need

ject to scorching in summer, especially during hot, dry periods.

A. h. baumannii, similar to *A. hippocastanum* but double-flowered and no fruit; subject to foliage scorch.

AILANTHUS ALTISSIMA (TREE OF HEAVEN)

Rather coarse, round-headed. Foliage of exotic appearance. Females have great clusters of green and red fruits somewhat like those of maples. Male flowers are very malodorous. The wood is weak and subject to storm damage. Self-sown seedlings can be a nuisance. Where better trees can be grown this ordinarily should not be planted, but it has its uses. It thrives under the worst possible city conditions, withstands inundations with sea water, is disease- and pest-free, and prospers in any soil that is not waterlogged, in sun or shade. Plant only female trees, and if possible have no males nearby. Under such conditions the females will bear only sterile seeds.

ALDER. See *Alnus*.

ALNUS (ALDER)

Chiefly valued for moist or wet soils. Most are rather short-lived.

Alnus cordata (Italian alder), 50 ft., round-headed. Leaves glossy. Will grow also on dryish soil. One of the best.

A. japonica, 60 ft., pyramidal. Dark green foliage. Will grow also in dryish soil. One of the best.

A. rhombifolia (white alder), 90 ft., round-headed. For Pacific Coast.

A. rubra (red alder), 60 ft., pyramidal head. For Pacific Coast. Much liked by tent caterpillars.

A. sinuata, 35 ft., often shrubby. Bright green foliage. Very hardy.

A. tenuifolia (mountain alder), 35 ft., oval or round-headed; they are often shrubby.

Aesculus carnea
(Red Horse Chestnut)

deep, fertile, well-drained but fairly moist soils. The fruits are attractive to small boys, therefore it is often wise to plant nonfruiting varieties. For bottlebrush buckeye (*Aesculus parviflora*), see page 418 in "Shrubs and Flowering Small Trees."

Aesculus carnea (red horse chestnut), 40 ft., flowers deep flesh-pink to watermelon-pink.

A. c. briotii, flowers scarlet; produces no fruit.

A. hippocastanum (common horse chestnut), 100 ft., flowers white with red and yellow blotches; foliage sub-

ASH. See *Fraxinus.*

ASPEN. See *Populus.*

BASSWOOD. See *Tilia.*

BEECH. See *Fagus.*

BETULA (BIRCH)
Generally short-lived, graceful trees
with attractive flower catkins in
spring and fine yellow fall foliage.
The bark of most of these trees
is highly decorative and especially
pleasing in winter when seen against
an evergreen background. They
are suitable for well-drained, reasonably moist soils and northern
climates. Any needed pruning should
be done in early summer. They are
very susceptible to infestations of
birch-leaf miner, which may be controlled by spraying with lindane.
Betula albo-sinensis, 90 ft., round-
headed. Bark orange-red; variety
septentrionalis has brownish-orange
bark.
B. lenta (sweet birch, cherry birch),
75 ft., round-headed. Bark like that
of cherry tree, brown; fine fall foliage
color.
B. mandschurica japonica (Japanese white birch), 60 ft., open, round-
headed. Bark white.
B. nigra (river birch, black birch),
90 ft., pyramidal. Bark reddish-
brown. Grows in wet soils, even in
places periodically inundated.
B. papyrifera (canoe birch, paper
birch), 90 ft., pyramidal. Bark white;
good fall foliage color. Less subject
to bronze birch borer; the best white
birch.
B. pendula (European white birch),
60 ft., pyramidal. Bark white. Very
subject to bronze birch borer, which
destroys the entire top of the tree.
Treat with DDT spray in early June.
B. p. dalecarlica, leaves finely
dissected.

B. p. fastigiata, narrow, columnar.
B. p. gracilis, branches pendulous;
leaves finely serrated.
B. p. purpurea, foliage purple in
early spring, dark green later.
B. p. tristis, round-headed; has
pendulous branches.
B. p. youngii, a decidedly smaller
tree than other varieties of *B. pendula;*
branches pendulous.

BIRCH. See *Betula.*

BLACK ACACIA. See *Robinia pseudoacacia.*

BLACK GUM. See *Nyssa sylvatica.*

BLUE BEECH. See *Carpinus caroliniana.*

BOX ELDER. See *Acer negundo.*

BROUSSONETIA PAPYRIFERA
(PAPER MULBERRY)
Broad, rounded head; height to 50
ft. Foliage dense; fruits red, early
summer. Thrives on poor, sandy or
gravelly soils and in cities. Hardy
about as far north as New York City.

BUCKEYE. See *Aesculus.*

CARPINUS (HORNBEAM)
Handsome trees that prosper in any
ordinary soil, including limestone
soils. Generally disease- and pest-free.
Carpinus betulus (European hornbeam), 60 ft., broad, round-headed.
Foliage yellow in fall. Stands shearing well and also makes a fine tall
hedge.
C. b. fastigiata, narrow-pyramidal
shape.
C. b. incisa, leaves deeply lobed.
C. b. pendula, branchlets pendulous.
C. b. purpurea, young foliage wine-
red.
C. b. quercifolia, leaves deeply
lobed, smaller than those of *C. b.
incisa.*

C. caroliniana (American hornbeam, blue beech), 35 ft., usually
with several trunks. Foliage colors
orange and red in fall. Very hardy.

CARYA (HICKORY)

Good shade trees but somewhat subject to storm damage. They thrive
in rich, fairly moist soils, are rather
slow-growing and are difficult to transplant unless root is pruned.

Carya glabra (pignut), 120 ft.,
oval-headed. Foliage yellow in fall.
Slow-growing. Tolerates dry soils.

C. ovata (shagbark hickory), irregular, narrow, upright. Foliage
golden-brown in fall. A good ornamental tree with conspicuously flaking bark and edible nuts.

C. pecan (pecan), 140 ft., round-
headed. Fall foliage yellow. The
fastest-growing hickory and a good
shade tree. Hardy as far north as
New York City. Special varieties are
planted for their edible nuts.

CASTANEA MOLLISSIMA
(CHINESE CHESTNUT)

Resistant to chestnut bark disease,
this bears edible nuts of good quality
provided that trees of at least two
different varieties are growing together. Dense, round-headed, 60 ft.
high. For well-drained ordinary soils.

Carya ovata
(Shagbark Hickory)

CATALPA

Coarse-foliaged trees bearing large
panicles of bloom in summer. For
ordinary, reasonably moist soils.

Catalpa bignonioides (Indian bean),
50 ft., round-headed. Flowers white,
with yellow and brown blotches.

C. b. nana (often wrongly called
C. bungei), a dwarf nonbloomer, usually grown as umbrellalike grafted
specimens on understocks of *C.
bignonioides* and often pruned back
hard each spring; such specimens are
rather ugly.

C. bungei. The tree to which this

name is correctly applied is rare.
See *C. bignonioides nana*.

C. hybrida, similar to *C. bignonioides* but a smaller tree with
smaller flower clusters.

C. ovata, 35 ft., broad-headed.
Flowers yellowish with orange and
violet markings.

C. speciosa (Western catalpa), 100
ft., pyramidal. Flowers white with
yellow and brown markings. Withstands heat and drought.

CELTIS (HACKBERRY)

Trees with elmlike leaves, for ordinary soils. The native *C. occidentalis* is not recommended because of its great susceptibility to the unsightly witches'-broom disease.

Celtis australis, 75 ft., round-headed. Adapted for hot regions and dry soils.

C. laevigata (sugarberry), 100 ft., round-headed, wide-spreading branches.

CERCIDIPHYLLUM JAPONICUM
(KATSURA TREE)
Wide-spreading, round-topped tree, usually with more than one trunk, up to 100 ft. Leaves heart-shaped, resembling those of redbud (*Cercis*); in fall they turn yellow and red. For fertile, fairly moist soil. Not much subject to pests or diseases.

CHINABERRY. See *Melia azedarach*.

CHINA TREE. See *Melia azedarach*.

CHINESE CHESTNUT. See *Castanea mollissima*.

CHINESE SCHOLAR TREE. See *Sophora japonica*.

CLADRASTIS LUTEA (YELLOWWOOD)
Round-headed, rather wide-spreading, up to 50 ft. Showy drooping racemes of fragrant, creamy-white wisterialike flowers in late spring. Foliage dense, turns yellow and orange in fall. Ordinary soil. If pruned in spring the tree "bleeds" (loses sap) profusely; delay any necessary pruning until early summer. Very hardy and handsome.

CORK TREE. See *Phellodendron amurense*.

CORNUS (DOGWOOD)
For other kinds, see page 422 in "Shrubs and Flowering Small Trees."
Cornus contraversa, 60 ft., branches

in distinct horizontal tiers. Flowers small, in flat clusters in late spring, followed by small black berries; foliage dark, lustrous green. Not susceptible to twig-blight disease. Thrives in any fairly good soil.

C. macrophylla, 45 ft., is similar to *C. contraversa* but has opposite instead of alternate leaves. Blooms later and is slightly less hardy.

CORYLUS COLURNA
(TURKISH HAZELNUT)
A good shade tree, especially for dryish soils. Up to 75 ft. tall, it is pyramidal and has attractive foliage. For other kinds of *Corylus*, see page 423.

COTTONWOOD. See *Populus*.

CUCUMBER TREE. See *Magnolia acuminata* and *M. macrophylla*.

DAWN REDWOOD. See *Metasequoia glyptostroboides*.

DOGWOOD. See *Cornus*.

ELDER. See *Sambucus*.

ELM. See *Ulmus*.

EMPRESS TREE. See *Paulownia tomentosa*.

FAGUS (BEECH)
Stately trees with attractive, smooth gray bark and neat foliage which colors beautifully in fall. They fill the surface soil with roots, and it is often impossible to grow anything under large specimens. The trees prosper in ordinary soil.

Fagus grandifolia (American beech), 90 ft., pyramidal. Densely foliaged; leaves turn brown and gold in fall. Does not transplant quite as easily as the European beech. Very hardy.

F. sylvatica (European beech), 90

ft., broad pyramidal, rather slow-growing. Densely foliaged; leaves turn warm bronze or brown in fall. Slightly less hardy than *F. grandifolia* and with darker gray bark.

F.s. asplenifolia, leaves deeply lobed or toothed, very narrow.

F.s. atropunicea (purple beech, copper beech), leaves copper-purple to dark purple. Various named horticultural forms are grown. Among the best are River's purple beech and Spaeth's red-leaved beech. When raised from seed the purple beech pro-

duces many poorly colored seedlings.

F. s. fastigiata (Dawyck beech), columnar and very slender (fastigiate). One of the very finest trees of this shape.

F. s. laciniata (fernleaf beech), leaves deeply cut and toothed.

F. s. pendula (weeping beech), branches pendulous, reaching to the ground; a wide-spreading, handsome tree.

F. s. purpurea-pendula (weeping purple beech), similar to *F.s. pendula* but with red-purple foliage.

F. s. tricolor, leaves white, variegated with green and pink; a slow, weak variety not easy to grow.

F. s. zlatia (golden beech), young leaves yellow, becoming green later.

FALSE ACACIA. See *Robinia pseudo-acacia*.

FRAXINUS (ASH)
Fast-growing, vigorous trees for ordinary, reasonably moist soils. Easy to transplant. Subject to scale insects, controlled by spraying with malathion.

Fraxinus americana (white ash), 120 ft., round-headed. Leaves turn yellow or dark purple in fall.

F. angustifolia, 70 ft., elliptic- or round-headed. Leaflets very narrow. Less hardy than *F. americana*.

F. a. Dr. Pirone, a newly named variety of promise.

F. excelsior (European ash), 120 ft., round-headed. Without colorful fall foliage.

F.e. nana (syn. *F.e. globosa*), really a very low dwarf variety, but usually grafted on understocks of *F. excelsior* to a dense globular head atop a clear trunk.

F.e. pendula (weeping ash) has pendulous branches.

F.e. Rancho, a horticultural variety.

F. oregona, 75 ft., rather narrow-headed. For Pacific Coast.

Fagus sylvatica pendula
(Weeping Beech)

F. ornus (flowering ash), 60 ft., round-headed. Bears showy clusters of fragrant white flowers in spring.

F. pennsylvanica lanceolata (green ash), 60 ft., round-headed. Foliage turns yellow in fall.

F.p.l. Marshall's Seedless, produces no seeds.

F. velutina, 50 ft., round-headed. Not hardy in the North. Adaptable for dry soils; tolerates alkaline soils.

F.v. glabra (Modesto ash), produces no seeds.

GINKGO BILOBA (MAIDENHAIR TREE)
An unusual tree of considerable botanical and ornamental interest. Its lobed, fan-shaped leaves resemble those of the maidenhair fern but are much larger. Attains a maximum height of 120 ft.; pyramidal in shape but erratic and variable in its branching. An excellent lawn specimen and city tree. The leaves become clear yellow in fall. Male and female flowers are on separate trees. Because the fruits are malodorous, it is best to plant male trees only; these should be propagated by grafting because it may not be possible to determine the sexes of seedlings until they are about 20 years old. The maidenhair tree thrives in any reasonably good soil. It is free of pests and diseases.

Ginkgo biloba fastigiata, narrow, columnar shape.

G.b. Lakeview, pyramidal or conical, male.

G.b. Mayfield, narrow, columnar, male.

G.b. Palo Alto, a male variety.

GLEDITSIA TRIACANTHOS
(HONEY LOCUST)
Attractive, lacy-foliaged, loosely round-headed, up to 120 ft. For ordinary soil; adaptable for city conditions. The typical kind has large, vicious, branched thorns on its trunk

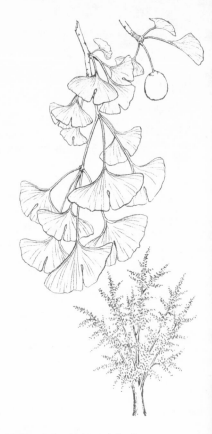

Ginkgo biloba (Maidenhair Tree)
A "living fossil" unrelated to other trees, enduring unchanged longer than any of them.

and branches, but thornless varieties are available and generally preferred. Slender pods are borne profusely by most varieties. The leaflets are small; they dry and blow away, so there is little or no need for raking in fall.

Gleditsia triacanthos inermis, a thornless variety.

G.t.i. Moraine, thornless; does not flower or produce pods.

G.t.i. Shademaster, straight, strong trunk; dark green foliage.

G.t.i. Sunburst; young leaves near ends of branches are yellow.

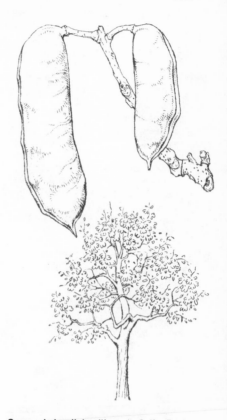

Gleditsia triacanthos inermis This variety
(Thornless Honey Locust) casts a light shade,
making it valuable for use on lawns.

Gymnocladus dioica (Kentucky Coffee Tree)
A survivor of the Great Ice Age, it is found
in isolated pockets untouched by the glaciers.

GYMNOCLADUS DIOICA
(KENTUCKY COFFEE TREE)
A sturdy, picturesque tree with
rounded head and ascending branches.
Has large seed pods which persist during winter. Foliage appears late in
spring. For fertile, fairly moist soils.

HACKBERRY. See *Celtis.*

HACKMATACK. See *Larix laricina.*

HAZELNUT, TURKISH. See *Corylus
colurna.*

HEARTNUT. See *Juglans sieboldiana
cordiformis.*

HICKORY. See *Carya.*

HONEY LOCUST. See *Gleditsia triacanthos.*

HOP HORNBEAM. See *Ostrya virginiana.*

HORNBEAM. See *Carpinus.*

HORSE CHESTNUT. See *Aesculus.*

INDIAN BEAN. See *Catalpa bignonioides*.

INDIAN LILAC. See *Melia azedarach*.

IRONWOOD. See *Ostrya virginiana*.

JACARANDA ACUTIFOLIA
(syn. J. MIMOSIFOLIA)
Beautiful tree, up to 50 ft., with ferny foliage and panicles of blue or violet-blue tubular flowers. Suitable for very mild subtropical climates. Jacarandas need sun and ordinary soil.

JAPANESE PAGODA TREE. See *Sophora japonica*.

JUGLANS (WALNUT)
Large trees with edible nuts, for moderately moist ordinary soils. Not easy to transplant when big.
   Juglans hindsii, 60 ft., round-headed. For mild climates only; popular on Pacific Coast.
   J. mandschurica, 60 ft., round-headed.
   J. nigra (black walnut), 140 ft., round- or oval-headed. Roots produce a substance harmful to other plants. Best in neutral or alkaline soils.
   J.n. laciniata, finely cut leaves.
   J. regia (English walnut, Persian walnut), 90 ft., broadly round-headed, dense. Less hardy than *J. nigra*.
   J.r. laciniata, finely cut leaves.
   J. sieboldiana cordiformis (heartnut), 60 ft., round-headed.

KALOPANAX PICTUS
Growing to 80 ft. high, this round-headed tree is very distinctive. Its lobed leaves may be 1 ft. across; in fall they turn reddish. The variety *maximowiczii* has more deeply lobed leaves. Free of pests and diseases. For ordinary soils.

KATSURA TREE. See *Cercidiphyllum japonicum*.

KENTUCKY COFFEE TREE. See *Gymnocladus dioica*.

LARCH. See *Larix*.

LARIX (LARCH)
Deciduous conifers of delicate beauty, especially when in new leaf in spring. For moist soils and cold northern climates. They are subject to several serious pests and diseases.
   Larix decidua (European larch), 100 ft., irregularly pyramidal.
   L. laricina (American larch, tamarack, hackmatack), 60 ft., pyramidal in shape.
   L. leptolepis (Japanese larch), 80 ft., pyramidal; perhaps the fastest grower.
   L. lyallii, 75 ft., pyramidal.
   L. occidentalis, 150 ft., narrowly pyramidal. Bark of older trunks cinnamon-red.

LINDEN. See *Tilia*.

LIQUIDAMBAR STYRACIFLUA
(SWEET GUM)
A handsome tree, up to 130 ft., broadly pyramidal, with glossy, sharply lobed maplelike leaves, brilliant crimson in fall. Rather difficult to transplant when large. Comparatively free of pests and diseases. For ordinary, rather moist soils.

LIRIODENDRON TULIPIFERA
(TULIP TREE)
A broad-pyramidal tree of distinction that grows to a maximum height of more than 150 ft. Tulip-shaped flowers, greenish-yellow and orange, are borne in summer. The variety *L.t. fastigiata* is narrow-pyramidal. For moderately moist, fertile soils. Subject to scale insects; controlled by spraying with malathion.

LOCUST. See *Robinia*.

MACLURA POMIFERA (OSAGE ORANGE)
Vigorous, thorny tree, up to 60 ft.,
with an irregularly rounded head. If a
male tree is nearby, female specimens bear large, irregular, rough,
orangelike fruits. Chiefly used for
windbreaks and hedges, especially in
the Midwest. Ordinary soil.

MAGNOLIA
Trees with conspicuous flowers, for
fertile, reasonably moist soils. Somewhat difficult to transplant, they
should be moved in spring with a ball
of soil. For kinds not listed here, see
pages 406 and 432.

Magnolia acuminata (cucumber
tree), 90 ft., pyramidal. Leaves
large; flowers greenish-yellow in early
summer.

M. denudata (yulan), 50 ft., round-
headed; flowers large, white, fragrant,
blooming in spring before leaves.

M. kobus borealis, 60 ft., round-
headed, fast-growing; flowers white,
in spring before leaves.

M. loebneri, 45 ft., pyramidal, fast-
growing; blooms when small; flowers
white, in spring before leaves.

M. l. Dr. Merrill, a superior horticultural variety.

M. macrophylla (large-leaved cucumber tree), 50 ft., round-headed;
leaves large, up to 3 ft. long. Flowers creamy white, fragrant, early
summer after foliage is fully developed. Needs location sheltered from
winds, which tear the leaves.

M. obovata, 90 ft., pyramidal;
flowers white, fragrant, late spring
after leaves develop.

MAIDENHAIR TREE. See *Ginkgo biloba*.

MAPLE. See *Acer*.

MELIA AZEDARACH
(CHINABERRY, CHINA TREE, PRIDE OF
INDIA, INDIAN LILAC)
A round-headed, rapid-growing,
spreading tree, up to 50 ft.; gives
heavy shade; for mild climates.
Flowers in panicles, purple or lilac,
fragrant, in spring, followed by yellow berries. Thrives in dryish soil.
The variety *umbraculiformis* (Texas
umbrella tree) has radiating branches
that form an umbrellalike head.

METASEQUOIA GLYPTOSTROBOIDES
(DAWN REDWOOD)
A deciduous conifer known only as a

Liriodendron tulipifera
(Tulip Tree)

fossil until 1945, when living specimens were discovered in China; specimens there exceed 90 ft. Narrow-pyramidal, fast-growing; thrives in ordinary soils.

MORUS ALBA (MULBERRY)

Morus alba Kingston, 30 ft., round-headed, fast-growing. Grows easily in ordinary soil; stands city conditions. Does not bear fruit (which in other varieties stains paving, clothing, etc., on which it falls).

M. a. tatarica (Russian mulberry), 30 ft., round-headed. Considered the hardiest variety but, like other mulberries, this kind is not especially ornamental.

MULBERRY. See *Morus alba*.

NYSSA SYLVATICA

(PEPPERIDGE, SOUR GUM, BLACK GUM)
Pyramidal, 90 ft.; leaves lustrous, leathery, turning brilliant orange and red in fall. A splendid ornamental, difficult to transplant except when small. May be grown in moist—even wet—soils.

OAK. See *Quercus*.

OSAGE ORANGE. See *Maclura pomifera*.

OSTRYA VIRGINIANA

(HOP HORNBEAM, IRONWOOD)
An attractive pyramidal tree, to 60 ft.; slow-growing. Bears clusters of bladderlike, light green fruits in summer. Rather difficult to transplant. For ordinary soils.

OXYDENDRUM ARBOREUM

(SOURWOOD, SORREL TREE)
A choice pyramidal tree attaining a maximum height of 70 ft., but usually lower, especially in the North; flowers small, bell-shaped, in drooping racemes like lily of the valley; summer. Leaves lustrous, leathery,

becoming brilliant red in fall. For reasonably moist acid soils.

PAPER MULBERRY. See *Broussonetia papyrifera*.

PARROTIA PERSICA

Usually with several trunks, this widespreading, round-headed tree attains an ultimate height of 50 ft. and is an effective ornamental. Free of pests and diseases. Foliage assumes bright yellow and red hues in fall. For ordinary soils.

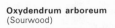

Oxydendrum arboreum
(Sourwood)

PAULOWNIA TOMENTOSA
(EMPRESS TREE)
A fast grower, up to 45 ft., round-headed, with large, heart-shaped leaves resembling those of *Catalpa*, and great panicles of funnel-shaped, fragrant lavender flowers in spring. Hardy into New England, but even in New York City the flower buds are often winter-killed so that there is no bloom the following spring. Ordinary, well-drained soil.

PECAN. See *Carya pecan*.

Platanus acerifolia
(London Plane)

PEPPERIDGE. See *Nyssa sylvatica*.

PHELLODENDRON AMURENSE
(CORK TREE)
A round-headed picturesque tree with deeply fissured corklike bark and stout branches. Foliage dark green. Greenish flowers in panicles are not conspicuous; but those of female trees, if a male is nearby, are followed by black berries, which are a little messy when they fall. For ordinary soil. Very hardy.

PIGNUT. See *Carya glabra*.

PISTACIA (PISTACHE)
Broadly round-headed, up to 50 ft. Foliage red and orange in fall; fruit borne by female trees if male is nearby, in clusters, red changing to purple. Slow-growing; withstands drought and heat; free of pests and diseases. For ordinary soils but very mild climates only.

PLANE TREE. See *Platanus*.

PLATANUS (PLANE TREE, SYCAMORE)
Large trees with bark that flakes off in patches. For ordinary soils, preferably those not excessively dry. The native sycamore, *Platanus occidentalis*, is not recommended because of its great susceptibility to twig blight (anthracnose).
 Platanus acerifolia (London plane), 100 ft., round-headed; branches massive, wide-spreading. Stands severe pruning well, also city conditions.
 P. orientalis (Oriental plane), 100 ft., less hardy and vigorous than *P. acerifolia*. Forms of *P. acerifolia* are often sold and grown as *P. orientalis*.
 P. racemosa, 100 ft., irregularly round-headed, usually with several trunks; picturesque. For mild climates only, such as California.

POPLAR. See *Populus*.

POPULUS
(POPLAR, COTTONWOOD, ASPEN)

Fast-growing trees of limited value because of their vigorous rooting systems, which are likely to invade and clog drains and lift paving. Their brittle, weak wood is subject to storm damage, and some kinds are much subject to disease. Useful in areas where few better trees can be grown. For ordinary soils.

Populus alba (white poplar, abele), 90 ft., irregularly round-headed; branches wide-spreading.

P.a. pyramidalis (syn. *P.a. bolleana*), narrow-pyramidal variety. Not as slender, but a good substitute for the Lombardy poplar; resistant to canker disease.

P. berolinensis, 70 ft., columnar or narrow-pyramidal. Useful in areas of severe winter cold and summer heat.

P. deltoides (cottonwood), irregularly round-headed; branches wide-spreading. Withstands hot, dry summers and cold winters.

P. fremontii, 90 ft., irregularly round-headed; branches wide-spreading. For dry, alkaline soils in mild climates.

P. lasiocarpa, 60 ft., irregularly round-headed; large leaves. One of the most handsome.

P. luteus, similar to *P. opulifolius*, but foliage is yellow through most of the spring and summer.

P. nigra italica (Lombardy poplar), 90 ft., narrow-columnar, very distinct. Should be planted only as a temporary tree because as it ages (at 20 years or so) it becomes very subject to canker disease, which kills its top, and for which there is no prevention or cure.

P. opulifolius, 9 ft., a rather coarse shrub best suited for unimportant locations.

P. sargentii (Great Plains cottonwood), 60 ft., round-headed, similar to *P. deltoides* but smaller.

P. tremuloides (quaking aspen), 90 ft., round-topped; foliage turns yellow in fall. Extremely hardy; best suited for planting in groups.

PRIDE OF INDIA. See *Melia azedarach*.

QUERCUS (OAK)

Mostly large trees of splendid qualities and long-lived, usually thriving best in fertile, reasonably moist soils. They are not free of pests and diseases. For evergreen kinds, see page 408.

Quercus alba (white oak), 100 ft. round-headed, wide-branched. Foliage in fall purplish-red to purple. One of the most majestic of trees; rather difficult to transplant.

Q. bicolor (swamp white oak), 60 ft., similar to *Q. alba* but with narrower head. Fall foliage brown to red. Suitable for moist soils.

Q. borealis (red oak), 70 ft., round-headed; fall foliage red. Grows rapidly and transplants easily; withstands city conditions well.

Q. cerris (Turkey oak), 100 ft., broad-pyramidal, a splendid ornamental. Foliage remains green in fall later than that of any other deciduous tree.

Q. coccinea (scarlet oak), 80 ft., round-headed; fall foliage brilliant scarlet. Difficult to transplant.

Q. falcata (Spanish red oak), 80 ft., round-headed; fall foliage orange-brown.

Q. garryana (Oregon oak), 100 ft., round-headed. Thrives on dryish soils. Suitable for Pacific Northwest.

Q. imbricaria (shingle oak), 60 ft., irregularly round-topped; fall foliage yellow-brown. Excellent for windbreaks and screens; may also be sheared to form hedges.

Q. macrocarpa (burr oak, mossy cup oak), 75 ft., broadly round-topped; leaves large.

Q. montana (chestnut oak), 90 ft., round-headed; foliage in fall dull orange-yellow. Grows well in dry soils.

Q. nigra (water oak), 80 ft., round-topped or pyramidal. A good tree for fairly mild climates.

Q. palustris (pin oak), 75 ft., pyramidal; lower branches drooping; foliage brilliant red in fall. One of the best oaks. Will not tolerate alkaline soils.

Q. phellos (willow oak), 60 ft., pyramidal or round-headed; leaves willowlike, becoming yellow in fall. A good ornamental; easy to transplant.

Q. robur (English oak), 90 ft., irregularly rounded; sturdy branching.

Q. r. atropurpurea (purple oak), leaves purple.

Q. r. Concordia (golden oak), young foliage yellow.

Q. r. fastigiata, narrow-columnar shape.

Q. r. pendula, branches pendulous.

Q. r. variegata, leaf margins white.

ROBINIA (LOCUST)
Light-foliaged trees that bear drooping racemes of pealike flowers in late spring. They are subject to borers and leaf miners. For ordinary soils.

Robinia pseudoacacia (false acacia, black acacia, yellow locust), 80 ft., oval or pyramidal; thorny; flowers white, fragrant.

R. p. decaiseana, flowers light pink.

R. p. inermis, without thorns.

R. p. umbraculifera (globe locust), compact, dense, globular head; usually grafted on tall stems of *R. pseudoacacia*.

R. viscosa (clammy locust), 40 ft., flowers pink.

SALIX (WILLOW)
A variable group adapted chiefly for moist soils. Wood is weak and subject to storm damage; roots are apt to clog drains. Susceptible to several serious diseases and pests. The weeping willows are useful waterside trees.

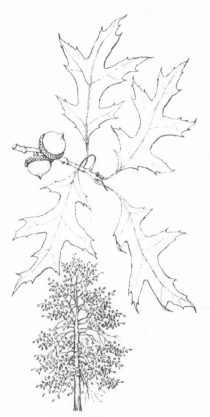

Quercus palustris (Pin Oak) The narrow leaves cast light shade; a popular lawn tree.

For the pussy willow, see page 442 in "Shrubs and Flowering Small Trees."

Salix alba chermesina (red-stem willow), branchlets bright red. 60 ft., pendulous or weeping, stems yellow.

S. babylonica, 30 ft., pendulous branches. Best weeping willow, not reliably hardy north of New York City.

S. blanda (Wisconsin weeping willow), 40 ft.; sometimes called Niobe willow, this has pendulous branches only about half as long as those of *S. elegantissima*.

S. elegantissima (Thurlow weeping willow), 40 ft.; pendulous branches

shorter than those of *S. babylonica.*
Much hardier than *S. babylonica.*

S. matsudana tortuosa, 35 ft.,
branches curiously spiraled.

SAMBUCUS (ELDER)

For other elders, see page 442.

Sambucus caerulea (blue elder), 50
ft., round-headed; flowers creamy
white in flat clusters, followed by
blue-black berries covered with whitish film. Wood weak and subject to
storm damage. For Pacific Coast.

SASSAFRAS ALBIDUM (SASSAFRAS)

A rather narrow, sparsely branched
tree up to 60 ft.; irregularly mitten-
shaped leaves turn brilliant orange
and scarlet in fall; fruits are small
bluish-black berries on red stalks.
Tolerates poor, gravelly soils. Difficult to transplant.

SOPHORA JAPONICA (JAPANESE PA-GODA TREE, CHINESE SCHOLAR TREE)

A broad, round-headed tree up to 75
ft., bearing panicles of creamy-white
pealike flowers in late summer, followed by slender pods. For ordinary
well-drained soils; stands city conditions well. The variety *pendula* has
pendulous branches. This weeping
kind rarely blooms.

SORREL TREE. See *Oxydendrum ar-boreum.*

SOUR GUM. See *Nyssa sylvatica.*

SOURWOOD. See *Oxydendrum arbo-reum.*

SUGARBERRY. See *Celtis laevigata.*

SWEET GUM. See *Liquidambar styra-ciflua.*

SYCAMORE. See *Platanus.*

TAMARACK. See *Larix laricina.*

TILIA (LINDEN, BASSWOOD)

Good shade trees which in summer
bear fragrant but not showy flowers.
For ordinary soils that are never too
dry. They may become infested with
aphids and other leaf insects, controlled by spraying with malathion.

Tilia americana (American linden,
basswood), 120 ft., round-headed,
less refined in appearance than
others listed here. Very hardy.

T. cordata (small-leaved linden), 80
ft., pyramidal; densely branched;
blooms midsummer; slow-growing.

Tilia cordata
(Small-Leaved Linden)

Tolerant of city conditions; very hardy.

T. euchlora (Crimean linden), broadly pyramidal; branches somewhat drooping; foliage lustrous bright green. A fine kind.

T. europaea, 100 ft., round-headed. A good city tree but susceptible to infestations of aphids. Remove suckers sprouting from burls on trunk.

T. petiolaris (weeping white linden), 80 ft., narrow-pyramidal; branches drooping; leaves white on undersides, very lively in a slight breeze.

Zelkova serrata
This disease-resistant relative of the elm shares that tree's graceful shape.

T. platyphyllos, 100 ft., rounded or broadly pyramidal; one of the largest-leaved kinds.

T. tomentosa (white or silver linden), 100 ft.; the leaves are white on the undersides.

TREE OF HEAVEN. See *Ailanthus altissima*.

TULIP TREE. See *Liriodendron tulipifera*.

TURKISH HAZELNUT. See *Corylus colurna*.

ULMUS (ELM)
Handsome shade trees now seriously threatened in many areas (which extend each year) by the deadly Dutch elm and phloem necrosis diseases. Very serious consideration should be given before planting them. One variety (Christine Buisman) of the smooth-leaved elm, *Ulmus carpinifolia*, appears to be resistant to these two diseases. Healthy elms deserve the best possible care in spraying, fertilizing and other operations. See *Zelkova serrata* as elm substitute.

WALNUT. See *Juglans*.

WILLOW. See *Salix*.

YELLOWWOOD. See *Cladrastis lutea*.

YULAN. See *Magnolia denudata*.

ZELKOVA SERRATA
An elmlike tree with small leaves that is related to the elms (*Ulmus*). Resistant to Dutch elm disease and phloem necrosis and a fairly good substitute shade tree for the elms. Attaining a maximum height of 90 ft., this is a round-topped, more or less vase-shaped tree with wide-spreading branches. It grows fast. In fall its foliage is yellow to reddish-brown.

CHAPTER 19

EVERGREEN TREES—
All-Year Greenery

Conifers of the North—Evergreens of the South—Selecting Trees and Site—Listing of Palms, Conifers and Broad-Leaved Evergreen Trees

EVERGREEN TREES serve as screens and backgrounds and as conspicuous elements that define landscape patterns during the months when deciduous kinds are without foliage. At all times they provide qualities that leaf-losing trees do not have, or do not have in the same degree. As a group they are noble in appearance. They bring to the garden a feeling of permanence and solidity, a richness of colors and textures that nothing else can.

They are perfect foils and contrasts for the deciduous plants; each complements the other. A garden without evergreens is almost unthinkable; but one of evergreens alone is likely to be oppressive, overpowering, perhaps a little gloomy. So consider evergreens, and especially evergreen trees, objectively. Introduce them to your garden after weighing the need for them and their possibilities. Study the garden carefully, in summer as well as winter, before planting.

WINTER-HARDY CONIFERS

Leaves are the chief organs through which plants lose moisture to the atmosphere, moisture which must be replaced by the roots if the plant is to continue to live. And roots have great difficulty doing this when the ground is cold or frozen. So evergreens north of New England have a tough time in winter. Only those with special adaptations to conserve moisture can, for the most part, survive. In cold climates—such as many parts of the northern U.S. and of Canada—the winter-hardy evergreen trees are those with needlelike leathery leaves that afford little surface to the drying effects of sun and wind, and have that surface covered with a nearly waterproof skin or waxy coating. These hardiest evergreen trees are all members of the great group botanists call conifers—which includes the firs, spruces, pines, junipers and many other familiar types.

TREES OF WARMER CLIMATES

As one goes southward, the number of evergreen trees that can be grown increases. In the East, by the time southern New England is reached, a few—pathetically few—broad-leaved evergreens may survive in favored locations, notably the American holly (*Ilex opaca*). At New York and Philadelphia the representation is larger, and at Washington, D.C., more varied still.

But to see the broad-leaved evergreen trees in greatest variety one must go to the Deep South, to California, or to some other area where frost is seldom or never experienced. In those climates, too, some conifers prosper, but it is the broad-leaved kinds that astonish us with their bold foliage and often magnificent flowers. Consider the glories of the Southern

Identification of Conifer Needles (Leaves)

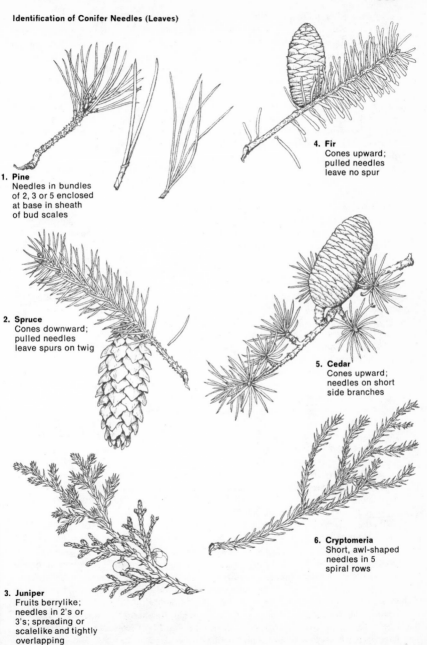

1. Pine
Needles in bundles
of 2, 3 or 5 enclosed
at base in sheath
of bud scales

2. Spruce
Cones downward;
pulled needles
leave spurs on twig

3. Juniper
Fruits berrylike;
needles in 2's or
3's; spreading or
scalelike and tightly
overlapping

4. Fir
Cones upward;
pulled needles
leave no spur

5. Cedar
Cones upward;
needles on short
side branches

6. Cryptomeria
Short, awl-shaped
needles in 5
spiral rows

magnolia (*Magnolia grandiflora*), the African tulip tree (*Spathodea campanulata*), the Moreton Bay chestnut (*Castanospermum australe*) and of a full-grown *Camellia japonica.* Nor must we overlook the magnificence of kinds not primarily grown for their flowers—the evergreen oaks and the eucalyptuses, for example. In the almost frost-free sections of the United States, too, are grown many examples of that special and distinctive group of evergreens, the palms.

SELECTING TREES AND SITE

Provided a little care is taken in selecting kinds suitable for the region, evergreen trees are not at all difficult. They should always be transplanted with good balls of earth about their roots and be kept well watered during dry periods, at least until they become well established. Many are surface rooters, and these especially should be kept mulched. None needs regular, systematic pruning except when sheared as a hedge or for some other formal purpose.

Because of the increasing scarcity of kinds of broad-leaved evergreen trees that prosper as one goes north, there is an ever-present and very understandable desire on the part of many gardeners to attempt to grow kinds to the very limits of their hardiness. If care is given to selecting locations sheltered from sweeping winds and perhaps strong winter sun, and if provision is made for good soil drainage, much can be accomplished. The soil near the foundation of a heated building may be warmer than that at a distance, and the building itself may provide protection from wind. Locations near the sea or other large bodies of water are likely to enjoy milder winters than those without such climate-modifying influences. By finding favored locations some gardeners have success with camellias even north of

New York City; it is in a favored location in an outdoor conservatory courtyard that the Southern magnolia or bull bay (*Magnolia grandiflora*) flourishes and blooms freely each year at the New York Botanical Garden.

Distinctions made between trees and shrubs are of necessity somewhat arbitrary. Kinds that under the most favorable conditions attain the dimensions of trees may be of shrub size in drier or colder regions or if faced with other unfavorable environmental factors. Those which are usually shrubs or shrublike sometimes become small trees under favorable conditions. So consider this chapter together with "Evergreen Shrubs," page 449. The heights given with the various kinds generally are maximums under ideal conditions (usually in native habitats). Most of the tall kinds are considerably shorter in cultivation.

PALMS

Palms are among the most distinctive and ornamental plants of the tropics and subtropics. Some are low and shrubby but many attain tree size, some very tall. Almost all are unbranched. Some have a solitary trunk, others several trunks. The foliage may be fan-leaved (with the blade of the leaf hand-shaped) or feather-leaved (divided in the manner of a feather), according to kind. Although the flowers are not especially interesting individually, they are in many cases produced in immense trusses that have some ornamental value, and are often followed by colorful fruit.

Palms suitable for the Southwest are listed, beginning on page 632, in "The Southwest." These, and many others, can be grown in Florida in favored locations. Noteworthy among additional palms for Florida are:

Cocos nucifera (coconut), 100 ft., graceful feather palm, trunk leaning; excellent by the sea. The fruits are the well-known, versatile coconuts.

Paurotis wrightii (everglade palm), 30 ft., fan-leaved, multiple-trunked; withstands poor drainage and sea spray.

Roystonea (royal palm), 60 ft., feather palm with erect, vertical trunk. The commonest is the Cuban royal palm, *R. regia.* Others are the Florida royal palm, *R. elata*, the Carib royal palm, *R. oleracea*, and the Puerto Rican royal palm, *R. borinquena.* All are stately avenue trees; all grow rapidly.

Sabal palmetto (cabbage palm), 80 ft., fan-leaved; the hardiest of the native palms.

CONIFERS

ABIES (FIR)

Tall, pyramidal, horizontal-branching trees of great beauty when young, but in cultivation often somewhat bedraggled-looking when 20 years old or more. Best adapted for areas of cool summers; they abhor city conditions.

Abies amabilis (Cascade fir), 150 ft., handsome, foliage dark green, lustrous. Recommended for Pacific Coast only.

A. cephalonica (Greek fir), 90 ft., foliage light green, dense. Hardy in southern New England.

A. concolor (white fir), 120 ft., stands dryness and high temperatures better than other firs. Hardy in southern New England.

A. grandis (giant fir), 300 ft., handsome. Recommended for Pacific Coast and Rocky Mountain regions only.

A. homolepis (Nikko fir), 90 ft., foliage dark green. One of the best. Hardy in the northern states.

A. lasiocarpa (alpine fir), 90 ft. Recommended for Rocky Mountain and Pacific Coast areas only.

A. pinsapo (Spanish fir), 70 ft., hardy about as far north as New York City.

A. veitchii, 75 ft., leaves dark green above, white on undersides. Hardy into Canada.

ARAUCARIA

Tall trees of very distinctive appearance; branches in widely spaced regular tiers.

Araucaria araucana (monkey puzzle). Flat, stiff, sharp-pointed leaves clothing sinuous stems provide a formidable obstacle to tree climbers. Of grotesque appearance; best suited for mild climates, hardy about as far north as Washington, D.C.

Araucaria araucana
(Monkey Puzzle)

A. bidwillii (bunya-bunya), very
handsome; foliage deep green. For
warmer sections of Florida and
California.

ARBORVITAE. See *Thuja.*

ATLAS CEDAR. See *Cedrus atlantica.*

BUNYA-BUNYA. See *Araucaria bidwillii.*

CALIFORNIA BIG TREE. See *Sequoiadendron giganteum.*

CALIFORNIA NUTMEG. See *Torreya
californica.*

CALLITRIS ROBUSTA (CYPRESS PINE)
Pyramidal, 90 ft., with jointed stems
and scalelike leaves. Grows rapidly
when young; useful as a windbreak.
For ordinary soils in warmer parts of
Florida and California.

CEDAR OF LEBANON. See *Cedrus libani.*

CEDRUS (CEDAR)
The true cedars (several other plants
are commonly called by this name)
are handsome and shapely; they need
fertile, well-drained soil.
Cedrus atlantica (Atlas cedar), 120
ft., wide-pyramidal, striking in appearance. Hardy as far north as
Washington, D.C.
C.a. glauca (blue Atlas cedar), foliage decidedly bluish. Hardy, in fairly
sheltered places, at New York City.
C. deodara (deodar cedar), 150 ft.,
pyramidal, rich green, branches pendulous. Hardy as far north as southern Virginia. Popular in California.
C. libani (cedar of Lebanon), 120
ft., pyramidal, narrow when young,
broad at maturity; green. This is the
classical cedar of Lebanon of the Bible.
A hardy strain; prospers as far north
as southern New England.

CHAMAECYPARIS (FALSE CYPRESS)
Numerous varieties of a few species
are grown and listed in nurserymen's
catalogues. These vary greatly in
height. Only a few are listed here;
for shrubby kinds see page 450 in
"Evergreen Shrubs." Some can be
grown throughout North America,
except in the hot, dry plains and deserts. They thrive in ordinary, well-
drained, nonalkaline soils—especially
well near the sea. Easy to transplant;
not too subject to insects or diseases.
Chamaecyparis lawsoniana, 120 ft.,
pyramidal. This and its varieties are
suited for the Pacific Northwest and
other regions of mild climate and
humid atmosphere only.
C.l. allumii, columnar, foliage steel-
blue.
C.l. argentea, foliage silvery-white.
C.l. glauca, foliage steel-blue.
C. nootkatensis (Nootka false cypress), 120 ft., narrow-pyramidal,
dark green. Suited for Pacific Northwest only.
C. obtusa (Hinoki false cypress), 120
ft., broad-pyramidal, slow-growing,
hardy far north. There are numerous
varieties, some dwarf and shrublike.
C.o. erecta, columnar, with erect
branches.
C.o. gracilis, pyramidal, compact;
branches slender, pendulous.
C. pisifera (sawara false cypress),
150 ft., narrow-pyramidal. This and
its varieties are most adaptable for
northern gardens and will grow in regions away from the coast.
C.p. filifera, branches slender,
threadlike.
C.p. plumosa, dense, conical;
branches feathery.
C.p. squarrosa, small tree or dense
shrub; foliage feathery, not in flat
fronds.
C. thyoides (white cedar), 75 ft.,
least attractive of the false cypresses.
Thrives in wet soil. Hardy in northern
New England.

CHINA FIR. See *Cunninghamia lanceolata.*

CRYPTOMERIA JAPONICA
Pyramidal, 150 ft., thrives best in humid regions not far from the sea and in climates as mild as that of Washington, D.C., or milder; although in sheltered places it may be grown as far north as southern New England. In the North its foliage turns bronze in winter. *C.j. lobbii*, which does not differ in appearance, is said to be slightly hardier.

CUNNINGHAMIA LANCEOLATA
(CHINA FIR)
Resembling *Araucaria* in appearance, this handsome, spreading tree, 75 ft., is generally adapted for California and the lower South; although in sheltered places it may be grown as far north as Washington, D.C. Soil ordinary.

CUPRESSUS (CYPRESS)
Mostly suited for the South and for California.
Cupressus arizonica, 45 ft., pyramidal, foliage bluish-green; rather difficult to transplant. Especially suited for the Southwest. One of the hardiest.
C.a. bonita, very blue when young.
C. macnabiana, 20 ft., pyramidal, often with several trunks. The hardiest true cypress, hardy in southern New England.
C. macrocarpa (Monterey cypress), 50 ft., pyramidal or rounded, foliage bright green. Excellent for shearing as a hedge and for seaside planting. It is hardy about as far north as Washington, D.C.
C. sempervirens (Italian cypress), 80 ft., pyramidal, dark green. Hardy about as far north as Washington, D.C.
C.s. stricta, extremely narrow and erect. One of the finest columnar evergreens.

CYPRESS. See *Cupressus.*

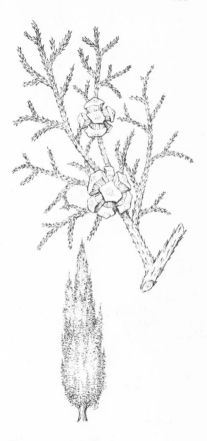

Cupressus sempervirens
(Italian Cypress)

CYPRESS PINE. See *Callitris robusta.*

DEODAR CEDAR. See *Cedrus deodara.*

DOUGLAS FIR. See *Pseudotsuga taxifolia.*

FALSE ARBORVITAE. See *Thujopsis dolobrata.*

FALSE CYPRESS. See *Chamaecyparis.*

FIR. See *Abies.*

394

GIANT SEQUOIA. See *Sequoiadendron giganteum*.

HEMLOCK. See *Tsuga*.

HIBA ARBORVITAE. See *Thujopsis dolobrata*.

INCENSE CEDAR. See *Libocedrus decurrens*.

JUNIPERUS (JUNIPER)
A large group best suited for porous, reasonably moist, alkaline rather than acid soils, although most grow fairly well in slightly acid earth. Some kinds serve as alternate hosts to cedar-apple rust disease, which also affects apples, crab apples, hawthorns, Juneberries and related plants; also subject to infestations of red spider mites. For shrubby kinds see page 451 in "Evergreen Shrubs."

Juniperus chinensis (Chinese juniper), 60 ft., pyramidal, variable in height, shape and color. Hardy in New England.

J.c. columnaris, narrow-pyramidal, silvery-green.

J.c. keteleeri, broadly pyramidal, dark green.

J.c. pyramidalis, narrow-pyramidal, blue-green.

J. drupacea (Syrian juniper), 50 ft., columnar, green. Hardy in mild climates only.

J. excelsa (Greek juniper), 60 ft., narrow-pyramidal, bluish-green. Not hardy in the North.

J.e. stricta, columnar, foliage blue; hardier than *J. excelsa*, but not hardy in the North. *J. chinensis pyramidalis* is often grown under this name.

J. monosperma (cherrystone juniper), 50 ft., grayish-green. Good for lower South.

J. rigida (needle juniper), 30 ft., graceful, green; branches pendulous.

J. scopulorum (Colorado red cedar), 30 ft., narrow-pyramidal, green or

Juniperus chinensis
(Chinese Juniper)

bluish; especially suitable for Rocky Mountain region, the Great Plains and the Southwest. Seedlings vary considerably in color. A number have been given varietal names such as Blue Haven, Chandler's Silver, Greenspire, Pathfinder, Silver Glow, Staver and Sutherland. For descriptions of these consult nurserymen's catalogues.

J. utahensis, 20 ft., yellowish-green. Suitable for Rocky Mountain and West Coast regions.

J. virginiana (red cedar), 80 ft., broadly pyramidal to columnar, green, olive-green or bluish. Will grow in

Picea abies
(Norway Spruce)

poor gravelly soils; extremely hardy. Many varieties of this variable kind have been named; some of the best of these are:

J.v. burkii, compact, narrow-pyramidal; foliage blue.

J.v. canaertii, pyramidal, dark green.

J.v. glauca, pyramidal, compact, silvery-blue.

J.v. pyramidiformis, pyramidal, green in summer changing to purple in winter.

J.v. schottii, narrow-pyramidal, bright green.

KETELEERIA FORTUNEI

Closely related to *Abies* (fir); 100 ft., pyramidal, becoming flat-topped with age. Ordinary soils. For lower South and similar climates only.

LIBOCEDRUS DECURRENS
(INCENSE CEDAR)

Handsome, 100 ft., columnar or narrow-pyramidal. For fertile, moderately moist soils. Resistant to pests and diseases. Hardy in sheltered places in southern New England.

MONKEY PUZZLE. See *Araucaria araucana.*

PICEA (SPRUCE)

Pyramidal, handsome trees for ordinary, well-drained, moderately moist soils. (For dwarf, shrublike kinds see page 451 in "Evergreen Shrubs.") Best suited for regions of cold winters and fairly humid atmospheric conditions; they are not resistant to extremes of heat and drought. Although best in sun, they tolerate more shade than most conifers.

Picea abies (Norway spruce), 150 ft., graceful, pyramidal, dark green; branchlets pendulous. Very apt to become rather decrepit, to lose its top or become thin at the top after the age of 30 years; makes good windbreaks and hedges; extremely hardy. Of tall varieties the following are especially noteworthy:

P.a. columnaris, narrow-columnar.

P.a. nigra, pyramidal, dense, very dark green.

P.a. pyramidata, a slender-pyramidal kind.

P. asperata (dragon spruce), 75 ft., dense, light green or bluish. The best spruce for seaside planting. Hardy in southern New England.

P. engelmannii, 150 ft., dense, bluish-green; tends to lose its lower branches as it ages. Very hardy.

P. glauca (white spruce), 75 ft.,

bluish-green. Is extremely hardy.

P.g. densata (Black Hills spruce), 40 ft., green or blue, dense and slow-growing. Extremely hardy.

P. omorika (Siberian spruce), 90 ft., narrow-pyramidal or columnar, dense; green with white undersurfaces to leaves. One of the finest spruces. Hardy in northern New England.

P. orientalis (Oriental spruce), 150 ft., dense, glossy, dark green; slow-growing. More subject to infestations of spruce budworm than many spruces.

P. polita (tigertail spruce), 90 ft., leaves stiff and prickly, green. Hardy in southern New England.

P. pungens (Colorado spruce), 100 ft., green to bluish, dense; attractive when young but likely to lose lower branches after 20 years or so; subject to infestations of spruce-gall aphid. Very hardy.

P.p. argentea, silvery-blue, often misnamed Koster's blue spruce. One of the finest color forms.

P.p. glauca, bluish-green.

P.p. kosteriana (Koster's blue spruce), silvery-blue; main trunk more or less prostrate; branches pendulous.

P.p. moerheimii, dense, compact, blue.

PINUS (PINE)

A large group containing many excellent and handsome kinds that will grow in a wide variety of soils; most need good drainage and, given this, prosper even in earth of low fertility; a very few grow in wet soils. Symmetrical when young, most pines assume highly picturesque forms with age.

Pinus aristata (bristlecone pine, hickory pine), 40 ft., often shrubby; freely branched. Hardy in southern New England but slow-growing; especially suitable for the Southwest.

P. banksiana (jack pine), 70 ft., useful only for poor, sandy soils where little else will grow. Extremely hardy.

P. bungeana (lacebark pine), 70 ft.,

round-pyramidal, often with more than one trunk; foliage light green; bark flaking off and showing beautifully colored decorative patterns. Slow-growing. Hardy in northern New England.

P. canariensis, 80 ft., handsome, bright green, rapid grower. For dry, rocky places in California and the deep South only.

P. cembra (Swiss stone pine), 70 ft., very dense and symmetrical when young; slow-growing. Extremely hardy.

P. cembroides edulis (nut pine), 25 ft., horizontally branched. Useful in Rocky Mountain area.

P. contorta (shore pine), 30 ft., dark green. For Pacific Northwest.

P.c. lactifolia (lodgepole pine), 80 ft., light green. Especially useful in Rocky Mountain region.

P. densiflora (Japanese red pine), 100 ft., broad, irregular head; bluish-green, becoming paler in winter.

P.d. umbraculifera (Japanese umbrella pine), 30 ft., low-growing with a broad, umbrella-shaped head.

P. flexilis (limber pine), 150 ft., dark green, very slow-growing. Useful in Rocky Mountain region; extremely hardy.

P. koraiensis (Korean pine), 90 ft., dark green, slow-growing.

P. monticola (Western white pine), 100 ft., narrow-pyramidal, bluish-green. For West Coast and Rocky Mountain regions.

P. nepalensis (syn. *P. excelsa*— Himalayan white pine), 150 ft. Wide-spreading, very graceful, blue-green. Hardy in southern New England but sometimes winter-damaged in far North.

P. nigra (Austrian pine), 90 ft., dark green, grows rapidly.

P. palustris (longleaf pine, Southern pine), 100 ft., attractive foliage. Suitable for the South. Hardy as far north as Virginia.

P. parviflora (Japanese white pine), 90 ft., wide-spreading; bluish-green, short leaves. Very decorative. Hardy in southern New England.

P. pinaster (cluster pine), 100 ft., glossy green. Well adapted for seaside planting. Hardy north to Virginia, and to New York City in sheltered places.

P. ponderosa (Western yellow pine), 100 ft., handsome tree; hardy in southern New England.

P.p. scopulorum (Rocky Mountain yellow pine), 75 ft. Hardier than *P. ponderosa*. Excellent for Rocky Mountain region.

P. radiata (Monterey pine), 60 ft., spreading branches, bright green; excellent for seaside planting; grows rapidly. Not hardy in the North.

P. resinosa (red pine), 75 ft., lustrous dark green. Subject to infestations of pine bark moth. Extremely hardy.

P. strobus (white pine) 100 ft., graceful, soft bluish-green foliage; fast-growing; one of the best. Transplants easier than many pines. Very hardy.

P.s. fastigiata, narrow-pyramidal or columnar.

P. sylvestris (Scots pine), 75 ft., bark in older specimens orange, foliage bluish-green. Extremely hardy.

P. thunbergii (Japanese black pine), 90 ft., irregular head, spreading branches. Exceedingly useful for seaside planting. Extremely hardy.

PODOCARPUS
Related to *Taxus* (yew); suitable for mild climates only.

Podocarpus elongata, 70 ft., bright green foliage of fine texture. For the warmest parts of the United States only.

P. macrophylla, 60 ft., dark green; a good hedge plant. Hardy north to North Carolina.

P.m. maki, has smaller leaves than *P. macrophylla* and is usually shrubby.

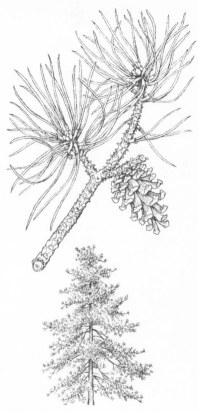

Pinus nigra
(Austrian Pine)

PSEUDOTSUGA TAXIFOLIA
(DOUGLAS FIR)

A splendid, pyramidal, dark green conifer, in its native western America attaining a maximum height of 300 ft., but much lower in cultivation. There are two types, that of the Pacific Coast and that of the Rocky Mountains—the much hardier *P.t. glauca*. This latter is more compact, slower-growing and bluish-green; is hardy in northern New England. Douglas fir thrives in porous soil that is never excessively dry. It may be sheared as a hedge and holds its needles well when cut as a Christmas tree. (See illustration, page 674.)

RED CEDAR. See *Juniperus virginiana*.

REDWOOD. See *Sequoia sempervirens*.

SCIADOPITYS VERTICILLATA (UMBRELLA PINE)

Handsome, narrow-pyramidal, of formal appearance, 100 ft.; leaves arranged on the branches like the ribs of an umbrella, dark, glossy green. For fertile, always reasonably moist soils; slow-growing. Hardy in southern New England.

SEQUOIA SEMPERVIRENS (REDWOOD)

Narrow-pyramidal tree, in its native Pacific Coast region attaining ultimate heights exceeding 350 ft.; the tallest tree in North America. Hardy as far north as Washington, D.C., but best adapted for the Pacific Coast. It grows in ordinary, well-drained, not excessively dry soil.

SEQUOIADENDRON GIGANTEUM (GIANT SEQUOIA, CALIFORNIA BIG TREE)

Narrow-pyramidal tree, somewhat less in ultimate height than *Sequoia sempervirens* (redwood), specimens of which are considered to be the oldest living trees (possibly 3000 to 4000 years) in North America. Somewhat hardier than the redwood, specimens of the giant sequoia have been grown in sheltered places in southern New England for many years; nevertheless the tree is best for the Pacific Coast.

SPRUCE. See *Picea*.

TAXUS (YEW)

These are among the most useful and distinctive of all evergreens. In addition to the tree types discussed here there are many low-growing bush or shrubby varieties (see page 452 in "Evergreen Shrubs"). The sexes of yews are on different trees and to insure that females produce their attractive red berries it is necessary to have a male nearby. They are trees for any ordinary, reasonably moist soil; they tolerate considerable shade, and may be sheared, pruned or even cut back hard with certainty that they will produce vigorous new growth. They are injured by mealybugs and black vine weevils. Deer are fond of the foliage, but, at least under some conditions, the leaves are poisonous to cattle.

Taxus baccata (English yew), 50 ft.,

Taxus cuspidata
(Japanese Yew)

pyramidal, dense, dark green, slow-growing. Less hardy than *T. cuspidata* and *T. media*, this tree may be grown in sheltered spots in southern New England.

T. brevifolia (Western yew), 50 ft., foliage dark yellowish-green. About as hardy as *T. baccata*.

T. cuspidata (Japanese yew), similar to *T. baccata* but hardy in northern New England and a faster grower. Seedlings grow tall and erect (cuttings made from side branches form spreading shrubs) and are usually sold as *T.c. capitata*.

T. media, 40 ft., broad-pyramidal, hybrid between *T. baccata* and *T. cuspidata;* about as hardy as *T. cuspidata* and very ornamental.

THUJA (ARBORVITAE)

Rather stiff trees with frondlike branchlets, slow-growing, intolerant of hot, dry environments and of city conditions; excellent for screens and tall hedges; some kinds assume rather sickly colors in winter. They are subject to infestations of red spider mites. In addition to the tree types described here there are many lower varieties; see page 452 in "Evergreen Shrubs."

Thuja occidentalis (American arborvitae), 60 ft., columnar or narrow-pyramidal; foliage discolors in winter; there are several color varieties which tend to discolor even more than the typical kind. Extremely hardy.

T. orientalis (Oriental arborvitae), 50 ft., pyramidal, bright green; tolerates heat and dryness better than *T. occidentalis*, but prefers environment that is humid and not excessively hot. Hardy as far north as New York City. Named garden varieties are described in nursery catalogues.

T. plicata (giant arborvitae), 200 ft., narrow-pyramidal; foliage rarely discolors in winter. For growing in the East, plants should be raised from seeds collected in the Rocky Moun-

tains instead of in the Pacific Northwest. Hardy in southern New England.

T. standishii (Japanese arborvitae), 40 ft., broad-pyramidal; foliage does not discolor in winter.

THUJOPSIS DOLOBRATA (HIBA ARBORVITAE, FALSE ARBORVITAE)

Similar to *Thuja* (arborvitae); 45 ft., pyramidal, dark green; requires a good, moist soil. Hardy about as far north as New York City.

TORREYA

Closely related to *Taxus* (yew), these trees thrive in ordinary soils.

Torreya californica (California nutmeg), 70 ft., glossy, dark green. Best suited for Pacific Coast.

T. nucifera, 70 ft., glossy dark green. It is hardy in southern New England.

T. taxifolia (stinking cedar), 40 ft., foliage glossy green, malodorous when crushed. Adaptable for the South.

TSUGA (HEMLOCK)

Graceful trees that stand more shade than most conifers, although they grow best in sun. They stand shearing and moderate pruning well and are excellent as hedges. They transplant readily and are subjects for deep, fertile, reasonably moist soils, in locations where they receive protection from sweeping winds. They do not thrive where hot, dry summers prevail, or under city conditions.

Tsuga canadensis (Eastern hemlock; Canada hemlock), 90 ft., pyramidal; one of the finest ornamental evergreen trees. Extremely hardy.

T. caroliniana (Carolina hemlock), 70 ft., pyramidal, branches somewhat pendulous; a magnificent tree. Slightly less hardy than *T. canadensis*. (See illustration, page 400.)

T. diversifolia (Japanese hemlock), 90 ft., pyramidal, often with more than one trunk; slow-growing. Hardy

Tsuga caroliniana
(Carolina Hemlock)

as far north as southern New England.

T. heterophylla (Western hemlock), 200 ft., narrow-pyramidal; best adapted for the Pacific Northwest.

UMBRELLA PINE. See *Sciadopitys verticillata.*

YEW. See *Taxus.*

BROAD-LEAVED EVERGREEN TREES

ACACIA

Attractive yellow-flowering trees that stand very little frost; for the warmer parts of the United States only. Quick-growing but short-lived.

Acacia auriculaeformis, 25 ft., flowers in short spikes.

A. baileyana, 25 ft., foliage finely divided, blue-gray; small flowers in racemes. Best for fertile soils.

A. decurrens dealbata (silver wattle), 50 ft., spreading, handsome; fragrant flowers in "strings" of small rounded clusters in spring. The hardiest kind.

A.d. mollis (black wattle), 50 ft., slender; foliage grayish-green; fragrant flowers in short "strings" of round clusters in summer. Withstands dry conditions.

A. melanoxylon (blackwood acacia), 50 ft., foliage dense, green; flowers cream, in racemes with few heads, in spring.

A. pendula (weeping myall), 25 ft., branchlets drooping; foliage bluegray; flowers not especially showy.

AFRICAN TULIP TREE. See *Spathodea.*

ARBUTUS MENZIESII (MADRONA)
Handsome tree up to 50 ft. or more high; foliage glossy green; flowers small, white, in panicles, followed by bright orange-red fruits. Difficult to transplant except when small. For West Coast only.

AUSTRALIAN PINE. See *Casuarina equisetifolia.*

BANYAN TREE. See *Ficus bengalensis.*

BEEFWOOD. See *Casuarina equisetifolia.*

BLACK OLIVE. See *Bucida buceris.*

BLACK WATTLE. See *Acacia decurrens mollis.*

BLUE GUM. See *Eucalyptus globulus.*

BO TREE. See *Ficus religiosa.*

BRACHYCHITON POPULNEUM
(KURRAJONG)
Sometimes called bottle tree because
of its swollen trunk, 60 ft.; leaves
somewhat like those of a poplar;
flowers small, white; withstands heat
and dryness; useful for windbreaks.
Hardy only in warmer parts of California and similar climates.

BRAZILIAN PEPPERTREE. See *Schinus
terebinthifolius*.

BUCIDA BUCERIS (BLACK OLIVE)
Dense, round-headed, 35 ft., slow-
growing, withstands wind. For southern Florida and similar climates.

BULL BAY. See *Magnolia grandiflora*.

CAJEPUT TREE. See *Melaleuca leucadendron*.

CALIFORNIA BAYBERRY. See *Myrica*.

CALIFORNIA LAUREL. See *Umbellularia californica*.

CALIFORNIA PEPPERTREE. See *Schinus
molle*.

CAMELLIA JAPONICA
Beautiful tree attaining a maximum
height of 40 ft., but usually lower and
often shrublike. Grown for its splendid flowers, which are borne in spring,
and its handsome glossy green foliage.
Hundreds of named horticultural varieties are cultivated, with single,
semidouble and double flowers—
white, pink, red and variegated. Consult catalogues for descriptions.
   Camellias thrive in sandy, slightly
acid soil that contains an abundance
of organic matter and is well drained,
but never excessively dry. They need
a little shade, and will stand a considerable amount of it. They grow especially well in the South and the Pacific Northwest, and are adaptable for

Acacia decurrens dealbata
(Silver Wattle Acacia)

other areas where winter cold is not
too severe. Although camellias are of
chief importance as landscape subjects from Virginia southward, in
sheltered places some varieties persist
outdoors as far north as Long Island
and, on the West Coast, to Seattle.

CAMPHOR TREE. See *Cinnamomum
camphora*.

CAROB. See *Ceratonia siliqua*.

CASIMIROA EDULIS (WHITE SAPOTE)
A useful shade tree, 50 ft., foliage

dark green; fruit as big as oranges, greenish-yellow, edible, delicious. For very mild climates only.

CASTANOPSIS (GIANT CHINQUAPIN)
Closely related to the chestnut, *Castanea*, this pyramidal tree grows up to 100 ft. high; flowers in spikes, creamy-white. Grows well in poor, dry soils. Hardy only in mild climates, such as those of California and Oregon.

CASTANOSPERMUM AUSTRALE
(MORETON BAY CHESTNUT)
Wide-spreading, 60 ft., with conspicuous yellow-orange to reddish flowers in summer. The globular seeds, somewhat larger than ordinary chestnuts, are roasted and eaten in Australia.

CASUARINA EQUISETIFOLIA
(AUSTRALIAN PINE, BEEFWOOD, HORSETAIL TREE)
Graceful, 90 ft., branches slender, pendulous; twigs green, jointed, leafless. Excellent for seaside. May be sheared as a hedge. For warm parts of Florida and California only.

CERATONIA SILIQUA
(CAROB, ST.-JOHN'S-BREAD)
Handsome, 50 ft., with glossy foliage and inconspicuous flowers followed by large beanlike pods containing sweet, edible pulp—supposedly the "locusts and wild honey" which sustained St. John in the wilderness. Suitable for regions where oranges prosper and for dry soils; difficult to transplant. Should always be moved with a ball of soil. The variety Cal.-Poly does not bear fruit.

CHRISTMASBERRY. See *Schinus terebinthifolius*.

CHRYSOPHYLLUM OLIVIFORME
(SATIN-LEAF)
Handsome, 25 ft.; leaves green above,

lustrous copper-colored on undersides. Slow-growing; suited only for frost-free climates such as that of southern Florida.

CIDER GUM. See *Eucalyptus gunnii*.

CINNAMOMUM CAMPHORA
(CAMPHOR TREE)
Dense, round-headed, 45 ft.; foliage lustrous, green above, silvery-blue on undersides; young foliage reddish. Difficult to transplant; use pot specimens for setting out. Thrives in southern California, central and southern Florida and similar climates. Requires well-drained soil. This is the tree from which camphor is extracted commercially.

CRINODENDRON
Trees with attractive bell-shaped flowers. For southern California and similar climates.
   Crinodendron dependens, 30 ft., flowers white.
   C. patagua, 30 ft., flowers red.

DAHOON. See *Ilex cassine*.

DIOSPYROS KAKI
(JAPANESE PERSIMMON, KAKI)
Round-headed, 45 ft.; when grown as a shade tree and not for its fruit, variety selection is unimportant. If the edible fruit is desired, seek the advice of the County Agricultural Agent, the state agricultural experiment station or other government source regarding varieties. Only a few produce fruit without pollination; others need both male and female trees planted in proximity to insure fruiting of the females. Suitable for subtropical California and the deep South only.

ERIOBOTRYA JAPONICA (LOQUAT)
Fragrant-flowered tree, 20 ft.; flowers white, in woolly panicles; leaves large, handsome; fruit orange-yellow,

edible. Needs full sun and deep, fertile soil.

EUCALYPTUS

A large group, particularly suitable for the Southwest and Pacific Coast.
Eucalyptus erythrocorys, 30 ft., flowers in clusters.

E. globulus (blue gum), 250 ft., narrow-pyramidal; foliage very blue on young trees, green on older specimens; grows very rapidly. It is good for windbreaks.

E. gunnii (cider gum), 40 ft., bark whitish; flowers white. One of the hardiest kinds.

E. maculata citriodora (lemon-scented gum), 150 ft., foliage strongly lemon-scented when bruised.

E. torquata, 20 ft., usually with more than one trunk; foliage grayish-green; flowers red, summer.

E. viminalis (manna gum), 200 ft., trunks and branches gray-white; branches pendulous; flowers white. One of the hardiest kinds; thrives in poor soils, grows rapidly.

EUGENIA

Small trees and shrubs which are well suited for Florida, California and similar climates.
Eugenia paniculata, 40 ft., round-headed; flowers white followed by rose-purple fruit useful for jelly making. Young foliage reddish. Will not stand sea spray.

E. uniflora (pitanga, Surinam cherry), 20 ft., foliage glossy; flowers white, fragrant, followed by edible, ribbed, deep red cherrylike fruits. May be sheared to form tall hedges and screens. This is suitable for seaside planting.

FICUS

These evergreen trees are often called figs because they belong in the same genus as the common fig, *Ficus carica*, a deciduous tree which produces the familiar edible fruits; however, they bear but little resemblance to that tree. Many grow to great size eventually. They stand little or no frost and are adapted to the warmest sections of the United States only.

Ficus bengalensis (banyan tree), 80 ft., spreading, round-headed; trunk and branches massive; foliage bold. Roots from branches extend to ground and eventually develop into secondary trunks. For southern Florida. Other species are often miscalled banyan.

F. benjamina, 60 ft., dense, round-headed.

F. elastica (rubber plant), 70 ft.

F. macrophylla (Moreton Bay fig), 70 ft., broader than high.

F. religiosa (peepul; bo tree), 60 ft., round-headed; leaves glossy, long-pointed. This is the tree under which it is believed that Buddha received enlightenment.

F. retusa, 60 ft., dense, round-headed.

FIG. See *Ficus*.

GIANT CHINQUAPIN. See *Castanopsis*.

GLOSSY PRIVET. See *Ligustrum lucidum*.

GORDONIA LASIANTHUS
(LOBLOLLY BAY)
Sometimes 60 ft. high, usually lower and often shrubby; head dense, more or less columnar; foliage attractive; flowers white, fragrant, borne over a long period in summer. Hardy north to Virginia. (See illustration, page 404.)

GREVILLEA ROBUSTA (SILK OAK)
Columnar, up to 150 ft.; with fernlike leaves and clusters of golden yellow flowers in spring. Grows well in poor soils. Withstands drought. (See illustration, page 404.) A much lower-growing species with red flowers, *G. banksii*, is sometimes grown.

Gordonia lasianthus
(Loblolly Bay)

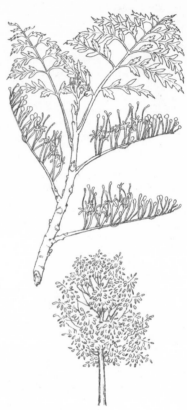

Grevillea robusta
(Silk Oak)

HARPEPHYLLUM CAFFRUM
(KAFIR PLUM)
Attractive, 30 ft., fast-growing; leaves
glossy; fruits as large as olives, dark
red, edible. For southern California
and Florida.

HOLLY. See *Ilex*.

HORSETAIL TREE. See *Casuarina equisetifolia*.

HYMENOSPORUM FLAVUM
(SWEET SHADE)
Pyramidal, fast-growing, coarse-

foliaged, 50 ft.; flowers yellow, fragrant, in profuse panicles, late spring
or early summer. Suitable for southern California and similar warm
climates.

ILEX (HOLLY)
A group of attractive small trees (for
shrubby evergreen kinds see page 462
in "Evergreen Shrubs") which have
female and male flowers on separate
plants. For females to berry, a male
must be nearby. The trees thrive in
ordinary, well-drained, neutral or
slightly acid soils. They stand shearing

and pruning well, and they make excellent hedges.

Ilex aquifolium (English holly), 60 ft., pyramidal, very dense; leaves glossy, usually spiny (there are kinds without leaf spines), in some varieties handsomely variegated with white or cream; berries in dense clusters, red, in some varieties yellow. One of the very finest evergreen trees, hardy in sheltered locations as far north as New York City (variegated-leaved varieties are more tender and thrive best in the Pacific Northwest). Many of the varieties are actually of hybrid origin and should, perhaps, be referred to *I. altaclarensis*. For descriptions of varieties consult catalogues of specialists.

I. cassine (dahoon), 30 ft., round-topped, often shrublike; berries dull red.

I. latifolia, 50 ft., round-topped; leaves large; berries dull red in crowded clusters. Best in light shade. This kind is hardy about as far north as Washington, D.C.

I. opaca (American holly), 50 ft., pyramidal, dense; leaves spiny, dull green; berries bright red (in variety *xanthocarpa*, yellow). A splendid tree. Although not quite as fine as *I. aquifolium*, it is hardier and may be grown in sheltered locations in southern New England. It drops its previous year's foliage at the time new leaves develop; is very subject to infestations of leaf miners. Many excellent varieties have been named; for descriptions of these consult catalogues of specialists.

I. pedunculosa, 25 ft., pyramidal, dense; leaves lustrous, without spines; berries bright red. A handsome kind, hardy as far north as southern New England.

I. pernyi, 25 ft., pyramidal; leaves small, lustrous, few-spined; berries small, red. Hardy in sheltered places as far north as New York City.

Ilex opaca
(American Holly)

I. rotunda, 30 ft., similar to *I. pedunculosa* but has larger leaves; grows rapidly. Hardy as far north as Virginia.

JAPANESE PERSIMMON. See *Diospyros kaki*.

KAFIR PLUM. See *Harpephyllum caffrum*.

KAKI. See *Diospyros kaki*.

KURRAJONG. See *Brachychiton populneum*.

LAGUNARIA PATERSONII

A pyramidal tree up to 50 ft. high, with dark olive-green leaves and hibiscuslike light pink flowers which bloom in late spring. This tree is well adapted for seaside planting in California.

LEMON-SCENTED GUM. See *Eucalyptus maculata citriodora.*

LIGUSTRUM LUCIDUM
(GLOSSY PRIVET)

Handsome, dense, more or less columnar, 30 ft.; leaves glossy; flowers small, white, in panicles; quick-growing and resistant to pests and diseases. The tallest evergreen privet; sometimes confused with the shrubby *L. japonicum.* Hardy as far north as Washington, D.C.

LOBLOLLY BAY. See *Gordonia lasianthus.*

LOQUAT. See *Eriobotrya japonica.*

LYONOTHAMNUS FLORIBUNDUS
(LYON SHRUB)

Attractive, up to 60 ft., often lower and shrubby; flowers small, white, in large clusters. The variety *asplenifolius,* with conspicuously divided leaves, is the kind most often cultivated. For California and similar climates only.

LYON SHRUB. See *Lyonothamnus floribundus.*

MACADAMIA TERNIFOLIA
(QUEENSLAND NUT)

Round-headed, sometimes with more than one trunk, 35 ft.; leaves glossy, spiny at edges; flowers white, in long racemes in spring; nuts edible. Grows slowly; needs deep, fertile soil; withstands dry conditions.

MADRONA. See *Arbutus menziesii.*

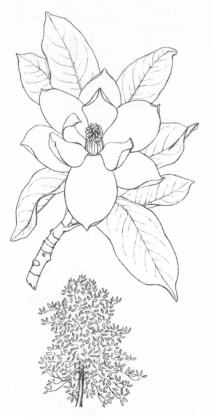

Magnolia grandiflora
(Bull Bay, Southern Magnolia)

MAGNOLIA

Magnolia grandiflora (bull bay, Southern magnolia), 80 ft., pyramidal; leaves large, glossy green, brownish on undersurfaces, very beautiful; flowers very large, white, fragrant, in summer. Stately; thrives best in deep, fertile soil. Several varieties, varying in leaf proportions, flower size and other details have been named. Hardy as far north as Washington, D.C., to Philadelphia in sheltered locations.

MANGIFERA INDICA (MANGO)

A magnificent round-headed shade

tree. Up to 40 ft. high, it has attractive foliage which when young is a lovely reddish-bronze. The finest edible fruits are produced by grafted or budded trees of choice horticultural varieties. For southern Florida and the warmest parts of California.

MANGO. See *Mangifera indica.*

MANNA GUM. See *Eucalyptus viminalis.*

MAYTENUS BOARIA (MAYTEN)
Graceful, 30 ft., branchlets pendulous; foliage light green. A handsome small tree for the Pacific Coast; useful for seaside plantings; hardy as far north as San Francisco.

MELALEUCA LEUCADENDRON
(CAJEPUT TREE, PUNK TREE)
Slender-pyramidal or columnar, 40 ft.; bark thick, spongy, whitish, peeling; foliage light green; flowers in spikes like bottlebrushes, creamy-white. Quick-growing, resistant to sea spray, grass fires, wind and drought. For California and southern and central Florida.

METROSIDEROS TOMENTOSA
(NEW ZEALAND CHRISTMAS TREE)
Broad, round-headed, 70 ft.; leaves glossy, dark green above, whitish on undersides; flowers dark red in dense clusters, in summer; tolerates sea spray. For California and Florida.

MORETON BAY CHESTNUT. See *Castanospermum australe.*

MORETON BAY FIG. See *Ficus macrophylla.*

MYRICA CALIFORNICA
(CALIFORNIA BAYBERRY)
Handsome small tree or shrub, up to 35 ft., leaves glossy dark green or bronze-green; purple berries are borne by female plants if a male is nearby; grows in sandy, more or less sterile soils; not easy to transplant. For the Pacific Coast. *M. cerifera*, which tends to be evergreen in warm climates, is listed on page 434 in "Shrubs and Flowering Small Trees."

NEW ZEALAND CHRISTMAS TREE. See *Metrosideros tomentosa.*

OAK. See *Quercus.*

OLEA EUROPAEA (OLIVE)
Round-headed, slow-growing, up to 25 ft.; foliage dark gray-green, silvery on undersides; flowers small, whitish, in panicles; fruits purple, the edible olive. Needs deep soil, stands dry conditions well. For warm climates only.

OLIVE. See *Olea europaea.*

PEEPUL. See *Ficus religiosa.*

PELTOPHORUM INERME
Adaptable to southern and central Florida, this handsome tree grows up to 40 ft.; has attractive dark green feathery foliage and, in spring and early summer, showy panicles of golden yellow flowers.

PITANGA. See *Eugenia uniflora.*

PITTOSPORUM
For the Southwest, Deep South and other warm climates. May be sheared to form hedges.
   Pittosporum eugenioides (tatara), 40 ft.; pyramidal or columnar; flowers yellowish, fragrant.
   P. phillyraeoides (willow pittosporum), 20 ft.; leaves willowlike on drooping branchlets; flowers yellow; berries yellow.
   P. rhombifolium (Queensland pittosporum), 80 ft.; flowers white; berries bright orange, attractive all winter.

PONGAMIA PINNATA
(POONGA OIL TREE)
Erect, up to 40 ft.; foliage handsome; flowers purplish to white, in loose racemes. For warm climates only.

POONGA OIL TREE. See *Pongamia pinnata*.

PRUNUS CAROLINIANA
(CHERRY LAUREL)
A dense tree, 40 ft., leaves glossy green; flowers cream-colored, small, followed by lustrous black berries. Stands shearing well, is a good hedge plant.

PUNK TREE. See *Melaleuca leucadendron*.

QUEENSLAND NUT. See *Macadamia ternifolia*.

QUERCUS
The evergreen oaks are all very handsome trees of majestic appearance.

  Quercus agrifolia (Coast live oak), 100 ft., round-headed; leaves holly-like, dull green. For California.

  Q. chrysolepis (California live oak, maul oak), 90 ft., spreading; round head; leaves spiny or smooth, bluish-green. Hardy in Oregon. For the Pacific Coast.

  Q. ilex (holly oak, holm oak), 60 ft., round-headed; leaves toothed or smooth, deep green. A hardy seaside tree; stands shearing and forms good hedges. Useful in the Southwest, on the West Coast and in the Deep South.

  Q. laurifolia (laurel oak), 60 ft., partly evergreen; dense, round-topped; leaves shiny, dark green. The variety *darlingtonia* (Darlington oak) is supposed to be more decidedly evergreen and more compact. For the South.

  Q. suber (cork oak), 50 ft., round-headed; bark is the cork of commerce; leaves glossy green. Hardy as far north as Maryland.

  Q. virginiana (live oak), 50 ft., wide-spreading, round-headed, with massive trunk and branches; much broader than high; leaves dark green, glossy. Hardy as far north as Virginia, but often deciduous or partly so near this northern limit.

RUBBER PLANT. See *Ficus elastica*.

ST.-JOHN'S-BREAD. See *Ceratonia siliqua*.

SATIN-LEAF. See *Chrysophyllum oliviforme*.

SCHINUS
Feathery-leaved trees that bear large clusters of bright red berries. They grow well in dry soils and are well suited for warm climates.

  Schinus molle (California peppertree), 40 ft., round-topped, wide-spreading; branchlets pendulous. Very subject to attack by a black scale insect which seriously infests citrus fruits; because of this its planting near citrus orchards is forbidden in some areas.

  S. terebinthifolius (Brazilian peppertree, Christmasberry), 40 ft., round-headed; attractive foliage. Somewhat more tender than *S. molle*.

SILK OAK. See *Grevillea robusta*.

SILVER WATTLE. See *Acacia decurrens dealbata*.

SPATHODEA CAMPANULATA
(AFRICAN TULIP TREE)
Adaptable for southern Florida and other frost-free or nearly frost-free climates only. Of upright growth, this tree attains a maximum height of about 40 ft. Throughout winter and spring it bears clusters of conspicuous large red flowers. In parts of California it is deciduous. For fertile, well-drained soils.

SURINAM CHERRY. See *Eugenia uniflora.*

SWEET SHADE. See *Hymenosporum
flavum.*

TATARA. See *Pittosporum eugenioides.*

UMBELLULARIA CALIFORNICA
(CALIFORNIA LAUREL)
Stately, round-headed, 70 ft.; foliage

glossy green, aromatic when crushed.
They require soils that are reasonably
moist.

WEEPING MYALL. See *Acacia pendula.*

WHITE SAPOTE. See *Casimiroa edulis.*

WILLOW PITTOSPORUM. See *Pittosporum phillyraeoides.*

CHAPTER 20

SHRUBS
AND FLOWERING
SMALL TREES

*Variety and Interest—Buying Quality
Nursery Stock—Preparation of the
Soil—Planting and Care—Propaga-
tion—Pests and Diseases*

DECIDUOUS SHRUBS and small trees,
grown for their fruits, flowers and foliage, are extremely important elements
in garden landscapes. This is particularly true in the North, where very few
broad-leaved evergreens prosper and
too much reliance upon needle-leaved
evergreens (conifers) can produce uninteresting and even funereal effects.
In milder climates, too, there is much
to be said for taking full advantage of
leaf-losing woody plants—using them
in groups, as single specimens, as
hedges and for other appropriate pur-

poses. Their changing aspects at different seasons bring variety and interest to garden plantings.

Deciduous plants are without foliage in winter; therefore most of these
small trees and shrubs provide interest during that season by branch patterns and traceries against snow and
sky. A few, such as certain colored-
stemmed dogwoods and blackberries
as well as *Kerria* and *Poncirus*, have
brightly colored barks which are displayed to best advantage during the
winter; others, such as witch hazels
and *Jasminum nudiflorum* (jasmine),
actually bloom toward the end of
that harsh season.

Shrubs herald the approach of
spring by magnificent floral displays.

Cornus kousa (Kousa Dogwood)

Syringa (Lilac)

Well before the first leaves unfold, the earliest azalea, forsythia, magnolia and many others are in full bloom. They are succeeded by flowering dogwood, spirea, lilac and mock orange, to mention but a very few of the vast number of spring-flowering shrubs and small trees. At a slower pace, changing displays continue all summer and even past frost, if the fall-blooming witch hazel, *Hamamelis virginiana*, is planted. The summer bloomers include hydrangea, shrub rose, rose of Sharon, chaste tree, stewartia and gordonia. Then there is the beauty of colorful fruits and berries, ranging from those of crab apple, hawthorn and cotoneaster to the unbelievable turquoise berries of sweetleaf, the violet of beauty-berry and the orange of sea buckthorn. Fall brings brilliant foliage colors to many of our plants—the winged-bark euonymus, the Virginia willow and

the Japanese barberry are among the most striking.

BUYING

Trees and shrubs normally live for many years, so it is worth buying good plants from a specialist nurseryman who is known for the quality of his produce. Many nurseries encourage visitors and allow them to mark particular plants for delivery later. It is best to visit nurseries while the plants are in flower.

Cheap trees and shrubs are advertised, and it is possible to buy a selection for only a few dollars; but in many cases these offers apply to the more common shrubs, which are easily propagated. The specimens may be very small and take years to reach a reasonable size. Specimens may also be incorrectly named. Not that bargains are not sometimes available; a nurseryman overstocked with particular items is likely to offer them at lower-than-usual prices, or he may make reductions as a sales promotional policy. Just be sure that the offer is made by a reliable dealer. In buying nursery stock one must, of necessity, rely to a great extent upon the reputation of the supplier.

Delivery of the Plants

Plants are usually delivered at the correct planting season, in most cases in early spring or early fall. By placing your order early, you will give the nurseryman an opportunity to make delivery on time. Orders received late are likely to be filled late.

Have the planting sites prepared well in advance of the arrival of the trees and shrubs. If they arrive during a wet period when it is impossible to plant, they can safely be kept in their straw or other packing for a week or even more, provided the wrappings are loosened and they are in a frostproof place.

Soak the roots of bare-rooted stock in water for an hour or two if they are very dry when unpacked. If it is not possible to plant within a week or so of delivery, heel in the plants temporarily. To do this, dig a trench (for small plants this need be no more than a V-shaped nick a few inches deep made with a spade) and place the roots in it; cover with soil and firm with the foot. It is best to heel in the plants where they are shaded and not subject to wind.

Where there is a delay in planting, balled and burlapped plants (those dug with a mass of soil about their roots, which is wrapped tightly in burlap and tied securely) should be stood close together in a sheltered, shady place with some leaves or straw heaped over the balls to keep them from drying.

Container-grown specimens that arrive in cans, plastic or fiber pots or small tubs may be stood together and kept watered until planting time.

SOIL AND SOIL PREPARATION

Most trees and shrubs succeed in any ordinary garden soil that will grow a fair selection of garden annuals, perennials, vegetables and a lawn. Some prosper in much poorer soils; others need fertile or moist conditions.

The question of acidity and alkalinity—that old bogey, soil pH (see page 741)—is often overemphasized by amateurs. The truth is that a soil satisfactory for a good selection of other garden plants (one with a pH between 6 and 7.5) will accommodate the vast majority of trees and shrubs. If the soil is alkaline, you cannot, of course, expect to cultivate definitely acid-soil trees and shrubs. Most of these, such as enkianthus, lyonia, rhododendron (including azaleas) and zenobia are in the botanical family *Ericaceae*; but even these and other acid-soil kinds, such as clethra and

Vaccinium corymbosum
(Highbush Blueberry)

Vaccinium corymbosum, get along quite well provided the soil is neutral or on the acid side of neutral and shows no alkalinity. Conditions can be improved for these by adding to the soil generous amounts of peat moss, compost or other decayed organic matter.

There seem to be no trees or shrubs that *must* have an alkaline soil, although there are many, such as lilac, butterfly bush and bluebeard, that grow best on such soils.

Because trees and shrubs are seldom moved, it is advantageous to do a thorough job of soil preparation. Specimens in deeply prepared ground grow more rapidly and are better able to survive periods of drought and other unfavorable conditions.

Spade the ground thoroughly for a good distance around the planting place. On both heavy and light soil, dig in well-rotted compost or other decayed organic matter, such as peat moss or humus. This provides the heavy soil with plant food and makes it more porous, and gives the light soil both food and moisture-retaining material. A dressing of superphosphate or bone meal mixed in is also likely to be beneficial.

It is best to prepare the soil a few weeks before planting so that the ground will settle down naturally; otherwise tread it until the surface is firm.

The Planting Holes

The planting holes must be of sufficient depth and width to accommodate the roots of the shrubs or trees when fully spread out. The bottoms of the holes should be spaded and organic matter mixed in and trodden firm before the plants are put into place. The plant must be set at the same depth as it was in the nursery, or perhaps an inch deeper, but no more. The soil line around the base

of the stem will serve as a good guide.

To avoid cramping the roots upward, it is often advisable to set the specimen on a mound of soil in the middle of the hole, spreading the roots out down the sides of the mound before filling in with soil.

After wet weather the soil is sometimes too sticky to use for returning around the roots. This applies particularly to clay soils, which pack down like concrete when they are firmed. To prevent this, keep some planting soil under cover so that it is dry enough to use when shrubs and trees are to be set out. The planting soil can be a mixture of ordinary garden soil, coarse sand and peat moss or well-rotted compost. Be sure not to use fresh manure, as this will damage the roots with which it comes in contact.

Staking

If the plant is to be staked—this is essential with large specimens and even with small ones in windy situations, until their roots are anchored— put the stake in position in the center of the hole *before* planting, so that there is no risk of damaging roots by driving in a stake later. Use stout stakes, driving them well into the ground.

Cedar and redwood stakes last for years; but whatever wood is used, it is advisable to treat the part that will be in the soil with a wood preservative of a copper-naphthenate type.

Treatment Before Planting

Roots shrivel very quickly if exposed to wind or sun; therefore keep bare roots covered with damp burlap or other suitable material while they are out of the ground. Before planting, see if there are any broken roots, which must be cut off with a knife or pruning shears. Reducing the size of the top by appropriate compensa-

Cercis siliquastrum (Judas Tree)

tory pruning (see page 416) is also important.

PLANTING

When planting shrubs and trees, it is important to allow each permanent plant sufficient space for its complete development, even though this means it will be surrounded by a patch of bare ground for a few years.

A plan often followed is to use fillers between the specimens that are to form the permanent planting. These are shrubs of lesser value and importance that can and will be chopped out (or transplanted) when the permanent plants need more room. Or, the spaces between the newly planted shrubs may be carpeted with ground covers. It is not wise to fill between the permanent plants with choice and perhaps expensive kinds, with the purpose of transplanting them when they begin to crowd. Best as fillers are plants that can be chopped out and discarded without heartbreak.

One person can quite easily plant

small specimens. Spread out the roots in the planting hole and then place a little good soil over them. Shake the shrub to insure that the soil sifts down among the roots, and then fill in more soil over the roots until they are covered. Firm this with the foot, and repeat the operation until the hole is filled. The plant will then be quite firm and upright. Leave a slight depression around the plant, or construct a "saucer" by establishing a raised rim of soil around the outer spread of the roots, to hold water.

At this stage, if necessary, tie the plant to the stake. Make the ties reasonably tight, crossing the strings between plant and stake; or bind a pad of folded burlap between stem and stake to prevent chafing of the young bark. Plastic tree ties or wire threaded through a piece of garden hose are also satisfactory.

It is advisable for two people to plant larger specimens, so that one can hold the plant and shake it when necessary and the other can fill in the soil and firm it. However, one person alone can plant them if the stems are tied loosely to the stakes while the soil is filled in and firmed.

After planting, rake the surface soil to remove footmarks.

Balled and Burlapped and Container-Grown Plants

Certain plants, such as azaleas, arrive from the nursery with their roots "balled and burlapped." If the ball of soil around the roots is intact, place the plant in the hole, cut the string and then slowly and carefully remove as much of the burlap as possible before filling in soil.

If the ball of soil shows signs of disintegrating, do not remove the burlap; simply place the shrub in its hole, cut the string and leave the enclosing burlap in place. It will eventually rot down and disintegrate in the soil, and in the meantime the roots of the plant will grow through it. In either case, do not spread out these balled roots.

Plants grown in cans and other containers are carefully removed from them and planted in the same way as balled and burlapped specimens. New soil is packed down around the sides of the root ball, while great care is taken not to break it or disturb the soil about the roots.

Planting in Grass

When shrubs and trees are planted in lawns or rough grass and it is impossible to dig a wide area around the planting hole, dig a deep hole and mix a generous amount of compost or well-rotted manure in the bottom. Mix this with the subsoil.

When shrubs are planted in circular beds cut from the turf, mowing is made difficult because the machine must be stopped frequently to mow around the edges of the beds. This difficulty is overcome if the shrubs are planted in a long, streamlined bed, wide in the center and narrowing to a point at each end.

AFTERTREATMENT

Most shrubs need little attention after planting, though the ties holding them to the stakes must be examined occasionally and loosened if they become so tight that the stems are restricted. Trees may need further ties as they grow.

Unless the soil is wet, a thorough soaking with water immediately following planting is in order. If mulching is to be done in spring, it may be advisable to postpone this for a few weeks so that it does not delay root action by keeping the soil cool.

Weeds must be kept down near the plants. Clear an area around each specimen; and if it is planted in grass, keep the grass cut short and make

sure it does not encroach on the cleared area around the stem.

Droughts may occur even in spring, and watering may be necessary in dry weather, especially during the first season following planting.

Watering

Established shrubs and trees may need watering during periods of drought. Be sure to soak the ground to the full depth of the roots, and then give no more until the soil is decidedly dry again. Frequent light sprinklings do little good.

Mulching

All shrubs and trees benefit from a mulch of rotted compost, rotted old manure or other suitable material, placed around them in late spring. This conserves moisture, smothers weeds and provides some nourishment.

Removing Dead Flower Heads

Shrubs that benefit from the removal of dead flower heads include azalea, cytisus (broom), tree lupine, lilac and zenobia. Remove the flowers soon after they have faded, so that new growths can develop properly. Do not delay until seedpods have formed.

PRUNING

Pruning is not essential for all small trees and shrubs, although many are improved by the annual removal of dead or crowded wood. Some shrubs need occasional, and others annual, pruning. Plants requiring annual pruning are divided into two main categories: those that produce flowers on the new wood formed in the current season, and those that produce flowers on wood formed in the previous season.

Shrubs Flowering on Shoots Produced In Current Year

These include *Caryopteris* (bluebeard),

Buddleia davidii, hardy fuchsias, *Hydrangea paniculata grandiflora*, *Indigofera gerardiana*, *Leycesteria formosa*, certain spiraeas and *Tamarix pentandra*.

In mild areas this pruning may be carried out at any time during the winter; but in colder climates and where there are frequent spring frosts that may damage young growths, it is best not to prune until the plants are almost ready to leaf out in spring.

Some plants, such as bluebeard, may be cut down each year to within a few inches of the ground; but others, such as *Hydrangea paniculata grandiflora* and the chaste tree, if treated in the same way, will not grow very large. If large specimens are wanted, build up a framework of trunk and main branches to the desired height and keep these permanently. Each winter or early spring, cut back the shoots formed the previous year to within a few inches of their bases. This forces them to produce new growths from the buds that are left, and these in turn are cut back the following year to within a few inches of their bases. In this way vigorous new flowering shoots are encouraged, but the plant itself does not increase much in size from year to year.

If the bush eventually grows too large, prune it more severely to keep it within bounds.

Other plants, such as certain dogwoods and blackberries which are grown for their winter stem color, should be cut down to the ground in late spring to induce them to produce new, brightly colored shoots.

Shrubs Flowering on Wood Produced in Previous Year

These include weigela, forsythia, jasmine, kerria, some spiraeas and mock orange.

Cut away as many as can be spared of the old shoots or branches that have flowered, and any very weak and crowded shoots, as soon as possible after the flowers have faded, in order to give the strong new shoots an opportunity to develop properly for blooming the following year.

Trees and Shrubs That Need No Regular Pruning

Among kinds that can safely be left unpruned for many years are: amelanchier, azalea, barberry, clerodendron, colutea, dogwood (except those grown for their colored stems), cotoneaster, cytisus (broom), daphne, witch hazel, hibiscus, sea buckthorn, jasmine, tree lupine, magnolia, tree peony, potentilla, currant, viburnum and zenobia.

These need no pruning unless they grow too large for the space allotted to them; then it is best, in the winter, to remove whole branches right back to their point of origin. Do not chop off bits of branches; this results in the rapid production of new shoots.

If frost kills or damages some growths, cut them back until sound wood is found. Do this in spring, after danger of freezing is past.

Removal of Suckers

Azalea, cytisus, lilac and *Viburnum carlesii* are a few of the plants that may produce suckers from belowground; these must be removed.

If the plant is known to be a particular variety grafted onto a stock root of a commoner sort (for example, named varieties of lilac grafted onto common lilac stock), the suckers will only produce flowers of the type normally produced by the stock, and may be vigorous enough to replace the grafted variety eventually. To remove a sucker, dig carefully to the root source and cut the sucker off.

Other plants, such as some clerodendrons and dogwoods, fuchsias, some hydrangeas, some hypericums, kerria, mock orange, roses on their own roots, rubus, salix and some spireas spread by means of sucker shoots produced from belowground.

Rehabilitation Pruning

It sometimes happens that an old and much neglected shrub—overgrown and densely crowded with branches, or tall, spindly and ungainly—must be pruned. Such drastic pruning should be done in late winter or spring. Only then, when the branches are bare of leaves, is it possible to determine which to cut out; only then is it possible to remove most or even all of the branches and still give the plant the opportunity of a full new growing season to renew itself.

In the case of early-blooming plants, such as redbud, lilac and mock orange, this means sacrificing at least one season's bloom, but it is well worth it. It is much better than waiting until after the plant has exhausted some of its energies producing foliage and flowers.

The recommendation is sometimes made to do such rehabilitative work gradually—to cut down part of a too tall and straggly lilac (for example) one year, part the next and the remainder in the third year. However, it is much better to do the whole job at once. Following such severe pruning, fertilize the soil, keep it well watered the first year and, if necessary, thin out some of the young shoots to allow good light and air circulation for those that remain.

Shrubs that make very few growths from the base and are naturally slow-growing, such as azalea, do not respond as well to severe pruning as many-stemmed specimens of more vigorous growth. And many small trees (flowering dogwood and Japanese maple, for example) take a long time to develop into sizable specimens if they are cut back nearly to the ground. In such cases, cutting back of the main branches and removal of unneeded ones will usually suffice.

With grafted plants (old lilacs often belong in this category), do not cut below the graft union, usually near soil level, and do not allow shoots to develop from below this point.

Compensatory Pruning

Inevitably, when a plant is dug for transplanting, it loses part of its root system. Unless the top is reduced in size, a smaller number of roots than before will be called upon to supply moisture and nutrients to the same number of branches and leaves. To compensate for this loss and to restore a balance between roots and top, it is advisable whenever possible to prune at planting time. This is especially important when trees and shrubs are planted bare-rooted. Such compensatory pruning usually involves reducing the branch system by about one third. Depending upon the type of plant, this is done by shortening the leader of the main trunk

Clerodendron bungei
(Glory-Bower)

and shortening the side branches, by cutting back all branches to more or less the same height, or by thinning out the branches that are the most poorly placed and weakest, and leaving the remainder unpruned or cut back lightly.

PROPAGATION

Many shrubs can be propagated from softwood cuttings taken in early summer and rooted in a propagating frame, or from hardwood cuttings taken in fall or early winter. It is also easy to detach the rooted suckers of some kinds of shrubs (not grafted ones) for propagation purposes.

The pliable branches of some types of shrubs often touch the ground and root where they touch. This is called natural layering. When well rooted, the layer can be detached and grown as a separate plant. The layering method is often adapted to propagate shrubs whose branches are low and supple enough to be brought to ground level. (See page 714.)

Most shrubs and trees can be raised from seed, although hybrids and improved horticultural varieties will not come true. The seeds of many trees and shrubs take more than a year to germinate, so do not give up until the seeds have been planted at least two years.

PESTS AND DISEASES

Various pests, such as aphids, leaf-rolling insects, sap-sucking pests, borers, scale insects and leaf- and shoot-eating caterpillars, attack trees and shrubs. In some years these attacks are more severe than in others. Trees and shrubs also suffer from a variety of diseases such as rots, molds, rusts and cankers.

The number of pests and diseases that may injure trees and shrubs is enormous. Fortunately, only a few are likely to be troublesome in any one garden. The gardener must learn to detect these particular enemies and then take prompt measures to curb or destroy them.

Small Trees and Shrubs for Bloom, Berries, Fall Color

ABELIA
In mild climates these are semi-evergreen. They succeed in ordinary soil, with sun or light shade. Prune in spring, to any extent desired. If shoots are winter-killed to the ground, live roots produce new shoots that bloom the same year.

Abelia chinensis, 4 to 6 ft.; flowers white, fragrant. Similar to *A. grandiflora*, but less hardy.

A. Edward Goucher, 4 to 5 ft.; rather large lavender-pink flowers. Less hardy than *A. grandiflora*.

A. grandiflora (glossy abelia), 4 to 5 ft.; leaves small, bronzy-green; flowers numerous, pinkish, tubular, with attractive, persistent, bronzy-pink sepals, in late summer and fall. Hardy at New York City and also hardy, with protection, in severer climates.

ABELIOPHYLLUM (WHITE FORSYTHIA)
Abeliophyllum distichum, 4 to 5 ft.; flowers white, resembling forsythia but smaller, in earliest spring. Hardy in sheltered locations in New England. Soil ordinary; full sun. Prune sparingly after flowering.

ACANTHOPANAX SIEBOLDIANUS

Thorny, 8 to 9 ft., attractive foliage remaining green late in fall. Soil ordinary; sun or shade. No regular pruning; when grown as a hedge, shear in spring and summer.

ACER (MAPLE)

Most maples are large trees. The Japanese maples and a few other kinds are small trees or shrubs grown for their decorative and often highly colored foliage. Most have no value as flowering or fruiting plants. Maples grow well in rich, deep soil, in sun, no regular pruning. For other kinds, see page 369 in "Shade Trees Enhance Your Grounds."

Acer campestre (hedge maple), 25 ft.; leaves small, green, not coloring well in fall. Suitable for screens and sheared hedges.

A. circinatum (vine maple), 30 ft.; leaves in fall orange and red. Popular on West Coast. Stands partial shade.

A. ginnala (Amur maple), 20 ft.; leaves small; fruit turns brilliant red in fall.

A. palmatum (Japanese maple), 20 ft.; foliage green or, more usually, red; in some forms much divided and lacy. Height differs greatly with variety, some varieties not exceeding 4 or 5 ft. When grown from seed there is considerable variation; many seedlings produce foliage inferior to that of their parents. Propagation by grafting insures perpetuation of the finest types, but sometimes grafted trees develop foliage scorch in summer as a result of incompatibility with the understock on which they are grown. For varietal descriptions, see nursery catalogues, or select specimens at a nursery after midsummer.

AESCULUS (BUCKEYE)

These relatives of the horse chestnut thrive in ordinary, not too dry soils, in sun. No regular pruning.

Aesculus parviflora (bottlebrush buckeye), 10 ft., broader than high, spreading by suckers. Spires of white flowers in summer. Very handsome.

A. pavia (red buckeye), 20 ft.; flowers in spikes, dark red, early summer.

A. splendens, 12 ft.; spikes of red flowers, late spring. One of the most handsome.

ALBIZZIA JULIBRISSIN (SILK TREE)

Spreading tree, 25 to 40 ft., called mimosa in South. Lacy foliage; flowers pink, in powder-puff clusters, in summer. Soil ordinary; full sun. No regular pruning. Hardy in sheltered places at New York City, variety *rosea* as far north as Boston.

ALDER, WHITE. See *Clethra*.

ALPINE CURRANT. See *Ribes alpinum*.

AMELANCHIER (JUNEBERRY, SERVICEBERRY, SHADBUSH)

Attractive spring-blooming, white-flowered small trees and shrubs that bear decorative fruits. They thrive in ordinary soil in sun or light shade. The flower display is usually of short duration. No regular pruning.

Amelanchier alnifolia, 7 ft.; short, dense flower clusters, fruit black. Spreads by suckers.

A. grandiflora, 25 ft.; large flower clusters, fruit red to black, edible. One of the best.

A. laevis, 35 ft.; flowers small, fruit red.

AMORPHA (FALSE INDIGO)

Shrubs for ordinary soil and sun. Spikes of blue, purple or purplish flowers, in spring. No regular pruning.

Amorpha canescens (leadplant), 4 ft.; grayish foliage.

A. fruticosa (bastard indigo), 15 to 20 ft.

A. nana, 1 ft.

ANTELOPE BRUSH. See *Purshia tridentata*.

ARALIA

Tall shrubs or trees of rather spindly growth with large, tropical-looking divided leaves and great clusters of tiny white flowers in summer, followed by small black berries; stems often spiny. Full sun or light shade; ordinary soil. No regular pruning is required.

Aralia chinensis (Chinese angelica tree), 30 ft.

A. elata (Japanese angelica tree), 40 to 50 ft., hardy into Canada.

A. e. aureo-variegata has yellow-variegated leaves.

A. spinosa (Devil's-walking-stick, Hercules'-club), 30 ft.; very spiny.

ARONIA (CHOKEBERRY)

Easy-to-grow shrubs with clusters of small flowers in spring. For sun or light shade. No regular pruning.

Aronia arbutifolia, 9 ft.; flowers white or pinkish, then red berries.

A. melanocarpa, 3 ft., flowers white, berries black.

ARROWWOOD. See *Viburnum dentatum*.

AZALEA. See *Rhododendron*.

BARBERRY. See *Berberis*.

BAUHINIA VARIEGATA (ORCHID TREE)

Suitable for southern Florida and similar climates. Flowers look somewhat like small lavender orchids. Ordinary soil; sun. No regular pruning is necessary.

BAYBERRY. See *Myrica pensylvanica*.

BEACH PLUM. See *Prunus maritima*.

BEAUTY-BERRY. See *Callicarpa*.

BEAUTY BUSH. See *Kolkwitzia amabilis*.

BERBERIS (BARBERRY)

Thorny shrubs, suitable for hedges and barriers. Flowers yellow; berries red, long-lasting. Foliage colors in fall. Sun or shade; ordinary soil. Prune in spring, when needed. For evergreen kinds, see page 454.

Berberis koreana (Korean barberry), 6 ft.

B. thunbergii (Japanese barberry), 6 ft.

B. t. atropurpurea, 6 ft.; foliage crimson.

B. t. Crimson Pygmy, 2 ft.; foliage red.

B. t. nana, 2 ft.

B. t. pluriflora (truehedge columnberry), 6 ft., upright growth habit.

BLACKBERRY. See *Rubus*.

BLACKCAP. See *Rubus occidentalis*.

BLACK HAW. See *Viburnum prunifolium*.

BLADDER SENNA. See *Colutea*.

BLUEBEARD. See *Caryopteris*.

BLUEBERRY, HIGHBUSH. See *Vaccinium corymbosum*.

BOXTHORN. See *Lycium halimifolium*.

BRIDAL WREATH. See *Spiraea prunifolia plena*.

BROOM. See *Cytisus, Genista*.

BUCKEYE. See *Aesculus*.

BUCKTHORN. See *Rhamnus*.

BUDDLEIA (BUTTERFLY BUSH)

Plant in deep, fertile soil, in sun.

Buddleia alternifolia, 12 to 15 ft., slender, arching branches bear tiny lilac-purple flowers along their length in late spring. The hardiest kind. No

Buddleia alternifolia (Butterfly Bush)

regular pruning; if any needed, do immediately after flowering.

B. davidii (syn. *B. variabilis*), 12 ft.; the most popular kind, available in many varieties having lavender, violet, blue, deep purple, reddish-purple or white flowers. Needs hard pruning to insure that it flowers freely and does not grow leggy. Cut back almost to the base each spring.

B. globosa (semievergreen), 15 ft.; with globular, bright orange flowers in midsummer. Needs little pruning. Suitable for very mild climates only.

BUFFALO BERRY. See *Shepherdia argentea.*

BUSH CLOVER. See *Lespedeza.*

BUSH HONEYSUCKLE. See *Lonicera.*

BUTTERFLY BUSH. See *Buddleia.*

CALLICARPA (BEAUTY-BERRY)
Grown for their attractive violet-to-

purple or white berries. Need fertile soil and sun. Prune hard and fertilize in spring. If winter-killed to the ground, new shoots from live roots will berry the first year.

Callicarpa americana (French mulberry), 6 ft.; hardy as far north as Virginia.

C. dichotoma, 4 ft.; hardy in southern New England.

C. japonica, 5 ft.; hardy in southern New England.

CALYCANTHUS
(SWEET-SCENTED SHRUB)
Dense bushes with fragrant reddish-brown flowers in spring. Soil rich, well drained; sun or light shade. No regular pruning.

Calycanthus fertilis, 10 ft.

C. floridus (Carolina allspice), 10 ft.

C. occidentalis, 12 ft.; hardy in mild climates only.

CARAGANA (PEA TREE)
Rather coarse, very hardy shrubs and small trees for well-drained soil and full sun. Flowers yellow, pealike. No regular pruning; when used as hedge, shear in spring.

Caragana arborescens, 20 ft.; good for hedges and windbreaks.

C. frutex, 9 to 10 ft.

C. pygmaea, 3 ft.

CAROLINA ALLSPICE. See *Calycanthus floridus.*

CARYOPTERIS (BLUEBEARD)
Small shrubs bearing blue flowers in late summer. They need full sun, but are not particular about soil. Prune almost to the ground each spring, but not the first year. If winter-killed to roots, new shoots bloom first year.

Caryopteris clandonensis, 2½ to 3 ft.; a hybrid with grayish leaves and bright blue flowers.

C. incana, 3 to 4 ft.; lavender-blue flowers.

CASSIA (SENNA)
Shrubs for sunny locations in mild climates. May be pruned in spring.
Cassia artemisoides (wormwood senna), 10 ft.; grayish foliage, pale yellow flowers.
C. corymbosa, 10 ft.; yellow flowers.

CEANOTHUS
Mostly plants for mild climates such as that of the Pacific Coast. These shrubs need full sun and well-drained soil. Prune when needed, after blooming. For evergreen kinds, see page 457.
Ceanothus caeruleus, 18 ft.; flowers blue to white, spring.
C. integerrimus (deer brush), 12 ft.; white, rarely pink or blue.
C. ovatus, 3 ft.; flowers white, late spring. Hardy in New England.

CERCIS
Attractive small trees with rosy-purple (or, in *C. canadensis alba*, white) pealike flowers produced abundantly when the rounded, heart-shaped leaves are just unfolding. Sun or partial shade; ordinary soil. No regular pruning. Cut back tall, straggly trees to 1 or 2 ft. from the ground.
Cercis canadensis (redbud), 30 to 40 ft.; hardy north to New York City.
C. chinensis (Chinese redbud), 30 to 40 ft., usually much lower; hardy at New York City.
C. siliquastrum (Judas tree), 30 to 40 ft.; hardy north to about Washington, D.C. (See illustration, page 413.)

CHAENOMELES (FLOWERING QUINCE)
Often listed under *Cydonia*, these sometimes semievergreen, dense shrubs bloom in early spring and bear fruit from which jelly can be made.
Chaenomeles japonica (dwarf Japanese quince), 3 ft.; flowers red. Requires little or no pruning.
C. lagenaria (Japanese quince), 6 to 8 ft.; flowers single or double, white, pink, red, orange-red. Nurserymen offer many named varieties. Prune occasionally, just after blooming, to remove old, worn branches and encourage strong new shoots.

CHASTE TREE. See *Vitex agnus-castus*.

CHICKASAW PLUM. See *Prunus angustifolia*.

CHILOPSIS (DESERT WILLOW)
Chilopsis linearis, 20 to 25 ft.; flowers trumpet-shaped, lilac, fragrant, in terminal clusters. Suitable for mild, dry climates. Soil ordinary; sun. No regular pruning.

CHIMONANTHUS
Sometimes called *Meratia*. For mild climates only, but may live in sheltered places as far north as Philadelphia. Ordinary soil; light shade. Little or no pruning.
Chimonanthus praecox, 10 ft.; flowers yellow with brownish stripes, fragrant, early spring.

CHINESE ANGELICA TREE. See *Aralia chinensis*.

CHIONANTHUS (FRINGE TREE)
Small trees with lacy flowers in late spring. For sun and moist, porous soil. No regular pruning.
Chionanthus retusa, 20 ft.; white flowers.
C. virginica, 30 ft.; greenish-white flowers. Blooms later than *C. retusa*.

CHOKEBERRY. See *Aronia*.

CHOKECHERRY. See *Prunus*.

CLERODENDRON (GLORY-BOWER)
Mostly mild-climate shrubs (the vines are not included here), for sun or light shade; ordinary soil. Pruning not regularly necessary but may be done in spring. Shoots arising from base

will bloom the same year, in summer.

Clerodendron bungei, 5 ft.; large, flattish clusters of pink flowers. Mild climates. (See illustration, page 416.)

C. fragrans pleniflorum, 5 to 6 ft.; fragrant, double, white flowers. For warm climates only.

C. speciosissimus (syn. *C. fallax*), 3 to 4 ft.; scarlet flowers. For warm climates only.

C. trichotomum, 8 ft.; fragrant white flowers in summer. The porcelain-blue berries, in autumn, are surrounded by the reddish-maroon calyxes which persist after the petals fall. Hardy in sheltered places at New York City. Spreads by suckers.

CLETHRA (WHITE ALDER)

Summer bloomers. For acid soils in sun or light shade. No regular pruning needed.

Clethra alnifolia (sweet pepperbush), 10 ft.; flowers white, fragrant.

C. a. rosea, flowers pale pink, fragrant.

C. barbinervis, 25 ft.; flowers white, somewhat fragrant.

COLUTEA (BLADDER SENNA)

Fast-growing, tough, rather coarse shrubs for poor, dry soil, in sun.

Colutea arborescens, 12 ft.; yellow pea-flowers in spring, followed by inflated, translucent pods.

C. orientalis, 6 ft.; bears coppery-red flowers from June to September.

CORALBERRY. See *Symphoricarpos orbiculatus*.

CORNUS (DOGWOOD)

A group of widely differing shrubs and small trees. The flowering dogwoods, *C. florida*, *C. kousa* and *C. nuttallii*, have their tiny true flowers surrounded by large, showy white, pink or red bracts. These varieties, and the yellow-flowered, early-spring-blooming *C. mas* and *C. officinalis*,

need little or no pruning. The shrubby kinds that have bright-colored stems are pruned hard in spring; the rest need no regular pruning.

Cornus alba argenteo-marginata, leaves edged with white; bright red stems.

C. a. sibirica, 6 to 9 ft.; bright red stems.

C. a. spaethii, yellow-variegated foliage; bright red stems.

C. florida (flowering dogwood), tree 30 to 40 ft.; hardy about as far north as southern New England. Bracts white; red berries in fall. Blooms before foliage expands.

C. f. rubra, large rosy bracts.

C. japonica, 15 ft.; very similar to *C. mas*.

C. kousa, tree 20 ft.; showy white bracts followed by fruit like strawberries. Blooms after leaves are expanded. Slightly less hardy than *C. florida*. (See illustration, page 410.)

C. k. chinensis is a name applied to forms with larger bracts.

C. mas (cornelian cherry), 15 ft.; small yellow flowers in late winter, followed by red berries.

C. nuttallii, tree as tall as 70 ft., but usually lower; large white or pinkish bracts; orange-red fruit. Suitable for Pacific Coast only.

C. racemosa, 15 ft.; creamy-white flowers; white berries.

C. stolonifera (red-osier dogwood), 10 ft.; bright red branches.

C. s. coloradensis, brownish-red stems.

C. s. flaviramea, bright yellow stems.

CORYLOPSIS (WINTER HAZEL)

Charming spring-blooming, yellow-flowered shrubs. Soil fertile, moderately moist; sun or light shade. No regular pruning. When overcrowded, thin out old branches after blooming.

Corylopsis glabrescens, 20 ft.; hardy into southern New England.

C. pauciflora, 6 ft.; hardy in sheltered places at New York City.

C. platypetala, 8 ft.; hardy in sheltered places at New York City.

C. spicata, 6 ft.; hardy in sheltered places at New York City.

CORYLUS (HAZELNUT)
Varieties of the European hazelnut are grown for their distinctive branching habits or their foliage. Bear conspicuous flower catkins in early spring. Thrive in ordinary soils, preferring those not too dry. For another *Corylus*, see page 376 in "Shade Trees Enhance Your Grounds."

Corylus avellana aurea, 15 ft.; foliage yellow.

C. a. contorta, 15 ft.; branches very twisted and contorted.

C. a. heterophylla, 15 ft.; leaves conspicuously lobed or cut.

C. a. pendula, 15 ft.; branches pendulous.

C. maxima purpurea, 25 ft.; foliage dark purple.

COTINUS (SMOKE TREE)
Shrubs or small trees with attractive foliage and masses of a gray "smoke" of hairs among the seeds. Ordinary soil; sun. No regular pruning.

Cotinus americanus, 30 ft.; has much less "smoke" than *C. coggygria*, but foliage colors beautifully in fall.

C. coggygria, 15 ft.; selected forms produce abundant "smoke." When raised from seed some individuals produce no "smoke" and others only a little. Plant only specimens propagated vegetatively from profuse-"smoking" individuals.

C.c. Notcutt Variety, rich purple foliage and purple "smoke."

COTONEASTER
Cotoneasters thrive in ordinary, well-drained soil in sun or light shade. All bear small pinkish-white flowers in spring, followed by ornamental berry-like fruit. No regular pruning. For evergreen kinds, see page 477 in "Hedges."

Cotoneaster adpressa, 1½ ft.; similar to *C. horizontalis*, but fruit ripens earlier and is bigger.

C. dielsiana, 8 ft.; graceful, large scarlet fruit and good autumn color.

C. divaricata, 6 ft.; has arching branches, red fruit.

C. frigida, 20 ft.; crimson fruit.

C. horizontalis, 1 to 2½ ft.; spreads horizontally and bears small leaves, twigs and branches arranged like herringbone; red berries and colorful autumn leaves.

C. multiflora calocarpa, 6 ft.; attractive flowers followed by red fruit.

C. racemiflora soongarica, 7 ft.; grayish-green foliage, attractive flowers, followed by red fruit.

C. simonsii, 10 ft.; deciduous or semievergreen, scarlet berries.

CRAB APPLE. See *Malus.*

CRANBERRY BUSH. See *Viburnum opulus, V. trilobum.*

CRAPE MYRTLE. See *Lagerstroemia indica.*

CRATAEGUS (THORN, HAWTHORN)
Small thorny trees with attractive flowers in spring, followed by clusters of small decorative fruits. Ordinary soil; sun or light shade. Good for hedges. No regular pruning except shearing when grown as hedges.

Crataegus crus-galli (cockspur thorn), 25 ft.; flowers white, fruit bright red, leaves glossy green. A good hedge plant.

C. douglasii, 30 ft.; flowers white, fruit black.

C. lavallei, 20 ft.; fruit orange-red, remains through winter.

C. mollis, 30 ft.; fruit large, pear-shaped, red.

C. monogyna biflora (Glastonbury

Crataegus oxyacantha paulii
(Paul's Double Scarlet Hawthorn)

thorn), 25 ft.; blooms in late fall—or winter in mild climates—as well as in spring.

C. oxyacantha (English hawthorn), 20 ft.; flowers white, fruit scarlet.

C. o. paulii (Paul's double scarlet hawthorn), 20 ft.; long-lasting, double red flowers.

C. o. rosea, 20 ft.; flowers pink.

C. o. rosea-plena, 20 ft.; flowers pink, double.

C. phaenopyrum (Washington thorn), 30 ft.; long thorns, leaves shiny, fruit red.

C. succulenta, 15 ft.; good flowers, red fruit.

CURRANT. See *Ribes*.

CYDONIA. See *Chaenomeles*.

CYTISUS (BROOM)
These pea-flowered shrubs have often fragrant flowers in early summer,

sometimes of one color but frequently with parts of the flower of different colors, such as yellow and crimson. Because of their green stems they have something of the appearance of evergreens. For full sun and dry soils. Plant out from pots when young. No regular pruning.

Cytisus albus, 1 ft.; white flowers.

C. battandieri, 10 to 12 ft.; silvery leaves and spikes of yellow flowers. Hardy in mild climates only.

C. beanii, 1½ ft.; golden-yellow flowers.

C. kewensis, 1 ft.; 4 or 5 ft. broad; pale yellow flowers; a lovely dwarf kind.

C. nigricans, 3 ft.; flowers yellow.

C. praecox, 6 ft.; yellow and cream flowers.

C. purpureus, 2 ft.; procumbent, flowers purple or purplish-pink.

C. scoparius, 5 to 10 ft.; flowers yellow.

In addition, many hybrid brooms are grown. Among the best are:

Burkwoodii, rich red flowers.

California, red, pink and cream flowers.

Daisy Hill, cream-tinted pink flowers.

Cytisus albus (White Broom)

Dorothy Walpole, crimson and rose flowers.

Lord Lambourne, crimson and yellow flowers.

Pink Beauty, pink flowers.

St. Mary's, white flowers.

San Francisco, rich red flowers.

DAPHNE
Most bear very fragrant flowers; many are rather difficult to grow. Well-drained soil and sun are appropriate. Many seem to thrive best if soil contains lime. No regular pruning. For evergreen kinds, see page 458.

D. burkwoodii, 3 to 4 ft.; spreading, fragrant, light pinkish-lavender flowers in spring. *D.b.* Somerset is an especially good variety.

D. genkwa, 3 ft.; flowers lilac, berries white.

D. mezereum (mezereon), 3 or 4 ft.; purplish-red flowers in late winter. There is a white variety, *alba.*

DAVIDIA INVOLUCRATA (DOVE TREE)
An unusual tree that seems to prosper in the Pacific Northwest and sometimes in the East, 40 to 50 ft. Each small cluster of tiny flowers has two conspicuous white bracts, one much longer than the other; but in the East specimens often fail to bloom. Hardy into southern New England. Ordinary soil; sun. No regular pruning.

DEER BRUSH. See *Ceanothus integerrimus.*

DELONIX REGIA (ROYAL POINCIANA)
For southern Florida and similar climates; 40 ft.; scarlet and yellow flowers, ferny foliage. Ordinary soil; full sun. No regular pruning.

DESERT WILLOW. See *Chilopsis.*

DEUTZIA
Free-flowering in late spring; easy to grow in ordinary soil and sun. Prune out dead wood, and thin overcrowded shoots after flowering.

Deutzia gracilis, 4 to 6 ft.; white flowers, bush compact.

D. grandiflora, 6 ft.; white flowers, the earliest to bloom.

D. lemoinei, 7 ft.; white flowers.

D. magnifica, 6 or 7 ft.; a profusion of double white flowers.

D. rosea, 6 ft.; pinkish flowers. *D. r. eximea* has larger flower clusters.

D. scabra, 10 ft.; clusters of single white flowers. This specimen and its varieties are charming shrubs, free-flowering and easy to grow.

D. s. candidissima, 8 ft.; pure white, double flowers.

D. s. Pride of Rochester, double white flowers; the backs of the petals are rose-flushed.

DEVIL'S-WALKING-STICK. See *Aralia spinosa.*

DOGWOOD. See *Cornus.*

DOVE TREE. See *Davidia involucrata.*

DYER'S GREENWEED. See *Genista tinctoria.*

ELAEAGNUS
Very hardy shrubs for well-drained soil and sun. No regular pruning. For the evergreen kind, see page 459.

Elaeagnus angustifolia (Russian olive), 20 ft.; handsome silvery-gray foliage; flowers fragrant; fruit yellow and silvery.

E. multiflora, 8 to 9 ft.; leaves, upper sides green, lower sides silvery; fruit red, oval, cherrylike.

E. umbellata, 12 ft.; flowers yellowish, fragrant; fruit red and silvery, edible.

ELDER. See *Sambucus.*

ELSHOLTZIA
Elsholtzia stauntonii, 5 ft.; dense

spikes of rosy-lilac flowers in fall. Ordinary soil; full sun. May be pruned to ground in spring. The foliage is fragrant.

ENKIANTHUS

Choice, small-leaved shrubs with little bell-shaped flowers before leaves appear. Foliage colors handsomely in fall. Acid soil, well drained but moderately moist; full sun or light shade. No regular pruning.

Enkianthus campanulatus, 20 ft.; flowers dull yellow or orange, veined pink or red.

E. perulatus, 6 ft.; flowers white.

EUONYMUS

Shrubs or small trees with attractive fruit and bright fall colors. Soil ordinary; full sun. No regular pruning; shear in spring and summer when grown as a hedge. See also page 460 in "Evergreen Shrubs" and page 478 in "Hedges."

Euonymus alatus (winged-bark euonymus), 10 ft.; stems with conspicuous corky wings.

E. a. compactus, 4 to 6 ft.; similar to *E. alatus*, but lower and denser.

E. americana (wahoo), 7 ft.; fruit warty, pink to red.

E. europaea (spindle tree), 20 ft.; fruit pink.

E. nana, 3 ft.; fruit pink.

E. yedoensis, 10 ft.; fruit pink.

EXOCHORDA (PEARLBUSH)

For ordinary soil, in sun. Prune out old, crowded and weak shoots after blooming time in the spring.

Exochorda giraldii wilsonii, 15 ft.; white flowers.

E. racemosa, 10 ft.; white flowers.

FALLUGIA

Fallugia paradoxa, 6 ft.; white flowers in spring; fruit with feathery, purplish plumes. Dryish, well-drained soil; full sun. No regular pruning.

FALSE INDIGO. See *Amorpha*.

FALSE SPIREA. See *Sorbaria*.

FLOWERING ALMOND. See *Prunus*.

FLOWERING APRICOT. See *Prunus*.

FLOWERING CHERRY. See *Prunus*.

FLOWERING CURRANT. See *Ribes*.

FLOWERING PEACH. See *Prunus*.

FLOWERING PLUM. See *Prunus*.

FLOWERING QUINCE. See *Chaenomeles*.

FONTANESIA

Fontanesia fortunei, 15 ft.; leaves shiny, small white flowers. Ordinary soil; sun. No regular pruning.

FORESTIERA

Forestiera neo-mexicana, 10 ft.; flowers inconspicuous. Moist soil; sun. No regular pruning.

FORSYTHIA

Yellow-flowered, spring-blooming shrubs. For ordinary soil in sun or light shade, but bloom best in sun. Immediately after flowering, prune out some of oldest branches to encourage the production of new wood for flowering the following spring.

Forsythia intermedia spectabilis, 10 ft. This is one of the best. The branches are wreathed in rich yellow flowers.

F. i. Lynwood Gold, larger flowers with broader petals, borne equally profusely.

F. ovata, 5 ft.; primrose-yellow flowers. The earliest to bloom.

F. suspensa sieboldii, 6 to 12 ft.; pale yellow flowers on slender trailing or hanging stems.

F. viridissima bronxensis, 2 ft.; compact; flowers pale yellow.

FORSYTHIA, WHITE. See *Abeliophyllum*.

Hydrangea macrophylla

FOTHERGILLA

Excellent spring-blooming shrub with good fall foliage color. The creamy-white, fragrant flowers are in heads like bottlebrushes. For ordinary, not too dry soil and sun; will tolerate light shade. No regular pruning.

Fothergilla gardenii, 3 ft.

F. major, 8 ft.

F. monticola, 6 ft., the largest flowered kind.

FRANKLINIA. See *Gordonia alatamaha*.

FRENCH MULBERRY. See *Callicarpa americana*.

FRINGE TREE. See *Chionanthus*.

FUCHSIA

Summer and autumn bloomers, mostly for mild climates. Flowers red, pink, white, purple and combinations. Rich, fairly moist soil; light shade. Prune fairly severely in spring.

Fuchsia magellanica, carmine and purple flowers.

F. m. riccartonii, the hardiest variety, succeeds in sheltered locations at New York City. Red and purple flowers. If winter-killed to ground and roots live, will send up new shoots which bloom first year.

In very mild climates many hybrid varieties are grown.

GENISTA (BROOM)

These are related to *Cytisus* and thrive in dry, stony soils in hot places. No regular pruning.

Genista aetnensis (Mount Etna broom), 12 ft.; fragrant yellow flowers. Hardy at New York City.

G. cineria, 2½ ft.; bright yellow flowers.

G. pilosa, 6 to 12 in.; prostrate, flowers yellow.

G. tinctoria (dyer's greenweed), 3

Fuchsia magellanica

ft.; flowers yellow. A double-flowered variety is *G. t. plena.* The hardiest kinds.

GLORY-BOWER. See *Clerodendron.*

GOLDEN CHAIN. See *Laburnum.*

GOLDEN CURRENT. See *Ribes aureum.*

GOLDENRAIN TREE. See *Koelreuteria paniculata.*

GORDONIA ALATAMAHA
Also called *Franklinia alatamaha.* This tree may attain a height of 25 ft. but is often lower and, in the North, shrublike. Handsome white flowers in late summer and fall. For fertile, reasonably moist soil and sun. No regular pruning.

HALESIA
(SILVER BELL, SNOWDROP TREE)
Small trees or shrubs with drooping, bell-shaped flowers in spring. Rich, well-drained, reasonably moist soil; sun or shade. These require no regular pruning.
   Halesia carolina, 30 ft.; flowers white.
   H. diptera, 30 ft.; flowers white. Not hardy in the North.
   H. monticola, 90 ft.; but usually smaller in cultivation, flowers white.

HAMAMELIS (WITCH HAZEL)
Witch hazels are not fussy about soil but prefer one not too dry; sun or light shade. Bloom in fall, winter or early spring. No regular pruning.
   Hamamelis japonica, 12 to 20 ft.; purple calyxes and yellow flowers in late winter, with petals slightly longer than those of *H. mollis.*
   H. mollis, 15 to 20 ft.; fragrant, narrow-petaled, yellow flowers in late winter.
   H. vernalis, 6 ft.; small, fragrant yellow flowers in midwinter.

   H. virginiana, 15 ft.; flowers yellow or brownish-yellow, in late fall.

HARDY ORANGE. See *Poncirus.*

HAWTHORN. See *Crataegus.*

HAZELNUT. See *Corylus.*

HE-HUCKLEBERRY. See *Lyonia ligustrina.*

HERCULES'-CLUB. See *Aralia spinosa.*

HIBISCUS
Mallowlike flowers, borne from late summer onward, are the attraction of these shrubs or small trees; for full sun and good soil. They can be grown without regular pruning; or previous year's shoots may be cut back close to their bases in spring and excess weak shoots thinned out. Pruned specimens produce the largest flowers. For a subtropical evergreen kind, see page 478.
   Hibiscus syriacus (shrub althea, rose of Sharon), 10 to 12 ft.; flowers pink, purple or white. There are

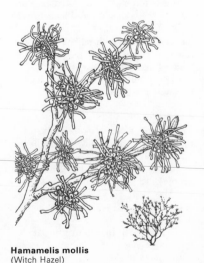

Hamamelis mollis
(Witch Hazel)

Hibiscus syriacus
(Shrub Althea, Rose of Sharon)

many named horticultural varieties; among the best are:

H. s. Admiral Dewey, double white flowers.

H. s. amplissimus, double pink flowers.

H. s. coelestis, deep blue single flowers.

H. s. Duc de Brabant, double red blooms.

H. s. elegantissimus, double white flowers marked with maroon in the center.

H. s. Jeanne d'Arc, flowers double, white.

H. s. monstrosus, flowers white with purple centers.

H. s. Snowdrift, fine single white flowers, a little earlier than most varieties.

HILLS-OF-SNOW. See *Hydrangea arborescens grandiflora*.

HIMALAYA HONEYSUCKLE. See *Leycesteria*.

HIPPOPHAË (SEA BUCKTHORN)

Hippophaë rhamnoides, 25 ft.; spiny, silvery-leaved. Soil ordinary; full sun. Provided a male plant is nearby, attractive orange berries are borne abundantly on the female plant and persist throughout the winter. No regular pruning.

HOLODISCUS

For sunny locations and well-drained soil, not excessively dry. Gracefully arching branches and small, creamy-white flowers in large pyramidal clusters in summer.

Holodiscus discolor (rock spirea), 18 ft.

H. dumosus, 8 ft.

HYDRANGEA

Summer and fall bloomers for deep, fertile, reasonably moist soils. Pruning varies according to kind.

Hydrangea arborescens grandiflora (hills-of-snow), 4 ft.; flowers white in great oval heads. Prune in spring. Sun or light shade.

H. macrophylla, 10 ft., and its many varieties are the hydrangeas with large globular heads of white, blue or pink flowers in summer. On alkaline soils, usually blue-flowered varieties produce pink flowers. Those most commonly grown have globular heads of all-sterile flowers. Attractive varieties called lacecaps have flat heads in which an outer ring of sterile flowers contrasts with the inner, small, fertile flowers. There are many fine named varieties of both sterile and lacecap types. For sun. Prune by cutting out old flowering shoots and weak growths immediately after blooming. Do not cut off strong new shoots that develop then. (See illustration, page 427.)

H. paniculata grandiflora (peegee hydrangea), 20 ft.; large panicles of creamy flowers, which turn pink as they age in late summer and fall. May be left unpruned or cut back to near bases of previous year's shoots in spring. Sun; will stand light shade. The fertile-flowered *H. paniculata* is dainty and attractive.

H. quercifolia (oak-leaved hydrangea), 6 ft.; handsome foliage that colors red in fall. Flowers in large pyramidal clusters. Best in light shade. Prune after flowering.

HYPERICUM (ST.-JOHN'S-WORT)
Attractive plants bearing golden-yellow flowers with a central brush of stamens in summer. Sun or light shade. No regular pruning. For evergreen kinds, see page 462.

Hypericum buckleii, 9 in.; suitable for ground cover.

H. frondosum, 3 ft.; flowers 2 in. across.

H. prolificum, 4 ft.; flowers ¾ in. across. Very hardy.

ILEX
For evergreen kinds, see pages 462 and 479. Deciduous kinds have colorful fall foliage, and the female plants bear attractive berries if a male is nearby. Good garden soil; sun or light shade. No regular pruning.

Ilex decidua (possum haw), 30 ft.; berries red or orange.

I. laevigata (smooth winterberry), 6 ft.; berries orange-red.

I. verticillata (black alder, winterberry), 10 ft.; red berries. Variety *chrysocarpa* has yellow berries. The berries are long-lasting.

INDIAN CURRANT. See *Symphoricarpos orbiculatus*.

INDIGO. See *Indigofera*.

INDIGOFERA (INDIGO)
Small-flowered summer bloomers for sun and well-drained soil. May be left unpruned or pruned in early spring. New shoots bloom first year.

Indigofera amblyantha, 6 ft.; lav-

ender-pink flowers over a long period.

I. gerardiana, 6 ft.; attractive short spikes of purple pea flowers after midsummer.

I. incarnata, 2 ft.; flowers pink and white.

I.i. alba, 2 ft.; flowers pure white.

I. potaninii, 5 ft.; flowers lilac-pink, produced over a long period.

ITEA VIRGINICA
(SWEET SPIRE, VIRGINIA WILLOW)
Excellent summer-flowering shrub, 9 ft.; for not excessively dry, fertile soil; sun or light shade. Has small white fragrant flowers in erect spikes. Foliage colors well in fall. Hardy at New York City. No regular pruning.

JAPANESE ANGELICA TREE. See *Aralia elata*.

JASMINUM NUDIFLORUM (JASMINE)
Spreading, branches lax, 10 ft.; flowers yellow, early spring. Ordinary soil; sun. No regular pruning.

JERUSALEM THORN. See *Parkinsonia aculeata*.

JETBEAD. See *Rhodotypos tetrapetala*.

JUDAS TREE. See *Cercis Siliquastrum*.

JUNEBERRY. See *Amelanchier*.

KERRIA
Kerrias are not particular about soil, are useful in sun or light shade. Prune after flowering, removing the old or weak shoots only.

Kerria japonica, 8 ft.; long green woody stems covered with single golden-yellow flowers in spring.

K.j. pleniflora, 8 ft., has globular double orange-yellow flowers.

KOELREUTERIA PANICULATA
(GOLDENRAIN TREE)
Summer-flowering tree, 30 ft. Small

yellow flowers in large panicles followed by bladderlike fruit. Ordinary soil; full sun. No regular pruning.

KOLKWITZIA AMABILIS (BEAUTY BUSH)
Spring-flowering, 10 ft.; with tubular pink flowers. Ordinary soil; sun. Prune by thinning out old and weak branches after flowering.

LABURNUM (GOLDEN CHAIN)
These lovely small trees have drooping racemes of yellow pealike flowers in spring. Ordinary soil; full sun. No regular pruning. Seeds are poisonous.
   Laburnum alpinum (Scotch laburnum), 15 ft.; the hardiest kind, hardy in southern New England.
   L. anagyroides, 20 ft.
   L. watereri, 20 ft.; a hybrid.

LAGERSTROEMIA INDICA
(CRAPE MYRTLE)
Commonly planted in the South, hardy as far north as Baltimore and, in extremely well-sheltered locations, at New York City; 20 ft.; blooms for long periods in summer. Flowers in showy panicles, white, pink or red. Ordinary soil; sun. May be left unpruned or cut back close to base of previous season's growth in late winter. Transplant with ball of soil.

LEADPLANT. See *Amorpha canescens.*

LESPEDEZA (BUSH CLOVER)
Summer bloomers for well-drained soil and sun. Flowers pealike. May be pruned hard in spring.
   Lespedeza bicolor, 10 ft.; flowers rosy-purple.
   L. japonica, 10 ft.; flowers pure white, late-blooming.
   L. thunbergii, 10 ft.; flowers rosy-purple.

LEYCESTERIA
(HIMALAYA HONEYSUCKLE)
   Leycesteria formosa, 6 ft.; green-

stemmed shrub with drooping clusters of white flowers surrounded by burgundy-colored bracts in summer. The flowers are followed by black berries, but the bracts remain. Hardy in sheltered places at New York City. Prune back hard in late winter. An attractive, easily grown shrub for ordinary soil in sun.

LIGUSTRUM (PRIVET)
Deciduous privets are used almost exclusively as hedge plants, yet when given room to grow and left unpruned they form useful shrubs for screening and windbreaks. Their peculiarly scented flowers are borne in small panicles in summer and are followed by bluish-black or black berries. Ordinary soil; sun, will stand shade. No regular pruning. For the evergreen kind, see page 465 in "Evergreen Shrubs."
   Ligustrum amurense (Amur privet), 15 ft.
   L. obtusifolium regelianum (Regel's privet), 5 ft.; very hardy.
   L. ovalifolium (California privet), 15. ft.
   L. quihoui, 6 ft.; late-blooming, for mild climates only.
   L. sinense, 12 ft.; for mild climates only.
   L. vulgare, 15 ft.

LILAC. See *Syringa.*

LOCUST. See *Robinia.*

LONICERA (BUSH HONEYSUCKLE)
Shrub-type honeysuckles thrive in ordinary soil in sun, will tolerate light shade. Flowers are small, funnel-shaped and followed by small berries in pairs. No regular pruning. For other kinds of honeysuckle, see page 479 in "Hedges."
   Lonicera bella, 6 ft.; flowers summer, pinkish; berries red.
   L. fragrantissima, 6 ft.; flowers white, fragrant; berries red.

432

L. involucrata, 3 ft.; flowers summer, yellow; berries purple-black.

L. korolkowii, 12 ft.; blue-green foliage; flowers pink, summer; berries orange-red.

L. maackii, 15 ft.; flowers white becoming yellowish, summer; berries red.

L. morrowii, 6 ft.; flowers white, changing to yellow, summer; berries red.

L. spinosa albertii, 4 ft.; flowers fragrant, pink, late spring; berries are reddish.

L. syringantha, 9 ft.; flowers spring, lilac-rose, fragrant; berries orange-red.

L. tatarica (Tartarian honeysuckle), 9 ft.; flowers late spring, pink to white; berries red. A vigorous, pest-free shrub.

LUPINUS (LUPINE)
Plant out from pots when young, in dry, sunny place. Must be staked, as it is not strong enough for windy sites. Suitable only for mild, cool climates, such as parts of Pacific Northwest. No regular pruning.

Lupinus arboreus (tree lupine), 6 or 7 ft.; short spikes of fragrant, yellow pea-flowers, summer.

LYCIUM HALIMIFOLIUM
(BOXTHORN, MATRIMONY VINE)
More or less sprawling shrub, usually spiny, 10 ft.; flowers purple, small, summer; berries orange-red. Ordinary soil; sun. No regular pruning.

LYONIA
Lyonia ligustrina (maleberry; he-huckleberry), 10 ft.; flowers late spring, white or pink. Soil acid, moist; sun or light shade. No regular pruning.

L. mariana (staggerbush), 6 ft.; flowers late spring, pink or white. Same requirements as *L. ligustrina.*

MAGNOLIA
Magnolias are aristocrats of shrubs

and flowering trees. Plant in well-drained, fertile soil that is not subject to extreme dryness. They need full sun. When transplanting, it is best to retain a ball of soil about the roots and to move in spring. No regular pruning. For an evergreen kind, see page 406. For other deciduous kinds, see page 381.

Magnolia cordata, 30 ft.; flowers yellow, late spring, after leaves are fully expanded. A small edition of the cucumber tree, *M. acuminata.*

M. liliflora, 10 ft.; flowers rosy-purple on outside of petals, white on inside, before leaves.

M.l. nigra, flowers dark purple outside, light purple within.

M. salicifolia, 30 ft.; not wide-spreading, leaves narrow; flowers white, fragrant, spring, before leaves expand.

M. sieboldii, 30 ft.; flowers white with red stamens, produced in succession over a long period in summer.

M. soulangeana, 20 ft., white flowers flushed purple at the base in spring, before leaves.

M.s. alba, white flowers.

M.s. lennei, flowers rose-purple outside and white inside.

M. stellata (star magnolia), 12 ft.; slow-growing; bears starry white flowers in early spring, before leaves. It flowers when the plant is very small. This is the hardiest magnolia.

M.s. rosea, delicate pink flowers.

M. watsonii, 20 ft.; flowers white with pink or red stamens, fragrant, midsummer.

MALEBERRY. See *Lyonia ligustrina.*

MALUS (CRAB APPLE)
Crab apples are small trees that bear a profusion of attractive flowers in spring and, in most cases, attractive fruit in fall. All grow well in most soils in sun. No regular pruning.

Malus angustifolia (Southern crab

Magnolia soulangeana

apple), 25 ft.; semievergreen; flowers pink, fragrant; fruit yellow-green.

M. arnoldiana (Arnold crab apple), 20 ft.; flowers pink, fading to white inside, fragrant; fruit yellow and red.

M. atrosanguinea (carmine crab apple), 20 ft.; flowers deep pink; fruit dark red; not very ornamental.

M. baccata (Siberian crab apple), 40 ft.; flowers white, fragrant; fruit red or yellow.

M. Dolgo, 35 ft.; flowers white; fruit red, ripening early, excellent for jelly.

M. Dorothea, 25 ft.; flowers crimson, semidouble; fruit yellow. Blooms when young and very regularly.

M. floribunda, 30 ft.; flowers deep pink, changing to nearly white, fragrant; fruit red and yellow. Blooms when young and regularly.

M. halliana parkmanii (Parkman crab apple), 15 ft.; flowers pink, double; fruit dull red, not attractive. Not as hardy as most crab apples; hardy in southern New England.

M. Hopa, 30 ft.; flowers pink, fragrant; fruit orange and red, useful for jelly-making.

M. hupehensis (tea crab apple), 20 ft.; flowers pink, fading to white, fragrant; fruit greenish-yellow to red.

M. ioensis plena (Bechtel crab apple), 25 ft.; flowers pink, double, fragrant; fruit green, sparsely borne. Extremely hardy but unfortunately subject to cedar-apple rust disease.

M. Katherine, 20 ft.; flowers large, pale pink fading to white, double; fruit dull red. May tend to flower profusely alternate years.

M. purpurea aldenhamensis, 25 ft.; flowers purplish-red, semidouble; fruit purplish-red; foliage purplish.

M. Red Jade, 15 ft.; pendulous branches; flowers blush-white; fruit bright red.

M. sargentii (Sargent crab apple), 8 ft.; broader than high; flowers white, fragrant; fruit small, dark red, remaining attractive for a long time.

M. scheideckeri, 20 ft.; flowers pale pink, double; fruit yellow or orange.

M. spectabilis riversii (River's crab apple), 20 ft.; flowers pink, double; fruit green, not ornamental.

M. toringoides, 25 ft.; late-blooming, flowers white, fragrant; fruit pear-shaped, yellow and red; handsome.

M. zumi calocarpa (redbud crab apple), 20 ft.; flowers pink in bud, opening to white; fruits bright red, very ornamental, long-lasting.

MAPLE. See *Acer*.

MATRIMONY VINE. See *Lycium halimifolium*.

MERATIA. See *Chimonanthus*.

MIMOSA. See *Albizzia*.

MOCK ORANGE. See *Philadelphus*.

MYRICA
Excellent for poor, sandy soils and full sun. Female plants produce a profusion of attractive gray waxy berries if a male specimen is nearby. No regular pruning. For evergreen kind, see page 407.

Myrica cerifera (wax myrtle), 34 ft.; hardy about as far north as New Jersey.

M. pensylvanica (bayberry), hardy north to Labrador.

NANNYBERRY. See *Viburnum lentago*.

NINEBARK. See *Physocarpus*.

ORCHID TREE. See *Bauhinia variegata*.

PAEONIA (TREE PEONY)
Tree peonies are among the most spectacularly beautiful of shrubs. They are not difficult to grow. Plant in deep, well-drained, fertile soil, containing lime, in fall, in sun. Do not transplant unless absolutely necessary. No regular pruning. Occasionally cut out old, weak branches.

Paeonia delavayi, 5 ft.; crimson flowers 3 to 4 in. across, with a ring of golden stamens, early summer.

P. ludlowii, 6 ft. or more; clear yellow flowers, early summer.

P. lutea, 3 ft.; yellow flowers in June, smaller than those of *P. ludlowii*.

P. suffruticosa (mountain peony), 3 to 6 ft. This bears red flowers in May; in common with all the peonies listed here, the much-divided foliage is always decorative. There are many named varieties and hybrids with semidouble or fully double flowers, often 6 in. across, in shades of white, red, pink or purple. Consult catalogues of specialists for these.

PARKINSONIA ACULEATA
(JERUSALEM THORN)
Thorny tree for subtropical climates, 30 ft.; flowers yellow, fragrant; leaves small. Ordinary soil; sun. No regular pruning except shearing when grown as a hedge.

PEA TREE. See *Caragana*.

PEARLBUSH. See *Exochorda*.

PHILADELPHUS (MOCK ORANGE)
The well-loved mock oranges are often called syringa, which is the Latin name of the lilac. Plant in fertile soil, in sun; they will tolerate light shade. Prune after flowering by removing some of the old flowered shoots.

Philadelphus coronarius, 10 ft.; a leafy shrub with small, creamy-white, very fragrant flowers.

P. cymosus, 6 to 8 ft.; includes several hybrids, with white flowers.

P.c. Atlas, flowers single.

P.c. Coquette, flowers single, very fragrant.

P.c. Perle Blanche, flowers single, very fragrant.

P. floridus, 8 ft.; flowers white, single, form a well-shaped specimen.

P. grandiflorus, 9 ft.; flowers white, single, not scented. Good growth habit.

P. inodorus, 8 ft.; flowers white, single, not fragrant. Good upright growth habit.

Philadelphus coronarius
(Mock Orange)

P. lemoinei, a group of splendid hybrids. Consult catalogues of nurseries for these.

P.l. Avalanche, 4 ft.; flowers white, single, very fragrant.

P.l. Belle Etoile, 6 ft.; flowers white, single.

P.l. Boule d'Argent, 5 ft.; flowers white, double.

P.l. Girandole, 4 ft.; flowers white, single.

P.l. Innocence, 8 ft.; flowers single, white, very fragrant.

P.l. Mont Blanc, 4 ft.; flowers white, single.

P. purpureo-maculatus, 6 ft. or more; white flowers with purple-blotched centers. The largest flowers are found among the hybrids.

P.p. Beauclerk, 6 to 8 ft.; white flowers with purple centers.

P.p. Sirene, 4 ft.; flowers white, single.

P.p. Sybille, 6 to 8 ft.; white flowers with purple centers.

P. virginalis, a hybrid group of which the following are excellent:

P.v. Bouquet Blanc, 6 ft.; flowers single, white.

P.v. Glacier, 5 ft.; flowers double, white.

P.v. Virginal, flowers double, white. This variety is at its best when pruned back hard, almost to ground level, after flowering.

PHYSOCARPUS (NINEBARK)
Easy to grow in ordinary soil in sun or semishade. Flowers are small, white or pinkish, in clusters. No regular pruning.

Physocarpus intermedius parviflorus, 4 ft.; a choice and more refined shrub than *P. opulifolius*.

PINXTER FLOWER. See *Rhododendron nudiflorum*.

PONCIRUS TRIFOLIATA (HARDY ORANGE)
A stiff, dense shrub or small tree, 35 ft.; with green spiny branches and dark green foliage. In spring the very fragrant small white orange blossoms appear and are succeeded by tiny inedible oranges, which are quite decorative. Hardy in sheltered places at New York City and even to Boston. Acid soil and sun. No regular pruning.

POSSUM HAW. See *Ilex decidua*.

POTENTILLA FRUTICOSA (SHRUBBY CINQUEFOIL)
These are very hardy shrubs which flower very freely all through summer. They are not fussy about soil, but do better in light soils in full sun. One of the best varieties is:

Potentilla fruticosa farreri, 2 ft.; with 1-in.-wide golden flowers.

Consult catalogues of nurserymen for many splendid named varieties.

PRINSEPIA SINENSIS

Thorny, up to 9 ft. tall, with red cherrylike fruit in summer. One of the first shrubs to leaf out in spring, and therefore interesting to use among or near very early-blooming shrubs, such as *Rhododendron mucronulatum* (azalea) and forsythia, which bloom before they leaf out. May be sheared to form a hedge; otherwise no regular pruning.

PRIVET. See *Ligustrum*.

PRUNUS

The *Prunus* genus is very large and diverse. It contains the cherries, plums, almonds, peaches and apricots, as well as evergreen kinds, which are treated on page 468. Those grown as hedges, both deciduous and evergreen, are listed on page 480. All grow well in ordinary soil, and most benefit from liming from time to time if the soil is acid. Little pruning is needed. See also "Fruits," page 304.

Flowering Almonds

Prunus glandulosa (flowering almond), 4 ft.; attractive shrub with small red cherry fruit. Although horticulturally regarded as a flowering almond, this is botanically a cherry.

P.g. albo-plena; flowers are white, double.

P.g. rosea, flowers pink.

P.g. sinensis, flowers pink, double.

P. tenella alba (dwarf Russian almond), 5 ft.; flowers white; fruit red cherries; very hardy.

P. triloba (flowering almond), 12 ft.; flowers white or pink, usually double in cultivated varieties.

Flowering Apricots

Prunus mume (Japanese apricot). A number of varieties, mostly 10 to 15 ft., are cultivated, including:

P.m. albo-plena, flowers white, double.

P.m. Bonita, flowers crimson and double.

P.m. Dawn, flowers soft pink and double.

P.m. pendula, flowers white, branches pendulous.

P.m. Weeping Red, flowers red, branches pendulous.

Chokecherries

Prunus maackii (Amur chokecherry), 40 ft.; flowers small, white; bark peels like that of birch trees. Extremely hardy.

P. padus (European bird cherry), 40 ft.; flowers white, fragrant, in drooping racemes; fruit small, black. One of the earliest to leaf in spring.

P.p. commutata, blooms earlier than other varieties.

P.p. plena, flowers double.

P.p. spaethii, large flowers.

P.p. watereri, longer racemes than other varieties.

P. virginiana, 25 ft.; flowers white; fruit dark purple. Very hardy. Much liked by tent caterpillars.

P.v. demissa and *P.v. melanocarpa* differ but slightly botanically.

Flowering Cherries

Prunus besseyi (Western sand cherry), 7 ft.; flowers white; fruit small, blackish-purple, edible; very hardy.

P. campanulata, 25 ft.; flowers rose-red; fruit red. Excellent for West Coast.

P. cistena (purpleleaf sand cherry), 7 ft.; flowers white; foliage reddish; fruit is dark purple, and the cherries are edible.

P. fruticosa (European dwarf cherry), 4 ft.; flowers white; fruit is small and red.

P. pensylvanica (wild red cherry), 35 ft.; flowers white; fruit small, red.

P. sargentii, 60 ft., usually smaller; flowers deep pink. Very hardy. One of the finest flowering cherries.

P. serrulata (Japanese flowering cherry), 20 ft. Most cultivated varieties of Japanese cherry belong here. Among the best varieties are the following (consult nursery catalogues for others):

P.s. Amanogawa, narrow, erect.

P.s. Fugenzo (syn. Kofugen), flowers large, pink, double.

P.s. Kwanzan, rather upright habit; flowers large, pink, double. One of the hardiest.

P.s. Shirotae, flowers large, white, double.

P.s. Shogetsu, a rather small tree; flowers pale pink, double.

P.s. Takinioi, flowers white, fragrant, single.

P. subhirtella (rosebud cherry), 30 ft.; flowers small, pink, appearing well before leaves.

P.s. autumnalis, blooms freely in fall as well as spring.

P.s. pendula, a pendulous or weeping kind.

P.s.p. flore-plena, a double-flowered weeping variety.

P. tomentosa, 9 ft.; blush pink; fruit, red edible cherries.

P. yedoensis, 45 ft.; flowers white or pink, slightly fragrant. Most of the trees around the Tidal Basin in Washington, D.C , are this kind.

P.y. perpendens, a weeping variety.

Flowering Peaches

Prunus persica (flowering peach), 20 ft. Several excellent varieties are cultivated, including:

P.p. albo-plena, flowers white, and double.

P.p. Burbank, flowers pink, double.

P.p. camelliaeflora, flowers red, double.

P.p. Helen Borchers, flowers large, clear pink.

P.p. Iceberg, flowers white.

Flowering Plums

Prunus americana, 25 ft.; flowers are white; fruit is red or yellowish.

P. angustifolia (Chickasaw plum), 12 ft.; flowers white; fruit red or yellow.

P. blirieana, 20 ft.; flowers light pink, double; fruit purplish-red; foliage reddish-purple. Prune fairly freely immediately after blooming to encourage vigorous growth.

P. cerasifera atropurpurea (syn. *P. pissardii*—Myrobalan plum), 20 ft.; flowers pink; fruit small, purple, edible; foliage reddish-purple. Prune fairly freely immediately after blooming to encourage vigorous growth. The variety Thundercloud has, perhaps, more intense foliage color.

P. maritima (beach plum), 6 ft., dense shrub; flowers white, single or double, followed by reddish-purple or, in variety *flava*, yellow plums that make excellent jelly. Especially suited for seaside planting.

PURPLELEAF SAND CHERRY. See *Prunus cistena*.

PURSHIA TRIDENTATA (ANTELOPE BRUSH)
Spreading shrub, 9 ft.; with bluish-gray, sparse foliage and rather inconspicuous yellow flowers in spring. Well-drained dryish soil; sun. Excessive wetness, especially in winter, kills this shrub. No regular pruning.

RASPBERRY. See *Rubus*.

REDBUD. See *Cercis canadensis*.

RHAMNUS (BUCKTHORN)
Mostly rather coarse shrubs or small trees with handsome, lustrous foliage, inconspicuous greenish flowers and berrylike fruit. They make good hedges and screens. Prosper in sun or light shade. No regular pruning is needed except for shearing when grown as hedges.

Rhamnus cathartica (common buckthorn), 12 ft.; fruit black. For dryish soil.

R. *dahurica*, 25 ft.; fruit black. For dryish soil.

R. *frangula* (alder buckthorn), 15 ft.; fruit red, changing to black-purple. For somewhat moist soil.

RHODODENDRON (AZALEA)

The plants commonly called azalea are included by botanists in the genus *Rhododendron*. Here we deal only with deciduous kinds; for the evergreens, see page 469. *Rhododendron* is a vast and varied group divided into several distinct types with numerous horticultural varieties in each. The work of breeding continues, and new varieties are named each year.

Deciduous azaleas are among the most magnificent of spring-flowering shrubs. Unfortunately they cannot be grown everywhere. First, they are acid-soil plants and need a pH of 5 to 6.5. They will grow at neutral, pH 7, but fail at higher readings. Also, they are essentially humid-climate plants. They do not succeed in the great inland areas of the continent, characterized by dry, hot summers or dry, cold winters. In the Northeast and Northwest many azaleas flourish. Different kinds vary considerably in their ability to survive low temperatures.

These plants form compact masses of fine roots, so should always be transplanted with a ball of soil. Early spring or early fall are the best times for moving them, although if great care is taken they can be successfully transplanted even when in bloom. The soil should be well drained and contain very generous amounts of organic matter, such as compost, leaf mold, peat moss or very old and very decayed manure (never use fresh manure). It should be always reasonably moist. Watering in periods of drought is very desirable, as well as a mulch of compost, peat moss, wood chips,

pine needles or other suitable material.

No regular pruning is needed, just the removal of occasional straggly growths that appear. Old, very overgrown specimens may be cut back hard in spring and if fertilized, mulched and kept watered, will renew themselves from the base; but this is a rather slow process, and it may take two or three years or more for a specimen so treated to attain flowering size.

Azaleas thrive in places sheltered from sweeping winds and where they receive just a little shade from the hottest sun. Excessive shade inhibits flowering and induces straggly growth. Provided they receive adequate moisture, they grow well in full sun.

These shrubs are likely to be infested with lacebugs, especially when grown in sun. The undersides of the leaves should be examined regularly, and at the first sign of infestation, spraying with malathion should be done. It is a good practice to pick off all faded blooms.

Species of Deciduous Azaleas

Rhododendron arborescens, 10 ft.; flowers white or pinkish, very fragrant, late spring; good autumn foliage color. Very hardy.

R. *calendulaceum* (flame azalea), 10 ft.; flowers yellow, orange to scarlet.

R. *canadense* (rhodora), 3 ft.; rosy-purple, early spring. For wet soils. Very hardy.

R. *mucronulatum*, 6 ft.; flowers rosy-purple. The earliest to bloom in spring. Foliage colors in fall. Very hardy.

R. *nudiflorum* (pinxter flower), 6 ft.; flowers pink to blush-pink (in variety *roseum*, bright pink), spring.

R. *obtusum kaempferi* (torch azalea), 7 ft.; a deciduous variety of a species that includes several evergreen, or at least partly evergreen, kinds, such as the Kurume azaleas (see page 470) and the varieties

Rhododendron
(Azalea)

amoenum and *hinodegeri*. *R. obtusum kaempferi* varies in flower color from pink and orange to red. These kinds are hardy as far north as southern New England.

R. occidentale, 10 ft.; flowers white to pinkish with a yellow blotch, spring. Useful for Pacific Coast gardens.

R. prunifolium, 9 ft.; flowers crimson, summer. Hardy about as far north as Philadelphia.

R. schlippenbachii (royal azalea), 15 ft.; flowers large, pink, fragrant, early spring; good foliage. Very hardy.

R. vaseyi (pinkshell azalea), 8 ft.; flowers light pink, spring; foliage colors well in fall. Thrives in moist soils but tolerates drier conditions. Very hardy.

R. viscosum (swamp azalea), 10 ft.; flowers white or blush-pink, fragrant, early summer; foliage colors well in fall. For moist or wet soils. Very hardy.

Hybrid Deciduous Azaleas

For the names of varieties and descriptions of the flower colors of the following fine hybrid azaleas, the catalogues of specialist nurserymen should be consulted.

Ghent azaleas: These hybrids, collectively *Rhododendron gandavense*, survive temperatures of -20° F. and are hardy well north into Maine. There are single- and double-flowered varieties in yellows, reds, pinks and combinations, as well as white. They grow 6 to 10 ft. high.

Knaphill and Exbury azaleas: These may be regarded as one hybrid group because the Knaphill varieties are the parents of the Exbury strain. They come in a wide range of colors from yellow through orange and pink to red, and include white and combinations. They grow 5 to 10 ft. and survive temperatures down to or below O° F.

Mollis azaleas: A group of hybrids somewhat less cold-resistant than the Ghent azaleas but which prosper in parts of New England. These azaleas, collectively *Rhododendron kosteriana*, are rather stiff shrubs with fragrant flowers in tones of cream, yellow, orange, pink and soft reds, as well as white. They are very sensitive to dry soil conditions in summer.

RHODOTYPOS TETRAPETALA (JETBEAD)
An easy-to-grow shrub, 6 ft., with white flowers in spring followed by glossy black hard berries which remain all winter. Soil ordinary; sun or light shade. No regular pruning.

RHUS (SUMAC)
Mostly coarse plants of secondary value in regions where better kinds can be cultivated; easily grown in ordinary soil in sun. No regular pruning. The plant sometimes called *R. cotinus* is dealt with under *Cotinus*.

Rhus aromatica (fragrant sumac), 3 to 4 ft.; flowers inconspicuous followed by attractive red fruits; foliage colors well in fall. Spreads by suckers. A good bank plant.

R. cistmontana, 6 ft.; flowers inconspicuous; fruit red.

R. copallina (shining sumac), 25 ft.; flowers inconspicuous; fruit borne by female trees, red; good fall color. Variety *laciniata* has finely divided leaves. One of the best of the sumacs.

R. glabra (smooth sumac), 20 ft.; flowers inconspicuous; fruits borne by female specimens, red; fine fall color. Hardy very far north.

R. typhina (staghorn sumac), 30 ft.; flowers inconspicuous; fruit, on

female plants, crimson; good fall color. Thrives in dry soil. The varieties *laciniata* and *dissecta* have finely divided leaves.

RIBES (CURRANT)
These should not be planted in areas where white-pine blister rust is prevalent because they are alternate hosts for this serious disease. Before planting, consult the local County Agricultural Agent or other government source regarding regulations. Ordinary soil; sun or light shade. No regular pruning except shearing when planted as hedges.

Ribes alpinum (alpine currant, mountain currant), 7 ft.; flowers inconspicuous; fruit on female plants if a male is nearby, red; foliage attractive. A good hedge plant. Thrives in shade. Very hardy. The male form is not susceptible to white-pine blister rust.

R. aureum (golden currant), 6 ft.; flowers yellow, showy; fruit black.

R. cereum, 3 ft.; flowers white or greenish; fruit red. Very hardy.

R. odoratum, 6 ft.; flowers yellow or reddish, showy, fragrant; fruit on female if male is nearby, black.

R. sanguineum, 10 ft.; flowers pink or red; fruit on females if male is nearby, bluish-black. Popular in Pacific Northwest.

ROBINIA
Attractive late spring-flowering shrubs with clusters of pealike flowers, for well-drained soils and sun. No regular pruning. For other kinds, see page 385 in "Shade Trees."

Robinia hispida (rose acacia), 6 ft.; flowers pink or purplish-pink.

R. kelseyi, 9 ft.; flowers pink; one of the best.

R. neo-mexicana, 6 ft.; flowers pink.

ROCK SPIREA. See *Holodiscus discolor*.

ROCKY MOUNTAIN FLOWERING RASP-
BERRY. See *Rubus deliciosus*.

ROSA (ROSE)
The hybrid tea and other bedding and
climbing roses are discussed in the
chapter "Roses," page 206; but
many kinds of roses are worth
growing as shrubs, either with other
flowering shrubs or as isolated specimens. These include the species roses
and also the so-called old-fashioned
roses, which are becoming popular.
These are offered and described in the
catalogues of specialists. Many of
these have a short period of flowering
in May or June; others flower until
well into the fall. Plant in deep, rich,
loamy soil, improved by the addition
of decayed manure or rotted compost.
Prune by thinning out in spring.

Rosa acicularis, 3 ft.; flowers deep
pink, fragrant.

R. alba semi-plena (white rose of
York), white flowers.

R. blanda, 6 ft.; flowers pink, often
thornless.

R. carolina (pasture rose), 3 ft.;
flowers pink.

R. centifolia (cabbage rose), 6 ft.;
flowers pink, very fragrant, double.

R.c. cristata (crested moss or Cha-
peau de Napoleon), pink flowers,
their stems covered with a mosslike
growth of hairs.

R. damascena (damask rose), 6 ft.;
flowers blush-white to red, very fragrant, double.

R. eglanteria (sweet brier), 6 ft.;
flowers single or double, pink; foliage
sweetly fragrant.

R. foetida (Austrian brier), 8 ft.;
flowers deep yellow with an unpleasant odor.

R.f. bicolor (Austrian copper), flowers copper-red.

R.f. persiana (Persian yellow),
flowers yellow, double.

R. gallica (French rose), 4 ft.; flowers deep red, very fragrant.

R.g. vericolor (syn. *R.g. rosamundi*),
striped red and white flowers.

R. harisonii (Harison's yellow), 6
ft.; flowers yellow, double.

R. hugonis (Father Hugo rose), 6
ft.; flowers yellow, early-blooming.

R. moschata (musk rose), 6 ft.;
flowers white, musk-scented.

R.m. nastarana, flowers pinkish.
Not hardy in the north.

R. moyesii, 8 ft.; flowers red; fruit
showy, pear-shaped, orange-red.

R. multiflora, 9 ft.; very vigorous;
flowers white; forms a dense thicket.

R.m. platyphylla (seven sisters rose),
flowers pink, double.

R. omeiensis pteracantha, 12 ft.;
flowers white; foliage attractive;
stems with conspicuous bright red
prickles.

R. primula, 8 ft.; flowers yellow,
very early.

R. rubrifolia, 6 ft.; flowers dark
red. Hardy far North.

R. rugosa, 6 ft.; flowers white or
pink, single or double. Excellent for
seaside planting. Hardy far North.
Several distinct varieties and hybrids
are grown.

R. spinosissima, 3 ft.; flowers white,
pink or yellow, double or single.
Many varieties are grown.

R. virginiana, 6 ft.; flowers pink.
Very hardy.

R. wichuraiana (memorial rose), 2
ft.; procumbent, flowers white.

R. xanthina, 9 ft.; flowers yellow,
semidouble.

ROSE. See *Rosa*.

ROSE ACACIA. See *Robinia hispida*.

ROSE OF SHARON. See *Hibiscus syriacus*.

ROYAL POINCIANA. See *Delonix regia*.

RUBUS (RASPBERRY, BLACKBERRY)
Of easy cultivation in ordinary soil;

most kinds are best in sun. Prune by removing old shoots after fruiting or, in the case of white-stemmed kinds, by cutting plants to ground in spring. Summer-blooming.

Rubus biflorus, white flowers, summer. Canes covered with white wax.

R. cockburnianus, purple flowers in summer. Canes covered with white wax.

R. deliciosus (Boulder raspberry, Rocky Mountain flowering raspberry), 6 ft.; flowers white; fruit purple, sometimes reddish-purple. The double-flowered *R.d. plena* is fine.

R. idaeus strigosus (American red raspberry), 5 ft.; flowers white; fruit red.

R. lasiostylus, purplish flowers, summer. Canes covered with white wax.

R. leucodermis, 5 ft.; flowers white; fruit black. Stems yellowish.

R. occidentalis (blackcap), 5 ft.; flowers white; fruit black.

R. odoratus (flowering raspberry), 8 ft.; flowers large, rosy-purple, fragrant. Thrives in moist soil and part shade.

R. ulmifolius bellidiflorus (double-flowered thornless blackberry), sprays of double pink flowers in July; an attractive bramble, though without the white stems.

RUSSIAN OLIVE. See *Elaeagnus angustifolia*.

ST.-JOHN'S-WORT. See *Hypericum*.

SALIX (WILLOW)

Willows are generally fast-growing and thrive in damp soil in sun. For other kinds, see page 385.

Salix alba chermesiana is really a tall tree but is kept low and shrub-like by pruning annually in spring to encourage development of its remarkable bright red young shoots, which are very conspicuous in winter.

S. caprea (goat willow), 25 ft., is the best of the pussy willows. The flowers of the male tree grow into especially large catkins if the tree is pruned back hard, almost to the ground, every few years.

S. discolor (pussy willow), 20 ft.; a native kind with smaller, less striking "pussies" than those of *S. caprea*.

SAMBUCUS (ELDER)

The elders are not particular about soil but thrive best in moist places in sun or light shade. No regular pruning. Fruit edible. For another kind, see page 386.

Sambucus canadensis, 12 ft.; flowers white; fruit black.

S.c. aurea, foliage yellow.

S. melanocarpa, 12 ft.; flowers yellowish; fruit black.

S. nigra (European elder), 20 ft.; flowers white; fruit black.

S.n. aurea, foliage yellow.

S. racemosa (European red elder), 12 ft.; flowers yellowish; fruit red.

S.r. aurea plumosa, finely cut golden leaves.

SAND CHERRY, WESTERN and PURPLE-LEAF. See *Prunus besseyi*, *P. cistena*.

SEA BUCKTHORN. See *Hippophaë*.

SENNA. See *Cassia*.

SERVICEBERRY. See *Amelanchier*.

SHADBUSH. See *Amelanchier*.

SHEPHERDIA

Rather straggly shrubs suitable for dry and alkaline soils in sun. Fruit may be used for jelly. No regular pruning.

Shepherdia argentea (buffalo berry), 18 ft.; thorny; silvery foliage; flowers inconspicuous; berries red or yellow. A male tree must be near females to insure the latter's fruiting.

S. canadensis, 8 ft.; flowers inconspicuous; leaves silvery beneath; fruit red or yellow.

S. sitchensis, 15 ft.; fruit red. Hardy.

SHRUB ALTHEA. See *Hibiscus syriacus.*

SHRUBBY CINQUEFOIL. See *Potentilla fruticosa.*

SILK TREE. See *Albizzia julibrissin.*

SILVER BELL. See *Halesia.*

SMOKE TREE. See *Cotinus.*

SNOWBALL. See *Viburnum opulus, V. tomentosum.*

SNOWBERRY. See *Symphoricarpos albus.*

SNOWDROP TREE. See *Halesia.*

SOPHORA VICIIFOLIA
Graceful shrub for poor, sandy soil and sun. No regular pruning. Has fine foliage and bluish or violet pealike flowers in early summer. For *S. japonica*, see page 386.

SORBARIA (FALSE SPIREA)
For deep, rich soils containing plenty of moisture, in sun. Prune out the old flowering shoots in late winter.

Sorbaria aitchisonii, 8 to 10 ft.; red stems and plumes of white flowers in summer.

S. arborea, 12 to 15 ft.; spectacular plumes of creamy flowers appear in summer.

SORBUS
Small or medium-sized trees grown mainly for their berries. Ordinary, well-drained soil and sun are suitable. No regular pruning.

Sorbus alnifolia, 45 ft.; a fine kind, well shaped; berries bright red; good foliage color in fall.

S. americana (American mountain ash), 30 ft.; similar to *S. aucuparia;* berries red.

S. aucuparia (European mountain ash), 45 ft.; feathery leaves; orange berries. Very hardy.

S.a. asplenifolia, leaves doubly toothed at margins.

S.a. fastigiata, narrow, columnar.

S.a. pendula, branches pendulous.

S. decora, 25 to 30 ft.; red fruit. Very hardy.

SOUTHERN BLACK HAW. See *Viburnum rufidulum.*

SPARTIUM (SPANISH BROOM)
Spartium junceum, 9 to 10 ft., has the effect of an evergreen because the long shoots remain green, although its leaves are rarely seen except on young plants. The main display of large, yellow, fragrant pea-flowers is in summer, but some flowers appear at almost any time. For well-drained soils in full sun. Prune established plants well back in spring to keep them bushy.

SPINDLE TREE. See *Euonymus europaea.*

Spartium junceum
(Spanish Broom)

SPIRAEA (SPIREA)

Spireas are easily grown in ordinary garden soil in sun or light shade.

Spiraea albiflora, 1½ ft., compact; flowers white, summer. Prune in early spring when needed.

S. arguta, 6 to 8 ft.; thin twigs wreathed in small white flowers in May. Prune, when needed, after blooming.

S. bumalda Anthony Waterer, 3 to 4 ft.; flat heads of carmine flowers from July to August. Prune severely in late winter.

S. cantonensis, 3 ft.; flowers white, spring. Prune, when needed, after flowering. Succeeds well in warm climates.

S. densiflora, 2 ft.; flowers pink. Prune, when needed, after blooming.

S. douglasii, 8 ft.; flowers, summer, deep pink. Prune, when needed, in late winter.

S. lucida, 3 ft.; flowers white. Prune, when necessary, after they finish blooming.

S. media, 5 ft.; Flowers white,

Spiraea Thunbergii

spring. Prune, when needed, after blooming.

S. prunifolia plena (bridal wreath), 6 ft.; small, double white flowers on its slender twigs in May. Prune, if needed, after blooming.

S. thunbergii, 5 ft.; white flowers in spring. Prune, if needed, after blooming is finished.

S. vanhouttei, 6 ft.; summer. Prune, when needed, after flowering.

STAGGERBUSH. See *Lyonia mariana*.

STAR MAGNOLIA. See *Magnolia stellata*.

STEPHANANDRA INCISA

Graceful, 7 ft.; finely cut leaves and rather insignificant clusters of tiny white flowers in spring. Useful as a hedge. Soil ordinary; sun. Prune out dead wood in spring; when grown as hedge, shear regularly.

STEWARTIA

Small summer-flowering trees and shrubs that grow satisfactorily in ordinary soil, not too dry, in sun. Large white flowers. No regular pruning.

Stewartia malacodendron, 12 ft.; not reliably hardy north of Virginia.

S. ovata, 15 ft.; large white flowers with yellow stamens.

S.o. grandiflora, similar to *S. ovata* but stamens purple.

S. pseudo-camellia, 50 ft.; flowers resembling single camellias.

STORAX. See *Styrax*.

STYRAX (STORAX)

Choice small trees and shrubs with white flowers in spring. Soil porous, fertile. No regular pruning.

S. japonica, 30 ft.; a wide-spreading small tree. Hardy into New England.

S. obassia, 30 ft.; flowers fragrant. Hardy at New York City.

S. wilsonii, 9 ft.; not hardy in North.

SUMAC. See *Rhus*.

SWEETLEAF. See *Symplocus paniculata*.

SWEET PEPPERBUSH. See *Clethra alnifolia*.

SWEET-SCENTED SHRUB. See *Calycanthus*.

SWEET SPIRE. See *Itea virginica*.

SYMPHORICARPOS
Easy to grow in ordinary soil, in sun or shade. Flowers inconspicuous. No regular pruning.

Symphoricarpos albus (snowberry, waxberry), 5 ft.; large white berries which, unless infected by a disease that in some areas causes them soon to turn brown, remain attractive for many weeks. Very hardy.

S. chenaultii, 3 ft.; fruit white, with side exposed to sun red. Less hardy than others.

S. orbiculatus (Indian currant, coralberry), 4 ft.; fruit red, coral-like. Very hardy.

SYMPLOCOS PANICULATA (SWEETLEAF)
Large shrub, 30 ft.; with clusters of tiny white fragrant flowers in spring, followed by bright turquoise-blue berries. For ordinary soil and sun. No regular pruning.

SYRINGA (LILAC)
Lilacs are well-loved shrubs, most of which grow from 8 to 12 ft. high and flower in spring. Prune moderately after flowering to remove dead flower heads; thin out any weak growths and remove all suckers from grafted specimens. It is important to prune in such a way that a succession of vigorous new wood is produced to replace the oldest branches. Tall, straggly specimens respond to cutting back to within 6 in. of the ground in late winter. If fertilized and kept watered, they develop into shapely shrubs in about two years. Fertile, well-drained soil with some lime, sun and a location where there is good air circulation are needed. They are subject to borers, scale insects and mildew disease. (See illustration, page 410.)

Syringa amurensis japonica (Japanese tree lilac), 30 ft.; large panicles of creamy flowers, summer.

S. chinensis, 15 ft.; flowers lilac-purple; variety *alba*, white flowers.

S. josikaea, 12 ft.; flowers lilac-violet; foliage glossy.

S. microphylla, 6 ft.; much broader than high; flowers pale lilac in small panicles; leaves small.

S. persica, 6 ft.; flowers pale lilac, in small panicles.

S. p. laciniata, similar to *S. persica* but has finely divided leaves.

S. villosa, 9 ft.; flowers rosy-lilac to white, summer. Very hardy.

S. vulgaris (common lilac), 20 ft.; flowers lilac or white, very fragrant. Numerous varieties and hybrids. The "French lilacs" of gardens are developments from this species. Both single and double-flowered varieties are available in a wide range of colors. Consult the catalogues of specialists.

Other hybrid lilacs of garden value in North America are the Preston hybrids—to which the group name *S. prestoniae* has been given, developed originally at Canada's Central Experimental Farm in Ottawa, by Miss Isabella Preston—and a group of hybrids developed by Mr. F. L. Skinner, Dropmore, Manitoba. Both groups are hardier than *S. vulgaris* varieties and many other lilacs.

TAMARISK. See *Tamarix*.

TAMARIX (TAMARISK)
These are graceful shrubs with feathery flower sprays on long, arching branches. Those that are commonly

grown reach 12 ft. or more but can be kept lower by pruning. They thrive in sandy, well-drained soil in sun.

Tamarix africana. The plant commonly grown under this name is *T. parviflora.*

T. hispida (Kashgar tamarisk), 4 ft.; prune back hard in late winter.

T. odessana, 6 ft.; prune back hard in late winter.

T. parviflora, 15 ft.; deep pink flowers in spring. Prune immediately after flowering.

T. pentandra, 15 ft.; pink flowers in late summer. Prune in the late winter or spring.

TARTARIAN HONEYSUCKLE. See *Lonicera tatarica.*

THORN. See *Crataegus.*

TREE LUPINE. See *Lupinus arboreus.*

TREE PEONY. See *Paeonia.*

TRUEHEDGE COLUMNBERRY. See *Berberis thunbergii pluriflora.*

VACCINIUM

These acid-soil plants are among the few shrubs that thrive in moist—or even wet—soils. They grow best in sun. No regular pruning.

Vaccinium corymbosum (highbush blueberry), 9 to 10 ft.; probably the best and well worth growing where it can be given the right conditions. It bears small pinkish flowers in spring; has large, shining edible blue-black berries. In fall, leaves turn red. Very hardy. (See illustration, page 411.)

V. parvifolium, 10 ft.; flowers pinkish; fruit red. Less hardy than *V. corymbosum.*

VIBURNUM

Viburnums are among the most useful garden shrubs. They are easy to

grow, have white or, rarely, pink flowers and, in many kinds, clusters of showy berrylike fruit. Plant in fertile, reasonably moist soil, in sun or light shade. No regular pruning. Their foliage blackens if sprayed or dusted with pesticides or fungicides containing sulphur.

Viburnum bodnantense, 10 ft.; fragrant pink flowers.

V. burkwoodii, 6 ft.; flowers in globular heads, white or pinkish, fragrant, early spring. A little less hardy than *V. carlesii,* which it resembles; stands fair amount of shade.

V. carlcephalum, 7 ft.; flowers in globular heads, white or purplish, fragrant, early spring. Very fine.

V. carlesii, 6 ft.; rounded clusters of fragrant white or pinkish flowers in early spring.

V. dentatum (arrowwood), 12 ft.; flowers creamy-white, late spring, followed by blue berries. Suitable for heavy shade and city conditions; very hardy.

V. dilatatum, 8 ft.; flowers creamy-white, in late spring, followed by very decorative bright red berries. Variety *xanthocarpum* has attractive yellow fruit. Both are splendid shrubs.

V. fragrans, 9 ft.; sweetly scented, with small clusters of pinkish flowers in winter or early spring. In climates harsher than that of New York City, flower buds may be winter-killed.

V. lantana (wayfaring tree), 15 ft.; flowers white, spring; fruit red, changing to black. Tolerates dry soil.

V. lentago (nannyberry), 25 ft.; flowers white, spring; fruit black. Very hardy.

V. opulus (European cranberry bush), 12 ft.; white flowers, spring; orange and red berries. Much subject to aphid injury.

V. o. nanum, 2 ft.; rarely flowers. Makes a good, low, sheared hedge.

V. o. roseum (snowball), 12 ft.; bears large, globular heads of white flowers; this variety has no berries.

V. pauciflorum, 5 ft.; flowers white, spring; berries red.

V. prunifolium (black haw), 15 ft.; flowers white; fruit red, becoming blue-black, edible. Fine for screens and hedges. Very hardy.

V. rufidulum (Southern black haw), 30 ft.; similar to *V. prunifolium*. Excellent for the South.

V. setigerum, 12 ft.; flowers white, summer; fruit red in large clusters, lasting for a long period. One of the finest of fruiting shrubs.

V. s. aurantiacum, fruit orange.

V. sieboldii, 30 ft.; flowers white; fruit red. changing to black; leaves dark lustrous green. A very handsome shrub or small tree.

V. tomentosum, 10 ft.; one of the finest viburnums. In bloom has the general appearance of flowering dogwood, with branches arranged in horizontal tiers along which are borne the flat heads of white flowers in late spring. The fertile inner flowers are surrounded by conspicuous, flat, sterile flowers; fruit red, turning black.

V. t. mariesii has larger flowers and is a broader bush.

V. t. Pink Beauty, attractive pink flowers.

V. t. sterile (Japanese snowball) has globular heads of all-sterile flowers; no fruit. Less subject to aphids than *V. opulus roseum*, which it resembles.

V. trilobum (cranberry bush), 12 ft.; flowers white; fruit scarlet, edible. Extremely hardy.

VIRGINIA WILLOW. See *Itea virginica*.

VITEX

Late bloomers for fertile soil in sun. Each year in late winter, prune back hard, close to ground if desired.

Vitex agnus-castus (chaste tree), 10 ft.; flowers lilac or lavender in spikes; foliage grayish, aromatic. Varieties with white flowers (*alba*) and pink

Weigela

flowers (*rosea*) are grown. Hardy in the North as far as New York City.

V. negundo incisa, 12 ft.; flowers lilac or lavender, in loose panicles; leaves finely cut. Hardy in southern New England.

V. n. macrophylla has broader foliage.

WAHOO. See *Euonymus americana*.

WAXBERRY. See *Symphoricarpos albus*.

WAX MYRTLE. See *Myrica cerifera*.

WAYFARING TREE. See *Viburnum lantana*.

WEIGELA

Spring-flowering shrubs which bear trumpet-shaped flowers in great abundance in various shades of pink or red. All grow well in good soil. Prune after the flowering is over to remove some of the old, flowered wood. Among the best of them are:

W. Abel Carrière, 6 to 7 ft.; rose-pink.

W. Bristol Ruby, 6 to 8 ft.; red. One of the hardiest; a good one.

W. Eva Rathke, 4 to 5 ft.; crimson.

W. florida variegata, 6 to 8 ft.; leaves silvery-edged; pale pink flowers.

W. Newport Red, 5 to 6 ft.; rich red.

WHITE ALDER. See *Clethra*.

WHITE FORSYTHIA. See *Abeliophyllum*.

WILLOW. See *Salix*.

WINTERBERRY. See *Ilex verticillata*.

WINTER HAZEL. See *Corylopsis*.

WITCH HAZEL. See *Hamamelis*.

XANTHOCERAS SORBIFOLIA
Choice shrub, 15 ft.; flowers in racemes, white with yellow or reddish blotch, spring. Needs fertile soil, sun. No regular pruning. Difficult to transplant.

XANTHORIZA SIMPLICISSIMA
(YELLOWROOT)
A shrub 2 ft. high that spreads by

Zenobia pulverulenta

underground runners and forms a mass of attractive foliage; flowers and fruit inconspicuous. Good as a tall ground cover; for sun or shade in moist soil. No regular pruning.

YELLOWROOT. See *Xanthorhiza simplicissima*.

ZENOBIA
Zenobia pulverulenta, 6 ft.; beautiful shrubs for acid soil, preferably sedge-peaty or sandy loam. Abundant clusters of bell-shaped flowers, similar to those of lily of the valley, summer. Leaves and branches covered with powdery, bluish-gray bloom.

EVERGREEN SHRUBS—
For Foliage and Flowers

Year-round Enjoyment—Importance in Garden Design—Hardiness—Winter Protection—Care and Pruning—Varying Heights of Shrubs and Trees—Conifers—Broad-Leaved Evergreen Shrubs

EVERGREEN SHRUBS include some of the choicest and most useful garden plants. They add character and quality to home landscapes, and are rewarding throughout the year. Some, such as dwarf spruces (*Picea*), plum-yews (*Cephalotaxus*) and yews (*Taxus*), without showy flowers, are valued for foliage and form. Others delight with magnificent floral displays as well as year-round leafage. What is more gorgeous than a splendid rhododendron in full bloom, or a sasanqua camellia? Yet others, for instance, holly mahonia (*Mahonia*) and heavenly bamboo (*Nandina*), bear attractive fruits or berries.

Like evergreen trees, shrubs that retain their foliage throughout the year provide strong elements in garden landscapes; they are especially emphatic in winter when deciduous plants are leafless. Their placement calls for special thought. Dotted about indiscriminately, they can cause a feeling of uneasiness. When they are located with a discriminating sense for garden design, they can help tie a planting together into a congruous whole.

Evergreen shrubs are of particular value as dividers between separate units of the garden. Serving as formal or informal hedges or planted in groups, they provide good backgrounds for deciduous shrubs and for perennial and annual flowers. Some kinds, such as rhododendron, mountain laurel and camellia, are sufficiently shade-tolerant to be used effectively as underplantings in thinned woodlands. For foundation plantings many kinds of evergreen shrubs are invaluable.

HARDINESS

In the milder sections of North America, most kinds of evergreen shrubs are hardy. As one travels north and into regions of colder winters the number that can be grown diminishes rapidly. In the East, the number of evergreen shrubs hardy north of Washington, D.C., is fairly limited; southward along the coastal plain the possibilities rapidly increase.

Gardeners in the North often go to great efforts to succeed, and in sheltered areas in favored localities, such as parts of Long Island and Cape Cod, they are often able to grow some kinds considerably north of where these would ordinarily be hardy. Their chances of surviving winters near the borderlines of their hardiness are increased by keeping the ground about them mulched, by making sure that they are kept well watered throughout dry periods in late summer and fall and by protecting them from sweeping winter winds by erecting screens of burlap or by spraying them at the beginning of winter and a second time, four to six weeks later, with an antidesiccant (antitranspirant) spray.

WINTER PROTECTION

A hazard to evergreens used in foundation plantings is caused by snow and ice dropping on them from roofs. Guards installed on the roofs, or deflecting "roofs" of wood erected over susceptible evergreens and supported by a stout wooden or iron pipe framework, afford protection, but the best way to avoid, as far as possible, such troubles is by planting sufficiently far out from the roof edge so that the evergreens will be clear of roof drop.

Accumulations of snow on the shrubs, particularly of the heavy, wet kind, can cause breakage. Remove soft snow by striking the plant gently with the flat side of a broom; frozen snow cannot be removed without damage to the plant.

CARE AND PRUNING

Evergreen shrubs are always transplanted with a good ball of earth intact about their roots. In cold sections spring transplanting is preferable to fall, but in regions where very long, cold winters are not experienced, late summer and early all are appropriate for this work. Much harm results from too deep planting. The top of the old ball should be set not more than an inch deeper than it was previous to digging, and less is better. Thorough watering and mulching should follow planting, and great care should be taken that the roots do not become excessively dry during the first year following transplanting.

Most evergreen shrubs require no systematic pruning, although some respond well to close shearing and may be used for formal hedges. Occasional pruning, to remove an ill-placed branch or to make the spec-

imen more shapely, may be desirable from time to time. Conifers should be trimmed only lightly. Most broad-leaved kinds may be cut back severely if they have become unshapely; if then fertilized and kept well watered, they will renew themselves from the cut-back branches and trunks. More detailed information regarding this is given in the descriptions in the lists which follow.

VARYING HEIGHTS OF SHRUBS AND TREES

The opening statements of "Evergreen Trees," page 388, apply with equal validity to evergreen shrubs. Read them carefully. There is no sharp line of distinction between trees and shrubs. Kinds that are very definitely trees in their natural habitats or in other favorable places may attain only shrub size under less congenial conditions. The heights given here with each kind generally refer to maximum or near-maximum development under the best conditions. In gardens they are often considerably smaller.

CONIFERS

ARBORVITAE. See *Thuja*.

CEPHALOTAXUS (PLUM-YEW)
Slow-growing yewlike shrubs of graceful habit, with dark green foliage and plum-shaped fruits; best with well-drained, sandy soils that never become too dry. They stand shade.

Cephalotaxus drupacea (Japanese plum-yew), 25 ft., survives in sheltered locations as far north as southern New England. Variety *pedunculata* (syn. *harringtoniana*) is hardier.

C. fortunei (Chinese plum-yew), 25 ft., is hardy in sheltered locations as far north as Philadelphia.

CHAMAECYPARIS (FALSE CYPRESS)
Here low-growing varieties of false cypresses are considered. For tree

types, see page 392. These thrive in ordinary, well-drained, nonalkaline soils, anywhere except in the hot, dry plains and deserts. They do well near the sea and are little subject to pests or diseases. Hardy in northern areas, these shrubs may be sheared lightly in spring.

Chamaecyparis obtusa (Hinoki false cypress). Has produced many distinct low varieties, including:

C. o. compacta, a broad, dwarf conical plant.

C. o. ericoides, rounded bush, foliage turns purple in fall.

C. o. filicoides, with fernlike foliage and narrow habit or shape.

C. o. gracilis, pyramidal, compact.

C. o. pygmaea, very dwarf, creeping or prostrate.

C. pisifera (Sawara false cypress) has a number of shrub-size varieties including:

C. p. minima, low and shrubby.

C. p. squarrosa, with feathery gray foliage.

FALSE CYPRESS. See *Chamaecyparis*.

HEMLOCK. See *Tsuga canadensis pendula*.

IRISH YEW. See *Taxus baccata stricta*.

JUNIPERUS (JUNIPER)
This group contains some of the most hardy and most useful evergreen shrubs, some spreading and low enough to be used as ground covers, others of more substantial height and effective in foundation plantings, planted in groups or as individual specimens, and as hedges. Junipers are all sun lovers. They prosper in ordinary soils, neutral or alkaline rather than acid, and stand dry conditions well. They may be pruned to keep them shapely, but do not lend themselves to such strict shaping as does *Taxus* (yew) or *Buxus* (boxwood).

For tree kinds, see page 394. There are numerous varieties of shrubby junipers.

Juniperus chinensis pfitzeriana (Pfitzer's juniper), 9 ft., spreading, flat-topped, graceful. Hardy in New England.

J. c. sargentii (Sargent's juniper), 1 ft., prostrate, creeping, forming broad mats of steel-blue foliage. Excellent for seasides.

J. conferta (shore juniper), 1 ft., spreading; good for sandy soils and seaside plantings.

J. horizontalis (creeping juniper), 1 ft., creeping, good ground cover.

J. h. Bar Harbor, 1 ft., procumbent, green.

J. h. douglasii (Waukegan juniper), steel-blue foliage.

J. h. plumosa (Andorra juniper), light green feathery foliage that turns purple in fall.

J. h. procumbens, very low and creeping, dark green.

J. sabina (savin juniper), 9 ft., upright.

J. s. tamariscifolia, 2 ft., feathery, very handsome.

J. squamata meyeri (Meyer's juniper), 6 ft., irregular outline, erect, steel-blue.

MUGHO PINE. See *Pinus mugo mughus*.

PICEA (SPRUCE)
There are many low varieties of *Picea abies*, the Norway spruce. The names of these are often confused and it is advisable, when possible, to see specimens in the nursery before purchase. They are very hardy to cold, but are not resistant to great extremes of summer heat or drought. They succeed best in full sun but will stand light shade. Sometimes vigorous branches, similar to those of typical *P. abies*, develop; these should be cut out. In height they are likely to vary from 3 to 8 ft. Among the best are:

Picea abies clanbrasiliana, 2 to 3 ft., forming broad mounds.

P. a. maxwellii, 8 ft., broader than high.

P. a. parsonsii, 5 ft., hemispherical but irregular in outline.

P. a. procumbens, 3 ft., broad, wide-spreading.

PINUS MUGO MUGHUS (MUGHO PINE)
The mugho pine varies considerably in form and ultimate height but scarcely ever exceeds 5 to 8 ft. It is usually broader than wide and of irregular outline. The plants are usually propagated by seeds and are so variable that it is advisable, when possible, to select specimens for planting at the nursery. This kind is extremely hardy and grows in any ordinary soil in sun. It is somewhat subject to infestations of scale insects.

PLUM-YEW. See *Cephalotaxus*.

Pinus mugo mughus
(Mugho Pine)

SPRUCE. See *Picea*.

TAXUS (YEW)
These are among the very finest of evergreens. The tree types are discussed in "Evergreen Trees," page 398. The introductory remarks in that chapter are applicable to the shrubby varieties as well as the taller-growing kinds. Among the lower-growing yews, the following are excellent; there are many others listed by nurserymen. Consult catalogues or visit nurseries before making selections.

Taxus baccata dovastonii, 15 ft., upright, dark green. Hardy in southern New England.

T. b. repandens, 3 ft., low, dense, with semiweeping branches. Hardy in New England. Hardier than other varieties of *T. baccata*.

T. b. stricta (Irish yew), 15 ft., upright with many rigid, spirelike branches, dark green, very handsome. Hardy north to Washington, D.C.

T. canadensis (Canada yew), 5 ft., usually lower, stands dense shade. The hardiest but the least attractive yew. Its foliage is yellow-green.

T. cuspidata (Japanese yew). Numerous varieties of this species are splendid plants. Specimens propagated from cuttings made from side branches instead of being grown from seeds form spreading bushes.

T. c. densa, 4 ft., low-growing, much broader than high.

T. c. nana (often sold as variety *brevifolia*), 10 ft., foliage somewhat duller than that of most kinds.

T. media hatfieldii, 10 ft., upright, pyramidal, dense, dark green.

T. m. hicksii, 12 ft., erect with many narrow-columnar branches, dark green.

THUJA (ARBORVITAE)
There are many low-growing varieties of arborvitae (for tall tree types, see page 399), and all have frondlike

branchlets. Many kinds turn yellow-ish or brownish in winter and all are intolerant of hot, dry locations and city conditions. They may be sheared in spring. The varieties of *Thuja occidentalis* (American arbor-vitae) are extremely hardy; varieties of *T. orientalis* (Oriental arborvitae) are hardy in southern New England. For descriptions of available varieties check nursery catalogues or visit nurseries that carry these plants.

Thuja occidentalis globosa (globe arborvitae), 5 ft., globe-shaped; foli-age bright green.

T. o. rubusta (syn. *T. o. wareana*), 12 ft., dense, bluish-green.

T. orientalis decussata, dwarf, shrubby.

T. o. globosa, dwarf, globose.

TSUGA CANADENSIS PENDULA
(SARGENT'S WEEPING HEMLOCK)
A graceful, slow-growing, widespread-ing variety with pendulous branches, which grows eventually to 12 ft. Especially effective beside a pool. For deep, fertile, not too dry soils; will stand some shade.

YEW. See *Taxus.*

BROAD-LEAVED EVERGREEN SHRUBS

ACACIA ARMATA (KANGAROO THORN)
Yellow-flowered, 10 ft., broader than tall; foliage green; withstands drought well and thrives in sandy soils. A good hedge plant. It is hardy in mild climates only; will not withstand much frost.

ADAM'S NEEDLE. See *Yucca filamen-tosa.*

ALEXANDRIAN LAUREL. See *Danaë racemosa.*

ANDROMEDA. See *Leucothë catesbaei, Pieris.*

ANISE TREE. See *Illicium.*

ARALIA. See *Polyscias.*

ARBUTUS UNEDO (STRAWBERRY TREE)
This shrub or small tree, about 15 ft. high, thrives in well-drained, some-what acid soil; is best suited for the West Coast. It bears small white flowers in fall, and when established carries orange strawberry-like fruits and flowers simultaneously. Easily kept in shape by occasional pruning. To insure pollination and fruit bear-ing, plant at least two specimens.

ARDISIA
For warm climates only, such as those of Florida and California. Shade-tolerant. Valued for their foliage and berries, attractive for a long time.

Ardisia crispa, 2 ft.; flowers whit-ish; berries red.

A. paniculata (marlberry), 18 ft.; flowers white, berries shining black. Stand sea spray well. Less hardy than *A. crispa.*

AUCUBA JAPONICA
Aucubas grow in any ordinary soil in light or deep shade. They are gen-erally hardy as far north as Washing-ton, D.C., but in sheltered locations will survive even as far north as New York City. They stand city condi-tions well and attain a maximum height of about 15 ft. and have hand-some, thick, glossy green leaves. Male and female flowers are on sep-arate plants; both sexes must be growing in proximity for the females to produce their bright red berries.

Aucuba japonica variegata (gold-dust tree) has bright splashes of gold on its leaves and attractive red ber-ries. It is a good shrub, useful for providing color all year.

AUSTRALIAN TEA TREE. See *Lepto-spermum laevigatum.*

454

AZALEA. See *Rhododendron.*

AZARA MICROPHYLLA
Graceful, 10 ft.; foliage handsome;
flowers greenish, fragrant; berries orange. For well-drained soils. Hardy as
far north as Washington, D.C.

BACCHARIS PILULARIS (COYOTE BUSH)
A native of dry hills and dunes in
California and Oregon, 2 to 5 ft.;
flowers white or yellowish. For the
West Coast.

BAMBOO
Bamboos are really giant grasses.
They belong to several distinct plant
genera, including *Arundinaria, Bambusa, Phyllostachys, Pleioblastus, Pseu-
dosasa* and *Sasa.* They are essentially
plants for mild climates (although a
limited number are hardy at New
York City), sheltered locations and
rich, moderately moist soils. Evergreen, but their foliage is often winter-
damaged in the North.

BANANA SHRUB. See *Michelia fuscata.*

BERBERIS (BARBERRY)
Thorny plants that bear a profusion
of yellow or orange-yellow flowers in
spring and attractive berries later.
Most evergreen kinds have distinctive
spiny leaves. All are easy to grow in
well-drained soil of moderate fertility,
not excessively dry. They may be
sheared as hedges. For leaf-losing barberries, see "Shrubs and Flowering
Small Trees," page 419.

Berberis buxifolia (Magellan barberry), 10 ft.; flowers orange-yellow,
berries dark purple. Variety *nana,*
1½ ft., rarely flowers or fruits. Excellent for hedges, these are hardy in
southern New England.

B. *candidula,* 2 ft., similar to *B.
verruculosa,* slow-growing.

B. *darwinii,* 8 ft., has prickly,
hollylike leaves, orange flowers and

Berberis darwinii
(Barberry)

bluish berries. Not hardy in North.

B. *gagnepainii,* 7 ft., makes a dense,
upright-growing shrub, with long,
narrow leaves, yellow flowers and
blue-black fruits. Hardy in southern
New England.

B. *julianae* (wintergreen barberry),
6 ft., very dense; berries blue-black.
Hardy in southern New England
and one of the hardiest of the evergreen barberries.

B. *mentorensis* (mentor barberry),
a partial evergreen only, this hybrid
is hardier than any of the completely
evergreen kinds and stands heat and
drought well. Its berries are dull red.

B. *stenophylla,* 8 ft., one of the
larger barberries, with large leaves
and yellow flowers on arching branches
in spring, and black berries. As far
north as Washington, D.C., it is
evergreen; although it survives farther north, it loses its leaves in the
cold of winter.

B. *triacanthophora,* 5 ft.; flowers
pinkish-white; berries blue-black;
hardy in southern New England.

B. verruculosa, 4 ft., leaves dark green above, white on undersurfaces; flowers comparatively large, yellow; berries black-violet.

BLUE BLOSSOM. See *Ceanothus thyrsiflorus*.

BOXWOOD. See *Buxus*.

BRUNFELSIA
For southern Florida and the Southwest, these grow well in a medium heavy soil and part shade; a fine display of conspicuous flowers.

Brunfelsia americana (lady-of-the-night), 8 ft.; flowers white, fading to yellow, fragrant at night.

B. calycina (yesterday, today and tomorrow), 3 ft., flowers rich purple, fading to lavender and finally white.

BUCHU. See *Diosma ericoides*.

BUSH POPPY. See *Dendromecon rigida*.

BUTCHER'S-BROOM. See *Ruscus aculeatus*.

BUXUS (BOXWOOD)
Shrubs, or sometimes small trees, valued for their dense, compact growth and very beautiful small, glossy leaves. They stand pruning and shearing well and are excellent hedge plants. In the South they are much prized and give character to many fine gardens. They grow satisfactorily in acid, neutral or alkaline soils provided they do not become excessively dry. Because they are shallow-rooted it is a mistake to dig or cultivate deeply near them. Annual mulching is decidedly beneficial. They are subject to damage by leaf miners, mites and a serious canker disease. In the North they are often harmed by severe winter cold; fine specimens are often protected over winter by screening them with burlap, branches of evergreens or plyboards. Care should be taken to allow for free air circulation about specimens so protected.

Buxus microphylla, 4 ft., slower-growing than *B. sempervirens*.

B.m. japonica, 5 ft., has somewhat larger leaves than *B. microphylla*.

B.m. koreana (Korean boxwood), 2 ft., hardy in southern New England, is the hardiest boxwood.

B. sempervirens (English boxwood, common boxwood), 20 ft.; foliage fragrant, especially in warm weather. Hardy in sheltered locations at New York City and in favored parts of southern New England, though sometimes damaged in severe winters.

B.s. angustifolia, usually treelike; leaves long and narrow.

B.s. arborescens, treelike.

B.s. argenteo-variegata, leaves variegated with white.

B.s. aureo-variegata, leaves variegated with yellow.

B.s. handsworthii, shrubby, upright-growing, excellent for hedges.

B.s. suffruticosa (edging boxwood), dwarf, compact, slow-growing; extensively used for very low hedges or edgings around flower beds, herb beds and in similar situations. Is often propagated by division.

CALICO BUSH. See *Kalmia latifolia*.

CALIFORNIA LILAC. See *Ceanothus thrysiflorus*.

CALLIANDRA INAEQUILATERA
(POWDER PUFF TREE)
Shrub or small tree, 15 ft., valued for its showy bright red "powder puffs" of flowers borne over a long period in winter. Adapted for warmest sections of the United States only. Also grown as *C. haematocephala*.

CALLUNA (HEATHER)
These plants are invaluable for providing color from July to October.

Calluna vulgaris
(Heather)

The flower colors vary from white through various shades of pink and crimson to dark crimson. Plants are from 3 in. to 3 ft. tall. Some varieties make good foliage plants, as their leaves are golden, bronze or pinkish in summer, often deepening in color in fall and winter. The foliage is fine and scalelike.

Callunas need sandy, peaty, acid soil that is poor in fertility and well drained but not excessively dry, and full sun. They should be sheared rather severely each spring before new growth begins. A mulch of peat moss is helpful.

Callunas are excellent as ground covers and for bank plantings in regions where they thrive. They are not suited for places where very hot, dry summers are experienced. Among the best of many varieties are:

Calluna vulgaris (Scotch heather), 2 ft., flowers rosy-lavender.

C.v. alba, 2 ft., white flowers.

C.v. aurea, leaves golden.

C.v. foxii forms a cushion only 2 or 3 in. high. It is not free-flowering.

C.v. H. E. Beale, 1 to 2 ft., long spikes of double rose-pink flowers.

C.v. plena, flowers double, pink.

CAMELLIA SASANQUA

This does not grow as tall as *Camellia japonica*, which is described earlier on page 401; its maximum height is about 20 ft. It requires the same cultural conditions as *C. japonica* and may be grown in the same regions, but it blooms earlier and is valued as a means of extending the blooming season of camellias. Many varieties of *C. sasanqua*, most, but not all, with single flowers, varying in color, according to variety, from white to deep pink, are described and offered in catalogues of specialists. This shrub is looser and less stiff than *C. japonica*. Its foliage is lustrous dark green.

CAPE JASMINE. See *Gardenia jasminoides*.

CARISSA

Carissa carandas (karanda), with smaller flowers than *C. grandiflora*, and black fruits, is cultivated in southern Florida. Excellent as a sheared hedge and for seaside planting in full sun.

C. grandiflora (Natal plum), is a thorny shrub, 18 ft.; foliage lustrous dark green; flowers conspicuous, waxy-white, fragrant; fruits plum-like, scarlet, edible. For full sun where there is little or no frost.

C.g. nana compacta, sometimes called "bonsai carissa," is low-growing, spreading and apparently without thorns.

CARPENTERIA CALIFORNICA

This California native, up to 10 ft. tall, bears few clusters of large, fragrant white flowers in summer. Best adapted for the Southwest and similar climates, it is intolerant of excessive wetness in winter. It needs porous soil and protection from winds.

CASSENA. See *Ilex vomitoria*.

CEANOTHUS
Evergreen kinds are natives, and hybrids of natives, of western North America. They are best adapted for gardens in California and elsewhere on the Pacific Coast. They thrive in well-drained soils in sun.
Ceanothus delilianus, 6 ft., blooms in summer. A hybrid kind that includes several distinct varieties such as Gloire de Versailles, flowers pale blue, and Gloire des Plantières, flowers deep blue. All may be pruned hard in early spring. Deciduous in fairly cold climates.
C. thyrsiflorus (blue blossom, California lilac), 25 ft.; flowers blue. One of the finest and hardiest of the evergreen kinds but subject to infestations of scale insects. Prune immediately after flowering.
C.t. griseus, has more compact flower heads and seems less attractive to scale insects.
C. veitchianus, 10 ft., a hybrid; flowers deep blue; one of the hardiest of evergreen kinds.

CESTRUM
Fragrant-flowered shrubs for warmest parts of the United States only.
Cestrum diurnum (day jessamine), 15 ft., flowers white, fragrant by day.
C. nocturnum (night jessamine), 12 ft., flowers greenish or cream-colored, very fragrant at night.
C. parqui (willow-leaved jessamine), 6 ft., flowers greenish, very fragrant at night; the hardiest kind.

CHAMAELAUCIUM UNCINATUM
Heatherlike shrub, 5 ft.; flowers white,

lilac or pink. For sandy, peaty soil in California and similar climates.

CHERRY LAUREL. See *Prunus laurocerasus*.

CHOISYA (MEXICAN ORANGE)
Choisya ternata, 6 ft., has bright green leaves; sweetly scented white flowers appear in spring and sometimes again in the autumn. Thrives in ordinary soil in sun. Prune to shape, plant after spring blooming. Hardy in southern Florida and southern California.

CHRISTMASBERRY. See *Heteromeles arbutifolia*.

CISTUS (ROCKROSE)
There are many species and varieties of cistus. Some are hardier than others, but all are best suited for areas of mild winters and dry climates, such as California. They will not stand much freezing. All have beautiful flowers over a long season, although

Choisya ternata
(Mexican Orange)

Cistus
(Rockrose)

individual flowers last for only a day. They thrive in the hottest, driest places, and in alkaline soils. They are ideal for large rock gardens.

Among the best are:

Cistus cyprius, 6 ft., white petals with crimson blotch at base of each.

C. hybridus, 3 to 4 ft., pure white flowers.

C. laurifolius, 6 ft., white, yellow-centered flowers. The hardiest kind.

C. purpureus, 4 ft., rosy-crimson petals with a deep maroon basal blotch.

CLEYERA JAPONICA. See *Eurya ochnacea*.

CODIAEUM VARIEGATUM (CROTON)
A popular tropical shrub in many varieties valued for the varied shapes and brilliant coloring of the glossy foliage. Flowers, not very showy, are white and are succeeded by red berries. Best in sun in ordinary soil. May be pruned as needed to keep shapely. For southern Florida, southern California and similar climates.

COPROSMA BAUERI (MIRROR PLANT)
Glossy-leaved, 20 ft., flowers whitish, followed, on female plants if a male is planted nearby, by orange berries. Excellent for sheared hedges and for planting near the sea in California and other mild climates. Variegated-leaved varieties are cultivated.

COYOTE BUSH. See *Baccharis pilularis*.

CROTON. See *Codiaeum variegatum*.

CRYSTAL TEA. See *Ledum palustre*.

CUPHEA HYSSOPIFOLIA
Small-leaved, much-branched shrub, 2 ft.; flowers small, purple, pink or white. For very mild climates only.

DABOËCIA
Heathlike shrub, flowers urn-shaped, nodding. For sandy, peaty, acid soils. Hardy in sheltered locations as far north as Long Island.

Daboëcia cantabrica (Irish heath), 1½ ft., numerous rose-purple flowers from June to fall.

D.c. alba, white flowers.

D.c. bicolor, both white and rosy-purple flowers on the same plant.

DAISY TREE. See *Olearia*.

DANAË RACEMOSA
(ALEXANDRIAN LAUREL)
An interesting shrub, 3 ft., for mild climates; flowers small, white, succeeded by red berries.

DAPHNE
Most daphnes bear very fragrant flowers. There are many kinds, some rather difficult to grow. Plant in well-drained soil. Easy to grow are:

Daphne blagayana, 9 to 10 in., a semiprostrate kind with very fragrant creamy flowers in spring, suitable for the rock garden; somewhat less hardy than *D. cneorum*.

D. cneorum, 9 in., spreading; flowers pink, in spring; hardy in southern New England. Acid, neutral or alkaline soils seem satisfactory, provided drainage is good. Varieties with white flowers and with variegated leaves are cultivated.

D. laureola (spurge laurel), 3 ft.; flowers yellowish-green, fragrant. Hardy to about Washington, D.C.

D. odora, 5 ft., flowers light rosy-purple, exceedingly fragrant, in spring. Hardy about as far north as Maryland. Variety *marginata*, leaves margined with yellow, may be hardier.

DAY JESSAMINE. See *Cestrum diurnum*.

DENDROMECON RIGIDA
(BUSH POPPY, TREE POPPY)
Native of California and best adapted for such climates; 8 ft., of stiff growth; leaves pale green; flowers golden-yellow. For dryish, sandy soils.

DIOSMA ERICOIDES (BUCHU)
Much branched, heathlike, 2 ft.; foliage fragrant; flowers small, white, very numerous. For sandy, peaty soils that are not excessively dry. Hardy only in mild climates.

DURANTA REPENS
(PIGEONBERRY, SKY-FLOWER)
Vigorous, quick-growing, thorny, 18 ft.; flowers in terminal racemes, light blue; berries yellow, remaining all winter. In variety *alba* the flowers are white. May be pruned in spring.

ELAEAGNUS PUNGENS
Somewhat spiny, broad shrub, 15 ft.; leaves leathery, silvery on under-surfaces, glossy green above. Most commonly grown are variegated-leaved varieties, such as *aurea*, leaves margined yellow; *maculata* with a central yellow blotch to each leaf; and *marginata*, leaves white-edged. Good for sun or part shade in ordinary soil;

withstands sea spray well. May be sheared as a hedge and kept in shape by cutting out long shoots that sometimes arise in summer. Although usually considered to be suitable for mild climates only, specimens have succeeded for many years in sheltered locations at New York City.

ERICA (HEATH)
Ericas, in mild climates such as occur in parts of the Pacific Northwest, will, if carefully chosen, provide the garden with flowers throughout the year. In many other areas, where winters are colder, kinds can be had in bloom from spring to fall. Most ericas must be grown in acid soil. Peat moss or leaf mold worked into the soil before planting is beneficial. Trim the plants with shears in spring (after flowering for spring and winter bloomers, ahead of blooming for those that flower in summer or fall) to encourage new flowering growths.

Three kinds will tolerate some soil alkalinity:

Erica carnea, up to 1 ft., rose-pink flowers in winter or spring, and its numerous varieties with pink, rosy-pink, carmine, red or white flowers.

E. darleyensis, 1½ ft., rosy-purple flowers in winter or spring.

E. mediterranea, 8 ft., rose-red flowers in spring, and several varieties having white or pink flowers, some more compact than the type plant.

Among the best of the acid-soil heaths are:

E. ciliaris (heath), 1 ft., rosy-red flowers in summer.

E. cinerea (twisted heath), 1 ft., in shades of red, pink, purple or white according to variety. Flowers June to September.

E. tetralix (cross-leaved heath), 9 to 18 in.; according to variety, white, purple, pink or crimson flowers from June to fall.

E. vagans (Cornish heath), 1 to 1½ ft., sprays of flowers in red, pink or white according to variety. August to fall.

The above-mentioned kinds are hardy in southern New England. Among kinds that succeed in acid soils in mild climates such as that of California are:

E. melanthera, 2 ft., flowers white or pinkish with black anthers, in winter.

E. ventricosa, 6 ft., flowers white, pink or red, spring.

ESCALLONIA

Most cultivated escallonias are evergreen, flowering in summer, excellent for near the sea where they may be used for hedges. A few are reasonably hardy as far north as Virginia, including the semievergreen *E. langleyensis*, but most are best adapted for Pacific Coast gardens. They grow rapidly and prosper in ordinary soils. Prune after flowering to cut away the flowered growths.

Escallonia C. F. Ball, 6 ft. or more, crimson flowers.

E. Donard Brilliance, 6 ft., crimson flowers.

E. Donard Seedling, 10 ft., with fragrant white pink-flushed flowers.

E. langleyensis (semievergreen), 6 ft. or more, with arching branches of bright red flowers.

E. macrantha, 10 ft., compact, flowers red.

EUCRYPHIA

These beautiful shrubs grow easily in most soils, except alkaline ones, if peat is added. Adapted for favored parts of the Pacific Coast only.

Eucryphia cordifolia, 10 to 15 ft., white flowers in late summer or fall.

E. glutinosa, semievergreen, 15 ft. or more, large white flowers in late summer.

E. nymansensis, 30 ft., is columnar

Euonymus japonicus

and bears great white, fragrant flowers with gold-tipped stamens in summer.

EUONYMUS

Handsome shrubs for sun or part shade in ordinary soils. They stand shearing well and are excellent for hedges. Leaf-losing kinds are:

Euonymus japonicus, 15 ft., foliage glossy green; hardy about as far north as Virginia. There are numerous varieties, some with handsomely variegated leaves.

E. kiautschovica (syn. *E. patens*), 10 ft., is partly evergreen and hardy about as far north as New York City.

EURYA OCHNACEA
(syn. CLEYERA JAPONICA)

Slow-growing and valued chiefly for its foliage, this camellia relative is hardy about as far north as Maryland. It stands part shade and is a fine foundation planting subject. Its max-

Fatsia japonica

imum height is perhaps 10 ft. It prefers a somewhat moist, acid soil.

FATSIA

Fatsia japonica, 12 ft., has large glossy, ivy-shaped leaves; a fine shrub for shade; large heads of milky-white flowers in fall, followed by blue berries. Not particular about soil and needs no regular pruning.

FEIJOA SELLOWIANA
(PINEAPPLE GUAVA)

Dense shrub with gray-green foliage, 15 ft., useful for hedges and for planting as specimens. The flowers, which are white to purplish with red stamens, are decorative and are followed by edible red-tinged green fruits. Grows well in sun or part shade in ordinary soil and succeeds near the sea. Selected named varieties are grown for their fruits. Hardy in the Deep South and Southwest.

FIRETHORN. See *Pyracantha.*

FLANNEL BUSH. See *Fremontia californica.*

FREMONTIA CALIFORNICA
(FLANNEL BUSH)

A native Californian and best adapted for growing there and in similar climates, 10 ft. Flowers yellow, showy. For sun and dryish soils.

FUCHSIA

Splendid flowering shrubs for outdoor cultivation in mild climates such as that of California; they remain evergreen or lose their foliage in winter depending upon the amount of cold to which they are subjected. With the exception of *F. magellanica riccartonii*, they will not stand much frost. Fuchsias need fairly good soil that does not become excessively dry, and light shade. They may be pruned fairly severely in spring. In addition to those listed below, there are innumerable garden varieties. They bloom throughout the summer.

Fuchsia magellanica, carmine and purple flowers; 15 ft.

F.m. riccartonii, a fairly hardy variety, red and purple flowers; 10 ft.

GARDENIA JASMINOIDES
(CAPE JASMINE)

A favorite for frost-free and nearly frost-free climates, this fine blooming shrub is highly valued for its very fragrant white waxy blooms, from late spring through summer, and its glossy deep green foliage. It needs deep, fertile, fairly moist soil that is slightly acid and full sun or just a little shade. Mulching the soil is helpful. It grows 4 or 5 ft. tall.

GARRYA ELLIPTICA (SILK TASSEL BUSH)

A native of the Pacific Coast region, this handsome 8-ft. shrub is well adapted for gardens in that region.

Male and female flowers are borne on separate individuals, the former in 8-in.-long, the latter in 4-in.-long greenish or yellowish catkins. For soils that are well drained.

GAULTHERIA
Fine shrubs for moderately moist acid soils and partial shade. They are not easy to transplant, so it is best to set out pot-grown specimens. For fairly mild climates, perhaps as far north as Washington, D.C.

Gaultheria miqueliana, 1 ft.; flowers small, urn-shaped, white or pinkish; berries white in clusters.

G. shallon (salal), 15 ft., spreading; flowers small, urn-shaped, white or pink; fruits purplish-black, edible.

GOLD-DUST TREE. See *Aucuba japonica variegata*.

GREWIA CAFFRA
Shrub or small tree with purple starlike flowers; for Florida, California and similar warm climates.

HAKEA SUAVEOLENS
Drought-resistant, round-headed, 10-ft. shrub for frost-free and nearly frost-free climates. It needs well-drained soil and sun. Its leaves are divided into slender, spine-tipped segments; flowers are small, white and fragrant.

HALIMODENDRON HALODENDRON (SALT TREE)
Shrub, 5 ft., branches spiny; leaves silvery; flowers pale purple, pealike. Very hardy and excellent for alkaline and saline (salty) soils.

HEATH. See *Erica*.

HEATHER. See *Calluna*.

HEAVENLY BAMBOO. See *Nandina domestica*.

HEBE (syn. VERONICA)
These shrubby, close relatives of veronicas are best suited for the Pacific Coast and similar climates. They thrive in full sun and are especially valuable for planting near the sea in well-drained, dryish soils. For long periods in summer they produce decorative spikes of flowers.

Hebe buxifolia, 4 ft., flowers white.

H. salicifolia, 10 ft., flowers white, tinged lilac.

H. speciosa, 5 ft., red-violet to purple-violet.

H. traversii, 6 ft., flowers white.

HETEROMELES ARBUTIFOLIA (TOYON, CHRISTMASBERRY)
Excellent for California and similar climates, 10 ft., leaves leathery, glossy green; flowers small, white, in clusters, followed by hollylike red berries in winter. May be grown in a variety of soils, even dry ones.

HOLLY. See *Ilex*.

HOLLY MAHONIA. See *Mahonia aquifolium*.

HYPERICUM (ST.-JOHN'S-WORT)
The evergreen kinds are mostly hardy, north to about Washington, D.C. (for deciduous kinds, see page 430 in "Shrubs and Flowering Small Trees").

Hypericum patulum henryi, 4 ft. It has 2½-in.-wide golden-yellow blooms. The hardiest variety of *H. patulum*.

H. Hidcote, 5 ft., an elegant hybrid, with large, saucer-shaped flowers.

H. Rowallane Hybrid, 7 ft. Probably the best evergreen hypericum. Its 2½- to 3-in.-wide flowers are borne in profusion.

ILEX (HOLLY)
Evergreen hollies include trees (see page 404 in "Evergreen Trees") and shrubby types. They are among the

finest of broad-leaved evergreens and many varieties are especially valued for use in landscape planting. They grow well in sun or light shade in a wide variety of soils. In most kinds male and female flowers are on separate individuals, and the sexes must be growing near to each other for the females to fruit. They make good hedges and stand shearing well.

Ilex cornuta (Chinese holly), 8 ft., broad, dense, round-topped; leaves very glossy, few-spined, almost rectangular; berries large, bright red, profuse. This holly produces berries without cross-pollination from a male planted nearby. Hardy north to Philadelphia, in sheltered locations to Long Island.

I.c. burfordii, 8 ft., an excellent, heavy-fruiting variety, with leaves broader at their tops than at their bases and usually with only 1 to 3 spines. A little less hardy than *I. cornuta*.

I. crenata (Japanese holly), 15 ft., dense; leaves small, like boxwood, glossy, dark green; berries black. Hardy in southern New England. Among the best of many varieties are:

I.c. convexa (often misnamed *bullata*), broader than high, with the upper leaf surfaces convex, is probably the hardiest variety.

I.c. Green Island, low, branching, flat-leaved.

I.c. helleri, 3 ft., small-leaved, much broader than high, very slow-growing.

I.c. Kingsville, dwarf, compact.

I.c. microphylla, small-leaved, one of the hardiest.

I. glabra (inkberry), 10 ft., slender-stemmed, rather loose and willowy; spreads slowly by underground runners; leaves glossy light green becoming purplish in winter; berries black. Distinct in appearance from other hollies, this hardiest evergreen kind needs moist—and will grow in wet—soils and in partial shade. A very good plant. Hardy far into the northern growing areas.

I. vomitoria (yaupon, cassena), 20 ft., shrub or rarely a small tree; leaves glossy, wavy-toothed; berries bright red, borne very profusely. Not hardy in the North.

ILLICIUM (ANISE TREE)

For slightly acid soils and part shade; foliage attractive, aromatic when crushed; flowers attractive. About as hardy as camellias, these are rarely troubled by diseases or pests.

Illicium anisatum, 12 ft., flowers greenish-yellow.

I. floridanum, 9 ft., flowers dark red.

INDIA HAWTHORN. See *Raphiolepis indica*.

INKBERRY. See *Ilex glabra*.

IRISH HEATH. See *Daboëcia cantabrica*.

IXORA

Magnificent flowering shrubs for the warmest parts of the United States only. They bear large clusters of small bright red, orange-red, or red flowers over a long period. Good, slightly acid soil, as well as sun or light shade, are required.

Ixora coccinea, flowers red.

I. macrothyrsa, flowers orange-scarlet.

I.m. Super King, flowers orange-scarlet in large clusters.

KALMIA

These belong to the same family as rhododendrons, and need acid, peaty soil. They are ideal planted on banks where the flowers can be seen from below. They grow well in part shade.

Kalmia angustifolia (sheep laurel, lambkill), 3 ft., a spreading bush. Its rose-pink or red flowers borne in June

Kalmia latifolia
(Mountain Laurel, Calico Bush)

are not as attractive as those of *K. latifolia*. Its foliage, eaten in large amounts, may poison livestock. For wet soils. Extremely hardy.

K. latifolia (mountain laurel, calico bush), 15 ft., one of the finest shrubs, with clusters of pink, basin-shaped flowers in May and June. Thrives in dryish or moist soils.

KANGAROO THORN. See *Acacia armata*.

LABRADOR TEA. See *Ledum groenlandicum*.

LADY-OF-THE-NIGHT. See *Brunfelsia americana*.

LAMBKILL. See *Kalmia angustifolia*.

LANTANA
For central and southern Florida and other areas where frosts are infrequent or unknown, these vigorous shrubs are satisfactory for dry soils and full sun and stand pruning well.

Lantana camara, 4 ft., prickly; flowers small, borne profusely in clusters, white, pink, rosy-purple, yellow, orange and red.

L. montevidensis, 3 ft., branches trailing, flowers rosy-lilac.

LAURESTINUS. See *Viburnum tinus*.

LAURUS
Laurus nobilis (sweet bay), 20 ft., often grown as a sheared, formally shaped ornamental tree in pots or tubs. If left unpruned it grows to a handsome bush. Its aromatic leaves are the bay leaves used for flavoring. The greenish-yellow flowers are small but are borne profusely in early summer and are followed by large black fruits. It thrives in ordinary soil, in sun or shade. Hardy about as far north as Washington, D.C.

LEDUM
For acid, moist or wet soils. Flowers small, white, in clusters in spring.
Ledum glandulosum, 6 ft.; for West Coast gardens.
L. groenlandicum (Labrador tea), 3 ft.; extremely hardy.
L. palustre (crystal tea, wild rosemary), 3 ft., similar to *L. groenlandicum;* very hardy.

LEIOPHYLLUM BUXIFOLIUM
(SAND MYRTLE)
A neat, 1½ ft. shrub, with small glossy, boxwoodlike leaves and clusters of small white flowers in spring. For acid, well-drained soils. Hardy as far north as southern New England.

LEPTOSPERMUM
Upright shrubs or small trees for California and similar mild climates. They prosper in sun, in well-drained sandy or peaty soils. They stand dry conditions well.
Leptospermum laevigatum (Australian tea tree), 25 ft.; flowers white.

L. scoparium, 18 ft.; flowers varying, according to variety, from white to deep red.

LEUCOPHYLLUM TEXANUM
Loose-growing shrub, 8 ft. high; leaves silvery-white; flowers bell-shaped, violet-purple in spring and summer. For warm, dry climates only. May be sheared as a hedge.

LEUCOTHOË
Attractive glossy foliage that becomes purplish-red in fall, on arching stems; has racemes of small, waxy white flowers in late spring. Well suited for acid soils that contain a fair amount of organic matter, and for shaded locations. Cut out old stems every two or three years. Mulch with compost, leaf mold or peat moss. Hardy in New England.
Leucothoë axillaris, 4 ft., very similar to *L. catesbaei* except for minor botanical differences.
L. catesbaei (syn. *Andromeda catesbaei*—drooping leucothoë), 4 ft.

LIGUSTRUM JAPONICUM
(JAPANESE PRIVET)
Sometimes confused with the taller-growing glossy privet, *Ligustrum lucidum*, the Japanese privet is hardy about as far north as Washington, D.C. It has glossy green leaves, spikes of small white flowers in early summer, and black berries. About 8 ft. high, sometimes more, it stands shearing well and forms a good hedge. It grows in any ordinary soil in sun or in part shade. Several varieties are grown, one of the most distinct being *L. j. rotundifolium* (syn. *coriaceum*) with closely spaced round leaves and a stiff manner of growth.

LOROPETALUM CHINENSE
A lovely spring-blooming relative of the witch hazel (*Hamamelis*), hardy about as far north as Virginia; 10 ft.,

flowers white or cream-colored. For well-drained, slightly acid, peaty soils; stands light shade.

MAHONIA
These are very decorative and are easy to grow in ordinary soil and in partial shade.
Mahonia aquifolium (holly mahonia), 4 ft., bears spikes of golden flowers in late winter and early spring, and has leaves that resemble those of the holly. Its blue-black berries are attractive. Hardy in southern New England. Sometimes called Oregon holly grape.
M. bealii, 7 ft., large, divided leaves and pale yellow flowers, which are heavy with the fragrance of lily of the valley, in spring. Berries are blue-black. Hardy about as far north as Long Island.
M. lomariifolia, 4 ft., the most decorative kind, has long leaves with as many as 20 pairs of leaflets, and tall spikes of deep yellow flowers in late winter. Hardy in mild climates only; best suited for West Coast.
M. nervosa (Oregon grape), 2 ft., flowers yellow; berries dark blue. Hardy in southern New England.
M. repens, 1 ft., spreading by underground runners; leaves dull green; flowers yellow; berries black. Useful as a ground cover.

MALVAVISCUS ARBOREUS (TURK'S CAP)
Popular in the Deep South, this relative of the hibiscus is about 10 ft. tall, has light green foliage and a profusion of drooping scarlet flowers which do not expand widely like those of *Hibiscus*. It stands shearing well, and makes a good hedge; thrives in ordinary soil; tolerant of sea spray.

MARLBERRY. See *Ardisia paniculata*.

MESCAL BEAN. See *Sophora secundiflora*.

MEXICAN ORANGE. See *Choisya*.

MICHELIA FUSCATA (BANANA SHRUB)
Hardy about as far north as Virginia, this fine shrub, up to 15 ft. high, in spring bears small yellowish-white flowers, edged with red, and having a distinct odor of bananas. It grows well in ordinary soil. Closely related to the magnolias, it is sometimes known as *Magnolia fuscata*.

MIRROR PLANT. See *Coprosma baueri*.

MOUNTAIN LAUREL. See *Kalmia latifolia*.

MURRAEA EXOTICA
(ORANGE JESSAMINE)
A fragrant-flowered relative of *Citrus*, of compact growth and 10 ft. tall; for southern Florida, southern California and other very mild climates. Its clustered white flowers are succeeded by bright red berries. For ordinary soil and sun. *M. paniculata* is very similar.

MYRTUS (MYRTLE)
The classic myrtle; other plants sometimes called by this name—such as running myrtle (*Vinca*), crape myrtle (*Lagerstroemia*), sand myrtle (*Leiophyllum*) and wax myrtle (*Myrica*)—are quite distinct.

Myrtus communis, 10 ft., has small, glossy leaves that have an agreeable fragrance when bruised; flowers small, white, in clusters, followed by blue-black berries. Excellent for shearing and forms good hedges. Needs sun and well-drained soil. Fine for seaside gardens. Hardy only in frost-free and nearly frost-free climates, but often grown in pots and tubs and wintered in cool greenhouses.

NANDINA DOMESTICA
(HEAVENLY BAMBOO)
Attractive, stems unbranched, bam-

boolike, 8 ft.; leaves large, fernlike, bronzy when young, red in winter; flowers small, white, in large panicles, followed by long-lasting red berries (in a variety, white berries). Thrives in ordinary soil in shade or part shade. Hardy about as far north as Virginia.

NATAL PLUM. See *Carissa grandiflora*.

NERIUM OLEANDER (OLEANDER)
Fast-growing, 20 ft., bearing clusters of single or double white, pink, purplish or red flowers throughout summer. The sap and fruits are very poisonous. This plant grows in ordinary, moderately moist soil in full sun, and is tolerant of wind, sea spray, city conditions and other adverse environments. It stands pruning (in early spring) well; old straggly specimens may be cut down to near the ground, others thinned out or the long previous season's shoots cut back severely. Hardy in the Deep South and similar warm climates. Often grown in pots and tubs and wintered under cool conditions indoors, in the North.

NIGHT JESSAMINE. See *Cestrum nocturnum*.

OCHNA MULTIFLORA
For climates such as that of southern California this 5-ft. shrub is excellent. It prospers in sun in ordinary soil, has small yellow flowers and fleshy black fruits which contrast with the bright red receptacle. Attractive a long time.

OLEANDER. See *Nerium oleander*.

OLEARIA (DAISY TREE)
Olearias grow best in a light soil, and are adapted for cultivation in California and sections of the Pacific Northwest.

Olearia haastii, 5 to 8 ft., multitudes of little white daisies in July and August; is the hardiest and will grow almost anywhere.

O. macrodonta, 5 ft., fragrant white flowers in summer, grows well near the sea.

O. stellulata, 4 to 5 ft., grows well near the sea; normally white-flowered but has forms with flowers in rose-pink, lavender or blue.

ORANGE JESSAMINE. See *Murraea exotica*.

OREGON GRAPE. See *Mahonia nervosa*.

OREGON HOLLY GRAPE. See *Mahonia aquifolium*.

OSMANTHUS
Attractive plants mostly for regions of mild winters. They thrive in ordinary soil in sun or part shade and have very fragrant flowers. The plant called *Osmanthus delavayi* is *Siphonosmanthus delavayi*.

Osmanthus fortunei, 10 ft., leaves hollylike, lustrous. Hardy north to about Virginia.

O. fragrans (sweet olive), 20 ft., flowers white or cream.

O. ilicifolius, 18 ft.; leaves spiny-toothed; flowers yellowish-green; berries blue-black. Several varieties, some with variegated leaves.

OSMAREA BURKWOODII
Interesting hybrid between *Siphonosmanthus delavayi* and *Phillyrea decora*. Grows well in ordinary soil. Leaves glossy, dark green; flowers ivory-white, fragrant. Hardy as far north as Virginia; about 8 ft. high.

PERNETTYA MUCRONATA
Pernettya mucronata, 2 ft., has tiny white flowers in spring, like those of the ericas, followed by decorative berries. It is a dense shrub with small evergreen leaves and wiry stems. Plant in acid, peaty soil in sun. The

Pernettya mucronata

berries vary in color according to the varieties. To be sure of berries, plant two or more varieties in proximity. Hardy to about Washington, D.C.

P.m. alba, pure white berries.

P.m. Bell's Seedling, dark red berries.

P.m. Donard Pink, with soft pink berries.

P.m. Donard White, pure white berries.

P.m. lilacina, rose-colored berries.

P.m. rubra lilacina, with purplish berries.

PHILLYREA DECORA
Handsome, 8 ft., hardy about as far north as Washington, D.C. Leaves glossy, bronze-green; flowers small, white, in clusters, followed by red berries which finally become black. For ordinary soils and full sun.

PHOTINIA SERRULATA
Vigorous shrub or small tree, 30 ft., for well-drained, ordinary soil and sun. Leaves reddish-bronze when young, green later; flowers small, white, in large clusters succeeded by red berries. Hardy to Washington, D.C.

PIERIS (ANDROMEDA)

Of great decorative merit, these thrive in well-drained, reasonably moist, moderately acid soils in light shade and should be mulched with peat moss, compost or other such material.

Pieris floribunda, 6 ft., flowers in erect panicles. Hardy as far north as New England.

P. forrestii, 6 ft., has brilliant red young foliage. Not hardy north of Washington, D.C.

P. japonica, 9 ft., flowers in drooping panicles; young foliage reddish-bronze. Hardy, in sheltered places, in southern New England.

PIGEONBERRY. See *Duranta repens*.

PINEAPPLE GUAVA. See *Feijoa sellowiana*.

PITTOSPORUM TOBIRA
(JAPANESE PITTOSPORUM)

Excellent as specimens and hedges in the Deep South and on the West Coast where mild winters prevail. About 9 ft., its foliage is attractive, as are the clusters of creamy-white fragrant flowers borne in May. It thrives in sun or shade in ordinary soil and tolerates seaside conditions well. A variety with variegated leaves is also cultivated.

POLYSCIAS (syn. ARALIA)

For southern Florida, southern California and similar warm climates, these are good screening shrubs and form good hedges. Erect in growth, they have green or variegated foliage. They grow well in poor soils in full sun or shade and tolerate seaside environments.

Polyscias balfouriana, 20 ft.

P. fruticosa, 8 ft.

P. guilfoylei, 8 ft.

PORTUGAL LAUREL. See *Prunus lusitanica*.

Pyracantha
(Firethorn)

PRIVET. See *Ligustrum*.

PRUNUS

Vigorous, for sun or shade in ordinary soils. Often used for screens and as hedges. Stands pruning well.

Prunus laurocerasus (cherry laurel), 15 ft., leaves glossy green; flowers fragrant, white, in spikes. Hardy as far north as Philadelphia.

P. lusitanica (Portugal laurel), 20 ft.; similar to and about as hardy as *P. laurocerasus*, but taller.

P.l. schipkaensis, 5 ft., is hardy as far north as Long Island.

PYRACANTHA (FIRETHORN)

Handsome fruiting shrubs, stiff and somewhat spiny, with clusters of small white flowers and quantities of very decorative berries. They are easily espaliered against walls and may be used as hedges. They grow well in ordinary soils in sun. Unfortunately they are subject to fireblight disease.

Pyracantha atalantioides (syn. *P. gibbsii*), 15 ft.; berries small, red, remaining attractive for a long period. Hardy about as far north as Washington, D.C.

P. coccinea, 8 ft., bright red berries; half evergreen or deciduous in the northern part of the area in which it can be grown. Hardy about as far north as Washington, D.C.

P.c. lalandii, 8 ft., berries orange-red, hardy to New York City.

P. crenulata, 15 ft., berries red, hardy as far north as Washington, D.C.

P.c. rogersiana, 10 ft., berries orange-red; hardy as far north as Philadelphia.

P. c. r. flava, 15 ft., berries yellow.

RAPHIOLEPIS

Attractive rounded shrubs for the Deep South, southern California and similar climates. They thrive in ordinary soils in sun or part shade.

Raphiolepis delacouri, 6 ft., flowers pink; a hybrid between the following two species.

R. indica (India hawthorn), 5 ft., flowers delicate pink or white.

R. umbellata (Yeddo hawthorn), 10 ft., flowers white, fragrant. The variety *ovata* has broader leaves.

RHODODENDRON (including AZALEA)

This large genus contains some of the finest ornamental evergreen shrubs and includes azaleas, which botanists consider not sufficiently distinct to be classed in a separate genus. Gardeners usually consider azaleas distinct from other rhododendrons; here they are grouped separately. Both groups need acid soil that contains abundant organic matter and is reasonably moist. Typical rhododendrons (the non-azalea types) generally have large clusters of showy flowers. They need shade from hottest sun, and protection from cold winter winds is desirable. Fairly high atmospheric humidity is favorable; these are not plants for hot, dry climates. A mulch of peat moss, compost or other suitable material is highly desirable. Of hundreds of species and varieties few are satisfactory in the East. Many parts of the Pacific Northwest afford ideal conditions. A selection is described here; for others, especially the numerous magnificent varieties and hybrids, consult catalogues of specialists.

Rhododendron carolinianum, 4 ft., compact; leaves rather small, flowers pale pink (in variety *album*, white). Needs moist soil. Hardy in southern New England.

R. catawbiense (Catawba rhododendron), 8 ft., compact, flowers rosy-purple, hardy in southern New England. The wild type has poor flower color, but hybrids of this are among the finest of rhododendrons and many are as hardy as the type. White-flowered *R.c. album* is very good.

R. decorum, 8 ft., flowers white or pale pink, is hardy in sheltered places in southern New England.

R. fortunei, 10 ft., flowers large, fragrant, white or pink. Many splendid hybrids of this have flower colors that include peach, apricot and other pleasing varieties of pink. Hardy in sheltered places in southern New England.

R. keiskei, 4 ft., leaves rather small; flowers clear pale yellow. Hardy at New York City.

R. macrophyllum, 9 ft., similar to

Rhododendron

R. catawbiense but adapted only for the Pacific Coast.

R. maximum (rosebay), 15 ft., very loosely branched; flowers pink, in rather small heads. The hardiest of the large-leaved rhododendrons and much valued for its foliage. Best in shade. Hardy far north; the hardiest kind.

R. racemosum, 4 ft., compact; has rather small leaves; flowers pink. Hardy in southern New England.

R. smirnowii, 8 ft., foliage attractive; flowers deep pink. Hardy in New England; one of the hardiest.

Rhododendrons of the azalea group usually have smaller and thinner leaves than other rhododendrons and generally smaller trusses of flowers. They appreciate light shade but grow well in sun provided that the soil does not become dry. They need no reg-

ular pruning, but some kinds may be sheared lightly after blooming to keep them compact. Among the best of the evergreen azaleas are the following groups.

Indian azaleas: Large-flowered; at their best in the Deep South. Both single- and double-flowered kinds are grown; flower colors include white, pink, red and mixtures. They are not hardy in the North. For selections of the many fine varieties that are available consult catalogues of specialists.

Kurume azaleas: These are hardy as far north as Philadelphia and, in sheltered places, somewhat farther north. They have small leaves and single or double flowers in pink, orange-red, red. They stand shearing well.

ROCKROSE. See *Cistus.*

ROSMARINUS (ROSEMARY)
Rosmarinus officinalis, 5 ft., has been cultivated since the 16th century for its aromatic gray-green leaves, and is often used as a low hedging plant. It bears violet-blue flowers in May and June. Plant in dryish, well-drained soil in full sun.
R.o. albus, flowers white.
R.o. Miss Jessup's Upright, flowers deep blue, more upright than the other varieties.
R.o. prostratus is a low-growing, sprawling variety.

RUSCUS ACULEATUS
(BUTCHER'S-BROOM)
A curious plant of stiff growth with spiny-tipped leaflike organs which are flattened branches and which bear tiny yellow flowers, males and females on separate plants; only if a male is located nearby will the female bear its red berries. Growing up to 2 ft., this shrub thrives in sun or shade and tolerates dry soils. It is hardy about as far north as Washington, D.C.

ST.-JOHN'S-WORT. See *Hypericum.*

SALAL. See *Gaultheria shallon.*

SALT TREE. See *Halimodendron halodendron.*

SAND MYRTLE. See *Leiophyllum buxifolium.*

SARCOCOCCA
Pleasing foliage plants, related to boxwood but quite different in appearance. They grow well in shade in ordinary soils not excessively dry. They spread by underground runners.
Sarcococca hookeriana humilis, 2 ft., shiny dark green leaves; flowers are white, berries black. They are har-

dy north to southern New England.
S. ruscifolia, 6 ft., flowers small, white, fragrant; red berries. Hardy in mild climates only.

SHEEP LAUREL. See *Kalmia angustifolia.*

SILK TASSEL BUSH. See *Garrya elliptica.*

SIPHONOSMANTHUS
(syn. OSMANTHUS) DELAVAYI
Excellent 6-ft.-tall shrub with glossy green foliage and waxy white fragrant flowers in spring, followed by black berries. For light shade or sun and ordinary soils. Hardy as far north as Washington, D.C.

SKIMMIA
Splendid for shade (in full sun becomes yellowish) and ordinary soils.
Skimmia japonica, 4 ft.; flowers yellowish-white, fragrant, in clusters; males and females on separate plants. Female plants bear handsome red berries if a male plant is nearby. Hardy as far north as Washington, D.C., and in very sheltered locations to New York City.
S. reevesiana, 1½ ft. Male and female flowers are on the same plant; berries dull red. Hardy as far north as New York City.

SKY-FLOWER. See *Duranta repens.*

SOPHORA SECUNDIFLORA
(MESCAL BEAN)
Shrub or small tree, 30 ft.; flowers in clusters, violet-blue, fragrant. Hardy in the Deep South only. For well-drained soils and sun.

SPANISH BAYONET. See *Yucca aloifolia.*

STENOLOBIUM (syn. TECOMA) STANS
(YELLOW BELLS, YELLOW ELDER)
For the warmest parts of the United

472

States only; this is a quick-growing shrub or small tree, 18 ft. It grows easily in ordinary soil in sun or shade. It blooms in fall and early winter, the showy yellow flowers borne in clusters. It should be pruned to shape in spring.

STRANVAESIA DAVIDIANA
Somewhat loosely branched, 8 ft.; flowers in flat heads, white, succeeded by pink berries. Satisfactory in ordinary soil in sun or light shade. Hardy north to about Washington, D.C. The variety *undulata* is slightly hardier.

STRAWBERRY TREE. See *Arbutus unedo.*

SWEET BAY. See *Laurus nobilis.*

SWEET OLIVE. See *Osmanthus fragrans.*

TERNSTROEMIA JAPONICA
Shrub or small tree, 18 ft., for mild climates as in the Deep South and southern California. Flowers pale yellow. Soil ordinary; sun or light shade.

THEVETIA NEREIFOLIA
(YELLOW OLEANDER)
For the far South only, 25 ft.; leaves resembling those of oleander; flowers yellow, fragrant. Grows well in sandy soils.

THUNBERGIA ERECTA
For the warmer parts of Florida and southern California only; 6 ft. tall, much branched. The flowers are dark purple-blue, appearing over a long season. It needs good soil and light shade.

TURK'S CAP. See *Malvaviscus arboreus.*

TOYON. See *Heteromeles arbutifolia.*

Viburnum tinus (Laurestinus)

TREE POPPY. See *Dendromecon rigida.*

VACCINIUM OVATUM
Beautiful foliage shrub, 10 ft.; for sandy, peaty soils in mild climates such as that of the Pacific Coast. Small white or pink flowers are followed by black berries. For sun or light shade.

VERONICA. See *Hebe.*

VIBURNUM
Beautiful shrubs that thrive in shade or sun in fertile, rather moist soils. With the exception of *V. rhytidophyllum* none is hardy in the North; they can be grown only in areas of mild winters.

Viburnum davidii, 3 ft., flowers white; berries black.

V. henryi, 10 ft., flowers white; berries red turning to black.

V. japonicum, 6 ft., leaves glossy green; flowers white, fragrant; berries red.

V. odoratissimum, 10 ft., leaves shining; flowers white, fragrant; berries red turning to black.

V. rhytidophyllum, 8 ft., leaves handsome; flowers yellowish-white; berries red turning to black. This shrub is hardy in sheltered locations at New York City.

V. tinus (laurestinus), 8 ft., bears 4-in.-wide clusters of pink-budded white flowers in the winter and early spring.

WILD ROSEMARY. See *Ledum palustre.*

WILLOW-LEAVED JESSAMINE. See *Cestrum parqui.*

YAUPON. See *Ilex vomitoria.*

YEDDO HAWTHORN. See *Raphiolepis umbellata.*

YELLOW BELLS. See *Stenolobium stans.*

YELLOW ELDER. See *Stenolobium stans.*

YELLOW OLEANDER. See *Thevetia.*

YESTERDAY, TODAY AND TOMORROW. See *Brunfelsia calycina.*

YUCCA
Especially adapted to dry, sunny locations and semidesert conditions; many kinds of these bold-foliaged plants are suited for gardens in the Southwest and West. They bear large panicles of showy, creamy-white flowers.

Yucca aloifolia (Spanish bayonet), 25 ft., has a distinct trunk. Varieties with variegated leaves are grown.

Y. filamentosa (Adam's needle), 3 ft., flower stems to 10 ft. tall. A variegated-leaved variety is cultivated. Hardy in New England.

CHAPTER 22

HEDGES—
Living Walls of Green

Adaptable and Attractive—Preparing the Site—Care—Shaping and Renovating—Broad-Leaved Evergreens and Deciduous Kinds—Coniferous Hedge Plants

HEDGES ARE USED to provide shelter and serve as windbreaks, to form screens and give privacy, to define areas and act as barriers; they also offer effective design elements in the landscape. They may consist of deciduous or evergreen shrubs or trees and, by reason of their colorful flowers, fruits or foliage, can greatly add to the garden display. Usually a hedge consists of only one kind of plant, but examples in which two or more kinds are interplanted are sometimes favored and can be very attractive. In height, to some extent depending upon the kind of plants

Hedge Shaping
Three suggestions for shaping hedges, each showing the ideal broad base, tapering toward the top. (Left) round-headed; (center) wedge-shaped; (right) flat-headed.

used, hedges vary from 1 to 15 ft. or more. They may be severely formal, strictly sheared to shape, or more or less informal, with minimum clipping or pruning.

Careful thought should be given to selecting the kind of plants to be used for a hedge. Obviously they must be adapted to soil and site. It would be hopeless to plant a hedge of sun-loving roses in a shady place or to set acid-soil camellias in a limestone bed. The plants selected should be reliably winter-hardy in the locality. Many plants on the borderline of hardiness are rendered more susceptible to cold as a result of repeated shearing. In the vicinity of New York City, the California privet, left untrimmed and allowed to grow as a tall shrub, winters perfectly through extremely hard winters during which sheared hedges of California privet are killed to the ground.

The ultimate height which free-growing specimens of the plant will attain is not always of prime importance. There are tall trees such as hemlocks which can easily be grown as hedges not exceeding 6 ft. in height. Other matters to consider

are appearance in winter as well as in summer, relative freedom from pests and diseases and the amount of clipping or shearing needed.

Unless immediate landscape effect is of first importance, it is usually best to set out fairly small and young plants rather than those of greater maturity. In this way, a hedge well furnished to its base with stems and foliage is more likely to be attained. When planting deciduous hedges, it is advisable to cut the plants back to within 6 or 8 in. of the ground at planting time. This encourages vigorous branching.

SPACING THE PLANTS

Hedge plants may be set in a single row or in a double row, with the plants in each line of the row alternating with those in the other line. Spacing will depend on the kind of plants, on their size at planting time and, to some extent, on their cost. Small-growing kinds such as Japanese barberry may be set 9 to 12 in. apart, while larger deciduous and evergreen plants may be spaced up to 2 ft. or even farther apart. Plants selected for an informal little-trimmed hedge may be set considerably farther apart.

When purchasing plants for a hedge, always get a few extra plants, and set them together in a group at one end of the row so that they can be used as replacement in case of any failure among the young plants in the hedge. They will grow to the same height and be used to the same conditions as the others.

PREPARATION OF THE SITE

Because hedge plants vie strongly with one another for moisture and nutrients, and because they are likely to remain in one place for many years, it is of the utmost importance to prepare the soil very thoroughly before planting and to make it as agreeable to plant growth as possible. This is worthwhile even though the hedge to be planted is of common material such as privet or barberry.

Clear a strip 4 to 6 ft. wide along the line of the proposed hedge and remove all perennial weeds. Plow, rototill or spade the ground to a minimum depth of 10 in. along the length of the strip, incorporating well-rotted compost or old manure in generous amounts and bone meal at the rate of 8 oz. per sq. yd.

Stretch a garden line down the prepared strip of ground to mark one side of a trench 1 to 1½ ft. wide that is to run down the center of the prepared strip. Dig the trench 1 ft. deep, throwing out the soil on either side. If there is a lawn on one side, place the soil on burlap or polyethylene to protect the grass, or throw all the soil on the other side of the trench. Fork over the bottom of the trench and mix in compost or other organic matter.

As the plants are set, replace the soil around the roots little by little and firm it with the heel. Firm planting is essential. Rake over the soil so that it looks neat and level, but leave a shallow trench or saucers around

the plants to make it easier to water them effectively the season following planting.

Newly planted hedges should not need support if the plants are small enough, and if the ground has been well firmed during planting. But wire-mesh fencing is sometimes helpful as temporary support in exposed places, or wires can be stretched taut between posts at either end of the hedge.

MAINTENANCE

Take great care of newly planted hedges for the first two or three years. Water whenever necessary. Replace any dead plants with those from the group at the end of the hedge.

Trim young plants when necessary for shaping and, in the case of formal hedges, sufficiently often to make sure that they branch freely; repeat as needed to insure a dense growth. Deciduous hedges will need more clipping than evergreens in the early stages, although all will need more frequent clipping when young than when they are established. Privet and *Lonicera nitida*, in particular, should be prevented from growing too high when young, otherwise the base of the hedge will be bare.

The trimming of established formal hedges will need attention at least once a year and in some cases oftener. Early summer is ordinarily a good time to cut hedges, with an additional trimming given, if necessary, as soon as the summer growth is complete. Informal hedges of early-blooming shrubs should be trimmed or pruned as soon as they are through flowering. Hedges of pines, spruces and firs should be trimmed while the candles of new growth are yet soft and before their leaves have unfolded.

Always keep the base of the hedge clear of weeds. A mulch of well-rotted compost, peat moss or other suitable organic material applied to clean soil

Ilex
(Holly)

helps to stifle weeds and keeps the ground cool and moist.

SHAPING AND RENOVATING

Train and shape hedges according to individual taste and requirements. Keep them broad at the base and, ideally, tapered slightly toward the top; never allow the top to become wider than the base—otherwise the lower parts are apt to die back.

Most overgrown, straggly hedges can be cut back severely in late winter or early spring to encourage the plants to break lower down and become bushy again. (But this treatment should not be followed with such subjects as hemlocks, spruces, pines and firs.) Following such a drastic pruning, fertilize the hedge generously and keep it well watered during periods of dry weather. The application of a spring dressing of a complete fertilizer is beneficial to any

hedge that is not making sufficiently vigorous growth.

For additional information on the plants in the following lists, see "Evergreen Trees," page 388; "Evergreen Shrubs," page 449; "Shade Trees," page 368; "Shrubs and Flowering Small Trees," page 409.

BROAD-LEAVED EVERGREEN AND DECIDUOUS HEDGE PLANTS

D = Deciduous   E = Evergreen

Many trees and shrubs make useful and attractive screens if planted in rows, but the following are particularly adaptable to close planting, and in many cases to close shearing. In stating height, the maximum given here is 15 ft. Some of the recommended kinds are trees and will exceed this height under favorable conditions if they are not kept well pruned.

ABELIA (D AND SEMI-E)

Abelia grandiflora, 4 to 5 ft., deciduous in the North, semievergreen in milder climates. Has attractive, glossy foliage which becomes bronze in fall, and pale pink flowers in summer.

ACANTHOPANAX (D)

Acanthopanax sieboldianus, 8 ft., thorny; foliage hangs late in fall. Grows well in shade and poor soils and stands city conditions well.

ACER (D)

Acer campestre (hedge maple), 15 ft.; hardy but less so than *A. ginnala*.

A. ginnala (Amur maple), 15 ft.; foliage colors well in fall. Extremely hardy and useful for gardens in far North; a good windbreak.

BEECH. See *Fagus*.

BERBERIS (BARBERRY) (D AND E)

The barberries are ideal for informal or formal hedges. The spiny stems provide both flowers in spring and well-colored foliage in fall.

B. stenophylla (E), 6 to 10 ft.; dark green spiny leaves; flowers yellow-orange in spring and blue grapelike berries late. Trim as flowers fade unless berries are desired. Not hardy in severe climates.

BUCKTHORN. See *Rhamnus*.

BUXUS (BOXWOOD) (E)

Among the best and choicest evergreen hedging plants. Boxwood hedges last for many years and provide an even background and an impenetrable but attractive barrier.

CARAGANA (PEA TREE) (D)

Caragana arborescens, 15 ft., small pealike flowers. Extremely hardy. Excellent as a windbreak on the plains of the northern states and Canada.

C. pygmaea, 4 ft., similar to *C. arborescens* but lower.

CARISSA (E)

Carissa grandiflora (Natal plum), 15 ft.; thorny, with handsome foliage and fragrant white flowers. Suitable for subtropical climates only.

CARPINUS (HORNBEAM) (D)

Carpinus betulus, up to 15 ft., good bright green leaves, prominently veined. A tree when allowed to grow naturally. Shear lightly in July when young and, once the hedge is established, fairly drastically in August.

CEANOTHUS (D AND E)

For mild climates the blue-flowered ceanothuses make ideal hedge plants.

CHOISYA (E)

Choisya ternata (Mexican orange), 3 to 5 ft., makes an excellent sweet-smelling, flowering hedge for mild climates. The abundant white flowers are borne chiefly in spring but occa-

Buxus
(Boxwood)

sionally appear again later. It flourishes in towns and in all types of soil, and can be pruned fairly hard after flowering.

COTONEASTER (D AND E)

The dark green foliage, which varies greatly from one species to another, is the chief attraction of cotoneasters. The small white flowers in summer are followed by handsome berries in autumn and winter.

CRATAEGUS (HAWTHORN) (D)

Crataegus crus-galli (cockspur thorn), 15 ft., a thorny plant that forms a stout hedge.

C. oxyacantha and its red form *C. o. coccinea*, 15 ft., good hedge plants. Can be closely clipped and shaped throughout the summer.

C. phaenopyrum (Washington thorn), 15 ft., a thorny plant with glossy foliage; produces a dense hedge.

CURRANT. See *Ribes*.

ELAEAGNUS (D)

Elaeagnus angustifolia (Russian olive), 15 ft., very hardy; excellent for windswept and seaside locations. Foliage willowlike, silvery. Needs full sun; withstands dry soils.

ELM. See *Ulmus*.

EUONYMUS (D AND E)

Euonymus alatus compactus (winged-bark euonymus) (D), 6 ft., forms a broad, tight hedge that requires minimum clipping. Foliage turns brilliant scarlet in fall. Not subject to insects or disease.

E. japonicus (E), 10 ft., has lustrous green leaves. Hardy in mild climates only. There are varieties with variegated foliage such as *E. j. albo-marginatus* and *E. j. aureo-marginatus*.

FAGUS (BEECH) (D)

Fagus sylvatica (European beech), 15 ft., makes a large, excellent hedge and can be closely clipped. Small plants 1 ft. high will grow quickly if given careful attention, reaching 4 ft. in four or five years. Do not clip for a year or two after planting, and then only lightly in July for a further two years. Established hedges should be clipped in August.

F. s. purpurea (copper beech), foliage almost pink when young and deepening with age to dark purple.

FIRETHORN. See *Pyracantha*.

FORSYTHIA (D)

Makes a good decorative informal hedge and provides a welcome splash of color in early spring.

Forsythia intermedia, 5 to 7 ft.; yellow flowers appear before leaves. Provide support for young plants by stretching wires tautly along the line

Forsythia intermedia

of the hedge. Can be clipped or left to grow more gracefully and pruned hard after flowering.

FUCHSIA (D)

In mild climates fuchsias make really decorative flowering hedges.

HAWTHORN. See *Crataegus*.

HIBISCUS (D AND E)

Hibiscus rosa-sinensis (E), 15 ft., good-looking foliage and large single or double white, pink or red flowers. Suitable for tropics and subtropics only.

H. syriacus (shrub althea, rose of Sharon) (D), 15 ft., bears single or double white, pink, red, lavender or blue flowers in summer. Best as an informal hedge. Prune in spring.

HOLLY. See *Ilex*.

HONEYSUCKLE. See *Lonicera.*

HORNBEAM. See *Carpinus.*

HYDRANGEA (D)
Hydrangeas can be used very effectively to make informal summer-flowering hedges.

ILEX (HOLLY) (E)
Long-lived evergreens, well worth planting for their well-groomed appearance. Holly flourishes in partially shaded places and in ordinary soil, but the ground should be well prepared before planting. (See illustration, page 476.)
Ilex aquifolium (English holly), shining dark green leaves, an excellent hedging plant.
I. cornuta (Chinese holly), 8 ft., handsome, glossy foliage.
I. crenata (Japanese holly), 8 ft., small-leaved, almost like boxwood.

LANTANA (D)
In semitropical and nearly frost-free climates, varieties of *Lantana camara* may be used as attractive hedges. They have clusters of white, cream, yellow or orange flowers and may be clipped to form tight barriers up to about 6 ft. high.

LAUREL. See *Prunus.*

LAVANDULA (LAVENDER) (E)
The fragrant gray-green lavender is ideal for informal low hedges or those bordering paths or driveways. Trim the hedge in spring.
Lavandula officinalis, 3 to 4 ft.; very sweet-smelling lavender flowers in July. Variety *alba* has white flowers.

LEADWORT. See *Plumbago.*

LIGUSTRUM (PRIVET) (D AND E)
Privets are tolerant of polluted air, wind, poor soil and considerable

neglect, and are therefore deservedly popular. They stand close shearing well. The evergreen kinds are hardy only as far north as Washington, D.C.

LILAC. See *Syringa.*

LONICERA (HONEYSUCKLE) (D AND E)
Lonicera maackii (D), 12 ft. holds foliage late into fall, extremely hardy, has red berries. A good hedge plant for northern gardens.
L. nitida (E), 4 to 6 ft., tiny dark green leaves. Makes a close hedge. Trim lightly for the first year or two, but several times during the growing season once the hedge is established. Not reliably hardy farther north than Washington, D.C.
L. tatarica (Tartarian honeysuckle) (D), 8 ft., very hardy, free of pests, a

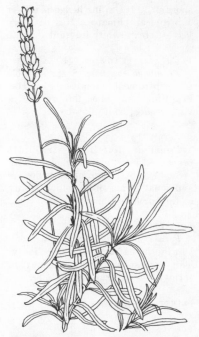

Lavandula officinalis
(Lavender)

fine hedge plant for northern gardens. Its foliage is bluish-green.

MACLURA (OSAGE ORANGE) (D)

Maclura pomifera, 15 ft., makes a dense, thorny hedge and succeeds on poor soil. Hardy to Massachusetts.

NATAL PLUM. See *Carissa grandiflora*.

OAK, SHINGLE. See *Quercus imbricaria*.

OSMANTHUS (E)

Osmanthus ilicifolius, 15 ft., a holly-like shrub of great ornamental value. For sun or semishade. Hardy in mild climates only.

PEA TREE. See *Caragana*.

PITTOSPORUM (E)

Pittosporum tobira (Japanese pittosporum), 9 ft., a fine hedge plant for subtropical climates. Has leathery leaves; cream-white fragrant flowers.

PLUMBAGO (LEADWORT) (E)

Plumbago capensis, 8 ft., suitable for subtropical climates only. Has beautiful pale blue flowers or, in variety *alba*, white flowers.

PONCIRUS (D)

Poncirus trifoliata (trifoliate orange), 15 ft., a thorny plant with green branches, fragrant white flowers and small orangelike fruits. Hardy as far north as Philadelphia.

PRINSEPIA (D)

Prinsepia sinensis, 8 ft., an excellent thorny barrier hedge, very hardy. The earliest shrub to leaf out in spring. Has red fruits in summer.

PRIVET. See *Ligustrum*.

PRUNUS (LAUREL) (D AND E)

Prunus caroliniana (cherry laurel) (E), 15 ft. Similar to *P. laurocerasus*

but leaves of this shrub are smaller.

P. laurocerasus (cherry laurel) (E), 15 ft., a shrub with thick leathery leaves, which makes an excellent windbreak. It flourishes in almost any soil and tolerates shade as well as sun.

P. l. schipkaenis, hardier and lower-growing than the type. Hardy as far north as Long Island, N.Y.

P. lusitanica (Portugal laurel) (E), 10 to 15 ft., has dark green, glossy leaves. Hardy about as far north as Philadelphia.

P. serotina (wild black cherry) (D), a very hardy tree with handsome foliage. Useful for windbreaks and hedges in northern gardens.

PYRACANTHA (FIRETHORN)
(E IN SOUTH, D IN NORTH)

All of the firethorns form attractive hedges. They are, unfortunately, subject to fire-blight disease.

QUERCUS (D)

Quercus imbricaria (shingle oak), 15 ft., a splendid hedge for the colder northern parts of the United States and southern Canada. It retains its dead brown leaves all winter.

RHAMNUS (BUCKTHORN) (D)

Rhamnus cathartica (D), 12 ft., foliage dark green. Extremely hardy, more or less spiny, provides a formidable barrier. Suitable for dryish soils; stands shade.

R. frangula (D), 12 ft., handsome, glossy foliage. Hardy far north, it thrives best in fairly moist soil; stands shade.

RIBES (CURRANT) (D)

Ribes alpinum (mountain currant), 6 ft., extremely hardy, especially useful for the coldest parts of the United States and southern Canada; withstands extreme heat, cold and drought well. Plant only the male (staminate) form, which is immune to white-pine blister rust. Stands shade and needs minimum shearing.

R. aureum (golden currant), 6 ft., very hardy and useful for northern gardens.

ROSA (D)

Several species of rose can be used to make attractive flowering hedges. The following, 5 to 8 ft. high, make attractive screens when left to grow somewhat naturally, and need only light pruning in spring.

Rosa hugonis, fine green foliage and single yellow flowers. An early bloomer.

R. moyesii, single dark red flowers followed by enormous pitcher-shaped fruits. Not hardy in regions of severe winters.

R. multiflora, a very vigorous white-flowered kind that is not useful where space is limited, but effective for enclosing fields and similar spacious areas.

R. rugosa, available in several varieties. All are excellent either as informal or as sheared hedges. One of the best plants for seaside gardens.

Floribunda roses make most successful and decorative hedges, 3 to 4 ft. high, and need very little pruning. Plant only one variety in a hedge, otherwise uneven growth will produce a poor effect.

ROSE OF SHARON. See *Hibiscus syriacus*.

RUSSIAN OLIVE. See *Elaeagnus angustifolia*.

SALIX (WILLOW) (D)

Salix purpurea nana (dwarf blue-leaf arctic willow), 3 ft., foliage bluish. Makes an attractive low hedge and is exceedingly hardy.

SYRINGA (LILAC) (D)

As hedges, most lilacs are at their best when grown informally with a minimum of pruning.

TAMARIX (TAMARISK) (D AND E)

Graceful, feathery plants, excellent for seaside districts. They thrive even in poor and alkaline soil and need full sun.

ULMUS (ELM) (D)

Ulmus pumila (Siberian elm), 15 ft., grows considerably taller if not

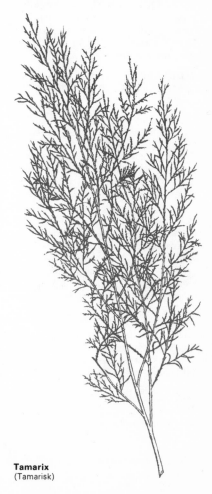

Tamarix
(Tamarisk)

pruned. Extremely hardy in the North; withstands drought, cold and winds well.

VIBURNUM (D AND E)

Viburnum prunifolium (black haw) (D), 15 ft., attractive foliage which colors well in fall; dense growth. Hardy in northern gardens. Excellent as a windbreak.

V. tinus (laurestinus) (E), foliage glossy dark green, showy heads of white or pinkish flowers. Makes a fine hedge which needs little or no clipping. Hardy in mild climates only. Avoid watering too much during summer.

CONIFEROUS OR NEEDLE-LEAVED EVERGREEN HEDGE PLANTS

ARBORVITAE. See *Thuja*.

CHAMAECYPARIS (FALSE CYPRESS) (E)
These form satisfactory hedges and screens. They should not be trimmed too severely—not back into old wood. Chamaecyparis thrive in any ordinary soil but are easily harmed by polluted atmosphere.

Chamaecyparis lawsoniana, 15 ft. Several of its varieties are useful in mild climates.

C. l. allumii, glaucous blue-green foliage and an attractive pyramidal habit.

CUPRESSUS (CYPRESS) (E)
Cupressus macrocarpa (Monterey cypress), a quick-growing and popular plant for screens and hedges in mild climates.

CYPRESS, FALSE. See *Chamaecyparis*.

HEMLOCK. See *Tsuga*.

JUNIPERUS (JUNIPER) (E)
The taller junipers are well adapted for planting as hedges. They are sun

Thuja occidentalis
(American Arborvitae)

Chamaecyparis lawsoniana allumii
(False Cypress)

lovers and stand exposed locations well.

J. communis (common juniper), foliage bluish, resistant to cold winds, slow-growing. Provides a tough barrier; is very hardy and especially suited to alkaline soils.

PICEA (SPRUCE) (E)
Spruce is particularly suited to cold, northerly regions. Although usually grown as a tall screen, spruce also makes an effective hedge up to 15 ft. tall. To plant as a screen, put in the young plants 6 to 8 ft. apart when they are 3 ft. tall. Remove alternate trees when branches overlap.

PINUS (PINE) (E)
Most pines form excellent screens, and several adapt themselves to growing as hedges.

SPRUCE. See *Picea.*

TAXUS (YEW) (E)
All of the yews, except the more or less prostrate, dwarf varieties, make excellent hedges and stand shearing well.

THUJA (ARBORVITAE) (E)
Thujas thrive on most well-drained soils but not on shallow, dry ones. They form excellent screens and good hedges; they grow quickly and can be clipped severely, but cuts should not be made back into old wood.

Thuja occidentalis (American arborvitae), foliage turns rusty red in winter, reverting to green again in late spring. When bruised, it emits a strong, tansylike odor, particularly when clipped. Perhaps the hardiest evergreen hedge plant.

TSUGA (HEMLOCK) (E)
These extremely elegant trees make excellent screens and trimmed hedges.

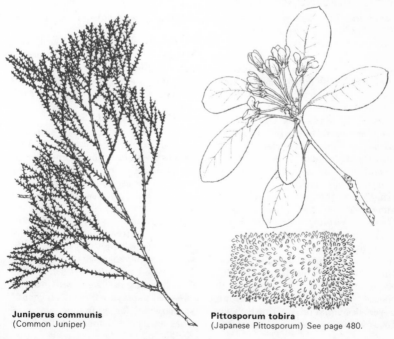

Juniperus communis
(Common Juniper)

Pittosporum tobira
(Japanese Pittosporum) See page 480.

They like a moist soil and humid atmosphere, and benefit from watering in dry weather. They are not adapted for windswept locations. When kept closely sheared, they have the general effect of a hedge of yew. All hemlocks except the dwarf varieties are excellent hedge and screen plants. Consult the catalogues of nursery specialists for varieties.

YEW. See *Taxus*.

CHAPTER 23

GROUND COVERS SAVE WORK

Decorative Carpets for the Landscape— Planting and Care—Propagation— Recommended Plants

GROUND COVERS ARE work savers— they reduce the cost of garden maintenance and if used advantageously add greatly to the decorative appearance of the landscape. Low-growing, they are used to carpet broad expanses, eliminating the need for grass mowing and reducing the necessity for weeding to an absolute minimum. They offer special advantages for covering banks that are difficult to mow, and for carpeting the ground in shady places unsuitable for the growth of lawn grasses. Of course, no other plant has all the virtues of grass as a living carpet for gardens; none bears the walking and playing on, or looks as uniformly neat. But, except for the special purposes mentioned, ground covers are equal or superior to lawns. In any case, a thriving carpet of a suitable ground cover is better-looking than a poor lawn.

Here we consider plants with wide tolerances, which are easy to propagate, relatively trouble-free and, given anything like reasonable growing conditions, prosper with minimum care.

LANDSCAPE ASSETS

Even where there are beautifully mowed lawns, the introduction of sweeps of carefully chosen ground covers provides a change of pace. They make the grass look better, just as nearby lawns flatter expanses of ground cover.

Each ground cover has its own special leaf pattern, its own shade of green, its own light-reflective qualities. In many cases their appearance from season to season varies more than does that of grass; some provide very effective displays of bloom. They have special value for tying together somewhat unrelated elements in the landscape picture. For instance, they reduce the "spotty" effect created by a new planting of shrubs with small specimens spaced at the distances they will need when mature. Ground covers can knit together taller plants of a foundation planting, and prevent soil from splashing onto house walls. They make wonderful transitions between solitary trees and shrubs, as well as between groups of trees and shrubs and lawn areas. Wisely used, they reduce restlessness and emphasize permanence in the landscape picture.

PLANTING

The preparation of the soil for planting ground covers should be as thorough as possible. A few kinds, such as sedums, thymes and achilleas (yarrow), will grow in poor soils with little or no improvement, but these and most others become established more quickly, cover the ground more rapidly and remain permanently attractive if they have a good medium in which to root. Turn the soil over to a depth of 6 in. or so with a spade, fork or rototiller, removing the roots of pernicious perennial weeds. Incorporate in it organic matter such as compost or manure, as well as a dressing of bone meal or superphosphate.

Either spring or fall is appropriate for setting out ground-cover plants, but on steep slopes spring is much to be preferred because then new growth starts quickly and roots soon ramify through the soil. There are erosion-controlling nettings and fabrics available which will not interfere with the rooting of small plants.

On steep banks it is sometimes practical to prepare only individual stations or planting holes for strong-growing ground covers that are to be spaced rather widely, as, for example, Hall's Japanese honeysuckle (*Lonicera japonica halliana*), trailing roses and small bushes.

For such station planting on steep banks, to reduce erosion, a splendid mulch is black polyethylene plastic film. This can be rolled out across the slope so that the edges overlap the strip above it in the opposite manner from that of shingles on a roof. Rainwater will thus be carried to the roots of the plants rather than over the plastic. The strips should be securely pegged into place. Plants are set through holes cut in the polyethylene film.

MAINTENANCE

Ground covers vary greatly in the rate at which they spread to provide an all-over carpet. One should establish good coverage the first year and complete coverage not later than the second. In the months immediately following planting, weeding should be thorough, and if dry weather threatens to limit ground-cover growth, water if possible.

During the first winter, freezing may heave the young plants out of the ground. Press them back into place without delay. Also, before the end of the first winter, plants that have failed to grow should be replaced.

Most established ground covers benefit greatly from an application of a general garden fertilizer early each spring. It should be applied when the foliage is dry and well watered in immediately.

In cold regions certain ground covers should have some winter protection. A covering of branches of evergreens, such as pines, is ideal. Heavy shelter that interferes with air circulation or with sufficient light is not recommended. By carefully selecting ground-cover plants that are completely hardy in the area, the chore of winter protection can be avoided.

Some kinds of ground covers, such as trailing roses and Hall's honeysuckle, require pruning or shearing every few years to keep them neat and within bounds.

PROPAGATION

Because plantings of ground covers usually involve large numbers of plants, their cost can be considerable even though the unit price is low. Most of the plants recommended here are easy to propagate, and once a basic stock is acquired, home gardeners may increase them easily.

Division and cuttings are the propagation techniques most commonly employed in multiplying ground-cover plants. Many can be propagated directly in an outdoor nursery bed located in a shady place, but success is much more certain with a simple cold frame. (A large box with a glass or polyethylene cover will do.)

RECOMMENDED PLANTS

D = Deciduous   E = Evergreen

ACHILLEA MILLEFOLIUM
(YARROW) (E)
A ferny-leaved plant that stands mowing well and is excellent for poor, dry soils in full sun; 2 to 3 in. high if mowed. Remains green even in very dry weather. Easily propagated by division and seed.

AEGOPODIUM PODAGRARIA
(BISHOP'S-WEED) (D)
A vigorous grower that can become an invasive weed in good soils and favorable locations; 6 to 12 in. high. Has rather large compound leaves, tiny white flowers in flat heads. For sun or shade. Propagate by division. A variety with variegated leaves, *A.p. variegatum*, is commonly grown.

AJUGA REPTANS (BUGLEWEED) (D)
A fast-growing spreading kind for sun or shade in any fairly good, not excessively dry soil. Leaves are glossy. In spring spikes of blue flowers, 9 or 10

in. tall, are freely borne. Propagate by division; 3 to 6 in. high.

ARCTOSTAPHYLOS UVA-URSI
(BEARBERRY) (E)
Small-leaved trailing shrub especially suited for poor, sandy, acid soils, in sun or light shade; 6 to 10 in. high. Has red berries. Collected plants are not easy to transplant. It is best to set out young pot-grown specimens. Propagate by cuttings or seed.

ARMERIA MARITIMA (THRIFT) (E)
A tufted, 6-in.-high plant with grass-like foliage. Small, tight heads of pink flowers on foot-long stems in spring. Excellent for sandy soils, in full sun, and for seaside gardens. Propagate by division or seed.

ASARUM (WILD GINGER) (E)
The evergreen wild gingers are better ground covers than the deciduous ones. Two similar kinds, *Asarum europaeum* and *A. caudatum*, are recommended and valued for their handsome heart-shaped leaves. They need rich, fairly moist soil and shade, and grow 6 to 8 in. high. Propagate by division and seed.

BARRENWORT. See *Epimedium*.

Asarum europaeum
(European Wild Ginger)

BEARBERRY. See *Arctostaphylos uva-ursi.*

BISHOP'S-WEED. See *Aegopodium podagraria.*

BROOM. See *Cytisus, Genista.*

BUGLEWEED. See *Ajuga reptans.*

CALLUNA VULGARIS (HEATHER) (E)
This, the heather of Scotland, is available in many varieties, differing in foliage character, flower color and height, which ranges from 6 in. to 2 ft. All are good. They need acid, reasonably moist, well-drained soil that is rather low in fertility, and full sun. Shear the plants back severely each spring. Propagate by cuttings, layers and seed.

CERATOSTIGMA PLUMBAGINOIDES
(PLUMBAGO LARPENTAE) (D)
This is one of the handsomest ground covers, 6 to 10 in. high, with green foliage that becomes bronze in fall. In late summer and autumn it bears blue flowers; it leafs out late in spring. For ordinary soil in sun or light shade. Propagate by division.

CONVALLARIA MAJALIS
(LILY OF THE VALLEY) (D)
Forms a mat of erect, paddle-shaped leaves that tend to become somewhat ragged-looking in fall; 6 to 10 in. high. In spring it produces racemes of fragrant, small, white bell-shaped flowers, sometimes followed by orange-red berries. It needs rich, fairly moist soil that contains an abundance of organic matter and light shade. Reduced flower production results from overcrowding. Replant and fertilize. Propagate by division.

CORONILLA VARIA (CROWN VETCH) (D)
A very vigorous plant, 1 to 2 ft. high, with compound leaves and heads of pretty pink pealike flowers in summer. Best suited for dry banks and similar areas in sun. Propagate by division and seed.

COTONEASTER (D)
Several low, spreading kinds are excellent ground covers; however, they are susceptible to fire-blight disease and to infestations of lacebug and red spider mites. They have small foliage and often attractive berries, thrive in ordinary soil in full sun or light shade, and are propagated by cuttings and seed. Among the best are:
Cotoneaster adpressa, 1 to 2 ft., red berries.
C. apiculata, 1 to 1½ ft., red berries.
C. dammeri, 6 to 9 in., red berries.
C. horizontalis, 1½ to 2½ ft., red berries.
C. microphylla, 6 to 12 in., has red berries.

CREEPING THYME. See *Thymus serpyllum*, p. 539 in "Rock Gardens."

CROWN VETCH. See *Coronilla varia.*

CYTISUS (BROOM) (D)
Several charming low-growing brooms are good ground covers for full sun and well-drained soil. They resent transplanting and so should be set out from pots. Their twigs are green, giving the effect of evergreens; their flowers are pea-shaped. Propagate by cuttings and seed. Among the best are:
Cytisus albus, 6 to 12 in., white flowers.
C. beanii, 1½ ft., golden-yellow flowers.
C. decumbens, 9 in., deep yellow flowers.
C. kewensis, 6 in., soft yellow flowers.
C. procumbens, 1 to 1½ ft., bright yellow flowers.

DEAD NETTLE. See *Lamium galeobdolon variegatum.*

DWARF FLEECEVINE. See *Polygonum reynoutria*.

EPIMEDIUM (BARRENWORT) (D)
There are several species and varieties of epimediums, all excellent for partial shade and moist, fertile soil. They take a long time to become established, and grow slowly, reaching a height of about 6 to 9 in. Their handsome foliage is beautiful in spring, green in summer and assumes rich bronze hues in fall. Small white, cream, yellow, lilac, pink or red flowers are borne in profusion in spring. Propagate by division and cuttings.

ERICA CARNEA (HEATH) (E)
An early-flowering heatherlike plant for poor, acid soils and full sun; 6 to 12 in. high. Flowers are pink, purplish, red or white, according to variety. Needs light winter protection in New England. Propagate by division, layers and cuttings.

EUONYMUS (D AND E)
Euonymus fortunei (E), two varieties: *E.f. coloratus*, with leaves that turn reddish-purple in winter; and *E.f. radicans*, with leaves green in winter. Both are rapid-growing viny plants for sun or shade and ordinary soil; 6 to 9 in. high. The first-named appears to be much less susceptible to infestations of scale insects than other euonymus. Both make pleasing ground covers and withstand adverse conditions. Propagate by cuttings.

E. obovatus (D), a fast-spreading viny plant, 1 ft., with leaves that will turn brilliant red in fall. Susceptible to scale insects. May be propagated by cuttings.

GALAX APHYLLA (E)
A choice plant for moist, rich, acid woodland soil and shade; 6 in. high. Has round glossy leaves which become a beautiful bronze in fall, and,

in spring, racemes of small white flowers. Propagate by division and seed.

GAULTHERIA (E)
Gaultheria miqueliana (E), suitable for mild climates. Has good foliage and white or pinkish flowers. For part shade in moist, acid soil; 1 ft. high. Propagate by division and seed.

G. procumbens (wintergreen) (E), a choice creeper for moist, acid soils and shade; 3 in. high. Has attractive lustrous leaves, small white bell-shaped flowers and edible berries. Propagate by division and seed.

G. shallon (salal) (E), especially adapted for West Coast planting. In rich soil or shade it is apt to grow too tall for use as a ground cover; but in sun and poor, dry soil it will retain a height of 2 to 2½ ft. Propagate by division and seed.

GENISTA (BROOM) (D)
The low-growing genistas resemble the cytisus broom, and require the same general treatment.
Genista pilosa, 6 to 12 in., yellow flowers.
G. sagittalis, 6 to 12 in., stems winged, flowers yellow.

Euonymus fortunei

HEATH. See *Erica carnea.*

HEATHER. See *Calluna vulgaris.*

HEDERA (IVY) (E)
Numerous varieties of English ivy, *Hedera helix*, are available; 6 to 8 in. high. One of the commonest used as a ground cover is the large-leaved *H.h. hibernica*. Two of the hardiest are *H.h. baltica* and *H.h.* 238th Street, which will grow in climates as severe as that of Boston. They thrive best in rich, loamy soil that does not become excessively dry, and in shade. Propagate by cuttings. In mild climates *H. colchica* and the Algerian ivy, *H. canariensis*, can be used in place of the English ivy. Both have larger leaves.

HONEYSUCKLE, HALL'S JAPANESE. See *Lonicera japonica halliana.*

HYPERICUM (ST.-JOHN'S-WORT)
(D AND E)
Among the finest ground covers for sandy, fertile soil and full sun or partial shade. Foliage is attractive, and over a long summer period large yellow flowers are freely produced. Propagate by division, cuttings and seed.

Hedera helix
(English Ivy)

Hypericum buckleii, 9 in., deciduous. Hardy about as far north as Philadelphia.

H. calycinum, 9 to 12 in., evergreen, hardy at New York City.

H. moserianum (goldflower), 2 ft., deciduous. This is less hardy than *H. calycinum.*

IVY. See *Hedera.*

JUNIPERUS (JUNIPER) (E)
Several low-growing junipers are useful ground covers for sunny places in well-drained soils. Propagate by cuttings. Among the best are:

Juniperus chinensis sargentii, 1 ft., steel-blue.

J. conferta (shore juniper), 1 ft., especially useful for exposed locations and poor soils.

J. horizontalis, 1 to 1½ ft., bluish-green.

J.h. douglasii (Waukegan juniper), 1 to 1½ ft., steel-blue becoming purplish in winter.

J.h. plumosa (Andorra juniper), 1 to 1½ ft., light green becoming purplish in fall.

J. procumbens, 2 ft., steel-blue, slow-growing.

J. sabina tamariscifolia, 2 ft., green.

LAMIUM GALEOBDOLON VARIEGATUM
(DEAD NETTLE) (D)
Vigorous grower with slender stems; leaves are variegated with white, has spikes of yellow flowers in spring; 6 to 12 in. high. For sun or light shade, ordinary soil. Propagate by cuttings and division.

LILY OF THE VALLEY. See *Convallaria majalis.*

LILYTURF. See *Liriope, Ophiopogon.*

LIPPIA CANESCENS (E)
Small-leaved creeper with little heads of white or lilac flowers; 2 to 4 in. high.

Suitable for sun and ordinary soil in mild, dry climates. Propagate by division and cuttings.

LIRIOPE (LILYTURF) (E)
Both *Liriope muscari*, big blue lily-turf, 1 to 1½ ft., and *L. spicata*, creeping lilyturf, 6 to 8 in., have grasslike foliage and are excellent for shade or sun in good soil. The former has spikes of purple, the latter of lilac or nearly white flowers in spring. Propagate by division.

LONICERA JAPONICA HALLIANA
(HALL'S JAPANESE HONEYSUCKLE)
(D OR SEMI-E)
A very vigorous vine, apt to become an aggressive nuisance unless strictly controlled. Best suited for difficult banks and similar places where there is no danger of it smothering perennials, shrubs, hedges and other garden plantings. Any ordinary soil in sun or shade. Grows 1 ft. high but will climb many feet if supports are available. Propagate by division and cuttings.

MESEMBRYANTHEMUM (E)
Low succulents for mild, dry climates, full sun and porous dry soils. Many are now called other names by botanists. White, pink, red, yellow or orange flowers that open in sunshine. Many kinds are grown; 6 to 12 in. Propagate by division or cuttings.

MONDO GRASS. See *Ophiopogon*.

MOSS PINK. See *Phlox subulata*.

MYRTLE, RUNNING. See *Vinca minor*.

OPHIOPOGON (E)
Similar to *Liriope* but less hardy. *Ophiopogon japonicus*, 6 to 9 in., often sold as "mondo grass," does not persist in climates more severe than that of Philadelphia. It forms a sod of dark grasslike leaves and has spikes

Pachysandra terminalis

of pale lilac flowers. The white lily-turf, *O. jaburan*, 1½ to 2 ft., is coarser and less hardy. Propagate by division.

PACHISTIMA CANBYI (E)
Handsome, small-leaved trailer for sun or shade and well-drained acid soil; 9 to 12 in. high. Propagate by cuttings.

PACHYSANDRA TERMINALIS (E)
A favorite carpeting plant that makes an interesting leaf pattern and has somewhat inconsequential spikes of white flowers; 6 to 8 in. high. For good soil and part shade. Propagate by cuttings and root cuttings.

PERIWINKLE. See *Vinca*.

PHLOX SUBULATA (MOSS PINK) (E)
A matting plant that looks somewhat like a very coarse moss, covered with magenta-pink, pink, white or lilac flowers in spring; 6 in. high. Old plants tend to die toward their centers, necessitating cutting back or re-propagating. In severe climates foliage turns brown in winter. For full sun and porous soils. Propagate by cuttings, division and seeds.

PLUMBAGO LARPENTAE. See *Cerato-stigma plumbaginoides.*

POLYGONUM REYNOUTRIA
(DWARF FLEECEVINE) (D)
A vigorous spreader with heart-shaped leaves and sprays of tiny pink flowers. For poor, dryish soils. In rich soils it becomes excessively rampant and 2 ft. or more high; in poor soils it remains about 1 ft. high. Propagate by division and cuttings.

POTENTILLA TRIDENTATA (E)
Has shiny, deep green, small straw-berry-shaped leaves and white flow-ers; 2 to 8 in. high. For full sun and acid soil. Spreads slowly. Propagate by division and seed.

ROSA (ROSE) (D)
A number of trailing roses are useful as ground covers, especially for exten-sive banks. They need ordinary soil and sun. Two of the best are *R.* Max Graf, 1 to 2 ft., with pink flowers, and *R. wichuraiana,* the memorial rose, 1 to 1½ ft., with white flowers. Propagate by cuttings.

ST.-JOHN'S-WORT. See *Hypericum.*

SALAL. See *Gaultheria shallon.*

SARCOCOCCA HOOKERIANA HUMILIS (E)
Handsome shiny-leaved plant easily kept to a height of 1 to 2 ft. by oc-casional shearing. Hardy into south-ern New England. Propagate by di-vision and cuttings.

SEDUM (STONECROP) (E AND D)
Several very popular sedums are excellent for sunny places in well-drained, ordinary soil. Easily propa-gated by cuttings and division. Among the best kinds for use as ground cov-ers are these:
Sedum acre, 2 in., evergreen, tiny leaves and golden flowers.

S. album, 6 in., evergreen, white flowers.
S. sarmentosum, 3 to 4 in., ever-green, yellow flowers.
S. spurium, 6 in., semievergreen, white or pink flowers.

SETCREASEA PURPUREA (E)
Handsome purple-leaved plant, 6 in. high, similar to wandering Jew (*Ze-brina pendula*). For ordinary soil in sun, and frost-free or nearly frost-free climates only. Propagate by cuttings.

STONECROP. See *Sedum.*

THRIFT. See *Armeria maritima.*

THYMUS SERPYLLUM. See page 539 in "Rock Gardens."

VINCA (E)
The hardiest is *Vinca minor* (peri-winkle or running myrtle), 6 in. high, with lustrous dark green leaves and lilac-blue or white flowers. More ten-der and suited only to areas of mild climates is *V. major* (large periwinkle), 8 in. high, with larger blue flowers. Both need rich soil containing abun-dant organic matter, and shade. Prop-agate by cuttings and division.

Vinca minor
(Periwinkle, Running Myrtle)

WEDELIA TRILOBATA (E)
Fast-growing trailer with bright yellow flowers; 6 to 8 in. high. For ordinary soil in sun or shade. Suitable for the Deep South only. Propagate by cuttings.

WILD GINGER. See *Asarum*.

WINTERGREEN. See *Gaultheria procumbens*.

YARROW. See *Achillea millefolium*.

CHAPTER 24

VINES—
Clingers and Climbers

Beautifying Unsightly Surfaces—Soil Improvement—Supports—Planting—Watering—Pruning—Evergreen and Deciduous Vines

THE MOST DELIGHTFUL vines, beautiful in flower, foliage and fruit, can be grown against upright surfaces. Walls and fences, tree stumps and sometimes unsightly posts and other objects can all provide ideal supports for climbing plants, and without taking appreciable growing space from the garden. Many vines are true climbers, some self-clinging by means of sticky pads or suckers, some twining, others clinging by means of tendrils. There are also some woody or semiwoody scramblers which grow successfully as vines provided they are kept tied to supports.

SOIL PREPARATION
Nearly all the plants described here will grow in any ordinary garden soil, but often the soil at the foot of walls is very poor and needs improving. It is best either to remove the soil to the depth of a foot or more and replace it with fresh soil mixed with moisture-retaining rotted manure, peat moss or compost as well as a

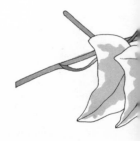

**Hedera canariensis
foliis variegatis**
(Variegated Algerian Ivy)

generous dressing of bone meal, or to dig wide, deep planting holes to be filled with the same mixture.

SUPPORTS

Except for self-clinging vines such as Boston ivy, English ivy and climbing hydrangea, put supports for the plants into place before planting. They may consist of plastic-covered wire netting of heavy gauge, or strongly made trelliswork, both held 3 to 6 in. away from the wall to minimize danger of damage from reflected heat and to allow room for thickening of the stems.

Do not plant self-clinging vines against surfaces which are painted periodically. Other types may be taken down when painting is done or may be grown on hinged trellises which may be moved away from the wall with the vines still attached to them.

PLANTING

Plant in early fall or early spring in well-prepared holes, leaving about 6 in. between the wall and the plant. Spread the roots roughly fanwise away from the wall and cover them firmly. When planting clematis, be es-

pecially careful not to kink the stems.

It is a good plan to provide small plants with a temporary support such as bamboo canes until they reach the wires or trellis. Also provide shade for their roots, either by putting a large stone over the soil which covers the roots, or by planting temporary plants such as annuals or bedding plants in front of them.

WATERING

Because of the overhang of the roof, the soil immediately surrounding a house often receives little rain. Especially during the first year or two after planting, therefore, water frequently and thoroughly, until the roots have spread well beyond the overhang of the roof.

PRUNING

Many wall plants grow rapidly and need pruning to keep them within bounds. This should be done in the spring, although it may become necessary to train new growths at other times of the year. When not wanted, forward-pointing growths can be removed. Clematis require special pruning methods and these are described below.

EVERGREEN AND DECIDUOUS VINES

D = Deciduous   E = Evergreen

ACTINIDIA (D)

These interesting twiners grow in sun or part shade and prefer rich, moist soil; resistant to pests and diseases.

Actinidia arguta, hardy to Massachusetts; has small white flowers and edible fruits.

A. chinensis, hardy about to Washington, D.C.; the largest-flowered kind; creamy flowers, edible fruits.

AKEBIA (D OR SEMI-E)

Akebia quinata, a twining plant, attractive in leaf and flower. The leaves are divided into five leaflets. The fragrant, brownish-purple flowers are in drooping clusters in spring. They are occasionally followed by sausage-shaped, violet-purple fruits up to 4 in. long. Useful for training over porches and arches. If growth tangles, cut to the base in winter.

ALGERIAN IVY. See *Hedera canariensis*.

ALLAMANDA (E)

Allamanda cathartica and its varieties are magnificent for gardens in the far South. Vigorous growers, they bear great clusters of golden-yellow trumpet flowers. Plant in full sun. Prune in winter.

AMPELOPSIS (D)

Ampelopsis brevipedunculata (porcelain vine), a vigorous tendril climber with attractive foliage and clear porcelain-blue berries in fall. *A.b. elegans* has beautifully variegated leaves.

ANTIGONON (E)

Antigonon leptopus (coralvine), a delightful slender vine which grows to 30 or 40 ft.; bears masses of small pink flowers, or, in variety *album*, white. Hardy in subtropical climates only.

ARISTOLOCHIA (D)

Aristolochia durior (Dutchman's-pipe), a rampant twiner. The large heart-shaped leaves are attractive. The green and yellowish-brown flowers, tubular in shape and bent like a meerschaum pipe, are unusual rather than colorful. Because it produces such rampant long growths, it is suitable for porches and pergolas.

AUSTRALIAN BLUEBELL CREEPER. See *Sollya heterophylla*.

BEAUMONTIA (E)

Beaumontia grandiflora (herald's trumpet), very vigorous, large-leaved vine with large, fragrant, trumpet-shaped white flowers. Suitable for subtropical climates only.

BIGNONIA (D)

Bignonia capreolata (trumpet flower), is grown in the South. Its trumpet-shaped flowers are yellow-red, sometimes darker. Not hardy in the North.

BITTERSWEET. See *Celastrus*.

BLACK-EYED-SUSAN VINE. See *Thunbergia alata*.

BOSTON IVY. See *Parthenocissus tricuspidata*.

BOUGAINVILLEA (E OR D)

In the far South and other warm climates these vigorous vines are popular for covering arbors and training against walls. Cultivated kinds are varieties of *Bougainvillea glabra* and *B. spectabilis*. They have very showy magenta, red, pink, bronze or white bracts which are often mistaken for petals. Plant in sunny locations. Prune in winter.

CAMPSIS (D)

These are self-clinging climbers with small aerial roots. They climb 15 to

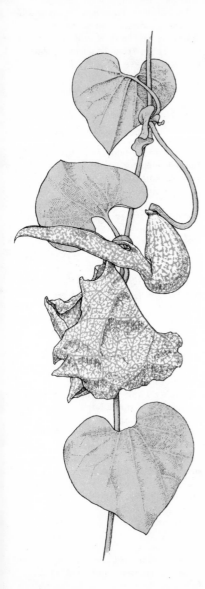

Aristolochia durior
(Dutchman's-Pipe)

20 ft. or more. They flower in summer and early autumn. If the lateral growths are pruned in autumn to two or three buds, not only will the plant be kept within its limits but flowering will be encouraged.

Campsis grandiflora (Chinese trumpet creeper), clusters of orange and red flowers; not hardy in the North.

C. radicans (trumpet vine), orange and scarlet flowers.

C. tagliabuana Madame Galen, salmon flowers.

CAROLINA YELLOW JESSAMINE. See *Gelsemium sempervirens*.

CAT'S CLAW. See *Doxantha unguis-cati*.

CELASTRUS (BITTERSWEET) (D)
Handsome vines with brilliant orange-yellow and red fruits in fall. Fruiting branches are much used in flower arrangements. They thrive without difficulty in sun or light shade in ordinary soil, but are very susceptible to infestations of scale insects.

Celastrus orbiculatus, 30 ft. Hardy into southern New England.

C. scandens, 20 ft. Extremely hardy.

CHINESE TRUMPET CREEPER. See *Campsis grandiflora*.

CLEMATIS (D AND E)
These attractive vines (see illustration, page 594) are not fussy about soil, but they usually thrive best when it contains lime. Keep their roots in the shade. If planted on the north sides of low walls, they find their way into the sun to flower. If planted on south or west sides of walls, shade their bases either by a low shrub or by placing a large flat slab of stone over the roots. Support them with wires or trellis. They are excellent for growing up dead trees.

Although clematis have a habit of dying back for no apparent reason, they are plants with which to persevere. Species and varieties worth growing and which need little pruning other than the removal of deadwood and the shortening of unwanted growths are:

Clematis armandii (E), leathery green leaves and large white flowers in spring. Not hardy in the North.

C. florida bicolor (D), white and purple flowers in summer. Not hardy in the North.

C. macropetala (D), violet-blue flowers in spring and early summer.

C. montana rubens (D), rosy-pink flowers in great profusion in May. Blooms on previous year's shoots. Do not prune in spring.

C. paniculata (D), tall climber, white, fragrant flowers in fall.

C. tangutica (D), thick-petaled, lantern-shaped yellow flowers blooming in September.

C. virginiana (D), flowers white, climbs to about 20 ft. A very hardy plant.

The pruning of the large-flowered hybrids differs with their various groups. The *patens* and *florida* groups need pruning immediately after flowering, by cutting back the stems that have flowered to a pair of buds.

In spring, prune the old growths of the *jackmanii* and *viticella* groups close to the base of the previous year's growth, and cut varieties of the *texensis* group back to live wood.

The *jackmanii* group includes varieties which bear large flowers from late summer to autumn.

The *viticella* group includes varieties which flower from July to September.

The *lanuginosa* group may be pruned after flowering in the same way as the *patens* and *florida* groups, when they will flower in spring, or they can be cut back hard like the *jackmanii* and *viticella* groups, to induce flowering in summer or early autumn.

CLYTOSTOMA (E)

Clytostoma calystegioides, suitable for the far South and other subtropical areas. A vigorous vine with panicles of large, attractive funnel-shaped lavender flowers.

CORALVINE. See *Antigonon leptopus*.

CREEPING FIG. See *Ficus*.

DOXANTHA

Doxantha unguis-cati (cat's claw), tendril climber with bright yellow flowers suitable for subtropical climates only.

DUTCHMAN'S-PIPE. See *Aristolochia*.

ENGLISH IVY. See *Hedera helix*.

EUONYMUS (E)

Euonymus fortunei and its varieties are the hardiest of all the evergreen vines.

E.f. radicans, a good self-clinging climber with inch-long leaves.

EVERLASTING PEA. See *Lathyrus*.

FICUS (E)

Ficus pumila (creeping fig), a self-clinger with small leaves, which on shoots lie flat against the surface up which it climbs. Mature flowering shoots stand out from the support and have larger leaves. Excellent in shade. For mild climates only.

FOX GRAPE. See *Vitis labrusca*.

FROST GRAPE. See *Vitis vulpina*.

GELSEMIUM (E)

Gelsemium sempervirens (Carolina yellow jessamine), a fragrant, yellow-flowered native of the southeastern states, as far north as Virginia. An attractive twining vine. Not hardy in the North.

HARDENBERGIA (E)

Hardenbergia comptoniana (lilac vine), has small blue or violet pealike flowers. Suitable only for frost-free or nearly frost-free climates.

HEDERA (IVY) (E)

Self-clinging, ideal for shady walls.

Hedera canariensis (Algerian ivy), large-leaved, less hardy than *H. helix.* (See illustration, pages 492–493.)

H.c. Canary Cream is handsomely variegated.

H. colchica, leaves very large, less hardy than *H. helix.*

H. helix (English ivy) is available in many varieties.

HERALD'S TRUMPET. See *Beaumontia.*

HIBBERTIA (E)

Hibbertia volubilis, tall twiner with handsome yellow flowers. Hardy in frost-free or nearly frost-free climates only.

HONEYSUCKLE. See *Lonicera.*

HOYA (E)

Hoya carnosa (wax plant), thick-leaved, stem-rooting vine with clusters of star-shaped delicate pink flowers, fragrant. A variegated-leaved variety is also grown. Needs subtropical climate.

HYDRANGEA (D)

Too few gardeners grow the delightful climbing hydrangea, *Hydrangea petiolaris*, a self-clinging, hardy plant, vigorous enough to cover the side of a house; it bears white heads of flat flowers in summer.

IVY. See *Hedera.*

JASMINUM (JASMINE) (D AND E)

None of the following is fussy about soil:

Jasminum nudiflorum (D), the beautiful winter jasmine, produces its bright yellow flowers in winter or earliest spring. Hardy at Boston, Mass.

J. officinale (D), the summer-flowering jessamine with fragrant white flowers, sometimes reaches 20 ft.; it is best in the larger-flowered form *affine*, the blooms of which are flushed with pink. Not hardy in the North.

J. polyanthum (E), fragrant white flowers. Hardy in mild climates only.

LATHYRUS (D)

The everlasting pea, *Lathyrus sativus*, is an attractive herbaceous perennial tendril-climber with white or pink sweet-pealike flowers.

LILAC VINE. See *Hardenbergia.*

LONICERA (HONEYSUCKLE) (D AND E)

These fragrant-flowered twiners, favorites for walls or fences, all do well in shade. The evergreen kinds often lose many of their leaves where winters are severe.

Lonicera heckrottii (D), flowers purple and yellow, borne for many weeks in summer.

L. henryi (E), dark green leaves, reddish flowers in June.

L. japonica aureo-reticulata (E), a pretty foliage plant with gold-netted leaves.

L.j. halliana (Hall's Japanese honeysuckle—E OR SEMI-E), creamy flowers, turning a deeper shade on maturity and borne all summer. A rampant grower which, unless restrained, can become a pest.

L. sempervirens (trumpet honeysuckle—D OR E), orange-scarlet scentless flowers appear over a long period in summer.

MENISPERMUM (MOONSEED) (D)

Menispermum canadense, attractive twiner, about 10 ft. tall, flowers small, greenish-white. Stands shade. Needs moist soil.

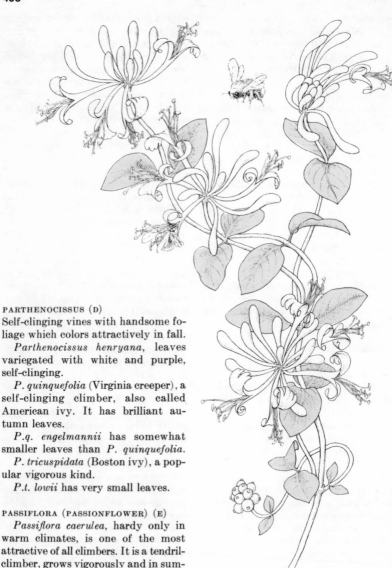

Lonicera
(Honeysuckle)

PARTHENOCISSUS (D)

Self-clinging vines with handsome foliage which colors attractively in fall.

Parthenocissus henryana, leaves variegated with white and purple, self-clinging.

P. quinquefolia (Virginia creeper), a self-clinging climber, also called American ivy. It has brilliant autumn leaves.

P.q. engelmannii has somewhat smaller leaves than *P. quinquefolia*.

P. tricuspidata (Boston ivy), a popular vigorous kind.

P.t. lowii has very small leaves.

PASSIFLORA (PASSIONFLOWER) (E)

Passiflora caerulea, hardy only in warm climates, is one of the most attractive of all climbers. It is a tendril-climber, grows vigorously and in summer bears numerous, spectacular, slightly fragrant flowers, blue, white and purple, the parts of which, according to legend, represent the instruments of the Crucifixion. It has handsome yellow egg-shaped fruits.

Passiflora caerulea
(Passionflower)

PETREA (E)

Petrea volubilis (purple wreath), a woody vine for cultivation outdoors in the far South. A strong grower, it has showy lilac or purple flowers.

POLYGONUM (D)

Polygonum aubertii, a rampant twiner and scrambler, suitable only for places where it can be allowed to spread. Bears trails of greenish-white or pinkish flowers in summer and autumn. Does best in sun.

PORCELAIN VINE. See *Ampelopsis brevipedunculata*.

POTATO VINE. See *Solanum jasminoides*.

PURPLE WREATH. See *Petrea volubilis*.

PYROSTEGIA (E)

Pyrostegia ignea, a tendril-bearing climber for the South and other subtropical places. Frequently planted to cover arbors and roofs. Bears an abundance of red-orange trumpet flowers.

SOLANUM (E)

Solanum crispum, purplish-blue flowers with prominent yellow centers reminiscent of the potato flower; the flowers are borne abundantly throughout the summer. For mild climates.

S. jasminoides (potato vine), a semi-evergreen with gray-blue flowers which start in mid-June and continue until autumn. Grows up to 20 ft. and is vigorous, requiring drastic pruning each spring. For mild climates.

S.j. album, a white-flowered variety.

SOLLYA (E)

Sollya heterophylla (Australian bluebell creeper), twining vine to 6 ft. tall with small nodding blue flowers. Hardy in subtropical climates only.

STAR JASMINE. See *Trachelospermum*.

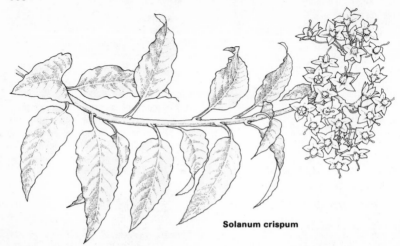

Solanum crispum

STIGMAPHYLLON (E)

Stigmaphyllon ciliatum, slender twiner with showy yellow flowers. Suitable for warm climates only.

THUNBERGIA (E)

Attractive twiners, hardy only in warm climates.

Thunbergia alata (black-eyed-Susan vine), flower is cream or orange-yellow with black throat. Often grown as an annual in northern gardens.

T. fragrans, flowers white, very fragrant.

TRACHELOSPERMUM (E)

Trachelospermum jasminoides (star jasmine), for planting outdoors in subtropical climates. A twining plant, it bears clusters of fragrant white star-shaped flowers.

TRUMPET FLOWER. See *Bignonia*.

TRUMPET HONEYSUCKLE. See *Lonicera sempervirens*.

TRUMPET VINE. See *Campsis radicans*.

VIRGINIA CREEPER. See *Parthenocissus quinquefolia*.

VITIS (D)

These do well in ordinary soil. The flowers are insignificant, but the plants are grown for the outstanding effect of their foliage.

Vitis coignetiae, leaves 1 ft. across, a beautiful tendril-climber. Very vigorous.

V. labrusca (fox grape), vigorous climber with large, thick, lobed leaves.

V. vulpina (frost grape), a high climber with large, rather shiny, mostly unlobed leaves.

WAX PLANT. See *Hoya carnosa*.

WISTERIA (D)

Wisterias are among the best of all vines and flourish in sun and in a good soil. They can be trained to cover very large areas and live to a great age but they are quite rampant and must be planted with caution. The following flower in spring and early summer:

Wisteria floribunda, a vigorous vine with very long flower clusters, white, purple or blue-purple according to variety.

W. sinensis, 1-ft.-long trails of fragrant mauve or white flowers. A favorite vine.

PART IV

Special Gardens

The pleasure and excitement of discovering new worlds lead many a gardener to create a traditional Japanese garden, to simulate woodland shade for wild flowers and ferns or to explore the possibilities of aquatic plants, mastering the skills needed to make them blossom on small, jewel-like pools.

Some of our most spectacular and interesting gardens are found where wind, sand and intense sun are hostile to the majority of plants. And determined growers surprise and beguile us by creating gardens on city rooftops, or by bringing rugged, rock-strewn slopes into bloom.

The specialist enjoys a number of advantages over others. He gets to know certain plants well by giving intimate attention to them. He keeps abreast of the latest varieties and joins societies devoted to singular phases of gardening. Without excessive study or strain, he can become an authority in his field of interest. Very often, even a few basic do's and don'ts make all the difference between frustration and joy in the cultivation of a specialty garden.

CHAPTER 25

WATER GARDENS

Place in Garden—Formal and Informal Pools—Winter Care—Planting and Stocking the Water Garden—Recommended Plants

A POOL OF WATER, miniature or larger, where aquatic plants bloom on the shining surface, adds great charm to a garden. It is easy to manage, lively and everchanging, and blends effectively with earth, rocks and plants. Many beautiful and unusual plants can be grown in a water garden. Virtually any receptacle capable of holding water is a potential pool, and there are water lilies small enough to live and flower in half a barrel.

If a pool is well constructed, if care is taken with the planting and if the right soil and aquatics (water plants) are chosen, water is easier to manage than a lawn. But the margin between success and failure is delicately poised. Great care is needed to hold the balance between clear water and a well-managed pool on the one hand, and slime, green water, rank smell and rampant aquatics on the other.

LOCATION

Most aquatics love the sun. The warmer the water, the more luxuriant the growth and the greater the number of blooms. Be sure to construct the pool some distance from trees or hedges so that dead leaves do not fall into it and foul the water. Alternatively, spread chicken wire over the surface of the pool during the few weeks when leaves are falling.

A very deep pool can be a disadvantage since depth may influence the temperature of the water, but a pool cannot be so shallow that the roots of hardy water lilies are in danger of freezing. From 12 to 18 in. of water above the crowns of plants is enough to induce free flowering and yet is sufficiently deep in many localities to safeguard the roots in winter. Where winters are severe, this depth of water will not give adequate protection—so that pools should be drained in winter (see Winter Care of Pools, page 505).

Water gardens are either formal or informal. Formal pools look better in conventional surroundings and do not blend with natural features such as wild gardens and rock gardens. Keep the vegetation in them low, concentrating on water lilies and submerged and floating aquatics.

An informal pool should not disclose its construction. The concrete or other material of which it is made can be hidden by keeping the outer edges below the level of the surrounding ground, and by the skillful use of bog and marginal aquatics to bridge the gap between the water and dry land.

TYPES OF POOLS

There are four principal types of pool construction to choose from: making a pool of concrete; installing a pre-shaped plastic or fiber-glass pool; adapting old containers such as tubs, baths and barrels; or lining an excavation with polyethylene sheeting.

Concrete Pools

These are the most popular and can be any size and shape. If properly constructed, they last for many years. A

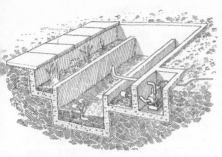

A Sunken Pool
This small concrete pool has a deep center
and side areas at a higher level, where shallow-
water aquatics may be grown. In a separate
watertight compartment, an electric pump
(to be covered by an edging stone) circulates
water from the bottom of the pool through
a pipe connected to a decorative fountain
in or at the edge of the pool.

concrete pool need not be the same
depth all over. Water lilies, submerged oxygenators (plants that provide oxygen in the water) and fish all
require deep water, but a shallow part
at one end or entirely surrounding the
deeper portion will provide a home for
marginal aquatics. This will reduce
the cost and labor of the excavation.

Maturing Concrete: Before a new pool is
stocked, be sure the concrete is matured. In its fresh, raw state, concrete
is exceedingly alkaline and harmful to
many plants and fish. There are three
ways of maturing it:
1. By keeping the pool full of water
for six months, then emptying and
rinsing it out before planting.

2. By painting the surface with one of
the special preparations that are
available for the purpose.
3. By neutralizing with acid the alkaline substances which come from the
cement. Any cheap product such as
commercial phosphoric acid serves
this purpose. Stir into the water
enough to show an acid reaction to
litmus paper 24 hours after adding.

Prefabricated Pools
These pools are usually made of fiber
glass and are available in all shapes
and sizes. To install, simply excavate
a hole into which the pool just fits,
level the rim, set the plants and fill
with water. Be sure that the depth of
the pool is sufficient to prevent deep
freezing in winter; a shallow pool has
to be emptied or protected at that
season. The edges can be concealed
by turf, creeping plants, rocks, flagstones or similar means.

Miscellaneous Containers
Tubs, old baths, stone troughs and
even galvanized tanks can be used for
water gardens. Old wooden wine or
beer casks sawed in half can also be
used, freestanding or sunk in the
ground. They need thorough cleansing
beforehand and should be kept filled
with water or the staves will shrink
and the tubs leak. If freestanding
casks are to be painted, do so only on
the outside surfaces.

Most receptacles present a better
effect when seen from above, so it is

A Tub as a Water Garden
Sink a tub or other small container
into the ground so that the plants
can be seen from above. Give the
pool a decorative outline by placing
pieces of stone or trailing plants
at the edges. The soil inside the
tub can be built up around the
rocks to give varying depths of water.

usual to sink tubs. If the rims are below ground level, small rocks and
low-growing plants can mask the outlines. A boggy surrounding area suitable for marsh plants or a rim of
rough, flat stones also hides the edges.

Polyethylene Sheeting

This is an inexpensive and simple
method of preparing a site for growing
aquatics; all that is needed is to excavate the area to the required shape
and depth, line the depression with
thick polyethylene sheeting, fill with
water and introduce the plants (in
boxes or baskets) and the fish.

There are two disadvantages to
polyethylene: A stab with a fork or
similar sharp tool spells disaster, and
if hot sun constantly plays on the material above the waterline, it is likely
to disintegrate and leak when the
pool is full. Protect the edges of plastic pools with pieces of rock or by
laying soil or paving stones up to the
water's edge, and always keep them
full of water.

OTHER WATER GARDENS
Stream Gardens

Rock and water are natural partners,
and in the garden, streams and waterfalls bring not only beauty but a mu-
sical splashing sound and sparkling
movement as well. A large area is not
essential, but the site must, of course,
be sloping. At the highest point, water
from a concealed source will trickle
slowly into a basin or cavity, to spill
over in a waterfall and collect in another basin, where it spills over again
before running, via a stream, to the
pool proper. Surprisingly little water
is needed to create attractive effects,
and there are several models of pumps
available which will recirculate the
water.

Remember that constantly moving
and forceful water is not good for
most aquatic plants, so that the source
of supply should be turned off at night
and be operated in small volume by
day. Also, the path of the water from
the top of a rock garden to the main
pool should not be too straight. In

A Raised Pool
Heavy-gauge plastic sheeting makes a pool that can be quickly erected. The top row of the
inner stone wall hides and holds in place the edges of the transparent sheeting. The plastic
stretches a little to take the shape of the earth base. When the pool needs emptying, the
water may be siphoned out. Rock-garden plants occupy pockets in the stone and earth walls.

nature, water takes the line of least resistance, meandering through soft ground and around obstacles in steady descent to the lowest reaches. Study such phenomena in the wild or visit appropriate gardens before starting to build a stream garden.

Bog Gardens

Many plants thrive in moist or wet soil yet cannot live completely in water. These are the bog plants, some of which are most colorful.

There are several ways of arranging for constant moisture during the active growing season. The area may be flooded periodically, which is quite successful if the floodwater can be trapped and held. But if it runs all over the garden, it is wasteful and ineffective.

A second method is to place 6 in. of drainage material such as broken bricks, stones or washed clinkers in the bottom of a 1-ft.-deep basin; cover this with a layer of sod laid grass-side downward and then with 10 to 12 in. of loamy soil. The plants' crowns will thus be in well-drained soil, but the roots will seek the water below.

WINTER CARE OF POOLS

During the winter months, all garden pools which are strong enough and sufficiently deep to avoid freezing solidly should be kept full of water. This is the best insurance against frost damage to plants and fish.

If possible, keep a hole open in the ice to give fresh air to any fish the pool contains. Do not bang the ice with a heavy hammer, as this can injure both fish and concrete, but float a ball or piece of wood on the surface, lift it out every day and gently chip away the ice around the hole.

In regions where small and shallow pools may freeze solidly if left filled with water, drain them in fall, fill them with dry leaves and cover them

with wooden shutters. Pile a foot or two of leaves on the shutters and hold in place with branches or chicken wire.

PLANTING

Water lilies, aponogetons (water hawthorns) and lotuses are hearty feeders and need a good, rich soil. Do not economize here, because poor soil results in a paucity of blooms, small stunted leaves and a general meagerness of growth. These plants need good, heavy loam, or clay soil enriched with one sixth of its bulk of decayed cow manure, which must be at least 12 months old and have been stored under cover to prevent the destruction of its nutrient properties by exposure to sun and rain. Other natural manures are unsuitable. If cow manure is unobtainable, the best substitute is one of the special fertilizers sold by dealers in aquatic plants, or coarse bone meal used in the proportion of a 5-in. potful to a wheelbarrow-load of soil. Mix thoroughly.

Do not introduce any of the organic materials normally associated with potting soils (see page 103). Leaf mold, compost, peat and similar substances may make good food, but during their breakdown they will charge the water with mineral salts. These will encourage algae, which in turn will discolor the water. If too much organic matter is present, putrid gases escape and can suffocate fish. Such destructive gases can sometimes be seen bubbling upward through the water.

Two Methods of Growing Water Lilies

There are two methods of growing water lilies in artificial pools. One is to place a 5- or 6-in. carpet of prepared soil over the bottom of the empty pool and plant directly into this material, later covering the bed with an inch or two of sand or gravel before running in the water. The disadvantage of this method is that when it is time to at-

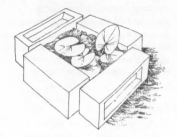

Planting in Containers

A basket is an ideal container for water-lily plants. When placing in the pool, raise it on bricks so that the crowns of the plants are just above the water.

Instead of a ready-made container, bricks placed on the bottom of the pool before it is filled may be used. Leave spaces between the bricks for water to seep through.

tend to or lift and divide the plants, the gardener churns up the mud, and the water loses the clarity that is one of its chief attractions.

When planting by this first method, make quite sure that the soil is in a moist—even sticky—condition. This insures firm planting, for dry soil does not bind effectively, and once water is added to it, the roots often become dislodged and float. Plant lilies according to the kind of roots they have. Place lilies with rhizomes (irislike roots) horizontally and set firmly, with the growing points of the shoots just protruding from the soil. Barely cover the top of the rhizome with soil. The other types (which include all the *marliacea* varieties) have a root something like celery. Plant these up to the collar, with the roots going straight down into the soil.

The second method is to plant the water lilies directly into containers. These can be made from galvanized wire, wood slats or concrete. Although not so long-lasting as other containers, wicker baskets, with their loose woven sides, allow the water to come into contact with the soil. If boxes of wood or concrete are used, make sure that there are holes in the sides and base.

Firm planting is even more essential for this method. Leave sufficient room in the basket to topdress the soil with an inch or two of sand or gravel. This prevents fish from disturbing the mud and clouding the water, and keeps debris from floating to the surface.

Care and Management: When planting by the first method is finished, run in just enough water to cover the tops of the lilies. After a few days, add another few inches, and continue in this way until the pool is quite full. This cautious procedure is necessary, for the water lilies, having sustained the shock of transplanting, may be checked or set back by the running in of a large amount of cold water.

When lilies are planted in baskets or containers, you may also fill the pool first—preferably some days previously—and stand the baskets on bricks or concrete blocks so that the crowns of the lilies are just below water level. As growth proceeds, lower these platforms gradually until the baskets rest on the bottom of the pool.

Planting Aquatics

Aquatics that grow at the margin of a pool do not need stimulants. The problem is to keep them compact and within bounds. Use plain, heavy loam in shallow troughs, and plant directly into these. Floating aquatics are simply placed on the water's surface.

Planting Oxygenators

Submerged aquatics as oxygenators (see page 516) have small rootstocks, and in soil-bottomed pools need only be weighted with a strip of zinc and then dropped into place. They soon form roots for anchorage.

Pools without soil need to have oxygenators introduced in the same way as the lilies—in containers. Fill shallow pans or boxes with soil and a little charcoal and insert the plants as cuttings. This is the simplest way to plant them, and they soon settle in when the containers are dropped into place.

WHEN TO PLANT

Spring, from March until the beginning of June, is the best time for planting water lilies and the stronger hardy aquatics, but floaters and oxygenators can be introduced at any time during the summer. Put in bog plants in early autumn or early spring.

LIVESTOCK IN THE POOL

Livestock added to the pool completes a balanced community. Fish and water snails feed on insects and debris and by their excreta fertilize the plants. The carbon dioxide they exhale provides the underwater plants, particularly, with one of the necessary ingredients for photosynthesis, or the making of food, and in turn the oxygen released during this vital process serves the needs of respiration in both plants and animals.

Fish keep down many enemies. In their ceaseless search for food, they destroy countless aphids, mosquito larvae and other pests, and also bring color and movement to the water garden. Surface-swimming fish are the only ones suitable for an ornamental pool, but do not introduce them until six or eight weeks after planting is completed. Of these, goldfish and their varieties and yellow orfs are the best and will live in harmony together. Do not overstock the pool with fish, because, if there is plenty of submerged vegetation, they will breed and multiply. Any dealer in fish will advise on the number required for a specific pool.

Artificial feeding is seldom necessary in an outdoor pool and in any case should not be overdone. Several times a week, give the fish as much food as they can consume in five minutes. If too much is provided, it drops to the bottom and ferments.

TROUBLES IN THE WATER GARDEN

Aphids

Aphids are the chief pest to attack water plants. A nicotine spray can be used only when there are no fish in the pool, because fish are allergic to it. Where fish are involved, dislodge the aphids from the plants with a powerful jet of water from a hose or syringe. They will then fall into the water and be devoured by the fish. Some of the aphids will always crawl back, and it is therefore important to repeat the operation on several consecutive days.

Another method of destroying these pests is to lay hoops or similarly shaped pieces of metal over the crowns of the water lilies to force the leaves and flowers beneath the water. By the next morning all the aphids will be drowned or consumed by fish.

Discolored Water

Green or cloudy water is the chief worry of the pool owner and is caused either by stirred-up mud or sediment or by microscopic plant life. Green water owes its color to myriads of tiny plants known as algae. These appear from airborne spores and multiply at a prodigious rate when the weather is sunny and the water contains plenty of mineral salts.

To combat the algae, cut down supplies of both sun and mineral salts.

This can be done most effectively by:
1. Adding no organic matter to the original planting compost (see Planting, page 505).
2. Removing rotting vegetable material such as dead flowers and leaves regularly.
3. Providing competition for the food in the pool by adding more plants.
4. Providing natural shade by introducing floating plants, such as water lilies and other surface aquatics.

5. Not introducing fish that live at the bottom of the pool.

CLEANING
From time to time, small pools need to be emptied and replanted, chiefly because the lilies exhaust the soil and the flowers become fewer and smaller. Occasionally, most of the plants need drastic division. Empty the pool, rinse it out and replant with fresh soil (see Planting, page 505).

Recommended Plants for Water Gardens

WATER LILY (NYMPHAEA)
Probably the first plants that come to mind when water gardens are planned are water lilies or nymphaeas. With their rounded, floating leaves—or pads, as they are called—and their conspicuous, many-petaled and often pleasingly scented flowers in a wide variety of colors, they are delightful pool dwellers. There are numerous varieties: the more vigorous will cover an area of 16 sq. ft. or more; the pygmy

kinds may be accommodated in 3 or 4 sq. ft. of water surface. All are easy to grow in positions where they receive full sun.

Water lilies are of two main types. The hardy kinds will live outdoors over winter even in the North if their roots are covered with a sufficient depth of water to prevent freezing (see Location, page 502).

Tropical types are splendid for summer flowering anywhere, but—

Nymphaea marliacea chromatella

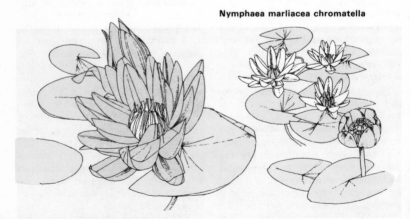

Nymphaea William Falconer (Water Lily)   **Nuphar** (Spatterdock)

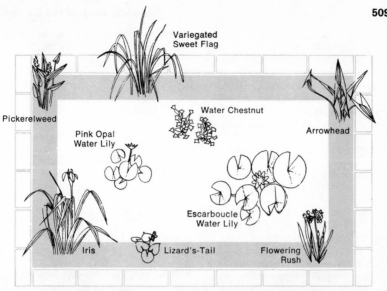

Variegated
Sweet Flag

Pickerelweed

Water Chestnut

Arrowhead

Pink Opal
Water Lily

Escarboucle
Water Lily

Iris

Lizard's-Tail

Flowering
Rush

An Arrangement for a Medium-Sized Water Garden
Submerged oxygenators (not shown in plan) should be planted in proportion to size of pool, allowing one oxygenator to each sq. ft. of water.

except in really warm climates—they must be replanted every year.

Hardy water lilies come in a wide range of colors except blue and purple, and their flowers usually float on the surface. Tropicals include blue and purple in the color range of their varieties, and their blooms are carried on stout stalks well above the surface. They are grouped as day bloomers and night bloomers.

The catalogues of specialists list and describe a great many varieties of both hardy and tropical water lilies.

LOTUS (NELUMBIUM)

Lotuses somewhat resemble water lilies, but both their handsome leaves and huge, fragrant flowers are carried on long stalks well above the water. They are easy to grow, if given rich soil and sun. Their curious pot-shaped seedpods may be dried for dramatic flower arrangements. They should be planted 2 in. deep in soil

that is covered by 8 to 9 in. of water.

Nelumbium flavescens, flowers cream-colored.

N. nelumbo (East Indian lotus), flowers pink or rose.

N. n. album grandiflorum, flowers pure white.

N. n. album plenum (syn. *N. n.* Shiroman), pure white double flowers.

N. n. roseum plenum, double pink flowers.

N. pentapetalum (American lotus), sometimes called water chinquapin, flowers yellow.

OTHER ORNAMENTAL AQUATICS

All the plants described in this section should be given very wet soil or shallow water conditions at the pool margin unless otherwise stated. All are propagated by division in spring.

ACORUS

This plant has something of the habit and foliage appearance of an iris; it grows from a stout rhizome and has strap-shaped leaves which are very aromatic when bruised. The brown flowers, which are more striking than beautiful, appear in late summer, on 3- to 4-in. fingerlike spikes protruding from the upper stems.

Acorus calamus (sweet flag), 2 to 3 ft., green flowers.

A.c. variegatus, green-and-cream-striped foliage; a good plant and worth a place in every water garden.

A. gramineus variegatus, 8 to 9 in., a dwarf form; has green-and-white-striped foliage.

ALISMA (WATER PLANTAIN)

Plants with plantainlike leaves and candelabra sprays carrying whorls of small white or pink-tinted, three-petaled flowers. The chief kind is *Alisma plantago-aquatica*, 2 to 3 ft.

APONOGETON

Aponogeton distachyus (Cape pond-weed, water hawthorn). The oblong leaves and white flowers with purple anthers borne on forked spikes and arranged in pairs float flat on the water's surface. The flowers are fragrant, with the scent of vanilla or hawthorn, and are produced in summer. The egg-shaped tubers should be planted in baskets and dropped into position. Not hardy—in the North it must be wintered indoors.

ARROW ARUM. See *Peltandra virginica*.

ARROWHEAD. See *Sagittaria*.

BOGBEAN. See *Menyanthes trifoliata*.

BUCKBEAN. See *Menyanthes*.

BULRUSH. See *Scirpus*.

BUTOMUS

Butomus umbellatus (flowering rush), 2 to 3 ft., has showy umbels or clusters of rose-pink flowers from June to September. The triangular, sword-shaped leaves are purplish when young but change to green later.

CALLA (WATER ARUM)

Calla palustris, 6 to 9 in., is a pretty North American native with small

Butomus umbellatus (Flowering Rush)

Caltha palustris (Marsh Marigold)

white calla-lily-like flowers in June and July and bright green heart-shaped leaves. Water snails fertilize the flowers, which develop into red berries in autumn.

CALTHA

Calthas have showy blooms and are valued for their early-spring flowering.

Caltha leptosepala, 8 to 12 in., bears solitary white buttercuplike flowers.

C. palustris (marsh marigold), 9 to 15 in., showy golden buttercuplike flowers on branching stems; smooth, heart-shaped leaves.

C.p. monstrosa-pleno, completely double and so floriferous that the leaves are hidden.

C. polypetala, a much taller species with branching stems 2 to 3 ft. high; blooms somewhat later. Watch that it does not become rampant.

CAPE PONDWEED. See *Aponogeton*.

CATTAIL. See *Typha*.

CORKSCREW RUSH. See *Juncus effusus spiralis*.

CYPERUS

These are attractive feathery plants with handsome scented leaves borne umbrellalike or moplike at the top of erect stems. None of the kinds listed is winter-hardy in the North.

Cyperus alternifolius (umbrella plant), 3 to 4 ft. A variety with green-and-white variegated foliage is sometimes cultivated.

C. papyrus (papyrus), 6 to 8 ft., very graceful and stately. This is the plant used by the ancient Egyptians for making paper.

FLOATING HEART. See *Nymphoides peltatum*.

FLOWERING RUSH. See *Butomus umbellatus*.

FORGET-ME-NOT. See *Myosotis palustris*.

GOLDEN CLUB. See *Orontium*.

HOUTTUYNIA

Houttuynia cordata, 1 to 2 ft., a Japanese plant with tapering, somewhat heart-shaped, bluish-green leaves and spikes of white flowers in July and August. The creeping rootstock thrives equally well in 2 to 4 in. of water or in wet mud.

HYDROCLEYS

Hydrocleys nymphoides (water poppy) has floating or sometimes erect leaves and three-petaled yellow flowers about 2 in. across. Not winter-hardy in the North.

IRIS

This large genus contains some truly aquatic members as well as a great number that thrive best under merely wet soil conditions, such as the Japanese iris. The kind mentioned here, however, can tolerate more and will grow in 3 to 4 in. of water all year.

Iris pseudacorus (yellow flag), 2½ to 3 ft. Stately, sword-shaped foliage and bright golden blooms in May and June.

JUNCUS (RUSH)

A large and extensive genus widely spread all over the world, but the majority are too weedy or insignificant for introduction to the water garden. Exceptions are:

Juncus effusus spiralis (corkscrew rush), 1 to 1½ ft. This variety is called "corkscrew" because the stems grow spirally.

J.e. vittatus, 2 to 3 ft. Its smooth, round stems are dark green, with a longitudinal golden band running up them, and are given a one-sided appearance by the crowded bunches of small brown flowers.

JUSSIAEA (PRIMROSE WILLOW)

Jussiaea repens, a trailing plant with small leaves, very smooth and shining, and large primroselike golden flowers, which are held just above water level, from July to September. Cuttings root easily in pans of loam in September and can be kept in a greenhouse until May to conserve the stock. Not hardy in the North.

LIZARD'S-TAIL. See *Saururus cernuus.*

MARSH MARIGOLD. See *Caltha palustris.*

MARSILEA
(CLOVER FERN, WATERCLOVER)

Marsilea drummondii, leaves resemble four-leaf clover, with white hairs.

M. quadrifolia is similar but without hairs. This is not winter-hardy in the North.

MENYANTHES

Menyanthes trifoliata (bogbean, buckbean), 6 in., a member of the gentian family with a spreading rootstock, grayish foliage and compound clusters of prettily fringed pink flowers from May to July. Grows well in shallow water or moist soil.

MYOSOTIS (FORGET-ME-NOT)

Myosotis palustris, 6 to 8 in., a well-known plant with bright blue flowers in May and June, suitable for wet mud or shallow water. Propagate by seed or cuttings.

MYRIOPHYLLUM (WATER MILFOIL)

Myriophyllum proserpinacoides (parrot's feather), 6 to 8 in. This species is useful for growing over fountains or rock-garden basins, for the stems are closely packed with whorls of needlelike leaves which hang down in feathery trails and turn up at the ends. They are green, with red tips in autumn, earning the plant the name "parrot's feather." The flowers are insignificant. A Brazilian plant that is usually grown outdoors only during the summer months, but which actually will live over outdoors even in quite severe climates if it is planted below freezing depth. It is also easily overwintered in a greenhouse from September-rooted cuttings.

NUPHAR

These are strong-growing aquatics akin but inferior to hardy water lilies; they should be grown only in situations where the latter plants would be unlikely to succeed, as, for example, in shade or very deep or running water. The rhizomatous roots are very invasive, and in deep water the submerged foliage is particularly handsome, with wavy margins and translucent membranous texture. Floating leaves are dark green and heart-shaped, and the flowers, which open all summer, are usually gold and smaller than water lilies.

Nuphar advenum (spatterdock), flowers 2 to 3 in. across, a native of North America.

NYMPHOIDES

Nymphoides indicum (water snowflake) has round leaves and fringed white flowers. Winter-hardy in warm climates only.

N. peltatum (floating heart), a pretty little plant which grows like a water lily with floating leaves and flowers. The leaves are round with wavy margins and heavily blotched with chocolate markings. The three-petaled flowers, which are produced from May to August, are yellow. Suitable for 6 to 18 in. of water.

ORONTIUM (GOLDEN CLUB)

Orontium aquaticum, 1 to 2 ft., has large, fleshy roots which need a good depth of soil. The big leaves—glaucous with a silver sheen—are so coated with wax that water runs from them like globules of mercury. The white spadix, covered with small yellow flowers from June to July, is particularly attractive. Suitable for 4 to 12 in. of water.

PAPYRUS. See *Cyperus papyrus*.

PARROT'S FEATHER. See *Myriophyllum proserpinacoides*.

PELTANDRA

The two species of peltandra bear dark green, arrow-shaped leaves on stems 1 to 2 ft. long and flower in July.

Peltandra alba, white flowers followed by scarlet berries.

P. virginica (arrow arum) is similar but has green flowers succeeded by green berries.

PICKERELWEED. See *Pontederia cordata*.

PONTEDERIA

Pontederia cordata (pickerelweed), 1½ to 2 ft., one of the best blue-flowered aquatics, with heart-shaped, smooth, shiny leaves on long stems and spikes of blue flowers all summer.

P.c. angustifolia may reach 5 ft. in one season and is the more prolific variety but less hardy than others.

PORCUPINE QUILL. See *Scirpus tabernaemontani zebrinus*.

PRIMROSE WILLOW. See *Jussiaea*.

RUSH. See *Juncus*.

SAGITTARIA (ARROWHEAD)

Sagittaria sagittifolia is interesting botanically. Its foliage is adaptable to various conditions. In deep water the leaves are completely submerged and ribbonlike; in water of medium depth they float and are rounded; and in shallow water they are borne 1 to 1½ ft. above the surface and are cut

to the center in triangular arrow shapes. The flowers are white, three-petaled and borne on spikes.

Sagittaria sagittifolia flore-pleno (also known as *S. japonica flore-pleno*), 1½ to 2 ft., a handsome double-flowered plant which flowers all summer. Do not plant under water more than 5 in. deep. (See illustration, page 514.)

SAURURUS

Saururus cernuus (lizard's-tail), grows from 12 to 16 in. and flowers most of the summer. A pretty plant for poolside planting in shallow water, with dark green, heart-shaped leaves borne on very slender stems and long, terminal spikes of fragrant, creamy-white flowers.

SCIRPUS (BULRUSH)

Scirpus lacustris, the true bulrush, 3 to 6 ft., has fat, round rushes, with bunches of brown flowers protruding from the upper parts of the stems in July and August. Will grow in running and fairly deep water.

S. tabernaemontani zebrinus (porcupine quill or zebra rush), 3 to 4 ft., stems alternately barred with broad bands of green and white, is more ornamental for the water garden. Check any tendency to revert to plain green by removing the offending stems.

SPATTERDOCK. See *Nuphar advenum*.

SWEET FLAG. See *Acorus calamus*.

THALIA

Thalia dealbata, 3 to 5 ft., one of the stateliest aquatics, has handsome, strongly ribbed blue-green leaves and panicles (pyramidal clusters) of purple flowers on long, arching stems in late summer and autumn. A native of the southern states, it is only hardy in mild climates or where the roots are planted sufficiently deep to be beyond the reach of frost. Container-grown

Sagittaria sagittifolia
(Arrowhead)

Pontederia cordata
(Pickerelweed)

plants may be sunk in the pool during the summer months and kept in a greenhouse or cellar over winter.

TYPHA (CATTAIL)

The flowers have pokerlike heads and flat, grassy foliage. Most typhas spread too much to be introduced to small or medium-sized pools, although the following are perfectly safe if planted in containers or confined in pockets to prevent root running.

Typha angustifolia, 6 to 9 ft., with much narrower leaves and flower spikes than the common cattail, *T. latifolia*.

T. minima, only 1 to 1½ ft. Tiny, purplish-brown poker heads in July.

UMBRELLA PLANT. See *Cyperus alternifolius*.

WATER ARUM. See *Calla*.

WATER HAWTHORN. See *Aponogeton*.

WATER MILFOIL. See *Myriophyllum*.

WATER PLANTAIN. See *Alisma*.

WATER POPPY. See *Hydrocleys*.

WATER SNOWFLAKE. See *Nymphoides indicum*.

YELLOW FLAG. See *Iris pseudacorus*.

ZEBRA RUSH. See *Scirpus tabernaemontani zebrinus*.

FLOATING PLANTS

Some floating plants, particularly lemna (duckweed), grow very rapidly and can prove a nuisance in the water garden. Unless they are tender enough to be killed in winter, it is unwise to introduce them to the outdoor pool.

AZOLLA

Azolla caroliniana, small floater with double fronds, ½ to 1 in. long, of palest green, which change color in autumn to russet-crimson. In warm weather it spreads rapidly, forming a complete carpet over the surface, but is never likely to become a permanent worry except where winter cold is not sufficient to kill any left outdoors.

CERATOPTERIS (WATER FERN)

Ceratopteris pteridoides, a true fern which floats and propagates by buds formed on its fronds. Not winter-hardy in the North.

EICHHORNIA (WATER HYACINTH)

Eichhornia crassipes has tough, glossy, heart-shaped leaves formed in a rosette around the crown of the plant, and the light blue flowers, with conspicuous "peacock-eye" markings on the lower petals, are borne on spikes.

The water hyacinth is a pestiferous weed in regions where it persists outdoors over winter. Where winter frost kills the plants, it may be used for summer decoration of pools and wintered indoors. A bowl with a little soil at the bottom will serve for this purpose and must be kept in a light but frost-free location. Because of the serious trouble this plant has caused by blocking waterways in the South, it is illegal to carry it across state lines.

PISTIA

Pistia stratiotes (water lettuce) forms floating rosettes of grayish-green, ribbed leaves. Not winter-hardy in the North.

TRAPA

Trapa natans (water chestnut), a plant with black spiny seeds the size of a large horse chestnut, which lie at the bottom of the pool all winter and germinate in spring to trailing stems 2 to 4 in. long with hollylike, floating leaves upheld by swollen, air-filled leafstalks. The flowers are small.

WATER CHESTNUT. See *Trapa natans*.

WATER FERN. See *Ceratopteris*.

WATER HYACINTH. See *Eichhornia*.

WATER LETTUCE. See *Pistia*.

SUBMERGED AQUATICS

The chief reasons for using submerged aquatics are to maintain water clarity (they compete with algae for food and light), to provide nurseries where fish can lay their eggs and to hide and protect the young fry from the cannibalistic tendencies of their parents.

Unlike plants in aquariums, these plants are rarely seen in a pool, so that daintiness, leaf texture and coloring matter little. Their most important function is oxygenation; some have been proved better than others in this respect. A few come to the surface and produce flowers that stand above the water to be insect-pollinated, but the majority have insignificant blooms fertilized by pollen brought by water currents. A few are deplorably weedy and will choke water lilies and other plants if given undisputed sway.

The following species are recommended and should be planted liberally as recommended in Planting Oxygenators (see page 507).

A 4-by-6-ft. pool will require some two dozen oxygenators; pools of other sizes should be stocked in roughly the same proportion.

ANACHARIS

Anacharis canadensis (waterweed), dark green, small leaves and brittle stems. A very good oxygenator.

CABOMBA (FANWORT, WATER SHIELD)

Cabomba caroliniana has glossy green, finely divided, fan-shaped leaves. A good oxygenator.

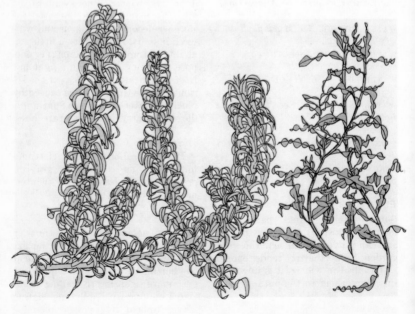

Lagarosiphon major　　　　　　　　　　　　**Potamogeton crispus** (Pondweed)

EELGRASS. See *Vallisneria*.

FANWORT. See *Cabomba*.

LAGAROSIPHON
Lagarosiphon major (syn. *Elodea crispa*) resembles a large curly-leaved anacharis; another good oxygenator.

POTAMOGETON (PONDWEED)
Most potamogetons are useful in pools and are entirely submerged, but beware of the floating species, *Potamogeton natans*. One of the best for pool cultivation is *P. crispus*, which has crisped, narrow green leaves.

VALLISNERIA (EELGRASS)
Vallisneria americana. Leaves are long, ribbonlike.

WATER SHIELD. See *Cabomba*.

WATERWEED. See *Anacharis*.

CHAPTER 26

ROCK GARDENS

Natural Effects—Selection of Rocks and Site—Waterfalls and Pools—Alpines, Low Native Plants and Specialties—Management and Protection—Winter Care—Pests—82 Rock-Garden Plants with 214 Species and Varieties

A ROCK GARDEN of the best kind depends for its inspiration on a natural feature—the outcropping of stone or boulders. To recreate and epitomize the grandeur of nature on the small scale suitable for a garden requires careful planning, not only in the choice of site, design and materials, but also in hiding all evidences of artificiality. Here, surely, true art lies in concealing art.

If you are favored by having natural rock outcrops on your property, well and good; but if you are going to construct a rock garden from scratch, choose, if possible, a site away from the formal parts of the garden, where the rock garden can blend with its immediate surroundings. To insure the success of the alpine and other low plants, give special attention to drainage, depth and character of soil, and the amount of sun and shade.

Highly effective rock gardens can be constructed on sites that are naturally uneven or sloping; they can, therefore, often solve the problem of what to do with oddly contoured or terraced areas. But excellent rock gardens can also be constructed on flat ground. It is worth visiting well-designed rock gardens to see how the various problems of layout have been met, and to walk over natural outcrops of rock in the hills, taking careful note of how the rocks lie.

FEATURES AND DESIGN

The size of the rock garden will depend on many factors, but because a well-cared-for garden calls for a good deal of detailed attention, it is usually better to keep it small. If the area is too large, it is likely to suffer from neglect, and few sights are sadder than an uncared-for, weedy rock garden. One incorporating special features, such as a waterfall and pool or a bank of ferns and woodland plants, requires somewhat more room, but even then it is well not to be overambitious.

In the design itself, proportions are highly important. Avoid using rocks that are too small or that are evenly sized. Try placing several smaller rocks together to create the satisfying illusion of a more massive piece. Remember that flat or gently sloping areas with little or no rock showing are just as important to the design as massive outcrops and rock-strewn slopes. They give relief to the eye and provide a sense of calm that contrasts pleasingly with the "busier" parts of the garden.

Such flat, rockless slopes and miniature valleys obviously should occupy areas between or below bold, rocky outcrops. A garden evenly studded with more or less similar-sized stones, "peanut-brittle" style, will prove uninteresting.

ROCKS AND SOIL

Select rocks that blend with the immediate surroundings. Sandstone and waterworn limestone are especially good because they are relatively soft and absorb and retain some moisture, but almost any type of natural rock can be used satisfactorily. Use the same type of rock throughout the garden. Weathered rocks are much to be preferred to newly quarried material.

If bold effects are planned, obtain large pieces of rock, weighing perhaps several hundred pounds each; smaller pieces will also be required to give variety. A piece of sandstone weighing 300 to 350 lb. may measure 2 ft. by 1 ft. by 1 ft.; a piece of granitic rock of the same weight is smaller.

The rock garden must have reasonably fertile, porous soil and very good drainage. If the natural soil is heavy, break up the subsoil thoroughly and work in plenty of sand, coal cinders or pieces of broken brick, as well as liberal amounts of peat moss, leaf mold, compost or other suitable decayed organic matter. The depth of soil should be adequate everywhere; 8 to 12 in. is

Good soil and especially good drainage are vital in a rock garden. A rubble base may be necessary. If the soil is very heavy, break it up and work in plenty of rubble. Then add better soil, preferably loam, and place a few large rocks so they protrude.

These rocks are incorrectly placed; they would not stick up vertically like this in a natural rock outcrop.

These rocks are correctly positioned; when set horizontally, they imitate the natural effect of stone strata.

not too much. It is a mistake to think that rock-garden plants thrive in shallow soils; a very few will—most will not. It may be desirable to modify the character of the general soil mixture in particular areas to meet the special needs of certain plants. Ground limestone may be mixed in for lime-loving plants, and acid peat moss where acid-soil plants are to be set. No fertilizer but bone meal is likely to be required.

CONSTRUCTION

The first step is to attend to any contouring of the ground that is needed. It is quite possible that shaping of the land or changing of grade will not be necessary, but often it is desirable to create high points and valleys, to modify slopes and to make provision for paths. This is especially true in creating a rock garden on a level site; by excavating some areas and using the material dug out to build up other parts, attractive grade variations can be attained. When extensive grade changes are to be made, first strip off the topsoil and stockpile it, contour the subsoil appropriately, and then replace the topsoil.

Begin construction by placing rocks in the lowest part of the garden first and working up and back. Remember that in natural rock outcrops the stones lie in strata, and most of their bulk is buried below soil level. Try to imitate this effect by laying the stones

so that any lines suggesting strata all run in the same general direction. (When these run at a slight angle to the horizontal, the most satisfactory effect is usually assured.) Position them, too, so that the weathered faces show. Both for safety and for effect, seat rocks firmly in the soil; pack them, where necessary, with soil and small stones, and tilt them slightly backward into the bank so rain will drain in to keep plant roots moist. As work proceeds, view it frequently from a distance, to get an overall impression.

Large, bold outcrops can be produced by placing two or more large pieces on top of each other; be sure that the pieces fit and do not overhang, or they may not be firm when in position. As long as the rocks are stable, it is not necessary that a large portion of each should be beneath the surface, but they should give the impression that what the eye sees is only the outcropping top of huge masses of bedrock that lie beneath.

If the rock garden is to be large, plan paths through it so that the plants can be admired and tended. Let the paths wind and turn as they would naturally. Do not let the rock garden finish abruptly, but allow it to trail off gradually, with occasional rocks showing here and there.

Pools and Streams

Where water is incorporated in a

Stones should lean into the soil so that rainwater will drain inward and keep the roots of the plants moist.

Stones placed like this are unstable and prevent sun from getting to the plants growing between them.

The soil will dry out and the plants suffer if stones are placed so that water can drain straight off them.

Plants growing between rocks set in this position will become "leggy" and drawn as they reach toward the sun.

large rock garden, it is usually allowed to run down into a pool or pools. If the water is to be recirculated, the feature should be situated conveniently close to a power supply and water source. Plastic pipe is ideal, as it is easy to install and maintain.

At the bottom of the lowest pool, an overflow or return pipe to carry the water back to the top of the rock garden will be needed. A manufacturer or dealer can supply the correct size and type of apparatus if a plan of the feature is provided, showing how high the water has to be pumped and how much will be circulating. For the sake of safety, a competent electrician should install the water pump.

House the pump near the highest part of the rock garden, and arrange

the outlet pipe so it is concealed by overhanging rocks. The water from this pipe can fall into the highest basin and overflow into others, creating a series of small waterfalls.

Construct the basins so that they tilt slightly into the rock-garden face and thus retain a proportion of the running water. If the front edge of each basin is perfectly horizontal, the water will flow over the entire edge to give a pleasing "sheet" effect.

Hide the sides of the basins with carefully placed overhanging rocks, and give each basin a rough face so that it has a natural, weathered look.

It is best to border the basins with rocks, using carefully selected, flat-faced pieces that can be cemented together. Keep the surface of the cement in the joints well below the top of the rocks so that it is not seen. It does not matter if open cracks or joints are obvious, as these would occur in a natural formation. If suitable rocks are not available, basins may be made of waterproof cement, of sheet lead or of sheets of plastic (see page 502 in "Water Gardens"). Give the pool at the bottom of the waterfall an irregular, natural-looking shape.

Many variations are possible in the design of a water feature. For instance, instead of waterfalls, a winding stream can be arranged to flow through the rock garden, starting from a high point and meandering down toward a pool at the bottom. But keep the size of the stream in proportion to the rock garden itself.

Moraines and Screes

Other settings for rock-garden plants, smaller and easier to produce than a full-scale rock garden, are often more suitable for a confined space. Interesting and colorful effects can be achieved with a moraine—a bed of small stones and grit which is supplied with water from below—or a scree—a similar but unwatered bed. Both features occur naturally.

To form the base of either feature, use crushed stone. Pieces should be at least ½ in. in size; include a few larger pieces of rock. Lay the chips to a depth of about 1 to 1½ ft. on a slight incline to give good drainage and a natural effect. Cover them with a thin layer of soil mixture, made of approximately 1 part good-quality loam to 10 parts crushed stone, plus 1 part peat moss and 1 part very coarse, sharp sand. To provide water below the bed for a moraine, it will be necessary to install metal or plastic water pipes, perforated with tiny holes and spaced 8 to 12 in. apart, at a depth of 9 or 10 in. beneath the surface. An excess of water should be avoided; keep the soil just moist.

CHOOSING ROCK-GARDEN PLANTS

The art of rock gardening originated from attempts to cultivate alpine plants in lowland gardens. Alpines naturally inhabit mountains at elevations above the level of tree growth. Charmed by the rare beauty of these plants and challenged by the difficulties many of them offered to cultivators, gardeners attempted to grow them by duplicating their natural environments as closely as possible. Only in part did they succeed, for while soils, available moisture and some other factors are subject to considerable manipulation, others (such as air pressure, length of the growing

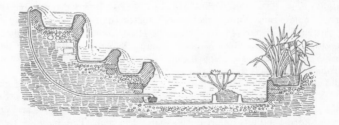

In a larger rock garden, a water feature adds interest. This diagram shows the basic elements: a succession of pools faced with rocks to give a waterfall effect, and a pipe from the lowest pool to the top (with an electric pump, not shown) so that the water can be used again and again.

season and intensity of certain light rays as they exist at high elevations) cannot be reproduced near sea level. Nevertheless, the development of certain rock-garden techniques has made it possible to grow a great many alpines in favored parts of North America, and at least some kinds can be grown almost everywhere except in the Deep South and in much of the Southwest.

As rock gardening increased in popularity, gardeners began to realize that many plants other than alpines—plants from the lowlands and plants of low stature found in woods and forests—were just as adaptable as alpines for growing in rock gardens and indeed could be most charmingly displayed there. This is a perfectly logical and proper development, for rocky landscapes are by no means confined in nature to the mountains; rock outcrops and plants that inhabit them are found in lowlands, in woodlands, in deserts, along riverbanks and at the seashore, in Arctic climates and in the tropics. Thus, there is no reason why a rock garden (meaning one in which rocks form the chief landscape feature and provide a suitable setting for plants of chiefly low stature) should not be featured in any climate.

Despite this, the term "rock-garden plants" as applied today is generally limited to kinds that are hardy in colder and humid sections and that are not harmed by being frozen for long periods. This is an acceptable interpretation; tropical or subtropical plants suitable for use only in mild climates are not included here.

In North America, the Pacific Northwest, the northern states and Canada afford the best opportunities for cultivating the widest selection of true alpines, as well as a great variety of other rock-garden plants. Much less favorable are those parts of the Middle West where very hot, dry summers prevail. In the U.S. Northeast and Central Atlantic areas, it is possible to grow a fair selection of alpines, together with a great many other rock-garden plants.

What to Plant

For the least trouble, choose only plants that are reasonably certain to prosper and remain a permanent part of your garden. Observe what other gardeners are growing in your area under conditions similar to those you have. Check the offerings of local nurseries. But avoid being trapped into planting invasive species of tremendous vigor and self-perpetuating qualities, no matter how beautiful you may think them to be. The plant that many a neighbor offers to share "because it grows so well with no trouble at all" may completely take over your rock garden and drive out choicer and more desirable kinds. What you need are plants that are permanent, grow with little trouble and do not spread too fast—or at least plants whose surplus growth can be easily curbed by pulling out.

You can have a very good-looking rock garden by confining yourself to plants of this kind, but your garden will be more interesting—and you will enjoy it more—if you attempt to grow a few others more challenging to your skill as a grower. No thrill is greater than that of succeeding with a plant known to be somewhat difficult. And you will possibly have in bloom plants different from those of your friends and neighbors.

Success with many choicer kinds is the reward of giving special attention to choosing planting sites and preparing the soil. The base of a north-facing rock may provide the shade and coolness that make all the difference to a saxifraga that would soon expire in a hot, sunny location; a moist soil near a stream or pool may suit a primula much better than would a drier location. Crushed limestone mixed freely with the soil may favor a gypsophila; old and very well-rotted manure will encourage a particular gentian or primula. Studying the idiosyncrasies of your plants and adapting your procedures to them will greatly increase your success.

You may even become a connoisseur of rock-garden plants, study them, read the literature about them, exchange correspondence and seeds with fans here and abroad, and attempt a great variety of choice and rare kinds. Rock gardening is a fascinating hobby demanding little heavy labor or money. Dedicated purpose and generous time, patience and interest are all that are needed.

Time of Planting

Plant the rock garden in either spring or early fall; it makes little difference which of the two seasons you choose. However, a rock garden planted in the autumn is unlikely to require much watering after the initial soaking unless the weather is unusually dry for more than a week at a time; it will then need a weekly soaking until the plants are sufficiently established to seek their own moisture. Spring planting necessitates more attention to regular watering.

Many young rock-garden plants are grown in pots and are supplied in them by the nurseryman; they can therefore be safely planted over a much longer period than plants dug from an outdoor nursery bed. But if they are not planted in either of the two recognized planting seasons, they will need extra care as to watering and shade until established.

ARRANGEMENT OF PLANTS

Most of the plants should fall into natural-looking groups and drifts of varying sizes. Here let a planting of houseleeks follow a long crevice; there have a creeping phlox or a dianthus tumbling over a cliff, repeating itself with one or two smaller specimens set near the cliff's base, as if they were chance seedlings from above. Plant a generous flat area or gentle slope with a creeping thyme or sandwort (arenaria), and space crocuses or other small bulbs irregularly in the area, for spring and fall display. If you have a pool or stream, group primulas near the water in light shade; do not space them uniformly as the polyanthus kinds are when used in formal beds, but at slightly varying distances, with the plants at one end of the group closer together than those at the other. Trailing off from the thinner end, one or more outlying plants may again suggest volunteers derived from wind-borne seeds.

The size of the plant group should be related to the extent of the rock garden. In a large garden, groups should be considerably larger than those in a small garden. For instance, three to five primulas or saxifragas may be perfectly in scale as a group in a small garden, whereas two or three times as many may not be out of place in an extensive garden.

Not all plants should be set in groups or drifts; at least a few single specimens should be used for variety. But do not overdo the single specimens; otherwise an uneasy, spotty effect will probably result.

You may want to include in your garden a few very dwarf trees and shrubs. Some of these are choice indeed and are quite effective when used as individuals. Offerings of dwarf spruce, juniper, thuja, false cypress, boxwood, cotoneaster, barberry, cytisus and others can be found in the catalogues of specialists. As background shrubs, less rare and

Collection of choice rock-garden plants, including campanula,
primrose, phlox, cyclamen (see page 234) and houseleek.

more familiar kinds, such as mugho
pine, mountain laurel, shrubby potentilla, weeping hemlock, andromeda
and the taller junipers, can be used
successfully.

PROTECTION AND CULTIVATION

When planting is completed, you may
want to mulch the surface of the soil,
at least in parts of the garden, with
crushed stone. This adds to the alpine or rock-country effect. The
stones should not be screened and of
even size, but should vary from pea
size to bean or walnut size, with perhaps a few pieces even larger. This
variation gives a more natural effect.
A crushed-stone mulch looks well in
the rockier areas and helps to keep
down weeds and retain moisture. In

shaded and wooded parts of the
garden and for some kinds of plants
(those that naturally inhabit woodlands), a mulch of compost, peat
moss or similar organic material looks
well and may be preferable. The mulch
will help to prevent plants set out in
the fall from being "lifted" by frost.
(If this happens, carefully press them
back into the soil as soon as the ground
has thawed and is no longer saturated.)

Winter Care

In regions where severe freezing and
thaws alternate through the winter
and where there is no certainty of a
continuous snow cover, as in the
northeastern United States, it is advantageous to provide rock-garden
plants with additional protection. The

best protection is afforded by branches of evergreens laid over the garden after the ground has frozen. Branches of Christmas trees are excellent for this purpose, and late December or early January is time enough to put the covering in place. Its purpose is not to keep the plants warm, but to help to keep the soil frozen and so minimize the harm alternate freezing and thawing do by tearing roots and heaving plants out of the ground. A covering also reduces the dehydration, with consequent "burning" of stems and foliage, and death that often result in late winter from exposure to strong sun and drying winds. A thin layer of salt-marsh hay, kept in place by brushwood, is also a satisfactory winter protection for a rock garden. Under no circumstances use materials that compact, remain wet and soggy and impede the free circulation of air. The covering should be removed gradually before the plants begin to grow in spring.

In humid areas where the ground is not frozen for most of the winter, as in much of the Pacific Northwest, plants with very soft, hairy leaves that persist through the winter may need slight protection during very wet periods; put a sheet or pane of glass over them, held in place by wire.

Drifting leaves from deciduous trees can also be a danger, as they often pile up in a corner between rocks, and distress plants that have to endure this soggy blanket; remove them at intervals. After high winds, watch carefully for leaves that may have drifted in from quite far afield.

Cutting Back

Perennial plants that make a great deal of soft growth, such as aubrietia, alyssum, rock cress (*Arabis*), sunrose (*Helianthemum*) and soapwort (*Saponaria*), should be cut back quite severely when they have finished flowering. This applies particularly to aubrietia, which soon grows into leggy, untidy mats, and flowers less profusely if it is not given an annual trim, and helianthemum, which lasts for years if properly tended, but which may perish in two or three years if left to straggle into loose bushes.

Weeding and Topdressing

Never let weeds get a strong hold in any part of the rock garden. A sturdy tuft of grass is a bad neighbor for a small plant, and it may be impossible to remove the weed without uprooting the plant as well.

It does not take long to weed and work over a small rock garden, cultivating and loosening the soil with an instrument such as a small hoe or hand fork. If this is done regularly, weeds will never become a problem.

Because there is a tendency for some rock-garden plants to grow out of the ground, and because in some areas the surface soil may be slowly eroded, topdressing (a layer of suitable soil mixture) should be added each spring wherever needed. Use a gritty mixture of topsoil, sand, crushed stone and leaf mold, compost or peat moss, together with a little bone meal; after loosening the surface, spread ½ to 1 in. of this mixture—under and among the plants and also between them.

PESTS

In some areas, slugs are a grave menace to rock-garden plants, as they like to eat the new leaves, flower stems and buds. They shelter beneath overhanging plants and in crannies between stones. An occasional inspection of these likely hiding places and keeping the garden clean and free from weeds will reduce the slugs to a minimum. An application of one of the several effective slug killers will deal with any that escape notice (see page 810 in "Plant Pests").

Sow bugs also can cause much damage, so sprinkle DDT dust in areas where they are troublesome.

Red spider mites are likely to be troublesome on a few plants, notably on certain evergreen shrubs and dwarf trees, such as junipers and spruces. To control these, use a miticide.

SUGGESTED PLANTS FOR THE ROCK GARDEN

Unless otherwise stated, the plants in the following list are sun-loving and easily grown in any well-drained soil. In addition to those listed here, others suitable for rock gardens are described in the following chapters: "Hardy Bulbs," page 227; "Ferns," page 265; and "Gardens in the Shade," page 540.

ACHILLEA

A large genus, containing a number of species well suited for rock gardens. These are invaluable plants for spring and early-summer flowering.

Achillea lewisii, sometimes called *Achillea* King Edward. Gray mats of ferny leaves and lemon-yellow flowers on 3-in. stems.

A. tomentosa, similar to *A. lewisii* but a little taller; bright green foliage and deeper yellow flowers.

A. umbellata, creamy-white flowers on 4-to-6-in. stems. Suitable for dry soils.

AETHIONEMA

Aethionema grandiflorum, about 1 ft., a delightful plant with pink flowers and bluish foliage.

A. pulchellum, similar to *A.* Warley Rose, but grows to 1 ft. or more and has rich pink flowers.

A. Warley Rose, 6 in., shrublike with masses of rich rose-red flowers in summer.

AJUGA (BUGLEWEED)

Low, spreading ground covers valued for their foliage and 6-to-8-in. spikes

of blue, purple, white or pink flowers, borne in early summer. They thrive in any soil not extraordinarily dry, and in sun or shade.

Ajuga genevensis, does not produce runners. A good bloomer; flowers blue or, in the variety Pink Spire, clear pink.

A. pyramidale, a vigorous plant which does not spread rapidly; handsome spikes of blue flowers.

A. reptans, spreads quite rapidly by runners. Flowers blue or purple or, in variety *alba*, white. Variety *variegata* has blue flowers, cream-edged leaves.

ALYSSUM

Alyssum saxatile (basket-of-gold), to 1 ft., golden-yellow flowers. An invaluable spring-flowering plant; use with care, as it can swamp smaller plants.

A.s. citrinum, identical with *A. saxatile* except for pale yellow flowers. Sometimes called *A.s.* Silver Queen.

ANDROSACE (ROCK JASMINE)

Among the androsaces are some of the loveliest alpine plants, but quite a few are difficult to grow. Easy ones are:

Androsace lanuginosa, trailing, silver-gray leaves and heads of flowers just flushed with pink, in summer.

A. sarmentosa, up to 5 in., mats of gray-leaved rosettes and round heads of deep pink flowers, in spring. One of the hairy-leaved alpines which may require winter protection in wet localities (see Winter Care, page 524). Varieties *chumbyi* and *watkinsii* are similar but of more compact growth.

ANEMONE

Many anemones are suitable for the rock garden. In addition to the species listed here, others are described on page 229 in "Hardy Bulbs."

A. pulsatilla (pasqueflower), 6 to 10 in., leaves silky and hairy, much dissected, large blue, lavender, purple or white flowers, in spring, followed by

Androsace lanuginosa
(Rock Jasmine)

attractive and decorative seed heads.

ANTENNARIA (PUSSYTOES)
These are gray-leaved carpeters as valuable for their foliage as for their tiny, tasseled flowers on 3-to-6-in. or sometimes taller stems, in spring.

Antennaria aprica, white or pink flowers.

A. microphylla, white flowers, slow-growing.

ANTHEMIS
Anthemis biebersteiniana, silvery, lacy leaves and yellow flowers.

AQUILEGIA (COLUMBINE)
Dwarf columbines are excellent for lightly shaded places. Reasonably moist soil is desirable, but excessive richness induces tall, gross growth not admired in rock gardens.

Aquilegia akitensis, 6 in., pale purple and creamy-yellow flowers.

A. flabellata nana, 6 to 9 in., foliage bluish-green, flowers lilac-blue and white. *A.f.n. alba* has white flowers.

ARABIS (ROCK CRESS)
These need minimum care and bloom freely in spring.

Arabis albida, 9 to 12 in., flowers white or sometimes pinkish. The double-flowered *A.a. flore-pleno* is especially good. There are also variegated-leaved varieties. This is a rampant grower.

A. blepharophylla, 6 to 10 in., flowers pink or purplish, fragrant.

A. procurrens, 6 to 8 in., flowers white. A trailing mat former, good for crevice planting.

ARENARIA (SANDWORT)
Arenaria laricifolia, 6 in., needle-like leaves, large white flowers. Often grown as *A. grandiflora*.

A. montana hangs over rocks in a cataract of snow-white flowers, in early summer.

A. verna caespitosa, a dense, rich green mosslike plant sprinkled with star-shaped flowers, in spring. A lightly shaded location is best.

ARMERIA (THRIFT)
Armeria caespitosa, dense cushions studded with stemless rose-red flowers, from spring onward.

A. maritima laucheana, 6 to 8 in., rosy-red flowers. An excellent variety.

ARTEMISIA (WORMWOOD)
These are grown for the beauty of their foliage. As soon as flower spikes begin to develop, they should be cut off. For hot, sunny places.

Artemisia frigida, 6 to 8 in., a dense mound of finely cut silvery foliage.

A. schmidtiana nana, 4 to 6 in., finely dissected silvery-white foliage.

ASTER
Aster alpinus, large lavender-blue, golden-eyed flowers on 6-to-9-in. stems in early summer.

ASTILBE (SPIREA)
Dwarf kinds of astilbe (often called spireas) are excellent for moist soil in light shade. They have plumy flower spikes in early summer.

Astilbe chinensis pumila, 6 to 8 in., flowers pink.

A. simplicifolia rosea, 10 to 12 in., flowers pink.

AUBRIETIA (AUBRETIA)
Flowers are lavender, purple or pink, most cultivated kinds being varieties of *A. deltoidea*.

BARRENWORT. See *Epimedium*.

BASKET-OF-GOLD. See *Alyssum saxatile*.

BEARD-TONGUE. See *Penstemon*.

BELLFLOWER. See *Campanula*.

BIRD'S-FOOT VIOLET. See *Viola pedata*.

BITTERROOT. See *Lewisia rediviva*.

BLUE-EYED GRASS. See *Sisyrinchium*.

BLUET. See *Houstonia*.

BROOM. See *Genista*.

BUGLEWEED. See *Ajuga*.

BUNCHBERRY. See *Cornus canadensis*.

CALAMINTHA
Calamintha alpina, 4 in., a mat-forming plant with small leaves and tiny white-lipped purple flowers.

CALLUNA (HEATHER)
Many garden varieties are splendid for sandy-peaty soil. White, pink and purple varieties.

CAMPANULA (BELLFLOWER)
Many kinds of campanula are available. They are colorful and easy plants

Campanula cochlearifolia
(Bellflower)

to grow, with bell-like or saucer-shaped flowers when spring and early-summer flowers are fading. A few of the best are:

Campanula carpatica, 9 to 12 in., blue or white flowers. Several named varieties of this species are available.

C. cochlearifolia (syn. *C. pusilla*), 4 to 6 in., blue or white flowers. Likes a limy soil.

C. garganica, a tufted, prostrate perennial, in many forms in blue or white.

C. portenschlagiana (syn. *C. muralis*), 6 to 9 in., deep purple-blue bells. Excellent for the rock garden.

C. poscharskyana, 6 to 8 in., spreading; nearly flat purple-blue flowers.

CANDYTUFT. See *Iberis*.

CATCHFLY. See *Silene*.

CERATOSTIGMA (PLUMBAGO)
Ceratostigma plumbaginoides, 6 to 10 in., spreading, mat-forming plant with green or bronzy foliage and deep blue flowers, for a long period in late summer and fall.

CHRYSOGONUM (GOLDEN STAR)
Chrysogonum virginianum, 4 to 8 in., slow-spreading clumps of hairy foliage and bright yellow flowers 1 to 1½ in. across, for a long period in summer. Prefers part shade.

COLUMBINE. See *Aquilegia*.

CORNUS
Cornus canadensis (bunchberry), 6 to 8 in., a low ground cover with handsome white flowers resembling those of flowering dogwood, followed by red berries. A capricious plant. Needs moist, acid soil and shade.

CORYDALIS
Corydalis cava (syn. *C. bulbosa*), 6 to 8 in., tuberous, flowers deep rose to purple.

C. lutea, 10 to 12 in., nontuberous; delicate fernlike foliage, golden yellow flowers.

COTONEASTER
Most cotoneasters are too large for a small rock garden, but the following flat-growing kinds are suitable for all but the smallest sites. They are evergreen dwarf shrubs which bear red berries.

Cotoneaster congesta, pinkish flowers.

C. microphylla, white flowers.

C.m. thymifolia, pinkish flowers.

CREEPING JENNIE. See *Lysimachia nummularia*.

CYMBALARIA
Low, trailing plants with small leaves and tiny snapdragonlike flowers. Suitable for somewhat moist, shaded places.

Cymbalaria aequitriloba, flowers pale mauve with reddish-purple throats.

C. muralis (Kenilworth ivy), a rather rampant creeper with lilac-blue flowers having yellow throats. Not hardy in severe winters.

C. pilosa, hairy-leaved, flowers lavender with yellow throat.

DAPHNE
Daphne cneorum, low shrub, bearing clusters of very fragrant pink flowers in spring. Needs well-drained sandy, peaty soil. Has white-flowered and variegated-leaved varieties.

DIANTHUS (PINK)
Dianthus loves sun and, with very few exceptions, lime, but it will grow quite well without the latter.

Dianthus alpinus, 3 in., large rose-red flowers in summer.

D. arenarius, 6 to 12 in., one of the earliest to bloom. Flowers white, fringed, very fragrant.

D. arvernensis, forms a gray-leaved mat; small pink flowers on 4-in. stems.

D. deltoides (maiden pink), 6 to 12

in. This species is seen at its best in one of the named forms, such as Brilliant, which displays countless small bright red flowers for many weeks.

D. gratianopolitanus (syn. *D. caesius*—Cheddar pink), 3 to 12 in., several fine garden forms, all with ash-gray leaves and good flowers in varying shades of pink and red.

D. neglectus (dwarf pink), 2 to 4 in., low cushions and large, deep pink flowers, in July and August. Hates lime and should be given neutral or acid soil. A choice plant.

D. Tiny Rubies, miniature mats of grayish foliage studded with deep pink carnationlike flowers on 3-in. stems.

DICENTRA

For partial shade and fertile, moderately moist soil.

Dicentra cucullaria (Dutchman's breeches), 6 to 10 in. Tuberous. Flowers white, yellow-tipped. Spring-flowering.

D. eximia, 9 to 15 in., fernlike foliage and deep pink bleeding-heart

flowers; bloom throughout summer.

D. oregana, 9 to 12 in., foliage glaucous blue, flowers cream, tinged with pink.

DOUGLASIA

Douglasia vitaliana, prostrate, with tiny leaves and, in spring, scented yellow flowers. For light shade and limy soil.

DRABA

These are spring-flowering cushion plants, for gritty soil and full sun.

Draba aizoides, 2 to 4 in., stiff evergreen rosettes, flowers yellow.

D. fladnizensis, 2 to 4 in., flowers greenish white.

DRYAS

Dryas octopetala (mountain avens), a creeping shrub with small oaklike dark green leaves and large rounded golden-eyed pure white flowers, in summer.

DUTCHMAN'S BREECHES. See *Dicentra cucullaria*.

Dianthus neglectus
(Dwarf Pink)

Dryas octopetala
(Mountain Avens)

EDELWEISS. See *Leontopodium alpinum.*

EDRAIANTHUS

Edraianthus pumilio, forms a lovely silver-gray hummock studded with pale blue bells in the spring. Requires sun and sharply gritty soil.

EPIGAEA (TRAILING ARBUTUS)

Epigaea repens, clusters of fragrant pink or white flowers on 3-in. stems, in spring. A charming trailer difficult to establish in gardens. For acid, sandy, peaty soil in shade.

EPIMEDIUM (BARRENWORT)

Excellent for semishade and woodland soil. All have splendid foliage, often highly colored when young, and sprays of small flowers on wiry stems, in spring.

Epimedium grandiflorum, 9 in., red, violet and white in same flower. Varieties *niveum* and *album* are white-flowered. Variety *violaceum* has light violet flowers.

E. versicolor, 9 to 12 in., flowers yellow and red. Variety *sulphureum* has yellow flowers.

ERICA (HEATH)

Dwarf shrubs and shrublets resembling heathers (*Calluna*). For sandy, peaty, acid soils. Many fine kinds.

Erica carnea, 1 ft., flowers red, in spring. Named varieties of this species are offered.

E. darleyensis, 1½ ft., flowers red, in spring.

ERIGERON (FLEABANE)

Erigeron compositus, tufted plant to 6 in. high, white or pinkish daisies.

E. karvinskyanus (syn. *E. mucronatus*), 6 in., myriads of white, pink or deep mauve daisies on low, bushy plants, from spring until late fall. Does best in rather poor, sandy soil or rock chinks.

ERINUS

Erinus alpinus, 2 to 4 in., flowers rosy-purple or white. Ideal crevice plant for shade. Not hardy where winters are very severe but often produces self-sown seedlings.

ERODIUM

These usually have pretty, rather ferny foliage, either gray or green, and bloom right through the summer into autumn. Flowers vary from white to deep pink and are marked with veinings of deeper color.

Erodium chamaedryoides roseum, 1 to 3 in., makes a flat dark green mat, starred continuously with small deep pink flowers on very short stems.

FESTUCA (FESCUE)

Festuca ovina glauca (syn. *F. glauca*—blue fescue), 6 to 9 in., a tufted ornamental grass with steel-blue leaves and panicles of creamy flowers.

FLAX. See *Linum.*

FLEABANE. See *Erigeron.*

FOAMFLOWER. See *Tiarella cordifolia.*

GENISTA (BROOM)

Dwarf shrubs good for sunny, somewhat dry places in well-drained soil.

Genista hispanica, 1 to 2 ft., spiny, flowers golden-yellow, early summer.

G. radiata, 1 to 2 ft., not spiny, flowers golden-yellow, in early summer.

G. sagittalis, 6 to 12 in. Branches conspicuously winged, flowers yellow, in early summer.

GENTIANA (GENTIAN)

Some gentians are difficult to grow.

Gentiana acaulis, 2 to 4 in., the big blue trumpet or stemless gentian of spring, which often blooms again in summer. Plant firmly in good loam.

G. andrewsii (closed or bottle gen-

Gentiana acaulis
(Trumpet or Stemless Gentian)

tian), 1 to 2 ft., flowers blue-purple, scarcely opening, in summer.

G. asclepiadea, 1 to 1½ ft., wand-like stems wreathed with dark blue flowers, in summer.

G. septemfida, clusters of deep blue flowers on 1-ft. stems, in late summer. Variety *lagodechiana* has prostrate stems and solitary flowers.

GERANIUM

This is another good genus for the rock garden, and there are many from which to choose. Recommended are:

Geranium cinereum subcaulescens, 4 to 9 in., brightest of all geraniums, with brilliant cerise, black-eyed flowers in profusion, in June.

G. dalmaticum, one of the best kinds, cheerful pink flowers on 4-in. stems, in summer.

G. sanguineum prostratum, grows flat on the ground, with wide saucer-shaped flowers of glowing pink from spring to fall.

GLOBULARIA

These are prostrate-growing, woody evergreen plants, studded in summer with fluffy blue balls of flowers on very short stems. *Globularia bellidi-folia* and *G. cordifolia* like the fullest sun, and are recommended.

GOLDEN STAR. See *Chrysogonum*.

GYPSOPHILA

Gypsophilas suitable for rock gardens are trailing or mat-forming plants with flowers of pink or white in June. Recommended are:

Gypsophila cerastoides, *G. repens*, *G. repens rosea* and *G.r. fratensis*.

HEATH. See *Erica*.

HEATHER. See *Calluna*.

HELIANTHEMUM (SUNROSE)

These dwarf plants make wiry bushes rarely more than 1 ft. tall, and are ideal for hot, sunny places in not-too-rich soil. They produce large, roselike flowers over a long period from May onward. Cut back hard at the end of the flowering season. Not reliably hardy where winters are very cold.

Helianthemum nummularium, many fine varieties, in a wide range of colors. Some varieties double-flowered.

HOUSELEEK. See *Sempervivum*.

HOUSTONIA (BLUET)

Excellent low, spring- and early-summer-flowering plants for fairly moist soils and shade.

Houstonia caerulea, 2 to 4 in., flowers blue, violet or white with yellow eye.

H. serpyllifolia, a trailing plant forming a mat, flowers deep blue.

HUTCHINSIA

Hutchinsia alpina, low, rounded cushions of divided leaves and pure white flowers, in spring. Needs a cool location with part shade.

HYPERICUM (ST.-JOHN'S-WORT)

Sun lovers with bright yellow flowers. Not reliably hardy in regions of severe winters.

Hypericum olympicum, low subshrub with stems from 6 to 9 in. long. Flowers yellow, July to September.

H.o. citrinum, pale yellow flowers.

IBERIS (CANDYTUFT)

Iberis sempervirens Little Gem is dwarf, with white flowers in summer.

I.s. pygmaea, a very dwarf variety, white-flowered.

IRIS

There are many dwarf irises for the rock garden. Recommended are:

Iris cristata, about 6 in., like a tiny orchid with blue and gold flowers, in May. The white-flowered variety, *I.c. alba*, is choice.

I. pumila, 3 to 8 in. Many named garden varieties are offered with flowers white, cream, yellow, blue or purple, in spring. Of easy culture.

I. verna, 6 to 8 in., flowers violetblue and gold or, in variety *alba*, white and yellow. Needs shade and a moist woodland soil.

JOHNNY-JUMP-UP. See *Viola tricolor*.

KENILWORTH IVY. See *Cymbalaria muralis*.

LEONTOPODIUM

Leontopodium alpinum (edelweiss),

Leontopodium alpinum (Edelweiss)

about 6 in., silver-gray flannel-like flowers in June and July. Easy to grow in sun and gritty soil.

LEWISIA

Lewisias grow up to 8 in., bloom in spring and early summer. Plant in crevices in very gritty, lime-free soil. There are many hybrids as well as the species listed below and others. All are choice and are rather difficult.

Lewisia columbiana, evergreen, white or pink flowers veined with red. In variety *rosea*, flowers are pink. One of the easiest to grow.

L. rediviva (bitterroot), narrow fleshy leaves, flowers pink or white. Foliage dies down after flowering.

L. tweedyi, evergreen, flowers almost 2 in. across, salmon-pink or apricot.

LINUM (FLAX)

Linum alpinum, 9 in., blue flowers in July and August.

L. flavum compactum, 9 in., yellow flowers in summer.

L. salsaloides nanum, a prostrate kind forming spreading mats, flowers white with lavender veins. Only moderately hardy.

LITHOSPERMUM

Lithospermum diffusum has dense carpets of gentian-blue flowers the whole summer through. Prostrate. Plant in neutral or acid soil.

LYSIMACHIA

For moist soils and part shade. Plants grow vigorously and may become a nuisance unless kept in check.

L. nummularia (creeping Jennie, moneywort), a prostrate fast spreader, flowers yellow, in summer.

MAZUS

Mazus reptans, 1 in., trailing plant with white- and yellow-centered lavender-blue flowers. Splendid for moist soil in light shade.

MENTHA

Mentha requienii, forms carpets of peppermint-scented green leaves and has tiny lilac flowers in summer. Plant in moist soil in shade. Not reliably hardy where winters are really severe, but often perpetuates itself by self-sown seedlings.

MITCHELLA

Mitchella repens (partridgeberry), small-leaved evergreen trailer having pairs of white flowers followed by red berries. Needs a fairly moist woodland soil and shade.

MOSS CAMPION. See *Silene schafta*.

MOSS PINK. See *Phlox subulata*.

MOUNTAIN AVENS. See *Dryas octopetala*.

OMPHALODES (NAVELWORT)

Omphalodes cappadocica, about 6 in., perennial, blue flowers from June to August.

O. verna, 2-to-8-in. gentian-blue flowers in spring. Grows best in a shady location.

OPUNTIA

Opuntia compressa (syn. *O. humifusa*), a low, spreading, perfectly hardy cactus. In summer bears 2-in. golden-yellow flowers. Needs full sun.

OXALIS

Some oxalises are weeds, but others are delightful rock plants. Among the latter are the following, none of which, unfortunately, are reliably hardy where winters are really severe.

Oxalis adenophylla, 4 to 6 in., crinkled gray leaves and rich pink funnel-shaped flowers, in May.

O. chrysantha, a carpet of gold for months from June on.

Oxalis chrysantha

PARTRIDGEBERRY. See *Mitchella repens*.

PASQUEFLOWER. See *Anemone pulsatilla*.

PENSTEMON (BEARD-TONGUE)

Rock-garden penstemons are colorful, mostly shrubby plants. Not all are reliably hardy in regions of severe winters. They are summer bloomers.

Penstemon cardwellii, 6 to 10 in., evergreen; purple flowers.

P. crandallii, 4 to 8 in., flowers blue.

P. hirsutus pygmaeus, 6 in., flowers pale lavender. One of the hardiest; not shrubby.

P. menziesii, 4 to 6 in., flowers purple.

PHLOX

Low-growing phloxes are easy to raise. Those listed are spring and early-summer bloomers.

Phlox divaricata (syn. *P. canadensis*), sometimes called wild sweet William. This is a creeping plant with erect flowering stems 8 to 12 in. high and blue-mauve or sometimes white flowers. Lovely for part shade and not-too-dry soil that contains much organic matter.

P. nivalis, a trailing kind somewhat resembling *P. subulata* but with larger flowers, pink or white.

P. procumbens, forms mats of dark green foliage and bears clusters of mauve-pink flowers on 6-to-8-in. stems. Thrives in semishade or sun.

P. stolonifera, a trailing species that forms dense mats of stems and foliage. Flowers pinkish lavender in clusters on 9-to-10-in. stems. At its best in full sun. Variety Blue Ridge has blue flowers; variety Pink Ridge, pink.

P. subulata (moss pink), forms tight, spreading mats or cushions of stems and foliage and in spring is covered with fragrant flowers that scarcely rise above the leaves. Many color variations. Easily grown, revels in full sun and dry soil.

PINK. See *Dianthus*.

PLUMBAGO. See *Ceratostigma*.

POLEMONIUM

Easy-to-grow, spring-flowering, ferny-leaved plants for rich, fairly moist soil and, preferably, part shade.

Polemonium carneum, 10 to 15 in., pink.

P. reptans, 9 to 12 in., blue flowers.

POTENTILLA

Potentillas are very numerous. Recommended for the rock garden are:

Potentilla alba, low mats of silvery foliage, flowers white, about 1 in. in diameter, in spring.

P. alpestris, low-growing with golden flowers, in summer and fall.

P. aurea, a creeper with yellow flowers, in early summer. A double-flowered variety is cultivated.

P. rupestris pygmaea, sometimes known as *P. r. nana*, 4 to 6 in., flowers white.

P. tonguei, prostrate, with apricot and crimson flowers, all summer.

P. tridentata, 4 to 8 in., mat-forming evergreen, flowers white. Thrives in poor and dryish soil in full sun.

P. verna nana, 2 to 3 in., dense cushions of foliage and freely produced yellow flowers, in spring.

PRIMROSE. See *Primula*.

PRIMULA (PRIMROSE)

There are many kinds of primulas, but some are very difficult to grow even in favored regions such as the Pacific Northwest, and are impossible, or nearly so, where hot, humid summer weather occurs. Among the easier kinds are:

Primula auricula, 6 to 8 in., occurs in many varieties and a great number of colors. Flowers fragrant and in clusters, leaves thick and usually white and mealy at margins.

P. chionantha, 1 to 1½ ft., fragrant white, dark-eyed flowers arranged in whorls or tiers, leaves dusted with golden meal. Likes a moist but well-drained soil and light shade.

P. cockburniana, 1 to 1½ ft., brilliant orange-copper flowers in whorls or tiers. Requires same conditions as *P. chionantha*.

P. cortusoides, 6 to 12 in., leaves

softly hairy, flowers rose-pink, in terminal clusters. Needs light shade.

P. denticulata, 6 to 12 in., lavender, rosy-lilac or white flowers in dense, globular heads. Delights in rich, moist, but well-drained soil and shade from strong sun.

P. farinosa. Clusters of pink golden-eyed flowers atop 4-in. stems, in spring. Likes moist but gritty soil.

P. japonica (Japanese primrose), 1½ ft., a bog primula, with purplish-red, pink and blush-colored flowers in tiers, in spring. One of the best. Needs a little shade.

P. juliae, 3 to 4 in., rich claret-crimson solitary flowers in abundance. Needs a reasonably moist, loamy soil and light shade. This species is a parent of many fine hybrids, many of which have been given varietal names.

P. rosea, 1 to 5 in., rose-red flowers in spring before all other primulas. Loves wetness and light shade.

P. vulgaris (syn. *P. acaulis*—English primrose), 6 in., flowers solitary, primrose-yellow, blue, lilac or pink. Some variations are given varietal names, and in some, flowers are double. One of the easiest to grow in any good loamy soil that contains abundant organic matter and is reasonably moist. Light shade is required.

PUSSYTOES. See *Antennaria*.

PYROLA (SHINLEAF)
Pyrola elliptica, 8 in., white flowers. Requires shade and woodland soil.

P. rotundifolia, similar to above and requiring same conditions.

RHODOHYPOXIS
Rhodohypoxis baurii, about 4 in., red flowers throughout summer. Likes sun and moist soil. Suitable only for regions where summers are cool and winters mild.

R. b. platypetala, a pure white counterpart of *R. baurii*.

Rhodohypoxis Margaret Rose

ROCK CRESS. See *Arabis*.

ROCK JASMINE. See *Androsace*.

ST.-JOHN'S-WORT. See *Hypericum*.

SANDWORT. See *Arenaria*.

SAPONARIA (SOAPWORT)
Saponaria ocymoides, trailing perennial with bright pink flowers, in summer. Easy to grow but a vigorous spreader.

SATUREJA
Satureja alpina, 4 to 6 in., small leaves. It bears purple flowers, in summer.

SAXIFRAGA
There are hundreds of different saxifragas, nearly all of which are good rock-garden plants. They are divided into 16 or 17 sections, the three main ones being, first, the kabschia section, which bloom in early spring in gritty, limy soil, with neat green or silver-gray hummocks studded with flowers of white, yellow or shades of red; second, the aizoon section, with silvery leaves and white, yellow or pinkish flowers; third, the mossy section,

which are carpeters with flowers of white to deepest red (but no yellow) and like protection from hot sun. Only a very few of these can be listed here.

Saxifraga aizoon, leaf rosettes silver-encrusted, flowers cream-colored, in early summer.

S. cochlearis, heavily silver-encrusted. Flowers on 6-to-8-in. stems, creamy white.

S. cotyledon, flat silver-encrusted rosettes and loose panicles of white flowers.

S. macnabiana, large rosettes, flowers white, spotted red. One of the easiest to grow of the encrusted saxifragas.

S. oppositifolia, rose-red flowers on carpets of dark green leaves, in early spring.

SCUTELLARIA (SKULLCAP)

Scutellaria alpina, 8 in., flowers purple and cream. Variety *nana* is more dwarf.

SEDUM (STONECROP)

Sedums are exceedingly easy to grow. They are useful for filling crevices and crannies as well as for use as ground covers. Flower colors are predominantly yellow and white, but pink- and red-flowered kinds occur. Nearly all love hot, dry situations and grow well even in shallow soil. Some tend to be invasive, however, and should not be planted except where they have ample room to spread without harming their neighbors, or where they can easily be kept in check.

Sedum acre, 3 to 4 in., evergreen mats of small leaves, masses of bright yellow flowers, in late spring. A fast grower.

S.a. minus, a dwarf, compact, slow-growing variety of *S. acre*.

S. album, vigorous grower forming mats 6 to 8 in. high, flowers white, in summer.

S.a. murale, similar to *S. album* but with purple foliage and pinkish flowers.

S. brevifolium, 2 in., evergreen, stems and foliage coated with white meal, flowers white, in summer.

S. cauticolum, a trailer with deep red hanging flowers, in fall.

S. dasyphyllum, evergreen carpets of blue-gray foliage, 2 in.; flowers are white-tinged-pink, early summer.

S. ewersii homophyllum (syn. *S. homophyllum*), 6 in., blue-gray foliage, pink flowers, in late summer.

S. gracile, 2 in., evergreen, flowers white, often red-spotted, in summer.

S. hispanicum bithynicum (syn. *S. glaucum*), 2 in., blue-gray foliage, flowers pinkish white, in late summer.

S. lydium, 3 in., foliage green or suffused with red, flowers white, in early summer.

S. middendorffianum, 6 in., forms neat clumps of green or bronzy foliage with yellow flowers, in summer.

S. sexangulare, 3 in., fast-spreading mats of evergreen foliage, flowers golden-yellow, in early summer.

S. sieboldii, arching or prostrate stems and rounded gray leaves with red edges, flowers pink, in late fall.

SEMPERVIVUM (HOUSELEEK)

A genus of easily grown, sun-loving plants which will thrive in the poorest soil as long as it is well drained. Their rosettes of fleshy leaves may be green, purple or red, or may combine all these colors. The star-shaped flowers may be white, cream, pink or red. In addition to the kinds described here, there are numerous hybrids, forms and varieties that have merit as rock-garden plants—their nomenclature is often confused.

Sempervivum arachnoideum (cobweb houseleek, so called because the reddish or green rosettes are crisscrossed with gray hairs). Bright rose-red flowers, in summer.

Sempervivum tectorum
(Common Houseleek)

tufted green perennial, with stemless
pink blossoms from June to August.
Rarely covers itself with flowers.

S. alpestris, 6 in., tufted, evergreen,
flowers white, in summer. A double-
flowered variety, *flore-pleno*, is also
grown.

S. caroliniana, 6 to 9 in., 1-in.-wide
pink flowers in clusters, in early summer. Also called *S. pensylvanica*, this
charming plant is excellent for light
shade.

S. maritima, 6 to 9 in., procumbent
stems, blue-gray foliage, white flowers
on ascending stems, in summer.

S. schafta (moss campion), 6-in.
tufts of green foliage, pink flowers, in
summer.

S. zawadskii, 6 to 8 in., clumps of
dark green stems and foliage, white
flowers in summer.

S. fauconnettii, rosettes tinged red,
leaves tipped with little tufts of hair,
flowers red on 8-in. stems.

S. soboliferum, rosettes bright green
becoming copper, 1½ in. across; pale
yellow flowers on 9-in. stems.

S. tectorum (common houseleek),
dark or light purplish-red flowers, in
summer.

SHINLEAF. See *Pyrola*.

SILENE (CATCHFLY)
Silene acaulis, about 2 in., a densely

SISYRINCHIUM
Sisyrinchium brachypus, 9 in., one
of the easiest, clear golden flowers, in
July and August.

S. californicum, 6 in., bright yellow
flowers, in autumn.

S. douglasii, 8 to 10 in., swinging,
bell-like wine-red flowers, in summer.

SKULLCAP. See *Scutellaria*.

SOAPWORT. See *Saponaria*.

SPEEDWELL. See *Veronica*.

SPIREA. See *Astilbe*.

STONECROP. See *Sedum*.

SUNROSE. See *Helianthemum*.

TEUCRIUM
Low evergreen shrublets.
Teucrium chamaedrys, 9 to 12 in.,
usually lax stems, small red-purple
flowers, in summer.

T. lucidum, 9 to 12 in., stems erect,
flowers red-purple, in summer.

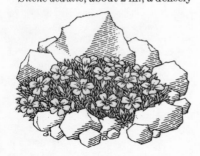

Silene acaulis
(Catchfly)

Sisyrinchium brachypus

THALICTRUM
These need semishade and moist woodland soil.

Thalictrum kiusianum, 3 in., delightful little variety, flowers lavender-purple, in summer.

T. minus, 10 to 15 in., fernlike foliage, flowers yellow.

THRIFT. See *Armeria.*

THYMUS (THYME)
Most of the thymes are showy and easy to grow. They tolerate dry soils and full sun.

Thymus serpyllum (creeping thyme), 1 to 3 in., mat-forming with purplish flowers, in summer.

There are many varieties, some with white, others with pink, red or crimson flowers. All are invaluable for planting in chinks between paving stones.

TIARELLA
Tiarella cordifolia (foamflower), 6 to 12 in., heart-shaped leaves and fluffy spires of white flowers, in spring. Plant in a shady corner.

TRAILING ARBUTUS. See *Epigaea.*

TUNICA
Tunica saxifraga (tunic flower), 6 to 9 in., wiry-stemmed, with small pink flowers, in summer. The variety known as *flore-pleno* has larger double flowers.

VERONICA (SPEEDWELL)
Some veronicas creep on the ground; others are more erect.

Veronica armena, 4 in., trailer with lacy foliage and blue flowers.

V. gentianoides, 6 to 8 in., tufts of glossy green leaves, flowers blue.

V. incana, 6 to 12 in., whitish-gray leaves, flowers blue.

V. latifolia prostrata (syn. *V. rupestris*), 6 to 8 in., prostrate, flowers blue. Variety *rosea* has pink flowers. Variety *nana* is more dwarf.

V. pectinata, gray woolly leaves on trailing stems, flowers blue or pink.

V. spicata, 9 to 12 in., flowers purple-blue or pink.

VIOLA (VIOLET)
Violas are free-flowering plants. There are numerous kinds. Many self-sow with great freedom. They need light shade and reasonably moist woodland soil.

Viola blanda, 3 to 5 in., white.

V. jooi, 3 in., pink flowers. For sun or light shade.

V. pedata (bird's-foot violet), violet and lilac.

V. priceana (Confederate violet), lavender-white and blue.

V. tricolor (johnny-jump-up), tiny pansy flowers of various colors. For sun or light shade.

VIOLET. See *Viola.*

WILD SWEET WILLIAM. See *Phlox divaricata.*

WORMWOOD. See *Artemisia.*

CHAPTER 27

GARDENS IN THE SHADE

Gradations of Shade—Tree and Building Shade—Care—Recommended Plants for Shady Areas

SHADE IN the garden can be a source of both pleasures and problems. Who is not grateful for relief from the glare and heat of summer's brightest sun? Yet too much shade brings only trouble to vegetable gardeners and to the budding horticulturist who craves a summer garden filled with colorful blooms.

As gardeners use the word, shade refers not to one condition but to many. It is not an exact term. The beginner learns that a certain plant thrives in shade, or in light shade, or in semishade, and tries to match plant and place, very often successfully.

There are numerous gradations from the gloomy areas beneath dense evergreens to the bright locations on the north side of a wall. Some areas receive a fair amount of direct sun early in the year but are protected later by the foliage of deciduous trees. In other places the sun's rays are filtered through foliage and reach the ground in a pattern of dappled light. Often a site will receive half a day of full sun either in the morning or in the afternoon and be completely shaded for the rest of the time.

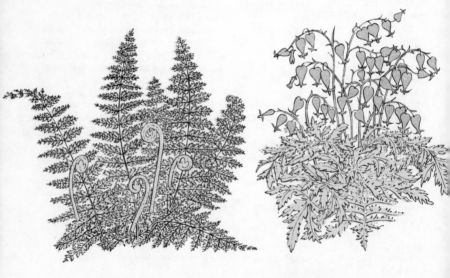

Dennstaedtia punctilobula
(Hay-Scented Fern)

Dicentra eximia
(Wild Bleeding Heart)

While all garden plants need light, some are more efficient users of the energy it supplies than others, and not all prosper under the same light intensities. Because gardeners can control to a great extent soil fertility, water, winter protection and other factors that affect plant growth, it is often possible to succeed with plants in cultivation under quite different light conditions from those of their native homes. Gardening is of necessity somewhat empirical, and this is especially true of gardening where shade is concerned.

Sometimes reflected light is of great importance. In city gardens, for example, locations to the north of high walls, which ordinarily would be classed as full shade, may be considered as light shade if considerable light is reflected from a nearby opposite wall that is painted white or one which is of some other strongly light-reflective color.

SHADE OF TREES AND SHRUBS

Another hazard arises if the shaded areas are under shrubs or trees. The introduced plants must compete for moisture and nutrients with the roots of the shade trees and shrubs. When it rains, the drip from overhead branches and foliage packs the surface soil. In the event that the soil is clayey, its physical qualities grow worse. Falling leaves may collect, especially in hollows, and may smother out the tender plants or increase their susceptibility to disease. Certain needles (leaves) of pines, hemlocks and other conifers result in a distinctly acid condition if they accumulate on the ground.

It is always worthwhile to improve exposure by removing any trees that can be spared or by thinning out branches, if this can be done without mutilating the specimens. Take off all possible lower limbs, so that light from the sides can reach the plants.

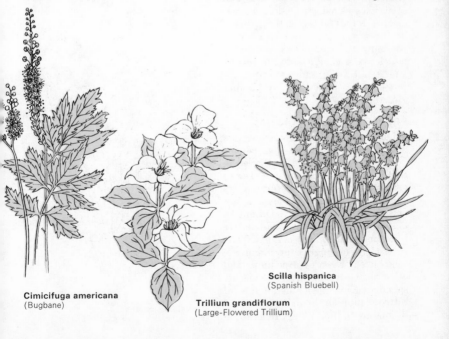

Cimicifuga americana
(Bugbane)

Trillium grandiflorum
(Large-Flowered Trillium)

Scilla hispanica
(Spanish Bluebell)

Many plants will grow under trees without much direct light from overhead.

Competition with tree roots is a condition that most woodland plants are naturally well equipped to meet. They do this chiefly by concentrating their own roots at levels not seriously invaded by those of the trees. But some trees, except when they are quite young, fill the soil to the surface with hungry, moisture-seeking roots so that scarcely any other plant can share the earth. Most maples are greedy, and so are beeches and many conifers. Under extreme circumstances, it is impossible to grow anything close to such specimens; this is often true of an old Norway maple. Similar conditions may be found near some surface-rooting shrubs such as lilacs and privets. Hardiest and toughest of underplanting for such a used-up place is *Euonymus fortunei coloratus*, which is often named *E. radicans coloratus*, and sometimes called purple-leaf winter-creeper. If that fails, then the gardener must resort to gravel or paving, or be content with bare soil or a covering of mulch material. Watering, fertilizing and topdressing merely stimulate the offending tree roots to vigorous growth.

Torenia fournieri
(Wishbone Flower)

PREPARATION OF SOIL

Where invasive surface roots are not a problem, a great deal can be done to prepare the soil for the reception of shade-tolerant plants. Dig in great amounts of humus-forming organic material such as compost, peat moss, sawdust and so on. Do not be misled by those who say that native woodland plants abhor manure. They revel in it, so long as the manure is well rotted. Even cypripediums and other native orchids luxuriate and respond well to a generous amount of rotted manure in the soil if other conditions are to their liking. In addition

Convallaria majalis
(Lily of the Valley) See page 176.

to humus-forming material, mix in a liberal dressing of bone meal.

Danger of damage to the soil caused by drip from overhanging branches and foliage is best prevented by maintaining a mulch of loose organic material on the soil surface. For this purpose, leaf mold works very well; equally effective are peat moss, compost, bagasse (the crushed, juiceless residue of sugar cane) or any one of the accepted organic mulches. A layer not more than an inch or two thick should be maintained at all times. Harm rather than good is likely to result if a leaf mulch is thicker. This is especially true of maple leaves, which pack on top of each other in close, flat layers, denying free air circulation to the soil and roots beneath. Soil acidity that naturally occurs under many conifers can, of course, be temporarily corrected by liming, but this may be detrimental to the trees. A better solution is to set in plants that tolerate acid soil and shade.

SOIL AT BUILDING SITES

A former building site may have shallow topsoil, inferior subsoil, buried builder's debris and perhaps an alkaline soil resulting from lime, plaster and cement that have been buried or washed down from mortar or plaster in walls. To check these conditions, excavate along the foundation to a depth of about 2 ft. (and whatever distance from the base of the wall that exploration determines advisable). Replacing existent poor topsoil with fertile earth may be the practical answer.

CARE OF PLANTS IN SHADE

The success of a shade garden depends, of course, upon providing water and good soil. In setting out shade plants in early spring or fall, give them adequate space. They should be allowed a little more room between individuals than needed for comparable plants in sunny locations. A maximum spread of foliage helps each plant to take full advantage of available light.

RECOMMENDED PLANTS

Plants suitable for growing in shade include permanent evergreen and deciduous shrubs, herbaceous perennials and bulbs (using the term in its broad sense to include tubers and other similar organs). Ferns (such as the hayscented fern illustrated on page 540) and other plants that are set out for the summer only are also recommended. Annuals for shade are few.

The following lists are not exhaustive; there are many other plants that will grow in varying amounts of shade. This is especially true in subtropical areas where numerous members of the botanical families *Araceae* (philodendron relatives) and *Marantaceae* (ginger relatives) grow well in shaded locations. For other shade-tolerant plants, consult "Ground Covers," page 484, and "Rock Gardens," page 517.

Deciduous Shrubs and Small Trees

Abelia grandiflora . . . glossy abelia
Acanthopanax sieboldianus . . .
                                      five-leaf aralia
Amelanchier . . . . . . Juneberry
Aronia . . . . chokeberry
Berberis thunbergii . . .
                                      Japanese barberry
Calycanthus floridus . . .
                                      Carolina allspice
Cercis canadensis . . . . . redbud
Chionanthus virginica . . fringe tree
Clethra alnifolia . . .
                                      sweet pepperbush
Comptonia peregrina . . . sweet fern
Cornus . . . . dogwood
Daphne mezereum . . . . mezereon
Enkianthus campanulatus
Fothergilla
Hydrangea quercifolia . . .
                                      oak-leaf hydrangea
Hypericum frondosum . . .
                                      St.-John's-wort

Hypericum prolificum . . .
St.-John's-wort
Ilex verticillata . . . . winterberry
Kerria japonica
Ligustrum. . . . . privet
Lindera benzoin . . . . . spicebush
Lonicera. . . . . bush honeysuckle
Philadelphus coronarius . . .
mock orange
Rhamnus . . . . buckthorn
Rhododendron (azalea)
Rhodotypos tetrapetala . . . jetbead
Rubus odoratus . . .
flowering raspberry
Stephanandra incisa
Styrax japonica . . . . . . storax
Symphoricarpos . . .
snowberry; coralberry
Viburnum
Xanthorhiza simplicissima . . .
yellowroot

Evergreen Shrubs

Abutilon . . . . . flowering maple
Ardisia crispa
Aucuba japonica . . . gold-dust tree
Berberis julianae. . . . . barberry
Buxus . . . . boxwood
Camellia

Coprosma baueri . . . mirror plant
Elaeagnus pungens
Euonymus fortunei vegetus
Eurya japonica
Fatsia japonica
Ilex . . . . holly
Kalmia latifolia . . mountain laurel
Laurus nobilis . . . . . sweet bay
Leucothoë
Ligustrum japonicum . . . . privet
Ligustrum lucidum . . glossy privet
Mahonia aquifolium . holly mahonia
Myrtus communis . . . . . myrtle
Nandina domestica .
heavenly bamboo
Osmanthus
Photinia serrulata
Pieris
Pittosporum tobira
Podocarpus macrophylla maki
Raphiolepis umbellata . . .
Yeddo hawthorn
Rhododendron
Rhododendron (azalea)
Ruscus aculeatus. . butcher's-broom
Sabal minor . . . . dwarf palmetto
Sarcococca
Severinia buxifolia . . . . boxthorn
Skimmia

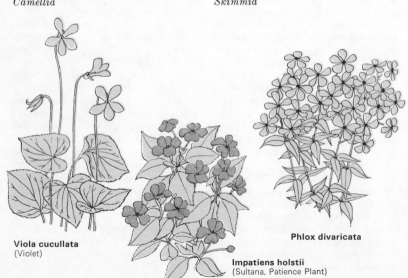

Viola cucullata
(Violet)

Phlox divaricata

Impatiens holstii
(Sultana, Patience Plant)

Taxus. . . . . yew
Trachelospermum jasminoides . . .
                  star jasmine
Viburnum rhytidophyllum

Vines

Actinidia arguta . . bower actinidia
Akebia quinata. . . five-leaf akebia
Aristolochia durior . . .
                 Dutchman's pipe
Gelsemium sempervirens . . .
        Carolina yellow jessamine
Hedera canariensis . . Algerian ivy
Hedera colchica
Hedera helix. . . . . . English ivy
Lonicera . . . . honeysuckle
Parthenocissus . . .
       Virginia creeper; Boston ivy
Polygonum aubertii . silver-lace vine
Pueraria thunbergiana . kudzu vine
Vitis labrusca . . . . . . fox grape

Annuals

Begonia semperflorens . . .
                   wax begonia
Impatiens holstii . . patience plant
Lobelia erinus
Nicotiana . . . . flowering tobacco
Torenia fournieri . wishbone flower

Vinca rosea . . .
        Madagascar periwinkle

Perennials

Aconitum. . . . . monkshood
Actaea. . . . . baneberry
Aegopodium podagraria variegatum . .
                 bishop's-weed
Ajuga. . . . . bugleweed
Amsonia tabernaemontana
Anemone japonica
Aquilegia . . . . columbine
Arisaema triphyllum . . .
             jack-in-the-pulpit
Aruncus sylvester. . . . goatsbeard
Asperula odorata . . sweet woodruff
Astilbe . . . . spirea
Bergenia cordifolia
Brunnera macrophylla
Caltha . . . . . marsh marigold
Campanula. . . . . . . bellflower
Ceratostigma plumbaginoides . . .
  (syn. *Plumbago larpentae*)
Chelone . . . . turtlehead
Chrysogonum virginianum . . .
               golden star
Cimicifuga . . . . bugbane
Convallaria majalis . . .
        lily of the valley

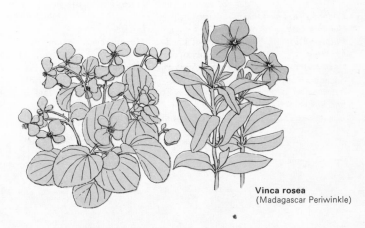

Vinca rosea
(Madagascar Periwinkle)

Begonia semperflorens
(Wax Begonia)

Corydalis lutea
Dicentra . . . . . . bleeding heart
Digitalis. . . . . foxglove
Doronicum . . . . . leopard's-bane
Eupatorium coelestinum . mistflower
Ferns
Filipendula . . . . . meadowsweet
Helleborus
Heracleum . . . . . . cow parsnip
Hesperis matronalis . dame's rocket
Heuchera . . . . coralbells
Hosta . . . . plantain lily
Hypericum calycinum . . .
                           St.-John's-wort
Iris verna
Lobelia
Lunaria biennis. . . . . . honesty
Lysimachia nummularia . . .
                           creeping Charlie
Mazus reptans
Mertensia virginica . . .
                           Virginia bluebell
Mimulus moschatus . . musk plant
Monarda didyma. . . . . bee balm
Myosotis . . . . . forget-me-not
Petasites fragrans . winter heliotrope
Phlox
Physostegia virginiana . . .
                           false dragonhead
Platycodon grandiflorum . . .
                           balloonflower
Podophyllum peltatum. . may apple
Polemonium
Polygonatum . . . . Solomon's seal
Primula. . . . . primrose
Pulmonaria . . . . . . lungwort
Smilacina racemosa . . . . . false
                           Solomon's seal
Stachys grandiflora superba . . .
                           betony

Stylophorum diphyllum . . .
                           celandine poppy
Thalictrum. . . . . . meadow rue
Tiarella cordifolia . . . foamflower
Tolmiea menziesii . . .
                           piggyback plant
Tradescantia virginiana . . .
                           spiderwort
Trollius. . . . . globeflower
Uvularia. . . . . bellwort
Viola . . . . violet, pansy

Bulbs

Begonia (tuberous)
Caladium (fancy-leaved)
Camassia
Chionodoxa luciliae . . .
                           glory-of-the-snow
Claytonia virginica. . spring beauty
Colchicum . . . . . autumn crocus
Colocasia antiquorum . . .
                           elephant's ear
Dicentra cucullaria . . .
                           Dutchman's breeches
Dodecatheon meadia. . shooting star
Eranthis hyemalis . . winter aconite
Erythronium americanum . . .
                           trout lily
Fritillaria . . . . fritillary
Galanthus nivalis . . . . snowdrop
Leucojum aestivum . . .
                           summer snowflake
Lilium. . . . . lily
Maianthemum canadense. . .
                           Canada mayflower
Muscari. . . . . . grape hyacinth
Narcissus . . . narcissus, daffodil
Ornithogalum . . star-of-Bethlehem
Scilla hispanica . . Spanish bluebell
Trillium

SEASIDE GARDENS

Characteristics of Gardens by the Sea— Spacing and Support of Plants—Improving Sandy Soils—Adaptable Plants

GARDENING BY THE SEA presents its own special problems and its own particular opportunities. Charming and delightful gardens *can* be had close to the ocean, and without heartbreaking expense or labor. The successful seaside gardener must of course select the kinds of plants that suit the environment, and he must modify that environment in keeping with his interest and according to his means.

Seashore garden sites have (1) very intense light, (2) strong and more or less continuous winds, (3) possible exposure to salt spray and (4) lack of adequate topsoil.

Because water has a tremendous capacity for retaining heat, which it absorbs and gives up rather slowly, the nearby presence of the ocean significantly modifies local climate. Minimum winter temperatures are higher than in inland areas; gardens by the sea warm up more slowly in spring and cool off less rapidly in fall. Thus they do not produce the earliest crops, but they continue productive and attractive after inland gardens have long since reached the end of the season. Seaside soils are often light in color, and this is another reason for the tardiness of spring growth near the sea. Light-colored soils reflect heat rather than absorb it; their temperatures are not quickly raised as warm weather arrives.

SUNLIGHT

Coastal regions are subjected to a great deal of brilliant sunshine, with

A secret of successful seaside gardening is shelter from persistent inshore winds. The hardiest and most resistant trees (as shown here, Japanese black pines) should be planted nearest to the shore to provide shelter for somewhat less tolerant kinds (also shown here, honey locusts), which, in turn, protect the hardier types of shrubs, such as Russian olives, and finally garden plantings.

intensive ultraviolet radiation. The highly reflective powers of water and of stretches of sand intensify the amount of light with which plants must cope. Light on the north side of a building, for example, is apt to be much more intense than that in a corresponding location inland. Truly shady places in a seaside garden—under a grove of trees or beneath dense bushes—are the exceptions.

Photographers soon learn to make necessary adjustments to light, and so must gardeners. The obvious approach is to depend almost exclusively upon plants that revel in brilliant sunshine, and they are not hard to find. Nearly all garden annuals, a vast number of perennials, most trees and a wide selection of shrubs are sun lovers. So are nearly all aquatic plants and many bulbs.

A seaside gardener is unlikely to succeed with ferns or other denizens of cool, shaded woodlands, but must depend upon plants which live naturally in open fields and meadows, in prairies, in semideserts and bordering the sea. This includes just about all of the gray- and silvery-foliaged plants we cultivate in gardens. Grayness of leaf, whether it results from hairiness or from a surface coating of wax, is a natural device to check excessive water loss and ordinarily is developed only among plants that grow in sunny places. For the same reason, succulent plants (those with thick fleshy stems or leaves) love the sun.

Both gray- and silvery-leaved plants and succulents are very distinctive in appearance. Used cleverly and in abundance, they can bring beauty and character to seaside gardens. They always look just right near the sea.

WIND

This, probably more than any other factor, determines what may and may not be grown near the sea. We are not now considering violent damage caused by storm or hurricane, but rather the cumulative effects of steady, persistent winds, usually from one direction, through most of the year. The chief effect is dehydration; water is removed from the aboveground parts of plants at an accelerated rate, so that the plant cannot absorb moisture from the soil in sufficient quantity to replace that lost by leaves, flowers and stems. Plants suffer as a consequence. Near the sea, fine sand, carried by the wind, virtually sandblasts vegetation and may cut off young shoots as effectively as a pruning knife.

The indirect consequences of more or less continuous winds are manifest in other ways. Often growth is slowed, and that which takes place is in a direction away from the wind. This is the reason for the compact and often "one-sided" appearance of trees and shrubs that grow near the sea. In extreme cases their tops appear to have been trimmed repeatedly through the years, and specimens that in less exposed locations would grow comparatively tall are stunted. They seem to hug the ground.

Plants exposed to wind may also produce smaller leaves. Thus they expose less surface from which moisture can be lost. Most plants that grow in windy locations naturally have minimal leaf areas, and many transplants to such a location also adapt by growing smaller foliage.

Shelter from wind is an absolute must if a considerable variety of plants is to be grown in a seaside garden. It is astonishing how well many ordinary garden plants prosper if they are grown on the leeward side of an effective windbreak. Without protection, only drought-resistant plants—the kinds botanists class as xerophytes and semixerophytes—are likely to survive. Plantings of drought resisters may be used as windbreaks. Walls and fences are also effective.

Coves and hollows protected by dunes or hills provide comfortable garden sites near the sea.

SPACING AND SUPPORT

Because plants in seaside gardens are usually smaller than the same kinds elsewhere, it is sensible to plant them closer together. This is as true of annuals, biennials and perennials as it is of trees and shrubs. When planted close together, individuals form a mutual protection society against the limiting effects of wind and strong sun.

Adequate support for tall-growing plants takes on special importance near the sea. Even though the garden is relatively well sheltered from the prevailing wind, occasional blows from other directions and short, sudden squalls can cause serious distress. A gardener may concentrate on low and bushy plants that withstand squalls without serious damage. However, he may need some tall, erect plants, such as hollyhocks, delphiniums and lilies, as accents in the garden or as cut flowers. He must not only set such plants in the most sheltered parts of the garden; he must see that they are staked and tied to insure their security.

SOIL

Many coastal areas lack good topsoil. The native soil often consists of little but sand. In other places, heavy clays or other difficult soil types prevail. The proximity of salt water need not inhibit the gardener. Except very close to the water's edge and where the underground water table is unusually high, the ground water is very unlikely to contain harmful amounts of salt. More limiting is the seaside soil's excessive porosity and inability to retain moisture, and its general poverty in plant nutrients. Traditional methods of improving and of maintaining comparatively infertile sandy soils should be employed vigorously by the seaside gardener. He must incorporate generous amounts of organic humus-forming materials, such as manure, peat moss, compost, seaweed, sawdust and the like, or of cover crops (green manures).

Because organic matter decomposes in soil, and in sandy soils at a markedly faster rate than in heavier media, its frequent replenishment is necessary. As it decays, the organic material releases nutrients which are used by the growing plants. It is practically impossible to add too much organic matter to this type of soil. A seaside gardener who works such soil must pay constant attention to building up its organic content. If he is fortunate enough to have anything heavier or more nutritious than sand, he should handle it in essentially the same way as is recommended for similar soils in inland gardens.

Because so many seaside soils are low in fertility, the application of fertilizers is a question of special importance. Certainly fertilizing is desirable and, indeed, necessary, but excessive fertilization can cause trouble; this is especially true of the use of too much nitrogen. If available in overly generous amounts, it encourages lush stems and foliage, a growth likely to be rather soft and thus especially unable to withstand the harsh conditions imposed by strong sun and wind. Plants by the sea are more durable if firm—not tender and luxuriant.

The fertilizing practices of the seaside gardener, then, should be directed toward encouraging steady, moderate, firm growth and discouraging any tendency toward the development of overvigorous shoots and foliage. "Little and often" is the golden rule to follow when fertilizing the sandy soils. By observing the plants themselves and their responses, the alert gardener soon learns when a little additional fertilizer is needed.

Mulching is very important for conserving ground moisture. Organic mulches also add valuable and much-needed nutrients. Peat moss, compost, buckwheat hulls and certain other mulches are dark in color and reduce the amount of harmful heat reflected by light-colored soil.

SALT WATER

Very few plants successfully live through wetting with salt spray or inundation by salt water. Those few have learned in their native habitats to adapt to rugged seaside conditions. Some are found along our coasts, but hardly any of our familiar flowers will stand up to such punishment.

PLANTS TO USE

By providing shelter from wind and salt spray and by conditioning the soil, the seaside gardener can grow many plants ordinarily cultivated in inland gardens. Important are the kinds of trees and shrubs that will withstand sand, wind and salty air without much aid, acting as windbreaks to shelter more tender plants.

Lists of plants adapted for coastal gardens in the Southeast, Southwest and Pacific Northwest are provided in the special chapters on gardening in those particular regions. The lists given here are of plants especially useful for seaside planting on the North Atlantic and Central Atlantic coasts. Plants that withstand the most severe exposures are marked with an asterisk.

Evergreen Trees

Chamaecyparis pisifera . . .
                    Sawara false cypress
Ilex opaca . . . . American holly
Juniperus virginiana. . . red cedar

Picea abies. . . . . Norway spruce
Picea asperata . . . dragon spruce
Pinus banksiana. . . . . jack pine
Pinus nigra. . . . . Austrian pine
Pinus rigida . . . . . . pitch pine
Pinus thunbergii . . .
                    Japanese black pine
Thuja occidentalis . . .
                    American arborvitae

Deciduous Trees

Acer pseudoplatanus . . .
                    sycamore maple
Acer rubrum . . . . . . red maple
Betula . . . . birch
Gleditsia triacanthos . honey locust
Platanus acerifolia . London plane
Populus. . . . . poplar
Quercus phellos. . . . . willow oak
Quercus velutina. . . . . black oak

Evergreen Shrubs

Ilex glabra. . . . . inkberry
Juniperus . . . . juniper
Pinus mugo mughus . . mugho pine
Rosmarinus officinalis . . rosemary
Yucca filamentosa

Deciduous Shrubs

Aronia arbutifolia . red chokeberry
Baccharis halmifolia. groundsel bush
Clethra acuminata . . . white alder
Clethra alnifolia . sweet pepperbush
Comptonia peregrina. . . sweet fern

Seaside Garden
Protection from wind and salt spray is offered here by fencing of corrugated fiber glass, with the garden laid out so that the more delicate plants have the added protection of smaller bays. Brick curbing retains the topsoil. Outside the fenced area, the drifting of sand is impeded by lath fencing. Plants which flourish without shelter are (foreground) Japanese black pine, juniper, (left center) yucca and (at rear) Russian olive, hydrangea, bayberry and roses; the ground cover is bearberry.

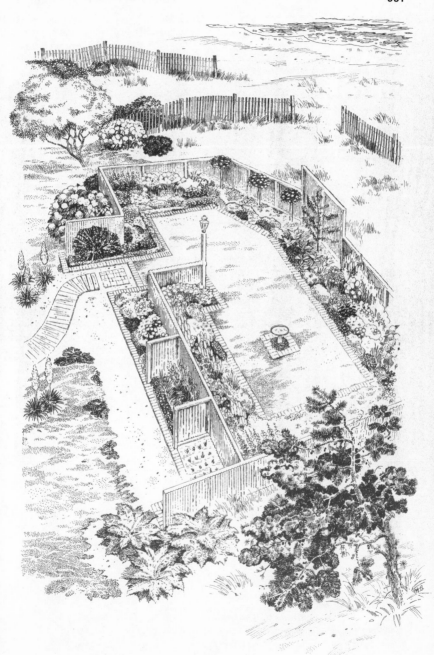

Cornus stolonifera . . .
           red osier dogwood
Cotoneaster
Cytisus scoparius . . Scotch broom
Elaeagnus angustifolia . . .
           Russian olive
Elaeagnus umbellata
Halimodendron halodendron . .
           salt tree
Hibiscus syriacus . . .
        shrub althea; rose of Sharon
Hippophaë rhamnoides . . .
           sea buckthorn
Hydrangea macrophylla
Hydrangea paniculata grandiflora
        . . . peegee hydrangea
Lavandula officinalis. . . . lavender
Ligustrum . . . . privet
Lonicera morrowii . . .
        shrub honeysuckle
Lonicera tatarica . . .
        Tartarian honeysuckle
Myrica pensylvanica. . . bayberry
Potentilla fruticosa
Prunus maritima . . . beach plum
Rhamnus . . . . buckthorn
Rhus . . . . sumac
Rosa multiflora. . . . . . . rose
Rosa rugosa. . . . . rose
Rosa virginiana . . . . . . rose
Salix humilis . . . . prairie willow
Santolina chamaecyparissus . .
        lavender cotton
Shepherdia argentea. . buffalo berry
Spiraea . . . . spirea
Syringa vulgaris . . . . . . lilac
Tamarix . . . . tamarisk
Vaccinium corymbosum . . .
        highbush cranberry
Viburnum cassinoides . . withe rod
Viburnum dentatum . . arrowwood

Vines

Ampelopsis quinquefolia . . .
        Virginia creeper
Clematis paniculata
Hydrangea petiolaris . . .
        climbing hydrangea
Lonicera japonica halliana . . .
        Hall's Japanese honeysuckle

Rosa wichuraiana . . memorial rose
Schizophragma hydrangeoides . . .
        Japanese hydrangea vine
Smilax .
Wisteria

Ground Covers

Arctostaphylos uva-ursi. . bearberry
Calluna vulgaris. . . . . . heather
Ceratostigma plumbaginoides
    (syn. *Plumbago larpentae*)
Juniperus, trailing kinds . . juniper
Lonicera japonica halliana . . .
      Hall's Japanese honeysuckle
Sedum
Thymus serpyllum . . .
        creeping thyme

Herbaceous Perennials

Althaea rosea . . . . . . hollyhock
Alyssum saxatile. . . basket-of-gold
Anchusa azurea
Aquilegia . . . . columbine
Arabis albida. . . . . . rock cress
Arenaria . . . . sandwort
Armeria . . . . thrift
Artemisia stelleriana. . dusty miller
Asclepias tuberosa. . butterfly weed
Chrysanthemum
Coreopsis . . . . tickseed

Althaea rosea
(Hollyhock)

Dianthus . . . . pink		*Cryophytum crystallinum* . ice plant		
Doronicum . . . . . leopard's-bane		*Dahlia*		
Echinops . . . . globe thistle		*Delphinium* . . . . larkspur		
Erigeron . . . . fleabane		*Dianthus barbatus* . . sweet William		
Eryngium maritimum . . . sea holly		*Eschscholzia california* . . .		
Gaillardia aristata . . blanketflower		California poppy		
Gypsophila paniculata . . .		*Euphorbia marginata* . . .		
baby's breath		snow-on-the-mountain		
Helianthemum . . . . sunrose		*Gaillardia* . . . . . blanketflower		
Hemerocallis . . . . day lily		*Gladiolus*		
Heuchera . . . . coralbells		*Gomphrena globosa* . globe amaranth		
Hibiscus moscheutos . . rose mallow		*Helichrysum bracteatum* . strawflower		
Iberis sempervirens . . .		*Iberis* . . . . candytuft		
evergreen candytuft		*Lantana camara*		
Iris		*Lobularia maritima* . sweet alyssum		
Limonium latifolium . . sea lavender		*Nigella damascena* . . love-in-a-mist		
Lythrum salicaria . purple loosestrife		*Papaver* . . . . poppy		
Nepeta mussinii		*Pelargonium hortorum* . . geranium		
Paeonia . . . . peony		*Petunia*		
Veronica		*Phlox drummondii*		
		Portulaca grandiflora . . . rose moss		
Annuals and Tender Summer Flowers		*Reseda odorata* . . . . . mignonette		
Abronia . . . . sand verbena		*Salvia*		
Ageratum		*Scabiosa atropurpurea* . . .		
Antirrhinum majus . . . snapdragon		sweet scabious		
Calendula . . . . . . pot marigold		*Tagetes* . . . . marigold		
Centaurea cyanus . . . cornflower		*Tropaeolum majus* . . . nasturtium		
Cleome spinosa . . . . spiderflower		*Verbena hortensis*		
Coreopsis . . . calliopsis; tickseed		*Viola tricolor* . . . . pansy		
Cosmos		*Zinnia elegans*		

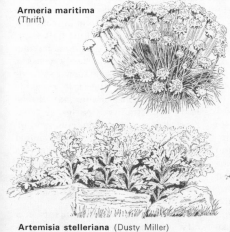

Armeria maritima
(Thrift)

Artemisia stelleriana (Dusty Miller)

Rosmarinus officinalis
(Rosemary)
See page 301.

CHAPTER 29

CITY GARDENS

*Lovely and Difficult—Scale of Design—
Kinds of Pavement—Soil—Ornaments
and Features—Roof Gardens—Recommended Plants—Tubs and Containers—Window Boxes*

A GARDEN in the city is especially appreciated; it brings the soul-satisfy-
ing freshness of leaf and blossom to a
world of cement and brick. But a city
garden is more difficult to plan and
manage successfully than other gardens; since its existence is always something of a miracle. The city gardener
must contend with air pollution, the
proximity of high buildings, poverty-
stricken soil, restricted space and inadequate sunshine. Nonetheless, he
can transform a dismal yard or even
a roof into a restful and lovely outdoor living room.

The plan should be simple and
practical. Generally speaking, the
center of the garden should remain
uncluttered. If the area is enclosed by
high walls, however, it is advisable to
place any flowers toward the center
for maximum sunlight. There should
be a focal point of interest—a small
pool, a sundial, a piece of sculpture.

PLANNING
The first step in its design is to measure the site and draw up a plan to
scale. This provides an opportunity
to visualize different schemes and
plan a definite procedure before clearing, digging and planting. Do not
forget to consider the walls of the
house, noting the position of any
doors and windows, for these will
have a bearing on the layout. Make

a note, too, of any natural features on
the site, such as trees, a group of
bushes, or a difference in levels. These
offer scope for interesting treatment.

PAVING OR GRASS
A city garden frequently consists of
only a small area bounded by walls
and heavily shaded. The most practical treatment is to transform it into
a formal, paved courtyard, using
either brick or flagstone. This is permanent, easy and inexpensive to
maintain, and always appears tidy,
with a clean surface that dries quickly.

Although grass is desirable, it is
seldom successful in a confined and
shady space. Where the site is open,
a small lawn is feasible, but plan it in
conjunction with a paved terrace
close to the house for sitting out.
Make it from good sod rather than
from seed, because birds raid the seed
and make dust baths in the soil.

For terraces and paths, an attractive material is flagstone in rectangular slabs laid in a suitable pattern or
in broken pieces as random paving.
Also satisfactory, and less expensive,
are rectangles of an artificial stone or
slabs of concrete tinted to resemble
flagstones. Bricks or tiles may also be
laid in attractive patterns—separately, together, or in combination
with other paving. The bricks should
be hard and well burned, and laid on
a bed of cinders, sand or concrete.

SOIL PREPARATION
AND IMPROVEMENT
The success or failure of plants in a
city garden depends upon the fer-

tility of the soil, which involves its texture as well as its richness. Complete resoiling by importing fresh topsoil to mix with the existing soil might be necessary. If merely digging up the planting area in the autumn, make sure that the subsoil is broken up. Leave the surface rough, and apply a dressing of lime at the rate of 2 to 3 oz. per sq. yd. Follow this about six weeks later with a dressing of manure, rich compost, humus or other bulk decayed organic matter.

The best way of restoring fertility to impoverished soil is to incorporate generous amounts of humus material while digging. Ideally, this should be rotted manure, but more easily available materials in a city are peat moss, commercial humus and, sometimes, compost. These should be supplemented by dressings of organic fertilizer and bone meal.

ORNAMENTAL FEATURES

Garden ornaments must be used with discretion, and their design and placement should be carefully considered. Arches, pergolas and shelters are usually impractical in a restricted space, but there may be room for a pillar or a well-sculptured figure at some strategic point; for a sundial or a birdbath; for vases and urns, either as ornaments in themselves or to hold plants; and for a seat on the lawn or terrace, under a tree or terminating a vista at the end of a path.

A birdbath is a particularly pleasing ornament for a city garden, while vases look attractive placed on the coping of a terrace wall or formal pool, on the terrace itself, or on either side of a low flight of steps.

In a formally designed garden, a small round, square or other geometric-shaped pool provides a focal point of great charm. A more natural layout, where the emphasis is on plants, provides greater scope in the shape and placing of a pool.

LIGHTING

Lighting of some sort is essential if the city garden is to be used as an outdoor living room on summer evenings. As in the case of garden furniture, utility should never be sacrificed for appearance, but the two can very often be combined.

Have one or two lights shining down on the terrace, and carefully arrange a few more low down in the borders. Another could perhaps be placed in the branches or at the foot of a tree. If the right plants are chosen for illumination, the result will be most effective. White and yellow flowers show up better than brightly colored ones, and all shrubs with gray, silver or shiny leaves light up to advantage, particularly if contrasted with neighboring dark evergreens.

All the lights should be controlled from a switch by the garden door of the house, and the cables need not be buried deeply, provided their position is known to those working in the beds and borders. A competent electrician should install the lighting.

FENCES AND HEDGES

One of the most important requirements for the city garden is privacy, and surrounding borders should therefore be designed to screen the view from both inside and outside, as well as to make an attractive backdrop.

Woven board fencing, bamboo and lattice screening and trelliswork panels will do much to cover ugly walls or mask an unsightly view. If a tall, dense screen is wanted, and only a narrow border is available, erect a high, wide-meshed lattice or trellis, and let it support a large-leaved vine or other climber.

Plants should also play their part as screening if the background is not

Spring Garden in the Old South

Graceful scrollwork in the antique
Spanish wrought-iron gate and railings suggested the sweeping curves in this garden
design. Fancy-leaved caladiums edge the
veranda, foreground. A spreading live oak,
draped with Spanish moss, shades the brick-
paved courtyard and fountain. The ground
cover is shaggy mondo grass, or dwarf lilyturf.
Typically southern are gardenias, left foreground, Carolina rhododendron and flowering
azaleas along the wall, opposite, crape
myrtle in the far corner and the two flowering Magnolia grandiflora trees. Such a garden might also display camellias. The border throughout is of begonias; it encloses
a bed of crinum lilies against the far wall.
On the wall itself is a creeping fig. The
strawberry jar is planted with succulents.

to become too austere. Place shrubs
or, if space permits, medium-sized
trees at strategic points. Recommended hedging shrubs for a screen
are yew, holly, *Lonicera nitida*,
pyracantha and privet. For a lower
hedge, use lavender, rosemary, barberry or boxwood, or floribunda roses
if a flowering hedge is wanted. All
these shrubs are also useful as partitions if the site is large enough to be
divided into more than one separate
enclosure.

Ideally, borders should be 5 to 6
ft. wide if shrubs are to be planted in
a single row, or about 8 ft. if planted
in a double row at staggered intervals. If groups of hardy perennial
flowers, such as campanulas, peonies,

perennial asters, day lilies and plume poppies, are planted between the shrubs, a border 8 to 9 ft. wide is advisable. The taller the shrubs are to grow, the wider should be the border. Choose simple outlines, for restricted space and the proximity of fences and walls do not allow much freedom in border planning.

ROOF GARDENS

Gardens in large cities are as likely to be located on a roof or on a small balcony as on the ground. Such sites pose problems, not the least of which is that of providing sufficient root room and soil. Basically, such gardens are of two types—those in which all the plants are grown in pots, boxes, tubs, planters and similar containers, and those with sizable soil beds, usually contained by masonry walls.

Before installing any off-the-ground garden, have a competent engineer or builder check supports of the roof or terrace. Masonry, pottery and even wood are heavy; so is soil, especially when it is wet, while trees and shrubs all add to the total load. Make sure that drainage facilities are adequate to carry away surplus water without damage to the building. Also, if you are a tenant, secure permission of the landlord in writing.

Masonry-enclosed beds are ordinarily 1 to 2 ft. deep. They should have a layer of 3 to 6 in. of cinder or other drainage material before they are filled with soil. Tubs, boxes and pots can be of any size that can be handled with reasonable ease. Planters should not be less than 9 in. deep; 12 in. or more is advisable. Usually of wood, like tubs and pots, they should have perforations in the bottom covered with drainage material.

With roof gardens, wind presents one of the most serious problems. A practical way of meeting this is by enclosing the area with a fence or other barrier. Apertures that allow some wind to pass through may prevent it from blowing down in a severe gale.

A mistake made by many roof gardeners is taking ordinary topsoil, without amendment, and expecting to grow satisfactory plants in it. This rarely succeeds. Even the biggest bed on a roof is just an oversized container—not really different from a pot, tub or window box. Unlike an on-the-ground garden, it has no direct contact with the subsoil, and so no exchange of gases, moisture, earthworm activities and so on.

Above all, soil for roof gardens must be permanently porous. If the topsoil tends to be clayey (heavy), lighten it by mixing in liberal amounts of crushed coal cinders (not fine ash) or perlite. Also add generous quantities of peat moss or humus, some bone meal and, if the soil is acid, a sprinkling of ground limestone.

In planning a roof garden, be sure to arrange for a handy faucet; carrying water from inside a building to a roof is no fun. If the garden is large enough, try to arrange for a tiny service area where tools, supplies and other implements can be kept at hand.

In climates subject to much winter

Roof Garden—July and August
This roof garden, with its two levels of raised beds, is designed for the gardener who wants to try his hand at a little bit of everything. A three-tiered fountain-pool dominates the graveled bed in the foreground with its sparse planting of succulents (sedums and hen-and-chickens) and papyrus. Weight problem on a roof is minimized by using extremely light, porous, volcanic rock. The rockery continues beyond the pool with a planting of silvery artemisia, euonymus and other rock-loving plants, beneath a clipped privet. Beyond is a long begonia-bordered bed of colorful annuals extending to the far wall, leading on at left to a bed of low-growing polyantha roses beneath a shrubby floribunda rose. Willow tree next to the pool, Russian olive at the far end and tubbed crab apple at left are all stoutly resistant to leaf-tearing winds and heat. Here they are partly sheltered by a windbreak of cedar stockade fencing. Tubbed yucca accents pool area.

freezing, protection of the roof garden during that season demands special care. Particularly with plants in containers, the soil may freeze solid throughout and remain in that condition for long periods. This is less likely to happen in soil beds because of their greater volume and because heat will be conducted to the soil from the building below. Long periods of solidly frozen ground are usually fatal to evergreens, since they are unable to replace moisture given off by their leaves. Even deciduous shrubs may be dehydrated to the extent that they are partially or wholly killed back. Hardy bulbs and perennials suffer too, making insufficient root growth.

Precautions against winter damage should consist of doing everything possible to prevent the soil from freezing solidly throughout and by trying to reduce loss of moisture from the aboveground plant parts.

Movable containers can be stood closely together in the least windy and most shady location, and be packed between and around with dry leaves, salt hay, straw or any other form of insulating material. Vermiculite is excellent if it is covered with sheets of polyethylene plastic to prevent it from becoming water-sodden. Permanent beds and containers too large to move should be mulched heavily and packed around with similar insulation. None of this should be done, however, until after the soil has frozen to a depth of an inch or two.

Toward the end of December, it is helpful to spray all trunks, branches and aboveground parts of plants with an antidesiccant plant spray and to repeat this a month later. It is also excellent practice to place evergreen branches over or around the tops of plants, and tie these into place so that they will not blow away, or enclose the plants in burlap. Evergreens must not be so heavily covered that their leaves do not receive a reasonable amount of light.

RECOMMENDED PLANTS

Under favorable conditions a very considerable selection of plants can be grown in city gardens, but because conditions there rarely approach the ideal, the lists given here are limited to kinds which are exceptionally tolerant and most likely to succeed. It is important, of course, to choose those that are winter-hardy in the region where they are planted. Some of the plants listed below are hardy in mild regions only.

Of all plants, evergreens find city conditions most difficult. Unlike deciduous plants and annuals, they retain their foliage for more than one season and thus accumulate even greater deposits of soot, oily particles, grime and other filth that interfere with their "breathing" and cut down seriously the amount of light they receive. Under the worst conditions, it becomes practically impossible to keep evergreens alive and healthy in places where at least a few deciduous plants will make a tolerable display.

Although some city gardens are heavily shaded by tall buildings, others are exposed to direct sun for a considerable portion of each day, and the inclusion of one or more trees to provide a certain amount of shade makes them more usable. Even in nonsunny gardens, it is pleasant to have trees near the boundaries to serve as screening and bring to the city something of the feel of the country. Deciduous trees, which lose their leaves in winter, prosper better than evergreens in the relatively polluted atmosphere of big cities. In cities where air pollution is not a great problem, a much wider variety of trees than is listed here may be grown.

Plants best suited for roof gardens and terraces are more limited in number than those adapted for city gardens generally. In the following lists, those kinds especially adaptable for roof gardens are marked with an asterisk.

Deciduous Shade Trees

Acer ginnala. . . . . Amur maple
Acer palmatum . . Japanese maple
Ailanthus altissima . tree-of-heaven
Catalpa
*Elaeagnus angustifolia . . .
Russian olive
Ginkgo biloba. . . maidenhair tree
Gleditsia triacanthos inermis . . .
thornless honey locust
Morus alba . . . . white mulberry
Platanus acerifolia . London plane
Quercus palustris. . . . . pin oak
Robinia pseudoacacia . yellow locust
*Salix babylonica . . weeping willow
Sophora japonica . Chinese scholar
tree; Japanese pagoda tree

Deciduous Small Flowering Trees

Albizzia julibrissin . . . . silk tree
Amelanchier canadensis . . .
serviceberry
Cornus florida   flowering dogwood
Cornus mas . . . cornelian cherry
*Crataegus crus-galli . . .
cockspur thorn
*Crataegus oxyacantha . . .
English hawthorn
*Crataegus phaenopyrum . . .
Washington thorn
Koelreuteria paniculata . . .
goldenrain tree
Laburnum watereri . . golden chain
Magnolia soulangeana . . .
saucer magnolia
Magnolia stellata . . star magnolia
*Malus . . . . crab apple
Parkinsonia aculeata . . .
Jerusalem thorn
*Prunus . . .
Japanese cherry, cherry plum,
flowering almond
Sorbus aucuparia . . .
European mountain ash

Evergreen Trees

Cryptomeria japonica
Eriobotrya japonica . . . . loquat
Magnolia grandiflora . . . bull bay
*Pinus nigra . . . . Austrian pine
*Pinus thunbergii . . .
Japanese black pine
Pseudotsuga taxifolia. . Douglas fir
Thuja . . . . arborvitae

Deciduous Shrubs

Abelia grandiflora . . glossy abelia
Acanthopanax sieboldianus
(syn. Aralia pentaphylla) . . .
five-leaf aralia
*Berberis thunbergii . . .
Japanese barberry
Buddleia davidii . . butterfly bush
Calycanthus floridus . . .
Carolina allspice
*Caragana arborescens . . .
Siberian pea tree
Chaenomeles japonica . . .
Japanese flowering quince
Clethra alnifolia . sweet pepperbush
Cotinus coggygria . . . smoke tree
Cotoneaster
Deutzia
Euonymus alatus . . .
winged-bark euonymus
*Forsythia
Fuchsia magellanica riccartonii
*Hibiscus syriacus . . .
rose of Sharon, shrub althea
Hydrangea macrophylla
Kerria japonica
*Ligustrum . . . . privet
Olearia haastii . . . . daisy tree
Philadelphus . . . . . mock orange
Rhodotypos tetrapetala. . . jetbead
Ribes . . . . currant
Spiraea . . . . spirea
Stephanandra incisa
Symphoricarpos albus . snowberry
Syringa. . . . . lilac
Viburnum
Weigela

Evergreen Shrubs

Ardisia crispa

Aucuba japonica variegata . . .
                        gold-dust tree
Bamboo
Berberis julianae . . . . barberry
Buxus sempervirens . . . boxwood
Camellia
Elaeagnus pungens
Euonymus fortunei vegetus
Euonymus japonicus
Fatshedera lizei
Fatsia japonica
    (syn. Aralia sieboldii)
Hebe
Ilex aquifolium . . . English holly
Ilex cornuta . . . . Chinese holly
Ilex crenata . . . . Japanese holly
Ilex opaca . . . . American holly
Kalmia latifolia. . mountain laurel
Laurus nobilis . . . . . sweet bay
Leucothoë catesbaei
Ligustrum japonicum. . . . privet
Ligustrum lucidum. . glossy privet
Mahonia aquifolium .holly mahonia
Murraea exotica . orange jessamine
Nandina domestica . . .
                    heavenly bamboo
Nerium oleander. . . . . oleander
Osmanthus ilicifolius
Pieris floribunda
Pieris japonica
Pittosporum tobira
Pyracantha. . . . . . . firethorn
Raphiolepis indica . . .
                    India hawthorn
Rhododendron
Skimmia japonica
Taxus . . . . yew
Yucca

Vines

Actinidia arguta. . bower actinidia
*Akebia quinata . . five-leaf akebia
Allamanda cathartica
Ampelopsis brevipedunculata . . .
                    porcelain vine
Antigonon leptopus . . . coral vine
Aristolochia durior . . .
                    Dutchman's-pipe
Bougainvillea glabra
Campsis radicans . . trumpet vine

Clematis armandii
*Clematis montana, and C. m. rubens
*Clematis paniculata
Clematis tangutica
Dioscorea batatas. . cinnamon vine
*Euonymus fortunei radicans
Ficus pumila. . . . . creeping fig
Gelsemium sempervirens . . .
                    Carolina jessamine
Hedera canariensis
Hedera colchica
Hedera helix . . . . . English ivy
Hydrangea petiolaris . . .
                    climbing hydrangea
Lonicera heckrottii . . honeysuckle
*Parthenocissus quinquefolia . . .
                    Virginia creeper
*Parthenocissus tricuspidata . . .
                    Boston ivy
Passiflora alata-caerulea . . .
                    passionflower
*Polygonum aubertii . silver-lace vine
Solanum crispum . . . nightshade
Syngonium podophyllum
Trachelospermum jasminoides . . .
                    star jasmine
Vitis coignetiae
Vitis labrusca . . . . . fox grape
*Wisteria

Ground Covers

Ajuga reptans . . . . . bugleweed
Convallaria majalis . . .
                    lily of the valley
Epimedium. . . . . . barrenwort
*Euonymus fortunei
*Hedera helix . . . . . English ivy
Hypericum calycinum
                    St.-John's-wort
*Iberis sempervirens . . .
                    evergreen candytuft
Lamium galeobdolon
    variegatum . . . . . dead nettle
Liriope spicata . . creeping lilyturf
Ophiopogon japonicus
    (syn. Mondo japonicum) . . .
                    dwarf lilyturf
*Pachysandra terminalis
Sarcococca hookeriana humilis
*Sedum . . . . stonecrop

Vinca major . . . large periwinkle
*Vinca minor . . . running myrtle

Herbaceous Perennials

Acanthus. . . . . . bear's-breech
Aconitum . . . . . . monkshood
*Ajuga reptans . . . . . bugleweed
Amsonia tabernaemontana
Anemone japonica . . .
Japanese anemone
Aquilegia . . . . columbine
*Arabis albida. . . . . . rock cress
Aruncus sylvester . . . goatsbeard
Aster . . . . . Michaelmas daisy
*Astilbe . . . . spirea
*Bergenia
Brunnera myosotidiflora
Campanula . . . . . . bellflower
Chrysanthemum, border varieties
*Coreopsis grandiflora . . . tickseed
Dicentra spectabilis . bleeding heart
Doronicum . . . . leopard's-bane
*Echinops ritro . . . . globe thistle
*Eupatorium coelestinum . mistflower
Ferns, all vigorous growing kinds
*Helenium . . . . . . sneezeweed
*Hemerocallis. . . . . . . day lily
*Heuchera sanguinea . . . coralbells
*Hosta . . . . plantain lily, funkia
*Iberis sempervirens . . .
evergreen candytuft
*Iris
Macleaya cordata . . plume poppy
*Oenothera . . . . evening primrose
Paeonia . . . . peony
Phlox
Physostegia grandiflora . . .
false dragonhead
Polemonium reptans
Polygonum . . .
jointweed; knotweed
Pulmonaria . . . . . lungwort
Rudbeckia laciniata hortensia . . .
golden glow
*Sedum . . . . stonecrop
*Sempervivum tectorum . . .
hen-and-chickens
Thalictrum . . . . . meadow rue
Tradescantia . . . . . spiderwort
Veronica . . . . speedwell

Spring-Flowering Bulbs and Bedding Plants

All the more common spring-flowering bulbs will thrive for at least two or three years in a city garden. The less sophisticated kinds, such as Spanish bluebell, star-of-Bethlehem, crocus, snowdrop, winter aconite, fritillary, grape hyacinth and narcissus, including daffodils, will continue to flower for many years if planted in borders and rough grass. Some of the tulips, such as *Tulipa kaufmanniana, T. fosteriana* and *T. praestans* Fusilier will do well in any sunny corner, especially if left alone for a few years in a location where the soil is fertile and subsurface drainage is good.

Spring bedding plants such as forget-me-not, English daisy, pansy, sweet William and primrose are invaluable for providing early color. There will be few casualties if all these are planted out in very early spring.

Summer-Flowering Bulbs and Bedding Plants

Later-flowering bulbs that flourish in a city garden include such lilies as *Lilium candidum, L. hansonii, L. henryi, L. regale, L. speciosum, L. hollandicum* and many of the newer hybrids like Enchantment, Royal Gold and Golden Clarion. The summer-flowering hyacinth, *Galtonia candicans*, is both easy and decorative in a border among shrubs, as also is *Lycoris squamigera*, the so-called hardy amaryllis. In regions where little frost is experienced, agapanthus, crinum and hymenocallis are excellent.

Among bulbs that are planted annually to provide summer bloom are tuberous begonia, tigridia, ismene and gladiolus. Caladium and colocasia may be handled the same way for attractive displays of foliage.

For city gardens, bedding plants, including such common ones as geranium, coleus, heliotrope, begonia and

lantana, are best bought from a reliable nurseryman or garden center. Buy and plant in the spring, but beware of forced plants that are available too early; they will suffer when they are planted outside.

Any of the annuals recommended on page 569 for window boxes can be grown, provided there is sun enough. For shady areas, the best are wax begonia, impatiens, balsam, torenia and nicotiana.

The only special care needed for summer bedding plants is to be sure that they have plenty of water during dry periods. Dwarf dahlia withstands city conditions admirably, as do begonia and such annuals as petunia, marigold, zinnia, sweet alyssum, four o'clock, calendula and nicotiana.

Small City Garden—May (above)
Flowering dogwood, tulips, azaleas and primulas bring color to this two-level garden. A border of pansies accents the hexagonal plan of the brick terrace. A background planting of rhododendron over andromeda and mountain laurel in a bed of pachysandra softens the formal design. A stockade fence of peeled cedar stakes insures privacy and lends a warm contrast to the brick. Virginia creeper climbs the wall in the corner.

Narrow City Garden—June (right)
Flowering in the foreground are peonies (right) and mountain laurel (left), while an apple tree shades the central area. A bed of plantain lilies and day lilies, opposite the climbing rose, partly screens the pool area. Beyond, a clump of birches and a flowering quince stand against the silvery, weathered pine boards of the fence. Border plants are marigolds, with begonias beneath the apple tree; creeping thyme grows in tufts between the stones. Ivy is on the wall at right.

TUBS AND CONTAINERS

Tubs, large pots and other suitable containers are frequently used to decorate patios and paved terraces and for growing plants where soil conditions are unfavorable. The placement of the containers can be rearranged periodically to produce new effects.

Preparation

Containers of oak, redwood, cypress and artificial stone are available ready for planting. Others can be made from large casks sawed in half. Treat the inside of each tub with Cuprinol, bore holes in the bottom for drainage and fix casters underneath for easy movement. If casters are not used, stand the tubs on bricks or wooden blocks to insure drainage and aeration. Paint the outside of the containers if they are of wood.

When the containers are in position, put a good layer of drainage material in the bottom of each, and fill them with coarse (not finely sifted), porous, fertile soil, pressed down firmly. Give the compost a good soaking, and allow it to drain before planting.

Maintenance

Regular watering is essential for all plants in containers, together with a biweekly application of dilute liquid fertilizer after the containers are well filled with healthy roots. Once a year, remove the top 2 or 3 in. of soil from permanently planted tubs and replace it with a fresh rich soil mixture. If practicable, replace the soil each year in tubs that are replanted annually. Make sure that the drainage is adequate, that all brackets and bands are sound and that the casters work easily. Give the tubs a coat of paint to freshen them up for a new season.

Plants for Tubs

Tubs and similar containers can be filled with permanent plants. However, if these are not hardy outdoors, they must be wintered in a cool, light cellar or similar place. If seasonal displays are desired, plant them afresh once or twice a year. Bulbs and bedding plants (see page 563), and annuals included in the list of plants on page 569 suitable for window and porch boxes, are satisfactory.

Among permanent plants that are suitable for growing in tubs are:
Acer palmatum . . Japanese maple
Agapanthus africanus . . .
                               lily of the Nile
Buxus sempervirens . . . boxwood
Cactuses and other succulents
Camellia
Clivia . . . . Kafir lily
Crinum
Fuchsia
Hydrangea macrophylla
Lantana
Laurus nobilis . . . . . sweet bay
Malus . . . . crab apple
Pelargonium . . . . . . geranium
Rhododendron
Rosmarinus officinalis . . rosemary
Viburnum rhytidophyllum
Viburnum tinus . . . . laurestinus
Strawberry jars (earthenware containers that have planting pockets in their sides) may be planted with strawberries, small cactuses and other succulents and a great variety of trailing plants, while the large opening at the top may be planted with geraniums, fuchsias, marguerites or with a dracaena or some similar single plant.

WINDOW BOXES IN CITIES

For the city dweller who would like a garden but lacks the space, window boxes provide at least a partial solution and the opportunity to indulge in some of the pleasures of gardening while being spared many of its problems. Window-box gardening is a compromise between indoor pot culture and outdoor gardening; it still requires

Plants in Tubs

In small gardens, where space is limited, tub-grown plants are useful because they can be moved about when change is desired. Here, a Japanese maple, trained as a standard, grows in an oak barrel. The other tub contains begonias, pelargoniums (geraniums) and petunias.

skill and care to bring plants to perfection. This is an instructive and entertaining form of gardening, resulting in gay and colorful adornments for a house.

Materials and Sizes of Boxes

The size and shape of the windows, the dimensions of the sills and the architectural style of the house itself will determine the type of window box. Red cedar and California redwood are the best woods, while other suitable materials are concrete, artificial stone, metals (other than copper) and various plastics.

Before painting any of these surfaces, apply an initial coat of sealing or priming paint. Make sure that the material is quite dry and free from dust before painting. The insides of wooden boxes should be treated with a preservative such as Cuprinol or asphalt paint. Be sure not to use any preservative, such as creosote, which is harmful to plant roots.

It is a good plan to line the boxes with zinc or other metal (except copper) or with heavy-gauge polyethylene plastic film, which will both prolong the life of the wood and retain moisture in the soil. It is necessary, of course, to provide drainage holes in the metal or plastic to permit surplus water to escape.

Prefabricated boxes are generally available in standard patterns, from 2 to 4 ft. long, about 8 in. deep, 7½ in. wide at the base and slightly wider at the top.

Filling Boxes

When a box is in position, spread a 2-in. layer of coarse cinders, crocks or gravel in the bottom, after first placing one large piece of crock or a piece of wire or plastic mesh over each drainage hole. Cover this material with a layer of rough leaves, hay, straw or grass sods turned upside

down, to prevent the soil from clogging the drainage. Then fill the box with really good soil, planting at the same time and finishing with the soil level at about 1 in. from the top.

A good soil mixture can be made from two parts loam, one part peat moss and one part sharp sand, with bone meal added at the rate of a pint to each bushel. If the loam is decidedly acid, some ground limestone or crushed limestone should be mixed in, unless definitely acid-soil plants are to be the occupants.

Plant spring-flowering bulbs in September or October. Plants which bloom in spring such as pansies, English daisies, wallflowers, forget-me-nots and primroses may be planted in fall in regions of mild winters, but where the soil is likely to remain frozen for long periods, it is better to wait until spring before planting these.

When bulbs and other spring bloomers have finished flowering, they can immediately be replaced by summer-flowering plants.

Maintenance

Since a window box has only a limited soil capacity, is exposed to wind and sun, and often sheltered from rain by overhanging eaves and other projections, it tends to dry out rather quickly. Regular watering is therefore necessary. Although the exact frequency of watering depends on a variety of circumstances, a good soaking every two to four days, preferably in the evening, is generally sufficient to keep the soil moist. However, more frequent watering may be needed in summer, and in spring the boxes may go somewhat longer without water. When it is given, be sure to soak the entire body of soil. An application of weak liquid fertilizer twice a month during the summer is a good stimulant. Always water before feeding, as liquid fertilizer may be harmful when applied to dry soil.

Stir the surface of the soil between the plants occasionally with a pointed stick or old kitchen fork to prevent the formation of a hard crust. When the plants are removed at the end of every spring and summer season, turn the soil over with a trowel or hand fork and mix in a dressing of fine bone meal or general fertilizer.

If possible, change the soil completely each year.

Recommended Plants

Ageratum, blue, white and pink; June to frost.

Alyssum saxatile (basket-of-gold), yellow; April and May.

Antirrhinum (snapdragon), various colors; June to October.

Arabis albida, white; March to May.

Begonia, white, pink, red, scarlet or yellow; July to frost. Wax begonias and tuberous begonias are best kinds for window boxes.

Bellis perennis (English daisy), white, pink or red; April and May.

Calendula, orange or yellow; June on.

Callistephus (China aster), various colors; July to frost.

Celosia argentea cristata (cockscomb), red and yellow; June to frost.

Cheiranthus cheiri (English wallflower), white, red, yellow, orange or pink; May. *C. allionii* (Siberian wallflower), orange; April to June.

Chionodoxa (glory-of-the-snow), blue, pink or white; March and April.

Chrysanthemum, border varieties, various colors; late summer and fall. *C. frutescens* (marguerite), white or yellow; June to August.

Coleus, variously colored handsome foliage; June to frost.

Convolvulus tricolor (dwarf morning glory), blue, pink or white; July to September.

Crocus, white, blue, yellow, orange or purple; early spring.

Dahlia (dwarf varieties), white, pink, red or yellow; July to frost.

Dianthus (pink), usually red, pink or white; July to September, South and West. *D. barbatus* (sweet William), various, often two-colored; May and June.

Fuchsia, white, red, pink and purple; July to frost.

Gazania, yellow or orange; June to frost.

Heliotrope, blue or white; July to frost.

Hyacinth, red, pink, white, purple, blue or yellow; March and April, except in the North.

Kochia, green or red foliage; July to frost.

Lantana, white, pink, lavender, yellow or orange; all summer.

Lobelia, blue or white; June to frost.

Mesembryanthemum, white, yellow, pink, red or purple; June to frost.

Myosotis (forget-me-not), blue, white or pink; spring.

Narcissus (including daffodils), white or yellow; spring.

Pelargonium (geranium), white, pink and red; June to frost.

Petunia, white, cream, pink, red, lavender, blue and purple; June on.

Phlox drummondii, white, pink, red or mauve; July onward.

Primula (primrose), yellow, cream, pink, red, purple and blue; spring.

Rose (floribunda varieties), white, pink and red; June to frost.

Salvia splendens, red, pink, white, purple; July to frost.

Scilla (squill), blue, white, pink or purple; spring.

Tagetes signata pumila (marigold), yellow or orange; July to frost.

Tropaeolum majus (garden nasturtium), white, yellow, orange or red; June to frost.

Tulip, various colors; April and May.

Verbena hortensis, blue, purple, pink, red or white; June to frost.

Viola, white, yellow, blue or purple;

spring. *V. tricolor hortensis* (pansy), various colors; spring.

Zinnia, white, orange, yellow, red, pink or purple; July to frost.

Shrubs for Winter

The most reliable plants for a window box in winter are small evergreen shrubs. Even these are poor in regions where the soil remains frozen for long periods, because the plants, as a result of sun and wind, lose moisture faster than the roots can replace it, and become dehydrated and die.

Among evergreens best suited for the purpose are boxwood, false cypress, English ivy, Japanese holly, junipers and yews.

CHAPTER 30

JAPANESE GARDENS

Imitative and Authentic Gardens— Achieving Perspective—"Strolling" and "Viewing" Gardens—Planning— Selecting Trees and Rocks—Suitable Plants

THE POPULARITY of Japanese gardens strongly reflects increasing interest in the unique horticultural arts of Japan. This interest is especially manifest on the West Coast, but it is gaining everywhere. The best American Japanese gardens are satisfying creations that interpret a great Oriental art in terms understandable to Occidentals. They are not merely imitative, but are selective and adaptive. Far too many of our Japanese gardens have been poorly conceived, however; they are travesties of the landscape art developed in Japan. They appear to be designed on the assumption that all that is necessary are pagodas, stone lanterns, bamboo screens and fences, arched bridges, a pool containing goldfish, and curiously shaped rocks, placed in an area that includes pines and other trees and shrubs contorted by pruning.

The first requirement of a Japanese garden is that it should closely integrate nature and the house. It must serve as a link between the natural and the man-made. Emphasis is placed on simplicity.

Stepping-stones and a water basin at the edge of the veranda are set in a bed of moss. Bamboo at right merges with bamboo sleeve fence. At center, polished black river pebbles simulate a mountainous torrent. Clipped azaleas, in foreground and along the watercourse, repeat and accent the shapes of rocks. Next to the stone lantern is a Japanese black pine, beyond the stream at right center is a maki (Podocarpus macrophylla maki) In the background, screening the weathered fence, are an evergreen oak and several camellias. A Japanese maple arches overhead, next to the veranda.

CHARACTER OF THE JAPANESE GARDEN

A whole philosophy is involved in the planning of Japanese gardens. They are intended for contemplation and meditation, as places where one may quietly appreciate and enjoy without distraction beauties of line, mass and texture in perfect relationship to each other.

Japanese gardens do not contain great collections of different kinds of plants or emphasize masses of color as do English gardens, or stress symmetry, lavishness and architectural qualities as do Italian gardens. Unlike those in America, gardens in Japan reflect few seasonal changes. Evergreens dominate the scene. Deciduous maples and azaleas may add touches of foliage color in fall; flowering cherries, Japanese iris and tree peonies, discreetly used, afford some spring bloom, but there is little else. Asymmetric balance, rather than symmetry, characterizes these gardens. There is no attempt to gain effects by repetition. Plants are not used in matched pairs, in rows or in formal beds; rocks are grouped purposefully with no bilateral symmetry.

An important point to remember about Japanese gardens is that they attempt to epitomize nature. Each represents in miniature an expanse of natural scenery, somewhat stylized and formalized and often with details suggested, rather than copied.

SCALE AND PERSPECTIVE

The mountains, hills, lakes, streams, waterfalls and seashores of Japan have inspired its traditional gardens. Scale and proportion are very important. Most Japanese gardens are created on comparatively small areas, and every effort is made to establish the illusion of space and distance. To help this, false perspectives may be realized by planting gradually smaller trees as the distance from the house or other viewing point increases. Larger rock groups may occupy the foreground; smaller ones are farther from the viewer. The nearer island in a lake may be larger than one slightly more distant and its vegetation taller. Paths and bridges are scaled to minimum usable dimensions, and such features as lanterns and pagodas are never out of proportion to their surroundings.

Similarly, the garden is made to appear vaster by the clever use of trees and shrubs that give an appearance of maturity and age, even though they are of moderate size. Such trees and shrubs are kinds that grow naturally this way or can be induced to do so by pruning. By locating brighter-colored plants toward the foreground and those of less insistence farther away, the feeling of distance is enhanced. This is true too when large, boldly leaved plants are restricted to near-to-the-viewer locations and the background planting is of finer-textured foliage. Spaciousness is further suggested by employing the horizontal lines of lakeshores, low roofs and surfaces of still water and of stretches of carefully tended sand or gravel.

TWO TYPES OF GARDENS

Japanese gardens may be "stroll" gardens or "viewing" gardens. Through the former, one walks along a path and enjoys a series of carefully planned landscape pictures from various points of vantage. The viewing garden is designed to be seen from one place only, perhaps through a window, and is often quite small.

A stroll garden may include one or more hills to represent mountains. Usually associated with the hills will be a stream or miniature lake or both, and perhaps a waterfall. A rocky island, planted with a low juniper or picturesque pine, may occupy an off-center position in the lake; sometimes two islands of varying size are used. From the chief viewing point, the hills are background to the water features. The path is contrived to lead the stroller naturally from vantage point to vantage point. Or the garden may be without hills or even water. Representations of these may be achieved by the skillful use of bold rocks and stretches of mowed turf, fine gravel, coarse sand or, possibly, "pools" or "streams" of flat, waterworn, oval or circular black stones. When gravel or sand is used, it is often raked to produce patterns—straight and placid, or swirling to suggest flowing water.

Viewing gardens are often gems. They are, in fact, three-dimensional pictures achieved with living plants and rocks and, sometimes, water, with perhaps a lantern or other artifact added. Every line, every mass, each particular texture is carefully studied and related to the whole. They are sculptured gardens, showing minimum change from season to season and with plant growth carefully controlled. The smaller the garden, the more important becomes the detail. To a perfect viewing garden nothing can be added, nor can anything be taken from it, without diminishing its effect.

PLANNING

Japanese gardens are enclosed, screened from the outside by plantings, fences or hills, but never so that these are obtrusive.

It is too much to expect that a Japanese garden designed by a Westerner, installed in North America and built of plants and materials available here, will have the same meaning and emotional significance, the same historical and religious associations for a Japanese as the gardens of his homeland. In North America, however, gardens can be based on the principles of design that the Japanese employ so effectively so that they are congruous with their surroundings and satisfying in their appeal, and not merely quaint or unusual. Japanese gardens here need not be copies of gardens in Japan; they should be Western expressions of a Japanese art.

Before beginning a Japanese garden, it is wise to read carefully one or more of the excellent books devoted to this subject and especially to study pictures of well-designed Japanese examples. So far as possible, the plants used should be native Japanese kinds, and the soil should be acid—at least slightly so. Few Japanese plants grow satisfactorily in alkaline soil. When selecting trees for the garden, remember that the Japanese like to see the trunks and branches. Careful pruning may improve a tree that is too symmetrical or too well clothed. Often more formal pruning or shearing tends to stylize azaleas and other shrubs.

SIGNIFICANCE OF ROCKS AND STONES

Although rocks are conspicuous in Japanese gardens, their use is quite different from that in Western rock gardens, where the aim is to duplicate natural rock formations as closely as possible. The rocks in a Japanese garden are considered individually as sculptural pieces, and either stand alone or are grouped for strong accents. The more rugged rocks symbolize mountains and cliffs, the rounded, waterworn boulders suggest riverbeds.

Stepping-stones arranged in a variety of interesting patterns provide charming paths that sometimes lead a stroller across water. Natural stone steps are often found on slopes. Bridges of many styles, of wood or stone, are installed only where they serve the purpose of spanning water or simulated water.

MAINTENANCE

Maintenance of a Japanese garden is largely a matter of housekeeping; it involves weeding, clearing away dead leaves, raking sand and gravel areas and keeping paths and lakes clean. There is little or no seasonal replanting. Pruning must be precise and frequent; trees and shrubs must never be permitted to grow out of bounds or out of character. Watering and disease and pest control are, of course, just as necessary in a Japanese garden as in any other.

RECOMMENDED PLANTS

Among plants best suited for Japanese gardens in North America are the following. Not all are hardy in all sections.

Evergreen Trees

Abies homolepis . . . . . Nikko fir
Abies koreana
Cedrus atlantica . . . Atlas cedar
Cedrus deodara . . . . . . deodar

Cedrus atlantica (Atlas Cedar)

Chamaecyparis obtusa . . .
              Hinoki cypress
Chamaecyparis pisifera . . .
         sawara false cypress
Cryptomeria
Cunninghamia lanceolata
Juniperus . . . . juniper
Pinus densiflora . Japanese red pine
Pinus mugo mughus . . mugho pine
Pinus parviflora . . .
         Japanese white pine
Pinus thunbergii . . .
         Japanese black pine
Sciadopitys verticillata . . .
         umbrella pine

Evergreen Shrubs

Ardisia crispa
Aucuba japonica . . . gold-dust tree
Bamboos
Camellia japonica
Camellia sasanqua
Cephalotaxus drupacea . . plum yew
Daphne odora
Euonymus japonicus
Fatsia japonica
  (syn. *Aralia sieboldii*)
Ilex crenata . . . . Japanese holly
Juniperus . . . . juniper
Laurus nobilis . . . . . sweet bay
Ligustrum japonicum . . . . privet
Ligustrum lucidum . . glossy privet
Mahonia bealii
Nandina domestica . . .
         heavenly bamboo
Osmanthus
Pieris japonica
Pittosporum tobira . . .
         Japanese pittosporum
Podocarpus
Raphiolepis umbellata . . .
         Yeddo hawthorn
Rhododendron (azalea)
Ruscus aculeatus . butcher's-broom

Deciduous Trees

Acer ginnala . . . . . Amur maple
Acer palmatum . . . Japanese maple
Acer palmatum dissectum . . .
        threadleaf Japanese maple

Cercidiphyllum japonicum . . .
                    katsura tree
Cornus kousa . . Japanese dogwood
Ginkgo biloba
Magnolia
Malus. . . . . crab apple
Prunus. . . . . . Japanese cherry
Punica granatum . . . pomegranate
Sophora japonica . . .
                    Japanese pagoda tree
Zelkova serrata

Deciduous Shrubs

Abelia grandiflora. . . glossy abelia
Acanthopanax sieboldianus . . .
                    five-leaf aralia
Berberis koreana   Korean barberry
Berberis thunbergii . . .
                    Japanese barberry
Cercis chinensis . . Chinese redbud
Chaenomeles japonica . . .
                    Japanese quince
Cotoneaster apiculata
Cotoneaster horizontalis
Enkianthus campanulatus
Enkianthus perulatus

Euonymus alatus compactus . . .
                    dwarf winged euonymus
Hamamelis japonica . . .
                    Japanese witch hazel
Hydrangea macrophylla
Paeonia suffruticosa. . . tree peony
Pyracantha . . . . firethorn
Rhododendron (azalea)
Rosa rugosa

Vines

Actinidia arguta . . bower actinidia
Akebia quinata. . . five-leaf akebia
Clematis montana rubens
Parthenocissus tricuspidata . . .
                    Boston ivy
Wisteria

Ground Covers and Perennials

Gaultheria miqueliana
Hedera helix. . . . . . English ivy
Iris kaempferi . . . . Japanese iris
Leiophyllum buxifolium
Pachysandra terminalis . . .
                    Japanese spurge
Primula japonica. Japanese primrose

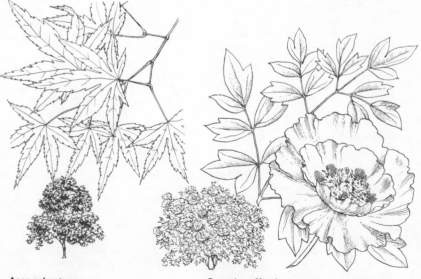

Acer palmatum
(Japanese Maple)

Paeonia suffruticosa
(Tree Peony)

CHAPTER 31

BONSAI

Achieving Sculptural Effects and the Illusion of Age—Containers—Suitable Plants—Planting—Care and Winter Protection—Repotting—Display

BONSAI are trees or shrubs grown in special containers according to certain classic forms established by the Japanese. The plants are trained to be objects of beauty, something of nature reproduced in miniature. From a few inches to two feet or more in height, they give the illusion of being fully grown and aged. The plant and the container must harmonize much as a painting and its frame.

The word "bonsai" comes from two Chinese characters, *bon* meaning "container" and *sai* meaning "to plant." The same word is used in both the singular and plural to designate the art, as well as all material grown in the bonsai style.

There are five basic styles: formal upright, informal upright, slanting, semicascading and cascading. Many substyles and combinations exist: clump, twin-trunk, multiple-trunk, sinuous, driftwood, windswept or root-over-rock. All are variations of the five classic forms.

All bonsai are sculptural, three-dimensional objects with well-defined front, back, left and right sides. When on display they are always viewed from the front, where a sparseness of foliage exposes the graceful or solid trunk line, a feature the Japanese enjoy very much. The back displays fullness, providing necessary depth.

Bonsai are created from seedlings, layerings, cuttings, nursery stock or naturally dwarfed native plants. From the beginning the tree is grown in a particular style and shaped by drastic pruning and wiring. Refinements in form—again by pruning and wiring—are continued throughout the life of the plant, although a well-proportioned, twiggy tree will develop in a few years' time.

TRADITIONAL STYLING

The creation of bonsai follows certain rules of design that dictate the final composition. They have been worked out and refined by the Japanese for generations. The component parts of a finished bonsai are container, surface roots, trunk, branches, twigs and leaves. The trunk is the focal point and is proportioned into three approximately equal parts. The bottom third is completely bare of branches; the middle is free of branches in the front but framed by branches at the sides and in the back. The top third shows branches on all four sides.

The branches of a bonsai are arranged in sets of three. Number one branch of the first triad is the lowest of the tree; it is trained to one side and slightly forward. Number two is slightly higher on the trunk; it is inclined to the opposite direction. Number three is often situated between the first two and extends to the back. This patterning is repeated up the trunk in spiraling groups of three. When the top third is reached, small branches are trained forward to cover the trunk. Limbs are always designed in an alternating pattern to avoid monotony. These principles are basic to good design; the beginner in bonsai should strive to follow them, but nature is not always accommodating and compromises often must be made.

THE ILLUSION OF AGE

Creating the illusion of age is one of the important aspects of bonsai. The shape of the trunk contributes to an aged look, and surface roots add to venerable appearance. They should radiate around the trunk on all sides, making a solid base on which the tree is supported.

Branch shape must also suggest an old tree. The limbs taper from the trunk slowly out to the end—a network of fine twigs. If the leaves or the needles on these twigs are too large, the illusion is lost. Trees grown as bonsai should have small leaves or needles which are in proportion to the trunk and branches. Large-leaved species with pleasing twig patterns are frequently grown for winter viewing, after the leaves have fallen. The overall composition, in any case, must suggest a large tree reproduced on a miniature scale.

CONTAINERS

The container is always selected to complement the mood and color of the bonsai. It must help to present the tree and never detract from it.

There are traditional colors that are used with certain species. Muted earth colors such as darker reds, browns and grays are used with evergreens, white or off-white with trees that have red or yellow flowers and fruits. Blue and green serve for plants with brilliant fall foliage. Black is used for trees with white flowers, white berries or variegated foliage.

Usually the individual bonsai dictates the shape of its container, although there are some general classic rules. Light, feathery plants are often planted in ornate glazed containers

that are decorated with designs of flowers and birds. Formal upright bonsai are planted in flat rectangular or oval pots, but heavy-trunked trees, particularly if they have thick foliage, appear to best advantage in bulky, deep, unglazed containers, which give them a stable, settled look. Deep round, octagonal or square pots enhance the beauty of semicascading or cascading bonsai (and in this style the tree is always planted exactly in the center of the container). Shallow round or oval containers lend an informal feeling to windswept bonsai or group plantings.

SUITABLE PLANTS

A few of the plants commonly used for bonsai are pine, spruce, juniper, maple, hornbeam, flowering quince and azalea. Some evergreen varieties are most frequently grown because their small leaves or needles are in proportion to the trunk and branches of a bonsai, and because they can be viewed throughout the year, at times when other specimens are not at their best. However, many deciduous species are grown for their flowers, fruits or fall foliage.

OBTAINING PLANT MATERIAL

Bonsai may be created from any woody or semiwoody plant, and there are several ways to obtain good material. Plants may be propagated from seed or cuttings, by layering or any other technique, or they can be found already grown in nurseries or in the woods. The selection of material is important. Many people believe that they must wait 20 or 30 years before they have a finished bonsai, but with the proper selection of material, a good bonsai can be created in a few hours.

Growing bonsai from seed is a lengthy proposition, although frequently it is the only way to include

1. Pinus parviflora pentaphylla
(Japanese White Pine)
The five-needle pine shown here is trained
in the semicascading style. Its trunk grows
straight up from the soil and then turns
downward; its lowest tip reaches below
the rim of the container.

2. Acer buergerianum (Trident Maple)
A curved trunk and slightly bent top
identify the informal upright style of
this bonsai.

3. Pinus thunbergii
(Japanese Black Pine)
In the formal upright style: the
trunk is straight and the top erect.

4. Pinus parviflora pentaphylla
(Japanese White Pine)
Cascading style: the trunk grows straight up
from the soil, then turns downward, and the
lowest tip reaches 1 ft. or more below the
container.

5. Picea glehnii (Saghalin Spruce)
The slanting style is distinguished by the
trunk tipped or curved toward either the left
or right, with the lowest branch spread in
the opposite direction to the main trunk.
The top is bent slightly forward.

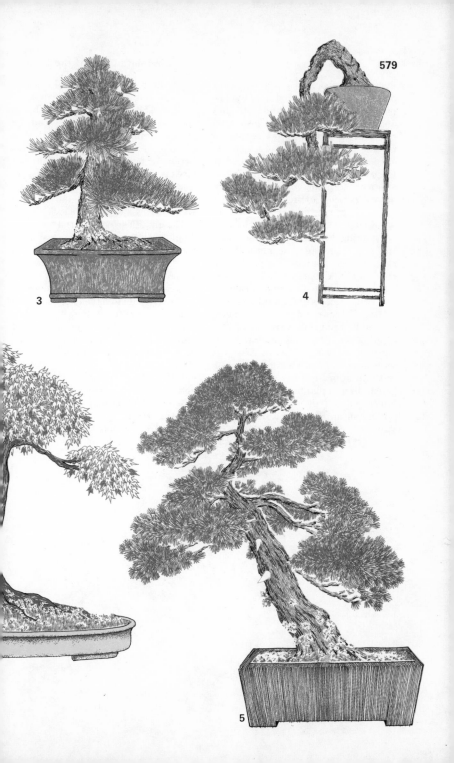

3

4 579

5

uncommon specimens in a collection. Seedlings are transferred to individual pots or to the open ground until they are fit for training. Seeds grown directly in the ground produce quicker results, but are less convenient to shape. Cuttings are also handled in the usual way, as nurseries propagate ornamental plant material. Once it has roots, the cutting is placed in a pot, and training is started when the material is woody enough for shaping.

Layering has one advantage that the other propagating methods do not: you can start with a well-developed tree in a short time. The rooted material will have the trunk, branches and twigs necessary for a fully formed bonsai. There are several simple methods of layering, all variants of two types, ground layering and air layering (see pages 714 to 716). After the roots have formed, the rooted portion of the tree or shrub is severed from its parent and planted in its own container, where it is grown just as any other bonsai. Training can begin as soon as the plant is established.

However, the most expedient way to obtain material for bonsai is in the form of nursery stock. The plant is fully established with a good fibrous root system, and training can be started immediately. Material that has been nursery-grown in cans is superior for bonsai, since the plant has already become conditioned to its reduced environment, and the procedures of root trimming and training will not cause excessive shock.

Natural dwarfed material collected from fields, mountains and seashore is excellent for bonsai. Weather and wind have already given the specimen some "training," frequently in remarkable shapes. However, collected material tends to have poor roots and must be replanted in the ground for a year or two until a fine network of roots develops. Then it may be planted in the container and trained.

INITIAL SHAPING AND TRAINING

Select a specimen which has inherent possibilities of becoming a fine bonsai. Set the tree at eye level and turn it slowly around, looking thoughtfully at all sides to determine which parts

1. Balled, burlapped dormant tree

2. Surface roots exposed

3. Drastic pruning eliminating opposite branches

4. Wiring branches for shaping

5. Root pruning

to train for the front, the back, the left and right sides. Now inspect the roots; take a blunt tool and dig away some of the soil to expose the large, heavy roots near the base of the trunk. They should be of good size and widely spread. After the roots have been exposed, the style can be settled upon and training can begin.

The traditional arrangement of branches is achieved by drastic pruning and wiring. Remove excess branches; shorten long ones. Then wind annealed copper wire around the trunk and branches, starting at the bottom of the tree with heavy wire and continuing out to the twig ends with lighter gauges. As the wire is applied, gently bend the trunk, branches and twigs into position. Bending the wire hardens it so that it keeps the branches in place. Select the size of wire according to the thickness of the trunk or branch. Leave it on the tree from six months to a year. If the tree grows quickly, remove the wires before they scar the bark, and then rewire. After six months or so, the woody portions of the branches will retain

their shape and the wire can be removed. Wiring is repeated as branches grow out and need shaping.

PLANTING

After the initial pruning and shaping, the tree is ready for planting in its container, which has been selected carefully to frame it. The drainage holes in the bottom of the pot are covered with plastic screen to prevent the soil from falling through. But before the soil is put in, several lengths of copper wire are looped U-shape through the drainage holes with both ends sticking up in the pot. They will eventually hold the plant in its place in the container. If the pot is small and has only one hole, the wire can be looped around a stick slightly larger than the hole. Then the bottom is covered to a shallow depth with very coarse sifted soil to provide good drainage. The main potting soil, which is also sifted, is spread over this— and the container is ready for the tree.

Root pruning is necessary to compensate for the drastic pruning in the upper parts of the plant and to en-

3

4

5

courage growth of fine, fibrous roots. Remove one third of the old soil from the root ball with a blunt tool. Cut back the long, loose roots, but retain fine rootlets that grow out of large roots near the trunk; they will sustain the plant while the new roots form.

Place the tree in its container, and settle it into place with a twisting motion. Pull the wire around the root ball, and twist it tight until the tree is held firmly in position. Cut off excess wire, and push the ends into the soil. Now fill in potting soil around the ball of roots so that no air spaces are left. After the potting soil has settled, brush away any excess and sprinkle sifted topsoil over the surface.

A cover of moss is grown on the topsoil to imitate nature and make the tree look more aged; it also prevents the soil in the container from being washed out during watering. Fresh, wet mosses and lichens give the grower the chance to arrange a natural underplanting with different shades and textures which enhance the composition. However, dried, powdered moss can also be sprinkled on and pressed down with a small trowel.

Now that the tree has been planted, it should be watered by placing the container in a basin and spraying from the top with a fine syringe. Be sure that enough water is given so that it flows from the drainage holes. The bonsai should be placed in a protected spot away from wind and strong sun for a period of three weeks until new growth begins to appear. The tree may then be placed in the sunshine and treated as any other.

ROUTINE CARE

Throughout its life, a bonsai needs special attention—at times, daily care—and it cannot be overlooked if the tree is to remain healthy and grow steadily more beautiful. A prime need is for fresh air and sunshine, which can best be supplied in the open. Bonsai are usually kept outdoors on tables. This affords free flow of air through the branches and facilitates watering, pruning and insect control.

Periodic pruning and trimming are extremely important, for treated otherwise, a bonsai quickly loses its shape, and there will be no chance to develop an intricate network of

1. Prepared container with plastic screen

2. Placement of tree fastened by copper wires

3. Poking in the potting soil

4. Planting moss on surface

5. Spray watering

1   2

branches. New growth on all bonsai is constantly trimmed. Deciduous trees have their new branchlets shortened, and in some species leaves are cut off healthy trees to promote branching and induce a new set of smaller leaves. Conifers may have their new shoots pinched back so that only four or five needles are left at the base.

A bonsai must be watered daily in spring and fall unless enough rain has fallen to take care of its needs, and in very dry and windy weather it may need water twice or three times a day. The tree should never dry out completely, as the damage caused may result in loss of the plant.

There are several ways to water. If the owner has the time, he can use a watering can with a fine nozzle, watering each tree in turn; but a garden hose with a fine spray attachment is easier. In either case, the plant should be checked to see that an excess of water drains out the bottom hole, indicating that the soil has absorbed a sufficient amount.

Bonsai must be fertilized to keep them healthy. The tree needs good foliage color, well-formed flowers or fruits and an intricate network of healthy branches. The easiest fertilizers to use are the water-soluble chemical compounds that contain trace elements. These are diluted by about half the strength recommended for plants grown more conventionally, because excessive feeding will encourage the growth of extra-long shoots which spoil the bonsai's shape. Deciduous and flowering trees are fertilized once a week from early spring to late summer, evergreens for three weeks in spring after their new needles have hardened and for three weeks in the early fall before dormancy.

Bonsai are subject to the same pests and diseases as larger trees and shrubs. Because of their diminished surroundings, it is even more necessary to keep them in top condition, healthy and free from pests. They should be inspected frequently. Spray with insecticide at any sign of infestation.

WINTER PROTECTION

In areas where winters are severe, bonsai need protection not from the cold so much as from high winds that cause the plants to die from parching.

4   5

The best way to winter them over is in a deep cold frame where they are protected from the wind, alternate freezing and thawing, soil-eroding rains, snow that may crack and break branches, and chewing rodents. The temperature remains fairly constant within a cold frame; if the trees go into shelter well watered, they should pass the winter in good condition.

If a cold frame is not available, the bonsai can be wintered in the ground. The pots are dug into the soil up to their rims, mulch is piled about halfway up the trunk, and a packing case is placed over the entire plant. This solution is particularly helpful to owners of only a few trees.

Frost-free structures adjacent to a heated dwelling, such as a porch or a lean-to plastic greenhouse, can be used if there is a window that can be opened to give heat in the coldest weather. The trees should be checked regularly for dryness and watered when necessary on days when the temperature is above freezing for several hours.

REPOTTING

Since a bonsai remains in a container for life, soil becomes a very important matter; the potted tree cannot extend its roots and find moisture or food like a tree grown in the ground. The roots do continue to grow, but they eventually become bound and can no longer absorb moisture or the nutrients that are needed for healthy growth. As a result, bonsai must be repotted whenever they become rootbound. Evergreens, since they are slow-growing in general, can be left in their containers for three to five years. Most deciduous trees need repotting each year or two. Willows and other rapid growers may have to be repotted twice a year. Early spring, when the tree comes out of its dormant period, is the best time for repotting. The tree is taken out of its container and, before re-

planting in new soil, one third of the old soil and roots is eliminated. In this way the trees are kept healthy.

The basic ingredients for bonsai soil are subsoil, sand, gravel, garden loam, leaf mold, compost and peat moss. They are sun-dried, sieved into various sizes and stored until use.

Subsoil is clay pellets, which are obtained by digging some 3 ft. below the soil surface. When first dug, the material is usually crumbly and not sticky. Dried into hard lumps, it is a basic ingredient of potting soil. Coarse sand or gravel is necessary for good drainage and root formation. Local gravel pits or construction companies are the usual sources. Leaf mold, compost or peat moss give acidity and nutrients. They are used in the proportions that each species requires. Garden loam is used with flowering and fruiting deciduous trees.

The bottom soil is made up of the larger lumps of clay, some leaf mold—each particle $\frac{1}{4}$ in. to $\frac{1}{2}$ in. wide—and some coarse sand. The main potting soil is made up of the same ingredients, with each particle about $\frac{1}{8}$ in. For topsoil, screen the basic mixture to obtain grains the size of table salt.

DISPLAY

Usually bonsai are brought inside only for display. Since they are viewed from the front and at eye level, they must be placed on a stand, shelf or table. The background should be light, plain muted color without design. Companion pieces such as stones, small containers of grasses, or lacquer boxes may be added to the display. A scroll is frequently hung behind the bonsai and to one side. But other objects are incidental to the tree; they must not be distracting. The display should communicate to the viewer a serene feeling of nature in miniature.

PART V

Regional Gardening

In New York a European ash will become a tall tree, but in Manitoba it will develop into a bushy shrub. Climate alone can account for such a difference. From Canada to Texas, the range of climates and soils, altitudes and exposures has an astonishing effect on plant life.

Five regions that differ from the great temperate territory of the United States are separately described in Part V: the northeast–north central states and adjacent Canada; the seaboard from Florida to Texas; southern California and the desert interior; the Rocky Mountain region; and the Pacific Northwest and British Columbia. These chapters deal largely with their special plants and the particular methods of cultivating them.

The regional boundaries are only approximate; one merges with the next. And within a general region, the growing conditions may also vary greatly. The western coastal strip contrasts with the interior valleys a few miles away; in the high "islands" of the Rockies, above 6000 feet, soils and temperatures are different from the plateaus and valleys below.

The home gardener in any of the five special regions can choose knowledgeably from among the plants suited to his locale, adapt his methods to his environment and deal imaginatively with its extremes—frigid north or salty seaside, desert or humid swampland.

CHAPTER 32

THE NORTHEAST-
NORTH CENTRAL REGION
and Adjacent Canada

*Gardening in the Northern Style—
Regional Variations—Areas of Hardi-
ness—Recommended Plants—Soils—
Planting and Sowing—Propagation—
Pruning—Wintering Woody Plants*

THE FARTHER north one goes from the favorable temperate region of the United States, the greater becomes the challenge in growing plants. This may diminish the number of gardeners, but it does not lessen their enthusiasm.

During the last two decades, in the North as elsewhere, more people than ever before have been able to purchase new homes. Landscaping the grounds has become a standard practice. Now, with the help of mechanized equipment, homeowners do their own maintenance work and frequently their own landscaping as well. The great advances made recently in the development of garden chemicals and equipment, coupled with an increased flow of good, informative literature, have made it possible to create gardens with less arduous labor and with a minimum of experience.

NORTHERN GARDENS

Until fairly recently, most North Americans copied the garden styles which their ancestors brought from Europe. We inherited the English love of growing flowers, the Scottish tendency to austerity and restraint, the French love of ornate detail; we gradually added to these a modern American and Canadian flair for showmanship, but no native style developed.

However, a distinctive northern garden style has begun to emerge. The front yard open to the street, suggesting a warm, neighborly quality, is a typical feature in towns and villages everywhere in America. A uniform planting of trees which provide shade on hot summer days is another attractive sight in suburban areas. Because the northern region is frequently snowbound, sometimes for weeks on end, special efforts must be made to condition plants to withstand the long cold siege from November to April, and then to help them shake off winter's icy grip.

In these snowbound areas, where deciduous trees and shrubs are bare of foliage for half the year and lawns become blankets of snow, numerous evergreens relieve the monotony of winter white. Where shelter from wind is imperative, enclosure by a hardy hedge or a fence is necessary for urban gardens; for rural homes a windbreak of two or three rows of hardy trees affords needed protection.

The idea of using the garden as an outdoor extension of living quarters has at last caught the imagination of gardeners in the North. Consequently, space is now designed to be used to its fullest advantage during the five months of the year when weather permits people to enjoy outdoor living in comfort.

General garden practices, such as soil management, planting and pruning, do not differ materially from those discussed in Part VI, "The Wonders of Plant Growing."

WINTER HARDINESS

Climate is the greatest limiting factor in the development of northern gardens. It not only determines what plants can be grown, depending upon their winter hardiness, but to a considerable extent the forms they will take and consequently their uses in the landscape. A European mountain ash, for example, will form a fairly open medium-sized tree in Ithaca, N.Y., but will develop as a large, compact shrub in Winnipeg, Manitoba. A Norway spruce will form a tall, graceful open pyramid where rain is plentiful and the site protected from wind; on the exposed seacoast or open prairie it grows as a compact, broad cone.

The hardiness of plants is not governed by temperature alone. Plant tissues are killed through desiccation by wind just as often as they are fractured by the expansive action of extreme cold, which makes ice crystals form between the cells from the moisture extracted from them.

Morden, Manitoba, experiences considerably lower temperatures than Ottawa, Ontario, yet *Philadelphus* (mock orange), *Prinsepia* and *Weigela* have often survived in the former place during winters when they were killed back in the latter. This was probably because warm, wet fall weather at Ottawa did not permit as thorough ripening of the wood as did the dry, cold fall at Morden.

Coniferous trees are unpredictable. Damage is usually caused by the desiccation of foliage and buds by wind and sunshine at times when low soil temperatures have reduced the ability of roots to absorb moisture. Often bad "burning" of foliage occurs on native species during mild, sunny winters, or when the plants are placed near a south- or west-facing light-colored wall.

There are so many variations in conditions that it is well for new gardeners to consult the nearest horticultural experiment station, garden club, or other source of local information to familiarize themselves with the kinds of plants which have succeeded in their locality.

REGIONAL VARIATIONS

The region discussed here is extremely varied in topography, soil and climate, particularly from east to west, where it covers approximately 1800 miles—from the Atlantic coasts of Nova Scotia and Maine to the prairies of the Dakotas. From north to south, it is about 300 miles wide, centering more or less on the international boundary east of the Great Lakes and extending north of Lake Ontario and Lake Erie.

Most of this region was glaciated. The Atlantic coast is rugged, with patches of thin, sandy, acid soil. But gardens will flourish where rivers have transported good soil from the hills to create rich valleys, such as those in southern New Hampshire, Vermont and New Brunswick. The valley of the Annapolis River in Nova Scotia is a rich garden spot.

In Maine and across the border in New Brunswick, huge crops of the best seed potatoes are grown. In eastern Quebec, there are large areas of muck soil on which vegetables grow to perfection. Ideal orchard land can be found near the foothills of the mountain ranges of New Hampshire, Vermont and northeastern New York.

588

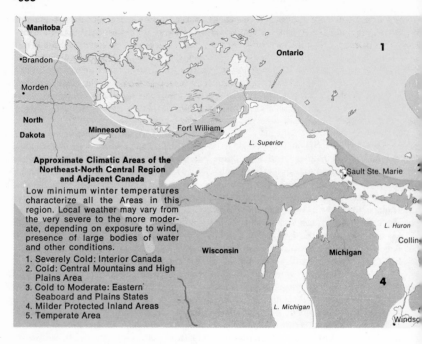

Manitoba

•Brandon

Ontario

1

Morden
•

North
Dakota   Minnesota   Fort William.

L. Superior

**Approximate Climatic Areas of the
Northeast-North Central Region
and Adjacent Canada**

Low minimum winter temperatures
characterize all the Areas in this
region. Local weather may vary from
the very severe to the more moderate, depending on exposure to wind,
presence of large bodies of water
and other conditions.

Sault Ste. Marie   2

Ge

L. Huron

Collin

Wisconsin   Michigan

1. Severely Cold: Interior Canada
2. Cold: Central Mountains and High
    Plains Area
3. Cold to Moderate: Eastern
    Seaboard and Plains States
4. Milder Protected Inland Areas
5. Temperate Area

4

L. Michigan

Windso

Except for the river valleys, the soils of eastern Ontario between the St. Lawrence and Ottawa rivers are unfavorable for gardening.

The Golden Triangle, from the southern end of the Georgian Bay of Lake Huron across to Toronto and down to Windsor (opposite Detroit), has the greatest concentration of population, industrial wealth and gardens in Canada. Here is rich, un-dulating farmland with a variety of good soils. For the most part, it has the mildest climate in eastern Canada.

The Central Area extends westward through unfavorable lands along the north shore of Lake Huron, through Michigan's Upper Peninsula, across Wisconsin and Minnesota to the rich prairie of the Red River Valley in North Dakota. This black prairie soil, a legacy from Lake Agassiz, which ex-isted 10,000 years ago, holds the agri-

cultural wealth of North Dakota and southern Manitoba.

AREAS OF HARDINESS

The Area map of the Northeast and North Central region generally di-vides this section into Areas which in-dicate the general hardiness of plants in the lists that follow. It is based on the Plant Hardiness Zone Map of the United States Department of Agri-culture. Such a map is only of limited help. Within the Areas there are vari-ations in temperature caused by ele-vation, air currents or proximity to large bodies of water. A garden on an exposed hillside where high winds sweep away snow and dry out twigs will probably suffer as much as one in a colder zone. A gardener in a cold Area who has a sheltered spot near a large lake will feel that the map does not represent his climate or the plants

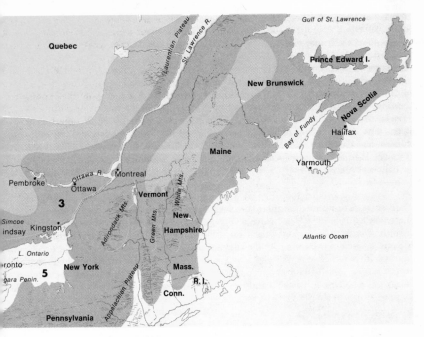

he can grow. In all the lists of suitable plants for the territory under discussion, the Area number will be given to indicate comparative hardiness.

Area 1

Lying almost entirely in Canada, this Area covers all of Quebec except the eastern coastal strip—which varies from 50 to 150 miles wide—and an interior zone where the temperature drops to −50° F. and below. All of Ontario is included except for the southeast and very thin strips along Lake Huron and Lake Superior. Plants that endure the minimum temperatures of −40° to −50° F. of Area 1 are listed on page 590.

Area 2

The northern part of Minnesota, all of Manitoba, most of North Dakota, the highlands of Maine, New Hampshire,

Vermont, New Brunswick and Quebec, where gardening is least likely to flourish, are included. All have temperatures of −30° to −40° F. at times.

Area 3

Here, where the average minimum temperature is between −20° and −30° F., the Area forms a strip of varying width along the shores of the Gulf of St. Lawrence, northern Newfoundland and New Brunswick. It extends into New England and northeastern New York and continues along the shores of the Georgian Bay to Lake Superior. Much of Wisconsin (except the west shore of Lake Michigan), the southern half of Minnesota and all of South Dakota are in this Area.

Area 4

The minimum temperature in winter is between −10° and −20° F. This

Area comprises the protected southern corners of Newfoundland, most of Nova Scotia, Prince Edward Island, the Bay of Fundy shore of New Brunswick, plus Maine, southern New Hampshire and southern Vermont, as well as a small portion around Montreal. It skirts northeastern New York, runs westward across central Ontario's Golden Triangle and includes the eastern tip of Michigan's Upper Peninsula and eastern and southern Wisconsin.

Area 5

The average minimum temperature is between –10° and 0° F. in Area 5. Mainly made up of small sheltered districts such as Halifax and Yarmouth in Nova Scotia, it runs along the Niagara Peninsula and the north shore of Lake Erie in Ontario and continues west into the temperate region.

HARDY PLANTS FOR NORTHERN GARDENS

The variety of trees, shrubs, vines and ground covers adapted for growing in Areas 1 and 2 is much more limited than those that can be grown in milder climates. Below are listed selections of the best plants for the coldest zones. Gardeners in the more favorable climatic areas of this region may confidently choose plants from the following chapters in this book: "Shade Trees," page 368; "Evergreen Trees," page 388; "Shrubs and Flowering Small Trees," page 409; "Evergreen Shrubs," page 449; "Hedges," page 473; "Ground Covers," page 484; "Vines," page 492; "Seaside Gardens," page 547.

Deciduous Trees
Hardy into Area 1

Acer negundo . . . . . . box elder
Betula papyrifera . . . paper birch
Salix alba . . . . . . white willow
Salix pentandra . . . laurel willow

Hardy into Area 2

Acer saccharinum . . . silver maple
Acer tataricum . . Tartarian maple
Betula pendula . . .
       European white birch
Celtis occidentalis . . . . hackberry
Crataegus crus-galli . cockspur thorn
Elaeagnus angustifolia . . .
       Russian olive
Fraxinus pennsylvanica lanceolata
       . . . green ash
Juglans mandschurica . . .
       Manchurian walnut
Larix decidua . . . European larch
Malus floribunda . . . . crab apple
Malus sylvestris . . . . apple
Populus alba . . . . . white poplar
Prunus maackii . Amur chokecherry
Prunus padus . . .
       European bird cherry
Quercus macrocarpa . . . burr oak
Salix alba chermesina . .
       red-stem willow
Sorbus americana . . .
       American mountain ash
Sorbus aucuparia . . .
       European mountain ash
Syringa amurensis japonica . . .
       Japanese lilac
Tilia americana . . American linden
Ulmus americana . . American elm
Ulmus parvifolia . . . Chinese elm

Deciduous Shrubs

The taller shrubs listed below, such as *Amelanchier grandiflora* (serviceberry), *Caragana arborescens* (Siberian pea tree) and *Syringa amurensis japonica* (Japanese lilac), are useful for boundary plantings in fairly large gardens and as occasional lawn specimens. In the northwestern part of the area, these shrubs do not grow as tall as in the East, but many are very useful as windscreens. Shrubs of medium height or lower are especially well adapted for small gardens.

Hardy into Area 1

Amorpha canescens . . . lead plant

Malus floribunda
(Crab Apple)

Caragana arborescens . . .
　　　　　Siberian pea tree
Caragana pygmaea . . . . pea tree
Cornus alba sibirica . . .
　　　　　Siberian dogwood
Cotoneaster adpressa
Cotoneaster horizontalis
Halimodendron halodendron . . . .
　　　　　salt tree
Hydrangea arborescens grandiflora
　　　　. . . hills-of-snow
Lonicera morrowii . . .
　　　　　bush honeysuckle
Prunus tenella. . .
　　　　dwarf Russian almond
Rosa acicularis. . . . . rose
Rosa blanda . . . . rose
Shepherdia argentea . . .
　　　　　buffalo berry
Symphoricarpus albus . . .
　　　　　snowberry

Betula pendula
(European White Birch)

Cotoneaster horizontalis
(Cotoneaster)

Viburnum trilobum . . .

cranberry bush

Hardy into Area 2
Acanthopanax sieboldianus . . .

five-leaf aralia
Amelanchier alnifolia. . .

serviceberry
Amelanchier grandiflora . . .

serviceberry
Amorpha fruticosa . . .

bastard indigo
Berberis koreana . . . . . barberry
Caragana frutex . . . . . pea tree
Cotoneaster acutifolia
Cotoneaster integerrima
Daphne mezereum . . . . mezereon
Euonymus alatus . . .

winged-bark euonymus
Euonymus alatus compactus . . .

dwarf winged-bark euonymus
Euonymus nanus
Forsythia ovata
Genista tinctoria . . .

dyer's greenweed
Hydrangea paniculata grandiflora. . .

peegee hydrangea

Lonicera maackii . . .

bush honeysuckle
Lonicera spinosa albertii . . .

bush honeysuckle
Lonicera tatarica. . .

Tartarian honeysuckle
Malus sylvestris . . . . apple
Physocarpus opulifolius . . ninebark
Prunus cistena . . .

purpleleaf sand cherry
Rosa harisonii. . .

Harison's yellow rose
Rosa rubrifolia . . . . . shrub rose
Rosa rugosa . . . . rose
Sambucus nigra . . .

European elderberry
Sambucus nigra aurea . . .

golden European elderberry
Sambucus racemosa . . .

European red elderberry
Spiraea arguta . . . . . . spirea
Spiraea billiardii . . . . . . spirea
Spiraea bumalda Anthony Waterer

. . . spirea
Spiraea media . . . . . . spirea
Spiraea trichocarpa . . .

Korean bridal wreath
Syringa amurensis japonica . . .

Japanese lilac

Daphne mezereum
(Mezereon)

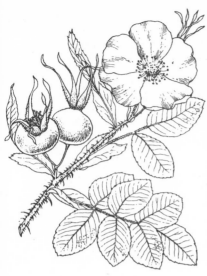

Rosa rugosa

Syringa microphylla . . . . . lilac
Syringa prestoniae . . . . . . lilac
Syringa vulgaris . . . common lilac

Coniferous Trees and Shrubs

Conifers provide the chief and indeed almost the only winter greenery in northern gardens. They are excellent for various landscape purposes. Very tall conifers form remarkably good windbreaks when planted in masses or in solid rows. They are also attractive as single specimens or as groupings in large parks and estates. None of the tall kinds is suitable for small gardens. However, somewhat lower-growing coniferous trees, such as *Abies lasiocarpa* (alpine fir), *Picea pungens kosteriana* (Koster's blue spruce), *Pinus banksiana* (jack pine) and *Tsuga canadensis* (Eastern hemlock), would be appropriate in small gardens in the drier western sections. The still lower-growing *Pinus cembra* (Swiss stone pine) and *P. mugo mughus* (mugho pine), *Picea glauca densata* (Black Hills spruce), *P. abies*

ohlendorffii (Norway spruce, variety), *Thuja occidentalis robusta* (American arborvitae, variety) and various *Juniperus* (juniper) would also prove satisfactory in small gardens in this section.

Ultimate height, of course, depends largely on the locality. As with deciduous trees, height is governed by the amount of precipitation, length of growing season and exposure to wind. A Norway spruce in the East, where rain is plentiful and winds moderate, will grow more than twice as tall as one in the dry, windswept western extremity of this region.

Hardy into Area 1
Picea abies . . . . Norway spruce
Picea glauca . . . . . white spruce
Picea glauca densata . . .
                        Black Hills spruce
Picea pungens glauca . . .
                        Colorado blue spruce
Picea pungens kosteriana . . .
                        Koster's blue spruce
Pinus sylvestris . . . . . Scots pine

Hardy into Area 2
Abies lasiocarpa . . . . . alpine fir
Juniperus horizontalis douglasii
      ' . . . Waukegan juniper
Juniperus horizontalis plumosa
                . . . Andorra juniper
Juniperus sabina tamariscifolia
                . . . juniper
Juniperus sabina Von Ehron . . .
                        juniper
Larix decidua . . .
                        European larch
Picea abies dumosa . . .
              Norway spruce, variety
Picea abies maxwellii . . .
              Norway spruce, variety
Picea abies ohlendorffii . . .
              Norway spruce, variety
Picea glauca conica. . .
              white spruce, variety
Pinus banksiana. . . . . jack pine
Pinus cembra . . . Swiss stone pine

Pinus mugo . . Swiss mountain pine
Pinus mugo mughus . . mugho pine
Pinus resinosa . . . . . . red pine
Pinus strobus . . . . . white pine
Tsuga canadensis . Eastern hemlock
Thuja occidentalis robusta . . .
American arborvitae, variety

Broad-Leaved Evergreens

The most useful plants of this class are all listed here as ground covers because no foliage will survive and remain green above the snow line except in Area 5. *Buxus microphylla koreana* (Korean boxwood) and *Mahonia aquifolium* (holly mahonia) are sufficiently tough for their wood to survive in Area 3, but their foliage burns badly. In Area 4, *Ilex crenata* (Japanese holly) survives.

Hardy into Area 3
Buxus microphylla koreana . . .
Korean boxwood
Mahonia aquifolium . holly mahonia

Hardy into Area 4
Ilex crenata . . . . . Japanese holly

Vines

Vines are useful for covering walls, fences and other supports. As screens for privacy, they also form gentle windbreaks.

Hardy into Area 2
Clematis ligusticifolia
Clematis serratifolia
Clematis tangutica . golden clematis
Lonicera sempervirens . . .
trumpet honeysuckle
Parthenocissus quinquefolia . . .
Virginia creeper
Parthenocissus quinquefolia engelmannii . Virginia creeper, variety
Vitis vulpina . . . . . frost grape

Hedges

For people who cherish privacy, hedges serve as excellent walls against

Clematis

the outside. They also partition one unit of a garden from another. As backgrounds for bright displays of color, they are ideal. Of course, hedges must be composed of species which are sufficiently hardy to withstand winter temperatures as well as the frequent clipping. The following species have proved most successful.

Hardy into Area 2
Acer ginnala . . . . . Amur maple
Caragana arborescens . . .
Siberian pea tree
Caragana pygmaea . . . . pea tree
Cornus stolonifera . . . .
red-osier dogwood
Cotoneaster acutifolia
Cotoneaster integerrima
Crataegus crus-galli . cockspur thorn
Euonymus nanus
Lonicera tatarica . . .
Tartarian honeysuckle
Picea glauca . . . . . white spruce
Pinus cembra . . . Swiss stone pine
Prunus fruticosa . . .
European dwarf cherry
Ribes alpinum . . mountain currant
Salix alba chermesina . . .
red-stem willow
Spiraea bumalda Anthony Waterer
. . . spirea
Syringa josikaea . . Hungarian lilac
Syringa vulgaris . . . common lilac
Ulmus parvifolia . . . Chinese elm

Ground Covers

Some low-growing shrubs or woody trailers form a sufficiently dense growth to hold the earth on a slope, or they develop into a thick mat in a shady spot where maintenance of turf is difficult. They are also grown in low masses as contrasting texture to turf and to lend interest to garden design.

Where snow coverage is uncertain, ground covers should be protected with evergreen branches or similar material in winter.

Hardy into Area 2
Arctostaphylos uva-ursi. . bearberry
Clematis alpina . . . blue clematis
Cotoneaster adpressa
Genista pilosa . . . prostrate broom
Juniperus horizontalis douglasii. . .
Waukegan juniper
Juniperus horizontalis plumosa . . .
Andorra juniper
Mitchella repens . . . partridgeberry

SOILS OF THE NORTH

Open, crumbly soil is a requirement for any garden. Winter can be used as an ally in improving a stiff clay. The freezing and thawing of the moisture in the soil has a shearing effect that does much to create a desirable granular, open texture. Therefore manure or other organic material should be dug into the soil in fall, and the surface left in a loosened state so that the maximum benefit from winter freezing and thawing is obtained.

Although the surface of the soil may be frozen and covered by snow so that one would think all root growing had ceased, this is not so. The deeper the snow, the warmer the soil remains. Roots continue to grow as long as the temperature remains above 35° F., and, although greatly reduced, bacterial action also continues. Because of this, the application in the fall of manure and of slow-acting fertilizers such as bone meal is good preparation for spring.

Applying quick-acting fertilizers in the fall is almost a total waste because the soluble salts are leached away before the roots can use much of them. A September application of fertilizer to lawns is an exception. Fertilizer applied to woody plants such as roses and fruit trees after the middle of July may render the plants more subject to winter injury by encouraging late growth of wood that will not be properly ripened before the onset of cold weather.

The farther north one goes, the shorter the period of bacterial activity in the soil, and consequently the longer it takes for organic matter to decompose. Thus, it takes compost heaps longer to produce a good product in the North than in more southern gardens. The use of an accelerator compound, available from garden-supply firms, stimulates bacterial activity and makes possible more rapid compost production.

In spring, the sunshine often appears deceptively hot before the earth has warmed sufficiently to encourage enough bacterial action to release soil nutrients necessary to give plants a needed boost. The use of an immediately available fertilizer such as 20-20-20, at 2 oz. of fertilizer to 5 gal. of water, about May 1 and again three weeks later, is beneficial.

PLANTING AND SOWING

Rose growers in Areas 4 and 5 stoutly uphold the advantages of fall planting; most growers in Area 3 prefer spring. In the northeastern region, the spring season is very short. There is not much time between the dates when frost disappears from the ground and summer heat sets in. If plants and labor are available for planting in the short spring, good results are obtained. Experience at Ottawa has shown 10 percent fewer casualties with spring planting than with fall planting. The danger lies in procrastination. Planting in late spring exposes the plants to blazing sun before the roots are established. Late fall planting, on the other hand, prevents plants from establishing good root systems because of the heaving of soil when it freezes.

The fall planting season is usually longer than the spring season, and there is not the same rush of other work to be done. Besides, October weather is usually more pleasant than is April's. We might sum up by saying that in the North, fall planting is more convenient for the gardener, and early spring planting is better for the plants.

Plants, of course, vary in their responses. Daphne, forsythia and lilac start to grow so early in spring that it is better to plant them in fall. Sorbus (mountain ash) and apple trees seem to transplant most readily when just coming into leaf, if they are well watered afterward. Birch, poplar and willow, all thin-barked trees, respond best when moved in spring.

Herbaceous perennials which bloom early usually establish themselves better when moved in September, while those which bloom after midsummer are better moved in spring. Most of the midseason bloomers can be moved either in spring or fall. For some, there are particularly appropriate times, such as iris in late July, oriental poppy in August and peonies in mid-September.

SOWING SCHEDULE

Although the dates when garden operations take place and when plants bloom vary markedly from Area to Area, there is a few days' difference between blooming dates in the south and north of the same zone because of differences in hours of daylight and the angle of the sun's rays. At Ithaca, N.Y., spring growth starts a few days ahead of that in Ottawa, Ontario; fall changes will be a few days behind. Plants which respond to longer daylight will bloom earlier in Ithaca, while short-day plants such as chrysanthemums and poinsettias will bloom earlier in Ottawa. This does not make much difference to garden operations. It does mean that, as you travel north, the blooming periods of different species and varieties become more closely bunched.

In the North, except for flowering

shrubs and trees, spring-flowering bulbs and early-flowering perennials provide the garden show until the end of June. Annuals must be timed to begin blooming in early July.

Annual flowering plants of different kinds take different lengths of time from sowing to producing a reasonable display of bloom. This varies from about 50 days for sweet alyssum to 120 days for pansies. In temperate regions, alyssum should be sown by the middle of May, and pansies by March 1 at the latest. Seed sowing out of doors by May 15 is usually safe in Area 3, but plants which require much longer from seed to bloom than alyssum must be sown indoors. A cold frame may afford sufficient protection for seeds in Area 5 by March 1, but not in Area 3, where indoor sowing is required at that date. Northern gardeners have to start more kinds of seed indoors than in warmer localities.

Sowing seed outdoors and setting out annual plants and vegetables is always a bit of a gamble because late spring frosts often come unexpectedly. However, the following table, based on 25-year averages, is quite safe:

Area	Sow Seed Outdoors	Set Plants Outdoors
5	April 20	May 10
4	May 1	May 20
3	May 10	June 1
2	*June 1	June 10
1	*June 15	June 25

*There are very few species practical to sow outdoors in these Areas.

PROPAGATION AND PRUNING

Another example of change in method due to climate is in the propagation of roses. Usually garden varieties are budded onto rootstocks of *Rosa multiflora* (memorial rose) because the plants grow more vigorously and carry more flowers than do those

budded onto roots of *R. canina* (dog rose). In Area 3, where hybrid tea roses must be completely protected anyway, plants budded on *R. multiflora* are popular. In Area 4, however, plants grown on roots of *R. canina* ripen their wood better in the fall and are therefore less subject to winter injury. They live longer and are consequently more practical.

Because of climate, pruning practices are also altered to some extent. Special attention is given to shaping plants in order to avoid a burden of ice and snow. It is a great mistake, for instance, to cultivate flat-topped hedges. A rounded or arched top will support much more weight without damage to the branches.

WINTER PROTECTION

It is impossible to avoid the cold. The purpose of winter protection is to prevent excessive fluctuations in the temperature of plants and the earth surrounding them—fluctuations which can cause alternate freezing and thawing. Another reason for winter protection is to conserve moisture within the plants without creating a soggy condition around them in which fungus molds will thrive.

Snow is the best insulating material for the protection of plants. During studies of the growth of tulips at Ottawa, soil-temperature recordings were taken at a depth of 6 in. below the surface of snow-covered and snow-cleared beds. Under only 6 in. of snow, the soil temperature never went below 27° F. when the air temperature was –22° F. In the snow-cleared beds on the same day, the soil temperature went to a low of 10° F. and the tulip bulbs died. If plants are snow-covered, there is no desiccation by wind, and air circulates sufficiently to prevent the sogginess that frequently occurs when leaves or chopped straw are used for protection.

Gardeners in Area 3 are reasonably sure of good snow cover, and no other mulch is needed on herbaceous plants in sheltered locations. In open, wind-swept sites, a snow fence or brush should be used to secure the snow on perennial beds.

In Areas 4 and 5, however, snow covering throughout the winter is not assured, and beds of perennials should be covered with a mulch. Fiber-glass or rock-wool insulation blankets have most nearly the same effects as snow. Either can be obtained in 1-in.-thick rolls and may be wrapped around rose bushes and placed over small seedbeds of pansies and Canterbury bells with good results. Unfortunately, they are more expensive than leaves or straw.

Straw, dry leaves or wood shavings are the usual materials used for covering borders. By the time spring arrives, they usually have formed soggy blankets that must be removed early to prevent damage to the foliage of arabis, chrysanthemum, foxglove and many other plants.

MULCHING TO CONSERVE MOISTURE

The practice of mulching shrubs and rose beds in midsummer to conserve soil moisture is also fairly general. But it is much more important and valuable in dry areas like the North Central region than in the Northeast, where rain is more frequent. Some materials used are peat moss, chopped corncobs, chopped straw, spent hops, wood shavings and sawdust. Their value is about in the order given. The lighter the color, the more the sun's rays are deflected. This helps to keep the soil cool, a condition particularly favorable to lilies and roses. Some mulches detract from the appearance of the plants, and, after all, it is for their appearance in the garden that most plants are grown.

Wherever any of these mulches is used, a general-purpose garden fertilizer should be sprinkled with it at the rate of 2 or 3 lb. for each cu. yd. of mulch. This will aid bacterial action; otherwise the bacteria will use nitrogen in the soil and temporarily reduce the supply available for plants.

WINTERING WOODY PLANTS

Antidesiccant sprays are available which create a thin film of wax or latex over the stems of woody plants and the foliage of evergreens. These sprays check evaporation of moisture, but they also, unfortunately, retard growth in spring.

The following methods are probably the usual form of covering and will at least give the gardener the satisfaction of knowing he has done what he could. In all areas, the stem bases of roses and large-flowered clematis are mounded with soil to a height of 8 or 10 in. in late fall before the ground freezes. No other cover should be put on until well after the ground freezes and the mice have found other quarters. Remove climbing rose and clematis from the trellises. Tie the stems in loose bundles to be covered later, and leave them on the ground. In November, cover them with straw or leaves and place an inverted trough of light-colored boards or boxes over them in order to shed rain and snow. In Area 3, all garden roses need more protection than the above. In addition, wrap them with fiber glass or place bell-shaped caps of Styrofoam over them, after they have been pruned in fall. If plants are in rows, place inverted troughs of light-colored plywood boards over each row.

Small conifers used around homes should be shaded from sun on the south and west by burlap screens tacked to wooden stakes. Wrapping them tightly in burlap or other material often causes damage. If they are planted where snow or ice may fall on them, installing "tents" of plywood will serve as protection.

Mice are a nuisance during winter. Wire-mesh guards should be placed around the trunks of apple trees, standard lilacs and standard roses, with the bottom edge of the guard buried in the earth. Spraying roses with lime sulphur before protection is put on, or using dusting sulphur, is a deterrent, though it does not kill the mice. A repellent product placed in open cans, on their sides, in bulb and perennial borders, is recommended.

Rabbits and deer are pests to young fruit and ornamental trees in Areas where they are present. Repellent sprays may be of some help applied in late fall, but, in general, fencing these animals out is surer than a spray.

GARDEN CALENDAR

The climatic conditions of the North-east–North Central region and adjacent Canada differ from those of the rest of the temperate areas of the United States and Canada largely in the degree of cold. The month-by-month calendar of garden work has therefore been incorporated in the general garden calendar beginning on page 851.

CHAPTER 33

THE SOUTHEAST AND GULF REGION

The Great Coastal Plain—Soils—Climatic Areas—Selected Plants—Palm and Rose Specialties—Garden Procedures—Planting-Time Calendar of Garden Work

ACROSS the South Atlantic and Gulf states from Norfolk, Virginia, to Brownsville, Texas, stretches a great coastal plain. This vast area encompasses all or portions of nine states—Virginia, North Carolina, South Carolina, Georgia, Florida, Alabama, Mississippi, Louisiana and Texas—with shores on the Atlantic Ocean or the Gulf of Mexico.

The terrain is flat or only slightly rolling, elevations nowhere rising above 600 ft. Behind the level land of the seaboard is part of an alluvial plateau; the southern tableland, called the Piedmont, merges into more rugged foothills which ascend to the Appalachian Mountains. Of utmost significance are the region's mighty rivers that have enriched parts of the Southland with silt through the ages.

The Atlantic and the Gulf of Mexico influence weather in the lower South so markedly that the region is classed as "cool subtropical" except for the lower seaboard of the Florida peninsula and the extreme southern part of Texas, between the Rio Grande and the Gulf of Mexico, which are called "warm subtropical." No part of the mainland United States is truly tropical; frosts are recorded periodically everywhere. Only the Florida Keys, tiny islets awash in tropic seas, are frost-free.

The oceanic climate of the southern Atlantic and Gulf states is characterized by high humidity; long, hot summers, during which there is abundant rainfall; and, most important, mild winters. Farther back, beyond the influence of the sea, winters are colder, summers hotter.

The mild weather of the southern Atlantic and Gulf states is disrupted when the jet stream, that immense river of wind that flows miles above the earth, swoops unusually far southward and brings frigid air from the Arctic. These sweeps of the jet stream occur periodically each winter, and push moist, warm air southward and eastward into the sea, replacing it with very dry, icy air. Temperatures may tumble 40° or more in a very short period, and suddenly it is winter in the lower South. Actually, there are at any one time usually only two or three days and nights of cold. In between these brief periods there are long periods of delightful springlike weather, during which gardeners can accomplish a great deal of work.

The sudden drop in temperature may injure plants which are completely hardy farther north, where they are prepared for winter by cold autumn nights. Minimum temperatures and their duration vary, but zero Fahrenheit is recorded infrequently, and in much of the sea-girt plain the earth never freezes at all.

RAINFALL AND SOILS

Southern gardens would have sufficient rainfall (about 50 in. yearly) if it fell regularly. Unfortunately, gardeners must be prepared for watering during droughts which recur regularly each winter and spring. Heavy summer rains leach away essential nutritional elements, so that southern gardeners must fertilize often but lightly during the warm months. Organic matter oxidizes rapidly under the subtropical sun, and so replacement of humus is a never-ending chore.

In some parts of the lower South artificial drainage is needed. Tiling, ditching or sometimes raising the levels of plant beds may be necessary to assure well-aerated root zones.

The great coastal plain of the Southeast, of marine origin, is made up of many diverse soils. While much of the land here is sandy and slightly acid, there are great deposits of clay and vast reaches of alluvial soil. On the other hand, the limestone formations of southern Florida and the river silts in the lower Rio Grande Valley are strongly alkaline.

CLIMATIC AREAS

Although there is considerable temperature change from year to year, the following Areas may be used as a general guide for plants and planting time. See the map opposite, and the regional plant lists beginning on page 604.

Area 1

Stretching from Norfolk, Va., across the Piedmont region into Texas, this is a warm, temperate Area but is occasionally subject to freezes down to 10° and 20° F.

Area 2

Comprising the lower Atlantic and Gulf maritime coasts, this Area is not subject to heavy freezes.

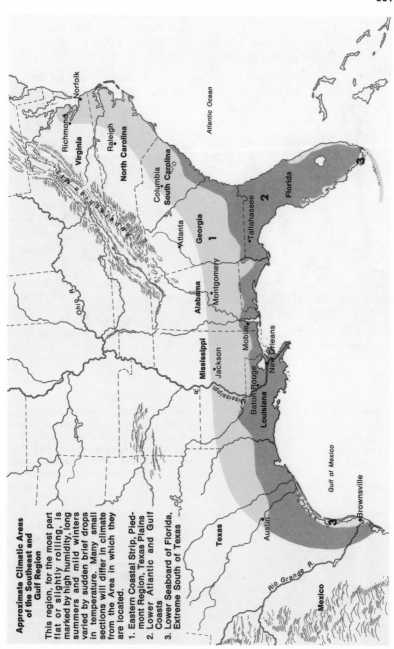

Approximate Climatic Areas of the Southeast and Gulf Region

This region, for the most part flat or slightly rolling, is marked by high humidity, long summers and mild winters varied by sudden brief drops in temperature. Many small sections will differ in climate from the Area in which they are located.

1. Eastern Coastal Strip, Piedmont Region, Texas Plains
2. Lower Atlantic and Gulf Coasts
3. Lower Seaboard of Florida, Extreme South of Texas

This Florida garden needs little maintenance. Beneath the banyan tree by the house are a bird-of-paradise flower, philodendron and crotons. Beyond is a screen of cabbage palm and traveler's-tree, beneath which are smaller plants: Aloe vera, fancy-leaved caladiums, crotons and philodendron. Grass is confined to a small plot. The foreground consists of a dragon tree and papyrus. In left foreground is a Chinese hibiscus. Along the sea wall are coconut palms and Aloe vera.

Area 3

The southern coasts of Florida and the southernmost coast of Texas, which are relatively frost-free, make up this Area.

GARDEN PLANTS OF THE WARM TEMPERATE AND "COOL" SUBTROPICAL SOUTH

Areas 1 and 2

Magnolias, live oaks, long-leaf yellow pines, hollies and cabbage palms are common in the lower South, and native flowering plants are justly famous. In springtime iris, lupines, coreopsis, phlox, tradescantias and others are breathtaking in their beauty, and autumn woods and fields are colorful with solidagos, liatris, rudbeckias, asters and sunflowers. Being native, these plants are completely adapted to climate and soils. Through long-time selective plant-breeding projects some have been developed into top-ranking garden flowers.

Choice Asiatic shrubs such as camellias, azaleas, firethorns and nandinas contribute beauty to man-made landscapes in this region. Deciduous plants play important roles, but in most gardens trees and shrubs with evergreen foliage predominate.

Because the mild winters do not offer sufficient hours of chilling temperatures, many cold-climate favorites are unsuitable for gardens in the lower South. Lilacs, peonies, gooseberries, horseradish and rhubarb do not thrive in the Southeast and Gulf states.

For a successful garden in the South the best plants are kinds that become dormant in the autumn, and remain so, without resuming growth during balmy days that appear between the short periods of low winter temperatures. Gardeners in the subtropics probably feel that they enjoy the best of two worlds. Temperatures never get too high or too low for the well-being of a great variety of plants, yet there is sufficient variation to give interest to each season. Palms,

broad-leaved evergreen trees and shrubs, flowering vines and evergreen lawns are a part of almost every home landscape.

Gardeners in the "cool" subtropics have learned to work with the climate, not against it. They have found that they can fit annuals as well as many kinds of bulbs and vegetables into seasons that meet their needs for both temperature and length of daylight.

"WARM" SUBTROPICAL AREA OF THE LOWER SOUTH

Area 3

There are two distinctive sections of the southern region—southern Florida and the lower Rio Grande Valley—that are classed as "warm" subtropical. Surrounded by warm seas on all sides but the north, the subtropical region of southern Florida is world-famous as a winter resort. It is also the year-round home of many Americans who have settled here because of the beneficent climate.

Southern Florida: Most of this flat land is just inches above sea level and at no point does it rise more than a few feet above the sea. Like other land masses adjacent to the South Atlantic, the Caribbean Sea and the Gulf of Mexico, southern Florida is on occasion attacked and sometimes even devastated by fierce winds of hurricane force. Damage is frequently reckoned in the millions of dollars, yet natives have learned through repeated experience how to rehabilitate their homes, gardens and orchards soon after the great winds subside.

The soil of southern Florida is composed mainly of sand, marl or oolitic rock (limestone). Surprisingly, plants thrive in these mediums, which do little more than serve as anchorage for roots. Organic matter, fertilizers and irrigation, all intelligently used, bring about this miracle. Because of the inadequate soil, consumption of domestic and imported peat mosses and commercial fertilizers is extraordinarily high in southern Florida.

Civilization has wrought havoc with southern Florida's natural water supply. Reclamation of land, dredging of canals and prodigious water consumption have resulted in salt-water intrusion in many wells. Some water is too saline for horticultural use. Fortunately, summer rains wash the sea salt down below the levels in which most feeder roots are found.

In spite of periodic frosts and infrequent deep freezes, many truly tropical plants are grown. Protection by banking with earth, covering, heating, intelligent pruning, watering and fertilization at the proper times helps to bring tropical exotics through cold periods. Royal palms, coconuts, mangoes and countless tender shrubs and vines abound.

Lower Rio Grande Valley: The second section of Area 3 in which climate, plant materials and gardening procedures differ from those of the lower South is extreme southern Texas. In the lower Rio Grande Valley the fertile, alluvial soils are strongly alkaline and high in salt content. In addition, strong, dry winds from the Great Plains and persistent breezes off the Gulf of Mexico create environments that are not ideal for tropical exotics. Since wind restricts plant growth, gardeners have had to devise windbreaks, both living and structural.

In southern Texas, just as in southern Florida (and southern California as well), gardening has become a leading hobby. Although many of the same kinds of plants are grown in these warm subtropical areas, it must not be assumed that their climates or gardening procedures are similar. In many respects they are quite different.

PLANTS FOR THE SOUTHERN AND GULF STATES

Deciduous Shade Trees

Acer	maple
Betula	birch
Celtis laevigata	sugarberry
Liquidambar styraciflua	sweet gum
Liriodendron tulipifera	tulip tree

Deciduous Flowering Trees

Albizzia julibrissin	silk tree
Cercis canadensis	redbud
Chionanthus virginica	fringe tree
Cornus florida	flowering dogwood
Koelreuteria paniculata	goldenrain tree
Lagerstroemia indica	crape myrtle

Magnolia
Oxydendrum arboreum . . sourwood
Parkinsonia aculeata . . .
           Jerusalem thorn
Prunus . . . . . . flowering plum
Prunus persica. . . flowering peach
Vitex agnus-castus . . . chaste tree

*For Sections Not Subject to Heavy Freezes
(Area 2)*
Bauhinia variegata . . . orchid tree
Jacaranda acutifolia

For Nearly Frost-Free Locations (Area 3)
Bombax malabaricum . . .
           red cotton tree
Cassia. . . . . senna
Delonix regia . . . royal poinciana
Pachira . . . . shaving-brush tree

Quercus virginiana
(Live Oak)

Evergreen Trees
Araucaria bidwillii . . bunya bunya
Callitris robusta. . . . cypress pine
Cedrus deodara. . . . deodar cedar
Chamaecyparis . . . . false cypress
Cinnamomum camphora . camphor tree
Cunninghamia lanceolata . China fir
Cupressus lusitanica . . .
           Portuguese cypress
Cupressus sempervirens . . .
           Italian cypress
Eriobotrya japonica. . . . . loquat
Ilex opaca . . . . . American holly
Juniperus virginiana . . . red cedar
Ligustrum lucidum . . glossy privet
Magnolia grandiflora . . . bull bay
Pinus . . . . pine
Prunus caroliniana . . cherry laurel
Quercus virginiana . . . . live oak
Thuja . . . . arborvitae

*For Sections Not Subject to Heavy Freezes
(Area 2)*
Bischofia javanica . . . . . . toog
Citrus

For Nearly Frost-Free Locations (Area 3)
Bucida buceras . . . . . black olive
Chrysophyllum oliviforme . satin leaf
Ficus bengalensis . . . banyan tree
Mangifera indica . . . . . . mango
Ravenala madagascariensis . . .
           traveler's-tree
Sapota achras . . . . . . sapodilla

Deciduous Shrubs
Berberis. . . . . barberry
Callicarpa americana . beauty-berry
Calycanthus . . sweet-scented shrub
Chaenomeles . . . flowering quince
Deutzia
Hibiscus syriacus . . rose of Sharon
Hydrangea
Ilex cassine. . . . . dahoon
Ilex decidua . . . . . possum haw
Lyonia ligustrina . . . . maleberry
Philadelphus . . . . . mock orange
Spiraea . . . . spirea
Viburnum
Weigela

Pyracantha coccinea . . . firethorn
Thuja orientalis . Oriental arborvitae

For Sections Not Subject to Heavy Freezes (Area 2)
Severinia buxifolia . . . . boxthorn

For Nearly Frost-Free Locations (Area 3)
Codiaeum . . . . croton

Vines

Antigonon leptopus. . . . coralvine
Campsis radicans. . . trumpet vine
Clytostoma callistegioides
Ficus pumila . . . . . creeping fig
Gelsemium sempervirens . . .
     Carolina yellow jessamine
Hedera . . . . ivy
Jasminum . . . . jasmine
Lonicera sempervirens . . .
     trumpet honeysuckle
Trachelospermum jasminoides . . .
     star jasmine
Wisteria sinensis . Chinese wisteria

For Sections Not Subject to Heavy Freezes (Area 2)
Bougainvillea
Pyrostegia ignea . . . . flame vine
Tecomaria capensis . . .
     Cape honeysuckle

For Nearly Frost-Free Locations (Area 3)
Allamanda cathartica
Petrea volubilis . . . purple wreath

Delonix regia
(Royal Poinciana)

Evergreen Shrubs

Buxus . . . . boxwood
Camellia
Chamaecyparis . . . . false cypress
Dracaena draco . . . . dragon tree
Eurya ochnacea . . . . . . cleyera
Ilex . . . . holly
Juniperus . . . . juniper
Ligustrum . . . . privet
Myrtus communis . . . . . myrtle
Nandina domestica . . .
     heavenly bamboo
Photinia
Podocarpus macrophylla maki

Hedge Plants

Abelia grandiflora. . . glossy abelia
Buxus . . . . boxwood
Camellia sasanqua
Elaeagnus
Gardenia jasminoides . Cape jasmine
Ilex cornuta . . . . Chinese holly
Ilex vomitoria. . . . . . yaupon
Ligustrum japonicum . . .
     Japanese privet
Pittosporum tobira . . .
     Japanese pittosporum
Prunus caroliniana . . cherry laurel
Rhododendron . . . . . . azalea

For Sections Not Subject to Heavy Freezes (Area 2)
Cuphea hyssopifolia
Eugenia uniflora . . Surinam cherry

For Nearly Frost-Free Locations (Area 3)
Ixora coccinea
Polyscias (syn. *Aralia*)

Plants for Seaside Gardens
(See also pages 550 to 553.)

Agave americana. . . century plant
Bumelia . . . buckthorn; ironwood
Elaeagnus
Ilex vomitoria. . . . . . . yaupon
Juniperus silicicola . . .
      Southern red cedar
Juniperus virginiana . . . red cedar
Myrica cerifera . . . . wax myrtle
Pinus palustris. . . . longleaf pine
Pittosporum tobira . . .
     Japanese pittosporum
Quercus virginiana . . . . live oak
Sabal palmetto. . . . cabbage palm
Serenoa repens. . . . saw palmetto
Trachycarpus fortunei . windmill palm
Yucca aloifolia . . Spanish bayonet

For Sections Not Subject to Heavy Freezes (Area 2)
Aloe
Carissa grandiflora. . . Natal plum
Casuarina equisetifolia . . .
      Australian pine
Chrysobalanus icaco . . . coco plum
Coccoloba floridana . . pigeon plum
Euphorbia
Nerium oleander . . . . . oleander
Raphiolepis indica . India hawthorn

For Nearly Frost-Free Locations (Area 3)
Coccoloba uvifera. . . . . sea grape
Cocos nucifera . . . . . . coconut

Annuals
Annual flowers provide color in gardens and make charming arrangements for indoors. Some are hot-weather kinds that grow and bloom best in summer, others are definitely cool-

Nerium oleander
(Oleander)

weather plants that thrive only in the fall through the spring.

PALMS
Nowhere in the continental United States are palms used in landscaping more successfully than in the southern Atlantic and Gulf states. Here these graceful trees, from dwarfs of a few feet to magnificent giants, are employed in distinctive compositions.

In southern Texas and southern Florida, an especially large variety, including gorgeous tropical exotics, thrive. Palms are used in many ways. Species of varying heights may be combined to form attractive groups. Tall palms make excellent framing trees, and can also serve in backgrounds. Native saw palmettos may be left near property lines to become integral parts of enclosing borders, and hardy dwarf palms make attractive accents in foundation arrangements.

Palms serve most dramatically as avenue trees. Tall, clean-growing, single-trunked specimens, set 25 to 30 ft. apart on both sides of avenues, make pictures long remembered.

Kinds for Planting

Among the best palms for planting in the Southeast are the following:

Arecastrum romanzoffianum . . . queen palm
Butia . . . . yatay or pindo palm
Chamaerops humilis . . . Mediterranean fan palm
Phoenix . . . . date palm
Rhapidophyllum hystrix . needle palm
Rhapis . . . . lady palm
Roystonea regia . . . . royal palm
Sabal palmetto . . . . cabbage palm
Serenoa repens . . . saw palmetto
Trachycarpus fortunei . . . windmill palm
Washingtonia . Washingtonia palm

Very tender kinds suitable only for essentially frost-free locations:
Adonidia merrillii . . . Manila palm
Cocos nucifera . . . . . . coconut

Kinds adaptable for areas warm enough for citrus:
Acrocomia . . . . . . grugru palm
Livistona chinensis . . . Chinese fan palm
Paurotis wrightii . . Everglade palm

Transplanting

Procedures used in transplanting palms differ from those recommended for woody trees.

Palms are transplanted in all sizes from small seedlings to finished landscape-size specimens. They may be transplanted at any time of the year, but the rainy season is most favorable. Root development is rapid at that time and palms rally from the transplanting operation most quickly. Just as for other plants, holes should be enriched with compost before planting.

The root ball taken with field-grown palms is much smaller in proportion than that habitually cut for typical woody trees. Frequently roots are trimmed within a foot or two of the trunk because it is recognized that new roots develop readily from the crown. In addition, palm roots

Roystonea regia
(Royal Palm)

emerge higher and higher above the crown, and it is therefore common practice to set palm trees slightly deeper than they grew previously.

When a palm is in place in its new location, fertile soil that was lifted from the prepared site is shoveled back while water is hosed in slowly to eliminate air pockets and to assure good contact between the roots and the particles of soil. Tramp the earth firmly into place, leaving a saucer around the tree to hold water. Fill this depression once a week if there is no rainfall.

Because of drastic reduction of the root system at digging time, the leaf surface should be reduced by half or two-thirds. With soft cotton cord, tie three leafless petioles around the youngest central leaves to protect these and the vital bud from which they grew. Most landscape palms have one single growing point, and horticulturists take every precaution to protect it from injury.

Fertilizer will not be needed during the first year, but at the beginning of the second rainy season apply about 2 lb. of a 6-6-6 mixture for each inch of trunk diameter. Lawn grasses should be kept back from the root zone until the transplanted palm becomes well established. Afterward many gardeners like the turf to grow close to the trunk.

Young palms will grow rapidly to mature landscape size if they are encouraged by proper cultivation and fertilization. It is advisable to keep circles of clean earth around young trees in lawns for a few years. A 5- to 7-ft. ring should be cultivated frequently with a scuffle hoe. An alternate method is to fork on a deep organic mulch. Once a week during dry spells, allow the hose to run slowly on the ground, and about once a month during warm weather apply a 6-6-6 fertilizer.

Palms that have been neglected can usually be reconditioned by piling rich compost into generous-sized holes dug at intervals around the trunk. Unlike woody trees, neglected palms never show increases in trunk diameters that occurred before reconditioning. Trunks formed above the pre-reconditioning height will be greatly expanded in thickness from the improved nourishment.

Most palms are resistant to diseases, insects and drought. Once they are established and of desired height, maintenance is limited to removal of brown leaves and fruit clusters with a sharp pruning saw. Tree-wound dressing is not used on palms.

ROSES

In the southern Atlantic and Gulf states it is customary to plant roses as soon as young plants become available in the market in November.

Long research at a leading southern university has demonstrated the superiority of *Rosa fortuneana* as a rootstock for roses which are to be grown in the lower South. A few specialty nurseries here produce container-grown specimens of leading varieties on this tenacious, disease-resistant, long-lived stock. Rosarians who have grown bushes on *R. fortuneana* stocks are universal in its praise.

CAMELLIAS

Together with the rose, magnolia and Cape jasmine, the camellia is prominent in the literature and tradition of the South. During antebellum days camellias were widely grown, and today century-old specimens are cherished in many southern gardens.

Interest in these handsome Asian shrubs was revived after World War II. Today, there are literally thousands of named varieties. The blooms of the camellia have few peers as flowers for personal adornment and exhibition. The glossy evergreen leaves and dense growth, long life, tolerance of shade and frost, and amenability to pruning account for the high esteem in which this plant is held.

Landscape Uses

Camellias of compact habit and lovely texture can often be used to fine advantage at strategic spots near the entrance to a home.

Conversely, the service area, smallest subdivision of the home landscape, usually is located close to the kitchen, carport and driveway. Screening from the outdoor living area and the street is essential. Camellias, slow-growing, reliable and evergreen, make ideal permanent barriers.

At the corners of a house where heavy masses are needed, tall, upright-growing varieties of *Camellia japonica* may be planted. Corner plants should never be allowed to grow as high as the eaves. Blank expanses of masonry, so characteristic of contemporary architecture, can be given dramatic treatment if camellias are espaliered (trained to grow flat) against them.

All types may be used to excellent advantage as shrubs for naturalistic borders. They should not be planted to the exclusion of other shrubs, but occasional groups may complement privets, viburnums and azaleas. Tall, columnar camellias, spaced at intervals in shrubbery borders, create more formal patterns.

Camellias in Formal Gardens

Camellias have long been used to define entrances to formal gardens. For this purpose pillarlike varieties of *C. japonica* are favored. So that pairs will grow evenly, they should be grown from cuttings from a single stock plant.

For formal enclosure, clipped hedges of *C. sasanqua* are without superior.

Space plants at 18-in. intervals in carefully prepared beds, and pinch new growth frequently to induce compactness. For hedges, cutting-grown sasanquas originating from one stock plant are best, because seedlings and grafted plants do not grow uniformly. Bulbs and annuals, planted in long flowing drifts in front of clipped sasanqua hedges, with a perfect winter lawn as foreground, complete a charming formal setting.

GARDEN PROCEDURES

Newcomers to the South find that they have much to unlearn in landscaping practices. Like the oldtimers, they will come to rely upon the really dependable species to form the permanent framework of their garden design. When they are tempted to try truly tender tropical exotics, they will treat them as temporary plantings, with the full knowledge that these colorful additions may die to the ground after the first winter frost.

Astute homeowners who select plants with care for complete hardiness in the South will be able to brag that their gardens endure zero temperatures without appreciable harm.

One line of defense against cold injury is to encourage maturity of tissues before freezing temperatures occur. During the autumn keep the soil just moderately moist so as not to promote vegetative growth. Nitrogen, the stimulator, is not used on shrubs, vines and trees in the fall except in the most nearly frost-free locations.

To help check growth apply a potassic fertilizer in late summer—or very early autumn, if you will—but do not expect benefit from potassium broadcast as late as Thanksgiving.

Planting Time

Spring, traditional season for tilling, is not best for planting in the lower

South; winter is much better. During July and August, days are much too hot and muggy for yard work. In some sections, the horticultural year starts in September–October, when hardy flowers and vegetables are sown and sites are readied for trees, shrubs and roses. During the first cool days of autumn, many homeowners broadcast seeds of hardy annual grasses for bright green winter lawns.

Transplanting

The modern practice of growing nursery stock in tin cans makes it quite customary and safe to transplant specimens any day of the year, and it reduces the necessity for cutting back in order to compensate for the loss of roots.

Woody plants are almost dormant in midwinter, so it is recommended that they be moved in December–January. Until that time, stake out planting sites and prepare them for new nursery stock. Dig holes somewhat larger than the root masses of the plants to be acquired, and carefully discard all lime-bearing building materials that may have been buried by the contractor's machinery. Throw a layer of compost or peat moss and a couple of handfuls of commercial fertilizer in each hole, and then fill it with fertile woods soil or compost, leaving a slight basin around the plant to gather water.

At planting time carefully shovel the rich earth aside, and set the nursery specimen in the hole at exactly the level where it formerly grew. Deep planting is a common error that must be avoided. See that roots assume, without bending and crowding, the same relative positions that they previously held. As rich earth is shoveled back, wash it in place with a gentle stream from the hose. Finish the job by treading and forming a saucerlike depression to hold water.

Fill this hollow once each week when there is no rain.

Protection of Plants

Recently transplanted woody trees should be protected against sun scald, excessive drying and borer attack by having their trunks wrapped from the ground upward to the branches. Spanish moss, commercial tree wrap, paper or similar material are suitable, and the covering may be secured with soft cotton cord. After foliage emerges, cut the string if it has not rotted, and loosen the wrapping or allow it to disintegrate in the weather.

Pruning to reduce leaf-bearing surfaces to compensate for the loss of roots is important. Cut back branches to make the transplants compact and shapely. Low branches are retained on shrubs, as are straight, central leaders of trees.

Fertilization and Mulch

Newly transplanted stock need not be fertilized during the first year, because of the high nutrient level of the medium into which it is set. During the second winter, drop commercial fertilizer into spade slits thrust at intervals through root zones. You may buy a special mixture formulated for the kind of plant you are concerned with, or you may safely use a general 6–6–6 blend. Trace elements will not be needed on fertile land and where animal manures have been used, but if your plot is sandy and devoid of organic matter, fertilizers fortified with trace elements may be useful. (See page 752 in "Fertilizers and Manures.")

Mulching is always recommended. A 4-in. blanket of oak leaves, pine straw or peanut hulls over plant beds acts as insulation to reduce fluctuations in soil temperature; it conserves moisture, and, as it decays, mild acids and elements of nutrition are released. Few weeds grow through such a deep organic mulch.

Some gardeners spread commercial fertilizer directly on the mulch and let it wash through to the root zone, but others prefer to drop it into spade slits as suggested above.

Pruning

In the maritime South, landscape trees, vines and shrubs grow rapidly and many require frequent, systematic trimming. Usually, informal, natural pruning, rather than shearing to geometric shapes, is preferred. Sharp, well-adjusted hand pruners are used to sever robust shoots near their points of origin close to the earth. New twigs of normal size will emerge to replace each excised branch.

Branch tips are reduced without regular pattern and in moderation, so that the planting will not have an artificial, barbered look. This light heading in, called pinching, is best done with thumb and forefinger while shoots are tender.

Spring-blooming plants such as bridal wreath, azaleas, abelias, hydrangeas, oleanders and a host of others are pruned immediately after blooming. Blossom buds are formed during long days, and these will be sacrificed if the shrubs are cut in late summer. Crape myrtle blooms on branches of the current season, so it is standard practice to prune this southern favorite after its leaves are shed in late autumn.

Prunus caroliniana or cherry laurel, privet, wax myrtle, podocarpus and juniper, none of which is grown for blossoms, are lightly headed back throughout each growing season.

Hedges require repeated shearing from March until autumn. Always do this while new growth is tender and succulent.

Occasionally it is necessary to remove parts of tender exotics that have been injured by low temperatures. It is suggested that the job be done within a few days after a cold wave.

Nick along a damaged branch with shears until an incision reveals healthy, green inner bark; then, somewhat below this point, clip through the branch with a clean, slanting cut. Leave plump, outward-pointing buds as new terminals. For small wood, use your hand shears, for larger branches select heavy loppers, and for members above 1 in. in diameter, sharp, wide-set pruning saws are accepted implements. After pruning is complete apply tree-wound dressing to all cuts larger than 2 in.

Azaleas, completely hardy in normal winters, may be severely injured when the temperature plunges suddenly after a warm, moist fall. The reason for this is a separation around the cambium layers which causes death of the branch. This type of azalea injury, called "split-stem," may not be noticed until the following summer.

Fertilization and Weed Control

In March, broadcast about 15–20 lb. of a 6–6–6 commercial lawn fertilizer over each 1000 sq. ft. Once every six weeks from June through September apply 2 or 3 lb. of sulphate of ammonia. Unless you work just before or during a rain, run the sprinkler promptly to prevent burning.

When permanent lawns are fertilized regularly, mowed frequently at the correct height and watered deeply and infrequently, weeds should not become a problem. However, sometimes weeds do invade lawns, particularly those of Bermuda and zoysia grasses.

If there are just a few annual weeds, hand-picking is recommended. If, on the other hand, invasion is widespread, it may be decided to spray with a 2, 4–D herbicide. The manufacturers' directions as to dilution and heaviness of application must be followed exactly.

Herbicides must always be applied through equipment that will not be used for insecticides, fungicides and fertilizers.

CALENDAR OF WORK
January

January, usually the coolest month in the lower South, is the time to graft, fertilize, transplant and prune. Bright, crisp weekends now are just right for yard work.

Prepare day lilies for spring flowering by dropping handfuls of 6-6-6 fertilizer in spade slits here and there among the clumps. Use about 5 lb. for each 100 sq. ft. of bed. Gardeners in warmer locations near the coast are enjoying first blossoms on calendulas, annual linarias, pansies and violas. The old flowers of these should be picked before seeds form, and the foliage should be protected against aphids, cabbage loopers and mites. When frost is forecast, damage to flower buds can be prevented by covering annuals with Spanish moss or excelsior. Order, for immediate or later planting, bulbs or roots of agapanthus, alstroemeria, amaryllis, calla, freesia, gladiolus, hyacinth, montbretia, ranunculus and watsonia.

Broccoli is now being harvested and young plants set out. Radishes should be sown every couple of weeks during the cold months. Turnip and collard greens must be picked while they are young and tender. Every southern garden should have a row of scallions: plant bulblets separately about 4 in. apart in rows 1 ft. apart. Sow outdoors seeds of beet, cabbage, carrot, chard, Chinese cabbage, collard, lettuce, mustard, radish and turnip.

The following may be sown outdoors in warm localities, indoors in colder sections: arctotis, begonia, bellis, brachycome, browallia, calendula, California poppy, calliopsis, candytuft, carnation, clarkia, cleome, cornflower, delphinium, dianthus, dimorphotheca, gaillardia, gilia, godetia, gypsophila, hollyhock, hunnemannia, larkspur, linaria, linum, lobelia, lupine, mignonette, nicotiana, nierembergia, petunia, phlox, poppy, salpiglossis, scabiosa, statice, stock, sweet alyssum, sweet pea, verbena and viola.

Strawberries are showing color. Keep crickets under control with poison bait. Cover the plants with plastic netting to protect ripening fruits from birds. Inspect deciduous fruit trees for scale infestations, and spray to eliminate them. If peaches, plums, blackberries and grapes have not been pruned, this task should be completed by the end of the month. Transplanting season for bare-root, deciduous fruit trees ends soon. Calamondin, kumquat and Satsuma orange, decorative little citrus relatives, can be grafted now on rootstocks of *Poncirus trifoliata*. Citrus trees must be banked with earth before a cold spell, and possibly assigned oil-burning heaters to ward off danger of frost damage. Order seeds of roselle and sow them in a flat, indoors. Shrubs not grown for their flowers can be cut back anytime. Established landscape plants should be fertilized toward the end of January.

February

This is the month of awakening plant life along the southern seaboard. Deciduous flowering trees are coming into bloom or are at their best, winter shrubs are showy, cool-weather bulbs are breathtakingly beautiful.

Annual flowers must be protected against insects and mites by spraying or dusting. There will be a frost or two sometime this month; be ready to put in place a protective covering of Spanish moss or excelsior. Plant gladiolus corms where gladioluses have not grown before. The following bulbs and roots can be ordered for immediate or later planting: agapanthus, alstroemeria, amaryllis, caladium, calla, crinum, dahlia, eucharis, freesia, gladiolus, gloriosa, hymenocallis, montbretia, tuberose, tulbaghia and zephyranthes. Sow these seeds outdoors: ageratum, sweet alyssum, China aster, blue lace flower, celosia, Chinese forget-me-not, chrysanthemum, early cosmos, dianthus, dimorphotheca, gaillardia, gypsophila, helichrysum, linaria, marigold, nasturtium, phlox, poppy, rudbeckia, schizanthus and verbena.

In the lower South do not sow vegetables successively where those belonging to the same botanical genus have been grown before.

Sow outdoors seeds of beet, cabbage, carrot, chard, Chinese cabbage, collard, lettuce, mustard, pea, radish and turnip. Sow in flats, indoors, seeds of eggplant, pepper and tomato. Now aphids may become numerous; be ready to dust or spray.

Since earliest days, southern homemakers have planted roselle as a substitute for cranberries. Seed sown indoors in February produces plantlets to set out after danger of frost has passed—for a harvest in time for Thanksgiving dinner.

Ripe strawberries should be ready for picking. They must be protected against crickets, birds and frost. Handpick weeds from the strawberry patch before they become well established.

In warmer parts spray peaches and plums to control curculios, and broadcast a complete fertilizer for orange trees this month. Fertilize orange trees lightly every six weeks, February through October. Pest-control firms will spray large, bearing citrus trees.

In nearly frost-free regions, set out papayas from cans toward the end of the month.

Flowering trees and azaleas are at their best. Transplant azaleas immediately after they have flowered or even while they are in full bloom, arranging azalea borders to secure the best possible color sequence.

March

The loveliest of months in many parts, owing to the beauty of azaleas, flowering trees, wisterias and spring bulbs. But danger of frost has not passed. For immediate or later planting, bulbs or roots of the following may be ordered: alstroemeria, caladium, calla, dahlia, eucharis, gladiolus, haemanthus, iris (native), montbretia, tuberose and zephyranthes. Outdoors, seeds of the following may be sown: China aster, blue lace flower, cosmos, cypress vine, gaillardia, morning glory and nasturtium. In flats indoors these seeds may be sown: balsam, celosia, dahlia, globe amaranth, helichrysum, marigold, portulaca, rudbeckia, salvia, torenia and zinnia.

Control the high incidence of soilborne pests by fumigation now. If inexperienced, call in a pest-control firm. Sow the seeds of eggplant, tomato and pepper indoors for planting out after danger of frost has passed. In warm areas corn may be sown toward the middle of March. The delectable yellow egg-shaped "plums" of the loquat are ripening now in all but the coldest sections. In the latter, stone fruits must be sprayed now on schedule, to control curculios.

Large azaleas may be cut back as drastically as necessary immediately after their blossoms fade.

April

In cooler parts of the coastal plain and back to higher ground, spring arrives; pink flowering dogwoods, crab apples, Kurume and native azaleas, wisterias and spring bulbs are most colorful. Killing frosts seldom occur in the lower South after the third week of this month.

Cannas, dahlias and fancy-leaved caladiums that have been stored over the cool months may be planted now. Naturalized bulbs should be fertilized. Spray gladioluses for thrips, sweet peas for spider mites, and roses for thrips and for leaf-spot diseases. Seeds of the following should be sown soon: ageratum, sweet alyssum, China aster, balsam, blue lace flower, celosia, cosmos, cypress vine, dahlia, gaillardia, globe amaranth, helichrysum, marigold, morning glory, portulaca, rudbeckia, salvia, sunflower, tithonia, torenia and zinnia.

April is tomato-planting time. Sow seed now, or acquire plants of a size suitable for planting. In the lower South growing tomatoes up stakes is the practice favored by amateur gardeners.

It is corn-planting time, too. The seeds or seedlings (sown indoors last month) may be planted outdoors now. Beans, okra and southern peas may be sown early in April.

A follow-up spray of stone fruits is now in order. Consult your local garden center or County Agricultural Agent about the exact timing. Severe pruning with sterilized shears after pear-blight infection is the only control for this bacterial disease. Pecan foliage should be covered with a protective coating of insecticide when it unfolds, and nut insects are repelled by spraying at the time of catkin-fall. Citrus trees should be fertilized every six weeks. Layering of trees and shrubs can be done this month. Cover gardenia foliage with a 2-percent white summer oil emulsion to kill white flies and remove sooty mold. Cape jasmines heavily coated with the black fungus will require two applications of this spray. Spider mites on citrus must be controlled. Leaf galls, growths on azalea and camellia leaves should

be handpicked and burned. If April is a dry month, soak plantings once each week. Winter grass needs periodic fertilizing and mowing.

May

Summer comes to the southernmost parts of the continent while spring still lingers in the cooler areas of the southern Atlantic and Gulf states.

It is day-lily season. Cool-weather annuals, rapidly passing from the scene, should be replaced with heat-tolerant kinds for the summer months. Seeds of the following may be sown: balsam, celosia, late cosmos, cypress vine, dahlia, gaillardia, globe amaranth, marigold, morning glory, portulaca, salvia, sunflower, tithonia, torenia and zinnia.

Cultivate, fertilize and irrigate regularly. Sow okra and southern peas. Eggplants, peppers and tomatoes may still be set out.

May is propagation time. If a mist system is used (see page 706), cuttings of most trees and shrubs root in about three to seven weeks. Cuttings of azaleas are ready when bristles on this year's shoots turn from yellow to reddish-brown. This occurs during this month and the next.

At signs of brown spots in St. Augustine grass, spray for chinch bugs.

Most homeowners get rid of old strawberry plants now. Thinning tree-fruits will increase the size of fruit and improve the flavor. Grapes and peaches need spray protection against rot diseases. All fruit trees must be sprayed for aphids, mites and chewing insects, and peach trunks may be sprayed with malathion to repel borers.

June

In torrid weather southern gardens show less flower color and are becoming green again, as flowering trees, shrubs, cool-weather annuals and bulbs finish blooming.

Set three or four plants of cleome and nicotiana near a screened porch, terrace or patio to provide evening fragrance. Heat-tolerant flowers are used to replace kinds that have to be pulled out now. Annual sunflowers, gaillardias, marigolds and zinnias are the principal kinds for cutting. Dig bulbs and tubers when their foliage turns yellow and store them over summer in a dry place. If gladioluses are still producing, protect them from thrips. Rose foliage always needs protection. Seeds of the following may be sown or young plants set out: balsam, late cosmos, cypress vine, gaillardia, marigold, morning glory, portulaca, sunflower, tithonia and zinnia.

Flower buds are forming in June; do not pinch out terminals any more this season. Tomatoes require pruning, tying, spraying and a generous organic mulch. Collards, some varieties of turnips and New Zealand spinach grow on into the hot weather to supply leaves for cooking. Okra, peppers and southern peas are in full production, and seeds of southern peas may still be sown.

Insect and weed control are important in the garden now. Spray malathion on peach trunks to keep borers away. To prevent "leggy" azaleas, cut out rampant, outsize canes. Control caterpillars that eat the foliage of azaleas by dusting with toxaphene as soon as the young caterpillars are discovered. Clip hedges periodically while their branch-tips are tender. Chinch bugs in St. Augustine turf must be killed when first brown spots appear.

July

Garden activities are now slowing down. Intense sun, hot days and high humidity prevail, yet weeds and insects must be controlled and lawns mowed and fertilized on schedule.

Crinums, gigantic bulbs of southern gardens, are attractive in the gar-

den and for using in flower arrangements. Cut blossoms from all annuals as soon as they fade to keep the plants in production as long as possible.

Day lilies that are crowded should now be lifted, divided into single fans and replanted in enriched beds.

Sow seeds or set out young plants of marigold, portulaca, wishbone flower (torenia) and zinnia.

Harvesting and pest control are the chief activities of vegetable gardeners this month. If you wish to raise a few home-grown yams, now is the time to start a bed. Sow southern peas.

Cover fig trees with netting to prevent damage by birds. Pecan trees should be sprayed with an insecticide. Grapes need periodic spraying for brown rot, and it is advisable to drape netting over bearing vines when the fruit begins to turn color.

Yellow spots in turf of centipede grass are likely to indicate iron deficiency. Stir iron sulphate or iron chelate into rainwater or lake water (city water is alkaline) and sprinkle the chlorotic area. Spraying St. Augustine grass for chinch bugs should be done repeatedly during warm months. Wisterias grown in tree form need pinching regularly to prevent the formation of long, twining branches.

Camellias should now be disbudded if exhibition-quality flowers are desired. Do not clip *Camellia sasanqua* hedges any more, or there will be no flowers this fall.

August

Seed, rose, bulb and fruit catalogues may now be studied in readiness for placing orders for fall gardening needs.

Compost piles can be started, or built higher, as suitable vegetable wastes become available. Chrysanthemums, cleomes, cosmos, dahlias and giant zinnias need to be staked.

Sow no seeds this month.

Suburban vegetable gardens in the

lower South need little attention except harvesting in August. Consider the need for having the vegetable soil sterilized. Purchase the *best* seeds of the most suitable varieties.

Secure netting with clothespins over muscadine vines to protect the crop from birds. Greatest harm to figs on sandy soil results from nemas or nematodes. Employ nemacides. A thick organic mulch is helpful for fig trees.

Dwarf fruit trees can be grown in containers on a sunny terrace. Tender subtropicals such as dwarf limes can be carried indoors when cold threatens. Fertilize citrus every six weeks.

Firethorns may be kept compact by pruning back long branches to just above the fruit clusters. In the hurricane belt, brace and guy young palms and other trees that have not yet established sturdy root systems. The earliest sasanqua camellias are now opening their flowers. Dust recently hatched caterpillars on azaleas before they can defoliate them. Lawn maintenance needs constant attention. Chinch bugs, sod webworms and army worms must be killed.

September

For many southerners, the garden year begins in September. Now is the time to start hardy annuals, bulbs and vegetables that thrive during the cool months ahead.

Beds must be readied for sowing and planting by cutting back summer growth and rototilling or spading under complete fertilizer and peat moss or compost. Chrysanthemums and other fall-flowering perennials may be given a final light application of a fast-acting, nitrogenous fertilizer to assure good-sized blossoms. Plant a few roots of the spectacular fall-flowering hybrid mallows in a moist, rich location. Full sun is needed.

The following may be ordered for immediate or later planting: bulbs of narcissus, ranunculus, cold-processed tulips and other "Dutch" bulbs. The following seeds may be sown: arctotis, begonia, bellis, brachycome, browallia, calendula, California poppy, clarkia, cornflower, delphinium, dianthus, dimorphotheca, gaillardia, gilia, gypsophila, hollyhock, hunnemannia, linaria, linum, lobelia, lupine, mignonette, nasturtium, nierembergia, petunia, phlox, salpiglossis, scabiosa, snapdragon, statice, stock, sweet alyssum, verbena and viola.

Make a layout on paper. If practicable, have the rows running north and south so that every plant receives maximum sunlight each day.

For the vegetable garden, rhubarb, chard, purple basil and curly kale, planted thickly, make splendid edgings for beds and walks.

Sterilized soil in which to plant seeds should be on hand at planting time.

Seeds and sets of the following, for immediate or later planting, may be ordered now: basil, beet, broccoli, cabbage, carrot, chard, Chinese cabbage, collard, endive, kale, lettuce, onion, parsley, pea, radish, spinach and turnip.

Muscadine grapes are still being enjoyed if the vines were covered earlier with netting. Oriental persimmons, sometimes called "kakis," especially some old seedling kinds, are very decorative. Most cannot be eaten until mushy-soft, except the Fuyu variety.

During the first cool spell spray camellias with 2-percent white summer oil emulsion to kill scale insects. Two applications under very high pressure are needed. Cut off crapemyrtle fruits that followed summer blooms.

Use great care when hoeing or cultivating around *Lycoris*; it is easy to overlook the slender green flower stalks that emerge from the ground before their flowers show color.

October

Cultivate between flower and vegetable seedlings started last month.

Seedlings in flats should be stimulated with a dilute solution of high-analysis fertilizer. When the plantlets are large enough to handle easily, set them out and shade them for a day or two; water them in with dilute liquid fertilizer.

Choose a cloudy day for transplanting tender seedlings. Broadcast cutworm bait along the rows; otherwise these hungry larvae will take a heavy toll.

Order, for immediate or later planting, bulbs of narcissus, ranunculus and cold-processed tulips. Seeds of the following may be sown: arctotis, begonia, bellis, brachycome, browallia, calendula, California poppy, calliopsis, candytuft, carnation, clarkia, cornflower, delphinium, dianthus, dimorphotheca, gaillardia, gilia, godetia, gypsophila, hollyhock, hunnemannia, larkspur, linaria, linum, lobelia, lupine, mignonette, nasturtium, nierembergia, pansy, petunia, phlox, salpiglossis, scabiosa, snapdragon, statice, stock, sweet alyssum, verbena and viola.

The rampant, cucumber-like vines of chayote are hung with fruits in various stages of maturity. Recommendations for September work in the vegetable garden apply this month also. Harden seedlings before transplanting them outdoors by lessening their supply of water.

With a scuffle hoe, thin vegetables sown outdoors last month.

During the last week of this month, sneak a few yams out from under a vigorous vine. Although sweet potatoes should grow until frost kills the vines, yam lovers want early samples of fine things to come.

Order seeds and sets for immediate planting of basil, beet, broccoli, cabbage, carrot, chard, Chinese cabbage, collard, endive, kale, lettuce, onion, parsley, pea, radish, spinach and turnip.

Strawberries are started now. Prepare the soil as suggested last month for annuals. If there is a high water table, plant in raised beds.

Twist kaki fruits gently from the tree and allow them to ripen on a window shelf. Give orange trees their last fertilization of the year.

For green winter lawns, sow seeds of a hardy annual grass during the first cool spell. Goldenrain trees, *Koelreuteria*, are in full bloom now. Seedlings transplanted to good garden soil soon develop into sizable specimens.

Look for volunteers of petunia, larkspur, linaria, arctotis and other annuals where plantings existed last season. These may be lifted and transplanted.

November

November is the month of the first frost in much of the lower South. Howling northers may bring temperatures in the thirties between Thanksgiving and December 15. Near the southern limits of the continent, frost comes much later.

Chrysanthemums should be at their best, their season ending about Thanksgiving. When frost threatens, budding plants can be lifted, set into containers and moved inside. Sweetpea planting time is here; sow heavy-producing spring-flowering varieties. These bulbs may be ordered for immediate or later planting: alstroemeria, amaryllis, freesia, hyacinth, iris, leucojum, Easter lily, narcissus, ornithogalum, ranunculus, sprekelia, tigridia, tulip and watsonia.

Seeds of the following may be sown: arctotis, begonia, bellis, brachycome, browallia, calendula, California poppy, calliopsis, candytuft, carnation, clarkia, chrysanthemum, cornflower, delphinium, dianthus, dimorphotheca, gaillardia, gilia, godetia, gypsophila, hollyhock, hunnemannia, larkspur, linaria, linum, lobelia, lupine, mignonette, nierembergia, pansy, petunia, phlox, salpiglossis, scabiosa, snapdragon, statice, stock, sweet alyssum, sweet pea, verbena and viola.

Chayotes must be harvested before frost. Dig sweet potatoes as soon as frost kills the vines. Vegetables that were started in September to be used as edgings in the garden should be set out at once. Plant them closer than if they were being grown for food production, about 6 in. apart. Tender plants, even during southern winters, need protection against pests, so put out cutworm bait and spray regularly for aphids, loopers, mites and other garden enemies. Sow seeds or plant sets of beet, broccoli, cabbage, carrot, chard, Chinese cabbage, collard, endive, kale, lettuce, onion, pea, radish, spinach and turnip.

This is planting time for fruit trees and bushes in the South. People plant pecans for their grandchildren, it is said. One pecan tree is sufficient; at maturity it will cast shade over an entire back yard. Citrus trees in cold locations must be protected by banking, or, in some cases, by oil heaters. Strawberries need to be blanketed with pine straw when frost is forecast. Late this month their first flower buds may appear. The fleshy calyxes of roselle are ready for jelly-making now.

Prepare planting sites for trees, shrubs and vines. Summer-blooming shrubs, such as crape myrtle, should be pruned as soon as their leaves fall. Be careful not to cut back spring-blooming kinds. Okra pods, pine, magnolia and sweet-gum cones, lotus pods, sea oats, pampas grass plumes and other dried plant materials can be gathered and hung in a dry place until needed for holiday decorations. Annual winter lawn grasses require constant grooming.

December

The twelfth month is one of little garden activity.

Successful hobby gardeners are proud to have produced Christmas-flowering calendulas, linarias, pansies and violas. Flower buds on these and other hardy species may be brought through frosts by covering with generous mounds of Spanish moss. Tulip-planting time has finally arrived. Set cold-processed bulbs, 6 in. deep, with a tablespoon of fertilizer mixed in below each bulb. These bulbs may be ordered for immediate or later planting: agapanthus, amaryllis, calla, crinum, dahlia, freesia, gladiolus, gloriosa, hymenocallis, Dutch iris, lily, montbretia, tigridia, tuberose, tulbaghia and watsonia.

Sow seeds of arctotis, browallia, calendula, California poppy, calliopsis, candytuft, carnation, Chinese forget-me-not, chrysanthemum, clarkia, cornflower, dianthus, dimorphotheca, gaillardia, gilia, godetia, gypsophila, hollyhock, hunnemannia, larkspur, linaria, lobelia, lupine, mignonette, nierembergia, pansy, petunia, phlox, poppy, salpiglossis, scabiosa, snapdragon, statice, sweet pea and verbena.

Enjoy salads of fancy loose-head, butter-head and rare little-leaf lettuce, raised from seed. Peas are not successful everywhere in the lower South, but every gardener should try at least a row.

Even in December cutworms destroy tender seedlings, so broadcast poison bait beside new transplants in the garden.

Sow seeds of basil, beet, broccoli, cabbage, carrot, chard, Chinese cabbage, collard, endive, kale, lettuce, parsley, pea, radish and turnip. Planting time continues. Select good but not large specimens of bare-root fruit trees. The Christmas holidays are an ideal time to prune deciduous fruits.

Short days, cool nights, occasional frosts have induced dormancy and leaf fall. Crisp, sunny weather is perfect for outdoor work. Muscadine grapes are trained along wires, and canes are headed in to spurs, each of which is allowed to carry about four buds. Figs are pruned severely because these deciduous plants fruit on wood of the current season's growth. Peaches and plums are pruned by shortening the branches that grow from the scaffold or main branches, by one third to one half. Pecans, citrus and other tropical and subtropical fruits are pruned only to remove crossing, diseased or broken wood.

Because firethorns and bottle-brushes do not transplant easily, small plants in gallon cans are best for planting. Have the nurseryman slit down through the metal, then, at the planting sites, remove the containers with great care. Plant at exactly the same depth that they grew previously. Small specimens of hollies in cans are also best for transplanting. But plants that have become pot-bound never become good landscape trees. Yaupon, one of the finest native shrubs of the South, is now available in the dwarf form, *nana*.

CHAPTER 34

THE SOUTHWEST

The Region of Mild Winters—Climatic Areas—Tropical Microclimates—Salty Soils—Frost Protection—Native and Other Plants—Calendar of Garden Work

GARDENING IS A WAY of life in the Southwest, where living space is generous even in large cities. With the high proportion of homeowners in this area, almost everyone has the opportunity to garden if he wishes to do so.

Climate in the Southwest ranges from near-tropical to alpine. In the Los Angeles area, for instance, tropical bananas and papayas may be growing within sight of snowy mountain valleys where the climate is similar to that of North Dakota.

The complexity of the climate in this region is shown by flowering that is advanced on the average of four days for every degree of latitude going south. But in addition to this, for every 400-ft. rise in elevation, flowering is retarded by four days. Thus spring not only comes in a surge along the south-to-north valleys, but in the mountains to the west it arrives everywhere abruptly and erratically, depending on the altitude.

Most of the population is concentrated in the flat valleys and plateaus, where mountain waters can be carried by streams or far-flung aqueducts. But even in the centers of dense population there are a multitude of climatic areas, varying from the coast to the high desert and intermountain plateaus. Only in the mountain terrain is there sufficient summer rainfall to maintain garden plants. The region is essentially an arid one, made fertile by irrigation.

THE MILD-WINTER REGION

A narrow strip of land on the Pacific Coast, extending from San Diego to the north, and west across the low deserts to Yuma and Phoenix, Arizona, has mild winters, kept so by the influence of the warming Pacific Ocean on one side and by high mountain barriers on the other, which act to check cold air from the interior. In summer the ocean cools the coastal strip; and the almost daily drift of high fog, screening the sun, moderates the temperature. Inland, universally high temperatures and low humidity rapidly exhaust the moisture of the soil. In the mild-winter areas without prolonged winter chilling, plants fail to become dormant. Some deciduous fruit trees bloom erratically over a long period. Ripe fruit and flowers on one plant at the same time are not uncommon after warm winters. The lives of some shrubs and many perennials which require a period of dormancy are shortened by the absence of enduring winter chill.

CLIMATIC AREAS

The Southwest may be divided into Areas which have different climates and soils. There are, of course, variations within these Areas, but each has distinctive features that determine its plant life.

Area 1

This extends from Morro Bay, Cali-

fornia, southward along the coast to Mexico. It includes the valleys that are not separated from the ocean by mountain ranges, such as the flower-seed-growing country around Lompoc and Santa Maria, coastal Santa Barbara County, the broad plain around Ventura and Oxnard, the Los Angeles basin, most of Orange County, the Mission Valley and the city of San Diego. The most nearly tropical area of the West, its day temperatures are uniformly in the low 50's in winter and 80's in summer. There are more hours between 65° and 75° F. than anywhere else in the continental United States.

Freezes seldom occur in the southern section and only every two or three years in the northern section, but tropical plants can be easily protected during these rather rare cold spells.

Light intensity is brilliant on clear days, yet fog and haze are so frequent in summer that many shade-loving plants can be grown in full sun in this coastal area. The long summer builds up sufficient heat by October or November to ripen varieties of mangoes that mature in June and July in Florida. Snow is almost unknown.

Area 2

Here are interior valleys known as the "inner coastal" region, which are separated by mountains from the ocean. In winter there is hardly ever any snowfall. This Area includes sections near Ojai and around Moorpark and Fillmore in Ventura County; the San Fernando, San Gabriel and La Canada valleys in Los Angeles County; as well as the section from Fallbrook to Escondido, in San Diego County—all in California.

In this subtropical climate citrus and avocados thrive but must be protected during severely cold nights, which may occur every winter. It is

622

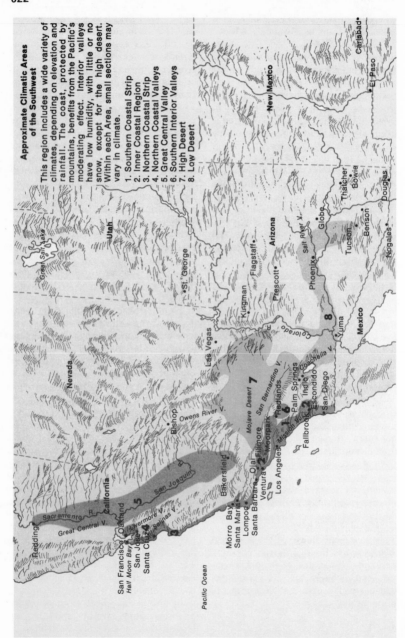

Approximate Climatic Areas of the Southwest

This region includes a wide variety of climates, depending on elevation and rainfall. The coast, protected by mountains, benefits from the Pacific's moderating effect. Interior valleys have low humidity, with little or no snow, except for the high desert. Within each Area, small sections may vary in climate.

1. Southern Coastal Strip
2. Inner Coastal Region
3. Northern Coastal Strip
4. Northern Coastal Valleys
5. Great Central Valley
6. Southern Interior Valleys
7. High Desert
8. Low Desert

warmer in summer and colder in winter than Area 1, but the extreme low is only 20° F. Careful location of plants in the garden and protective measures against severe cold make it possible to grow tropicals, such as bougainvillea and hibiscus, that would otherwise succumb.

Lower humidity deprives gardeners of the opportunity to raise many kinds of plants, but the successful cultivation of some varieties of roses, crape myrtles and other plants that are especially subject to powdery-mildew disease is one reward. Summer-bearing varieties of avocados are usually more dependable because of the frequency of cold, wet weather when Fuerte and other spring-bearing varieties are blooming. Failure of pollination because of wet weather results in disappointing yields of the spring-bearing kinds.

Area 3

From Morro Bay northward along the coast is a narrow band that widens at Santa Cruz and Half Moon Bay and includes most of San Francisco and Oakland. The ocean has a tremendous effect on the climate, moderating the winter chill and tempering the summer heat with fingers of fog that extend landward for a considerable distance in summer.

The cool weather favors the growing of Brussels sprouts and artichokes; carnations and stocks are the cut-flower growers' favorites. Here (at Santa Cruz) most of North America's supply of tuberous begonias is grown, and the climate is perfect for fuchsias, azaleas and rhododendrons.

Winter temperatures average 48° F., summer temperatures about 60°. The sun shines only 65 percent of the year, and snow in winter is rare.

Area 4

In the north, the coastal valleys are slightly warmer in both winter and summer: the Salinas Valley, the leeward side of the peninsula south of San Francisco to San Jose, the Santa Clara and Livermore valleys and part of the Bay Area. This is where most of the country's summer lettuce is produced, but winter temperatures are low enough to permit cherries and other deciduous fruit trees and flowering shrubs to grow. Snapdragons, pansies and sweet peas continue to bloom throughout the winter.

Summer temperatures average 70° F.; in winter, temperatures go as low as 20° F. but average about 50° F. It snows once every few years.

Area 5

This is the Great Central Valley (San Joaquin) where winter fog of weeks' duration serves to differentiate it from the low desert. It stretches from Bakersfield in the south to Redding in the north. Hillsides and mountain slopes that provide good air drainage permit the growth of citrus. A long growing season favors cherries, Japanese plums, apricots, figs and grapes; peaches, nectarines and pears are also extensively grown. Walnuts and almonds are the most popular nut trees. Winter temperatures down to 16° F. allow the growth of forsythias, weigelas, lilacs and peonies and provide adequate winter chilling for peaches, pears and cherries. The early onset of the long season of hot weather curtails the growing of cool-season annuals and shrubs—such as primroses, stocks, pansies, azaleas, pieris and heather—but there are many compensations for this disadvantage.

Area 6

Valleys more distant from the ocean, such as the Pomona and the San Bernardino—including Riverside and Redlands—form this Area. Snow is rare except over 3000 ft. The temperature fluctuates greatly in summer and winter. Highs of 116° F. are attained every summer, with night temperatures in the low 60's. In winter it is common for day temperatures to reach 80°, with nights down to 20°. The hot weather sets in abruptly in June and continues until October.

In this Area citrus need protection night after night in winter, but hot summer weather is ideal for navel oranges, as well as pomegranates and persimmons. A greater variety of fruits can be grown here than anywhere else in North America.

Area 7

The high desert is colder than the interior valleys. Snow stays on the ground for several days in winter, and citrus cannot be grown. This Area includes the Antelope Valley north of Los Angeles and most of the Mojave Desert, as well as scattered valleys in Arizona near Phoenix and south of Tucson. Such Arizona towns as Benson, Bowie, Douglas, Thatcher, Kingman, Globe and Nogales share this climate, as well as Carlsbad, N. Mex., and El Paso, Tex.

Apples, cherries, pears and peaches grow well here, mostly under irrigation, and peonies and lilacs may be cultivated. Day and night temperatures differ by 35° to 40° F. Winter temperature drops to 10°, eliminating subtropical plants from this region.

Area 8

The low desert extends from Palm Springs and Indio in the Coachella Valley in California, and Yuma, Phoenix and the Salt River Valley, to Tucson in Arizona. It is characterized by high temperatures throughout the year, moderating somewhat in winter. Extremely low temperatures of short duration can occur, but the average minimum is around 36° F.

Citrus, especially grapefruit, are grown; oranges are often given part shade, as are roses. This is the only Area in the United States where dates can be grown. Cool-season vegetables and flowers are planted in October. The long growing season favors Thompson seedless grapes, cotton, watermelons, tomatoes and sweet corn. In winter, lettuce, carrots and spinach are produced. Warm temperatures and maximum hours of sunshine make winters almost ideal here, but summers are made bearable only by air conditioning. Snow in winter is very unusual.

HARDSHIPS FOR TROPICALS

At the same time rather low temperatures, not only in winter but even in spring and summer, drastically limit the kinds of tropical plants that can be grown. Infrequent freezes occur in normally frost-free areas, and many tropical plants have enzyme systems which are harmfully affected even when temperatures do not drop below 36° F. The greatest losses in southern California are among tropical plants which succumb to root-rot diseases caused by cold soil. Easily affected are many of the most desirable tropicals: the flamboyant tree (*Delonix regia*), ixoras, many varieties of hibiscus, allamandas and the African tulip tree (*Spathodea campanulata*). Mangoes need more extensive heat than California with its cool nights can provide. Gardenias can be grown only in the warmest locations of the coast.

By utilizing the coldest and the warmest spots in the garden for plants that need either extreme, it is possible to increase the number of kinds of plants that can be grown successfully. "Microclimates" of the garden can be created by the skillful gardener who uses windscreens or plants near a warm whitewashed south or southwest wall to hold heat; in a sun-baked patio, lemons, oranges or grapefruit can be grown.

In the desert to the west, the sun is brilliant and unbroken by clouds. Humidity is reduced to such a low point that keeping tender plants alive when desert winds blow is a tough job. A climate must be created with sprays, mists, foggers and frequent watering. Even so, maidenhair fern, piggyback plant, fuchsias and tuberous begonias suffer drastic setbacks or die altogether with the best care. Such weather conditions limit the growth of rhododendrons through all the Southwest except central California.

SOILS

Most of the densely populated sections of the Southwest are on alluvial soil—bottomlands, floodplains, terraces or gently sloping alluvial fans of the rivers. They are found in central and southern California, and along the Colorado River and its tributaries in both California and Arizona. The climate is arid to semiarid. The natural vegetation is largely the tenacious chaparral of the West, except along streams. These soils become very productive under irrigation.

In places other than these rich alluvial stretches, the soils of the Southwest have little humus, and high concentrations of salt abound.

Vast areas are desert soils with a brownish-gray surface that grades down into a layer of hardpan called "caliche." Red desert soils have the same characteristics but differ in color and are mostly covered with creosote bush and cactuses including giant saguaro, mesquite, palo verde and Joshua trees. Furthermore, with the high temperatures that prevail most of the year, bacteria and funguses are always active, breaking down and even destroying any organic matter that does exist. In the Southwest, soils are not leached by frequent rains and

are apt to be saline. The ruin of salty soil can be aggravated by irrigation water, which has a high soluble-salt content. Frequent summer irrigation and constant evaporation build up salts in the soil in a way similar to that of lime accumulating in a tea kettle. This will raise the alkalinity of the soil to a point much too high for many garden plants.

In these parts of the Southwest, gardening is a great challenge. Care in watering and a buildup of humus in the soil give it more body and increase its water-holding capacity. Organic matter helps heavy soils by binding particles together, improving water drainage and aeration (see "The Soil," page 726, and "Fertilizers and Manures," page 749). Soils can be made more acid by thoroughly mixing in a small amount of soil sulphur. Usually a cupful is enough before planting a shrub or small tree, and 10 lb. is sufficient for 1000 sq. ft. of lawn or flower bed (see pages 741 to 742 concerning soil alkalinity).

PROTECTION FROM FROST

Frost warnings are broadcast nightly by radio stations when cold threatens. In the home garden, vegetables and flowers may be protected by hot-kaps—waxed-paper covers used on tomatoes, watermelons and other vegetables and flowers. These hold sufficient heat in to prevent frost damage. An asphalt mulch is sometimes used for spraying on the soil surface. This absorbs heat, warms up the soil and so encourages early germination and growth of the warm-season crops planted in winter or early spring.

Ornamental plants may be protected from frost with a covering of opaque cloth or black plastic film suspended over the shrub or tree. Leaves in direct contact with the cover will freeze. If an electric light bulb is turned on underneath the covering, many kinds of plants will survive severe cold without damage.

Similarly, tender plants under a roof overhang are less likely to freeze than specimens of the same kinds in the open, because the roof traps heat that radiates from the soil on a clear night. Another protection useful for vegetables and ground covers is to turn on sprinklers in freezing temperatures. This works on the principle that when water turns to ice, heat is released which the plants readily absorb, thus preventing damage to them. This method cannot be used on trees and shrubs, because the ice formed is likely to break branches.

Frost-damaged plants should thaw out slowly to prevent the most severe injury. If the plants are in containers they should be moved to a shaded, cool place. If they cannot be moved, sprinkle them with water and provide protection from the sun. When sun hits frozen parts, damage is greatly increased.

Do not prune plants immediately after they have been injured by the cold. Wait until they begin to grow again and all danger of frost is passed. Then cut back to green shoots. Some plants you may think are dead will grow again from the roots.

COMBATING HIGH TEMPERATURES

The best way to modify high temperatures is to provide shade and supply a mulch which is kept moist at all times. The water evaporating from the moist surface has a cooling effect.

An automatic mister that turns on periodically creates comparatively cool temperatures in which tuberous begonias and fuchsias can be grown, even in the hottest climates.

Plants themselves help to create humid atmospheric conditions by means of the moisture they transpire. For this reason they are easier to grow massed than as single specimens.

Hot sun burns an exposed fleshy fruit. Keeping fruit trees well foliated is the best precaution against this injury. Heat damage often occurs when the rate of transpiration is checked by watering. The amount of heat absorbed is then greater than that lost by evaporation.

NATIVE PLANTS AND THE SOUTHWESTERN LANDSCAPE

In the Southwest, native plants are grown chiefly because of their drought resistance and their easy culture, which demands no watering all year long. Most of them begin to look a little bedraggled in summer and are not considered prime subjects for year-round beauty. But these tough plants can solve a slope problem where no water is available for irrigation. Some are widely grown and have great cultural adaptability. Others can withstand little or no summer moisture but are killed by root-rot diseases when drainage is not perfect. Natives of the coastal area have different requirements from the plants of the desert or those of the riverbanks.

Most are adapted to soils low in humus, and the natural soil does not have to be amended to grow them. They get along on small amounts of fertilizer elements—heavy fertilization is usually harmful.

CACTUSES AND SUCCULENTS

These, which often achieve dramatic size, are frequently used in landscap-

In this desert garden, the flagstone terrace is flanked at the right by an arrangement of succulents and cactuses. Beyond, naturalized cactuses merge with the open desert. Among these are barrel cactus, prickly pear, cholla, spidery ocotillo and giant saguaro. Close to the terrace at left is a Yucca elephantipes. Stones are carefully set to prevent walking into the more vicious varieties—cholla, especially.

ing throughout the Southwest. Of the three branches of the cactus family, two are widespread as natives. The first group, *Opuntieae*, to which the prickly pears belong, generally requires full sun, sparse to moderate supplies of water, and sharply drained, sandy soil that is rather poor in fertilizer elements. All members of this group are stem succulents, easy to propagate from cuttings which root quickly in sand.

The second group, *Cereeae*, is so varied that no general cultural requirements can be given, but among those native to the Southwest the torch (*Cereanae*), hedgehog (*Echinocereanae*), barrel (*Echinocactanae*), melon (*Cactanae*), and pincushion (*Coryphanthanae*) cactuses grow best in full sun and in sandy soil with little water.

Other kinds of cactuses, notably the tree-dwelling types such as epiphyllums, need soil rich in humus or coarse organic matter, abundant water and semishade for best growth. Climbing cactuses, which include night-blooming species, also require rich soil, shade, much water and protection from freezing. Epiphyllums are used mostly in hanging baskets and are grown in lathhouses with orchids, begonias and ferns. All grow outdoors in the Southwest in Areas 1 and 2.

Succulent members of the amaryllis and lily families, both native and introduced kinds, such as agaves and aloes, are extremely useful for landscaping in the Southwest and are used as specimen plants. The agaves, of which the century plant is an example, die after blooming, but usually require about ten years to flower. The century plant is too large for the average garden. Agaves and aloes are of easy culture, needing only a small amount of water and protection from severe cold to thrive.

Other succulent plants with similar

requirements which are also used as specimens include: *Kalanchoë beharensis*; jade plant, *Crassula argentea*; some of the larger echeverias such as *E. gibbiflora*; several species of *Aeonium*; and *Fouquieria splendens*, the ocotillo. The curiously contorted *Euphorbia lactea cristata* is sometimes used as a living sculpture.

Sedums, smaller echeverias and a great variety of mesembryanthemums are prized as ground covers because of their low maintenance requirements. They need little water and little or no fertilizer to grow and spread. All mesembryanthemums need full sun, but some sedums and echeverias grow better in shade, especially in the desert.

Succulents of many kinds are used as ground covers and include *Othonna crassifolia*, little pickles; and *Kleinia repens*. A trailing variety of *Portulacaria afra* is also used, as is the widely planted annual, portulaca or rose moss.

In Palm Springs and other desert areas, but rarely elsewhere, the total landscaping is often devoted exclusively to cactuses and other succulents. Naturalistic groupings of these around protective rocks together with a few native desert trees, give interesting desert-landscape effects.

DECIDUOUS TREES

Most deciduous trees that grow throughout North America succeed in the Southwest but some, such as flowering dogwood, cannot be grown except at high elevations, and others—horse chestnut and laburnum, for example—struggle in southern California but succeed elsewhere. Many are not adapted to desert conditions—birch, hawthorn and maple among them.

Well-Adapted to Desert:
Acer negundo . . . . . . box elder

Albizzia julibrissin . . . . silk tree
Catalpa bignonioides. . Indian bean
Fraxinus uhdei. . . . . shamel ash
F. velutina . . . . . . Arizona ash
Gleditsia triacanthos . . .
honey locust
Liquidambar styraciflua . . .
sweet gum
Melia azedarach . . . . chinaberry
Pistacia chinensis. . . . . pistache
Pterocarya stenoptera . . .
Chinese wingnut
Robinia pseudoacacia . . .
yellow locust
Salix . . . . willow
Tamarix parviflora . . . . tamarisk

EVERGREEN TREES
These are especially numerous in the Southwest. A few are conifers; most are broad-leaved kinds, many beautiful in bloom.

Broadleaf Kinds
Well-Adapted to Desert and Other Areas:

These are comparatively few. In addition to the kinds listed below they include *Agonis flexuosa*, the desert willow, which grows to 40 ft. tall, has willowlike leaves and white flowers, and *Tamarix aphylla*, the athel tree, 15 ft. tall, with evergreen branches and twigs and numerous tiny pink flowers.
Casuarina equisetifolia . . .
beefwood or Australian pine
Ceratonia siliqua . . . . . . carob
Schinus molle . . .
California pepper tree
S. terebinthifolius . . .
Brazilian pepper tree

Conifers
Because the northern part of our continent is composed of almost solid stands of pine, larch, fir, spruce and hemlock, we commonly think that all conifers are cold-resistant, forgetting that in large sections of the tropics and subtropics conifer forests exist which

have never been subjected to cold and have little or no resistance to freezing.
Araucaria araucana . . .
monkey puzzle
A. bidwillii . . . . . bunya bunya
Cedrus atlantica . . . . Atlas cedar
C.a. glauca . . . . blue Atlas cedar
C. deodara. . . . . . deodar cedar
C. libani . . . . cedar of Lebanon
Cupressus arizonica . . .
Arizona cypress
C. sempervirens. . . Italian cypress
Pinus canariensis . . .
Canary Island pine
P. radiata . . . . . Monterey pine
Podocarpus elongata
P. macrophyllus
P.m. maki

In addition to the conifers listed above and those described beginning on page 391 in "Evergreen Trees," the following are important kinds in the Southwest:

Araucaria excelsa (Norfolk Island pine) has precisely placed branches like the points of a star. It can withstand heat but not much cold. It tolerates seacoast exposure, and can survive to grow 70 ft. tall, but only along the coast.

Pinus halepensis (Aleppo pine) is the best pine for the desert. It has sparse, gray-green needles and great tolerance of heat, drought, salinity and dry, hot winds, as well as seacoast conditions.

P. pinea (Italian stone pine), a beautiful pine which takes the shape of a giant umbrella. It withstands desert winds and will thrive in a heavily watered lawn.

SHRUBS
The greatest difference between the shrubs of the Southwest and those of most other areas of the United States is the fact that they are primarily evergreen. In fact, deciduous shrubs, no matter how beautiful, are usually

accorded second place in favor of year-round foliage.

Descriptions of suitable shrubs for the Southwest not described below will be found in "Evergreen Shrubs," page 450, in "Shrubs and Flowering Small Trees," page 417, and in other parts of this book.

ARCTOSTAPHYLOS (MANZANITA)
Evergreen shrub or small tree, 12 ft. or more tall; flowers small, urn-shaped, in drooping panicles, white or pink.

ATRIPLEX BREWERI (SALT BUSH)
Three to six ft., foliage silver-gray. This and some other species are well suited for exposed sunny locations and saline soils.

BACCHARIS PILULARIS (COYOTE BUSH)
Five ft., leaves toothed; flowers small, in clusters, whitish. For dry, sandy soils.

COCCOLOBIS UVIFERA (SEA GRAPE)
Evergreen, 20 ft., leaves large, rounded, handsome; flowers in dense racemes, greenish white; fruits like bunches of grapes, purple, used for jelly. Excellent for seaside.

CORREA
Evergreen, somewhat fuchsialike plants, 3 to 4 ft.; flowers tubular, red, white or yellowish. *C. speciosa*, flowers bright red, is one of the best. Suitable for dry, sandy soils.

DENDROMECON RIGIDA
(BUSH POPPY; TREE POPPY)
Evergreen, 6 to 8 ft. tall; flowers large, poppylike, golden yellow. Suitable for dry, sunny conditions.

DOMBEYA
Large-leaved evergreen, 6 to 20 ft. tall, with dense hanging clusters of pink or white flowers.

ERIOGONUM
Evergreen, 3 to 6 ft., with white or pink flowers, adaptable for exposed, dry locations.

HIBISCUS ROSA-SINENSIS
(ROSE-OF-CHINA)
Evergreen, 15 to 25 ft.; flowers red, pink or white, in some varieties double. Variety *cooperi* has handsomely variegated leaves.

LAVATERA ASSURGENTIFLORA
Ten ft., flowers rose-purple. Well adapted for sunny, exposed locations.

LEUCOPHYLLUM TEXANUM
Eight ft., leaves silvery; flowers purple. For sunny, exposed locations.

MACKAYA BELLA
Four ft., flowers large, tubular, lavender-colored.

PUNICA GRANATUM (POMEGRANATE)
Attractive in foliage and flower. Varieties range from 3 to 18 ft. in height and have white, red or pink flowers, in some varieties double.

RHUS LAURINA (LAUREL SUMAC)
Evergreen; foliage aromatic; flowers greenish-white, in dense panicles; fruits whitish with a waxy coating. Suitable for hot, dry locations.

TECOMARIA CAPENSIS
(CAPE HONEYSUCKLE)
Evergreen, more or less climbing; flowers funnel-shaped, orange-scarlet, in clusters. Very handsome.

TETRAPANAX PAPYRIFERUM
(RICE PAPER PLANT)
Evergreen, 15 ft.; leaves large, lobed, green above, white beneath. Flowers in large panicles, fuzzy, cream-colored.

TIBOUCHINA SEMIDECANDRA
Evergreen, 10 ft.; flowers large, flat,

a fine purple. For partial shade and rich, reasonably moist soil.

XYLOSMA SENTICOSA
Evergreen, 3 ft., spiny; flowers inconspicuous.

TREELIKE PLANTS
Some plants are called trees but do not truly belong in this classification. Among them banana, beaucarnea, dracena, nolina, giant bird-of-paradise and yucca are especially suited for use on sunny patios.

BANANA
Two varieties of bananas are grown in the mildest Area of the Southwest. One produces sprouts or suckers and keeps renewing itself after flowering.

Musa ensete (Abyssinian banana) develops a single stalk and graceful, arching leaves. It grows up to 20 ft. tall and dies after flowering and fruiting, without producing sucker growths. It is propagated from seeds. Bananas need generous fertilizing and watering to keep them growing rapidly. This way old, ragged leaves that are removed are quickly replaced with new ones. One variety of the Abyssinian banana has handsome red leaves and is a choice plant for a tropical accent. It will come back after freezes of down to 15° F., but the foliage is browned at 28°.

BEAUCARNEA
To the genus *Beaucarnea* belong a group of yuccalike plants with swollen, bulbous trunks and tufts of grasslike leaves at the ends of their branches. Young plants grow erect and unbranched, but older specimens may have multiple trunks. In the grotesque trunk are water-storage tissues that will keep the plant alive when it is severed from its roots, so that transplanting presents no problem. Beaucarneas are killed at 20° F.

CORDYLINE AUSTRALIS (DRACENA)
A palmlike plant with thick clusters of radiating leaves at the end of each branch. When young, the plant grows as a single trunk with a single tuft of leaves 18 to 36 in. long and 1 to 2 in. wide; leaves are light green, blue-green or bronze. Branched clusters of small white flowers appear in summer but are relatively unimportant. This plant grows rapidly to 15 to 30 ft., withstands heat and drought, tolerates any soil. Not affected by wind or seacoast conditions and is free of pests and diseases. The long taproot must not be damaged if transplanting is to be successful. It is hardy to 10° F. and thrives in coastal and desert climates.

NOLINA
This yuccalike plant has leaves that, when faded, hang down and create a shaggy skirt. The leaves are 3 ft. long and only ¾ in. wide. A 2-ft. flowering stalk of whitish flowers is produced in summer. Nolina is about as hardy as beaucarnea.

STRELITZIA NICOLAI
(GIANT BIRD-OF-PARADISE)
Of tropical appearance, its banana-like leaves are strong and not apt to shred in high winds. The stem becomes treelike and after 15 to 20 years reaches 25 ft. in height. White flowers with a blue tongue are produced continuously in warm areas. It needs rich soil and plenty of water for maximum growth. Hardy to 25° F.; grows in protected locations in Palm Springs, Calif., and Phoenix, Ariz. (See illustration, page 632.)

YUCCA
Yuccas are good specimen plants, many having a decided desert aspect, including the Joshua tree, *Yucca brevifolia;* and the Spanish dagger, *Y. gloriosa.*

Strelitzia nicolai
(Giant Bird-of-Paradise)

Y. elephantipes. This species from Mexico needs a very warm climate. Its wide shiny leaves, always lax and often pendant, are bright green, with purple tones in winter. It needs considerably more water than the desert species but should have sharp drainage. In the desert it may be favored by some shade. As with all yuccas, the blooms are magnificent. It is damaged by frost at 22° F. (See illustration, page 627.)

PALMS

For more information on palms, see page 390 in "Evergreen Trees" and page 607 in "The Southeast."

Fan-leaved Kinds

CHAMAEROPS HUMILIS
(MEDITERRANEAN FAN-LEAVED PALM)
Native from Spain to Sicily and from

Algeria to Morocco. This species is not as wind-resistant as the windmill palm (see *Trachycarpus*, page 633) but withstands the desert climate better. Some shade should be provided in extremely hot locations.

ERYTHEA
Erythea armata (Mexican blue palm). Native to the desert areas of Baja California. Leaves shed, allowing a clean, smooth trunk. Very sturdy and well adapted to hot, dry conditions, living without irrigation after becoming established.

E. brandegeei (San Jose palm). Native to Baja California. It is taller, more slender and faster-growing than the others. The fruits, covered with puffy shells, are a nuisance.

E. edulis (Guadalupe palm). Native to Guadalupe Island, off the coast of Mexico. It grows faster than the Mexican blue palm and attains 60 ft. in the desert with good soil, ample water and nutrients. Fruits of both species cause litter.

E. elegans. Less than 6 ft. tall. The leaves are almost as blue as those of the Mexican blue palm. This species, from Sonora, Mexico, is of great decorative value for small gardens, especially when several are planted together.

LIVISTONA (FOUNTAIN PALM)
This palm is native to Australia, China, Malaya and the Philippines. All varieties need rich, moist but well-drained soil. They are self-cleaning, shedding their leaves as soon as the leaves die.

Livistona australis grows slowly but attains 60 ft.; has gracefully drooping leaf tips. This species will withstand 18° F. and grows well in Palm Springs, Calif., and Phoenix, Ariz., and as far north as San Francisco.

L. chinensis, the Chinese fountain palm, is almost as hardy but is not as well adapted to desert conditions—where it is better in shade, especially when young.

RHAPIS (LADY PALM, BAMBOO PALM)

The common fan-leaved variety needs shade; its leaves turn yellow in sun. In the desert, it needs added humidity when temperatures are excessive. Forms natural clumps much like bamboo and is sometimes used as a substitute for bamboo in shaded areas. Needs rich, moist soil and protection from wind.

Rhapis humilis, tall and most attractive; under ideal conditions grows to 12 ft.

R. excelsa grows to only 5 ft.

TRACHYCARPUS FORTUNEI (WINDMILL PALM)

Native of China and Japan. It will withstand briefly temperatures down to zero, and grows better in cool coastal areas than in the intense heat of the desert. Extremely wind-resistant. The windmill palm needs a deep, fertile soil, abundant water and good drainage.

WASHINGTONIA

Washingtonia filifera (fan-leaved palm). Found in canyons in western Arizona and southern California, this is the only native of the Southwest. Favored as a street tree in many cities, including Phoenix and Tucson, Ariz., it grows from Las Vegas, Nev., to Globe and Nogales, Ariz. Hardy below 15° F. when established and mature, but it is damaged by temperatures below 25° F. when young.

W. robusta (Mexican fan-leaved palm). Extremely slender, of great vigor, growing 2 ft. or more a year in a favorable location and attaining heights of 100 ft.: hardy to 15° F. Grows better than *W. filifera* in humid regions near the coast, but is also at its best in the desert.

Feather-leaved Kinds

ARCHONTOPHOENIX CUNNINGHAMIANA (KING PALM)

Known as *Seaforthia elegans*, this is truly an elegant tree with a slender, smooth trunk and a broad leaf base that bulges slightly and completely hides the ugly transition zone between old and new fronds. It withstands only 10 degrees of frost under favorable circumstances when mature. It requires rich, moist soil and mild fertilizing. Abundant water while growing is necessary, but in cold winters this palm withstands dryness well.

ARECASTRUM ROMANZOFFIANUM (QUEEN PALM)

Often sold as *Cocos plumosa*, it is one of the most common feather-leaved

Archontophoenix cunninghamiana
(King Palm)

palms in Los Angeles and San Diego, and is native to South America. Variable in cold resistance and height. It grows best in the coastal sections of California and is hardy to 18° F. but young plants are often damaged at 25°. High temperatures (above 100°) burn the fronds. Sheltered and shaded specimens grow at Palm Springs, Calif., Phoenix and Tucson, Ariz. Short-lived (about 60 years) and subject to damage from smog.

BUTIA CAPITATA

Known in the trade as *Cocos australis*, this is a tough palm from Brazil and Uruguay that takes temperatures down to 12° F., remaining undamaged when citrus is severely injured. It withstands heat and drought but must be supplied with water for good growth. The leaf bases make a particular pattern that identifies this tree. The arched fronds are blue. Short-lived palm (30 to 40 years), about 20 ft. tall.

CARYOTA (FISHTAIL PALM)

Caryota ochlandra. Fishtail palms are generally considered to be borderline subjects in California but this one from China has survived at 26° F.

C. urens (wine palm). A mammoth tree to be avoided in settled areas because the heavy fronds, 15 ft. long, crash down with great force. The tremendous trunk is often 5 ft. in diameter and the tree is 60 ft. high when mature. It survives from San Francisco to Tucson, Ariz.

CHAMAEDOREA

A group of bamboolike palms from Central America, these make beautiful clumps in the shade.

Chamaedorea costaricana grows to 10 ft. and is hardy to 25° F.

COLLINIA ELEGANS

This native of the Guatemalan jungles needs full shade for best growth and can survive little frost. An ideal container specimen, it suckers prolifically. Known also as *Neanthe bella*, this is a dwarf palm.

HOWEA FOSTERIANA (KENTIA PALM)

A native of Lord Howe Island in the South Pacific, this palm is best known as a pot plant. It survives outdoors if given the protection of an overhang.

PHOENIX (DATE PALM)

Phoenix canariensis (Canary Island date palm). Quite hardy, surviving temperatures down to 15° F. from San Francisco to Tucson in all soils except cold, heavy soil where water stands. The massive trunk is topped by huge fronds up to 15 ft. long. It withstands sea winds and salt spray, and can tolerate saline soil. This voracious feeder needs abundant water and heavy fertilizing for best growth.

P. dactylifera (commercial date palm). Widely used for ornament outside the area where it is grown for fruit production, mostly because date groves are being subdivided and huge trees are available for transplanting. Same requirements as the Canary Island date but considerably less cold resistance. Long hours of 100° F. weather is needed for dates to set, and abundant water must always be available.

P. reclinata (Senegal date palm). Best choice for the average garden and ideal for the pool patio. The slender, curving trunk of the true species does not appear in plants grown from seed resulting from hybridization with *P. canariensis*. It grows rapidly when young and is inclined to produce suckers which slow down growth of the main stem. Hardy to 24° F. when young, it will withstand to 20° when mature. This palm grows best from Santa Barbara southward to San Diego and eastward to Riverside,

Calif. A clump makes an excellent planting near a pool.

P. roebelenii (pygmy date palm). A very refined small tree, 3 to 6 ft. tall. It is produced locally for use as a house plant since the favorite species, *Collinia elegans*, is subject to damage by smog. It can be grown in a pot, transferred to a planter in the patio and eventually planted in the garden, where it makes a graceful specimen.

RHOPALOSTYLIS

Rhopalostylis baueri, a better and more stylish tree than *R. sapida*; has a heavier trunk and more graceful, arched leaves. This species, from Norfolk Island, thrives from Santa Barbara to San Diego but is very rare.

R. sapida (shaving-brush palm), well named as its fronds are upright on the end of a handlelike stem. A native of New Zealand, it thrives in Santa Barbara, where it attains 30 ft. in height.

CYCADS

The supposed connecting link between ferns and conifers is a group of plants called cycads, which are raised extensively in the gardens of the Southwest.

The most primitive seed plants—remnants of the Coal Age—they need moist, rich soil and a full-sun location at the coast, shade in the desert and inland. Their dramatic accents make them conspicuous in the most lavish landscapes.

Cycas revoluta (sago palm) is the most hardy but exceedingly slow-maturing. It withstands 15° F. and grows from San Francisco to Tucson, Ariz. In its long duration of life on earth, this plant has endured many hardships and will survive much neglect. It is a native of Japan.

Dion edule, hardy to 20° F., is the most distinguished of the cycads. It needs shade and is an excellent plant

for growing in containers. This is a native of Mexico.

VINES

Vines are of special importance in the Southwest because they can bring shade to special spots. Most are vigorous growers and need more than average amounts of water and fertilizer during the growing season. Fortunately, in this region there is a wide array of tropical vines from which the gardener can choose. See also "Vines," page 492.

SEMITROPICAL PERENNIALS

Certain nonwoody perennials used in landscaping in the Southwest are rarely seen outdoors elsewhere in the country, except in Florida. These include the gingers, bamburantas, New Zealand flax, philodendrons (not the vines but the self-heading types), *Liriope* and the bird-of-paradise or *Strelitzia reginae*.

ALOCASIA MACRORHIZA

A better choice for ornamental use than Elephant's Ear (see *Colocasia* below), this plant has leaves that are large but more leathery and less subject to wind damage.

BAMBURANTA

More than one kind of plant is offered by nurseries under this name.

Bamburanta arnoldiana or *Hybophrynium braunianum*, a native of the Congo; grows to 3 ft.

Ctenanthe compressa; grows to 2 to 3 ft.

Ct. oppenheimiana (giant bamburanta); grows to 6 ft. The ctenanthes are natives of Brazil. All are adapted for growing in shade and all are tropical in effect.

COLOCASIA ESCULENTA
(ELEPHANT'S EAR, OR TARO)

Before philodendrons became abundant, the best bold-leaved tropical accent was the Elephant's Ear. Known as taro, it is the source of poi in the Hawaiian Islands. In frost-free areas, it is evergreen but can be killed to the ground by the slightest frost. (See also page 252 in "Tender Bulbs.")

GINGERS

Two kinds of plants called gingers are commonly grown—the ginger lily (*Hedychium*) and the shell ginger (*Alpinia*). Vigorous tropical plants, they have erect 4- to 6-ft. stems with colorful flowers in terminal clusters. Given a warm place, good light but not full sun except at the coast, and plenty of water, they will bloom in summer or fall. Great fragrance of flower and aromatic leaves are their outstanding characteristics.

All gingers need rich soil, high in humus, for best growth. Sharp frost will kill them to the ground but new shoots appear in spring. When the stalks have flowered they should be cut back to the soil level.

Alpinia speciosa (shell ginger), the most cold-tolerant of all gingers, withstanding 15° F., it must grow for two years before it blooms. The buds are coral-pink and open to reveal a yellow flower mottled with red.

Hedychium coronarium (garland flower) has white flowers.

H. flavum. Blooms are yellow to orange.

H. gardnerianum (kahili ginger), yellow blooms. This is the most easily flowered of the gingers and quite hardy to cold.

LIRIOPE

Liriope spicata and *L. muscari*, both described on page 490 in "Ground Covers Save Work," are useful for gardens in the Southwest.

PHILODENDRON

House-plant fanciers who know the common philodendron as a vine will have a difficult time relating it to the giant arborescent or treelike outdoor kinds. Yet they belong to the same genus, and are natives of the South American subtropics. Their ability to survive in the open, grow in full sun and stand without support differentiate them from the vining species. Most will endure 28° F. without a sign of injury but foliage burn occurs when the temperature drops to 22°. Cut-leaved varieties such as *P. selloum* and its hybrids have greater sun tolerance than those with entire leaves. These bold-leaved plants grow best in a coarse medium kept moist but not wet, and will respond very quickly to fertilizer.

PHORMIUM TENAX
(NEW ZEALAND FLAX)

This is a plant of very distinctive appearance much used by landscape architects in the Southwest. It will survive in any exposure and almost any soil but needs fertility and moisture for rapid growth. Grows to 6 ft. and has stiff, sword-shaped leaves that stand erect at first and later often become bowed or drooping. Curious mahogany-colored flower stalks appear in spring and stand well above the leaves, bearing dark red flowers. The stalks are used in flower arrangements. There are several varieties, of differing height and foliage color.

STRELITZIA REGINAE
(BIRD-OF-PARADISE)

The adopted flower of the city of Los Angeles, it is a perennial about 3 ft. high with colorful, long-lasting flowers that resemble the head of a tropical bird. They are produced more or less continuously but most commonly from October to April. Full sun is required for best bloom. The plant survives neglect but responds to water and fertilizer. Taking about five years to bloom, it will flower more quickly in a container than in a garden bed, surviving temperatures down to 20°.

DICHONDRA
Ground covers have become popular in the Southwest as lawn substitutes; dichondra is by far the most important. Best adapted to the area around Los Angeles, it thrives in shade in the desert. It grows wherever temperatures do not drop below 25° F. but revives following cold in such places as Las Vegas and Lancaster. The entire planting is killed if the soil freezes.

Dichondra is a low, dense, turfing plant belonging to the morning-glory family. Propagated by runners, it seeds heavily and naturalizes itself in lawns throughout the Los Angeles area. One pound of seed is sufficient to sow 1000 sq. ft. Planting is limited to the warm season (April to October), when germination occurs in ten days or less. A mulch must be applied to keep the soil moist. Water twice a day while seed is germinating.

Recently a weed-killer (diphenamid) has been developed that prevents weed growth without affecting the germination of dichondra. This has made the establishing of a dichondra lawn very simple.

GRASSES AND BAMBOOS
Beautiful, but quick to get out of hand, is the pampas grass, *Cortaderia selloana*, 6 to 8 ft. tall. The handsome white flower plumes appear in August from clumps of thin, arching, saw-toothed leaves. It grows only in the coastal area, southern interior valleys and the low desert.

Bamboos are divided into two groups: the clumping and the running types. The latter are planted only in containers or enclosed areas, because running bamboos can be weeds of the worst sort and will come up through an asphalt driveway.

One of the running types withstands down to –20° F. and can easily be grown anywhere in the Southwest. This is the yellow groove bamboo, *Phyllostachys aureosulcata*, which grows to 30 feet tall with stems up to 1½ inches in diameter. Most other kinds survive zero temperatures and include black joint bamboo, *P. niger* and the giant timber bamboo, *P. bambusoides*. Dwarf bamboo, *Pleioblastus viridi-striatus vagans*, both the green and the variegated, is a good plant near pools or in a paved area.

The clumping bamboos are less hardy, most of them being killed by temperatures from 15° to 20° F., and one, the male bamboo, *Dendrocalamus strictus*, is killed below 27°. Another giant species is *Bambusa oldhamii*, which grows to 50 ft. with stems up to 3 in. in diameter. It is hardy to 20°. *B. multiplex* includes the Alphonse Karr and Golden Goddess varieties that are 15 to 30 ft. and 8 to 10 ft., respectively. The hardiest of the clumping types is *Sinarundinaria murieliae*, which grows 12 ft. tall and survives zero temperatures.

BULBS
Several hardy bulbs offer problems when grown in the Southwest, but tender bulbs, for the most part, can be grown with ease. Among hardy bulbs, tulips are the most difficult; they usually survive no more than one season. In the warm-winter sections, varieties must be carefully selected to get tall stems and satisfactory flowers even the first year. In general, the most vigorous varieties do best, and these include the darwins, cottage, lily-flowered, parrot and the new orchid-flowered varieties. Most of the single early, early and late double, breeder, mendel and triumph varieties do not do well in southern California and the low desert areas. Among the species, only the lady

tulip, *Tulipa clusiana*, will naturalize itself readily.

Scillas, daffodils and narcissuses naturalize easily, even in the warmer areas, but crocuses, both autumn- and spring-flowering, are not satisfactory and hyacinths rarely bloom for more than one year. Lily of the valley, glory-of-the-snow, winter aconite and snowdrops are limited to the cold winter areas.

The Southwest more than makes up for these losses, however, when it comes to tender bulbs and roots that can be grown without lifting. These include:

Agapanthus umbellatus . . . .
                 lily of the Nile
Alstroemeria . . . . . Alstremaria
Amaryllis belladonna . . .
                 belladonna lily
Clivia . . . . Kafir lily
Cyclamen
Freesia
Gladiolus
Lachenalia . . . . . . Cape cowslip
Nerine
Sparaxis . . . . wandflower
Tigridia . . . . tigerflower
Watsonia

Most commercial production of ranunculuses and anemones is in southern California and these are generally suitable for the whole Southwest. It is worth noting here that, though not strictly bulbs, the evergreen varieties of day lilies are favored throughout this area and bloom continuously in warm weather.

EVERGREEN FRUIT TREES

The cherimoya, the litchi and the mango are too far from their tropical home climates to be anything but curiosities. Others are well adapted to large areas of the Southwest.

AVOCADO

Two types of avocados are grown in the Southwest—the Mexican and the Guatemalan. The most popular, however, is a cross between these two, named Fuerte. It is best suited to the interior valleys, which are not troubled by cold, wet weather when the tree blooms in February and March. Buds and blossoms are damaged with temperatures of 27° F., but if it survives cold periods unscathed it can withstand more freezing weather with only a blackening of the vessels in the fruit to show for it.

Mexican varieties have greater cold resistance; the Guatemalan have almost none. Both thrive on fertile, well-drained soil, amply supplied with water at about three-week intervals during the summer.

CITRUS

The least cold resistance of all citrus species is found in the lemon, although Meyer lemon and ponderosa lemon, both hybrids, have been grown where temperatures drop below 20° F. True lemons, *Citrus limonia*, are damaged at 28°. Hot, dry winds quickly defoliate lemons and they must be protected for best growth.

Sweet orange has more resistance to cold than any other citrus except the kumquat. It has survived temperatures as low as 15° F. Fruit will not mature in the cool coastal districts, however, and the coastal and interior valleys are best suited to its growth. The navel orange requires more heat and is best adapted to the area around Riverside, Calif.

Grapefruit, *C. paradisi*, needs still greater total heat and matures well only in the low desert from Coachella Valley to Phoenix. Grapefruit is less damaged by temperatures over 115° F. than either oranges or lemons.

Kumquat, *Fortunella*, the fruits of which are eaten whole—peel and all— are a type of citrus that thrives in all parts of California and Arizona except in the mountains. They have survived temperatures down to 10° F.

None of the citrus fruits are well-adapted to lawn planting, as frequent watering causes their leaves to drop.

MACADAMIA

The macadamia is tolerant of poor drainage, and many avocado trees that succumb to root rot on wet soils are being replaced with this tropical nut. It is very ornamental, reaching a height of 35 ft., and can be grown wherever avocados grow.

OLIVE

Picturesque when grown on the dry, sterile soils typical of the Southwest, the olive survives temperatures as low as 10° F. and can be grown almost anywhere except on the high desert and intermountain plateau. Trees in the hot interiors produce the best quality and heaviest crops.

LESSER-KNOWN EVERGREEN FRUIT TREES

CASIMIROA EDULIS (WHITE SAPOTE)

A good lawn tree, damaged at 25° F. but more tolerant of wet soil than citrus fruits. In San Francisco it survives but grows very slowly.

ERIOBOTRYA JAPONICA (LOQUAT)

A beautiful ornamental, and hardier than most subtropical trees, its habit of blooming in the winter causes the flowers to be destroyed by frost in cold areas. It is not a tree for the desert, where summer temperatures are too high. Loquat is well adapted to lawn planting.

FEIJOA SELLOWIANA (PINEAPPLE GUAVA)

Does best in rich, moist soil but withstands drought very well. It is a subtropical fruit, prefers cool locations, is well adapted to coastal California from San Diego to San Francisco,

but it will grow in the desert region to Tucson, Ariz. and in areas with temperatures above 10° F.

SEASIDE GARDENS

In the Southwest, as elsewhere, some plants are especially well adapted for gardens by the sea. Those listed below are among the most suitable. See also pages 550 to 553 in "Seaside Gardens."

Trees

Acacia
Casuarina equisetifolia . . .
           beefwood or Australian pine
Eucalyptus
Lyonothamnus floribundus
   asplenifolius . . Catalina ironwood
Melaleuca leucadendron . . .
               cajeput tree
Metrosideros tomentosa . . .
       New Zealand Christmas tree
Myoporum laetum
Pinus radiata. . . . Monterey pine
Pittosporum

Shrubs

Atriplex . . . . saltbush
Callistemon . . . . . . bottlebrush
Carissa grandiflora . . Natal plum
Cistus . . . . rockrose
Coccolobis uvifera . . . . sea grape
Coprosma baueri . . . mirror plant
Cotoneaster
Dodonaea viscosa . . . . hopbush
Erica . . . . heath
Escallonia
Grevillea banksii
Griselinia littoralis
Hakea suaveolens
Hebe andersonii
Hibiscus tiliaceus . . . . . mahoe
Lantana camara
Leptospermum
Ligustrum . . . . privet
Melaleuca . . . . . . bottlebrush
Nerium oleander . . . . . oleander
Pittosporum
Raphiolepis
Rosmarinus officinalis . . rosemary

Ground Covers

Armeria. . . . . . sea pink, thrift
Ceratostigma plumbaginoides
  (syn. *Plumbago larpentae*) . . .
              blue leadwort
Ficus pumila . . . . . creeping fig
Fragaria chiloensis . . . strawberry
Gazania
Juniperus . . . . juniper
Lantana montevidensis . . .
              trailing lantana
Limonium. . . . . statice
Lonicera . . . . honeysuckle
Mesembryanthemum
Ophiopogon japonicus . . .
              dwarf lilyturf
Pelargonium peltatum . . .
              ivy geranium
Portulacaria afra
Rosmarinus officinalis . . rosemary
Santolina chamaecyparissus . . .
              lavender cotton
Sedum

VEGETABLES

The largest commercial vegetable-growing areas in the United States lie within this region, so there is little interest in growing home vegetables here.

The wide variation in climate dictates the time of planting; the growing season is long and irrigation is a necessity. In Area 1, hot-weather crops such as tomatoes, corn, beans and the cucumber family encounter difficulty. Tomatoes often must be sprayed with a plant hormone to get blossoms to stay on and form (seedless) tomatoes. But the cool-season vegetables may be planted any time of the year, and repeated plantings will give continuous supplies of fresh vegetables. In Area 2, cool-season vegetables are planted from September to March and warm-season kinds from March to July.

In Area 3 it is impossible to grow tomatoes, snap beans, cantaloupes, corn, eggplant, okra, peppers, pump-

kins and squash except in the warmest locations. However, all cool-season vegetables thrive, including artichokes, beets, broccoli, Brussels sprouts, cabbage, carrots, cauliflower, celery, lettuce, onions, peas, radishes and spinach.

Area 4 includes the greatest summer-producing lettuce area in the United States and much of the country's supply of carrots also comes from there. Area 5, on the other hand, produces most of the warm-season vegetables supplied during the summer months; Area 6 furnishes these vegetables to local areas. In the high desert (Area 7) cool-season vegetables are planted from March to April and warm-season ones during May and June. Most of the United States' winter supply of cool-season vegetables comes from Area 8, and many of the hot-weather vegetables are also produced here in summer. Cool-season crops requiring a long season, such as Brussels sprouts and celery, cannot be grown easily in this area.

GARDEN CALENDAR OF WORK

January

January opens the bare-root planting season in the Southwest, when all kinds of deciduous plants may be set out. The best-known of these—bare-root roses—must have sun for at least six hours a day, shelter from wind, and be out of range of tree roots. Other plants usually planted bare-root include strawberries, blackberries, raspberries and certain perennial flowers, such as gerberas. If you haven't already set out winter-blooming annuals, now is the time to do so. Sweet alyssum, pansies and violas, calendulas, pinks, Iceland poppies and snapdragons are offered in garden-supply stores. Perennials such as marguerites, English primroses, English daisies and bergenias are available in January and are dependable sources of winter color.

The roots of camellias and azaleas in full bloom are now semidormant; bushes can be planted immediately.

Do not transplant fuchsias, hibiscus, citrus, avocados or any tropicals that might freeze if their new growth starts too soon.

Prune peaches and nectarines heavily to encourage fruit production.

February

This is the time to prune roses. In the Southwest, roses should not be pruned as severely as they are in cold-winter areas where dormancy is more complete. A good general rule is to prune hybrid teas no lower than 24 in., grandifloras no lower than 30 in. and to do little more than remove old blossoms from floribundas.

Fertilize grass lawns and all garden plants except newly planted roses, camellias, azaleas and tropical plants that develop succulent new growth which may be harmed by frost.

Prepare for spring planting by digging large quantities of organic material into the planting beds. Dress dichondra lawns with good compost or humus.

In many sections of the Southwest, frost damage is likely this month. A degree or two of frost can be prevented from doing damage to ground covers and vegetable crops by running sprinklers slowly all night. Do not prune plants damaged by frost until they have sprouted; then, after all danger of frost is passed, remove dead tissues.

Sow quick-growing annuals, such as sweet alyssum and violas, in tulip and daffodil beds.

Prune fuchsias growing in baskets to the edge of the container and cut those in ground beds back one-third. Mulch them with a two-inch layer of peat moss. Repot established fuchsias.

This is the month to purchase begonia and dahlia tubers.

March

March is the last month to purchase bare-root roses, fruit and shade trees.

Seeds of hot-weather annuals such as marigold, petunia, aster, zinnia and celosia, should be sown in flats indoors in the colder areas and directly into the outdoor ground where they are to grow in milder areas. Most other annuals can be planted directly into the flower beds this month throughout the Southwest. Soil preparation is the most important step in planting annuals. Dig the soil deeply; to the humus-deficient soils of the Southwest, add copious amounts of composted organic material. In desert areas, cover the soil with a sheet of polyethylene film until the seedlings emerge.

Pile soil or mulch over newly planted bare-root roses that do not sprout immediately. A paper collar will hold the material around the canes. Remove the collar and soil as soon as the buds begin to swell.

Dahlia and begonia tubers may be planted this month; keep them in a warm place until they sprout. Gladioluses and iris may be planted now. Repeated plantings of gladioluses keep flowers coming all year.

Prune flowering almond and flowering quince after they have bloomed. Flowering fruit trees may be pruned when in full bloom. Cut back poinsettias so that only one or two buds are left on each stem.

Although grass lawns may be planted any time in the Southwest, fall and spring are preferable for planting cool-season grasses. In desert areas, apply a half-inch layer of mulch evenly over the seed bed unless you can water the seed every two or three hours during the day in the first week after planting.

April

April is the best month to plant tropical and subtropical shrubs and trees that need warm soil for root growth. These include citrus and avocados, hibiscus, bougainvilleas, tropical palms, bananas and *Dracaena terminalis.* Certain tropical plants used as ground covers, such as weeping lantana, gazania, verbena and alternanthera, grow best when planted now.

When setting out bougainvillea, do not break the root ball but leave it in its container with the bottom of the container cut out.

Spray roses and other plants whose tender shoots may attract aphids. Be alert for these insects and spray when they first appear.

Fertilize camellias and azaleas, and all other garden plants and lawns. Use cottonseed meal to fertilize acid-loving plants.

At a reliable nursery select rooted cuttings of carnations and chrysanthemums ready to be set out. The carnation cuttings will be accompanied by flowers, so you will be able to choose the colors you want.

Dichondra needs almost constant attention from now until fall. Fertilizers with diphenamid and those with an insecticide added simplify dichondra care.

Snails are active in the garden almost every month but busiest in the moist, cool spring. Apply baits.

Annuals, such as marigolds, petunias, celosias, portulacas, salvias, China asters and zinnias may still be set out in the cooler areas.

May

May is a good time to start gladioluses, dahlias and tuberous begonias. Add 25-percent composted humus to the soil and place a stake for each dahlia.

Apply weed controls to dichondra lawns.

Colorful perennial plants, such as pelargoniums, gerberas, pinks and Shasta daisies, are available; plant now for continuous flowering through the summer.

Prune spring-flowering shrubs, such as spirea, weigela, forsythia, flowering quince and flowering almond.

Thin peaches, plums and apricots when the fruits are about $\frac{1}{2}$ in. in diameter. Leave one peach for every 6 in. of branch and one apricot or plum for every 3 in. of branch.

Pinch fuchsias, chrysanthemums, carnations and any annuals you wish to remain more compact.

Watch for aphids on roses and spray to control mildew.

If you have not already done so, set out ageratums, asters, petunias and marigolds.

June

In most areas of the Southwest, June heralds the dry season and watering becomes a major chore. Regular and thorough irrigating helps avoid problems and, contrary to the opinion of many, overhead watering is good occasionally because it helps to control mildew and red-spider damage. However, it should be done only in the morning, because if plants go wet into the evening, fungus diseases may be encouraged.

Dichondra lawns must be watered twice a week, grass lawns once a week and Bermuda grass every ten days to two weeks. In hot desert areas where the soil is light, the frequency must be increased. Shrubs must be watered for at least two hours daily and trees overnight, letting the hose run slowly into the irrigation basin. Mature trees do not require water more frequently than once a month.

A thick application of mulch can reduce the frequency of watering appreciably and help to control weeds as well. Mulch is especially important with roses, camellias, azaleas and all plants for which a comparatively high humidity is desirable. Camellias and azaleas are very shallow-rooted and can be permanently damaged by allowing the surface soil to dry.

It is not too late to plant asters, petunias and zinnias in the ground. Even though you set these plants out last month, set more out now for prolonged blooming. Do not plant asters in the same location in which they were planted last year unless you set wilt-resistant varieties.

Heavy soils in many areas of the Southwest become compacted and may be aerated at this time. Equipment can usually be rented that will cut small holes in the lawn and allow air and water to penetrate. Bluegrass and dichondra lawns are most apt to suffer if the soil is compacted. After aerating, dress these lawns with composted organic material.

Ground covers planted this month will spread more quickly than those planted at any other time: Verbena, weeping lantana, dichondra, bougainvillea, mesembryanthemum, and star jasmine.

Fuchsias can be purchased in full bloom for planting in beds or in hanging baskets.

Palms and bamboos are planted most successfully this month. This is true also of many tropical fruits—including papayas, sapotes, cherimoyas, bananas and litchi.

Mildew on tuberous begonias may appear this month and must be controlled by spraying.

After delphiniums have finished blooming, cut the plants back to just above the soil line and they will probably bloom again.

July

It is impossible to exaggerate the importance of a mulch during this hot, dry season. All plants benefit from a generous mulch that is kept moist.

Cut chrysanthemums back to 1 ft. from the ground to keep them from becoming too tall. Do not pinch them later than the end of this month, however.

Within reason, the more roses and fuchsias are fertilized, the more they bloom. This is not the case with many other plants, such as dahlias and camellias, which produce fewer blooms if overfertilized.

Take measures to control ants before they become a nuisance. Ant control is important because they carry aphids, scale insects and mealybugs and pasture them out on your favorite plants. Ants harm beneficial and protect harmful insects.

Before leaving for vacation, place polyethylene plastic bags around all house plants after watering them thoroughly. Do not allow the plastic to come in contact with the leaves.

August

Soil alkalinity becomes an acute problem this month in many areas of the Southwest because of alkaline irrigation water which, on evaporation, leaves an accumulation of salts in the soil. Acid-loving plants are the first to show signs of distress, but eventually all plants may be affected. Iron sulphate, aluminum sulphate or liquid lime sulphur applied to the top of the soil will penetrate and correct alkalinity. The harmful salts can be leached out by heavy watering, but the fertilizer salts will be lost as well and must be replaced after the leaching.

Lawn and ground-cover insects and diseases often become prevalent in August and control measures must be taken. Crabgrass makes its appearance in lawns and should be controlled at once.

Crape myrtle blooms this month and can be obtained in tree or shrub form at the nursery.

Low humidity damages many plants; this especially affects camellia buds, tuberous begonia and fuchsia flowers. Sprinkle these plants often to raise humidity and make sure sufficient mulch is present to protect their shallow roots.

September

Plant sweet peas, calendulas, snapdragons, pansies and stocks for fall and winter flowers. Seed them where they will grow in the garden or sow in flats and set them in a cool, shady location. Cover the flats with plastic film to prevent the soil surface from drying out.

Replace summer flower beds of tuberous begonia with bulbs of cyclamen. Pull out summer annuals and replant, after revitalizing the flower beds with a thick layer of composted humus worked deeply into the soil.

Prune out stems of *macrophylla* hydrangeas that have flowered. Do not cut nonflowering stalks, as they will produce flowers early next year.

Divide bird-of-paradise plants any time they are not in bloom. Cut pie-shaped segments out of the plant for replanting but do not dig up the entire plant or you will retard its flowering.

September is the warmest month of the year in most of the Southwest, with hot desert winds and low humidity. Leaves dry out faster than they can be supplied with water through the roots. Citrus trees are especially susceptible and react by dropping their leaves. Water trees deeply to prevent this type of injury.

Withhold fertilizer from azaleas, camellias, fuchsias—indeed, from most plants except roses and the grass and dichondra lawns.

October

Shop this month for the best selection of narcissus, hyacinth and tulip bulbs.

Easiest to naturalize in the Southwest climate are the daffodils and scillas, which should be given particular prominence. Store tulips in the refrigerator until late November to insure one year's satisfactory bloom. Better adapted to this part of the country are the tender bulbs, such as freesias, wandflowers, Cape cowslips, African corn lilies, veltheimias and nerines. Enrich the soil with compost before planting the bulbs.

This is the best time to plant native California shrubs. Wild-flower seeds scattered now will turn waste places into blazing color next spring.

Sweet peas, snapdragons, calendulas and stocks set out this month will give winter color in sunny locations, while pansies, cinerarias and primroses bring sparkling color to the shade garden.

Be sure to continue watering lawns, trees and shrubs until the fall or winter rains arrive.

Chrysanthemums are blooming profusely, and this is the best time to make selections. Plant in containers or in the soil for further bloom. They can be used to fill holes that the season brings to the flower borders. After they bloom, cut them back.

November

Set out annuals if you haven't already done so and plant tulips that have been chilled in the refrigerator. Plant lilies this month and finish up other bulb planting. Shop for *sasanqua* camellias, which are in full bloom in nurseries. They can be transplanted most easily at this time. Harvest dahlia and tuberous-begonia tubers and store them in dry vermiculite after they have thoroughly dried.

Some camellia varieties set buds too heavily and should be disbudded. Remove a few buds of different sizes to maintain long blooming periods.

Plant bare slopes with a mixture of

rye grass, purple vetch and bird's-foot trefoil to prevent erosion by winter rains. Perennial ground covers planted now will hold slopes permanently as soon as they have time to grow.

Most shrubs can be planted this month to secure an extra season's growth. Winter rains provide watering, and the roots grow in the cool season.

Cymbidiums are forming flower spikes this month and should be staked before the flowers open.

December

This is the best month to prune deciduous shade trees. Cut back the fruiting canes of boysenberry and other small cane fruits.

Preemergent controls should be applied now to prevent the appearance of crabgrass next spring.

Prune red-berried plants, such as holly and pyracantha, and use the clippings for Christmas decorations.

Plant Cuthbertson-type sweet peas now for spring blooms.

Flowering and fruiting peach trees are very susceptible to peach leaf curl. Spray them to control this disease.

This is the best month to plant conifers.

CHAPTER 35

THE ROCKY MOUNTAIN REGION

Gardens of the Rocky Mountains— Climatic Areas—Soils—Landscaping —Watering—Garden Calendar of the Year—Plants

THE ROCKY MOUNTAIN region is still relatively unexploited. A hundred years ago hunters, adventurers, livestock men and miners came here to try their fortunes. Eventually some of them did strike it rich. Towns and then cities rose in what had been wilderness. To display their new wealth, some of those who had amassed fortunes built enormous mansions surrounded by splendid gardens, particularly in the towns and cities. Today most of these isolated strongholds of vast wealth have vanished, to be replaced by thousands of communities with modest areas set aside for small, pleasant gardens.

Like so many of the pioneers whose origins were European, these early settlers brought with them familiar plants from their old homes. But many of the plants did not take well to the new setting and perished. Gradually, however, trial and error proved that it was possible to adapt quite a few of the old favorites to the new conditions.

As recently as 20 years ago, this area was horticulturally undeveloped to a large extent, but garden clubs have steadily increased in number and influence. Now the Rocky Mountain section is recognized as a distinct region, with problems and opportunities differing from those of older horticultural regions, but with a good gardening future. As more plants that will prosper are introduced and better methods of cultivation are learned, gardens comparable to any in Canada or the United States will be developed here.

The Rocky Mountains extend from Alaska to New Mexico. The portion we are considering extends from southern British Columbia and Alberta through Montana, Idaho, Wyoming, Utah and Colorado, into New Mexico. Although the region is dominated by high mountains, about 80 percent of the population lives at the foot of the mountains, where the growing season is longer, the land more level. Denver, which is about a mile above sea level, is the midpoint; the seasons gradually shorten as we go north or to higher elevations; they lengthen as we move south or to lower elevations. By either descending 1000 ft. or going southward about 365 miles, we find that the growing season is extended by about one week. Moving north or higher into the mountains has the opposite effect. In Missoula, Mont., and Santa Fe, N. Mex., some of the same kinds of shade trees may be successfully grown, but at different altitudes within a few miles of these cities, the climate is so different that these shade trees barely survive.

Altitudes in this region range from 2000 ft. along the larger rivers to over 14,000 ft. in the high mountains. The precipitation ordinarily increases with elevation so that most of it falls as snow in the mountains. Without the runoff from the melting snow in summer, much of the region would be little more than desert. The low humidity that results from many sunny days, combined with an abundance of water from the mountains for irrigation, creates satisfactory conditions for gardening.

CLIMATIC AREAS

In addition to the differences in latitude and altitude, distinct changes become evident as we go eastward to the high plains and westward to the mesa-canyon-desert country. A narrow valley at 7000 ft., warmed by the sun and protected from winds, may grow the same plants cultivated in an open valley 2000 ft. lower. Local climatic sections, known as microclimatic pockets, are numerous all over the region. For the purpose of selecting plants for various landscaping (see lists at the end of this chapter), this whole Rocky Mountain region may be divided roughly into four principal climatic Areas.

Area 1

The Northern Area—Montana, Idaho, Wyoming and lower Canada, much of which lies between 3000 and 9000 ft.—has a relatively short season, except along the very low valleys. Humidity is generally high, and the precipitation is greater than in other Areas to the south. Cheyenne, Wyo., has a climate decidedly more severe than that of Denver, and some mountain plants grow there that cannot be grown in Denver. Missoula, Mont., while much farther north than Cheyenne, is lower and enjoys a climate that permits the cultivation of a wide selection of ornamental plants. Pocatello and other communities in Idaho vary considerably in climate but generally have a rather short growing season.

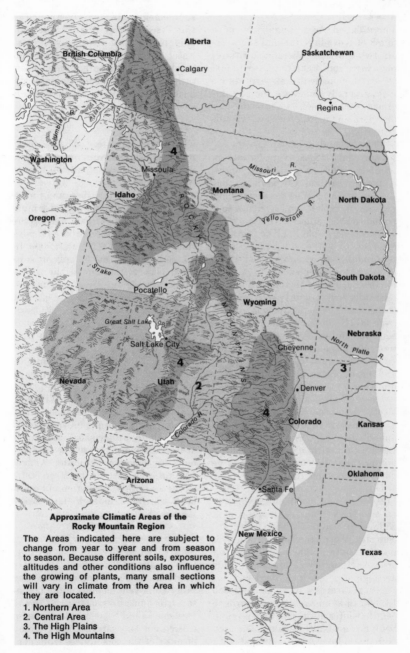

Approximate Climatic Areas of the Rocky Mountain Region

The Areas indicated here are subject to change from year to year and from season to season. Because different soils, exposures, altitudes and other conditions also influence the growing of plants, many small sections will vary in climate from the Area in which they are located.

1. Northern Area
2. Central Area
3. The High Plains
4. The High Mountains

Area 2

The Central Area roughly includes much of Nevada, Utah and the western two thirds of Colorado. Altitudes may vary from 4000 ft. to over 14,000 ft., but for horticultural purposes we may generally eliminate the sections above 9000 ft. because there are very few permanent residences above this altitude.

This Central Area has a growing season which varies considerably in number of days. (For most gardeners, it might mean more to indicate that the season varies from long enough to grow corn, melons and apricots to a period so short and cool that only leaf and root vegetables, oats and grasses are grown.)

Rainfall also will vary from 12 in. or less in the lower valleys to 30 or 40 in. in the higher altitudes. There is relatively low humidity over most of the Area. Temperatures may range from 90° F. and above in summer to –20° in winter. This section at the foot of the mountains and in the valleys has most of the population, and most of the general farming is done here.

Denver, the largest city of the Rocky Mountain region, is situated at the eastern edge of the mountains and western edge of the plains. Salt Lake City, with a climate slightly milder than in Denver, raises a large variety of ornamental plants.

Area 3

In the High Plains, extending in a wide strip from North Dakota to central Texas, the precipitation is low (possibly averaging 20 in.) and erratic. Humidity is low and winds are high.

Temperatures will frequently reach 100° F. in summer and may drop to –40° in winter in the northern section. Soils are generally alkaline but rich and productive when supplied with supplementary water. Over much of the Area, many plants are not able to survive unless given extra water and the protection of a windbreak. The growing season is often rather long. Grasses dominate the natural vegetation. Population is sparse.

Area 4

The High Mountain Area extends from the Selkirk and Monache ranges in Canada southward all the way to New Mexico.

The region is now becoming more and more important as a greater number of all-year homes and resorts are being built in sections where the altitude is between 6000 and 9000 ft. These occur, of course, only in scattered pockets throughout the Rocky Mountain region. There is a normal four-season climate, but the growing period is very short at these altitudes, limiting ornamental plants to hardy perennials, annuals and native trees and shrubs.

The precipitation and humidity are much greater and soils are generally less alkaline here than in the plains, plateaus and valleys below. With consistent snow cover, gardeners may winter over many plants that would not normally be hardy where temperatures often dip to –30° or –40° F., even in southern Colorado. Annual precipitation varies from 30 to 50 in. in the vast forested sections to a low of 6 to 10 in. in high, near-desert regions.

SOILS

Soils vary considerably with altitude and location. They may be very sandy or stiff clay or gumbo, and they range from very shallow in the mountains to quite deep along the rivers. Because rainfall has been limited in this region for centuries, the reaction of most of the soils ranges from neutral to very alkaline. These soils are naturally low in organic matter and nitrogen. The addition of nitrogen and phosphorus is always beneficial, but supplementary potash is usually unnecessary. The addition of a little iron sulphate is often helpful. Lime is rarely needed. Proper soil preparation and intelligent watering practices will solve about 75 percent of Rocky Mountain region garden problems, particularly plant diseases and ordinary pests.

Hot sun, low humidity and alkaline soil considerably affect the prevalence of diseases and pests. In general, diseases such as black spot of roses are much less frequent than in moister areas. A number of insects, however, such as the elm scale, find this climate hospitable.

LANDSCAPING IN THE ROCKIES

As elsewhere in North America, the design of gardens in the Rocky Mountain region must be adapted to fit the climate. One of the basic tasks in managing a garden in this region is to establish a degree of control over climatic effects. Most garden problems stem from limited precipitation. With less rain and snow and many more sunny days than in most parts of the United States, there is less natural moisture. Roots of plants can be kept moist, and slightly tender plants may be helped to survive, by proper shading, protective wrapping, trimming and mulching. Extremes of heat, cold, light, wind and precipitation may be minimized to make the garden more enjoyable.

In the last few years, many fine garden-design ideas from England, Spain, Japan and Mexico have been adapted to the Rocky Mountain region. Foreign plants are, however, often subject to damage from the region's dryness and hot sun in winter, even more than from the cold.

Many native Rocky Mountain plants make excellent ornamentals and are available from local nurseries. These should be used in landscape plantings whenever possible. Other plants from regions where the climatic conditions are similar to those of the Rocky Mountains may be seriously considered. As some plants may require special planting techniques, ask your nurseryman if special instructions are needed, and follow his advice carefully.

Tall shade trees may need bracing to prevent wind damage until new roots are established. Wrapping the trunks of such tender-barked trees as mountain ash and lindens is often very helpful.

A number of materials that are part of the natural landscape are often employed to enhance the beauty of a garden. Where flagstone is available, it can be used in the construction of terraces, walks and walls. Weathered and lichened rocks, common in the Rocky Mountains, can create wonderful rock gardens. Interesting formations of naturally weathered stumps and logs add a dramatic touch, and stone chips and aggregates derived from variously colored rocks are popular surfacing materials in modern gardens. In high mountainous areas, nothing blends more naturally with the landscape than garden structures made of native logs.

WATERING

Watering practices are among the most important cultural techniques for gardeners in the Rocky Mountain region. One of the principal inhibitors of satisfactory plant growth in both the lower mountain and plains Areas is insufficient snow or rain. But various factors determine the frequency and amount of watering needed. Soils vary in their ability to retain moisture. The slope of the ground and mulch or cover crops make a difference in the amount of water absorbed and also in the rapidity with which it is lost by evaporation. Certain plants need more water than others. Exposure, temperature and atmospheric humidity also influence the amount of water needed.

The best way to decide whether to water is to test the soil in various locations. For lawn areas, running a pencil or screwdriver into the ground is usually a satisfactory test. If it goes in easily, the chances are the ground is moist enough.

To discover whether enough water is being given to the larger trees and shrubs, it may be necessary to dig test holes to a depth of a foot or more, depending upon the depth to which the roots go. Unless this is done, some stretches of ground thought to be properly watered may be wet only half as deep as necessary, and other spots may be too wet.

Many towns and cities have ordinances prohibiting the use of an open hose for the irrigation of a garden or lawn. This method, however, when properly controlled, wastes much less water than sprinkling and gives better results. In the sprinkling process, much water is often lost through evaporation. A thorough watering of trees three or four times a year which soaks down to the farthest roots is of much greater value than more frequent lighter waterings.

PLANTS OF THE ROCKY MOUNTAINS

Lawns

Nothing has been discovered in the way of living ground covers suitable for general use in the dry, sunny Rocky Mountain region that is more attractive, cheaper to install or easier to maintain than a good lawn. (For general instructions, see the chapter "Lawns and Their Maintenance," pages 344 to 367.)

Hardy Roses

In recent years it has been proved that most of the Rocky Mountain region lends itself to the production of fine roses. Of course, special care is required to grow them successfully. They should be planted in the same way as trees and shrubs, but it is well to cut their stems to 8 or 10 in. and to mound them with good soil up to a height of 4 to 5 in. These mounds must be removed when new growth starts. The bulge at the base of a budded rose, which indicates where the graft-union has been made, should be set about 1 in. under the soil. Roses will grow in full sun, but in the Rocky Mountain region they thrive better in about half to three-quarter sun and with some protection from wind. They should not be planted near the south side of a building or wall because such locations are usually too hot.

Roses are probably the best-loved garden flowers, and kinds to suit every taste can be grown in the Rocky Mountain Areas. Among the most popular are hybrid teas, grown mostly for their large individual blooms. Floribunda roses, with smaller flowers in clusters, are a little hardier and more free-flowering than hybrid teas and can be planted for their landscape effects.

The grandifloras, in a class between the hybrid teas and floribundas, are a vigorous-growing group, with large but clustered blooms. Climbing roses have been popular in the Rocky Mountain region for many years. They may be trained on fences, pergolas, gates and walls or left to grow as shrubs. The true climbers, such as Paul's Scarlet Climber, Blaze, Don Juan, New Dawn, Golden Showers and City of New York are hardy here, but most of them bloom only in June. The many climbing sports of hybrid-tea varieties give repeat bloom throughout the summer but are generally not as hardy. Miniature roses are becoming more popular each year. These low plants, with their thimble-sized blooms, are very attractive and just as hardy in the Rockies as the hybrid teas. June-blooming shrub roses are old-time favorites and should be used more often as shrub borders. Harison's Yellow, Persian Yellow, Austrian Copper, *Rosa hugonis*, prairie rose and some varieties of *R. rugosa* are all attractive when grown in this way. The most recent roses to become popular are the "fence" roses, which combine some of the hardiness of shrub roses with the everblooming qualities of the hybrid teas. Red Robin, Robin Hood, County Fair and Red Glory are a few of the varieties most commonly grown.

Herbaceous Perennials

As ornamentals, there is not much difference between the hardy herbaceous perennials recommended for the Northern Central and mountain areas of the Rocky Mountains and those for other temperate regions of North America. Because their tops die down each fall, these plants are protected with snow cover, and Rocky Mountain winters do not affect them seriously. (See "Practical and Permanent Perennials," page 154.)

Annuals and Bulbs

Annuals that will thrive in Rocky Mountain gardens include most of those cultivated in other cool, temperate parts of North America. (See "Annuals for Color and Cutting," page 119.) However, the growing season is short over most of the region and atmospheric humidity is low, so it is not practical to start seed directly outdoors. To assure a long season of bloom, seed must be sown indoors a few weeks in advance of the date for setting the young plants in the garden. Almost all hardy spring-flowering bulbs will do very well in the Rocky Mountain region if they are planted at least 50 percent deeper than is usually recommended for the same kinds in other regions. But they should not be planted against the south side of a house or any other place exposed to prolonged, intense sun. If they are planted shallowly or in spots that become too warm too soon, they will be affected by warm spells of weather early in the season and will often be frozen by later cold snaps. If planted deeply, they not only bloom longer each season but persist for a greater number of years. All kinds of tulips and narcissuses prosper. The small early bulbs such as scilla, grape hyacinth, crocus, chionodoxa (glory-of-the-snow) and star-of-Bethlehem are all good. Hyacinths last for a few years, but eventually the bulbs deteriorate and need replacing. The newer hybrid lilies thrive satisfactorily. (See "Hardy Bulbs," page 227.)

Such summer-flowering bulbs as gladiolus, canna, and dahlia may also be grown as in other cool, temperate parts of North America.

Native Wild Flowers

Many wild flowers native to the Rocky Mountain region can be adapted to cultivation here. Unfortunately, seeds of most kinds are not readily available and are often difficult to collect. This is regrettable, since many of the native wild flowers make nice additions to a flower garden. Some especially adaptable and attractive are: allium, antennaria, beard-tongue, columbine, evening primrose, false Solomon's seal, gaillardia, iris, monarda, pasque-flower, prickly poppy and sunflower.

Ferns

Because of the generally low humidity of soil and atmosphere here, ferns are not common, but with proper preparation of the soil and provision for shade, several can be grown—especially male fern, lady fern, cinnamon fern and interrupted fern.

Fruit

Some of the lower valleys of the Rocky Mountain region are especially adapted to the growing of apples, pears, sweet cherries, peaches and apricots. Watermelons, cantaloupes and pumpkins also do well in the lower valleys. The dry climate and low humidity produce high-quality fruit where irrigation is available.

In the higher sections, 5000 to 6000 ft., only a few fruits will produce fairly regularly. Some of the early apples such as Cortland, McIntosh and Jonathan sometimes bear. Pears at this height are seldom worth the space they take. Early varieties of peaches will often bloom and bear in protected places. Sour cherries such as Montmorency, English Morello and Early Richmond usually bear regularly. Of the hybrid plums, Waneta is the best for quality. Sometimes Greengage, Omaha, Damson and Italian prune give good crops. Apricots usually bloom too early and then suffer severely from frost damage. Gooseberries and currants bear occasionally. The everbearing Indian Summer raspberry produces a reliable crop, and so do strawberries. Concord and Portland grapes bear crops every few years only, but the hybrid Beta will produce every year. Nanking cherries, chokecherries, sand cherries, elderberries, serviceberries and buffalo berries often bear well.

Vegetables

In the lower valleys all common vegetables can be grown satisfactorily.

Aquilegia caerulea
(Colorado Columbine)

Squash, cabbage, beans and sweet corn are of good quality. Other good vegetables are asparagus, rhubarb, peppers, cauliflower, broccoli, Brussels sprouts and celery. Carrots, beets, turnips and other root crops grow well when planted either early or late in the season even at comparatively low altitudes, but produce the best quality at higher elevations. Lettuce, spinach, potatoes and radishes may be grown successfully in the higher altitudes, where there is a shorter season and a cooler climate.

GARDEN CALENDAR FOR THE ROCKY MOUNTAIN REGION

The seasons described in this calendar are those of the Central Area and are typical of Denver. Spring comes later by a week or more in the mountains of the Central Area and in the Northern Area, and later by two weeks or more in the high mountains of the Northern Area.

January

The weather is likely to be colder than elsewhere in southern Canada and the United States. Now is the time to list changes you would like to make, and outline your garden plan for the year ahead. Break up the Christmas tree and use its branches for shade around evergreens or as mulch around roses or perennials.

Check to see whether you have given winter protection: shading tender evergreens, wrapping tender-barked trees, erecting shields against snow and covering tender perennials. January is the traditional time to prune grapes. When you have the pruners out, you might also do some necessary shaping of shrubs and trees. Fruit trees, too, may need a careful pruning. But pruning of maples, birches and walnuts should be left until they are in leaf; the cuts "bleed" less then. Make hardwood cuttings of

grapes and deciduous shrubs now. Bury them in moist sand or soil where they can callus and be ready for planting out in nursery rows the following June.

February

The theme for gardeners this month should be planning. Study magazines, books and catalogues and exchange experiences with other gardeners and with nurserymen to learn what kinds of plants will be successful in your garden. Not all the handsome pictures in the catalogues show plants suitable for your climate.

Check plants, especially those on the south side of the house, to see if they need watering. In such locations, natural precipitation is seldom enough to keep the soil around plants sufficiently moist. Of course, you cannot water until the ground thaws.

It is pleasant to bring a few branches of flowering shrubs indoors and put them in water to encourage them to break into early leaf and bloom. Forsythia is excellent for this purpose.

Check house plants. Some may need repotting, others a little fertilizer; some may have to be discarded. It is a good idea to examine stored bulbs again. Dahlias especially may have become too dry, too damp, or conditions may be too warm or too cold for them.

Checking your winter protection of plants may enable you to save them from destruction by storm and ice or from dehydration.

March

The weather is probably favorable now to start transplanting trees and shrubs. Plants moved while they are completely dormant usually grow better than those moved later.

If you can obtain bare-root roses and the soil is in suitable condition, plant them this month. Mound a few inches of soil around them, and leave this in place until they begin to break into leaf.

Be sure to dig holes of really ample size for all plants, and pack the best soil available around their roots. Twenty-five percent peat moss mixed with the backfill soil will help newly planted trees and shrubs to a good start.

Inspect your garden carefully while there is still no bloom and little foliage to influence your judgment, and decide if anything can be done to improve its winter interest.

Bring tuberous begonias out of storage and start them into growth in peat pots or flats of peat moss. An early start allows for more weeks of summer bloom.

If any plants harbor scale insects, now is the time to apply a dormant spray. The temperature must be above 40° F., and there must be no severe wind at the time of application. Do not be deceived by the first few good days of the season. This is not the time to remove all winter protection from plants, because it may be needed more during the next four weeks than it has been all winter. However, if it lies especially thick or heavy on bulbs or other plants that show signs of new growth, it should be gradually lightened or thinned. Traditionally, sweet peas should be planted on St. Patrick's Day, but a few days one way or the other do not matter.

April

The important task this month is to do all essential transplanting. It will be too late after plants are in bloom. Moved early in the season, a well-cared-for tree or shrub with good roots will reestablish itself more quickly and grow much more vigorously than one planted late and carelessly.

If bare-root plants are delivered in bad weather, be sure that they are temporarily stored where there is free circulation of air around their tops, but see that their roots are kept covered and moist until they are set in the ground.

Pansies may be planted now. They can stand considerable frost.

The early, hardy vegetables—onions, spinach, lettuce, radishes, beets and peas—may be seeded outdoors.

Start petunia, marigold, zinnia, tomato and pepper seeds indoors. Under average conditions, young plants will be just large enough to set in the garden when the danger of frost is over. Days when the sun shines warmly and the ground is not sloppy underfoot afford a good opportunity to work off premature spring fever by doing some tree pruning.

Check juniper and piñon pine for infestations of aphids. Also, unless a dormant spray was applied earlier, look for scale on dogwood trees, as well as on lilac, cotoneaster, viburnum and euonymus. If any pests are present, take prompt remedial measures. Apply preemergence treatments for crabgrass.

May

Finish all bare-root transplanting before the middle of the month. Then, if you don't mind taking the risk, you may set out some tender annuals. If the weather remains favorable, such early plantings will be two weeks ahead of similar plants set out in June; should they be seriously harmed by late frosts, you can make another planting. Conservative gardeners, however, wait until the first week in June to plant out petunias and other tender annuals. Soon the summer routine of water-weed-cultivate-spray-prune will be in full swing.

If there are bare spots in the lawn, May is a good time to renovate them by loosening and fertilizing the soil and sowing a little grass seed. Rose pruning in the Rocky Mountain region consists of little more than cutting out the dead wood. If the shoots are shriveled and brown, the chances are they are dead and may be removed at any time. Most hybrid tea roses are killed to near ground level by spring. The parts protected by mounds of earth since fall should be alive.

June

Now is the time to give all established plants that will benefit from the treatment a dressing of a complete fertilizer. The main nutrient needed in this region is nitrogen.

Prune most spring-flowering shrubs just after they have finished blooming; they will now have time to develop new growth and buds for next year's bloom. Many shrubs need just a thinning out of old stems each year.

Pines may be shaped by shortening the "candles" of new growth before the leaves spread; only the current year's growth should be sheared from junipers. Formal hedges, espaliered shrubs or trees and other strictly shaped plants are most beautiful when they are sheared frequently. Some perennials, such as delphiniums and Shasta daisies, may be encouraged to produce a second blooming in fall if their first flowers are now cut back as soon as they are finished. Seed of warm-weather crops—such as sweet corn, beans and melons—may be sown early this month.

Inspect the garden every few days for first signs of damage by insects. If any is detected, spray or dust at once.

July

As the weather gets warmer, you may regret not having anticipated the need for more shade trees in the patio and play areas. Plans for such contingencies should be made in early fall or spring. Plants without shade may dry out quickly in hot weather. The garden generally will need more water now than in April, but the old rule applies: Water thoroughly when needed, but not oftener than necessary.

Spider mites are usually active in hot weather. Thorough spraying or dusting with a good miticide at the very first sign of infestation gives satisfactory control. Check phlox, hollyhocks and shrub roses for rust diseases. Dusting with sulphur helps to prevent damage. Mildew may suddenly appear on roses, zinnias and some other plants. Spray them with a fungicide.

In the region's alkaline soils, the gardener must be continually on the alert to discover and treat chlorotic plants. A symptom of this deficiency disease is yellowing of the leaves, with the veins usually remaining green. It is most often caused by an inability of the plant to get enough iron. Apply iron in the form of a sulphate or chelate; repeat if necessary.

August

If there is little bloom showing, check your own as well as other gardens and list the plants that are still blooming. Include these in your garden scheduling for future Augusts. You may bring in—from a nursery or a reserve bed where you have been growing them especially for this purpose—chrysanthemum plants in full bud or flower with soil attached to their roots. They will wilt at first, but, thoroughly watered in, they will be bright and sturdy by the next morning and remain attractive for a long time.

Iris can be transplanted now, and Oriental poppies must be, if you are planning to move them. Consider adding to your garden at this time new varieties of Oriental poppies in some of the many new colors now available. Cut down hollyhocks when they are about through blooming.

Prepare the soil for sowing new bluegrass lawns.

At this time of year, ants may become troublesome. A little chlordane dusted over their nests or hills will keep them under control.

September

New lawns may be seeded any time this month and until the middle of October. If planted now, they often do better than when planted in spring. Weeds are much less of a problem. Many hardy perennials may be divided and transplanted in September. This will give them ample time to become established before the onset of winter.

If hedges and lawn edges are trimmed and dead stems taken out of shrubs and perennials, the garden will be neater all winter, and there will be less danger of harboring diseases and insect pests. It is well to let up a little on regular watering and to allow woody plants to ripen their growth before the winter. Most native plants, under cultivation, will require this treatment.

If frost comes this month, there are many little chores to be done. Tender bulbs, such as dahlia, canna, gladiolus, tuberose and tuberous begonia, must be dug and stored for winter. Bring pumpkins and squash into a cool place. Collect and dry bundles of culinary herbs for winter use.

Repot, cut back and bring indoors house plants that have been outdoors under trees or shrubs all summer. It is well to spray them with an insecticide first, to avoid bringing pests indoors. As cooler weather arrives and woody plants display their fall colors, make note of those you like best for future planting.

October

Plant hardy bulbs, such as tulip, hyacinth, narcissus, crocus, squill, snow-drop and grape hyacinth, as soon as they are available. Throughout the region, they should be planted at least 50 percent deeper than is usual in regions of milder winters. Remember, it is for such mild sections that recommendations as to planting depths are ordinarily made. If you expect them to last several years, don't plant spring-flowering bulbs on the south side of a building. Erratic spring weather with a few early warm days induces the leaves to come through the ground, and then, very frequently, a cold spell will damage the plants.

Start a few narcissus, hyacinth, tulip and other hardy spring-flowering bulbs in pots and cover them with sand, ashes or sawdust in a cold frame, where they are left to root; bring them indoors during the winter, a few at a time, to brighten the house.

After woody plants have shed their leaves and all other plants are dormant, the ground should be thoroughly soaked. The moisture provided may not last all winter if there is much sunshine, but it will help for a couple of months at least.

Red-twig dogwood, viburnum and sometimes euonymus are often covered with aphids just before the leaves drop. They are building up a big population to attack the tender leaves early next spring. A preventive spray now is worthwhile.

November

Mound soil around hybrid tea roses before the ground freezes solid. If you wait for all the rose foliage to fall, there may not be loose soil available.

As deciduous trees and shrubs and perennials become dormant, they may be transplanted if this is desirable. Moving plants in fall is slightly riskier than spring transplanting, but if the winter happens to be favorable, some time is saved from the annual spring rush. In the higher altitudes, fall planting is often necessary; by the time the frost is out of the ground in spring, all stock from nurseries at lower altitudes is in leaf and not in condition for transplanting.

If you set out trees with tender bark, such as linden, mountain ash and thin-barked maples, it is advisable to wrap the trunks to avoid winter burning. Construct shades of lath and burlap to set at the southwest of tender plants. Cut back long limbs broken by snow. Brace or tie up multi-stemmed junipers subject to damage from massed-up snow.

Start into growth large amaryllis bulbs that have been dormant for several weeks, so that they will be in bloom for Christmas or soon after.

Bring in carrots and turnips now and bed them in a box of sand stored in a cool place.

While the extreme cold lasts, time will be well spent cleaning and fixing all garden tools for the coming season.

December

Order new catalogues now, so that you will have them to study in January or at least as soon as they are available.

If there are rabbit tracks in the snow, the trunks of all fruit trees and shrubs belonging to the *Rosaceae* or rose family—such as plums, apples and pears—should be protected with wire netting or repellent chemicals.

If some of your evergreens have become overgrown, trim them back moderately and use the trimmings for Christmas decoration.

Check house plants frequently for infestations of aphids, spider mites and mealybugs.

PLANTS FOR AREA 1: THE NORTHERN ROCKY MOUNTAIN AREA

In the lower valleys throughout Wyoming, Montana and Idaho and adjoining Canada, most of the ornamental plants recommended for the Central Rocky Mountain region (see pages 658–661) may be grown. But farther north and at higher altitudes, the growing season becomes shorter and the weather more severe, so only the hardiest plants survive. On the other hand, there are plants that do not thrive farther south. The atmospheric humidity is often greater and the soil more acid. A list of the more common woody plants native to Glacier National Park in Montana (see page 662) suggests many ornamentals. Herbaceous perennials, annuals and hardy bulbs that can be grown here are essentially the same as for other Rocky Mountain Areas.

Evergreens

Abies grandis . . . . giant fir
Abies lasiocarpa . . . . . alpine fir
Juniperus scopulorum . . .
              Colorado red cedar
Picea engelmannii . . .
            Engelmann spruce
Pinus albicaulis . . whitebark pine
Pinus contorta murrayana . . .
              lodgepole pine
Pinus flexilis . . . . . limber pine
Pinus monticola . . .
        Western white pine
Pinus ponderosa . . .
       Western yellow pine
Pseudotsuga taxifolia . . Douglas fir
Tsuga heterophylla . . .
       Western hemlock

Low Evergreens

Arctostaphylos uva-ursi . . bearberry
Juniperus . . . . juniper
Pachistima myrsinites
Taxus brevifolia . . . Western yew

Deciduous Trees

Betula papyrifera . . . paper birch
Crataegus douglasii . . .
        Western thorn apple
Larix . . . . larch
Populus . . . poplar; quaking aspen

Deciduous Shrubs

Acer glabrum douglasii . . .
           Rocky Mountain maple
Alnus sinuata. . . . . alder
Amelanchier alnifolia . serviceberry
Betula glandulosa . . . . . . birch
Cornus stolonifera . . .
           red osier dogwood
Elaeagnus commutata. . .silverberry
Ledum glandulosum . . Labrador tea
Lonicera involucrata . . honeysuckle
Menziesia glabella
Potentilla fruticosa
Prunus virginiana melanocarpa . . .
           Western chokecherry
Rhamnus alnifolia . . . buckthorn
Ribes . . . . currant
Rosa . . . . rose
Rubus . . . . raspberry
Salix . . . . willow
Sambucus melanocarpa. . elderberry
Shepherdia canadensis . . .
           Canada buffalo berry

Sorbus . . . . mountain ash
Spiraea . . . . spirea
Symphoricarpos albus . . .
           snowberry; waxberry
Vaccinium . . .
           blueberry; whortleberry
Viburnum pauciflorum . . .
           highbush cranberry

PLANTS FOR AREA 2: THE CENTRAL ROCKY MOUNTAIN AREA

(Colorado, Utah, Nevada and adjoining territory)

Conifers

Conifers or needle evergreens dominate most of the native forests of the
Rocky Mountain region and should
be used wherever they are appropriate
in ornamental landscape plantings.
Abies concolor . . . . . . white fir
Juniperus . . . . juniper

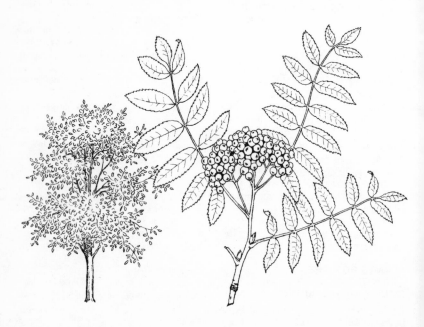

Sorbus aucuparia (European Mountain Ash)

Picea pungens. . . . Colorado spruce
Pinus. . . . . pine
Pseudotsuga taxifolia . . Douglas fir

Hardiest Shade Trees

Trees that provide shade add to the comfort and beauty of gardens. Because of the limited precipitation and generally alkaline soil in the Rocky Mountain region, trees planted here must be kinds that are tolerant of these conditions.

Acer negundo . . . . . . box elder
Acer saccharinum. . . . silver maple
Celtis occidentalis . . . . hackberry
Fraxinus pennsylvanica lanceolata
         . . . green ash
Gleditsia triacanthos inermis . . .
         thornless honey locust
Gymnocladus dioica . . .
         Kentucky coffee tree
Morus alba tatarica . . .
         Russian mulberry

Populus sargentii . . . cottonwood

Small Ornamental Trees

Trees that are too small to be used primarily for shade but have ornamental bloom, fruit or foliage are especially worthwhile.

Ailanthus altissima . tree of heaven
Catalpa
Cercis canadensis . . . . . redbud
Cladrastis lutea . . . yellowwood
Crataegus crus-galli . cockspur thorn
Crataegus mollis. . . . . . hawthorn
Crataegus oxycantha . . .
         English hawthorn
Crataegus phaenopyrum . . .
         Washington thorn
Crataegus succulenta . . hawthorn
Elaeagnus angustifolia . Russian olive
Koelreuteria paniculata . . .
         goldenrain tree
Malus . . .
     flowering crab apple; orchard apple

Picea pungens glauca (Colorado Spruce)

Prunus . Newport plum; sour cherry
Robinia neo-mexicana . . . . locust
Sophora japonica . . .
                    Japanese pagoda tree
Sorbus aucuparia . . .
                    European mountain ash
Syringa amurensis japonica . . .
                    Japanese lilac

Broad-Leaved Evergreens

The list is limited; most kinds require a protected location.
Buxus microphylla koreana . . .
                    Korean boxwood
Ceanothus velutinus
Cercocarpus ledifolius . . .
                    mountain mahogany
Euonymus fortunei
Mahonia
Pachistima myrsinites
Pyracantha . . . . firethorn
Yucca

Deciduous Shrubs

Newcomers to Rocky Mountain gardening must make a complete readjustment when selecting shrubs. The brilliant-flowered kinds cultivated in areas with greater rainfall are lacking. However, there is available a quite extensive selection of shrubs of different leaf textures, flower and foliage colors and other characteristics that make it easily possible to provide plenty of variety in landscape plantings here.
Acanthopanax sieboldianus
    (syn. *Aralia pentaphylla*)
Acer . . . . maple
Alnus tenuifolia . . mountain alder
Amelanchier . . . . . serviceberry
Amorpha . . . . lead plant
Aralia spinosa . . . . Hercules' club
Berberis . . . . barberry
Betula fontanalis . . . . water birch
Buddleia . . . . . . butterfly bush
Caragana . . . . pea tree
Caryopteris incana . . . . bluebeard
Cercocarpus montanus . . .
                    mountain mahogany

Chaenomeles . . .
                    Japanese flowering quince
Chionanthus virginica . . fringe tree
Colutea arborescens . . bladder senna
Cornus . . . . dogwood
Cotoneaster
Elaeagnus
Euonymus
Exochorda . . . . pearlbush
Fallugia paradoxa
Fontanesia fortunei
Foresteria neo-mexicana
Forsythia
Hibiscus syriacus . . .
                    shrub althea; rose of Sharon
Hippophaë rhamnoides . . .
                    sea buckthorn
Holodiscus dumosa
Hydrangea
Hypericum . . . . St. John's-wort
Jasminum nudiflorum . . . jasmine
Kolkwitzia amabilis . . beauty bush
Lespedeza thunbergii . . bush clover
Ligustrum . . . . privet
Lonicera . . . . honeysuckle
Lycium halimifolium . . .
                    matrimony vine
Philadelphus . . . . . mock orange
Physocarpus opulifolius nana . . .
                    ninebark
Potentilla fruticosa . . . . cinquefoil
Prinsepia sinensis
Prunus
Purshia tridentata . . antelope brush
Rhamnus cathartica . . .
                    common buckthorn
Rhodotypos kerrioides . . . jetbead
Rhus . . . . sumac
Ribes . . . . currant
Robinia hispida . . . . rose acacia
Rosa . . . . rose
Rubus . . . . raspberry
Salix discolor . . . . . pussy willow
Sambucus canadensis . American elder
Shepherdia argentea . . buffalo berry
Sorbaria . . . . false spirea
Spiraea . . . . spirea
Symphoricarpos . . .
                    coralberry; snowberry
Syringa . . . . lilac

Tamarix hispida . . . . . tamarisk
Viburnum
Vitex negundo incisa
Xanthoceras sorbifolia

Plants for Hedges

The following are a few plants that are most suitable for clipped hedges. Almost any shrub or small tree may be used for an informal hedge under some conditions.

Evergreen Hedges

Juniperus chinensis hetzi . . juniper
Juniperus chinensis pfitzeriana . . .
Pfitzer's juniper
Picea pungens. . . Colorado spruce
Pinus nigra. . . . . Austrian pine
Pinus ponderosa scopulorum . . .
Rocky Mountain yellow pine
Pinus sylvestris. . . . . Scots pine

Tall Deciduous Hedges

Acer ginnala . . . . Tatarian maple
Elaeagnus angustifolia . Russian olive
Morus alba tatarica . . .
Russian mulberry
Ulmus pumila . . . . Siberian elm

Vines

Campsis radicans. . . trumpet vine
Celastris scandens . . .
shrubby bittersweet
Clematis
Euonymus fortunei
Hedera helix. . . . . . English ivy
Lonicera . . . . honeysuckle
Parthenocissus quinquefolia . . .
Virginia creeper
Polygonum aubertii . silver-lace vine
Rosa . . . . rose
Vitis. . . . . grapevine
Wisteria

Ground Covers

For the Central Rocky Mountain Area, no ground cover is easier to maintain than a good bluegrass lawn, but in many places a lawn is not appropriate and some other kind of ground cover

is needed. A number of native plants are suitable for this purpose, as well as other cultivated kinds.

Aegopodium podograria variegatum . . . . bishop's-weed
Ajuga reptans . . carpet bugleweed
Antennaria . . . . pussytoes
Arctostaphylos uva-ursi. . bearberry
Convallaria majalis . . .
lily of the valley
Eriogonum umbellatum
Hedera helix. . . . . . English ivy
Lysimachia nummularia . . .
moneywort
Mahonia repens
Phlox subulata . . . . . moss pink
Polygonum reynoutria
Rosa, trailing kinds. . . . . rose
Sedum . . . . stonecrop

PLANTS FOR AREA 3: THE HIGH PLAINS AREA

Quite a large proportion of the Rocky Mountain region extends into the high plains where the population is small. Here it is especially important to select plants that will tolerate the great extremes of heat, cold wind, alkaline soils and drought.

Evergreens

Juniperus scopulorum . . .
Colorado red cedar
Juniperus utahensis . . . . juniper
Pinus cembroides edulis . . nut pine
Pinus ponderosa scopulorum . . .
Rocky Mountain yellow pine

Deciduous Trees

Acer negundo . . . . . . box elder
Celtis occidentalis . . . . hackberry
Elaeagnus angustifolia . . .
Russian olive
Gleditsia triacanthos inermis . . .
thornless honey locust
Populus sargentii . . . cottonwood
Salix discolor. . . . . pussy willow

Deciduous Shrubs

Amorpha fruticosa . . bastard indigo

Caragana arborescens . . .
               Siberian pea tree
Cotoneaster acutifolia
Ligustrum . . . . privet
Prunus americana. . . . wild plum
Prunus virginiana demissa . . .
               chokecherry
Rhamnus cathartica . . .
             common buckthorn
Rhus aromatica . . fragrant sumac
Ribes aureum. . . . golden currant
Rosa . . . . rose
Spiraea . . . . spirea
Syringa . . . . lilac
Tamarix hispida . . . . tamarisk
Yucca filamentosa . Adam's needle

PLANTS FOR AREA 4:
THE HIGH MOUNTAINS

Here, native trees and shrubs are the most dependable woody plants for landscaping. They include—among evergreens—Douglas fir, several pines, larches, firs, spruces, thujas and junipers. Among attractive deciduous trees are mountain maple (*Acer glabrum*), alders, birches, serviceberry (*Amelanchier*), mountain ash.

Native shrubs worth considering include silverberry (*Elaeagnus commutata*), deer brush (*Ceanothus velutinus*), snowberry (*Symphoricarpos albus*), chokecherry (*Prunus melanocarpa*), currants (*Ribes*), *Potentilla fruticosa* and willows (*Salix*).

Many perennials and annuals can be grown, as well as all hardier and short-season vegetables. Because of the short growing season, most annuals are best started early indoors, then set out as soon as the weather is warm.

Plants of Glacier National Park, a publication of the National Park Service of the United States Department of the Interior, lists and describes a wide variety of trees, shrubs and flowering plants, many worthy of trial in the High Mountains Area.

CHAPTER 36

THE
PACIFIC NORTHWEST
And British Columbia

Climatic Areas—Soils—Calendar of Work—Plants for the Pacific Northwest

THE PACIFIC NORTHWEST extends from northern California to Alaska and from the Rocky Mountains to the Pacific. It includes that portion of the United States and Canada affected by the warming Japanese Current, which flows across the Pacific and up into the Gulf of Alaska, profoundly influencing the climate.

This does not mean that the region has a uniform climate. Differences are marked and often erratic from the Pacific to the Rockies, up and down the mountains and across the valleys. Interest in home gardening is extremely high throughout the Pacific Northwest, partly because of the long growing season. The moderate climate makes it possible to grow a tremendous variety of plants, affording the gardener an almost endless choice (for list of plants see pages 680 to 682).

The region does not have a special horticultural tradition of its own, based on local conditions and a West Coast manner of living. Unlike southern California, it still reflects to a great extent British and Western European influences. A fair share of the population consists of families who emigrated from those countries, among them many highly trained gardeners. A strong and ever-growing influence of the Orient is, however, now being felt. This results from the Americans and Canadians of Japanese and Chinese ancestry who call the West Coast home, and from the increased trade and social contacts across the Pacific. This mingling of Western European traditions and styles with those of the Orient may bring about a kind of gardening characteristic of the Pacific Northwest.

CLIMATIC AREAS

It is possible, from studying weather records and plant life, to break up the region into four Areas within which temperature and rainfall are similar.

These run more or less lengthwise north and south, unlike those of the Atlantic Coast, which tend to run east and west. Even dividing the Pacific Northwest into these four Areas does not indicate the considerable variations within each Area.

Area 1

This exposed coastal strip is approximately 1000 miles long, and extremely narrow in some sections. Even so, the climate is consistently moderate. The length of the growing season ranges from about 300 days in the south to about 225 days in the north. And the rainfall shows a great variation—from about 12 in. in parts of the south to more than 150 in. in isolated sections of the north.

Winter lows are rarely much below freezing, though the northern portion comes under the influence of the Arctic air mass which periodically covers the north coast and may even extend as far south as the mouth of the Columbia River.

Area 2

The cities of Seattle and Bellingham, Wash., and Vancouver and Victoria, British Columbia, are some that lie in this Area, which is an extremely important garden section of the Northwest. Here the growing season ranges from 150 to 250 days. Summer temperatures are moderate, seldom above the 70's in the north and the 80's in the south, with consistently cool nights. Winter lows depend on the protection of the gradual movement of air from the Pacific, coming as a steady procession of rainstorms. Rarely, the Arctic front moves down to meet moist Pacific air, creating very heavy snowfall, particularly in the mountains. Most precipitation, from 30 to 80 in. per year, falls from mid-September to mid-March. Dry summers are the rule.

Area 3

Quite similar to Area 2, this section differs from it mainly in the heat and dryness of its summer and the freedom from extreme winter cold. The growing season averages well over 200 days around Portland and extends to over 300 in parts of northern

664

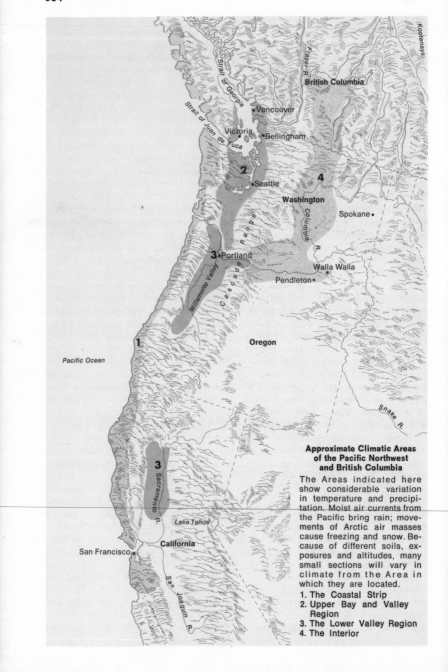

**Approximate Climatic Areas
of the Pacific Northwest
and British Columbia**

The Areas indicated here
show considerable variation
in temperature and precipitation. Moist air currents from
the Pacific bring rain; move-
ments of Arctic air masses
cause freezing and snow. Because of different soils, exposures and altitudes, many
small sections will vary in
climate from the Area in
which they are located.
1. The Coastal Strip
2. Upper Bay and Valley
   Region
3. The Lower Valley Region
4. The Interior

California. Winter brings varying amounts of rainfall, depending on elevation and proximity to the mountains. The extreme northern portion of this area may be affected by the Arctic air moving down the Columbia basin and into the Willamette Valley. It is not as vulnerable, however, to this extreme cold as Area 2. Winter mean temperatures are higher.

Area 4

The Interior, as most of Area 4 is called, is the great fruit-producing section of the Pacific Northwest. Winters are relatively mild, but the higher elevation causes snowfall rather than rain. The growing season may be shortened by late spring frosts, which can be very damaging to fruit blossoms. All sections have adequate frost-warning service, so that protective measures may be taken. Total precipitation is light, from 12 to 25 in., and the success of the fruit crops depends on irrigation. Summer temperatures are fairly high, but nights are dependably cool as on the coast.

SOILS

A good gardener may always modify his soil to suit the plants he wants to grow, but some understanding of the conditions of the Area is helpful.

Most of the soils of Area 2 and the northern section of Area 1 are characteristic of the coastal rain forest. These are shallow, often gravelly with glacial till, sometimes containing huge granite boulders. Underneath is a varying layer of impervious hardpan. This condition creates winter drainage problems. The high winter water table has resulted in shallow roots of the natural forest cover. That is why isolated trees seldom survive a clearing operation in new subdivisions. It is difficult to retain the coastal forest character along with intensive development of any new area. The wise

decision usually is to clear completely, modify the soil, correct the drainage as required, then replant.

Coastal river valleys may have extensive areas of deep, fertile alluvial soil, and there are large deposits of good-quality peat in some valleys. Area 3 consists primarily of deeper loam soil, naturally more fertile than much of the rain forest to the north.

One characteristic which these first three Areas have in common is acid soil. This is the greatest natural section of the continent for growing ericaceous plants such as rhododendrons, azaleas and heathers, and the climate of these Areas suits a wide range of these and other acid-loving plants.

Most of the soils in the lower interior and intermountain regions, many of them of volcanic origin, are slightly to heavily alkaline. Cold winters here usually rule out the cultivation of the more tender ericaceous plants in any case.

CALENDAR OF WORK

Because of the great variations of climate and soil in the Northwest, garden activities in the various areas differ widely at times through the year.

January

January is the month of greatest contrasts in the Pacific Northwest. While Area 4 is still in the cold grip of winter, spring comes to much of Area 1, and, in an unusual season, the first touch of spring will also appear in Areas 2 and 3. It is camellia-blooming time in the southern parts of the region. For this evergreen section of the Northwest which has such a long growing season, January may be the only spring month.

A steady pattern of Pacific storms sweeps across the coast, bringing rain and moderate temperatures to the coast and snow to the interior valleys.

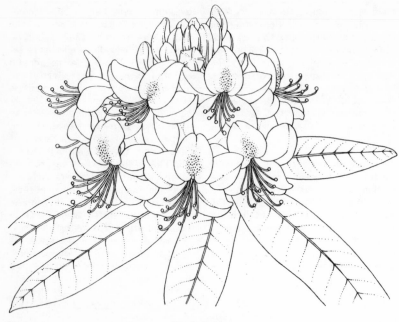

Rhododendron

During this critical month the Arctic front may move down the northern half of the area, causing serious damage. The cold air may suddenly pour down the river valleys, over the coast mountains and out the coastal inlets. The change, accompanied by dry north and northeast winds, can be so sudden that it has a desiccating effect on plants ill prepared for winter. When the change is more gradual, snow may cover the region as the Arctic air mixes with that of the moist Pacific. The white blanket is a strong protective device. Nevertheless, gardeners must be on the alert at this season. Heavy masses of soft snow can break branches if left to accumulate.

Despite fluctuating weather, the West Coast garden is never without color this month. The many red-berried cotoneasters, hollies and fire-

thorns hold their fruit through the winter, and pieris (andromeda) and laurestinus buds are ready to burst.

In the extreme south, gardeners should take advantage of the spring weather to do a good garden cleanup. Many perennials may be divided now. Although the planting season has been extended greatly by the use of container-grown nursery stock, this is still the best month to transplant shrubs and trees. Topdress and fertilize lawns, taking advantage of the rains which should come this month and help wet them down.

Other Areas of the region are still in winter. A few tasks, however, may be undertaken: trimming broken branches and removing heavy snow loads. Some pruning of deciduous trees and shrubs may be done in all Areas. Emphasis should be placed on improving appearances and cutting out dead and broken branches, leaving most of the flowering-shrub pruning to be undertaken immediately after blooming.

It is not too late to prepare for the cold snap and snow which may arrive later this month in Areas 2 and 3. Rosebushes should be mounded with soil or mulched to protect the buds. Camellia bushes, if planted in southern exposures, may be wrapped with burlap. This affords little protection from the cold but prevents rapid changes in leaf and bud temperatures, which damage plant tissues. Tall forms of *Chamaecyparis* may be neatly tied up to prevent damage from the weight of snow.

In frost-free sections of the Northwest, the soil of the vegetable garden may be prepared. In all Areas, this is seed-catalogue month. It is not too early to order the best varieties of seeds from reliable sources. Make a plan of the vegetable garden (see p. 276 in "Vegetables"). Start lettuce, cabbage and cauliflower in cold frames toward the end of the month for earliest crops.

Winter pruning of fruit trees should be completed this month in the mildest sections; elsewhere anytime before March will do. Grapes can be pruned in most of the region. In the milder sections this should already have been done.

February

Through much of the Pacific Northwest there will be more winter, but soon the early blooms of *Daphne mezereum*, *Pieris japonica* (Japanese andromeda), *Viburnum tinus*, *Rhododendron mucronulatum* and *Camellia japonica* will appear. In sheltered corners of the garden, hardy dwarf cyclamen will soon be flowering, accompanied by miniature blue iris. Snowdrops, winter aconites and rifts of crocuses follow, and the tiny species narcissuses precede their larger cousins by a few weeks.

Impatient gardeners in Area 4 may now start their cleaning up of the garden. They can do what gardeners in milder areas did in January: order new plants and seeds and work on garden plans. In the milder Areas, final dormant pruning of deciduous plants should be completed; climbing roses may be thinned out and retied.

Deciduous shrubs and trees are still dormant enough to transplant. Fertilize deciduous trees; drill holes in the soil under the tips of the branches near the best feeding roots, and fill them with fertilizer (see page 369).

Turn over the compost in preparation for lawn topdressing. Use some of it with peat moss or well-rotted manure to improve the soil of flower and shrub borders. This treatment is particularly important in regions of heavy winter rainfall, for the excess moisture will have leached out most available nutrients. Apply a side-dressing of complete high-nitrogen fertilizer to be washed in with spring rains. In the mildest parts of the Pacific Northwest, gardeners may get an early start by direct outdoor seeding of hardy annuals. Sweet peas can be sown wherever there is no frost in the ground. Place the seed 1 to 2 in. deep in fertile soil which has been well built up with decayed manure or compost.

Activity should be under way in the vegetable garden in all sections where there is no frost in the ground, particularly in Areas 1 and 3. It may still be too cool for planting in Area 2, where there are frequent white frosts at night, but soil preparation, at least, should be possible.

Sow seed of early vegetables, such as broad beans, leeks, radishes and parsley, outdoors, starting early in the month in the extreme south and progressing to Area 2 toward the end of the month. Where outdoor activity is impossible, get a head start on the season by making use of a hotbed or warm frame.

February is planting time for bush and cane fruits in the milder areas. Currants and blueberries should be pruned now, although this could have been done earlier. Strawberry beds should have an application of complete fertilizer. Check for frost damage and press in firmly plants dislodged by heaving. Fruit trees may still be pruned and fertilized. This may be the last month to apply a dormant fruit spray.

March

One characteristic of West Coast gardening is the variation from season to season in blooming dates. There may be up to six weeks' difference in the time of flowering of the very early shrubs and bulbs, particularly in the northern section of Area 2, but also in Area 3. Regardless of this, March is sure to bring its quota of bloom to gardens throughout the moderate sections of the Northwest.

In the south, camellias and early rhododendrons are at their best; *Pieris japonica* and *Viburnum tinus* open their pure white blooms; narcissuses, grape hyacinths and species tulips put on a month-long show. The purple-leaved flowering plum, so popular on many residential streets, is a mass of delicate pink flowers.

March may also be a treacherous month in the interior, where sharp spring frosts may damage the flowering buds of the soft fruits. Smudge pots must be ready for frost warnings.

March may be a month of sunshine, with night temperatures just cool enough to hold back spring growth, or it may be a month of rain and moderate temperatures, conducive to spring growth and early flowering.

Interest in broad-leaved evergreens is increasing rapidly in the moderate sections of the Northwest. Once a region of conifer forests, it is admirably suited for coniferous shrubs and trees. When planting conifers, be sure that adequate drainage has been provided; little else is required. When planting shrubs such as rhododendrons, azaleas, pieris, enkianthus and heathers, use peat moss liberally.

Shrubby ground covers have become popular for use on banks and for underplanting trees and shrubs: *Hypericum calycinum*, with bright yellow flowers all summer long; all varieties of English ivy, running myrtle and Japanese spurge for shade. The popular heath family—Scotch heather, spring-flowering heaths, pernettya, bearberry, dwarf vacciniums, salal and other gaultherias—contribute many splendid ground covers. To decrease the competition for food from larger shrubs, broadcast a little complete plant food over the ground covers.

Gardeners who have the fine bentgrass lawns so popular on the West Coast should use a power rake or some type of special machine to remove last year's thatch. This may leave the lawn unsightly for a short period, but it will recover with the coming of spring rains. Lawns should receive a good dressing of balanced fertilizer.

Outdoor seeding of early vegetables may proceed in the moderate-climate coastal section, but where danger of spring frost is great, early vegetables should be started indoors.

It is the last call for spring pruning in the fruit garden. Along the coast, a final dormant spray may be applied if buds have not already burst. Set out new strawberry plantings; give existing strawberry beds a thorough spring cleanup. Rhubarb beds will respond to a good nitrogen feeding given now. Grape and loganberry and boysenberry canes should be tied up securely.

April

Signs of winter are finally disappearing even in the colder sections. On the coast, spring continues with a steady succession of blooms: daffodils and early border perennials, wallflowers and winter pansies; low, colorful, shrubby Japanese azaleas, early species of rhododendron, Japanese cherries, early crab apples and, most interesting of all, because it is characteristically "West Coast," Western flowering dogwood (*Cornus nuttallii*), with its huge white bracts. A larger tree than the eastern American flowering dogwood (*C. florida*), it is less winter-hardy and can be grown only in Areas 1, 2 and 3 of the Northwest. Even in its native region, this dogwood does not take kindly to cultivation. Since it is particularly hard to establish, do not grow it in an exposed location. This is the best time to move dogwood, even if in full bloom.

In the milder sections, early bedding-out annuals that have been started indoors may be set out after they have been well hardened off (i.e., gradually accustomed to the cold). Wait another month to do this in the northern part of Area 2.

It is garden-preparation time in Area 4, a month or more behind the coastal region.

April is the best month for pruning bush roses, even though they may have already started into growth. Early-flowering deciduous shrubs should be pruned as soon as their blooms are past their best. Keep in mind the long growing season ahead, and prune now to encourage production of new branches.

Spring-flowering heaths may be sheared back after they are through blooming, summer-blooming heathers before they start into new growth.

Hydrangeas which bloom on shoots of the current season's growth—*H. paniculata* and its variety *grandiflora* (known as the peegee hydrangea), *H. arborescens grandiflora*, the hills-of-snow hydrangea—*Spiraea* Anthony Waterer and other summer-blooming shrubs should be drastically pruned this month, if they have not been previously cut back. Do not prune the blue-, pink- and white-flowered varieties of the summer-flowering *H. macrophylla* because their flower buds were set last fall.

Plant out rooted or divided chrysanthemums now. Start the first of a long succession of gladiolus plantings which will provide all-summer bloom.

Except for the mildest sections of the Northwest, April is not too late for planting evergreens. If the soil is warm, root growth will start.

Along the coast, herbaceous perennials should be divided and new plants set out. This is the last opportunity this spring to make changes in the perennial border.

Winter rains will have leached out most of the available nutrients from coastal soils. April is the time for a general application of a complete fertilizer, if not done last month.

As bulbs finish blooming, nip off the flower heads but leave all of the foliage. Give rock-garden plants a light application of fertilizer worked into the soil around them.

Lawns should be given an application of screened compost or good loam, raked in well and watered if needed. Avoid sand and peat for topdressing; they may bring problems later in periods of drought, and they have little or no nutrient value.

April is a good month for starting new lawns in all coastal sections. Bluegrasses are increasing in popularity in West Coast grass mixtures, but the finest lawns are still made from bent grasses and fescues.

As the soil warms up this month in the milder sections, continue sowing vegetables outdoors. A second planting of potatoes may be made this month, while farther north and into Area 4, it may be time for a first planting. Early cabbage plants, onions and other vegetables which have been started indoors may safely be set out at the beginning of this month in the south and later in the month in the more northern section of the coast. Early varieties of sweet corn may be sown in the milder sections, but wait until May or June in other regions.

Follow the spray calendar recommended for local conditions in applying necessary fruit sprays throughout this month. Apples and pears, in full bloom in most regions this month, should have some of their blossom thinned to prevent too heavy a fruit set. Prevent rotting by removing straw mulch from strawberries in places where it has been applied.

May

May is still a spring month through most of the Pacific Northwest. Bulbs are in bloom in Area 4; it is late-spring-flowering time in Areas 2 and 3, and early summer in the south and parts of Area 1.

Once again, weather is a controlling factor, for it may be sunny and warm or wet and cool. Regardless of the weather, May is bound to be a busy time for the West Coast gardener.

In all Areas, there is plenty of color. Highlights of the month in most gardens will be rhododendrons and azaleas. Many of the best hybrids are in bloom now. Take special note of these; there may be such a diversity of colors that clashes in the color scheme are inevitable. To avoid such disharmony next year, plan appropriate placement of varieties now. May is the month for rhododendron flower shows—as fascinating as are the bet-

ter-known rose and gladiolus shows.

Unless the season has been particularly early, the last of the spring-flowering trees, laburnums and English hawthorns, now come into bloom. Late-flowering deciduous spring shrubs are at their best, filling the garden with color a month or more before roses and most perennials appear.

Prune early-flowering deciduous shrubs, which need this treatment when they have finished blooming. A good rule is to thin out one third of the oldest canes at ground level; then cut back one third of all remaining branches by one third of their length. This applies to forsythia, spirea and weigela, as well as to the later-blooming mock orange and deutzia.

Conifers may need a little judicious pruning to keep them in shape.

Rhododendron and azalea pruning should be confined to pinching off the old flower heads when they have finished blooming and removing occasional disfiguring branches. Pines may be kept compact by "snuffing out the candles," or pinching back the new shoots.

Lilacs do best in the acid coastal soil if lime is alternated one year with a complete fertilizer the next, both applied in May, after flowering. Prune lilacs lightly immediately after they are through blooming, removing all very weak shoots; also pick off all faded blooms.

Spray for holly leaf miner this month, when the adult insects are emerging from the leaves.

If the season has been early, give lawns a second light application of fertilizer, using ammonium sulphate, ammonium nitrate or a special lawn fertilizer. Water in well.

Cannas and dahlias should be planted now. Geraniums and begonias, set out early in the month in the south, should not be planted until late

May in the cooler coastal areas and even later in the interior. Continue planting a succession of gladioluses.

Strawberries should be fruiting this month in the earlier sections of the Northwest, but it may be well into June before they ripen in the northern half of the coastal region. Cover the beds with netting to protect from birds as the fruit ripens. Keep all blossoms picked off new strawberry plantings to give them strength for heavier bearing next season. To prevent mold, spray all strawberry beds with captan before the berries start to ripen.

Mulch bush fruits to make picking easier next month. Tree fruits demand little attention this month. Diligently continue the dusting or spray program suitable for your local conditions.

June

Weather records for the Pacific Northwest in June show confusion about what might be considered "normal." It should be a month of sunshine, which is almost always assured in the extreme southern area, but not necessarily in the north.

Grass must be cut; flower and shrub borders need weeding. But the pressure of spring work is past, and now is the time to look at the garden again with a critical eye. The spring garden was planned to be looked at. The summer garden must be planned as an area to be lived in. From early June onward, herbaceous plants can help to create such an intimate atmosphere. Put these plants to advantageous use in controlled planting areas such as patios, in tubs, boxes or other containers, as well as in more natural arrangements in perennial beds and borders.

The climate of the Pacific Northwest is admirably suited to herbaceous perennials. One of the reasons they have become so popular in the region is because they provide a color link between spring-flowering and summer-flowering shrubs and annuals.

The garden is not without shrub color. Many of the large late-blooming rhododendrons are at their best in June, and low evergreen *indica* azaleas are particularly showy when massed. Varieties of *Hydrangea macrophylla* start blooming now, as do *Escallonia rubra* and *Cistus laurifolius*.

Pruning is one of the important garden tasks this month. The rush of spring growth is over, and most coniferous and broad-leaved evergreen hedges should be trimmed.

Most coniferous and small-leaved hedges may be sheared, but laurels, holly and other large-leaved hedges should be pruned, each branch being cut back as necessary without slicing through individual leaves. Flowering trees should be pruned sparingly— remember that they require much less pruning than their fruit-producing relatives. Wall shrubs and climbers also need further pruning and training.

Continue pruning deciduous flowering shrubs as their bloom passes. These include mock orange, deutzia and weigela this month.

Roses bloom in succession from south to north through June. Disbud some of them to produce superb flowers. Keep up a regular rose-spray program; apply at least every ten days, using both insecticide and fungicide or an all-purpose spray.

The whole garden should receive one or more complete sprays or dusts this month, using a general-purpose spray or dust.

As the blue-flowered varieties of *Hydrangea macrophylla* come into bloom, intensify the blue of the flowers, if pale, with a mixture of iron sulphate and aluminum sulphate, watered well into the soil.

Almost everything in the Northwest garden needs fertilizer this month. Side-dress annual plantings with a complete fertilizer, watered in well.

Lawns need their early-summer application of nitrogen to carry them through the dry months ahead. In June apply a weed killer.

This is the first month for taking summer cuttings. Shrubs which start growth early will now have half-ripened wood, suitable for use as cuttings. These include cistus and some deciduous shrubs, including brooms.

Geraniums and begonias often turn out best if left until June before planting out.

This month is maintenance time in the vegetable garden. Weeds must be kept under control; seedlings must be thinned; potatoes and other hill crops should be earthed up. In many sections it is finally warm enough to sow sweet corn. Tomatoes, celery and other vegetables started and kept indoors can be set out. Continue regular sowings of radishes, lettuce and other salad greens.

The natural seasonal drop of the stone fruits will usually do the job of fruit thinning, but if necessary, thin the remaining fruit to assure good size and quality.

Weed control is especially important this month in new strawberry plantings and around bush and cane fruits as well.

Continue the spray program as required.

July

Visitors to the Pacific Northwest are impressed by the brilliance of flower color in July. Even roses, blooming on in the south since June or coming into their own in the north, seem to be more perfect in color and sweeter in scent than elsewhere.

The reason for this is the weather, the frequent cause of many Pacific Northwest plant peculiarities. July is normally dry, with moderate temperatures. Nights are invariably cool, and

sunny days often alternate with light overcast and occasional drizzle. This type of weather seems to produce the superb color and scent in flowers.

Topdress each bush in the rose garden with a complete fertilizer and water it in well, then cover with a mulch.

Among the garden favorites which thrive under these conditions are clarkias and stocks. Some of the heat-loving annuals do poorly in the coastal regions, or at least take much longer to come into flower than in warmer regions. Gardens in the interior are assured of more heat, but they, too, share the benefits of cool nights.

Summer shrubs are at their best in July. Sweet-scented Spanish broom is a favorite, blooming from now until late autumn. The peegee (*Hydrangea paniculata grandiflora*) blooms after the blue-, pink-, and white-flowered varieties of *H. macrophylla*. Ceanothuses, fuchsias, escallonias, lavender and the many varieties of Scotch heather are at their best this month.

Cutting roses or removing spent blooms will encourage subsequent bloom. Most hybrid teas will continue to bloom and will provide good fall display if you prune carefully now. Other pruning tasks include hedge trimming, if this was not done last month.

In the rock garden, prune or shear back low shrubs and unruly alpines, and improve the soil where needed. Spring-flowering bulbs will have finished their growth and may be dug, cleaned and stored. Tulips should be lifted each year, but daffodils and other narcissuses may stay in the ground until they show signs of crowding. Continue taking cuttings of half-ripened shoots this month, for shrub replacements. Tiny tip cuttings of ericas root readily at this time.

This is the month to prepare for winter gardening. Sow seed of winter pansies, violas, wallflowers and forget-me-nots. Sow either in a cold frame or in a sheltered, shady spot in the garden.

Keep all bent-grass and bent-fescue lawns closely clipped, but raise the mower blades now for other grasses. Fine lawns will stay green through dry periods if watering is regular and thorough. It is not too late for a summer application of nitrogen fertilizer, if this was not done last month.

Fall crocuses and colchicums should be planted.

Divide bearded iris. If there is a low spot in your garden, Japanese iris will grow well there. They like plenty of moisture at least during the spring and summer growing period. Flooding is not necessary, though, and any moist situation will be satisfactory.

Early peas, beans, lettuce and radishes will be ready, and the first carrots, young and tender, will be delicious. Thin out rows of beets; cook together the tops and roots of the thinnings for a tasty dish. The main crop of early potatoes should be dug this month. Plant the last of your vegetables. These will include Chinese cabbage and another crop of carrots, lettuce, radishes and beets. Fall cabbages, cauliflowers, Brussels sprouts and broccoli should be sown now. They can stand a moderate amount of frost and may survive the coming winter if it is not too severe. Plant out the last batch of celery plants this month. Pull soil away from onions now, to allow them to mature.

Bush fruits need attention after crops are harvested. Remove the canes which have fruited, and prune back or thin out others, keeping the bushes neat and compact. A regional exception to this rule is the raspberry: pruning is usually left until spring, for winter protection.

Do not neglect to water small fruits

through a dry spell. Spray or dust fruit trees regularly, according to the spray calendar recommended for your local area. Continue with light summer pruning, as necessary.

July is the best time for budding. Topwork fruit trees to change variety and to insure pollination. Varieties may also be budded on seedling understocks.

August

August is the best month to sit and enjoy West Coast gardens. The autumn procession of storms across the coast have not yet started, and garden floral display continues unabated. Annuals still provide brilliance of color. Summer-blooming heathers may be over their best flowering by the end of the month, but abelia, ceanothus and buddleia are at their peak.

This is also the month when *Cornus nuttallii*, the Western dogwood, blooms again. Its early fall performance is, however, most unreliable; it seldom has fall blooms in the wild. Its habit of breaking dormancy half a season ahead of normal flowering time seems to depend on the amount of care it gets under cultivation. Extra summer watering is the most important contributing factor.

If, for vacation, you are going to leave your garden unattended, make sure that your plants get a good spray before you leave. Use a mixed fungicide-insecticide-miticide spray or dust on most shrubs and trees, including conifers. Watch for the appearance of mildew on roses and phlox, which are the worst sufferers in August from fungus disease.

Young wallflowers should be planted in protective plant bands now, ready for bedding out in a month or so. Winter pansies should be planted out in flats or in plant bands and kept in a cold frame or sheltered spot in the

Pseudotsuga taxifolia
(Douglas Fir)

and varieties of *Hydrangea macro-phylla*. Prune these hydrangeas carefully, for, unlike their hardier relatives (peegee and hills-of-snow hydrangeas), their buds set this fall for next summer's bloom. Simply remove the old flowering shoots, shape as necessary and retain stout new growths, especially those that originate near the base of the bush.

Dahlias, at their best this month, will respond to another fertilizing now. This will enable them to continue blooming until late fall in coastal gardens.

August is exhibition time. Gladioluses, dahlias, roses and annuals should be timed to be at their best for showing this month.

Bare ground is unsightly and, because of the heavy winter rains in the Pacific Northwest, nutrients are wasted by excess leaching from unoccupied ground. Work out new combinations of plants as cover for bare ground. Try an underplanting of evergreen ground covers with wide-spaced deciduous shrubs. The opposite, too, can be interesting: low deciduous plants as a footing for a few well-spaced broad-leaved evergreens. These combinations are relatively self-maintaining.

While established lawns need regular watering and cutting, this is the month to prepare for fall seeding of new lawns. Remember that once the lawn is seeded, the surface is "sealed off." Incorporate plenty of organic matter in the seed bed, preferably well-decayed manure and peat moss. Seeding the last week in August should be just right to take advantage of fall rains.

It is not too late to sow lettuce, radishes and other quick-maturing crops. Early August is still time to set out plants of late cabbage and to sow Brussels sprouts. Broccoli should mature within three months, so it may

garden until time to bed them out. There is still time for a final seeding of some favorite herbaceous perennials, if given the protection of a cold frame where moisture and shade can be favorably controlled.

As heathers and lavender finish blooming, cut them back promptly. Prune into shape cistus, ceanothus

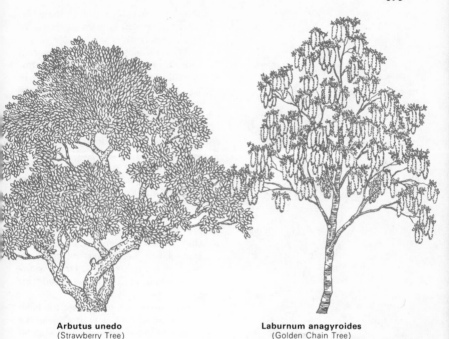

Arbutus unedo
(Strawberry Tree)

Laburnum anagyroides
(Golden Chain Tree)

be sown early this month in sections of the Northwest where the danger of winter setting in by November is slight.

This is harvest time for early varieties of peaches, apricots and apples. There is still time for budding, as suggested for July. Grapes may need a light pruning to let light in to the fruit at this time. Canes of raspberries and blackberries which have finished fruiting may be cut to the ground this month.

September

In general, sunny days and cool nights prevail during September, one of the most pleasant months in the Pacific Northwest. The pattern is almost certain to be broken, however, by periodic storms which cross the coast and bring rain to coastal areas and cloud to the interior. Growing conditions continue to be ideal. Rainfall might even be heavy enough so that sprinklers can be put away for the season. Cool nights at higher elevations in the interior bring an occasional frost that can kill many annuals.

In gardens throughout most of the Pacific Northwest, bloom is provided by a profusion of dahlias, late gladioluses, early chrysanthemums, annuals which may be able to stand the rain, roses which take a new lease on life, and late-summer shrubs which may continue to bloom into late autumn.

Extra color is provided by the many red- and orange-berried shrubs, so typical of the West Coast home landscape. On the rocky slopes overhanging the ocean and on the lower slopes of the coastal mountains, the native

Lilium hollandicum
(Holland Lily)

broad-leaved evergreen arbutus is particularly colorful, with its load of bright red fruit.

This is the month spring-flowering bulbs appear on the market, but few need to be planted as early as this in the Pacific Northwest. Lilies, however, should be planted as soon as they are received. The climate is ideal for lilies, and many new varieties have originated in the Northwest. It is not too early to plant many of the earliest-blooming bulbs and corms, such as crocuses, which put on their floral display in January and February near the coast.

Some annuals do not stand up to fall rains. Once finished blooming, they should be removed so that the ground can be prepared for winter bedding plants or bulbs. Divide some of the oldest clumps of perennials this month.

September is a good time for lawn renovation. This is usually done in the spring, but recovery is almost as good this month, because fall rains and moderate temperatures hasten the establishment of new roots. (For procedures, see "Lawns and Their Maintenance," page 344.)

Late-summer cuttings of some shrub favorites may be taken this month. They must be kept in a cold frame for the winter. Roots may not develop on many of them until the spring of next year.

It seems early, but September is a good month to transplant broad-leaved evergreens and conifers. Growth is not too active now, and they should become well established before winter sets in.

The vegetable harvest continues. Carrots and beets will be ready. Onions may be pulled to dry and store. Early cabbage, cauliflower and celery will be ready for harvesting. Dig the main crop of potatoes. Sweet-corn varieties continue to mature in the warmer sections of the Pacific Northwest. It may be some weeks before harvest time for sweet corn in the cooler coastal districts, depending on the amount of summer heat in the months just passed. Tomatoes are slow to ripen on the coast if the season has been cool. Vine crops—citron, cucumber, pumpkin, squash, melon—will be mature this month in sections of the Northwest which had enough summer heat. Along the coast, however, these will not ripen before October.

It is harvest time for many apple varieties. Use a stop-drop spray on McIntosh and other apple varieties. This will hold the fruit on the trees until maturity. Some varieties are very slow to mature in the cooler coastal sections of the Pacific Northwest. Boysenberry and blackberry canes should be pegged down for over-winter layering.

October

Frost is rare throughout much of the Pacific Northwest this month. The interior, though, with higher elevations and less protected by the moderating influence of the Pacific, may expect frequent frost. A succession of bloom, on the other hand, is characteristic of coastal gardens through the long autumn.

All sections of the Northwest are affected by the rhythmic pattern of storms which travel across the coast throughout the month. Heaviest rains are in the coastal valleys and the western slopes of the Coast and Cascade ranges. Although cloud persists into the interior, most of the moisture has been dropped before the moist Pacific air has crossed the mountains, so total precipitation this month is relatively light in these sections.

There is plenty of compensation, however, for this pattern of weather on the coast. Days of rain are followed

by days of sunshine. The air is crisp and clear on these bright days, and conditions are ideal for the many fall tasks in the garden.

For a continuity of flowers, replace summer varieties with biennials, such as wallflowers, winter pansies and forget-me-nots. Interplant these hardy biennials with some of the spring-flowering bulbs. This is general bulb-planting time, although many gardeners prefer to wait another month before planting tulips in the milder sections of the Pacific Northwest.

Soil preparation is particularly important when bulbs are to be left in the same place for several years. While there is not the same need for deep planting in moderate-climate sections of the Northwest as in colder areas, a good rule to follow is to set the bulbs at a depth of 2½ times their diameter.

Fall planting is in full swing on the coast, so now is a good time to plan changes for the home garden if any improvements are to be made. With a little foresight and imagination, that tired old backyard can be turned into an outdoor living room to be enjoyed next summer.

Gladioluses should be lifted, dried and stored. Gardeners in the interior must dig up all dahlia tubers this month. Gardeners on the coast, however, should enjoy another month of bloom from theirs unless the season is exceptionally cold.

Hardy chrysanthemums are a special feature in West Coast gardens this month. Blooming can be prolonged if they are covered with polyethylene to keep off the rain.

Lawns will stand up to winter conditions best if they are given a good topdressing now.

Winters are too wet for outdoor pit storage in the Pacific Northwest, so gardeners must rely on a cool, not-too-dry, well-ventilated basement or shed for storing potatoes and most of the root crops harvested this month. After asparagus tops have been cut off, cover the bed with well-decayed manure. Fork it into the soil. Rhubarb should be divided and replanted now, or new two-year-old clumps may be purchased for setting out. Fall crops from the home garden include spinach, head lettuce, cabbage, celery, broccoli and Brussels sprouts.

Fruit trees are seldom dormant enough this month for planting in the Pacific Northwest. With prospects of an open winter ahead, though, there is plenty of time for this task. Most bush fruits, however, may be moved at this time.

Gardens in mild climates do not require excessive winter protection, but where it is colder, small fruits should be mulched with manure or compost. On the coast, where heavy winter precipitation is inevitable, applications of manure or good compost at this time help to keep up the fertility level. To increase plantings of raspberries and blackberries, take root cuttings now. It is harvest time for late pears and most late apple varieties on the coast.

November

Weather again plays a major part in regulating garden activities this month. Perhaps nowhere else on the continent is the weather so consistently unpredictable! Although the regular pattern of October storms may continue through November, weather records show a surprising number of bright, sunny days during this period. In some seasons these even dominate November weather. However, it is during these high-pressure spells, when the weather should be perfect, that coastal regions get fog. There is continuous sunshine at higher elevations, but all low areas may be fogged in completely for days on end. At times like these, coastal gardeners wish for a good Pacific storm to clear the air. This will come in due course.

Prolonged clear spells may bring frost to the coastal garden. Winter sometimes arrives suddenly, when Arctic air moves down quickly over the coast in November. Such occasions are fortunately rare, but sections of the Northwest farthest from the coast may get their first real taste of winter at this time. Nights are invariably cool, and gardeners should watch for snow on nearby mountains to remind them when the last tender flowers and plants must be taken indoors.

It is past normal fall-pruning time, but some berried shrubs may be trimmed now to enhance their fruiting effects. Prune rosebushes lightly, delaying heavy pruning until spring. Watch for brown patch and other fungus diseases of turf this month. A spray, promptly applied, using one of the special fungicides for turf diseases, will keep these problems in check. The last of the season's herbaceous perennial flowers—asters and chrysanthemums—bloom through November. When these have finished, they should be cut down and the plants mulched, as should other perennials, with compost, leaf mold or manure.

Many deciduous shrubs and trees are sufficiently dormant now for transplanting.

Westerly gales often alternate with periods of good weather. The gales pose a severe threat to some trees, particularly in exposed coastal sections. Tree wood just does not harden up as well as it does in the East. Tree roots are shallow in the rain forests and uprooting may occur; there is little one can do to prevent this. However, check trees for weak crotches, where long periods of wet weather tend to produce rotting. Brace limbs where necessary. Call in an expert if trees need this type of attention. Care provided now may prevent splitting during heavy winds or after a heavy fall of wet snow.

November is not too late for bulb planting. Dahlias must be dug and stored, even if they are still blooming well. Dahlias and gladioluses may winter over in the ground in some coastal areas, if the winter is moderate, but it is seldom worthwhile to take this chance.

Gardeners in the mildest section may plant sweet-pea seed late this month, but in most of the Northwest it is better to let this task wait until spring.

Take cuttings of many foliage plants for rooting in the propagation frame. Petunias, sown indoors now, will provide attractive pots in April.

This is the principal month for putting late vegetables into storage. Beets, carrots, parsnips and turnips keep well when cold but not too dry. Turnips keep best if not covered, but the others should be stored in boxes of sand. Check squash and pumpkins that were stored last month and discard any which do not appear to be keeping well. Cabbages and Brussels sprouts should be kept outside as long as possible; then they should be stored in a cool place.

Bring indoors a good supply of potting soil this month. Keep a supply of peat and sand on hand to mix with the soil for making up seed-sowing and potting soils.

During severe winters, strawberry losses are great in northern coastal sections of the Pacific Northwest. In spite of the temptation to mulch heavily to prevent winter killing, it is seldom wise to follow this practice because of the inevitable, prolonged wet season through winter. Rotting frequently occurs, and losses from this cause may be more severe than from the cold.

December

The pattern of regular winter storms from the Pacific has resumed this month. However, the cold continental air mass frequently moves down from the northeast. December temperatures are seldom extremely low, but the colder air, meeting the moist air from the ocean, may result in a heavy snowfall, damaging shrubs and trees. The snow will also give protection to the garden during the almost inevitable cold snap which January brings. An open month is the rule, nevertheless, in most moderate-climate sections of the Northwest.

The landscape is very much alive this month. Many broad-leaved evergreens are ready for spring, with flower buds plump and firm, a characteristic of rhododendrons and azaleas; or they are showing color, as in *Pieris japonica* and laurestinus (*Viburnum tinus*).

Winter-blooming heaths are flowering. *Camellia sasanqua* is in bloom and, in sheltered places, *Garrya elliptica* is putting out its long winter catkins. *Fatsia japonica* blooms this month, bearing strange yellow-green spikes among dark green palmate leaves. *Daphne laureola*, too, is at its best, with its greenish flowers clustered under the curled dark foliage. *Skimmia japonica* combines white flowers with loads of red berries. Holly berries are at their brightest, ready for cutting for Christmas. Fruits of cotoneaster, stranvaesia, pyracantha and pernettya add a festive touch to the December landscape.

Most of the vigorous conifers, including varieties of *Chamaecyparis lawsoniana* and *C. pisifera*, profit from a light pruning and, as a result, will provide a good supply of greens. Cut the branches of holly carefully, and remember that this is a pruning operation. Next season's crop will depend on how drastic the prun-

ing has been this month. All cut holly
should be treated with a hormone dip
or spray to prevent leaves and berries
from dropping. Stranvaesia and many
of the evergreen cotoneasters may be
cut more freely than holly, without
danger of spoiling their shapes. Cut
out dead branches and shape deciduous shrubs, but do not cut out too
much spring-flowering wood. Cut
flowering branches, in full-bud stage
this month, of *Pieris japonica* and
Viburnum tinus. They will open in a
short time if placed in water indoors.

If it is an open winter, planting
may continue through December.

Make preparations for spring in the
vegetable garden where the ground is
frost-free. A good application of manure or compost, well dug or cultivated in, will make easier an early
start with spring work.

A light pruning of fruit trees and
bushes to cut out deadwood and generally to improve their appearance is
wise now. Peach trees must be sprayed
to control peach leaf curl. A general
dormant spray on all fruit trees should
be applied at this time. Take dormant
cuttings of currants, gooseberries and
grapes. Store the prepared cuttings in
bundles in peat, sand or sawdust in a
cold frame or sheltered spot outdoors,
for spring planting.

PLANTS FOR
THE PACIFIC NORTHWEST

The number of kinds of plants that
can be grown in the Pacific Northwest
is immense. The following lists give
some indication of the great variety
and name some of the best; there are
many more of equal merit. Not all
listed are hardy in all parts of the
region. Gardeners should use as a
guide in making selections the plants
successfully cultivated in other local
gardens and the kinds offered by nurseries. Visits to arboretums, botanical
gardens and public parks will reveal

an astonishing wealth of really fine
plants.

Deciduous Shade Trees

Acer . . . . maple
Betula pendula . . .
    European white birch
Carpinus betulus . . .
    European hornbeam
Catalpa speciosa . . Western catalpa
Cercidiphyllum japonicum . . .
    katsura tree
Fagus sylvatica . . European beech
Ginkgo biloba . . . maidenhair tree
Gleditsia triacanthos inermis . . .
    thornless honey locust
Juglans . . . . walnut
Liquidambar styraciflua . sweet gum
Liriodendron tulipifera . . tulip tree
Platanus acerifolia . . London plane
Populus nigra italica . . .
    Lombardy poplar
Quercus . . . . oak
Robinia pseudoacacia . . black locust
Salix babylonica . . weeping willow
Sorbus aucuparia . . .
    European mountain ash
Tilia cordata . . small-leaved linden

Flowering Trees

Aesculus carnea . red horse chestnut
Cercis siliquastrum . . . Judas tree
Cornus nuttallii . . .
    Western flowering dogwood
Crataegus oxyacantha . . .
    English hawthorn
Davidia involucrata . . . dove tree
Fraxinus ornus . . . . flowering ash
Laburnum anagyroides . golden chain
Magnolia
Malus . . . . flowering crab apple
Oxydendrum arboreum . . .sourwood
Paulownia tomentosa . empress tree
Prunus . . .
    flowering cherry, plum and apricot
Styrax japonica . . . . . . storax

Evergreen Trees

Abies . . . . fir
Araucaria araucana . monkey puzzle

Cedrus. . . . . cedar	*Spiraea* . . . . spirea
Chamaecyparis . . . false cypress	*Stewartia* . . . . . pseudo-camellia
Cryptomeria japonica	*Syringa vulgaris* . . . . lilac
Cunninghamia lanceolata . China fir	*Tamarix pentandra* . . . tamarisk
Cupressus macrocarpa . . .	*Vaccinium parvifolium*
Monterey cypress	*Viburnum*
Juniperus . . . . juniper	*Weigela florida*
Libocedrus decurrens . incense cedar	
Picea. . . . . spruce	**Coniferous Evergreen Shrubs**
Pinus . . . . pine	*Cephalotaxus drupacea* . . .
Pseudotsuga taxifolia . . Douglas fir	Japanese plum yew
Sciadopitys verticillata. umbrella pine	*Chamaecyparis* . . . . false cypress
Sequoiadendron giganteum . . .	*Cryptomeria japonica*
giant sequoia	*Juniperus* . . . . juniper
Taxus brevifolia . . . Western yew	*Picea abies*. . . . . Norway spruce
Thuja. . . . . arborvitae	*Pinus mugo mughus* . . mugho pine
Thujopsis dolobrata . Hiba arborvitae	*Taxus* . . . . yew
Tsuga. . . . . hemlock	*Thuja*. . . . . arborvitae

Deciduous Shrubs

Broad-Leaved Evergreen Shrubs

Caryopteris incana. . . . bluebeard	*Abelia chinensis*
Chaenomeles lagenaria . . .	*Arbutus unedo* . . . strawberry tree
Japanese quince	*Aucuba japonica* . . gold-dust tree
Corylopsis pauciflora	*Azara microphylla*
Cotinus coggygria. . . . smoke tree	*Berberis* . . . . barberry
Cotoneaster	*Buxus sempervirens* . . . boxwood
Cytisus . . . . broom	*Calluna vulgaris* . . . . heather
Daphne mezereum. . . . mezereon	*Camellia*
Deutzia	*Ceanothus*
Elaeagnus angustifolia . . .	*Cistus laurifolius*. . . . . rockrose
Russian olive	*Cotoneaster*
Enkianthus campanulatus	*Daphne*
Euonymus alatus . . .	*Elaeagnus pungens*
winged-bark euonymus	*Erica carnea* . . . . heath
Forsythia	*Escallonia rubra*
Fuchsia magellanica	*Euonymus fortunei*
Holodiscus discolor . . . rock spirea	*Fatsia japonica* (syn. *Aralia sieboldii*)
Hydrangea	*Hypericum patulum*
Kolkwitzia amabilis . . beauty bush	*Ilex* . . . . holly
Leycesteria formosa . . .	*Kalmia latifolia* . . mountain laurel
Himalaya honeysuckle	*Lavandula officinalis* . . . lavender
Magnolia	*Leucothoë catesbei* (syn. *Andromeda*
Paeonia suffruticosa. . . tree peony	*catesbei*)
Philadelphus. . . . . . mock orange	*Ligustrum* . . . . privet
Rhododendron . . . . . . azalea	*Lonicera*. . . . . . . honeysuckle
Rhus typhina . . . staghorn sumac	*Mahonia aquifolium* . holly mahonia
Ribes sanguineum . . .	*Myrica californica* . . .
flowering currant	California bayberry
Rosa . . . . rose	*Nandina domestica*. heavenly bamboo
Spartium junceum . Spanish broom	*Olearia haastii* . . . . . daisy tree

Osmanthus ilicifolius
Osmarea burkwoodii
Pachistima myrsinites
Pernettya mucronata
Phillyrea decora
Photinia serrulata
Pieris
Prunus
Pyracantha . . . . firethorn
Raphiolepis umbellata ovata . . .
                     Yeddo hawthorn
Rhododendron
Rosmarinus officinalis . . rosemary
Sarcococca hookeriana humilis
Siphonosmanthus delavayi
  (syn. *Osmanthus delavayi*)
Skimmia japonica
Stranvaesia davidiana
Vaccinium ovatum
Viburnum

Ground Covers

Arctostaphylos uva-ursi . bearberry
Calluna vulgaris . . . . . heather
Ceanothus thyrsiflorus . . .
                       blue blossom
Cotoneaster
Cytisus kewensis . . . . . . broom
Daphne cneorum
Erica carnea . . . . heath
Gaultheria
Hypericum moserianum . gold flower
Juniperus . . . . juniper
Pachysandra terminalis . . .
                     Japanese spurge
Vinca minor . . . . running myrtle

Hedge Plants

Berberis thunbergii . . .
             Japanese barberry
Berberis wilsoniae . . . . barberry
Buxus sempervirens . . . boxwood
Chamaecyparis pisifera . . .
                      Sawara cypress
Cotoneaster simonsii
Cupressus macrocarpa . . .
                   Monterey cypress
Ilex . . . . holly
Ligustrum . . . . privet
Lonicera nitida

Osmarea burkwoodii
Prunus laurocerasus schipkaensis
               . . . cherry laurel
Pyracantha coccinea . . . firethorn
Taxus baccata . . . . English yew
Thuja . . . . arborvitae
Tsuga heterophylla . . .
               Western hemlock

Vines

Actinidia chinensis . . . . yangtao
Akebia quinata . . five-leaf akebia
Aristolochia durior . . .
                 Dutchman's-pipe
Campsis grandiflora . . .
           Chinese trumpet creeper
Clematis
Euonymus fortunei minimus
Hedera helix . . . . . English ivy
Hydrangea petiolaris . . .
               climbing hydrangea
Parthenocissus
Passiflora caerulea . . passionflower
Polygonum aubertii . silver-lace vine
Wisteria

Plants for Seaside Gardens

For other suitable kinds, see pages
550 to 553 in "Seaside Gardens."
Arbutus menziesii . . . . madrona
Berberis wilsoniae . . . . barberry
Cedrus . . . . cedar
Cistus laurifolius . . . . rockrose
Crataegus lavallei . . . . hawthorn
Cupressus macrocarpa . . .
                   Monterey cypress
Cytisus . . . . broom
Elaeagnus
Escallonia rubra
Gaultheria shallon . . . . . . salal
Genista
Hebe traversii
Myrica californica . . .
              California bayberry
Olearia haastii . . . . . daisy tree
Pinus contorta . . . . . shore pine
Quercus garryana . . . Oregon oak
Rosmarinus officinalis . . rosemary
Salix . . . . willow
Vaccinium ovatum

PART VI

The Wonders
of Plant Growing

Contrary to popular belief, luck plays but a small part in gardening. Green thumbs are developed, not inherited. The ability to grow plants comes from a deep understanding of the soil, the environment and of the plants themselves. Much that the gardener learns can be gained by personal experience and personal lore without ever reading a book or taking a course in botany— this is evidenced by the achievements of unlettered peoples in many places and many ages. But modern gardeners have the organized knowledge that has been painstakingly assembled by researchers and practical growers.

Gardening is more rewarding if the gardener knows how plants are structured, how they "feed" and grow, how they reproduce. He will certainly be more successful if he learns of the microscopic life teeming in the soil, and how to condition it so that plants will flourish.

The wise gardener takes advantage of such scientific information, then turns to his garden, windowsill or greenhouse with new ability and appreciation. By observing what he has learned, he will benefit in experience as much as his plants will benefit in vigorous life.

CHAPTER 37

HOW PLANTS LIVE—
And How They Grow

The Nature of Plants—Seeds—How Roots Work—Stems—Leaf Forms—Photosynthesis — Transpiration— Flowers and Fruit

PLANT LIFE was the first life on earth. Carbon remains of the first primitive plants which lived in the sea have been found in rocks over two billion years old. It was not until 400 million years ago that plants appeared on land. These were simple, without roots and as yet leafless, but their presence on land made possible the emergence of animal life from the sea by providing a source of food. All the brilliant and complex variety of the plant kingdom has evolved from these first land plants.

A plant is generally considered to be a green, living thing with roots in the soil and with stem, leaves and flowers aboveground. Yet a plant is not necessarily green, and it may have no roots, leaves or flowers. Flowering plants comprise only one of the 13 divisions into which botanists classify the vegetable kingdom. The other divisions consist of more lowly and less evolved plants, such as bacteria, algae, diatoms, funguses, mosses, liverworts, horsetails and ferns.

All plants are made up of living cells, are capable of drawing energy from inorganic substances and have no specialized sense or digestive organs. The simplest consist of a single cell able to live, breathe, feed, grow and reproduce by itself. Many bacteria and algae are in this group. But in the course of evolution plants have become increasingly complex, the most highly evolved being the flowering or seed-producing plants. These have a well-defined structure of root, stem, shoot, leaf, flower and seed.

Cultivated plants, with very few exceptions, belong with the flowering plants and ferns, but other kinds inhabit gardens and make their presence known. The green coatings that grow on flowerpots in greenhouses and on trees in woodlands are algae; tiny flat bodies with little "cups" on top that grow on soil in damp places are liverworts; mosses are well known and often desirable; horsetails are weeds of waste places. Funguses are very familiar as mushrooms of many shapes, colors and sizes, and as disease-producing organisms in the form of mildews, rusts, leaf spots and rots. Some bacteria also cause plant diseases, while some (as well as other kinds of lowly plants) are responsible for maintaining soil fertility.

SEEDS

Seeds of different plants vary greatly in size, shape, texture and color, but all have the same basic structure. Within a protective seed coat lie the embryonic plant and, except with orchids, a store of food material that provides first nourishment for the young plant. Seeds contain comparatively little moisture, and most may be stored dry for long periods.

To germinate or begin to grow, a seed needs air, moisture and warmth. Seeds of tropical plants need higher temperatures than those of plants native to the temperate zones. The first growth to emerge in this process is the young root or radicle, which grows rapidly.

ROOTS

The root system anchors the plant in the soil and absorbs nutrients needed for growth. In some plants the root is also a storage organ, which enables the plant to survive a winter and grow again the next season. The working and growing part of a root is the fragile whitish flexible tip, which is usually torn off when a plant is removed from the soil.

Just behind the tip is a zone where fine whitish hairs grow out from all sides. These vary in length from microscopic size to ¼ in. or more. New hairs are formed constantly as the root grows; but at no time is the ac-

tive hair zone more than a fraction of an inch long. Collectively, the root hairs form the "mouth" of the plant. It is their job to take in oxygen, moisture and nutrients.

The soil water is a thin "soup" of water containing dissolved mineral salts which the roots absorb by complex processes not yet fully understood. The most important is osmosis, whereby water and the dissolved substances filter through the membrane walls of the root cells and root-hair cells and pass into the cells of the plant itself.

The root systems of individual plants vary according to their kind and to the texture and structure of the soil and the plant nutrients it contains. A dense clay offers more resistance to root development than a light, sandy soil. Roots branch more freely

Root Tip
This fragile, whitish tip is the growing part of the root.

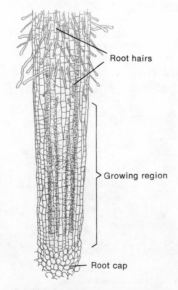

Section through a root tip (enlarged)

Root Hairs
The root hairs form the "mouth" of the plant, taking in moisture (shown by arrows) from the soil.

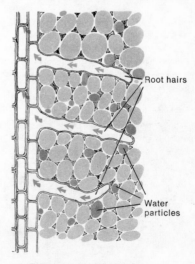

Diagram (enlarged) showing root hairs, particles with air spaces and pockets of water

and extensively in the latter. Most soils are better aerated and more fertile near the surface, so the feeding roots tend to be more numerous and active in these areas. Nevertheless, many roots do penetrate deep into the soil.

Roots that do not originate from the seed or the root system are called adventitious roots. Such roots form naturally on philodendron and blackberry shoots and on the underside of English ivy stems. The ability to produce adventitious roots is exploited when plants are propagated by cuttings and layers (see pages 704 and 714 in "How to Raise New Plants").

STEMS

The downward growth of a plant's primary root from its seed is swiftly followed by the upward growth of its primary shoot. The embryo stem grows to the light as eagerly as the embryo root grows down into the soil. At first it is white or yellowish, but once exposed to light the stem tissues quickly turn green, as the light energizes within them the formation of a green pigment, chlorophyll. From this moment the new plant can synthesize its own food and feed its growing tissues. Roots, except aerial roots of certain tropical plants such as orchids, do not have chlorophyll.

The stem provides the channels through which the water solution absorbed by the roots is carried to the leaves, and the food then produced in the leaves is circulated to all other parts of the plant.

Stems carry the leaves and flowers into the air and light, and therefore in most plants grow erectly and have

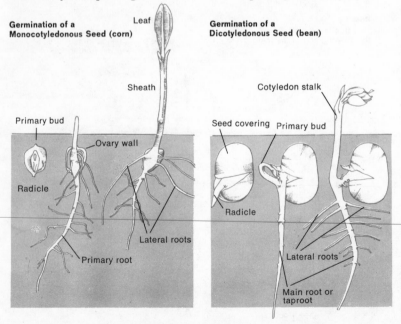

Germination of a Monocotyledonous Seed (corn)

Leaf

Sheath

Primary bud

Ovary wall

Radicle

Lateral roots

Primary root

Germination of a Dicotyledonous Seed (bean)

Cotyledon stalk

Seed covering   Primary bud

Radicle

Lateral roots

Main root or taproot

Plants with seeds containing one embryonic seed leaf or cotyledon are called monocotyledons; they have many tufted roots of equal length. Plants with two embryonic leaves are dicotyledons; they have a central taproot and side, or lateral, roots.

strong woody cells to make them self-supporting. But in others the stems grow among neighboring plants or up supports, either by twining as in the honeysuckle, by tendrils as in the pea, by adhering with aerial roots as in English ivy or by hooking with prickles as in the blackberry.

In certain plants the stem is modified and grows underground. The tubers of the potato are really modified stems. Other plants with underground stems, known as rhizomes, are lily of the valley and iris.

LEAVES

Leaves are of many sizes, shapes and textures. *Magnolia macrophylla* may have leaves up to 3 ft. long, while those of a heath (*Erica*) may be ¼ in. or less.

Leaf shapes vary astonishingly. Botanists divide them into simple, single leaves like those of a cabbage, and compound leaves like those of celery. The latter are again divided into two groups—those which are palmate like the horse chestnut, and those which are pinnate like the ash. Leaves may grow in opposite pairs, in whorls of more than two leaves at the same level, or singly (alternately) on the stems. See the illustrations on pages 688 and 689.

Although often very thin, a leaf blade is made up of several layers of cells. Enveloping the whole leaf is a single layer of clear, transparent cells which form a skin, or epidermis. This is covered with a waxy cuticle, virtually air- and waterproof.

The lower surface of the leaf, in the majority of plants, is perforated by tiny holes—100 times smaller than those made by a fine sewing needle. Through these, moisture is given off in the process of transpiration, and gas diffusion between the outer atmosphere and the interior of the leaf takes place.

Leaves and Plant Nutrients

The great function of plant leaves is a unique chemical process known as photosynthesis. The leaves use the energy of light to make sugars and other complex foods from the simple raw materials of the water solution absorbed by the roots and from the carbon dioxide absorbed by the leaves from the air. These foods nourish the plants and, in turn, all living organisms which depend on plants for their food.

The key to the process is the substance contained in the leaves that makes them green—chlorophyll. This absorbs light rays, chiefly the red, blue and violet, and converts them into a form of energy for the manufacture of the plant's food.

Colored-Leaved Plants

Some plants—such as coleus and Japanese maples—have red foliage, but this is caused by certain pigments which mask the presence of green chlorophyll without impairing its efficiency. On the other hand, plants with yellow or white variegation in their leaves, like variegated English ivies, have little chlorophyll, and their efficiency is impaired. Such plants need good culture to do well.

Light

Chlorophyll-containing leaves, photosynthesis and light go together. Without light, leaves turn white, and growth ceases. The more intense the light, up to an optimum which varies for different kinds of plants, the greater the rate of photosynthesis.

Temperature

Temperature affects plants and influences the rate of photosynthesis. This decreases in very cold and very hot weather, but varies with the kind of plant.

For most of the plants grown out

Classification of Leaf Shapes

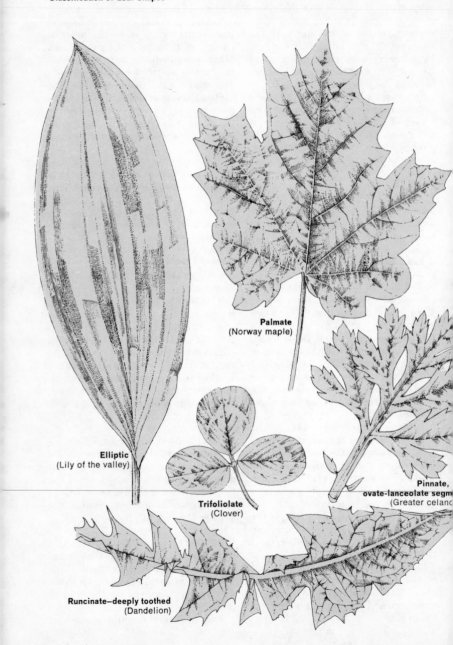

Palmate
(Norway maple)

Elliptic
(Lily of the valley)

Trifoliolate
(Clover)

**Pinnate,
ovate-lanceolate segm**
(Greater celand

Runcinate—deeply toothed
(Dandelion)

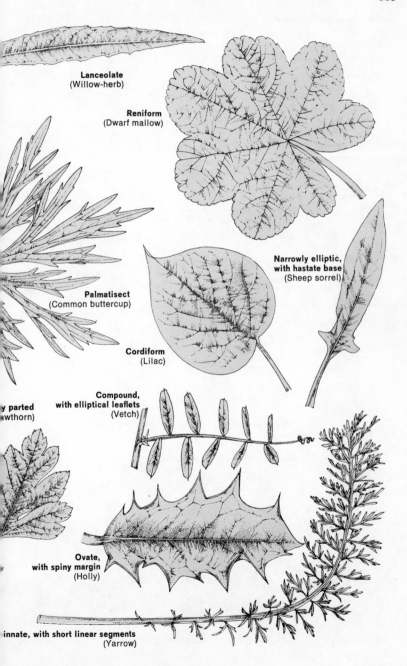

689

Lanceolate
(Willow-herb)

Reniform
(Dwarf mallow)

Palmatisect
(Common buttercup)

Cordiform
(Lilac)

Narrowly elliptic,
with hastate base
(Sheep sorrel)

ly parted
awthorn)

Compound,
with elliptical leaflets
(Vetch)

Ovate,
with spiny margin
(Holly)

innate, with short linear segments
(Yarrow)

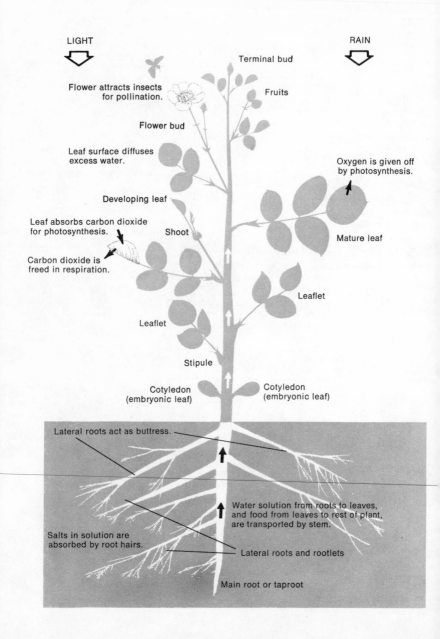

LIGHT

RAIN

Terminal bud

Flower attracts insects for pollination.

Fruits

Flower bud

Leaf surface diffuses excess water.

Oxygen is given off by photosynthesis.

Developing leaf

Leaf absorbs carbon dioxide for photosynthesis.

Shoot

Mature leaf

Carbon dioxide is freed in respiration.

Leaflet

Leaflet

Stipule

Cotyledon (embryonic leaf)

Cotyledon (embryonic leaf)

Lateral roots act as buttress.

Water solution from roots to leaves, and food from leaves to rest of plant, are transported by stem.

Salts in solution are absorbed by root hairs.

Lateral roots and rootlets

Main root or taproot

of doors in temperate climates, photosynthesis becomes noticeably active somewhere about 40° F. and quickens progressively as the temperature rises to about 90° F. At higher temperatures than that, it diminishes.

Respiration

Photosynthesis results in the setting free of oxygen into the air. But this process should not be confused with the breathing or true respiration of the plant. All living cells in plants and in animals respire all the time, and in much the same way. Oxygen is used to convert food materials into new tissue and energy, and in the process carbon dioxide is liberated. In plants, the two processes of photosynthesis and respiration go on at the same time, even in the same cells.

The carbon dioxide freed in respiration is used in photosynthesis, together with more taken from the atmosphere. During darkness, photosynthesis stops, and traces of carbon dioxide may be released into the air, but in nothing like the quantities to justify the superstitious removal of flowers or plants from a sickroom at night because their respiration might poison the atmosphere.

Water and Transpiration

A plant invariably tends to take up more water than it can use. The excess is given off by the leaves in the process called transpiration.

The rate of transpiration is not constant. It increases as temperatures rise and in dry or windy conditions, and slackens in cool, humid or rainy weather. It is greatly reduced at night when photosynthesis stops.

If the root hairs are unable to absorb sufficient water quickly enough to replace that lost by transpiration, growing tips, leaves and stems wilt. Without water, the plant will gradually die as its cells dry out.

Adaptations of Leaves

Against the ever-present danger of drying out, many plants have evolved safeguards. Plants native to hot, dry conditions often are without leaves but have stems which function as such, as in cactuses, or develop thickened leaves with capacity for water storage, as in succulents such as houseleeks. On the other hand, plants that grow in damp places, such as *Caltha palustris* (marsh marigold), tend to have large soft leaves to allow them to transpire freely. In warm regions with continuous water, leaves may do their work the year round. Plants in these regions do not shed their leaves, but are evergreen.

FLOWERS

All living things can reproduce their own kind. The smallest single-celled plants, the algae and bacteria, reproduce by dividing themselves. Ferns and funguses form tiny specialized cells called spores, which are highly resistant to adverse growing conditions. They rest almost indefinitely during poor growing periods, ready to sprout as conditions improve.

The most highly evolved plants reproduce themselves by forming flowers, the primary purpose of which is to form and contain the male and female organs of reproduction and to facilitate their union. From such a union comes the seed of a new generation.

Flower Construction

In some cases the individual flower has four kinds of parts, all growing from a common base, called the receptacle, at the head of the stalk or peduncle. On dissecting such a flower as that of the buttercup, working from the outside in, the first parts to be removed are the sepals, collectively called the calyx. Petals, usually colored, will be found just inside—all the petals together forming what is

Examples of Flower Heads

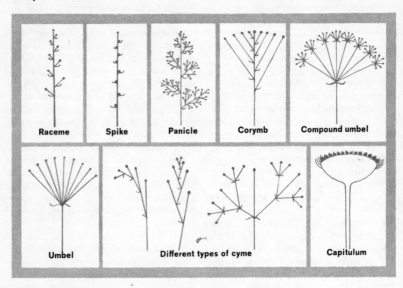

Raceme Spike Panicle Corymb Compound umbel

Umbel Different types of cyme Capitulum

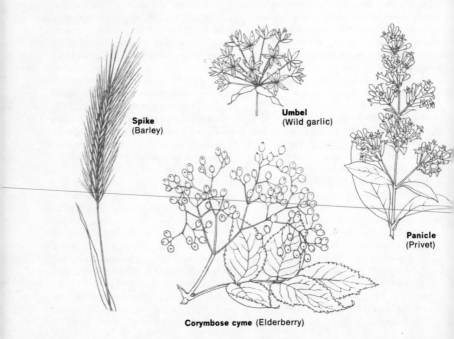

Spike (Barley)

Umbel (Wild garlic)

Panicle (Privet)

Corymbose cyme (Elderberry)

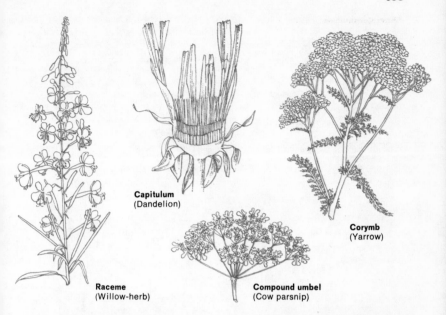

Capitulum
(Dandelion)

Corymb
(Yarrow)

Raceme
(Willow-herb)

Compound umbel
(Cow parsnip)

known as the corolla. Sepals and petals combined make up the perianth.

Taking off the petals reveals the male sex organs, known as stamens. Each stamen has a stalk or filament at the top of which is attached a sac or anther, containing the pollen grains which are the male cells of the plant. The stamens are collectively known as the androecium (male part).

With the stamens removed, a central structure, the pistil or gynoeceum (female part), is revealed. This structure will be found to be made up of smaller stalked bodies, apparently fused together. These are carpels. Each carpel is made up of a hollowed swelling (ovary) at its base, with a small stalk (style) arising from it and having a sticky top (stigma). In the swelling are tiny round bodies—the female cells, known as ovules.

Not all flowers have all four kinds of parts; one or more may be lacking, and in some flowers other parts may be present.

The vital parts of the flower are the stamens and carpels, since they produce the pollen and the ovules, which contain the gametes, or sex cells. The majority of plants have flowers containing both stamens and carpels. But on certain plants the flowers contain only one kind of sex organ. The function of flowers is to produce pollen grains and ovules and, by bringing about their union, eventually to produce seed.

Fertilization

To effect a union, pollen grains must alight on the stigma or carpel. If ripe and from the same species of plant, the pollen grains germinate and each grows a long tube which reaches down the style to the ovary. There a male nucleus from the pollen unites with the female nucleus of the ovule. Once fertilized, the ovule swells rapidly and builds up the food stores and protective tough outer coat that make it into a seed.

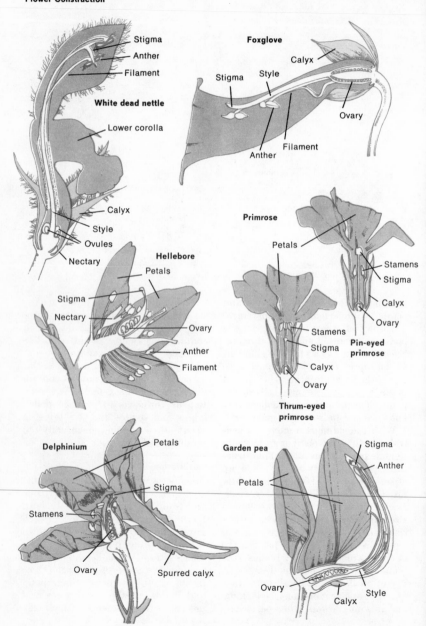

White dead nettle — Stigma, Anther, Filament, Lower corolla, Calyx, Style, Ovules, Nectary

Foxglove — Calyx, Stigma, Style, Ovary, Anther, Filament

Hellebore — Petals, Stigma, Nectary, Ovary, Anther, Filament

Primrose — Petals, Stamens, Stigma, Calyx, Ovary; Pin-eyed primrose — Petals, Stamens, Stigma, Calyx, Ovary; Thrum-eyed primrose

Delphinium — Petals, Stigma, Stamens, Ovary, Spurred calyx

Garden pea — Stigma, Anther, Petals, Ovary, Style, Calyx

Pollination

Pollination is the prelude to fertilization and is the process of getting pollen grains onto the receptive stigmas. In many plants equipped with both stamens and carpels, the anthers shed their ripe pollen on the stigmas and the plants are said to be self-pollinated. When the pollen of one plant is transferred to the stigma of another similar plant, what is known as cross-pollination takes place. This usually gives a stronger and more robust offspring; it is common in nature and often resorted to in scientific plant breeding.

FRUIT

After the fertilized flower sheds its petals, the ovary containing the seed or seeds develops into a fruit. Fruits take very different forms. The dry, hard hazelnut and the soft, succulent tomato are unlike in appearance but alike in origin. Both are fruits developed from a matured ovary, with their seed enclosed in a fruit wall known as the pericarp. The fruit serves as a nursery for the maturing seed, and a protective covering and a mechanism for the seed's dispersal when ripe. Fruits as food have great value, of course, to animals and man.

The Development of an Apple

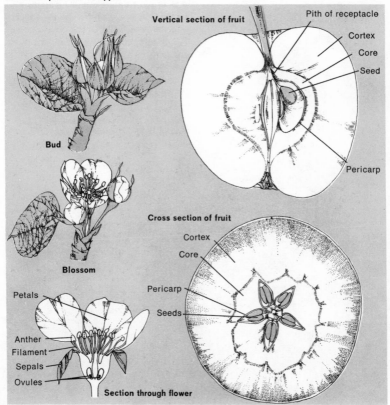

Vertical section of fruit

Pith of receptacle

Cortex

Core

Seed

Pericarp

Bud

Blossom

Cross section of fruit

Cortex

Core

Pericarp

Seeds

Petals

Anther

Filament

Sepals

Ovules

Section through flower

HOW TO RAISE
NEW PLANTS—Propagation

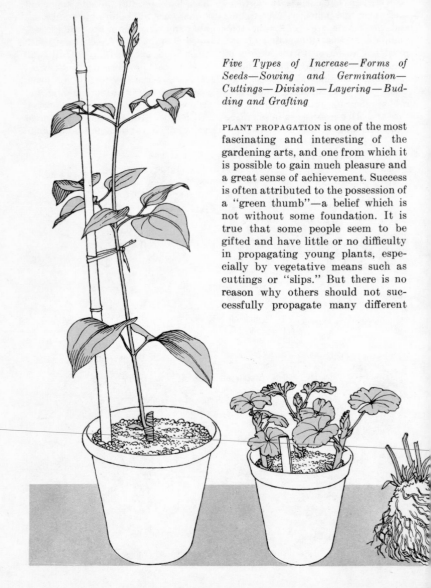

Five Types of Increase—Forms of Seeds—Sowing and Germination—Cuttings—Division—Layering—Budding and Grafting

PLANT PROPAGATION is one of the most fascinating and interesting of the gardening arts, and one from which it is possible to gain much pleasure and a great sense of achievement. Success is often attributed to the possession of a "green thumb"—a belief which is not without some foundation. It is true that some people seem to be gifted and have little or no difficulty in propagating young plants, especially by vegetative means such as cuttings or "slips." But there is no reason why others should not successfully propagate many different kinds of plants, provided certain essentials are borne in mind and well applied.

The methods by which plants may be increased are many, but generally they may be grouped under five main headings: Seeds, Cuttings, Division, Layering, and Budding and Grafting. The first is known as seminal propagation, and the other four as vegetative propagation. Propagation by seeds, cuttings, division and layering are the methods that mainly concern the beginner, although, with experience, budding and grafting are not beyond the scope of those whose enthusiasm is not dampened by possible early setbacks and failure.

Only by working with plants and observing their habits and modes of growth can the gardener know certainly which method of propagation to apply to any given plant. Annuals, biennials and many perennials are often grown from seed, but a great many improved horticultural varieties of perennials cannot be reproduced truly in that way and must be increased by division or other methods. Many trees, vines and shrubs, in-

cluding bush fruits, may be started from cuttings, while such plants as the strawberry, which produces stolons or runners, can have their "daughter" plants severed from them in the summer.

Nature's most common method of reproduction is by seed, and wherever practicable it should be used. Not only is it an easy means of securing a large number of young plants, but plants raised from seeds are often healthier and less prone to disease. They are completely "newborn," having been derived from the fusion of two cells, one male and one female. Seedlings raised from a plant of mixed parentage (a hybrid) will not produce plants that are identical to either parent, in habit, form and color of flowers, but many modern highly selected hybrid strains produce plants that are remarkably similar to each other. The gardener should, therefore, obtain seeds only from reliable sources—that is, from seedsmen who are experts and who offer only the best strains and varieties of seeds.

Vegetative propagation includes

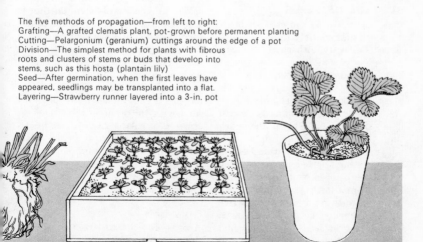

The five methods of propagation—from left to right:
Grafting—A grafted clematis plant, pot-grown before permanent planting
Cutting—Pelargonium (geranium) cuttings around the edge of a pot
Division—The simplest method for plants with fibrous
roots and clusters of stems or buds that develop into
stems, such as this hosta (plantain lily)
Seed—After germination, when the first leaves have
appeared, seedlings may be transplanted into a flat.
Layering—Strawberry runner layered into a 3-in. pot

the many and varied methods by which parts of living plants other than seed are used to generate new plants. Plants that are propagated by vegetative means have a separate existence, but they are not completely new plants in the way that seedlings are, because their characteristics are exactly the same as those of the parent plant. For example, if division is used to propagate a given variety of iris, the part divided from the parent will grow in the same way and be identical in habit, form and color of flowers to the original plant. This is also true of cuttings taken from chrysanthemums, begonias and most other plants. The resulting sizes may vary, however, because of the season or the richness or poorness of the soil.

Propagation by Seeds

Seeds are usually the best method of raising quantities of the many kinds of plants required for spring and summer bedding displays, such as snapdragons, zinnias, marigolds, stocks, asters and petunias. Many greenhouse plants, like calceolaria, cineraria, schizanthus, primula and cyclamen, are also raised in quantity from seed. It is the only method of propagation for annuals and biennials, which flower, seed and die in either one or two years. Most vegetables are raised from seed, and so are many lawn grasses.

STORAGE OF SEEDS

If seeds purchased from a seedsman are not sown immediately they should be stored correctly, otherwise the percentage of germination will not be as high as it should be. The seed is a resting stage in the life history of the plant and, although dormant, is alive and capable of developing growth if it is subjected to warmth and moisture. Under natural conditions seeds fall from the parent plant and spend their resting period among fallen leaves and loose soil, often being frozen or in a fairly low temperature; when warmth and moisture arrive with the spring, germination starts. The storing of seeds under dry and warm conditions is, therefore, un-

suitable and can result in loss of viability or growing power. Store packets of seeds in a cool, airy place—not in an airtight container. The ideal spot is one of fairly even temperature, warm enough to dispel dampness.

TYPES OF SEEDS

Seeds vary considerably, not only in size and shape, but also in their formation.

Small, Dustlike Seeds

Begonia, calceolaria and lobelia provide examples of these seeds, which should be sown thinly on a surface of soil or other suitable medium that is very fine and perfectly level. Many gardeners do not cover such tiny seeds but merely press them into the surface. If any covering is given it should be a mere sprinkling of fine sand or sandy soil. To make thin sowing easier, mix a small quantity of fine, dry sand with the seeds in the packet to serve as a carrier and to insure an even spread as the seeds are scattered. If sowing indoors, cover each receptacle with a pane of glass to conserve moisture, and put a sheet of paper on top to exclude the light.

Fleshy Seeds

Acorns and beans are two of the fleshy seeds. Some fleshy seeds become hard externally and have a hard skin or seed coat, especially if they have been stored for any length of time. They should be soaked in water, preferably tepid, for 24 hours or more before sowing. This will soften the seed coat and help the process of germination to start.

Hard-Coated Seeds

Seeds such as those of morning glory, dark-colored sweet pea, various nuts, including walnuts and almonds and others having a hard outer shell, need presowing treatment to insure reasonably quick germination. If sown without treatment the seeds may remain dormant for a long time or fail to germinate.

To make sure that the hard seed coats do break down and that moisture enters to start the seeds germinating, chip the outer casing of the seeds with a knife, or file or rub them on a rough surface. The filing or chipping should be done carefully and *on the opposite side* to the "eye" of each seed, or the embryo or "germ" may be damaged.

On most seeds the eye can be seen fairly easily, because it is the point where the seed was attached in the seedpod.

Oily Seeds

There are seeds which have an oily content, and because of it do not retain their viability as long as other seeds. Good examples are those of carrot, parsnip, celery, castor bean, magnolia and camellia. Do not store these seeds in a warm place or for any longer than is necessary, because once the oil dries up, the seeds shrivel and will fail to germinate. For this reason it is unwise to retain parsnip and carrot seeds for a second year: the old seeds are likely either to fail completely or to provide very poor germination.

Composite or Multiple Seeds

Some plants produce several seeds together within a dry or fleshy case. The beet is a good example of a dry case which contains several seeds. Thin sowing or sowing in little hills is essential for these, as three or four seedlings usually arise from each multiple seed.

The cotoneaster, holly, hawthorn and crab apple are some of the shrubs and trees that produce fleshy and often highly colored fruits with a number of seeds embedded in the pulpy mass.

STRATIFICATION

Certain seeds will not germinate until they have been subjected for some weeks or even months to low temperatures and humid conditions similar to those which occur in nature after they drop from the parent plant and are covered with fallen leaves and other forest debris.

To simulate this natural winter environment, gardeners employ a technique called stratification. A usual method is to fill a wooden box with alternate layers of seeds and moist sand, or sand and peat moss, and then to bury the box 6 in. deep in a well-drained, shaded location outdoors. Fleshy fruits—such as those of holly, cotoneaster and hawthorn— are stratified without removing the pulp that surrounds the seeds they contain. As a precaution against mice and other rodents, it is wise to enclose the box in fine wire mesh. When very small seeds are being stratified they may be spread between layers of cheesecloth before they are buried in the sand, to make finding them at a later date easier.

An alternate method is to stratify seeds by mixing them with slightly moist sand, or a mixture of sand and peat moss, and keep the mixture in closed—but not completely airtight—

jars in a refrigerator. Temperatures of 34° to 40° F. are satisfactory for most seeds requiring stratification.

Most seeds stratified in fall will germinate the following spring, but some kinds—for example, hollies—do not germinate until the second spring after they are stratified. When the time for germination arrives, seeds should be separated from the sand or sand and peat moss by sifting or by hand picking. They should be sown in pots, pans, flats, cold frames or directly outdoors.

SOWING SEEDS

There are three essentials for the successful germination of seeds of all types—moisture, warmth and air. In addition, the great majority of seeds germinate best in darkness, but there are a very few which respond best when exposed to light. The depth of sowing is governed by the size of the seed, and, as a general rule, seeds should be covered by a layer of soil that is equal to once or twice their own depth. There are some seeds, however, that should be sown deeper, because they have a tendency to push up to the surface as they germinate. Beans, for example, should be sown 2 to 3 in. deep, and peas should be sown 1 to 2 in. deep. Most small seeds need only a very light covering of fine soil.

Outdoor sowing should be in properly prepared soil or seedbeds. It is useless to sow seeds in loose, freshly dug soil. Always firm the surface by treading or rolling, then rake it evenly to remove stones and create a fine tilth, or surface covering of crumbs. On heavy, claylike soils add sand, fine coal cinders or other gritty material— as well as peat moss, commercial humus, well-decayed compost or other suitable organic matter—to the surface to make it easily crumbled.

The actual times for sowing vary according to region, season and soil conditions, and no hard-and-fast rules can be laid down, but do not sow until the weather is right and is expected to remain reasonably favorable to the growth of the kinds of seeds that are to be sown.

Once the seedbed has been prepared, the seed drills, little shallow trenches in which seeds are sown, should be drawn. Using a carpenter's rule graduated in feet and inches, measure off the prescribed distances between the rows on opposite sides of the plot, and place small stakes to mark the ends of the rows. Then stretch a good strong garden line (a plastic clothesline is ideal) across the plot from stake to stake, and draw out the seed drill along one side of the line to the correct depth.

For making shallow drills, use a stout stake or the handle of a broom, rake or hoe. The end of a pencil will make an ideal drill for smaller seeds such as cabbage and lettuce. For larger seeds a small draw hoe or a triangular warren hoe can be used. Flat-bottomed drills should be drawn, particularly for the larger seeds, because they allow an even distribution. If the drills are V-shaped, the seeds will run together at the base of the drill.

Watering is usually unnecessary out of doors except during prolonged dry periods. If the ground is very dry, water it well a day or so *before* the seeds are sown, or, better still, water along each drill a short time before scattering the seeds. The latter method is very helpful, especially for seeds that may take a rather long time to germinate.

Moisture is essential for germination, but the ultimate success of a crop depends on the thin sowing of the seeds. Thick sowing results in enfeebled seedlings because of overcrowding and lack of light; and much time and patience will be required to thin out the overcrowded young plants in order to leave the proper growing space for those that remain. There are usually far more seeds in a packet than are required, and it is a great mistake to sow them thickly in order to use all of them. Successive sowings are an advantage with short-duration crops.

After sowing, cover the seeds by using the back of a rake, then gently firm the soil over the seeds along the lines of the drills. Label each kind distinctly and give the date of sowing and any other particulars that may be helpful.

SOWING IN PATCHES

Seeds can be sown by broadcasting or scattering them over a prepared patch of soil, where informal groups of flowering plants such as annuals are grown in a border, or where seeds of biennials or perennials are sown in frames. This method is particularly easy and, provided the seeds are sown thinly and the plants are later thinned out and kept weeded, gives good results. The final result is very natural and pleasing where flowering plants are concerned.

SOWING SEEDS INDOORS

There are various methods of seed sowing that apply to plants raised in greenhouses and cold frames, but the necessary requirements for germination—moisture, warmth and air—are the same as are those for sowing out of doors.

Sowing in a greenhouse is done under controlled conditions so that the question of climatic interference does not arise. Very high temperatures are *not* essential, nor are they conducive to the best results. Generally speaking, the seeds of many greenhouse and garden plants that are started indoors for later planting out need a temperature of only 55° to 60° F.

Seeds of tropical plants appreciate 10° to 15° higher temperatures.

Pots, Pans and Flats

Seeds can be sown in pots, seed pans or flats (shallow boxes or trays). Sheets of glass and pieces of paper (newspaper will do, but thick brown paper is better) are needed to cover the receptacles until germination takes place. The glass is placed over the top of the receptacle to prevent rapid drying out and lessen the need for frequent watering, and the paper is placed over the glass to exclude light and insure a nearly uniform temperature.

Preparation of Pots

Hygiene is most important. Pots and pans that have already been used should be well washed, scrubbed and air-dried. New pots should be soaked in water for a few minutes before use, to allow the clay to absorb some moisture; otherwise the pots will absorb the moisture from the potting medium and the plants will suffer. Well in advance of their being needed, treat wooden flats with a preservative which is known to be harmless to the roots of growing plants when used for this purpose.

Drainage

It is very important to provide good drainage. Fill the seed pots to one quarter of their capacity with clean broken clay pots, called crocks, and give seed pans a good layer of these crocks over the drainage holes. On top

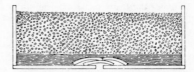

Seed-Flat Drainage
Cover space between bottom boards with large crocks.

of the crocks use clean moss, dried leaves or fibrous material shaken from partially decayed grass sod, to prevent the soil clogging the drainage holes.

With seed flats a layer of large crocks over the spaces between the bottom boards is all that is needed, but the bottom of the flat should be covered with leaves or fiber before the flat is filled with soil.

Seed Soil

The seed soil should be an open sandy mixture, consisting of approximately two parts sifted loam (good topsoil) and one part each of peat moss, or of sifted leaf mold, and sand. For certain plants a higher proportion of organic material or a larger amount of sand may be used to meet special needs. If possible, home-mixed seed soils should be sterilized by steam, by baking or by using a chemical preparation sold for this purpose.

Fill the pots, pans or seed flats with the soil mixture to within ½ in. of the top; moderately firm it with the fingers (not thumbs) to get an even surface; and finally level it with the edge of a wooden plant label, ruler or any similar strip of wood. Not until the surface is quite level should it be finally firmed with a presser, and then only lightly. (A presser is a flat piece of board with a short handle attached.) Next, water the soil-filled receptacles with a watering can fitted with a fine spray, or stand them in a sink, tub or similar container and fill it with water to just below the rims of the pots or other containers. Allow the water to rise through the soil and moisten the surface, then lift out the seed receptacles and allow them to drain. A thoroughly moist soil before planting provides the best conditions for germination and prevents the need for frequent watering while the seeds are germinating.

Soil Substitutes

Substitutes for soil are often used for indoor seed sowing. Most popular of these are vermiculite, perlite and milled (pulverized and sifted) sphagnum moss. The latter is especially advantageous when sowing seeds of plants such as snapdragons, which are subject to loss from damping-off, a disease caused by a fungus. It spreads rapidly over the surface of the soil, attacking the lower part of the stems and causing the seedlings to collapse and rot. When sphagnum is employed as a sowing medium this trouble is eliminated or very greatly reduced. Because none of these soil substitutes provides needed nutrients, it is important to compensate for this either by transplanting very promptly when the first true leaves of the seedlings are well developed or by watering every few days with a dilute solution of a complete, quickly available fertilizer. Any of the liquid brands especially prepared for house plants are likely to be satisfactory.

One other point to remember is that seedlings transplanted from a soil substitute to real soil are called upon to make a considerable adjustment to their new environment. This they can do most satisfactorily if the soil into which they are set is decidedly sandy and if it is not pressed too firmly about their roots.

Seed Sowing

The actual sowing is governed by the same rules as for outdoor sowing. Scatter flat seeds—such as those of lilies, amaryllis, and grevillea—thinly and evenly over the soil or other medium, and press each seed gently on one side with a pencil or pointed stick to set it on edge. This insures better germination than if the seeds are allowed to lie flat. Afterward, gently cover the seeds with fine, sandy soil or with the soil substitute that is being used, to a depth about equal to that of the diameter of the seed, and firm the surface lightly. Extremely fine, dustlike seeds, such as those of begonia and lobelia, may be merely pressed into the surface without any covering of soil or soil substitute.

All seeds sown indoors should be sown thinly. Overcrowded seedlings (or those in cold, wet soil, such as heavy clay) are prone to "damping-off" (see also page 791 in "Plant Diseases"). Any seedlings that are allowed to become thin and drawn are apt to succumb to this fungus disease, which is also encouraged by a damp atmosphere, lack of light and inadequate circulation of air. Also known as preemergence rot, this may be prevented by the use of a preemergent fungicide. Spray a little of the dust into the packet of seeds before sowing, and shake it well.

Germination

Watch carefully for the appearance of the seedlings and, as soon as they are plainly visible, remove the glass and paper. At this stage, light and the normal air conditions of the greenhouse or cold frame (see below) are essential.

Avoid drafts, as a current of cold air can do a lot of harm and even result in the loss of the seedlings. Shade the seedlings from strong sunshine during the hottest part of the day to prevent them from wilting. Unnecessary exclusion of light is harmful and can only result in spindly growth, so make sure that the shade is removed except in sunshine too strong for the well-being of the young plants.

SOWING IN COLD FRAMES

If cold frames are used and the seeds are sown in pots, pans or flats and placed inside the frame to germinate, the procedure is much the same as the one already prescribed, the only differ-

ence being that there is no artificial heating and therefore the growth of the seedlings may be slower. See page 84 in "Your Own Greenhouse."

When large numbers of young plants have to be raised—as is often the case with biennials and perennials, for instance—a seedbed may be prepared directly in the cold frame, thus dispensing with the need for pots, pans and flats. If the seedbed is carefully prepared and the cold frame is properly ventilated, a great variety of plants can be propagated in this way. The advantage of a cold frame as compared with sowing in unprotected outdoor beds is that the operation is under better control, because there is little interference from the weather and pests, and earlier crops can be obtained.

When sowing in a cold frame, sow the seeds directly into a bed of soil with a reasonably firm, fine tilth, prepared in much the same way as an outdoor seedbed. Seed drills can then be drawn from back to front of the frame, or the seeds can be sown broadcast. The seeds are sown and covered as is done when making sowings directly outdoors. Afterward the covering sash is placed in position, with adequate ventilation afforded if the weather is hot, and the glass (or plastic) sash shaded. Shade is removed and ventilation is increased as soon as the seedlings show through the soil.

TRANSPLANTING

The next step is the first transplanting of the seedlings. Do this as soon as they produce their first true leaf, when they will be large enough to handle. The earliest "leaves" to appear are the cotyledons or seed leaves, and their shape is normally simple and different from that of the normal leaves of the plant. The true leaves appear from between the cotyledons and can easily be recognized by their more characteristic shape, which varies according to the kind of plant.

The first transplanting needs to be done carefully, because the seedlings can easily be damaged by careless handling. Young and tender, they cannot yet be moved to the outdoors. Set them into flats or pans filled with a light, fertile soil. This soil may be similar to that used for seed sowing but coarser (it will be fine enough if it passes through a ¾-in. mesh sieve or screen) and more fertile. The required fertility is assured by mixing thoroughly with it 1 pt. each of steamed bone meal and pulverized sheep manure, or their equivalent in other fertilizer, to each bushel.

When transplanting the tiny plants, use a small pointed stick or dibber in one hand to make the hole in the soil. Pick up the seedling—by a leaf, not by its stem—with the other hand and place it carefully in position. Then gently firm the soil around the roots with the dibber. For very small and rather delicate seedlings, such as those of the begonia, a small V-notched stick made from a label can be used to lift up the tiny seedlings and place them in the holes. Space out the seedlings evenly, allowing about 2 in. between them in the row and 3 in. between rows. (See illustration.)

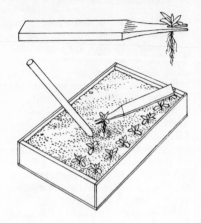

Transplant small seedlings with a V-notched stick.

To insure that the operation checks the growth of the seedlings as little as possible, always transplant seedlings into damp soil and do the work in the greenhouse or in a warm workroom.

Let seedlings continue to grow in their pans or flats under the same conditions and gradually accustom them to more and more air until they are ready to withstand outside conditions. This is called "hardening off."

Most seedling plants can grow in flats until the leaves touch, but at this stage it is wise either to pot them singly or to transplant them outdoors.

Vegetative Propagation

CUTTINGS

For many plants this is the quickest, easiest and cheapest method of propagation, one that provides a sure way of perpetuating a kind or variety in the exact likeness of the parent plant. This is why cuttings are in common use, especially for the raising of plants with double flowers and those that have colored or variegated foliage. Generally the term "cuttings" refers to any portions removed from the stem, leaves or roots of the parent plant which, if properly prepared, inserted and cared for, will produce new plants.

Equipment

Knife: The first priority is a good sharp knife that should not be too large or too small for the hand, with a thin, straight-edged blade. There are various suitable forms of knives on the market; the gardener's budding knife is very useful and most suitable for making cuttings. A safety-razor blade mounted in a suitable handle is useful for making soft cuttings, such as those of chrysanthemum, dahlia and similar nonwoody plants. Such a tool is also very useful for preparing cuttings to reproduce many of the small rock-garden plants.

Pruning shears: A good pair of pruning shears will be needed, especially where cuttings are to be taken of woody plants—that is, shrubs and trees. As with the knife, the blade of the pruning shears must always be sharp to insure a clean cut.

Dibbers: For the insertion of the cuttings several dibbers of varying sizes are needed. They should be made of hardwood and not be too sharply pointed. Dibbers are pegs used for making holes in the rooting medium in which the cuttings are planted and for firming the medium about the cuttings. An eraser-tipped pencil makes a good dibber for cuttings that are not very thick.

Propagating frame: This is usually a small wooden frame in a greenhouse, with a glass sash (or a sash covered with transparent polyethylene plastic film) fitted to close down over it. The sash is attached to the back of the frame with hinges so that it does not move out of position when lifted at the front. The frame can vary from an ordinary box covered by a pane or panes of glass to an elaborate span or lean-to type of frame specially constructed by a carpenter. Whatever its form and size, the purpose of a propagating frame is to make it possible to maintain an atmosphere that can be controlled to the correct temperature and humidity. Thus the movement of

air about the cuttings is reduced in order to keep them in a turgid—unwilted—condition while they root.

The bottom of the propagating frame may be covered with a layer of cinders, gravel, sand or similar material upon which pots, pans and flats containing the cuttings are stood; or the frame can be partly filled with the rooting medium and the cuttings inserted directly into it.

If a propagating frame in a greenhouse is not available, much the same results may be had by standing the receptacles in which the cuttings are planted in a covered terrarium or aquarium (fish tank) or under a glass bell jar, or by placing over them a framework of wood or wire covered with transparent polyethylene plastic film. The purpose is, of course, to protect the cuttings from drafts and to insure that a humid atmosphere is maintained around them.

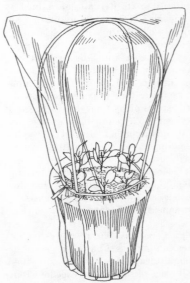

Cuttings under Polyethylene
The polyethylene bag is supported by a wire or bamboo frame to keep the plastic clear of the foliage.

Hotbed: Many cuttings, especially those of tropical plants, root more surely and more quickly if the medium in which they are planted is maintained in a temperature 5° to 10° F. above that of the atmosphere. This is accomplished by providing what gardeners call "bottom heat" in a propagating bed, a "hotbed" (see also page 85 in "Your Own Greenhouse"). Bottom heat is most easily provided by laying, 4 or 5 in. beneath the surface of the rooting medium, a gridiron pattern of electric heating cables made especially for this purpose and connected with a thermostat.

Mist systems: One of the most significant improvements in the field of propagation is the development of practical mist systems. These consist of one or more nozzles that bathe the cuttings and their surroundings with a foglike mist of water at regular intervals, or at intervals determined by a device sensitive to the relative humidity of the atmosphere close to the cuttings.

Cuttings planted under mist systems are never subjected to drying conditions and so do not lose moisture faster than it can be replaced by the stems or by their developing root systems. Therefore they prosper under maximum light and do not require shading—as do most cuttings planted without the benefit of a mist system. This results in faster root development. Another advantage is that they are less subject to diseases caused by funguses and bacteria.

Rooting mediums: Sharp sand—but not sea sand unless it has been very thoroughly leached or washed to remove all trace of salt—is an excellent rooting medium for most cuttings, but they must be removed from it as soon as they are well rooted, because sand contains little or no nourishment.

A mixture of equal parts sand and peat moss gives good results, particularly if the cuttings have to be left in the frame or receptacles for a time after the roots have formed. This mixture also provides especially good conditions for cuttings of azaleas and other acid-soil plants. Other rooting mediums that are popular and effective are vermiculite and perlite. Like sand, these contain no nutrients, and cuttings rooted in them should be transplanted to soil as soon as they have rooted or, alternatively, should be given occasional applications of dilute liquid fertilizer.

Hormone preparations: Scientific research has produced chemical growth substances known as hormones, and these in liquid or powder form can be used as an aid to the quicker and better rooting of cuttings. There are different types for the treatment of softwood, half-ripe and ripe-wood cuttings. The hormone preparations, under various proprietary trade names, can be obtained from stores selling horticultural goods, and should be used strictly according to the manufacturer's directions.

Various utensils: A conveniently sized watering can with a set of fine spray nozzles (flat and round) is essential for watering. A syringe capable of delivering a very fine (atomizer-type) spray of water should also be available. Such a fine spray is necessary for damping the cuttings and keeping the inside of the frame moist. Receptacles (pots, pans and flats) of varying sizes are needed for different batches of cuttings. The advantage of using the receptacles is that even after the cuttings are inserted they can be rearranged in the frame or removed, if necessary, without disturbing other batches of cuttings which may be in different stages of development.

Types of Cuttings

Stem cuttings: These are pieces of growth taken from the aerial parts of the parent plant, and can be either side shoots or the tips of main shoots. They can be of softwood, half-ripe wood or ripe wood. Softwood cuttings are made from the young, tender growth; half-ripe cuttings are made from semiripened shoots that have been growing for some time and have become slightly woody or firm (usually about midsummer); ripe-wood or hardwood cuttings are made from mature wood at the end of the growing season. Cuttings of hardwood are chiefly used for the propagation of trees and shrubs.

All stem cuttings are prepared by removing the lower leaves from the piece that has been cut from the parent plant, and then cutting across the stem just below a joint or node (see illustration below, left). The cuttings ordinarily should be 3 to 5 in. long. In the case of ripe-wood cuttings they can be made with a "heel" of the older wood attached at the base and be up to 10 or 12 in. long (see illustration below, right). The method of inserting these cuttings and the general rules to be followed when inserting all types of cuttings appear on page 710.

Leaf-bud cuttings: These are made from half-ripe wood and consist of one leaf with a dormant bud at its base and also a portion of the stem. They are inserted in the same way as stem cuttings, but with the leaf and bud just above the surface of the rooting medium. This type of cutting is used particularly for the propagation of camellias and some other evergreens, and has the advantage of providing a greater number of young plants from one piece of growth than are provided by a stem cutting. Geraniums are easily increased by means of leaf-bud cuttings.

Bud or eye cuttings: These are similar to leaf-bud cuttings but with no leaf attached, and are made from dormant ripened wood in autumn or winter. Ornamental and fruiting grapevines may be propagated from this type of cutting. Make each cutting of woody stem—with a single dormant bud or eye—about $1\frac{1}{2}$ in. long. Take off a strip of bark and wood on the side opposite to the bud, then insert the cutting horizontally, with the bud just at the level of the rooting medium. Label it and keep it moist and in a humid atmosphere until a tiny shoot begins to sprout.

Leaf cuttings: Quite a number of plants, particularly greenhouse plants, can be propagated from leaf cuttings. Begonia, gloxinia, African violet, sedum, the piggyback plant, streptocarpus and echeveria are examples. Remove the leaves from the parent plant, keeping the leafstalk attached, and, after cutting the end of the

Making Cuttings
(Left) Softwood or half-ripe cuttings are made by slicing just below a joint. (Right) On ripe wood, a "heel" may be left at the base of the cutting.

Leaf-Bud Cuttings of Blackberry

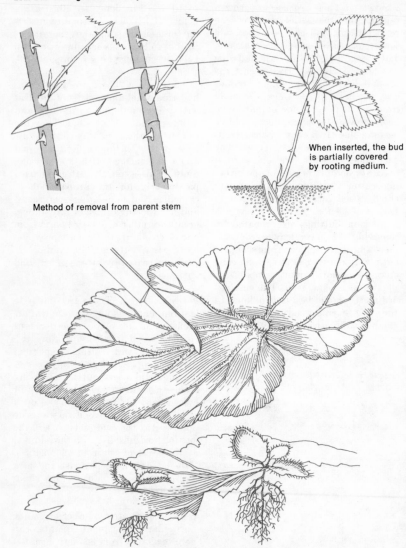

When inserted, the bud is partially covered by rooting medium.

Method of removal from parent stem

Leaf Cutting of Begonia rex-cultorum

(Above) Make cuts in the main veins on the bottom of the leaf.

(Below) Young plantlets form on top of leaf above where the veins were cut, and root into medium below.

stem cleanly, insert it into the sand
or other rooting medium so that the
leaf blade lies at an angle of about
45° with the surface. A young plantlet
will rise from the base of the cut leafstalk after little roots have formed.
Lay the leaves of large-leaved begonias of the *B. rex-cultorum* type on
a bed of sandy peat after the main
veins on the back of the leaf have been
severed—with a sharp knife or razor
blade—where they join other veins.
The young plantlets will develop
where the veins were cut and will root
into the medium beneath them. By
this method a number of young plants
can be obtained from a single leaf.

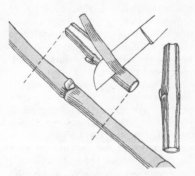

Bud or Eye Cuttings
These are made from a woody stem with
dormant buds. Cut a 1½-in. piece
including a bud, and remove a strip
of bark on the side opposite the bud.

Root cuttings: There are many plants,
both shrubby and herbaceous, that
can be propagated by root cuttings:
for example, perennial phlox, verbascum, hollyhock, romneya, *Anemone
japonica*, eryngium, gaillardia, anchusa and oriental poppy. The method
is simple. Lift a complete plant during
the dormant season and cut sections
of the larger and more fleshy roots
into pieces called "thongs" about 2 to
3 in. long. Cut the end of the root
nearest the crown of the plant (the
top) straight across, and cut the other
end on the slant. The different types
of cuts make it easy to distinguish the
top ends of the thongs from the lower.
For more woody plants, the ends may
be dipped in a rooting-hormone powder obtainable at garden supply stores.

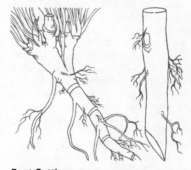

Root Cuttings
Cut pieces of fleshy roots 2 to 3 in. long,
each with square top and tapering base.

Insert the root cuttings into pots or
flats of rooting medium with the
straight cut just at surface level. Then
plunge the receptacles into beds of
ashes or peat moss until the cuttings
have rooted and growing points or
crowns have formed at their top ends.

During early spring plant the cuttings out in rows in nursery beds or
borders to continue growing and form
flowering plants for the next year.
When large numbers of root cuttings

Slips
Take slips of carnations or pinks
by pulling out the tips of shoots
with the finger and thumb.

are being handled, they may be set directly into beds of sand outdoors or in a cold frame and left to root there until the following spring, when they may be transplanted to nursery beds in the open garden.

It is unnecessary to distinguish the ends of the root cuttings of some plants, particularly the perennial phlox. The selected roots can be cut into 1-in. lengths, laid horizontally on sandy soil and lightly covered with sand. If they are placed in a cold frame or greenhouse, a young plantlet will develop from each piece of root.

Slips: Hardy carnations and pinks may be propagated by pieces of the young tip growth called slips. This type of cutting needs no trimming. Hold the growth or shoot in one hand and then pull out the tip of the shoot with the other hand. Insert the slip in a suitable rooting medium in a propagating frame or at the edge of a pot containing a similar material that is kept covered with a polyethylene bag.

Inserting the Cuttings

It is important to realize that, no matter how well the work of preparing the cuttings is done, they will not root properly unless they are inserted correctly.

The natural healing of a wound in plants is much the same as in animals, because new tissue is formed to grow over and cover the damaged area. Thus, when a cutting is made or prepared by cutting it cleanly just below a joint or node, the cells that are damaged by the knife cut die and, as a result, a corky layer of tissue, called "callus," is formed. Under favorable conditions the callus forms a ring around the edge of the wound. From it roots grow out, anchor themselves into the rooting medium and produce root hairs which absorb moisture and

nutrients, thus providing the cutting with the means to continue a separate existence.

Sometimes, however, cuttings will make a lot of callus formation at the expense of roots—in fact they will appear to be growing yet will produce only a drumstick-like end to the part below soil level and no sign of a root. This may be caused by too high rooting-medium temperature, or by a coarse rooting medium which allows too much air to penetrate to the base of the cutting. The use of very coarse sand has been found to cause excessive callus formation. To overcome this difficulty, shave off the excessive callus with a razor blade or small, sharp knife. This will often cause roots to form quickly after the cutting is reinserted.

Certain kinds of plants, notably many evergreens of the cone-bearing type, are much given to excessive callus development. Many plants in this group are very slow to root even under circumstances that are very favorable.

The method of insertion is very much the same for all kinds of stem cuttings but differs somewhat according to the rooting medium used. The prepared ends should be set in the rooting medium so that the cutting does not hang in a hole with an air space or void beneath it. If the medium is pressed around the cutting at the surface and left loose at the base, the cutting will fail to root because of the air space below. Insertion to a depth of 1 in. or 1½ in. is usually ample for the average cutting, but the larger ones need a greater depth, certainly sufficient to give them stability. Leafless hardwood cuttings made from fully ripened wood are commonly planted to at least half their depth in the rooting medium. When inserting cuttings, use a dibber with a blunt end to make the hole. Push it to the required depth and put the cutting in so that its end rests firmly on the base of the hole. Then fill in by pushing the medium around the cutting. If vermiculite or perlite is used for rooting, do not pack it, but if sand—or sand and peat moss—is the rooting medium, make it firm by gently ramming at the side of the cutting with the dibber. After inserting, always sprinkle well with a watering can fitted with a fine spray, to settle the soil and make it firm around the cuttings.

Cuttings in Outdoor Beds

Hardwood or ripened cuttings, of which those of climbing roses, hardy shrubs and bush fruits are typical, are prepared from ripened growth during late summer or autumn, about the time the leaves fall. They should be about 10 to 12 in. long and may have a heel of older wood at the base.

In mild climates these hardwood cuttings may be planted directly in the ground as soon as they are made, but where severe winters prevail, a better plan is to tie them together in bundles of about 25 and bury them outdoors under an 8-in. layer of sand. In early spring they are removed from the sand, the bundles untied and the cuttings inserted in beds of well-drained soil.

Insertion of this type of cutting into prepared beds is not difficult, but the soil should be fine and firm. Cut out a narrow trench with a spade and, if the soil is inclined to be heavy, sprinkle some coarse sand along the bottom of the trench. Then space the cuttings 3 or 4 in. apart against the vertical side of the trench with their lower ends firmly on the bottom of the trench. Fill in the soil and make it firm by treading or ramming. At least two thirds of each cutting should be in the soil; a greater proportion is often advantageous.

Leave the cuttings in the bed for a year, by which time they will be well rooted. The bed requires little attention, and need be watered only if the weather is very dry. Growth starts in early spring, and its rate and extent will generally indicate the success or failure of the cuttings. If they are successful, leave the bed undisturbed for the summer, but keep weeds in check. During the autumn transplant the young plants into well-prepared ground, for they must have ample space to develop their true habit of growth. Put them in rows 2½ ft. apart and leave 1½ to 2 ft. between the plants, to allow easy access between them for hoeing and cultivating, and for staking and tying if necessary. According to type and variety and its mode of growth, the young plant can remain in the nursery bed for one or two years, but it is unwise to delay transplanting into the permanent location for longer than is necessary.

DIVISION

Division is the simplest and one of the most obvious methods of increase, particularly when it is not possible or wise to propagate by seed, because it is necessary to have only a shoot or young growth with roots attached in order to form another plant that will be exactly the same as the parent. The method requires a number or mass of shoots or buds growing together which can be pulled apart or severed with a knife to form individual portions, with roots or rudiments and a crown, that will develop into complete new plants. Plants which grow from a single stem or crown cannot be propagated in this way. Most plants which have a fibrous rootstock, such as perennial asters, phlox, heleniums and chrysanthemums, are readily increased by division. But the method is not always easy with other plants.

The division of most plants is carried out during early spring when growth is active, and it is only necessary to retain sufficient rhizome or underground stem to supply the immediate needs of the divided portion until it has rooted and is established. However, some plants, such as irises and peonies, are divided later in the season.

Shrubby plants can be divided only if they have a compact habit and produce new growth by branching or making suckers from below ground. Examples of such shrubs are *Kerria japonica*, *Hypericum calycinum* (St.-John's-wort), *Xanthorhiza*, forsythias and some spireas.

Rhizomes

Plants with underground stems or with rhizomes that grow on or just below the surface of the soil—such as bearded iris, Solomon's seal, obedient plant (*Physostegia*), Chinese lantern (*Physalis*) and bee balm (*Monarda*)— lend themselves to increase by division. When dividing plants of this type, select the strong-growing portions from the outside of the clump or

Divide the rhizome of bearded iris so that the new growth is removed with a portion of the rhizome attached.

group and discard the central portions which are old and worn out. Divide and replant bearded irises soon after the flowering is over—July is generally the best time. In this class of iris, the new growth is formed at the end of the rhizome, or swollen, creeping stem. It should be removed from the parent plant by cutting with a strong knife about 2 or 3 in. back from the growth. This will provide a section of rhizome with roots attached which, when planted horizontally and just below soil level, will allow for the quick establishment of the new plant. Modern varieties of bearded irises usually are best when divided every second year so that strong growth and fine flowers are maintained.

Plants with Woody Crowns and Growth Buds

Of perennial herbaceous plants with a compact semiwoody crown from which numerous growth buds arise, the lupine and delphinium are perhaps the best-known examples. Division of such plants needs to be done carefully in the early spring if it is to be successful. In many parts of North America the successful propagation of delphiniums and perennial lupines by division is scarcely practicable, and it is usual to rely upon sowing seeds to obtain new plants.

Lift the parent crown and shake it clear of the soil, if necessary removing the soil by washing the crown in water. It is then easier to divide sections from the crown, with buds or shoots attached. Plant the divided portions separately, or first establish them in pots, and then plant out later after a good root action has been formed.

Tubers

Tuberous-rooted plants, such as peonies, need special treatment and careful handling when being divided.

Divide peonies during the early autumn. The eyes or growth buds can easily be seen on the tubers, and each division should consist of an eye and a tuber. If large numbers of a certain variety are needed, plant them out in well-prepared soil in a nursery bed with the eye about 2 in. below the soil level. But if only a doubling or trebling of stock is required, lift an established crown and divide it into several portions, each having at least three eyes or growth buds, by using two hand forks back-to-back pushed well between the roots. Then gently lever them apart to avoid snapping too many rootlets.

Peonies unfortunately dislike root disturbance and often several years will elapse before newly divided crowns flower freely, so do not dig them up unless it is necessary and new or increased stock is required.

The potato is another example of a tuberous plant which can be divided by being cut into pieces, each with an eye or bud attached.

Few beginners propagate tuberous-rooted begonias by division of the tuber, although the method is simple if the tubers are placed in a greenhouse or propagating frame to start them into growth before dividing them. Put them in shallow flats, barely cover them with peat moss or sandy leaf mold, and growth buds will appear, producing stout, strong shoots. It is then easy to see where to cut the tuber into portions, each with one or more growth buds attached. Dip the portions into powdered charcoal, powdered sulphur or fermate to dry up the cut surfaces, and then either pot them singly or space them out in flats to continue growing. The *multiflora* class of tuberous begonia, popular as summer bedding plants, forms large, irregularly shaped tubers that will produce many growing shoots, so that many plants can be obtained by dividing only one tuber.

Offsets

Another large and varied group of plants, which includes tulips, daffodils, crocuses, gladioluses, and the bulbous irises, produce their annual growth and flowers from a bulb or corm. These plants do produce seeds and can be propagated by them, but often three to five years elapse before the seedlings reach flowering size, and even then selected varieties do not reproduce true from seeds. This group has, however, an alternative means of increase by the production of offsets. These are complete but smaller new plants that are produced alongside and attached to the parent bulb or corm, the number of offsets produced varying with different species. Daffodils have what is termed a "mother bulb"; this is one large bulb with two or three offsets which produce a number of shoots and flowers. The offsets on daffodils, tulips and other bulbs can be planted separately to form bigger bulbs, but only the larger of them will flower in the first year.

Suckers

Suckers are shoots that grow from the roots or underground stems of some plants, often near their bases. In many cases they are a nuisance: for instance, roses; grafted trees of lilac, plum and apple; and certain large trees—some poplars are notorious for producing unwanted suckers. But in other plants the sucker growths provide a quick and sure means of reproduction. A good example is the raspberry, which produces sucker growths that often appear several feet away from the parent plant. The growths can be severed in the autumn and lifted with roots attached.

Spireas and some roses, such as *Rosa rugosa*, are easily increased by suckers.

The use of suckers for increasing stock should be exercised with discre-

714

tion, because certain grafted trees produce sucker growth from the rootstock and these suckers ultimately produce plants like the stock. Suckers of the peach, for example, when—as often—grafted onto a plum rootstock, would produce plum, and suckers of pears grafted onto quince would produce quince.

LAYERING

This is another easy and sure way of propagating a number of flowering and fruiting plants to insure that they are the same as the parent. Layering occurs naturally in many plants (as forsythia), and is the term used to describe the rooting of a stem while it is still attached to the parent plant. The "runners" of the strawberry and the tip rooting of loganberry and blackberry are well-known examples.

Natural layering also occurs with large trees and shrubs, and examples can be seen in public parks and gardens. Beeches and horse chestnuts with low branches sweeping the ground will layer themselves. Generally the rubbing of the branch against the ground causes an injury to the bark. Then, from the healing of the wound and contact with the soil, roots form to anchor the branch, which eventually grows to become a secondary tree beside the parent. The layering of rhododendrons and other ornamental shrubs is sometimes done into large boxes of prepared soil placed beneath the branches to be layered. The advantage of a box is that once the layer is rooted and severed from the parent plant, it can be moved without disturbing the new roots.

Other plants, particularly strawberries and clematis, are layered by pegging the growth into pots filled with gritty soil and plunged into the ground near the parent plant. Loganberries and blackberries can be treated in the same way.

Layering
Layer strawberry runners into small pots sunk directly into the soil. They may also be layered directly into the ground, but transplanting is not so easy.

Border or hardy carnations are propagated by layering. The operation is carried out toward the end of summer. It is important to remember that it is the new season's growth, or nonflowering shoots, that are layered, and that strong plants are needed to withstand the winter.

Layering carnations or any other type of plant which lends itself to this means of increase is just as easy as taking cuttings and, because the layers are still attached to the parent plant, there is more certainty of their rooting.

Equipment

A good sharp knife with a thin blade is needed, as well as a trowel, a hand fork and a supply of layering pins or pegs made from 6-in. lengths of galvanized wire bent double and shaped like a hairpin. Good, fresh soil made up with a mixture of loam, peat moss or sifted leaf mold, and coarse sand is also necessary. This soil mixture should be moist, but not so wet that it will bind together when pressed.

Method

After midsummer select a strong, healthy plant with good growth that is free from pests and diseases. Lightly loosen the soil around the plant with the hand fork, being careful not to disturb or break the roots. Then, if the natural soil tends to be poorly drained, spread a layer of the prepared soil around the plant to form a ridge or mound 2 or 3 in. higher than the normal soil level, and make it fairly firm. This is particularly necessary if the soil is heavy and inclined to be wet. Arrange the soil so that the growths to be layered can readily be anchored into it. On light soils that are well drained the use of prepared soil is not so necessary, although it is wise to add some peat moss or sifted leaf mold and incorporate it well with the natural soil. This increases the humus content and is good for the layered plant when the roots are formed.

Select the best and most suitably placed shoots and prepare them as follows: Strip off all leaves from the part of the stem to be put in the soil (usually two or three pairs of leaves are removed). Then with a sharp knife cut into the stem to about half its thickness, just below a joint from which the leaves were removed. Extend the cut up the center of the stem for about 1 in. so that a tongue is formed, and trim the end of the tongue if the cut is not clean. Then bring the shoot down, keeping the cut open, and press the tongue into the soil. The whole of the cut portion will thus be in contact with the soil and should be secured there with a layering pin placed nearer to the plant than the cut and pressed firmly into the soil. Treat each growth to be layered in the same way and then make sure that the cut portions of the layers are covered with a generous amount of the prepared soil. Next, water the area with a sprinkler to soak thoroughly all of the new soil as well as the layers beneath. This watering is essential because it settles the soil around the layers and gives the final firming.

The method used particularly for layering shrubs closely copies the natural process. The shoot or branch is bent or twisted where it is to make contact with the soil so that the bark is damaged and the tissue is split. The splitting of the wood checks the flow of sap and causes the formation of callus or healing tissue from which roots will usually emerge. In addition to pegging down the layered shoot or branch it is advisable to secure the tip to a small stake, tying it as nearly as possible in an upright position. This prevents damage to the shoot, makes sure that it grows straight, and prevents it from swinging up into its old position before the roots have formed.

If the weather is dry, regular watering is necessary, because it is essential that the ridge or mound of soil does not dry out. In order to prevent this, it is helpful to cover the area around the layered branches with polyethylene plastic film weighted down with a few stones. After about six weeks inspect one of the layers by gently lifting it to see if roots have formed. Some layers will be in advance of others, but experience will soon help the gardener to decide when plenty of roots are formed. When all the layers are rooted, sever them from the parent plant by cutting the stem between the layer and its parent, but leave the layered plants in place for a time to recover from the severing and to become fully established on their own roots. After a week or so, lift the plants and set them separately in pots varying in size according to the plants, or plant them out into well-prepared soil in a bed or border. Some shrubs, particularly evergreens such as rhododendrons, may take a year or more before layers made of them are sufficiently rooted to be removed from the parent plant.

Air Layering With Polyethylene

Air layering in its original form was practiced in China centuries ago. A stem or branch was partly severed by making an upward cut from just below a joint, and after a small wedge had been inserted to keep the cut open, sphagnum moss or some other moisture-holding medium was wrapped around and over the cut and tied with string. If the moss or other material was kept constantly moist, roots eventually grew out into it, and after a while the air layer was removed and potted separately to provide a separate plant.

In the past, various modifications of this method have been used, chiefly to propagate greenhouse plants. But the success of air layering depended on the sphagnum moss or other material being kept constantly moist, and this was only possible in greenhouses where the atmosphere was moist and regular attention could be given to syringing and watering. The necessity for constant dampening is no longer a problem if polyethylene plastic film is used to surround the layer and its rooting material. Air layering is therefore a method which can be used with every chance of success, particularly for those plants which are difficult to propagate by the more usual methods of seed, cuttings or division.

The best time for air layering depends on the season and to some extent on the locality, but most ornamental shrubs and trees growing in the open should be air-layered in spring when the sap is rising and flowing freely. Plants growing in greenhouses can be air-layered from late winter to midsummer.

Method

The branch to be air-layered should not be too tender nor too old. Mature one-year-old wood is the most suitable, but there are exceptions with different kinds of plants. Firm wood is better than pithy wood and should usually be about as thick as an ordi-

nary pencil. With thick-stemmed tropical plants such as dumb canes, dracaenas and philodendrons, they commonly are considerably stouter.

The operation is not difficult to perform. Make the cut with a sharp knife, starting just below a leafstalk or joint and penetrating nearly half-way through the stem, then turning upward for about 1½ in. Treat the cut surfaces with a hormone or root-promoting substance if you wish, although many kinds of plants root freely from air layers without this aid.

Wedge open the cut with a bit of moss. Then pass a tube of polyethylene over the growing part of the branch, slide it over the cut and secure its lower end with adhesive tape. Pack the tube with broken-up moist sphagnum moss until it covers the cut portion and extends several inches above it. Then bind the top of the tube with adhesive tape. Support the layer by tying the layered branch to a bamboo cane or to another nearby branch. Inspect the layer from time to time to make sure that the plastic film is unbroken and that the layer itself is secure.

If the sealed layer is kept airtight, the moss that is surrounding it will remain moist throughout the season and until roots have formed. When these can be seen through the polyethylene, cut the layer from the parent plant, take away the polyethylene and moss carefully, and pot the new plant in sandy soil in the usual way. Keep the new plant in a very humid atmosphere in a cold frame or greenhouse until well established; then gradually harden it to more normal conditions and, if it is a kind that is hardy, plant it out in the spring.

BUDDING AND GRAFTING

This is a method of propagation that differs from other methods in that it is a joining together of two living por-

Air Layering with Polyethylene

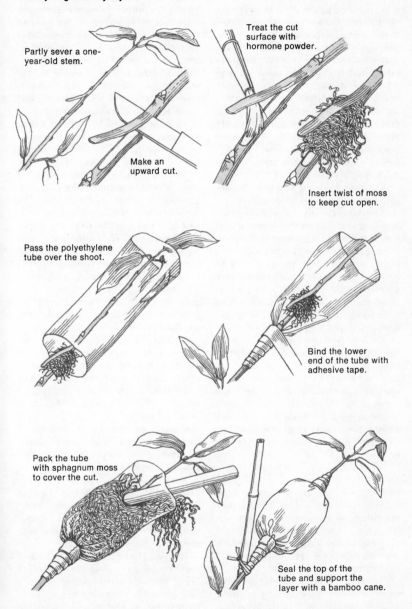

Partly sever a one-year-old stem.

Make an upward cut.

Treat the cut surface with hormone powder.

Insert twist of moss to keep cut open.

Pass the polyethylene tube over the shoot.

Bind the lower end of the tube with adhesive tape.

Pack the tube with sphagnum moss to cover the cut.

Seal the top of the tube and support the layer with a bamboo cane.

tions from two separate plants to form a permanent union. One is part of a plant with roots and is called the "stock"; the other is a piece of the previous year's wood of another plant and is called the "scion." When properly joined to the stock, the scion supplies the aerial parts of the new plant—that is, the branches, leaves, buds, etc. It is essential that the stock and scion be compatible. This usually means that they should be of the same botanical genus, but sometimes different genera within the same botanical family can be grafted.

Although budding and grafting are separate methods of propagation carried out at different times of the year, budding is in fact only a form of grafting; the principles governing the joining together of the two parts are the same, although the material used to produce the growth part of the new plant is different. A single bud and a small piece of bark or rind to join to the stock are used for budding, whereas a piece of growth or shoot (the scion) to join to the stock is used for grafting. Some amateur gardeners propagate roses and fruit trees by budding or grafting; once the essentials are understood and after some practice, anyone can become efficient at one or both methods. Cactuses are among the easiest of plants to graft; the popular Christmas cactus is often grafted onto *Pereskia*.

The Stock

Stocks used for grafting should be chosen with care and with particular attention to any special characteristics they may have. In some cases the type of stock used influences to a very significant extent the growth of the scions grafted upon it.

Different types of stocks for fruit trees have been developed by research stations for their suitability to certain varieties and to the ultimate mode of growth of the tree. The various stocks for apple trees are therefore classified into groups or types. The dwarfing stocks have a restricted root action and, when they are worked with any variety of apple, produce small and dwarf trees, which will fruit early in life. Another group produces trees that are semidwarf in habit, and those with a vigorous rooting system produce large trees. Rootstocks which are immune to pests like the woolly aphid (see page 816) have recently been developed and selected.

There are various stocks for plums. The most commonly used is the Myrobalan (*Prunus cerasifera*) but in regions where this is not hardy, *Prunus americana* is favored. The Japanese varieties of plum are often budded on seedling peach stocks, and this same stock is also often preferred for plums to be grown in sandy soils. The sand cherry (*Prunus besseyi*) is used as a dwarfing stock for plums. Peaches are usually budded onto seedling peach stocks.

Quince stock is used for pears because the rooting system is less vigorous than that of the common pear, a stock that is used only when very large trees are needed. The types of quince stocks are known as Malling A and Malling C.

Cherries are budded onto stocks of the mazzard or wild sweet cherry (*Prunus avium*) and onto the mahaleb stock (*Prunus mahaleb*).

For roses various types of stocks are available that are easily raised either by seeds or cuttings. The most popular is *Rosa multiflora*. Most of the tree roses are grown on stems of the Japanese rose, *Rosa rugosa*.

It is essential that the stocks be well rooted and fully established before being worked, and also free of pests and diseases. When the stocks have been obtained and have been established in the garden, the method of working and the form of union (that is, budding or grafting) can be decided upon.

BUDDING

Successful budding depends not only on the way the budding is done, but also on when it is done and on the type of material used.

When to Bud

The growth—or "wood," as it is called—produced in the current season is used. Budding can therefore be carried out in summer, when there is an abundance of sap and the bulk of the season's growth has been made but has not yet become hard and woody. No rules can be laid down with certainty as to exact dates to carry out the operation, because so much depends on the season. There are several simple tests to determine the right choice of wood to be made. With roses, for example, if the thorns snap off easily and cleanly—leaving a clean, moist scar—the wood and buds are in good condition for budding.

With the stock it is easy to make a trial cut, and if the bark or rind separates readily from the wood and there is plenty of sap, the stock is ready. During a dry season, however, such a condition, particularly with the stock, is not always easy to obtain. Stocks that are dry at the roots, so that the bark will not part or lift from the wood, must be thoroughly watered a week or so before they are worked. Whether roses, fruit or ornamental trees are being budded, the essentials are the same, except that roses (aside from those to be grown in "tree" or "standard" form) are budded below ground level, and fruit trees and most ornamentals above ground level.

Materials

For budding and grafting, the tools and materials required are:

1. A pail of water for keeping the "budwood" fresh and moist until it is required.
2. A bowl or similar receptacle to hold water into which the prepared buds can be placed to keep them damp.
3. A hand fork or trowel to remove soil from the base of stocks if they are being worked below or near to ground level, as, for example, bush roses.
4. A budding knife with a long, thin handle flattened at the end to lift the bark of the stock.
5. Ties, which may be rubber bands, moist raffia or soft string.
6. Wax or rubberized tape.

Method

There are three distinct operations: (a) the preparation or cutting out of the bud, (b) cutting the incision in the stock into which the bud is to be inserted and (c) the insertion and tying in of the bud.

Cutting out the bud is perhaps the most difficult job, for unless the bud is properly prepared the whole operation will fail. The best buds are those near the base of the bud stick, which is a piece of the current year's growth. First cut off the leaves, leaving the stalks of the leaves to act as handles for the buds. Starting with the lower bud, cut in about $\frac{1}{2}$ in. below the leaf-stalk and draw the knife upward to come out about 1 in. above the bud. A little wood is cut out behind the bud and this can be removed or not.

The second operation is simple. A T-shaped cut is made in the bark of the stock at a point where it is smooth. Make a long upward cut with the point of the knife and a short crosscut at the top of it, just deep enough to sever the bark.

Lift the flaps of the T-cut with the knife handle and slide the prepared bud down beneath the flaps of bark so that it fits snugly against the wood of the stock. Then press the bud down

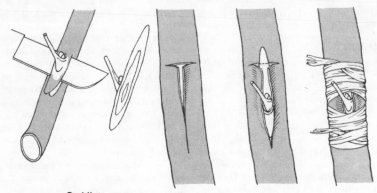

Budding
(Left to right) Cutting the bud from the bud stock; bud with petiole or leafstalk and shield of bark, ready for insertion; T-cut incision in bark of stalk; bud inserted in T-cut; tied with damp raffia.

until the base of the T-cut begins to split a little, which is a sign that the bud is firmly inserted. Trim off the remaining part of the shield of bark above the bud, level with the top of the T-shaped cut, and tie the bud into place with a rubber band, moist raffia or soft string. Start the tie a little below the bud, binding the cut firmly but not so tight as to cause a strangling effect. Finish just above the T-cut and tie securely. No further protective covering is needed, and the stocks are allowed to continue to grow without restriction for the rest of the season. The actual cutting back of the stock is not done until early spring.

Aftercare
Make sure that the stocks do not suffer during the dry weather; and prevent the growth of weeds. About a month after inserting the buds, examine the stocks. If the buds are swelling, as is likely, draw a sharp knife up the back of the raffia, string tie or rubber band, cutting it sufficiently to cause it to ease and part.

During early spring examine the buds, and if they are alive cut back or

"head back" the top of the stock to a point about 1 in. above the bud in the case of roses, and some 6 in. above the bud for fruit and other trees. This longer snag of stock can be used as a stake for the new growth when the

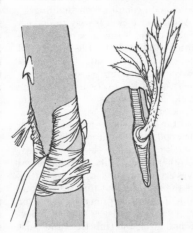

Budding Aftercare
(Left) Cut the back of the tie a month after budding to allow swelling of the bud and stock.
(Right) Stock headed back and bud growing out the following spring.

bud grows out, to prevent damage by wind.

This method is known as shield budding. There are several other methods, such as patch budding, flute budding and ring budding, which are more involved and not commonly practiced or recommended.

GRAFTING

Many methods of grafting, some very elaborate, have been employed to make the cuts on both stock and scion, so that the operation appears to be very involved. Therefore only the simpler methods are described here, and the others are listed for reference.

Whichever method is used, the essentials for a successful union are the same. The vital part of both stock and scion is the cambium—the thin layer of tissue lying between the bark and the wood, clearly visible as a green line when a young living stem is cut through diagonally. The fusion or joining together of the cells of the cambium layers of both scion and stock makes grafting possible, so it is essential that these layers be placed in direct contact with each other if the union is to be successful.

Whip-and-Tongue Grafting

Generally used where the stock and scion are of approximately the same thickness, this method is employed by nurserymen for grafting young fruit trees. First cut down the stock to about 4 in. above ground level, and on the smoothest side make a slanting upward cut about 1½ in. long, followed by another smaller downward cut starting just below the top of the upward cut, to form a tongue. Prepare the scion, which should be about 4 in. long, by making a corresponding slanting cut at the basal end and a second small upward cut from just above the base of the slanting cut, again to form a tongue. Cuts on the scion should correspond with those on the stock, but in reverse. Place the

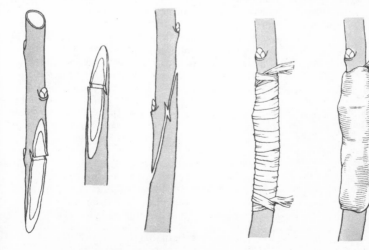

Whip-and-Tongue Grafting
(Left to right) Scion with slanting cut and tongue; stock with similar cuts; scion and stock in contact; secured by tying with raffia; covered with grafting wax.

tongue of the scion gently into the tongue of the stock, making sure that the bark and cambium layers of scion and stock are opposite to each other. Press the scion down until the two long, slanting cuts are flush. The tongue will then hold the graft firmly in position.

Make sure that the cut surfaces are in even contact. To form a union the cambium layers must meet on one side, if not on both. Where the stock is larger than the scion, careful attention must be given to this. Then bind the cut surfaces together with rubber ties or moistened raffia and apply grafting wax to cover and seal the graft area, excluding air and moisture. The cut top of the scion should also be given a coat of grafting wax to keep out moisture.

Splice Grafting

Similar to whip-and-tongue grafting, but simpler because no tongue is made. Make two slanting cuts of corresponding size, one on the stock and the other on the scion. Then place the cut surfaces together, making sure

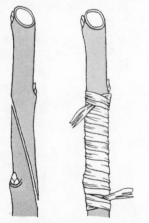

Splice Grafting
(Left) Scion and stock showing the long, slanting cuts
(Right) In position and tied with raffia

that the cambium layers are in contact on one side at least, if the stock is larger than the scion. As there is no tongue, hold the splice firmly in place while the tying is done. Afterward wax the graft as already described. The limitation of this method is that the splice can easily move while it is being tied, with the result that the vital contact of the cambium layers may be lost and the graft fail to grow.

Crown or Rind Grafting

In the reworking or rejuvenating of old fruit trees, "crown grafting" refers to a limb or branch that has been cut back to expose a circle of wood and a ring of bark, which when worked with a number of scions around the edge gives a crown effect.

Head back the larger branches of the tree to a convenient point, usually 1 ft. or so above a crotch. After trimming the bark and wood to make them smooth, prepare a number of scions by making long, slanting cuts of about 1½ in. Then make a cut in the bark of the prepared limb extending down the side for about 2 in. from the edge of the bark. By slightly lifting the edges of the bark where the cut is made, a prepared scion can easily be pushed down inside the bark, with the flat surface of the slanting cut resting against the inner wood of the stock. The scion is held firmly in position by the tension of the thick bark of the limb or branch, and it is easy to bind the graft with raffia or with soft string and then cover the whole cut area with grafting wax. The number of scions inserted around the edge of a headed-back limb will depend on its size, but usually two scions are sufficient, one opposite the other.

Cleft Grafting

This method of crown grafting used to be popular because, when properly done, it was easy and reliable although

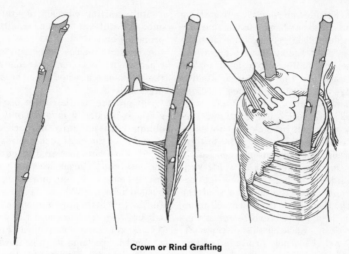

Crown or Rind Grafting

Make scion with slanting cut; insert scion between bark and wood;
after tying with raffia, cover top and side with grafting wax.

Cleft Grafting

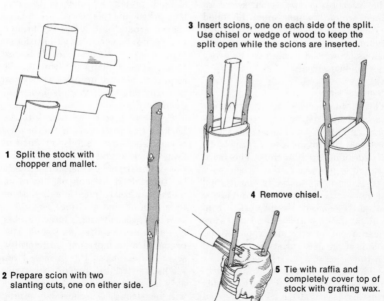

1 Split the stock with
chopper and mallet.

2 Prepare scion with two
slanting cuts, one on either side.

3 Insert scions, one on each side of the split.
Use chisel or wedge of wood to keep the
split open while the scions are inserted.

4 Remove chisel.

5 Tie with raffia and
completely cover top of
stock with grafting wax.

rather crude and rough. Cleft grafting is used on cut-back stocks that are considerably larger in section than the scion. Split the stock with a grafting chisel or small axe to a depth of 3–4 in., and use the tool or a wooden wedge to keep the split open until one or more scions (several, for a large stock) are ready for insertion. Prepare the scion by making two slanting cuts, one on either side, to form a wedge-shaped base. Then insert the scion in the cleft or split, with one side of the bark of the wedge corresponding to the split bark of the stock. Usually, if the stock is 2 in. or more in diameter, two scions are inserted, one on each side of the cleft, where they are held firmly in position by the pinching effect of the split stock. It is wise, however, to bind the stock with raffia or soft string, and then cover the entire surface and sides of the graft with wax. The splitting of the stock across its center and the insertion of two scions leave an open wound, which must be filled with wax to make the grafts airtight and prevent water entering. If both scions grow, the weaker is cut away the following year.

Frameworking

This is another way of rejuvenating an old fruit tree, but the tree is prepared differently and numerous scions are used to provide a new framework of side and tip branches. The main branch system of the tree, with the exception of badly positioned branches, is retained to provide a suitably spaced framework from which all side branches and twigs are cleared completely and replaced by scions of the new variety to be grafted on the tree.

The various methods of frameworking are known as stub grafting, side grafting, inverted-L bark grafting and slit grafting.

Stub grafting consists of grafting onto the stubs of spurs or small side branches and as close as possible to the main branch of the fruit tree, whereas in the other three methods the scions are inserted into the main branch itself.

Slit grafting is the easiest of these methods because it involves only one oblique 2-in. cut into the bark with the point of the knife just meeting the wood. The scion, prepared by cutting the basal end to form a wedge with the cuts about 1 in. or more long, is pushed into the slit cut of the bark and, with a little pressure, embeds itself between the bark and the wood. At the same time the scion can be positioned by pushing it up or down to obtain the angle required for the side branch it is to form. As the scion is held firmly in position by the bark, no tying is required, but the cut is sealed with grafting wax to make it airtight and waterproof.

Each prepared branch of the tree is worked in this way, the scions spaced around and along the branch to provide an even and well-positioned framework of side branches. It is wise to put on more than will ultimately be required, because unwanted ones can be easily cut out if there is danger of overcrowding.

Frameworking by grafting into the bark can be done only if the bark is reasonably thick, usually on wood of 2-in. diameter and over. The extremities of the branches therefore have to be tip-grafted by one of the other methods already mentioned, that is, by crown or rind grafting.

With frameworking a large number of scions are required and should be prepared with more buds, preferably seven or eight, as the growth from scions inserted into an old tree—probably having a vigorous root system—will be strong. If scions containing only three or four growth buds were to be used, strong growth would result from them and would only overcrowd the tree. Long scions with up to eight buds will not grow so strongly and will only produce growth from the top two or three buds, while the lower buds will produce short spurlike growth bearing fruit buds. In this way the newly grafted tree is productive within a few years.

Methods of Frameworking

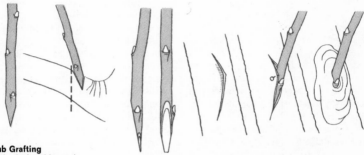

Stub Grafting
Method of making scion
and inserting it into stub.
Note line of final cut
to remove branch after
scion has been set in place.

Inverted-L Graft
(Left to right) Preparation of scion;
inverted L-shaped cut in bark of stock;
scion inserted and held in place by a small
thin nail; graft entirely sealed over
with wax to prevent the entry of water.

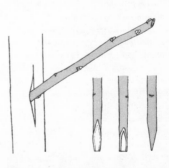

Side Grafting
Scion prepared with two
cuts, one of them more
slanting than the other.

Slit Grafting
Scion inserted in oblique cut in bark.
The scion is cut to a wedge shape
as shown on the right.

CHAPTER 39

THE SOIL—
Well Managed, It Rewards You Richly

Soil Profile—Elements—Textures and Tilth—Living Organisms and Humus—Moisture—Acidity—Drainage

THE ROOTS of many plants are not confined to the so-called "topsoil"; they penetrate deeply into underlying layers. To learn the conditions their roots have to meet, it is necessary to dig down to about 3 ft. or even more to disclose the soil "profile."

Most soils dug in this way show a series of definite layers, one above the other, with different colors and textures. These layers have been produced through the centuries by the action of climate, vegetation and animal life on mineral matter, and are known collectively as the soil profile. This is important in soil classification. The main things to look for when examining a profile are depth, texture, structure, color and drainage.

A soil profile usually consists of two or more layers lying parallel to the land surface. For instance, often a foot of sandy soil overlies several feet of clay soil. The upper layer, which is generally called the topsoil, is, as a rule, darker in color than the lower layers because of its higher content of decaying vegetation and animal matter (humus). In this upper layer, life in such forms as bacteria, funguses, insects and other small organisms is most abundant. Being near the surface, it receives the rainfall first, so that its nutrients are washed down and lost more easily than in deeper layers. In addition, the humus slightly acidifies the soil water, so that its solvent power is increased and a number of salts are washed out. It is in this way that lime is lost, so even in shallow soils overlying limestone it is not unusual to find the upper layer acid. On steep slopes the upper layer is commonly thin, and on building sites it is often completely destroyed by the builders, or covered over with raw, barren earth from excavations.

THE SUBSOIL

This is the name usually given to the layer below the topsoil. It is harder to dig when dry, and often is stickier when wet, owing to its higher clay content, much of which has been washed out of the topsoil. The subsoil often has a brighter color, due to the washing down of red oxides of iron and other materials, which in some cases collect and cement the soil particles together into hard continuous layers known as pans. These, of course, very effectively prevent roots from penetrating any farther and may seriously interfere with drainage.

GEOLOGICAL BASE

Below the topsoil and the subsoil—the layers which constitute the true soil—lies the mineral matter of geological origin which may or may not be the parent material of the soil above. This mineral matter may be

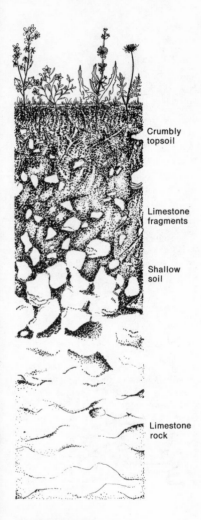

Crumbly topsoil

Limestone fragments

Shallow soil

Limestone rock

Limestone Soil
This is often shallow and stony; it is alkaline. A wide variety of plants, including most fruits and vegetables, can be grown on it, but it is quite unsuitable for definitely acid-soil plants such as rhododendrons. Drainage is satisfactory, but many limestone soils dry out in summer. With plenty of humus and regular fertilizing, they can be made into useful soil. Organic matter rots very quickly and must be replenished frequently.

solid bedrock or it may be loose and porous to great depths. It may result from the breakdown of hard rocks, or it may have been moved to its present position by water, wind or ice. Both this layer and the one above are poorer in humus and in organic life than topsoil, and when spaded should be brought to the surface only a little at a time to avoid spoiling the topsoil. Deep topsoils hold more moisture and nutrients than shallow ones. Plants will grow in shallow soils but, just as when grown in pots, they need more frequent fertilizing and watering than when grown in deeper soils.

WHAT IS SOIL?

The soil has five main components: mineral or inorganic particles; dead and more or less decayed organic matter of vegetable and animal origin; water (usually called the "soil solution" because it contains traces of various salts which have been derived from the weathering of rocks and the decay of organic matter); air, which fills voids between the soil particles that are not occupied by water; and teeming hordes of living insects, worms, minute animals such as protozoa, as well as funguses, bacteria and other primitive life. All these constitute the population which gives the soil its animate or living nature.

FRAMEWORK

The proportions of the major components vary greatly from garden to garden and even with depth in the same soil. Inorganic soil particles occupy only about one half of the total bulk of most soils, and do not fit together tightly like the pieces of a jigsaw puzzle but have spaces between them. These inorganic or mineral particles are the residue of the rocks from which the soil is derived, and have resisted the action of weathering. As they are the most unchanging part of the soil, they really represent its skeleton, or framework. Many of these particles, such as grains of sand, can be seen quite easily, but others, such as the smallest particles of clay, can be examined only with an extremely powerful microscope. Indeed, in the case of colloidal clay, only the electron microscope can distinguish the ultimate particles.

TEXTURE

Soil scientists find it convenient to classify mineral particles into fractions or separates, according to size. These they call coarse sand, fine sand, silt and clay. Soil layers rarely consist of one fraction only, but usually contain a mixture of all four. The proportion of sand, silt and clay in each soil layer determines the soil "texture" and, as many recommendations for the management and improvement of garden soils are keyed to it, the texture should be judged by the gardener. The texture in most soils changes from layer to layer, the subsoil generally containing more clay than the surface soil above it or the deeper layer below it.

Samples of soil can, of course, be sent to a laboratory for analysis, but with a little practice the gardener can learn to estimate the relative amounts of sand, silt and clay by rubbing a pinch of moist soil between thumb and forefinger.

SAND

Sands feel harsh and gritty, and the particles scarcely hold together at all, even when moist. Soils containing a high proportion of sand are called coarse-textured soils. They are well aerated, "light" and easy to spade or plow, but they hold little moisture and nutrients and therefore, for good plant growth, need constant replenishment with water, as well as comparatively frequent fertilizing.

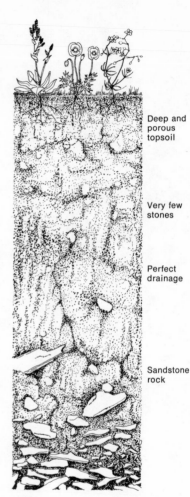

Deep and porous topsoil

Very few stones

Perfect drainage

Sandstone rock

Sandy Soil
Deep and easily worked, sandy soil is suitable for most garden plants. It is derived from sandstone, and its chief drawback is its low water-holding capacity This defect can be overcome by liberal watering and heavy dressings of bulky organic materials to prevent drying out. Regular liming counteracts acidity and helps to maintain fertility.

SILT

Silt feels smooth, soft and floury and is intermediate in size between sand and clay. Being smaller than sand grains, the particles pack together with smaller air spaces or voids between them, which slows up the movement of air and water in the soil. Thus very silty soils drain slowly and remain moist for long periods. They are difficult soils to improve, since neither liming, frost nor cultivation will granulate them or reduce their stickiness. Large dressings of bulky organic materials mixed into them make working them easier.

CLAY

As opposed to light, sandy soils, clay soils are termed "heavy" because they are hard to work and to cultivate. Clay particles are quite different from sand particles. They are not merely fragments of the original rock, but are a secondary product of rock weathering, and are exceedingly fine—at least 1000 times smaller than sand particles. Their peculiar structure gives unique properties to clay and is responsible for the impenetrability and stickiness of soil. Most gardeners think of clay as a nuisance, for excessive amounts of clay lead to a very bad structure, but it does play a vital role. In proper amounts it can act as a conditioner by binding soil particles into granules—a property which is normally associated with the condition known as "good tilth."

Clay particles are able to retain chemical elements dissolved in the soil solution surrounding them. Many of these elements are plant nutrients and, when so held, are readily available to plant roots. Thus clay and humus (which is very similar to clay in some ways) serve as nutrient storehouses. The clay has holding qualities because its particles are so small, and the

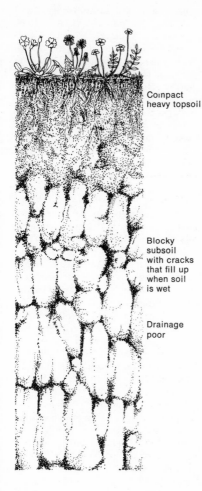

Compact heavy topsoil

Blocky subsoil with cracks that fill up when soil is wet

Drainage poor

Clay Soil
Although the top layer of granular soil is quite good, the raw clay lumps in the subsoil make a poor medium for roots and impede drainage, especially in winter and early spring. This soil is unsuitable for root vegetables and some other crops but will grow most plants if subsurface drainage is improved so that the structure channels and cracks are preserved.

humus because of its spongy nature.

Soils with a high clay content are notoriously difficult to handle. Compression occurs if they are cultivated when wet; compact lumps are formed and these dry out into stony clods. When dry clays are moistened, the colloidal matter (ultramicroscopic sticky particles) swells and tends to block their pores and make them impassable to water. Heavy clays, therefore, become easily waterlogged or "puddled." When the clay dries it shrinks again, forming the great deep cracks so often seen in heavy soils in the summer.

TYPES OF SOILS

Sandy soils are not necessarily all sand, nor are clay soils necessarily all clay. In between these two extremes, both of which would be most unfavorable to plant growth, there are a number of different textural classes. These can be placed in three broad groups—coarse soils, medium-textured soils and fine-textured soils.

Coarse Soils

The coarse-textured soils, which include sands, loamy sands and sandy loams, are valuable not only for their ease of cultivation but for their ability to produce early crops because they warm up quickly in spring. Soon after wet weather ends, they can be cultivated—hoeing and sowing can be carried on.

Poor drainage is rarely a problem. But it is often only a few days after rain that these soils dry out, and unless there is a good water supply, young seedlings may soon die of drought. Bulky manures and composts incorporated with them rot quickly, and some plant nutrients are rapidly washed out of reach of plant roots. Lime is readily washed out also, thus making such soils prone to acidity.

Coarse soils are improved by heavy applications of manure, compost and other spongy humus-forming materials, and by fertilizing on a little-and-often schedule. The addition of clay in reasonable amounts can work wonders provided the two soils are mixed thoroughly. But this treatment is rarely practicable, and it is usually necessary to depend on organic matter in large amounts for the improvement of sandy soils.

The practice known as green manuring (see page 764) is of great benefit to coarse-textured soils.

Medium-Textured Soils

In the medium-textured soil group are loams which contain sand, silt and clay in such well-balanced proportions that none produces a dominating influence. When moist they feel neither gritty, silty nor sticky, and when a moist lump is rubbed with the thumb only a rough smear is left. They are among the most fertile soils, and with proper management almost any crop can be grown in them. They are apt to become cloddy when worked too soon after rain, but break down into a good tilth fairly easily when dry.

These soils are easy to manage, for they do not need any of the careful treatment required by either coarse- or fine-textured soils. It is well, of course, to add organic matter and fertilizers regularly to maintain the humus and nutrient content at desirable levels, and liming may be needed periodically to correct excessive acidity.

Fine-Textured Soils

As the amounts of silt and clay in the soil increase, so the soil becomes more difficult to work. Such soils are slow to drain; the rain lies about in puddles for a long time and the soils, being wet, are cold and delay spring sowing and planting.

Care must be taken to choose the right time to cultivate them, for if they are spaded or worked while they are too wet their structure will be ruined for the whole season. When wet they are like modeling clay, and when dry like concrete. They must be worked just at the right time, when they are neither too wet nor too dry. The advantages of these soils are that they do not dry out as quickly as sandy soils do, and though plants may take longer to establish themselves in them, once they are established large yields of high-quality crops can be expected.

Corrective treatment may necessitate artificial drainage as well as the mixing in of coarse organic matter—peat moss, compost or strawy manure—or inorganic conditioners like coal cinders or gritty sand, in order to open up the soils and so let air into them and water through them. Where possible, spade or plow clay soils in the autumn and allow them to remain in a rough surface condition throughout the winter so as to expose the biggest surface area possible to frost action, which will pulverize the lumps into smaller pieces by the spring.

To decide whether a soil is clay or not, roll a little when moist between thumb and finger. Clay will roll into long, slender, wormlike cylinders which bend into a ring without fracturing, and will polish if rubbed lightly with the thumb. Silt, although often simulating the heaviness of clay, feels smooth and lacks its stickiness. Clay soils are not necessarily acid. If, however, they do become acid, comparatively large quantities of lime are necessary to counteract the acidity.

STRUCTURE

The structure of the soil is just as important as its texture. A careful examination of an undisturbed side of a soil pit will show a very distinct anatomy or structure in many soils.

In some soils the particles are clumped together into what resembles the crumbs of a loaf. Other soils may appear to be made up of angular blocks or clods. These predominant shapes of the soil, or aggregates, as they are called, indicate its "structure." It is believed that some kind of natural cement must be present to bind the soil particles together and keep them in these shapes; clay, as well as humus and various oxides of iron, are the chief elements.

The soil can be likened to a city of many inhabitants, and like any city it has its own system of communications. Some of the main routes are the work of earthworms, of which there may be more than a million in an acre of soil. Their tunnels often penetrate to a depth of 5 or even 6 ft. or more, and allow water and air to permeate the soil. They may largely determine the layout of root systems.

Plant roots, too, make their own contribution toward the breaking up of the soil by running in between the blocks of soil formed by the earthworms' tunnels and preventing them from sticking together again. This is most noticeable with freshly broken-up grassland. Grass is one of the best agents for producing a good structure, which is one of the reasons for sowing it in fields to renew croplands. The more fibrous the root system, the greater the effect.

To find out whether a soil has a good or bad structure, dig out a spadeful of undisturbed soil, let it drop onto a hard surface and then notice how it shatters. A moist soil of good structure should come apart in rounded porous crumbs, but a poorly structured soil will break into blocklike clods with flattened surfaces and sharply angular sides. A cloddy, lumpy soil, its pores almost invisible, is a sure sign of soil compaction or structure deterioration.

Bad Tilth
In poorly structured soil, blocklike lumps are difficult to break up.

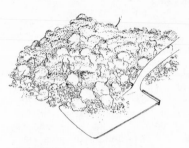

Good Tilth
Soil with a good structure is crumbly, like that found in a meadow.

CRUMBS

The individual particles of an ideal garden soil are grouped together into granules or crumbs, and soil scientists consider that the best size of crumb lies anywhere between about ⅕ in. to ⅟₂₀ in. in diameter. Therefore, one aim in cultivating the soil is to try to achieve a good crumb structure. The crumbs, being porous, soak up the soil water and retain part of it in their tiny internal pores. But there are also large pores between them which allow the rapid penetration of heavy rains and provide rapid drainage for superfluous water, thus reducing surface runoff and the danger of erosion of the soil.

TILTH

A granular or crumb structure is associated with good tilth—a rather vague but useful term used in connection with the fitness of the soil for the growth of plants. A tilth that is ideal for lettuce is not necessarily ideal for beans or other larger seeds and mature roots which can live in coarser soil. But it is not sufficient to have a good tilth just at the surface and a cloddy, lumpy soil below. What is really required, but is sometimes difficult to achieve in practice, is a good system of large pores running right down to bedrock or to the water table, through which fresh air can circulate, and where water is held to meet the needs of the roots.

Maintaining a Good Tilth

To produce a good tilth and keep it once it has been produced are two different arts. A principal enemy of soil structure is exposure to heavy rain, when the raindrops are harmful and batter the crumbs into their individual particles, which then clog the pores after muddy water has subsided. When this clod layer dries, a hard crust forms, varying anywhere from a fraction of an inch to several inches thick, and acts as a barrier to development of seedlings. Therefore, where there is poor germination the soil conditions should be examined. Walking, wheelbarrowing and trucking on wet soil are also powerful agents of destruction, and clay soils which are low in humus soon become compacted and massive if stirred or walked upon when wet.

Tilth formation may also be to some extent the handiwork of certain soil microorganisms whose gums and sticky substances help to bind the particles together. These feed on organic matter, which explains in part why organic matter is such an important element in soil.

The traditional method for building and maintaining tilth is to work in bulky organic manures that rot down into humus, which is a valuable soil conditioner. But to do appreciable good a large amount of organic matter is required, for most bulky organic manures consist largely of water. For instance, a ton of farm manure may consist of 1500 lb. of water and 500 lb. of dry useful matter. Consequently, for any substantial improvement to be made, a good thick (2- to 4-in.) layer of manure, compost, peat moss or similar material should be applied all over the soil and mixed thoroughly with it.

Grassing down is nature's restorative, but unfortunately a number of years in grass are needed before a badly damaged soil fully recovers. The porosity of heavy clay soils can, of course, be increased by mixing in coarse materials such as grit and well-weathered coal cinders, with a view to opening the soil and improving aeration. The mixing of clay into sandy soils helps to bind the sandy-soil particles together into groups and improve their moisture-holding capacity. But as the structure of sandy soils is very easily broken down by rainfall, it is probably better to insure that they are always covered by a crop. Even annual weeds on sandy soils will act as a blanket during the winter and take the first impact of the raindrops, and weeds will, of course, absorb nutrients which would otherwise have been lost in drainage. If the weeds are dug in, in the early spring, an improvement in the soil structure will usually be noted.

Much better than relying upon crops of annual weeds to protect sandy soils is the practice of growing on them a crop of winter rye to be spaded or plowed under in late winter or early spring. Thus nutrients are saved from leaching, the organic content of the soil is increased and good tilth is encouraged. This green-manure crop of winter rye is sown early

enough in fall to insure a 2- to 4-in.-high growth before winter closes in.

It is important that the living conditions for plant roots should be really good. If soil structure is not good the best results will not be obtained from fertilizers and manures, for if the voids or pores in the soil are too small for roots to enter, they cannot explore every nook and cranny, however rich the soil may be in nutrients. Fertilizers, when applied to a soil in poor tilth, cannot be used to their best advantage.

COLOR

Color is a useful guide to soil drainage. Yellow soils often suggest leaching—that is, the washing out of nutrients—as do the gray soils in upland areas. When soils are completely waterlogged their colors become gray or grayish-blue; if they contain much humus they may become black, when waterlogged, due to the formation of iron sulphides. Poor drainage, which is quite common in many soils of heavy texture or in those with hard layers below, cannot always be detected at the surface. If there is any doubt about drainage, dig a few scattered holes 2 or 3 ft. deep, fill them with water and then wait for about 24 hours. If the water disappears within an hour, then the soil is well drained and will be good for all garden plants that require well-drained soils, but if it does not disappear within 24 hours, only shallow-rooted plants can be expected to survive.

Well-drained soils have a pleasant, uniform brown color to a depth of at least 2 ft.; any sign of bluish or rusty mottling below the surface is always suspicious. Where the drainage is bad in winter but improves in summer, rust stains and deposits appear.

Color also provides some indication of the amount of humus in the soil. Brownish-black and dark brown colors

Shallow
compact
topsoil

Lumpy
subsoil

Wet layer

Rusty,
iron-colored
lumps,
indicating
bad drainage

Wet Soil
Plant roots are likely to be suffocated
in this soil when they reach the wet
layer, unless drainage tiles are placed
about 2 to 3 ft. below the soil surface
and are connected to a lake, pond,
sewer or other outlet in such a way
that superfluous water is carried
away, thus permitting air to enter the
soil. The only plants which will
tolerate this soil are bog and
waterside plants.

usually show a good humus content,
but blackness in topsoil in low ground
may indicate bad drainage, particularly if peat moss is present as well.
And in low ground, if the soil surface
is nearly black-gray or grayish-green,
then again poor drainage is clearly
indicated.

It is important to identify such
conditions in advance in order to decide whether they are bad enough to
justify artificial drainage or not. If
the soil is really badly drained, tile
drains for removing the excess water
may need to be installed. In cases
where water comes primarily from
adjoining higher land, an intercepting
ditch or drain may be all that is necessary. Where drainage is not feasible,
only those plants which can tolerate
wet roots can be grown. Or, alternatively, it is possible to use beds raised
above the surrounding level.

It is winter crops, deep-rooted
plants and rapidly growing young
plants that are most prone to serious
damage by poor drainage. Some soils
that are well drained during the
summer and wet only in the spring
will grow annual plants, but roots of
perennials cannot live over the winter
in them.

ORGANIC MATTER

The soil in an acre may contain up to
100 tons or even more of organic
matter, which is made up of plant
and animal debris. Although plants
take a part of their sustenance from
the soil, they also return to it leaves,
decayed stems and roots. And all the
numerous organisms living in the soil
also play their part in producing this
organic matter.

Most soils rarely have enough organic matter unless green crops are
regularly grown for digging in. This
is why bulky composts, manures and
other sources of organic matter are
needed to make good the deficiency.

Living Soil Organisms

The soil is teeming with hordes of small creatures belonging to both the animal and vegetable kingdoms. Vast numbers of earthworms, insects, protozoa and other small animals are at home in the soil, as well as tiny microscopic plants such as bacteria, funguses, algae and actinomycetes. Those of microscopic size are generally called microorganisms, and there may be billions of them in a small lump of soil, a fact which is difficult to believe without seeing them through a powerful microscope.

Not all soils contain the same kinds and numbers of microorganisms, but most rich garden soils contain numerous bacteria. Nearly all of these are beneficial. In fact, were it not for microorganisms the earth might still be covered with rocks only, and would be without its greatest natural resource—the soil.

Uses of Organic Matter

With its teeming millions of workers, the soil is very much like a factory, and the workers—that is to say, the bacteria and many other types of living organisms—all require the food and energy which organic matter provides. Not only does the organic matter provide nutrients for the soil organisms and for plants, but it also improves the physical condition of the soil. In heavy soil it has an opening effect, and prevents soil particles from settling into a solid mass. Roots can run better in soils which have plenty of organic matter. And—more important—in well-drained soils the organisms that decompose organic matter produce substances that lead to granulation and a better structure. Hence the clay soils are made more fluffy and porous, and thus are able to give the roots better opportunities to spread.

Organic matter adds "body" to sandy soils and acts like a sponge in holding moisture. It also holds nutrients. There is little benefit in watering a very sandy soil if there is nothing in it to hold the moisture. Bulky organic materials, such as sawdust, animal manure and peat moss, when applied to the surface of the soil as a mulch, help to control temperature, to reduce losses by evaporation and to keep down weeds.

Organic matter is also a chief source of nitrogen in the soil. Manure or compost derived from a wide range of plants gives a balanced supply of slowly available nutrients.

HUMUS

The bulk of organic matter added to the soil is not decomposed completely within a few weeks or months. Usually a resistant residue of partly decomposed matter remains, which continues to break down very slowly.

This residue is humus: a dark brown or sticky substance, quite different in appearance and properties from the fibrous and bulky material which forms it, and quite different, also, from the commercial material sold as "humus"—really a kind of peat. This commercial humus decays in the soil and leaves a residue of true humus, which also eventually decomposes completely. Not only humus is important as an improver of the soil; so too is the strawy or fibrous material from which it is produced, as well as the products that are formed in the process of breaking down. Constant replenishment of bulky organic materials is necessary in order to maintain the richness of soil for growing healthy flowers and vegetables.

Fresh organic materials vary widely in their breakdown rates and in the amount of plant nutrients, especially nitrogen, that they release. Some contain fairly large amounts of protein or other nitrogen-bearing matter, and these decompose readily. In fact the breakdown processes may go so rapidly and furnish so much nitrogen for plant growth that these materials are regarded primarily as fertilizers. Castor-bean pomace, cottonseed meal and other vegetable-seed remains have the same property. Grass remains decompose very quickly, and so does straw, but the latter is low in protein and so provides very little nitrogen. Most peat mosses decompose slowly and provide only minor supplies of nutrients.

In a fertile soil the organic matter contains about 10 times as much carbon as nitrogen. But leaves, straw, old stems and most of the plant materials commonly available are dry, coarse, and contain much more carbon—they may have 40 times as much carbon as nitrogen. When added to the soil they are not only hard to mix in evenly, but they need a large amount of moisture. Their excess carbon provides the bacteria with a great deal of energy food which acts rather like sugar and helps the soil population to increase enormously. But the soil population also needs nitrogen and phosphates, and these it takes from the soil. To compensate for this, add nitrogen and phosphatic fertilizers when burying undecayed vegetable refuse such as freshly fallen leaves, sawdust and very strawy manures; otherwise the plants will be temporarily deprived of the nitrates they need for growth. Better still, break down this refuse or strawy manure in a compost heap, the purpose of which is to produce an organic matter approximately like that in a fertile soil.

It is a mistake to bury bulky manures too deeply. Always mix them with the topsoil either by placing them against the sides of the trenches when digging; or, provided they are well rotted, by incorporating them

with a rotary cultivator; or by forking them into the soil where the rows are to be sown or planted.

Some people who do not believe in plowing or spading claim to have obtained good results by simply using heavy organic mulches without incorporating them into the soil, but the usual practice is to work the material into the surface to a depth of 6 to 10 in. The nutrients in organic manures are of no direct use to plants until they have been broken down into simpler substances. For example, the protein which is a source of nitrogen in animal manure is of no use at all until it is converted into nitrates, when it can be taken up by the plants. And if there were no microbes in the soil, manure and organic fertilizers such as dried blood and bone meal would yield no nutrients at all.

DECOMPOSITION

Of the many different organisms that break down organic remains, earthworms start the ball rolling by eating debris and partially decomposing it. It is thus reduced to a suitable condition for attack by the microorganisms. During the processes of decay, the dead plant tissues are broken into simpler forms, such as ammonia and carbon dioxide, some of which are broken down further and then become available for the growth of numerous kinds of plants.

In addition to the decomposition of inorganic and organic residues by microorganisms, some special bacteria fix free nitrogen from the air so that it becomes available for the growth of plants. Some nitrogen-fixing bacteria live on the roots of peas, beans, clover and other legumes, and create the characteristic nodules which are so often seen when such plants are lifted from the soil. That is why it is beneficial to bury the roots of plants belonging to the legume family; by so

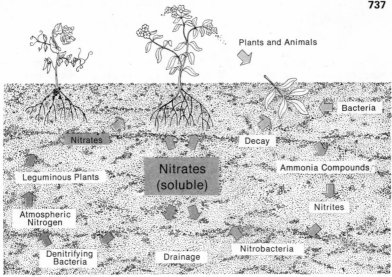

The Nitrogen Cycle
Nitrogen from the atmosphere reaches the soil and plants, and then animals; nitrogen from plant and animal remains is processed by microorganisms and released to plants in the soil.

doing the nitrogen content of the soil is appreciably increased.

Other kinds of bacteria convert ammonia into nitrites, and still others the nitrites into nitrates, which then become available for plant growth. Sulphate of ammonia, used as a fertilizer, depends upon these bacteria for its availability as a nutrient.

There are also mycorrhiza funguses living on the roots of many plants from which they receive at least part of their food. In return they may act as water absorbers for their hosts, and may supply them with certain useful chemicals. But there are harmful as well as useful organisms existing in the soil. Most obvious of the harmful ones are, perhaps, insects such as grubs, but probably much more important are the microscopic and nearly microscopic ones such as the nematodes, funguses and bacteria of kinds which cause plant diseases.

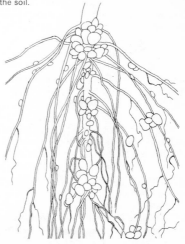

Roots of Leguminous Plants
Small nodules or tubercles form on the roots of peas, beans and other leguminous plants. They contain nitrogen-fixing bacteria which absorb nitrogen gas from the air in the soil and convert it to a form available to plants. In return, the plant provides some of the food required by the bacteria.

Not all soil organisms live on vegetable matter. Some are predatory, living on other soil organisms, so that the crowded community of microorganisms in the soil is rather like a jungle. Many species prey upon others, and the waste products of one become the food of others. Soils rich in organic matter also breed certain molds and bacteria which reduce the numbers of funguses that cause plant diseases, as well as producing powerful antibiotic substances.

Activity of Soil Organisms

The activity of microorganisms varies with the season of the year, usually being greatest in the spring and autumn and least in the summer and winter. Fortunately the spring peak of activity coincides with the maximum growth of plants, and is probably one of the reasons why certain kinds of manures are most effective when applied in spring. Nutrients released by bacterial action are set free into the soil in the greatest amounts at the time they are most needed. So, when fertilizing crops, do not forget the microorganisms. There are so many below the ground, busily feeding, that in an acre of dairy-farm land the weight of livestock below the surface may be as great as the weight of livestock feeding above the ground. The soil organisms have first call on any nutrients which may be applied; the green plants really get what is left over.

In boggy areas, where the ground is waterlogged and often acid, bacteria do not thrive, and consequently plant remains are not entirely decomposed. The operation of breaking down tissues is then taken over by funguses, which can tolerate greater acidity than the bacteria. This results in a slow accumulation of partially decayed vegetable matter that, when compressed, forms peat.

SOIL MOISTURE

The soil is permeated with pores or cavities which are filled with air, water or both. Too much water or too little water are the chief problems facing the gardener, so that the control of water is essential except in places where there are plants that can put up with wet, dry or alternately wet and dry conditions. Many plants are not so adaptable.

THE WATER TABLE

When water falls, either as rain or from a sprinkler, some of it penetrates the ground and is retained by the soil. The soil surface is saturated immediately after rain, but in a well-drained soil this state is only temporary. The surplus water runs away down the worm tracks, crevices and large pores until it reaches rock or some other hard, impermeable layer, upon which it collects, forming a permanently waterlogged layer. The upper surface of this waterlogged layer is known as the "water table." It is very similar to an underground lake.

The water table may be a few feet or even a few inches from the surface, or it may be a hundred feet or more down. In soils by rivers the water table may be at the surface during the winter, and so these soils will be marshy. Waterlogged soils hold no free air and therefore roots of ordinary land plants cannot grow in them because they become suffocated. On sloping ground where the subsoil is very compact, some of the drainage water often appears at the bottom of the slope, forming a marshy place. If the water table is too near the surface, only a small depth will be left for plants to grow in and, as a result, they will be short, shallow-rooted and stunted.

In most places the water table rises and falls but is nearest the surface in

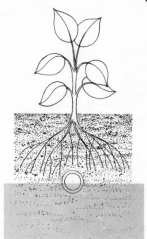

Water Tables
Root restriction occurs
when natural drainage is too slow
and the water table is high.

When drainpipes are
laid, the water table is lowered and
a larger root system can develop.

the winter. Ideally it should be about 4 ft. below the surface. Some of the deeper roots can then obtain moisture directly from the very moist soil layer which lies immediately above the water table.

WATER RETENTION

Sometimes rain merely runs off the surface without penetrating the soil. This "runoff," as it is called, occurs on crusted soils and can be very serious on slopes, where it is always necessary to guard against erosion.

The soil retains water. A sandy soil will hold about 2 gal. per sq. yd. to a depth of 1 ft., whereas a clay soil will hold much more, possibly up to 5 gal. per sq. yd. to a depth of 1 ft.

Plants keep drawing on the water held by the soil. A tomato plant, which even on a dull, humid day uses about a quarter of a pint of water, on a sunny day will take up about 16 times as much. The 2 gal. in a sandy soil will not, therefore, last long, particularly as some of the water

which is held by the soil is not available at all. A proportion of the water in the soil is retained very firmly against the action of roots, the force holding the water being known as the moisture tension. As roots gradually exhaust the available water, they have greater difficulty in overcoming increasing moisture tension. In the smallest pores water is held with greatest tenacity—often so tightly that plants are unable to extract it. When they fail to take up sufficient water for their needs they wilt, even though the soil in which they are growing may still contain quite a lot of moisture.

WHEN TO WATER

It is generally thought that the time to water is when about half the water that could be retained in the soil has gone. To find out this stage exactly is very tricky and requires instruments, but the chart presented on the next page will give some guidance.

When watering, do not sprinkle

MOISTURE CHART			
APPEARANCE AND FEEL OF SOILS			
Amount of Available Soil Moisture	Coarse Texture: Sandy Loam	Medium Texture: Fine Sandy Loam, Loam, Silt Loam	Fine Texture: Clay Loam, Clay
None	Loose, falls through fingers.	Small lumps which break down into powder. Powdery.	Cracked surface, hard, baked appearance.
Less than half water retention	Looks dry, will not form a ball when squeezed.	Crumbly, but will form a ball when squeezed.	Forms a ball quite easily.
Half to three quarters water retention	Forms a ball that crumbles easily.	Forms slightly pliable ball. Smears when rubbed between thumb and finger.	Forms a ball and long threads when rolled between palms of hands.
Three quarters and over water retention	Forms a ball that crumbles easily. Ball easily broken by pressure. Dark color.	Forms very pliable ball. Sticks to hands, particularly when clay content is high.	Very sticky. Forms long threads which can be bent into a ring. Dark color.

just the top of the soil. Always give enough water to wet the soil to a depth of at least a foot, otherwise it will merely evaporate from the surface and do little real good. Sprinkling which merely wets the surface without penetrating to any considerable depth only encourages roots to grow to the surface, so that they suffer severely during hot spells by becoming scorched. A dry, sandy soil needs at least 4 to 5 gal. per sq. yd. to moisten the soil properly to a depth of 1 ft. Watering during hot periods should be done in the evening when evaporation by the sun will be at its lowest. However, watering throughout the day, even in sunshine, is better than allowing plants to suffer from lack of sufficient moisture.

The best way to prevent undue loss of moisture from dry soil is to mulch it with a layer or blanket of rotted material, lawn mowings, straw, sawdust or black polyethylene film, which is put on the surface of the soil to prevent evaporation. Its function is primarily to keep roots cool and moist, but when it consists of organic material it also acts to some extent as a fertilizer.

Although some experiments have seemed to give no support to the belief, most practical gardeners are convinced that soil moisture is conserved by frequent shallow surface cultivation, especially if done as soon as practicable after each rain and irrigation. In any case, such stirring of the surface soil eliminates weeds, prevents caking and promotes growth.

CHEMISTRY OF THE SOIL

At least sixteen chemical elements are necessary for the growth of plants. Carbon, hydrogen and oxygen find their way into the plants from the atmosphere or from soil water.

Those that occur in compounds in the soil are nitrogen, phosphorus, potassium, calcium, magnesium and sulphur, manganese, iron, boron, zinc, copper, molybdenum and chlorine. Although all these elements are essential for healthy growth, some are needed in greater amounts than others. Boron, manganese and some others are regarded as trace elements, because plants need very small amounts of them, but they are just as essential as nitrogen, phosphorus and potassium, which the plants require in much larger amounts.

The soil is like a bank with large reserves of nutrients, though these reserves are not all available for immediate use. They are gradually released by weathering processes, and are then dissolved in the soil solution, from which plants obtain most of their nutrients.

Although the exact method whereby plants take up their nutrients is still a mystery, it is known that they absorb them in liquid rather than in solid form, by means of root hairs growing a short distance behind the root tips. These root hairs make very intimate contact with soil crumbs—a fact readily seen when a seedling is lifted from a seed bed.

The elements most often lacking or seriously deficient in the soil are nitrogen, phosphorus and potassium—the chief fertilizer elements. The other elements are usually present in sufficient quantities, and it is only in special conditions that they have to be provided.

SOIL TESTING

Before using fertilizers it is best to have soil tested to determine its nutritional level. Soil tests can be arranged through a County Agricultural Agent or other local resource.

In order to provide a sample of soil from the garden, take a small amount from 10 to 12 different places, going down to a depth of 6 in., using a trowel. Put the sample into a pail, mix the whole mass together and then take enough of the mixture to fill a pint carton. If any part of the garden or lawn differs from the rest, that part should be sampled separately.

When mailing a sample of soil to the adviser, give as much information as possible about the previous growth and soil treatment. He will then be better able to give accurate recommendations for the immediate and future treatments of your soil. It is helpful, too, to say what plants you intend to grow next.

The fall is generally considered the best time for sampling, since the soil is then in a more normal condition after cropping, and if an application of lime is recommended it will have all winter to act in the ground.

ACID OR ALKALINE SOIL

At the time the soil is tested for nutrients, tests are also made to find out how acid or alkaline it may be. A sour soil is one that is acid; a sweet soil is alkaline. The degree of acidity or alkalinity is expressed by the scale of pH values, ranging in the case of soils that are likely to be cultivated as gardens from 4.0 to 8.5. The neutral point is pH 7.0, that is, the soil is neither acid nor alkaline. All figures *lower* than 7.0 denote acidity, and all figures *higher* than 7.0 denote alkalinity.

There is probably a best pH value for each plant species, but most plants will grow well in soils with fairly wide ranges of pH values. There are exceptions, however. The lowest pH that rhododendrons will thrive in would be disastrous for peas, beans and lettuce. Scabiosa, hart's-tongue fern and most clematis prefer a pH value of

7.5. They fail in conditions that are decidedly acid.

Acid Soils

Just why some crops grow poorly in acid soils is not fully understood. Phosphates become locked up and potassium and magnesium leach more easily from acid soils. Iron and aluminum may be released in too large amounts, thus causing toxicity or poisoning, and this, together with the inactivation of most of the beneficial microorganisms, may be the cause. But soil acidity need be no problem, since liming materials are a simple cure and easy to use.

Alkaline Soils

It is much more difficult to accomplish the acidification of an alkaline soil than the alkalization of one that is acid. Sulphur will help to make the soil acid, but do not use it without first taking expert advice.

Lime

Of the many kinds of liming materials, ground limestone is probably the best form to use. It lasts longest and does not "burn" growing plants. Hydrated lime is also very popular, being fine and more concentrated than ground limestone. It is used not only to correct acidity but also to improve the soil structure and to help to make certain nutrients more available to the plants.

The rates of application of lime depend upon the soil types. A clay soil needs 1½ times as much lime to correct the same degree of acidity as would a sandy soil. So it is always advisable to have soil tested first and not just to apply lime because a neighbor is doing so. He may be making a great mistake, since over-liming can lead to the locking up of nutrients and can cause chlorosis and other deficiency diseases.

Apply lime to the surface of the soil after spading or plowing, and then rake it in. It can be applied at any time of the year, but is likely to wash into the soil quickest with autumn rains. To obtain an even application, delay raking in until the soil is fairly dry.

Gypsum

Because lime (calcium carbonate) reduces soil acidity or increases its alkalinity, under some circumstances its use is not practicable, as, for instance, when the gardener wants to grow acid-soil plants.

Much the same physical improvement of the soil as results from liming can be had by applying gypsum (calcium sulphate) at about the same rate. Gypsum does not reduce soil acidity. It is especially useful for reducing stickiness or pastiness of clay soils and for helping to rehabilitate soils that have been flooded with seawater.

Soil Drainage

Most trees, bushes and other plants will not grow in waterlogged soil and, if excess moisture cannot get away because of an impermeable subsoil, some form of drainage must be provided.

A simple test, to be made in early spring or at any time following a rainy period when the soil is well charged with moisture, is to dig a series of holes 2½ to 3 ft. deep. Heap soil around them and cover so that surface water cannot drain in; if water soon fills the holes to within about 2 ft. of the surface and stands for more than a day or two, additional drainage is required.

In most cases the installation of a system of underground agricultural drains provides the only satisfactory solution, but before this is undertaken it is well to examine the subsoil carefully. It sometimes happens that a thin layer of clay or hardpan, overlying a porous substratum, is holding the water. In that case, relief can often be found by breaking through this layer with a subsoil plow, by double digging or, under exceptional circumstances and under the direction of experienced operators, by the use of dynamite. Such measures are not effective if there is a considerable depth of impervious material.

The first thing to determine before embarking on any land-drainage scheme is where the excess water is to go. The outlet must be lower than the lowest point of the drainpipe system to be installed. A pond, a stream, a ditch or downward-sloping land may provide the simple and obvious answer, or it may be possible to connect with an existing storm sewer. Where no such facility exists, the construction of a dry well must be considered. Unless the dry well connects with reasonably porous soil it may not prove satisfactory, and sites occur where the provision of additional subsurface drainage is simply not practicable. Investigate very thoroughly the disposal problem that an installed drainage system necessitates, and make sure that a practical solution is available before committing yourself to considerable labor and expense which may prove futile.

There are various ways of laying drains, and the layman would be well advised to ask a landscape architect, or perhaps a local surveyor, for advice on the most suitable method.

Land is most effectively drained by means of pipes laid below the soil.

These pipes are obtainable in fixed lengths and may be either of earthenware, composition or permeable concrete. The lengths of earthenware pipe are laid with a ⅛-in. gap between their ends through which the water can seep. But the roots of trees sometimes grow through these gaps, so that after a time the drains may become completely blocked. This trouble can, however, usually be obviated if permeable concrete piping is used, as the lengths can be cemented together.

SIZE OF DRAINPIPES

The main drain, which should be of 6-in.-diameter piping, should run the length of the land to be drained, from the highest to the lowest part of the plot.

The side or branch drains are of 4-in. diameter. They are put in to meet the main drain at an angle of 60° in a herringbone pattern, but no two lateral drains should join both sides of the main drain at the same point.

Though the drains can be laid 3 ft. deep, in many cases they need be no more than 20 in. deep. The depth depends to a certain extent on where the impermeable layer of clay lies, and therefore where the water is held up.

Dig truncated-V-shaped trenches for the drainpipes, as shown below.

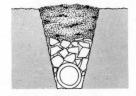

Cross section of drainpipe in position. The truncated-V-shaped trench should be at least 20 in. deep, and the pipe should be covered with rough clinkers, broken bricks or coarse gravel, so that water can trickle through quickly.

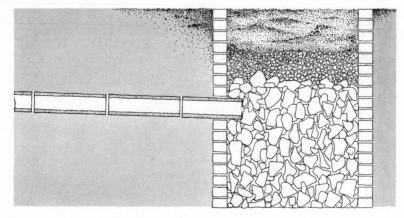

A dry well should be built if there is no ditch or other suitable outlet at the lowest point of the garden. It should have openwork masonry sides and be covered, or filled for most of its depth with coarse clinkers or brick rubble.

Lay the main drain first, and then set the laterals in place. Always begin at the outlet, the lowest point in the drainage system, and work backward and upward. Never give a steep slope to the pipes. A fall of 3 to 6 in. in each 100 ft. of running length is adequate. To check that the pipes have the right fall, put pegs into the bottom of the trenches, and place a board across them with a builder's level laid on it. This should be done regularly as the work proceeds.

DRY WELL

If a dry well must be provided, it should be dug 4 to 5 ft. deep and at least 4 ft. wide. The sides should be supported by open brickwork, field-stone or concrete blocks, arranged so that water can easily seep between them and out into the soil, and the hole may be filled with large clinkers, brick rubble or similar material. Over the well place a slab of concrete or stone and a layer of earth.

Cover the drainpipes with gravel, rough clinkers or broken bricks to allow the water to trickle through

quickly. Then put the soil back (subsoil underneath, topsoil on top), leaving the surface slightly raised to allow the soil to settle to the right level.

ALTERNATIVE METHOD

If drainpipes are not to be used, then drainage trenches can be dug. These trenches should be 2 ft. deep, the main trench being 1 ft. wide and running to the lowest part of the garden. The side trenches should be narrower and should run obliquely into the main trench. Fill the bottom 6 or 8 in. of all the trenches with large stones, big clinkers, brickbats or similar material through which the water can percolate. This method is less likely to be successful than well-installed drainpipes.

WHEN TO INSTALL

Drainage work in the garden is better done in the late autumn, or even winter, when the ground is not frozen. More time is available, as there are few other gardening jobs to do, and the interference with growing plants will be at a minimum.

CULTIVATING THE SOIL
How to Insure Best Results

Machine Cultivation—Patterns of Spading—Types of Hoes—Other Tools—Mulching

THE SOIL PROVIDES an anchorage for plants as well as a reservoir of needed moisture and nutrients. Water and other elements that the plant transforms into foods are absorbed through the roots. As a general rule the more extensive and vigorous the root system, the more satisfactory will be the growth and health of the plant. Roots need oxygen in addition to water and other nutrients, and this they obtain from the air that is in the soil.

The soil, then, is an extremely important part of the plant's environment, and because it is one very susceptible to manipulation, every gardener must learn how to cultivate and manage it advantageously. Gardeners are rarely able to locate their plots on ideal soils; circumstances other than the character of the soil normally determine where one lives and raises plants. Fortunately, almost any soil can be improved and brought into fertile condition by intelligent management, and the maintenance of the soil fertility also largely depends upon understanding its nature and characteristics and knowing how best to cultivate it.

Here we shall consider the manipulative operations connected with the management of garden soils. Fundamentally they consist of:
1. Plowing, rotary tilling or spading to a depth of 8 in. or more to bury surface portions of the soil and bring new parts to the surface where they will be affected by sun, wind, rain and freezing, to mix in organic matter and other aids to growth, to bury weeds, to improve drainage and to increase the amount of air in the soil.
2. Forking or harrowing and raking immediately before sowing or planting to develop a condition or tilth most favorable to the crops that are to be planted.
3. Shallowly cultivating the surface with a hoe or cultivator to destroy weeds, to admit air and to conserve moisture.
4. Mulching to control weeds, to conserve moisture, to modify soil temperatures and sometimes to provide nutrients.

PLOWING

Except when extensive areas are being prepared, tractors are not ordinarily used in gardens. They are essentially agricultural rather than horticultural implements. Nevertheless, it is sometimes convenient or advisable to plow ground in preparation for vegetables, new lawns and landscape operations; an experienced worker should operate the equipment. Plow only when the soil is not excessively wet, and so that weeds are buried and manure (or other material to be turned under) is covered. If topsoil is shallow, depth of plowing should be such that an inch or two of subsoil (not more) is brought up and mixed with the topsoil.

ROTARY TILLING

Rotary tillers are among the most useful of garden machines. They make possible deep soil cultivation without hard physical effort. Because of the great amount of work that can be accomplished with them in a very limited time, the gardener is often able to make ready the ground and complete a planting during a brief spell of favorable weather—a task which would be impossible to accomplish with hand tools.

For deep soil preparation, to a depth of 6 to 8 in. or more, a heavy-duty rotary tiller is needed. The lighter machines made especially for amateur gardeners are not powerful enough for this work although they are very useful for shallower soil operations and for surface cultivation. In many areas rotary tillers and operators can be hired on a piecework basis or by the hour.

Whichever arrangement is entered into, take care that the operator attains an adequate and uniform depth. These machines have two speeds, and maximum depth is reached only when the machine is working at its slower speed. In hard ground it is often necessary to go over the area twice to achieve the required depth. Do this by tilling a strip as wide as the machine, then returning immediately along the *same* strip. Repeat this on the next strips until the area is finished. Always work by strips; never rototill the *entire* area before going over it a second time. In this way you can always walk beside the tiller on firm ground and will not step on the first tilling.

SPADING

The soil should be turned over to a depth of 8 to 10 in. During this process any weeds that are growing on the surface should be buried.

When spading a plot, first make a

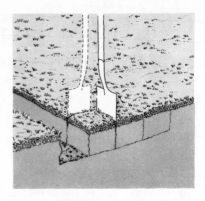

First strip removed; second strip about to be turned over

Two strips turned over; third strip about to be turned over

trench or ditch—1 ft. wide and about 10 in. deep—at one end of the area. Put the soil from this trench in a heap at the other end of the plot, so that when the plot has been dug, the soil from the first trench is nearby to fill in the last trench.

Then spade over a 6-in. strip of soil bordering the trench, throwing it forward and at the same time turning it upside down, so that surface soil and weeds are buried and previously covered portions of soil are brought to the top. Thus a new trench of the same dimensions as the first will be opened. This process is repeated until the end of the plot is reached, when the soil first excavated is used to fill the last trench.

Spading is done by plunging the blade of the spade into the soil at right angles to the trench, and then plunging it parallel to the trench so that a rough square chunk of soil the width of the spade is cut out. It is then simple to lift the chunk of soil, invert it and throw it forward into the trench alongside. If available, put some well-rotted compost or manure at the bottom of the trench before the soil is thrown in. Apply this at the rate of at least a pailful to a running yard of trench.

It is very important when spading to leave the surface as level as possible, but this should be accomplished by properly spreading the soil directly from the spade. Forking and raking the surface to achieve fineness should be delayed until immediately before seeding or planting is to be done.

SPADING FORK

A broad, flat-tined fork is best for digging very heavy clay soils.

The object of forking is to help break down the soil in the top 4 or 5 in. and thus aerate it. Plunge the fork into the soil at an angle of about 50°, lift the soil and if possible invert it when dropping it back. It is useful to put a line across the plot and then to fork over an area about 3 ft. wide right across, then move back the line another 3 ft. and work over this new area—and so on until the whole plot has been forked.

ROLLING OR TREADING

After the land has been forked in the spring it may be necessary to roll it with a light roller in order to consolidate the soil a little and to prevent it

from being "puffy." If land is too loose it may dry out too quickly and the plant roots may be unable to get proper anchorage and to collect moisture and nutrients they need. Both forking and light rolling are often necessary; with a light roller the soil will be left less firm than it was before forking was started.

Rolling also helps to break down any lumps of soil and to leave the surface level, thus making it easier to carry on the next operation—raking.

If a light roller is not available, then the plot can be trodden carefully from one end to the other. When doing this, adopt a sideways and shuffling motion so that the whole of the land is evenly firmed.

RAKING

The purpose of raking is to break down the top $\frac{1}{2}$ in. or 1 in. of soil into particles that will be finer than grains of wheat. Raking normally follows the forking and light rolling or treading which has made the soil level, and the fine tilth it produces is then a suitable medium in which to sow seed.

Raking is done by running the teeth of the rake evenly and at the same depth through the soil, in a backward-and-forward motion, and also to the left and right if need be. If raking is done carefully no mound of soil will be left when the end of the plot is reached. Any large stones, twigs, roots or other debris are picked out as the work proceeds.

HOEING AND CULTIVATING
Scuffle Hoe

Scuffle hoeing of bare ground between growing plants (except such notorious surface-rooters as azaleas, camellias and rhododendrons) should be done, if possible, every week from spring to fall. There is no point in waiting until there are weeds, for if the hoeing is done regularly the weed seedlings will

Scuffle hoe (left) for eliminating sprouting weeds; draw hoe (right) for larger weeds, and for making "drills" for planting seeds

be killed just as they start to germinate. Move backward while hoeing, so that all footmarks are removed.

Use this hoe between rows of vegetables and herbs, between plants in the perennial beds and between roses.

The Draw Hoe

The common garden or draw hoe is required when weeds are 2 or 3 in. high. Use it with a chopping and dragging action so that it cuts through the soil and weeds and chops the weeds out.

Hand Cultivator

Growth is encouraged and water absorption and water retention of the soil improved by keeping the top inch or so of surface in a loose condition at all times. This creates and maintains a soil mulch. Hoeing, which is done primarily for the suppression of weeds, accomplishes this purpose. Pronged hand cultivators, both long-handled and short-handled, are also employed to keep the surface soil loose. They are less effort to use than hoes but are not

as effective in eliminating weeds. They are especially appropriate for working areas between growing plants that are essentially weed-free.

MULCHING

Mulching is the application of a layer of suitable material over the surface of the ground, first to reduce the evaporation of moisture from the soil, and second to smother annual weed seedlings and so prevent them from growing. A third objective, that of providing additional nutrients, depends of course upon the kind of mulch material used. Mulches are sometimes used also to protect the roots of plants from cold or heat. They may be put along rows of strawberries to keep the fruit clean.

For soft (bush or cane) fruits a mulch in the form of clean straw 1 ft. deep is often used all over the ground. For the flowering-shrub border, use compost, bagasse, sawdust, peat moss, peanut shells, leaves, buckwheat hulls or other suitable available material to a depth of 3 to 5 in. For perennial borders, rose gardens, etc., any of the mulch materials mentioned except straw is suitable. Which to use largely depends on cost, appearance and availability.

Wide strips of black plastic film, heavy roofing paper and some other inorganic materials are also used as mulches—though organic materials are preferable, as they gradually decay and so add humus to the soil.

Do not apply a mulch too early in the season or it will retard the warming of the soil. It also lowers the night temperature of the air immediately above it, a point of importance where plants of doubtful hardiness are concerned. Make sure that the soil is moist before applying the mulch. Remember that a mulch, while conserving soil moisture, may act as a barrier to light rain.

FERTILIZERS AND MANURES—
Wisely Used They Work Wonders

Organic and Inorganic—Signs of Need—Types of Chemical Fertilizers—Organic Fertilizers—Hints on Use

THE WORDS "fertilizer" and "manure" are often used synonymously, but a fertilizer is preferably considered to be a substance that supplies in more concentrated form than do animal manures one or several of the three nutrients—nitrogen, phosphorus and potassium—most needed by plants. Fertilizer does not provide in any great bulk the humus-forming organic materials that animal manures do. A fertilizer is used primarily as a source of nutrients, a manure as a source of these as well as for the soil-building qualities of its organic matter.

Fertilizers are applied at the rate of a few ounces per square yard, manures at the rate of several pounds per square yard. All fertilizers should be used carefully, as they can produce unwanted effects. While they supply nutrients that improve crop growth and quality, they also increase the concentration of dissolved substances in the soil solution. If this occurs excessively, it becomes difficult or impossible for the roots to absorb the water and nutrients they need. It is therefore important to remember that overdoses can cause serious wilting, even the death, of plants. So do not give more than the recommended amounts. The same harmful effects can, of course, result from applying too great an amount of fresh manure to the soil.

FERTILIZERS
Nonprotein Organic

The chemist regards all carbon compounds as organic. At one time the only sources of such materials were plants and animals—organisms that were alive or had been alive. It is now possible to make carbon-containing compounds artificially (the first to be synthesized was urea), with the result that we have both natural and synthetic organic nitrogen fertilizers. The synthetics may be referred to as "nonprotein organics" to distinguish them from the "protein organics" derived from plant and animal sources. The two nonprotein organics used as fertilizers—urea and calcium cyanamide—unlike the protein organics, are readily and rapidly soluble in water. They contain a much higher percentage of nitrogen but add no humus-forming material to the soil. From the gardener's point of view these synthetics have more of the characteristics of inorganic than of protein organic fertilizers.

Inorganic

Inorganic fertilizers are manufactured or are derived from mineral deposits. They may be used either by themselves to supply a specific nutrient, or they may be combined to become a mixed or so-called complete fertilizer.

SIGNS OF FERTILIZER NEED

Experienced gardeners learn to recognize—from many indications presented by the soil and by the plants that grow in it—when various nutrient elements are in short supply and when they are present in excessive amounts.

The ability to judge fertilizer requirements by these means is helpful and useful in day-to-day practice, but soil tests provide a more certain way of determining the basic soil deficiencies. They provide the information with which to plan a sound, overall fertilizing program. Soil tests can be arranged through the local County Agricultural Agent or other similar local resource. Among the practical indicators of probable nutrient deficiencies are the following.

Nitrogen

Nitrogen is likely to be in short supply if:
1. The topsoil is badly eroded or has been stripped in building operations.
2. The soil is very sandy.
3. The soil is very acid.
4. The soil lacks a reasonable humus content.
5. The soil has a grayish color.
6. Large amounts of undecayed organic material such as straw, sawdust or green manure have recently been mixed with it.
7. Foliage is yellowish and stunted.
8. The leaves of trees fall early (and not as the result of excessive drought).
9. Plants tend to flower and seed prematurely.

Nitrogen is likely to be in adequate or excessive supply if:
1. An abundant supply of humus is in the soil.

2. Vigorous stem and leaf growth make a rich green color.
3. Plants are delayed in reaching their flowering and fruiting stages (mature slowly).

Phosphorus

Phosphorus is likely to be lacking if:
1. Subsurface drainage is poor.
2. The soil is of very fine texture.
3. The soil is very acid.
4. The soil is lacking in adequate amounts of humus.
5. The plants remain stunted even when fertilizers supplying nitrogen and potash are applied.
6. The leaves of plants, especially tomatoes and corn, assume a purplish color.

Phosphorus is likely to be available in adequate amounts if:
1. Plants grow with normal vigor and mature at the normal time.
2. Good root systems are developed.

Potash

Potash is likely to be lacking in adequate amounts if:
1. The soil is very sandy.
2. The soil is grayish in color.
3. The soil is chiefly muck or peat.
4. Older leaves become mottled or yellowish between the veins and scorched at their margins.

Potash is probably present in adequate supply if:
1. Plant growth is normal and vigorous and the plants develop good root systems.
2. The foliage shows no obvious symptoms of potash deficiency.

WHAT TO BUY

Once the results of a soil test and the needs of the plants to be raised are known, you may buy the fertilizers from garden-supply dealers in the form of crystalline powders or in pellet or granular form, the latter being easier to store and spread. There are also some brand-name fertilizers that are sold as liquids.

Although manures may sometimes be obtained from farmers and a good supply of wood ashes may be saved at home, it is generally more convenient, and usually necessary, to purchase supplies.

The analyses that are shown on container labels are useful guides to the effectiveness of fertilizers—and are the guarantee of the minimum percentages of nitrogen, phosphorus and potassium that they contain. The phosphorus content is expressed as P_2O_5 (phosphoric acid), potassium as K_2O (potash) and nitrogen as N. For example, nitrate of soda has an analysis of 16 percent nitrogen, which means that 100 lb. of this fertilizer has 16 lb. of nitrogen in it.

Urea, however, has 46 percent nitrogen, so about one third of the quantity of urea is needed to provide the equivalent amount of nutrient that is contained in nitrate of soda.

Inorganic fertilizers are not simply nutrients but are salts having two portions—namely, the nutrient or wanted portion, and the unwanted portion. One cannot be had without the other.

In nitrate of soda the unwanted portion is sodium, which can easily spoil the tilth of heavy soils if this fertilizer is applied too generously. A reasonable amount of sodium benefits beets, but is apt to spoil the quality of potatoes. To insure the best results and to do this economically, it is important to select the right fertilizer and, when using brand-name products, to follow the manufacturer's directions.

Some advocates of the use of only protein organic fertilizers maintain that inorganic and the nonprotein organic fertilizers are harmful to plants and to man—who eats the plants. They say that the nutrient elements are made synthetically or are derived from purely mineral substances, often obtained by the combination of strong acids and alkalis. But there is no scientific evidence to show that crops grown with nonprotein fertilizers are inferior in quality or lower in nutritional value than those grown with fertilizers derived from plant and animal products.

Complete and Mixed Fertilizers

Nitrogen, phosphorus and potash can be provided by making separate applications of, say, sulphate of ammonia for nitrogen, superphosphate for phosphorus, and sulphate of potash for potassium.

Alternatively, the gardener can mix these three fertilizers together and spread in one application. But a commercial fertilizer that comes ready-mixed saves a good deal of trouble and can be relied upon to be uniform throughout. Many manufacturers have their own brands and specify for which plants they are to be used. The best are made from the fertilizers already described. Those that include ammonium phosphates are more concentrated than those based on superphosphate.

Content of Commercial Fertilizers

When a fertilizer contains nitrogen, phosphorus and potash, it is called a "complete" fertilizer; when only one or two of these are included, it is an "incomplete" fertilizer. The law requires that all fertilizers sold be clearly labeled with an analysis giving the percentage of nitrogen, available phosphoric acid and available potash. The figures of the analysis denoting these percentages always appear on the containers. The first figure denotes the percentage of nitrogen (marked N), the second figure the percentage of soluble phosphoric acid (marked P) and the third figure the percentage of available potash (marked K). If one of the three major elements is lacking in a fertilizer a zero appears in its place; thus 5-0-10 means 5 percent nitrogen, no soluble phosphoric acid and 10 percent potash.

When selecting mixed or complete fertilizers, take note of the ratio of N, P and K as well as the actual percentage of each. Fertilizer ratio is the analysis reduced to its simplest terms. For example, the 5-10-5 fertilizer has a ratio of 1-2-1. A 10-20-10 fertilizer has the same 1-2-1 ratio but is twice as concentrated; 50 lb. of a 10-20-10 will provide as much nutrient value as will 100 lb. of a 5-10-5 fertilizer.

Extra figures are added to the analysis in some geographic areas, where soils are known to be deficient in certain trace elements as well as in the three standard nutrients that are needed (N, P and K)—and these trace elements are guaranteed to be present in the fertilizer. In Florida, for example, fertilizers with an analysis of 4-6-8-3-1-½ are used. The last three figures mean that 3 percent magnesium oxide, 1 percent manganese oxide and ½ percent copper oxide will also be contained in the fertilizer.

LIQUID FERTILIZERS

Liquid fertilizers are becoming more popular for supplying nutrients for plants, particularly house plants and those grown in home greenhouses.

The modern commercially prepared liquid fertilizers, marketed as concentrated solutions or as solid mixtures for making into concentrated solutions, are consistent in composition and convenient to use. The main constituents of most liquid fertilizers are potassium nitrate, monoammonium phosphate, and ammonium nitrate or urea. These are mixed in various proportions to give a wide

range of different analyses to suit the needs of most crops and soils.

Liquid fertilizers are not necessarily better than solid kinds. A gardener who is skillful in using solid fertilizers will no doubt obtain results just as good as those he would get with liquids and vice versa. But liquids are popular because of the ease and speed with which nutrients can be applied in balanced form to meet the immediate requirements of plants. They also save time in fertilizing and watering, since these are done in one operation. They sink evenly into the soil, where they are quickly absorbed by the roots.

Application

Liquid fertilizing may be more expensive than using solids. Concentrates sold in bottles have to be diluted with water according to the manufacturer's instructions, which should be carefully adhered to.

If a big area is to be covered, buy a diluter attachment for a garden hose. The liquid fertilizer is poured into it. Dilution and spraying of the fertilizer take place when the hose is connected to a running faucet.

LEAF FERTILIZING

Plants can absorb nutrients through their leaves when they are sprayed with dilute solutions of fertilizers. Radioactive tests show that micronutrients applied in this way can be in the sap stream within one hour after application. Thus, the long journey from the root to the leaf is avoided and nutrient deficiencies may be corrected rapidly.

Fertilizing through leaves, called foliar fertilizing, may be preferable to soil dressings for plants with poor or diseased root systems. This is useful for giving a boost to growth during dry weather when there is little soil water in which to dissolve fertilizers. Deficiencies of manganese, iron and other nutrients in plants growing in alkaline soils can be quickly corrected by means of suitable substances which are applied as leaf sprays.

To strengthen and increase leaf growth, a spray containing urea at the rate of 1 oz. per 2 gal. water will be sufficient to cover 25 to 30 sq. ft. of soil fully covered with foliage. Potassium nitrate, when applied at the same rate, will help to harden soft, sappy tissues without checking growth. Excellent brand-name fertilizers adapted for foliar application are available.

Apply the sprays when the plants have developed enough leaves to insure a reasonable amount of leaf absorption, and then spray once a week or according to the manufacturer's instructions.

Use a fine, mistlike spray to cover both sides of the leaves. Keep the spray moving the whole time to insure that the plants receive a reasonable and equal amount of liquid. Add a wetting agent at rates according to the manufacturer's instructions when spraying plants with shiny leaves; otherwise the liquid will run off the leaves without being absorbed.

SEPARATE APPLICATIONS

If there are special soil conditions requiring the use of individual nutrients, or if you wish to make your own mixtures, the following are usually available on order from garden-supply houses.

Nitrogenous Fertilizers

Nitrate of Soda (16 percent N): This is a quick-acting stimulant for applying to growing crops in spring and summer, particularly when plants have been checked by cold weather or pest attacks. Provided the soil is moist, the effect can usually be seen within a few days of application. Nitrate of soda is suitable for use on acid and peaty soils, but may harm the tilth of clay soils if applied too freely. It has a slight alkalizing effect. The usual rate of application is $\frac{1}{2}$ to 1 oz. per sq. yd. It may also be used as a liquid fertilizer, dissolved in water at the rate of $\frac{1}{2}$ oz. per gal.

Sulphate of Ammonia (21 percent N) This is slightly slower-acting than nitrate of soda, usually becoming available to plants within 10 to 14 days of application in the summer, but taking a somewhat longer time in cold weather. Although suitable as a topdressing on a wide range of crops and lawns, it is generally best used in combination with other fertilizers to make up a complete or mixed dressing. It tends to make the soil acid and thus is often most useful on well-limed or alkaline soils. It can be employed as a liquid fertilizer in the same way and same rate as nitrate of soda.

Nitrate of Potash (15 percent N, 36 percent K_2O): This is a very useful topdressing for supplying both nitrogen and potash, and is applied at 1 to 2 oz. per sq. yd. in spring and summer. It is very quick-acting. It also makes a useful liquid fertilizer when 1 oz. is dissolved in 2 gal. water.

Urea (46 percent N): The most concentrated of nitrogenous fertilizers, this has its nitrogen in a form that rapidly becomes available to plants. When applied repeatedly it has a slightly acidifying effect. It is used at the rate of $\frac{1}{8}$ to $\frac{1}{4}$ oz. per sq. yd. It may be dissolved in water at the rate of $\frac{1}{8}$ oz. per gallon and employed as a liquid fertilizer.

Ureaform fertilizers are synthetic combinations of urea and formaldehyde. Their advantage is that the nitrogen they contain is released slowly over a period of many weeks or months, and thus they more nearly resemble animal manures in this respect than does any other nonprotein source of nitrogen.

Calcium Cyanamide (21 to 22 percent N): This fertilizer, often called cyanamid, contains a high percentage of lime and, being alkaline, reduces soil acidity. Its original form is harmful to plant life (it is actually used as a weed killer) but when mixed with moist soil, in from two to seven days it is converted into urea and hydrated lime, both valuable. Calcium cyanamide, then, must always be thoroughly mixed with the soil well in advance of planting. It is used at the rate of $\frac{1}{2}$ to 1 oz. per sq. yd.

Phosphatic Fertilizers

Superphosphate (16 to 20 percent soluble P_2O_5): This is the most popular fertilizer for supplying readily available phosphates before sowing or planting. It is applied at the rate of 2 to 3 oz. per sq. yd., usually in combination with other fertilizers. It can be used at any time of the year without fear of its being washed out, but is most usually applied during the spring and summer. Double superphosphate (32 percent P_2O_5) is applied at approximately half the rate of ordinary superphosphate. Treble superphosphate (40 to 47 percent P_2O_5) is employed at about one third of that rate.

Ground Phosphate Rock (30 to 40 percent P_2O_5): Although this contains about twice as much phosphoric acid as ordinary superphosphate, that important nutrient is relatively unavailable in this form. Because of this, the use of ground phosphate rock should be regarded as a means of building up the phosphorus content of the soil over a period of many years rather than as a method of rapidly improving soil fertility. The more finely the phosphate rock is ground, the more quickly available is the nutrient element it contains. It may be used at the rate of 6 to 8 oz. per sq. yd. For most garden purposes superphosphate must be considered preferable to ground phosphate rock.

Basic Slag (8 to 12 percent P_2O_5): This is a slow-acting phosphatic fertilizer. It gives best results on acid soils in wet climates when applied in the autumn at the rate of 4 to 6 oz. per sq. yd. Its lime content helps to correct acidity. Little is used in North America; comparatively small amounts are manufactured in Alabama.

Potassic Fertilizers

Sulphate of Potash (48 percent K_2O): This is the most popular potassic fertilizer and is safe for all plants. It can be applied at any time of the year at 1 to 2 oz. per sq. yd. without fear of loss by drainage. It is generally combined with other fertilizers to provide a mixed or complete fertilizer before sowing or planting. It is also used as a topdressing for crops that have to occupy the ground for a long time.

Muriate of Potash (48 to 62 percent K_2O): This fertilizer is more concentrated than the sulphate form. Although suitable for a wide range of plants, it may damage strawberries, currants and tomatoes. Normal rates of application are 1 to 2 oz. per sq. yd.

PROTEIN ORGANIC FERTILIZERS

Organic fertilizers other than the nonprotein ones (urea and calcium cyanamide) are of animal or vegetable origin, often being derived from slaughterhouse refuse and vegetable wastes such as seed residues. They are mainly used for supplying nitrogen, but some animal products contain bone residue, which gives phosphates also, and many supply some potash as well as various trace elements.

The nitrogen in these fertilizers is in the form of protein, which is not immediately available to plants. Soil organisms change it into exactly the same nitrates as are available in inorganic and nonprotein organic fertilizers. This class of fertilizer—dried blood and bone meal, for example—does produce some humus, but it does not provide a sufficient amount to have a significant effect at normal rates of application.

If the soil is acid, too wet or too cold, protein organic fertilizers will not break down properly, since these are the conditions that are unfavorable to bacteria; unless bacteria are working properly, the nitrogen in the fertilizer will not be released.

Although protein organic fertilizers are generally thought to be slow-acting, the nutrients in dried blood, fish meal and several others become available quite quickly in warm, moist and well-limed soils. But the speed of action also depends upon how finely ground they are. Dusty forms of hoof and horn meal work almost as quickly as dried blood or even sulphate of ammonia, whereas coarse forms may take years to become exhausted. Among the advantages claimed for the protein organics are, first, that they are longer-lasting than other fertilizers and, second, that they give a steady supply of nitrogen rather than a concentrated supply for a brief period only, and so are less likely to encourage rank growth even if applied at the wrong time.

A fairly heavy dressing of nitrogen in the form of hoof and horn meal, say 4 oz. per sq. yd., can safely be given before sowing, whereas the equivalent amount of nitrate of soda would cause damage.

Nitrogen in protein form is less likely to be leached out of heavily watered soils.

Protein organics are often preferred to other types of fertilizers because they are much less likely to scorch foliage they fall upon, a decided advantage when a topdressing has to be given to crops with creeping stems and spreading leaves.

But the protein organics are comparatively expensive and have no precise or fixed composition. While sulphate of ammonia always has about 21 percent of nitrogen, the nitrogen content of dried blood may vary from 7 to 14 percent. Some waste materials may show quite a high percentage of nitrogen, but this may not be of any value in the year of application because of very slow breakdown. Leather wastes and some plastic wastes are of this nature.

Kinds

Dried Blood (7 to 14 percent N): This has a quick and sustained action in warm soils. It is very useful for applying to plants with spreading foliage and is very suitable for greenhouse plants. The best samples are fine, dusty red powders. Dried blood is used as a rule only for topdressing growing plants at the rate of 2 to 3 oz. per sq. yd. or for feeding pot plants at the rate of about 1 tsp. for a 9-in. pot.

An almost completely soluble form can be used at the rate of 1 tbsp. to 1 gal. water as a liquid fertilizer.

Hoof and Horn Meal (7 to 15 percent N): This is available in various particle sizes. Fine grinds, that is to say from $\frac{1}{8}$ in. to dust, are quick-acting and at the same time have a lasting effect. But coarse grinds ($\frac{3}{8}$ in.) and hoof parings are very slow-acting. Fine grinds are used for mixing in potting soils to supply nitrogen. Hoof and horn meal, at the rate of 2 to 4 oz. per sq. yd., is generally worked into the ground before sowing or planting.

Heat-Dried Activated Sewage Sludge (4 to 6 percent N): Dried and processed sewage sludge is sold by some municipalities as a fertilizer. It is powdery, and quite safe and inoffensive to handle. It is mainly used for supplying nitrogen, but it contains an appreciable amount of available phosphoric acid and smaller amounts of potash and trace elements. It also contributes a little organic matter. Milorganite is one of the best known of these products; others are Akra-Soilite, Humite, Nitrohumus, Nitroganic, San-Diegonite and Tol-e-gro.

Bone Meal (3 to 5 percent N, 20 to 35 percent P_2O_5): Raw bone meal can be obtained in coarse, medium and fine grades, the latter being fairly quick-acting. Bones crushed to $\frac{1}{4}$- and $\frac{1}{2}$-in. particles are slow in action and will supply phosphates for two years or more; fine bone meal becomes soluble as the organic acids in the soil act upon its dusty particles. The slow and steady availability of nutrients from bone meal, and the absence of harmful unwanted portions, make it a very safe fertilizer for young plants. The usual rate of application is 4 to 8 oz. per sq. yd., and it is used either by itself or with other fertilizers. The small amount of nitrogen that it does contain is as a rule quite quickly available.

Steamed bone meal, because of the steaming treatment to which it has been submitted and because it is ground fine, acts more quickly than raw bone meal, but its effect is exhausted within a year. It contains less nitrogen (1 to 2 percent) than raw bone meal, but its phosphoric acid

content is higher (22 to 30 percent).

Guano: Guano used to be the term applied to droppings of seabirds, which were collected from uninhabited islands off Peru, but it now applies to various kinds of natural manures, including the droppings of bats, seals and turtles, and usually includes remains of dead bodies of the birds or animals—feathers, bones, hides, etc. Guano is normally applied in the spring, two to three weeks before sowing or planting, or as a topdressing, at rates of 2 to 4 oz. per sq. yd.

Fish Meal: This and other fertilizer products are obtained from fish wastes, and are usually supplemented with inorganic fertilizers and sold as fish manures under brand names. These fish manures are quick-acting, giving a sustained supply of nitrogen and phosphorus. They are generally used at the rate of 2 to 4 oz. per sq. yd., and are best applied a few days before sowing or planting.

Some fish fertilizers have a strong odor. The percentage of nitrogen in fish meals ranges from 5 to 10 and that of phosphoric acid from 2 to 6.

Tankage: This product of slaughterhouses is a processed meat meal that contains 9 to 11 percent nitrogen and from merely a trace to $3\frac{1}{2}$ percent phosphoric acid. It is a most excellent fertilizer. The product called bone tankage may contain up to 6 percent nitrogen and from 7 to 20 percent phosphoric acid. Tankage is used in the same manner as dried blood.

Cottonseed Meal (6 to 9 percent N, 2 to 3 percent P_2O_5, $1\frac{1}{2}$ to 2 percent K): This is a very good protein organic fertilizer. The nitrogen is released slowly over a long period. The rate of application is usually 3 to 7 oz. per sq. yd.

Castor-Bean Pomace (5 to 6 percent N, 2 percent P_2O_5, 1 percent K): This is an excellent fertilizer. It is poisonous if eaten by animals. It is applied at from 4 to 8 oz. per sq. yd.

Pulverized Manures: Dried and pulverized sheep, goat, cattle and poultry manures are favorites of gardeners and are very useful and easy to apply. Poultry manure contains 5 to 6 percent nitrogen, 3 to 6 percent phosphoric acid and 1 to 2 percent potash; the others mentioned analyze 1 to 2 percent nitrogen, 1 to 2 percent phosphoric acid and 2 to 3 percent potash. The dried and pulverized poultry manure may be used at 2 to 4 oz. per sq. yd., and the others at about twice that rate of application.

Wood Ashes: Wood ashes contain varying amounts of potash according to the materials burned. The richest wood ashes come from the burning of hardwoods, but all wood ashes are valuable as sources of potash. They should be collected and stored as soon as they are cool enough to handle, and then kept perfectly dry; otherwise the potassium carbonate will be washed out. About 4 to 8 oz. per sq. yd. are required to give as much potash as there is in sulphate of potash applied at 1 oz. per sq. yd. Heavier dressings tend to cake the soil surface and destroy tilth. Wood ashes are inclined to make the soil alkaline.

BULKY ORGANIC MANURES

Fertilizers are not complete substitutes for manures or other bulky organic materials; they are supplements.

Many soils deteriorate when the humus level falls too low, and bulky manures and other types of organic materials may be used to prevent and correct this. But manures are difficult to obtain easily or at a reasonable price. Farm manure is the droppings of horses, pigs or cows, the litter used for their bedding and the urine which has been soaked up by it.

Horse manure is the richest and the driest. A heap of horse manure soon starts to steam, thus showing that rapid fermentation is taking place. It is therefore called a hot manure. Fresh horse manure from riding or racing stables is often merely urine-soaked straw with a few droppings, which dwindles to a very small heap when it is stacked.

In cattle yards, as straw is added daily and is trodden into the manure, a very much denser material is obtained. One cu. yd. of cattle manure can weigh as much as 1500 to 1600 lb. in contrast to a similar measure of fresh racing-stable manure—which may weigh less than half a ton. Cattle manure is wetter and lower in nutrients than horse manure, and decomposes more slowly in the soil, which makes it especially valuable for sandy soils.

Similarly, pig manure is slow-acting and long-lasting. Because it is slow to ferment it is a cold manure and therefore unsuitable for the making of hotbeds. When fresh it is caustic and liable to burn the roots of young plants. It is best composted with straw or garden refuse and then allowed to decompose for three months before use.

Composting Animal Manures

The quality of manure varies according to the kind of food the animals have been eating. Animals fed on rich food produce a richer dung, but breeding animals and those with young retain more of the nutrients in their bodies, to the detriment of the manure.

Old manure which has been stacked for several months is safer to use for most purposes than fresh manure, and the nutrients are more readily available. Although farm manure is purchased mainly for its humus-forming properties, it supplies a considerable amount of plant nutrients. One ton of cattle manure will give about 8 lb. nitrogen, 4 lb. phosphoric acid and 8 lb. potash, much of which is accessible to plants soon after application. Make allowances for these nutrients when working out fertilizer plans. Pig manure provides slightly less total nutrients than cattle manure, good horse manure about 75 percent more.

Farm manure also usually contains quite large amounts of magnesium and calcium and all the trace elements. A good dressing of farm manure will remain active for at least three years and probably longer. But after buying it do not leave it in loose heaps; make a solid, compact pile well trampled down, with the center higher than the edges. This will cut losses to the minimum. But even with the best storage, one third by bulk will be lost in the first three months of storage, since organisms convert some of the dry matter into gases which escape into the atmosphere.

Application of Manures

Manure is used to best advantage when mixed in the topsoil by forking or rotary cultivation. If plenty is available, lay it in the bottom of the trench when spading, but do not apply more than can be dug in at any given time. To give a really good dressing, completely cover the ground with a 2- to 3-in. layer—which is equal to about 10 to 15 lb., or a good pailful, per sq. yd.

Poultry Manure

Poultry and pigeon manures are at least four times as rich in nitrogen, two to three times as rich in phosphorus and about as rich in potash as cattle manure, but they provide very little humus. They tend to make clay soil stickier and acid. Poultry manure can be applied fresh but is better stored. It is easier to handle mixed with half its bulk of fine dry soil and sand, and can be used for topdressing growing crops. Always keep it under cover to avoid loss of nutrients in the rain. Apply at the rate of 2 to 3 lb. per sq. yd., but do not place it close to the roots of growing plants since it is likely to damage them.

If trouble is taken to dry and pulverize the droppings of poultry, a high-grade fertilizer will be obtained. Apply this at the rate of 4 to 8 oz. per sq. yd. well in advance of sowing, or as a topdressing. The potash content of poultry manure is low and is best balanced by adding 1 part by weight of sulphate of potash to 12 parts by weight of dried poultry manure.

PEAT

Peat is a useful alternative to manure for providing bulky organic matter. Although it may contain twice as much nitrogen as manure, most of it is inaccessible to plants. The phosphate and potash content is usually one tenth that of farm manure. It can only be regarded, therefore, as a soil conditioner and not as a fertilizer. It breaks down more slowly than manure, keeping the soil loose and thereby improving the aeration and drainage. As peat is weed-free and easy to spread. it is more convenient to use than manure, particularly in greenhouses. There are various types of peat, the two most commonly used being peat moss and sedge peat. The material sold commercially as humus is ordinarily a form of sedge peat. The only way to find out which is best for any particular soil or purpose is to try both types on the garden and watch the results. There are good and poor peats. Bad peat is black, greasy, and becomes sticky and adhesive when wet, whereas the best types are brown and spongy or fibrous, or are black and fluffy and of comparatively light weight. Peat can be bought in bales or in plastic bags as well as in bulk.

Application of Peat

For digging, ½ to 1 bu. (3 to 6 lb.) per sq. yd. of peat is needed to provide a good covering. For potting soils it is usually mixed with loam and sand in approximately equal amounts. Never mix in dry peat when preparing potting soil; it will merely take up moisture badly needed by the plants. Dry peat swells in potting soils and upsets the firm potting of the plants or seedlings. If spread thinly on the soil surface or on the potting bench, it can be moistened with a fine spray of water before incorporation with the soil. A coarse grade—with large particles—is best for a sandy soil, and a fine grade best for a clay soil. Because peat supplies such small amounts of available nutrients it is important to supplement it by the intelligent use of fertilizers.

COMPOST

Composting is the predigestion or partial decomposition of organic residues. There are several methods of composting, as described in the chapter "Composting and Green Manuring" (page 761). Well-made compost may be almost equal in value to farm manure and is applied at the same rate. For the best results it is often desirable to insure additional nutrients by using fertilizers as well as compost.

OTHER MATERIALS
Sawdust

Sawdust, when properly handled, builds up the humus content in the soil, but before being mixed in should always be composted. Never use fresh, undecomposed sawdust, because it temporarily robs the soil of nitrogen. To obtain the best results, mix three parts by bulk of sawdust with one part by bulk of well-rotted animal or poultry manure, and leave it in a heap for 12 months. Calcium cyanamide or sulphate of ammonia may be added to speed up rotting at the rate of 1 lb. per 20 lb. sawdust. Leave the whole heap moist. Sawdust is not a fertilizer, since its nutrient content is very low. The usual rate of application is 10 to 15 lb. per sq. yd.

Old sawdust is ideal for mulching fruit bushes, shrubs or other widely spaced plants. It eventually breaks down into humus when dug in at the end of the season.

Leaf Mold

Leaf mold or leaf soil taken from the top few inches of woodland soils or made by composting fallen leaves is excellent humus-forming material and one of the finest of soil conditioners, particularly when it is derived from deciduous trees and shrubs. Compost fallen leaves in heaps. If placed in shallow heaps not more than 2 to 3 ft. high, a fibrous mold will result after about a year. Apply this at 5 to 6 lb. per sq. yd. and use it for mixing with potting soil in the same way as peat moss is used for that purpose.

Hop Manures

Spent hops, which sometimes may be obtained from breweries, are helpful for improving the physical condition of the soil, but are low in nutrients. In a wet state they contain about as much nitrogen as cattle manure (0.5 to 0.6 percent) and from two to four times as much phosphate (1 to 2 percent P_2O_5), but they contain only traces of potash.

Seaweed

For those who live in coastal areas seaweed is a cheap, excellent fertilizer.

Spread at the rate of 10 to 12 lb. per sq. yd. and dig in immediately. It will then provide nearly as much nitrogen and up to three times as much potash as an equivalent dressing of cattle manure, but it contains very little phosphorus. Seaweed breaks down rapidly into humus, and is free from weed seeds and disease organisms.

GENERAL HINTS ON USING FERTILIZERS AND MANURES
Application
1. Apply solid fertilizers to the soil before sowing or planting, or as topdressings during the growing period.
2. Spread fertilizers as evenly as possible all over the soil surface. Small amounts are more easily distributed if mixed with dry, sifted soil or sand.
3. Because they will injure most garden seeds, do not scatter fertilizers down the seed drill.
4. Fertilizer spreaders mounted on wheels insure even distribution.
5. Always cultivate or rake in the fertilizer lightly to avoid caking on the surface.
6. The recommended rates of application must be closely adhered to.
7. It is a good plan to weigh out the required amount for, say, 5 sq. yds. Put the fertilizer into a can or other convenient container and make a mark on the inside to show the level. Then spread the fertilizer evenly over 5 sq. yds., to give a good guide as to the distribution for the rest of the plot.
8. Water in newly spread fertilizer during dry weather.
9. In general, the closer the plants are set, the more fertilizer should be applied. Some vegetables, however, have sparse root systems that are unable to explore the soil fully and contact the fertilizer that has been mixed in it. Therefore, when the rows are about 2 ft. or more apart, the best results will often be obtained by placing the fertilizer in bands. on either side of each row and a few inches below the level of the seed or of the roots of transplanted plants. About half the normal amount of fertilizer will be required for band placement, as this method is called.
10. Mix phosphatic and potassic fertilizers thoroughly with the topsoil by forking or by rotary cultivation, so that they will be available in the root zone, where there is more moisture. These fertilizers do not move appreciably from where they are first placed in the soil.
11. When manure or compost has been dug in, the amount of fertilizer that is applied can be reduced by one quarter for light dressings of manure; by half for medium dressings of manure; by three quarters for very heavy dressings (15 to 20 lb. per sq. yd.) of manure.
12. Light, sandy soils will generally need more potash than loamy or clay soils, depending on the needs of the plants or crop to be grown. In rainy localities or heavily watered soils some of the nutrients, particularly nitrogen, will wash into the deeper layers, out of reach of shallow-rooted plants. Topdressings of nitrogen help to counteract this loss.

Storing
Some fertilizers are difficult to store for long periods because they tend to absorb moisture from the air and either become a sticky or solid mass or burst their bags. However, since fertilizers are cheaper when bought in bulk, one tends to buy more than is required immediately—so it is a good plan to pour the fertilizer into a plastic bag and label it. Store this inside a can or other container and keep it covered. Do not leave bags of fertilizer touching each other on shelves, against brick walls, or in damp sheds, for if the fertilizers go solid or sticky they never regain their original condition.

CHAPTER 42

COMPOSTING AND GREEN MANURING
In Modern Garden Practice

Composting

THE WORD "compost" is used by gardeners to denote two quite different substances. The first is a mixture of soil, peat moss and sand or similar materials used in potting and generally called a potting compost. The second is vegetable waste of all kinds which has been properly rotted down in a heap or pit, often with an activator, and in consequence has formed a blackish-brown crumbling material very similar to humus. It is this kind of compost that is dealt with here.

In the past, gardeners were able to obtain large quantities of animal manure, and so composting was not generally practiced. But under present conditions such manures are no longer readily available to many gardeners, and one of the finest—probably the finest—substitutes is good compost.

WHAT TO USE

Many things can go into the compost heap: the vines of peas and beans, soft hedge clippings, peapods, tea leaves and coffee grounds, banana peel, fluff from the vacuum cleaner, straw, lawn mowings, fallen leaves and even well-soaked newspapers. It is important not to use obviously diseased plant material.

Whatever the material, it is advisable to encourage it to rot down properly by using some type of activator. This may be animal excreta, the droppings from birds such as poultry or, when these are not available, fish meal or a brand-name activator. The compost heap is built up in layers of the vegetable waste with a sprinkling of the activator and soil in between the layers.

It is often easier to make a bottomless bin of boards or of chicken wire into which the vegetable waste can be collected and raked level. The size of the bin will depend on the size of the garden. For a garden of half an acre the bin may be 6 ft. by 6 ft., with perhaps a reserve bin nearby. For a garden of an acre it may be 8 ft. by 8 ft. and have two reserve bins alongside.

There is all the difference in the world between a rubbish heap and a compost heap. A rubbish heap is merely a collection of vegetable waste, and may well be the breeding ground for pests and diseases, as well as a place where weed seeds are stored but not killed. In a properly made compost heap the temperature will rise

Bottomless Compost Box for the Small Garden
Build a compost box with three fixed sides, and construct the front so that
loose boards can be slipped into position as the box is filled.

to 180° F. It is then that the actino-mycetes (rod-shaped bacteria) break down the more resistant proteins and carbohydrates in the heap. The temperature may remain high for a month and then, as the heap cools, the bacteria complete the task of breaking the organic material down until it is first-rate compost.

GENERAL METHOD OF MAKING

For a good compost heap, the layers of refuse should be 6 to 8 in. thick and should be trampled down moderately firmly. If the material is very dry, water may be applied before the activator is put on. If it is necessary to use very tough material such as cabbage stumps, it is best to break them up first on a chopping block to pulverize them. They should then be intermingled with grass mowings or similar material to help build up heat. Healthy soft growth, but not woody material, can be included. Woody

matter should be burned and the ashes collected, to be stored dry for use as fertilizer. Never burn any soft material unless it harbors soil-borne diseases; to do this is a great waste of potential compost.

If you use a brand-name commercial product, apply the activator as recommended by the manufacturer. If you use unprocessed animal or bird manure as an activator, simply sprinkle a layer an inch or so thick on top of every 6-in. thickness of compacted compost material. If you use dried and pulverized sheep manure, dried blood or fish meal, add it to the heap at the rate of about 3 oz. per sq. yd. of each new 6-in. layer. If the garden soil is known to be decidedly acid, sprinkle ground limestone, at the rate of 4 oz. per sq. yd., over every compacted foot of compost material, in addition to the activator.

Build up the heap gradually day by day and week by week as the vegetable waste becomes available. Keep the top of the heap slightly concave to catch rainwater. When the heap reaches a height of, say, 6 ft., put a 6-in. layer of soil on the top as a capping to help keep in the heat.

If very soft materials are used, such as lawn mowings and cabbage leaves, provide a ventilation shaft by driving a post of 3- or 4-in. diameter into the ground at the center of the bin or pit, pile the vegetable waste around it layer by layer and activate in the normal way. When the heap reaches the correct height, pull out the post, thus leaving an air shaft through the middle; or use a double roll of chicken wire about 1 ft. in diameter in place of the post and leave it in the heap. This is seldom necessary for small heaps but is quite a good practice for heaps that are 12 ft. by 12 ft. or larger.

Some gardeners believe that the compost heap should be turned at the end of three months, but the heap rots satisfactorily without any attention at all. It will probably be ready for use at the end of six months, though it need not be used for one, two or more years. If the outsides have not rotted down properly, cut them off with a spade—just as the black part of a burned cake is cut off with a knife—and put them on the reserve compost heap to complete their decay.

When the compost is ready to use, it should look like earthy mold or moist peat. It should be dark brown or black, perfectly sweet-smelling and show no traces of the original materials. Eighty-five percent of it should pass easily through a $\frac{3}{4}$-in. sifting screen.

When it is properly made, compost can be quite as valuable as manure, for in addition to containing actual plant food it is alive with millions of microorganisms. It will also contain most of the minor minerals, known as trace elements, which all plants require for healthy growth.

These are the principles of compost making. There are two other methods that are sometimes used.

The first is the Indore Method. For the small garden make a bottomless box to contain a heap 4 ft. by 4 ft., and 3 ft. 4 in. high. Such a heap will provide 2 cu. yd. of good compost, weighing 1 ton. Bolt or screw three sides of the box together, and make up the front with loose boards slipped into position as the box is filled. Where possible, make a reserve bin.

Cut all the vegetable waste into lengths of a few inches and put it into the box with one third or one quarter of the same volume of manure. Incorporate a little soil at the same time. If manure is not available use hoof and horn meal or dried blood at the rate of 1 to 2 percent of the dry vegetable waste.

When the box is full, make three holes vertically through the mass with an iron bar to improve the supply of air. Cover the top with sheets of plastic or other material to keep out the rain. After six weeks dig the material out and stack it on a convenient site where it can ripen for another six weeks. Four tons of compost per year can be made in one of these 1-ton boxes.

The second method is to make the bins with old boards (old railway ties are excellent, as they are thick and help to retain the heat), chicken wire or bales of straw. The straw can later be put on the heap.

Make the bins 6 ft. by 6 ft. with open ends for ease of access, and intersperse the 6-in. layers of waste with fish meal or dried sheep manure at 3 oz. per sq. yd. Whenever available add the urine and excreta from any animals that are kept. Once a week or so, in the summer, give the heap a good watering. When it is 4 ft. high plunge a long-tined spading fork into it in several places and move it backward and forward to provide aeration.

At the end of six months the heap will be ready for use. Skin off the top 9 in. or so and also the sides, if they are not fully decomposed, and put them into the reserve bin for further rotting.

If the garden soil is acid, use hydrated lime in addition to the fish meal or sheep manure as the activator, at the rate of 4 oz. for every 2 cu. ft. of waste.

HOW TO USE COMPOST

Apply compost at the rate of at least a large pailful to the sq. yd. each year. Mix it thoroughly with the topsoil to a depth of 6 to 10 in. with a spading fork or rotary tiller, or apply it as a topdressing or mulch on the surface of the ground. The worms will pull much of it in, greatly enriching the soil as they consume and excrete it. Their tunnels aerate the ground. With the use of compost the soil will not dry out so readily, the tilth will be improved and there will be ample humus to encourage the growth of seedling plants.

Green Manuring

To give land a rest is a good thing. Even as far back as Old Testament times the practice was to rest the soil every seven years.

In a large garden a good plan is to rest one seventh of the area devoted to vegetables and cut flowers every year, and to sow this seventh with a green manure or cover crop which can be dug or plowed in at the end of the season. A more intensive program of green manuring, consisting of turning under two, three or more successive cover crops, may be employed to condition poor soil or to rehabilitate an area in preparation for lawn making or landscaping.

But green manuring, done wrongly, can have bad temporary results. For when crops are sown and are dug into the land in a fresh condition, the soil organisms immediately begin to work on the green plants and break them down. In doing so they exhaust the land of nitrogen, for they have to make use of a good deal of this nutrient to build their own bodies and those of their rapidly increasing progeny. Fresh green ma-

nuring, therefore, will normally result in a reduction—for the time being—of the available nitrogen content of the soil.

Notable exceptions are when leguminous plants, such as the annual lupine, quick-growing cowpeas and soybeans, are used for green manuring. These legumes have nitrogenous nodules on their roots, so that when they are dug in, the soil suffers no nitrogen starvation. But, even with leguminous plants, undigested organic substances may remain in the soil to damage the roots of the next crop.

Because green-manure crops do not give as quick results as good composted vegetable refuse, they are less frequently used in ordinary gardens than under commercial conditions. It takes considerable time to grow a green-manure crop. Then, after it has been dug or plowed under, six weeks or more elapse before it is properly rotted down and is ready for plant roots to use. During this period it is better not to plant or sow in the turned-over plot.

The best results with green manuring are achieved under the following conditions:

1. The land is properly drained so that sufficient air is present.
2. The soil is adequately limed so that it is not acid.
3. An activator is applied at the time the green crop is turned under in order to provide additional nitrogen with which the organisms can start work.
4. The soil is warm.

GREEN-MANURE CROPS

Because gardening is an intensive cultivation, it is rarely possible to devote considerable areas for lengthy periods to the growing of cover crops to turn under. Cover cropping or green manuring is therefore less extensively practiced by gardeners than by farmers. Nevertheless, its possibilities must not be overlooked. Ordinarily the gardener's green manures must be kinds that grow quickly and can be incorporated with the soil in a few weeks or, at most, a few months from the time of sowing. Only under exceptional circumstances can he consider a crop—such as alfalfa or red clover—that will occupy the ground for a year or more. There are many satisfactory green-manure crops for gardens. Among them are:

Buckwheat

A rapid-growing warm-weather crop. Sow from spring through midsummer and turn crop under when it is about 8 in. high. If successive sowings are to be made on the same ground (to insure addition of maximum amounts of organic material during the summer), allow ten days between turning under one crop and sowing another.

Hairy Vetch

Sow inoculated seed (seed which has been treated with bacteria to promote nitrogen fixation) in early fall. Thrives best on sandy, well-drained soil that is about neutral. Turn under in late spring. Is leguminous and adds nitrogen to the soil.

Ryegrass

Annual ryegrass (not to be confused with rye) is very useful. It may be sown in fall or spring (or even in summer) and may be kept mown to provide a very acceptable temporary lawn until it is turned under.

Soybeans

A rapid-growing summer annual, to be sown about the time it is safe to plant corn. Must be turned under before the vines become excessively tough and woody—that is, when the beans in the pods are about half developed. Is leguminous and adds nitrogen to the soil.

Cowpeas

These serve the same purposes and are handled in the same way as soybeans. Leguminous.

Winter Rye

This is an excellent winter crop. Winter-rye seed is sown in late summer or fall and the crop is ready for turning under in late winter, well before the time comes for sowing regular garden crops.

Because of this, winter rye is one of the most convenient cover crops for the gardener. It can ordinarily be used in vegetable and cut-flower gardens and on temporarily vacant beds without interfering with spring planting.

CHAPTER 43

PRINCIPLES OF PRUNING
Understand Before
You Snip or Cut

*Balance of Top and Roots—Severe
Cutting and New Growth—Encouraging
Shoots—Proper Times for Pruning—
Tools—Hints*

PRUNING serves both practical and
esthetic ends and is designed to develop and reveal the best qualities of
a plant. It entails the cutting away of
any parts that are not required, and
is particularly applicable to shrubs
and trees.

The chief aims of pruning are:
1. To keep the plant healthy by cutting away all dead, diseased, injured
or weak shoots as soon as possible.
2. To regulate growth, either to re-
strict a plant to an allotted space or
shape, to enhance its natural habit, to
keep it neat and shapely or to increase its vigor.
3. To develop to the full those qualities, whether of form, foliage, flower
or fruit, for which the plant is being
grown.

PRINCIPLES

The basic principle lies in the fact that
the removal of a part of a plant modifies the remaining growth, and prun-

Heading Back
The shoots are pruned just above
well-placed buds.

Thinning Out
Shoots and weak laterals growing into
or crossing main branches are removed
to admit light and air.

Pruning Terms

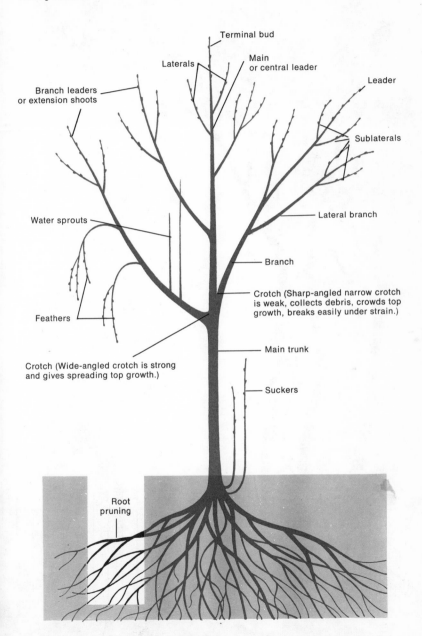

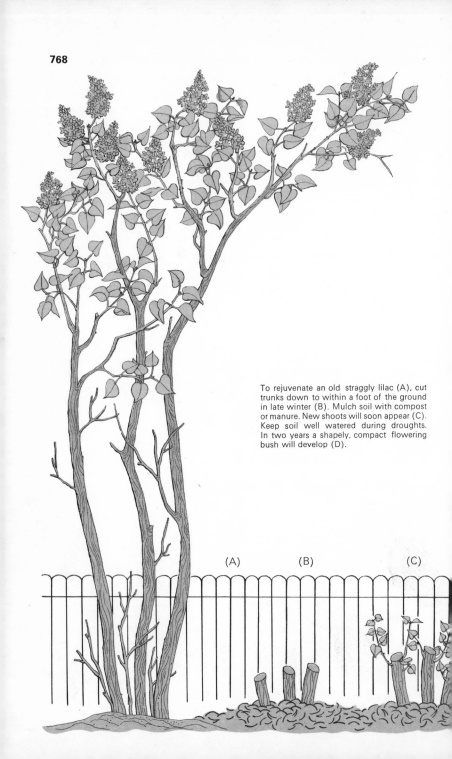

To rejuvenate an old straggly lilac (A), cut trunks down to within a foot of the ground in late winter (B). Mulch soil with compost or manure. New shoots will soon appear (C). Keep soil well watered during droughts. In two years a shapely, compact flowering bush will develop (D).

(A)   (B)   (C)

ing will not be successful unless the way in which the pruned plant is likely to use its growth energies is intelligently anticipated.

A characteristic woody plant has a branching root system underground and a framework of stem and branch, clothed with leaves, aboveground. In the established shrub or tree the roots and leaves have usually arrived at an economical working balance, and curtailment of either will disturb this balance. When top growth is cut away there are fewer leaves for the roots to support and, because of this, less plant food is manufactured to nurture root action. Consequently, the root system adjusts itself by becoming proportionately less extensive and less active. Conversely, any pruning of the roots checks the top growth.

The reaction of a plant to pruning takes place during periods of active growth (usually spring and summer) and the adjustment is often more gradual than immediate. To appreciate what the reaction may be, the branching framework of the stems and roots must be regarded as a structure in which the food reserves that are manufactured in the growing season are stored.

When top growth is removed, some of the food reserves are lost, but those in the roots are undiminished, so that there is a tendency for the roots to initiate a vigorous reaction, shown by new stem growth. Just how vigorous this reaction is and the form it takes depend partly on the manner of pruning and its timing.

Hard pruning usually results in a strong growth reaction, and a shoot that is cut back severely will attempt

(D)

Prune wisteria in early summer by shortening the leafy, viny shoots to about seven leaves.

In late winter, prune back the shoots shortened the previous summer to a length of 2 to 4 in.

The flowers of wisteria develop from buds produced near the bases of the cut-back shoots.

to produce more leaf-bearing shoots or wood growth quickly. This reaction can be advantageously used when it is desired to build up a strong branch framework in young plants, or to make a plant produce strong new growth. If the shoot is pruned lightly, or not pruned at all, food reserves in the shoot are left more or less intact and are used to induce new growth in the buds—the undeveloped branchlets.

The development of buds is apparently controlled by certain growth-regulating substances in the plant, sometimes called "plant hormones," but it varies according to the species or variety of plant. Development is also affected by the food reserves available when new growth is made, and can be greatly influenced by pruning.

REGENERATION

Plants differ widely in their reaction to pruning and their ability to regenerate thereafter. Some kinds readily make new shoots even if most or all of the top growth has been cut away. Lilac, holly, yew and hawthorn have this facility, and old, ailing plants can often be rejuvenated by drastic pruning. Other plants, such

as magnolia, broom and camellia, when once well established, resent severe pruning and may even be killed by it. Woody plants usually regenerate most readily when pruning is confined to the young shoots of the current or previous year's growth.

WHEN TO PRUNE

The timing of pruning is important, as it affects both the growth response and the health of the plant.

Most deciduous shrubs and trees can be pruned when dormant—that is, between leaf fall and bud burst (during the autumn and winter), but there are two broad exceptions to this rule. First, stone fruits and related ornamental trees of the *Prunus* genus (such as flowering almond and cherry), maple, walnut and other trees liable to bleed profusely or to develop diseases if pruned hard in winter, may be pruned as soon as in full leaf in June or early July. Second, spring- and early summer-flowering shrubs, such as forsythia, flowering currant and deutzia, can be pruned after flowering because they produce their flowers best on shoots matured in the previous year.

Prune evergreens and most conifers

just before new growth begins in spring. Winter pruning may cause the tree to die back as a result of injury by the weather. When the growth of pine, spruce and fir must be restricted, it is best done by cutting back, from one third to two thirds, the "candles" or young shoots before their needles (actually their leaves) have expanded.

Carry out pruning to restricted shapes for hedges or topiary work in the growing season as growth dictates. Most hedges can be kept neat with a

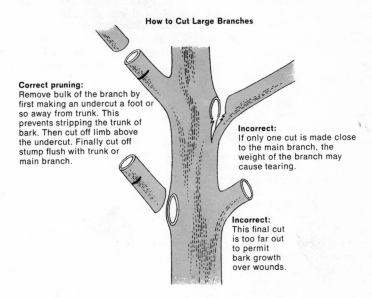

How to Cut Large Branches

Correct pruning:
Remove bulk of the branch by first making an undercut a foot or so away from trunk. This prevents stripping the trunk of bark. Then cut off limb above the undercut. Finally cut off stump flush with trunk or main branch.

Incorrect:
If only one cut is made close to the main branch, the weight of the branch may cause tearing.

Incorrect:
This final cut is too far out to permit bark growth over wounds.

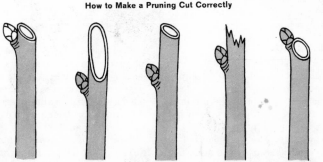

How to Make a Pruning Cut Correctly

Correct cut is made cleanly and close to the bud.

Cut slants too sharply.

Cut is too far above the bud.

Jagged cut damages the living cells.

Cut is too close to the bud.

June and late-August trimming; a few need cutting more frequently, while informal hedges or well-established walls of beech, hornbeam, holly, boxwood or yew thrive on one annual cutting in the summer.

Summer Pruning

Summer pruning is done in July and August and entails the removal of leaves that are actively at work; it has an almost immediate effect on the root-leaf balance. If the pruning is carried out too early in the season and growth is then checked, the plant tries to put out new shoots and leaves, which can exhaust and weaken it.

Summer pruning is practiced chiefly on espaliered and ornamental trees by removing a few inches from the growing tips of new shoots as their wood begins to harden in late summer. It is an especially useful practice for encouraging the blooming of wisterias that produce great amounts of growth but few or no flowers.

PRUNING TOOLS

Pruning tools must be razor-sharp and clean-cutting. A pruning knife used expertly with the support of the thumb is excellent, but well-designed pruning shears are satisfactory. Use a pruning saw for large cuts, then clean and smooth the rough surface of the cut with a knife.

GENERAL RULES

In practice it is necessary to study and appreciate the habits and requirements of the species and varieties of the plants to be pruned, but in all pruning there are four precepts which should be kept in mind:

1. Cut cleanly. The living cells of the shoots are concentrated in and about the greenish, slightly slimy area, called cambium, just inside the bark. Try not to damage these cells, as the healing of the cuts and the develop-

ment of new growth are dependent on them.

2. Cut just above a healthy bud or node. It is here that cambium and growth cells are most concentrated and where the energies of the plant will be diverted. Start the cut opposite to and slightly above the base of the bud and slant it very slightly upward to finish just above the bud.

3. Remember that the growth reaction will be strongest in the terminal and uppermost buds left after pruning. When pruning for new growth, make the cut above a bud facing in the direction the new shoot is required to grow. Pruning retards the growth of dormant buds lower on the branch, and to stimulate such buds into growth a method of bark-nicking is recommended. A notch of bark is removed from just above a bud from which new shoot growth is required, or below a bud from which flower development is desired.

4. Remove unwanted shoots or branches at their base or at their junction with a large branch. This is necessary when thinning out growth from which regeneration is not required. Tangled branches must be removed to enable light and air to reach the plant. Make the cuts flush with the bark of the major branch that is left or with the trunk of the tree so that no stubs remain. If stubs are left they do not heal but encourage pests and diseases. In removing dead, diseased or damaged shoots it is essential to cut back to where healthy, clean tissue is exposed, preferably at the base. Until healing is complete, cuts can be protected by a coating of tree-wound paint.

After pruning, clean, healthy cuttings can be used for the base of a compost heap, but it is advisable to burn large limbs, dead and diseased wood and add their ashes to the compost heap.

PART VII

Enemies of the Garden

A great hazard of discussing plant diseases, pests and the prevalence of weeds is that a gardener, looking over the long and formidable lists, may decide that his adversaries are too numerous for a single human being to contend with. It may strike him that cultivating the soil and raising plants is tantamount to providing a banquet for hungry hordes of borers, cutworms, moths, mites and beetles or arranging nice, comfortable beds for energetic crops of annual and perennial weeds. That diseases and pests do attack on occasion and that weeds are hardy and prolific is undeniable. However, today nearly all enemies can be controlled.

A gardener needs only to be acquainted with the diseases and pests that are likely to affect his particular plants. He need not prematurely accumulate an arsenal of sprays or dusts which happily he may never find reason to use. No gardener can expect to be spared the unwelcome presence of weeds, but he can learn to recognize them as seedlings and he can make life so miserable for them that they will not take hold. The practice of good gardening and proper cultivation of the soil is always the best assurance against attacks of any kind. Plants that are well nourished in a favorable environment tend to fend off enemies by their own vigor. A gardener combats destructive forces whenever he intelligently answers the needs of his plants, be it for fertilizing, irrigation, mulching or pruning.

CHAPTER 44

PLANT DISEASES
How to Control Them

Conditions That Cause Disease— Types of Diseases—Ways to Combat Trouble—Sprays—Diseases General Among Plants—Diseases of Specific Flowers and Vegetables

PLANTS, just as much as animals, may suffer from various diseases which can injure or kill them. All types—from annuals, perennials and bulbous plants to shrubs and large trees of every kind—can be attacked, so that a knowledge of the early signs of infection and of the way in which a disease can be combated is a valuable asset.

New varieties of plants are being produced all the time by various methods of selection and inbreeding. Some of these are highly bred, but highly bred plants are not necessarily highly resistant to disease, and with these in particular the *prevention* of disease can assume great importance. Much research work is, therefore, devoted to the prevention and curing of plant ailments.

Where one particular type of plant is grown in quantity, often on the same ground year after year, an outbreak of disease can cause serious losses. Such a disease finds ample opportunity to live on its particular host plant during the summer, and will usually have some method of persisting through the winter. It may remain in the soil, and although the soil may be only slightly contaminated at first, the trouble may build up to serious proportions. This is most likely to arise in greenhouses and cold frames,

and in flower beds that are replanted each year with the same or similar types of plants. Eradication may require treatment of the soil when unplanted, in early spring or late fall.

With growing crops, swift action may be needed to prevent serious losses. The more common troubles which can affect plants should be easily recognized and the appropriate remedy applied. Outside advice may be quickly available, but with fast-spreading diseases early treatment has great advantages.

The term "plant disease" refers not only to foreign organisms (parasites) which can injure or kill a plant, but also to anything—except insect damage—which may check the growth of a plant, cause abnormal growth or cause the death of part or all of the plant. Consideration must therefore be given not only to invasion by parasitic organisms, but also to cases where plants fail to thrive because of unsuitable soil, incorrect temperature, injury from fumes and sprays or excessive liming. Fruits and vegetables— such as apples, pears, potatoes and carrots—continue to live even when stored and can suffer from various difficulties which either reduce their food value or destroy them entirely.

Plant diseases may be divided into two main groups: nonparasitic diseases, which are not infectious; parasitic diseases, which are infectious. The latter may be subdivided into two classes: fungus and bacterial diseases; virus diseases.

PARASITIC DISEASES

Funguses

Fungus diseases are those caused by parasitic funguses, and with them are grouped the very similar bacterial diseases.

Parasitic funguses are mostly microscopic. They invade higher plants and grow in their tissues (cells), which they kill and then absorb the contents for food. They penetrate and grow in the plant cells by means of fine fungal threads (hyphae), and spread from plant to plant by means of spores (the equivalent of seeds in higher plants). The spores are formed at the ends of special threads, often inside special fruit bodies, and they are produced in enormous numbers. When released, they are carried by wind currents or water (by splashing) to healthy plants, where they alight, germinate, grow into the tissue and thus spread the disease.

Most of the fungus parasites overwinter on the plant or in the soil by forming a type of thick-walled spore or some other structure which is resistant to adverse weather.

These fungus parasites may be roughly divided into two types. The first—which includes the powdery mildews (common on many plants such as roses, delphiniums, lilacs and zinnias)—produces an obvious and superficial whitish growth on the surface of the leaves, stems and petals. This growth is made of fungal threads and spores, which cover the leaf surface and feed by sending down a kind of sucker (haustorium) into the surface cells (epidermis) to absorb nourishment. In the second type, the parasite grows down deeply into the internal tissues, sending up threads to produce spores at the surface. The first type is easy to check, but unfortunately most fungus diseases belong to the second.

Bacteria

Bacteria which attack plants are much smaller than parasitic funguses, but infect in a similar manner by living in, and killing, the tissues. Some species form resting spores. They are able to persist by remaining in plant debris or in dormant cells in the tissue of seeds, corms, bulbs, etc.—a method that is also used by some fungus parasites.

Viruses

With virus diseases, the exact identification of the parasite is difficult. Viruses are so small that they cannot be seen through the ordinary microscopes used to detect and study fungus and bacterial parasites. They can be photographed by means of the modern electron microscope, but even so they are something of a mystery. Undoubtedly plants suffering from virus disease have some form of infectious agent in their sap, but in many cases its exact nature has not been identified. It is, however, known to be very small and to multiply within the plant's cells, so that it is usually distributed throughout the tissues.

Results of Virus Infection: Plants, unlike animals, do not seem to produce antibodies to fight viruses, although in some cases they are able to resist to a certain extent. Thus, more than one virus can exist in a plant at the same time. For some plants, though not many, virus attack means sudden death, but usually infected plants become more crippled and degenerate with the passing of each season.

Seeds of most virus-infected plants are usually free from virus; so, by saving seed, clean stock can be obtained again. This method is, however, suitable only in the case of fairly short-lived plants.

Special care has to be taken, for example, to exclude the risk of virus

Apple Bitter Pit

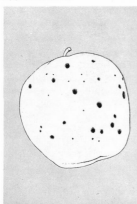

Damage: Dark, sunken spots and brown areas are seen in flesh.
Control: No remedy known—do not pick too early.

Apple Black Rot

Damage: Brown to black decay of fruit with spots appearing on leaves and cankers on stems.
Control: Spray leaves with captan, maneb or zineb; remove mummied fruits and cut out stem cankers.

Apple Canker

Damage: Wood decays, bark peels.
Control: Scrape and cut out cankers. Treat cuts with a paint containing phenyl mercury acetate.

Apple Fire Blight

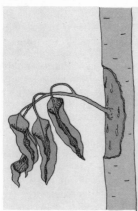

Damage: Blossoms and leaves turn brown, then black. Fruit yield reduced.
Control: Spray during blooming period with Bordeaux mixture, a fixed copper or streptomycin.

Apple Powdery Mildew

Damage: White coating appears on shoot tips.
Control: Prune. Spray with Karathane or Phybam.

Apple Scab on Fruit

Damage: Dark olive-colored raised spots are seen.
Control: Spray with captan o Phybam in spring.

ple Scab on Leaves	Apple Scab on Shoots	Cherry Black Knot

mage: Olive-drab moldy ▸ts appear.
ntrol: Spray with captan or ybam in spring.

Damage: Blisters show on young wood.
Control: Prune out scabby wood.

Damage: Black rough swellings are seen on branches; dieback of twigs and branches.
Control: Prune out infected parts, then spray in spring with copper or sulphur fungicide.

ape Powdery Mildew	Grape Black Rot	Lemon Scab

mage: Powdery white ▸osit appears on leaves and ts.
ntrol: Spray leaves with ▪athane or sulphur.

Damage: Fruits turn black and wrinkled. Reddish-brown spots on leaves.
Control: Spray with ferbam or zineb.

Damage: Warty areas or protuberances are seen on fruit.
Control: Spray with Bordeaux mixture or a fixed copper.

infection from clean stocks of fruit trees and bush fruits, which are all propagated vegetatively as increase by seed is not feasible.

Symptoms of Virus Infection: The symptoms of virus infetion are very varied. Common signs are stunted growth and mottled patterns on the leaves (often referred to under the general term "mosaic"). Other signs are ring-like markings on the leaves (ring spots); curling or distortion of leaves and shoots; "breaking" of flowers (white streaking in the color of the petals); abnormal production of shoots (proliferation); and many other abnormalities. Infection usually results in all the cells of the plants being invaded by the virus, although shoots already developed are not usually much altered. New shoots and leaves, however, begin to show abnormal symptoms as they grow.

The symptoms of the same virus may vary in different plants—or even in different varieties of the same species. For example, some varieties of dahlias affected by the so-called mosaic or stunt virus may be quickly and severely crippled, while other varieties, similarly affected, show no outward signs of the disease. The latter varieties are referred to as "tolerant carriers" and therefore should not be planted near a very susceptible variety.

Plant viruses injected into the bloodstream of animals, such as rabbits, may produce antibodies, with the result that animal antiserum can be prepared and used in the detection of a specific virus. If the animal antiserum is mixed with a dilute suspension of the virus from the sap of a plant, a cloudiness (precipitate) will appear.

Reactions such as this are used extensively in the identification of some plant viruses and can be of great

value in the work of virus classification. No generally accepted method of classification has, however, been adopted. In describing plant diseases, scientists usually use the name of the host plant first and follow this with the most obvious symptoms caused by the virus: for example, beet curly-top virus and tomato ring-spot virus.

The Spreading of Virus Diseases: Aphids are mostly responsible for the spread of virus diseases, although a few are spread by leafhoppers, thrips, mealy-bugs and whiteflies. These insects are referred to as insect "vectors." When feeding, they may take up the virus from the sap of virus-infected plants and transmit it to healthy plants. Many insect pests, therefore, present a double threat to the gardener's success.

Viruses can also be transmitted by the propagation techniques of budding and grafting. This is a very common way in which diseases increase and spread, so that the use of clean stocks is essential for propagation of new plants.

Only rarely does a virus travel with the seed, and then only in a minute percentage: examples are tomato black ring, cherry necrotic ring spot and bean mosaic. It is thought that there are many different strains of virus and that these, like other parasitic organisms, may vary greatly in their virulence toward different hosts.

Some viruses remain in and contaminate the soil in which virus-infected plants have been grown. Raspberries are a case in point, and although it is not understood exactly how the soil is contaminated, it is certain that there are some fields where raspberries cannot be grown with profit because the young shoots will become infected with virus from the soil.

Prevention of Disease

CONTROL MEASURES

The methods used to control plant diseases are many and varied, but the best protection is to know the needs of the crop being grown and to practice good cultivation so that the plants make healthy, vigorous growth. Robust plants have some resistance to disease, but those weakened by adverse conditions are more likely to be attacked by parasitic funguses.

Many factors favor the spread of disease: buying cheap seed of poor quality from which weak seedlings are raised; growing plants too close together; acid soil; poor light in greenhouses; overfeeding with chemical fertilizers; high temperatures. So far as fungus diseases are concerned, there is no substitute for good culture. Spraying, dusting, fumigating and seed treatments, important as they are, are only secondary.

Virus diseases present a rather different problem, for even well-grown plants can be severely affected.

Good Culture

The following are some of the factors of good culture, so important in the maintenance of clean, disease-free crops: good soil drainage and correct soil preparation—if necessary, such humus-forming materials as peat and leaf mold can be added, or a drainpipe can be installed, to improve the drainage.

The plants' supply of fertilizers should be increased, if this is desirable, so that plant nutrients are available whenever needed; the ventilation of cold frames and greenhouses should be adjusted so that the excessively warm and humid conditions which encourage plant parasites are never experienced. Careful pruning will provide more air circulation in the outdoor garden; stagnant air encourages such destructive diseases as apple scab and downy mildew of blackberry and black raspberry.

Crop Rotation

Crop rotation is important in keeping down disease. If the same kind of crop is grown in the same ground for several years in succession, two undesirable things happen. First, the same plant nutrients are being taken continually from the soil, and second, if the particular crop being grown has a disease that lives over in the soil, then the disease will be encouraged to build up in the ground.

Plant parasites live on small pieces of crop debris (for example, on fragments of stem, root and so on), and most, to insure their survival in winter, produce some special fruit body of a hard, resistant nature. Routine soil preparations may spread infected material, and the ground becomes heavily infested.

But most diseases are confined to a particular crop and can be "starved out" of the soil if different crops are grown in rotation. In the greenhouse, where crop rotation may not be practicable, soil pasteurization (often miscalled sterilization) is essential.

Weeds

Weeds act as alternate host plants to many fungus diseases, which persist on them and then move on to cultivated plants. For instance, shepherd's purse may carry the clubroot disease of cabbages, wallflowers and other cruciferous plants; wild celery spreads the serious leaf-spot disease to cultivated celery. Plantains may carry the virus of spotted wilt; ground cherry may harbor the mosaic virus, which affects peppers and tomatoes.

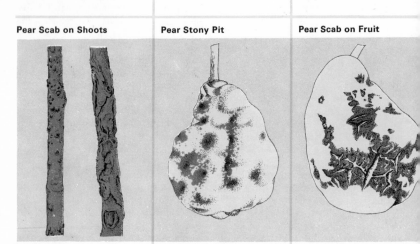

Peach Chlorosis

Damage: Leaves are yellow to almost white.
Control: Improve drainage, acidify soil and treat soil or spray leaves with iron chelate (Sequestrene of Iron).

Peach Leaf Curl

Damage: Leaves become distorted, yellow and dark red.
Control: Spray trees while dormant with ferbam.

Peach Mildew

Damage: White powdery deposit on shoot tips of young fruits.
Control: Spray early in season with lime-sulphur, 1 part to 100 parts water.

Pear Scab on Shoots

Damage: Blisters show on young wood.
Control: Prune out scabby wood. Spray with ferbam, sulphur or ziram.

Pear Stony Pit

Damage: Fruit is pitted with hard brown areas in flesh.
Control: Destroy infected trees.

Pear Scab on Fruit

Damage: Dark spots appear.
Control: Spray with ferbam, sulphur or ziram.

Bacterial Canker

age: Spots on leaves,
y appearance, yellowing
dieback of whole branches.
trol: Prune infected twigs
oranches. In California,
y with Bordeaux mixture
n leaves are dropping.

Plum Brown Rot

Damage: Fruits have whitish
concentric rings and mummify.
Control: Cut out dead wood.
Remove any "mummified" fruits.
Control plum curculio (weevil).
Spray with captan.

Plum Pockets

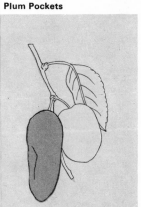

Damage: Fruits appear puffy,
enlarged into whitish or reddish
swollen bladders.
Control: Spray with Bordeaux
mixture in spring before flower
buds open.

Silvered Leaves

age: Leaves silver.
cted branches have brown
in wood when cut.
trol: Cut out affected
ions; treat wounds with a
ective paint; feed tree
rously.

Plum Silver-Leaf Fungus

Damage: Silvery film shows on
leaves and there is a cankering
of wood.
Control: Cut out all dead
wood. Encourage good
cultivation. Treat all large cuts
with a protective paint.

Walnut Blight

Damage: Black spots appear on
nuts, green shoots and leaves.
Control: Spray with fixed
copper, streptomycin or
Agrimycin 500 during
blossoming period.

Hygiene

Destroy all weeds and infected material. Remove and burn all dead and decaying plant material, especially from cold frames and greenhouses. Remove and burn dead and dying branches from trees and shrubs and cover the wounds with a good tree paint. Make sure that disease-carrying packing material and infected vegetable debris are not added to the compost heap.

Pruning Cuts

Paint with protective material—such as an asphaltum-based tree paint—all large pruning cuts of ½-in. diameter or over. This is especially important if the cut is low down on the tree or shrub, for if a fungus does gain entry, all the growth above this point may eventually be killed.

If a large branch tears away, trim the wound by cutting and chiseling to obtain a smooth surface. Should a large cavity be left, it may be necessary to paint its surface with preservative fluid such as creosote. The cavity should be left open, not filled with cement or other materials.

Spacing

Spacing plants so that each has sufficient room may seem a small point, but hygienically it is important. Thickly sown seedlings are always subject to the familiar "damping-off" disease (see page 703 in "How to Raise New Plants"). If transplanted too closely together into seed flats, they may still be crippled by various mildews and molds. Very close planting of older plants or "massing" in beds may encourage powdery mildew to attack perennial phlox, and gray mold to attack calendulas, primulas and zinnias.

New Stock

Examine any new plants which have been purchased. Disease is more obvious on active plants than on dormant ones, but with the latter, there may be signs that all is not quite normal. Young cabbages may have slightly swollen roots due to attack by clubroot; young apple trees may already show symptoms of apple canker; young roses may have galls on their roots or canker in their stems; and many bulbs or corms such as tulip, freesia and gladiolus may have discolorations on their flesh—inside the outer rough scales—caused by the presence of disease parasites. With a valuable or valued stock of plants, isolate any new arrivals until new growth shows that disease is unlikely to be present. This is especially worthwhile with house plants and those for the greenhouse.

Sanitation, Disinfection and Fumigation

A more direct approach to plant health involves strict sanitation and disinfection of greenhouses, frames, flats, pots and even garden tools. These measures should be practiced at all times without waiting for a disease to be spread or suspected.

Clay pots and other containers also may carry harmful funguses. These should be washed free of any soil and vermin and then dipped into a disinfectant such as dilute formaldehyde, copper naphthenate or diluted Clorox. It is well to rinse off the pots with clean water before using them.

Once each year, the inside woodwork, glass and other washable surfaces of the greenhouse should be scrubbed with strong soap and hot water. When walls and other surfaces—except glass—have dried, they should be painted or whitewashed. The frames holding the glass should be scraped and painted every third or fourth year. Be sure not to use paints containing mercury (used to keep molds down on painted surfaces) because these will release mercury fumes that are very toxic to roses and many other greenhouse-grown plants.

Weeds around greenhouses and under greenhouse benches should be destroyed, because these may harbor such funguses as botrytis and powdery mildews, as well as harmful insects. A flame gun can be used to burn off the tops of weeds. Weed killers may also be used, but with great care. Some are so volatile they may affect cultivated plants. Also, do not spray weed killers on heating pipes, because they may be vaporized when the heat is turned on and thus harm the desirable plants.

The soil under greenhouse benches is frequently infested with the *Rhizoctonia (Pellicularia)* fungus. If the open end of the watering hose is dropped on the ground after use, some of the infested soil may adhere to the open end and then be washed into beds or pots of clean plants.

Wooden benches in the greenhouse and the wooden sides of cold frames and flats may also harbor parasitic funguses. Flats and greenhouse benches can be treated with steam at the time soil is being pasteurized. Or they may be treated with chemicals. Among the chemicals most commonly used are copper naphthenate and formaldehyde. The former requires a much shorter period before the benches or frames can be used; the latter may require several weeks. The materials are harmful to plants and annoying to workmen, and must be handled with care.

Soil Pasteurization

The soil in greenhouses and even in some beds outdoors can be treated to destroy disease-producing organisms. This process is known as soil sterilization, but in reality, it is only partial sterilization and hence is more correctly called soil pasteurization. Soils which are "sick"—those which contain disease organisms—can be rejuvenated by pasteurization. Particularly in greenhouses, the continued good health of plants susceptible to root diseases requires this kind of disease control.

Soil can be pasteurized by means of steam. Full information is available from government sources, such as the United States Department of Agriculture's Technical Bulletin 443 and county agricultural agents. Of course, small amounts of soil can be pasteurized by baking in an oven, and treated soil can be bought in garden-supply stores. Such soil is used for pot plants, and for transplants in the early stages of growth, so they may have a better chance of escaping disease infection.

Chemicals are used to free soils of harmful organisms. Formaldehyde is frequently employed to pasteurize small quantities of soil, especially for flats or pots. To treat a standard greenhouse flat filled with soil, first sprinkle a mixture of 1 tbsp. of formaldehyde and 5 tbsp. of water over the soil surface and thoroughly mix in. Cover the flat and let stand for 24 hours. Then sow seeds in the flat in the regular manner and water thoroughly. Larger amounts of soil can also be treated with formaldehyde, but in such cases, a far longer period (a month or more) must pass before it is safe to set plants in this soil.

A mixture of captan, Terraclor and ferbam can be used as a drench to kill harmful funguses in the soils of greenhouse growing benches. Details on the use of chemicals for disinfecting soils can be obtained from county agricultural agents, state and federal plant pathologists, or other government sources.

Another way to grow seedlings without the danger of seed decay or damping-off (rot of seedlings at the

Blackberry Dwarf Virus

Damage: Numerous small stunted shoots appear.
Control: Destroy affected plants immediately.

Currant Leaf Spot

Damage: Small black spots on the leaves, which fall in severe attack.
Control: Spray with Bordeaux-cottonseed-oil mixture early in June and in July after harvest.

Fig Mosaic

Damage: Leaves are discolor and distorted. Fruits have ligh areas and rusty spots.
Control: Spray to control fig mite. Do not use infected plar for propagation.

American Gooseberry Mildew

Damage: White coating at shoot tips and on fruits.
Control: Spray with lime-sulphur, 1–50, with a spreader, just after bloom.

Gooseberry Anthracnose

Damage: Small black spots appear on leaves in severe attacks.
Control: Spray with Bordeaux mixture with a spreader, just after leaves appear and again after harvest.

Gooseberry Rust

Damage: Orange blisters are seen on leaves, fruits, etc.
Control: Spray with Bordeau mixture just before flowering starts. Eliminate sedges (Care: species)—alternate hosts.

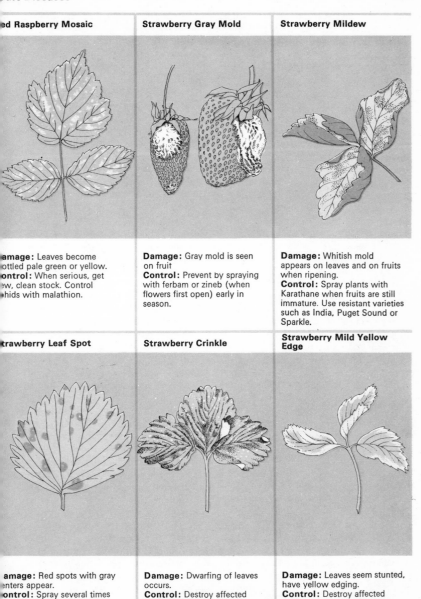

ed Raspberry Mosaic

amage: Leaves become
ottled pale green or yellow.
ontrol: When serious, get
ew, clean stock. Control
phids with malathion.

Strawberry Gray Mold

Damage: Gray mold is seen
on fruit
Control: Prevent by spraying
with ferbam or zineb (when
flowers first open) early in
season.

Strawberry Mildew

Damage: Whitish mold
appears on leaves and on fruits
when ripening.
Control: Spray plants with
Karathane when fruits are still
immature. Use resistant varieties
such as India, Puget Sound or
Sparkle.

trawberry Leaf Spot

amage: Red spots with gray
enters appear.
ontrol: Spray several times
arly in season with Bordeaux
ixture.

Strawberry Crinkle

Damage: Dwarfing of leaves
occurs.
Control: Destroy affected
plants. Control aphids. Select
runners from healthy plants
only.

Strawberry Mild Yellow Edge

Damage: Leaves seem stunted,
have yellow edging.
Control: Destroy affected
plants. Control aphids. Select
runners from healthy plants
only.

soil line) is to use some medium other than soil. Sphagnum moss and vermiculite are the soil substitutes most frequently employed (see page 702 in "How to Grow New Plants").

The former, a coarse, spongy bog-plant material (not to be confused with peat moss), may be bought in specially prepared form for use as a seed-sowing medium. Pour it into cleaned flats, moisten it and sow the seeds on the surface. When tiny seeds (azalea, petunia, snapdragon, etc.) are sown, cover the flat with a pane of glass to retain the moisture until the seedlings appear. For larger seeds, a cover of the moistened material itself, no more than $\frac{1}{4}$ in. thick, is sufficient.

Vermiculite is a mineral mica which has been heated to 2000° F. until it expands like popcorn over a flame, and becomes a sponge which can absorb eight times its weight of water. The intense heat used in its preparation leaves it absolutely germ-free. The special garden grade of vermiculite is suitable as a medium in which to root cuttings and sow larger seeds. A more finely sifted grade must be used for smaller seeds, which sift down too deeply when coarser material is used.

Seed Treatments

Always buy seed—and the term in this sense includes bulbs, corms, tubers, etc., which can carry disease in the dormant state—from reliable firms which do their utmost to supply clean, disease-free material. Despite all precautions, though, some diseases which travel on seeds are missed, and once infected seeds are sown, the diseases have the opportunity of spreading. With some crops, precautions are taken by treating the seed before sowing with a proprietary seed dressing.

A parasite or fungus may infect a seed in one of two ways: it may live on the surface, quite superficially, so that it can be killed easily; or it may penetrate deeply and live in a dormant state inside the tissues (cells) of the embryo plant.

In the first case, the seeds can be disinfected by steeping them in a weak solution of formaldehyde, copper sulphate or other suitable chemical, or alternately by dusting them all over with organic mercury compounds (New Improved Ceresan or Semesan), thiram (Arasan), red copper oxide (Cuprocide) or zinc oxide (Vasco 4).

In the second case, treatment is more difficult. But good results are obtained against several important diseases by steeping the seed (bulb, corm, etc.) in hot water. The temperature and time of immersion varies with the different crops. For example, seeds of cabbage can be rid of black-rot and leaf-spot bacteria and the fungus which causes black leg by steeping the seed in hot water for 25 minutes at 122° F. Early and late blight funguses and the bacterial blight organism can be destroyed in celery seed by soaking the seed for 30 minutes at 118° F. Details on chemical and hot-water seed treatments for vegetables are available in the United States Department of Agriculture's Farmers' Bulletin 1862.

With many diseases, even some of the internal type, good results are obtained by coating the diseased mother corm, bulb, etc., with a fungicidal dust, so that when the corm is planted, the parasite is unable to grow out through the chemical into the surrounding soil. Thus it cannot infect the young growth or the young, developing corm. This method is of great value in keeping stocks of such corms as gladiolus free from disease. It is often possible to sow treated seeds or to plant treated corms in heavily disease-contaminated soil and get good seasonal results, although the disease still remains in the soil.

CHEMICALS USED AS SPRAYS

To protect plants from disease parasites, chemicals must, without harming the plant, kill the fungus parasite or stop its spores from germinating. For many years, the principal substances used as fungicides have been copper and sulphur and occasionally mercury. They are still important, but there are now many modern organic sprays. These are very good, but they are more specific in their action and so do not have such a widespread application as the older chemicals. Hundreds of new synthetic organic compounds are being examined and tested each year, and there is still much to learn in this field of study. Even the substances known as "antibiotics" in human therapeutic practice—penicillin, streptomycin, griseofulvin, etc.—have been and are being tested against various plant diseases. In special cases they have proved successful.

The plant—including the undersurface of the leaves—is covered by spraying with a protective film of the fungicide. Attacked plants cannot always be cured, but those not yet affected can be protected. Hence, the importance of early detection.

With most fungicidal sprays, it is best to include a "wetter" or "spreader." This has the effect of causing the fluid to spread and stick more closely to the leaves. Some well-known spreaders and stickers are casein, calcium caseinate, ordinary wheat flour, powdered skim milk and soybean flour. Emulsified mineral oils are also used as spreaders and stickers. Commercial spreaders and stickers widely available include Du Pont Spreader-Sticker, Triton B 1956, Spred-O-Stick and Wilt-Pruf. Dilute according to directions on the package.

Many modern insecticides can be mixed with these fungicides so that both can be applied at the same time. An excellent combination spray for fruit trees contains the following ingredients per gallon of water: 3 level tbsp. of 25-percent malathion wettable powder (W.P.), 3 of 50-percent methoxychlor W.P., 2 of 50-percent captan W.P. and ½ level tbsp. of Kelthane. For vegetables, carbaryl (Sevin), 50-percent W.P., 3 tbsp, may be substituted for methoxychlor. Where mildew is a problem, folpet (Phaltan) may be substituted for captan.

The "systemic" type of fungicide enters the plant tissues and by its presence in the cells prevents, or at the very least minimizes, any attack.

Many different names are in use for the same or similar fungicides. Some names are proprietary; others are based on the name of the chemical composing the fungicide. This is sometimes confusing, but the reader can refer to *Pesticide Handbook*, published annually by College Science Publishers, State College, Pennsylvania, or to *Guide to the Chemicals Used in Crop Protection*, Canadian Department of Agriculture, London, Ontario.

Method of Application

There is a wide choice of machines suitable for applying the sprays and dusts used as fungicides. Liquid sprayers vary from hand models with 1-qt. capacity to large tank sprayers mounted on wheels. Hose-end sprayers are popular and easy to use. Choose one having sufficient capacity to spray all the plants without repeated refilling.

The nozzle should deliver the spray as a fine mist in the shape of a cone so that the fungicide falls on the plant as a fog and a film of fluid covers the foliage. Spray when there is little or

Antirrhinum (Snapdragon) Rust

Damage: Brown pustules are seen on leaves and stems.
Control: Grow resistant varieties or spray with maneb or zineb.

Carnation Ring Spot

Damage: Pale spots show with dark pustules in rings.
Control: Destroy infected plants. Disinfect cutting knife frequently, because virus can be spread via infected sap.

Carnation Rust

Damage: Brown pustules on stems and leaves.
Control: Avoid syringing in greenhouse, ventilate properly. Dust plants with zineb, or a mixture of ferbam and sulphur.

Chrysanthemum Fasciation

Damage: Cauliflower-like mass of stunted shoots occurs at stem base.
Control: Destroy infected plants. Pasteurize or use fresh soil for clean cuttings or plants.

Chrysanthemum Powdery Mildew

Damage: Powdery-white deposit shows on leaves.
Control: Spray with Actidione PM, Karathane or folpet (Phaltan).

Chrysanthemum Rust

Damage: Chocolate-colored spots on undersurface of leaves.
Control: Spray with maneb or zineb and destroy affected leaves early.

...mping-Off in Stock ...edlings

...amage: Seedlings collapse at ...il level, wither and die.
...ntrol: Sow thinly and ...aintain good growing ...nditions. Use pasteurized ...il just before planting ...edlings, or plant seeds in ...ted sphagnum moss.

Delphinium Black Spot

Damage: Dull black spots on leaves.
Control: Spray with copper fungicide regularly.

Gladiolus Dry Rot

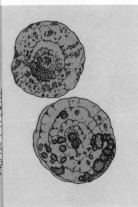

Damage: Dark spots appear on corms. Infected plants turn yellow and die prematurely.
Control: Plant in well-drained soil. Treat infected soil with Terraclor, methyl bromide or Mylone. Treat corms with New Improved Ceresan.

...adiolus Scab

...amage: Sunken brown spots ...pear on corm base.
...ontrol: Reject badly scabbed ...rms—change site each ...ason.

Cyclamen Gray Mold

Damage: Rotting of flower and leaf stalks occurs.
Control: Improve ventilation and spray with ferbam or zineb.

Hellebore Black Leaf Spot

Damage: Leaves have dark brown or black spots.
Control: Spray with copper fungicide.

no wind and, if possible, just before a rainy spell. Be careful not to breathe the spray, as some substances are harmful to the lungs.

The importance of keeping sprayers clean cannot be overemphasized. Wash them well after use, clean the nozzle or nozzles and place the empty machine upside down to drain. Sprayers put away with fluid still in them may be ruined during the winter by rust or corrosion.

"Dusters" for small gardens are available in plastic containers which, when squeezed, produce a fine cloud of dust.

RESISTANT PLANTS

Some plants are slightly resistant to disease, while others are completely immune. A plant may be immune to one disease but very susceptible to another. For example, potatoes that are resistant to scab (*Actinomyces scabies*) can be easily attacked by blight (*Phytophthora infestans*). (Illus. p. 802.) Despite this, the production of resistant varieties marks an important step forward in checking disease and is probably the simplest method of doing so.

The work of producing resistant varieties is not easy, because they must stand comparison with susceptible varieties in quality of flower or flavor. Breeding for quality and flavor combined with a high degree of resistance goes on continuously, but there is always the chance that resistant plants will suddenly succumb to a new strain of the disease parasite. Then the search for new resistant plants starts all over again. This is why the study of crop-protective measures such as spraying must always continue.

CONTROL OF VIRUS DISEASES

The only spray treatment likely to be needed for the control of virus dis-

eases is that designed to keep down insects, for these are the virus carriers. Burn plants with suspected virus symptoms to eliminate sources of infective material. The infected plants will not recover, and it is useless trying to save them. Support this effort—especially in greenhouses—by regular spraying or fumigation to keep down insects. Annuals—which are, of course, propagated by seed—in general keep free of virus infection. Take cuttings from healthy plants only, and wipe or dip the knife used to prepare them in disinfectant.

REGULATORY CONTROL

In the United States, federal quarantine laws prevent the importation of soil, certain plants and plant products because of the danger of introducing new diseases or insect pests into the country. Some states also have laws which prohibit the movement of certain fruits, vegetables, trees and shrubs into these states from other states that are known to harbor harmful organisms. For example, states free from the virus disease of peach, known as X-disease, do not allow the entry of peach trees from states known to harbor this highly fatal disease.

The movement of plants between nurseries and gardens in America cannot be regulated easily, but voluntary schemes are available for growers and nurserymen to encourage them to raise and sell clean stocks. The best known is probably the seed-potato certification program. The grower has his stocks rigorously inspected during the growing season, and if all is well he is granted a certificate which indicates that the stock is true to type and free from virus infection. Encouragement is thus given to the purchase of certified fresh potato seed, and the crippling effect of virus and the lower crop yield which is often obtained from home-saved seed are avoided.

Similar voluntary schemes exist for plants such as strawberries, raspberries and peaches. Government plant pathologists supply information concerning which varieties are covered by such programs and are certified to be free from virus infection.

A Guide to Plant Diseases

DISEASES THAT AFFECT MANY KINDS OF PLANTS

Damping-Off and Foot Rot

(*Pythium* and *Phytophthora* species) Damping-off is a common trouble of very young seedlings, causing them to collapse at soil level, wither and die. It can also occur among young plants at a later stage when they are transplanted into boxes or pots. It is then known as foot rot. This is caused by a fungus at the base of the stem or in the root, and often comes from thick sowing and too wet soil conditions. (Illus. p. 789.)

Control: It helps to treat infected soil with such materials as Panodrench, PCNB (Terraclor) or Semesan, or to dust the seeds with a fungicide, but it is essential to use good compost and provide suitable growing conditions both for the seeds and for the young plants.

Crown Gall and Leafy Gall

Crown gall is the result of infection by *Erwinia tumefaciens;* leafy gall, by *Corynebacterium fascians.*

Crown gall takes the form of a sphere varying in size from a pea to a baseball. It is hard with a smooth or rough surface, and it usually occurs on the roots. Sometimes, however, it may show on aerial shoots of blackberry, roses and other plants.

Leafy gall is a cauliflower-like mass of shortened shoots, growing usually at the base of the plant stem. It is usually rather soft. On sweet peas, the shoots are very flattened, stunted and not so numerous.

Although crown gall may be seen on many herbaceous plants—asters, chrysanthemums, etc.—it mostly attacks the roots of trees and shrubs—roses, apple and other fruit trees and even some conifers.

Control: Any plants showing signs of leafy gall should be burned, and no cuttings should be taken from them except possibly in the case of pelargoniums (geraniums), where the cutting material comes from upper shoots well away from the infected base of the stem.

Gray-Mold Fungus

(*Botrytis cinerea*) Gray mold causes much trouble in greenhouses because it likes humid conditions, can live on dead and decaying matter (that is, it is a facultative saprophyte) and can survive almost anywhere. Given the right conditions, it can do enormous damage to cuttings of such plants as salvias, pelargoniums (geraniums), dahlias and chrysanthemums in greenhouses and to the flowers of zinnias, carnations, sweet peas, etc. Pot plants such as cyclamens, calceolarias, lilies and pelargoniums often suffer from this disease.

Even on outdoor plants, botrytis can quickly enter a wound or dead bud in soft stems of roses and other shrubs, killing the branch. In wet summers, and particularly if they are closely planted, petunias, clarkias,

Hollyhock Rust

Damage: Undersides of leaves are covered with orange-red or white pustules.
Control: Gather and burn infected parts in fall and early spring. Spray with ferbam or zineb three or four times at two-week intervals.

Iris Leaf Spot

Damage: Pale circular spots appear on leaves (not usually serious).
Control: Keep beds well cleared of old leaves in spring. Bordeaux mixture or zineb sprays will control severe infections.

Lilac Blight

Damage: Shoots and flowers become blackened and wither.
Control: Cut out affected parts. Spray with Bordeaux mixture.

Michaelmas Daisy (Aster) Mildew

Damage: Plants looks as if covered with flour.
Control: Spray with Actidione PM, Karathane or Phaltan.

Narcissus Basal Rot

Damage: Bulbs become brown, soft and shiny. Encouraged by wet soil.
Control: Choose well-drained site; treat bulbs with New Improved Ceresan.

Narcissus Yellow Stripe

Damage: Yellowish or light green stripes appear on the young leaf. Not so severe on some varieties.
Control: Discard affected plants in spring. Inspect when leaves are about 8 in. high.

ony Botrytis Blight	Phlox Mildew	Plane-Tree Anthracnose

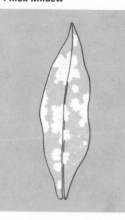 

mage: Young shoots decay,
s are blighted.
ntrol: Gather and burn
veground parts in fall.
ay several times in spring
h Bordeaux mixture, ferbam
ineb.

Damage: White powdery
coating appears on leaves.
Control: Spray with Actidione
PM, Karathane or Phaltan.

Damage: Leaves turn brown in
spring; twigs and small branches
may be killed outright.
Control: Spray with an
organic mercury just as buds
begin to swell in spring. Prune
infected twigs and branches.

ododendron Bud Blight	Rose Leaf Black Spot	Rose Mildew

 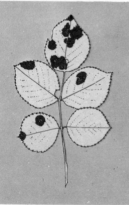 

mage: Buds wither and
n turn grayish.
trol: Spray with Bordeaux
ture before blossoming and
nonthly intervals after
ssoming.

Damage: Black spots on leaves.
Control: Spray with Phaltan,
Manzate or ferbam.

Damage: Whitish powder on
leaves and stems.
Control: Spray with Actidione
PM, Karathane or Phaltan.

godetias, zinnias and similar bedding plants may be killed. It is the stems of these plants which are attacked.

Tomato, strawberry and raspberry fruits are destroyed as they ripen; the same fate can overtake apples and pears in storage. Imported grapes and other fruits may suffer seriously if conditions in transit are not correct.

Moist air seems to be the factor of utmost importance to this disease. If the humidity is high, the gray-mold fungus will flourish through an extraordinarily wide range of temperatures. (Illus. p. 789.)

Control: Keep down humidity as much as possible by prudent ventilation and watering. Avoid syringing and overhead watering, allow plenty of space between plants, and do not let temperatures become too cool.

Honey Fungus
(*Armillaria mellea*)

The honey fungus is an underground parasite which attacks the roots of trees and shrubs. It rarely shows aboveground, except when it produces its honey-colored clusters of mushrooms on old stumps or at the base of trees which it has killed. When it has done this, it sends out long, black, shoestringlike strands (rhizomorphs), which may be many feet in length. These grow through the soil to attack other trees.

Some people claim that it can only attack roots which have been injured or which are weakened by some other cause. Others believe it to be a more serious parasite. It is widespread and causes many losses; few trees or shrubs are known to be immune. Where soil conditions are adverse—excessively wet, for instance—the honey fungus seems to flourish, rather than in good, well-drained soils.

It is risky to clear woodland of old scrub and use the land immediately for young fruit trees. Honey fungus on old tree stumps and pieces of root may attack the young trees.

Control: Where trees are killed by this parasite, remove the stumps and all possible roots for burning. If this cannot be done, make a trench in a circle around each dead stump and throw the soil inward. Then fork over the soil inside the trench and saturate it with ½ pt. phenyl mercury acetate in each 100 gal. of water. Another control is to drench the base of infected trees with carbon disulphide.

Mildews

Downy Mildews: These mildews grow deeply into the plant and produce a velvety, moldlike growth on the surface to release their spores. They include many serious difficulties of flowers and vegetables. Among vegetables, they attack cabbages and other crucifers, cucumbers and other gourds, lettuce, onions, peas and spinach. Among flowers, there are similar mildews which attack China asters, godetias, flax, lupines, snapdragons, veronicas and other plants.

Control: It is the young plants that are seriously affected by these mildews, and a timely spray with zineb (Dithane Z-78) is often required. At no time allow the plants to suffer dryness at the roots.

Powdery Mildews: The powdery mildews are a group of funguses which include many genera, but all are closely related, and all resemble one another in the way they grow on the host plants they attack. They are the type of disease most often seen in ordinary gardens. (Illus. pp. 776, 777.)

Their habit of growth is fairly conspicuous. They produce a white powdery coating on the leaves, shoots and sometimes fruits of their hosts. This white covering consists of a network of threads of the mildew fungus sending down its suckers to feed in the epidermal (outer) cells. On many of the threads long chains of spores are produced. These are cut off in regular succession and released in enormous numbers to spread disease. Such mildews are commonly seen on roses, delphiniums, clematises, cyclamens, hawthorns, lilacs, zinnias, peas, cucumbers, strawberries, gooseberries, grapes, apples, young oaks, plane trees and many other plants.

Before the arrival of winter, the white coating develops small dotlike bodies (perithecia), which survive the winter and produce another kind of spore to begin the disease again in spring.

Control: Moist conditions and drafts often encourage these mildews, especially in greenhouses and cold frames, but dryness at the roots is also an encouraging factor. This appears to lower the plants' resistance to mildew and should be guarded against by watering and mulching. The best sprays to use against this kind of mildew include Actidione PM, Karathane and folpet (Phaltan).

Rust Diseases

Rust diseases are easily recognized: they commonly show on leaves and stems as yellow-brown or orange-colored pustules. These have a rusty appearance, from which they take their common name.

They are highly specialized and produce spore stages of different kinds in a definite order. The rusts are interesting, because although some produce all their spore stages on the same plant (autoecious rusts), many produce them on different plants (heteroecious rusts). In the latter, the parasitic-rust fungus is said to use alternate hosts, a factor of great importance when considering control measures. It is of extreme importance to know the alternate host and the method by which the fungus lives and persists on its different host plants.

Some common examples of rust diseases are mint rust (*Puccinia menthae*), which produces all its spore stages on mint plants (illus. p. 799), and currant rust (*Cronartium ribicola*), which has some spore stages on the leaves of black currant in summer but also lives and produces other spores on the white pine and similar five-needled pines. The stage on the latter is known as blister rust because of the orange-yellow fungus which emerges from the bark.

Control: Rust diseases are checked by occasional applications of Bordeaux mixture, ferbam, sulphur or zineb. The white-pine blister-rust fungus can be controlled by painting the affected areas with a mixture of Actidione BR in fuel oil or spraying the basal third of the trunk with this mixture, in the way directed by the manufacturer.

In autoecious rusts, where the parasite lives on one kind of plant, control is fairly simple by spraying or destroying diseased plants.

With heteroecious rusts, it may also be necessary to learn from your County Agricultural Agent, or other government resource, the identity of the alternate host, and either destroy it or treat it by spraying.

Silver Leaf (*Stereum purpureum*)

This disease is well known but not well understood. The main symptom is the silvering of the leaves, but this is not entirely reliable, because other agencies such as cold and aphid attack can sometimes cause foliage to become silvered. In trees or branches

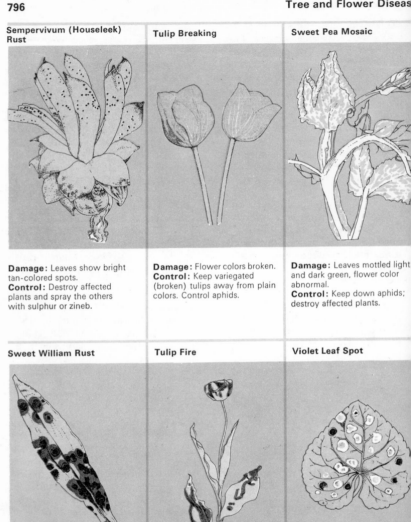

Sempervivum (Houseleek) Rust

Damage: Leaves show bright tan-colored spots.
Control: Destroy affected plants and spray the others with sulphur or zineb.

Tulip Breaking

Damage: Flower colors broken.
Control: Keep variegated (broken) tulips away from plain colors. Control aphids.

Sweet Pea Mosaic

Damage: Leaves mottled light and dark green, flower color abnormal.
Control: Keep down aphids; destroy affected plants.

Sweet William Rust

Damage: Chocolate-brown pustules on leaves.
Control: Dust with a mixture of ferbam and sulphur or with zineb.

Tulip Fire

Damage: White patches on leaves, buds blighted, plants stunted.
Control: Spray with captan or zineb every week (during rainy springs), starting when leaves are 4 in. tall.

Violet Leaf Spot

Damage: Greenish-yellow spots with burnt-umber margins
Control: Gather and burn infected leaves in fall. Spray with maneb or zineb if necessary

affected by the true silver-leaf fungus, a brown irregular stain can usually be seen in the wood when the infected branch is cut across. The real proof is the appearance of the typical purple-colored fungus outgrowths, but these appear only on dead wood.

Plums are most susceptible to this disease, but it also affects apples and other fruit trees. (Illus. p. 781.)

Occasionally it attacks shade and ornamental trees. It is most commonly found and most serious in the Pacific Northwest.

Control: Infection can occur only through a wound, and the way to prevent this disease from gaining entry is to treat all wounds with a good protective paint and to burn all dead wood. Remove all brush from the orchard.

DISEASES WHICH NORMALLY ATTACK ONE OR TWO KINDS OF PLANTS ONLY

As many diseases as possible are mentioned briefly under this heading or shown in the illustrations. They are listed under their respective hosts.

Fruit Diseases

BLACKBERRY
Orange Rust: Orange spores on leaf undersurface. Destroy infected plants. Use resistant varieties such as Eldorado, Russell, Snyder and Ebony King.

GOOSEBERRY
Dieback: Branches die back and wither when near fruit harvest, owing to botrytis infection through wound or dead side shoot. Cut off behind point of infection and paint over cuts with a protective paint.

PEACH
Leaf Curl: Spray with ferbam when trees are dormant. (Illus. p. 780.)

PEAR
Mildew: White coating on shoot tips. Cut these off and spray tree with Karathane.
Brown Rot: Fruit turns brown and develops white pustules. Cut out dead spurs and shoots when pruning. Bury deeply all rotten fruits. Keep the storage area clean and do not store bruised fruit. Pick and store when dry and wrap better-class fruits in special wrappers. Try to prevent injuries from wasps and birds. Control codling moth.
Cankers: Scrape and cut out cankers and cover cuts with a good tree paint.

RASPBERRY
Gray Mold: Check by spraying fruit with zineb or ferbam early in season.
Virus: Mosaic shows as yellow blotches or spots and crinkling of leaves. Some varieties are only slightly affected and may still bear fruit. If crippled, they must be discarded.

Tree and Flower Diseases

ALMOND
Leaf Curl: Swollen and malformed reddish blisters on leaves. Spray with ferbam when trees are dormant.

ANTIRRHINUM (SNAPDRAGON)
Downy Mildew: Furry gray mold on leaf undersurfaces. Destroy crippled plants, feed, and spray with zineb.

ASTER (MICHAELMAS DAISY)
Wilt: Browning and withering of leaves from bottom of plant up. Take short cuttings in early spring and plant out on fresh site in April.

BEGONIA
Bacterial Wilt: Brown spots on the leaves and on stalks: branches wilt and die. Cut off affected parts; spray with Bordeaux mixture and dip cuttings in it.

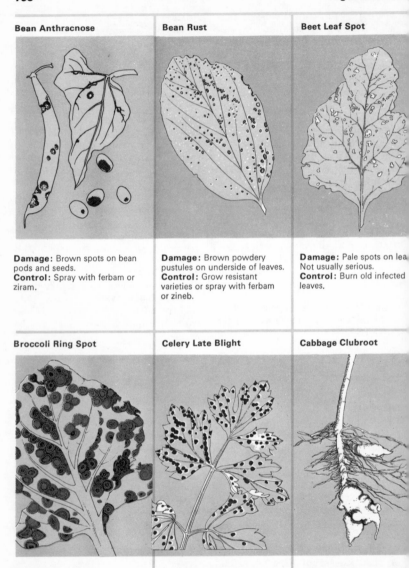

Bean Anthracnose

Damage: Brown spots on bean pods and seeds.
Control: Spray with ferbam or ziram.

Bean Rust

Damage: Brown powdery pustules on underside of leaves.
Control: Grow resistant varieties or spray with ferbam or zineb.

Beet Leaf Spot

Damage: Pale spots on lea Not usually serious.
Control: Burn old infected leaves.

Broccoli Ring Spot

Damage: Brown spots surrounded by concentric rings.
Control: Burn old infected leaves. Rotate plantings.

Celery Late Blight

Damage: Brownish-black spots on leaves. Seed-borne.
Control: Buy clean seed. Spray with Bordeaux mixture early, even on young plants still in flats.

Cabbage Clubroot

Damage: Roots swell and s unpleasant. Plants do not th and wilt in hot sun.
Control: Lime soil heavily weeks before setting out pla Treat infested soil with Terra

uce Gray Mold	Lettuce Mosaic	Mint Rust

age: Gray molded decay ants, usually at ground

trol: Treat soil with clor mixed with captan.

Damage: Leaves yellow, plants are dwarfed.
Control: Use virus-free seed, destroy infected plants and control aphids.

Damage: Thickened shoots have orange-colored cups.
Control: Dust with sulphur, harvest plants early.

n Mildew	Onion Neck Rot	Onion White Rot

age: Leaf tips turn yellow wilt.
trol: Spray with zineb.

Damage: Neck of plant becomes soft and brown.
Control: Harvest carefully. Dry under cover, store below 37° F.

Damage: White fungus on roots.
Control: Treat soil with steam, Mylone or Vapam.

CALLISTEPHUS (CHINA ASTER)
Foot Rot: Often encouraged by wet conditions. Pasteurize soil before setting out new plants.
Wilt: Very serious; attacks stem halfway up and prevents flowering. Also contaminates soil. Grow resistant varieties.

CAMELLIA
Dieback, Canker: Branch tips die back, leaves wilt. Elliptical cankers on old wood. Prune infected tips, remove cankers surgically. Spray with Bordeaux mixture.
Leaf Blotch: Grayish blotches in young rooted cuttings. Cut off affected parts and spray with captan.
Yellow-Mottle Virus: Yellow mottling, blotches and speckles appear on the leaves, but the disease is not an important one.

CARNATION
Leaf Spots: Spray for these with Bordeaux mixture.
Stem Rot: Leaves turn yellow and wither. Destroy affected plants and use steam-pasteurized or treated soil for the cuttings.

CHEIRANTHUS (WALLFLOWER)
Clubroot: Large swellings on roots. Leaves wilt. Treat soil with PCNB (Terraclor).

DAHLIA
Spotted Wilt: Ring pattern on leaves. Control aphids. Root only small stem-tip cuttings if the stock plants are affected.

DELPHINIUM
Black Root Rot: Treat seed in hot water. Drench crowns with Bordeaux mixture. Poorly aerated and wet soils favor the disease.
Virus: Leaves become mottled and flowers are stunted. Destroy the infected plants.

ELM
Dutch Elm Disease: In June or July leaves on a branch turn yellow, wilt and turn brown, but remain on the tree. The tree shows dead branches in its crown (is stag-headed) and then dies. No control known. Spraying with DDT or methoxychlor gives some protection.

EUONYMUS
Mildew: Often serious in Midwest and South. Spray with Karathane.

FREESIA
Virus: Leaves show pronounced striping. Best to destroy heavily infected stock and plant new stock. Do not plant near beans or gladioluses.

GARDENIA
Canker: Destroy infected plant. Set cuttings in pasteurized rooting medium, or dip cuttings in ferbam, potassium permanganate or Semesan.

GLADIOLUS
Dry Rot: Black lesions on corms. Dip in New Improved Ceresan before planting. Plant on a fresh site each season. (Illus. p. 789.)

GLOXINIA
Virus (Spotted Wilt): Circular brown bands appear on leaves. Destroy diseased plants.

GODETIA
Gray Mold: Rare on this host. Spray with zineb if necessary.

HYDRANGEA
Mildew: Spray with Karathane.

IRIS
Ink Spot: On bulbous irises, black inky patches on bulbs, which should be burned. Plant in new location. Spray with Bordeaux mixture.
Leaf Spot: Not usually serious if

beds are cleared of old leaves, etc., in spring. Spray with Bordeaux mixture, maneb or zineb. (Illus. p. 792.)
Soft Rot: Soft rotting of rhizomes of bearded iris. Remove dead parts. Control borers. Drench infested soil with Semesan.
Virus: Chiefly on bulbous iris. Leaves show mottling and flowers show "breaking." Burn affected plants.

JUNIPER
Cedar Apple: Swollen branches producing white hornlike fruiting bodies containing brown spores. Cut off and burn affected parts. Spray with cycloheximide (Actidione).

LABURNUM
Twig Blight: Cut out and burn affected parts.

LARCH
Canker: Orange fungus bodies on the cankered areas. Remove and burn infected trees promptly.

LILAC
Blight: Blackens young shoots and flowers, causing them to wither and droop. Cut out affected shoots. Spray with Bordeaux mixture. (Illus. p. 792.)

LILIES
Botrytis: Spots and brown patches on leaves. Spray early with Bordeaux mixture and repeat at 10- to 14-day intervals.
Virus: Mosaic is common. Destroy infected plants and keep down aphids.

MAPLE
Tar Spot: Black spots on leaves—not usually serious. Burn old leaves. Spray with an organic mercury or a copper compound in early May.

MECONOPSIS
Downy Mildew: Serious in seedlings. Spray with zineb. Provide good culti-

vation. Destroy the infected plants.

OAK
Mildew: Can be serious on young oaks. Spray with Karathane.

PRIMULA
Virus: Mottling on leaves. Very common on all kinds of primulas. Destroy affected plants. Spray for aphids with malathion or lindane.

RHODODENDRON
Dieback: Terminal buds and leaves turn brown and die. Prune affected twigs to sound wood; spray with Bordeaux mixture. (Illus. p. 793.)

ROSE
Canker: Remove the brown cankered shoots by pruning.
Chlorosis: Leaves become pale, owing to iron deficiency. Apply Sequestrene.
Leaf Black Spot: Spray with captan. Pick off infected leaves. (Illus. p. 793.)

SPRUCE
Rust: On needles—in the U. S. Pacific Northwest. The alternate host is rhododendron. Do not, therefore, grow rhododendrons on a site that is near spruce.

STOCK
Foot Rot: Plant collapses. Too much water around roots. Destroy plants. Treat soil with PCNB (Terraclor).
Virus: Flower "breaking" and mottled leaves. Often spread from infected crucifers (cabbage family). Destroy infected plants.

SWEET WILLIAM
Rust: Sometimes serious enough to need spraying of young plants with a mixture of ferbam and sulphur, or with zineb. (Illus. p. 796.)

TAGETES (MARIGOLD)
Foot Rot: Favored by wet soil condi-

Parsnip Canker

Damage: Brown rotten patch is seen on root.
Control: Plant in well-drained soil. Spray with copper fungicide or zineb every ten days starting in August.

Pea Powdery Mildew

Damage: White powdery coating on leaves, stems and pods.
Control: Use mildew-free seed or resistant variety.

Pea Pod Spot

Damage: Brown sunken spo with darker margins.
Control: Use well-drained se and practice four-year rotation Buy western-grown seed.

Potato Blight on Leaves

Damage: Dark green water-soaked spots.
Control: Spray with Bordeaux mixture, maneb, nabam or zineb.

Potato Blight on Tubers

Damage: Browning of skin, brownish-red rot beneath.
Control: Spray with Bordeaux mixture, maneb, nabam or zineb.

Potato Scab

Damage: Scabby growths on tuber.
Control: Acidify soil with sulphur. Treat soil with Terraclor or Vapam.

tato Wart	Spinach Downy Mildew	Tomato Buckeye Rot

mage: Wartlike growths
ear on tuber (rare in the
ted States).
ntrol: Treat soil with copper
ohate, then lime. Grow
atoes on same land only
ry fourth year.

Damage: Often serious, this
grows deeply into plant.
Control: Plant thinly on
well-drained soil. Use
resistant varieties.

Damage: Brown concentric
zones on fruit.
Control: Mulch the soil
surface to prevent water
splashing, stake plants, or spray
with captan or maneb.

mato Blossom-End Rot	Tomato Leaf Mold	Tomato Magnesium Deficiency

mage: Brown decay at
ssom end of fruit.
ntrol: Water during dry
lls; add calcium oxide to
or spray leaves with 1
cent calcium chloride; mulch
surface.

Damage: Leaves have velvety
brown spots.
Control: Spray with ziram.
Choose resistant varieties.

Damage: Orange-yellow
patches on leaves.
Control: Several sprayings
with Epsom salts, 3 oz. in 1 gal.
water at two-week intervals.

tions. Plant in clean soil or pasteurize infested soil.

TULIP

Fire: Scorching of leaves and spotting on petals. Soil is contaminated. Pasteurize infested soil. Choose good bulbs and spray with zineb or captan early in spring on young foliage. (Illus. p. 796.)

Virus: "Breaking" in flowers—plants are not much affected. Control aphids. Keep plants of broken (variegated) colors away from those of plain colors. (Illus. p. 796.)

VIOLA (VIOLET)

Root Rot: Fungus invades roots, turning them reddish or violet. Pasteurize soil or plant in new soil.

Scab: Reddish spots with white centers change to raised scabs on leaves and stems. Spray with zineb.

Smut: Swollen blisters on shoots. Leaves contain black powdery spores. Spray plants that remain with Bordeaux mixture, after affected plants have been destroyed.

WILLOW

Canker: Brown spots on leaves. Small cankers on shoots. Cut away cankered wood and burn it. Spray with Bordeaux mixture or use resistant varieties.

Rust: Yellow spots appear on the leaves. Stems become cankered. Spray the young trees early with Bordeaux mixture.

ZINNIA

Bacterial Wilt: Seedlings die as result of infected seed. Destroy. Use clean or treated seed in pasteurized soil.

Gray-Mold Blight: Brown spots on leaves, cankers on stems. Flowers blighted. Treat seeds in hot water. Spray plants with Bordeaux mixture or ferbam.

Vegetable Diseases

ASPARAGUS

Rust: Premature yellowing of leaves, rusty pustules on stems. Use resistant varieties.

BEAN, BUSH

Anthracnose: Brown spotting on stems and pods is often caused by infected seed. Spray with ferbam or ziram. (Illus. p. 798.)

Foot Rot: Frequently due to planting too often on same site. Rotate crops.

Virus: Mosaic can be carried in the seed. Destroy infected plants. Use resistant varieties.

CABBAGE FAMILY (CRUCIFERS)

Clubroot: Thickened, swollen roots prevent good growth. Apply lime for crucifers, treat soil with PCNB (Terraclor). (Illus. p. 798.)

Downy Mildew: Common but rarely serious. Yellow patches on leaves. Spray young plants with zineb and be careful to keep them from becoming overcrowded.

Ring Spot: Brown spots with concentric rings. Rotate crops.

Virus: Several kinds, some infecting flower crops such as wallflower, stock and candytuft. Destroy all plants affected. Keep down aphids.

CUCUMBER

Bacterial Wilt: Sudden wilting of leaves and drying of stems. Control cucumber beetles.

Downy Mildew: Spray with maneb.

Virus: Mosaic green mottling in leaves. Destroy affected plants when young. Keep down insects. Use resistant varieties.

LEEK

Smut: Blisters full of black powder on leaves and bulbs. Water the drills when sowing with formalin, ¼ pt. in 4 gal. water; or apply Arasan dust with the seed.

LETTUCE
Gray Mold: Rotting at soil level. Treat soil with Terraclor mixed with captan. (Illus. p. 799.)
Mildew: Give good ventilation and use resistant varieties.
Mosaic: Prevent aphid infestations. Use virus-free seed.

ONION
Mildew: Serious. Spray with zineb. (Illus. p. 799.)
Smut: Blisters full of black powder on leaves and bulbs. Water drills when sowing with formalin, ¼ pt. in 4 gal. water, or apply disinfectant dust with seed.
White Rot: White fungus destroys roots. Treat fallow soil with steam, Mylone or Vapam. (Illus. p. 799.)

PEAS
Foot Rot: Change the site each season.

POTATO
Blackleg: In June, base of the stem blackens and leaves yellow. Use certified seed. Plant whole tubers or disinfect cutting knife frequently.
Dry Rot: Shriveling of seed tubers. Do not plant infected stock. Use certified seed.
Virus: Several serious ones. Avoid by planting fresh certified seed each year. Use mosaic-resistant varieties. (Illus. pp. 802 and 803.)

RHUBARB
Crown Rot: Black rotten areas below crown. Change site and get fresh plants.

SWEET CORN
Smut: Some ears and other plant parts swell and are full of black powdery spores. Cut out and burn infected parts while young.

TOMATO
Blight: Symptoms the same as potato blight. Appears on outdoor plants only. Spray with Bordeaux mixture, maneb, nabam or zineb.
Blossom-End Rot: Brown decay at blossom end of fruit. Mix calcium oxide in soil prior to planting or spray leaves with dilute calcium chloride. Water well when dry. (Illus. p. 803.)
Cracking: Caused by alternate wet and dry conditions.
Flower Drop: Caused by dry soil conditions or very cool nights at flowering time. Spray with hormone product which prevents dropping.
Leaf Mold: Spray with ziram. Use resistant varieties such as Globella, Improved Bay State or Improved Vetomold. (Illus. p. 803.)
Virus: Several viruses known causing severe mosaic, streak and malformations. Destroy plants. Control aphids.

TURNIP
Clubroot: See Cabbage Family.
Virus: Yellowish-green mottling on leaves. Protect seedlings from peach and cabbage aphids by spraying or screening seedbeds.

CHAPTER 45

PLANT PESTS
How to Detect and Destroy

Conditions for Invasion—Use of Pesticides—Plant Pests: General Garden, Vegetable, Fruit, Indoor, Ornamental and Tree

PLANTS ARE A SOURCE OF FOOD for many types of insects and other small creatures, and there are few plants which are not attacked by them. In some cases the attacks may be sporadic and unpredictable, but the more serious pest attacks can be expected to cause damage to certain plants year after year. Their severity usually depends on the weather conditions of the current and previous seasons. A wet summer and fall results in the destruction of many Japanese-beetle larvae in the soil, thus reducing the beetle population the following year. A hot, dry summer favors the development of red spider mites.

The variation in the range of pests found in different localities is probably due to the climate, but is also influenced by the available shelter from the weather, the type of soil and the kind of vegetation growing near the garden.

No single garden, therefore, is likely to harbor all the pests mentioned in this chapter, and preventive measures should be taken only if pests are known to be present and are causing appreciable damage. It is wise to learn to recognize the more common types of pests feeding on the plants and, during a few years of experience, to build up an idea of the degree of damage caused by those which attack regularly.

Pests can usually be divided roughly into three categories:
1. Those which cause so little damage that control is unnecessary.
2. Those which normally cause little damage but may increase in numbers under certain conditions, such as hot weather, rain, etc. Keep these pests under observation and deal with them if they show signs of increasing.
3. Those which cause severe damage every year. If possible, take preventive measures before they appear, or destroy them as soon as they are seen on plants.

If these points are kept in mind, pesticides need not be used unnecessarily, and the beneficial insects, of which there are large numbers, will have a chance to exert a modicum of natural control over the pests.

BUYING PESTICIDES

A great many pesticides are available, and each one may be sold under a variety of trade names. Every pesticide label must supply the following: the name and address of the manufacturer or the person for whom the pesticide was made; the name, brand or trademark under which it is marketed; the weight or volume of the contents; the correct ingredient statement; if highly toxic to man, a warning indicated by skull and crossbones and an antidote suggestion; a warning or caution statement as to whether it may harm man, animals or plants and adequate directions on how to use it.

CAUTIONS IN
USING PESTICIDES

Before using a pesticide read the label carefully.

Do not use more pesticide than is recommended or the plants may be damaged.

Avoid spraying when the temperature is above 85° F. Some pesticides are likely to damage plants under such conditions.

Avoid spraying open flowers, so as to safeguard bees and other pollinating insects.

Do not spray in windy weather when the spray might drift to open blooms or to fruit and vegetables ready for picking.

Most pesticides are poisonous to human beings, and it is unwise, therefore, to smoke or eat while applying them. They are also poisonous to domestic animals.

Allow seven days to elapse between the spraying and harvesting of edible plants sprayed with DDT, Diazinon, Kelthane, malathion or methoxychlor; allow three days for edible plants sprayed with nicotine sulphate; and allow one day for those sprayed with carbaryl, rotenone and pyrethrum. Rotenone and pyrethrum are non-poisonous to human beings, but, as with the other materials recommended, do not use them near ponds or streams containing fish. Aldrin, chlordane, dieldrin and Toxaphene should not be used on edible plant parts.

After spraying, store all pesticides out of reach of children, wash utensils used and wash hands thoroughly.

General Garden Pests

The information in the following pages will enable the gardener to recognize and deal with the more important and troublesome pests.

General garden pests are described below beginning on this page; for vegetable pests, see page 811; fruit pests, see page 816; greenhouse and houseplant pests, page 825. The pests of ornamental plants and shade trees are described beginning page 829.

It is impossible to include all the pests which may be found. Should any of the less common ones suddenly appear in larger numbers than usual, help can be obtained from the advisory services of the gardening press, insecticide manufacturers, county agricultural agents, botanical gardens, state and federal Departments of Agriculture and, in Canada, from government experimental farms, experimental stations and experimental substations.

ANTS

Ants of various species, especially the black ant, are responsible for many types of damage. In borders and rock gardens their underground nests loosen the soil around the roots of plants, causing them to wilt and die. On lawns and terraces the small piles of loose soil around the entrances to their nests are unsightly. Ants may also swarm over plants infested with aphids and feed on the honeydew excreted by these pests, but they rarely damage the plants directly, although they may sometimes injure the blossoms when hunting for nectar. They also feed on ripe fruit, particularly when it has already been damaged by Japanese beetles or wasps. (Illus. p. 808.)

Control: Inject malathion or chlordane into the holes with an oil gun such as is used for automobiles, or use an aerosol can for this purpose.

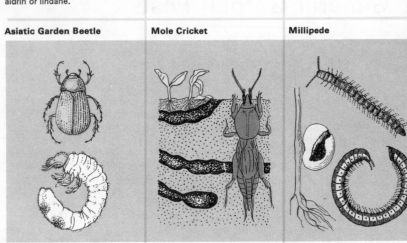

White Grub

Damage: Attacks roots of grasses, vegetables and other crops.
Control: Treat land with chlordane or dieldrin. Water established plants with liquid aldrin or lindane.

Ant

Damage: Loosens soil around roots; plants wilt; associated with aphids.
Control: Chlordane or dieldrin.

Cutworm

Damage: Gnaws collar of plant; plants collapse; eats roots and tubers.
Control: Dust surface of soil with DDT.

Asiatic Garden Beetle

Damage: Adult feeds at night on leaves of China aster and other plants. Larva feeds on grass roots.
Control: Spray leaves with arsenate of lead or treat soil with chlordane or dieldrin.

Mole Cricket

Damage: Makes tunnels in upper 2 in. of soil, thus cutting roots of seedlings and lawn grasses.
Control: Apply chlordane to soil.

Millipede

Damage: Feeds on roots and seeds; attacks newly sown seeds of leguminous crops.
Control: Spray soil surface with carbaryl or Diazinon.

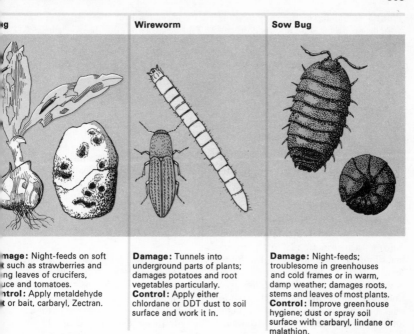

Wireworm

Sow Bug

mage: Night-feeds on soft t such as strawberries and ng leaves of crucifers, uce and tomatoes.
ntrol: Apply metaldehyde t or bait, carbaryl, Zectran.

Damage: Tunnels into underground parts of plants; damages potatoes and root vegetables particularly.
Control: Apply either chlordane or DDT dust to soil surface and work it in.

Damage: Night-feeds; troublesome in greenhouses and cold frames or in warm, damp weather; damages roots, stems and leaves of most plants.
Control: Improve greenhouse hygiene; dust or spray soil surface with carbaryl, lindane or malathion.

BEETLES, ASIATIC GARDEN
The adult stage is a chestnut-colored beetle that feeds at night on the leaves of many garden plants. When day comes it buries itself in the soil near the base or in the vicinity of the plant on which it feeds. The larval stage is a white grub which, like the Japanese beetle grub, feeds on grass roots. (Illus. p. 808.)

Control: Spray plants on which the beetles feed with arsenate of lead, 4 level tbsp. in 1 gal. of water. Control the grub stage by working into the soil either chlordane or dieldrin, as suggested for other white grubs.

CUTWORMS
Cutworms are fat brown or greenish caterpillars which feed on the surface of the soil at night, gnawing the stems

and leaves of plants at ground level and hiding just under the surface or among long vegetation during the day. If the stems are damaged, the plants wilt and collapse. Cutworms attack many types of vegetables as well as ornamental plants, such as marigolds, chrysanthemums and rock-garden plants. (Illus. p. 808.)

Control: Dust the ground under attacked plants with 2½ lb. of 5 percent DDT dust per 1000 sq. ft.

MILLIPEDES
Millipedes are often mistaken for wireworms because they also have shiny, cylindrical bodies, but they can be distinguished by their numerous short, bristlelike legs and by their peculiar habit of coiling up like a watch-spring when disturbed. They grow to

about 1 in. in length, and vary in color from cream to black. They feed on the roots of many plants, will destroy the sown seeds of peas and beans, and may also tunnel into the roots of beets, carrots, parsnips, potatoes and turnips. Fruit such as muskmelons, tomatoes and strawberries, which touch damp ground, may also be invaded by them. (Illus. p. 808.)

Control: Spray the soil surface with either carbaryl or malathion, as directed by the manufacturer.

MOLE CRICKETS

Two species of mole cricket, one native and the other introduced from Europe, are present in North America. The crickets are 1½ in. long, brownish above, paler underneath and covered with velvety hairs. They live underground during the day and come out at night to pulverize garden beds and plants growing in them. Roots of ornamental and food-plant seedlings as well as those of grasses are cut. Mole crickets also cut off stems aboveground (somewhat like cutworms). They eat seeds of some plants and make holes in underground roots and stems. (Illus. p. 808.)

Control: Treating the soil with chlordane as described for white grubs will control these pests. Also effective is a poison bait containing dry bran or corn meal, cottonseed meal, calcium arsenate, molasses and water.

SLUGS AND SNAILS

Slugs and sometimes snails can be very destructive creatures in the garden. They attack many types of plants, particularly low-growing ones whose foliage touches the soil, by eating holes out of the stems, leaves and petals. The damage is often confused with that done by caterpillars and other insects, but slugs and snails usu-

ally leave trails of slime on the plant. These pests are abundant in wet, cool conditions, especially on soils containing plenty of humus and in shaded gardens. They feed at night, and during the day they hide beneath vegetation or under the surface of the soil.

Strawberries are the only fruits which are likely to be seriously damaged by slugs, although raspberries and gooseberries may sometimes suffer. The pests eat large cavities out of the flesh of the fruits, and the young foliage is also attacked. In the vegetable garden they often eat holes in lettuce, spinach and cabbage. (Illus. p. 809.)

Control: Spread bait containing metaldehyde, available in garden supply stores, in small piles on tin lids or broken pieces of clay pots. Or dust the infested area with 15 percent metaldehyde dust. This should not be applied to parts of plants that are to be eaten by humans. Zectran, a systemic insecticide, is also effective for combating slugs, as is carbaryl.

SOW BUGS

Sow bugs are the gray or brownish creatures with oval, armor-plated bodies that are found in the dark, damp places of every garden, hiding under stones, under loose bark and in tangled vegetation. They cause serious damage only in the sheltered, humid conditions of cold frames and greenhouses, or if they are present in large numbers. At night they feed on the roots, stems and leaves of most plants. (Illus. p. 809.)

Control: Eliminate the dark, damp hiding places frequented by the pests during the day; or, if this is impossible, dust or spray the hiding places and infested areas with carbaryl, lindane or malathion.

WHITE GRUBS

These are the larvae of the May beetle (*Phyllophaga*) and related beetles. The largest of them grow to 1½ in. long, and all species have whitish, C-shaped bodies with brown heads. They feed on the roots of grass, corn, cereals, potatoes and other crops. The adults feed on leaves of many shade and ornamental trees. (Illus. p. 808.)

Control: Apply either chlordane or dieldrin to white-grub-infested soil and work it into the top 4 in. Where turf is present, apply to the surface and wash the chemical in with a sprinkler attached to a garden hose. Apply 5 lb. of 5 percent chlordane, dust or granulated, or 26 oz. of 5 percent dieldrin, granulated, to each 1000 sq. ft. of turf. In years when May beetles abound, spray valuable shade trees with arsenate of lead or carbaryl, as directed by the manufacturer.

WIREWORMS

Wireworms, the cylindrical, golden-yellow larvae of click beetles, grow to 1 in. long and, unlike the millipedes with which they are often confused, have only three pairs of legs at the front of the body. They are present in the soil of most gardens but not always in sufficient numbers to be troublesome. They feed on the roots of a wide range of plants and tunnel into potatoes and other tubers. They may attack bulbs and corms. (Illus. p. 809.)

Control: In eastern states, apply 2 lb. of 5 percent chlordane dust to each 1000 sq. ft. of soil surface and thoroughly work it into the upper 6-8 in. Do not apply this material within one year before planting carrots or parsnips. In western states, apply 2 lb. of 10 percent DDT dust for each 1000 sq. ft. about six weeks before planting and work it into the top 6-8 in.

Vegetable Pests

APHIDS (greenfly, blackfly, etc.)

These are the most abundant pests in the garden, and most plants, including vegetables, are likely to be attacked by one or more species. A close watch should be kept for them, and even if only a few are seen, they should be destroyed immediately, as they can multiply very quickly, especially when the weather is warm. Aphids, sucking the sap from a plant and congregating on the tender young growth, can quickly cripple it and cause general stunting. Many species also transmit virus diseases, which can reduce a crop or wipe it out altogether.

The most important species which attacks vegetables is the bean aphid, greenish-black in color, found on beans, beets and spinach (illus. p. 812). The potato aphid is glistening pink and green, about $\frac{1}{16}$ in. long, with long cornicles. The cabbage aphid has a mealy, grayish-white appearance and is found in tightly packed colonies on the leaves of cabbage, broccoli, Brussels sprouts, cauliflower, collards, kohlrabi, kale, radish. It must be controlled in the early stages of infestation because, once it has invaded the inner leaves of cabbage hearts and Brussels sprouts, it is difficult to reach with insecticides, and it makes the plants practically inedible. The lettuce aphid is green and transmits a virus which produces severe stunting in lettuce.

Control: Spray or dust with malathion

Bean Aphid

Damage: Smothers young growth, particularly broad beans.
Control: Spray with malathion or nicotine sulphate.

Mexican Bean Beetle

Damage: Leaves and beans are chewed by both larvae and adults.
Control: Crush eggs on lower leaf surface. Spray thoroughly with carbaryl or rotenone.

Corn Earworm

Damage: Larvae feed on the silk and tips of ears of sweet corn.
Control: Spray with carbaryl.

Imported Cabbage Worm

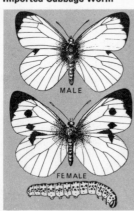

MALE

FEMALE

Damage: Eats leaves, sometimes leaving only skeleton of leaf.
Control: Spray with rotenone or Bacillus thuringiensis when caterpillars are still young.

Carrot Rust Fly

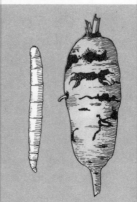

Damage: Maggots tunnel into roots of carrots, parsley and celery. Carrot leaves turn reddish.
Control: Apply Diazinon to furrow at planting time.

Celery Worm

Damage: Chews leaves of celery, carrot, parsley and parsnip.
Control: Spray or dust with rotenone or pyrethrum.

a Beetle

mage: Attacks cabbage and ...d plants. Peppers the leaves ...n tiny, round holes. Beetles ...p when disturbed.
...ntrol: Spray or dust with ...aryl or rotenone.

Onion Maggot

Damage: Maggots burrow into bulbs of developing plants; bulbs rot; leaves turn yellow and collapse.
Control: Spray leaves with malathion or Diazinon when flies appear.

Pea Moth

Damage: Caterpillar feeds inside the pods, eating into the peas.
Control: Sow early or spray with malathion at flowering time and repeat in 10 days.

...ato Beetle

...mage: Leaves are chewed ...both adults and larvae.
...ntrol: Spray foliage with ...aryl.

Golden Nematode

Damage: Infests potato roots, causing them to rot. Lower leaves wither and drop. Poor yield.
Control: Treat infested soil with DD mixture, Vapam or Mylone.

Squash Bug

Damage: Sucks sap from leaves and causes vines to wilt and die.
Control: Spray infested plants with carbaryl or malathion.

or nicotine sulphate, repeating the application as necessary.

BEETLES
Flea Beetles

There are several species of flea beetles that attack garden plants, particularly cabbages, radishes, turnips, tomatoes, eggplants and peppers. They are black, or black and yellow insects, $\frac{1}{10}$ in. long; they leap off the plants onto the soil when disturbed. The beetles eat small holes in the leaves, which eventually look as though they have been peppered by small shot. The worst damage occurs on seedlings—often killed off. (Illus. p. 813.)

Control: Spray or dust the seedlings at weekly intervals with carbaryl or rotenone until the rough leaves are well developed, when the plants should be able to withstand later attacks.

Potato Beetle

Also known as the Colorado beetle, the voracious pest attacks not only potato, but also eggplant, tomato, pepper, nicotiana and petunia. The adult is yellow with 10 longitudinal lines on its wing covers and black spots on its thorax. The larvae—the most gluttonous feeders—are red, fat, humpbacked grubs. There are two generations each season in the North and three in the South. (Illus. p. 813.)

Control: Spray susceptible plants with carbaryl at the rate of 2 to 4 level tbsp. in 1 gal. of water. Mix the carbaryl in a little water to make a paste, then add water to make a gallon. Make a second application seven to ten days later; repeat if necessary. Keep spray mixture well agitated.

CATERPILLARS
Cabbage Worm

The imported cabbage worm is a most serious pest of all members of the cab-

bage family. The caterpillar stage is green and velvety smooth with alternating light and dark longitudinal stripes. The adult is the white butterfly, with three or four black spots on the wings and a wingspread of nearly 2 in. The caterpillars eat holes in the leaves, starting on the outer ones, and leaving nothing but the skeleton of main veins. (Illus. p. 812.)

The caterpillars of the less common cabbage moth, yellowish-green on the underside and dark, brownish-green on the back, are more difficult to control than the cabbage worm because they tunnel into the interior of cabbages and destroy the hearts. They also attack onions, lettuce and peas.

Control: If possible, crush the yellow eggs which are laid singly or in clusters on the undersides of the leaves. The best control is obtained when the caterpillars are young. As soon as damage is seen, spray or dust with rotenone. A spray or dust made from *Bacillus thuringiensis* is also effective.

Celery Worm

Green with a black crossband on each body segment and two soft, forked orange horns just back of its head, it chews the leaves of celery, caraway, carrot, dill, parsley and parsnip. The adult is a swallowtail butterfly with two rows of yellow spots on its black wings. (Illus. p. 812.)

Control: Handpick and destroy the worms where only a few plants are involved. Spray or dust young plants with arsenate of lead, and older plants, as they approach harvest, with rotenone or pyrethrum.

Cutworm

Cutworms attack many types of vegetables, especially brassicas (turnip, rutabaga, cabbage, Brussels sprouts and kale) and lettuce. (See page 808.)

NEMATODES (EELWORMS)

Nematodes, or eelworms, are so small that they are not normally visible to the naked eye, but they can, nevertheless, cause serious damage to certain plants and are difficult to eradicate. As chemical control is difficult and very expensive at present, the most practical control is to starve out the eelworms by not planting their food plants on infested soil for a number of years.

Golden Nematode

This nematode, also known as the potato-root eelworm, feeds on the roots of potatoes and causes them to rot. The growth of such potatoes is poor, the lower leaves wither and drop off, and on infested land the yield of tubers dwindles progressively each year. (Illus. p. 813.)

Control: Do not plant potatoes on infested land. Treat infested soils with DD mixture, Vapam or Mylone, as directed by the manufacturer.

Stem and Bulb Nematodes

These sometimes attack onions, causing them to become swollen and puffy at the base with distorted, twisted leaves ("onion bloat"). The plants later start to rot. These pests also feed on many other bulbs, as well as ornamental plants and vegetables. (They are discussed in greater detail on page 837.)

Control: Do not grow any of the food plants on infested soil for three years. Treat infested soil with DD mixture or Telone, as recommended by the manufacturer.

PEA MOTH

Pea-moth caterpillars are pale yellow with black heads and can cause serious damage in some localities. They are found inside the pods, feeding on the peas, and produce what are known as "maggoty peas." (Illus. p. 813.)

Control: In areas where this pest is prevalent, sow early varieties of peas to escape the worst of the damage. Spray late peas at flowering time with malathion and repeat in ten days.

ROOT MAGGOTS

The larvae of certain flies are common and destructive pests of vegetables in many areas. The maggots are small, whitish, peg-shaped creatures without legs or visible heads, which feed on the roots of vegetables.

Cabbage Maggot

These eat away the lateral roots of cabbages and related plants, and then tunnel in the main root. Attacked plants are retarded in growth and may wilt and die. This pest also tunnels in the roots of broccoli, cauliflower, radishes and turnips.

Control: Cover seedbeds with cheesecloth to prevent flies from laying eggs. Before setting plants out, dust stems with a mixture consisting of 8 oz. of calomel and 3 oz. of cornstarch. Large acreages of crucifers are treated by spraying or dusting the bases of newly set plants with chlordane.

Carrot Rust Fly Maggot

Tunneling in the roots of carrots, parsley and celery, they cause the roots to be deformed and the plants stunted. The foliage of carrots may become reddish. Attacked seedlings are often killed in dry weather. (Illus. p. 812.)

Control: Apply ¾ oz. Diazinon per 1000 sq. ft. to seed furrow at planting time. Do not apply after planting.

Onion Maggot

Burrowing into the bulbs of onions

and shallots, they cause the leaves to turn yellow and collapse and the bulbs may be reduced to a soft, rotting mass. Dig up affected plants immediately and also the soil around them because the maggots will often move on to feed on healthy plants. (Illus. p. 813)

Control: When flies appear, spray the foliage with malathion or Diazinon several times at 4-day intervals and repeat 10 to 14 days later. Do not spray malathion-treated onions within 3 days before harvest or Diazinon-treated ones within 10 days before harvest.

SLUGS

Slugs attack lettuce, spinach, cabbage and celery. (See page 810.)

SQUASH BUG

The squash bug attacks all members of the cucumber family but prefers squash, pumpkin, gourds and melons in that order. While feeding, this bug injects a toxic substance into the vine, causing a wilt disease. After wilting, young vines turn black and crisp and then die. In older vines only one or two runners may wilt—the remainder of the plant will not be affected. (Illus. p. 813.)

Control: Practice strict sanitation by removing all rubbish that may offer protection for the bugs during the winter. Control the young squash bugs by spraying with carbaryl or with sabadilla.

TOMATO HORNWORM

The tomato hornworm is a bright green caterpillar that grows to 4 inches in length. A green horn with black sides projects at its rear and accounts for its name. It feeds on tomato, tobacco, eggplant and other members of the *Solanaceae*. The adult stage, a sphinx moth, emerges in May and June to deposit greenish-yellow eggs on the undersides of the leaves. Caterpillars hatching from the eggs feed for three to four weeks.

Control: In small gardens, handpick and crush the caterpillars. Where large numbers of plants are grown, spray with carbaryl.

WIREWORMS

Wireworms attack potatoes, carrots and turnips. (See page 811.)

Fruit Pests

APHIDS

By sucking the sap, aphids can cause devitalization and reduction of crop on all types of fruit. The eggs are laid on the bark in the autumn, and infestation starts when they hatch in the early spring. The young insects are usually hidden deep in the folds of the developing leaves, but their presence is often betrayed on sunny days by ants, which run up and down the trunk feeding on the sugary honeydew excreted by the pests. If aphids are not dealt with in the early stages, they will quickly multiply and cluster on the young shoots and on the undersides of young leaves, often causing them to become severely distorted and, in some cases, badly discolored as well.

It is possible to deal here with only a few of the more common species of aphids which infest fruit, but, with few exceptions, notably the easily recognized woolly apple aphid, the control measures recommended are adequate for all species. (Illus. p. 826.)

Apples are attacked by the green apple aphid (illus. p. 822) and the rosy apple aphid (illus. p. 823), pests which cause curling of the young leaves at the tips of new shoots. The latter species also attacks young fruits, causing them to become stunted and misshapen. The purplish-brown woolly apple aphid is distinguished by the masses of white "wool" which cover the colonies. This species feeds on bark and causes the formation of swollen tumors, which later tend to split as the wood grows and thus allow disease organisms to enter.

Currants are attacked by the whitish currant blister aphid, which causes the formation of raised blisters on the leaves. These blisters are usually a reddish brown, but on black currants they may be yellow. (Illus. p. 818.)

The leaves of currants and gooseberries are frequently chewed by the imported currant worm, a green larva with a black head and body spots. (Illus. p. 818.)

Pears are not so likely to be damaged by aphids as other fruits, but the woolly pear aphid may occasionally be troublesome.

Plums are often severely crippled in the spring by the leaf-curl plum aphid, which causes the leaves to become tightly curled and coated with sticky honeydew (illus. p. 823). Later in the summer the foliage may be attacked by the mealy plum aphid, which covers the undersides of the leaves. It is a pale green species with a white powdery covering. It does not cause leaf-curling but may cause the leaves to fall prematurely. (Illus. p. 823.)

Raspberries may be damaged by green European raspberry aphids, which congregate at the tips of the canes, causing curling of the young leaves (Illus. p. 819.)

Strawberries are very prone to aphid attack, especially by the dark green melon aphid, which causes the leaves to become twisted and the flower trusses stunted, and by the strawberry aphid, a pale creamy-colored insect that is an important carrier of virus diseases.

Control of woolly apple aphid: Spray with lindane or malathion at the pink-bud stage of apple blossoms. Colonies seen after blossoming should be sprayed with malathion or Diazinon.

Control of other aphids: Kill the overwintering eggs on fruit trees, currants and gooseberries by spraying with a superior-type self-emulsifying petroleum oil on a mild day in spring just before growth starts. Scale insects and eggs of mites will also be destroyed by this treatment. During the growing season spray as follows:

Tree fruits—malathion or nicotine sulphate between bud-burst and the appearance of green blossom buds.

Currants—malathion or nicotine sulphate just before the flowers open (late "grape" stage).

Raspberries—malathion to the lower leaf surfaces when aphids are seen.

Strawberries—malathion or nicotine sulphate just before flowering and again after picking.

Outbreaks of aphids during the summer should be handled by spraying or dusting with malathion or nicotine sulphate.

APPLE MAGGOT

The apple maggot is also known as railroad worm, perhaps because it tunnels through the fruit by rasping and tearing the pulp into brown winding galleries. Early varieties of apples become soft and rotted; later varieties have corky streaks in the pulp and the surface is pitted and distorted. The adult stage resembles the housefly but is smaller in size. (Illus. p. 822.)

Currant-Bud Mite

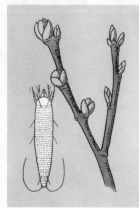

Damage: Invades buds of black, native and flowering currants. Buds swell and wither. **Control:** Cut and burn infested shoots. Dust or spray with sulphur in early spring.

European Fruit Lecanium

Damage: Sucks sap of plums, peaches and soft fruits. **Control:** Spray with a superior-type, self-emulsifying petroleum oil in spring just before growth starts.

Blueberry-Stem Gall Wasp

Damage: Causes kidney-shaped galls, first green, then reddish-brown on stems. May reduce fruit yield. **Control:** Remove and burn galls in winter.

Currant Blister Aphid

Damage: Causes raised, reddish-brown or yellow blisters on leaves of currants. **Control:** Spray the leaves, particularly the lower surfaces, with malathion or nicotine sulphate early in the growing season.

Imported Currant Worm

Damage: Larvae, in groups, devour leaves. **Control:** Spray with malathion or rotenone.

Clover Mite

Damage: Infests leaves of gooseberries, raspberries and many tree fruits, causing yellowing and premature dropping. **Control:** Spray with Kelthane and repeat every 10 days as needed.

m Curculio	European Raspberry Aphid	Eastern Raspberry Fruit Worm

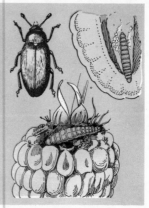

mage: Causes misshapen, tty fruits or worm-infested s.
trol: Spray with arsenate ead or methoxychlor.

Damage: Feeds at tips of canes; young leaves curl.
Control: Spray with malathion when pests appear.

Damage: Grubs feed first on outside of developing fruit, then inside fruit.
Control: Apply 1-percent rotenone dust just after blossom buds show and again just before blooms open.

Control: Gather and dispose of fallen fruits of the early varieties twice each week. After the flies appear, spray with a special lead arsenate spray (2 oz. lead arsenate and 2 oz. hydrated lime in 2 gal. of water). Do not apply this spray within one month of harvest.

BORERS

Borers are the caterpillar or grub stage of moths or beetles that invade woody or herbaceous stems. There are many kinds affecting fruit, ornamental and shade trees and shrubs. Borer attack is more prevalent in trees that have been weakened by excessive drought, sunscald or other means.

Flat-headed Apple-Tree Borer

The inner bark, cambium, sapwood and heartwood of apple and many other fruit and deciduous shade trees are ruined by this borer. It kills many fruit and shade trees the first season

after transplanting. Injury is more severe in dry seasons and with exposure to too much sun as a result of excessive pruning.

Control: Wrap the trunk of newly planted trees with burlap, especially prepared crepe paper (Tree Wrap), or spray with an antitranspirant such as Wilt-Pruf. With a penknife or stiff wire, crush borers already in the tree. Spray or paint trunks and larger branches with DDT three times at two-week intervals, starting in early May.

Peach Borer

This is the most destructive pest of peach trees. It also attacks plums, wild and cultivated cherries, apricots and some shrubs in the genus *Prunus*. Amber-colored jelly or gum exuding from the trunk base usually indicates that the borers—white, brown-headed worms—are at work beneath the bark. Their attacks are usually fatal unless control measures are applied. (Illus. p. 823.)

Control: Dig out and crush borers with a penknife in trees already invaded by them. Prevent reinfestation by painting or spraying the trunk base with DDT, three times at two-week intervals, starting in early July. In early September, spray the trunk base with lindane.

CANKERWORMS

Cankerworms, also known as inchworms or measuring worms, feed on the leaves of apple and other fruit trees, on oak, elm and other shade trees. They often let themselves down from trees by a thread of silk.

Fall Cankerworm

This is one of the most serious tree pests throughout the northern parts of the United States and Canada. Brownish above, green below, it has three white stripes along the body. This pest is known as the fall cankerworm despite the fact that it appears in the spring and early summer. The adult female has no wings. Hence, in order to deposit its eggs in the treetops, it must climb up the trunk in the fall. The adult moth of the spring cankerworm, a close relative, climbs the tree to deposit eggs in the spring.

Control: Band the trunk with a sticky substance known as Tree Tanglefoot in early fall to trap most of the female moths attempting to climb the tree. Trees should be banded in early spring in areas where the spring cankerworm is a problem. In seasons of heavy infestations, spray susceptible trees either with arsenate of lead, 1 lb. in 30 gal. of water, or with carbaryl (Sevin), as recommended by the manufacturer, in late April or early May.

CATERPILLARS

Caterpillars of one type or another are common pests on fruit, particularly tree fruits, and those which feed on the foliage can reduce the leaf area so much that crops suffer a severe check. Some will attack the fruit itself.

Codling Moth Caterpillar

These are among the most common and destructive of apple pests and, together with the larvae of the apple maggot, are responsible for the condition known as "maggoty apples." The codling caterpillar is pink-colored and enters either near the "eye" of the fruit or by a hole in the side, which is often surrounded by a red ring. It burrows into the apple and feeds around the core. If attacked apples do not fall prematurely, the mature caterpillars descend the trunk from late August onward and hibernate in cracks and crevices in the bark. (Illus. p. 822.) The control measures are quite different from those used against the apple maggot, and it is therefore important to be able to distinguish between these two pests.

Control: Spray with carbaryl, as directed by the manufacturer. Repeated use of carbaryl for caterpillars will cause a buildup of mites. Do not use carbaryl during blossoming time because it is toxic to bees.

Tent Caterpillar

Also known as appletree tent caterpillar, this species builds ugly nests or "tents" in the crotches of trees in spring from which the young forage during the day. It prefers to feed on the leaves of wild black cherry, chokecherry and apple, but when food is scarce it feeds on birch, elm, hawthorn, maple, oak, pear, plum, willow and other fruit and ornamental trees. (Illus. p. 822.)

Control: Spray with carbaryl when young caterpillars begin to feed in spring. Detach and burn egg masses in winter; later on, remove tents during the evening when caterpillars have returned from foraging.

EASTERN RASPBERRY FRUIT WORM

A most destructive pest of raspberries and loganberries, it is also known as the raspberry beetle. The adult, a light brown beetle about $\frac{1}{16}$ in. long, feeds on the blossoms, buds and leaves. The larva, a slender white grub, bores into the fruit, making it unfit for human consumption. (Illus. p. 819.)

Control: Apply 1 percent rotenone dust just after the blossom buds show and again just before blooms open.

LEAFHOPPERS

Leafhoppers are small, active, winged insects, less than $\frac{1}{8}$ in. long. They fly readily when disturbed. The young are wingless, usually yellow or green. They feed mainly on the lower surfaces of leaves, sucking out the juices.

Apple Leafhopper

This is a common pest of apple trees east of the Rocky Mountains. It sucks out leaf juices, causing the foliage to turn pale in late summer and early fall. The green upper-leaf surface is flecked with white spots, and the lower surface is covered with dark bits of excrement as well as white cast-off skins. This species also infests roses. (Illus. p. 822.)

Control: Spray with DDT when leafhoppers are first seen. Do not spray within one month of harvest.

MITES
Clover Mite

This species infests the leaves of apple, apricot, cherry, peach, pear,

gooseberry, raspberry and other fruit trees and fruit bushes, as well as many shade and ornamental trees and lawn grasses. It also may migrate from lawns into homes in great numbers in autumn and cluster in sunny windows. (Illus. p. 818.)

Control: Spray susceptible trees with Kelthane and repeat every ten days as needed. Where the pests may move from the lawn into homes, spray a 10-ft.-wide band of grass along the outside walls of the house with Kelthane in early fall. To clean up mites that already have entered the house, use chlordane in aerosol form.

Currant-Bud Mite

Microscopic in size and invisible to the naked eye, this mite invades the buds of black native and flowering currants in vast numbers; the buds become globular and swollen to about twice their normal size. Infested buds usually wither and die without producing leaves, and the general effect is a progressive reduction in the yield of fruit. (Illus. p. 818.)

Control: Cut and burn infested shoots. Dust or spray with sulphur in early spring.

Red Spider Mite

Red spider mites are very small creatures that suck the sap on the undersurface of leaves. They are distantly related to insects and spiders, and in spite of their name their color is more usually orange-green than red. Although the adults are smaller than a pinhead, they can, when present in large numbers, cause considerable damage and general weakening of the plant. (Illus. p. 826; see also p. 829.)

European Red Mite

Particularly harmful on apple, plum, pear and prune, its attack in the early

Apple Maggot

Damage: Causes brown, winding galleries in pulp, and pitted and distorted fruit.
Control: Gather and burn fallen, infested fruit. Spray with lead arsenate-hydrated lime.

Apple Leafhopper

Damage: Sucks juices from leaves, causing stippling or yellowing.
Control: Spray with DDT.

Apple Borer

Damage: Bores into inner bark, cambium, sapwood and heartwood of apple and other fruit and shade trees.
Control: Spray several times with DDT.

Codling Moth

Damage: Caterpillars burrow into fruit, feeding at the core.
Control: Spray with carbaryl.

Tent Caterpillar

Damage: Chews leaves of wild black cherry, apple and other fruit and ornamental trees. Makes ugly nests in branch crotches.
Control: Spray with carbaryl.

Green Apple Aphid

Damage: Causes curling of young leaves and distortion of new growth.
Control: Spray with a superior-type self-emulsifying petroleum oil when tree is still dormant in spring, and with malathion in May.

ealy Plum Aphid

amage: Attacks underside of
aves in summer, causing them
fall prematurely.
ntrol: Spray with a superior-
e self-emulsifying petroleum
while tree is dormant in
ring and with malathion in
ay.

Oystershell Scale

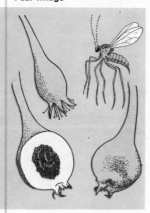

Damage: Sucks sap. Found on
most tree and bush fruits, as
well as ornamentals, especially
lilacs.
Control: Spray with oil and
malathion as for mealy plum
aphid.

Pear Midge

Damage: Maggots feed inside
young fruit, causing abnormal
swelling.
Control: Spray with DDT just
before sepals separate and again
7 days later.

af-Curl Plum Aphid

amage: Attacks young
ves, curling them tightly and
ating with sticky honeydew.
ntrol: Spray with a superior-
e self-emulsifying petroleum
while tree is dormant in
ly spring, and with malathion
May.

Peach Borer

Damage: Chews cambium and
sapwood, causing death of tree.
Control: Spray with DDT in
July and August, followed by
lindane in September.

Rosy Apple Aphid

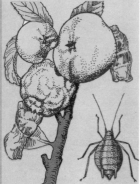

Damage: Causes curling of
young leaves and distortion of
fruit.
Control: Spray with a superior-
type self-emulsifying petroleum
oil in spring when tree is
dormant, and with malathion in
May.

stages causes the leaves to become dull and speckled finely with yellow. Later the foliage may take on a silvery appearance, owing to air entering the damaged cells, followed by bronzing and premature leaf fall.

Control: To kill the overwintering eggs, spray with a superior-type self-emulsifying petroleum oil in spring when trees are dormant. During the summer, spray starting early June with Kelthane or Tedion twice at 14-day intervals. Apply the spray to the undersides of the leaves.

PEAR MIDGE

The pear midge is a small fly that lays its eggs in the flowers of pear. The legless white maggots that hatch out bore into the young fruit and feed inside. The fruit then becomes abnormally swollen and rounded, and when cut open it reveals a blackened cavity containing the maggots. The fruit later falls, cracks and decays, allowing the mature maggots to escape. (Illus. p. 823.)

Control: Spray with DDT just before sepals separate and again seven days later. Infested young fruit should be picked off and destroyed before they fall.

SAWFLIES

Sawfly larvae resemble the caterpillars of moths, and the damage done by the two types of pest is very similar.

European Apple Sawfly

A common pest of apple. Its larvae are often confused with those of the codling moth.

Attacks by sawfly larvae are usually seen first in May, and they eat more of the flesh than does the codling caterpillar, which attacks in July and feeds mainly on the core.

Apples infested by sawfly larvae have an obnoxious smell when cut open, and fruits attacked by these larvae often display long "ribbon" scars on the surface, the result of the young larvae burrowing under the skin.

Control: Spray tree with rotenone at petal-fall stage and again one week later.

Cherry Fruit Sawfly

On the Pacific Coast this pest attacks cherry, plum, prune and sometimes apricot and peach. The larvae, white with brown heads, enter partly developed fruit and feed on the seeds. Infested fruits wither and drop.

Control: Spray with lead arsenate just before the blossoms open.

Raspberry Sawfly

Feeding on the undersides and edges of leaves of raspberry, loganberry, blackberry and dewberry, this occurs in the northern United States but is more common on the Pacific Coast. The adult flies are black with yellow and reddish markings; the larvae are pale green.

Control: Spray with lead arsenate just before the blossoms open and with rotenone after the fruit is set.

SCALE INSECTS

Scale insects, which are usually found only on neglected fruit trees and bushes, are described in detail beginning page 828.

European Fruit Lecanium

This is chestnut-brown, about ⅛ in. long and convex. It may be found on the bark of plums, peaches and soft fruits. (Illus. p. 818.) The oystershell scale, much flatter, is gray and shaped like a miniature oyster. It is found mainly on apple trees but can occur on almost any tree or bush fruit. (Illus. p. 823.)

Control: Spray with a superior-type self-emulsifying petroleum oil in the spring when trees are still dormant and with malathion in May and June.

SLUGS

Slugs attack strawberries, raspberries and gooseberries. (See page 810.)

Greenhouse and House-Plant Pests

Many of the outdoor pests mentioned in this chapter, such as slugs, sow bugs, millipedes, thrips, leafhoppers, aphids, caterpillars and leaf miners, are also found in the greenhouse. Different species of these pests may be encountered, but the control measures are the same, with the added advantage that in some cases insecticides can be applied as a smoke, thus saving much time and labor. This section will therefore be confined to those species which are generally found primarily under glass.

BLACK VINE WEEVIL

Also found on outdoor plants, this weevil has a curved white grub that is an important pest of house plants. It kills cyclamen and begonia by tunneling into the corms and tubers. (Illus. p. 827.)

Control: Mix DDT or chlordane dust with the potting soil. Some control can be obtained on established outdoor plants, such as yews, by drenching with liquid dieldrin.

GREENHOUSE WHITEFLY

Although some species of whitefly are found out of doors, on bush fruits and rhododendrons principally, the most common and troublesome is the greenhouse whitefly. The adults, which resemble miniature moths, are pure white and about ½₀ in. long, and can be found clustering on the undersides of leaves of a wide variety of plants. They flutter about when disturbed. The young, which are flat, scalelike creatures, difficult to see because of their small size and transparent greenish color, are also found on the undersides of leaves. The pests suck the sap, causing lack of vigor, wilting and, on some plants, yellow mottling of the leaves. The foliage also becomes sticky with honeydew excreted by the insects, and sooty molds are then likely to grow on this material. (Illus. p. 827.)

Control: Spray with lindane or malathion to control the immature stage. Adult flies are difficult to kill.

MEALYBUGS

Mealybugs are pale pink or yellow insects covered with a white mealy substance. They congregate in sheltered corners of the plants, such as leaf axils, and suck the sap. Like many sucking insects, they excrete large quantities of honeydew, and the leaves may become covered by sooty molds. They are normally found indoors and in the greenhouse where they can infest a wide variety of plants. Some species, such as the *Taxus* mealybug (illus. p. 835), the citrus mealybug and the Comstock mealybug, are serious pests of outdoor plants.

Japanese Beetle

Damage: Feeds on leaves of
fruit and shade trees, ornamental
plants and some vegetables.
Control: Spray all susceptible
plants, except Boston ivy, with
carbaryl.

Fall Webworm

Damage: Feeds on leaves of
fruit and shade trees and makes
large, webbed nests at tips of
branches.
Control: Spray with carbaryl.

Woolly Apple Aphid

Damage: Forms white, woolly
patches on twigs. Feeds on bark
and causes swollen growths.
Control: Use lindane or
malathion at pink-bud stage
and repeat as needed.

Pests of the Greenhou

Cottony Taxus Scale

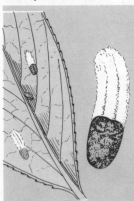

Damage: Many kinds of plants
weaken and become sticky and
covered with black mold.
Control: Spray with malathion
as needed.

Chrysanthemum Gall Midge

Damage: Causes cone-shaped
galls on leaves and stems.
Control: Pick and burn infected
leaves. Spray with lindane when
adult flies appear.

Red Spider Mite

Damage: Yellow speckling
spreading until whole leaf turn
yellow and dies.
Control: Spray with Kelthane
or Tedion.

enhouse Whitefly

mage: Plants wilt and show
nished vigor. May become
k and sticky.
ntrol: Spray with lindane
nalathion to control larval
e.

Long-Tailed Mealybug

Damage: White, cottony
substance on leaves and stems.
Leaves become sticky and black.
Control: Spray with malathion
or carbaryl and repeat as
needed.

Oleander Scale

Damage: Plant loses vigor and
turns sticky. Black molds appear.
Control: Spray with malathion
or summer oil to control
crawling stage.

ot-Knot Nematode

mage: Conspicuous
llings on roots.
atrol: Pasteurize soil with
t or treat with Vapam.
card heavily infested soil.

Brown Soft Scale

Damage: Plant loses vigor.
Black sooty molds appear.
Control: Wash with soapy
water. Spray with nicotine-
white-oil emulsion or with
malathion.

Black Vine Weevil

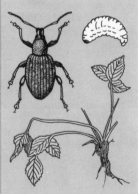

Damage: Tunnels into roots of
cyclamen, primrose and other
pot plants.
Control: Mix DDT or chlordane
with potting soil.

Control: Indoor and greenhouse infested plants can be sprayed with malathion from time to time as needed. Cactuses and other succulents, ferns and poinsettias are sensitive to malathion and should not be sprayed with this insecticide. Carbaryl also controls mealybugs but should not be applied to Boston ivy. Mealybugs on *Taxus* can be controlled with dimethoate.

NEMATODES
Tomato-Root Nematode
These nematodes attack tomatoes grown in the greenhouse as well as outdoors. Infested plants make poor growth because of the damaged roots, and the foliage droops and is purple on the underside. Such symptoms can, however, be the result of bad root action due to other causes, and expert advice should be sought if nematodes are suspected.

Root-Knot Nematode
These nematodes produce similar symptoms on tomatoes, but they are comparatively easy to identify by the tiny, hard, elongated swellings that appear on the roots. Many other greenhouse plants may be attacked by this eelworm, especially cucumber, begonia, coleus, carnation and gardenia. (Illus. p. 827.)

General symptoms are the retarding of growth and pale yellow foliage which tends to wilt in warm weather. The shape and consistency of the root swellings vary on different plants.

Control: A few ornamental plants such as gardenia and boxwood, already infested with root-knot nematodes, can be rid of the infestation by dipping bare-rooted plants in Zinophos. Fallow soil in the home garden can be treated with Garden Dowfume or DD mixture. Root-knot larvae free in soil can be killed with Nem-

agon or V-C 13, but these will not kill all the nematodes inside the root knots or nodules. The most effective way to rid greenhouse soils of root-knot and other nematodes is to heat (steam) the soil. Vapam and VPM Soil Fumigant are chemical substitutes for heat, but these too must be used prior to planting crops.

SCALE INSECTS
Scale insects resemble small, discolored blisters on the stem or leaf and are often not recognized as insects. Their bodies are protected by a tough scale that varies in shape and color according to the species, and they remain motionless for most of their lives, sucking the sap through elongated mouth parts thrust into the plant tissues. Infested plants lose their vigor owing to loss of sap and, as honeydew is excreted, they are likely to be disfigured by sooty molds. In severe cases leaves may turn yellow and drop off and plants may die eventually.

Some important outdoor species, already discussed, are also common in the greenhouse, where conditions are ideal for this type of insect.

Cottony Taxus Scale
About ⅙ in. long, it is oval and easily recognized by the white woolly mass pushed out behind it. This scale attacks orchid, camellia and magnolia as well as *Taxus* (yew) outdoors. (Illus. p. 826.)

Oleander Scale
A round flat whitish scale about 1/12 in. in diameter, it attacks the foliage of lemon, orange, acacia, oleander, ferns and many other plants. (Illus. p. 827.)

Brown Soft Scale
It is the most frequently found greenhouse species, is very flat, oval, about

⅛ in. long and yellowish-brown in color. It attacks citrus, fig, grape, ivy and many other tender plants, and is found on the undersides of the leaves, usually near the midrib. (Illus. p. 827.)

Control for scale insects: Wipe or brush off as many of the older scales as possible with soapy water. Then spray with malathion, carbaryl or a white-oil emulsion, as directed by the manufacturer.

RED SPIDER MITE

The red (or two-spotted) spider mite, one of the most serious greenhouse and indoor house-plant pests, is extremely small, and a strong magnifying glass is required to see it clearly, but it breeds quickly and can cause a lot of damage in a short time.

It attacks most plants, feeding on the underside of the leaves where it lays its round, reddish eggs, and the leaves become finely speckled with yellow marks that spread until the whole leaf turns yellow and withers. When plants are heavily infested, the mites spin fine webbing over the leaves. These pests will also infest outdoor plants, particularly those growing in sheltered places or against walls. (Illus. p. 826; see also p. 821.)

Control: Spray with Kelthane or Tedion, repeating the treatment seven days later. The mites dislike humid conditions, and frequent syringing or hosing with water will help to prevent serious infestations.

Pests of Ornamental Plants and Shade Trees

Many of the pests that attack fruit trees—including aphids, cankerworms, leafhoppers, Japanese beetles, fall webworms, tent caterpillars, scales and spider mites—attack shade trees, shrubs and other ornamental plants.

APHIDS

A great variety of aphids attack ornamental plants and shade trees, but the damage done is usually less spectacular than on fruit, because leaf distortion is not so common. The stems of young growth are twisted, but the aphids cause most damage by robbing the plants of large quantities of sap—causing poor growth, wilting and the formation of dwarfed, misshapen flowers. The leaves of infested plants are often made sticky by the honeydew excreted by the insects, and this sweet liquid is a medium for the growth of harmless, but disfiguring, black molds.

Many of the fruit-infesting aphids mentioned earlier also attack flowering cherries, crab apples, currants, etc., causing similar symptoms. These can be dealt with by the same methods as those recommended for control on fruit trees.

The more important and widespread species that attack ornamental plants include the black bean aphid, which infests dahlias, nasturtiums, poppies and zinnias and also feeds on vegetables; the chrysanthemum aphid, a reddish-black species, which attacks chrysanthemums (illus. p. 830); the peach-potato aphid, green, yellow or pink in color, which attacks snapdragons, China asters, phlox, sweet peas, chrysanthemums and many other plants; and the rose aphid, a large green or red aphid, which infests the shoots and flower buds of roses and scabious.

Chrysanthemum Leaf Nematode

Damage: Leaves turn brown and die.
Control: Treat soil with sodium selenate or demeton (Systox).

Tarnished Plant Bug

Damage: Brown-rimmed pinholes on young leaves, causing subsequent tearing and distortion. Blooms misshapen.
Control: Spray with carbaryl. Repeat at 14-day intervals.

Chrysanthemum Aphid

Damage: Growing tips are distorted.
Control: Use malathion, lindane or nicotine sulphate.

Chrysanthemum Leaf Miner

Damage: Leaves are marked by twisting tunnels made by grubs.
Control: Handpick and destroy infested leaves. Spray with carbaryl, lindane or malathion.

Cyclamen Mite

Damage: Deforms leaves of African violet, delphinium, snapdragon, strawberry and other plants.
Control: Spray with Kelthane or Dimite before leaves are deformed.

European Earwig

Damage: Eats both leaves an flowers at night.
Control: Apply chlordane or lindane dust along fences or house foundations or spray th infested areas with carbaryl.

…nymus Scale	Gladiolus Thrips	Holly Leaf Miner

…age: Sucks leaf juices. …es turn yellow and drop; …s die back.
…trol: Use dormant oil spray …rly spring and malathion …rbaryl in May and June.

Damage: White or yellowish mottled areas on leaves and petals.
Control: Spray with DDT and repeat several times at weekly intervals.

Damage: Yellow-brown blisters form on leaves.
Control: Handpick and burn infested leaves before adults emerge. Spray with DDT or carbaryl when flies emerge in spring or with lindane or dieldrin in mid-July.

… Borer	Lilac Leaf Miner	Onion Thrips

…age: Bores holes in trunk …ac, ash and other trees.
…trol: Spray or paint trunk … DDT three times at 2-week …vals starting in early May.

Damage: Small yellow caterpillars mine, then roll and skeletonize leaves.
Control: Spray with lindane, malathion or carbaryl.

Damage: A flecking of carnation and rose blooms occurs and a streaking of leaves of many ornamental and food plants.
Control: Spray ornamentals with DDT or malathion.

Control: As soon as aphids are seen on the plants, spray or dust with malathion, lindane or nicotine sulphate, repeating the application as necessary.

BAGWORMS

These are caterpillars that build a covering over their bodies as they grow, and carry the spindle-shaped bags around with them. The young worms appear in May and feed on the leaves of evergreens such as arborvitae, juniper, hemlock and pine, and on deciduous trees, including plane trees, maples, locust, linden and citrus trees.

Control: Spray with lead arsenate, carbaryl or malathion in the spring as soon as the young caterpillars start to feed.

BEETLES AND WEEVILS

The grubs of some beetles, such as wireworms and white grubs, are described on page 811. Damage is usually less common on ornamental plants than on fruits and vegetables. The following may, however, be met with.

Japanese Beetle

Metallic green with coppery wing covers and about ½ in. long, it is one of the most common pests in the eastern United States. It feeds on nearly 300 kinds of deciduous fruit and shade trees, shrubs and garden flowers, as well as a few vegetables. The larval stage lives in the soil, where it eats the roots of turf grasses, causing the grass to turn brown in spring and fall. (Illus. p. 826.)

Japanese Weevil

Another serious pest of ornamental trees and shrubs, it is about ¼ in. long, from light to dark brown in color with striations on the wing covers and with a broad abdomen and short snout. Its wing covers are fused, and

hence it cannot fly. Some of its favorite hosts are azaleas, California privet, Japanese barberry, mountain laurel, roses, deutzia and lilac.

Black Vine Weevil

Already described as a greenhouse pest (see page 825), it is also a serious pest of outdoor plants such as yews. (Illus. p. 827.)

Water-Lily Leaf Beetle

A dark brown beetle, its blackish larvae are common pests of water lilies. They eat elongated holes in the leaves and they also attack the flowers, disfiguring them and causing early decay. (Illus. p. 835.)

Control: Spray Japanese-beetle-infested plants with carbaryl as soon as they appear. Repeat the treatment every five to seven days as needed. Spray Japanese-weevil-infested plants with chlordane, dieldrin or heptachlor. Water-lily leaf beetles are more difficult to control, especially if fish are present in the water. Submerge the leaves for several days with iron hoops or nets to get rid of the beetles. If fish are present, they must be removed before an insecticide such as malathion is applied to control the larvae.

CATERPILLARS

Fall Webworm

These caterpillars feed on the leaves of more than 100 kinds of fruit, shade and woodland trees. The pale green or yellow caterpillars have a dark stripe down the back and a yellow stripe along each side. (Illus. p. 826.) They make nests or webs over the ends of branches rather than in the crotches (as does the tent caterpillar).

Gypsy Moth

Brown, hairy caterpillar; nearly 2 in. long, with five pairs of blue tubercles along the back followed by six pairs of red tubercles, they feed on a wide variety of fruit and shade trees, preferring apple, alder, basswood, birch, hawthorn, oak, poplar and willow.

California Tent

This caterpillar resembles the ordinary tent caterpillar in that it also constructs tents or webs in the branch crotches. This species infests oaks most commonly on the West Coast, but also feeds on apple, apricot, California coffeeberry, currant, hazel, plum, prune, redbud and willow.

Variable Oak-Leaf

Greenish yellow with variable markings, it devours the leaves of oaks, especially white oak, basswood, walnut, elm, hawthorn and persimmon in the South.

Control: Caterpillars can be controlled by spraying with carbaryl, starting when the young begin to feed. Repeat the application in seven to ten days as needed. Large forest areas can be treated with DDT applied by airplane and in concentrated form. Care must be taken not to allow the spray to drift to streams or to cultivated or habitable areas. DDT should not be applied to food crops almost ready for harvest.

EARWIGS

Earwigs are often found hiding under flat stones, in long vegetation and other damp, dark places. They feed by night on the leaves and flowers of garden plants, such as chrysanthemums, cinerarias and dahlias. Occasionally they climb fruit trees, especially apricot and peach, to dine on the ripening fruit. (Illus. p. 830.)

Control: Keep the garden clear of piles of rubbish and rotting vegetation, which provide shelter. Apply chlordane or lindane dust along fences or house foundations, or spray the ground and lower parts of susceptible plants with carbaryl.

LEAFHOPPERS

The apple leafhopper has already been described on page 821. Many other species occur on a wide variety of plants.

Rose Leafhopper

A small, pale yellow insect resembling an aphid, it is, however, able to jump quickly when disturbed. It sucks the sap on the underside of the leaf, causing a distinctive coarse mottling near the midrib, which spreads until the yellowing is extensive and may cause premature leaf fall in dry weather. (Illus. p. 834.)

Six-Spotted Leafhopper

Also known as the aster leafhopper, this is a very serious pest of flowers and vegetables because it spreads a virus disease known as aster-yellows. Among the flowers, China asters are most susceptible, whereas lettuce and celery are favored among the vegetables. Virus-infected leaves turn yellow and plants are stunted. Seeds of some affected plants are sterile. (Illus. p. 835.)

Control: Spray with carbaryl or DDT to reduce the leafhopper population. This practice, however, will not eliminate aster-yellows entirely. Commercial growers of China asters enclose their plantings with cheesecloth early in the season to keep out the leafhoppers.

LEAF MINERS

Leaf miners are the larvae of flies and small moths, which feed on the internal tissues of leaves between the upper and lower surfaces. There are two main types of mines: linear mines, which are winding tunnels growing

Rhododendron Lacebug

Damage: Leaves are stippled yellow; brownish flecks appear on lower surface.
Control: Spray with lindane, malathion or carbaryl when bugs are hatching in late spring.

Rose Leafhopper

Damage: Leaves are stippled white in early spring and again in fall.
Control: Spray with lindane or carbaryl in spring and fall.

Rose Chafer

Damage: Feeds on flowers of roses and peonies and on leaves of many other plants.
Control: Spray with DDT or lead arsenate to control chafe feeding on leaves of ornamentals.

Rose Slug Sawfly

Damage: Leaves are skeletonized.
Control: Spray with lead arsenate when roses are in full leaf.

Rose Scale

Damage: Round, dirty-white bodies encrust the canes and suck out juices.
Control: Spray with lime sulphur in spring before growth starts.

Ermine Moth

Damage: Caterpillars spin s webbing over young shoots trees and shrubs and feed insi webbing.
Control: Prune and burn webbed shoots. Spray with malathion or carbaryl.

Curculio

age: Adults drill holes in
of wild and cultivated
.

rol: Spray with DDT
e buds open.

Stem and Bulb Nematode

Damage: Gradual deterioration
of bulbous plants. If cut across,
bulb shows signs of decay.
Control: Treat narcissus bulbs
in hot water four hours at
110° F., or destroy.

Spruce Gall Aphid

Damage: Small pineapple-
shaped swellings appear at
base of new growth on Norway
and white spruce.
Control: Spray with lindane
or malathion when trees are
still dormant in late March or
early April.

Spotted Leafhopper

age: Leaves turn yellow;
s are stunted. Spreads
-yellows virus disease.
rol: Destroy diseased
s. Spray with DDT. Grow
ptible plants, such as
a asters, under cheesecloth.

Water-Lily Leaf Beetle

Damage: Grubs disfigure
leaves and flowers with
elongated holes.
Control: Control is difficult.
Submerge leaves for several
days by holding them down
with hoops or nets. Remove fish
and dust leaves with malathion.

Taxus Mealybug

Damage: Sucks plant juices,
weakens plant and causes leaf
yellowing.
Control: Spray with
dimethoate when pests are seen.

wider as the larva grows; and blotch mines, which are blisterlike cavities eaten out by one or more larvae. The damage is whitish at first and later turns brown as the injured leaf tissue withers. A large number of garden plants may be attacked by leaf miners, but only in a few cases are the plants severely checked and disfigured.

Chrysanthemums, cinerarias and other related plants are often attacked by the chrysanthemum leaf miner, particularly when they are raised in greenhouses. The linear mines of this pest usually start on the edge of the leaf, where they may not be noticed at first, and then quickly invade the rest of the leaf, so that the whole leaf is destroyed in severe cases. (Illus. p. 830.)

The holly leaf miner forms yellowish-brown blisters on the leaves of holly. (Illus. p. 831.)

Mines of the blotch type are made on lilac and privet by the lilac leaf miner, and if the attack is severe the shrubs look very unsightly when the damaged leaves shrivel. (Illus. p. 831.)

Control: If possible, remove the mined leaves by hand and burn them. Otherwise, spray with lindane, malathion, DDT or carbaryl two to three times at 14-day intervals, starting as soon as the damage is seen.

LEAF ROLLERS

These caterpillars roll up leaves and feed in the protected area. Basswood, box elder, hickory, locust and redbud are attacked by different species. The oblique-banded leaf roller, however, attacks a wide variety of trees, shrubs and flowers. Among trees are apple, ash, basswood, dogwood, hawthorn, horse chestnut, maple and oak.

Control: Spray susceptible trees with lead arsenate, carbaryl or malathion before the leaves are rolled.

LEAF TIERS

Several species of insects tie leaves together with strands of silk and continue to feed inside the protected area. One species attacks beech, another holly and another oak. The last can completely defoliate pin and scarlet oaks within two weeks in the spring. Another species, the omnivorous leaf tier, attacks a wide variety of ornamental plants as well as fruits and vegetables.

Control: Spray with carbaryl or malathion as soon as the caterpillars begin to feed in the spring and before the leaves are tied together.

NEMATODES
Chrysanthemum Leaf Nematode

This is a common pest of chrysanthemum, perennial aster, pyrethrum and related plants. The lower leaves are the first to show symptoms. Brown patches appear between the main veins of the leaf, and these darken and spread until the whole leaf shrivels and falls. As the infestation proceeds upward, the buds may be attacked and "blinded"; and the flowers are often dwarfed and misshapen. The worst attacks take place when conditions are wet or humid. (Illus. p. 830.)

Control: Commercial growers control the chrysanthemum nematode with parathion sprays, but this chemical is too dangerous to be handled by amateur gardeners. Available for amateur growers is a material known as P-40, which contains 2 percent sodium selenate impregnated on superphosphate. This is spread over the soil around chrysanthemum plants in the spring, and scratched in. The selenium is absorbed by the plant into the leaves, where it kills any nematodes present. Selenium is a very poisonous material and should always be handled with great care.

Food crops should not be grown in soils treated with this material. Demeton is also widely used by commercial chrysanthemum growers.

Stem and Bulb Nematode

A common pest of daffodil, iris, hyacinth, bluebell and snowdrop, this nematode also attacks begonia, gladiolus, onion, parsnip, strawberry and many weeds. The stems and leaves of infested plants are distorted, dwarfed and discolored by yellow streaks. Daffodils and snowdrops may also have small yellowish swellings on the leaves. When the bulbs of attacked plants are cut across, dark rings are seen where some of the scales have begun to decay. The final result of the nematode attack is the gradual deterioration and death of the plant. (Illus. p. 835.)

Control: The nematodes in lightly infested bulbs can be killed by immersing the dormant bulbs for four hours in water kept at a constant temperature of 110° F., but, as special apparatus is required to do this successfully, it is easier to destroy the stock of bulbs and plant fresh ones in clean ground. Avoid growing possible host plants on contaminated ground for at least three years.

Phlox Stem and Bulb Nematode

A different race of stem and bulb nematode infests phlox. Leaves of attacked plants become narrow and crinkled; stems may be twisted and split.

Control: Gather and burn infested phlox and other susceptible plants. Fumigate infested soil or set plants in a new location.

PLANT BUGS
Chinch Bug

This bug is black with white wings when mature, reddish when young. These sucking insects cause great damage to lawn grasses, especially during dry summers.

Tarnished Plant Bug

This is a common pest of asters, chrysanthemums, dahlias and other garden flowers, as well as many vegetables, particularly celery. This sucking insect liberates a toxin into the plant which causes shoots to blacken or flowers to be deformed. (Illus. p. 830.)

Control: Spray susceptible plants with carbaryl when the bugs are first seen. Repeat at seven- to ten-day intervals to maintain effective control.

RHODODENDRON LACEBUG

This lacebug is cream-colored when young, while the adults are shiny black with broad, lacelike wings. The leaves become finely mottled with yellow and sickly in appearance, and the undersides, where the small, flat bugs can be seen, are stained with rusty-brown excrement. (Illus. p. 834.)

Control: Spray the undersides of the leaves with lindane, malathion or carbaryl in late May or when the damage is first seen. Give two or three applications at ten-day intervals.

SAWFLIES

Sawfly larvae resemble moth caterpillars but have more legs. Like caterpillars, many species eat pieces out of the foliage of the plant and in severe cases may strip it completely.

The rose slug sawfly attacks roses, and the damage caused is distinct from that of other species. The yellowish, semitransparent larva of this species feeds only on one surface of the leaf, leaving the other to turn brown and wither, which results in the appearance of brown blotches on the foliage. (Illus. p. 834.)

Other common sawflies include the introduced pine sawfly, the larval stage of which feeds on white pine and other five-needled pines; the curled rose sawfly, which feeds on wild and cultivated roses; and the European spruce sawfly, which feeds on white, red, black and Norway spruces. The latter may cause complete defoliation, resulting in the death of the tree.

Control: Spray susceptible trees with lead arsenate, malathion or rotenone when the sawfly larvae begin to feed.

SCALE INSECTS

These insects are described more fully on page 828. Out of doors they are usually found on woody plants, and those species found on fruit trees are also common on some ornamental shrubs. The stems of cotoneaster, hawthorn, flowering currant, mountain ash and other trees and shrubs may become infested by European fruit lecanium and oyster-shell scale.

Rose Scale

A flat white scale that is found encrusting the stems of roses, especially in sheltered places. (Illus. p. 834.)

Euonymus Scale

This is a common pest of euonymus, pachysandra and American bittersweet. Occasionally it infests English ivy growing near euonymus, and in Florida it is found on camellias. The adult female is dark brown and is shaped like a miniature oyster shell. The males are very thin and pure white in color. (Illus. p. 831.)

Oleander Scale

Especially common on oleander and ivy, it also infests many kinds of fruit and ornamental trees and shrubs, particularly in the South. The females are circular, pale yellow, somewhat flattened and about $\frac{1}{10}$ in. in diameter. The males are much smaller, and they are pure white. (Illus. p. 827.)

Control: Rose scales can be controlled with a lime-sulphur spray applied in spring when the plants are still dormant. Lime-sulphur should not be used near houses, walls or fences because it will stain.

Euonymus scales are more difficult to control. Infested plants should be sprayed when dormant with a superior-type self-emulsifying petroleum oil. During the growing season in May and June they should also be sprayed with carbaryl or malathion to control the young, crawling stage.

Oleander scales can be controlled with carbaryl, malathion or summer oil.

THRIPS

Three species of thrips damage outdoor ornamental plants. The gladiolus thrips is found on gladiolus, and sometimes on delphinium, hollyhock and freesia. (Illus. p. 831.)

The onion thrips is found on roses, peonies and other plants. These minute insects suck the sap of the leaves and flower petals, leaving white or yellow spots on the feeding areas, and if the attack is severe, the flowers may be misshapen or may wither before they have had a chance to bloom. (Illus. p. 831.)

The privet thrips attacks the foliage of privet bushes and hedges, causing the leaves to turn uniformly gray and dusty-looking.

Control: Spray with nicotine sulphate and soap or with pyrethrum-rotenone insecticide.

TUSSOCK MOTHS

The name is derived from the fact that the caterpillar stage has tussocks of hairs on its body. There are several species but the most common one is the white-marked tussock moth, which is primarily a pest in cities—where it feeds on the leaves of elm, maple, horse chestnut, poplar and willow as well as on fruit trees. The leaves are skeletonized, only the veins remaining. The caterpillars are hairy, have red heads with two pencil-like tufts of long black hairs projecting like small horns.

Control: Spray with lead arsenate, carbaryl or malathion as soon as the young caterpillars begin to feed in the spring. In the southern parts of the country there are as many as three generations each year. Hence sprays may have to be applied again later in the season.

CHAPTER 46

KEEP YOUR GARDEN WEED-FREE
The Means and the Methods

Practicing Good Culture—Weeding— Chemical Weed Killers for Lawns, Paths, Ornamental Plants and Vegetables—Methods of Application—Safety Precautions—"Treatment for Weeds" Chart

THE SUPPRESSION of weeds in gardens is of the utmost importance. If they are not kept under control, a garden will soon become a wilderness. Weeds compete with cultivated plants, interfere with air circulation and serve as nurseries and breeding grounds for many otherwise avoidable pests and diseases.

Most of them are species which prefer to grow in disturbed ground or in an open situation where there is little competition from other plants.

Their capacity for producing and distributing seed is such that there will always be new crops of weeds to replace those that are removed by the gardener.

Annual weeds die and renew themselves from seed each year, but the perennials have persistent underground parts and live indefinitely. In all cases it is important to prevent weeds from forming seeds, but this is especially critical in the case of weeds of annual duration. If they are not eliminated until after they have distributed their seed, comparatively little good is done: the start for next year's crop is already assured. If they are destroyed before they seed, there will be no future problem except from seeds that blow in or are brought in some other way. In practice some annual weed seeds find their way into the garden each year; therefore the fight to eliminate these pests is a never-ending one, but it can be reduced greatly by preventing them from setting their seeds among plants in the garden or nearby.

PRACTICING GOOD CULTURE

Although the practice of killing weeds by chemicals has made giant strides since World War II, these are by no means the only weapons in the gardener's arsenal. In fact, in small gardens, chemical weed control may well take second place to older methods of attack, such as hoeing and weed pulling, and even in large gardens complete reliance should not be placed on dusts and sprays.

One important method of keeping down weeds is to provide environmental conditions that are more favorable to the plants you want to grow than to the weeds. This is particularly true of lawns. A large population of ground ivy, chickweed or sheep sorrel in sod clearly indicates that soil conditions are not optimum for the growth of grass. Killing the weeds will bring only temporary relief—fewer weeds but no more grass—and eventually a full crop of weeds again. By following the best practices of draining, fertilizing, liming, mowing and whatever else may be needed to encourage the growth of vigorous grass for a fine lawn, these weeds will be reduced or eliminated altogether.

METHODS OF WEEDING

Hoeing and hand pulling when there has been recent rain and the ground is moist still remain the most effective methods of weeding under some circumstances. For instance, hand pulling is effective in removing young intruders from among seedling vegetables and flowers that are growing closely together; for weeding pots, flats and cold frames; and for eliminating weeds that cluster closely around the bases of trees, shrubs and other plants.

Hoeing—especially with the scuffle hoe and its modern counterpart, called the swoe—is perhaps the simplest and most effective mechanical means of destroying weeds. These tools require little effort to use; their blades slice through the ground an inch or less beneath the surface and cut off all growth with which they come in contact. The best results are achieved by using them repeatedly throughout the growing season and never permitting the weeds to grow more than an inch or two high. Hoeing should be done when the ground surface is fairly dry.

Even the most vigorous and persistent perennial weeds will be eliminated if care is taken to cut off every shoot as soon as it appears, provided that this process is continued through one full growing season.

Digging out the roots of persistent perennial weeds is often necessary when new ground is being transformed into a garden. The young growths that spring from the roots that inevitably remain can be destroyed as soon as they appear, employing either a scuffle hoe or swoe or pulling by hand.

When flower beds and vegetable patches are dug annually, many weeds are eliminated by turning the soil so that the surface layer and the weeds or weed seeds it contains are well buried under the freshly dug earth.

Smothering weeds by mulching the soil surface is especially effective with annual weeds and is helpful with many perennials. All kinds of organic mulches, including peat moss, buckwheat hulls, bagasse and wood chips are useful, and so is black polyethylene plastic mulch. Even if a few weeds do develop in a mulch, it is not difficult for the gardener to pull them by hand.

CHEMICAL WEED KILLERS

Nowadays weeds associated with a wide range of vegetable, fruit and flower crops can be controlled by chemical means.

These chemicals have been produced primarily for the commercial grower, however, and they are most useful when large areas of a single crop are grown. In the normal garden many different crops are produced in a small area, and the weed killer suitable for one crop may have disastrous effects on another. Nevertheless, there are times when chemicals can be used safely in the home garden, and this saves a great deal of hand labor. The recommended dosage should not be exceeded, or the plants may be damaged.

LAWNS

Growth-Regulator Weed Killers

The discovery of the selective action of the growth-regulator weed killers 2,4-D and MCPA in 1942 first demonstrated the great economic potentialities of chemicals for weed control. It was found that these compounds could kill many broad-leaved weeds among crops of the grass family. A single application kills such weeds as plantain, creeping buttercup and sorrel; others, such as dandelions and gill-over-the-ground, need to be treated again four to six weeks later; and a few, such as white clover, are more susceptible to a related compound, silvex. Combinations of 2,4-D and 2,4,5-T are more effective against some weeds than either compound used alone.

Best conditions for application: Growth regulators are most effective if applied when the temperature is between 70° and 85° F., when little or no wind is blowing, and when no rain is expected for at least several hours. On lawns where bent grass and clover are to be maintained, 2, 4-D should be used at a quarter to a half the rate recommended for lawn weed control. Silvex will kill dichondra and white clover, and dichondra is also sensitive to 2,4-D. Lawns of St. Augustine grass require special weed-control treatment. Details can be obtained from state agricultural experiment stations or other government sources.

Methods of application: Silvex, 2,4-D and 2,4,5-T are obtainable under many different trade names, some of which are included in the charts on pages 842 to 845.

Apply these carefully at the rate suggested by the manufacturers, either with a sprayer or a watering can fitted with a sprinkler. The advantage of using a watering can is that there is less danger of the spray drifting onto sensitive plants. It does, however, distribute the chemical less evenly than a sprayer, and the rates recommended for application by means of a watering can are usually higher than those for spraying. For spot treatment of lawn weeds, some growth regulators are now available in aerosol containers.

A somewhat more comprehensive description of lawn weed control is presented on page 364 in the chapter "Lawns and Their Maintenance."

Precautions: 2,4-D and related compounds can be used safely on well-established lawns but can injure young grass seedlings and newly laid sod. Do not apply for six months after sowing grass.

Most flowers, fruits and vegetables are extremely sensitive to growth-regulator weed killers. Take great care

TREATMENT FOR WEEDS

Crop	Type of Weed	Appropriate Chemicals*	Some Trade Names**	Type of Action	Notes and Precautions
ASPARAGUS	Annual	monuron simazine	Telvar Geigy Simazine	Residual	Apply in spring before spears emerge.
	Quack grass and Bermuda	dalapon	Dowpon	Translocated	Apply after grass is 4"–6" tall. Repeat if necessary.
BULBS (tulips, daffodils)	Annual	CIPC	PPG Chemicals Chloro IPC	Root absorption; prevents cell division	Apply to clean ground before shoots appear.
		amiben	Weedone Garden Weeder	Residual	Kills weed seedlings as they sprout.
BUSH FRUITS (brambles, blueberries, grapes)	Annual	simazine	Geigy Simazine	Residual, soil-acting	Apply to clean ground; prevents establishment of seedlings.
CABBAGE	Small annual	CDAA CDEC DCPA	Randox Vegedex Dacthal	Residual	After planting out, kills small seedling weeds.
CARROTS, CELERY, DILL, PARSLEY, PARSNIPS	Annual except ragweed	dry-cleaning fluid CDEC	Stoddard Solvent Vegedex	Scorching	Kills small weeds; apply after seedlings have 2 true leaves. Flammable.
ONIONS	Annual	CIPC	Chem. Chloro IPC PPG Chemicals IPC, W.P. Superkill Chloro IPC	Soil-acting; prevents cell division	Controls purslane, chickweed, smartweed. Apply after 6" tall or at 3-4-leaf stage.
		CDAA	Randox	Residual	Apply up to 2 days before emergence. Controls grasses, pigweed, purslane.
PEPPERS	Annual	amiben	Vegiben Granular	Residual	Apply within 4 weeks of transplanting.
		diphenamid	Dymid Enide	Residual	Apply to clean soil after plants are established.

(Treatment for Weeds, cont'd)

Crop	Type of Weed	Appropriate Chemicals*	Some Trade Names**	Type of Action	Notes and Precautions
POTATOES	Annual	linuron	Lorox	Residual	Do not use on sandy soil.
		dalapon	Dowpon	Translocated	Do not use on red-skinned varieties.
ROSES, PEONIES, ESTABLISHED SHRUBS	Annual	simazine, amiben	Geigy Simazine, Weedone Garden Weeder	Residual	Apply to clean ground; prevents establishment of seedlings.
		CIPC	PPG Chem. Chloro IPC	Root absorption; prevents cell division	Apply to clean ground before weeds appear.
		trifluralin	Treflan, Greenfield Grass and Weed Control	Residual	Apply during dormant period.
SQUASH, PUMPKINS		amiben	Vegiben	Residual	Treat at planting time.
STRAWBERRIES	Annual	sesone, dacthal	Amchem Sesone	Soil-acting	Apply to clean soil after plants are established.
	Broadleaf	2,4-D amine	Weedar 64, Weedkiller "66"	Growth regulator	Apply after picking but before runners form.
TOMATOES	Annual	amiben	Vegiben Granular	Residual	Apply to clean, moist soil.
		diphenamid	Dymid, Enide	Residual	Apply before weeds germinate.
		PEBC	Tillam	Volatile	Work into soil immediately after transplanting.
VINE CROPS (cucumbers, muskmelons, watermelons)	Annual	NPA, CDEC	Alanap-3, Vegedex	Soil-acting	Apply immediately after sowing.

*Some of the chemicals listed are available only in bulk for commercial growers.
**Inclusion of a trade name in this list does not imply that the product is superior to others which may not be listed.

TREATMENT FOR WEEDS

Situation	Type of Weed	Appropriate Chemicals	Some Trade Names**	Type of Action	Notes and Precautions
LAWNS	Broadleaf weeds: dandelion, plantain	2,4-D and/or 2,4,5-T	Greenfield broadleaf weed killer; Super-D Weedone Weed-B-Gon Weed-No-More Weedone Lawn Weed Killer	Selective; kill most broadleaf weeds but not grass. Growth regulators; distort growth.	Most ornamentals, fruits and vegetables sensitive. Use separate applicator. Avoid drift to susceptible plants.
	Clover, chickweed	silvex (2,4,5-TP)	Acme Chickweed Clover Killer Kansel Weedone Chickweed Killer Weedone Clover Killer		Treat chickweed in fall or spring.
	Hard-to-kill weeds: knotweed, sheep sorrel	dicamba (banvel-D)	Scott Turf Builder Super-D Weedone	Growth regulator; absorbed primarily by roots.	Keep away from trees and shrub roots.
	Grassy weeds: crabgrass	dacthal treflan zytron	Amchem Crabgrass Killer Greenfield crabgrass killer Heritage House Spring Crabgrass Preventer	Preemergence control.	Use in early spring before crabgrass seedlings emerge.
		calar sodar PMA	Clout, Ortho Crabgrass Killer; Tat-C-Lect Weedone Crabgrass Killer	Postemergence control.	Best used during cool, moist weather.
	Perennial grasses: muhlenbergia, tall fescue, quack grass	amitrole	Weedone Spot Grass and Weed Killer	Prevents chlorophyll production. Semiselective.	Disappears from soil rapidly.
PATHS, FENCE ROWS, WASTE AREAS	General weed growth	simazine	Simazene	Sterilant absorbed by roots; remains in soil all season.	Apply to clean cultivated ground; prevents weed-seed germination.
		amitrole and simazine	Amizine* X-All*	Translocated plus residual herbicide.	Kills existing plants and prevents reestablishment for a season.

(Treatment for Weeds, cont'd)

Situation	Type of Weed	Appropriate Chemicals	Some Trade Names**	Type of Action	Notes and Precautions
PATHS, FENCE ROWS, WASTE AREAS (cont'd)	General weed growth (cont'd)	diuron monuron	Karmex Telvar	Sterilants absorbed by roots; season-long control.	Controls most shallow-rooted weeds. Avoid application over roots of desirable trees.
	Bindweed	2,4-D and/or dicamba	Esteron 99 Super-D Weedone Weedone LV-4	Growth regulators.	Avoid drift to desirable plants. Respray if necessary.
		benzac	Benzac 354	Nonselective sterilant.	Absorbed primarily by roots. Will injure or kill desirable plants in treated area.
	Brambles, incl. dewberry	2,4,5-T	Esteron 2,4,5-T Weedone 2,4,5-T	Growth regulator.	Spray thoroughly. Treat regrowth. Protect sensitive plants.
	Poison ivy, honeysuckle, thistle	amitrole	Amchem Poison Ivy Killer Amino Triazole Weed Killer Weedazol; Weedone Spot Grass and Weed Killer	Absorbed by leaves; excellent translocation.	Slow but efficient. Leaves often turn white.
	Quack grass and other weed grasses	dalapon	Dowpon	Translocated; pre- and post-emergence. Nonselective.	Mix spray immediately before application; corrosive to iron. Remains in soil 60 days or longer.
		amitrole	Amchem Poison Ivy Killer Amino Triazole Weed Killer Weedazol; Weedone Spot Grass and Weed Killer	Absorbed by foliage; inhibits regrowth.	Dig whitened growth under. Respray a green growth.
	Trees (cherry, sumac, sassafras, ailanthus)	2,4-D and/or 2,4,5-T	Esteron Brushkiller 2,4,5-T Weedone Brushkiller 32 Weedone 2,4,5-T	Growth regulators. Selective.	Desirable plants may be sensitive; avoid spray drift.

*Amizine and X-All are combinations of amitrole and simazine which are very effective in controlling weeds in driveways, patios, tennis courts, fence lines and stone walls.
**Inclusion of a trade name in this list does not imply that the product is superior to others which may not be listed.

that these plants do not come in contact with them, either through drift of spray droplets or through failure to clean a watering can or sprayer thoroughly after it has been used for weed control.

If possible, use the equipment with which weed killers are applied for that purpose only.

If this is not possible, then the sprayer should be cleaned either with activated charcoal or with household ammonia, the former being faster-acting. Put 1 oz. of charcoal and 1 to 2 oz. of household detergent in $2\frac{1}{2}$ gal. of water and agitate thoroughly. Operate sprayer with this mixture in it for about two minutes to clean. Then rinse thoroughly with clear water.

If ammonia is used, mix 2 tbsp. in 1 qt. of water. Fill the sprayer with the solution and spray a small quantity through the nozzle. Allow the remainder to stay in the sprayer overnight. Then pour out the ammonia solution and rinse the sprayer twice with clear water.

Weeder Bars

One way of avoiding problems of drift and contamination is to use one of the weeder bars on the market. A weeder bar has a waxy base impregnated with weed killer, so that when it is dragged over a lawn the chemical rubs off on the foliage.

Coverage of weed foliage is less complete than with liquid application, however, so that results are more variable. And, even though no drift is possible, contamination can still occur through waxy material adhering to the soles of shoes, tools and hands, and in this way being transferred to plants with which it should not come into contact.

Moss

The presence of moss in a lawn usually indicates excessive compaction of the soil, poor subsurface drainage, overly acid soil or lack of plant nutrients. See page 365 in "Lawns and Their Maintenance," for ways to control moss in lawns.

PATHS, PATIOS, ETC.

Residual Chemicals

Prevent the establishment of weeds on paths by applying a residual, soil-acting herbicide such as simazine or monuron (see charts on pages 844 and 845).

These chemicals are insoluble and tend to stay near the surface of the soil, where they kill the weeds as they germinate. At medium rates of application, their action persists for six to twelve months. But they must penetrate some distance into the soil to exert their full effect, and they act best when the soil is already moist or when rain follows shortly after application.

At the higher rates of application recommended for the destruction of perennial weeds, the herbicides may persist for two years, but care must be taken to insure that no roots of susceptible trees or shrubs are below the treated area. Plums and other stone fruits are among the fruit trees particularly likely to suffer damage.

Sodium Chlorate

Weeds which make paths unsightly can be killed with sodium chlorate, used alone or mixed with one of the residual herbicides to increase the duration of potency. Apply as a spray or as a fine powder on the leaves of the weeds.

Sodium chlorate will kill many annual and perennial species. If applied in spring, it acts rapidly and can persist for about six months. Its principal disadvantages are that the chemical and any organic material soaked in it are highly inflammable when dry; they have sometimes been known, even, to ignite spontaneously. The fire risk can be reduced by using one of the formulations containing a fire-retarding agent.

When there is a draining movement in the soil—for example, on sloping ground in wet weather—plants growing alongside the treated path can suffer damage from the chemical washing down the slope.

Grass Killers

Where quack grass or other grasses are the principal weeds of uncropped ground, they are best controlled with dalapon. This chemical is applied as a solution in water and enters the plant mainly through the leaves. It is most effective when it is applied in spring, as growth is most rapid then, or in autumn.

With quack grass a certain amount of regrowth often follows the application if the ground is left undisturbed; there is less regrowth when the ground is dug over or cultivated deeply two to six weeks after spraying. Except under very dry conditions, susceptible crops may be safely sown six weeks after dalapon treatment, as long as the ground has been deeply cultivated.

Many garden plants are subject to injury by dalapon, but it has relatively little effect on broad-leaved weeds; such weeds as buttercups, docks and dandelions often take over a lawn or garden after quack grass has been killed.

Amitrole is another possible grass killer. It has more effect on these other weeds than dalapon and is also extremely effective in eradicating mugwort and poison ivy.

Perennial Weeds

For fence lines where docks, thistles, bindweed and other perennials have gained a hold, and where there is no danger of damaging nearby suscepti-

ble plants, use amitrole or 2,4-D. Either will kill the weeds down to ground level, but a single application will rarely give a complete kill of the roots. If nettles or brambles predominate, the brush killer 2,4,5-T is more effective.

Painting a solution of the chemical on the leaves of weeds is laborious, but it may make possible the treatment of small areas, especially those too closely surrounded by sensitive plants to allow other methods of application to be used.

PLANTINGS
Fruit

Perennial weeds in apple orchards can be controlled with growth regulators, but take care to keep the chemical off the tree foliage. Do not carry out this treatment during the blossoming period. Dalapon can also be used to kill quack grass under well-established apple and pear trees, but is not safe under plums and cherries.

Control annual weeds among established plantings of bush and cane fruits through the summer by applying low rates of simazine (1 to 2 lb. per acre of active material) to clean ground in the spring. Simazine is fully effective only if the soil is moist, and it should, of course, be kept off the fruit plants as much as possible. Take care also not to exceed the dosage recommended. Higher rates, when they are applied for several years, may lead to a buildup of chemical in the soil and so cause trouble with subsequent crops.

If quack grass has infested fruit plantings, dalapon may be used as a control, but it should be employed only during the dormant season; even then there is a risk of damage with some crops.

Most broad-leaved annual weeds and many annual grasses in raspberry and blackberry patches can be controlled with simazine. Similar weeds in strawberry beds can be controlled with a mixture of sesone and Dacthal. Details are presented in the chart on page 843.

Ornamental Plants

Few safe herbicidal treatments have yet been developed for use among flowers. But with bulbs, an autumn or winter application of CIPC (Chloro IPC), or a mixture of CIPC and diuron made before the shoots appear, will prevent the emergence of weeds until well into the spring. CIPC is especially effective against chickweed and annual grass.

Roses have shown a high degree of resistance to simazine, and therefore this material may be used between rosebushes to control most annual weeds.

Vegetables

A number of chemical methods of weed control have been developed for use with vegetable crops. In the average garden, however, any one vegetable is rarely grown in a large enough area for advantage to be taken of these methods, and the herbicides in question are not usually marketed in small enough quantities to be practical for home-garden use.

The following crops can be sprayed successfully: asparagus, beets, cabbage, carrots, celery, onions and vine crops. The appropriate chemicals are given in the chart on pages 842 and 843.

GENERAL INSTRUCTIONS

Methods of Application

The technique used by the gardener to apply a herbicide is relatively unimportant as long as the correct amount of chemical is distributed evenly over the area being treated. Many types of small sprayers are suitable; those with plastic containers are usually cheaper than those made of metal, and some are designed especially for small-scale garden use. In many cases, a watering can fitted with a fine sprinkler will be found adequate.

It is most important to follow as closely as possible the instructions supplied with the herbicide. With some chemicals the margin between the dose which will kill the weeds and that which will injure the crop is small, so measure out the required amounts carefully.

The amount of water used to apply the weed killer is not so important, provided distribution is even. But with those chemicals which are taken up through the foliage, the amount of water used in proportion to chemicals must not be so high that there will be excessive runoff. The gardener's work may then prove to have been wasted.

Safety Precautions

The chemicals that have been mentioned are all of low toxicity to man and animals, but it is a sensible precaution to keep the concentrated materials well out of the reach of children and away from foodstuffs. The supply of weed killers should also, of course, be kept well away from seeds and fertilizers.

Dispose of used containers in such a way that any remaining chemical will not find its way onto growing plants. Sodium chlorate is highly inflammable and needs to be treated with special care.

As many garden plants are highly susceptible to chemical weed killers, take every precaution to insure that the weed killers make contact only with the weedy area being treated. Always avoid spraying such solutions in windy weather.

Charts indicating the treatment for most types of weeds appear on pages 842 to 845.

SUPPLEMENT

Calendar of Work—
Great Temperate Zone

Glossary—
Including Terms for Beginning Gardeners

Index

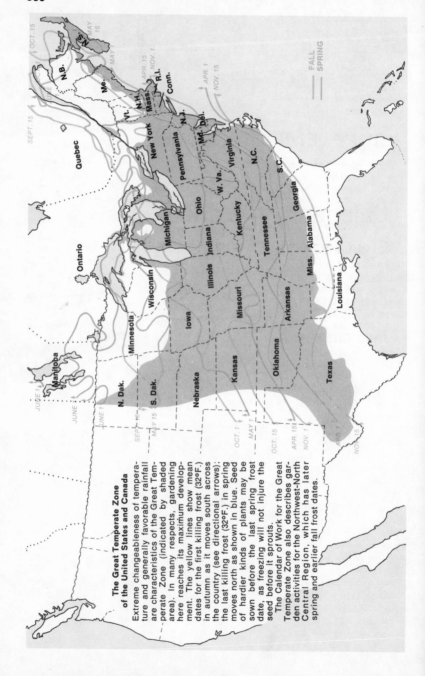

The Great Temperate Zone of the United States and Canada

Extreme changeableness of temperature and generally favorable rainfall are characteristics of the Great Temperate Zone (indicated by shaded area). In many respects, gardening here reaches its maximum development. The yellow lines show mean dates for the first killing frost (32°F.) in autumn as it moves south across the country (see directional arrows); the last killing frost (32°F.) in spring moves north as shown in blue. Seed of hardier kinds of plants may be sown before the last spring frost date, as freezing will not injure the seed before it sprouts.

The Calendar of Work for the Great Temperate Zone also describes garden activities for the Northwest-North Central Region, which has later spring and earlier fall frost dates.

CALENDAR OF WORK—
Great Temperate Zone

THIS CALENDAR serves the great temperate region stretching from New England to North Dakota and from Virginia across Tennessee to Arkansas and Oklahoma. With allowance for earlier seasonal dates of a week or two, which are noted in parentheses in the Calendar, it also may be used for the cold-winter Areas discussed in "The Northeast–North Central Region and Adjacent Canada" (see map on pages 588–89). Naturally, over such a vast terrain, differences exist in the kinds of plants that can be grown and in the appropriate times for carrying out some gardening operations. But the differences are less than might be supposed. In general, procedures are similar throughout the zone. Near its southern limits winter is shorter and less severe and spring comes earlier. But late spring frosts there are apt to be troublesome, and the fall is prolonged. As one goes westward from the East coast, summers are usually hotter and drier. There are not, of course, strict lines of demarcation between climatic regions. The temperate territory we are discussing merges into the Rocky Mountain region in the west and, in the south, into that of the Southeast.

The time to carry out gardening operations in Area 5 of the Northeast–North Central region does not vary much from suitable dates for southern New England and New York. Differences are most noticeable in early spring and in late fall.

Early in the season, blooming dates are affected. Crocuses in Area 5 of the Northeast–North Central region often finish blooming by April 1, while in Area 3 they may be at least two weeks later (see map, opposite). An early or late spring may make a difference of ten days in blooming dates from year to year; by the end of May there is a difference of only a few days. By the end of June differences are scarcely noticeable. Plants which bloom in midsummer seldom vary much in their blooming dates from one year to another or from Canada to Virginia.

JANUARY

There is little to be done in the garden now besides removing snow from trees and shrubs (especially evergreens) likely to be damaged by the weight of accumulations. Shake or brush off newly fallen snow before it becomes wet and heavy and before it freezes. Any attempt to remove ice from branches will result in broken ones. Guard against snow slides from roofs, which very easily break branches when the wood is cold and brittle.

If salt has been used on sidewalks or drives, carefully pile the salted snow away from nearby plants.

Be sure house plants receive maximum light. Do everything possible to humidify the air. Standing potted plants on trays filled with pebbles kept wet is helpful; so is spraying the foliage with water on bright days.

In greenhouses, be careful not to give too much water, and watch temperatures carefully. Dry off poinsettias that are through blooming. Bring in the first batch of hardy bulbs, such as early narcissuses, hyacinths and tulips, for forcing. Sow seed of annuals for early bloom indoors, also seed of perennials such as *Aquilegia* (columbine) and delphinium, to bloom outdoors in summer.

FEBRUARY

Spring catalogues have arrived. Study them and place orders as soon as possible. Rely chiefly on popular varieties, but do order small quantities of a few new items for trial and for variety.

Tramp down the snow around the trunks of young fruit trees to deter mice from burrowing under the snow to chew the bark. If adequate wire guards were put in place in November, this step can be omitted.

February is a busy month in the greenhouse. Sow seed of begonias, lobelias and other outdoor annuals that need a long season of growth. Bring more bulbs indoors for forcing.

It is time to take the first cuttings of geraniums, lantanas, heliotropes, fuchsias and abutilons from plants that have been wintered in the greenhouse, and to start into growth stock plants of chrysanthemums from which cuttings will be taken later.

Inspect gladioluses as well as dahlias and bulbs, corms and tubers stored indoors over winter. Prune grapes on a sunny day.

MARCH

This is a busy month in gardens except in the coldest areas. Gardeners can get a two-week start on those who live in such cold regions as Area 3 of the Northeast (see map, pages 588–89) — and who must usually wait until April to start outside work. Those who garden south of Area 5 of the Northeast can begin even earlier.

This month fruit trees may be pruned and examined for oystershell and San Jose scale. These pests may also be present on cotoneasters, dogwoods and lilacs. To control them, dormant-strength lime sulphur or commercial preparations should be used before the leaf buds swell.

Shrubs that need spring pruning can be given this attention as soon as the severest winter weather is over, but it is easier if the pruning is postponed until just after their buds start to swell (which in some parts will not be until April or, in Area 3 of the Northeast and northward, early May).

Spring-flowering bulbs planted on the south or west side of a building often cause concern when shoots appear before the snow has gone from other places. Mulching aggravates this. Shoveling snow over the bed, before the foliage appears, protects it.

As soon as the snow has melted and the ground is no longer frozen deeply, remove the upper winter covering from roses and leave only the mound of earth; this should be taken down about two weeks later. Also remove leaf and straw mulches, which may mat and cause mildew, from bulb, perennial and rock-garden plantings.

Seed of ageratums, verbenas, snapdragons, petunias, annual carnations and other annuals that take 70 to 90 days to bloom should be started indoors or in the greenhouse early in March. They make a display outdoors sooner if given an early start. The sowing of quicker-maturing kinds such as marigolds, asters, stocks and zinnias, needing about 60 days from seed sowing to setting out in the garden, may be made 10 to 20 days later.

The timing of operations during March and April depends a great deal on the differences between climatic Areas. For gardeners throughout the temperate region, however, mid-March to mid-April is the time to sow indoors the seed of the majority of annuals and common vegetables. Cabbage, cauliflower, pepper, eggplant and tomato need to be started early so that good-sized plants can be set out in May or early June. Sowing dates will vary with the kind of plant and the geographical location.

Tuberous begonias should be started into growth about the middle of March, to provide plants to be set out

Calendar of Work

in June. In gardens in the southern part of this range, also start cannas and caladiums. For pot culture start tubers of gloxinias.

Take cuttings of coleus, blood-leaves and chrysanthemums and, if needed, more cuttings of fuchsias, flowering maples and geraniums, from stock plants started in February.

In southern New England and farther south, peas may be sown outdoors and onion sets planted.

APRIL

In the more temperate areas, snow usually disappears from the lawn in March or early April and, particularly if its departure is slow, may leave a trail of fungus damage in its wake, known as "snow mold." Treating the lawn with a mercurial fungicide the previous fall would probably have prevented this. If patches of the disease are present, they should be brushed vigorously with a steel leaf-rake to prevent the mold from smothering the turf.

As soon as the surface is dry enough, established lawns will benefit from being swept and topdressed with sifted rich topsoil if the surface is uneven or eroded. The application of a lawn fertilizer is also now in order. If a new lawn is planned, sow it at the first favorable opportunity.

Lose no time in spading beds that are to be planted with perennials, biennials and annuals. Beds made ready in advance make it possible to take every advantage of good planting weather in the days ahead.

Inspect the emerging tips of tulips for scorched spots which may be evidence of the disease known as "tulip fire" (*Botrytis tulipae*). Daffodils may show "burned" foliage if the bulbs are infested with lesser or greater bulb flies. Infested bulbs should be burned.

As soon as the frost leaves the ground, woody plants should be set out. (Gardeners in Area 5 of the Northeast may have about three weeks in which to do this, those farther southward a full month or more; but snow in Area 3 usually lies on the ground until the third week in April, and leaf buds often do not expand until early May. Spring planting time lasts a week or ten days after thaw in this Area. Further delay leaves too short a period to develop bloom before frost.)

Remove earth mounds from roses as soon as the frost is out of the ground and attend to needed pruning and fertilizing. If the fungus disease known as "black spot" (see illustration, page 793) is prevalent in the locality, spray the plants and the surface of the soil with dormant-strength lime sulphur (as the manufacturer directs) before the leaf buds swell.

For northern gardens, start cannas and dahlias indoors during the last week of April.

Remove the straw covering from strawberries after all danger of hard freezing is past. All dead tips of raspberry canes should be removed now, and healthy canes may be cut back to a height of 2 ft.

Complete the removal of winter covering from the rock garden. Push back into the soil any plants heaved out by frost. Spread a topdressing of new soil or compost and set out young plants where needed.

Carefully check perennials and replace any that have been winter-killed. If new perennial plantings are to be made, attend to this without delay. Clump-forming perennials can be divided and replanted before they have made much new growth.

As soon as the ground is dry enough to be worked to form a good seedbed, hardy vegetables—spinach, radishes, lettuce and carrots—can be sown outdoors, and seed of many hardy annuals can also be sown. Among suitable kinds are larkspur, coreopsis, gypsophila, gaillardia, cornflower, annual chrysanthemum, clarkia, godetia and love-in-a-mist.

Transplant into flats the seedlings of annual flowers sown indoors last month. Pot tuberous begonias, gloxinias and cannas that are well started.

Continue to insert cuttings of chrysanthemums, as well as of geraniums, fuchsias, abutilons and other plants for indoor flowering pot plants. This is a good time to propagate—by cuttings and air layering—many tropical foliage plants such as dracaenas, dieffenbachias, crotons and philodendrons.

Examine all permanent greenhouse and house plants carefully, trim to shape and repot or topdress as necessary. Other specimens that have filled their containers with healthy roots and are in active growth will benefit from weekly or biweekly applications of dilute liquid fertilizer given from now until fall. Keep newly potted plants shaded from bright sun and in a humid atmosphere for at least three to four weeks after potting. As the sun gains increasing strength, additional shading will be needed by many greenhouse plants.

MAY

In Area 5 of the Northeast region (see map, pages 588–89) gardening work will still be about ten days ahead of that in colder zones. By now even gardens in Area 3 should be cleaned and lawns ready for the first application of fertilizer. New planting of trees and shrubs in the coldest areas should be well in progress. Planting of most herbaceous perennials should be completed by May 10; evergreens may be planted so long as they have not made appreciable new growth.

As a mild gamble in Areas 3 and 4, sow most vegetable seed and seed of

quick-blooming annuals, such as alyssum, clarkia and godetia, outdoors about May 10. On the rare occasions when late frost threatens, cover these young plants at night with paper tents. Seeds of beans, corn and melons like warm soil and should not be sown until a week or so later. Most gardeners in Areas 3 and 4 wait until the last week in May or the first in June before doing this, to avoid danger of late spring frost.

In the Great Temperate Zone, first sowings of tender vegetables—such as beans, corn, squash and cucumbers—should be made as soon as the ground is warm enough. Second sowings of earlier vegetables will provide successive harvests.

Gardeners usually plant out annuals about the middle of May. Gladiolus corms and summer-flowering bulbs may be planted outdoors from the beginning to end of this month, depending upon locality; and from the middle to the end of the month is a good time to plant out the sprouted roots of cannas and dahlias. Tuberous begonias, started indoors, should not be planted outside until the end of May or later.

Seedlings of annual flowers raised indoors in flats should be put in a cold frame early in May. Then cover them at night and expose them to sun and air during the day for a week or two before they are set out in the garden after all danger of frost is over.

Dig up and burn all tulips that have striped or feathered flowers caused by virus infection. Insects can spread the disease to other tulips or other susceptible plants.

If tulip bulbs are to be saved after blooming, take the bulbs up at the end of the month and, for the present, plant them thinly in a trench so that the tops can remain as long as they are green. Later, cut off the tops and dry and store the bulbs in a cool, airy place for planting again in the early fall where they are to bloom the following spring. In regions which have hot, dry weather in June, the most economical method is to leave tulips in the ground for three seasons of bloom and then discard them and buy fresh bulbs. If this is done, annuals may be planted between the tulips. The tulip tops should be left until they have died completely. They may then be cut flush with the ground or removed with a sharp tug.

Pinch the tops of annuals such as snapdragons early in May to make them branch.

Only a few shrubs should be pruned in early spring—the kinds that bloom after July 1 on wood of the current season's growth. Bush roses (hybrid tea roses, hybrid perpetuals and floribundas), peegee and hills-of-snow hydrangeas are the commonest. Buddleias (except *B. alternifolia*), clethras and lespedezas (bush clover)—all of which must be treated as herbaceous subjects in Areas 3 and 4 of the Northeast—are others. Kerrias, sorbarias and late-blooming spiraeas should have any weak or dead stems removed. Spring-flowering shrubs, such as forsythias, spiraeas, mock oranges, deutzias and weigelas, should be pruned, if necessary, immediately after flowering.

Deciduous hedges which have been badly neglected may be severely cut back in spring to encourage renewal growth. Those which have been well cared for should not be trimmed until June, after they have achieved good growth.

JUNE

This is the month for roses. Watch now for harmful pests, and spray or dust regularly to keep them under control. When the temperature rises above 70° F. during the day, it is a good time to use weed killers on lawns.

The press of spring work is over;

annual and vegetable gardens have already been planted, but successive sowings of some kinds, such as beans and beets, can be made. There is time to trim the edges of beds, stake and tie tall plants that need support against wind, and attend to other chores.

Any annuals and other bedding plants not yet planted should be set out by the second week of June.

Many rock-garden plants can be cut back as soon as blooming is over and be either lifted and divided, or have cuttings of fresh growth taken from them to produce a stock of young plants.

Woody plants in northern gardens, with a few exceptions, have made most of their growth by the end of June, so the third week in June is the best time to trim most hedges. They may still make enough new growth to hide the cut ends but not enough to require a second trimming. Privets, yews and arborvitaes may be trimmed a second time.

The majority of shrubs which bloom before the end of June should have a few old branches removed close to the base when bloom is finished. This keeps them within bounds, allows light to reach the interior parts and improves next year's show of bloom.

People interested in growing shrubs from softwood cuttings will find mid-to-late June an excellent time for cuttings (see page 707).

Tulip bulbs will be ready to lift by the end of June in the northern areas. In the cool, moist climate of the eastern seacoast, they will ripen later but they will be larger. In most parts of the Great Temperate Zone, June is hot. This encourages the formation of many small lateral bulbs rather than large central ones.

Make successive plantings of gladioluses to insure as long a season of bloom as possible. Tigridias, tuberoses and dahlias may be planted.

Seeds of perennials and biennials should now be sown to start new plants for the next spring. Cover the seedbeds with lath shades to reduce light intensity.

As soon as the last cutting of asparagus is made, cultivate and fertilize the bed.

Now that the weather is warm and settled, most house plants may be stood outdoors, in sun or light shade according to their individual needs. Bury the pots to their rims in sand or fine gravel. Fertilize regularly and repot when necessary.

JULY

Garden chrysanthemums should not be pinched back to encourage bushy growth after mid-July, or bloom will be affected.

The first blooming of roses is almost over and, even in northern regions, they will be in flower during the first week of July. Prune rambler-type climbers as soon as they are through flowering.

Daffodil foliage will be ready to cut from the beginning to the middle of the month. Old clumps of bearded iris should be lifted, divided and replanted sometime during July. It is better to wait until the end of the month or until August before dividing Siberian iris.

Heavy watering once or twice a week is likely to be needed during this usually hot period. Watering should be followed by shallow cultivation to keep the surface soil loose in order to reduce evaporation. Mulches of peat moss, chopped corncobs or other suitable material eliminate the need for surface cultivation.

July produces an early harvest of annual flowers as well as peas, bush beans, spinach and beets.

In northern sections, second crops of quickly maturing flowers and vegetables may be sown. (Area 3 of the Northeast does not have a long enough fall to make this worthwhile, except for New Zealand spinach, beet tops and lettuce.)

Delphiniums should be cut back after their first bloom. They will flower again in September or October.

With the coming of hot weather, raise the mower blades so that the grass is not cut lower than 2 in. Use selective weed killers to control crabgrass and other weeds.

Sow pansies after the middle of the month. Transplant seedlings of other biennials and perennials sown last month.

Most house plants benefit from being placed outdoors during the summer, in sun or shade according to their individual needs. Bury the pots to their rims in a bed of cinders, fine gravel or sand and pay attention to regular watering, fertilizing and pest control as well as staking and tying. Repot any specimens in need of this.

AUGUST

This is such a popular month for vacations that gardens often suffer. But the work of watering, weeding, staking and tying must go on, as must the cutting of annual flowers and harvesting of vegetables. Spraying for the control of insects and diseases should be a week-to-week operation.

Oriental poppies become leafless by the middle of August, and this is when to transplant them.

The third or fourth week in August or early in September is a good time to seed new lawns and patch old ones. During late August and early September there is usually ample rain—in the East at least—to give the seed a good start. (Seeding after September 10 in Northeast Area 3 is too late.)

Madonna lilies and autumn crocus may be purchased and planted now. Order hardy bulbs for fall planting.

Seeds of perennials and biennials

sown in June or early July should have produced good seedlings. Transplant into outdoor beds or cold frames to remain over the winter.

Cuttings may be taken from many rock-garden plants, such as arabis (rock cress), aubretia, androsace (rock jasmine), phlox, sedum and dianthus (pink). These should be placed in cold frames for the winter.

Shrub cuttings taken in June will probably be rooted by the end of August; leave them undisturbed in a cold frame for the winter.

Harvesting early crops in the vegetable garden is in full swing in August. As new garden or lawn areas are cleared, sow winter rye as a cover crop to be turned under later.

SEPTEMBER

If planting is to be done this fall, prepare the beds without delay.

Good open weather usually characterizes fall in the North, but new plants need considerable time to prepare for winter. (For this reason it pays to plant conifers in Area 3 of the Northeast in late August and herbaceous perennials early in September so that they will have four to six weeks in which to establish new roots before the soil temperature falls below 35° F.) Planting can be continued later. The drop in temperature, which effectively stops root growth, usually happens in November—earlier in the northern parts than in the southern parts of this territory.

Spring-flowering bulbs, particularly of crocus and narcissus, should be planted in September. Tulips root more quickly; with them early October planting is fairly safe in northern gardens, and farther south still later planting is advocated. Early November planting is advisable for tulips in the vicinity of New York City. Delay results in serious losses unless a thick mulch of leaves or straw

is placed over the new planting. In the South, tulips planted in early November are satisfactory.

House plants that have summered in the garden should be brought in before the first early frost. Even if tender kinds are not frozen, cool nights may harm them. Coleus, geraniums and other tender plants which are to be saved over winter, as "mother plants" from which to take cuttings in the spring, should also be taken indoors at this time.

Killing frost comes to some parts of the region this month, to other parts not until October or November.

Cannas, dahlias, tigridias, tuberoses, montbretias and tuberous begonias may be left until their tops are slightly damaged by frost; this assures the gardener of the benefit of late bloom if frost is delayed. As soon as the tops are killed, cut them back close to the ground and dig up the roots. Turn them upside down and leave them in the sun for a few hours to drain the stems and dry the soil. Then spread them thinly in a dry, airy place at room temperature until they are thoroughly dry, which will be about a month later. Remove the remainder of the tops and soil, place in polyethylene bags and store them in temperatures appropriate to their kinds.

Start cleaning up flower beds as soon as the tops of the plants lose their ornamental value. Cut the tops of herbaceous perennials an inch or two above the ground and the tops of annuals just below ground, so that the roots will be left to rot and improve the soil texture.

Clean stakes and tie them in bundles to use next year.

Hedges which continued to grow after they were trimmed in June should receive a light trimming the first week in September.

Pot astilbes, hostas and any other

perennials that are to be forced during the winter. Sink the pots to their rims in a cold frame and water moderately until their foliage dies naturally.

Parsley, chives, basil and other herbs may be potted now and taken indoors before severe frost threatens, to provide winter pickings.

OCTOBER

As the fall clean-up proceeds in October and November, continue to add garden refuse to the compost heap.

Deciduous trees and shrubs which have lost their leaves or will soon do so may now be transplanted in those Areas where fall planting is good practice. Gardeners usually favor fall planting (but most people in sections as cold as Area 3 of the Northeast prefer to plant in spring).

Early October is the time to pot hardy bulbs that are to be grown indoors. To enable them to establish good root systems, it is necessary to give them a period of cool storage (45° F.) for 10 to 12 weeks after planting. If "prepared" bulbs (kinds treated especially to produce early flowers) are used, the cool-storage time may be reduced to eight weeks. In the North a dependable way to provide storage conditions is to dig a trench 15 to 18 in. deep, place a board in the bottom and stand the pots on this so that the roots cannot push through into the soil. Then water the pots and surround and cover them with 8 in. of coarse sand or cinders. Peat, sawdust or vermiculite may be used if a slanted roof is erected to keep these materials from becoming soggy from melting snow and then frozen in.

Most gardeners lift their gladioluses and other tender bulbs during late October, rather than run the risk of having to do this after the ground freezes. The method of preparing them for storage is the same as de-scribed for other summer-flowering tubers lifted last month.

Late vegetables must be stored. Onions and squash need dry, quite warm storage; cabbages, potatoes, beets and carrots, comparatively cool (35°–40° F.) and fairly humid conditions. (Climbing roses and large-flowered clematis in Area 3 of the Northeast should be taken down from trellises now.)

NOVEMBER

Even in the southern parts of the temperate territory all planting of deciduous trees and shrubs should be completed this month. All herbaceous perennials (except chrysanthemums) that have not been cut back earlier may be cut down now. Cutting chrysanthemums down may stimulate new growth at the base if there is a mild fall, and these new shoots will be killed during winter.

This is the month to mound soil about the bases of roses and to put in place mulches and other forms of winter protection.

Wire mouse-guards are a necessary precaution around fruit trees. Burlap screens should be placed around conifers that may be "burned" or dried out by winter weather.

Make sure that cold frames containing plants are snug for the winter and that, where needed, mats or other protection are at hand with which to cover them on cold nights.

By the end of November outdoor garden activity has ended and the northern gardener moves operations indoors.

DECEMBER

Those without a greenhouse might assemble a fluorescent lighting unit in the basement. Pots of bulbs, African violets, gloxinias, seedling annuals and many other plants can be grown under even one four-tube fixture.

GLOSSARY
Including Terms for Beginning Gardeners

ACTINOMYCETES: A group of micro-organisms.

ADVENTITIOUS ROOTS: Those that develop spontaneously from above-ground parts of plants, such as stems.

ALGAE: A group of lower plants without true stems, roots or leaves. The group includes seaweeds.

ALPINE: A plant that grows naturally at elevations above levels where trees grow. Also, a term used when referring to elevations above timberline.

ANDROECIUM: The stamens of a flower, collectively.

ANTHER: The pollen-bearing part of a stamen.

AREOLES: Small, specialized areas of a surface, such as those from which the spines of cactuses arise.

AUTOECIOUS RUST: A rust-disease fungus that passes through all stages of its life in the same host plant.

AXIL: The angle formed between an axis (such as a branch) and any organ growing from it.

BAGASSE: Residue of sugarcane after the juice has been extracted.

BARE-ROOT: Refers to the condition of a plant dug up for transplanting without a ball of soil retained about its roots.

"BEDDING" PLANTS: Plants set out in ornamental flower beds for one season.

BITUMEN: Asphalt or mineral tars.

BLACKTOP: Asphalt surfacing used for driveways, paths and roads.

BOTRYTIS: A group of funguses that cause certain plant diseases; also, a disease caused by such a fungus.

BRACT: A specialized leaf, sometimes highly colored, from the axil of which a flower develops; the red parts of a poinsettia "flower" are bracts.

BROADLEAF WEED: Any weed belonging to the great group of plants called dicotyledons.

BROMELIAD: Any member of the pine-apple family (*Bromeliaceae*).

BROWN ROT: A fungus disease causing decay and brown discoloration, usually of fruits.

BUDDING UNION (or BUD UNION): The part of the stem where the scion joins the stock following propagation by budding.

BULBILS: Small bulbs which develop on the stems of some plants, as in tiger lilies.

BULBLET: A small bulb that develops from a larger bulb.

BUNCH GRASS: A type of grass that grows in bunches.

CALYX: The outer circle of floral parts, composed of sepals.

CAMBIUM: A thin layer of tissue under the bark, consisting of cells capable of dividing themselves and forming new layers of wood, bark or other tissue.

CANE: A thin stem that tapers only slightly, like that of the raspberry and bamboo.

CANKER: A well-defined area or lesion on a woody stem caused by a disease organism.

CAUDEX: The thickened woody base of a plant.

CHLOROPHYLL: The green coloring matter in plants.

CHLOROSIS: An unhealthy yellowing of foliage resulting from a deficiency of chlorophyll.

CLEAN CULTIVATION: Keeping the surface of cultivated ground from caking, and removing weeds by hoe, hand cultivator, etc.

CLONE: A group of plants derived by vegetative propagation from one original plant.

COLLOIDAL CLAY: Clay composed of extremely fine (ultramicroscopic) particles.

COMPOST: Partially decayed organic material prepared and used for soil improvement.

CONIFER: Cone-bearing trees, such as pines, firs and spruces.

CORM: A solid bulblike organ, usually subterranean, such as that produced by crocuses and gladioluses.

CORNICLE: Wax-secreting tubes of certain insects, such as aphids.

COROLLA: The petals of a flower, collectively.

CORONA: A structure between the corolla and stamens that is found in plants such as narcissuses and passionflowers.

COTYLEDON: The first or "seed" leaves of a plant grown from seed.

CROSS-POLLINATION: Transference of pollen from the anthers of the flower of one plant to the stigma of the flower of another.

CROTCH: The angle formed between two branches that join.

CROWN: A root system's top and center—from which stems or leaves develop in many herbaceous perennial plants; also, the top or head of a tree.

CRUCIFEROUS: Belonging to the mustard family (Cruciferae).

CRUMBS (in soil): Small, easily separated fragments composed of smaller particles which adhere together.

CUTICLE: Skin or epidermis.

CUTTINGS: Parts of a plant—usually stems, leaves or roots—prepared and used for propagation.

CYCAD: A palmlike tropical plant.

DECIDUOUS: Leaf-losing, not evergreen.

DEFOLIATION: The premature falling off of leaves. May be caused by disease, insects, or too much or too little moisture.

DIBBER: A tool used in soil to make holes for transplanting small plants.

DICOTYLEDON: A plant that has two seed leaves, for example, beans, peas.

DIG IN: To bury during the operation of spading.

DIOECIOUS: Bearing male and female flowers on separate plants.

DISBUD: To remove unwanted buds.

DIVISION: A portion of a plant (generally consisting of roots and buds or aboveground sections) used for propagation; also, the act of preparing such divisions.

DRAW HOE: A hoe handled by drawing it toward the operator.

DRY WALL: A wall built without mortar or cement.

EMBRYO: The rudimentary plant within a seed.

EPIDERMIS: Outer skin.

EPIPHYTIC: Growing upon another plant without taking nourishment from it.

ESCAPES: Plants, once cultivated in gardens, which have "escaped" domestic confines and established themselves in the wild.

ESPALIER: A plant trained with its trunk and branches flattened in one plane; also, to train it in this manner.

EYE: An undeveloped bud of a plant.

EYE OF SEED: The point of attachment where the seed joins the ovary wall or placenta.

FACULTATIVE SAPROPHYTE: A fungus or other organism that ordinarily lives on dead organic material but has the ability to exist also as a parasite on living plants.

FANGY (of roots): Forked.

FASTIGIATE: Narrow, with erect branches that are close together.

"FITTING" THE SOIL: Preparing the soil for planting.

FOLIAR FERTILIZING: Fertilizing plants by spraying on them nutrient solutions to be absorbed by the foliage.

FOOT ROT: A rot disease that affects the basal parts of a plant.

FORCING: Methods of inducing the maturing of fruits, vegetables and flowers ahead of their normal seasons.

FRIABLE: Loose and crumbly.

FROND: The leaf of a fern, cycad or palm.

FUNGICIDE: A material that inhibits the growth of or destroys funguses.

GALL: An abnormal growth or swelling caused by insects, funguses or other organisms.

GAMETES: Sexually reproductive cells.

GENERA: The plural of genus.

GLAUCOUS: Having a blue-green waxy surface.

GRAY MOLD: A fungus disease characterized by the grayish moldy appearance of affected parts.

GREEN MANURING: Turning under living plants for the purpose of improving soil fertility.

GROWTH REGULATOR: A chemical that speeds or slows growth.

GYNOECIUM: The entire female portion of a flower.

HARDEN OFF: Gradually to accustom a plant to more rigorous conditions, as in transferring it from indoors to outdoors.

HARDWARE CLOTH: Fine wire mesh.

HARDINESS: The ability of a plant to winter outdoors in cold climates without protection.

HARROW: To break up the soil surface by dragging over it an implement (harrow) designed for this purpose.

HAUSTORIUM: Rootlike sucker of parasitic plants.

"HEAD BACK": To prune the main branches back severely.

HEARTWOOD: The harder and usually darker-colored wood that forms the interior portion of a tree trunk or branch.

HEEL IN: To plant close together temporarily.

HERBACEOUS: Refers to seed-bearing plants that die to the ground each year, commonly used when describing perennials.

HETEROECIOUS RUST: A disease-causing fungus that lives at various times in its life cycle on different hosts.

HIGH-ANALYSIS FERTILIZER: A fertilizer containing high proportions of nutrient elements.

HOE, WHEEL: A hoe fitted with a wheel.

HOE, SCUFFLE: A hoe operated in a to-and-fro motion with its blade just below the soil surface.

HOTBED: A bed of soil heated by fermenting material, hot-water pipes or electric heating cables.

"HOT CAPS": Small paper or plastic tents used for protecting young plants.

HUMIDISTAT: An instrument for measuring relative humidity of the atmosphere.

HUMUS: Organic matter in an extremely advanced state of decay.

HYBRID: A crossbreed between two different species; sometimes applied to any crossbreed.

HYDRAULIC SEEDING: A method of sowing grass seed by spraying it in a stream of water.

HYPHAE: The threadlike filaments that form the vegetative part of a fungus.

INFLORESCENCE: A complete flower cluster.

INORGANIC FERTILIZER: A fertilizer that does not contain carbon compounds.

INSECT VECTORS: Insects that carry and distribute disease-causing microorganisms.

KEEL: A ridge growth on a part of a plant, like the keel of a boat.

LARVA: The immature or grub stage of an insect.

LEAF CURL: A disease that causes curling of leaves.

LEAF MOLD: Compost formed of leaves.

LEGUME: Any plant belonging to the pea family (*Leguminosae*).

LIFTING: Digging up and removing a plant from the soil.

LOAM: Soil that contains both clay and sand.

LOBE: A partial division or segment of a leaf or other organ.

MICROCLIMATE: The climate of a small area which differs from that of the general surrounding region because of special conditions.

MICROORGANISMS: Living organisms of microscopic size, especially bacteria and protozoa.

MIDRIB: The central rib or vein of a leaf or other organ.

MILDEW: A fungus that produces a thin whitish covering on the surface where it grows.

MONOCOTYLEDON: A plant with a single seed leaf, for example, a leaf of grass.

MORPHOLOGY: The science that deals with the form and structure of plants.

MOSAIC VIRUS (of plants): A type of virus which produces a mosaic pattern or mottling of the foliage.

"MOTHER" BULB: A mature bulb that has developed offset bulbs.

MOTHER PLANT: A plant from which propagations are taken.

MULCH: A layer of loose material spread over the ground surface.

MUTATION: A fundamental change in heredity that produces a new plant basically unlike the parent, or that produces part of a plant that differs significantly from the main body.

NATURALIZE: To establish plants as if they grew by chance—as daffodils in a woodland—so that they persist with a minimum of care.

NATURAL LAYERING: The spontaneous rooting of stems in contact with the ground.

NEMATODE: One of a group of very small wormlike creatures, for example, eelworms.

NITRATES: Certain salts of nitric acid, which are used as oxidizing agents in the manufacture of fertilizers.

NITROGEN CARRIER: A material, usually a fertilizer, that contains the element nitrogen.

NURSE GRASS: A quick-growing, temporary grass included in lawn-seed mixtures to give rapid coverage and to protect the more permanent grasses from soil erosion and other adverse conditions.

OBOVATE: The reverse of ovate; oval with the point of attachment at the small end.

OFFSET: Small bulb or other portion of a plant that can be detached for propagation.

ORGANIC FERTILIZER: A fertilizer containing carbon compounds.

OSMOSIS: Diffusion through a semipermeable membrane; thus, moisture is taken up by roots and carried from cell to cell throughout the plant.

OVERWINTER: To provide conditions that enable plants to live through the winter.

OVULE: Female reproductive element within the ovary which, when fertilized, becomes a seed.

PALMATE: Lobed, divided or arranged like the fingers and palm of a hand.

PAN: A layer of hard, impervious material below the soil surface, as in "hard pan."

PANICLE: A loosely branched flower head.

PASTEURIZE: To sterilize partially.

PEAT MOSS: Peat formed from sphagnum moss.

PEDUNCLE: The main stem of a flower or flower cluster.

PELTATE: Term used to describe a leaf that has its stalk attached to the center of the leaf, for example, lotus.

PERIANTH: The sheath that holds both petals and sepals of a flower.

PERICARP: The wall of a fruit.

PERITHECIUM: Receptacle that contains spores.

PHOTOSYNTHESIS: The process by which green plants convert inorganic elements into organic compounds by using the energy of light.

PINCH BACK: To snip off the soft tip of a shoot, usually with the fingers.

PINNATE: With parts arranged on both sides of a common axis in the manner of a feather.

PISTIL: The whole female organ of a flower.

PLANT BAND: Small "circlet" of paper or other material inserted usually in seed flats to separate young plants and facilitate later transplanting.

PLUG: A small piece of grass sod or turf used for planting lawns.

POLLEN: Dustlike grains that contain male fertilizing cells, borne by the anthers of a flower.

POLLINATION: The transfer of pollen from stamen to stigma.

POLYETHYLENE: A plastic that permits the passage through it of air and other gases but not of moisture.

PROLIFERATION: Multiplication of growth in excess of that which is normal.

PROPAGULES: Buds, shoots or runners capable of being used for propagation.

RECEPTACLE (of flower): The widened end of the stem which bears the parts of a flower.

RESPIRATION: The process by which living organisms "breathe," absorbing oxygen and giving off waste products (particularly carbon dioxide).

RHIZOME: A thick underground or surface-creeping stem.

RHIZOMORPH: A rootlike branched strand of fungus.

RING SPOTS: Circular markings on foliage resulting from fungus, virus or other causes.

ROOTSTOCK: The root system and basal stem of a plant which is grafted to another and more desirable kind; also, the thickened rhizomes of some plants.

ROSETTE: Cluster of leaves crowded on a stem and spreading in all directions.

RUN (plants start to run): To produce vining stems.

RUNNER: A slender stem that grows along the surface of the ground and bears young plants, such as that of strawberries.

SAPWOOD: The more recently formed wood of a dicotyledonous tree.

SCAFFOLD BRANCHES: The main branches of a tree, especially of a fruit tree. See illus., page 307.

SCAPE: Leafless flower stem arising directly from the ground or from a very short main stem.

SCION: A shoot grafted onto the understock or base and root system of a related plant.

SEED DRILL: A shallow trench in which seed is sown; an implement for making seed drills.

SEPALS: The parts that compose the calyx or outer ring of organs of a mature flower.

SERRATED: Toothed like a saw.

SET: To plant; also, a young bulb, tuber or other propagation ready for planting.

SHEATH: An organ which wholly or partly encloses another organ at its base.

SILT: Finely grained sediment suspended in, or deposited by, water.

SOFTWOOD: Stems that have not yet become hard or woody.

SPHAGNUM MOSS: A particular kind of moss that grows in bogs.

SPRIG: A piece of a stolon (underground stem) used in the propagation of some lawn grasses.

STAMEN: The male organ of a flower.

STAMINATE: Having stamens (usually applied only to flowers without pistils).

STEM-ROOT: Roots that develop from a stem.

STIGMA: The area (usually terminal) of a pistil that receives the pollen.

STOCK PLANTS: Plants retained for purposes of propagation.

STOLON: A horizontal stem that roots and produces new plants along its length or at its apex.

STRATIFICATION OF SEED: A process whereby seeds are kept cold and moist for a period before germination.

STUNT VIRUS: A virus disease that causes the stunting of a plant.

STYLE: The part of the pistil between the ovary and stigma.

SUCKER: A shoot that arises from below ground level rather than from the stem or trunk of a bush or tree.

SWOE: A type of scuffle hoe.

SYNTHETIC ORGANIC FERTILIZER: An organic fertilizer manufactured synthetically.

TANBARK: A residue of bark that has been used for tanning leather, suitable for mulching or for walks.

TENDER PLANT: A plant that cannot be expected to survive freezing temperatures.

TENDRIL: A slender organ by which some plants attach themselves to supports.

TILTH: The physical condition of the soil in relation to the plant growth; the results of tillage.

TOLERANT CARRIERS (of disease): Plants that carry certain diseases but are not seriously harmed by them.

TRACE ELEMENTS: Chemical elements present in exceedingly small quantities.

TRANSPIRATION: The exhalation or giving off of water vapor.

TRUSS: A compact cluster (as of flowers).

TUBER: A thickened underground stem; sometimes also applied to thickened underground roots.

TUBERCLES: Small tubes or tuberlike bodies.

TUBEROUS: Having tubers.

UMBEL: A flower head with branches arranged like the ribs of an umbrella.

UNDERSTOCKS: The root systems and base stems of plants upon which other plants are grafted.

UNLEACHED WOOD ASH: Wood ashes that have not been washed out, as by weathering.

VARIEGATED: Having various colors in regular or irregular patterns.

VEGETATIVE PROPAGATION: Propagation by means other than seeds or spores.

VIABLE: Capable of growing.

VOLUNTEER: A garden plant which has seeded itself and sprouted unexpectedly.

WETTING AGENT: A substance added to water that increases its ability to wet surfaces, especially those that are waxy or oily.

INDEX

IN THIS INDEX appears the Latin or scientific name of each plant as well as the common name or names by which it is popularly known. Sometimes the same common name, such as "mimosa," will be used for several different plants in various parts of the United States and Canada. Occasionally the scientific name is more widely used than the common one. The "rosebay" of the woodland hills of the Carolinas is known everywhere else as rhododendron, its Latin name.

Very often the scientific name labels a plant whose species encompass a wide range. *Delphinium* is applied to related plants that differ considerably in appearance, from the modest larkspur to the towering blue spikes which we know by the common name delphinium. So we use the popular name to indicate just one of the plants which are scientifically known under the same name.

All of this may seem confusing, but there are ways to find a path through the maze. The scientific names are, by and large, precise and clear, known over the world by botanists. Only in the scientific world is *Rosa* a rose. When Shakespeare wrote that "a rose by any other name would smell as sweet," he was not concerned with compiling an index for a complete garden book. Here you will find "moss rose" as well as "rose moss." The "moss rose" is a rose. "Rose moss" is neither moss nor a rose. Scientifically it is *Portulaca* and luckily most of us

have come to know it by that name.

The more we come to accept the scientific name, the more accurate we will be in gardening, especially in ordering plants from a nursery. The nurseryman will know what plant we mean and we will receive what we want. But this is not the whole story. Trees and vegetables, especially, are so widely known by their common names that even the botanist may not refer to a maple as *Acer* or a potato as *Solanum tuberosum*. But when ordering a certain kind of maple, the gardener will find it best to spell out *Acer palmatum* if he wishes to receive the delicate Japanese maple rather than the towering sugar maple (*Acer saccharum*)—which will produce maple sugar by the time his children have grandchildren.

This is a gardener's index rather than a botanist's. For convenience, each name is listed under its last noun rather than the first word of its name. So "rose moss" will be found under "moss, rose" and "moss rose" will be found under "rose, moss."

In using this index, it is best to note the scientific name when you read the text, and refer to the page numbers listed under it as well as under the common name. The Latin or scientific name will often be the guide for a pleasant botanical journey, revealing the less familiar forms of plants that will decorate your garden as beautifully as Shakespeare's sweet-smelling rose or the rosebay of the Carolinas.

A

Aaron's rod, 204
Abele, 384
Abelia, 417, 476, 543,
 561, 575, 606, 612,
 673, 681; glossy, 417,
 543, 561, 575, 606
Abeliophyllum, 417
Abies, **391**, 574, 593, 657,
 658, 680
Abronia, 121, 553
Abutilon, 19, 50, **91–92**,
 97, 554, 852, 854
Acacia, (112), **400**,
 (401), 453, 639; black,
 385; blackwood, 400;
 false, 385; pests, 828;
 rose, 112, **440**, 660
Acalypha, 97
Acanthopanax, 338, **418**,
 476, 543, 561, 575, 592,
 660
Acanthus, (111), **162**, 563
Acer, 368, **369**, 372, **418**,
 476, 550, 561, 566, 574,
 (575), (578), 590, 595,
 604, 628, 658, 659, 660,
 661, 662, 680
Achillea, **162**, (162), 485,
 486, **526**
Acidanthera, **249–50**
Acidity, 541, 543, 728,
 (728), 738, **741–42**;
 greenhouse, 103;
 perennials, 155; shrubs,
 411–12; soil, 119–20,
 276, 305, 346–47, 363;
 tests, 346–47
Aconite, winter, 227, **234**,
 (235), 546, 563, 638, 667
Aconitum, **163**, 545, 563
Acorus, 509–10
Acroclinium, 137
Acrocomia, 608
Actaea, 545
Actinidia, **494**, 545, 562,
 575, 682
Adam's needle, (112),
 473, 662
Adder's-tongue, **234–35**
Adiantum, 52, (266), **267**,
 270
Adonidia, 608
Adonis, 121–22
Adromischus, 62
Aechmea, (13), 19
Aegopodium, 339, **486**,
 545, 661
Aeonium, **62**, 628
Aeration, greenhouse, 104;
 lawns, 361; soil, 747
Aeschynanthus, 19, 97
Aesculus, **372–73**, (373),
 418, 680
Aethionema, **122**, **526**
African violet. See Violet,
 African

Agapanthus, (109), **259**,
 (259), 563, 566, 613,
 614, 619, 638
Agave, 57, **62**, 607, 628
Ageratum, 92, **122**, (122),
 157, 220, 553, 569,
 614, 615, 642, 852;
 golden, 141–42
Aglaonema, **19**, (51), 52, 97
Agonis, 629
Agrostemma, 193
Agrostis, 47, **122–23**, **354**,
 356
Aichryson, 62
Ailanthus, 339, **373**, 561,
 659, 845
Air circulation, 305;
 greenhouse, 81, 84, 86
Air layering. See Layering
Air plant, 70–71
Ajuga, **163**, **486**, **526**, 545,
 562, 563, 661
Akebia, **494**, 545, 562,
 575, 682; five-leaved,
 545, 575, 682
Albizzia, **418**, 561, 604,
 605, 629
Albuca, 262–63
Alder, **373**, 658, 662; black,
 430; Italian, 373;
 mountain, 373, 660;
 pests, 833; red, 373;
 white, 373, **422**, 550
Alfalfa, 765
Algae, 365, 684, 691, 735;
 in pools, 507–08
Alisma, 510
Alkalinity, 305, 347, 363,
 543, 600, 604, 625, 643,
 648, 649, 655, 659, 661,
 (727), **741–42**; shrubs,
 411–12
Allamanda, 97, **494**, 562,
 606, 624
Allium, **228–29**, 263, 299,
 300, 651
Almond, 108, **318**, 623, 699;
 diseases, 797; dwarf,
 (111); dwarf Russian,
 436, 591; flowering, 101,
 436, 561; pruning, 641,
 642, 770
Alnus, **373**, 658, 660
Alocasia, 635
Aloe, 57, **62–63**, (63),
 (64), (602–03), 607, 628
Alonsoa, 123
Alpine plants, 116, 517,
 521, 672; greenhouse, 77
Alpinia, 636
Alstroemeria, (113),
 259–60, 613, 614, 618,
 638
Alternanthera, 642
Althaea, **164**, 221, 552,
 (552)
Althea, shrub, **428–29**,
 (429), 478, 561, 660

Aluminum plant, **40**,
 (49), 97
Aluminum sulphate, 643,
 671
Alyssum, (122), **123**, **164**,
 220, 340, 525, **526**, 552,
 569, 854; sweet, (110),
 120, **141**, 553, 564, 597,
 613, 614, 615, 617, 618,
 619, 640, 641; perennial
 border, 157
Amaranth, 121, ·**123**;
 globe, (114), **135–36**,
 553; perennial border,
 157; sowing, 614, 615
Amaranthus, 121, 123
Amacrinum, 260–61
Amaryllis, 24, **33**, 109,
 260, 628, 638, 657;
 greenhouse, 101; hardy,
 241, 563; planting, 613,
 614, 618, 619
Amelanchier, 323, 415,
 418, 543, 561, 590, 592,
 658, 660, 662
Amianthium, 229
Ammonia, (737)
Ammonium nitrate, 670,
 752
Ammonium sulphate, 670
Amorpha, **418**, 590, 592,
 660, 661
Ampelopsis, **494**, 552, 562
Amsonia, **164**, 545, 563
Anacharis, 516
Anagallis, 123
Anaphalis, 164
Anchusa, (110), (111),
 123, **164–65**, (165), 552;
 cuttings, 169, 709
Androecium, 693
Andromeda, **468**, 524,
 (564), 666, 681;
 Japanese, 667
Androsace, **526**, (527), 857
Anemone, (110), (111), **165**,
 229–30, (230), **257**, 267,
 526–27, 545, 563, 709;
 American wood, 229;
 European wood, 229;
 Japanese, (115), 117,
 165, 563; rue, 230;
 yellow wood, 230
Anemonella, 230
Anethum, 300
Angelica, 294, 295,
 297–98, (297)
Angelica tree, Chinese,
 419; Japanese, 419
Angraecum, 99
Anise, 298; tree, 463
Annual flowers, **119–54**,
 331, 543, 545, 607, 613,
 614, 615, 616, 617, 618,
 619, 640, 641, 644, 648,
 651, 654, 657, 676, 790,
 851, 852, 853–54; cool-
 weather, 615; cutting,

444, **469–70**, (556–57),
(564), (570–71), 572–75,
577, 602, 606, 623, 641,
642, 643, 644, 665, 668,
670, 671, 679, 681, 747;
deciduous, 438–40;
Exbury, 438–40; flame,
438; Ghent, 439;
greenhouse, 85, 92,
101, 104; Indian, 470;
Japanese, 669; Knaphill,
439–40; Kurume, 92,
(115), 438–39, 470, 614;
mollis, 440; pests, 615,
617, 832; pruning, 612,
615; propagation, 706,
786; royal, 439; swamp,
439; torch, 438–39;
transplanting, 614
Azara, **454**, 681
Azolla, 515

B

Babiana, 257
Baboon flower, 257
Baby blue-eyes, 144
Baby's breath, (136), **137**,
184–85, 553
Baby's tears, **33**, 50
Baccharis, **454**, 550, 630
Bachelor's button, **128**,
(128), **221**
Bacillus thuringiensis,
(812), 814
Bacteria, 625, 684, 691,
726–27, 735–37, (737);
black rot, 786; compost,
762; diseases, 774, 775,
786, 797, 804;
greenhouse, 106
Bagasse, 543, 748
Bagworm, 832
Balled and burlapped
plants, 413–14, (580)
Balloonflower, (114), (115),
198, 546
Balloon vine, 127
Balm, 294, **298**; bee, 158,
194, 298, 546, 712;
fragrant, 298; Molucca,
144; Oswego, 298
Balsam, (114), **138**, 564,
614, 615, 616;
planting, 616
Balsam apple, 144
Balsam pear, 144
Bamboo, 50, (114), (115),
343, 454, 562, 570, 574,
637, 643; black joint,
637; clumping, 637;
dwarf, 637; giant timber,
637; heavenly, 449, **466**,
544, 562, 574, 606, 681;
male, 637; running, 637;
yellow groove, 637
Bamburanta, **635**; giant,
635

Bambusa, 454, 637
Banana, shrub, 466, 620,
631, 642, 643;
Abyssinian, 631
Banana shrub, 166
Banyan, **403**, (602–03), 605
Baptisia, 170
Barberry, (113), (114), (115),
415, **419**, 454–55, (454),
474, 475, 476–77, 523,
(543), 544, 557, 561, 562,
575, 592, 605, 660, 681,
682; Japanese, 410, 419,
474, 543, 561, 575, 682;
Korean, 419, 575; Ma-
gellan, 454; mentor, 454;
pests, 832; wintergreen,
454
Barley, (692)
Barrenwort, 488, **531**, 562
Bartonia, 143
Basella, 125–26
Basil, 114, 294, 296, **298**,
(298); planting, 617,
618, 619; potting, 858;
purple, 617; sweet, 298,
(298)
Basket flower, **128**, 256
Basket-of-gold, **164**, **526**,
552, 569
Basswood, **386–87**, 833,
836
Bauhinia, **419**, 605
Bay, 296; bull, 390, 401,
406, (406), 561, 605;
loblolly, 403, (404);
sweet, 104, (110), (111),
464, 544, 562, 566, 574,
605
Bayberry, **434**, (550–51),
552; California, **407**,
681, 682
Bean, (274), 279, **280–82**,
640, 653, 655, 673, 698,
700, 854; broad, 667;
bush, 281, 856; castor,
108, **148–49**, 699, 736;
disease, (798); Indian,
375, 629; lima, 277,
281; mescal, 471; pests,
798, 804, 810, 811,
(812); pH value for,
741; pole, (274), 281,
(282); snap, 277, 281;
sowing, 615, 855
Bearberry, **486**, (551), 552,
595, 657, 661, 668, 682
Beard-tongue, (112), **197**,
534–35
Bear's-breech, **162**, 563
Beaucarnea, 631
Beaumontia, 494
Beauty-berry, 410, **420**,
605
Beauty bush, **431**, 660, 681
Beds, flower, 155, 156, 157,
334, 357; plants for,

563–64
Beech, 50, 340, **376**, 478,
542, 714; American,
376; blue, 375; copper,
377, 478; Dawyck, 377;
European, 376, 478,
680; fernleaf, 377;
golden, 377; pests, 836;
pruning, 772; purple,
377; weeping, 377, (377);
weeping purple, 377
Beefwood, **402**, 629, 639
Beet, 276, 277, **281**, 640,
653, 654, 673, 676, 679,
699; disease, (798);
greenhouse, 99; harvest-
ing, 856; pests, 810,
811; sowing, 613, 614,
617, 618, 619, 855, 856;
storing, 858; weed con-
trol, 848
Beetle, 806, (808), 809,
811, (812), (813), **814**,
819, 821, (826), 832,
(835); Asiatic garden,
(808), **809**; black vine,
398; click, 811; Col-
orado, 814; flea, (813),
814; Japanese, 366, 806,
807, 809, (826), 829,
832; June, 366; May,
811; Mexican bean,
(812); potato, 814;
raspberry, 821; water-
lily leaf, 832, (835)
Begonia, 14, 18, (20), **22**,
52, 77, 92, 97, 103, (113),
(114), **126**, **230**, 250,
331, 545, (545), 546,
(556–57), (558–59), 563,
564, (564–65), (567), 569,
623, 625, 626, 628, 641,
642, 643, 644, 670, 672,
852, 854, 857; cuttings,
698, 707, (708), 709–11;
diseases, 797; pests, 825,
828, 837; sowing, 613,
617, 618; tuberous, 106,
250–51, (250), 546,
563, 654, 656, 713, 852;
wax, 92, 120, 126, 545,
(545), 564, 569
Belamcanda, 170
Bell, Canterbury, (110),
221, 598
Bellflower, **171–72**,
221, **528–29**, (528), 545,
563; chimney, 221; tus-
sock, (110), (111)
Bellis, **221**, 569, 613, 617,
618
Bells, cathedral, 130;
yellow, 471
Bells of Ireland, 144
Bellwort, **204**, 546
Beloperone, **22**, **92**
Berberis, (113), (114),
(115), **419**, **454–55**,

Bold type indicates main entries; parentheses denote illustrations.

Bold type indicates main entries; parentheses denote illustrations.

Bold type indicates main entries; parentheses denote illustrations.

820, 833, 839; Siberian,
481, 661
Elodea, 517
Elsholtzia, 425–26
Embothrium, 113
Emilia, 134
Empress tree, **383,** 680
Endive, 100, **286,** 617,
618, 619
Enkianthus, 411, **426,**
543, 575, 668, 681
Epidendrum, 98
Epigaea, 531
Epimedium, 488, **531,** 562
Epiphyllum, **67,** (68), 628
Episcia, 29
Eranthis, 234, (235), 546
Eremochloa, 357
Eremurus, 180–81
Erica, (110), (111), 411,
459–60, 488, **531,** 639,
672, 681, 682, 687
Erigeron, **181, 531,** 553
Erinus, 531
Eriobotrya, **402–03,** 561,
604, 605, **639**
Eriogonum, **630,** 661
Erodium, 531
Erwinia, 791
Eryngium, **181, 553,** 709
Erythea, 632
Erythronium, **234–35,**
546
Escallonia, (113), **460,**
639, 671, 672, 681,
682
Eschscholtzia, **134,** 553
Espalier, 331, 655
Eucalyptus, 95, **403,** 639
Eucharis, **261,** 614
Eucomis, 261
Eucryphia, (113), **460**
Eugenia, **403,** 607
Euonymus, 50, (115), **426,**
460, (460), 478, 488,
(488), 496, 542, 544,
(558–59), 561, 562,
574–75, 592, 595, 654,
656, 660, 661, 681, 682;
diseases, 800; pests,
831, **838;** winged-bark,
410, 426, 478, 561,
592, 681
Eupatorium, **181,** 546,
563
Euphorbia, **29,** 56, 57,
67–68, (68), 95, **134,**
182, 553, 607, 628
Eurya, **460,** 544, 606
Evergreens, 85, 339, 560,
593–94, 653, 657,
658, 661, 669, 851;
bonsai, 577; broad-
leaved, 594, 629, 660,
668, 676, 681–82; cut-
tings, 710; layering,
715; low, 657; pruning,
770–71; antidesiccant

spray, 598
Evergreen shrubs, **449–73,**
544–45, 550, 561–62, 574;
broad-leaved, 453–73,
594, 602–03, 606;
hedges, 661; seaside, 550
Evergreen trees, **388–409,**
605, 657; broad-leaved,
388, 390, 400–09,
602–03, 629; Japanese
gardens, 574; less hardy,
388–89; low, 657; sea-
side, 550; selection, 390;
winter-hardy conifers,
388
Everlasting, **137–38, 153–
54, 164;** pearly, 164;
Swan River, **138**
Exochorda, **426, 660**

F

Fagus, **376–77,** (377), 478,
680
Fairy ring, 367
Fallugia, 426
False cypress. See
Cypress, false
Fanwort, 516
Fasciation, chrysan-
themum, (788)
Fatshedera, **29–30,** 95, 562
Fatsia, 30, 95, 97, **461,**
(461), 544, 562, 574,
679, 681
Faucaria, 68, (69)
Feijoa, **461, 639**
Felicia, 134–35
Fence, 336, 340, 343, 555;
lath, (550–51)
Fenestraria, 69
Fennel, 293, 294, **300;**
Florence, **286**
Fennelflower, 146
Ferns, 13, **265–73,** 546,
563, 652, 684, 691; ball,
52; bird's-nest, 52, 271;
Boston, 272, (272);
bottle gardens, 50, 52;
brake, 273, (273);
Christmas, 269;
cinnamon, **269,** 562;
cliff, 272; clover, 512;
coffee, 272, 512; com-
mon polypody, 269;
deciduous, 265; elkhorn,
272; fertilizing, 266;
greenhouse, 86, 95, 97,
103; hardy, 265–69;
hare's foot, 272;
hart's-tongue, **269,** 741;
hay-scented, **268,** (540);
holly, 270, **271;** indoor,
269–73; interrupted,
269, 652; lady, **267,**
652; maidenhair,
American, 52, (266);
267, **270,** 625; delta,

52, 270; male **268,**
(268), 652; New York,
268; ostrich, 269;
parsley, American, 267,
(267); pests, 828;
planting, 265–66;
propagation, 266–67;
rabbit's foot, 271;
royal, 269; sensitive,
269; spiny wood, 268;
squirrel's-foot, 270, **271;**
staghorn, 272, (273);
sweet, 543, 550; sword,
270, **271;** water, 515;
wood-ash, 265
Ferocactus, 69
Fertilizers and manures,
305, 485, 583, 585,
595, 596, 598, 611,
612, 613, 615, 617, 618,
619, 667, 730, 733, 736,
749–60, 853, 854;
aquatics, 505; city
gardening, 555;
commercial, 751;
complete and mixed,
305, 669, 670, 751, 752;
compost, 762;
greenhouse, 97, 103,
104; inorganic, 361–62,
749–50, 751; lawns, 666,
670; liquid, 566, 568–69,
702, 706, 752; nitrogen,
362, 673, 736, **753–54,**
764; nonprotein organic,
749, 751; organic, 347,
361, **735–36,** 757–58;
overdosage, 749;
phosphatic, 736, **754;**
potassic, **754;** protein
organic, 749, 751,
754–57; storage, 760;
synthetics, 749;
ureaform, 753
Fertilizing, 216, 266, 505,
693, 695; bonsai, 583;
deciduous shade trees,
369; house plants, 17;
lawns, 346, (348), 358,
361–63; leaf, 752; perennials, 156, 160; sea-
side gardens, 549–50;
vegetables, 278
Fescue, 531, 669; red, **354;**
fine, 344, 348, 351, **354,**
356, 362; tall, 348, 354,
356, 364, 365
Festuca, **354, 356,** 531
Feverfew, 143
Fiber-glass, greenhouse,
80; mulch, 350, 598;
pools, 502–03
Ficus, (12), **30–31,** (49),
50, (51), 52, 55, 97, **403,**
496, 562, 605, 606, 640
Fig, **320,** (320), 403, 616,
623; brown turkey,
(320); creeping, **31,**

Bold type indicates main entries; parentheses denote illustrations.

Bold type indicates main entries; parentheses denote illustrations.

Bold type indicates main entries; parentheses denote illustrations.

Bold type indicates main entries; parentheses denote illustrations.

Bold type indicates main entries; parentheses denote illustrations.

Bold type indicates main entries; parentheses denote illustrations.

Weed-control applications
(continued):
Simazene, 844
Simazine, 842–43,
846–48
Smartweed Killer, 842
sodar, 844
sodium chlorate, 846
Solvent, 842
Spot Grass and Weed
Killer, 844
Telvar, 842, 845
Tillam, 843
Treflay, 843, 844
Trifluralin, 843
Turf Builder, 844
2,4-D, 841, 843–45
2,4,5-T, 841
2,4,5-TP, 844–45
Vegedex, 842–43
Vegiben, 842, 843
Weedar 64, 843
Weedazol, 845
Weed-B-Gon, 844
Weeder bar, 846
Weedkiller "66," 843,
855
Weed-No-More, 844
Weedone, 842, 843, 844,
845
X-All, 844
zytron, 844
Weevil, 825, (827), 832;
black vine, 825, (827),
832; Japanese, 832
Weigela, 415, 447–48,
(447), 561, 587, 605,
642, 670, 671, 681;
pruning, 855
Wetters, 787
Whitefly, 106, 615, 778,
825, (827)
White torch, (58)
Whortleberry, 658
Willow, 340, 385, 442,
481, (558–59), 595, 629,
658, 662, 682; desert,
421, 629; diseases, 804;
dwarf blue-leaf Arctic,
481; goat, 442; laurel,
590; niobe, 385; pests,
820, 833, 838; prairie,
552; primrose, 512, 513;
pussy, 442, 660, 661;
red-stem, 385, 590, 595;
Thurlow weeping,
385–86; Virginia, 410,
430; weeping (111),

(115), 385–86, 561, 680;
white, 590
Willow-herb, (689), (693)
Wilt, 797, 800, 816;
verticillium, 305, 324
Wilt-pruf, 787, 819
Windflower, 165, 229,
(230)
Window box, 566–70;
tender bulbs, 250, 251
Window plant, 69, 72
Wind protection, 333, 339,
549, 648; evergreens,
390; perennials, 155;
roof gardens, 558,
(558–59); seaside, (547),
548–49, (550–51);
trees, 381, 384
Wingnut, Chinese, 629
Winterberry, 430, 544
Winter creeper, 542
Wintergreen, (112), 488
Winter protection, 485,
613, 858; bonsai, 583–84;
perennials, 160; roses,
217; severe climates,
597–98, 649, 653;
tender bulbs, 249
Winter sweet, (115)
Wireworm, (809), 811,
816, 832
Wishbone flower, 152,
(542), 545, 616
Wisteria, (115), 500, 552,
562, 575, 606, 614,
616, 661, 682; Chinese,
(115); pruning, 770,
(770), 772
Witches' broom, 376
Witch hazel. See Hazel,
witch
Withe rod, 552
Woodruff, 125; sweet, 545
Worm, army, 617;
cabbage, (812), 814;
celery, (812), 814;
currant, 817, (818);
Eastern raspberry fruit,
821; inch, 820;
measuring, 820; rail-
road, 817
Wormwood, 298, 528
Wound dressing, 612

X

Xanthoceras, 448, 661
Xanthorhiza, 448, 544

X-disease, 790
Xeranthemum, 153–54
Xerophytes, 548
Xylosma, 631

Y

Yam, digging, 618;
planting, 616
Yangtao, 682
Yarrow, 162, (162), 485,
486, (689), (693)
Yatay, 608
Yaupon, 463, 606, 607,
620
Yellow edge, strawberry
mild, (785)
Yellowroot, 448, 544
Yellowwood, 376, 659
Yesterday, today and
tomorrow, 455
Yew, 398–99, 449, 451,
452, 483, 545, 557, 562,
681; Canadian, 452;
English, 398, 682;
Irish, 452;
Japanese, (398), 399,
452; pests, 825, 828,
832; pruning, 770,
772, 855; Western, 399,
657, 681
Youth-and-old-age, 154
Yucca, (112), 473, 550,
(551), (558–59), 562,
607, 626, (627), 631–32,
660, 662
Yulan, 381

Z

Zantedeschia, 264
Zea, 154
Zebrina, 44, (49), (51),
52, 97
Zelkova, 387, (387), 575
Zenobia, 411, 414–15,
448, (448)
Zephyranthes, 262, 814
Zephyr flower, (113), 262
Zigadenus, 248
Zinc, 507, 741
Zinnia, 91, (112), 154, 157,
553, 564, 570, 614, 615,
616, 641, 642, 643, 654,
655, 775, 791, 794, 795,
804, 852; creeping, 150
Zygocactus, 57, 77